ISAIAH 13–27

Other Continental Commentaries from Fortress Press

Genesis 1–11
Claus Westermann

Genesis 12–36
Claus Westermann

Genesis 37–50
Claus Westermann

Theology of the Psalms
Hans-Joachim Kraus

Psalms 1–59
Hans-Joachim Kraus

Psalms 60–150
Hans-Joachim Kraus

Song of Songs
Othmar Keel

Isaiah 1–12
Hans Wildberger

Obadiah and Jonah
Hans Walter Wolff

Micah
Hans Walter Wolff

Haggai
Hans Walter Wolff

Matthew 1–7
Ulrich Luz

Galatians
Dieter Lührmann

Revelation
Jürgen Roloff

HANS WILDBERGER

ISAIAH 13–27

A Continental Commentary

Translated by
Thomas H. Trapp

FORTRESS PRESS
MINNEAPOLIS

ISAIAH 13–27
A Continental Commentary

English translation first published by Fortress Press in 1997.

Translated from *Jesaja, Kapitel 13–27*, published by Neukirchener Verlag, Neukirchen-Vluyn, in 1978 in the Biblischer Kommentar series.

Copyright © Neukirchener Verlag des Erziehungsvereins GmbH, Neukirchen-Vluyn, 1978. English translation copyright © 1997 Augsburg Fortress.

Publication of this volume was assisted by a grant from Pro Helvetia, the Swiss cultural foundation.

Biblical quotations from the New Revised Standard Version Bible are copyright © 1989 by the Division of Christian Education of the National Council of Churches of Christ in the United States of America and are used by permission.

Library of Congress Cataloging-in-Publication Data

The Library of Congress has catalogued this series as follows:

Wildberger, Hans, 1910–
    [Jesaja. English]
    Isaiah : a commentary / Hans Wildberger.
       p.   cm.—(Continental commentaries)
    Translation of: Jesaja.
    Contents: [1] Isaiah 1–12
    ISBN 0-8006-9508-9 (v. 1; alk. paper):
    1. Bible. O.T. Isaiah—Commentaries. I. Title. II. Title:
Isaiah 1–12. III. Series.
BS1515.3W53613   1990
224'.1077—dc20

                91-8874
                CIP

Isaiah 13–27: ISBN 978-0-8006-9509-5

Manufactured in the U.S.A.   AF 1-9509

Contents

v

Contents

Foreword to the Second Volume

Chapters 13–27 of the book of Isaiah, the subject matter for the second volume of my commentary, form a distinct unit in a certain sense. They deal with the theme of Israel and the nations, moving on then to the theme of God's reign as king, as proclaimed in the Isaiah Apocalypse. These chapters are not given the same focused attention by scholars as is given to the study of the first part of Isaiah. General readers of the Bible are also not as drawn to read this material as they are to give attention to the previous chapters. Part of the reason for this is that Isaiah, the son of Amoz, speaks in relatively few passages within this section —though not nearly as few as some scholars would have us believe—but this relative lack of attention is also caused by the fact that certain sections of this material are the result of a very complex history of development. It is very difficult to date and to understand this material within its religio-historical and theological settings. There are roadblocks along the path that are very often impossible to surmount. In spite of this, I would say that this commentary demonstrates that study of this part of Isaiah will be most rewarding. Indeed, a careful reading promises to be both stimulating and satisfying for the person who is willing to devote attention to this part of the book as well.

The informed reader will notice right away that this study was written paying close attention to and in dialogue with current research. But the reader is asked to remember that the individual subsections of this book were completed between one and two years before they appeared in print in fascicle form. After the first volume of this commentary appeared, the significant commentary by Otto Kaiser was published, which could be consulted from chapter 15 on. I have learned much from my study of his views and my dialogue with him, in general as well as in many particulars, but I have not been persuaded to agree with his general conclusions.

Thanks must be offered: to the Schweizerischen Nationalfonds zur Förderung der wissenschaftlichen Forschung (The Swiss National Fund for the

Foreword to the Second Volume

Advancement of Scholarly Research), without whose considerable financial support it would not have been possible to continue this work; to the publishers and editorial team of the Biblischer Kommentar, especially to Prof. Dr. Dr. S. Herrmann in Bochum, for the gracious guidance provided and for many helpful suggestions; to my former assistant Felix Mathys, now serving as a pastor in Dielsdorf, who worked on this project up to chapter 16, and to Fräulein VDM Ursula Herter, who has served in the same capacity since that time. They have spared no effort in getting me the necessary research materials and in seeing to it that the manuscript was readied for typesetting. They also provided stimulation and suggestions that affected the work in significant ways.

In addition, the commentary on chaps. 28–35 is already quite far along. The work on the historical materials recorded in chaps. 36–39 should be finished rather soon. Moreover, the third volume will also include the overview of the entire book, which many are eagerly awaiting, and will include a discussion of the composition and transmission of chaps. 1–39, a characterization of the prophet and his message, and an analysis of the secondary materials in the book, as well as the theology contained therein. Once more, I ask the reader to be understanding about the fact that the discussion of the book as a whole has had to be postponed until the commentary on each section could be completed.

I dedicate this volume to my beloved partner on life's journey, who eagerly took an active interest in "my Isaiah" and sacrificed much on account of that effort, but who now will not be able to enjoy seeing the entire work come to completion.

מֶלֶךְ בְּיָפְיוֹ תֶּחֱזֶינָה עֵינֶיךָ
תִּרְאֶינָה אֶרֶץ מַרְחַקִּים:

"Your eyes will see the king in his beauty;
they will behold a land that stretches far away."
—Isaiah 33:17

Zurich, February, 1978
Hans Wildberger

Translator's Preface

When I set out to translate the three volumes of Hans Wildberger's commentary on Isaiah 1–39, I decided to make every effort to make it read as if Wildberger were speaking English. But I have sought to be as careful as possible in giving nuance to the ideas that he presents. I wanted the results of Wildberger's thirty years of labor to be available also to those who did not have a deep background in the study of foreign languages. So I chose to add to the workload by translating every foreign word. The meanings for the words in the biblical languages are quoted from the New Revised Standard Version, except when dealing with the material from Isaiah 1–39. In the Isaiah material, the meaning of the Hebrew word matches Wildberger's own translation. I was also aware of the fact that students of the biblical materials want up-to-date bibliographies. Here I beg a little more time. I plan to update the very significant bibliographical material that is presented in Wildberger's third volume during the time that it will be going through the editorial process. Please remember that this is one work in three volumes.

I am at work on the third volume. It covers Isaiah 28-39 in about 475 pages and then contains about 250 pages of concluding material. It is unfortunate that the publication of the second volume was delayed by circumstances beyond the control of anyone connected with the project. It is hoped that the final volume will not be so delayed.

Technical matters have changed radically since I began the first volume. The day that I was officially asked to translate this work was the day our family bought its first computer. The first and second volumes were done on that machine. The first was typeset manually. This second volume was typeset using the disks, but all of the foreign language terms and diacritical marks had to be written into the original translation manuscript by hand. The third volume will be typeset with all the foreign language fonts included as it is translated. This ought to speed up the process of editing and publication.

I appreciate being asked to translate these volumes. It is an awesome amount of work. I have been helped with some of the foreign language terms by members of the Department of Religion and Theology at Concordia University-

St. Paul. Many still-more difficult terms, from Akkadian, Ugaritic, Arabic, and Syriac, were deciphered with the help of Mark Hillmer of Luther Seminary in St. Paul. Bruce Eldevik, librarian at Luther Seminary, has also helped me track down items for cross-referencing. Gary Lee did a very careful job of editing and helped me see where refinements had to be made. I thank them all.

I must also thank my family. My wife Kathy has shouldered an extra load with our family during the many hours that I have been at work on this. My children Matthew, JoAnna, and Daniel have spent their grade school, high school, and college years with this project as an extra member of the family and all have given me their encouragement and support.

Hans Wildberger studied the concept of history in the book of Isaiah. He perceived that the text maintained again and again that God was at work, even though unseen, in the events of history. Those who would shape their lives according to what God was already doing would be at peace and would be helped through rough times. Those who believed that they had to take matters into their own hands, by oppressing fellow citizens or seeking treaties with other nations to help them survive, would continue to make matters worse. Some day, God would finally gather the faithful together and celebrate a banquet, one at which all who recognized God's lordship would be at peace and all who fought God would perish. Such words continue to need to be heard. Such a framework for life continues to provide hope in this world. Wildberger has helped me to hear Isaiah and Isaiah has helped me hear God's voice. For that, I am thankful.

I have a little confession to make. I spent hours tracking down whatever I needed or wanted to check. But three items eluded me. I cannot find where Pliny talks about the mouth of the Nile being like a sea. The reference to Pliny in the commentary is incorrect. I paged through all the volumes of his *Natural History* twice without being able to find the source. I have stared for a long time at a description of Egyptian fishermen, trying to understand what Wildberger describes as he looks at a depiction of the fishermen at work. I am not sure exactly what technique is being used. I have consulted Egyptian scholars for help and hope that I have translated this accurately. The reference work that depicts this activity is unclear about exactly what is being done. And I was not able to track down a Scandinavian saga about how a certain group celebrated the enthronement of their king. Any help on these matters will be appreciated.

I was involved in many fascinating little side trips in this work. It showed me that Wildberger left no stone unturned. He listened much and read much in order to present a work that was the result of study, rather than a work that anticipated the conclusion beforehand and just set out to make the facts fit. One can appreciate the wide range of secondary research topics by consulting the indices.

It is my hope that this work will be read and studied. It is well worth the effort.

Thomas H. Trapp
St. Paul, Minnesota
August, 1997

The Oracles against the Nations

Literature

C. C. Torrey, "Some Important Editorial Operations in the Book of Isaiah," *JBL* 57 (1938) 109-139. L. J. Liebreich, "The Compilation of the Book of Isaiah," *JQR* 46 (1955/56) 259-277, and 47 (1956/57) 114-138. J. H. Eaton, "The Origin of the Book of Isaiah," *VT* 9 (1959) 138-157, esp. 150ff. N. K. Gottwald, *All the Kingdoms of the Earth* (1964). J. H. Hayes, "The Oracles Against the Nations in the Old Testament," diss., Princeton Theological Seminary (1964). G. Fohrer, "Entstehung, Komposition und Überlieferung von Jesaja 1–39," *Studien zur alttestamentlichen Prophetie (1949–1965)*, BZAW 99 (1967) 113-147, esp. 127-129, 132f. B. Margulis, "Studies in the Oracles against the Nations," diss., Brandeis (1967). J. Becker, *Isaias—der Prophet und sein Buch*, SBS 30 (1968) 63-66. J. H. Hayes, "The Usage of Oracles against Foreign Nations in Ancient Israel," *JBL* 87 (1968) 81-92. S. Erlandsson, *The Burden of Babylon*, Coniectanea Biblica, OT Series 4 (1970) 43-105. O. Kaiser, *Isaiah 13-39*, OTL (1974; this was not available until after work on chapters 13–14 was completed).

[**Literature update through 1979:** Calvin, *Sermons sur le livre d'Esaïe ch. 13–23*, ed. G. A. Barrois, Suppl. Calv. 2/1 (1961). G. E. Wright, "The Nations in Hebrew Prophecy," *Encounter* 26 (1965) 225-237. Y. Hoffmann, *The Prophecies against Foreign Nations in the Bible* (Hebrew) (1977). P. Höffken, "Untersuchungen zu den Begründungselementen der Völkerorakel des Alten Testaments," diss., Bonn (1977).]

The message about Babylon in 13:2ff. is introduced in v. 1 as a מַשָּׂא (verdict). This designation serves as a noteworthy formal indicator in the superscriptions at the beginning of each of the units found in chaps. 13–23: see 13:1, concerning Babylon; 15:1, concerning Moab; 17:1, concerning Damascus; 19:1, concerning Egypt; 21:1, concerning the wilderness of the sea (?); 21:11, concerning Dumah (?); 21:13, in the desert plain; 22:1, concerning the valley of vision (?); 23:1, concerning Tyre. In addition, the message about the Philistines is identified as a מַשָּׂא (verdict) in 14:28ff. Outside the complex of materials found in chaps. 13–23, this superscription is found elsewhere only in 30:6. This use of the same designation to introduce each of the individual sections in chaps. 13–23 binds them all together and shows that this was formed into a single, large unit, constructed intentionally by a redactor.

Further evidence for this is provided by the content of the individual sections: on the one hand, this section deals with oracles against the nations (though 22:1-14 is directed against Jerusalem). One must admit that this superscription is not in every passage where one would expect it if a rigid plan had been adhered to throughout (14:24; 17:12; 18:1; 20:1). On the other hand, 22:1-14, 15-19, and 20-25 are out of place in a collection of oracles directed against the nations. This set of circumstances can be explained only by recognizing that the redactor did not assemble this collection from separate individual units that were at his disposal. Instead, this material must have had a complicated earlier history of development. One comes to the same realization when considering the question about the source of each of the original units. On the one hand, current research considers relatively few sections in chaps. 13–23 as Isaianic: most likely 14:24-27, 28-32; 17:1-7; chap. 18; chap. 20; 22:1-14, 15-18 (see G. Fohrer, BZAW 99 [1967] 127). General agreement has also been reached concerning those passages which, on the other hand, are considered "not genuine": 13:1—14:23; chaps. 15f.; chap. 21. Passages about which there is disagreement include 17:12-14 (see O. Eissfeldt, *The Old Testament: An Introduction* [1965] 313); 19:1-4 and 11-14 (see Procksch, 243ff.); 23:1-14 (see W. Rudolph, FS Baumgärtel [1959] 166-174). The question about authenticity, as well as questions about secondary insertions and supplements, will be dealt with at the appropriate time in connection with the discussion of the individual units.

Provisionally, it is suggested here: when taken as a whole, Isaiah 13–23 is composed of messages delivered by Isaiah that are primarily directed against foreign peoples, and of a collection of oracles against the foreign peoples that comes from the exilic-postexilic era. One must presume that later additions were inserted into both sets of material. Since all the passages that clearly do not come from Isaiah are introduced with the superscription מַשָּׂא (verdict), it would seem likely that the redactor of the "nongenuine" messages against the foreign peoples had a מַשָּׂא (verdict) collection that had been assembled before this time. He would have combined this material with a small collection of messages from Isaiah, to which he himself would have affixed the label מַשָּׂא (verdict) at certain points as he worked through the entire complex of material. The stimulus and justification for bringing this material together may have been suggested by the use of מַשָּׂא (verdict) in the superscription in 14:28, which might have been written by Isaiah himself; in any case, it goes back to a very old level of transmission of the material. The question about why the collection of מַשָּׂא (verdict) sections would have been united with one that consisted of sections of prophecy from Isaiah might be answered by assuming that someone wanted to accord these מַשָּׂא (verdict) messages the authority of the great prophet who had been active during the Assyrian era.

2

Babylon's Downfall and
Israel's Return Home

Literature
H. Grimme, "Ein übersehenes Orakel gegen Assur (Isaias 13)," *TQ* 85 (1903) 1–11.
K. Budde, "Jesaja 13," FS W. W. von Baudissin, BZAW 33 (1918) 55–70. L. Alonso-
Schökel, "Traducción de Textos poéticos hebreos, Is 13," *CB* 17 (1960) 170–176. R.
Bach, *Die Aufforderungen zur Flucht und zum Kampf im alttestamentlichen
Prophetenspruch,* WMANT 9 (1962). F. C. Fensham, "Common Trends in Curses of
the Near Eastern Treaties and *kudurru*-Inscriptions Compared with Maledictions of
Amos and Isaiah," *ZAW* 75 (1963) 155–175. D. R. Hillers, *Treaty-Curses and the Old
Testament Prophets,* BibOr 16 (1964). P. D. Miller, "The Divine Council and the
Prophetic Call to War," *VT* 18 (1968) 100–107. S. Erlandsson (see literature to Isaiah
13–23). O. Kaiser (see literature to Isaiah 13–23).

Concerning משׂא: H. S. Gehman, "The 'Burden' of the Prophets," *JQR* 31
(1940/41) 107–121. P. A. H. de Boer, "An Inquiry into the Meaning of the Term משׂא,"
OTS 5 (1948) 197–214. R. B. Y. Scott, "The Meaning of *massā'* as an Oracle Title,"
JBL 67 (1948) v–vi. Erlandsson, 64f.

Concerning the Day of Yahweh: see *Isaiah 1–12,* p. 97. Additional literature
includes: M. Weiss, "The Origin of the 'Day of the Lord' —Reconsidered," *HUCA*
37 (1966) 29–72. G. Eggebrecht, "Die früheste Bedeutung und der Ursprung der
Konzeption vom 'Tag Jahwes,'" diss., Halle (1966); see *TLZ* 93 (1968) 631f. R. W.
Klein, "The Day of the Lord," *CTM* 39 (1968) 517–525. H. P. Müller, *Ursprünge und
Strukturen alttestamentlicher Eschatologie,* BZAW 109 (1969) 72–85. K. D. Schunk,
"Der 'Tag Jahwes' in der Verkündigung der Propheten," *Kairos* 11 (1969) 14–21.
H. W. Wolff, *Joel und Amos,* BK XIV/2 (1969) 38f. (Engl: *Joel and Amos,*
Hermeneia [1977] 33f.). C. Carniti, "L'espressione 'Il giorno di Jhwh': origine ed
evoluzione semantica," *BeO* 12 (1970) 11–25. G. W. Ahlström, *Joel and the Temple
Cult of Jerusalem,* VTSup 21 (1971) 62–97. J. G. Heintz, "Aux origines d'une
expression biblique: *ūmūšū qerbū* in A.R.M., X/6,8?" *VT* 21 (1971) 528–540. F.
Stolz, *Jahwes und Israels Kriege,* ATANT 60 (1972) 158–161 (including much back-
ground literature).

[Literature update through 1979: H. Goehring, "The Fall of Babylon—Historical or Future? A Critical Monograph on Is 13:19-20. Abridged by the Author,"
Grace Journal 2/1 (1961) 23–34. A. Caquot, "Hébreu ע־מ, Gr. Aithiopes," *Mélanges
Marcel Cohen* (1970) 219–223. R. V. G. Tasker, *The Biblical Doctrine of the Wrath
of God* (1951). W. Kuhnigk, "שבת hi. 'zerschlagen,'" Biblica et Orientalia (Pontifical
Biblical Institute) 27 (1974). N. H. Snaith, "The Meaning of שׂעירים," *VT* 25 (1975)
115–118. K. W. Allen, "The Rebuilding and Destruction of Babylon," *BS* 133 (1976)
19–27.

Concerning משׂא: J. A. Naudé, "maśśaʾ in the OT with Special Reference to the Prophets," *OTWSA* 12 (1969) 91–100.
Concerning the Day of Yahweh: F. C. Fensham, "A Possible Origin of the Concept of the Day of the Lord," *Biblical Essays* (1966) 90–97. P. D. Miller, Jr., "The Divine Council and the Prophetic Call to War," *VT* 19 (1968) 100–107. H. P. Müller, *Ursprünge und Strukturen alttestamentlicher Eschatologie,* BZAW 109 (1969), esp. 69–85. E. Haag, "Der Tag Jahwes im Alten Testament," *BibLeb* 13 (1972) 238–248.]

Text

13:1 The verdict concerning Babylon, which Isaiah, the son of Amoz, saw.

2 Upon a barren[a] hill erect the battlefield[b] signal,
   with loud voice shout to them,[c]
motion with the hand, so that they come
   through the gates[d] of the freely willing ones.

3 I myself have commanded . . .[a]
   . . .[a]my consecrated ones,
indeed summoned to my wrathful (judgment[b]), my valiant warriors,
   who shout for joy because of my majesty.[c]

* * * *

4 Listen,[a] an uproar[b] on the mountains,
   as it sounds when many people are there;
listen, a roaring[b] of kingdoms,[c]
   of nations, which are gathered together.
Yahweh of Hosts musters
   the host for the war.

5 They come[a] from a very distant land,
   from the heaven's rim,[b]
Yahweh with[c] the implements[d] (for the execution) of his malediction,[e]
   to devastate the whole land.

* * * *

6 Start singing the lament, for the Day of Yahweh is near,[a]
   As a devastation from the devastator[b] it approaches.

7 Because of this, all hands will go limp,
   and every human heart despairs

8 [and they will stand aghast].[a]
They will have cramps and pains,[b]
   they will writhe as does one who is giving birth.
One will stare blankly[c] at the other;
   each one's face is flaming red.[d]

* * * *

9 Behold, the Day of Yahweh[a] comes, gruesome it is,
   with[b] frothing rage and glowing anger,
to make the earth into a ghastly wasteland,
   when[c] he eradicates the sinners from upon it.

10 Then the stars[a] of heaven [and the Orions within it][b]
   do not allow their light to stream forth;[c]
the sun is dark, when it comes forth,
   and the moon does not permit its light to shine.

* * * *

11 I requite the world for the evil[a]
  and the transgressors for their offensive behavior.
  And I bring to an end the haughtiness[b] of the proud,
  and the high-mindedness[b] of the tyrants I bring low.
12 I make human beings rarer than fine gold[a]
  and the children of Adam[b] as the gold of Ophir.

* * *

13 On account of that heaven trembles,[a]
  and the earth jumps startled from its place,
  at the frothing rage of Yahweh of Hosts,
  on the day of his glowing anger.
14 And as gazelles that have been scared off,
  and like a herd that no one is able to keep together,
  each one turns away toward his own people,
  and each one flees into his own land.
15 Whomever anyone meets by chance[a] at any time will be pierced
    through,
  and whomever someone happens to seize by chance[b] will fall by
    a sword.
16 [a]Their children will be crushed
  before their eyes;[a]
  their houses[b] will be plundered,
  and their wives[c] will be raped.

* * * *

17 Behold, I rouse up against them
  the Medes,[a]
  who pay no attention[b] to silver
  and take no pleasure in gold.
18 And the bows of the young men 'will be smashed,'[a]
  . . .
  and they will not have mercy on the fetus,
  'and'[b] their eyes will show no pity[c] toward the children.

* * * *

19 And it will happen to Babylon,[a] the most elegant of kingdoms,
  the pride-filled magnificence of the Chaldeans,[b]
  as it happened to Sodom[c] and Gomorrah,
  when God overthrew them.[d]
20 Never again will it[a] be inhabited,[b]
  never again resettled,[b] from generation to generation.
  And no nomads[c] will camp out in tents[d] there,
  and no shepherds will permit (their herds) to lie down there.[e]
21 Only demons[a] will lie down there,
  and their houses will be filled with owls.
  And ostriches will dwell there,
  and goat-demons will hold their dances there.
22 [a]Wild dogs[b] will find shelter for themselves[c] in 'their'[d] fortress,
  and jackals in the delight-filled palaces.
  Their time has drawn very close,
  and their days will not be prolonged.

* * * *

14:1 [For Yahweh will have pity on Jacob and will elect Israel once again
  and will transplant them into their homeland. The resident aliens will

5

attach themselves to them and will associate themselves with the
house of Jacob.] 2 [They will take peoples and bring them to
their place, and the house of Israel will make them male slaves and
female slaves, as their own inherited possession on Yahweh's land.
And they will take away the[a] captured ones, who had earlier placed
them in confinement, and over those who had been their taskmasters they will be rulers.]

13:2a נִשְׁפֶּה (barren) is a niphʿal participle from שׁפה; cf. Arabic *safā* = bare, sweep
smooth (by means of the wind); Aramaic *spʾ* = smooth out. הַר־נִשְׁפֶּה thus refers to the
bare top of a hill, which does not have any trees or shrubbery growing on it, upon
which a battlefield signal would be clearly visible even if someone were standing a
great distance away.

2b Concerning נֵס (battlefield signal), see *Isaiah 1–12*, p. 239, on 5:26.

2c It has been suggested (*BHK²*) that one should read לָחֶם (war) instead of לָהֶם (to
them). But לֶחֶם is never used in the OT with the meaning "war," as presumed in this
proposal. Further, the referent for the suffix on לָהֶם (to them) is not obvious; it is possible that it should be eliminated from the text. But it is more likely that it is used on
purpose, so that a definite tension is created, as one anticipates finding out who is
being issued this order.

2d פִּתְחֵי נְדִיבִים (gates of the freely willing ones), dependent on בֹּא (come), is difficult. One expects a preposition after בֹּא (come); at this point, the discussion cannot
yet be about troops entering Babylon, since this is only speaking about mustering out
the troops. Instead of פִּתְחֵי ("gateway" or, better yet, "splendid gateway," in the sense
of a plural of amplification; see Joüon, *Gr* §§136f.), the Gk reads ἀνοίξατε (you
[pl.], open), so that it seems it read the imperative פִּתְחוּ (open). In this case, one mentally would have to supply the object חֶרֶב (sword) to the verb (פְּתַח חֶרֶב, "draw out the
sword"), as is read by Procksch; Kissane, I, 160; and R. Bach, 58, note 1; see Ezek.
21:33; Ps. 37:14. In spite of this, it is recommended that one stay with the transmitted text.

3a If this is supposed to be an entire line of a verse, v. 3 is too short; and צוה, in the
sense demanded here, "send for," is used elsewhere only with a simple accusative
object. For this reason, I. Eitan (*HUCA* 12 [1937] 60f.) suggests that there is a relationship between צוה in the present passage and Arabic *ṣawwata* or *ṣāta* = burst forth
with a loud sound. Others suggest that לְאַפִּי (to my wrathful [judgment]), now found
in v. 3b, should be placed immediately after צִוֵּיתִי (I myself have commanded), and that
the לְ (to, for) just before מְקֻדָּשַׁי (my consecrated ones) be dropped altogether: "I have
summoned my holy ones for my wrath (my wrathful judgment)." However, the fact
that מְקֻדָּשַׁי (my consecrated ones) is translated twice in the Gk (ἁγιάζω αὐτούς, "I will
make them holy," and ἡγιασμένοι εἰσί, "they will be made holy") would lead one to
suppose that the error was made at a still earlier time. This would mean that the object
is missing in the first colon and the predicate has been lost from the second.

3b Based on what it assumed was meant, the Gk translates לְאַפִּי as πληρῶσαι τὸν
θυμόν μου (to execute my wrath).

3c The Gk translates עַלִּיזֵי גַאֲוָתִי as χαίροντες ἅμα καὶ ὑβρίζοντες (at the very same
time rejoicing and acting insolently), on the basis of which Guthe translates this "my
rejoicing ones and proud ones." One could justify this translation since the suffix on
גַאֲוָתִי (my majesty) could be treated as governing the entire genitive construction, and
this translation is an exact parallel to מְקֻדָּשַׁי (my consecrated ones) and גִבּוֹרַי (my
valiant warriors). However, גַאֲוָה refers to the majesty of Yahweh himself.

4a Concerning קוֹל (here: listen; lit.: voice, sound), when used as an exclamation, see Joüon, *Gr* §125s.

4b The terms "uproar" and "roaring" are used in an attempt to reduplicate the rhyming sound of the Hebrew words הָמוֹן and שָׁאוֹן.

4c MT reads the construct state מַמְלְכוֹת (kingdoms of); in contrast, the Gk reads φωνὴ βασιλέων καὶ ἐθνῶν (sound of kings and nations) (in which case βασιλέων, "of kings," is an error that developed within the Greek text, which originally would have read βασιλείων, "of kingdoms"), which leads to the conclusion that the noun should be pointed as an absolute form. But both the Targ (מלכוון, kingdoms) and Syr (*mlkwt*, the kingdom) have it right as well, reading the absolute form.

5a It has been suggested that the singular participle בָּא (he who is coming) should be read here, but the plural form בָּאִים (lit.: those who are coming; here: they come), even though it functions grammatically without a referent, maintains for a moment longer the tension about the identity of the one who is approaching with such great might.

5b מִקְצֵה הַשָּׁמַיִם means "from the end of the heavens," i.e., at the point where heaven and earth seem to touch one another.

5c The ו is a so-called *waw concomitantiae* (*waw* of concomitant circumstances); see Ges-K §154, note 1b.

5d כְּלִי normally means "implement, tool" but also can be used as a designation for a "weapon"; see, e.g., 2 Sam. 1:27 כְּלֵי מִלְחָמָה (weapons of war). Here, however, when reference is made to the "war implement" of Yahweh, the host coming from a distance is meant.

5e Concerning זַעַם ([for the execution] of his maledicton), see *Isaiah 1–12*, p. 416, on 10:5, and see זְעוּם יהוה = "cursed by Yahweh" in Prov. 22:14 (NRSV: he with whom Yahweh is angry).

6a It is not advisable that one eliminate יהוה (Yahweh) (because of meter!); vv. 9 and 13 also speak of the Day of Yahweh, and this section uses terms that certainly are commonly used when the יוֹם יהוה (Day of Yahweh) is mentioned.

6b Concerning שֹׁד (devastator), see 16:4 and 22:4. There is no doubt that this is intended as a play on words with שַׁדַּי (Shaddai), which, according to this suggested relationship, would have been treated as a derivative of שָׁדַד, "devastate, lay waste, assault."

8a If it is part of the original text, וְנִבְהָלוּ (and they will stand aghast) must be taken with v. 7b, as is done by the Masoretes, but then that line is too heavy metrically. The same holds true if it is considered to be part of v. 8a. Moreover, one would then have to interpret צִיר in the sense of "messenger" (see the Gk: πρέσβεις, "elders"), but this is highly unlikely when used in conjunction with חֵבֶל (birth pains), just as G. R. Driver's suggestion is also unlikely, that one should derive the word from a postulated root *צרר (see Arabic *maṣārru*, "bowels"), with the meaning "inner parts" (*JSS* 13 [1968] 43). It is possible that וְנִבְהָלוּ (and they will stand aghast) is the remnant from a line of the verse that has now been lost, but it is more likely that it is a gloss to v. 7b.

8b Commentators have differing opinions about whether צִירִים וַחֲבָלִים (cramps and pains) should be taken as the subject or the object of the verb יֹאחֵזוּן (they will have): (subject: Hertzberg, Steinmann, Leslie, Fohrer, et al.; object: Hitzig, Dillmann, Feldmann, Duhm, Marti, Gray, Procksch, et al.). That the verb has no suffix, as one would have expected, speaks in favor of the second option: "they get cramps and pains." אֹחֵז can certainly be used in the sense of "get, come into"; see Job 18:20 and cf. Jer. 49:24.

8c According to the lexica, the *qal* of תָּמַה means "be astounded, dumbfounded," every other time it is used. It is possible that יִתְמָהוּ should be pointed in this present passage as a *hithpaʿel;* in any case, the meaning that is common for the other passages where the *hithpaʿel* is used, "facing one another dumbfounded," has to be the right one in this passage as well.

8d The double use of פָּנִים (face) in v. 8b has raised questions. The Gk translates: πρόσωπον αὐτῶν ὡς φλὸξ μεταβαλοῦσιν (their face, as a flame, undergoes a change) and therefore must have read a verb instead of פְּנֵי (face of). It is possible that one should simply alter פְּנֵי to read פָּנוּ, in which case one must attempt to translate it something like: "their face changes itself in flames." Since this emendation and translation are questionable, it is suggested that one stay with the transmitted text.

9a Concerning the suggestion that one should eliminate יהוה (Yahweh) from the text, at this point as well, see textual note 6a.

9b Once again, the *waw concomitantiae* is used; see above, textual note 5c.

9c Concerning the use of a simple ו (*waw*) to give expression to a temporal relationship, see Joüon, *Gr* §166i.

10a כִּי־כוֹכְבֵי (then the stars of) is removed by some commentators, who suggest that the colon is too long. But this phrase, which functions as the subject of יָהֵלּוּ (stream forth) in v. 10aβ, is absolutely necessary (besides this, one cannot object on metrical grounds if כִּי, "then," is not counted as a stressed syllable).

10b כְּסִיל (in the singular!) appears elsewhere in the OT (Amos 5:8; Job 9:9; 38:31) with the meaning "Orion." The plural, used together with כּוֹכְבֵי־הַשָּׁמַיִם (the stars of the heavens), is most unusual. The Gk reads καὶ πᾶς ὁ κόσμος τοῦ οὐρανοῦ (and the entire cosmos of the heavens). Ehrlich (*Randglossen* IV, ad loc.) suggests reading יְכַסֶּה עֲלֵיהֶם (he covers them over); however, this is a very radical alteration of the text. KBL suggests reading the plural as "Orion and its constellations," while others translate this "the constellations of Orion," but Orion itself is a constellation. Perhaps the plural of כְּסִיל is supposed to convey the generalized meaning "constellations." Since the sun and moon are mentioned in v. 10b, one would expect a simple mention of the stars in v. 10a. Therefore וּכְסִילֵיהֶם (and the Orions within it) is probably an ancient scholarly gloss.

10c Qᵃ inserts יָאִירוּ (they shine forth), which can be nothing other than an explanatory gloss to clarify יָהֵלּוּ (stream forth), when it is inserted immediately before אוֹרָם (their light).

11a Since עָוֺן (offensive behavior) has been furnished with a suffix in the second half of the line, it has been suggested that רָעָה (evil) should be altered to read רָעָתָהּ (its evil)—but this is not correct, since the רְשָׁעִים (transgressors) indeed should be faulted for their offensive behavior, but the same is not true for "the world." Of course, this does not mean that the world should not also play a role in acknowledging the guilt of the evildoers.

11b Using "haughtiness" and "high-mindedness" is at least an attempt to replicate the sound of the substantives גְּאוֹן and גַּאֲוָה, which are from the same verbal root.

12a פָּז does mean fine gold, contra KBL (chrysolithe [olivine]); see G. Gerleman on Song of Sol. 5:11 (BK XVIII [1965] 173); Gk: τὸ χρυσίον τὸ ἄπυρον (gold that has not been refined with fire).

12b The translation of אָדָם as "children of Adam" is used simply to avoid repeating "human beings" in English.

13a The use of the first person in אַרְגִּיז (I cause to tremble) is surprising, since Yahweh is referred to in the third person in v. 13b. The Gk reads θυμωθήσεται (it [heaven] will be made angry), which seems to suggest that it read the form as יִרְגְּזוּ (they [the heavens] will be agitated). It is possible that the first person form could have been inserted here in an effort to adjust the reading to flow smoothly after vv. 11f.

15a מצא refers to "meeting someone" by chance, as opposed to having the express purpose of "locating" someone; cf. Ugaritic *mẓa* "come across" (Aistleitner, *WB* no. 1649), and see E. Jenni, *THAT* I, 922f., for a discussion of the controversy surrounding the question of the etymology of the word.

15b In other passages, ספה in the *niphᶜal* means "be swept away." In the present passage, הנספה must refer to those from a group of people who are fleeing, to those who could be swept away = seized (Buhl: he who is caught). Ehrlich (*Randglossen* IV, ad loc.) suggests altering the text to read הנס, "the one who is fleeing" (so also *BHK³*), but this would furnish a poor parallel term for הנמצא (whomever anyone meets by chance) in the first colon.

16a–a It is possible that the first line of v. 16 is not preserved in its entirety, but it is also possible that ועלליהם (their children) and לעיניהם (their eyes) are each to be read with two stressed syllables.

16b It has been suggested that בתולתיהם (their virgins) should be read instead of בתיהם (their houses), which would seem to offer a better parallel for נשיהם (their wives). But it is certainly plausible that women would have been raped whenever houses were plundered; see this same sequence of terms in Zech. 14:2; cf. also Deut. 28:30.

16c *Qere* and Qᵃ read תשכבנה (they shall be lain with) instead of תשגלנה (they shall be violated). Their intention was that the offensive word שגל, "violate," should be avoided, even though שכב in this context conveys the same meaning. The same alteration is suggested by the Masoretes for Deut. 28:30; Jer. 3:2; Zech. 14:2; cf. *b. Megillah* 25a: "Passages written with unclean expressions are changed to more seemly readings"; in addition, see R. Gordis, *The Biblical Text in the Making* (1937) 30f. S. Feigin (*AJSL* 43 [1926/27] 44–49) should be consulted on the meaning of שגל, which he connects with Akkadian *šigirtu* (pl.: *šigrēti*) = harem wife. Cf. B. Landsberger (VTSup 16 [1967] 198–204), who explains the substantive on the basis of Akkadian *ša ekalli* (those of the palace), but distinguishes this from the verb form שגל.

17a It is possible that the line has been shortened here as well. And yet את־מדי (the Medes) receives particular emphasis if it is read as having two stressed syllables.

17b Qᵃ reads יחשוב (he pays [no] attention); in spite of this, it does read the third plural יחפצו (they take [no] pleasure), which means that there is a case of haplography of the ו (*waw*) on the end of the first verb.

18a The second colon seems to have been lost, but the first colon is also hardly in good shape: it sounds strange that bows "smash." But both E. J. Young and Erlandsson point out a parallel for this in the Tukulti-Ninurta Epic: *giškakku ᵈašur tiba dapna mušharmiṭa šalamda iddi* (W. G. Lambert, *AfO* 18 [1957/58] 40): "The rod of Assyria knocked down the aggressor, the assaulter, the destroyer, making dead bodies"; but *kakku* is a rod, just exactly what one normally uses when one smashes something. The Gk reads: τοξεύματα νεανίσκων συντρίψουσιν (bows of the young men will be shattered), and thus reads the construct form קשתת (bows of) (without the ו!, and), which has caused some commentators to point תרטשנה as a *puᶜal* instead of a *piᶜel*: "The bows of the young men will be smashed," which finds support in the Syr (*qeštātā daᶜlayme nettabrān*, "the bows of the young men will be broken"). Since the second colon is missing, it is not possible to be confident about any suggested solution. Concerning the pointing of תרטשנה (will be smashed), see Joüon, *Gr* §52c.

18b Some MSS of the Gk, Syr, Vulg presuppose the reading ועל (and . . . toward).

18c Concerning the irregular third feminine singular form of תָחוֹס instead of the regular form תָּחֹם (both: show no pity), see Joüon, *Gr* §80k.

19a בבל (Babylon) is considered a gloss by some exegetes (on account of meter!), sometimes even by those who concede that in fact it is Babylon which is being threatened with extermination.

19b The suggestion that כשׂדים (the Chaldeans) should also be eliminated on text-critical grounds, so that the oracle can be interpreted as a reference to Assyria (see H. Grimme, 2f.), is certainly not acceptable.

19c Concerning the way סדם (Sodom) and עומרה (Gomorrah) are written in Qᵃ, see *Isaiah 1–12*, p. 20, textual note 1:9b.

19d מהפכה (overthrow) is a verbal abstract noun and, as such, governs the accusative; see also Jer. 50:40; Amos 4:11.

20a The subject has to be Babylon.

20b In the *qal*, particularly when it refers to cities, ישׂב (BDB: sit, remain, dwell) can mean something roughly equivalent to "be inhabited"; see Jer. 17:25; Ezek. 26:20; Zech. 9:5; 12:6; Sir. 16:4. The same is true of שׁכן (BDB: settle down, abide, dwell); see Jer. 33:16; 46:26. The usage can be explained by the fact that the name of a city also can be used as a way to designate its inhabitants.

20c The Hebrew is ערבי (Arab), but this need not be taken in the technical sense to refer to the Arabs as a people; rather, it identifies the people according to their lifestyle.

20d יהל has been explained by Hitzig as a *hiphʿil* from נהל, meaning "lead [others] to get a drink," whereas others have explained it as a *piʿel* from אהל (= יְאַהֵל, "he will pitch a tent"); see KBL, Ges-K §68k. Nonetheless, it is more likely that it is a *qal;* see *BHS* and compare this with וַיֶּאֱהַל (and [he] moved his tent) in Gen. 13:12, 18.

20e The Gk reads ἀναπαύσονται (they will [not] rest themselves there), Targ ישׁרון (dwell), Vulg *requiescent* (they will rest), which means that all of them presume that the *qal* form ירבצו (they will lie down) was the proper textual reading. Qᵃ inserts a י after the medial ב, which ensures that the verb is read as a *hiphʿil*, certainly correct, since the main point is that land where a city once stood would not even be used as a pasture.

21a Some have objected to rendering ציים as "demons." Some translate it as "animals of the desert regions" (see Ges-B); others read "wild cats," on the basis of Arabic *ḍayûna*.

22a Manuscript B (Vaticanus) begins chap. 14 already at 13:22; the Vulg begins the next chapter at v. 22b.

22b According to KBL, איים should be translated "(uncanny) islanders, demons"; *HAL* offers the traditional translation "jackal."

22c In general ענה (here: will find shelter) has usually been linked to ענה IV, "sing, howl" (in contrast to ענה I, "answer"); cf. Arabic *ǧannā*, "sing" and rabbinic Hebrew עני, "song of lament." I. Eitan (61f.) (see textual note 3a), citing the Gk (κατοικήσουσι, "they will settle in"), suggests interpreting the present usage of ענה on the basis of Arabic *ǧaniya*, "spend some time (at a particular place)," which would provide a good parallel for שׁכן (will dwell) in the previous line. In spite of this, Budde may be correct when, on the basis of the substantive מָעוֹן (refuge, habitation) (which designates the dwelling places of jackals in similar curses in Jer. 9:10; 10:22; 49:33; 51:37), he suggests there was a root עון, "dwell" (*Der Segen Mose's Deut. 33* [1922] 16, on Deut. 33:28; see also F. M. Cross and D. N. Freedman, *JBL* 67 [1948] 210, note 87; and Zorell, *Lexicon*, on עון). In this passage, ענה (find shelter for themselves) is a third feminine singular perfect, which is not uncommon when used with a plural; see Joüon, *Gr* §150g.

22d Note that there is no *shewa* under the מ in בְּאַלְמְנֹתָיו (thus in Codex L). The masculine suffix is to be replaced by the feminine suffix; אַלְמְנֹת (here: fortress) is just a linguistic variant of the common term אַרְמְנֹת (citadels). It is not very likely that the word means "tower dwelling," as suggested by L. Köhler (*Kleine Lichter* [1945] 30ff., based on a derivation from the root רום, "be high, exalted"); it is much more likely that it is related to רמה, "cast" (cf. Akkadian *ramû*, "establish a residence"). The word means "palace"; the translation used above has been selected so that the English word "palace" can be used for translating הֵיכָל, which follows right after this.

14:2a Concerning the use of ל with the accusative, see Joüon, *Gr* §125k; its usage is distinctive of a later stage in the development of the language, being particularly common in Chronicles.

Form

In a way that is analogous to the superscriptions at the beginning of the messages directed against the nations that follow, the one at the beginning of the message concerning Babylon would simply have read מַשָּׂא בָּבֶל (verdict concerning Babylon). Thus the relative clause that expands this by adding the words "which Isaiah, the son of Amoz, saw" is purely redactional. The present form of the text is comparable to what is found in 1:1 and 2:1. One notes that Isaiah is introduced as if he had not been proclaiming any messages before this time. This can only be explained by presuming that chap. 13 stood, at one time, at the beginning of a separate collection of messages, one that would have included the material now found in chaps. 13–23.

As is also the case in 1:1 and 2:1, the prophet is introduced by using his name and his father's name. As in those chapters, the use of the verb חזה (saw) creates the impression that the message to be proclaimed here is a written description of what was actually a vision. But nothing in chap. 13 leads one, with certainty, to the conclusion that the person who composed this had seen a vision; and the poem that follows in 14:4a, introduced as a continuation of the message that precedes it, is called a mocking song (מָשָׁל). It is a stylistic trait of such superscriptions that a message of this type is called a vision and simply makes the claim that what is introduced in this way is to be considered a revelation from God. This furnishes further evidence for the tendency, observable also elsewhere, to attribute anonymous passages to well-known prophets.

However, in a way that differs from 1:1 and 2:1, the prophetic message itself is not entitled a חזון (vision) or דבר (message), but rather a מַשָּׂא (verdict, utterance, oracle). This term derives from the root נשא, "lift, carry." Thus in some passages it means "burden," and some also translate it as "burden" (or "burden message") in 13:1. In most cases, this meaning seems to correlate well with the fact that a catastrophe, some sort of destruction, punishment, or judgment from God is imminent when a prophetic proclamation carries the superscription מַשָּׂא (as is true right in the book of Isaiah). Yet the versions differ in the way they translate this term. The Gk uses the terms ῥῆμα (word), ὅρασις (vision), and ὅραμα (spectacle); Aquila always renders it ἄρμα (burden, load); Sym and Theod render it λῆμμα (what is received) (on this, see Ziegler, *Isaias*, 96f.); Vulg translates it *onus* (load, burden). Thus one must ask whether מַשָּׂא, when used as a title for prophetic messages, should be treated as a derivation of the root נשׂא (lift) or should rather be explained on the basis of a connection with the formula נשׂא קוֹל, "raise one's voice" (the verb standing by itself is also used in this sense; see Num. 14:1; Isa. 3:7; 42:2; Job 21:12), in which case it ought to be translated with some expression such as "utterance." נשׂא עליו את המשׂא הזה in 2 Kings 9:25 can hardly be translated in any other way than "he uttered this oracle against him." In Lam. 2:14 that which is מַשְׂאוֹת שׁוא (false and misleading), by means of which the (false) prophets have misled "the daughters of Zion," has to refer to promises of salvation; and apparently a play on words in Jer. 23:33ff. involves both meanings of the word, "utterance" and "burden." The use of מַשָּׂא (oracle) in super-scriptions in Nah. 1:1; Hab. 1:1; Zech. 9:1; 12:1; and Mal. 1:1 shows that, in later times, the word practically became synonymous with דבר יהוה (message from Yahweh) (see also 2 Chron. 24:27 and cf. the extensive explanation offered by K. H. Graf, *Der Prophet Jeremia* [1862] 315, in which he justifies why he translates this as "utterance"; in addition, see the literature citations at the beginning of this section).

The question must be raised about the extent of the material to include under the heading מַשָּׂא בבל (verdict concerning Babylon) and whether chap. 13 (and 14:3–23) is really directed against Babylon. The next superscription is not encountered until 14:24. In 13:2–22 the name Babylon occurs only in v. 19, but there is no justification for using textual arguments to question whether it belongs there. Verse 17, "Behold, I rouse up against them the Medes," has normally also been interpreted as referring to Babylon (in which case "the Medes" are understood usually to be a reference to the Persians), and some also suggest that "gates of the freely willing ones" (v. 2) makes reference to Babylon (popular etymology identified the Babylonians as those connected with *bâb-ili* = "gate of God"; on this, see R. Borger, *BHH* I, 177); however, the text, translation, and interpretation are very uncertain in this case.

The short inserted section 14:1–3 is obviously directed against Israel. According to 14:4a, however, the song in 14:4bff. is addressed to the king of Babylon and the addendum to this song mentions Babylon once again in 14:23. There is no doubt that the final redactor thought that 13:2—14:23, in its entirety, was to be treated as material governed by the superscription מַשָּׂא בבל (verdict concerning Babylon). In spite of this, it is easy to see that the prophecy that begins in 13:2ff. already reaches its conclusion in 13:22 and should be considered initially as a single unit by itself. It is also beyond doubt that the prophecy in 14:4b–22 (23) originally formed an individual unit as well; the bracketing in 14:3 is the result of redactional activity; the two sections are to be attributed to different authors. It has been common that 14:1–4a, not just 14:3, be treated as providing the link (and introduction) with 14:4bff. Yet it has long been noted that this short section is hardly a single homogeneous unit: vv. 1 and 2 are composed in third person style; vv. 3 and 4a address Israel using the second singular form. As will be shown below (see p. 33), 14:1f. is actually an addendum to 13:2–22, and the redactional point of transition, which introduces 14:4bff., does not begin until 14:3.

The question about the unity of the material must also be discussed concerning 13:2–22. After Duhm, and even more so after Marti had already performed radical surgery on the present form of the chapter, K. Budde (BZAW 33 [1918]) contended that there had been an extensive reworking of the text, with the result that a message directed originally against Babylon had now been recast as a description of an all-encompassing world judgment and final judgment. As the text was undergoing this expansion, the major alterations would have been in those passages that announced the Day of Yahweh. However, this thesis simply does not survive close scrutiny. Budde's alterations to the text are arbitrary and are based on the faulty notion that the concept of the יום־יהוה (Day of Yahweh) can be understood only within a universal-eschatological context and therefore would have been out of place if found in a message directed against Babylon. By contrast, Kissane is of the opinion that chap. 13 was addressed originally to Israel itself, speaking thus about punishment at the hand of the Assyrians, who would have been given the task of carrying out that punishment at that very time. The Babylonians and Chaldeans would have been referred to in v. 19 only after mention of the Assyrians had been suppressed, in other words, when the text was reinterpreted. Borrowing from Kissane's observations, Erlandsson seeks to interpret the main section of the poem as a prophecy against the Assyrians, in which case, however, vv. 19–22 would have to be taken as a unit by itself, which, as the text itself states explicitly, would have been directed against Babylon, the very Babylon that existed at the time of Isaiah and that experienced the darkest hour in its troubled history when it was destroyed by Sennacherib in 689 B.C. This would mean that the Babylon known from the early Persian period, the one that usually comes to mind when commentators speak of Babylon, the one that Cyrus had spared, would not have been the city addressed in this passage.

One must freely admit to these exegetes, and to those who come to the defense of their points of view, that one cannot treat the superscription "verdict concerning Babylon" as completely trustworthy and that it alone is not sufficient to settle the question about who is addressed in this announcement of coming disaster. It is worth noting that the name Babylon is first used in v. 19, yet that does not justify removing it from v. 1 because it is metrically superfluous, nor, following the same line of argumentation, does it justify suggesting that the Chaldeans were first mentioned when the text was reworked. But the most important reason for not acceding to those who have doubts about this text is provided by the inner unity demonstrated in this chapter. On the one hand, vv. 2–5 pose the question about what type of military power Yahweh would summon from a distant land to execute his wrathful judgment. The answer is provided in v. 17: it would be the Medes. On the other hand, vv. 7–16 pose a question for the reader who wishes to know which people or which city would be crushed by this unheard-of judgment from God. The answer is first provided in v. 19. It is true that it was the Persians, not the Medes, who took power away from ancient Babylon; indeed, they did not destroy that city of Babylon when they took over. The first difficulty can be eliminated by the observation that there are references to the Medes in Greece and Egypt (see H. Bengtson, *FWG* 5 [1965] 13), as well as in the OT, in passages where we would expect a reference to the Persians, based on the way we identify which nations are in control; the transfer of power from Medes to Persians in Iran was viewed more as a change of dynasty than that one world power was freeing itself from another. It is also possible that the Medes and Persians were confused simply because of a lack of precise knowledge about the history (see A. T. Olmstead, *History of the Persian Empire* [1948] 37). No matter how this might be explained (on this, see below, p. 18), there is no solid reason for maintaining that either the first (so Erlandsson) or the second (so Kissane) part of the poem speaks of Assyria instead of Babylon. It is even more unlikely that Kissane is correct when he suggests that vv. 2–7 and vv. 11–16 refer to Israel and/or its enemies. One cannot detect a significant break in the train of thought after either v. 7 or v. 11. No matter how complicated the development of the sections in the unit of material that forms this threat, it is just as certain that the thoughts in this poem form one single unit.

By contrast, 14:1f. forms a reflective piece, which someone from a later time appended to the threat when considering what it meant for Israel. (There is no doubt that the next section begins first with 14:3; see below, pp. 47f.) The author who composed chap. 13 did not have in mind just Israel and its humiliation by Babylon, but wrote with a view toward all the peoples of the world who had groaned under the troubles that this world power inflicted on them; his interest is directed toward the end of its oppressive world domination, not just toward the hope that Israel would be restored so that it could exist independently.

Based on its content, the chapter is a prophecy of disaster concerning a foreign people, just like so many others included in the complex of transmitted texts that have been attributed to the prophets. The threat is cast in the form of an announcement of the Day of Yahweh, which points to Yahweh as the harsh judge of the evil on the earth (concerning the concept of יום יהוה, "Day of Yahweh," see *Isaiah 1–12*, pp. 112f. and H. P. Müller, 72–85). In the OT the Day of Yahweh is mentioned most frequently in descriptions of the day of wrath that comes upon Israel's enemies and consequently also upon those who are enemies of its God: Jer. 46:2–12; Ezek. 30:1–8 (Egypt); Isaiah 34 (Edom; see also Obad. 15a). Disaster for its enemies implies that salvation will come for Israel, and on some occasions that correlation is stated in so many words. For that reason, the Day of Yahweh is a day for which one would yearn in times of oppression, a day of light (Amos 5:18f.). In the opinion of the "Writing Prophets," however, it is almost exclusively a day of judgment against Israel; see the passage just cited from Amos 5 and, in addition, Isa. 2:12–17; 22:5; Zeph. 1:2–18 (see also 2:3); 3:6–8; Ezekiel 7; Joel 2:1–11. That means that the concept of the Day of Yahweh has been reinterpreted by these prophets, whereas, in a passage like Isaiah 13, though it is relatively young in comparison with these others, it still seems to be used in the original sense. The Day of Yahweh is the day on which God appears so that he can settle accounts with Israel's enemies (see Judg. 5:4). Verses 2–5 portray the way in which Yahweh musters the troops. The warriors whom he calls up for service are his own champions, those whom he identifies as his dedicated ones (concerning מְקֻדָּשִׁים, consecrated ones, see קַדְּשׁ מִלְחָמָה, prepare war, in Jer. 6:4; 51:27; Joel 4:9; concerning the motif "summons to battle," see Bach, 62; and Müller, 74f.). In vv. 6f. a summons to raise a cry of lament (with reason provided) is attached to the description of the mustering of Yahweh's army, a day of confession commonly being called for when it was apparent that the entire community was in a distressed state (see H. W. Wolff, "Der Aufruf zur Volksklage," *ZAW* 76 [1964] 48ff. [= TBü 22, 392–401]). In this case as well, the poem remains within the framework of holy war ideology (see Zeph. 1:11). It is possible that the prophecy could come to an end with v. 16. Up to this point, however, the author has simply assembled various elements of a pattern that has been followed many times, along with traditions that have been used in oft-repeated formulations, leading to an impressive portrayal of a judgment from God. For him, however, that was no scholarly exercise or religious babbling. Beginning with v. 17, this description of the Day of Yahweh that seems so disconnected from historical events becomes quite real in a most surprising way.

Strophes and Meter: According to Duhm, the poem is to be divided into six strophes, each of which is made up of seven bicola, with each bicolon composed using a three-stress + two-stress pattern. However, one must force the text into this scheme of six strophes (Fohrer handles it this way also), and each of these lines can be analyzed as having this particular number of syllables only after one agrees to eliminate major sections of the text from vv. 7, 19, and 21. Since one hardly ever encounters strophes in the OT that are constructed on a strictly regular pattern, one should forgo a risky and extensive manipulation of the received text here as well. On the contrary, one should take note of the individual units of thought, as they are identified in the translation above.

It is also hardly possible to treat all the lines of text as if they have three-stress + two-stress cola. The first section, vv. 2f., begins with a rich sound in v. 2a with a three-stress bicolon (3 + 3), but then continues with five-stress cola (in v. 3a, one probably ought to presume that there has been textual damage). The second section, vv. 4f., is composed of five-stress cola. The third section, vv. 6–8, the summons to a cry of lament, is composed using heavy six-stress cola, assuming that וּנְבֹהֲלוּ (and they will stand aghast) at the beginning of v. 8 is to be eliminated. The fourth section, vv. 9f., uses three-stress + three-stress bicola (אָכְזָרִי, "it is gruesome," in v. 9a, belongs to the first colon; וַחֲרוֹן אַף, "glowing anger," is to be accented with only one stressed syllable). The fifth section, vv. 11f., has three-stress + three-stress bicola. The sixth section, vv. 13–16, begins with three-stress + three-stress bicola in vv. 13–15; v. 16 is very difficult, with v. 16a possibly being a five-stress colon (with a double stress on וְעֹלְלֵיהֶם, "their children," and on לְעֵינֵיהֶם, "before their eyes"), but v. 16b is a two-stress + two-stress bicolon. That did not happen simply by chance. The poem comes to an initial conclusion with the announcement about the worst things that could possibly happen, that the children would be crushed and the women would be raped; it would take more time to pronounce these words, which has the effect of making sure that the full impact of this disaster can be heard. The seventh section, vv. 17f., begins with a five-stress colon in v. 17; both of the words in אֶת־מָדַי (the Medes) receive a stress, which clearly points out the weighty nature of the subject, as one finally hears what has been long anticipated, the name of "the enemy." After this, the description returns to the three-stress + three-stress bicolon pattern (it would seem that the second colon, which belongs with v. 18a, must have been lost somehow). The eighth section, vv. 19–22, is composed of three-stress + three-stress bicola, with the exception of v. 19a, which is a seven-stress colon. It is also necessary that the proper emphasis is accorded to the mention of Babylon. In this case, that is accomplished through the use of the longest line possible in Hebrew metrics.

Thus chap. 13 furnishes us with a very artistically formed poem, which uses variety in the number of stresses in each line, in order to make the understanding of the poem easier by supplying helpful accents.

Setting

Almost without exception, recent scholarly activity has treated Isaiah 13 as post-Isaianic (concerning this, see the introductions to the OT and the commentaries). But voices are not completely silent when it comes to those who seek to treat the text as having originated with Isaiah. It is obvious that this would be hard to maintain simply because the world power at the time of Isaiah, the one that posed such a great threat and was so greatly feared, was hardly Babylon, but rather was Assyria. For this reason, Grimme promulgated the thesis, after he removed בָּבֶל (Babylon) and כַּשְׂדִּים (Chaldeans) in v. 19, that the poem was spoken against Assyria and came from "the days of agitation that followed immediately after Sargon's death, which opened the possibility for the peoples of the Near East that they might be able to be free from the Assyrian yoke in the near future." Reference already has been made to the similar theses offered by Kissane and Erlandsson (see above, p. 13). Of course, Erlandsson does acknowledge that, at the very least, vv. 19–22 are directed against Babylon, but he interprets that section as having been composed at the time when Isaiah sought to warn Judah against reliance on Babylon (compare this with the delegation sent to Hezekiah by Merodach-Baladan, Isaiah 39)—just as he had sought to divert efforts to make diplomatic contact with the Philistines, Ethiopians, and Egyptians. These "attempts to save the text for Isaiah" do not meet with any success. It is certainly correct that Isaiah came out in opposition to a coalition that would link Judah and Babylon, but this would not have provided him with sufficient grounds for announcing the final end of Babylon. Most importantly: in Isaiah's time, Babylon simply did not play the significant role that is attributed to the group that is addressed in Isaiah 13.

The thesis that vv. 2–18 ought to be understood as an announcement of judgment from Isaiah himself, but against Assyria, is just as unlikely. It is certainly true that Isaiah could have proclaimed that Assyria would stumble in its dealings with Judah, but he would have hardly predicted a collapse for this great world power that would be comparable to the catastrophe envisioned by the author as coming upon the world power described in chap. 13. In the discussion of the form of this material, it has been shown already that Isaiah does

16

use the form of speech that would be employed by someone speaking about the Day of Yahweh, but that he radically recasts it (see above, p. 14).

Erlandsson believes he has marshalled enough evidence to show that the vocabulary used in Isaiah 13 is Isaianic. One cannot deny that some passages have similarities to terminology used by Isaiah. To a certain extent, that can be explained by recognizing that Isaiah had some acquaintance with the words used in connection with the Day of Yahweh, and therefore with holy war terminology as well. This would lead one to presume that the author of Isaiah 13 was familiar with Isaiah's messages as they had been passed down. It may be that certain phrases from 5:26 were in mind and did play a role when 13:2–5 was formulated (compare שְׂאוּ־נֵס, "erect the battle field signal," with יִשָּׂא נֵס, "for he will raise up a signal"; גּוֹיִם נֶאֱסָפִים, "of nations which are gathered together," with לְעָם, "for a people"; מֵאֶרֶץ מֶרְחָק, "from a very distant land," with מֶרְחָק, "from afar"; and מִקְצֵה הַשָּׁמַיִם, "from the heaven's rim," with מִקְצֵה אָרֶץ, "from the ends of the earth"). Yet it must be observed that נֵס שְׂאוּ (erect the battlefield signal), to cite one example, appears in post-Isaianic passages (11:12 and 18:3) as well, which means that this cannot be used as an indicator proving that the term has to be linked to Isaiah. One ought to be convinced to proceed cautiously by the simple observation that, even though Isaiah 13 does refer to Yahweh Sebaoth (of Hosts), which Isaiah himself was fond of using, it does not use any of the other names for God that this prophet used; conversely, the chapter makes frequent use of שַׁדַּי (Shaddai), which is used throughout the book of Job as a way to refer to God (concerning the names that Isaiah uses for God, see H. Wildberger, "Gottesnamen und Gottesepitheta bei Jesaja," FS Shazar [1973] 699–728). In addition, there are also many striking points of comparison with Zephaniah: compare 13:9 with Zeph. 1:18 and 2:2, and Isa. 13:13 with Zeph. 3:8. Whether that argues in favor of this chapter being dependent on Zephaniah must remain in the realm of speculation, since the apparent relationship can be explained by Zephaniah also having been very familiar with Day of Yahweh terminology.

However, if one does not think it is possible that this chapter has come down to us from Isaiah, then the question is all the more urgent. What situation might provide the setting for Isaiah 13? As a rule, scholars have directed their attention to events connected with the demise of the Neo-Babylonian Empire. However, since Cyrus did not permit Babylon to be destroyed after he conquered the city (on this, see the so-called Cyrus Cylinder, *AOT* 368ff.; *ANET* 315f.), Erlandsson suggests, as has been explained above, that this reference would have to have been to Sennacherib's destruction of Babylon (see *ARAB* II, §§339–341). As a matter of principle, however, it is not permissible to attempt to date such predictions on the basis of whether they were fulfilled or even when they were not fulfilled. The catastrophe that befell Babylon at the hand of Sennacherib received not the slightest mention in the OT. One suspects that the silence is due to the fact that Israel felt itself neither threatened nor oppressed by Babylon. The latest date for the passage, now as before, remains the year 538. It is true that v. 17 speaks not of the

Persians but of the Medes being the great enemy of Babylon. One cannot, out of hand, reject the possibility that the Persians are meant anyway (see above, p. 14). But one must keep in mind that Ezekiel does speak about the Persians (27:10; 38:5), yet he never mentions the Medes. Thus the possibility is still worth mentioning that the author of Isaiah 13 may have written at a time before the Persian leader Cyrus seized control of the empire of the Medes and that the destruction of Babylon at the hand of the Medes may indeed have been anticipated. No doubt there were fears in Babylon that the rivalry with the Medes could result in a battle for world domination. Already previously, the very successful Nebuchadnezzar had seen to it that a massive, protective, Median wall was built north of Babylon, in order to protect the city from incursions from the Medes who lived to the north (see H. Schmökel, *HdO* II/3, 314), and it is possible that Nabonidus assisted in Cyrus's rebellion against Astyges (ibid., 318). At the very latest, when Cyaxares went up against Alyattes of Lydia at the Halys (585 B.C.) it would have become clear to the politically observant populations throughout the Near East that a very dynamic power had made its appearance on the stage of recorded history when the Medes arrived, one that could envelop Babylon in a life-or-death struggle. That this altercation was finally initiated not by the Medes but rather by their successors, the Persians, had more to do with the unexpected weakness demonstrated by the last king of the Medes, Astyges, and the majestic appearance of the Persian king Cyrus (on this, see also Scharff and Moortgat, *Ägypten und Vorderasien* [1950] 454f.). One cannot reject the possibility that, instead of just before 539, chap. 13 might have been formulated already at an earlier time and might be understood as a reaction to the conquest of Jerusalem by Nebuchadnezzar, which at the time of composition was not too far in the past. After the death of Nebuchadnezzar, Babylon plunged into a severe political crisis, which gave the Medes a chance to seize Elam from Babylon. With that, they stood, one might say, before the gates of Babylon.

Commentary
[13:2, 3] *The Task of the Consecrated Ones*
Yahweh speaks. In v. 2 he calls on messengers or heralds to go out among the peoples of the world in order to cause them to come near, to be his helpers in the battle that was close at hand. In v. 2 he makes the point that he himself is the one who has summoned the consecrated ones. When seeking to understand what is meant by the concept of the heralds, one should picture Yahweh being surrounded by servants, whom he could send forth to carry out his instructions (on this, see the discussion at 6:8, *Isaiah 1–12*, pp. 254f. and pp. 270f.; in addition, see Ps. 104:4; Zech. 1:11f.; 6:5-8). As can be seen in Judg. 4:6, Yahweh can also use those who function as prophets in order to deliver his notice of a call to arms.

At first, his warriors are referred to in v. 2a only as להם (to them). Some have suggested that this ought to be altered, perhaps to read לגוים (to the nations) (see Budde, 63; and above, textual note 2c). One ought not be put off by the fact that the Medes, or some other people, are not mentioned by name, since 5:26-29, which is very similar to this passage, does not identify the enemy either; cf. also 10:27b-32. It is necessary simply to point out that powers are at hand that have put themselves at Yahweh's disposal. Instead of mentioning them by name, they are identified in v. 3 with titles. First, they are Yahweh's מְקֻדָּשִׁים (consecrated ones); they direct Yahweh's war and therefore are his holy ones (see Josh. 3:5; Jer. 51:27f.; Joel 4:9), since, as his warriors, they have to undergo certain rites that involve abstaining from particular activities; cf. Deut. 23:10-15; 1 Sam. 21:5; 2 Sam. 11:11; and see F. Stolz, *Jahwehs und Israels Kriege*, ATANT 60 (1972) 25ff., 140. Second, they are his גִּבּוֹרִים (valiant warriors); on this see Ps. 103:20: the גִּבֹּרֵי כֹחַ עֹשֵׂי דְבָרוֹ (mighty ones who do his bidding), and Joel 4:9. Finally, they are the עַלִּיזֵי גַאֲוָתִי (the ones who shout for joy because of my majesty), concerning which one might consult Zeph. 3:11. It is likely that the most decisive title is that which was already mentioned in v. 2: they are the נְדִיבִים, the "freely willing ones," who make themselves available to Yahweh so that he can execute his wrathful judgment. Unfortunately, פִּתְחֵי נְדִיבִים is beset with textual difficulties and both the translation and meaning are somewhat uncertain. It was mentioned above (p. 12) that this might be an allusion to Babylon (gate of the nobles), but this is unlikely; at this point, where initially it merely speaks about summoning the troops, it can hardly already be referring to an entry into Babylon. And it makes no sense at this point, where there is such hesitation even to mention Babylon by name, that its gates would be identified as those of the nobles or princes. One must interpret נְדִיבִים in the sense in which it is used in Judg. 5:2, 9: these are the "freely willing ones," who make themselves available when Yahweh summons them to do his bidding. This interpretation causes problems with the meaning of פִּתְחֵי; it must refer to something like the entrance into the camp, the place where all the troops bivouac, so that one would have to imagine that those who were freely willing would have to go through some gateway, understanding that whoever passed through this entrance would be declaring himself ready to go into battle.

There are three ways in which Yahweh's messengers are to lead the "freely willing ones": by erecting a battle standard (on נֵס, see *Isaiah 1–12*, p. 239; cf. Jer. 51:27), by calling out with a loud voice, and by signaling with one's hand (on this, see the related expression הֵנִיף יָד, "swing the hand," in 10:32). The נֵס (battlefield signal), up on a bare hill, can be seen at a great distance; it is more likely that it points to the path upon which the troops are to forge ahead, so that they are able to reach Babylon, rather than the point where the troops of Yahweh are to assemble (5:26; 11:10; Jer. 51:27). צִוָּה (here: command) can be used as a technical term for raising an army; see *Isaiah 1–12*, on 10:6; cf. Judg. 4:6; Jer. 34:22; Isa. 45:12; 47:7; Lam. 1:17. Instead of this term, v. 4 uses the synonym פָּקַד *pi'el* (muster) (hapax legomenon, with Yahweh as the subject; in the *qal*, the same holds true for its use in Jer. 15:3; with a human subject, see Exod. 30:12; Num. 1:3; Josh. 8:10; and often elsewhere; see Akkadian *peqetti umâni*, "mustering," and, concerning this term, see E. A. Speiser, *BASOR* 149 [1958] 21ff.; J. Scharbert, *BZ* 4 [1960] 212; Jer. 51:27 speaks of a מפסר, i.e., conscription officer), whereas v. 3b uses the common verb קרא (summoned); on this term, see Joel 4:9. The גבורים (valiant warriors) are commissioned as the tools that will execute the divine wrath (לאפי, "to my wrathful [judgment]"). Just as, according to 10:5, the Assyrians are the "rod of anger," so in this case it is the Medes who are Yahweh's tool. They know no mercy (v. 18), but that does not preclude Yahweh from using them to serve him.

The holy war concepts employed here are radically "recast, in a strange way": in the original sense, the freely willing ones, who are at Yahweh's beck and call, would have to have been his own "holy ones" and "heroes," as is the case with Barak and his people in Judg. 4:6. Here, however, it is a foreign people, one that carries out the judgment not against Israel, as in 10:5, but rather against those who were Israel's oppressors. The prophetic understanding of history is clearly presumed, namely, that Yahweh also can make use of foreign peoples as he carries out his plans within the historical sphere, though the idea is modified. The author would find Deutero-Isaiah to be like-minded, since the latter viewed Cyrus as one who had a mandate from Yahweh to act for the benefit of his people.

[13:4f.] *Mustering the Troops*

According to Judg. 4:6, the prophetess Deborah summoned Barak to proceed up to the top of Mount Tabor with his ten thousand men from Naphtali and Zebulun. One would assemble for war at a place that offered safety and a good opportunity to observe the expected deployment of the enemy troops in the surrounding countryside. Thus v. 4 speaks of the "uproar on the mountains," which is precisely what is heard when those who are coming for battle stream in. It may be that this was meant as a specific reference to the mountains of Media, which are northeast of Babylon. (The capital city of the Medians was Ecbatana, present-day Hamadan.) But it is also possible that "assembling on the hills" is nothing more than a traditional motif, to which one ought to attach no further importance. In either case, one wonders whether the plurals, "kingdoms" and "nations," are nothing more than elements of the forms of speech found in such a prophecy or whether they should be pressed to see if further details might emerge. It is indeed true that the Median (as also the Persian) Empire, both inside and outside the borders of Iran, included a variety of ethnic groups. Each Persian king called himself a "king of kings" (just as the shah of Iran used to have the title *shah-in-shah*), and they proudly made a great effort to provide, on their inscriptions, a list of all the subject peoples who had been brought into submission and united during their reign (concerning Assyria, see *Isaiah 1–12*, pp. 419f.). It was common for warriors from widely divergent backgrounds to be serving together in the troops of ancient monarchs (on this, see also Isa. 17:12; 22:6; 29:5-8). In addition to the Medes, Jer. 51:27f. mentions the kingdoms of Ararat, Minni, and Ashkenaz, that is, Uraraturians, the Manneans (from south of Lake Urmia), and the Scythians. The double use of קול (here: listen) and the alliteration between המון (uproar) and שאון (roaring), with their gloomy sounding vowels, paints the picture of the muffled sounds of the machinery of war being moved into place (cf. the same vocables in 17:12; 29:5-8).

The hosts of peoples come from distant lands, some even from the most distant regions of the settled world. In 5:26 Isaiah spoke about the Assyrians as "a people from afar" (emended text) and about the "end of the earth." Formulas of this type are common; see Deut. 28:49 (Sargon speaks of the *Madaya rūqūti*, "distant Medes"; see C. G. Gadd, *Iraq* 16 [1954] 200; as does Sennacherib, Taylor Prism II, line 30; additional examples are in *AHW* 995). To be sure, *end of the heavens* in 13:5 means the same thing as *end of the earth*, but the way it is formulated is shaped by the notion that Yahweh was able to summon the heavenly hosts to fight in his battles. According to Judg. 5:20, the stars fight side-by-side with the hosts of Israel, and Josh. 5:13f. speaks of Yahweh's host (צבא) and about its commander, who carries the drawn sword in his hand; concerning this image, see Hab. 3:3-5 and Isa. 40:26 (on this text, see P. D. Miller, 105); 2 Kings 6:16f.; 7:6; Ps. 68:18. Ancient Israel thus reckoned with the possibility that cosmic or heavenly powers could intervene to assist Israel's warriors, or, more specifically yet: human and heavenly powers were able to work in consort when in battle (Miller, 100f.). Thus it is most fitting to presume that, according to v. 4b, Yahweh himself is the one who musters the troops who are going to war (whereas, according to Jer. 51:27, an officer for marshaling the troops was to be appointed).

In v. 5, this force is called the כלי־זעמו (implements [for the execution] of his malediction) (cf. לאפי, "to my wrathful [judgment]," in v. 3; and עברה, "frothing rage," חרון, "glowing," אף, "anger," in v. 9; for the meaning of זעם, "malediction," see *Isaiah 1–12*, p. 416). The plural of כלי oscillates between the meanings "tool" and "weapon." According to v. 5bβ, the battle force's task is לחבל כל־הארץ (to devastate the whole land). As happens often elsewhere, the question must be raised about whether ארץ should be translated as "land" or "earth." If someone believes the first part of the chapter has a direct relationship with events in Babylon, then this word has to be translated "land"; yet Babylon is a world power, hence the judgment takes on cosmic proportions, so that the meaning "the whole earth" is certainly also in the picture (see below, on v. 9b). In and of itself, the last judgment, which includes all humanity, is not visualized in these events. Concerning חבל (devastate), see *Isaiah 1–12*, p. 444, on 10:27a.

[13:6-8] *Call to Lament, with Reason*

הילילו (start singing a lament) is the most commonly used term for summoning people to a communal lament when circumstances have reached a critical stage (see Isa. 14:31; 23:1, 6, 14; Jer. 4:8; 25:34; 49:3; Ezek. 21:17; Joel 1:5, 11, 13; Zeph. 1:11; Zech. 11:2 [on this, see Wolff, *ZAW* 76 (1964) 55 = TBü 22, 398; BK XIV/2, 23f. (Engl: *Joel and Amos*, 21)]). The "howling" does not serve the purpose of mourning about misfortunes that have already taken place or putting one's own personal pain into words, but is used in the hope that one might still be able to ward off a disaster that still looms, hoping still to motivate the deity to be lenient by making a loud agonizing cry. One would show one was serious about the lament by fasting (Joel 1:14; 2:15; and often elsewhere). As Wolff has demonstrated, the "call to communal lament" is a genre all its own. Naturally, this is usually addressed to Israel. If, as here, it is directed toward a foreign people, then it would be intended in an ironic sense (compare the ironic song of lament for the dead in 14:4bff.). Obviously, there is virtually no prospect that gathering together to confess sins would be able to ward off the coming end; the purpose is plainly to dramatize the scene depicting the terribly harsh type of misfortune that was to break in against them.

This particular genre generally includes three formal elements: first, there is an introduction, using the imperative (in this case, it has been condensed as much as possible by use of the single word הֵילִילוּ, "start singing the lament"); then, those who are addressed are identified by the vocative; finally, introduced by כִּי (because), the reason for the lament is made clear. As is also the case from time to time elsewhere, the second structural element is missing here, not because the person being addressed in this situation is obvious but because the tension about exactly who will suffer in the coming disaster is not to be resolved until later.

The reason for the lament, however, is the threatening nearness of the Day of Yahweh, with all the terror which accompanies that event. In addition to the noun clause קָרֹב יוֹם יְהוָה (the Day of Yahweh is near), the perfect form of the verb is used in יוֹם יְהוָה בָּא (here: the Day of Yahweh comes) in v. 9 (both ways of formulating this thought occur together in Joel 2:1). It is a fixed element in this particular literary form for one to observe that the Day of Yahweh is near; cf. Ezek. 30:3; Joel 2:1; 4:14; Zeph. 1:7, 14. G. von Rad (*OTTheol* II, 119–125) suggests that this terminology belongs to expressions of hope connected with holy war. The passage in Zephaniah shows that this certainly does not appear first in the postexilic era and that it is not originally connected, in any way, with the expectation that an eschatological upheaval is close at hand.

Verse 6b puts into words exactly what is to be expected when the Day of Yahweh comes: "devastation approaches from the devastator." This same clause occurs in Joel 1:15; it may indeed be a familiar play on words, current in that day, in which the ancient name for God, שַׁדַּי (Shaddai), continued to be used because of its presumed association with שָׁדַד (devastate).

Concerning the original meaning of שַׁדַּי (אֵל) ([El] Shaddai), see F. Stolz, *Strukturen und Figuren im Kult von Jerusalem*, BZAW 118 (1970) 157ff.; M. Weippert, "Erwägungen zur Etymologie des Gottesnamens Šaddaj," ZDMG 111 (1961) 42–62 (but see ZDPV 82 [1966] 305, note 172); in addition, see L. R. Bailey, "Israelite *'ĒL ŠADDAY* and Amorite *BĒL ŠADĒ*," *JBL* 87 (1968) 434–438. The most insightful explanation relates this word to Akkadian *šadû*, "mountain" (Enlil is referred to by means of the term *šadû rabû*, "great mountain").

The Gk translates this present occurrence as θεός (God); Vulg as *Dominus* (lord) (on the Gk, see G. Bertram, "Die Wiedergabe von *schadad* und *schaddaj* im Griechischen," *WO* 2 [1954–1959] 502–513; idem, "ΙΚΑΝΟΣ in den griechischen

Übersetzungen des ATs als Wiedergabe von *schaddaj*," *ZAW* 70 [1958] 20–31). It may be that the presumed derivation of שַׁדַּי (Shaddai) from שדד (devastate) has influenced the Gk version in the book of Job to translate שַׁדַּי as παντοκράτωρ (almighty), in which case, of course, the meaning has undergone a change, so that it means "almighty" instead of "assaulter," whereas Aquila and Sym translate this with ἱκανός (sufficient), a rendering related to the rabbinic interpretation of שַׁדַּי, suggesting that it came from שֶׁ + דַּי = "the one who is sufficient of himself." But Gen. 49:25 states that El Shaddai blesses with בִּרְכֹת שָׁדַיִם וְרָחַם (blessings of the breasts and of the womb), which means that, in that passage, שַׁדַּי is related to שָׁדַיִם, "breasts" (see Stolz, 158f.; and M. A. Canney, *ExpTim* 34 [1922/23] 332). Apparently, Israel never was completely sure of the meaning attached to the name שַׁדַּי [Shaddai] and therefore felt free to suggest a variety of original meanings. The great importance attached to both παντοκράτωρ (almighty) and ἱκανός (all-sufficient) in the doctrinal teachings about God, in both Judaism and Christianity, cannot be dealt with in greater detail at this point.

[13:7] The announcement about the Day of Yahweh and the general reference to the devastation that would accompany that day could have brought the summons to sing a woeful lament to an end. However, introduced by עַל־כֵּן, "because of this," further details about the implications of this event are now sketched out—not simply the bare events, but rather the psychological shock that it would cause (see passages such as Jer. 4:19; Ezek. 21:12; Nah. 2:11). It is a recurrent theme in announcements of judgment that hands go limp (see Jer. 6:24; 50:43; Ezek. 7:17; 21:12; cf. Zeph. 3:16). רָפָה יָדִים often means simply "stop doing something" (Neh. 6:9; 2 Chron. 15:7), but, psychologically, it can also mean "lose one's courage" (2 Sam. 4:1). The parallel in v. 7b, "every human heart melts," means the same thing (see Josh. 2:11; 5:1; 7:5; Isa. 19:1; Ezek. 21:12; Nah. 2:11; Ps. 22:15).

[13:8] It would seem that an expander felt it necessary, in using נִבְהָלוּ (they will stand aghast) at the beginning of v. 8, to add specific details to this generally well-understood metaphor. One also finds widespread use of the imagery about the "travail" and "labor pains" that come to a woman who is about to give birth (יוֹלֵדָה): Ps. 48:6f.; Jer. 6:22-24 = 50:41-43; 22:23; 30:6; 49:24; Mic. 4:9 (see also Hos. 13:13; Isa. 21:3; 42:14; Mic. 5:2). This wide distribution shows that the idea has its roots in the oracles against the foreign nations and that it was possibly used initially to describe the expression of terror on the part of those attempting to storm the city of God (thus Ps. 48:6f.).

Concerning צִירִים (cramps) in its literal sense, one should see how it is used in 1 Sam. 4:19 (see also Dan. 10:16 and Isa. 21:3); the OT speaks about the חֲבָלִים (pains) of a woman who is about to give birth only in its transferred meaning (Jer. 13:21; 22:23; 49:24; Hos. 13:13).

תמה actually means "be astonished" but is used also in a secondary sense to mean "go numb," sometimes as a result of being astonished but other times, as in the present passage, because one is filled with terror (Ps. 48:6; see the *hithpaʿel* Hab. 1:5; Isa. 29:9).

Verse 8b has caused much trouble for commentators, since human beings are more likely to grow pale rather than get a flaming red face when they are terribly frightened. But it is certainly possible that growing pale when in terror and becoming red in the face when agitated are both reactions that can be described and used interchangeably and both can certainly serve as external indicators pointing to a deeply upsetting event. In addition, the face becoming bright red is also used as part of the typical vocabulary describing the Day of Yahweh in Nah. 2:11b (even though a different vocabulary is used there: פְּנֵי כֻלָּם קִבְּצוּ פָארוּר (all faces grow pale); however, note also וְלֵב נָמֵס (hearts faint) in v. 11a; Joel 2:6b is similar, using חיל (be in anguish, writhe) in v. 6a.

[13:9f.] *The Coming of the Day of Yahweh*

Verses 6-8 interrupted the train of thought in the poem; up to v. 5, nothing was mentioned beyond the assembling of the צְבָא מִלְחָמָה (host for the war), and one would have expected that this would have continued with a description about how this army was set into motion. Instead of that, vv. 9f. reach back into the mythological vocabulary connected with the Day of Yahweh, since one point is to be made very plainly: Babylon is not simply going out of existence because of a confrontation with other peoples; instead, the event unfolds within two different dimensions, in which case the vertical is finally the most crucial.

Concerning the "formula of presentation," הִנֵּה (behold), see *Isaiah 1–12*, p. 128. This formula signals that the actual beginning of the prediction is found in v. 9. One should interpret this use of הִנֵּה (behold) in conjunction with its use in v. 17, which announces the same events described here, though there the scene focuses on the horizontal plane. In the midst of the unfolding of world history, Yahweh brings his own work to completion.

One notes the use of the perfect בָּא (here: comes) (not a participle; see Ezek. 7:12 and W. Zimmerli, BK XIII/1, 167f. [Engl: *Ezekiel 1*, 202). The events that will take place in the future are presented as events that have already taken place. It is striking that both עֶבְרָה (frothing rage) and חֲרוֹן־אָף (glowing anger) are mentioned in parallel with יוֹם יהוה (the Day of Yahweh); one might say that the wrathful activity of Yahweh is personified (see *Isaiah 1–12*, pp. 232f.; on עברה, "frothing rage," see ibid., pp. 416f.). The phrase חֲרוֹן־אָף (glowing anger) is used quite frequently in the OT (although Isaiah himself never uses it) and is not really a pleonasm, since חרון means not "wrath" but rather "passion" (the word is used in the OT only in an anthropopathic sense, always with reference to God).

Grouping several terms for wrath together serves to underscore its intensity, balanced by the use of the adjective אַכְזָרִי (gruesome it is) to stress the massively destructive power of the Day of Yahweh. In other cases where similar circumstances are described, the "wildness" of the enemy is portrayed (see Jer. 6:23=50:42). The parallel phrase in the just-mentioned Jeremiah passage discloses what "wild" means, that לֹא יְרַחֵמוּ (they have no mercy). This same idea is used in v. 18 to characterize the Medes.

In v. 9b, we read לְשׁוּם הָאָרֶץ לְשַׁמָּה (to make the earth into a ghastly wasteland). One must ask, at this point as well, whether אֶרֶץ should be understood as a reference to the "earth" or the "land." On the one hand, according to vv. 20-22, Babylon itself, though certainly not the entire "earth," is to become a desert. On the other hand, one cannot help but notice that concepts that describe the Day of Yahweh are mixed together with phraseology that speaks of Yahweh's coming as judge of the whole earth, as found in the "songs of ascent to the throne." The judgment against Babylon, which the author announces at the outset, is now expanded and shaped so as to proclaim a far-reaching judgment over the whole earth. This viewpoint is not a new one. Isaiah himself had already announced a "day for Yahweh" against all human arrogance (2:12; see also 14:26). According to Zeph. 1:17, that day is to be all-inclusive, against all human beings; and, according to v. 18 (certainly a secondary passage), it will thus encompass the entire earth.

The same is true for Ezekiel (30:3), since the Day of Yahweh that will affect the Egyptians will, at the same time, be an עֵת גּוֹיִם (lit.: a time of nations), a time when accounts will be settled with all peoples (see also Zimmerli, BK XIII/1, 169 [Engl: *Ezekiel 1*, 203f.] on Ezek. 7:2); and the book of Obadiah states that the judgment on insignificant Edom will be expanded to become a day "against all the nations" (Obad. 15). The reference to a specific group apparently does not automatically exclude the possibility that this might have worldwide ramifications; a paucity of geographical terminology and the fluid meaning of אֶרֶץ (land, earth) make it easier to assume a widening of the circle of those who would be punished.

Concerning שַׁמָּה (ghastly wasteland), see *Isaiah 1–12*, p. 199. It is stereotypical of ancient Near Eastern treaties that include threats of curses to say that the land would become a wasteland (e.g., "Treaty Between Ashurnirari V of Assyria and Matiʾilu of Arpad," (i) and (v), *ANET* 532f.).

The coming of the Day of Yahweh is accompanied by cosmic phenomena: sun, moon, and stars all lose their customary brightness. This concept is not new either; cf. Amos 5:18, 20; 8:9f.; Jer. 4:23; Zeph 1:15; Ezek. 32:7; Joel 2:10; 3:4. "Darkness" had been included as a backdrop for a theophany of Yahweh since ancient times (Ps. 97:2; Deut. 4:11; cf. also Hab. 3:11, among other passages). However, none of these pre-apocalyptic passages is yet at the point of describing a cosmic catastrophe, the complete destruction of the entire world; basically, images that have been developed in past times are used once again in order to describe Babylon's demise as if it were an event that brought about the return of a chaotic situation. What happened once upon a time to Sodom and Gomorrah (v. 19) is now going to happen to Babylon, which does not mean that order and the basic functioning of the entire world would grind to a complete halt.

[13:11f.] *The End of the Wicked and the Proud*

These two verses are formulated as a direct address from Yahweh. Thus, already on a formal level, they are given special prominence and report the central message. In 10:3 Isaiah himself had spoken about the יוֹם פְּקֻדָּה, "the day of affliction" (though he does not use the verb פקד, "visit punishment upon"; see נחם, "revive my activity, ease oneself by taking vengeance," and נקם, "avenge oneself," in 1:24), and פקד, in the sense of "bring one to account for actions, requite" is common in announcements of disaster (Amos 3:2, 14; Hos. 4:9, 14; Isa. 10:12; Zeph. 1:8; in the last passage this term is connected with the Day of Yahweh; see also *Isaiah 1–12*, pp. 214f.). Corresponding to the universal character of the Day of Yahweh as announced here, the afflictions will be inflicted on the entire earth (תבל), but it is significant that each one's evil seeks out its own judgment, and specific reference is made to the רשעים (transgressors), used in parallel with "world." Concerning עון (offensive behavior), see *Isaiah 1–12*, p. 22. תבל (world) is not used by Isaiah himself (nor is it used in Deutero-Isaiah), but it is common in secondary additions to the book: 14:17, 21; 18:3; 24:4; 26:9, 18; 27:6; 34:1. It is a loanword from Akkadian (see H. Zimmern, *Akkadische Fremdwörter* [1915] 43, *tābālu;* root: אבל) and refers more specifically to the (dry) mainland. The word is originally rooted in the creation traditions: Pss. 19:5; 24:1; 90:2; 93:1; Prov. 8:26, 31, among other passages, and is selected regularly whenever mention is made of Yahweh's coming in judgment: Pss. 96:13; 97:4; 98:7, 9, among other passages, since the creator is the judge as well.

Whereas v. 11a had spoken about רעה (evil) and עון (offensive behavior) as the reason for the "avenging," now v. 11b offers a variation: it is the גאון (haughtiness) of the זדים (proud) and the גאוה (high-mindedness) of the עריצים (tyrants). The author seems to tie in directly with Isaiah, according to whom the Day of Yahweh comes on all who are haughty and lifted up (גאה and רם) (2:12), a day on which all pride (גבהות) of human beings will be brought low (2:11); see also גאוה (arrogance) and גדל (haughty disposition) in 9:8, and cf. 10:12. Isaiah's vocabulary also includes עריץ (tyrants) (see 29:5); however, this word is a favorite of the expander as well: 25:3, 4, 5; 29:20. It is more surprising to find the parallel זדים, "proud, impudent," a term that has its roots in the psalms and proverbs (see also Mal. 3:15, 19). In 10:5-15, where Isaiah describes the pride of the Assyrians, we are provided with specific details about what is meant by it, and Deutero-Isaiah (chap. 47) also furnishes details articulating the reasons for the judgment. By contrast, the author of this present announcement of judgment provides no sketch to fill in the specific details of the evil perpetrated by Babylon or about its pride. He is convinced of Babylon's guilt; it would be a complete waste of time to bother with explaining it further. However, the threats are terribly severe. The populace will be frightfully decimated (v. 12); human beings will be "rarer than fine gold." יקר, in and of itself, means "having value, to be expensive," but here, as makes good sense, it means "be rare." It is possible that the verb was chosen because of alliteration with אופיר (Ophir) (on this, see Alonso-Schökel, who speaks of a "juego fonético *ʾôqîr—ʾôpîr," Estudios de Poética Hebrea* [1963] 408; see also I. Eitan, *HUCA* 12 [1937] 61, who believes that there is a play on words, which has its roots in the meaning of the words, assuming that there is a causative form of יפר, which means "consider valuable." However, there is no evidence for a root with this meaning). Concerning פַז (fine gold), see G. Gerleman, BK XVIII, 173; אוֹפִיר (Ophir) apparently should be sought either somewhere in southwest Arabia (?) or on the east coast of Africa (Somalia?). "Gold from Ophir" is a proverbial expression (כתם אופיר, "gold of Ophir," is used also in Ps. 45:10; Job 28:16; זהב אופיר, "gold of Ophir," in 1 Chron. 29:4). Yet gold from Ophir is not simply a legendary sum, but is actually used when making purchases, as an ostracon from *tell qasîle* demonstrates (ש . . . . לביתחרנ . אפר . זהב: "Ophir gold to *bēt ḥōrōn*, thirty shekels"; see B. Maisler (B. Mazar) *JNES* 10 [1951] 266). It is possible that כתם (gold) is a Nubian word (KBL).

[13:13-16] *The Terror of the Day of Yahweh*

Whereas v. 7 touched only indirectly on the way the Day of Yahweh was to have a devastating effect, by portraying the consternation of those who would be affected directly, vv. 13-16 now speak of the event itself by using images that describe the reality of the event in drastic terms, but not as if one were writing up an official report. With harshest severity, the Day of Yahweh is defined as the "day of his glowing anger" (see Zeph. 1:15; 2:2, 3), the day on which Yahweh's frothing rage has free rein.

The first motif is that of the quaking of heaven and earth, a common expression when such portrayals of the Day of Yahweh are presented; see Isa. 34:4; Joel 3:3f.; Zech. 14:3f. From most ancient times, characterizations that present a theophany of the appearance of Yahweh include the earth quaking when he comes, and it is likely that the description of the Day of Yahweh has been adopted from that source; see J. Jeremias, *Theophanie*, WMANT 10 (1965) 99f.

The second motif speaks about how human beings will scatter and flee from one another, comparing this with the way a herd of gazelles disperses or the way sheep scatter when they have no shepherd (concerning נדח, "disperse," and קבץ, "gather," see *Isaiah 1–12*, pp. 493f.). The image does not fit well with v. 12, which seems to imply that there will be destruction, not simply a scattering. However, since the text has been transmitted with many fragmentary insertions included, one can hardly expect a smooth reading, constructed so that no seams show. Verse 14b interprets the flight as fleeing back toward one's ancestral home, in which case one would be moved to think about the residents of Babylon, since that population was composed of groups of people that had come from many different places (see Jer. 50:16; 51:44). Aeschylus speaks about the πάμμεικτος ὄχλος (thoroughly mixed population) of Babylon (*Persai* 53). Babylon was a city of merchants; one might also remember that this mixture included soldiers (see Jer. 46:16) and deportees. Those who remain behind, mainly the indigenous Babylonian population, seeking to keep a hold on their native land, would be apprehended and brought down; see Jer. 37:10 and 51:4. The depiction of the fury of the enemy in v. 16a, directed against the children as well, comes once again from the supply of typical phrases used in such portrayals; see Nah. 3:10; Hos. 10:14; 14:1; 2 Kings 8:12 (always speaking of עללים, "small children," who have no means of defending themselves and whose annihilation is completely senseless; see also Ps. 137:9). According to the present context, the suffix on עֹלְלֵיהֶם (their children) must refer back to "those who are pierced through," mentioned in v. 15, but then the suffix on עֵינֵיהֶם (their eyes) does not fit, since those already pierced through are fortunately spared from having to watch as that hideous destiny comes and their children are destroyed. But one would be led astray if one concluded (with Marti) that part of v. 16aβ has been lost: one should not expect a continuity of thought in this discourse.

The motif that describes the plundering of houses and the raping of wives brings this hideous description to a conclusion (both phrases have been used in Zech. 14:2 to furnish details about the destiny awaiting Jerusalem). שׁגל (violate, ravish) (see Deut. 28:30) is the term used to describe the completion of the act of sexual intercourse. Naturally, the author chose this "gutter" term because of the connotation it conveys, which is the reason why the Masoretes consciously substituted another term (see textual note 16c).

[13:17-18] *Rousing the Medes*

Finally, we discover who is to prepare the macabre end for Babylon (concerning the new beginning, with הִנֵּה, "behold," see above, p. 24). One must leave open the question about whether, as is generally presumed, מָדַי should be taken as a reference to the Persians or is actually about the Medes, especially in light of what has already been mentioned above (pp. 13f.). Thus the name, as it is in Hebrew, must simply be taken as such in English (Old Persian: *māda;* Akkadian: *maday;* Greek: Μῆδοι). Just as Jeremiah calls Nebuchadnezzar the "servant" of Yahweh (25:9; 27:6; 43:10) and Deutero-Isaiah identifies Cyrus as his shepherd (44:28) or even his anointed (45:1), summoning them to bring Yahweh's plans to fruition (44:27f.), and as Isaiah considers Assyria to be a tool of Yahweh in his hand, in the same way the Medes are called to carry out Yahweh's plan against Babylon. *They* are Yahweh's "freely willing ones" (vv. 2f.). And just as Yahweh had called Cyrus (45:3, 4), so he does the same with the Medes here (see קָרָא, "summoned," in v. 3). Verse 17 also uses the word הֵעִיר (rouse) in the same sense (see also Jer. 50:9; 51:1, 11; Joel 4:7; Isa. 45:13; Ezra 1:1-5; cf. also how הֵקִים, "raise up," is used in Amos 6:14; Hab. 1:6; Ezek. 34:23; Zech. 11:16). Verse 17b characterizes the Medes as follows: "They pay no attention to silver and take no pleasure in gold." According to the present context that does not mean that they did not know the value of silver and gold—since they certainly would not have completely ignored such booty when they were plundering—rather, it means that they would not be swayed to cease from carrying out their military objectives by offers of gold (gifts, tribute money). At various times, that tactic was indeed used, as one notes, for example, in Zeph. 1:18; and Herodotus (1.105) reports that it was even a successful ploy at times: Psammetichus persuaded the Scythians to retreat from the border of Egypt by offering them such gifts. Further, Xenophon reports that Cyrus says to the

28

Medes: οὔτε χρημάτων δεόμενοι σὺν ἐμοὶ ἐξήλθετε (and you shall not go out with me in order to gather money) (*Cyropaedia* 5.1.20).

Too many questions remain about the exact wording of the text of v. 18a to allow much to be said about it specifically. But the (shortened) verse apparently intends to say that the Medes are also the most courageous opponents, able to go into battle equipped with the best weapons.

The bow is the Median weapon par excellence (Herodotus, 7.61f.; Xenophon, *Cyropaedia* 2.1.7). The Medes do not even spare the fruit of the womb. This motif in no way simply reflects the fantasizing of the author. The OT repeatedly reports that pregnant women were "slit open" (2 Kings 8:12; 15:16; Amos 1:13; Hos. 14:1); this practice was common among those who waged war in the ancient Near East (Greece included; on this practice in general, see Wolff, BK XIV/2, 195 [Engl: *Joel and Amos*, 161]). From the outset, one should not even entertain the possibility that the enemy might recover from this destructive blow. One notes, however, that the term בנים (children) in v. 18b parallels פרי־בטן (here: fetus; lit.: fruit of the womb), which poses the question about whether "fruit of the womb" might not simply mean "descendants." However, since slashing the women open parallels smashing children in both Hos. 14:1 and 2 Kings 8:12, the alternate meaning is unlikely.

A subtle point is made in the way v. 18bβ is formulated: "Their eyes will show no pity." The expression is common (e.g., Ezek. 5:11; 7:4, 9; 8:18) and presumes that even a soldier who has his mind set on harsh actions would normally be moved to be gentle when looking into the face of a child.

[13:19-22] *Babylon's Destiny*

Whereas one might say that vv. 9-13 described rather abstractly the events that would accompany the Day of Yahweh and that vv. 17f. portrayed the excessive fury that the Medes brought into battle, vv. 19-22 now speak directly about what will happen to Babylon itself. It is said that it is the "most elegant of kingdoms, the pride-filled magnificence of the Chaldeans." Here this refers to the Babylon of the Neo-Babylonian-Chaldean kingdom, established by Nabopolassar and Nebuchadnezzar and brought to an end by the Persians, under the leadership of Cyrus, in 539 B.C. Just as is true for the authors of Jeremiah 50–51 and Deutero-Isaiah (chap. 47), the author of Isaiah 13 anticipates that there will be a complete destruction of the city. In this, he was to be disappointed. One might conclude that this prophecy took shape at a time when the political lineage of those kings who succeeded Cyrus had not yet appeared on the scene. This would certainly be the case if the Medes are the actual opponents of Babylon in Isaiah 13.

Deutero-Isaiah calls Babylon the mistress (גְּבֶרֶת) of kingdoms (47:5); v. 19 says that Babylon is the most elegant of kingdoms (צְבִי). According to Isa. 28:1, 4, there were other occasions when one could describe capital cities as "the elegance" of their land (see also Ezek. 25:9). Since Babylon had united many peoples under its scepter and had heaped up the treasures of many nations within its midst, it would be fitting to say that it is the most elegant of all the kingdoms. At the same time, however, Babylon is also said to be the "magnificence of the Chaldeans." Already in the eleventh century an Aramean sheik had conquered and temporarily controlled Babylon; and, in roughly 850 B.C., the Chaldeans, who were one of the Aramean groups, had established a settlement in the southern part of Mesopotamia, in what was once known as Sumer. From that base of operations, Chaldea's mighty expansion caught Babylon in the undertow. Mardukaplaiddin (Merodach-Baladan in the OT), who frequently occupied the attention of the Assyrians from his base in Babylon, was an Aramean from the country of Bīt-Yakīn; it was because of the efforts of the Chaldeans that Babylon could repeatedly stand in opposition to the Assyrians, until finally Nabuaplausur (Nabopolassar), having sealed a treaty with the Medes, finally dealt the deathblow to the Assyrians. Thus Babylon was indeed "the pride-filled magnificence of the Chaldeans"; it is because of them that this city ascended to the status of a world power and was able to shape a rich cultural heritage.

The author announces that Babylon will share the same destiny as befell Sodom and Gomorrah. Already at the time of Amos and Isaiah, the destruction of these two places had become a standard example when describing the sudden and total annihilation of cities (see *Isaiah 1–12*, p. 31; and Hillers, 74-76). When this event is described, it virtually always includes the use of the same phraseology, including the term מהפכה (overthrow), which is all the more surprising, since this term is not used in Genesis 18–19. One might conclude, on the basis of Zeph. 2:9, that the fixed formula was originally employed in the oracles against the foreign nations and was appropriated from that original setting for usage in announcements of disaster that were spoken against Israel (Amos 4:11; Deut. 29:22; see also Deut. 32:32).

The details about what it means for Babylon to experience the same destiny as did Sodom and Gomorrah are described in vv. 20-22. However, what lies ahead is not described by using the outline of the events from the story about Sodom. Instead, motifs are employed from the rich arsenal of maledictions that are used typically throughout the ancient Near East, especially in the maledictions included to ensure compliance with treaties; on this, see Fensham and Hillers. Some features of what could happen if someone rebelled are also found on *kudurru* stones and in the annals of kings. Thus, for example, Ashurbanipal describes the destruction of Elam as follows: "I completely silenced, in their common land, the hustle and bustle of human beings, the sounds cattle and sheep make as they move along, the jubilant shouts of celebrations. Instead, wild donkeys, gazelles, animals of the field, as many varieties as exist, I allowed to settle down as if they were in a green meadow (*ušarbiṣa!*)" (*Annalen,* Rm VI, 101ff.; Streck, VAB VII, 56ff., expanded on the basis of *AHW;* see the entry for *parganiš*). Such expressions are also found elsewhere in the OT oracles against the foreign nations, as well as in Deuteronomy 28 and Leviticus 26, in threats against Israel, which would come to pass if they did not live within the framework of the Yahweh covenant. Some of the individual motifs have also been recast in the prophetic announcements of disaster, which were uttered against Israel.

First of all, in v. 20, one confronts the motif of the annihilation of unspecified inhabitants, which would be so complete that no one would ever replace them. In the belief that an irrevocable curse hovered over a place that had been completely ruined, being set into motion once again if someone attempted to resettle there, people strenuously avoided such places. The curse against Jericho cost Hiel his firstborn son (1 Kings 16:34). Abimelech sowed salt on the destroyed city of Shechem so that it would be made forever uninhabitable (Judg. 9:45; on this, see F. C. Fensham, "Salt Curse in the OT and the Ancient Near East," *BA* 25 [1962] 48-50). Once again, it is Ashurbanipal who writes about Elam: "For a whole month (plus) 25 days I laid waste the districts of Elam. I spread salt (and) *siḫlû*-thorns over all of it" (*Annalen*, Rm VI, 77ff.; Streck, 57). The motif is used in the OT as well; cf. Isa. 34:10; Jer. 4:29; 50:40; 51:43; Zeph. 2:15. Isaiah himself uses this motif, directing it against the cities of Judah, in 6:11.

The author of Isaiah 13 takes it up another notch: no shepherd will ever even allow his flock to pasture there and no nomad will tent there, even though nomads traditionally will set up their tents temporarily in any place where the land is not completely desolate, since they cannot always be choosy when they are seeking places to camp.

The exegetes are undecided about whether one should treat ערבי as a reference to a sociological group (nomads or bedouin) or as the name of a particular group of people (Arabs). In Jer. 25:24 the מלכי־ערב (kings of Arabia) are mentioned only after other groups of people whom we would include among the Arab people; Ezek. 27:21 is similar; cf. Jer. 3:2. At the time of Nehemiah, Arabs are already settled in Palestine (2:19; 4:1; 6:1); and in the era when Chronicles was composed they are permanent neighbors of Israel, just as the Philistines are (2 Chron. 17:11; 21:16; 22:1; 26:7 *Qere*).

Instead of human beings, a mob of creatures that avoids being seen in the light inhabits these places that have been ruined. First of all, demons are mentioned, ציים (appearing also in 34:14, parallel to שעיר, goat demons).

This word should most likely be associated with ציה, "very dry region, area that has no water." The Arabs themselves, in a later era, considered the places that had been ruined to be inhabited by demons: "The genii are the successors, the ghostly shadows of extinct nations. They reside in places that once were inhabited but that are now deserted and without human inhabitant, in places that are thought to be hexed" (J. Wellhausen, *Reste arabischen Heidentums* [1897²] 150; see also E. Zbinden, *Die Djinn des Islam und der altorientalische Geisterglaube* [1953] passim; and O. Keel, *ZAW* 84 [1972] 432f.). Vergil mentions dancing satyrs (*Eclogue* 5.73). Ghosts especially like to dance at cemeteries and at places that have been utterly ruined, where human beings would be frightened by the spooky apparition; cf. Mengis, "Geistertanz," *Handwörterbuch des deutschen Aberglaubens* III (1930/31) 556f.; in addition, idem, "Geisterort," III, 541f.; "Spuk," VIII (1936/37) 344-348.

Unfortunately, the exact identification of the types of demons and the specific names for the types of animals remain mostly uncertain. According to Ges-Buhl, the hapax legomenon אח refers to a creature that howls, possibly an "owl, an eagle owl"; KBL refers to Aharoni, *Osiris* 5 (1938) 469: the "eagle owl," *Bubo bubo aharonii.*

On the basis of Arabic *waʿnatun,* יענה has been taken to mean "stony, rocky region, desert," and consequently the בת־היענה are the desert dwellers par excellence (Aharoni, ibid.), that is, the ostrich (which the Arabs call *ʾabu eṣ-ṣahārā,* "father of the desert"; see Ges-Buhl).

The meaning of אײם is also disputed. KBL suggests "uncanny islanders, demons," but others translate it as "jackals" or "wild dogs." We use wild dogs in our translation here so that we can save the term "jackal" to translate תן, which follows right after this (*Canis aureus*).

Thus, on the one hand, the author includes animals that live in deserted regions and, on the other hand, those that attract attention because of their sinister nature: one finds oneself in a region that anyone who has been well advised either would avoid in the first place or leave again as quickly as possible. One ought not be surprised that scholars are unclear about specific details as to whether this refers to demonic beings or animals; human beings in ancient times did not make a sharp delineation between animals and demons or apparitions.

In addition, one might note how the predicates have been selected with great care: where the shepherds do not want to allow their herds to camp down, there only the demons are encamped. The owls practically fill the fallen walls full. The "daughters of the desert" have a place to dwell in what formerly was a district of the city but has now become a desert, which fits their needs for a suitable place to live. It fits amazingly well, in this macabre scene, that it is specifically the (hairy) goat demons who have a place where they can dance their dances. Wild dogs, which are noted for their sinister howling, now find shelter in the palaces where sweet music had resounded once upon a time, and jackals would be found in the chambers in which one would have heard the echoes of the sounds of joyful pleasure at an earlier time. The author has succeeded in capturing the macabre atmosphere that would be found among the piles of ruins as he portrays this future scene.

Verse 22b could be an addition, occasioned by the historical fact that Babylon's demise was not as sudden as had been expected (thus Buhl). Because there were some who impatiently would have been asking questions, it must be underscored once again: its (Babylon's) hour is drawing near. Yet, as one can see from what happens to Isaiah himself (5:19) and to some of the other prophets (Hab. 2:3; Ezek. 7:7; and especially 12:21-28 or Isa. 60:22: "I am Yahweh; in its time I will accomplish it quickly"), the prophetic predictions always had to reckon with the problem of a "delay," which could result in some people questioning whether the message the prophets proclaimed was trustworthy (see Zimmerli, BK XIII/1, 276f. [Engl: *Ezekiel 1,* 280f.]). They must have been under increasing pressure when, as the author of Isaiah 13 indicates here, they specifically quoted the phrase in order to reiterate קָרֹב יוֹם יְהוה (the Day of Yahweh is close). But one must also consider the possibility that the author, being aware of the risky nature of the prediction that he was making, was attempting to anticipate in advance and answer a wide variety of probing questions from skeptics. Of course, in and of themselves, the parallel passages do not support the theory that this is simply a later insertion into the text.

When considering v. 22bα, one must remember that the way of thinking reflected in the OT maintains that everything has its time; see G. von Rad, *Wisdom in Israel* (1972) 138ff. For Babylon also, that is, for its demise, an appointed time has been fixed, which cannot be hurried but must be awaited patiently (on this, see *ūmūšu qerbū* in ARM X/6, line 8; cf. J. G. Heintz, 535f. However, this point takes away some of the effect of קָרוֹב (close). The same idea is actually conveyed in v. 22bβ, "their days will not be prolonged": if one presses for details, one cannot pin down when "their days" will come; faith has to hold onto the expectation that it will come at the appointed time; it has to come when Yahweh wills it so.

[14:1 + 2] *The Addendum*

It is within the realm of possibility that a redactor, who got hold of a copy of the poem about Babylon, thought some reference to Israel's destiny should have been included. The insertion of Isa. 14:1f. takes care of this. To him, it was obvious that the judgment against Babylon was the flip side and the necessary prelude to Yahweh's dealing in mercy with his people. By means of the introductory כִּי (for), he appends his thoughts to the poem, but apparently pays less attention to the whole chapter than he does to the last verse. The end of Babylon will come; that is a given. One should therefore not harbor any doubts that Israel's destiny would also take a turn for the better.

Form

Of course, questions have been raised about whether both verses have come from the same hand. Verse 1 is a closed unit, both in terms of form and thought; Israel is referred to in the third person. It is a wonderful thought that resident aliens would attach themselves to the people at the very time when their restoration was to come and would thus join with them, and it is evident that others also want to be part of its restoration. However, even a superficial reading shows that v. 2 continues the previous thought in a very awkward way. The suffix on לְקָחוּם (they will take them) cannot refer back to the גֵּרִים (resident aliens); instead, even though it is in the plural, it must refer back to Israel. Little is gained by adopting the frequently suggested alteration of עַמִּים (peoples) to עִמָּהּ (with them), since that change makes the referent of the suffix on מְקוֹמָם (their place) unclear. Nonetheless, if it were necessary, v. 2aα could be understood as a continuation of the thought expressed in v. 1: the change in fortunes is to be so radical that Israel, which up to the present moment had been trodden down, would now be led home in triumph by the peoples. However, v. 2aβ provides a change in the direction of what will unfold that is almost impossible to reconcile with the preceding. Israel, enslaved up to this very moment, will take these peoples who have accompanied them in a friendly manner and will subject them to an ongoing bondage as male and female servants. Nonetheless, G. Quell (see below, literature on 14:3-23) attempts to defend the unity of vv. 1-4a: there is "an individuality that comes through this inferior style and through the developing thought that appears incoherent" (136). No one will be able to deny that, and, for this reason, one can hardly have confidence in any conclusion one reaches. As frequently happens in the book of Isaiah, however, an addition is supplemented by still another addition (see passages such as those at the end of chap. 6 or the complex section 7:18-25), and the same thing has happened here as well.

Setting

There is no way to determine when the two verses were composed. It is possible that they were written before the exile came to an end, especially if Isa. 13:2-22 is to be dated in the early exilic period. Verse 1 sounds very much like Zechariah (see immediately below, commentary on v. 1). It is not explicitly stated that Israel's return home would originate in Babylon; mention of the "peoples," without any further identification, would suggest rather that this comes from a time when the Jews had already been scattered far and wide in the diaspora. The content reminds one of Isa. 11:11-16. If that is the case, like "Assyria" in Isa. 11:16, "Babylon" would have been used by the expander of chap. 13 as a code name for the current ruling world power. The second addition would have to have been formulated during a time when the Jews of the diaspora were undergoing times of severe oppression.

Commentary

[14:1] The author of the first addition considers Yahweh's mercy toward his people to be the most important driving force within world history. According to Quell (140 [see literature to Isa. 14:3-22]), he uses the "most powerful word that can be used to describe love in the Hebrew language," the word רחם, the denominative of רחם, "mother's womb," which describes the deeply emotional way a mother turns to her child, who is absolutely dependent on her care, a child who is completely unable, at the moment, to love her back in the way she loves (see 49:10; 54:8, 10). One can be certain that the ancient confession about Yahweh is in the background, that he is the אל רחום וחנון (a God merciful and gracious) (Exod. 34:6; Deut. 4:31; Joel 2:13; Jonah 4:2; Ps. 78:38, and often elsewhere in the Psalm literature). This particular terminology is selected because it is rooted in ancient "dogma"; the reference to such a deep love brings to mind the "utopia" dimension of Israel's faith, which holds firmly to the belief that God will remain faithful to his people, despite all evidence to the contrary.

For this reason, it is all the more astonishing that it continues as it does: "and will elect Israel once again." Israel's belief that it had been specially chosen had been confronted with a grave crisis when the Davidic kingdom fell apart and the temple was lost (on this, see H. Wildberger, "Die Neuinterpretation des Erwählungsglaubens Israels in der Krise der Exilszeit," FS W. Eichrodt [1970] 307–324). Evidence for that crisis is most obvious in the deuteronomistic history. The emphasis that the second Isaiah places on presenting clearly to Israel that it has been elected helps us to become aware of how difficult it was to overcome serious doubts about this statement. Should Israel not have been rejected? Some believed that, in reality, the end of Jerusalem and its temple were to be interpreted in this light (2 Kings 23:27). Along with Zechariah (2:16; see also 1:17), in opposition to this type of defeatism, the author of the present passage turns and announces that their election will be seen in a visible way once again. Of course, it would seem theologically impossible to suggest that election could have been rendered invalid and then would come on the scene once again. The one who attests to this hope in Jer. 33:23-26 also gives assurances that it is wasting time trying to answer those who babble on that Israel's two families have been rejected. As he continues, it becomes clear why the author of Isa. 14:1 had to say this as he did. For him, election is related intrinsically to possession of the land. To be elected again means to be brought in and settled in the land (the אדמה) once again. If Israel is not dwelling permanently in the land, then its election has apparently been rendered meaningless (cf. e.g., the connection between election and the gift of the land in Deut. 4:37f.).

When considering the expression וְהִנִּיחָם עַל־אַדְמָתם (and he will transplant them into their homeland), one might question whether וַהֲנִיחָם (cause to rest) (see Deut. 3:20) should be read instead, which would bring into the picture the concept that the land that had been given as an inheritance was a מנוחה (resting place) (see Deut. 12:9), though one does find הניח על־א׳ (leave on its own land) in Jer. 27:11 and Ezek. 37:14 as well.

If Israel is once again in its ancient homeland, then it will bloom and thrive, so that the גרים (resident aliens) who dwell in its midst will long to develop a closer relationship to Israel. Zechariah (2:15, also using the term נלוה, "join oneself to"; see also 8:20-23 and cf. Exod. 12:38) expresses this same hope. Zechariah does not mention the גרים (resident aliens) but speaks of the "many peoples"; yet he also thinks of those who live among the people of Israel in the land, stressing that it is, in fact, *Israel's* land. In conjunction with נלוה (join oneself to), which is rather vague, a clearer point is made with נספח (associate themselves with), which in the final analysis must have some connection with מִשְׁפָּחָה, "clan" (KBL, 1002). נספח does not have to mean "become part of one common clan," in the sense of an intermarriage; as the sense in Zech. 8:23 indicates, it refers instead to being brought into the social structure of Israel, which would also result in being included in the Yahweh community (see how the *hithpaʿel* is used in 1 Sam. 26:19). The Gk translated this גרים as γιῶραι, "the sojourners," instead of the more commonly used προσήλυτοι (proselytes), evidence that some were urging others to agree with their aversion to the assimilation of foreigners. But it is still a long way from this to Rabbi Ḥelbo, who used 14:1 as evidence for his opinion that

accepting proselytes was as bad as having leprosy, since he related the word
מְצֹרָע (leprosy) to the root סָפַח (attach oneself to) (*b. Qiddušin* 70b).

[14:2] The expander who adds v. 2 was also of the opinion that there should
be no way for "the resident aliens" to be attached to the Yahwistic community. The "peoples," which means in this passage the nations in the midst of
whom Israel lived in the diaspora, would bring Israel back to its own territory. It may be that the author had Isa. 49:22 in mind (see also 66:20): Israel
experiences the honor of having an escort as it is on its way home; in fact,
Isa. 49:23 mentions kings and sovereigns who would take care of them with
the same conscientiousness as someone would when helping a child to reach
maturity. However, the train of thought takes an unexpected turn: Israel will
take "nations" along so that they will be available to serve them as slaves
after they arrive back in their homeland. Psychologically, it is not beyond the
realm of possibility that a certain element of a population that has been
enslaved and has now achieved its freedom would be sorely tempted to give
free rein to its own long-suppressed desires to be in control. From a theological perspective, it is more than just a possibility. But one must know more
about the exact situation in which these words were originally composed if
one is to render a legitimate assessment. One must ponder this thought:
"Like many others, this prophecy is only there for a time when there was an
acute emergency" (Quell, 145 [see literature to 14:3-23]). But this also
means that such a prediction should under no circumstances be adopted as a
general guiding principle for personal conduct.

"They will capture those who had earlier placed them in confinement,
and they will be rulers over those who had been their taskmasters." The
author wants to show that righteousness will be set in motion when the complete turn of events, which is expected from God, is finally set in motion.

Purpose and Thrust

Poetically, this is a magnificent and impressive portrayal, fashioned by some
anonymous individual in the exilic era to describe the downfall of the world
power, Babylon. But it is significant that the exegesis of this passage has
raised questions about whether it is Babylon or rather some other world
power—or possibly "world power" in the generic sense, hiding behind various names and yet able to manifest itself—that was in the mind of the author.
Except for the single mention of Babylon and the Chaldeans in v. 19, the
poem contains no reference that would force one to interpret this section
specifically as a prophecy about the great city on the Euphrates. For the
author, in fact, it was not so important that Babylon, in its concrete historical
form, was going to fall but rather that the fall of Babylon was a typical example of the downfall of all tyrannical conglomerates that rule by raw power.
For this reason, it is not completely off the mark when, in later times—as is
seen already in the work of the expanders who added 14:1 + 2—"Babylon"
was used simply in a symbolic sense. In this section of material, one would
be able to hear the message announcing the end of all the dominions that

either opposed God or were not even human powers. Countless generations
have held onto the hope, each in its own time, when confronting such powers that were wickedly oppressive, that each one's "Babylon" would someday collapse.

Babylon is to be shattered by the Medes, a newly established power
that was on the rise. At the same time, "Babylon's time has drawn very
close" means that the time for this other people to gain power has arrived as
well. We have established above that it is virtually impossible to determine
whether the reader should treat "Medes" as referring to the Persians, which
is the most common solution, or should rather take this to be a historical reference to the Medes proper. This uncertainty is not significant when one is
attempting to assess the theological value of this text. What is happening at
that moment on the center stage of history is not so important; rather, it is
significant that this event has signaled that the Day of Yahweh is arriving on
the scene. As the Lord of history, he can use his sovereignty over all earthly
powers, just as one would move the pieces on a chess board, in order to
accomplish his own objectives. The Medes are his mighty warriors; indeed,
they are his holy ones and thus they are identified by the ancient name of
honor that was applied to those who fought for Yahweh, the "freely willing
ones." No matter what their own personal objectives are, they are the "implements (for the execution) of his malediction" (v. 5). As the hidden yet the
only real authoritative Lord of history, Yahweh carries out his judgments as
world powers battle one another, effecting his own righteousness even as the
power-hungry and ambitious rulers further their own agendas.

Although the theme "establishment of divine rule" is not explicitly
mentioned, it is implicitly still the most important point, since a lasting
impression is left by the detailed description about the wrath of Yahweh and
the horrible nature of the judgment that would accompany it, meaning that
any act of mercy would be out of the question. One cannot escape the conclusion that the theological description of Yahweh, which forces one to
examine the wider implications of a central theme in the OT, states that God
himself is creator of the heavens and the earth and thus does not relate to the
foreign nations solely as a "destroyer." One must begin by reflecting on three
points that are made here if one does not wish to do a disservice to the
author. First, this prediction must have come from a time when the peoples
of the inhabited world were suffering untold agony under the tyranny and
economic exploitation of Babylon. Second, it is surprising that Israel is never
mentioned in the entire long poem, quite different from the way the topic is
handled later by the author of Jeremiah 50–51, who used Isaiah 13, in addition to many other passages, as a "quarry" (see K. Budde, *Jahrbücher für
Deutsche Theologie* 23 [1878] 441; and Rudolph, HAT, ad loc.). This means
that the text does not deal with "avenging" all that had been done specifically
to Israel, but rather is a reaction to this people's widespread evil activity
(רעה) and wrongdoing (עון). At a minimum, there are allusions to their
wicked behavior in v. 11b: "haughtiness of the proud" and "high-mindedness
of the tyrants." The "sinners" were to be annihilated from the face of the

earth (v. 9). Third, this text asserts that judgment comes because this world power had set itself up in the place that could be occupied only by the one who is lord over all the peoples; they availed themselves of power over other human beings that could not be reconciled with God's own rule as king over all. This means that the Day of Yahweh would have to come over the whole earth, since the honor and holiness of God had been damaged in a way that could not be allowed.

The Day of Yahweh, the main event that this text predicts, is viewed in wholly negative terms. It was to bring dreadful disaster for Babylon and its entire land (vv. 19-22), finally extending so as to affect the whole world (תבל). Chapter 13 furnishes us with a meaningful advance in Israel's trek on the way toward an apocalyptic understanding of history—to be sure, not as much in what it actually says as in the way it was interpreted in the history of both Judaism and Christianity. Taken by itself, and understood from within its historical context, it mentions neither a world judgment nor a final judgment. The original context, out of which the Day of Yahweh developed, had nothing to do with what would happen eschatologically. Besides this, the reader learns nothing about what was to happen "afterward"; the author feels bound to stay within the framework of the disaster that he envisions would break out very soon. He knows as little about a new era breaking into history, one that would have different ground rules from the one in which he was living, as he does about the breaking in of a radically different, completely new world—at least he says nothing about such a possibility.

The author makes no mention about how Israel would experience this catastrophe and how it would be able to survive it. Unlike Deutero-Isaiah, we hear virtually nothing about how the end of Babylon would usher in the glorious return home for the people of God. Verse 14 merely mentions that there will be flight, "each one toward his own people," "each one into his own land." It is possible that the author was also, and maybe primarily, thinking about the Jewish exiles (those in the *Gola*) who were sitting in Babylon. Jer. 51:6 calls to them: "Flee from the midst of Babylon, save your lives, each of you! Do not perish because of her guilt." That passage also mentions no triumphal rehabilitation for Israel, but at least the possibility that one can save one's life, though a person would have to abandon everything for which one had worked so hard.

It makes sense that such a piece could not be handed down without someone appending further observations. The expander who added 14:1 had good intentions when seeking to draw out the positive implications for Israel. There is not a single word about satisfaction, to say nothing of sheer joy, in the misfortune of others as this tyrannical power is destroyed, no fanaticism that could tend in the direction of letting someone think that Israel would inherit control over the world; there is only the simple assurance that Israel can have hope for the future, since it can count on divine mercy. Based on what the rest of the passage had to say, that was enough. The ancient promise which declared that Israel could live in the land (אדמה) was going to be put in force once again. A second aspect is included as well: those who were living in the land with them—those whom no one would wish would leave and certainly no one would suggest the possibility that they should be "forcefully removed"—they would no longer continue to be treated coldly, at a distance, but would join in with the returnees because they would be convinced that it was an incomparable advantage to be able to be treated as if one were a natural citizen, born into the house of Jacob. At the same time, this assurance would include an implicit warning to Israel that it ought not attempt to shut out the "foreigners" but should include them within their fellowship.

That the expander who included v. 2 was not pleased with this picture of the future, but sought instead to correct it, shows that there is both great danger and a loss of true significance when the ramifications of one's faith and the way that forges a new relationship to the "other" come to be recast ideologically, in the context of a suspicious, elitist demeanor.

The Downfall of the World Ruler
and the End of Babylon

Literature

W. H. Cobb, "The Ode in Isaiah xiv," *JBL* 15 (1896) 18–35. P. Lohmann, "Die anonymen Prophetien gegen Babel aus der Zeit des Exils," diss., Rostock (1910). F. A. Vanderburgh, "The Ode on the King of Babylon, Isaiah XIV, 4b-21," *AJSL* 29 (1912/13) 111–125. H. Jahnow, *Das hebräische Leichenlied*, BZAW 36 (1923) 239–253. A. Dupont-Sommer, "Note exégétique sur Isaïe 14:16-21," *RHR* 134 (1948) 72–80. G. Quell, "Jesaja 14:1-13," FS F. Baumgärtel, Erlanger Forschungen A 10 (1959) 131–157. S. Erlandsson (see literature to Isaiah 13–23). O. Kaiser (see literature to Isaiah 13–23).

Concerning the text: P. Lohmann, "Jes 14:19," *ZAW* 33 (1913) 253–256. J. T. Hudson, "Isaiah xiv. 19," *ExpTim* 40 (1928/29) 93. L. Köhler, "Isaiah xiv. 19," *ExpTim* 40 (1928/29) 236f.; and ibid., 41 (1929/30) 142. H. M. Orlinsky, "Madhebah in Isaiah XIV 4," *VT* 7 (1957) 202f. J. Carmignac, "Isaïe 14:11," FS H. Bardtke (1968) 39f.

Concerning vv. 12-15: N. A. Koenig, "Lucifer," *ExpTim* 18 (1906/1907) 479. S. A. Hirsch, "Isaiah 14:12," *JQR* NS 11 (1920/21) 197–199. S. Schiffer, "Un chant de triomphe méconnu sur la mort de Sanchérib," *REJ* 76 (1923) 176–182. S. Mowinckel, *Die Sternnamen im AT, NTT* 29 (1928). S. H. Langdon, "The Star Hêlēl, Jupiter?" *ExpTim* 42 (1930/31) 172–174. B. Alfrink, "Der Versammlungsberg im äussersten Norden (Is. 14)," *Bib* 14 (1933) 41–67. K. L. Schmidt, "Lucifer als gefallene Engelmacht," *TZ* 7 (1951) 161–179. J. de Savignac, "Note sur le sens du terme *ṣaphôn* dans quelques passages de la Bible," *VT* 3 (1953) 95f. P. Grelot, "Isaïe XIV 12-15 et son arrière-plan mythologique," *RHR* 149 (1956) 18-48. Idem, "Sur la vocalisation de הילל (Is. XIV 12)," *VT* 6 (1956) 303f. M. Dahood, "Punic *hkkbm ʾl* and Isa 14:13," *Or* NS 34 (1965) 170–172. A. Ohler, *Mythologische Elemente im Alten Testament* (1969) 175–177. U. Oldenburg, "Above the Stars of El: El in Ancient Arabic Religion," *ZAW* 82 (1970) 187–208. F. Stolz, *Strukturen und Figuren im Kult von Jerusalem*, BZAW 118 (1970). J. W. McKay, "Helel and the Dawn-Goddess," *VT* 20 (1970) 451–464. R. J. Clifford, *The Cosmic Mountain in Canaan and the Old Testament*, HSM 4 (1972) 160–168. F. Stolz, "Die Bäume des Gottesgartens auf dem Libanon," *ZAW* 84 (1972) 141–156. P. C. Craigie, "Helel, Athtar and Phaethon (Jes 14:12-15)," *ZAW* 85 (1973) 223–225 (this could not be consulted before finishing this section).

[Literature update through 1979: H. L. Ginsberg, "Reflexes of Sargon in Isaiah after 715 B.C.E.," *JAOS* 88 (1968) 47–53. C. E. L'Heureux, "El and the Rephaim: New Light from Ugaritica V," *HTR* 65/4 (1972) 599. H. Ferenczy, "Scheol. Untersuchung des Begriffs," diss., Vienna (1975).

Concerning the text: J. H. Tigay, "Toward the Recovery of *Poḥar, 'Company,' in Biblical Hebrew," *JBL* 92 (1973) 517–522 (on 14:13). C. E. L'Heureux, "The Ugaritic and Biblical Rephaim," *HTR* 67 (1974) 265–274. P. H. Vaughan, *The Meaning of* בָּמָה *in the Old Testament: A Study of Etymological, Textual and Archaeological Evidence*, SOTSMS 3 (1974) (on בָּמָה in 14:14). J. C. de Moor, "Rāpiʾūma—Rephaim," *ZAW* 88 (1976) 323–345.

Concerning vv. 12-15: R. L. Alden, "Lucifer, Who or What? (Is 14:12; cfr. Lk 10:18)," *BETS* 11 (1968) 35–39. M. Granot, "'For Dust Thou Art'" (Hebrew with English summary), *BetM* 50/3 (1972) 310–319. A. van den Branden, "Il Dio Eljôn," *BeO* 16 (1974) 65–68. O. Loretz, "Der kanaanäische Mythos vom Sturz des Šaḥar-Sohnes Helel (Jes 14:12-15)," *UF* 8 (1976) 133–136.]

Text

14:3 [On that day, on which Yahweh has provided you rest from your hardship and from your privation and from the hard forced labor, which had been laid on you,[a] 4 then you will begin to sing and you will say:]

I Ah, how the despot came to an end,
    the 'tyrant'[a] came to an end.
5 Yahweh has smashed[a] the rod of the evildoer,
    the staff of the one who held power,
6 who struck down peoples in seething rage,[a]
    [b]uninterrupted blows,[b]
trampled down[c] nations in anger,
    following[d] them relentlessly.[e]
7 Now the whole earth reposes and rests,
    each person breaks forth in ringing shouts of jubilation.[a]
8 Even the juniper trees[a] are themselves rejoicing over you,
    the cedars[b] of Lebanon:
"Since you laid yourself down to sleep,
    the one who fells[c] the trees does not climb up to us any longer."

     * * * *

II 9 The realm of death[a] down below was in an uproar
    [b]because of the encounter with you,
that you showed up,[b]
    on your account the spirits of the dead roused up[c]
    all the rulers[d] of the earth;
there raised up from their thrones
    all the kings of the nations.
10 [a]. . . they all commence
    and speak to you:
"Even you have become weak[b] just like us,
    are now just (exactly) the same as we are!
11 Your splendor has plunged down into the realm of death,
    the (noisy) sound of your harps.[a]
Maggots are[b] 'the couch' beneath you
    and worms are your blanket."[c]

     * * * *

III 12 Ah, how you have fallen from heaven,
    you radiating star,[a] son of the first morning light!
'Ah,'[b] as if smashed to bits upon the earth,
    the one who conquers[c] 'all' peoples!
13 You had obviously thought to yourself:

41

"I will ascend to heaven,
higher than God's[a] stars;
  I will set up my throne,
  I will set myself up atop the mount of the meeting place[b] (of the
    gods)
  in the most distant region of the north.
14 I rise up on the heights of the clouds,[a]
  install myself on the same level with the Most High."
15 Yet you are hurled down into the realm of death,
  into the grave of the uttermost distant region.

      *   *   *   *

IV 16 Whoever catches sight of you, peers at you intently,[a]
  checks you out in a most careful way[b]:
"Is this the man who stirred up the world,
  caused kingdoms to tremble?"
17 He turned the earth into desert,
  and he demolished 'their'[a] cities.
As for its prisoners, he did not [b]allow access to
'the house,   18   which he keeps closed to them.'

      *   *   *   *

V   All together, the kings of the peoples[a]
  rest in honor, [b][each in his own house];[b]
19a yet you are cast out, 'have no grave,'[a]
  just like a stomach-turning 'miscarriage,'[b]
covered with those who have been slain, with those pierced through
    by the sword,
  [c]...as a trampled carcass.
19b[c] With those who travel down to[d] the stones of the pit,[e]
20 there is no pact making for you [in the grave[a]],
since you have completely wrecked your land,
  murdered your people.
No longer, in all eternity, will mention be made[b]
  of this wicked family line.[c]

      *   *   *   *

21 [Prepare for his sons the slaughtering bench
  because of the guilt of their fathers![a]
They shall not ascend to an important position and conquer the
  earth
  and fill the wide world full with cities.[b]]

      *   *   *   *

22 [Thus I will raise myself up against them; that is the utterance of
Yahweh of Hosts; and will obliterate from Babylon renown and remnant,[a] offspring and family line; that is the utterance of Yahweh of
Hosts.   23   I make it into a possession of the hedgehogs and into
puddles of water and sweep it away with the broom of annihilation;
that is the utterance of Yahweh of Hosts.]

3a בַ עֲבֹדָה עָבַד means "impose on someone work done by slaves" (Exod. 1:14; Lev.
25:39), so that עָבַד הָעֲבֹדָה בָ means "work done by slaves is performed by," which
means that this present passage, taken literally, would have to be translated: "and
from the work of slaves, which was done through you." Rather than עֻבַּד (which had
been laid [on you]), for this passage, Gesenius, ad loc., would read עֲבֻדָּה (slave

work); however, instead of this, it should be treated as an impersonal passive (quoting Gray: "wherewith it was worked with thee"; cf. Naegelsbach, *Hebräische Grammatik*, 1862², §100, 2).

4a מרהבה can hardly be the correct reading. The versions have widely divergent readings: Gk: ἐπισπουδαστής, "one who presses"; Syr: *mḥpṭn'*, "one who exhorts, incites"; Vulg: *exactor*, "one who drives out"; OL: *incitator*, "vehement one"; Targ: תקוף חייבא, "power of the sinner"; Sym, Theod: φορολογια, "levying of tribute." One would probably not be right if one related this word to Aramaic דהב (= Hebrew זהב), "gold," which would mean that מרהבה would convey the sense "greed for gold" or "riches." The same conclusion must be reached concerning H. M. Orlinsky's suggested derivation from a root רבא, resulting in the meaning "power, strength, oppression," doubtful particularly because the meaning of Ugaritic *db'at* and Hebrew רבאך, occurring in Deut. 33:25, has not been satisfactorily clarified (on Deut. 33:25, see F. M. Cross, "Ugaritic *DB'AT* and Hebrew Cognates," *VT* 2 [1952] 162ff.). Since the time of J. D. Michaelis, the text has generally been emended to read מרהבה, "storm," and this reading seems to be supported by Q^a, which has the identical consonants: מרהבה (Dahood: "overbearingness") (on this, see F. Nötscher, *VT* 1 [1950] 300; G. R. Driver, *JTS* 2 [1951] 25; M. D. Goldmann, *AusBR* 1 [1951] 10f.; and M. Dahood, *Bib* 48 [1967] 432, with reference to Isa. 3:5). Yet one must note that both the Gk and Syr presuppose that there is a *nomen agentis* (a noun identifying the agent); the parallelism with נגש in v. 4aβ would also anticipate this type of noun; and, most importantly, the verb רהב is found in Hebrew (*qal* and *hiph'il*) but there is no evidence for any use of the substantive מרהבה (BDB: boisterous, raging, behavior). Thus the *hiph'il* מרהיב (tyrant, stormer) (or, if need be, the *pi'el* מרהב, "tyrant, stormer") should be read here, which necessitates that שבתה (came to an end) (third feminine sing.) be altered to read שבת (also: came to an end) (third masculine sing.).

5a The first colon in v. 5 is too long, which arouses suspicion in this poem, which is constructed with a noticeably regular *Qina* meter. Thus, already from the time of Staerk (*Das assyrische Weltreich . . .* [1908] 227) and Guthe, the suggestion has been made to remove יהוה (Yahweh) and to read a passive, either נשבר (be broken) or שבר (be shattered) instead of שבר (smash) (on this, see Jahnow, 239). Since the word יהוה (Yahweh) is not used as a name for God elsewhere in the poem, this suggestion is attractive; it is likely that there was a secondary alteration to the text. However, since this does not deal with a misreading but would have been a conscious addition to the text, this name for God ought not, under any circumstances, be removed on the basis of text-critical considerations.

6a Concerning עברה (seething rage), see *Isaiah 1–12* for discussions of Isa. 9:18 and 10:6.

6b–b מכת בלתי סרה (uninterrupted blows) is an adverbial accusative (הכה מכה is a *figura etymologica* ["the addition of an object in the form of a noun derived from the same stem"; Ges-K §117p]). Concerning בלתי [a particle of negation], cf. Joüon, *Gr* §125b.

6c Vulg reads *subicientem* (subjecting); Gr: παίων (striking); the suggestion made in *BHK³* to alter this to read רדף (pursuing) is unnecessary.

6d The parallelism between v. 6a and 6b would lead one to expect a word derived from the root רדה (have dominion, rule) instead of the *hoph'al* participle מרדך (having been pursued) (or is it possible that this was meant to be taken as a substantive?). The Gk does not appear to have read this word at all, but the Syr offers the reading *w^erādep* (and pursuing), and the Vulg, *persequentem* (following constantly), which would lead one to conclude that they read a participle, either *qal* or *pi'el*, from רדף

(pursue). But the Targ says in v. 6b: מפלח בתקוף עממין מפלח ולא מנע (that made the nations serve in anger [or: by force], making them serve and restraining not), which makes one wonder whether we still should presume for this passage, where we read מרדף (follow), that originally there was a word derived from the root רדה (have dominion), possibly reading something like מרדה, "step, trample down." Nonetheless, since the substantive מרדה occurs nowhere in the OT, one still would be better off to follow the Syr and Vulg and read either ורדף (and following) or מרדף (following).

6e חָשָׂךְ is hardly a pausal form of the perfect; not only would the parallel in v. 6a (סרה, turning aside, being interrupted) speak against this, but also the fact that בלי [one of the particles of negation] is never used directly before a perfect (cf. KBL). Since the substantive form חֶשֶׂךְ (refraining) is not found elsewhere, it may be that the infinitive חֲשֹׂךְ (to refrain, relent) should be read; for another view, see Joüon, *Gr* §160m.

7a For פצח, KBL suggests the meaning "be serene," and on this basis Fohrer translates פצחו רנה as "they break forth with serene rejoicing." However, it is difficult to determine the exact meaning, since this vocable, with the exception of Ps. 98:4, where it parallels רנן (give a ringing cry) and זמר (make music), occurs only in the book of Isaiah and then only with רנה (ringing cry) (but note that Akkadian *piṣû* means "white, be bright").

8a According to KBL, בְּרוֹשׁ does not mean "cypresses," as it has traditionally been interpreted, but rather the "Phoenician juniper," *Juniperus phoenicea L.* (which looks very much like a cypress); see Immanuel Löw, *Die Flora der Juden* III, 33–38.

8b Concerning ארז (cedar), see *Isaiah 1–12*, p. 116.

8c The appearance of כרת (fell, cut down) in this text certainly has nothing to do with the name of the Ugaritic hero in the KRT texts (as was suggested by A. Kapelrud, *Joel Studies* [1948] 26ff., a suggestion rejected by Quell, 148).

9a The Hebrew word שְׁאוֹל (Sheol) never has the article.

9b–b Literally: "to meet your coming."

9c The form of עוֹרֵר (roused up) is not the perfect but rather the infinitive absolute of the *poʿel* of עור (rouse oneself, awake). For this reason, הֵקִים should also be pointed as an infinitive absolute (thus: הָקֵם, "raised up").

9d The Hebrew vocable עתּיד normally means "ram, he-goat"; to explain the meaning "rulers" in this present passage, cf. Zech. 10:3, where it parallels "shepherds" and where, at the same time, one also finds the shepherd-flock metaphor.

10a The first colon is too short; there must be a gap in the text. But the suggestions to fill out the colon with הִנֵּה (behold) or הֵמָּה (they) (see *BHS*) or בשׂמחה (with rejoicing) (see Marti) are little more than unsubstantiated conjectures.

10b Driver (*JSS* 13 [1968] 43) suggests deriving חֻלֵּיתָ from Ugaritic *ḥly*, "was alone," and Arabic *ḥalâ*, "was vacant, disengaged," and not from חלה, "be sick, weak"; this alteration is unnecessary, since the traditional rendering makes good sense.

11a Instead of נְבָלֶיךָ (your harps), Qᵃ reads נבלתך (your corpse). If this were the correct reading, then המית, as is normally the case with הָמוֹן (roar, crowd, abundance), would have to mean "ostentatious display, pomp" (on this, see Driver, 43). J. Carmignac believes that the Qᵃ text reads המות (the death) (cf. θανατος, "death," in Theod!) and suggests the translation: "(in) death, your corpse . . ."; however, "corpse" is not used as a parallel term for נאון (splendor).

11b Concerning examples of incongruence between the substantive and the verb, when the verb is in the first position, see Joüon, *Gr* §150j (Duhm and Jahnow read יצוע, "couch, bed"; Marti reads יצוע, "couch of").

11c Instead of מכסך (your [pl.] covering), some MSS and Qᵃ read מכסך (your [sing.]

covering); in any case, the verb form is in the singular, though this does not require any adjustment to the text; see Meyer, §47.

12a On the one hand, questions have been raised about the reliability of the Masoretic pointing; KBL and others refer to Arabic *hilālun*, "new moon," and suggest pointing הֵילֵל as הֵילֵל (see also *BHS*). On the other hand, Grelot (*VT* 6 [1956] 303f.) interprets this word on the basis of the root הלל, "shine" (Arabic *halla*, "be radiant"; Hebrew, in the *hiphʿil*, "let shine") and links הֵילֵל with the Akkadian adjective *ellu* (from *halilu* → *elilu*) "clean, shining" (on the manner in which one would write "e" with י as a *mater lectionis*, see Grelot, 303). The Gk translates הֵילֵל as ἑωσφόρος (bringer of morn); Vulg as *lucifer*.

12b Once again the first colon has only two accented syllables. It has been suggested (see *BHS*) that this line, like v. 12a, should begin with אֵיךְ (ah) (Cheyne, Marti, Staerk, Guthe, Duhm, et al.).

12c חלש, "weaken, subdue," has an accusative object every other time it occurs. Since the Gk in v. 12bβ reads ὁ ἀποστέλλων πρὸς πάντα τὰ ἔθνη (the one who is sending to all the nations), the על (upon) that immediately precedes גוים (peoples) could have been miscopied from a text that originally read כל (all). Gunkel has a different solution, taking חלש as an intransitive, "lying motionless," and changing גוים, "peoples," to read גויות, "corpses" (*Schöpfung und Chaos* [1895] 132); see McKay, 453, note 4, who also suggests that this verb has an intransitive meaning, on the basis of Job 14:10, but that is a textually uncertain passage; see also A. Guillaume, *JTS* 14 [1963] 91f., who refers to Arabic *halasa* (waste away) and believes, on that basis, that it is possible to translate חלש in this passage as "plunder completely."

13a Some have wondered whether אל (here: God's [stars]) might better be left untranslated, treating it as a personal name, particularly since עליון (Elyon, the most high) follows in v. 14. However, since the present context of the poem places this word within material that gives witness to faith in Yahweh (see above, textual note 5a), אל (El) is a reference to Yahweh, just as עליון (Elyon) is. To be sure, in many passages אל (El) is used in the sense of a superlative (Fohrer, for example, renders this: "the highest stars"; on the whole topic, see D. W. Thomas, "A Consideration of Some Unusual Ways of Expressing the Superlative in Hebrew," *VT* 3 [1953] 209–224). But Dahood (170f.) refers to the close connection between El and the stars; see, e.g., Job 22:12f. and cf. Ps. 147:4 and Isa. 40:26. Most importantly, the use of עליון (Elyon) in v. 14 provides sufficient reason for staying with reading אל (El) as a reference to "God."

13b According to the context, מועד (meeting place) must refer to the assembly of the gods (cf. Ugaritic *phr mʿd*, "group of the assembly," and Akkadian *puhur ili*, "assembly of the gods," *AHW* 876). It is apparently used so frequently in this sense that the genitive, אלהים (of the gods), does not even have to be supplied (Ugaritic does use *phr bn ilm* [II AB, III 14] and *phr ilm* [*UT* 21:2], both meaning "assembly of the gods").

14a The construct form בָּמֳתֵי (the heights of) occurs six times in poetic passages of the OT. As the reading from Qᵃ indicates (בומתי), the form is not from an original root במה but from a postulated form *בָּמֶת (see *HAL* 131).

16a שׁגח *hiphʿil* refers to looking at something, intending to inspect it with a critical eye.

16b התבונן = "handle oneself in such a way as to show that one is intent on learning the true nature of something, turning one's attention to a matter."

17a Since תבל (earth) (always used in poetic contexts and never with the article) is feminine, the form should be read either וְעָרֶיהָ (and 'her' cities) or, if one follows the Gk (καὶ τὰς πόλεις, and the cities), וְעָרִים (and cities) (Ehrlich, *Randglossen* IV, 56).

17b–18a Changing פָּתַח (he opened) to פִּתַּח (he loosened, freed), based on the Gk (ἔλυσε, "he loosened") and Syr (*šᵉrāʾ*, "he loosened"), some translate this: "who did not release his captives so they could go back home." However, בַּיִת (house) never carries the meaning of "homeland," and בַּיְתָה never means "toward home" but always "in the house." In addition, the meter of the passage is not as it should be; therefore, taking כֹּל (all) from the beginning of v. 18 with this part of the line (the word actually does not fit well so close to כֻּלָם, "all together, all of them," anyway), then v. 17b is to be emended as follows: לַאֲסִירָיו לֹא פָתַח בֵּית הַכֶּלֶא (for his prisoners, he did not open their house of imprisonment); and מַלְכֵי גוֹיִם (kings of the peoples), at the beginning of v. 18a, should be moved to, and joined with, the next line.

18b–b אִישׁ בְּבֵיתוֹ (a man in his house) is to be treated as a later insertion into the text.

19a The Gk reads: ἐν τοῖς ὄρεσιν = בֶּהָרִים (in the mountains), which some (see *BHK³*) think is a damaged reading, from what would originally have read בַּהֲרוּגִים (in the killing), but that is unlikely, since הֲרֻ(וֹ)גֵי follows in the next line, where it is absolutely necessary. Yet the text could hardly have in mind that the "tyrant" had been thrown out of his grave [so MT], but rather that he had been cast out on the ground, unburied (see Jer. 22:19). Thus the reading should be מִקֶּרֶב (without having a grave) (a מִן privative).

19b The reading נֵצֶר (sprout) is uncertain; Gk: ὡς νεκρὸς ἐβδελυγμένος (as a nausea-causing corpse); Sym: εκτρωμα, "miscarriage," like Aramaic יַחַט (abortion), could presuppose that the reading was originally נֵפֶל (miscarriage, abortion) in the Hebrew. Aquila reads ιχωρ (putrified blood, discharge of a woman after childbirth), which may suggest that his original text was נָצַל (spoiled), commonly used in rabbinic Hebrew. It would seem that Jerome used the same textual reading, translating it *sanies (polluta)* "corrupted blood from a wound, which has run down." L. Köhler (236f., and 142) suggests that one should read נֶשֶׁר (eagle) here (KBL also), but such a comparison would not help at all, since one would normally never have the opportunity to throw eagles away. But one cannot be satisfied with נֵצֶר (sprout) in the transmitted text either, since no one would ever ask whether a sprout of a plant ought to be buried, whether it was detestable or not. The closest to the original is still probably the proposal (based on a suggestion by Schwally, *ZAW* 11 [1891] 257f.) that the text be emended to read נֵפֶל (miscarriage), which does have textual support from Targ and Aquila. A miscarried birth is abhorred because it is believed that some evil forces have been at work and may have caused such an event. נֵפֶל נִתְעָב (stomach-turning miscarriage) furnishes a good parallel for כְּפֶגֶר מוּבָס (as a trampled carcass) in v. 19b.

19c–c יֹרְדֵי אֶל־אַבְנֵי־בוֹר (those who travel down to the stones of the pit) has apparently been displaced and should follow the phrase that now follows it in MT, properly being the first colon of the next line of text.

19d Concerning the participle in the construct state before prepositional phrases, see Joüon, *Gr* §121n and §129m.

19e "Stones of the graves (cisterns)" makes no sense, unless given further explanation; one cannot be completely certain about the text in its present form. Yet the suggestion, based on Sym (θεμελιους, "foundations") and with reference to Job 38:6, that one read אֶל אַדְנֵי, "to the foundations" (see *BHK³*), is not even close to the original meaning, but rather shows just how perplexed exegetes are at this point.

20a בַּקְבוּרָה (in the grave) is probably a gloss, added to explain the puzzling אַבְנֵי בוֹר (stones of the pit).

20b Driver (44) considers יְקָרֵא (mention will be made) to be a variant form of יִקָּרֶה and translates this line "the brood of evildoers shall no more appear," which makes no more sense than does the text as it now stands.

20c Many commentators are not pleased with זרע מרעים (seed of evildoers) as it stands; they would rather read the singular מֵרַע (from the evildoer), on the basis of the Gk (σπέρμα πονηροῦ, seed of the evil one) and the Syr (*zarʿāʾ bîšāʾ*, "the evil seed"); it is suggested that the plural would have been read here because the textual tradition was influenced by 1:4 (Marti). But 1:4 itself (see *Isaiah 1–12*, p. 23) shows that זרע מרעים does not mean "generation descended from rogues" but rather "generation made up of rogues."

21a Instead of the plural אבותם (fathers), the Gk reads the singular (τοῦ πατρός σου, "of your father" or, according to the Hexapla, αὐτῶν, "of their father"). M. Dahood (*Bib* 44 [1963] 291) thinks אבות (fathers) could be read as a *pluralis excellentiae;* Rinaldi (*BeO* 10 [1968] 24) rejects this suggestion, maintaining that עון אבות is a set phrase: "guilt of the fathers." Thus the text certainly ought not to be altered.

21b The fear that the sons of evildoers could fill "the surface of the continent" with cities does not seem to provide some commentators with a good enough reason to explain why the sons are to be slaughtered. Here the Gk reads πολεμῶν (wars) but (according to Gehman, *VT* 3 [1953] 399) this is an inner-Greek corruption of the text, based on a misreading of πόλεων (of cities) = ערים (cities). Some have suggested that it should originally read צרים, "enemies" (Gesenius, ad loc.) or have conjectured that the text might have read עיים, "ruins" (so *BHK³*). Still others think that this might be a gloss. Since v. 21 is a late addition, it might be that ערים (cities) is original; maybe the author was thinking about founding cities in regions where various peoples had been brought under subjection.

22a Instead of שְׁאָר (remnant), Syr reads *šᵉʾer* (see *BHK³*) "flesh," in the sense of "blood relative." Qᵃ reads שארית (remnant), which might be correct, since שם (renown, name) and שארית (remnant) also occur together in 2 Sam. 14:7. However, there is no need to make such an alteration to the text, since שְׁאָר and שארית are completely interchangeable and can hardly be differentiated from one another and given distinguishable meanings (see H. Wildberger, "שאר," *THAT* II, 844–855).

23a An infinitive absolute form dependent on a substantive makes this suspicious; yet in this particular, undoubtedly late passage, it ought to be left as is, especially since the infinitive absolute of the *hiphʿil* can easily be used as a substantive (see, e.g., הַשְׁקֵט, "quietness," in Isa. 30:15 and 32:17; and cf. Joüon, *Gr* §123b2).

Form

[14:3, 4a] The *parashiyyot* (paragraph) divisions in the MT make clear that a new body of material begins with v. 3. This cannot be a completely decisive factor for modern scholarship; however, observations dealing with both form and content also show that a new section begins with v. 3: The expander of the material in the book of Isaiah often used the formula ביום ההוא (in that day) or והיה ביום ההוא (and it will happen in that day) as a way of appending his material (on this, see *Isaiah 1–12*, pp. 118ff.). Here we find a slight variation (והיה ביום הניח, "on that day, on which he [Yahweh] has provided rest"), but the function of the formula is the same. A new theme brings with it new content in vv. 3, 4a as well, since a "mockery saying" is now introduced, speaking about the king of Babylon, who had not been mentioned until this point. Verses 3, 4a form a link between the section in chaps. 13:1—14:2 and the mocking song in vv. 4bff.

[14:4b-21] Present-day exegetes have reached broad consensus, on the basis of both form and content, that the song about the downfall of the world ruler in vv. 4b-20(21) is a single unit. On formal grounds: according to the study of the history of genres, this is a mocking song, formed by modifying a song of lament for one who has died (see below, pp. 50f.). Metrically, this section clearly differs from the material surrounding it; it is composed using five-stress bicola, which stay true to the pattern in a manner rarely duplicated elsewhere (see below, pp. 52f.). If v. 21b has been transmitted in its original textual form (see above, textual note 21b), it is a three-stress + three-stress bicolon. By itself, that fact is not enough to raise questions about why a poem that follows a very regular pattern would deviate from the meter of the verses that precede it. However, other factors show that v. 21 can hardly be part of the original poem. By the end of v. 20, the lament for the dead has clearly come to a conclusion: the tyrant is dead and it has been stated with certainty that no one would speak about his sons ever again. It is incredible that a summons to take part in slaughtering them would follow in v. 21. Verse 20 uses the second singular to address the tyrant; v. 21 speaks about *his* sons. In addition, there is a complete departure from the pattern of a lament for the dead in v. 21. Commentators conceal the difficulty posed by the transition from v. 20 to v. 21 by translating v. 20b as if it were a jussive (see, e.g., Quell, 155), to which the imperative in v. 21 would then be connected without sounding somewhat disjointed. However, v. 20b (לֹא!, "no longer") is an indicative statement, after which the passionate outburst in v. 21 comes as a total surprise.

[14:22f.] Everyone agrees that vv. 22f. are an addition to the song. The way in which they are composed discloses that both verses have been written in prose. In contrast to *BHK³*, *BHS* attempts to read poetic lines here as well, but what results from this effort is simply that some "lines" have an arbitrary meter but have absolutely no *parallelismus membrorum*, which is typically an identifying characteristic of Hebrew poetry. In terms of form, this is a prophecy of disaster, and the threatened disaster is not going to come upon the "evildoer" who has been the subject of the song, but rather upon the city of Babylon. As is the case with vv. 3, 4a, these closing sentences, which have been appended, are intended to link this song with the oracle against Babylon in 13:1—14:2. Because of this, it is a reasonable assumption that both of these sections, vv. 3, 4a and vv. 22, 23, are to be attributed to the same redactor, who was able to preserve this magnificent poem in vv. 4bff. within the biblical tradition.

Setting

(Concerning the authenticity of 14:4b-20[21] and the time when it was written, see below, pp. 53ff.)

[14:3, 4a, 22-23] The framework constructed around the song itself presumes that the oracle against Babylon in chap. 13 is already part of the text; the author wants to emphasize further the threat against Babylon and say still more about it by using the lament for the dead. It is less certain whether he already knew of the addition to chap. 13 as well, that is, what is presently found in 14:1, 2. It would seem, however, that he based v. 4 on 14:1 and made a special effort to connect this verse with the verb נוח *hiphʿil* (cause to rest), even though he uses it in a different sense. If one accepts this solution, then the resulting questions about dating revolve around the difficulties of explaining what is meant by "Babylon." Since 13:2-22 is exilic, 14:1 is already postexilic (Zechariah's era?), and 14:2 is more recent yet, then still another level of activity would have to be posited for the framework surrounding 14:4b-21. Procksch dates the work of the redactors to the time between Zechariah and Ezra. But is there any reason to presume that an oracle against Babylon would have been composed at that time? One could make the observation that Babylon had not as yet been destroyed in the Persian era and that the direct fulfillment of chap. 13 was still a real possibility. But Babylon had been robbed of its power and it would have made no sense to threaten them once again with their demise. Therefore the name "Babylon" must function as a symbolic name used to identify the "world power" for this redactor, who initially had the Persian Empire in mind. There is apparently not a single threat against this empire in the entire OT (that is, if one looks beyond the prophecies of Haggai and Zechariah, which do not mention the Persians by name). That cannot be explained simply by presuming that Israel had accepted the Persian rule, at least after the time of Haggai/Zechariah. This odd state of affairs can be explained by the fact that pseudonyms are used when referring to this kingdom. This technique might have come into vogue after human beings who spent time studying the rise and fall of a number of world powers learned that, in addition to whatever was unique about a particular world empire that happened to be in control at the moment, with its own plans and important figures, in the final analysis one could also identify general characteristics that would apply to each and every "world power." After people came to that conclusion, an important element in the apocalyptic view of the world appeared as well.

Commentary

[14:3, 4a] Verses 3 and 4a identify the time when one should begin to utter the מָשָׁל (parable, poetic teaching) as the time when Yahweh "has provided rest" for Israel. הֵנִיחַ (provide rest) comments further on the idea of הִנִּיחַ (transplant, bring to rest) found in v. 1, regardless of whether the author read הֵנִיחַ (provide rest) there as well or whether he recast it so that it would have the meaning of הֵנִיחַ (provide rest [instead of: transplant]). In the more ancient traditions of Israel, "provide rest" meant: in the process of taking the land, allow oneself to be delivered from the anxieties of a nomadic way of life in order to be settled permanently in one place (see passages such as Deut. 3:20; Josh. 1:3); an even more ancient idea behind this offered the possibility that one might live at rest and peace "from all the enemies round about," in the land that had been inherited (see, e.g., Deut. 12:10; 25:19; Josh. 23:1; on this motif, cf. G. von Rad, "There Remains Still a Rest for the People of God: An Investigation of a Biblical Conception," *The Problem of the Hexateuch and Other Essays* [1966] 94–102). In the present passage, "rest" is further defined by its opposites: "hardship, privation, and hard forced labor." No mention is made of returning to the homeland, and it would certainly make sense to assume that an Israelite living in Palestine is speaking, probably at a time when there was groaning because of the oppressive rule of some foreign entity. עצב, "pain, affliction," seems to be most commonly used in late OT texts; see Ps. 139:24; 1 Chron. 4:9; in the latter passage, it refers to birth pains, but in the present passage it obviously speaks of afflictions that accompany oppression. רגז (be agitated, quiver) can certainly be used when describing the wrath of Yahweh (see Hab. 3:2), but in several Job passages is refers to the general unrest that comes in human life. Finally, in addition to the general sense of "work" and "service," עבודה can be used in a special sense, to describe "forced labor," more specifically, to describe Israel's bondage in Egypt (Exod. 1:14; 2:23; 5:9, 11; 6:9; see also 1 Kings 12:4). It is easy to insert the adjective קשה (hard) when speaking about this negative aspect of work. In this way, the deliverance from "Babylon" is promised to Israel here, set forth as a parallel to the deliverance from bondage in Egypt— an indication that Israel was able to find the strength from time to time to believe and to hope, looking back to its salvation history. Rest would come to Israel when and because the tyrant of the people was dead. The mocking song that followed would speak of that.

Form

[14:4b-21] Verse 4a describes the song as a משל. The word actually means "likening, comparison" (see Akkadian *mašâlu*, "be like"; Arabic *mitlun*, "the equivalent"); it can be used as a neutral term, "saying, proverb," but can also be used in the special, technical sense of a "mocking saying"; the משל is the one who speaks mocking words (Num. 21:27; see also Isa. 28:14). By their very nature, such sayings are short (see the משלי שלמה, "proverbs of Solomon," Prov. 1:1); simply for these reasons, the designation משל does not adequately describe the poem in vv. 4b-21 as a whole. Modern scholars have known for a long time that the song obviously contains elements from the song of the lament for the dead; see particularly Lohmann and Jahnow. The key term that identifies the lament for the dead is איך (how) in v. 4b, and it is also found in v. 12b. Because of the mention of איך נפל (how you have fallen) in v. 12b, one should compare this with the song of David, in which he laments the death of Saul and Jonathan (2 Sam. 1:19, 25, 27).

To cite an example from a completely different cultural tradition, one can compare this passage with the satirical funeral dirge of Seneca, sung for Emperor Claudius, which also has some other striking parallels: "For he that is dead had a wit most keen, was bravest of all that on earth have been. Racehorses are nothing to his swift feet: Rebellious Parthians he did defeat; swift after the Persians his light shafts go: For he well knew how to fit arrow to bow, swiftly the striped barbarians fled: With one little wound he shot them dead. . . . He chained by the neck as the Romans' slaves. He spake, and the Ocean with trembling waves. . . . Once ruler of fivescore cities in Crete, must yield to his better and take a back seat" (*Apocolocyntosis* 12, quoting the W. H. D. Rouse translation in the Loeb Classical Library; see also Jahnow's rendition, 250f.).

A typical element in a lament for the dead is a contrast between the then and the now; see 2 Sam 1:23; Isa. 1:21ff. (on this, see *Isaiah 1–12*, pp. 59ff.); Ezek. 31:3ff.; and 32:2ff., and note how the poem of Seneca just cited contrasts past and present. It is only natural that one would seek comfort when someone died, in the hope that there would be those who would follow after to continue the work begun by the one who died or that the nature and honor of the dead person would live on in them.

Thus mourning women in the Sahara sing to the widow of a sheik: "He is not dead, he is not dead, he has left his brothers as survivors. He has left you with children; they will be a protecting wall for your shoulders. He is not dead; he is not dead" (Jahnow, 249).

In complete contrast, the present song purposely recasts the typical motifs to say the opposite: "No longer, in all eternity, will mention be made of this wicked generation" (v. 20b). Additional motifs will be discussed in detail in the exegesis of the individual verses. The song thus uses many of the motifs normally found in a lament for the dead, but the lament is recast to convey mockery. Scholarship has called this a "mocking prophetic funeral dirge" (see O. Eissfeldt, *The Old Testament: An Introduction* [1965] 96f.) or a parody on a lament for the dead (see Jahnow, 231).

However, the term מָשָׁל (mocking saying) is certainly used appropriately to identify certain elements of the song. As a comparison with Isa. 37:22-29 shows, Israel also knew about the mocking song that heaped scorn on disempowered enemies. It is easy to see that both songs have the same motifs (cf. particularly 37:24 with 14:13). This poet who fashioned 14:4bff. was certainly not the first to use *Qina* (lament) meter in a *mashal* (comparison, proverb, mocking saying) and direct this against a people or a political opponent. On this point as well, the clearest examples are in Ezekiel: 19:1-4; 27:2-10, 25b-36; 28:12-19; see also 31:1-18. It is significant that what Isaiah calls a מָשָׁל (mocking saying) in 14:4 is termed a קִינָה (*Qina*, lament) in Ezek. 27:2; 28:12; 32:2, 16 (and that מָשָׁל, "taunt song," and נְהִי, "bitter lamentation," are used together in Mic. 2:4). "Just as in the life of the individual, the mocking saying represented a weapon of great power, so the mocking song was a terrible political weapon, which provided protection and security for one's own people" (Eissfeldt, *Introduction*, 93). If one would clothe this mockery in the attire of a lament for the dead, then that would significantly elevate its potency. In the final analysis, this usage reflects back to a time when it was thought that such words had magical power. The person who has had this lament for the dead spoken over him has already been transferred, in effect, into the realm of the dead; even if he is still "alive," he has been robbed already of all his power. One would have to pay no more attention to such a person than one would pay to someone already dead.

Such a conclusion brings with it certain consequences for the exposition of the text that have usually not been considered properly. In common usage, songs of lament for the dead are normally sung when the person who is being mourned has already died. For that reason, it is common to use the perfect tense. That is the case here as well. However, to sing a mocking song of lament for the dead makes no sense after the subject of the song has died, if the purpose of singing such a lament for the dead person is to do battle against one's political opponent. In addition, the parallels mentioned above from Ezekiel deal, without question, with powers who had not yet passed from the scene in defeat and—as is particularly obvious with Tyre—never did come to the final end that had been expected in the lament for the dead spoken over them. Duhm already noticed correctly: "In spite of the perfect forms, we have a prediction" (see Marti as well). After an exhaustive study that sought out a ruler who would fit the description provided in vv. 4ff., Lohmann came up empty and came to the same conclusion (see 25-42).

Exegetes have expended a great deal of effort to demonstrate that the poem is to be divided into five strophes, each with seven lines (cf. the textual reconstruction offered by Lohmann, 19f., and Marti's divisions: vv. 4b-8, 9-11, 12-15, 16-19, 20f.). However, this view can be adopted only if one is willing to make questionable alterations to the transmitted text and if one agrees with arbitrary subdivisions (on this, see Eissfeldt, *Introduction*, 97f.). Therefore it is best here to avoid using the term "strophe" and simply to speak of sections. Section I, vv. 4b-8, "laments" the end of the tyrant and speaks about how the whole earth can finally breathe a sigh of relief now that he has fallen. Section II, vv. 9-11, portrays his reception into the realm of the dead and his fate within it. Section III, vv. 12-15, describes the plunge taken by someone who had stormed the heavens themselves, now going down "into the grave of the uttermost distant region." Section IV, vv. 16-17, supplies a graphic depiction of the thoughts of those who stand before the corpse of the evildoer. In section V, vv. 18-20, this person himself is addressed: he cannot even look forward to an ordinary existence among those who are in the same condition as he is in Sheol. This is followed by the assertion that he will not have any future through the lives of his descendants on earth either, which forms the conclusion, since the summons to murder his sons, in v. 21, has to be treated as a later addition to the text, as was explained above.

Meter: In a lament for the dead, the *Qina* meter is appropriate, that is, the five-stress colon (3 + 2). In fact, this song is composed with an amazingly regular pattern of five-stress cola. One exception is found in v. 5a; however, on this, see above, textual note 5a. In v. 9 מכסאותם (from their thrones) receives two stresses; on the first colon of v. 10, see above, textual note 10a; the same holds for v. 12 (see above, textual note 12b); in the phrase הזה האיש (is this the man) in v. 16b, only איש (man) is accented; in vv. 17-19, irregularities in the textual meter are probably caused by intrusions into the text, so that one could proceed confidently with a restoration that reads these verses as having five-stress cola as well. Thus the only verse that does not fit this pattern is v. 21b (on this, see above, p. 48).

Even on purely formal grounds, the diction found in this poem is extremely lively: in v. 8 the cedars speak; in v. 10b the Rephaim have their say; in vv. 13f. the tyrant himself is quoted; and finally, in vv. 16f. the Rephaim have their say once again. Verses 13f. provide an excellent example of the so-called courtly monologue (G. von Rad, *OTTheol* II, 180, note 10), a form that the OT prophets used when they wanted to place words into the mouths of foreign kings, as part of the way they showed the character of those rulers. Another element that makes this come alive is the use of the second singular form of address, beginning with v. 8, which is also used in the sections that describe the action.

Setting

[14:4b-21] It was established above that the framework which the final editor constructed around the song was not from Isaiah. If one accepts that v. 4b is correct in identifying this as a mocking song against the king of Babylon, then this song could not have originated with Isaiah. In Isaiah's day the Babylonian kings, insofar as they were able to assert their authority over against Assyria, never wielded the type of power under which the entire world would have had to groan and sigh. And it is just as unlikely that someone in Israel, at that time, would have rejoiced in the downfall of Babylon, since that could only have meant that one would have been driven even more intensely into the clutches of Assyria, would have been even more completely helpless and without ally. In its present position, however, this song can only have been linked to a ruler of Babylon in a secondary way. The song itself has no indicators that would assuredly connect the detailed descriptions with Babylon per se. Some have suggested that the mention of נֵצֶר (miscarriage) in v. 19 is a play on Nebuchadnezzar's name, but this would remain uncertain even if there were no textual difficulties at that point. In addition, it is at least possible that that word, which is hard to understand in its present context, was inserted into the text secondarily, precisely because it could function as a reference to this Babylonian. Therefore it is highly likely that one should conclude that this song was originally composed with someone in mind who was a non-Babylonian. If Isaiah were the source of this composition, then the subject could only be an Assyrian king. That solution is what Cobb proposes, based on the historical allusions, the style, the vocabulary, and the literary character, as he attempts to make a case for Isaiah as the source of the composition. Schiffer, along with others (see Winckler, *Altorientalische Forschung* I, 193f.; but see 410ff. and KAT[3] 74f.), believes that Sennacherib is being addressed and also argues in favor of its authenticity. However, even if it were true that one could come up with further arguments favoring the view that this refers to an Assyrian king, it would still be impossible for one to consider Isaiah as the author. Isaiah had announced that Assyria would be laid waste outside the walls of Jerusalem, but not that it would be completely, absolutely destroyed. It is incomprehensible that a poem of this length, composed by him, would include not a single mention of God's name. Even though Isaiah was conversant with the Jerusalem traditions, he himself never used עליון (Elyon) as a designation for God. It is not enough to point out that certain vocables that Isaiah uses are also found here (see the statistics on word usage gathered by Erlandsson, 129ff.; for arguments to the contrary, see Wildberger, *JSS* 17 [1972] 152f.), since other words are undoubtedly late: Gray identifies פצח רנה (each person breaks forth in ringing shouts of jubilation) in v. 7; בור as the "underworld" in v. 15; השׁגיח (peer at intently) in v. 16; בל (not) in v. 21; Vanderburgh also adds to this list נמשׁל, in the sense of "liken," in v. 10.

In general, there are parallels between these terms and the book of Jeremiah, but parallels are most common between this vocabulary and exilic-postexilic prophecy, with the most frequent connections being found in the secondary portions of the book of Isaiah, e.g.: שׁבת (rest, v. 4) in 24:8; 33:8; עור (rouse up, v. 9) in 10:26; 13:17; and eight times in Deutero-Isaiah; רום *hiphᶜil* (I will set up, v. 13) in 10:15b; 13:2; 37:23; and six times in Deutero-Isaiah; פגר (carcass, v. 19) in 34:3; 37:16; שׁמים (heaven, vv. 12f.) in 13:5, 10; 34:4f.; 37:16; and twenty-one times in chaps. 40–66; in authentic Isaianic passages only 1:2; מדבר (desert, v. 17) in 16:1, 8; 21:1 (bis); 27:10; 32:15f.; 35:1, 8; and eleven times in chaps. 40–66.

If this material does not come from the time of Isaiah, it is going to be difficult to determine its exact date of composition. In general the preexilic prophets identify the subject about whom they are speaking when they are discussing foreign peoples. That the author of this poem does not provide such detail could be explained by the simple fact that he had no specific historical personage in mind about whom he wanted to make a statement (in addition, there is no mention about the opponent of this tyrant), but rather intended this as a statement about anyone who could fill the role of being a representative of world power in general, just as the final editor uses "Babylon" as a code word for any world authority. Of course, one should still try to determine some historical point of reference; even apocalyptic does not speak of situations that are removed completely from the historical arena. But it does suggest that the specific person about whom it originally was spoken would be unimportant in the final analysis: what is important is the type of person, not the actual historical individual. Thus it does not affect the exegesis negatively, in any significant way, that attempts to determine the historical setting for the song have not brought any assured results.

Scholars have been much perplexed about the identification of this personage: in addition to Sargon (A. Jeremias, *The Old Testament in the Light of the Ancient Near East* [1911] II, 270; Feldmann; Winckler; see the earlier discussion in this section) and Sennacherib (once again, see the earlier discussion in this section; in addition, see also commentaries by Cheyne, Mauchline, Eichrodt), others have suggested the last Assyrian king Ashur-uballit II (P. Rost, FS Meissner, MAOG 4 [1929] 175–179, though he suggests that this king is nothing but a personification of Assyria in general), Nebuchadnezzar (F. Delitzsch, Bredenkamp, Bruno, Steinmann, Procksch, Montagnini), Nabonidus (Langdon, 174; Lohmann, 36ff.; Jahnow, 242; Dillmann [?]; Marti; Duhm; König), and even Alexander the Great (Torrey, BZAW 41 [1925] 286, and *JBL* 57 [1938] 116f.). Others distinguish between various stages of expansion to the text, and still others do not focus on one individual but think this is a personification of a world power (P. Rost [1929]: Assyria; Hitzig, Knobel: Babylon). Once again, others yet explicitly forgo making any identification at all.

In the final analysis, the wide variety of suggestions simply points out that a question has been confronted that can produce little more than idle speculation. The anonymity of the evildoer and the absence of tangible historical links must be respected; these realities have made it easier to reactualize the details of this song, over and over again, within the context of new historical circumstances. If one would be permitted an educated guess, the most likely candidate would be Nebuchadnezzar. He has the "typological profile" that one would use to describe a tyrant, and Israel was deeply involved with him and his actions. The poem has close parallels in Ezekiel, but seems to be older. That Nebuchadnezzar did not come to the end which the poet had hoped for is no argument against this identification, since the song is a lament for the dead that was sung before the person died.

Scholarly research has also been very involved with another special problem. W. F. Albright already expressed his opinion that the poem presented a Canaanite epic (*JPOS* 14 [1934] 156) and has found much agreement for this view (thus Quell, Fohrer, et al.). The poem obviously contains material that has been reworked, using mythological ideas originating among non-Israelite peoples; and, since the Ugaritic texts were discovered, it has become clear that these myths came to be known in Israel via the Canaanites. However, it is an oversimplification to assume that the poem, for that reason, was not produced in its present form originally by someone within Israel. The parallel texts in the book of Ezekiel have reworked extensively the same mythological material (above all, see 28:12ff.; concerning the relationship between these materials and passages from Ezekiel, see Lohmann, 67ff.), yet no one has suggested that they were composed by someone from outside the Israelite community. There must have been a tradition in Israel, which had been worked and reworked many times, according to which the pride and downfall of foreign rulers was depicted by using graphic portrayals that originated in heathen myths; indeed, these would have been most appropriate when used in the form of speech now identified as "satirical songs of lament for the dead" (see B. Margulis, 290ff.). Already quite early in their history, the Hebrews integrated El and Elyon as names of the deity, as they described faith in Yahweh; the concept of an assembly of the gods and of a divine mountain of assembly is also known in other passages; the mythological elements connected with the cedars in Lebanon are no less common in biblical texts, and the people of Israel certainly used the concept of Sheol. Admittedly, no other passage refers to the myth about the downfall of Helel ben Shachar (Helel, son of the dawn). At least for the present, however, that myth has not been discovered elsewhere in Canaanite materials either. Therefore, based on the content itself, no case can be made that this poem has particular elements that would prove that it could not have originated within Israel. That some would say it is "heathen according to its origin" (see Quell, 156f.) could have been strongly influenced by the observation that the poem does not, at first glance, mention anything about Yahweh's involvement in the matter. However, that lack does not provide enough evidence to show that it includes elements which are unique to Canaanite religious traditions either. El and Elyon are mentioned only superficially. Beyond that, the mythological elements deal simply with images that refer to events that regularly take place within the earthly realm. That is not to say that the poem is utterly meaningless in terms of religious matters. But its religiosity is found in its proclamation of a righteousness that plays out in the real world and that is on the same level as what one would find in the rest of the OT, particularly in the context of wisdom teaching.

Commentary

[14:4b-8] *The End of the Tyrant and the Rejoicing of the Whole World*

[**14:4b**] As is appropriate, this lament for the dead begins with איך (how) (see *Isaiah 1–12*, p. 62). The one who is being lamented is called a נגש (despot) and a מרהב (tyrant). As it now stands, the tyrant is not specifically addressed as "king," which means that the author, for example, could have had a very powerful commander of troops in mind. Title and position play just as small a role as name and nationality. Concerning נגש (despot), see the earlier discussion in 3:5 (*Isaiah 1–12*, p. 132), and 9:3 (ibid., p. 397). Both נגש (despot) and רהב (tyrant) are used together in 3:5 as well. The Hebrews were certainly focusing in on the association with Rahab when they used מרהב, the designation for the monster of chaos (see Pss. 51:9; 89:11), but they also used it as a symbolic name for Egypt (see Isa. 30:7; Ps. 87:4). Already at this point, they have conjured up the conceptual world of mythology, since the common terms for atrocities, as they are normally described, were not considered strong enough for conveying this type of hideousness. However, the activity of the evildoer now has come to an end, has come to rest. שבת (rest), in the *qal, niphʿal,* and *hiphʿil,* is used frequently in lamentations (Lam. 5:14f.), in announcements of judgment (Isa. 17:3; Ezek. 6:6; 30:18; 33:28), and in curses (Lev. 26:6; Deut. 32:26). The subject of the verb is normally God and thus the *hiphʿil* is used most frequently. In other situations someone laments that joy, once expressed in song and music, has now come to an end (Jer. 7:34; 16:9), but it is also expressed that pride will come to an end (Isa. 13:11; Ezek. 30:18, 33:28).

[**14:5f.**] Although שבה (rest) is intransitive and does not identify the individual who is active in bringing about these events, v. 5 mentions that this is Yahweh. It has been explained already (see p. 43) that this could hardly have been in the original text. It is both significant and noteworthy, however, that someone felt it necessary to make this into a "Yahwistic" piece (in this connection, one might compare this to the completely different type of message about Babylon in chap. 13). It involves a particular stage of development corresponding roughly to the action-consequences relationship known from the realm of OT wisdom material, set in motion when sentences were uttered by Yahweh as the bearer of blessing or disaster. Within the writings of Isaiah himself, one encounters this "synthetic view of life" pattern of thought about the way the world functions, so that, whenever he speaks of wrath, it is as if it has a nature and existence all its own (on this, see *Isaiah 1–12*, pp. 232f.). But the context always makes clear that "wrath" also, in these cases, refers to the power of Yahweh that he exercises within the historical realm. Those who passed on the traditions contained in this poem thought it sufficient to insert the name of Yahweh, in order to present this as further evidence of Yahweh's righteousness within history. The final editor, who inserted vv. 22f., altered the text significantly by having Yahweh himself speak, thus heavily emphasizing Babylon's gloomy downfall being the result of Yahweh's own active intervention.

Concerning שֵׁבֶט (rod) and מַטֶּה (staff), one should compare the usage in 9:5 and 10:5. Like the שֵׁבֶט (rod), the מַטֶּה (staff) is a symbol of the power of the one who is ruling. It is hardly pure chance that the author uses these two parallel terms together, as does Isaiah himself. Fohrer sees this (as with the use of the names for God) as a clear indication that there has been Israelite reworking of what was originally a non-Israelite song. Indeed, it could be that the entire verse was inserted as part of a reworking, but by itself this would not force one to conclude that this song was originally Canaanite. But that hypothesis is not convincing also because the vocabulary in v. 6 is found in passages attributable to Isaiah himself (מַכֶּה, "smiting," and מַכָּה, "blow"; עֶבְרָה, "seething rage," and אַף, "anger"; גּוֹיִם, "peoples," and עַם, "nation"), without anyone having argued that any of those verses should be considered as interpolations. Concerning עֶבְרָה, "seething rage," see 9:18; 10:6; concerning אַף, "anger," see 5:25; 9:11, 16, 20. The alliteration between מַכֵּה and מַכַּת, בִּלְתִּי and בְּלִי, רֹדֶה and מֻרְדָּף underscores the unceasing number of blows being struck by this merciless tyrant. רֹדֶה, no doubt related originally to the root רדד, "trample down, subjugate," is a verb that clearly portrays the great force wielded by the ruler.

[14:7f.] Verses 7 and 8 speak about the effect that the downfall of the tyrant has on the world, which has been plagued by his horrible acts of oppression. This unfolds in two phases: first, "the whole earth" simply comes to rest all at once (one might note that נוח, "repose," is used, not שׁבת, "rest"). The taskmaster is no longer there; the oppressed forced laborers who had been mercilessly driven without any letup finally have the chance to take a break and catch their breath. Only then are they aware of the significance of the ruler's downfall; at that time the fact that they have been freed sinks in. At that moment they break out into lively songs of jubilation. The phrase פָּצַח

רנה (ringing shouts of jubilation) is a favorite of Deutero-Isaiah (44:23; 49:13; 54:1; 55:12; פצח, "break forth," occurs alone elsewhere only in Ps. 98:4 and Isa. 52:9).

It is not enough for the author simply to say that human beings rejoice, as he tries to describe the unrestrained feelings unleashed at this time of jubilation. The juniper trees and the cedars of Lebanon join in; all creatures are made part of the great joyous celebration. The background for this is the thought that all creatures in the entire cosmos are part of one great unity (see also 11:6-8), which means that there is, as yet, no perceived line of demarcation between human beings and the rest of what had been created and had life. But at this point the motif is used simply as a stylistic device to express the tremendous import of this event for the human beings who had been enslaved.

[**14:8b**] In an indirect way, the author portrays the joy that the trees have as they are permitted to address the one who has fallen: "Since you laid yourself down to sleep, the one who fells the trees does not climb up to us any more"; the word שׁכב is often chosen when describing "lying" in the grave and in the underworld, and it is certainly not just by chance that parallels occur in both Ezekiel (31:18; 32:21, 27-30) and Deutero-Isaiah (50:11), but see Job 7:21; 14:12; 20:11 as well; in addition, cf. Judg. 5:27; Isa. 43:17; Lam. 2:21. The use of כרת would lead one initially to think that these are simply woodsmen who fell the trees; undoubtedly, many climbed up into the mountains of Lebanon to do just that. The "cedars of Lebanon" were proverbial in the OT from time immemorial (see Isa. 2:13 and also Judg. 9:15; Pss. 29:5; 104:16). They are often mentioned in other places, along with junipers, to refer to wood used in construction (1 Kings 5:20ff.; 2 Kings 19:23f.; Ezek. 27:5; 31:8). A wide variety of texts from the ancient Near East frequently mention harvesting trees in the Lebanon for use in construction projects.

It will suffice to cite just one example, that from Nebuchadnezzar's report about his march toward Lebanon: "At that time, the Lebanon, the [Cedar] Mountain, the luxurious forest of Marduk, the smell of which is sweet, the hi[gh] cedars . . . my *nâbû* Marduk [had desired] as a fitting adornment for the palace of the *ruler* of heaven and earth, (this Lebanon) over which a foreign enemy was ruling and robbing (it of) its riches—its people were scattered, had fled to a far (away region). . . . I constructed a straight road for the (transport of the) cedars. I made the Arahtu flo[at] (down) and carry to Marduk, my king, mighty cedars, high and strong, of precious beauty and of excellent dark quality, the abundant yield of the Lebanon, as (if they be) reed stalks (carried by) the river. Within Babylon [I stored] mulberry wood" (cited from *ANET* 307; see *AOT* 395). In addition, concerning descriptions of other points of contact with Mesopotamia, see *ANET* 275, 291; from Egypt, see *ANET* 27b, 240b, 243, 252f., with notes 8, 254c; from Ugarit: II AB, VI, 18ff. (= *ANET* 134). For a portrayal of rulers from Lebanon who were felling trees for the pharaoh, see *ANEP* nos. 327 and 331; see also Dalman, *AuS* I, 82ff., and figs. 28–31.

It might not seem necessary to include information from the realm of mythology in order to make sense of this passage. However, in recent times that has been done, and with good reason. F. Stolz set forth a thesis that the background for this text must be established in light of the concept of a garden of God located on the top of the Lebanon, planted by El, a concept that Israel used in a variety of ways after reflecting on the idea theologically (141–156). As a matter of fact, in a chapter that presents several parallels that are similar to Isaiah 14, Ezekiel 31 speaks about a garden of God on top of Lebanon, with ארזים (cedars) and ברושים (fir trees) among the types of trees growing there, and mentions the trees of Eden in vv. 16 and 18. The pharaoh is likened to one of these trees of God, the box tree. Because of its height (it stretches its treetop way up into the heavens, v. 18), the box tree serves as a symbol for arrogance. The pharaoh was to be delivered over by Yahweh "into the hand of someone from among the peoples who is very powerful" and cast down, along with the trees of Eden, into the subterranean region, where he is to be forced to lie among the uncircumcised. However, it is a rather strange concept that trees of the garden of God should be felled and must travel down into the underworld. Unlike this description, Isaiah 14 presents an insightful depiction of the myth: a foolhardy rascal climbs up into the Lebanon, forces his way into the garden of God, and commits the sacrilege of touching the trees of El (see ארזי אל, [NRSV: mighty cedars], in Ps. 80:11). It is not the "tree," as in Ezekiel, but the intruder who is driven by hubris, who is to be handed over into the power of one who is stronger, one who would deal with him on the basis of his evil nature. The correctness of this analysis is supported by Isa. 37:24bff.: "With my many chariots I have gone up the heights of the mountains, to the far recesses (ירכתים!) of Lebanon; I felled (כרה!) its tallest cedars, its choicest cypresses; I came to its remotest height, its densest forest." The myth has been radically altered in Ezekiel, but it is still in its more original form in Isa. 14:8. (Ezekiel's alteration follows more closely that of Isaiah; see Isa. 2:13 and also 10:34, where the trees of Lebanon are symbols of human presumption.) There is no question that, from the very first, the trees of the garden of God were symbolic of life and fruitfulness (see Kapelrud, *Joel Studies*, 27f.). If the evildoer climbs up to them in order to fell them, he is trying to take hold of the elements that constitute life itself. It posed a deathly threat to the "whole earth" when this impious one forced his way to the junipers and cedar trees in the garden of God. Only when this background has been fully appreciated can one understand completely why the whole world would break out in singing at the downfall of this evildoer.

[14:9-11] *The Despot in Sheol*

With the explanation of v. 8 just offered, it is easy to see how vv. 9-11 continue the same pattern of thought. The intruder who entered the garden of God is thrust down into the underworld, just as it is reported about the pharaoh in Ezek. 31:15ff.; and there, like that other ruler, he is also afflicted with a wretched fate. In Isa. 14:9ff., however, the destiny of the one who has been cast down is depicted much more dramatically. First, we get the report of the reaction of those living in the underworld (v. 9). The arrival of the tyrant creates quite a sensation; it provides a measure of satisfaction for the "shades" in the underworld, since this one who had seemed to be invincible must now finally participate in their own miserable existence in the grave. Taken literally, the author speaks about Sheol as if it were a person itself. It is clear that שאול (Sheol), as is true throughout the OT, has no article (the same is true, for example, of תהום, the Deep) because some elements of the mythological concepts still survive, according to which שאול (Sheol) is described as a deity from the underworld. In the present passage, the author uses mythological terminology in poetic speech, but that does not mean that he is attempting a remythologizing. שאול (Sheol) is no longer a deity; it is nothing more than a poetic personification of the place where the dead reside.

The etymology of שאול (Sheol) is still widely disputed; the word seems to be used only in Hebrew. As W. F. Albright (*Oriental Studies,* FS P. Haupt [1926] 143–154) and W. Baumgartner (*TZ* 2 [1946] 233ff.) have shown, it may still have some connections with Akkadian *suʾaru,* the designation for Tammuz's abode in the underworld, whereas L. Köhler (KBL and *TZ* 2 [1946] 71–74) suggests a derivation from שאה (desolate), with the inserted letter ל (see Arabic *sûʾ* and *sûʾa,* "disaster"). Even less likely is the suggested derivation from a root *šwl* = Arabic *safala,* "be low," or from שאל, "ask, question," which would give שאול a meaning something like "place where one must give an answer." No one has followed the lead of E. Dévaud, who suggested a derivation based on the Egyptian way of describing the other side as *sḥ.t—ỉ ꜣrw,* "domain of the rush plants" (*Sphinx* 13 [1910] 120f.; see Erman-Grapow, *Wörterbuch der ägyptischen Sprache* I, 32; IV, 230). Out of sixty-five occurrences of שאול (Sheol) in the OT, the Gk translates sixty-one as ᾅδης (Hades), which means there was certainly a close relationship between the Israelite concept of Sheol and the Greek concept of Hades (Vulg translates שאול (Sheol) as *infernum* or *inferi* a total of sixty-five times); concerning the realm of the dead (Akkadian *erṣet lâ târi*) as depicted by those who lived in areas surrounding Israel, see. W. Zimmerli, *Ezechiel,* BK XIII/2, 784 (Engl: *Ezekiel* 2, 172f.).

As elsewhere in the OT, the inhabitants of the underworld are described with the technical term רפאים (Rephaim) (see also the threat against those who desecrate graves, that they will find no places of rest among the רפאים, "Rephaim," as found on two Phoenician coffin inscriptions, *KAI* 13:8; 14:8). In Isa. 26:14 and Ps. 88:11 this designation parallels מתים (the dead). But "dead," in our common way of thinking, that is, beings whose existence has been obliterated fully and completely, is not what is meant. They, in fact, "pass their time" in Sheol; see also Prov. 9:18; Job 26:5; or, to use another expression, they are in אבדון (Abaddon), which is what Ps. 88:12 calls the place where the dead reside. But also: they "pass their time" in the darkness; one can even speak of the assembly, the קהל, of the Rephaim, Prov. 21:16.

The etymology and original meaning of the term "Rephaim" is controversial as well. The question is made more complicated by the fact that the OT sometimes mentions the רפאים (Rephaim) with reference to a legendary, pre-Israelite population group that inhabited Palestine (Gen. 15:20, and often elsewhere). Their members were known for being particularly tall (see Deut. 3:11), for which reason the Gk calls them γίγαντες (giants) (Vulg: *gigantes*). So that one, in principle, does not have to try to distinguish these two meanings, some have suggested that the Rephaim were possibly originally giants, half gods, bringers of fruitfulness, later becoming beings who inhabited the underworld (in Isa. 14:9 they would still have been the elite among those who dwelt in the subterranean region), and that, finally, the word would have functioned as a general term for describing all the inhabitants of Sheol. After the content of the Ugaritic texts became known, the discussion started afresh as to whether there was a relationship between the seven mythical creatures called *rpum* in Ugarit and the biblical רפאים (Rephaim). J. Gray ("The Rephaim," *PEQ* 79 [1949] 127–139) views the *rpum* as the descendants of an ancient race of kings, which in later times still would have held the important position of being those who guaranteed fruitfulness. It is possible that they are part of the entourage of Baal. Since this explanation for the *rpum* is still uncertain, however, for the time being one would do well to leave this out of the discussion about the Rephaim mentioned in the OT. But the other question must also remain open, as to whether the Rephaim who inhabit the underworld have anything to do with the Rephaites from remote antiquity. On the one hand, it is possible that the Ugaritic name *rpum* could be related to Hebrew רפא, "heal"; and it is likely, on the other hand, that רפאים (Rephaim), referring to those who inhabit the subterranean region, can be related to the root רפה, "sleep, be unoccupied." They are also described as weak; see v. 10. In any case, this etymology would fit splendidly if one were to use the text before us to describe more about what was experienced by those who dwell in Sheol.

Under normal circumstances, the Rephaim lie on their beds, almost as rigid as if they were dead. Sheol must rouse them up (עורר), raise them up from their thrones (הקים), at which point life comes back into them for a time, though they soon sink back into their lethargic state once again. For this reason, the land of the dead can also be called דוּמָה (land of silence) (Pss. 94:17; 115:17). Once in a while there is talk of a marked difference in the fates of the dead (see Ezek. 32:26ff., and, on that passage, see Zimmerli, BK XIII/2, 784ff. [Engl: *Ezekiel 2*, 172ff.]); there are positions of honor and disgraceful regions. Thus, according to this present text, the עתודי־ארץ (rulers of the earth) are still seated on thrones; by contrast, the scoundrel has nothing but maggots as his bed, about which he can do nothing but wrap himself in a blanket made of worms. The others sit on thrones because, once upon a time, they were kings on earth. It is not explicitly said that some rulers within this group had once been defeated on earth by this tyrant, but that is likely. The erstwhile opponents are naturally very interested in the downfall of their conqueror. One must wonder whether the parallelism between רפאים (Rephaim) and עתודי־ארץ (rulers of the earth) should be taken in the strict sense; if this is the case, it would support the opinion expressed above that the Rephaim initially formed an elite group within the realm of the dead. However, this special meaning for רפאים (Rephaim) cannot be proved; it is more likely that עתודי־ארץ (rulers of the earth) identifies more precisely the sense of what is conveyed by the more general term רפאים (Rephaim). Verse 9b replaces this term with a simple מלכי־גוים (kings of the nations). Concerning כסא (couch, throne), see *Isaiah 1–12*, p. 261; on עתוד (rulers), see above, textual note 9d.

The power of nations was often represented in ancient times through the use of animal imagery; note how animals are used on coats of arms even today.

Now these inhabitants of the land of silence commence to speak. Obviously, ענה in this instance does not mean "give an answer," but rather (according to KBL and Ges-Buhl ענה IV) "strike up a song" (cf. 13:22); naturally, in the present passage, this is a mocking song. A similar mocking song is sung about an enemy in 37:22-29 (= 2 Kings 19:21-28) (see above, p. 51), where it is put in the form of a message from Yahweh. However, typical elements of this tradition were already altered in Judg. 5:15b-17 and 28-30.

When גם אתה (even you) is used at the beginning of the song, it accentuates that the residents of the underworld gloat maliciously in triumph. Whoever has to suffer under the arrogance and violent actions of another gets ready for the pleasure that comes when that opponent falls as well: "even you have become weak just like us." This "just like us" is to be understood as the complete reversal of the motif normally expressed in a song for the dead, where the one who has died is mourned as one who was like no other (Jahnow, 245). He seemed to be stronger than anyone else; now he is also just as "weak" as all the other Rephaim. His majesty, which had filled him with immeasurable pride (גאון can mean both), has gone down with him to Sheol; on this, see 5:14. To invite others to view his "majesty," which once surrounded him, "the sound [lit.: noisy swishing] of your harps" is summoned. Having someone available to play music is one of the indispensable elements of prestige typically found in a king's palace, and music to accompany eating is part of palace etiquette; see 2 Sam. 19:36; Dan. 3:5; and cf. Isa. 5:12; Amos 5:23.

Concerning נבל (harp), see *Isaiah 1–12*, pp. 200f. For this great evildoer, there is nothing in Sheol except a pitiable couch formed solely by worms. The concept of the underworld is developing, taking on the nature of the place where retribution is to be carried out; it is becoming hell. רמה has usually been translated as "maggot" (KBL, Ges-Buhl: "decayed, putrid, worms" [a collective]); רמה are found in spoiled food (Exod. 16:24), but also in sick bodies (Job 7:5), and especially in corpses in graves (Job 21:26; Sir. 7:17; 10:11). Thus it is hard to distinguish this word from the term תולעה (worms) (see Exod. 16:20), but one can say that this description about decaying has less to do with what happens to someone's body when sick and more to do with the biological phenomenon that accompanies decomposition. It is the grave, not Sheol, that v. 11b is describing. The concepts connected with the grave and Sheol, which really need to be distinguished from each other, are often used in the OT without close attention to that distinction; instead of שאול (Sheol), v. 15 speaks of בור, "the pit," and v. 19 of קבר, "the grave."

[14:12-15] *The Downfall of Helel*

[14:12] The exegesis of the preceding passage has shown that the author of the song made use of motifs from a myth about the garden of God on Lebanon, with its magnificent trees, which the evildoer wanted to fell. Apparently, the author united concepts from that myth with that of another,

62

similar in content, in vv. 12f. Some background needs to be furnished for this: Helel, son of Shachar, was a powerfully valiant warrior, who had the audacity, in his arrogance, to place himself on an equal level with Elyon. He wanted to ascend, on the heights of the clouds, into heaven, higher than all the other stars of God, on the mountain of assembly in the far north, so that he could take the throne as king over the universe. But the final end of this sacrilegious grasping for the stars was a downfall into Sheol. We are able to tell still more: a battle took place; he was challenged by the one whose power and majesty he sought to appropriate for himself, El Elyon. A broad, general consensus has been reached that this myth has its roots outside Israel, but it cannot be found in any form, neither in Canaanite materials nor in those from Israel's wider circle of neighbors. The decisive point about how the myth has been altered is that it has been "historicized," which means that it now has been made to refer to a historical personage and its motifs now have taken on the character of images used within poetic speech (concerning the problem in general, see A. Ohler, 175ff.).

This section begins once again with אֵיךְ (how), characteristic of the *Qina* (lament) pattern (concerning נָפַל, "fall," see above, p. 50). At the same time, however, מִשָּׁמַיִם (from heaven) shows that the one being mourned is not one who would typically have been expected to die; the comparison with Helel ben Shachar makes that crystal clear. The *crux interpretum* is, first, that we do not know who Helel is. The Gk translates הֵילֵל בֶּן־שָׁחַר (Helel ben Shachar) as ἑωσφόρος ὁ πρωὶ ἀνατέλλων (bringer of morn, the one who makes the dawn to rise up); Vulg: *Lucifer, qui mane oriebaris* (Lucifer, you who will rise in the morning). We are not completely in the dark when it comes to Shachar. In a wide variety of settings, documented by studies in history of religion, there is a divinity of the dawn, a figure that is sometimes loved, sometimes feared. Some vestiges of this belief can be detected in the OT. For example, Ps. 139:9 refers to the wings of the morning, and Job 3:9 and 41:10 mention its eyelids; one can say that it glances away in Song of Sol. 6:10, and one can awaken it according to Pss. 57:9; 108:3. Indeed, Ps. 110:3 seems to talk of the womb of Shachar. At the same time, Phoenician personal names show that Shachar was considered a deity (ברשחר, Bar [son of] Shachar, עבדשחר, Ebed [servant of] Shachar, and שחרבעל, Shachar Baal; the OT itself mentions אחישחר (Achi [my brother] Shachar) (see R. de Vaux, *RB* 46 [1937] 547, note 3). One of the Ugaritic texts (SS) portrays the procreation of Shachar by El and his birth from one of El's consorts, at which point comparisons have been made with Shalim, the god of the evening dusk. The way Shachar is used in personal names in Ugarit provides further evidence that it was considered a deity (see F. Stolz, 182, note 10).

By contrast, the identification of Helel has proved most difficult (concerning earlier attempts, see McKay, 451ff.). Arabic *hilâlun* means "new moon"; hence many choose to read הִלֵּל (instead of הֵילֵל, Helel) and treat this as a reference to the new moon (see, among others, Ges-Buhl, KBL, *BHS*). N. A. Koenig, taking the opposite approach, thinks הֵילֵל refers to the old moon, the one that is just about ready to dis-

63

appear. But whether this is the new moon or the old moon, to consider either the son of the dawn makes no sense. To compensate for this problem, some alter שׁחר to read שׂחר, which refers to the moon (god) in some Semitic languages, thus: "new moon, son of the (old) moon." However, it is better to avoid complicating the uncertainty of the identification by altering a good Hebrew word שׁחר (dawn); the problem is really with the identification of הילל (Helel). In the first place, there is hardly any doubt that what is referred to with this term is linked somehow to the well-known Hebrew root הלל (shine) (see above, textual note 12a). In Akkadian, *ellu* and the feminine *ellîtu*, both from the same root, are epithets for the female astral deity (so Grelot, *VT* 6, 303). This means that הילל is not as much a name as an epithet for a deity. That Ishtar, in Babylon, is called *ellîtu*, "the glowing one," does not help us much, since הילל has to be a reference to a male deity. Already back in 1883, however, O. Gruppe suggested the possibility of some interplay with the Greek fable of Phaëthon (W. Baumgartner, *Zum Alten Testament und seiner Umwelt* [1959] 157; in addition, see Duhm, and H. Gunkel, *Schöpfung und Chaos* [1895] 133f.). Grelot (*RHR*) was convinced that φαέθω means "shine," as does הלל and that Φαέθων (Phaëton) is the name of one of the horses that pull the wagon of Eos (*Odyssey* 23.275). Φαέθων (Phaëton) also can be the name for the sun itself or for the son of Helios. In Hesiod, *Theogony* 986f., Φαέθων (Phaëton) is the son of Eos, and this name refers to the Venus star; in addition, *Theogony* 378 tells about how Eos gave birth to the morning star ἑωσφόρος (he also can be called φωσφόρος = Lucifer). On this basis, Grelot concludes that הילל בן־שׁחר (Helel ben Shachar) is the same deity as Φαέθων (Phaëthon), son of ἕως (Eos). Concerning the other Phaëthon, son of Helios and of Clymene, it is said that he, in a reckless act of daring, tried to steer the wagon of the sun with its fiery horses through the clouds, taking his father's place. That was above his level of competence; Zeus had to intervene in order to avoid a worldwide catastrophe. He thrust the foolhardy wagon driver to the ground with a bolt of lightning (see Grelot, *RHR*, 30–32). It is possible that the account of this myth was transferred, being linked after that with the other Phaëthon, the son of Eos. If one can make that assumption, then the relationship with Isa. 14:12ff. is immediately apparent. Just as Φαέθων, son of Eos, is an appellative for the morning star ἑωσφόρος, so הילל could be considered an epithet of the Canaanite morning star ʿAttar (as suggested earlier by W. F. Albright, *Archaeology and the Religion of Israel* [1968] 84 and 86; and more recently once again in the vigorous argument presented by Oldenburg, 199ff.).

One ought not conceal the difficulties posed by this thesis. Eos is a female deity, whose beauty captivated the Greeks, whereas Shachar was a male deity, with little doubt about his wild ways. In Ugarit, ʿAttar is the son not of Shachar but rather of El (III AB, C 15ff.; but see NK 25, 27 and cf. F. Stolz, 187f.), and Shachar and Shalim seem to be two hypostases of ʿAttar's. We do not learn anything about Phaëthon's desire to establish his throne higher than the stars of God nor that he wanted to establish himself atop God's mountain of assembly; and we also learn nothing about his being cast down into the kingdom of the dead. That which the Ugaritic texts tell us about the story of ʿAttar (cf. also Clifford, 160ff.) does not match up (contra McKay) with the myth of Phaëthon. Indeed, the attempt has been made to smooth out the differences. Thus McKay believes that he can find examples from throughout the OT to show that the dawn was thought of as a female figure (with reference to Psalm 110, which mentions her womb, and Song of Sol. 6:10, which apparently describes Shachar as a wife, as well as other examples). However, that eliminates only one of the problems. If one wants to follow through and suggest that Helel ben Shachar = Phaëthon, son of Eos, then one would have to assume that various significant alterations took place within the myth on its travels from the point of origin in Greece as it moved toward Canaan, though no evidence in the ancient Near Eastern mythological materials presently available can show us how the specific shifts in the story occurred. One must also consider the possibility that other myths affected the way the story now stands. Certain elements of the Helel myth remind one of the Greek story of the "revolt of the giants." According to Apollodorus Mythographicus (*Bibliotheca* 1.6.1, ed. J. G. Frazer, Loeb Classical Library 121 [1961] 42), the giants, sons of Ge (earth) and Uranos (heaven), hurled toward the heavens both rocks and tree trunks that had been set on fire. But in a wild battle the gods were able to ward off the attack on their dwelling place, Zeus and his lightning bolts, along with Heracles and his bow, leading in the counterattack. Here also there is no mention of anyone being cast down into the underworld. Finally, reference has been made to the story of the Aloeids. The earthly giants Otus and Ephialtes had attempted to mount up into the heavens, trying to get there by piling Mount Pelion upon Mount Ossa and then both of those upon Mount Olympus, but Apollo killed them with arrows (for a description and the original sources, see Toepffer, Pauly-W I/2, 1590f.). Without a doubt, these myths are composed as a way to deal with the stabilizing of world order. Certainly, the Helel myth had the same function. However, this "concept of world order" is known so far and wide that one should be very hesitant about presuming "direct dependence," even though there may be a phenomenological relationship.

Helel ben Shachar, as the phrase נגדעת לארץ (as if smashed to bits on the earth) suggests, must have been involved in a rough battle; Phaëthon is shot by a lightning bolt from Zeus; the Canaanite myth must have originally told about how Helel went up against El, the head of the pantheon of Canaanite gods. But this text no longer says anything about that. The world ruler, who is the subject of the present discussion, does not come to ruin because of a battle against a deity who puts him back in his place; his downfall is self-inflicted, caused by his own arrogance.

[14:13] Helel, with whom the tyrant is compared, was undoubtedly a lesser deity, but he got it into his head to set up his throne above the stars of El. As the head of the pantheon, the creator of the heavens and the earth, El had his own throne above the stars, in the heavens. In Ugarit, one could confess: "El of the heavens, El, who created the mountainous regions" (I D 220), and the OT also speaks of אל השמים (God of heaven) (Ps. 136:26; Lam. 3:41; cf. Ps. 57:3f.). In Jerusalem, where El traditions were first incorporated into the description of faith in Yahweh, it is a fixed element, when speaking of God, to say that God looks down from the heavens (Isa. 18:4; Ps. 14:2, and often elsewhere). One significant problem for understanding the text is connected with the mention of the "mount of the meeting place" in v. 13b., about which it says explicitly that it is to be sought in the "most distant region of the north." Two distinct traditions, one about the mountain of the gods in the north and the other about heaven, have apparently been merged. The same thing happened in Greece, where "Olympus" and "Heaven" were originally separate, but before long they became synonymous (see E. Oberhummer, Pauly-W 18/1 [1939] 277–279).

Materials from many eras and settings in the Near East make clear that הר־מועד refers to the mountain on which the deities assemble themselves, under the lordship of El (for the Akkadian material, see Alfrink, 44ff.). In South Arabia, mention is made of *ʾEl fḥr*, which apparently means "El of the (divine) assembly" (see Oldenburg, 130). This expression is not found elsewhere in the OT; according to Ps. 74:8, the מועדי אל (meeting places of God) are the sanctuaries, and מועד (lit: meeting place) is simply another name for the temple in Ps. 74:4 and Lam. 2:6; in addition, the אהל מועד is well known as the tent of meeting, the "tabernacle." In spite of this, the concept of a meeting of the gods is found throughout the OT (see *Isaiah 1–12*, pp. 254f.) and the Ugaritic texts provide evidence that this idea was common throughout Canaan (see *pḫr bn ilm*, "assembly of the gods," II AB, III 14; *pḫr mʿd*, "the group of the assembly," III AB, B 14; *pḫr ilm*, "assembly of the gods," *UT* 17:7 and 21:2). It is true that the extant literature from Ugarit does not speak about a "mountain" of assembly. But it does mention the *ṣrrt ṣpn* (or *mrym ṣpn*), "the height of Zaphon." Yet that which is called the mountain of Baal in this reference (what was known as *mons Casius* in classical antiquity, presently known as *ǧebel el aqraʿ*, north-northeast of Ugarit on the Mediterranean) cannot be the same as the mountain where the gods assemble, since that could be located only at the place where El dwells. For that reason, it is unlikely that the occurrence of צפון (north) in this passage should be taken as a reference to the Ugaritic mountain of the gods (for a different view, see O. Eissfeldt, *Baal Zaphon, Zeus Kasios und der Durchzug der Israeliten durchs Meer* [1932] 14, who suggests that ירכתי, with reference to Isa. 37:24, means "summit, peak"). One can come to that conclusion on the basis of the Ugaritic epithet *il ṣpn*, El Zaphon (*UT* 17:13); a stele calls him *il kn ṣpn*, "El, who has established Zaphon" (R. Giveon, *RSO* 40 [1965] 197ff.; see Stolz, 145), and text III AB, B 20 (which also ought to be reinserted into lines 2, 14 as well) mentions a *ǧr ll* (not, as in Gordon, *UM* 137:20, *ǧr il*), in which case *ll* is the name of El's mountain. Thus, for the Ugaritic El, it is a residence on a distant, high mountain in the north, in which case there might be links between it and the world mountain, which those who lived in Mesopotamia sought in the mountain range northeast and east of the alluvial plain (on this, see H.-J. Kraus, *Psalmen I*, BK XV, 342f. [Engl: *Psalms 1–59*, Continental Commentary (1988) 462f.]; in addition, see O. Eissfeldt, "Die Wohnsitze der Götter von Ras Schamra," *KlSchr* II, 502–506). This idea that El had his dwelling place in the most distant region of the north must have been known in Jerusalem as well, which could lead someone who equated Zion itself with the mountain of the gods to identify Mount Zion in the "most distant region of the north" (ירכתי צפון) as the dwelling place of the great king (Ps. 48:3). In addition, the Greek Mount Olympus, residence and home of the gods, is also in the "north"; see Oberhummer, op. cit.; and cf. *Iliad* 1.494ff.; 11.75ff.; 15.21.

[14:14] After discussing the heavens (v. 12) and the mount of assembly in the most distant region of the north (v. 13), the author now continues with the "heights of the clouds" (cf. also Ezek. 31:10). Just as the identification of the place צפון (north) in v. 13 does not refer to the residence of El, but seems to be about where Baal lives, במתי עב (in the heights of the clouds) seems best understood as a reference to Baal, the "cloud rider," rather than about El. However, v. 14b explicitly mentions Elyon. Here we have a situation similar to that in Psalm 29, just to cite one example, which has motifs that one would normally attribute to Baal, the storm god, but which are assigned explicitly to El. In fact, there is no question that El Elyon of Jerusalem was worshiped as the storm god (Ps. 18:14; 1 Sam. 2:10; cf. also Stolz, 152ff.).

As one notices already in Gen. 14:18ff., עֶלְיוֹן (Elyon) was used as an appellative for El in pre-Israelite Jerusalem. As time passed and the Israelites adopted the ancient Jebusite festivals, אֵל עֶלְיוֹן (El Elyon) or even simply עֶלְיוֹן (Elyon) became an epithet for Yahweh, now portrayed as the one who was enthroned on Zion, the mountain of God; cf. יהוה אֵל עֶלְיוֹן (Yahweh El Elyon) in Gen. 14:22; יהוה עֶלְיוֹן (Yahweh Elyon) in Pss. 7:18; 47:3; אֱלֹהִים עֶלְיוֹן (Elohim Elyon) in Pss. 57:3; 78:56. Apart from Gen. 14:18ff. and numerous passages in the Psalms, Elyon occurs otherwise only in Num. 24:16; Deut. 32:8; Lam. 3:35, 38. These are all texts, one might conclude, that originate in Jerusalem; in the OT, no other designation for God is so closely linked to special traditions originating in Jerusalem. But this name is also found elsewhere in the ancient Near East. A Sfire inscription speaks of אֵל (El) וְעֶלְיוֹן (and Elyon) (*KAI* 222:A 11; supposedly this does not refer to two gods, but rather the name and epithet of the same god are used, one right after the other). Philo of Byblos (in Eusebius, *Praeparatio Evangelium* 1.10.14f.) speaks of Ἐλιοῦν καλούμενος Ὕψιστος (Elyon, the one called Most High) (on this, see M. H. Pope, *El in the Ugaritic Texts*, VTSup 2 [1955] 56f.; and Stolz, 136). In South Arabia there is mention of ʾl tʿly (God is supreme), and the Koran praises Allah as ʾallahu taʿālay (Allah is exalted) (see Oldenburg, 189f.; for other regions where there is some evidence that the name was in use, see Stolz, 134f.). In contrast to the other ways it is employed, the reference to Ἐλιοῦν in Philo points specifically to the biblical Elyon. The addition of ὕψιστος (most high) immediately afterward is apparently intended as the Greek way to translate עֶלְיוֹן (Elyon). Without a doubt, the name is from the root עלה, "ascend, be high" (the afformative -ōn or -ān is a common ending on the names of deities; see, for example, Shulman in relation to Shalim; the Gk translates this as ὕψιστος, "most high"; Targ as אֱלָהָא, "God"; Syr as rwmʾ, "high"). However, the word is not a superlative, as is ὕψιστος (most high), but simply identifies the deity as the "high one" (cf. *excelsus*, "elevated," when used with *altissimus*, "most high," in the Vulg, with the renderings in the Targ and Syr; one should also note the wordplay between אֶעֱלֶה, "I rise up," and עֶלְיוֹן, "Elyon," in v. 14; in addition, the use of אֶעֱלֶה, "I rise up," in v. 14 picks up on the use of יעלה, "climbing up," in v. 8). It is not surprising that a god would be praised as "high." Therefore both nominal and verbal elements of the word עלה (go up) are found in theophoric names in regions that use the Semitic languages (see Stolz, 135, note 198); in the OT one can observe that usage in the name Eli (עלי). Without any question, the use of this epithet identifies the deity as the lord of the heavens, which is exactly what is corroborated by the context of v. 14. (The corresponding designations also are used widely in Hellenistic and Roman settings and describe the deity who is the head of the pantheon; naturally, more than any other, this is Zeus; see M. Simon, "Theos Hypsistos," FS G. Widengren I [1972] 372–385; G. Bertram, "ὕψιστος," *TDNT* VIII, 614–620.)

Based on the Greek story of the revolt of the giants (and also the revolt of the Titans), one would expect that the evildoer would go up to heaven, cast Elyon down, and want to take his place. That is not said; the OT makes no mention of anyone seeking to dethrone God, but does know of humans and titans who "wanted to be as God"; the evildoer wants to be just like God (דמה, *hithpaʿel;* one might compare this with the four times the verb is used in the related song in Ezekiel 31). Songs of lament for the dead commonly speak about the uniqueness of the one who had died. This present text satirically recasts the motif: the one who stormed heaven wanted to be like the "high one."

[14:15] But Helel is cast down into Sheol. Verse 15 repeats the content and sometimes the actual words from v. 11 and thus underscores the central point that the poet wants to make. The gloomy sound of שְׁאוֹל תּוּרָד (realm of death) corresponds to the macabre scene; יַרְכְּתֵי־בוֹר (uttermost distant region) is contrasted with יַרְכְּתֵי צָפוֹן (most distant region of the north) in v. 13. This expression is usually translated: in the deepest depth of the pit, or something similar. However, that would cause one to miss the wordplay with יַרְכְּתֵי צָפוֹן (most distant region of the north) in English. It does not have to be the deepest depth; it could just as well refer to the most remote region of the underworld. A בוֹר is a cistern, but here, parallel with שְׁאוֹל (Sheol), it is a designation for the realm of the dead, as is also true in other passages; see N. J. Tromp, *Primitive Conceptions of Death and the Nether World in the Old Testament,* BibOr 21 (1969) 166ff. In the past it was suggested that this was related to an Akkadian word *būru,* but that word does not exist; see W. von Soden, *UF* 2 (1970) 331f. The formula יֹרְדֵי־בוֹר (those who go down into the Pit) is common; see 38:18; Ezek. 26:20; 31:14-16; 32:18, 24, 25, 29, 30, and often elsewhere; see Ugaritic *yrdm arṣ* (he goes down into the earth), I* AB V 15–16. Thus Sheol is thought of as a place under the earth, shaped like a cistern (see O. Keel, *The Symbolism of the Biblical World: Ancient Near Eastern Iconography and the Book of Psalms* [1978] 69ff. and illuss. 66–68, 78). Reference is made to the billows that tumble down on those who pass their time there. Concepts are apparently used that refer to the depths of the sea, in which the powers of chaos have not yet been subdued; see Keel, op. cit., 70f.; and see 2 Sam. 22:5ff. (= Ps. 18:5ff.); Pss. 40:3; 88:7f.; Job 26:5.

[14:16f.] *In Front of the Corpse of the Evildoer*

[14:16] In v. 16a the author begins to speak once again. The only issue that needs to be resolved deals with the identity of those who listen to the message about the fallen world ruler. Some suggest that the scene continues to be played out in Sheol and that v. 16a also describes how its inhabitants inspect the new arrival, giving full expression to their mockery in v. 16b. But that would do little more than offer a poor repetition of vv. 9-11. It is much more likely that the setting of the scene shifts as v. 15 shifts to v. 16: v. 16a speaks about human beings who come across the corpse of the ruler who once was so proud but who now lies unburied and simply dumped somewhere. A battlefield scene may furnish the background: someone would pace it and would make an attempt to identify the fallen; a careful examination would bring one to the discovery that, among those who had been slain, who had been pierced through with the sword (v. 19b), this powerful man had also been killed, this one before whom the entire earth had trembled. One would peer intently; the normal verb ראה (see) would not do here. This verb describes careful observation, which would not simply make a positive identification but would be so intense that not even the slightest detail would go unnoticed, so that one could enjoy this triumph as fully as possible. For the use of שׁגח (peer intently) in the *hiphᶜil*, cf. Song of Sol. 2:9. Similarly, התבונן conveys the idea of the way someone acts when focusing complete attention on some thing or some person. The rhetorical question in v. 16b (which becomes a descriptive portrayal in v. 17) characterizes the feelings of those doing the observing in their own words, recognizing by careful examination and reflection that everyone finally passes on and that human arrogance finally shows itself to be without power. At the same time, it portrays the astonishment about how rapidly and how completely this change in fortune has taken place. רגז (stirred up) describes both physical ("the earth quaked," 1 Sam. 14:15) and also emotional convulsing (see v. 9), being used most frequently to describe what happens when someone shakes out of fear (e.g., in Exod. 15:14). The *hiphᶜil* in this present passage covers both types of situations. רעשׁ (cause to tremble) means almost the same thing, although it is more commonly used for physical situations; it is especially used when world empires forcibly displace others by means of brute force through the use of the politics of power (see Hag. 2:6f., 21, where the shaking affects the entire cosmos).

[14:17] However, both the devastation wrought on earth and the destruction of cities mentioned in v. 17 definitely result from military might being unleashed. חרס (demolish), the opposite of בנה, "build," is a very strong word, one that describes the demolition of a city; cf. 2 Sam. 11:25; 2 Kings 3:25; Jer. 1:10; 24:6; 42:10; 45:4.

Verse 17b adds a detail that is even more specific: he is not one to release his prisoners. It is rare to find a בית הכלא (house of confinement) mentioned in the OT; it occurs only within the context of political activities. Prisoners of war, if they had not been killed along the way, had to perform the duties of slaves or were deported elsewhere. Only those individuals who were high up the ladder would have been considered candidates for being put into prison, in cases where one would have been hesitant to bring about their death or where it would have been thought politic to keep them around, since some positive factors could make them useful in certain political circumstances. They also served as hostages, to keep the groups of people who were loyal to them in line; think, for example, about what happened to Jehoiachin, 2 Kings 25:27-30.

[14:18-20] *The Humiliating End, Without Comfort or Hope*

[14:18] The antithesis to the tyrant's merciless treatment of others is depicted in the humiliating destiny following his death. Whereas other rulers rest in the grave "in honor," no one even bothers to take care of his corpse. It is left exposed to the elements and to the beasts of prey, just as one might dispose of a stomach-turning miscarriage, which one would not handle carefully by disposing of it with reverence, because one would be afraid of the powers that were at work to keep the fetus from being born alive, or as one might leave a corpse rotting right where the body fell. There is a certain tension between this section and that which immediately precedes it, according to which a place of repose was readied for the tyrant in Sheol. Yet concepts about Sheol and the grave can be used together; going back and forth from one to the other poses no great problem.

For human beings in ancient times, it was a great comfort to count on having an appropriate and fitting burial. "Remain where thrown, without a grave," would be a great humiliation for anyone. Whether or not they thought every time about the reason for desiring a proper burial, there was a belief that one who had not been buried would have no rest; cf. Jer. 22:19; 36:30. However, if one had confidence that one would someday "be gathered together with one's fathers (or family members)," then the sting of death would be removed. One notes that the same word is used for "lying" in the grave (שׁכב) as for lying in bed while one sleeps. Such a rest in the grave is provided for "the kings of peoples," but it is used most specifically when describing those who died in battle against the evildoer. One ought not press the כֻּלָּם (each) too much; its function is to accentuate the contrast between their status and the unique despair that accompanies the death of the great tyrant. They rest "in honor"; he carries the shame of a "dishonorable" burial. Apparently an expander added: אִישׁ בְּבֵיתוֹ (lit.: each in his house). Does בֵּית mean "grave" here? Hardly; it should be taken literally: sovereigns were buried in an area near their palaces (cf. the formula: "and was buried in the city of his father David," 1 Kings 11:43; see also 1 Kings 2:34: "he was buried at his own house"; on this, cf. Noth, WAT, 154f. [Engl: *The Old Testament World* (1966) 169]). Even this prospect would give one comfort when anticipating one's own death. Just as one, at some future time, would rest in the family burial place with one's ancestors, one would also remain closely bound to one's descendants, with whom one also had close ties, indeed, in whom one's existence would continue. If one thought of oneself as part of a collective group, as was common in ancient times, then each individual was no more than a temporary expression of the life force within that clan.

[14:19f.] Introduced by וְאַתָּה, "yet, you," these verses set forth a contrast between a comforting and honorable end of life for "all the kings of the earth" and the humiliating end of the tyrant: "cast out, having no grave." The OT normally speaks of the corpse being "cast forth" in situations in which no one is able to bury someone who has died or else no one wishes to do so (cf. 1 Kings 13:24f.; Isa. 34:3; and often elsewhere). Naturally, that would often be the case after a battle, but it could also be because someone intentionally wanted to disparage the one who died; see Jer. 22:19 and cf. 36:30.

Unfortunately, the text of v. 19aβ (כנצר נתעב) is corrupted and one cannot be sure about the emendation suggested above, reading כנפל נתעב (just like a stomach-turning miscarriage). Like many others, Fohrer opts for staying with the MT and says this means: "as a family member who has been expelled, a lost son, for whom no one cares" (the way one might speak of a "wild shoot" or of the "black sheep of the family"). Support for this interpretation is cited by pointing to the use of נצר (sprig) in 11:1; there, however, it is used to describe something pure and fitting that comes forth from a root. One might compare Ps. 58:9; Job 3:16; and Eccles. 6:3 to see how נפל (miscarriage) is used. The word תעב (stomach-turning) conveys the sense of what is currently identified, by those who study a variety of religions, as "taboo." That sense fits perfectly in the context; no one would want to have anything to do with the corpse of the tyrant, since one would fear that the evildoer could still cause a disaster, even in death, and "stick it to" whomever had any contact with his body.

The continuation, v. 19aγ-bβ, shows that the author clearly has in mind a death in battle. The ruler lies underneath a pile of others who had been slain. One ought not say (as Procksch does) that the meaning of לבוש (covered with) is incomprehensible; bitter scorn is involved with this expression: a ruler is otherwise always dressed in most magnificent clothing; now, the tyrant has nothing left as "clothing" except those blood-drenched soldiers who have been "pierced through by the sword." Ezekiel promises approximately the same thing to the pharaoh: "you shall lie among the uncircumcised, with those who are killed by the sword" (31:18; see also v. 17 and 32:20ff.); there it is worse yet, since those "killed by the sword," חללי חרב, are also uncircumcised; however, it is even more important there that the scene changes, since the fate of the ruler is described within the context of the underworld; one's fate on the field of battle leads to one's destiny in Sheol.

The author adds a second comparison: כפגר מובס (as a trampled carcass). This does not fit exactly with the first comparison, but then this is not a blow-by-blow account of the events of the day; rather, it employs a variety of images to depict the humiliation that has come on the one who died.

At this point, vv. 19bα and 20aα continue with still another motif: just as the evildoer has been denied burial in a grave, he will also be denied the chance for fellowship down below with those who are like himself, who reside by the אבני־בור (stones of the pit). One wonders what this expression is supposed to mean; attempts have been made to reshape the text in order to make some sense of the phrase. However, all the proposed solutions remain unsatisfactory, which means one still ought to try to make some sense of the words as they stand. Duhm says: "The poet refers to the disgraceful way the enemies disposed of the body, dumping it into the grave and tossing stones on top of it; cf. 2 Sam. 18:17." But this fantasy-filled explanation ignores the fact that ירד בור (go down into the grave) is a fixed formula, used to describe the descent into the underworld; see above, p. 68. Possibly the stones served as pillows for the head of those who would sleep there (cf. Gen. 28:11), or maybe it refers to stone slabs that some might have thought were used to pave the surface of the underworld.

[14:20aβ] Verse 20aβ seems to state explicitly the reason for the tyrant's dismal end. Yet one is in for a surprise: one would already have come to the conclusion that the entire world could breathe a little easier because he had gone down in battle (vv. 3f.), since he had upset the entire world and had made it into a desert (vv. 16ff.). But now one reads: "You have completely wrecked your land, murdered your people." One might argue that the poet thought that all the suffering he had inflicted on the other peoples was not, in the end, as horrible as the destruction he had inflicted on his own land, with his plans for conquering the world. As appealing as this idea might be, however, one must assume that a poet of the OT would have thought, first and foremost, of the suffering and the distress that had been inflicted on Israel. Instead, it is more likely that v. 20aβ simply furnishes the reason why the scoundrel would be refused admission to Sheol, in order to be reunited with his fellow citizens in the "pit." He had completely wrecked their land, brought his own fellow citizens (עַמְּךָ, "your people") to their death; this means that his single-minded arrogant lust for power was carried out at the expense of both land and people. Thus he is an outcast in the underworld, never to have the chance of associating even with his own people.

[14:20b] Just as the dead can no longer reach back to contact those still alive, there is also to be absolutely no hope when he looks toward the future. "In all eternity" no mention will be made of this evil family line to which the tyrant belongs. It is not said that it will go unmentioned because it will no longer even exist; rather, it will be absolutely unimportant in the future.

[14:21] Verse 21 offers a completely different perspective. The gap between these two verses is often smoothed over by translators who read here: "may they be [or: may they continue to be] mentioned no longer," which is impossible (see above, v. 20b). Yet if one continues to treat this as an indicative statement, the passionate outburst in v. 21 makes no sense. To help explain הָכִינוּ מַטְבֵּחַ (prepare the slaughtering bench), compare Zeph. 1:7: הֵכִין יְהוָה זֶבַח (Yahweh has prepared a sacrifice). What is said there about the way Yahweh acts in judgment, employing the motifs connected with holy war, is now said when calling for this judgment to be put into effect. The poem in vv. 4b-20 portrays the imposing narration of the events that bring nemesis (retribution); there is scant mention of human involvement as well as little mention of divine intervention. But here human beings are summoned to be involved in a major way, in making sure that righteousness will have the upper hand. Whenever a ruler was overthrown in the ancient Near East, there was a concerted effort to exterminate his family as well, so that no family member could come back and claim to have a legitimate right to regain power; cf.

KAI 223:C 13ff.: "The gods of this treaty will all snatch away . . . Mattiʿel and his son and his grandson and his descendants." For the OT see, e.g., 1 Kings 15:28f.; 2 Kings 10:17. If אבותם (their fathers) has been transmitted correctly, the guilt is not precisely identified as that of that one tyrant only, but is linked to the entire dynasty. But since it is a common and oft-repeated formula that the sons are to suffer the consequences of the guilt of the fathers (see Exod. 20:5; 34:7), one ought not try to be too specific about what might be intended when such a formula is used. Rinaldi (*BeO* 10 [1968] 24) is correct when he calls attention to the way the suffix refers back to the entire expression when it is used in a genitive relationship; thus, technically, it should be translated: "because of the guilt of their fathers."

It makes good sense that one would have a mass execution of the sons in order to hinder any plans that they might have to resurrect the ancient goal that their family would subdue the whole world. However, the second reason, that the sons of the tyrant might not have the opportunity to "fill the wide world full with cities," seems, completely anachronistically, to anticipate modern postulates about protecting the environment. One might question whether the text has been transmitted correctly in this case as well. Nevertheless, in the Greek and Roman era, the establishment of cities was a most effective tactic for gaining absolute control over a land that had been conquered. Yet one would not wish to place this addition to the text at so late a date. Anyway, the Assyrian and Persian rulers already had attempted to magnify their own glory through the establishment of cities or had adopted this approach as a way to establish secure borders for their country. The original inhabitants certainly did not favor foreigners being brought in to settle in their land, thus imposing themselves on the natives and robbing them of their self-rule.

[14:22f.] The concluding material, which provides a frame around this poem, vv. 22f., formally presents a threat against Babylon, as if spoken by Yahweh himself. The scoundrel and his dynasty are no longer on the scene, in spite of the mention of עליהם (against them) in v. 22aα; this preposition with suffix does not effectively establish a transition with the preceding description of wicked individuals. This author is thinking only about the end of the city itself, which to this point had not been mentioned at all. As was explained above (p. 49), it is likely that "Babylon," as used here, refers no longer to the capital city of the Chaldeans but rather to whatever great power was in control during the time when this was written; in the final analysis, this would have been understood as a code word for any imperialistic world power. The formula for an utterance of God, נאם־יהוה (utterance of Yahweh), especially when it is simply tacked on, is a favorite way expanders of OT texts sought to legitimize their prophetic claims (on the formula itself, see *Isaiah 1–12*, pp. 66f.).

וקמתי עליהם (Thus I will raise myself up against them) is the direct opposite of the call to prepare for a slaughter in v. 21; form-historically, we are in a completely different setting.

The destruction of Babylon is to be thorough: שם ושאר ונין ונכד (renown and remnant, offspring and family line) (one notes the alliteration, first of all between שם, "renown," and שאר, "remnant"; second, between נין, "offspring," and נכד, "family line"; Procksch tries to imitate this: "Name und Neige, Kind und Kegel!").

שם does not mean only "name" but also "reputation, renown, importance"; cf. passages such as Gen. 11:4; Isa. 63:12. שאר, "remnant," is a concept with many shades of meaning; when it is used, a judgment is certainly involved—only a "remnant" remains from an entire people, indeed, maybe it is only the "smallest of remnants," but this could still be a hopeful sign, that at least there are some who remain; see *Isaiah 1–12*, pp. 296f.; and H. Wildberger, "שאר," *THAT* II, 844–855. When mention is made of the finality with which a judgment has been carried out, then it is specifically said that even those who have escaped death up to this point are going to be killed as well. שם (renown) and שאר (remnant) (or שארית, remnant) are used together in a fixed formula; see Zeph. 1:4; 2 Sam. 14:7. The formulaic aspect is even more pronounced when נין (offspring) and נכד (family line) are linked; these two words are found in the OT only when used together: Gen. 21:23; Job 18:19; Sir. 41:5; 47:22. The etymology of נין is not clear; in Ps. 72:17 the verb form נין possibly means "sprout." The Gk translates both terms with just one word, σπέρμα (seed); Aquila reads γονην (offspring), Sym ἀπογονον (descendant); Vulg: *germen et progeniem* (shoot and progeny); Targ: בר ובר־בר (child and child's child).

[14:23] The city itself will be covered over by a swamp (אגם, "puddles of water" = Akkadian *agammu*, "pool with bulrushes," Arabic *mâʾun ʾâǧimun*, "puddles with bulrushes always in them").

Whenever someone established a settlement in the low-lying flatlands of Mesopotamia, there was always a danger of inundation, and a significant number of cities were destroyed by catastrophic floods. It is not easy to harmonize this with the statement that the city district would also become the hunting ground for the hedgehogs; the hedgehog is not found in swamps. But קפד (hedgehog) is apparently one of the stock terms when one portrays the complete annihilation of a populated area; cf. 34:11; Zeph. 2:14. In addition, one cannot be sure about identifying this as a hedgehog. The word should indeed be treated as related to קפד (*piʿel:* "roll together"; Arabic: *qafada* = "bind [the head binding] on tightly"; it should be noted that the hedgehog is called *qunpud* [with a fricative *d*!] in Arabic; some identify this in the Zephaniah passage as the "[short-eared] owl" [see KBL]). Thus, whether it is a hedgehog or an owl, it is certainly no domesticated animal or grazing animal but is some sinister creature instead (cf. 13:21ff.). The region in the vicinity of the city will not so much as be grazed, not even by a sheep that is there just for a time (cf. passages such as Mic. 3:12).

Whereas it is true that one often expected that an area once inhabited would become populated by wild and sinister creatures, typical of similar portrayals predicting destructions and commonly found in similar threats within curses (see above, pp. 32f.), it is unique that one would include what is predicted in the closing sentence: "and sweep it away with the broom of annihilation"; this is hard to render in English, because both the substantive and the verb (both hapax legomena) derive from טיט, meaning "mud, filth, slime," in the other passages where it is used.

Purpose and Thrust

The exegesis of the individual verses has confirmed the analysis given above. First of all, vv. 4b-20 are to be treated as a separate unit. The song is written in the form of an ironic lament for one who has died, recast so that what is uttered takes the form of a song mocking a fallen enemy. If one studies this song after it is removed from the framework furnished by vv. 3, 4a and 21, 22f., then one sees no points of contact in the text that could help in identifying historically which ruler might have been in the author's mind. Even though one need not doubt that the author had some historical personage in mind (see above, pp. 53f.), the author apparently tries to describe that which would be typical of any one of the leaders who held such a high position.

Exegetes generally agree that this is one of the most magnificent pieces of poetry in the OT. "This song for the dead [is first] among equals when it comes to clarity in organization, variety of images, power of thought, passionate feelings. The downfall of the tyrant produces an aftereffect: in the silent world of nature, where trees now get a chance to speak; in the underworld, whose dead kings sing a gruesome choir piece; for the prophet, who illuminates the unfolding drama of the one who had acted outrageously against God, showing both arrogance and downfall, between his zenith and nadir, with electrifying speed; for the human observers, who watch an inglorious decline, among whom are the members of the choir who sing the closing chorus, at which point the passion of the piece reaches its high point" (Procksch). Even when compared with the magnificence of the formal aspects, the theological themes are no less impressive. These correspond to the way wisdom understands the world, and perhaps one could expect to discover that the author was a member of a group that was familiar with the worldview of wisdom. (One might compare passages such as Prov. 8:22-31, a poem showing that wisdom teachers were also familiar with and could use mythological materials and knew how to use these to suit their purposes.) The central theme, a common wisdom topic, is about the judgment against the hubris of human beings who reach for the stars and break into a world reserved for God alone. Wisdom teaching speaks about how pride (גאוה) causes human beings to fall (Prov. 29:23) or that pride (גאון) comes before destruction and a haughty spirit before a fall (Prov. 16:18). It proclaims that the path of life for a wise person leads upward, in order to avoid Sheol below, but that Yahweh will tear down the house of the proud (גאים) (Prov. 15:25). That Isaiah 14 does not utter its wisdom teaching in short phrases but rather in the form of a song that also employs many mythological expressions shows only that this passage belongs to late wisdom. Wisdom speaks regularly about human pride, but even an ancient passage such as Judg. 9:7-15 shows that criticism of kingship was not impossible. One might say it something like this: wisdom expected much from the king; cf. this with passages such as Prov. 16:10-15; wisdom was quick to criticize whenever the king did not live up to its expectations, particularly when he failed to be the protector of the poor (see, e.g., Prov. 29:4, 14; 31:4f.; Eccles. 4:13; 10:16f.); it knows that he is dependent on Yahweh for his position (Prov. 21:1); and it brings a critical eye when destructively exorbitant demands are placed on the people (Prov. 29:4). Within the scope of its discussion, however, the poem is not far from the message delivered by Isaiah (see 2:9-17; 9:7-9), and the way Isaiah depicted the arrogance of the Assyrian king in 10:5-15 might have inspired the present author. Yet it is more likely that one could explain the reason for the thematic and verbal points of contact by suggesting that Isaiah himself was stimulated by and adapted thought patterns from wisdom. It fits with wisdom's worldview that the poem, at least in what has been suggested was its original form, does not speak at all about Yahweh: the arrogant one comes to destruction just because of his own hubris. Mythological ideas have been used successfully to show in fitting detail both his pride, which led him with reckless flair to overstep the bounds established for all human beings, and his rapid fall to ruin. The very fact that no specific historical contact point can be detected allows the poem to function on and on, as a contemporaneous protest against every tyranny and, at the same time, to give an emphatic witness, rarely found elsewhere, to the confidence of a faith that believes that oppressive violence will always come to ruin because it cannot keep itself in check. It is also quite amazing that the song has no pretensions about being composed for Israel alone. As is common in the way wisdom teaching is presented, it is for all peoples, all who had been forced to suffer untold agonies, who now had the chance to rejoice at the downfall of the tyrant; it is for all the oppressed of humanity, pure and simple. Even if the conclusion cannot be corroborated that this song has its roots beyond Israel, it is still worth noting that some maintain that this is the case. That fact is also seen in points of contact that can be found between the poem and Isaiah, since there is evidence neither for humans feeling sorry for themselves nor for human hatred. How can a human being make a place for hatred when seeing the majestic way in which righteousness steers a steady course? The author detected some of the tragic element found in such personages who attempt to storm the heavens.

A reinterpretation is furnished by the verses that frame the poem, making it into a prediction against "Babylon" and into a promise for enslaved Israel: a promise for Israel in v. 3, which is loosely linked to vv. 1-2, and a prediction against Babylon in the conclusion, vv. 22f. The main point is no doubt that Israel can have hope. That point is obscured by the circumstance that 14:3ff. are presently also read in light of the rubric of the superscription מַשָּׂא בָּבֶל (verdict concerning Babylon) that heads 13:1. Verse 3 may have been crafted intentionally, with great care by the author, making use of the poem that had already been written and that was now before him, since הֵנִיחַ (provide rest) in v. 3 furnishes a link with נָחָה (reposes) in v. 7; רֹגֶז (privation) may have some connection with מרגיז (stir up the world) in v. 16. From the song itself, the expander took the assurance that human arrogance finally brings its own destruction to fashion a statement of hope for freedom and deliverance for Israel. However, he does not believe that the cause for the change in fortune is found within the framework of world order, into which it had been foreordained "that the trees do not grow up into the heavens," but rather in the activity of Yahweh, who would give his people the promised gift of "rest" and would thus deliver them from their bondage. It is possible that this man himself is the one who inserted into the song, in v. 5, the word "Yahweh," thereby expressing his own theological understanding of history.

The final editor not only gave the poem a Yahwistic tone but also inserted his personal "eschatological" view of history. Israel's time of affliction and privation would come to an end; a time would come in which all world power would be completely annihilated; then all the ancient, grandiose, and as yet unfulfilled promises of God for his people would become completely real, and Israel would finally come into its "rest."

Yahweh's Irrevocable Decision

Literature

H. Donner, *Israel unter den Völkern*, VTSup 11 (1964) 145f. B. S. Childs, *Isaiah and the Assyrian Crisis*, SBT 2/3 (1967) 38f. V. O. Eareckson, "The Originality of Isaiah XIV 27," *VT* 20 (1970) 490–491. O. Kaiser (see literature to Isaiah 13–23).

Text

14:24 Yahweh of Hosts has thus sworn:
 Surely,[a] as I have contemplated,
  thus, it has happened;[b]
 Just as I have decided,
  thus, it has come to be.[b]
25 I shatter Assyria in my land,
  and on my mountains I trample it down.
 [Then its yoke will depart from them,
  and from their shoulders[a] its burden will depart.][b]
26 That is the decision, determined
  for the whole earth,
 and that is the hand
  stretched out over all peoples.
27 For Yahweh of Hosts has determined it,
  who will thwart it?
 And his hand is stretched out,[a]
  who will turn it back?

24a On the use of אם־לא (if not) in sentences containing an oath, cf. Joüon, *Gr* §165c.

24b היתה (it has happened) and תקום (it has come to be) are feminines used in a neuter sense; cf. Joüon, *Gr* §152c. It is worth noting that a change of tense takes place, from the perfect היתה (it has happened) to the imperfect תקום (it has come to be). Donner (145) translates the first as a preterite: "thus it has happened," but תקום, as a future: "And it shall come to be"; other renderings are similar. Donner thinks that the first half of the verse is supposed to show that Assyria, according to Yahweh's plan, has attained the status of a world power, but that the second half is to show the judgment that is to come because of its hubris. However, this analysis is contradicted

78

by the explicit parallelism and does not help much with making sense of the passage; cf. 7:7: לֹא תָקוּם וְלֹא תִהְיֶה (it will not happen and will not succeed). Duhm, Marti, Gray, Fohrer, and others treat הָיְתָה as a prophetic perfect and consequently translate it either in the present or in the future. But then one would expect to find קוּם (come to be, stand) in the perfect as well. The Gk reads ἔσται (will be), which has caused Procksch to alter הָיְתָה (it was) to read תִהְיֶה (it will be), which is the reading in Q^a as well.

25a The Gk reads ὤμων (from shoulders) instead of שִׁכְמוֹ (his shoulder), and many extant copies add αὐτῶν (their); see also OL, Syh, Syr, Targ, Vulg, Ethiopic, Arabic. Because of the plural suffix on מֵעֲלֵיהֶם (from [upon] them), one would expect the plural שִׁכְמָם (their shoulders) (see also *BHS*). However, v. 25b is practically a word-for-word quote from 10:27 (see below, p. 80); for this reason, one should not expect the suffixes to match perfectly.

25b Instead of סֻבֳּלוֹ (its burden), the Gk reads τὸ κῦδος αὐτῶν, "their glory," but H. S. Gehman (*VT* 3 [1953] 399) points out that this is a corruption of the text within the Greek, which would originally have read τὸ κῆδος αὐτῶν, "their trouble." This points to a tendency within the Gk to spiritualize the original intent of the passage (Sym, Theod translate literally: βάσταγμα, "burden").

27a The article is missing from הַנְּטוּיָה (stretched out) in the Syr (cf. M. Lambert, *REJ* 50 [1905] 261), making it possible to treat נְטוּיָה (stretched out) as a predicate, which would fit better here in light of the parallelism.

Form

This message is furnished with an introduction (v. 24a), which undoubtedly is original. Therefore a new section begins with v. 24. If, as Erlandsson and others before him have suggested, one believes that the מָשָׁל (taunt) in vv. 4b-23 is directed against the king of Assyria, or even that chap. 13 also was directed originally against Assyria, then at the very minimum the identity of the person addressed would have been the same throughout both chapters. In spite of this suggestion, 14:24-27 should be considered a self-contained unit, since a completely different situation is presumed here (see v. 25a), namely, Assyria's downfall on the mountains of Judah.

Little else needs to be said to show that another new unit begins with v. 28; the exposition of the text also will show that the two sections are virtually unrelated, meaning that their present order does not reflect a chronological sequence.

One cannot say for sure why this section was appended to the conclusion of 14:23. It is highly unlikely that the redactor wanted to place it under the superscription "verdict concerning Babylon," as has been suggested by Erlandsson (166) (see literature to Isaiah 13–23). One might presume that he simply wanted to include a prediction about Assyria within his collection of oracles against the foreign nations and that he obviously was aware of the close ties between Assyria and Babylon.

Verse 25b should be treated as an insertion by a later hand (so, e.g., Duhm, Marti, Gray, Fohrer). One can see that this is the case just by noting its form: it has to be read as an inverted seven-stress colon (3 + 4), which is rare in and of itself and has no parallel anywhere within the context. The line is reminiscent of 10:27 and 9:3. The reason for the insertion is the same as that which caused 14:1f. to be added onto 13:1-22: someone sought in vain a direct statement about what it was to mean for Israel that its powerful enemy would come to its end or that it would have its plans go for naught.

Based on references to Job 9:12; 11:10; 23:13, V. O. Eareckson has defended the view that v. 27 offers a later expansion using wisdom terminology. Although rhetorical questions are closely related to wisdom formulations, that does not provide one with sufficient reason to deny that Isaiah could have authored them; on this, see B. S. Childs, 128, 136.

If one analyzes the content, this is a prediction of disaster against Assyria. On formal grounds, it is to be divided into two parts: a first part, cast in the style of an oath of Yahweh, and a second, speaking about Yahweh in the third person, which might be described as prophetic reflection about the divine oath that had just been uttered. Childs speaks of a "summary-appraisal," pointing out that this type of concluding evaluative assessment also occurs at the end of other sections in Isaiah (17:14b; 28:29), apparently styled along pedagogical lines and betraying Isaiah's familiarity with wisdom diction (see *Isaiah 1–12*, pp. 201f., and often elsewhere). This leads to the conclusion that one ought not treat this second part as secondary. It is not uncommon, in other settings as well, for one to find a divine message combined with a prophetic reflection (see H. Wildberger, *Jahwewort und prophetische Rede bei Jeremia* [1942]). What is more surprising is the content of this "prophetic speech": in this passage one cannot say that this material provides an explicative, causal, or adversative reflection about the message from Yahweh (see Wildberger, op. cit., 102ff.), but rather, it has some sort of an empowering function. It confirms the trustworthy nature of the message that has gone forth at some time in the past. The same reason that motivated Isaiah to introduce the prediction not simply as a message of Yahweh but set into the framework of an oath of Yahweh, namely, the desire to make sure that the message would be accorded a full hearing and would be trusted absolutely, apparently also motivated the one who added this material to include this reflection. This message must have been uttered during a most precarious time, when someone wanted to counteract a very deep skepticism.

Meter: Verse 24a is an introductory formula; for this reason, it is not considered as part of the metrical structure. But אם־לא (surely, if not) should be taken with the first line of the poem, which is to be read as a five-stress colon (contra *BHK*; see also scholars such as Donner and *BHS* as well). Verse 24bβ is a two-stress + two-stress bicolon; v. 25a, a five-stress colon; v. 25b, an inverted seven-stress colon (? see above, p. 79); v. 26, 2 five-stress cola; v. 27a, a five-stress colon; v. 27b, a two-stress + two-stress bicolon. This short line, which would have been spoken a bit more slowly, identifies the momentous conclusion.

Setting

Seldom does anyone today question that this message originated with Isaiah. In the past many influential exegetes considered it to be a later addition; see

B. Stade, *ZAW* 3 (1883) 16; H. Oort, *TT* 20 (1886) 193; Gray; Mowinckel,
Jesaja, 114; and others. Marti provided the most cogent reasons for denying
that this passage was authentic: Isaiah's own message included the expectation that judgment would be set in motion against Judah and Israel, but not
against other peoples; for him, the judgment of the world was not merely the
reverse side of the salvation story, as those who came later viewed it; Isaiah
would not have been interested in calling for belief in a judgment of the
whole world; Isaiah's conception of God would not have brought him to
conclude that the setting for the judgment (in Jerusalem) would automatically mean that Yahweh was the instigator; in fact, this section of material
did not even make use of Isaianic phraseology (so Stade), though it does
have many close parallels to other parts of the book of Isaiah; finally, the evidence provided here about a coming judgment of the world sounds simply
too theoretical to be part of one's faith. On the basis of these remarks, Marti
considered this passage to be the proclamation of a universal, final judgment,
in fact, an apocalyptic event. If this were the case, it comes as no surprise
that strong doubts would be voiced about its authenticity. But Marti's exposition is false: what is described is a stunning defeat that Assyria was going
to suffer on the mountains of Judah, which means that the locale's identity
did not go unstated because of some ideological concern, but simply because
it was a historical fact that Assyria's army had pressed forward all the way to
Jerusalem. It goes without saying that Isaiah would have seen far-reaching
consequences coming from this violent intrusion, simply because, as Donner
(169) described it, "this place, namely, the land in which Israel resides, [is]
thought to have a special destiny throughout its history, with worldwide ramifications when something happened there, of greater import than one could
ever put into words." In addition, Marti is limited by his doctrinaire conclusion that Isaiah expected nothing for Judah/Israel except judgment. It is clear
in this passage, if anywhere at all, that it is a most "unfair oversimplification"
to think that the preexilic (writing) prophets were, by their very nature, nothing other than harbingers of the judgment that was to come upon the people
of Yahweh, an opinion that even today hinders a true understanding of the
prophetic movement for all too many. In the final analysis, Isaiah is not
the one who announced judgment but is rather a messenger who spoke of the
righteousness of Yahweh that would prevail not only in Israel but also in
the world at large.

Now, however, the question is raised about how to date this section,
taking into account the various phases of Isaiah's activity. Procksch thinks
that 14:24-27 provides the final conclusion to the "awesome tenth chapter"
(after removing 10:16-23, 33f., believing they were written later), which
would mean that 14:23 at one time followed immediately after 10:32. Yet
that is most unlikely, even if at one time there actually was a closer literary
link between chap. 10 and this present passage (many think this passage
should follow immediately after 10:15), which means that the question about
an exact date has not been answered yet. With some degree of confidence,
10:5-15 can be dated to the time period after 717; a possible solution was

offered above that would date 10:27bff. in connection with the events surrounding the revolt of Ashdod (713–711) (see *Isaiah 1–12*, p. 451). Like 10:27bff., 14:25 presumes that the Assyrians are in the land, but there is no way this passage belongs to that time period. In the earlier passage, events revolve around a massive threat to Jerusalem; here it involves the downfall of Assyria "on my mountains." This could refer to nothing other than Sennacherib's invasion of Judah, at which time, after the fall of all the cities of Judah (see the Sennacherib Prism, *TGI*² 67–69; *ANET* 287f.), Jerusalem was hemmed in completely by the Assyrian forces. Without a doubt, one would have thought the people of Jerusalem abnormally overconfident if they had believed that a change for the better was on the horizon. It is easy to explain how Isaiah, with such unprecedented vigor, could have been moved to assert that the decisions which God had made could be trusted, without wavering. In spite of all the announcements of disaster that passed his lips during earlier phases of his activity, in 701 he was supremely confident that deliverance could be expected. To accept this conclusion would be considered questionable if this were the only passage containing such a hope; however, other passages, undoubtedly "genuine," also anticipate the "miracle" of divine intervention in the final moment (see 29:5-7; 30:31-33; 31:4ff.).

Commentary

[14:24] Concerning the way one formulates a message from Yahweh as a promise of Yahweh, sworn with an oath, cf. 5:9 (emended text) and *Isaiah 1–12*, pp. 198f. The OT authors have no compunctions about saying that Yahweh swears. This is formulated so as to accentuate Yahweh's אמת, his constancy, reliability, faithfulness. Normally, mention is made of the *one to whom* God swears an oath or what it is *by which* he swears (by his holiness, Amos 4:2; his "soul," Amos 6:8; by the pride of Jacob, Amos 8:7; and by similar means). In the present passage, one does not find the partner identified, since what is to be sworn is simply to be stated; the one who is the guarantor of the oath, willing and able to back it up (human beings swear by their god), is not mentioned, since Yahweh is able to swear only by his own self (see the ways to get around this in Amos and Jer. 22:5; 49:13); an oath uttered by God is in a category by itself, not restricted by having to conform to the rules that humans must follow. In 5:9 (if emended correctly), an addition to the text says that Yahweh had placed his oath "in the ears" of the prophet, which means that Isaiah says he heard this. Implicitly, the same claim is accentuated and highlighted in this passage, providing the reason why the prophet might even venture to speak with such unheard-of certainty about God's unalterable decision, all appearances to the contrary.

At the center of this message, assurance is offered that Yahweh has come to a specific עצה (decision) and that one could place unequivocal trust in the fulfillment of what has been decided. In order to understand this message correctly, one must be careful to be precise about the meaning of this term (see *Isaiah 1–12*, pp. 202f.). Some have felt comfortable translating this as "plan," meaning thereby that Isaiah thought Yahweh had a comprehensive plan about how the history of the world should unfold. This is way off the mark; Isaiah certainly does not think that history has been planned, from the very beginning, with a definite goal in mind, which would leave prophecy with nothing to do but take the wraps off an eternally designed plan. "Planning" (יעץ), as it is done by מֶלֶךְ (King) Yahweh, is described by using the analogy about the "planning" carried out by a king, who from time to time, in light of a certain configuration of events, has to make some decisions. Thus his "planning" is always directed toward responding to a particular time in history and does not stretch out into a future that is not yet on the horizon. Unfortunately, one cannot avoid misunderstandings that come when it is rendered in English as "decision," used both in the title and translation, since definite theological overtones have been associated with this idea; it is too easy to assume this word refers to what is "eternally" predestined.

Taking all this into account, יעץ means to "conclude" or "decide" in v. 24. דִּמָּה (contemplated) functions as a parallel term to this verb in the first half of the verse. The *qal* of דמה means "be like"; the *pi'el* means "compare, ponder," and, in the estimative sense, "consider suitable," in which case it also could mean "plan" (see E. Jenni, *THAT* I, 451ff.). These two verbs are as good as any for expressing the idea that Yahweh's decisions are the result of deliberations that take into account all the variables that affect a concrete decision. Whatever happens, happens because in Yahweh's judgment it is the most appropriate for that moment in time. For observations about the use of היה and קום in parallel ("happen" and "come to be"), see 7:7 and *Isaiah 1–12*, p. 300.

[14:25a] Verse 25a provides a brief synopsis of the content of such a momentous decision on Yahweh's part: he will "shatter" Assyria. If one does not question the authenticity of the passage, there is no doubt that this statement assesses Assyria's destiny within the context of Sennacherib's campaign against Jerusalem. That Isaiah does not say specifically "before Jerusalem," but rather says "in my land" and "on my mountains" points to the reason for God's decision: Assyria functioned as "my rod of anger" and "my staff of malediction" (10:5); it had been given the assignment of "chastising" Israel/Judah, but when it took possession of Yahweh's people and land it went beyond what had been authorized (10:13; see also v. 12). Thus 14:24-27 lies completely within the framework of the judgment that one sees predicted against Assyria already in 10:5ff. The land in which Israel lives is Yahweh's land; whoever invades the land has to settle accounts on that matter with Yahweh himself. This concept might have taken shape within the context of the traditions about the taking of the land (better yet, the "tradition about the giving of the land"); see 2 Sam. 7:23; 1 Kings 8:36; Hos. 9:3; Jer. 2:7 (my land = my נחלה); 16:18; Joel 2:18; Ezek. 36:5, 20; Ps. 83:2. However, since Isaiah betrays little awareness of the tradition about the taking of the land, this concept could have another background, which holds that the land that surrounds Jerusalem is thought to be holy since, as the place where Yahweh dwells (see 8:18; 31:9), it is his own special possession.

This interpretation would not be quite as tenuous if the text read "my mountain" instead of "my mountains." It is not impossible that it should have been pointed as a singular or that the plural הָרַי (my mountains) is to be taken as a plural of amplification. Then one would automatically think of Zion, Yahweh's holy mount (הר קדשׁי in 11:9; on this, see *Isaiah 1–12*, p. 481). Concerning such formulaic expressions, which declare that the mount of God cannot be stormed by enemies, cf. Pss. 48:5ff.; 76:4. Since Isaiah has shown familiarity with the concepts linking Zion and the mountain of God and elsewhere already has betrayed his views during the crisis in 701, showing that this concept framed his thinking, this interpretation of his remarks would be the most likely. Yet one must stay with the translation "mountains," since the Assyrians had not actually encamped on Zion but rather on the mountains round about, which shared in the splendor, honor, and holiness of Mount Zion. What the prophet has to say in this concrete situation is given a solid foundation in the transmitted accounts, which were available to all and certainly well known in Jerusalem; tradition and prophetic charisma are not at odds with one another. This same situation provides the background for 7:2-9, where the ideology of kingship (and Zion traditions!) provides the backdrop for the promise of deliverance.

[14:25b] The expander inserts a description about the yoke being removed and about being freed from the burden, both of which he adapted from materials that were given shape by Isaiah, in order to show what the overthrow of Assyria would mean for Israel: the end of foreign rule. He was probably speaking about the oppressing powers of his own era, the Babylonians (or the Persians?). This additional promise would not have fit particularly well in the presumed historical context: Sennacherib's withdrawal from Jerusalem had spared Judah and its kings from the worst, but it did not bring with it freedom from Assyria and the end of vassal treaties, for which Hezekiah had certainly yearned when he initiated his revolt. Of course, Isaiah would not have identified himself with the high hopes of Hezekiah and his partners.

[14:26f.] With v. 26 one comes to the beginning of Isaiah's "reflection" on the oracle that he had received, to what has been termed the "summary-appraisal" form (Childs). Isaiah was either obligated or thought it necessary to underscore exactly that *that* was Yahweh's goal and that he would inevitably attain it. The decision had been made; Yahweh's hand was already "stretched out"; thus זאת (that) is used twice. Concerning the phrase היד הנטויה (the hand is stretched out), see 5:25; 9:11, 16, 20; 10:4; and cf. *Isaiah 1–12*, p. 233. In those passages, the hand is still stretched out against Israel; here, it is against Assyria. That is part of the ambivalence within the preaching of Isaiah that prohibits one from trying to force him into the mold of being either a prophet of salvation or a prophet of disaster.

However, this reflecting does modify the message that has been proclaimed in one important way, in that the prophet adds "for the whole earth" and "over all peoples." Isaiah seems to have a universal judgment of all peoples in mind. One could follow Kissane's suggested way of making the text flow smoothly by taking אֶרֶץ (land) in v. 25 as a reference to the whole earth and the mountains of Yahweh as a reference to all the mountains in the world, since they all would be Yahweh's mountains, because he created them! But the OT does not use this vocabulary in this way (הָרַי, "my mountains," 49:11, is certainly a textual error). Procksch also notes the problem but thinks that he can solve it by presuming that this does not discuss a judgment against all the peoples, but that it refers to all who now are able to be freed because Assyria is being destroyed. "Just because of the close ties that the image of the outstretched hand has elsewhere with the idea of judgment, . . . one ought not conclude . . . that this refers to a punishing judgment against all the peoples of the world." After they had experienced their own punishment at the hands of God's scourge, Assyria, they were now to be set free. This apparently elegant solution proves deceptive: יָעַץ עַל means "make a decision against" in only one passage and נָטָה יָדוֹ עַל actually means "stretch out his hand *against* someone." The fact remains: the judgment "on my mountains" applies primarily to Assyria, but it is a matter of consequence for "the whole world" and one that finally would involve "all peoples." Hyperbole is being used in the way these passages are formulated (Duhm) and one ought not press for details; yet Isaiah does expect that the overthrow of Assyria in Judah will have far-reaching effects throughout the world. To be sure, the prophet does not have in mind a catastrophe that is to come at the end of time, the "final judgment," but also not simply a trivial episode of merely local interest. Related passages, such as 28:22 (cf. also 29:5-8), show that Isaiah thinks in broad categories, being in fact the first prophet who works with the equation: history = world history (in chaps. 1, 2, his contemporary Amos focuses only on Israel's immediate neighbors). There is little doubt that the newer, worldwide horizon appears in Isaiah because he sees Yahweh as the מֶלֶךְ (king), whose "glory shouts out, that which (always) fills the whole earth" (6:3), but also simply because it was the first time during his lifetime that a state, i.e., Assyria, which could even lay claim to the title "world power," actually set out determinedly, seriously, to make themselves just that. In this regard, the author of chap. 13 followed the same line of argument as Isaiah, insofar as he also used the judgment concerning Babylon as a way of showing that "the world" as a whole would be brought down as well.

Purpose and Thrust

The short section is important in a variety of ways. First, it shows how Isaiah assessed each particular situation in which his people found themselves, as the relationships between the major powers continued to change, as the history of the world unfolded, in a *unique and special way*. The constant factor within his proclamation about political issues did not consist in repeating the same judgment against this world power over and over again (on this, see 10:5-15). One must certainly take this into account if one wishes to speak of Yahweh as the lord of history in the way that this prophet did.

To go still further, one can demonstrate that Isaiah assesses the matters of the moment on the basis of specific key points that were fundamental to his faith: his point of departure, here as elsewhere, is the theology of Zion, the solid foundation on which his faith was built (cf. 7:7ff.; 28:16; 29:7; 31:8f.). Trust in God's promises about Zion and protection for her inhabitants is not without problems and could lead to a dangerous self-confidence, certainly an issue because this point of view shaped the way in which the people in Judah/Jerusalem thought about the future. But it is clear enough in all that Isaiah proclaimed that he did not treat this as a free pass, intended to allow one blissfully to exude confidence, come what may, and did not treat this as an opportunity where one could stop worrying about having to "turn back" or "believe." It would miss the point completely for one to presume that he underwent a radical change, deep within, or even that he had "converted," becoming a prophet of salvation during the last period of his activity. Yet one should bear in mind that even Isaiah, in the face of a final threat to his people, felt compelled to base his reaction on the salvation traditions, without first issuing some disclaimers to guard against the possible misuse of his words.

Finally, it is of the greatest importance that we are able to follow the path taken by Isaiah in this passage, to see how the prophets of Israel learned to think in universal terms and how they understood Yahweh as the lord of history.

There is no doubt that Isaiah's proclamation, at the time of the crisis of 701, helped Jerusalem to endure until the Assyrians finally broke off their siege. It was certainly no triumphant victory, won by Judah—Isaiah does not say that either—and the Assyrians were still far from the time when their power reached its maximum. But the fact that Jerusalem did not suffer destruction at that point is amazing enough, in and of itself, being seen even by Isaiah's contemporaries as a "miracle" of God; this was taken as evidence that proved the validity of the prophet's message.

Zion, Refuge of the Wretched

Literature

K. Fullerton, "Isaiah 14:28-32," *AJSL* 42 (1925) 86–109. W. A. Irwin, "The Exposition of Isaiah 14:28-32," *AJSL* 44 (1927/28) 73–87. C. C. Torrey (see literture to Isaiah 13–23). J. Begrich, "Jesaja 14,28-32: Ein Beitrag zur Chronologie der israelitisch-judäischen Königszeit," *ZDMG* 86 (1932) 66–79 (= Begrich, *GesSt*, TBü 21 [1964] 121–131; cited here from *ZDMG*). H. Donner (see literature to 14:24-27). H. Tadmor, "Philistia under Assyrian Rule," *BA* 39 (1966) 86–102. B. S. Childs (see literature to 14:24-27) 59f. J. de Savignac, "Les 'Seraphim,'" *VT* 22 (1972) 320–325. O. Kaiser (see literature to Isaiah 13–23).

[**Literature update through 1979:** K. Aartun, "Hebräisch ʿānī und ʿānāw," *BeO* 28 (1971) 125f. O. García de la Fuente, "La cronología de los reyes de Judá y la interpretación de algunos oráculos de Isaías 1–39," *EstBib* 31 (1972) 275–291 (on chaps. 7–11; 14:28ff.). K. R. Joines, *Serpent Symbolism in the Old Testament: A Linguistic, Archaeological, and Literary Study* (1974) (on שׂרף in 14:29). H. W. Hoffmann, *Die Intention der Verkündigung Jesajas*, BZAW 136 (1974) 64ff. B. Beck, "Kontextanalysen zum Verb נבה," FS G. J. Botterweck (1977).]

Text

14:28 [a]In the year that King Ahaz[b] died, the following verdict was issued:
29 Do not rejoice, entire[a] land of the Philistines,
   that the staff is broken, which struck you![b]
  For from the root of the snake comes forth a viper,
   and its fruit will be a winged seraph.
30 [There, 'like lambs,'[a] the insignificant ones graze,
   and the poor lie down in safety.]
  It[b] will affect you fatally through hunger, down to the root,[c]
   and will bring down whatever of yours (yet then) still remains.
31 Howl,[a] gate! Cry out aloud, city!
   Despair,[b] entire[c] land of the Philistines!
  For, from the north, smoke[d] comes,
    and [e]not a single one from among those who have been summoned runs away.[e]
32 [a]What therefore shall one answer the messenger of the people?[a]
  "Yahweh has founded Zion,
   and the wretched of his people have refuge with him."[b]

87

28a The Syr precedes this message with the superscription *mšqlʾ dplšt* = פלשת משא (verdict about Philistia), which is certainly not original but does provide an indicator to show that all the individual sections of material that were gathered together into a משא collection were assembled only gradually.

28b J. A. Bewer (in the W. R. Harper Remembrance Volume II [1908] 224–226) suggested that וָאחזה (and I had a vision of) should be read instead of אחז היה (Ahaz, there came) and later repeated this suggestion two more times (*AJSL* 54 [1937] 62; and FS A. Bertholet [1950] 65f.; see also Torrey, 110). One could agree with this reading if one were convinced that the introduction in v. 28 is original but that vv. 29-32 could not possibly have been composed in the year that King Ahaz died. Yet what help is the reference to the year of some king's death if the name of the king is not there? (Note that the name of a king is mentioned in a similar passage that establishes a date in 6:1.)

29a Here, and in v. 31, it is written כֻלֵּך (lit.: all of you [fem.]); in 22:1 and Song of Sol. 4:7 it is כֻלֵּך (all of you [also: fem.]); cf. Joüon, *Gr* §94h.

29b The Gk reads שבט מכך as a construct clause: ὁ ζυγὸς τοῦ παίοντος ὑμᾶς (the yoke of those striking you). In this case, the "one doing the striking" would be the enemy power, i.e., Assyria, and the "yoke, staff," would be its king. By contrast, most recent exegetes interpret מכך (which struck you) as being in apposition to שבט (the staff), which would be possible even though there is no article on the participle.

30a It has been difficult to make sense of בכורי דלים (firstborn of the poor). Although Donner (110, note 1) thinks that it might have been a commonly used metaphor, many have suggested alternate readings (Lowth: בְּכוֹרי, "my firstborn ones"; Koppe: בְּכָרי, "in my meadows"; Dillmann: בִּכְרי, "my firstborn"; Marti: בְּהָרי, "in my mountains"; others: בְּהָרי, "in my mountain"). Begrich (72) suggests כְּכָרים, "as lambs," which at least makes some sense when used with the verbs רעה (graze) and רבץ (lie down) (in all the places where כר is thought to mean "meadow," the text is suspect).

30b The first person form המתי (I will cause death) does not coordinate with the third person יהרג (and he will kill). המתי (I will cause death) presumes that Yahweh is speaking, but there is no other place in this entire section where Yahweh speaks in the first person. Qᵃ reads אהרוג (I will kill), which Bredenkamp already had suggested as the likely reading; however, it would be better to follow the Gk (ἀνελεῖ, "he will kill"; see also Targ and Vulg), so that this should be read המית (he will kill) (the י was transposed); for another solution, see Driver, *JTS* 2 (1951) 25.

30c One wonders if it is correct to find שרש (root) read here, since it was used in a markedly different context just previously, in v. 29. In addition, one expects to find a word that would be parallel to שארית (remnant). The Gk reads τὸ σπέρμα σου = זרעך (your seed) (see also OL), which is certainly not impossible; however, this appears to be the way the translators solved a difficulty they themselves found in the text. Irwin, (79) considers the possibility that the word should be altered to read שֹׁריך (your ruler[s]), but finally concludes that שרש has the same meaning, that is, "nobility." But שרש never has that meaning anywhere else, and it does not seem clear why the nobility alone would starve, while the rest of the people were to be killed. The translation "generation," as in the Zürcher Bibel, is highly unlikely. The best one can do is to stay with שרש and not look for any other meaning beyond the basic sense "root." It may be that the word was chosen so that there might be a rhyming sound between ושארית (remnant) and שרש (root). It is a common stylistic element in predictions of disaster, such as this, that comments are made about those who still remain after the destruction that takes place during a catastrophe (see H. Wildberger, art. "שאר," *THAT* II, 844–855).

31a Concerning the feminine הֵילִֽילִי (you [pl.] howl) (שַׁעַר, "gate," is masculine), cf. BrSynt §16g (the feminine is to be linked with עִיר, "city," which follows).
31b נָמוֹג (despair, melt in terror) is an infinitive absolute, used instead of the imperative (see Joüon, *Gr* §123u).
31c According to Donner (111), כֻּלֵּךְ (all of you) is a gloss, being inserted here in addition to its use in v. 29. With this solution, he reads v. 31a as having cola that follow a 2 + 2 + 2 pattern. In reality, the syllables are to be accented to read 3 + 3 in each bicolon (זְעַקִי־עִיר, "cry out aloud, city," being read as one stressed syllable).
31d G. R. Driver (*JSS* 13 [1968] 44), noting Aramaic עֲשִׁין (strong) and its presumed Hebrew form עָשַׁן, "be hard" (which he posits for Ps. 80:5), and with reference to the enemies of Yahweh in Isa. 28:2 as the חָזָק וְעָמִץ (mighty and strong ones), suggests reading either עָשֵׁן or עָשִׁין here, meaning "strong," instead of reading עָשָׁן, "smoke." But this meaning for עשׁן cannot be substantiated and the transmitted text makes good sense as is (cf. passages such as Jer. 1:13f.; Ezek. 1:4; or the similar images in Jer. 46:20; 47:2).
31e-e בּוֹדֵד has generally been understood to mean something such as "separating oneself from" (בדד means "be alone"; Arabic: *badda*, "separate, split apart"). Qᵃ reads מוֹדֵד. G. R. Driver (*JTS* 2 [1951] 26) considers this to be the original reading and translates it "deserter." By contrast, Donner adopts the same variant reading (after eliminating the ב prefix from מוֹעֲדִים, "their assemblies") but translates it "and no one counts their hosts." But מדד means "measure," not "count," and Donner's way of interpreting מוֹעֲדִים is not itself without problems. In the OT there is no occurrence of a substantive מוֹעֵד that could having a meaning such as "group, troop" (or even "place of meeting"; see KBL). For this reason, Begrich was bold enough that he altered this to read וְאֵין נֹדְדִים עַמּוּדָיו (and his pillars do not become shaky) and also others favor reading עַמּוּדִים (pillars, columns), since one speaks of army columns even in modern languages (Marti). But עַמּוּד never has this meaning. One cannot be sure enough to adopt the suggestion to read בְּמוֹ־עֵדוֹ (at the time of his going forth) (based on Arabic *ʿadwun* = Latin *impetus*, "attack"; see BHS). The later Greek translations (see Ziegler) read: ἐν τοῖς συντεταγμένοις αὐτοῦ (among those whom he has set up in battle array), which, according to B. Kedar-Kopfstein (*Textus* 2 [1962] 144f.), could be based on a posited Hebrew בִּנֹעֲדָיו. In addition, on the basis of the Vulg, which reads *effugiet* (he escapes) for בּוֹדֵד, he suggests that the Hebrew also would have read נוֹדֵד, arriving at the translation: "none is fleeing among his summoned troops." נֹדֵד is used elsewhere of those who "are fleeing in battle"; see Isa. 22:3, and esp. 21:15. But this conjecture is also not convincing enough for it to be accepted as the correct solution. For an emendation suggested on the basis of the Targ, see S. Speier, *Tarbiz* 34 (1964/65) 194f.
32a-a The first line of v. 32 (if, indeed, it is supposed to be a line of the verse) is too short. Possibly it is supposed to be a prosaic introduction to v. 32a. Yet, apart from the question about the meter of the line, one has the impression that this is the first half-verse of a line that has been damaged and that the rest was lost: the subject of יַעֲנֶה (he will answer) is missing; reading the plural יַעֲנוּ (they will answer) improves little. Some (Duhm, Guthe, Begrich, Leslie, et al.) suggest inserting עַמִּי (my people). Still others favor inserting מַלְכִּי (my king) (Procksch, on the basis of the Gk), but βασιλεῖς is the word used in the Gk to translate מַלְאֲכֵי (messengers of). Yet מַלְאֲכֵי גוֹי (messengers of a people), as the text now reads, does not make sense either. The Gk seems to have used a text that read the plural גוֹיִם (peoples), even though mention had been made earlier of one nation only, the Philistines. Some think that גוֹי (people) has been used to replace what would have originally read either פלשת or פלשתים

(Philistines) (see Donner), altered during a time when someone wanted to interpret the text apocalyptically, in the sense of "heathen people." Since there is so much uncertainty about all of these alterations and expansions to restore the text, one does best to stay with the original textual reading, so as not to allow oneself to be led to a faulty conclusion from the outset.

32b For וּבָהּ (and in her), Qᵃ reads וּבוֹ (and in him). Irwin (83) had already come up with the suggestion to point this וּבוֹ (and in him), so that the referent would be not Zion but Yahweh. But this change is not needed; the text makes clear that Isaiah means the same thing when speaking about either Yahweh or Zion.

Setting

The superscription in the Syr, "verdict concerning the land of the Philistines," shows that vv. 28-32 are to be considered as an integral part of the complex of materials in chaps. 13–23, along with the other messages directed against the other foreign peoples. The redactor wanted to insert a message spoken against Israel's western neighbor to precede the message against their eastern neighbor. In the final analysis, however, that does not alter the fact that the passage is addressed to Jerusalem/Judah, not to the Philistines.

   The first problem in interpreting this passage is whether the introduction, v. 28, which dates this message to the time of the death of Ahaz, is original or whether it was inserted at a later time by a redactor. If it does come from another hand, then the natural question would be whether the date is valid. This answer is obviously related to the decision about whether the main passage itself, vv. 29-32, should be treated as Isaianic.

   For this reason, one must begin with the question about the authenticity of vv. 29-32. In this regard, hardly another passage in the book of Isaiah has used up as much printer's ink as this one, without a consensus having been reached even after all that. Those who do not believe that this is truly from Isaiah begin with vv. 30a and 32b. Since v. 30a is certainly a later addition (see below, p. 94), we will limit our discussion to v. 32b. On the one hand, suspicions about this verse have been raised by the fact that the theology of Zion is so blatant (see, e.g., Fullerton or Duhm), but also on the other hand because of the use of the term עָנִי (the wretched of) (in v. 30a, דַל, "insignificant," and אֶבְיוֹן, "the poor"), which would call for an interpretation here that would be wholly foreign to the way Isaiah thought, being much more appropriate only from the time of Trito-Isaiah on, namely, that the term is used to identify the pious adherents who belong to the people of God. The first argument carries no weight; one can make no mistake about it, and it is almost universally acknowledged today: Isaiah made frequent use of motifs connected with Zion theology; see above, concerning v. 25.

   What remains is how to understand the word עָנִי. Isaiah certainly uses the word. In 3:14f. he clearly uses this term as a way to designate those who are economically oppressed, and he speaks in a similar way when using עֲנִיֵּי עַמִּי (the poor of my people) in 10:2 and עֲנִיֵּי־אֶרֶץ (the poor of the land) in 11:4 (text emended). In 14:32, however, such a meaning cannot be assigned to the word. The Gk already detected this and translated it: οἱ ταπεινοὶ τοῦ λαοῦ (the humbled of the people) (possibly having a text that read עָנָו עַם, "humble ones of the people"). But the Vulg translates this term as *pauperes*, thus staying with the "profane" meaning of עָנִי. Among modern scholars, Begrich (76) tried to solve it as follows: the "poor" would have been the lowest level of society, a view that presumes that the upper level had been done away with (or exiled). That would make no sense in the present context; if this is the correct interpretation, how could Isaiah expect the palace to offer this answer to the Philistine messengers: it is true that the upper level of society in Jerusalem will be lost, but the socially deprived will survive the destruction unharmed, and that is enough to give us hope. Procksch explains: "not the entire people, but, in fact, the wretched have refuge in Zion. Thus we find a reference here to Isaiah's concept of a remnant" (a similar suggestion was offered already by J. Meinhold, *Der Heilige Rest* [1903] 128ff.). However, the concept of a remnant does not play as central a role in Isaiah as Procksch thinks it does (see *Isaiah 1–12*, pp. 435f.); furthermore, one must ask why the remnant would be designated specifically as "the poor." One would have an even harder time agreeing with Baudissin, who explains these individuals to be: "the wretched, that is, the people of Yahweh," which means that all the people of Judah are promised deliverance (W. von Baudissin, *PrJ* 149 [1912] 210; similarly: Guthe, Duhm). Instead, the solution to the problem must be sought in the direction suggested by Donner: "The concept 'poor, wretched,' which was used originally in a social sense, is on the road to becoming another way to refer to the 'pious'" (113). Thus those who have questioned the authenticity of the passage have at least identified one thing for sure: עָנִי has undergone a significant change in meaning. The only question is whether one might be able to attribute this significant change in meaning to Isaiah himself. Undoubtedly, he would not have said: Judah/Jerusalem is safely hidden on Mount Zion. He had said explicitly to Ahaz in 7:9: "If you do not believe, then you will not remain," even though the logical consequence of 7:2ff. would suggest that one could rely on the stability of the Davidic dynasty (and Jerusalem) with absolute certainty. It sounds much the same in 28:16: not everyone, but the "one who trusts need not panic."

When the formula עַמּוֹ עֲנִיֵּי (wretched, humbled of his people) (or maybe originally עַמּוֹ עַנְוֵי, humble ones of his people) is used, the same restriction must apply as is implicit in the use of הַאֲמִין (believe) in 7:9 and 28:16. Because of this, עָנִי (wretched) is in fact is a religious term. For this reason, "pious" would be an inadequate translation. The opponents of the עֲנִיִּים (wretched ones), who have gone to seek help in Zion, are the arrogant politicians, who believe that they can control the situation by means of diplomatic skill or military action. Without question, the arrogant would more likely belong to the upper level than to the lower level of society. Yet one's social-economic status is not the issue; Fohrer is right: as in 7:9, Isaiah is calling for complete trust in God alone, and he formulates the answer that is to be delivered to others as a confession, to be repeated again and again: we believe!

If one acknowledges that vv. 29-32 are substantively from Isaiah, then one cannot deny that v. 28 also could have come from Isaiah himself or, at the very least, that it correctly identifies the time period during which this message was delivered in public. The form of this verse is very similar to 6:1a and 20:1a. A first person report is introduced in 6:1a that could go back to Isaiah himself, and hardly anyone questions the accuracy of that dating. The function of 20:1a is to introduce a message from Yahweh, and there is no question about the accuracy of that dating either—the content of the following verses makes that clear and the date is indispensable for making sense of the message (see v. 5), even if the originality of that material has been questioned. One could be confident about reaching the same conclusion concerning this material in 14:28 if the "staff" that struck the Philistines but is now broken could be identified as the Judean king Ahaz, who is mentioned in the introduction. This conclusion, which was commonly accepted in the ancient exegetical tradition (Jerome, Thomas Aquinas, et al.; see Knabenbauer), is still advocated by some today (Irwin). But it is unlikely; we know nothing about Ahaz ever having oppressed the Philistines, and it makes no sense—whatever the consequence of this interpretation might be—that Isaiah would have been interested mainly in saying that the successor to Ahaz, Hezekiah (or, as the case may be, the messiah; see Targ), would "strike" the Philistines with even greater intensity. Instead, this must have something to do with the death of an Assyrian ruler. Yet that does not mean that the specific dating, to the year in which Ahaz died, as furnished in vv. 29f., could not still be valid. Many have been bothered by the use of משׂא (verdict), which Isaiah himself does not use elsewhere. The formula היה המשׂא הזה (the following verdict was issued) is even more surprising, since vv. 29ff. are not cast in the form of a message from Yahweh (though this would be the case if והמתי, "and I will cause death," in v. 30b, would be altered to read והמית, "and he will kill"). Nevertheless, that may be the very reason why אלי (to me), which one would expect here, is missing, and why this is identified instead as a משׂא (verdict). Some exegetes suggest that the term משׂא (verdict) was first used when these messages were inserted into the collection of the oracles against the nations, as a replacement for another term that previously stood at the beginning (Begrich, 68). But the one who assembled these together would certainly have simply taken the commonly used superscript, משׂא פלשׁת (verdict against Philistia) and placed it at the beginning of the passage that had come down to him (as can be seen in the Syr). Since one cannot find a good reason why a later redactor would have dated this message to the year in which King Ahaz died, and since היה המשׂא הזה (the following verdict was issued) is hardly a favorite formula of the expanders, quickly coming to mind whenever they wrote, the originality of the introduction ought not be called into question (a solution followed by Fohrer, Childs, Donner, Eichrodt)—presuming, of course, that vv. 29-32 actually make sense during the time of Ahaz.

For many exegetes such a solution would not make sense—and no doubt that is why they question the originality of v. 28 or even of the entire section, vv. 28-32. If, as has just been explained, v. 29 refers to the death of

an Assyrian ruler, then the change in rulers in Assyria would have to correspond to the transfer of rule from Ahaz to Hezekiah in Judah. During Isaiah's
period of activity, three different rulers took the throne, and vv. 29–32 have
been linked to each of these three by one scholar or another (see Donner):
727: Tiglath-Pileser III/Shalmaneser V (Schrader, Duncker, Barth [see Don-
ner], Gray, Begrich; see also Fohrer); 722: Shalmaneser V/Sargon II (Bredenkamp, Cornill, Giesebrecht, Procksch); 705: Sargon II/Sennacherib
(Driver, Kuenen, Smith, Bewer, et al.). However, since the message of Isaiah
was occasioned by Philistine envoys who probably were soliciting others to
join a conspiracy against Assyria, Donner suggests that the only time period
which would apply was "the situation during the years 722–720" (111), at
the time when Hanno of Gaza rebelled, a revolt quashed by Sargon in 720.
But that suggestion remains uncertain. For example, Fohrer focuses on the
time when Ashdod rebelled, 713–711 (even though he still chooses to have
v. 29 refer to the death of Tiglath-Pileser, which had happened more than ten
years earlier). Thus, in this regard, no definite conclusion can be reached. We
would be able to make progress only if we were sure about the chronology
of the Judean kings during the time of Isaiah. Those who consider the introduction (v. 28) to be original and postulate that Ahaz died in 715 (see Isaiah
1–12, pp. 3f.; and cf. Wright, Mauchline, Leslie, Moriarty, Bright [*A History
of Israel*, [1981³] 281ff.], and others) think that this is the time when preparations were being made for Ashdod's rebellion. That remains doubtful, since
no Assyrian king died or was overthrown at that time. The movement toward
rebellion that began in 705, when the throne changed from Sargon to Sennacherib, merits no consideration if one considers v. 28 to be accurate, since
Ahaz was certainly long dead by that time. The only dates remaining are
those that give an early date for the death of Ahaz. Jepsen and Hanhart suggest 725. At that time the death of Tiglath-Pileser could still have been having an effect on the Philistine cities. The dates of Pavlovský and Vogt would
match up better still (see *Isaiah 1–12*, p. 4), according to which Ahaz died in
728/727 (similarly Begrich, in 727/726, and Young, in 727, and many others
as well). This conclusion is the most likely by far. It was during the time of
Tiglath-Pileser III that the Philistines experienced the harshest mistreatment
from the Assyrians. In 734, certainly even before Ahaz had appealed to the
Assyrian king for help (on this, see *Isaiah 1–12*, pp. 298f., and cf. Tadmor,
88), the Assyrian army had set out from Phoenicia. Gaza, the ringleader of
the rebellion, was conquered and plundered; its king, Hanno, fled to Egypt
(though, as an Assyrian vassal, he was later reinstalled in his position). After
Gaza had been conquered, Tiglath-Pileser pushed forward as far as the "city
located on the brook of Egypt" (presently known as *wādi el-ʿarīš*). One year
later, after they already had pressed on into Galilee, the Assyrian troops
advanced once again along the coastline, as far as Ashkelon. At that time, the
Assyrians resettled an Arabic tribe, the *Idibiʾlu*, as "Warden of Marches on
the border of Musur [Egypt]" in the southern part of the Philistine territory
(see *ANET* 282, and Tadmor, 89f.). Thus the Philistines had reason enough to
rejoice when Tiglath-Pileser died. However, we do not know whether the

Philistines attempted in their territory, after his death, to extricate themselves from the oppression of Assyria—though this apparently is assumed as the background of v. 32a. It is possible that such a plan evaporated quickly; however, we have little to go on concerning the events that occurred during the time of Shalmaneser (see *FWG* 4 [1967] 58).

In addition to questions about vv. 28 and 32b (see above, pp. 90f.) that deal with the authenticity of the passage, v. 30a has problems as well. The content is also a factor here. Is it possible that Isaiah had advocated the type of piety mentioned here? Whoever considers v. 32b to be from Isaiah hardly will exclude that possibility automatically. However, in a way that simply cannot justify its being treated as part of the original text, v. 30a interrupts the flow between vv. 29b and 30b, both of which speak of the disaster coming upon the Philistines. In order to eliminate this problem, many commentators, who want to "save" the passage for Isaiah, reassign v. 30a to a position either immediately before or after v. 32b (see Begrich, Childs, Donner; cf. Bruno as well). But apparently a reader, or someone reworking the text, felt compelled to include the דלים (the insignificant) and the אביונים (poor), as well as the עניים (wretched). He may have written his additional note in the margin, that note being inserted into the text still later but at the wrong place.

Form

The section is made up of two parts: vv. 29-31: the land of the Philistines should not rejoice but should lament; and v. 32: the answer that one should give to the (Philistine) messengers (in Jerusalem). Part one itself is to be divided into two parts, introduced by אל־תשׂמחי (do not rejoice) and הילילי (howl). Naturally, however, these two challenges are to be taken together; part two cannot be separated from part one either (Fullerton), since that would leave the first part hanging in the air. Because of the textual uncertainties in v. 32a it is simply not possible to arrive at a completely accurate assessment about the exact details concerning how all this fits together.

In terms of the form-historical analysis, v. 31 is plainly a "summons to a communal lament" (on this, see H. W. Wolff, *ZAW* 76 [1964] 48–56, specifically, 54 [= *GesSt*, TBü 22, 392–401, specifically, 399]; and see above, on 13:6). הילילי (howl) and זעק (cry out) (see Jer. 4:8; 25:34; 49:3, among others, on the first term; and Ezek. 21:17; Joel 1:14, on the second) are almost "characteristic fossil evidence" for such a form (also being used together in parallel in Jer. 25:34; Ezek. 21:17; זעק, "cry out," can also be used instead of צעק, "cry out aloud"; see Jer. 49:3 and cf. Jer. 22:20). Besides the summons in the imperative, the other formal elements are there as well (see Wolff, 51 [= 396]): mention is made of the one who is summoned, being identified not in two different ways, as is the norm, but with three different appellations, plus the reason for the summons introduced by כי (for, because). A similarly constructed parallel precedes v. 31b in v. 29, though the summons in that verse is quite different, having the imperative in the form of a negative. Yet such a method of verse construction is found in other examples of communal laments as well (most clearly, in Isa. 23:1-14 and Joel 1:5-14); what we have here is simply a loose adaptation of the form.

The form of the piece also helps make sense of v. 32. The people who have gathered together for a service of lament are eager to hear an answer, one that would settle them down. In terms of the content, the response offered in v. 32b may not be much different from the types of answers that were given to the people who had gathered together at the sanctuary. About this, one must be clear, however: as he set forth his proclamation, Isaiah exercised his own discretion about how he would use the forms that were available to him and the motifs that were connected with those forms. The summons to take up a lament for the Philistines served the function of appealing to those who were in leadership positions in Jerusalem to fall in line, to give up on relying on any sort of joint political adventure with the Philistines, to place their confidence in Yahweh alone, who was the only one who could protect them from danger.

Meter: three-stress + three-stress bicola are found in vv. 29-31 (יֵצֵא, "comes forth," in v. 29b, receives no stress; וּשְׁאֵרִיתְךָ, "what of yours still remains," in v. 30b, receives two stresses). Verse 32a is either a fragment or is constructed in prose and is not to be analyzed metrically. Verse 32b, making the important main point, has to be read as 2 four-stress + four-stress bicola.

Commentary

[14:28] Enough has been said about the introductory v. 28 already; see above, p. 92.

[14:29, 30b] The Philistines are warned not to mistake the seriousness of their situation. The term that was used regularly when identifying their land is chosen for addressing the Philistines directly: פְּלֶשֶׁת (Akkadian: *Palastu, Pilišta,* or *Pilistu*). The Israelites did not feel any close ties with this people, who had come from the Aegean, had entered the land with lightning speed, and had taken over the role of serving as the custodians of the Canaanite culture. The reason Israel developed into a nation was because of the danger that they might come under Philistine domination. Only when Israel and Judah were being threatened by the Assyrians did they consider working together with the Philistines. That this type of political alliance offered the only possible means of defense made the risk for Judah all the greater. As the campaigns of Tiglath-Pileser through the coastal regions and on to present-day *el-ʿarīš* make clear, Assyria was not nearly as interested in Judah as it was in controlling a route along the coast that would give it access to Egypt. As long as Jerusalem did not endanger this access route, Assyria could basically leave them alone, permitting continued sovereignty. Thus Isaiah's stance in this case should be considered politically wise and farsighted as well. Yet we do not learn anything about whether he offered these observations on the basis of political reasoning; his warning about not entering into a treaty with the Philistines, which was of vital interest to Egypt as well, was based solely on religious grounds (v. 32b).

The addition of כֻּלֵּךְ (all of you) after פְּלֶשֶׁת (Philistia) can be explained by the fact that this little country of the Philistines was divided up into smaller city-states: Ashdod, Ashkelon, Ekron, Gaza (and at times also Gath). The conflict with Assyria shows that they did not always act with a united front and with equal input. Different cities took the lead at different times. At the time of Tiglath-Pileser, Gaza was the central player in the rebellion.

Concerning the joy that accompanied the death of a tyrant, cf. discussions such as the one above dealing with 14:7f.

The text mentions that the "staff is broken, which struck you," a reference to the death of Tiglath-Pileser if one accepts the chronological solution suggested above. Concerning the imagery connected with a staff, see the discussion at 10:5 and 14:5ff.

Before Tiglath-Pileser, Assyria had lived through a period of weakness; one might easily have expected that the kingdom would once again fall quickly into a period of weakness after his death, as quickly as it had risen during his rule. Isaiah could not agree with this expectation, though that certainly would have been the considered opinion of seasoned diplomats: "from the root of the snake comes forth a viper" (צֶפַע is a hapax legomenon; however, see צִפְעוֹנִי, "young viper," in 11:8, which means the same thing; according to F. S. Bodenheimer, *Animal Life in Palestine* [1935] 186f., this is the *viper vipera xanthina*). "Root of the snake" seems an odd expression; damage to the text is not out of the question. But it is a proverbial type of utterance. Since a son or a successor could be called a "sprout," as in 11:1 and Dan. 11:7 (emended text), it would not be that far removed to call the father, or the predecessor, the "root." "Root of the snake" thus should be understood in the sense of an epexegetical genitive: "root, which is a snake." Wherever mention is made of a root, it is common to have this associated with "fruit" as well (see Isa. 11:1; Ezek. 17:9; Hos. 9:16; Amos 2:9, among others): "and its fruit will be a winged seraph." On the Eshmunʿazar inscription, those who might consider desecrating the coffin are threatened: "May they neither have a root below nor fruit above" (*KAI* 14: 11f.). When the word pair "root"-"fruit" is used, the totality of the destruction is underscored.

The suffix on פִּרְיוֹ (its fruit) does not refer back to the צֶפַע (viper) (so Procksch), which would mean having to wait to compare dead Tiglath-Pileser with a seraph who was identified as the successor to the dead king's own replacement; rather, v. 29bβ parallels v. 29bα.

One ought not try to press this imagery to make every detail fit logically: a seraph is certainly not a צֶפַע (viper); instead, according to Num. 21:6ff., it is Nehushtan, which is also called a שָׂרָף (seraph), a נָחָשׁ (snake), but a winged serpent as well. In 30:6 Isaiah also speaks of a שָׂרָף מְעוֹפֵף (flying serpent); there it is a sinister creature of the desert. Concerning the ideas connected with seraphim, see *Isaiah 1–12*, pp. 264f., on 6:2. The seraphim described in that passage also are able to fly; in that passage one does not get the impression that they are dangerous, since their function there is to sing praise to Yahweh (concerning the ambivalent nature of the seraphim, cf. now J. de Savignac). In the present passage, the שָׂרָף (seraph) poses a greater threat than does the צֶפַע (viper), which is dangerous enough as it is (see also Deut. 8:15). Winged seraphim are not simply dangerous animals but are demonic beings, from which it is difficult to protect oneself in any case (however, compare this with the story about Nehushtan in Numbers 21, in which the cultically worshiped seraph functions as a palladium or safeguard against all seraphim). Since Nehushtan was still known to be in the temple at the time of Isaiah (see 2 Kings 18:4), one can suppose that Isaiah and his listeners were familiar with stories that told of the danger of the seraphim.

The point of this imagery is clear: the successor to the dead tyrant will place the Philistines in an even more precarious position. One might remember the statement of Rehoboam: "My father disciplined you with whips, but I will discipline you with scorpions" (1 Kings 12:11). We are not aware of specific details about Shalmaneser V being an even more demanding overlord for the Philistines than was his predecessor. But that would not preclude dating the text to the time that has been suggested already. Isaiah is no fortune-teller and the point of what he says does not revolve around exposing what will happen in the future, but rather that he might warn his contemporaries: protect yourself from illusions, which are nothing but the product of wishful thinking, even though at the moment it seems as if such dreams might indeed appear realistic, with Assyria seeming to have been shaken to the roots by the death of its ruler. In hindsight, taking the long view of things, Isaiah was right on the mark: the worst troubles that Assyria would bring against the land of the Philistines were still to come: in 720 Gaza fell and Raphia (Akkadian *rapiḫu;* known today as *refaḫ;* see Tadmor, 91; *ANET* 284f.; *TGI*² 62), located to the south, was destroyed completely by Sargon. It was Ashdod's turn in 711; in 701 Sennacherib took possession of Ekron. Truly, the death of Tiglath-Pileser did not provide the land of the Philistines with a way to have their burdens lightened.

[14:30b] Verse 30b describes what is to be expected in greater detail. First, וְהֵמִית בָּרָעָב שָׁרְשֵׁךְ (and it will fatally affect you through hunger, down to the root). The subject of הֵמִית (it will fatally affect you) has to be the צֶפַע (viper)/שָׂרָף (seraph); this is the way the successor to the Assyrian throne is characterized. If the text has been transmitted correctly (see above, textual note 30c), the Philistines were going to be affected deeply by hunger-related problems—by circumstances that come during wartime—until their very existence would be threatened. The Israelites had apparently noted that the stump of a tree or a vine could still produce new shoots (6:13; 11:1; 37:31; Job 14:7f.). As long as the root "had life," hope remained. If the root was destroyed as well, then the end would have come; see the curse quoted above from the Eshmunʿazar inscription, p. 96. Even if a "remnant" would remain, that also would be "devoured" by the sword (הָרַג, "kill," is used frequently when describing the way death is inflicted in battle by means of a sword:

Gen. 34:26; Josh. 10:11; Amos 9:4; according to Job 20:16, the word is used in a special sense as well for describing the bite of a serpent). One also might compare this with Ezek. 5:12: a third dies because of pestilence and by being exterminated as a result of hunger, a third falls to the sword, and a third is scattered by the wind (cf. also vv. 16f.; in addition, see Jer. 15:9, 22f.; 24:8-10; 25:27ff., among other passages).

[**14:31**] This verse is the summons to communal lament. For a discussion of הֵילֵל (howl), see above, p. 21, on 13:6. The parallel word זעק ("cry out aloud") can hardly be distinguished from it (and the same goes for צעק, "cry out aloud"); the יְלָלָה (howling) corresponds to the זְעָקָה (outcry) (as also זַעַק, "cry," and צְעָקָה, "outcry"). Both terms can be used in a more narrow, cultic sense as well as in the more generalized "profane" way. Finally, one does not "howl" and "cry out in lament" just within the context of official worship services, called specifically for the purpose of lamenting. However, based on what was explained earlier about the formal category "summons to a communal lament," it may be that Isaiah—naturally only in an ironic sense— might have been summoning the Philistines to set up a special worship service for the purpose of holding a communal lament. One would suppose that the Philistines also were familiar with these types of events; it is certain that "days of confession of sin" were common in the entire ancient Near East during times of need (cf. H.-J. Kraus, *Klagelieder,* BK XX, 8ff.; examples are provided in *SAHG* 183ff., 203ff.). That both verbs הֵילֵל (howl) and זעק (cry out aloud) have been used is necessary because of formal considerations connected with *parallelismus membrorum.* But their use also functions stylistically to underscore the urgency of the summons. In the present passage, however, a third imperative is used as well, technically an infinitive absolute (נמוֹג, "despair") (cf. passages such as Exod. 15:15). The verb מוג (melt) does not seem to belong to the vocabulary commonly associated with the summons to a communal lament, and it is not supposed to depict how someone would react when scared to death; instead, it describes the inner doubts that come upon a person who expects that evil things might happen. For that reason, there is no justification for trying to demarcate clearly between an official cultic action and an individual being agitated personally. Days on which sins are confessed are not brought to a conclusion just by celebrating a set, official ritual, but rather are the means whereby an individual is able to get his or her own terror out into the open. In spite of this, it must not be forgotten: one does not simply "lament" in order to express one's hurts publicly but rather in the expectation that the harsh fate on the horizon might thereby be diverted elsewhere.

It is easy to understand why the call for זְעָקָה (crying out loud) would be directed toward "the city": the inhabitants of the city are the ones who constitute the members of the cultic community. To wonder about which specific city is being addressed (Procksch: Gaza) would be a mistake; it would be intended for whichever city heard the summons to cry (the Gk reads πόλεις, "to the cities"). First, the summons is addressed to those in the שַׁעַר (gate), i.e., those who are assembled in the open area just inside the gate, to whom one would naturally turn at first, but who in fact are representatives of the inhabitants of the city. That Isaiah uses the feminine הילילי (howl), even though שער (gate) is masculine, shows that he is already thinking in terms of summoning the עיר (city [feminine]), that is, all the inhabitants of the entire city. However, what takes place in each individual city should be replicated in all the cities of the land of the Philistines (see פלשת כלך, "Philistines, all of you").

The reason for this is simple: "For, from the north, smoke comes." Wherever troops pass through in wartime, communities are set on fire. Still today, the burn layers detected in Palestinian archaeological excavations leave a deep impression about the ravaging that took place, also during the time when the Assyrians were invading (i.e., in Lachish; see H. Bardtke, *Bibel, Spaten und Geschichte* [1969] 93; or, concerning *tell bēt mirsim*, see W. F. Albright, *The Archaeology of Palestine* [1960] 129f.). There is no doubt that צפון refers here to nothing other than a direction on the compass (for another view, cf. A. Lauha, *Zaphon: Der Norden und die Nordvölker im Alten Testament,* AASF B 49/2 [1943] 57f.). The Assyrians set out either from Damascus or from the Phoenician coastal plain and then marched along the coastline until they arrived down at the Egyptian border (cf. the reports from Tiglath-Pileser and Sargon, *ANET* 282ff.; and, concerning these, see *FWG* 4 [1967] 54, 60).

The uncertainties within the text itself make it more difficult to understand v. 31bβ. Yet the intention is apparently to make clear that the enemy forces will not lose their effectiveness because of a lack of discipline or even because some of the troops might desert, which undoubtedly was not all that rare among mercenary forces in ancient times.

[14:32] This verse is the answer to the messengers of the people. Apparently this message from Isaiah was occasioned by the arrival of Philistine envoys in Jerusalem, who were there seeking to gain allies who would support an action of rebellion against Assyria by suggesting that the time was ripe. Ahaz, who had just died, had previously made himself a subject under Tiglath-Pileser during the course of the threat that Israel and the Arameans posed to Jerusalem (see 7:5ff.). Apparently, he remained a loyal Assyrian vassal because of his conviction that this would be the best way to protect his own interests as the ruler on the throne. This political stance was certainly not accepted by everyone, and it makes sense that, after the death of the king, some would have tried to check out the possibility of determining whether Judah could be included in the anti-Assyrian front. Later political decisions on the part of Hezekiah show that he was open to being swayed in this direction. In 733 Isaiah had taken his stand in vehement opposition when Ahaz turned to Tiglath-Pileser, either to seek help or to offer to subject himself as a vassal (7:4). Now, just six years later, his no to the anti-Assyrian faction was no less forceful. He had not taken the time to author some official party doctrine—which means that the reason for not acting, on both occasions, was solely within the religious realm. "Yahweh has founded Zion" is the way it is stated here. This means that Judah ought not sign any treaties in an attempt to guarantee its safety. On the one hand, this answer corresponds exactly to what could have been furnished in the text if he would have continued his thought in 7:9a by saying: ". . . for the head of Judah is Jerusalem, and the head of Jerusalem is the Davidic king" (or, Yahweh). Some have objected that, even according to Isaiah himself, as is demonstrated in 29:1, David, not Yahweh, is the one who established Jerusalem, not Yahweh (Duhm, Marti). But 29:1 does not deny Yahweh's involvement, even though distinguished scholars keep on saying so. On the other hand, 1 Kings 5:31 says that builders laid the foundation for the temple, and Zech. 4:9 says that the hands of Zerubbabel "laid the foundation of this house" (cf. also 1 Kings 6:37; 7:10; Hag. 2:18; Ezra 3:11; 2 Chron. 3:3). But the fact that humans established the temple or laid its foundation stone in no way eliminates Yahweh as the one who, in the final analysis, established his sanctuary. In addition, one must be aware that nowhere else in the OT—except for Isa. 28:16, a passage whose authenticity is questioned—is the verb יסד used to say that he established the temple. In that other passage, יסד (lay [a foundation stone]) is used with a transferred meaning (similar to 54:11 as well), but this shows that Isaiah could expect that his listeners knew what this concept meant. This way of thinking is implicit in widely different contexts in the OT; one might note how the Song of the Sea ends in Exodus 15: "you brought them in and planted them on the mountain of your own possession, the place, O Yahweh, that you made your abode, the sanctuary, O Lord, that your hands have established" (כוננו; see also Pss. 48:9; 68:10; 87:5; and, on the entire topic, F. Stolz, *Strukturen und Figuren im Kult von Jerusalem,* BZAW 118 [1970] 169ff.); or one might compare this concept to the ἱερὸς λόγος (holy oracle) in 2 Samuel 24. Of course, in 14:32 Isaiah does not speak of the establishment of the temple but rather about Zion's founding. As with 8:18 ("Yahweh of Hosts, who dwells on Mount Zion") or with 31:9 ("whose fire is in Zion, and whose furnace is in Jerusalem"), one is left with the impression that Isaiah uses "dogmatic" sentences from official theology about Zion, which undoubtedly took shape within Jerusalem's cultic liturgical celebrations. In addition, the passage just cited from the Song of the Sea makes clear that "mountain," "abode," and "sanctuary" are alternate ways of saying the same thing. Yahweh has established a residence on Zion (Ps. 74:2); Zion is the holy mountain precisely because that is where Yahweh's dwelling place is located (Ps. 43:3); his abode was established in Salem and his dwelling place in Zion (Ps. 76:3), to cite just some of the relevant passages. Zion is God's seat of government and the cultic center (on this, cf. Fohrer, "Σιων," *TDNT* VII, esp. 307–311). Concepts about an impregnable mountain of God are used in a transferred sense and reapplied. The enemies storm against the city in impotent rage, Pss. 46:7, 10; 48:5-8; 76:4-10; Isa. 30:30; 31:4; cf. also 14:25; 17:12-14. Thus why would Jerusalem have any need of help from the Philistines!

At least for a moment, Isaiah appears as one who believes a theology which states that one could expect an era of salvation to continue uninterrupted, shocking commentators time and time again, which means that they have not been able to treat this word of Isaiah as authentic. But such a solution cannot be justified. It is impossible to remove references to a Zion theology from his messages. Most importantly, a careful examination will make clear that he ensures that the concept will not be misunderstood (see above, p. 91).

The verb חסה (have refuge) is rooted in the language of the Psalms: the one who is praying admits now and again that refuge has been taken with Yahweh: but, to be sure, with Yahweh, not on Mount Zion. "God is our מחסה" (refuge), Ps. 46:2; cf. also Pss. 14:6; 61:4; 62:9, and often elsewhere. Or else one might say: "He [Yahweh] hides me in his shelter, . . . he conceals me under the cover of his tent," Ps. 27:5; cf. also Isa. 4:6; Ps. 31:21. By contrast, when Isaiah speaks of Zion, unlike the quoted psalmists, who were speaking of the individual being protected in the time of one's personal needs, he highlights the inviolability of the city itself, even when threatened by mighty foes.

There is also no exact parallel elsewhere for the comment that it is precisely the עניי עמו (wretched of his people) who will find refuge there, and Isaiah certainly took care to formulate it exactly in this way. The ones who speak are not human beings in general, not even simply Judah/Jerusalem, with no further qualifying statements, but the people of God who seek this type of refuge because they have confidence, who will "dwell there in safety." When interpreting v. 32b, one ought not ignore passages such as 30:15: "in returning and rest you shall be saved" (cf. J. H. Hayes, *JBL* 82 [1963] 425f.). Isaiah definitely makes use of vocabulary that is found in the cultic lyrics. Yahweh is the protector for the oppressed, the hope of the wretched (e.g., Ps. 10:12, 18); the poor trust in him, seek him out (Ps. 9:10). (Some of these psalms certainly were composed after the time of Isaiah; however, there is no doubt that the way these words are used originates in preexilic times.) For more on עניי עמו (wretched of his people), see above, p. 91.

[14:30a] The expander who adds v. 30a intends to supply even more specific details to the ideas expressed in v. 32b. One supposes that he would not have intended to speak about his own דלים (insignificant ones) and אביונים (poor) in the same way that Isaiah thought of the עניי (wretched). Both terms are honorific titles, applied to those who truly were pious, those who had become the true community of God; cf. E. Gerstenberger, *THAT* I, 24; and G. J. Botterweck, *TDOT* I, 40 (who admittedly accepts the conclusions that Duhm reached about this section).

Purpose and Thrust

In a way similar to 7:1-9 and other related passages, Isaiah also attempts to exercise his influence with those who are making the concrete political decision discussed in 14:28-32. He remains true in this passage to the same approach that he uses elsewhere in other circumstances, in which he tries to keep Jerusalem/Judah from having dealings with the world powers (since, of course, Egypt was the driving force behind the Philistine effort). He justifies his message with forceful theological reasons, supporting his arguments with nothing but the "utopia" of the faith. Of course, the reflections offered above, in relation to the power plays in the political realm during his era, show that he did not go off half-cocked, totally ignoring the actual circumstances. In addition, one can be sure that the faith also protected him from a dangerous misreading of the events and made it possible for him to be at an advantage when appraising the situation, clearly distinguishing his views from the wishful thinking of many who were politicians by profession. Yet one must never overlook the fact that he was not supplying a recipe that could be used in every possible circumstance. A quick glance at his contemporary, Micah, would warn us about this: he spoke about Zion in a much different way. Chiefly, one must reflect on the following: Isaiah has no intention of simply calming someone down; his message was motivated by his deep concern about whether Israel would also be willing to take a risk in faith, whether the "poor" among Yahweh's people could summon the strength to protect their place of safety solely because they knew that they would be protected, since Yahweh willed it so.

If the suggested dating set forth above (somewhere around 727) is correct, for once Isaiah got someone to listen to him. At least, we do not know anything about Judah having given in to the Philistines' advances at that time. Since the Philistine territories apparently initiated no revolt in those days, one might conclude that the no which their messengers received in Jerusalem, as the reply to their overture, might have motivated the Philistines themselves to hold off on their plans. Sadly, however, one observes that the people did not choose to stay permanently on track and believe as Isaiah had encouraged them to do, as is seen so horribly at a somewhat later date, during the time of Hezekiah.

Words Concerning Moab

Literature

F. Hitzig, *Des Propheten Jonas Orakel über Moab kritisch vindicirt und durch Über-setzung nebst Anmerkungen erläutert* (1831). F. Schwally, "Die Reden des Buches Jeremia gegen die Heiden. XXV.XLVI–LI," *ZAW* 8 (1888) 177–217. H. Bardtke, "Jeremia der Fremdvölkerprophet," *ZAW* 54 (1936) 240–262. L. Alonso-Schökel, *Estudios de Poética Hebrea* (1963). W. Rudolph, "Jesaja XV–XVI," *Hebrew and Semitic Studies Presented to G. R. Driver* (1963) 130–143. G. Fohrer, "Vollmacht über Völker und Königreiche: Beobachtungen zu den prophetischen Fremdvölker-sprüchen anhand von Jer 46–51," FS J. Ziegler II (1972) 145–153.
Concerning textual criticism: F. Nötscher, "Entbehrliche Hapaxlegomena in Jesaia," *VT* 1 (1951) 299–302. J. Reider, "Contributions to the Scriptural Text," *HUCA* 24 (1952/53) 85–106. E. Ullendorff, "The Contribution of South Semitics to Hebrew Lexicography," *VT* 6 (1956) 190–198. G. R. Driver, "Notes on Isaiah," *BZAW* 77 (1958) 42–48. A. Guillaume, "A Note on the Roots ריע, ירע, and רעע in Hebrew," *JTS* 15 (1964) 293–295. D. Dimant, "Targum Jonathan to Isa. XVI.6 and Jer. XLVIII.29f.," *JSS* 18 (1973) 55–56. Ch. Rabin, "Hebrew *baddīm* 'Power,'" *JSS* 18 (1973) 57–58.
Concerning the history and language of Moab: For the Mesha Inscription, see *KAI* 181 (further literature citations there). J. Simons, *Handbook for the Study of Egyptian Topographical Lists Relating to Western Asia* (1937). F. M. Cross and D. N. Freedman, *Early Hebrew Orthography* (1952). H. W. F. Saggs, "The Nimrud Letters, 1952—Part II," *Iraq* 17 (1955) 126–160. H. Donner, "Neue Quellen zur Geschichte des Staates Moab in der 2. Hälfte des 8. Jahrhunderts v. Chr.," *MIO* 5 (1957) 155–184. M. Noth, "Moab," *RGG³*, IV, 1065f. A. H. van Zyl, *The Moabites*, POS 3 (1960). S. Segert, "Die Sprache der moabitischen Königsinschrift," *ArOr* 29 (1961) 197–267. S. Mittmann, "Das südliche Ostjordanland im Lichte eines neuassyrischen Keilschriftbriefes aus Nimrūd," *ZDPV* 89 (1973) 15–25.
Concerning the archaeology and geography of Moab: A. Musil, *Arabia Petraea, I: Moab* (1907). N. Glueck, *Explorations in Eastern Palestine* I, *AASOR* 14 (1933–1934) 1–113. Idem, *Explorations in Eastern Palestine* III, *AASOR* 18–19 (1939). R. de Vaux, "Notes d'histoire et de topographie transjordaniennes," *VivPen* 1 (1941) 16–47. H. S. Nyberg, "Studien zum Religionskampf im Alten Testament," *ARW* 35 (1938) 329–387. N. Glueck, "Some Ancient Towns in the Plains of Moab," *BASOR* 91 (1943) 7–20. Idem, *Explorations in Eastern Palestine* IV/1, *AASOR* 25–28 (1951). A. Schwarzenbach, *Die geographische Terminologie im Hebräischen des Alten Testaments* (1954). F. V. Winnett and W. L. Reed, *The Excavations at Dibon (Dhībân) in Moab*, *AASOR* 36–37 (1964). R. Rendtorff, "Zur Lage von Jaeser," *ZDPV* 76 (1960) 124–135. K. H. Bernhardt, "Beobachtungen zur Identi-

fizierung moabitischer Ortslagen," *ZDPV* 76 (1960) 136–158. A. Kuschke, "Jeremia 48:1–8: Zugleich ein Beitrag zur historischen Topographie Moabs," FS W. Rudolph (1961) 181–196. Idem, "Historisch-topographische Beiträge zum Buche Josua," FS H. W. Hertzberg (1965) 90–109. W. Schottroff, "Horonaim, Nimrim, Luhith und der Westrand des 'Landes Ataroth,'" *ZDPV* 82 (1966) 163–208. H. Donner and H. Cüppers, "Die Restauration und Konservierung der Mosaikkarte von Madeba," *ZDPV* 83 (1967) 1–33. E. K. Vogel, "Bibliography of Holy Land Cities," *HUCA* 42 (1971) 1–96. A. D. Tushingham, *The Excavations at Dibon (Dhībân) in Moab, AASOR* 40 (1972). R. S. Boraas and S. H. Horn, *Heshbon 1971,* Andrews University Monograph 6 (1973) = *AUSS* 11 (1973).

[**Literature update through 1979:** I. Zoller, "Note Esegetiche (Isaia XV, 2a [among the passages cited])," *GSAI* NS 2 (1930) 244f. K. Seybold, Das davidische Königtum im Zeugnis der Propheten, FRLANT 107 (1972) (on 16:1–5).
Concerning the history and language of Moab: E. Lipiński, "מואב = maqtal rad.wʾb 'the broad land,' synon. ad מישור," *Or* 40 (1971) 326f. M. Miller, "The Moabite Stone as a Memorial Stela," *PEQ* 106 (1974) 9–18.
Concerning the archaeology and geography of Moab: W. L. Reed, "Elealeh: The Archaeological History of Elealeh in Moab," FS F. V. Winnett (1972) 18–28.]

Text

15:1 [Verdict concerning Moab.]
    Truly, overnight[a] it was destroyed,
      Ar[b]-Moab was destroyed,
    truly, overnight it was destroyed,
      Kir-Moab was destroyed.[c]
  2 [a]'The daughter of Dibon has gone up'[a]
      to cry on the offering high places;
    on[b] Nebo and on[b] Medeba
      Moab starts a howling.[c]
    Every head is shaved bald,[d]
      [e]every beard is clipped[f] off.
  3 In their side streets they wear sackcloth,[a]
      on their[b] roofs 'they have laments for the dead,'[c]
    in their places 'they howl'[d] all together,[e]
      (and) they[f] melt into tears.
  4 And Heshbon and Elealeh raise up their cry for help;
      even as far as Jahaz their voices were heard.
    For that reason Moab's 'loins'[a] 'tremble violently';[b]
      its spirit 'considers itself to be most wretched.'[c]

          *   *   *   *

  5 My heart[a] cries for help for Moab,
      'its'[b] fugitives are (dispersed) as far as Zoar[c] [to third Eglath].[d]
    Yes, onto the mountain tracks of Luhith,
      one ascends thereupon with weeping;
    yes, upon the road toward Horonaim,
      they raise[e] the downfall shriek.
  6 Yes, the waters of Nimrim
      will become a desert region,
    since the grass is withered, the plants gone,[a]
      nothing green is there any longer.
  7 Therefore, whatever is still left,[a]
      and whatever anyone had put aside[a]

over the willow brook,
  they will take them away.
8 Truly, the cry of murder crosses through[a]
  Moab's entire territory;[b]
its cry[c] reaches even as far as Eglaim,
  and as far as[d] Beer-elim[e] [its cry].[c]
9 [Truly, the waters of Dimon,[a] they are filled with blood,
  for I bring upon Dimon[a] new disaster;
[b]for the escapees of Moab a lion,
  and terror for the remnant.[b]]

    *   *   *   *

16:1 Send[a] [b]a ram
  of the sovereign[b]
from the rock in the desert[c]
  to the mount of the daughter of Zion:
2 [And it will happen: as fleeting birds,
  a startled nest,
the daughters of Moab will be
  at[a] the fords of the Arnon.]
3 Give[a] a suggestion,
  hand down[b] a decision,[c]
throw, as the night, your shadows
  at the zenith of noontide!
Hide the scattered,
  do not betray the refugee!
4 As protected citizens, in your midst, they ought to sojourn,
  those who have been 'dispersed'[a] from Moab!
Be[b] for them a hiding place,
  when the devastator appears!
When[c] the hardship[d] is at an end,
  the devastation[e] is gone,
[f]assault has been cleared[f] out of the land,
5 then, in truth, a throne will be established,
  and on it will sit, permanently, [a][in David's tent],[a]
one who establishes righteousness, striving[b] for justice,
  certainly proficient[c] in righteousness.

    *   *   *   *

6 We heard about Moab's pride[a]
  which pushes on in with great pomp,
about its haughtiness, its pride, and its presumption,
  [b]about its untrue idle babbling.[c]
7 Therefore Moab howls[a] [on account of Moab],[b]
  each one howls,
for the grape cakes[c] from Kir-hareseth
  'they'[d] whimper, completely crushed.

    *   *   *   *

8 Truly, the garden terraces of Heshbon are 'devastated,'[a]
  the grapevines of Sibmah are withered
where,[b] in fact, the lords of peoples
  once had been overcome by its choice grapes.[b]

They reached even as far as Jazer,
  roamed even out into the desert;
its runners grew rapidly,
  marched forth as far as the sea.[c]
9 Therefore I will cry, as[a] Jazer cries,
  for the grapevines of Sibmah,
will soak[b] you with my tears,
  Heshbon and Elealeh.
Since, for your summer fruit and your harvest produce,[c]
  cheering has ceased.
10 There, joy and shouts of jubilation will be harvested
  away from the groves of trees,
and in the vineyards one hears joyful shouts no (longer),
  'and'[a] the call for rejoicing stays far away.
In the winepress, one [the winepresser][b] treads out no wine,
  for the cheering 'an end has been prepared.'[c]
11 [a]Therefore my insides are riled up concerning Moab [as a lyre][a]
  and my innards concerning Kir-heres.[b] . . . [c]

* * * *

12 [And it is going to happen: when Moab [appears,[a] when it] makes
the effort[b] to get itself up to the offering high places and comes to
pray in its sanctuary, it will not be able to make anything happen.]

* * * *

13 [That is the message that Yahweh spoke at an earlier time about
Moab. 14 Now, however, Yahweh has indeed said: in three years,
as are years of one who does day labor,[a] Moab's majesty, together
will all of its great bustling, will have become despicable, and its
remnant[b] will become [c]minutely small, completely powerless.[c]]

15:1a Instead of בְּלֵיל (in the night of), Qᵃ reads בלילה (during the night). If בְּלֵיל is
correct, then it has to be translated: "during the night in which Ar was destroyed,
Moab was brought to silence" (concerning לֵיל in the construct state preceding a relative clause, see Joüon, *Gr* §129q, §158d). Correspondingly, v. 1bβ would have to be
translated in a similar fashion. However, קִיר (Kir), as the name of a Moabite city, is
never mentioned in the OT without some additional information that further identifies the location. One also expects מוֹאָב (Moab) to be mentioned, to identify עָר (Ar)
more specifically; cf. Num. 21:15; Deut. 2:18. For this reason, one should alter לֵיל
(night of) to read לַיִל (night) (cf. Qᵃ and Vulg: *quia nocte vastate est Ar Moab conticuit*, "because by night it has been devastated, Ar-Moab has become silent"), unless
one simply should take לֵיל as being in the absolute state (see König, *Lehrg.* §337y).
1b For עָר מוֹאָב (Ar-Moab), the Gk reads ἡ Μωαβῖτις (Moab/the Moabites).
1c The second נדמה is translated by Aquila, Theod as εσιωπησεν (was silent), by
Sym as εσιωπηθη (has been silenced), by Vulg as *conticuit* (has become silent).
Because of the parallelism in the present passage, however, it is better to stay with
the traditional translation "be destroyed" (contra KBL and L. Köhler, *Kleine Lichter*
[1945] 32–34; see also *Isaiah 1–12*, pp. 249f., on 6:5).
2a–a עלה הבית ודיבן makes no sense. It is possible that הבית is a garbled form of a
place-name (Dillmann and Kittel). Targ: סליקו לבתיא דדיבון = "they have gone up to
the houses of Dibon." Syr: *slqw lbytᵓ drybwn* (they have gone up into the house of

Ribon). On the basis of Jer. 48:18 (יֹשֶׁבֶת בַּת־דִּיבֹן, "enthroned daughter Dibon"), it should be read עָלְתָה בַּת דִּיבֹן (the daughter of Dibon has gone up).

2b עַל never means "in" (a city), as Fohrer translates this passage. One could translate this "over," in the sense "concerning the matter of" or something similar to that (thus Naegelsbach, Kissane, Bewer, Hertzberg, et al.). But that would mean that both cities, Nebo and Medeba, would have been destroyed by an enemy. In fact, the invasion took place in the southern part of the country, but it was in the north that the cry of lament was uttered. Therefore עַל must mean "on" in this case, namely, "on the offering high places" (Delitzsch, Orelli, Marti, Dillmann, Gray, Duhm, Steinmann, Eichrodt, Young, Kaiser).

2c The form יְיֵלִיל (begins to howl) is also found in v. 3 and 16:7; cf. אֵילִיל (I wail) in Jer. 48:31; יְיֵלִילוּ (they wail) in Hos. 7:14; תְּיֵלִילוּ (you shall wail) in Isa. 65:14. Such forms ought not, as is usually the case (see the *BHS* apparatus), be "normalized" (by reading יְיֵלִיל, etc.), but can be explained by observing that an attempt was made to preserve both the preformative letter and the first root consonant, or an attempt was made to reconstruct such a form; cf. Ges-K §70d.

2d The pointing on רָאשָׁיו (his heads) is not common; nevertheless, it could be an original, dialectical variant. However, the suffix hangs in midair (or, if its referent is בַּת־דִּיבֹן, "daughter of Dibon," it ought to be a feminine suffix), which means that the Qᵃ reading ראושו (his head) does not help either. Some MSS simply read the singular ראש (head); see also Jer. 48:37 and the Gk (ἐπὶ πάσης κεφαλῆς, "upon every head").

2e Qᵃ and some MSS (see also Syr, Targᶠ, Vulg) read וְכָל (and every).

2f Gkᴮ and many MSS have the reading גְּדוּעָה (shave off, hew off), which can be explained as an attempt to use a more common word instead of the infrequently used technical term for clipping the beard, גְּרֻעָה (contra Driver, *WO* 1 [1947] 29); cf. Ezek. 5:11.

3a Concerning שַׂק, "sackcloth," cf. W. Hönig, *Die Bekleidung des Hebräers* (1957) 102–111.

3b The suffixes in v. 3 are not consistent. The two feminine forms could both refer back to the city (Medeba?), the masculine forms to Moab as a people. However, one would have to presume that all the suffixes originally had the same referent. Since מוֹאָב (Moab), as a people, is masculine and, as a land, is feminine, both solutions are possible; however, since there is mention of Moab as a people in v. 2bα, masculine suffixes are more likely original (contra בְּחוּצוֹתֶיהָ, "in her side streets," in Qᵃ; cf. Driver, *JTS* NS 2 [1951] 25; but supported by יֵרֵד, "going down, melting [into tears]," in v. 3bβ). The feminine forms would have come into existence because the early masculine forms were written with a ה (*he*) (as is the case on the Mesha Inscription).

3c The second colon in the first line is too short; a verb is missing; the side streets are obviously not located on the roofs. Driver (*JTS* 41 [1940] 163) suggests inserting קֵעוּ (just before עַל, "on"), which he understands, in the sense in which the Syriac *qᶜ* is used, to mean "cry out loudly." The Gk reads κόπτεσθε (you [pl.] beat your breast), whereas Jer. 48:38, in a similar context, reads מִסְפֵּד (lamentation), so that one could possibly read here כָּפְדוּ (they bewail) or some other verb that conveys the same meaning (Rudolph suggests reading יֵהֶמוּ, "they will wail," or הָמוּ, "they wailed"; see also Kaiser).

3d Concerning יְיֵלִיל (howl), see above, note 2c.

3e Concerning the suffix on כֻּלֹּה (all together), see Joüon, *Gr* §146j.

3f KBL claims that יֵרֵד בַּבֶּכִי in the present passage should be translated: "going up and down with tears." However, instead of this, it is to be treated as a metaphor, sim-

107

ilar to the well-known ירדה עיני דמעה = "my eyes run down with tears" (see Jer. 13:17 and cf. Lam. 1:16; 3:48).

4a Instead of חֲלֻצֵי, "equipped for military service," the Gk reads ἡ ὀσφὺς here, thus having read חֲלָצֵי, "loins."

4b It might be due to the misunderstanding caused by misreading חלצי that the questionable reading of the verb as יָרִיעוּ developed; this reading does correspond to the pointing חֲלֻצֵי, but does not make any sense within the wider context: who, in such a situation, would still want to shout out a battle cry! The Gk reads γνώσεται (he will know) (cf. also Syr). For this reason, some have speculated that the original verb would have been from the root ידע (know) (Gray; D. W. Thomas, 55); a different solution is suggested by A. Guillaume, 293–295. In fact, יָרִיעוּ should be explained as a mistake in copying, either from יִרְעוּ, "they quiver," or from רָעֲדוּ, which has the same meaning (ירע: Marti, Duhm, Feldmann, Kissane, Ziegler; רעד: Kaiser).

4c If it is correct that one ought to read יִרְעוּ (they tremble violently) in v. 4bα, then one runs into trouble in v. 4bβ, where the MT reads the very same verb. Qᵃ reads ירע, which F. Nötscher (299) derives from רעע (be evil); one might compare יֵרַע לְבָבוּ (carry a grudge) in Deut. 15:10 and 1 Sam. 1:8 ("your heart is sad"), as well as וַיֵּרַע לְמֹשֶׁה (it went ill with Moses) in Ps. 106:32.

5a Some commentators have replaced לבי (my heart) (thus Duhm, Bruno, Marti) with לבו (his heart) (Gk: ἡ καρδία, "the heart"; Targ: בליבהון, "in their hearts"), but first person speech from the author, who is also actively involved in the destiny that has come upon Moab, appears additionally in 16:9, 11.

5b For בְּרִיחֶהָ, Qᵃ reads ברחוה, "in his spirit"; Syr reads *brwḥh* (in his spirit); cf. the Gk: ἐν [ἑ]αυτῇ (in herself) and Theod: συν τω πνευματι αυτης (together with her own spirit). Possibly one should read either ברִיחֶהָ (with her fugitives) or ברִיחוֹ (with his/its fugitives) (cf. Driver, *JSS* 13 [1968] 44; and see above, note 3b), in which case ברִיחַ (fleeing), used elsewhere in the OT only as an adjective, could be explained here as being used as a collective substantive (fleeing ones).

5c Qᵃ: צעור (z^{e}ôr).

5d עֶגְלַת שְׁלִשִׁיָּה (Eglath-shelishiyah) seems to be a gloss to צֹעַר (Zoar). It is uncommon to find two place-names in the same colon, and the lines would then be too long. It is possible that the identification of these places, presumably interpolated into this text from Jer. 48:34, forced out a verb that was originally read here. By altering עֶגְלַת (Eglath) to read עֵין אֶגְלַיִם (cf. v. 8), then translating "one-third as far as En-eglaim," Fohrer attempts to make some sense of the text, but this remains in the realm of speculation. Concerning the ending יָּה- instead of ית- with feminine ordinal numbers, see Joüon, *Gr* §101b.

5e The rare form יְעֹעֵרוּ (raise) has been analyzed as a *pilpel* from עוֹר (= יְעַרְעֲרוּ); cf. Ges-K §72cc. Since this form does not exist anywhere else, however, it seems better to suggest that it be treated as a *pi'lel*: יְעוֹרְרוּ; the *hiph'il* of the same root has also been suggested: יָעִירוּ (*BHS*) (others [see *BHS*] think it might be a passive *pi'lel* from רוּעַ, which would result in the reading: יְרֹעָעוּ).

6a Kaiser suggests removing כְּלָה דְשֶׁא (the plants gone), because it makes the line too long metrically. That is not necessary if one reads the two words as having only one stress.

7a עשה (lit.: he made) functions as a relative clause in relation to יתרה (what is left); however, the singular does not agree with the plural יִשָּׂאוּם (they will take them away), which means that something must be altered, changing either the first term to read עָשׂוּ (they made) or the latter term to read יִשָּׂאֵם (he will take them away), the first being preferable, since otherwise one also would have to emend פקדתם (what anyone has put aside) to read פקדתו (what he put aside) (cf. Driver, *JTS* 38 [1937] 40).

8a נוּק: II *hiphⁱil* = "wander around in a circle" or "(in all directions) wander through."

8b גבול can mean not only "border" but also "territory." The latter meaning is more accurate for this passage. Unfortunately, to date, Eglaim and Beer-elim have not been identified geographically with certainty (on this, see below, p. 137).

8c The second יללתה (its cry) is missing in the Syh and should be removed as a dittography. Once again, however, there are problems with the suffix (see above, notes 3b, 5b). One must also point this with a normal masculine suffix: יללתוֹ (his/its cry).

8d The Gk reads ἕως τοῦ φρέατος (as far as the well [Beer]), which would seem to suggest that its text had the preposition עד ב in this colon as well (Vulg: *usque . . .*, "all the way . . ."; Syr: *wlbʾrʾ*, "and to Beer"). Then one might presume that the passage read ועד ב/ (and as far as Beer) originally, unless one would accept the interpretation suggested by Joüon (*Gr* §132g) that sometimes the preposition, though not used again, is to be treated as governing the second colon as well as the first.

8e The conjecture first offered by Marti, and accepted by many, to read ובאראלים = "and in Erʾelim," is useless and unlikely, since no mention is made anywhere of a settlement with this name.

9a For דימון (Dimon), Qᵃ reads: דבון (Dibon); Vulg: Dibon (Gk: Ρεμμων, Remmon: Syr: *rybwn*, Ribon). Since there is no known city in Moab with the name Dimon (or Ribon) (the Dimonah in Josh. 15:22 is in Judah), it would make the best sense to follow Qᵃ. Yet for the very reason that Dibon is a well-known locality it is hard to understand why someone would have replaced it with the place-name Dimon, an otherwise unknown city. Trustworthy MSS of the Gk read δειμων (Deimon; thus GkᴮB), others δεμμων (Demmon) or δημων (Dēmon); and Targ, Aquila, Sym, Theod all presume a reading דימון (Dimon), so that, plainly, one ought not alter the MT (on this matter, cf. the extensive discussion by Orlinsky, *IEJ* 4 [1954] 5–8, and FS Albright [1961] 117ff.). It is still possible that Dimon is the same as Dibon, since it is easy to understand how the ב and מ could be used interchangeably; in addition, the Dimonah mentioned in Josh. 15:22 is at the same place as the Dibon mentioned in Neh. 11:25 (see KBL, Zorell, Ges-Buhl).

9b–b There is complete uncertainty about the original text at the end of v. 9. For אריה (lion), the Gk reads καὶ Αριηλ (and Ariel), which makes no sense in the context. As a parallel to אריה (lion) in v. 9bα, J. Reider (87) suggests that one should read שחל, "lion" or "young lion" (KBL) at the end of v. 9bβ, a word that would have been lost due to haplography because of the first word in 16:1, שלחו (send). G. Hoffmann ("Versuche zu Amos," *ZAW* 3 [1883] 104) took a different approach, emending אריה (lion) to read אראה: "I have a vision," and, correspondingly, altering אדמה (land) to read אדמה, which supposedly means: "I speak a parable." But then one would have to have mentioned something about the content of the vision and parable as well. In light of the Gk Αριηλ (Ariel), Procksch conjectures an original איליל, "I lament"; instead of לשארית (for the remnant): לשאריתו, "for his remnant"; instead of אדמה (land): אדמעה "I must cry." One cannot completely rule out the possibility that the text originally read something like this, but these are no more than suppositions. For this reason, it seems preferable to stay with this text as much as possible, in the form in which it has been transmitted, following Kissane, Rudolph, Eichrodt, and others (see also *BHS*), by reading אימה (terror) at the very end of the verse instead of אדמה (land). There is no convincing evidence, however, that one ought to build on this conjectured

אֵימָה (terror) to emend the earlier word אַרְיֵה (lion) to read יִרְאָה, "fear" (cf. Rudolph), or אֲנִיָּה, "mourning" (so Kissane).

16:1a For the imperative שִׁלְחוּ (send [pl.]), eastern MSS read שָׁלְחוּ (they sent); Gk: ἀποστελῶ (I will send); Syr: ʾšdr (I will send); Targ paraphrases this: יהון מסקן מסק למשיחא דישראל (They shall bring tribute to the Anointed One [or, Messiah] of Israel). None of the numerous suggested alterations (שָׁלְחוּ, "they were sent"; אֶשְׁלַח, "I will send"; [וְ]שָׁלְחוּ, "[and] they sent"; אֶשְׁלְחָה, "I will indeed send") can claim to be correct, since one is left with the unavoidable impression that the text of the entire original verse has been damaged.

1b–b For כַּר מֹשֵׁל־אֶרֶץ (ram, ruler of the land), the Gk reads: ὡς ἑσπετὰ ἐπὶ τὴν γῆν (as a four-footed animal on the earth), thus having treated the transmitted text as if the word divisions would have resulted in the reading: כְּרֶמֶשׂ לָאָרֶץ (as a creeper on the earth). However, that a creeping animal should be sent "to the mount of the daughter of Zion" makes no sense. Other suggestions (מַלְאֲכֵי אֶרֶץ: "messengers of the earth," or אֶשְׁכָּר מֹ אֹ: "tribute of the ruler of the land") are much too uncertain. (The conjectured אֶשְׁכָּר, "tribute," was first offered long ago by Cheyne; on this, see Ezek. 27:15; Ps. 72:10; and Akkadian iškaru = "regularly sent tribute money.") In spite of much hesitation, one ought to stay with the MT. Instead of מֹשֵׁל (sovereign), some have suggested לַמֹּשֵׁל (to the sovereign) or לְמֹשְׁלֵי (to the sovereigns of). However, the MT does not have an impossible reading: the Moabite ruler is known as one who himself possessed many herds (see 2 Kings 3:4).

1c מִדְבָּרָה calls for attention, since the translation "into the desert" makes no sense. The readings of the Gk: πέτρα ἔρημος (rock of the desert); Syr: kʾpʾ dmdbrʾ (rock of the desert); and Vulg: de Petra deserti (from the desert of Petra) have given rise to the emendation סֶלַע הַמִּדְבָּר (rock of the desert). According to Ges-K §90d, מסלע מדברה may indeed be translated "from the rock in the desert."

2a One notes that there ought to have been a preposition before מַעְבְּרֹת (the fords of). Sym reads: απαγομεναι περαν αρνων (led away beyond Arnon), which has brought forth the suggestion to read מֵעֵבֶר (= מֵעֵבֶר) ("from beyond," BHS; see Gray). It is more likely that one should assume that a ב was lost just before מַעְבְּרֹת (the fords of) because of haplography (Syr: bmʿbrtʾ, "at the fords of").

3a Kethib: הָבִיאוּ (you [masculine pl.] shall bring); Qere: הָבִיאִי (you [feminine sing.] shall bring). As one can see from שִׁיתִי (throw [feminine sing.]) and צִלֵּךְ (your [feminine sing.] shadows) in v. 3aβ, the Qere reading is preferable, being followed by some of the MSS and versions. Qᵃ הביי (you [masculine pl.] shall give) at least leads one to suppose that the text should perhaps read הבי (you [feminine sing.] shall give) (from the root יהב). In the present situation, it makes no sense to talk about "bringing a decision"; nowhere else in the OT does one find the phrase חביא עצה, but one does find יהב עצה (give [your] advice) (Judg. 20:7; 2 Sam. 16:20).

3b On the basis of many MSS and Gkᴬ, Syr, Targ, Vulg, one should read עֲשִׂי (hand down [feminine sing.]) here, instead of עֲשׂוּ (hand down [masculine pl.]); cf. note 16:3a.

3c There is no need to replace פְּלִילָה (decision) with פְּלֵיטָה (escapees) (Ehrlich, Randglossen, IV, 60), which also contradicts the parallelismus membrorum within the bicolon.

4a Instead of נִדָּחַי (my dispersed ones), with support from 2 MSS, from the Gk (οἱ φυγάδες Μωαβ, "the fugitives of Moab") and from the Syr (mbdrʾ dmwʾb, "the wilderness of Moab"), some read נִדְחֵי (dispersed of); "'my dispersed one, Moab' is the result of an eschatological interpretation" (Kaiser).

4b The rare form הֱוִי (become [feminine sing.]) (from הוה, "become"; see Gen. 27:29;

Neh. 6:6; Eccles. 2:22; 11:3) "might correspond to the Moabite way of speaking" (Procksch).

4c Dillmann and Kittel, among others, would like to insert an עַד before כִּ ("until it happens that"), in which case v. 4b would be a postscript to v. 4a. However, v. 4b should be considered as the introductory clause for v. 5.

4d הַמֵּץ (the extortioner) is an uncertain reading. Qᵃ reads either הַמוֹץ or, more probably, חמוֹץ (see E. R. Rowlands, *VT* 1 [1951] 228), which would be pointed חָמוֹץ (the ruthless). Targ (מעִיקְאָ = "oppressor") would presume this same reading (or another conjecture that has already been suggested, חָמֵץ, "ruthless one"). However, one would be more likely to find an abstract term with שֹׁד (devastation), so that it is recommended that one stay with the MT anyway, rendering מֵץ, on the basis of the way מִיץ is used in Prov. 30:33 ("press"), as something like "pressure." The sense would be the same as that suggested by Driver (*JTS* 38 [1937] 40), who, instead of הַמֵּץ (the extortioner), reads the *hiphⁱil* infinitive הָמֵץ, "acting in an extortionate way."

4e Instead of שֹׁד (devastation), one can presume that it should read השֹׁד (the devastation) (haplography of the ה). If one would favor altering הַמֵּץ (the extortioner) to read חמוֹץ (ruthless one), or something similar, then one would have to read שֹׁדֵד (devastator) here, which is unlikely, since v. 4a already ends with this word.

4f–f Qᵃ reads the singular תַם (clear out), which is the same reading reflected in Gk, Syr, and Vulg. Taking the other approach, some commentators make the singular רֹמֵס (assault) into a plural, but this would hardly be right in light of the singular forms in v. 4bα. After what has immediately preceded, one would not expect the *nomen agentis* to be mentioned, which means one can follow Driver (*JTS* 38 [1937] 40) and read רְמֹס (assault, oppression) instead of רֹמֵס (assault).

5a–a בְּאֹהֶל דוד (in David's tent) makes the line too long metrically (being an interpretive gloss). For בְּאֹהֶל the Gk reads ἐν σκέπῃ (in a shelter), but this is apparently a copying mistake for what probably read ἐν σκήνῃ (in a tent) originally.

5b It would make better sense to eliminate the ו (and) from before דרש (striving for). Apparently, דרש משׁפט (striving for justice) and מהר צדק (proficient in righteousness) provide more detailed descriptions of the שׁפֵט (one who establishes righteousness).

5c מהר is the "expert, specialist"; cf. E. Ullendorff, 195. There is no need to change this word to read שׁחר, "looking diligently for."

6a גֵּא (pride) is a hapax legomenon; 2 MSS, Qᵃ, and Jer. 48:29 all use the common form גֵּאֶה, which is probably the original form here as well.

6b Jer. 48:30 reads וֹלֹא (and not); however, the ו is a dittography.

6c On the basis of the Arabic, Ch. Rabin (52ff.) suggests translating בַדִּים as "might" (Vulg: *fortitudo*, "strength, bravery"; in Jer. 48:30: *virtus*: "valor, bravery"). However, the traditional translation "idle babbling" is closer to the parallel terms. Concerning this text, see D. Dimant (55f.) as well.

7a Concerning the unique form יְיֵלִיל (howls), see textual note 15:2c, above.

7b לְמוֹאב (to Moab) should be eliminated not only on metrical grounds but also because it is completely unnecessary.

7c Instead of אֲשִׁישֵׁי (raisin cakes of), Jer. 48:31 reads אַנְשֵׁי (people of); Targ: אֲנָשׁ (humankind); this is clearly a smoothing out of the reading. Driver's suggestion (BZAW 77 [1958] 43), that one interpret אֲשִׁישֵׁי in light of Arabic *ʾaṭṭa* = "live comfortably," and translate this: "ye shall moan for the luxurious dwellers in Kir-hareseth," is not compelling.

7d The second person plural in תהגו (you whimper) appears unexpectedly, since no such form is found anywhere else in the entire section of the text that deals with

Moab. One MS reads יהגה (he moans) (see also Targ), but a better solution would be to follow the conjecture הגו (they whimper) (ה is a dittography).

8a The first line in v. 8 seems too long, and אמלל (grow weak, languish) does not make sense with שדמות (fields of). Ges-K §145u explains that the form is the singular אמלל because שדמות is a collective, but one still suspects that there has been some damage to the text. Kaiser would eliminate שדמות (fields of) altogether and read the feminine אמללה (languishes). However, the parallel expression נפן ש׳ (vines of Sibmah) makes that unlikely. Driver (*JTS* 38 [1937] 40) reads כשדמות and translates "as the fields of Heshbon, (so) doth the vine of Sibmah languish." In this case, however, the first colon in the first line would be too short. The Targ has quite a different reading: "Behold, the armies of Heshbon have been plundered (אתבזיזא), the divisions of Sibmah have been beaten." That would be closer to what should be read here, since there also would be a verb for נפן ש׳ (vines of Sibmah); this verb might have been שדדו (devastated), which would make it possible to move אמלל (withered) over to the second colon of that line.

8b–b Fohrer translates this: "The lords of the nations dashed its grapes to pieces"; others read something similar to this, which means that they treat שׁרוּקֶיהָ (BDB: its vine tendrils or clusters) as an object (so Gesenius, Naegelsbach, Fischer, Bewer, Kaiser, et al.). Yet grapes are not "dashed to pieces," and the rendering "grape tendrils," as some translate this, is not really what שׁרוּקִים means (but cf. שׁרֵקָה, "choice vine," in Gen. 49:11). In addition, in the more immediate context, the discussion is not about Moab's enemies but about the superior quality of its vineyards. Therefore שׁרוקיה (its choice grapes) must be the subject of the sentence (so Hitzig, Delitzsch, Dillmann, Marti, Duhm, Steinmann, Eichrodt, et al.); בעלי גוים (lords of peoples) would have been placed at the beginning, in what has been called a *casus pendens* relationship (as for the . . .). Isa. 28:1 (הלומי יין, "overcome with wine") shows that the verb הלם (hammer, strike down) also can be used when talking about grapes or wine.

8c Fischer translates this: "spanned across the sea"; others, similarly; this is a grotesque image, even if this phrase refers to the Dead Sea and not to the Mediterranean.

9a Gk: ὡς τὸν κλαυθμόν (as the weeping), but this does not mean that one ought to change the reading from בבכי (with the weeping of) to כבכי (as weeps), and one is not forced by the MT to presume that the author himself was a citizen of Jazer.

9b אריוך is an impossible form (on this, see Ges-K §75dd and Bauer-Leander §57t"); Qᵃ reads ארזוך (your cedarwood), which is a corruption of ארוך (to be pointed אֲרַוֶּךְ, "I will soak you").

9c Jer. 48:32 read not קציר, "harvest produce," but rather בציר, "vintage," but this change in the text is doubtful, since alliteration was apparently intended between קִץ (summer fruit) and קציר (harvest produce).

10a Many MSS, Qᵃ, Targ, Vulg (cf. Gk, Syr) presume ולא (and there is no), which certainly should be read in the original (cf. the metrical structure).

10b הדרך (the winepresser) is missing in the Gk, correctly so, as can be seen by the metrical structure. Concerning the indefinite subject, "one," cf. Joüon, *Gr* §155d.

10c Since the first person pronoun is never used with Yahweh as the referent in the rest of the passages dealing with the Moabites, it is probably not correct in this passage either. On the basis of the Gk (πέπαυται, "it has been made to cease"), the *hoph'al* הֻשְׁבַּת (an end has been prepared) should be read here.

11a–a Zürcher Bibel: "for this reason my heart laments for Moab"; others read something similar. It is very difficult to find the right words to depict the vivid sense of Hebrew המה, while being sensitive to the way this might be conveyed in present-day speech, and yet also to be able to find a verb that can describe both the sounds made by one's "insides" and by a "lyre"; in addition to this, כְּכִנּוֹר (as a lyre) is probably a gloss (cf. the meter). Concerning translating כִּנּוֹר as "lyre," see *Isaiah 1–12*, pp. 200f.

11b Instead of חֶרֶשׂ (Heres), two MSS read: חָרֻשׁ (make new; Gk: ὃ ἐνεκαινίσας, "the one made new"); on this, see below, pp. 146f. Since Jer. 48:31, 36 also read קִיר־חֶרֶשׂ (Kir-heres), it ought not be altered to read קִיר־חֲרָשֶׂת (Kir-hareseth), even though it is obviously the same city mentioned in v. 7.

11c After קִיר חֶרֶשׂ (Kir-heres), a verb has been lost, possibly יֶהְגֶּה (whimper); see v. 7; it may have been lost through haplography (see וְהָיָה, "and it is going to happen," at the beginning of v. 12).

12a נִרְאָה (make an appearance) can be used when referring to appearing at holy sites for the purpose of carrying out a cultic act. When it is used in this sense, however, the *niphʿal* has replaced what would originally have been expressed using a *qal* ("look on the face of God" or something similar); on this, see *Isaiah 1–12*, p. 43, on 1:12. In the present passage it ought to be removed, along with the preceding כִּי (when) (as a dittography of כִּי־נִלְאָה, "when it makes the effort, gets weary"). Without trying to find more complex reasons, we can say that such a solution makes good sense simply because נִרְאָה (appear), when standing alone (i.e., without the original accusative object that would always accompany the *qal* form), is never used this way in the special cultic sense just described.

12b Qᵃ reads בָא (comes), instead of נִלְאָה (make the effort).

14a It is also possible to translate this term "mercenary" (see Jer. 46:21).

14b Instead of וּשְׁאָר (and the remnant), the Gk reads: καὶ καταλειφθήσεται = וְנִשְׁאַר (and that which has been left); see also Syr, Vulg.

14c–c This reads literally: "a little, a trifle, not strong." Instead of כַּבִּיר (strong, mighty), Qᵃ reads: כָּבוֹד (glory) (cf. Gk: ἔντιμος, "honored"), but this is a copying mistake, occasioned by the כָּבוֹד (majesty) that had just preceded it.

Form

Both chapters 15 and 16 are included under the superscription מַשָּׂא מוֹאָב (verdict concerning Moab). They achieve their unity because they both deal with Moab, whereas the Philistines are discussed just before this and Damascus is discussed immediately afterward. Moab is addressed directly in 15:2, 4, 8, 9, and 16:2, 4, 6, 11, 12, 13, 14; in addition, the localities mentioned in chaps. 15f. are all located in a region east of the Dead Sea, extending somewhat to the north of the northern end of the Dead Sea and somewhat to the south of the southern point of the sea and along the entire edge of the inhabited land to the east. That is the territory which Moab, during the course of its thousand-year history, attempted to control, sometimes with greater, sometimes with lesser, success. To some extent, Moab was successful in controlling only the territory between the Dead Sea and the desert, from *wādi el-ḥesā* up as far as the Arnon. The region to the north of this was claimed by Israel from time to time.

Exact details about the chronology of the individual sections of both chapters are not only difficult to determine but are the subject of widely divergent suggested solutions. For this reason, a short overview will be provided first, to survey the basic information available to us concerning Moab's history. As is also true for the Israelites, the Moabites were not aboriginals in their land, but had immigrated into their territory at some point in time (cf. Deut. 2:9). Where they came from is not known. Their language is best known to us as it is recorded on the Mesha Inscription (for text, translation, and commentary, see *KAI* 181; *ANET* 320f.; for an illustration, see *BHH*, illus. 23b). As is also true of Hebrew, this language is West Semitic, and is closely related to Hebrew (see Cross, 35–44; and van Zyl, 161ff.). The Moabites probably either adopted the language of the Canaanites after they became sedentary or they adapted their own Semitic dialect, which they brought along, to that of the Canaanites. The traditions in the OT are all in agreement that this neighboring people had already come into their land before Israel arrived (cf. Num. 21:25ff.; 22; 23). Exactly when this happened is beyond what we know at this time. It is possible that the *šw-t-w* who are mentioned in the Egyptian Execration texts (about 1800 B.C.) are identical with the Moabites, on the basis of the parallelism between Moab and the בְּנֵי־שֵׁת (Shethites) in Num. 24:17 (see Helck, 46, 50). A "land of *šw-t*ᶜᶜ," which might be identified with Moab, is also mentioned in the grave of *ḥnmw-ḥtp* at Beni Hasan (13th century). But it is not certain whether one ought to equate, or at least to what extent one can equate, the *šw-t-w* with the Moabites, and it is not likely that the Moabites would have been in the land that was later named after them already around 1800; it would be more reasonable to suppose that the *šw-t-w* were the pre-Moabite population who lived in the region east of the Dead Sea. The name Moab itself does appear in a list of Ramses II in the temple of Luxor (*m-i-b;* see Simons, *Handbook,* list XXII d 10).

The OT account of Balaam seems to be set in the historical framework of the time of the judges (M. Noth, *A History of Pentateuchal Traditions* [1972] 71–79); it was no doubt inserted at a later time into the traditions about the immigration of the Israelite tribes. But it is correct insofar as it reports that there was kingship in Moab before Israel arrived at the point where it established a monarchy. In spite of this, Moab did not have the pleasure of celebrating their control over this land unmolested. The song that mocks Moab in Num. 21:27-30 speaks of a massive strike engineered against Moab by the Ammonite king Sihon of Heshbon. We learn that the tribe of Benjamin had to pay tribute to King Eglon of Moab in the "time of the judges," but that Ehud's leadership led to throwing off the overlordship of Moab. No assured results are yet available concerning the assessment of the historicity of the note in 1 Sam. 14:47, which says that Saul, among others, also waged war against Moab (see H.-J. Stoebe, KAT VIII/1, 275–278). The same is true concerning 1 Sam. 22:3f., according to which David, as he was fleeing from Saul, brought his relatives to the Moabite king in Mizpeh so that they might be protected. As David built up his kingdom, Moab was placed in subjection (2 Sam. 8:2-12; 1 Chron. 18:11; cf. also 2 Sam. 23:20 and possibly—the translation is uncertain—1 Chron. 4:22).

We do not know what happened to Moab when the kingdom of David fell apart after the death of Solomon. It probably extricated itself from the overlordship of Judah and Israel. After a time, Omri, the king of the Northern Kingdom (886/885–875/874), was successful in taking control over large regions of the Moabite territory. "(Now) Omri had occupied the land of Medeba, and (Israel) had dwelt there in his time and half the time of his son (Ahab), forty years" (Mesha Inscription, lines 7f., *ANET* 320). In addition to Medeba, according to the Mesha Inscription, Omri apparently also conquered all the important localities north of the Arnon, insofar as the region claimed by Moab had not already come into the possession of the Israelites, as had Ataroth (see Mesha Inscription, line 10). The king of

Israel imposed a heavy tribute on Mesha himself as well (2 Kings 3:4). But one day Mesha gave notice to the Israelite king that he would no longer be subject to him. In response, Joram of Israel and Jehoshaphat of Judah set out on an expedition to punish the Moabites, a campaign that originated in the south, proceeded "by the way of the wilderness of Edom," and moved into the center of the Moabite territory. The campaign finally came to a halt just before they came to Kir-hareseth and eventually had to be abandoned altogether. When Mesha glories in the great success that he has had against Israel ("I have triumphed over him [the son of Omri] and over his house, while Israel hath perished forever," Mesha Inscription, line 7, *ANET* 320), one would not be mistaken in assuming that this refers to what happened after the debacle of the Israelite/Judean campaign against Moab.

Amos alludes to a quarrel between Moab and Edom (Amos 2:1-3), which ended in a Moabite victory. Since the Edomites had achieved their independence (2 Kings 8:20) from Joram of Judah (850/849–843/842) but were later made subjects (2 Kings 14:7) during the time of Amaziah (797/796–769/768, the dates of his reign are disputed), and then once again were able to reestablish their independence at the time of the Syro-Ephraimitic War (2 Kings 16:6, conjecture), it would seem that the incident mentioned by Amos would probably fit into the period between Joram and Amaziah, when Moab enjoyed independence, and could have even taken place during the reign of Mesha (who, according to van Zyl, 144, ruled approximately from 870 to 840).

Nothing is known about the fate of Moab during the next one hundred years. But then it was caught in the undertow, as were Israel and Judah, as Assyria expanded its empire. Along with Ammon, Ashkelon, Judah, Edom, and Gaza, it is mentioned in a tribute list of Tiglath-Pileser III (dated to 728; see *AOT* 348, text II, R 67, line 10) and in a letter (no. XVI), found in Nimrud (*kalḫu*), which adds the detail that Moab, like Muṣur, Gaza, Judah, and Ammon, had to pay taxes (text in Donner, *MIO* 5 [1957] 159ff.; and Saggs, 134f.). It would seem that Moab, as well as Ahaz of Judah (2 Kings 16:7-16), had still been able to make arrangements for payments to the Assyrians at that time and had thereby avoided having its country conquered. Nonetheless, there were invasions by nomads from the desert region on the eastern border. Possibly to be dated to the time of Tiglath-Pileser as well, Donner refers to still another letter, also found in *kalḫu* (no. XIV). It reads as follows, according to Donner's translation (including his expansions to the text; for the Akkadian text, see Donner, 156ff.; and Saggs, 131ff.): "'To the king, my lord: Your slave *qurdi-aššur*. May the king, my lord, be in good health. The messenger of *aya-nūrī*, the man from ᴷᵁᴿ*d/ṭa-ab/p-i-la-a-a*, by the name of *ezazu*, brings a sealed missive in his hands to the palace. The matter . . . concerns the inhabitants of the city of Moab (ᴷᵁᴿ*ma-a-ba-a-a*), the ones whom the people of the land of Gidir (ᴷᵁᴿ*gi-di-ra-a-a*), as they moved into the land of Moab (ᴷᵁᴿ*ma- a-ba-[a-a]*) and left it once again, had laid low.' I believe that what this is all about can be interpreted in the following way: 'I have just now placed it into the hands of my messenger; he will bring it to the palace. On the 29th day of the month *šabāṭu*, they took it away.'" The sender of the letter, *qurdi-aššur*, is certainly identical with the *qurdi-aššur-lāmur* who is mentioned in other letters found in the same place, an Assyrian official who was stationed either in or near Tyre. This is apparently just a letter that was to accompany one written by *aya-nūrī*, which is no longer extant. That he is apprising the Assyrian officials about events in Moab leads one to conclude that he had either an official or a semi-official area of responsibility. In any case, we find out that people from the land of Gidir (*šunu ša* ᴷᵁᴿ*gi-di-ra-a-a*) have overrun both the cities and the countryside of Moab.

Unfortunately, we cannot determine who these Gidiria are or where they come from, and the same is true about what *aya-nūrī*, whose message *qurdi-aššur* had sent to *kalḫu*, would have called home. Some have taken the gentilic ᴷᵁᴿ*d/ṭa-ab/p-i-la-a-a* as a rough approximation of *daybānāya* = Dibonite (Saggs, 132)—a rather adventuresome way to try to link these two bits of information. More recently, Mittmann offered the opinion that the locality from which *aya-nūrī* came would have been what is presently known as *eṭ-ṭafīle*.

The mention of the Gidiria has caused the OT place-names Gederoth and Geder/Beth-gader to be brought into the debate, but it makes no sense that a small Judean settlement would have wanted to, or would have been in a position to, carry out an expedition against the capital city of Moab. Others have also called attention to the nomadic tribe of Kedar (Saggs, 133), but the identification is highly unlikely on linguistic grounds. Mittmann (20ff.) suggests that the Gidiria would have been a class of people who lived in the southern Transjordanian region, who were never fully integrated into the Moabite population, whose home territory would have been in the *wādi jedēra* (in a valley that branches off in the south from the *sēl el-mōjib*) or maybe even more likely in the *wādi el jedīre* (which is what the middle portion of the *wādi en-numēra* is called). However, since many personal names include the element גדר (*gdr*), one ought to be cautious here as well. One should most likely consider this group to have been one of the many who posed a threat from the desert regions, whom Moab, in the course of its history, would have confronted time and again.

At the time of the Ashdod rebellion (713–711), just as was the case with Judah and Edom, Moab also considered joining in an attempt to attain its former independent status once again, though it did finally make a decision to pay its tribute when the payment was due (see Sargon's prism inscription A, lines 27ff., *AOT* 351; cf. also text K 1295, *ANET* 301, dated to the period between Sargon and Esarhaddon). In the same way, in the Taylor Prism, Sennacherib reports that the Moabite kings, among others, had brought *kamusunadbi* gifts and had kissed his feet, even before Jerusalem was placed under siege. Late in the history of the Assyrian Empire, at the time of Ashurbanipal, there is one final mention of a Moabite king, *muṣuri*, who is a vassal of the Assyrians. In addition, this last great Assyrian ruler also mentions in his annals that he had to carry out a punitive expedition against the Arabs, for which the Moabite territory served as the stage for the battle (Rm VII, 107–116; Streck, VAB 7/2). At the time when Ashurbanipal was occupied by wars with Shamashshumukin of Babylon, Arabs invaded Moab, though King *ka[ma]shaltā* (reading uncertain) was able to defeat them and was able to take their survivors into custody, along with their king, Ammuladi from Kadri (= קדר, Kedar) (Annals Cylinder B, VIII, 37–44), at which time Moab had played the part of a loyal defender, looking out for the affairs of Assyria. The reports in the OT agree with this description about their behavior, so that, after the downfall of Jehoiakim of Judah, the Neo-Babylonian ruler Nebuchadnezzar, along with those from other places, also sent forces from Moab to inflict punishment (2 Kings 24:1ff.). Furthermore, we learn from Jer. 27:3 that envoys from Moab appeared in Jerusalem at the time of Zedekiah; this shows that Moab also was in on that rebellion against Babylon that led to the final downfall of the Davidic state. This time as well, Moab seems to have escaped unscathed (cf. Jer. 40:11). Josephus (*Antiquities* 10.9.7) had information that Nebuchadnezzar, in his twenty-third year (582), during a campaign against Coele-Syria, "made" the Ammonites and Moabites "obedient." It might be that this is the historical situation for which the threat was spoken against Moab in Ezek. 25:8-11 (see

Zimmerli, BK XIII/2, 595 [Engl: *Ezekiel 2*, 15]). Yet one must be somewhat suspicious about this report, since Josephus includes this campaign in the eastern Jordanian territory in the context of a description about a campaign that was carried out against Egypt, concerning which we have no further information.

In the time that follows, traces of the Moabites fade into the night. M. Noth (*RGG*[3]) thinks that the land was laid low by nomadic invasions during the sixth century. But even if matters progressed to the point where Moab lost its identity as a people, one might still say that it had an ongoing literary existence within the OT (Ezra 9:1; Neh. 13:1, 23; Pss. 60:10; 83:7; 108:10; Isa. 25:10f.; Dan. 11:41); Moab's downfall seems to have become a prime example when someone wanted to depict the final destiny of godless peoples. At the end of the fifth century, and beyond, the Moabite territory came under the control of the Nabateans, an Arabic tribe that forced its way into the inhabited regions and took permanent possession of whatever they seized from ancient Israel's neighbors to the east.

Moab considered itself to be the people of Chemosh (Num. 21:29; Jer. 48:46; cf. the name of Mesha's father, כמש[ית], Chemosh[ith], and the royal names *kamusunadbi* and *kamashaltā*). Chemosh drives out the enemies; inhabitants of conquered cities are offered to him (Mesha Inscription, lines 11ff., 16f.). The Mesha Inscription also mentions עשתר כמש (Ashtar-Chemosh; does this refer to the same deity? line 17). This leads one to suppose that Chemosh may be a parallel figure to the OT "Molech," who had his own sanctuary in the Hinnom Valley (cf. 2 Kings 3:27 and, on that, see V. Maag in *Kulturgeschichte des Alten Orient*, ed. H. Schmökel [1961] 582f.). If correct, that would offer some explanation about the harsh rejection that the Moabites experience in the OT (see Deut. 23:3f.). In the same vein, the pericope about Israel's harlotry, which they committed with the Moabite women in the cult of Baal-Peor (Num. 25:1ff.; Hos. 9:10), shows that Israel, conscious of its relationship with Yahweh, was intent on keeping a careful distance from the Moabites.

[16:13f.] The two chapters about Moab certainly do not present us with a single literary unit; instead, units with a variety of styles and original settings are assembled into a portrayal of Moab that is like a mosaic. However, the analysis is very difficult and, at the present time, has not led to a generally accepted solution. The only point about which there is general agreement is that 16:13f. is a postscript. By setting up an antithesis between מאז (at an earlier time) and ועתה (now), the expander points out with his own words that this is an addition. In light of the relatively happy mood that can be detected in at least some of what he noted had been predicted for the future of Moab, he feels obligated to announce that Moab is going to have to face a harsh blow, which would bring them close to being completely destroyed, with little chance for recovery.

[15:9] A careful examination makes it apparent that both chapters also include other fragments, which have indicators showing that individual sections of material were not simply linked together, but that commentary was added to these sections by a second hand as well. First, it is apparent that 15:9aβ-b lies outside the boundary of the subject matter of the rest of the chapter. Verses 1-8 raise a lament concerning Moab, because disaster has already started to come upon the people. In v. 9aβ-b, however, there is an announcement of judgment, which presumes that Moab had already been severely smitten at an earlier time: "For I bring upon Dimon . . . נוספות"; נוספות means literally "more to be added to what has already come," which itself betrays that a later hand was at work, adding something here. The "I" who speaks is Yahweh, who had not appeared at all in what precedes. Our reflections about this, as expressed above (see textual note 15:9a), have led to the conclusion that "Dimon" refers to none other than the well-known city Dibon. This alternate form of the name might be another indication that one should understand this message as having come from someone who lived at a later time. Indeed, v. 9aβ-b has generally been considered an addition (so Marti, Feldmann, Fohrer, Kaiser, et al.). As a rule, however, many have still taken v. 9aα with that which precedes. But, here as well, the Dimon form of the name would suggest that it comes from a different source. And that is not all: the כי (truly) at the beginning of v. 9 is at odds with the כי (truly) uttered at the end of v. 8. In terms of content, v. 9aα would provide a poor conclusion to the preceding poem. Finally, Dimon/Dibon is not centrally situated in the geographical region that is being discussed. This means that the entire v. 9 is to be considered as an addition to what precedes it (so also Duhm).

[15:1-8] A further question must now be posed, about whether vv. 1-8 are to be considered as one unit.

[15:1-4] Verses 1-4 lament Moab's destiny, more specifically, that of Ar-Moab and Kir-Moab (in which case it is likely that Ar-Moab should also be considered to be the name of a city; see below, p. 131); no doubt these are two representative localities within the country, whose devastation had brought sadness and consternation on the entire land of Moab. However, the only cities mentioned are those which are northeast of the Arnon: Dibon, Nebo, Medeba in vv. 2f.; Heshbon, Elealeh, and Jahaz in v. 4a. Verse 4b, one might say, summarizes it all: the cries of woe and cries for help had completely broken Moab, affecting it deep within itself. In terms of the way it is constructed, this is an obvious, self-contained unit.

[15:5-8] Between vv. 4 and 5 there is a clear break: the feelings of the speaker are completely shrouded in vv. 1-4; in v. 5, however, the author speaks from the heart, deeply moved with sympathy for the fugitives of Moab. For this reason, some commentators (see textual note 15:5a) alter לבי (my heart) to read לבו (his heart), which would smooth the transition from v. 4 to v. 5. Nevertheless, from v. 5 on, in contrast to vv. 1-4, one finds oneself in a different geographical setting: one is no longer in the region of Moab northeast of the Arnon, which had been spared, but rather among the fugitives, who had sought to escape from the region that had been destroyed by going south or southwest (concerning the location of Zoar, the Ascent of Luhith, Horonaim, and the waters of Nimrim, see below, pp. 135f.). The "willow brook" is certainly the *wādi el-ḥesā,* the mouth of which is located at the southern end of the Dead Sea. The only difficulty is that one can hardly fix the location of Eglaim and Beer-elim at the southernmost point of the Moabite country; yet these are not localities that the fugitives pass through; instead, these demarcate the most distant points that hear Moab's cry for help. This means that the section 15:5-8, unlike vv. 1-4, has fugitives as its main interest; it describes their pitiful lot in life and speaks of the cries of lament that echo back and forth, with the author not trying to hide how deeply it has affected him.

Even if vv. 1-4 and vv. 5-8 are to be considered as two separate units of material, both of them still could have come from the same author, and there is nothing that would deny the possibility that they refer to the same situation. The fugitives mentioned in vv. 5-8 could have been the ones who were driven out when Ar-Moab and Kir-Moab were conquered.

[16:1-5] A new section begins with 16:1. Unfortunately, the text has not been preserved intact, and one cannot place as much confidence in the text, as emended, as one would wish. In a way that is more decisive here than usually is the case elsewhere, the interpretation is prejudiced by the very way one translates the verse. By the way it has been rendered here, it would seem that the text says that the Moabites—i.e., authoritative representatives of the people—have sent some of the rams, which were owned by their sovereign, through the land of Moab and on up to Jerusalem, as an act of submission or at least as a plea for assistance.

However, there is no way that v. 2 continues the train of thought in v. 1. Some (Duhm, Feldmann, Kissane, Hertzberg, Leslie, Fohrer) rearrange it and place it at the end of chap. 15. But the transition from 15:9 to 16:2 would be too rough; 15:9 does not lead one to expect anything after it. Thus 16:2 must be considered a gloss, inserted into the text at a place where it did not fit.

By contrast, v. 3 does provide a fitting continuation for v. 1. The feminine forms, הָבִיאִי (give) (so *Qere*), etc., show that the "daughter of Zion," mentioned in v. 1, is asked to provide counsel and make decisions in this time of great need, and is approached with a request that asylum be granted in Jerusalem (vv. 3b, 4a). One would expect that an answer to these requests would follow this. Some believe that this answer is found in v. 6. That would mean that the response was a blunt no: Jerusalem could not promise to give any help, since Moab deserved whatever fate it received, because of its own presumptuous attitude. Beyond this, because of the כִּי (truly) that begins v. 8, it would be difficult to separate vv. 6 and 7 from one another. That vv. 6 and 7 belong together can also be seen when one considers the content of the passages: Moab has had a haughty disposition and therefore it will now have to "howl." More than anything else, however, that vv. 6f. should be considered separately from 16:1, 3-5, has found welcome support in the text of the message about Moab recorded in Jeremiah 48, which admittedly is itself based on Isaiah 15f., in fact making use of Isa. 16:6-12 but not vv. 1-5. It is difficult to comprehend why the one who came later, who speaks in Jeremiah 48 and who was so eager to use material from Isaiah 15f., would not have warmly welcomed the chance to use these verses as well, as he actualized the traditions that came down to him.

If v. 6 (or vv. 6ff.) cannot be considered as the answer to vv. 3, 4a, then one must suppose that the answer is already provided in vv. 4b, 5. Some object that these verses would supply a most vague answer to a very specific, concrete request from Moab, by pointing to some undefined time and situation in the future. That there would be some time up ahead when a righteous judge (in Moab or in Jerusalem?) would sit on the throne, with all the oppression and devastation in the past, sounds almost like a harsh insult in light of their terrible circumstances, when comfort could be given only by a massive infusion of immediate material aid. Would Jerusalem not have to give a clear promise to be at their side, to help drive out Moab's enemy or at least to give assurances that those who were seeking asylum could find safe haven with them? For this reason, it is no wonder that some commentators eliminate vv. 4b and 5 as a secondary insertion (Marti, Kaiser), a decision that is naturally almost forced on someone who concludes that the answer to vv. 3 and 4a has to be found in v. 6. If v. 6 begins a new section, however, then the elimination of vv. 4b-5 would leave the request in vv. 3-4a without an answer. The exegesis of the individual verses (see below, pp. 140ff.) will demonstrate that 16:1, 3-5 can be considered a self-contained, relatively late insertion into the text, which means that one ought to avoid any attempt to understand this material within the framework of the other passages about Moab in chaps. 15f.

[16:6-11] The last question about the composition of chaps. 15f. deals with whether, or to what extent, 16:6-12 forms a unit. Surprisingly, in 16:6 a "we" speaks, just a little after 15:5, in which an "I" had made an appearance. It is not beyond the realm of possibility that Moab howls because of its pride, with its laments having been uttered because its vineyards were destroyed. But the geographical scenery has changed. After Kir-hareseth is mentioned in v. 7, only localities in the north of Moab are mentioned in vv. 8 and 9. In v. 11 Kir-heres (which is identical to Kir-hareseth) comes into view once again, and Moab is parallel to Kir-hareseth (Kir-heres) in both vv. 7 and 11. However, it is still unlikely that vv. 6-11 form a single unit. Although a "we" speaks in v. 6, an "I" speaks in both vv. 9 and 11 once again. The use of עַל־כֵּן (therefore) in v. 9 does not fit well with לְכֵן (therefore) in v. 7. Most importantly, however, there is a completely different attitude over against Moab that must be considered: vv. 6f. state clearly that Moab deserved its fate; vv. 8-11 articulate the deep sympathy the author has for Moab. It would seem possible that vv. 8-11 are a later addition to vv. 6f., coming from an author who felt compelled to describe the whole situation in greater detail. He would have used vv. 6f. as a starting point, and one would not be completely wrong in thinking that it might be the author himself who furnishes the commentary; knowing someone is at fault does not preclude having compassion.

Do the sections 16:6f. and vv. 8-11 deal with the same situation as 15:1-4 and 5-8? In 16:6f., as in vv. 8-11, the author makes observations about the fate of the cities in the north. Heshbon, which itself is located farther north than the mouth of the Jordan, is the most southerly of the localities mentioned—if one does not take Kir-hareseth into account for the moment. Kir-hareseth, situated south of the Arnon, is apparently mentioned only because it, as the capital city, represents Moab as a whole; and the author, even though his prime concern at this point is the destiny of the northern province, naturally also looks at what will happen to the capital city. Thus, in contrast to the sections in chap. 15, 16:6-11 presumes that a blow has been struck that has affected all of Moab deeply. It is possible that the devastation of Moab, which is mentioned in chap. 15, also extended even up into the northern reaches of the land. However, one must also consider the possibility that 16:6-11 is to be dated to a different time within the history of Moab. Because we have such a limited knowledge of its history, and so few of the details that are provided can be cross-checked historically, the questions raised here cannot be answered with certainty.

[16:12] Yet one can be sure that 16:12 is a later addition, related to what precedes it, at least in somewhat the same way as 15:9 stands in relation to 15:1-8. On purely formal grounds, this is demonstrated by the use of the introductory formula וְהָיָה כִי (and it is going to happen) (see 10:12; Jer. 3:16; and the commonly used formula וְהָיָה בַּיּוֹם הַהוּא, "and it will happen on that day").

[16:13f.] Concerning vv. 13f., see above, p. 117.

The analysis of these two chapters produces the following results:
I.   15:1a   Superscription
II. a. 15:1b-4   A lament concerning Moab, particularly the devastation of Ar- and Kir-Moab.
     b. 15:5-8   Lament in the "I" form, about Moab, particularly about the fate of the fugitives.
        15:9   Addition: A threat of judgment against Dimon.
III.   16:1, 3-5   Moab seeks help from the daughter of Zion and the answer delivered to them. This is a [later] insertion into already existing messages about Moab.
        16:2   An inserted threat directed toward the "daughters of Moab."
IV. a. 16:6f.   Moab's pride, the reason for its being afflicted.
     b. 16:8-11   Lament in the "I" form, about Moab's fate.
        16:12   Addition: Threat against Moab.
V.   16:13f.   One final gloss to the passages dealing with Moab: Threat against Moab.

According to this analysis, then, the section 16:1, 3-5 stands in the center of the two chapters, a fact that one must take into account when setting forth the interpretation of the entire collection of passages (cf. Alonso-Schökel, 416ff.).

On the basis of the results of this analysis, more specific points can be made about the form (including the metrical structure) when the individual units are studied in greater detail. One point must be clearly kept in mind. Though one might expect it in messages against foreign peoples, the passages that form the basic core of these two chapters do not consist of threats of judgment against Moab; in the main, they are made up of songs that lament some disaster that has come already rather than announce a disaster yet to come. It is only when the additions 15:9; 16:2, 12, are inserted, and when 16:13f. is appended, that the מַשָּׂא (verdict) against Moab takes its present shape, which would have brought about its inclusion into the group of messages against foreign peoples now found in chaps. 13–23.

Setting

Researchers who have studied these passages have considered it particularly problematic that there has been little success in identifying the historical background of these two chapters that deal with Moab, at least the original material, with any degree of certainty. The dates that have been suggested stretch all the way from the time of Joash of Judah (836/835–797/796; thus König) to the time of John Hyrcanus (135–104, the time of the Nabatean invasion of Moab; thus Duhm).

Since the time of Hitzig, on the basis of 2 Kings 14:25, some have wondered whether Jeroboam II might have been Moab's opponent and whether the author might have been the prophet Jonah ben Amittai from Gath-hepher. This verse reports that the successful ruler of the Northern Kingdom had reconquered the land east of the Jordan, as far as the יָם־הָעֲרָבָה (Sea of the Arabah). Amos, who apparently refers to this same event, speaks in 6:14 of the נַחַל הָעֲרָבָה (Wadi Arabah), which some have sought to identify as the lower portion of the wādi el-qelt, whereas others have thought this would have been the wādi kefrēn (van Zyl), which originates in the mountains east of the Jordan and joins together with the wādi ḥisbān (which itself also has been suggested as a possibility), to flow toward the Jordan, being known in this last stretch as the wādi ġarbe, which then discharges into the Jordan 5 km. north of where the Jordan itself flows into the Dead Sea. In any case, one must understand עֲרָבָה (Arabah) as a reference to the low-lying ground along the Jordan, in the area northeast of the Dead Sea, and the יָם־עֲרָבָה (Sea of the Arabah), mentioned in 2 Kings 14:25, cannot be identical with the נַחַל הָעֲרָבִים (the willow brook) that is brought into the discussion in Isa. 15:7; this means that Jeroboam came to a halt at the northern border of Moab. In addition, the two chapters do not give any hint that Israel is the opponent of Moab. For the same reason, there is no evidence that would lead one to believe that Judah might have been the opponent, and a certain sympathy that is expressed for Moab would speak against this possibility from the outset. It is also rather likely that one can eliminate great powers from consideration, when seeking to identify who was threatening Moab; such a power would have certainly been identified, and then there would have been more than a devastation; instead, it would either have been said that Moab was subjected under such a power or that Moab would have come to an end altogether. The most likely conclusion, at least based on what seems to be in the background of 15:1-8, is that a nomadic tribe from the Arabian desert had carried out a raid.

Naturally, to set this into a historical context is thus related to the way one answers the question about the authorship. Among modern exegetes, in addition to Delitzsch, Orelli, Kissane, Fischer, Steinmann, and Young, more than anyone else, Procksch and Hertzberg have come out in favor of identifying at least a core passage as attributable to Isaiah. For Procksch, the pièce de résistance for his argumentation is 16:1-5, especially v. 5, which is closely related to the "Christmas message" in 9:1-6. The praiseworthy restraint, the features that hint at rather than give graphic details, and the avoidance of the divine name in a message addressed to Moabites, who would not know the God of history, would make good sense. The central message of Isaiah would be found in 16:4b, 5. That would be Isaiah's response to the request from the Moabites (16:1-4a), and this plea would have made sense only in light of the events described in the lament in chap. 15. Procksch is obviously aware that this lament does not correspond to the way Isaiah speaks in other passages, but thinks that that would not have been expected anyway, since the song of the fleeing Moabites would have been put in their mouth. However, 16:6-12, with its sharp, repulsive tone, would have been composed later than the time of Isaiah; Procksch speculates that this latter section (or at least its original form) might be attributable to Jeremiah.

Though most attractive, the interpretation offered by Procksch does not stand up to closer scrutiny. It is true that Isaiah turns his attention to the destiny in store for other peoples, but only when it would have an impact on the destiny of Israel or when Israel was in danger of being sucked in by these peoples into making decisions that would be clearly wrong (cf. 14:28-32; 17:1-7; 20:1-6). One cannot possibly conceive of laments, such as what is found in chap. 15, coming from the mouth of Isaiah. There is no hard evidence to show that such laments were quoted by the prophets (R. H. Pfeiffer, *Introduction to the Old Testament* [1948] 444), who thus would have been making use of original Moabite poetry (the "we" of the Moabites is missing). Above all else, however, there is no way that 16:4b, 5 could come from Isaiah, and this would still be the case even if דוד באהל (in David's tent) were a gloss. If this note were original, then Isaiah would have expected that a ruler from the line of David, or even a Moabite, as the counselor of that Davidic ruler, would take charge in the neighboring land. Not a single other message from Isaiah gives rise to any such expectation. The "messianic" predictions, in 9:1ff. and 11:1ff., give no indication that the rule of the future Davidic sovereign would extend beyond the borders of Israel (for the opposite viewpoint, cf. Pss. 2:8; 72:8-10). Even if דוד באהל (in David's tent) is removed, which means one could assume that 16:4b, 5 might refer to a Moabite ruler, then one really gets into difficulty. There is no way that Isaiah would have thought that Yahweh could have carried out his rule through a Moabite representative (however, cf. Deutero-Isaiah, 45:1).

From time to time, following Hitzig, scholars have also attempted to consider at least 16:13f. as from Isaiah, attributing all of what precedes this to another, earlier prophet, whose words Isaiah included and on which he commented. That is impossible: no prophet in the preexilic era ever quoted from the words of an earlier prophet and then reinterpreted those words, simply to serve his own purposes. The content itself excludes the possibility that Isaiah spoke vv. 13f. Since Jeremiah must also be excluded from consideration (contra Bardtke; see the following excursus), even though there is a definite relationship between Isaiah 15f. and Jeremiah 48, we have to relinquish the quest of identifying the author or authors of the Moabite passages. As regards the date when the various anonymous speakers uttered their messages, one must stay within the realm of speculation. We will provide the details of the possible solutions as we discuss each of the individual sections. Here a few of the chronological suggestions for dating can be mentioned: Eichrodt: about one hundred years before Isaiah; Dillmann: the time of Uzziah; Fischer, Hertzberg, van Zyl: at least some of this is Isaianic, eighth/seventh century; J. Bright, *Peake's Commentary on the Bible:* about 650; Leslie: about 450; Marti: fifth century; Duhm: the end of the second century. It is noteworthy that the most recent commentators are the most cautious: Fohrer: not from Isaiah, but most of it is from a later time, that is, from the postexilic era; Kaiser avoids suggesting any date whatever and believes that there is no way one could even be sure whether 15:1-8 (9aα) refers to a specific historical event or else that the text depicts eschatological events. Still, one must ask whether it can help to compare this material with the related chapter, Jeremiah 48.

Isaiah 15f. and Jeremiah 48: the points of correspondence in the vocabulary are shown in table 1 (cf. the discussion of the problem in F. Schwally, 207f.; Procksch; Rudolph, FS Driver; Schottroff, 184). Such close agreement, which goes so far as to have many of the same words, cannot have happened simply because both passages deal with a common theme, Moab, nor simply because both passages make use of the terminology commonly found in songs of lament. There are only three possible ways to explain this agreement, each of which has been offered by one exegete or another: (a) the author of Jeremiah 48 knew Isaiah 15f., or at least the major portion of that material, and added to it a further interpretation (e.g., Schwally, 207f.; Duhm; Rudolph, FS Driver, and HAT 12³; Schottroff, 184; Kaiser; Alonso-Schökel, 420ff.); (b) the Isaiah passage is dependent on Jeremiah 48 (thus, particularly, the view of Bardtke, esp. 247f.); (c) both variant passages made use of a third, possibly non-Israelite, source (e.g., Gray; Pfeiffer, *Introduction,* 444; van Zyl). Bartdke has not convinced many to accept his thesis that the messages against the foreign peoples in Jeremiah 46–51, in their basic form, were composed during the first phase of Jeremiah's activity. However, in addition to it being highly unlikely that Jeremiah went through a period of activity when he spoke as a prophet of salvation, a comparison of the way Isaiah 15f. and Jeremiah 48 are constructed would speak against this solution. Within Isaiah 15f., in contrast to Jeremiah 48, there is a clear outline, with corresponding divisions within the material. In a way similar to Jeremiah 51f., Jeremiah 48 is a conglomeration of literary reminiscences and does not have a point-by-point relationship with these two chapters in Isaiah (see table 3, and cf. Fohrer, FS Ziegler, 149f.; Alonso-Schökel, 420). That author is a compiler, who makes use of all the quarries available within the OT, without giving it a second thought.

The comparison between Isaiah 15f. and Jeremiah 48 shows more yet. First, the Jeremiah chapter is presented primarily as a threat against Moab. Thus one would presume that whoever composed it would have been happy to make use of the additions contained in Isaiah 15f., which set forth threats against Moab. But precisely these verses remain unmentioned. One could explain this only by assuming that the compiler did not find these verses in the text that was before him and that, instead of this, he inserted his own expansions into the basic text of Isaiah 15f., in his own way. Second, if one ignores 16:6 for the moment, then no reason is given in the Isaiah chapters for why the disaster has come on Moab. That fits nicely; songs of lament do not need to include the reason for the punishment. It is different when it comes to threats of judgment; it is consistent with that type of material that great effort is expended in the Jeremiah passage to stress the reason, that being that Chemosh has been worshiped (v. 13; cf. also vv. 7 and 46). Finally, the judgment announced in Jeremiah 48 is comprehensive and total (if one steps away for a moment from what is said in v. 47, which is a secondary addition), whereas that described in Isaiah 15f. is only partial, even if it does portray a harsh blow being struck, which fits with the intention of Isaiah 15f. to detail a disaster that has already occurred, unlike Jeremiah 48, which announces a coming judgment.

These observations make clear that Jeremiah 48 depends on Isaiah 15f. What remains is the third possibility, that a common "source" is behind both sections of material about Moab. That is not likely. Even if one attempted to reconstruct this source, one would be forced to follow the arrangement now found in Isaiah 15f. and to reconstruct its original by making use of these two chapters.

Thus if one can consider Isaiah 15f. to be the prototype for Jeremiah 48, the comparison of the passages brings with it another noteworthy result, that the verses in Isaiah 15f. that we identified earlier as later expansions (15:9; 16:2, 12, and also 16:13f.) are also missing altogether from the version found in Jeremiah. Admittedly, some (thus Rudolph, HAT 12³, 281; and Schottroff, 184) think that they can establish a relationship between 16:12 and Jer. 48:35. But the content of these two verses is quite dissimilar. The author of Jeremiah 48 may have found 15:1f. as it now stands, but he preceded that with his own introduction, since his purpose was to present an announcement of judgment. There is no apparent reason for 15:6b-8 not being used in Jeremiah 48. Possibly the most interesting observation is that 16:1, 3-5 are missing in the parallel passage in Jeremiah as well. Did that author avoid using this passage because he wanted to proclaim disaster for Moab instead of salvation? It does not seem that it would have been that hard for him to find some way to adapt these verses to his conception of what would come. For this reason, it is more likely that these verses were also inserted into the text of Isaiah 15f., into the message against Moab, but only after that passage (at least in its basic form) had been used for Jeremiah 48.

The comparison of the two traditions about Moab helps us to reach the conclusion that the composition of Jeremiah 48 is the terminus ad quem for the time when the basic material in Isaiah 15f. came into existence. This knowledge does not help us much, however, since there is also radical disagreement about the dating of Jeremiah 48 as well; no one suggests that Jeremiah is the author of that material. If it is true that Nebuchadnezzar did engage in a campaign against Ammon and Moab in his twenty-third year (582) (see above, pp. 116f.), it is possible that someone in Judah made use of the ancient laments of Moab and recast them to become threats of judgment against this neighboring people. Because Judah probably would have had to swallow hard, in the face of humiliating jabs sent its way from Moab after the Davidic state came to an end, since Moab at first was able to hold its own in its relationship with Babylon, those who were still in Jerusalem would have followed the events of the downfall of Moab as an independent state with interest, if not with some measure of satisfaction. But that is no more than a hunch. From the time of Tiglath-Pileser even to the end of the ancient state of Judah there were many occasions when consideration was given to join with Moab, as also with the Philistines and other small states in the Palestine/Syria region, to carry out common schemes of rebellion against the mighty power headquartered in Mesopotamia. Jeremiah 48 can hardly come from this time period. But it is possible that the original passages in Isaiah 15f. might come from this time. One might say that, during the latter days of the kingdom, they all paddled in the same canoe with Moab and would also have been deeply affected if their near neighbors were debilitated. Based on the dates known to us from Moab's history, one might at least consider it possible that 15:1-8 describes the raid of the Gidiria people against Moab (see above, pp. 115f.); but, just as likely, it could be another raid about which we have no information, coming most likely during the waning days of the Judean kingdom, which would have given cause for someone to compose this lament.

[15:1b-4] *The Lament about the Downfall of Ar- and Kir-Moab*

Form

There is no doubt that this is a lament. Repeated attempts have been made to make sense of this section as if it were a lament uttered before the fact, so that it would serve the same function as an announcement of judgment (see above, the "ironic lament for the dead," uttered when the tyrant was overthrown, in 14:4bff.). One can come to such a conclusion only by failing to recognize that the threats in 15:9 and 16:2 and 12 are additions to the text, by means of which the songs of lament are first made into threats of judgment. Of course, 15:1b-4 is a unique type of lament song. Information is provided about the downfall of just two, no doubt very important, Moabite cities, but the rest of the passages relate information about the way the people in northern Moab carried out their mourning rites.

Meter: Verse 1: 2 three-stress + three-stress bicola; v. 2: 3 five-stress cola; v. 4a: a three-stress + three-stress bicolon; v. 4b: presumably a seven-stress colon (or, in any case, at least a full five-stress colon). It is noteworthy that the gap between vv. 1 and 2, noted in the structure of this poem, is also apparent in the change in rhythm. But there is also a break between vv. 3 and 4 (note the imperfect consecutive at the beginning of v. 4a). Finally, attention is drawn to the end of the poem by use of the heavy seven-stress colon.

Setting

Concerning the setting, see above, pp. 122ff.

Commentary

[15:1] קִיר (Kir) is related to Hebrew קִרְיָה (city) (cf. Arabic *qiryatun*, "village"; Phoenician *qart* [thus in קְרְתחדשת, *qrtḥdst*, and מלקרת, *mlqrt*]; cf.

Table 1

Jeremiah 48

כֻּלֹּה רֹאשׁ קָרְחָה וְכָל־זָקָן גְּרֻעָה [37]
עַל־כָּל־יָדַיִם גְּדֻדֹת וְעַל־מָתְנַיִם שָׂק
עַל גַּגּוֹת מוֹאָב וּבִרְחֹבֹתֶיהָ כֻּלֹּה מִסְפֵּד [38]
כִּי־שָׁבַרְתִּי אֶת־מוֹאָב כִּכְלִי אֵין־חֵפֶץ בּוֹ נְאֻם־יְהוָה

כִּי מֵי נִמְרִים מְשַׁמּוֹת יִהְיוּ [34a]

עַל־כֵּן יִתְרָה עָשָׂה וּפְקֻדָּתָם [5]
מֵחֶשְׁבּוֹן עַד־אֶלְעָלֵה עַד־יַהַץ נָתְנוּ קוֹלָם [34b]

כִּי נָתַתִּי בַּמִּדְבָּר קוֹל בֶכִי [36b]

Isaiah 15

מַשָּׂא מוֹאָב [1]
כִּי בְּלֵיל שֻׁדַּד עָר מוֹאָב נִדְמָה כִּי בְּלֵיל שֻׁדַּד קִיר־מוֹאָב נִדְמָה
עָלָה הַבַּיִת וְדִיבֹן הַבָּמוֹת לְבֶכִי [2]
עַל־נְבוֹ וְעַל מֵידְבָא מוֹאָב יְיֵלִיל
בְּכָל־רֹאשָׁיו קָרְחָה כָּל־זָקָן גְּרוּעָה
בְּחוּצֹתָיו חָגְרוּ שָׂק [3]
עַל גַּגּוֹתֶיהָ וּבִרְחֹבֹתֶיהָ כֻּלֹּה יְיֵלִיל יֹרֵד בַּבֶּכִי
וַתִּזְעַק חֶשְׁבּוֹן וְאֶלְעָלֵה עַד־יַהַץ נִשְׁמַע קוֹלָם [4]
עַל־כֵּן חֲלֻצֵי מוֹאָב יָרִיעוּ
נַפְשׁוֹ יָרְעָה לּוֹ
לִבִּי לְמוֹאָב יִזְעָק [5]
בְּרִיחֶהָ עַד־צֹעַר עֶגְלַת שְׁלִשִׁיָּה
כִּי מַעֲלֵה הַלּוּחִית בִּבְכִי יַעֲלֶה־בּוֹ
כִּי דֶּרֶךְ חוֹרֹנַיִם זַעֲקַת־שֶׁבֶר יְעֹעֵרוּ
כִּי־מֵי נִמְרִים מְשַׁמּוֹת יִהְיוּ [6]
כִּי־יָבֵשׁ חָצִיר כָּלָה דֶשֶׁא יֶרֶק לֹא הָיָה
עַל־כֵּן יִתְרָה עָשָׂה [7]
וּפְקֻדָּתָם עַל נַחַל הָעֲרָבִים יִשָּׂאוּם
כִּי־הִקִּיפָה הַזְּעָקָה אֶת־גְּבוּל מוֹאָב [8]
עַד־אֶגְלַיִם יִלְלָתָהּ וּבְאֵר אֵילִים יִלְלָתָהּ
כִּי מֵי דִימוֹן מָלְאוּ דָם כִּי־אָשִׁית עַל־דִּימוֹן נוֹסָפוֹת [9]
לִפְלֵיטַת מוֹאָב אַרְיֵה וְלִשְׁאֵרִית אֲדָמָה

— : (underlined) means that the texts demonstrate very close agreement

------ : means there are some differences between sections that are generally in agreement

Table 2

Jeremiah 48	Isaiah 16
No parallels in Jer 48	16:1-5

No parallels in Jer 48

Jeremiah 48

29 שָׁמַעְנוּ גְאוֹן־מוֹאָב גֵּאֶה מְאֹד גָּבְהוֹ וּגְאוֹנוֹ וְגַאֲוָתוֹ וְרֻם לִבּוֹ׃

30 אֲנִי יָדַעְתִּי נְאֻם־יְהוָה עֶבְרָתוֹ וְלֹא־כֵן בַּדָּיו לֹא־כֵן עָשׂוּ׃

31 עַל־כֵּן עַל־מוֹאָב אֲיֵלִיל וּלְמוֹאָב כֻּלֹּה אֶזְעָק אֶל־אַנְשֵׁי קִיר־חֶרֶשׂ יֶהְגֶּה׃

32 מִבְּכִי יַעְזֵר אֶבְכֶּה־לָּךְ הַגֶּפֶן שִׂבְמָה נְטִישֹׁתַיִךְ עָבְרוּ יָם עַד יָם יַעְזֵר נָגָעוּ עַל־קֵיצֵךְ וְעַל־בְּצִירֵךְ שֹׁדֵד נָפָל׃

33 וְנֶאֶסְפָה שִׂמְחָה וָגִיל מִכַּרְמֶל וּמֵאֶרֶץ מוֹאָב וְיַיִן מִיקָבִים הִשְׁבַּתִּי לֹא־יִדְרֹךְ הֵידָד הֵידָד לֹא הֵידָד׃

34 מִזַּעֲקַת חֶשְׁבּוֹן עַד־אֶלְעָלֵה עַד־יַהַץ נָתְנוּ קוֹלָם מִצֹּעַר עַד־חֹרֹנַיִם עֶגְלַת שְׁלִשִׁיָּה כִּי גַּם־מֵי נִמְרִים לִמְשַׁמּוֹת יִהְיוּ׃

35 וְהִשְׁבַּתִּי לְמוֹאָב נְאֻם־יְהוָה מַעֲלֶה בָמָה וּמַקְטִיר לֵאלֹהָיו׃

Isaiah 16

6 שָׁמַעְנוּ גְאוֹן־מוֹאָב גֵּא מְאֹד גַּאֲוָתוֹ וּגְאוֹנוֹ וְעֶבְרָתוֹ לֹא־כֵן בַּדָּיו׃

7 לָכֵן יְיֵלִיל מוֹאָב לְמוֹאָב כֻּלֹּה יְיֵלִיל לַאֲשִׁישֵׁי קִיר־חֲרֶשֶׂת תֶּהְגּוּ אַךְ־נְכָאִים׃

8 כִּי שַׁדְמוֹת חֶשְׁבּוֹן אֻמְלָל גֶּפֶן שִׂבְמָה בַּעֲלֵי גוֹיִם הָלְמוּ שְׂרוּקֶּיהָ עַד־יַעְזֵר נָגָעוּ תָּעוּ מִדְבָּר שְׁלֻחוֹתֶיהָ נִטְּשׁוּ עָבְרוּ יָם׃

9 עַל־כֵּן אֶבְכֶּה בִּבְכִי יַעְזֵר גֶּפֶן שִׂבְמָה אֲרַיָּוֶךְ דִּמְעָתִי חֶשְׁבּוֹן וְאֶלְעָלֵה כִּי עַל־קֵיצֵךְ וְעַל־קְצִירֵךְ הֵידָד נָפָל׃

10 וְנֶאֱסַף שִׂמְחָה וָגִיל מִן־הַכַּרְמֶל וּבַכְּרָמִים לֹא־יְרֻנָּן לֹא יְרֹעָע יַיִן בַּיְקָבִים לֹא־יִדְרֹךְ הַדֹּרֵךְ הֵידָד הִשְׁבַּתִּי׃

11 עַל־כֵּן מֵעַי לְמוֹאָב כַּכִּנּוֹר יֶהֱמוּ וְקִרְבִּי לְקִיר חָרֶשׂ׃

12 וְהָיָה כִי־נִרְאָה כִּי־נִלְאָה מוֹאָב עַל־הַבָּמָה וּבָא אֶל־מִקְדָּשׁוֹ לְהִתְפַּלֵּל וְלֹא יוּכָל׃

Table 3

Parallels that are not found in Isa. 15f.   Jeremiah 48

Hebrew (left)	Reference	Hebrew (right)
פַחַד וָפַחַת וָפָח עָלֶיךָ יוֹשֵׁב הָאָרֶץ:	Isa. 24:17f.	⁴³ פַחַד וָפַחַת וָפָח עָלַיִךְ יוֹשֵׁב מוֹאָב נְאֻם־יְהוָה:
וְהָיָה הַנָּס מִקּוֹל הַפַּחַד יִפֹּל אֶל־הַפַּחַת		⁴⁴ הַנָּיס מִפְּנֵי הַפַּחַד יִפֹּל אֶל־הַפַּחַת
וְהָעוֹלֶה מִתּוֹךְ הַפַּחַת יִלָּכֵד בַּפָּח		וְהָעֹלֶה מִן־הַפַּחַת יִלָּכֵד בַּפָּח
כִּי־אָבִיא רָעָה אֶל־אַנְשֵׁי עֲנָתוֹת שְׁנַת פְּקֻדָּתָם:	Jer. 11:23b	כִּי־אָבִיא אֵלֶיהָ אֶל־מוֹאָב שְׁנַת פְּקֻדָּתָם נְאֻם־יְהוָה:
כִּי־אָבִיא עֲלֵיהֶם רָעָה שְׁנַת פְּקֻדָּתָם נְאֻם־יְהוָה:	Jer. 23:12b	
		⁴⁵ בְּצֵל חֶשְׁבּוֹן עָמְדוּ מִכֹּחַ נָסִים
		כִּי־אֵשׁ יָצָא מֵחֶשְׁבּוֹן וְלֶהָבָה מִבֵּין סִיחֹן
וְמָחַץ פַּאֲתֵי מוֹאָב וְקַרְקַר כָּל־בְּנֵי־שֵׁת:	Num. 24:17bβ	וַתֹּאכַל פְּאַת מוֹאָב וְקָדְקֹד בְּנֵי שָׁאוֹן:
כִּי־אֵשׁ יָצְאָה מֵחֶשְׁבּוֹן לֶהָבָה מִקִּרְיַת סִיחֹן	Num. 21:28f.	
אָכְלָה עָר מוֹאָב בַּעֲלֵי בָּמוֹת אַרְנֹן:		⁴⁶ אוֹי־לְךָ מוֹאָב אָבַד עַם־כְּמוֹשׁ
אוֹי־לְךָ מוֹאָב אָבַדְתָּ עַם־כְּמוֹשׁ		כִּי־לֻקְּחוּ בָנֶיךָ בַּשֶּׁבִי וּבְנֹתֶיךָ בַּשִּׁבְיָה:
נָתַן בָּנָיו פְּלֵיטִם וּבְנֹתָיו בַּשְּׁבִית לְמֶלֶךְ אֱמֹרִי סִיחֹן:		
וְשַׁבְתִּי אֶת־שְׁבוּת מִצְרַיִם	Ezek. 29:14aα	⁴⁷ וְשַׁבְתִּי שְׁבוּת־מוֹאָב בְּאַחֲרִית הַיָּמִים נְאֻם־יְהוָה
וְאַחֲרֵי־כֵן אָשִׁיב אֶת־שְׁבוּת בְּנֵי־עַמּוֹן נְאֻם־יְהוָה:	Jer. 49:6	עַד־הֵנָּה מִשְׁפַּט מוֹאָב:
	and 49:36	

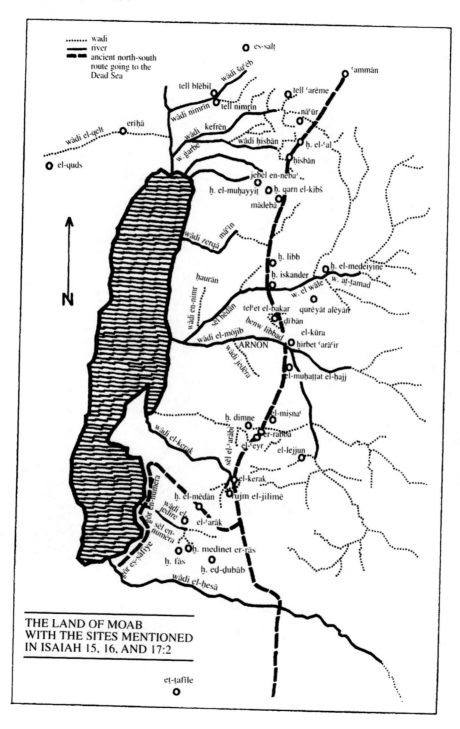

THE LAND OF MOAB
WITH THE SITES MENTIONED
IN ISAIAH 15, 16, AND 17:2

also קר, "city," in the Mesha Inscription, line 11, and in the place-name קְרִיֹתן,
Qaryaten, in line 10). Therefore קִיר-מוֹאב means "the city of Moab," that is,
its capital city, which would not always have been in the same location during its entire history. Scholars generally presume that its location should be
placed at *el-kerak*, in the center of the southern region of the Moabite territory, along the upper course of the *wādi el-kerak* (cf. Targ: כרכא דמואב, "the
city of Moab"; Abel, *Géographie* II, 418f.; and van Zyl, 69–71; the description of the present site can be found in Musil, 45ff., with illustrations). But
one cannot be certain that this is the correct identification (cf. Kaiser). Yet
there is even greater uncertainty about the meaning of עָר מוֹאב (Ar-Moab).

עָר is presumably related to Hebrew עִיר (city) (also written עָר in Phoenician),
which would mean that עָר מוֹאב would also mean "the city of Moab." One might wonder whether this refers to the same place as Kir-Moab (Q^a reads עִיר מואב, "city of
Moab," both times; see also Buhl, ad loc.), but this is highly unlikely. For עִיר מואב,
the Gk reads: ἡ Μωαβῖτις, "the Moabite" (for קִיר-מוֹאב, Kir-Moab, it reads: τὸ τεῖχος
τῆς Μωαβίτιδος, "the wall of Moab"), which means it uses עָר to describe a region,
not a city. One would also think it refers to a region when reading Deut. 2:18 and
Num. 21:15 (see the parallels, which read גבול מואב, "territory of Moab"), and, on the
basis of Deut. 2:9, עָר is the region inhabited by the בְנֵי-לוֹט (sons of Lot). In the present passage, however, the parallelism makes it unlikely that this would refer to a general region, and a city must also be intended in the reference found in Num. 21:28.
(Nonetheless, some suggest altering עִיר מואב, "city of Moab," in Num. 22:36 to read
עָר מואב, Ar-Moab; see *BHK*, KBL, *BHS*. One wonders whether it should be pointed
as עִר, "city," in every passage. Since the Moabite language makes no attempt to
include the matres lectionis in its writing, it is possible that pointing this as עָר was an
obvious misunderstanding on the part of someone who was writing the Hebrew.) It is
not hard to understand how the name for the city also could be used in a wider sense,
to refer to the region that it itself dominated. Today עָר מואב is most commonly identified as the town presently known as *er-rabba*, between *el-kerak* and the *sēl el-mōjib*
(known in the Greco-Roman era as Ραββαθ Μωαβ-Ἀρεόπολις, Rabbath Moab-
Areopolis), which Jerome (Corpus Christianorum, Series Latina LXXIII/I, 5.175)
identifies, when referring to the Greek name Ἀρεόπολις, as *ciuitas Ar* (the city of
Ar). Musil (381) supposes that the ancient name עָר could still be reflected in the
present-day *el-ʿeyr* (just a little south of *er-rabba*). But the identification of עָר with
Ἀρεόπολις (Areopolis) is not assured, and the pottery that has been found in *er-
rabba* does not include any evidence for a settlement having been there in the Iron
Age. For this reason, others have sought to identify the locality in some place that
could satisfy these last-mentioned requirements where pottery remains from the era
have been found: *el-miṣnaʿ* (Abel, *Géographie* II, 39; van Zyl, 71–72) or possibly
even *muhaṭṭat el-ḥajj* (Rudolph, FS Driver, 133). But these also are nothing more
than guesses.

The כ at the beginning of each of the first two lines of 15:1 does not
function as a causal conjunction but rather, as is common, as a deictic particle: "behold, truly, yes indeed"; cf. the way כ (truly) is replaced in Jer. 48:1
with הוֹי (woe). שֻׁדד (destroyed) is commonly used in laments about a whole
people; see 23:1, 14; Jer. 4:13, 20; 9:18; 49:3, 10; Joel 1:10. The same

applies to דמה‎ (destroyed); see Jer. 47:5; Ezek. 32:2 (in a קינה‎, "lament," mourning the pharaoh); Obad. 5 (cf. Hos. 4:6; 10:7). The only concrete detail is the information that this was a nighttime raid, which was the only chance nomads would have in trying to overpower a well-fortified city.

[15:2-4] The names of the localities mentioned in vv. 2-4 bring us into the northern region of the country, which remained undamaged. First, דיבן‎ (Dibon) is present-day *dībān*, on the main highway running from north to south through the land (the *via Traiana* of the Roman era) that ends up at the capital city of King Mesha, located 5 km. northeast of the *sēl el-mōjib*, 15 km. east of the Dead Sea. (In Josh. 13:17, the Gk reads Δαιβων, Daibon. The Mesha Inscription reads דיבן‎, Dibon. Since the Moabite language does not make any use of the *matres lectionis*, the name in Moabite may have been pronounced Daibān or Daibōn.) After conflicts with the Moabites (Num. 21:30), the city was "erected" by Gad (Num. 32:34; 33:45f.), but was lost to the Moabites after a series of border skirmishes between the two. Mesha expanded Dibon (Mesha Inscription, lines 21–25; the קרחה‎, Qarḥoh, mentioned there must have been a "suburb" of Dibon). For reports on the excavations at *dībān*, see Winnett and Reed, and Tushingham.

Second, נבו‎ (Nebo) is mentioned. Since the time of Musil (346), this city has been identified as present-day *ḥirbet el-muḥayyiṭ*, 2 km. south of the *jebel en-neba'*, to the east of the northern end of the Dead Sea, on the edge of the point where the higher elevations of Moab begin (see Rudolph, HAT 12[3]; van Zyl, 89; Vogel, 63). According to Num. 32:37f., along with Heshbon, Elealeh, Sibmah, and other sites, it belonged to the area settled by the Reubenites. Mesha reports (Mesha Inscription, lines 14–18) how he conquered it, at the command of his god Chemosh: "So I went by night and fought against it from the break of dawn until noon, taking it and slaying all."

The third name mentioned, Medeba, is also well known, present-day *mādebā*, southeast of Nebo, 35 km. south of Amman. The Mesha Inscription spells it מהדבא‎; the ה‎ must be a consonant (Segert, 216f.). Gk[A] in Josh. 13:9 and Gk[B] in 1 Chron. 19:7 read Μαιδαβά, Maidaba. This locale is well known in scholarly research because of a Byzantine mosaic map of Palestine found there in the Greek Orthodox church building (on this, see Donner and Cüppers; Abel, *Géographie* II, 381f.; and van Zyl, 88). Medeba is also considered to be part of the Reubenite territory in the OT (Josh. 13:9, 16), but it was lost to Israel (cf. Num. 21:30). According to 1 Chron. 19:6ff., David reportedly fought in front of Medeba against a coalition of Arameans and Ammonites, but the textual reading is not certain. Mesha (lines 7f.) reports that Omri had overpowered the entire region around Medeba and had dwelt there "in his time and half the time of his sons, forty years." During his (Mesha's) days, however, Chemosh dwelt there. Apparently the place had suffered much during these wars that were waged back and forth; Mesha also mentions it among the cities that he built up (once again) (line 30).

Not far from Medeba one finds two more of the cities mentioned in v. 4: Heshbon, present-day *ḥisbān*, 9 km. north-northeast; and Elealeh, present-day *el-ʿāl*, another 3 km. farther in a north-northeasty direction from *ḥisbān*. In the OT Heshbon is identified as belonging to Reuben (Josh. 13:17) and yet also to Gad (Josh. 13:26; 21:39). According to Num. 21:27, it was the residence of Sihon, the king of the Amorites, who had retaken all of the land as far as the Arnon, which had been under the control of the previous king of Moab. There is no way to confirm this historical reference but it is not unlikely, since there were city-states in this region (on

132

this, see S. Herrmann, *A History of Israel in Old Testament Times* [1981²] 101ff.; for further resources that provide information about Heshbon, cf. Vogel, 37; for the excavation reports, see Boraas and Horn).

In addition to 16:9 and Jer. 48:34, Elealeh is mentioned otherwise only in Num. 32:3, 32 (here as a Reubenite city; see Abel, *Géographie* II, 312; and van Zyl, 93). H. S. Nyberg (336) suggests that the name is constructed by combining the names אֵל (El) and עלה (*ʿalah*), to be explained as following the same pattern of construction as אֵל עֶלְיון (El Elyon) or Arabic *allāhu l-ʿalīyu*. But a better solution is offered by A. Schwarzenbach (201), who suggests that there is a reduplication of the root על (with a dissimilation of the first ע to א), so that the name would furnish a reference to "high ground." The city is located in a fertile plain (see Musil, 248, 390); from time to time it would have shared the same destiny as the more important city, Heshbon.

For a long time there was great disagreement about the identification of Jahaz (in Josh. 13:18; 21:36; Judg. 11:20; Jer. 48:21; 1 Chron. 6:63, the הֹצָה, "Jahzah," form of the name is used). In earlier times, its location was sought at *ḥirbet libb*, on the main road, on the promontory above the *wādi zerqā māʿīn* (so R. de Vaux; 20; and J. Simons, *The Geographical and Topographical Texts of the Old Testament* [1959] §§298, 441) or at *ʿalēyān* (van Zyl, 80f.). Rudolph (HAT 12³, 285) suggested that it was *ḥirbet iskander*, on the *wādi el-wāle* (on the main road about 30 km. south of Heshbon and 7 km. northeast of Dibon) and, since earlier archaeological conclusions seemed to have been invalidated, many agreed (see K. H. Bernhardt, 157f.; A. Kuschke, 93, with note 20; Schottroff, 182; Kaiser). This concludes the grouping of the cities, beginning with Dibon and going throughout the Moabite territory, all north of the Arnon. In Josh. 13:18 Jahaz is counted among the cities of Heshbon, and, according to Deut. 2:32; Judg. 11:20, it was on the southern edge of the territory that had come under the control of Sihon. In Josh. 21:36, however, it is considered to be part of the territory of the tribe of Reuben. Mesha mentions that the king of Israel (Omri?) had built the city and had encamped there during the campaign against Moab but that he was expelled from there by Chemosh. "And I . . . took it in order to attach it to (the district of) Dibon" (lines 18–21).

Verses 2-4 provide a graphic description of the way worship services of lament were carried out during times of war. When such a service is held, the main objective is not to give voice to one's own personal anguish; instead, it is an official, solemn activity, almost an official state function. For this reason, one also does not lament in one's own house, but climbs up instead to the city's high place, where its offerings are offered (בָּמָה). In Dibon this would have been the sanctuary that Mesha mentions, which he erected in קְרִחֹה (*qeriho?*), as a sign celebrating the deliverance (lines 3f.). Corresponding to this, the "crying" or "howling" is part of the lament ritual (cf. Joel 2:12; Jer. 3:21; 9:9; 31:15f.), whether it is a service of confession of sins or follows someone's death. The verb הֵילִיל (howl) is a technical term for the cry of lament raised during that ritual (see above, pp. 21f., at 13:6). But the traditional rites also include cutting the hair of one's head and beard. Literally, v. 2bβ says: "on each one of their heads there is a bald place." According to some, the Hebrew word for baldness, קָרְחָה, has been chosen because it would remind one of the name of the part of the city that has just been mentioned, קְרֹחָה, Qarḥoh or *qeriḥo;* cf. Abel, *Géographie* II, 418; *KAI* II, 172; and cf. Kaiser. But if that were the case, then the mention of this "baldness" would have to be more closely connected with mention of Dibon—ignoring altogether the fact that neither the author nor his hearers would have known the Mesha Inscription as well as the modern commentators of the book of Isaiah know it. קְרֹחָה and קָרְח are both simply terms that are part of the vocabulary of the lament; see Amos 8:10; Isa. 3:24; Mic. 1:16; Jer. 47:5; Ezek. 7:18; 27:31. Yet except for Jer. 48:37 and 41:5 (מְגֻלְחֵי זָקָן, "their beards shaved"), there is no other mention of cutting off one's beard during the lament ritual; rather the beard was hidden from view (עָטָה עַל שָׂפָה, "cover their lips," Mic. 3:7; Ezek. 24:17, 22). But this ritual action is not hard to understand when considered as a parallel to completely shaving hair off one's head. It is also common that wearing sackcloth is mentioned in connection with lament.

The main purpose of these rites (see Gen. 37:35; 1 Kings 20:31; 21:27; 2 Kings 6:30, and often elsewhere) would chiefly involve one's clothing: one would make oneself unrecognizable, so that the demons of death would not be able to recognize the person; on this, see W. Hönig, *Die Bekleidung des Hebräers* (1957) 109f.; H. Jahnow, *Das hebräische Leichenlied,* BZAW 36 (1923) 22–24; O. Böcher, *Dämonenfurcht und Dämonenabwehr,* BWANT 90 (1970) passim. These mourning rites were carried out right in the open, and were seen by everyone, since the person would wear שַׂק (sackcloth) in the side streets, would howl loudly in the streets, and would hold laments for the dead up on the roofs. According to Jer. 19:13; 32:29; and Zeph. 1:5, cultic activities could be held up on the roofs. סָפַד (bewail) is a special word, used to describe a lament for the dead (see, e.g., Gen. 23:2; 50:10; 1 Sam. 25:1; 28:3); however, it can also be used in a more general sense, e.g., someone laments when fields have been destroyed (32:12) or when a city has fallen (Jer. 4:8).

Even though vv. 2f. might leave us with the impression that a death is being lamented, that is, that Moab has come to an end, v. 4 shows that such is not the case: Heshbon and Elealeh "cry" (זָעַק)—that can only be a cry for help (cf. passages such as Joel 1:14ff., in connection with a summons to lament in 1:13). But that means: the mourning rites carried out in the cities of northern Moab are intended to guard them against the spread of the disaster. One does "penitence" in order to divert the divine wrath that one has brought on oneself for whatever reason. The louder one cries, the quicker one can expect to get a favorable hearing from the deity. In any case, the people in Heshbon and Elealeh would not already have screamed so loudly that someone would have been able to hear the wailing 30 km. away in Jahaz—which is obviously not enough of a reason for raising questions about the correctness of where Jahaz has been located geographically in the above discussion. The sorry state of the text in v. 4b does not permit one to come to any conclusion with confidence. In any case, it would seem that a description is given about the violent, deep shock that this had caused throughout all of Moab.

[15:5-8 (9)]   *The Lament about the Fugitives of Moab*

Form

The second song, 15:5-8, describes the desolate situation south of the Arnon, where those who had been deeply shaken by the terrible news were trying to save themselves by making a desperate attempt to escape. As a detailed study of the place-names will show, with the possible exception of Beer-elim, all the localities are south of the Arnon.

When studying 15:5-8, one may appropriately pose the question about whether this is a lament spoken in advance of the event, somewhat similar to what is found in Jeremiah in the "war songs" (cf., e.g., Jer. 4:19-22). But the specific mention of the various localities would not fit well with this suggestion, and nothing is said that would make it appear that the enemy was just then appearing on the scene. This dilemma about whether it refers to the past or the future would obviously be assessed differently if v. 9 were considered to be part of the original text.

Meter: Verse 5: 3 five-stress cola. עגלה שלשיה (to third Eglath) is a gloss, עד־צער (as far as Zoar) is to be read with one stress only, as is also the case with יעלה־בו (one who ascends thereupon) and זעקת־שבר (the downfall shriek). Verse 6a: a five-stress colon; כי (yes), as in the two preceding lines, is to be treated as a deictic particle, and thus receives a stress; but that same particle, in its use at the beginning of v. 6b, is unstressed, since there it serves the function of a causal conjunction (since). Verse 6b: a six-stress colon (3 + 3; כלה דשה, "the plants gone," is given only one stress; לא, "nothing," is not stressed). Verses 7 and 8a: once again, these are five-stress cola (ופקדתהם, "and what anyone had put aside," and ישאום, "they will take it away," in v. 7, each receive two stresses). Verse 8b: a three-stress + three-stress bicolon. The addition in v. 9 should be read as a three-stress + three-stress bicolon. Placing two stresses on the single word that comes in the second colon of both v. 7a and v. 7b underscores the tragic nature of the flight and the weight of the heavy load of their belongings, which they have to drag along. The three-stress + three stress bicolon in v. 8b marks the end of the poem; the six-stress colon in v. 6b marks the midpoint, drawing together some of the observations before the reasons for further actions are given (על־כן, "therefore").

Setting

The same historical setting behind 15:1-4 should be presumed to be the background of 15:5-8.

Commentary

[15:5-8] The decisive bit of information, which points out the exact geographical situation, is provided when one identifies the "waters of Nimrim" (v. 6) correctly. If one does not notice that a new section begins with v. 5, then one would probably be inclined toward thinking this is the present-day *wādi nimrīn* (= *wādi šuʿēb*), which flows into the Jordan Valley opposite Jericho (cf. *tell nimrīn*, on the road from

Amman, past *es-salṭ*, toward Jericho, at the place where the river emerges from the mountains). Num. 32:3 speaks of a place called נמרה (Nimrah), known in 32:36 and Josh. 13:27 as בת נמרה (Beth-nimrah). It has been identified (see M. Noth, *Numbers*, OTL [1968] 240) as *tell blēbil*, northeast of the just-mentioned *tell nimrîn*, which itself was first settled in the Roman era. N. Glueck has been the most vociferous (*AASOR* 18–19, 213) in identifying this נמרה (Nimrah) as the מי־נמרים (waters of Nimrim) mentioned in Isa. 15:6 (*BASOR* 91 [1943] 11–13; and *Explorations in Eastern Palestine IV/1 AASOR* 25–28 [1951], esp. 367, with note 1048). But Knobel and Diestel raised objections to this identification already; all the other localities mentioned in vv. 5–8 are found in the south of Moab, far from the *wādi nimrîn*. It is possible that the word *nimrîn* is related to נמר, "panther," but it more likely that it is connected to Akkadian *namru*, "bright, clear," and to South Arabic *nmry*, "reservoir with clear water" (see F. Perles, *Analekten zur Textkritik des Alten Testaments* NF [1922] 92). Today one pays special attention to places where clear water is found, and nothing in the ancient world would suggest that the situation was any different, meaning that a variety of places might all have been identified with such a term, because they had clear water. On the basis of the parallel passage in Jer. 48:34a, A. Kuschke looked for a place that would have been about as far away from Zoar as Jahaz is distant from Elealeh and Heshbon and used this point of reference to suggest *ḥaurān*, northwest of the *wādi en-nimr*, which flows into the *sēl hēdān* (FS W. Rudolph, 188ff.). But surface examinations of the area have yielded negative results (see Schottroff, 164ff.). Musil (68, 74) had already suggested that this might refer to the valley of the *sēl en-numēra*, which flows out into the spit of land known as the *ǧor en-numēra* (just a little north of the southern end of the Dead Sea), and this conclusion has been generally accepted by recent scholars (Schottroff, 201f.; Rudolph, HAT 12³; Kaiser).

The identification of the נחל הערבים, the "willow brook," in v. 7, is also controversial. As already mentioned (p. 122), this would not have referred to נחל הערבה (Wadi Arabah), which is north of the Dead Sea. Because of the similarity in the sound of the names, Musil (157, 170) thought this might be the *sēl el-ʿarābi* (west of *er-rabba*), but this wadi is too insignificant for it to have been mentioned, and it is simply too far away from the other localities named in the text. The same is true of van Zyl's suggestion (56) that it might be one of the tributaries of the Arnon. It is most common today to suggest that this stream should be identified as the *wādi el-ḥesā*, which flows from the southeast and empties into the Dead Sea at its southern end (see the discussion in Schottroff, 183f.). Of course, objective data to support this identification are not available, but what is important for an understanding of this present passage is that the "willow brook" should no doubt be sought in the south of Moab.

As for the other localities mentioned here, one can do no better than accept educated guesses, some of which are more obvious than others.

Zoar has been sought in the *ǧōr eṣ-ṣāfiye*, at the southeastern end of the Dead Sea; in descriptions about the lowest parts of the Jordan Valley, Zoar seems to be the southernmost point (Gen. 13:10; Deut. 34:3), and it is mentioned together with Sodom and Gomorrah (Gen. 19:22f.). Later traditions, including the *Onomastica* of Eusebius and the Medeba mosaic, place it at the southern end of the Dead Sea (see Abel, *Géographie* II, 466; and van Zyl, 65f.). However, no clearly identifiable remains of any Iron Age settlement have as yet been found in this region.

There is even less certainty about the location of the mountain tracks of

Luhith and that of Horonaim. According to Eusebius, Luhith was on the road that ran, in Roman times, from Areopolis (*er-rabba*) toward Zoar (see Schottroff, 204f.). One might suppose that a stretch of road ran along the same line through this territory already many hundreds of years earlier. It would be on this route, parts of which cannot be identified with certainty along its whole length and parts of which have not been studied systematically, that Luhith and Horonaim were once located. The road runs quite a distance down into the south of Moab. Musil (72, 75) suggested that Luhith might be either *ḥirbet fās* or *ḥirbet medīnet er-rās* and that Horonaim might be *el-ʿarāq* (75), having found general acceptance for these conclusions. At the same time, van Zyl also suggests that Luhith was *ḥirbet medīnet er-rās* but that Horonaim was *ḥirbet ed-ḍubāb* (65). Schottroff (207) thinks it more likely that Horonaim is *ḥirbet el-mēdān* and finds no acceptable suggestion for the location of Luhith.

After more thorough study of the route of the Roman road has been made and after further clarification of the archaeological remains at each of the sites where ruins have been located, one ought to be able to be much more certain. Based on what has been suggested up to the present, one can say that the fleeing Moabites hoped to reach Zoar and would have been passing through the southwestern corner of the Moabite territory, which means that nothing stands in the way of concluding that they were fleeing from the area around Ar- and Kir-Moab. One could circle around the southern end of the Dead Sea from Zoar and go on up into the Judean territory (see 2 Kings 3:8f.), but one could also go further to the south and go on into the Edomite territory. The road shown on the Peutinger tables [Tr.: the Roman Empire charts of rivers, roads, and settlements] goes from Rababatora through Tamara and up to Aelia Capitolina (Jerusalem). (Rababatora is formed by uniting Raba = *er-rabba* and Battora = *el-lejjūn*, which is 15 km. east-southeast of *er-rabba*; Tamara is the same as the OT Tamar, Ezek. 47:19, in the south of Judah.)

The localities mentioned in v. 8b do not have to lie along this path of flight. As v. 4 shows, there was no hesitation about including some places that could not possibly have heard the cries for help. Some have sought to identify Eglaim as *rujm el-jilimē*, near *el-kerak* (Simons, *Geographical . . . Texts*, §1259; Kaiser makes the error of writing this *ğimilē*) or somewhere else in the general vicinity of this city (see van Zyl, 69, and the literature cited there).

Beer-elim has frequently been equated with the Beer mentioned in Num. 21:16, which some think ought to be sought in the *wādi aṭ-ṭamad*, a valley that branches off from the *wādi el-wāle* (Abel, *Géographie* I, 461; Simons, *Geographical . . . Texts*, §441; van Zyl, 85f.). This identification was originally made by Musil (298f., 318, note 11; cf. Glueck, *AASOR* XIV, 13), who gets even more specific and suggests that this is *el-Medeiyineh*, on the left bank of the wadi (see illustrations and the plan of the site, figs. 136f.). He bases his identification on the fact that *ṭamad*, "watering hole," provides further information about a place, as does Hebrew באר (Beer), that terebinths (אילים) grow in this wadi, and that this is the only place north of the Arnon where the water comes out of the ground in the way it is described in Num. 21:16ff. But many places include the element באר (Beer), also many valleys have terebinths, and the third point he makes is extremely hard to verify. It is better to look for Beer-elim much closer to Eglaim. Some have even offered the suggestion that this should be read "as far as Eglaim and as far as Beer-elim," interpreting it as the equivalent of the well-known way to use the shortcut, when describing the entire territory of Israel, by calling it the land "from Dan to Beer-sheba," so that they attempt to place Eglaim in the south and Beer-elim in the north of Moab. That is a false interpretation: there is no "from-to" in the text, and the *wādi el-wāle* is nowhere near the northern border of Moab.

[15:5] In addition to the fact that different geographical localities are mentioned here, this material in vv. 5-8 shows itself to be distinct in relation to the preceding lament in vv. 1-4 in that the author lets it be known that he also is deeply moved inwardly by the fate that has come to Moab: "My heart cries for help for Moab." Even more specifically, as is shown by the continuation of this thought, he is concerned for the fugitives who try to flee toward Zoar. It is possible that laments can be raised without any indication that the speaker is speaking in the first person. Except for 16:9f., the closest parallels to the present passage are in the poems of lament in Jeremiah: apparently Jeremiah made use of a form of the song of lament that was very well known to his listeners. But many more of the elements commonly used in this form of speech have been employed by this author in Isa. 15:5 and 16:9 than are used by Jeremiah. Yet it is still important to note that, even though he is certainly a Judean, he is deeply moved by the disaster that has overtaken Moab.

Concerning weeping as one flees, see 2 Sam. 15:30. On the road to Horonaim, they raise a זְעַקַת־שֶׁבֶר (downfall shriek). Once again, the same type of activity is mentioned by Jeremiah, who speaks regularly about the kind of שֶׁבֶר (destruction) (Jer. 4:6, 20; 6:1, 14, and elsewhere) that comes on a whole people; cf. also Lam. 2:11; 3:48; 4:10.

[15:6, 7] Naturally, it is certainly realistic that those who, according to v. 7, are fleeing would haul along as many of their worldly goods as possible, but it is not as easy to understand why it is portrayed that the entire region around Nimrim is utterly laid waste, though it does seem that the intention is to depict the complete withering of all plant life. Nonetheless, it is unlikely that the whole verse ought to be bracketed out. It is possible that this is supposed to convey the idea that the fugitives (and their herds) need so much of the water in the Nimrim that the fields in the vicinity would be deprived of the necessary flow of water and therefore would just dry up. Fohrer makes reference to 2 Kings 3:25 to suggest that the enemies had blockaded the springs so that there was no access to the water. In reality, it just means that images are being used from the stock phrases that the author would have available from songs of lament, even though these might not correspond exactly to the details of the particular situation.

[15:8] The section comes to a close with v. 8. It makes no more mention of the fugitives' circumstances, but rather refers to the fact that the entire land of Moab is filled with cries for help. נָקַף II *hiphʿil* does mean to "go in a circle," but it also can simply mean "go in all directions" (see KBL), so that it is not necessary for Eglaim and Beer-elim to be situated anywhere near the other localities mentioned in this section.

[15:9] If, as some argue, v. 9aα should be considered the real conclusion of

this section, then one would have to look for the location of Dimon somewhere in the south of Moab. If the whole text of v. 9 is an addition, however,
then there is no reason not to equate Dimon with Dibon, as was suggested
above. However, then it is apparent in this passage that a completely different situation forms the background of the addition, which the author of the
verse would clearly know (cf. נוֹסָפוֹת, "new disaster"; on this, see above,
p. 118). It may be that the author makes observations about the disaster that
came as Nebuchadnezzar carried out his campaign against the states east of
the Jordan, including Moab, in 582. The "waters of Dimon" might be the
wadis dividing the two city hills from the *el-kūra* plateau, the *ḥenw libbād* to
the west and the *telʿet el-baqar* to the north (see Musil, 377, fig. 178). But it
is also possible that the pool which Musil described, east of the city wall,
existed already in ancient times. The city gate was located close to this pool,
so that much heavy fighting might have taken place at that site. If the entire
v. 9 is separated from what precedes it, as suggested here, the use of נוֹסָפוֹת
(new disaster) would not mean that there was going to be another catastrophe, in addition to the disaster depicted in v. 9aα; rather the כִּי clause (for)
would provide the reason why the waters of Dimon were filled with blood;
the נוֹסָפוֹת (new disasters), which were coming upon Dimon, would simply
differentiate them from the earlier ones that had affected Moab according to
vv. 1-8, particularly new in relation to the suffering that had come upon
Dibon, according to v. 2. Apparently, at the time of the expander, Moab had
already been damaged severely, with earlier catastrophes having left only a
few פְּלֵיטָה (escapee[s]) and שְׁאֵרִית (a remnant), following the pattern that the
few who survived and escaped from a catastrophe would be decimated once
again (see Lev. 26:36); for more on the terms פְּלֵיטָה (escapee) and שְׁאֵרִית
(remnant), see *Isaiah 1–12*, at 4:2f. (pp. 167f.) and 10:20 (p. 436). One notes
that the addition in 16:14 also deals with the destiny in store for Moab's remnant.

A severe plague also can be brought to a country by wild animals, so
that it is part of the age of שָׁלוֹם (peace) in the time of salvation that they either
will disappear or else be tamed (cf. Lev. 26:6; Hos. 2:18; Isa. 11:6-8). Here
we are told that lions are threatening Moab. The context suggests that this is
figurative; the lion is a fierce enemy; see Jer. 4:7; 50:17; cf. Isa. 5:29;
1 Chron. 12:9. The parallel אֵימָה (terror [conjectured]) refers to the terror that
comes to someone when animals threaten (Job 39:20; 41:6; Dan. 7:7). The
concept can be personified easily: Deut. 32:25: "In the street the sword shall
bereave, and in the chambers אֵימָה (terror)"; see also Ps. 88:16; Job 9:34;
13:21; 33:7. Of course, that does not change the fact that Yahweh is the one
who sends terror against the enemies; see Exod. 23:27: "I will send my terror in front of you." This is meant in a concrete sense in Isa. 15:9, that Yahweh sends a terror-causing enemy; cf. Hab. 1:6f.: "I am rousing the
Chaldeans . . . dread (אָיֹם) and fearsome are they."

[16:1, (2), 3-5] *Seeking Asylum and a Promise of Salvation*

Form

If one eliminates 16:2 from consideration (see above, p. 119), then 16:1, 3-5 have the following train of thought: Moab is requested to send a delegation to Jerusalem (v. 1), there to ask advice and seek asylum for its fugitives (vv. 3a, 4). As already explained (p. 120), vv. 4b, 5 are to be understood as Jerusalem's answer. After the time of need is past, a throne in which one can place trust will be established, by means of which justice and righteousness will be assured. Thus in brief: a summons to turn to the "daughter of Zion," the request that comes to the city, and a promise of salvation.

Commentary

[16:1] The uncertainties in the text and how to translate it make it impossible to be confident about understanding v. 1. But one can at least say that the verb שלח (send), whether in the perfect or the imperfect masculine plural, speaks about a gift being sent, specifically a ram—a sign either of loyalty or of submission. On the one hand, according to v. 1bβ, they should turn toward—or had already turned toward—the "mount of the daughter of Zion." On the other hand, v. 1bα seeks to identify the place from which the delegation set out: מסלע מדברה. That apparently means "from the rock in the desert" (see above, p. 110), a puzzling bit of information, since there are many rocks out in the desert; one would anticipate something more specific, unless סלע is a proper noun, which one would suspect, simply on the grounds that הר בת־ציון (mount of the daughter of Zion) seems to furnish a term that is paired up with סלע מדברה (lit.: rock in the desert). However, we have no knowledge of any place in Moab by the name of סלע (Sela), though we do know of הסלע (Sela), the capital city of the Edomites (2 Kings 14:7; Judg. 1:36), later known as Petra, the Nabatean city (more specifically, the massif of rock known as *umm el-biyāra*). If this Edomite Sela is the one that is meant, then one would have to conclude that important individuals fled there from Moab and set out from there to seek help in Jerusalem, a view that has received some support from time to time (cf. Gesenius, Hitzig, Fischer, Young). At the same time, however, comments in Jer. 48:28 would not support this interpretation: "Leave the towns and live בסלע (= "in the rocks"; thus the Zürcher Bibel). Hence מסלע מדברה means: get away from the rocky terrain that is the desert land, which borders on Moab, to which one would now and then have to flee during times when enemies brought oppression, though one would not be able to find a permanent dwelling place in such terrain.

The most problematic matter, however, is how one ought to understand משל־ארץ (sovereign of the land). Is the "sovereign" the Moabite or Judean ruler and is משל־ארץ (sovereign of the land) a genitive, dependent on כר (ram), or is it considered an accusative of direction? If the latter is the case, then a preposition would have to be used, even if the person being sent this gift is mentioned explicitly in v. 1bβ. For this reason, כַּר מֹשֵׁל־אֶרֶץ has to be translated "ram of the sovereign." In this case, the sovereign has to be the one in Moab. The question remains about who speaks and who is addressed. One might suppose that the author fashions this as a discussion among Moabite leaders, whereby the vote favors turning toward Jerusalem for help. It is also possible that he himself is hereby offering that suggestion to the Moabite leaders.

Setting

The question must now be posed about the situation during which this section would have taken shape. Does it even refer to a particular historical event? It is odd that the one being addressed by means of this "gift being sent" would be designated as the "mount of the daughter of Zion." One would normally address a plea to Jerusalem for help either to the king or, if this message was sent after the Davidic kingdom was no more, to those who were in charge of the "civilian protective forces" in Judah. It would seem, however, that the author has in mind the situation anticipated in Isa. 2:2-4: the peoples will stream to Zion and seek guidance there, not from the political leaders but from Yahweh. The author gives it his own peculiar slant: one is to seek counsel from the "daughter of Zion," i.e., the Yahwistic community or its leaders, the priests, whose center of activity is on Mount Zion. Thus 16:1, 3-5 does not depict a scene to be interpreted, at least partially, in connection with the Moabite poems now found in 15:1-8 or even 16:6ff.; instead, this is a "vision" of the future, which took shape in postexilic Israel, within the context of the eschatological hope for the future. The author knows his "Bible"; that the "gift" of Moab is specifically to be a ram from its ruler is reminiscent of 2 Kings 3:4, according to which Mesha of Moab, a well-to-do breeder of sheep, sent yearly tribute to the king of Israel, consisting of the wool from one hundred thousand כָּרִים (lambs) and from one hundred thousand אֵילִים (rams). If this is a vision about the future, it makes sense that there are only vague indications about the identity of the "sovereign of the land" and about the "rock in the desert," and finally, that this does not get more specific, having little more than a general reference to the "mount of the daughter of Zion."

Commentary

[16:3] By means of the symbolic action of sending a ram from the flocks of the ruler of the land, the Moabites are to seek counsel and a place of refuge for those people of Moab who had been scattered. In the other two passages where this turn of phrase occurs (Judg. 20:7; 2 Sam. 16:20), הָבוּ עֵצָה (give a suggestion) calls for looking for advice in the midst of a tense military situation.

פְּלִילָה (decision) is a hapax legomenon; פְּלִילָיָה, a closely related word used in Isa. 28:7, refers to an opinion offered by a priest or a prophet (one notes that the word is used there parallel to רָאָה, "vision"). Both fit well in the context; someone is seeking assurance that it is possible to be granted asylum, and the priests, in charge of providing asylum at the sanctuary, would be responsible for making the decision.

In the sanctuary, one is protected in the same way that one finds protection from the burning rays of the sun in some shady place. This explains why it would be said that one could be confident in the shade provided by God or in the shadow of his wings (Pss. 91:1; 17:8; 36:8; 57:2; 63:8). This thought is expressed in a unique way in the present passage: "throw, as the night, your shadows at the zenith of noontide." At noontime, when the sun is at its high point, the shadows in Palestine are very short; it would be most pleasant if, from time to time, one were able to hide in the full shadows of night at the time when the midday sun was its hottest. It is that type of complete protection which Moab sought for its scattered (נִדָּחִים; on this, see *Isaiah 1–12*, p. 493). The Jews of the diaspora were known as "the scattered" during the postexilic era (Deut. 30:1; Isa. 11:12; 27:13; 56:8; etc.), but here it is those who have been driven out of their land during military activity (cf. 13:14); in the second half of the verse each one is simply called a נֹדֵד (an escapee) (cf. the imagery of the עוֹף נֹדֵד, "the fleeting bird," in 16:2).

[16:4] A more precise form of the request for granting a place of safety (סתר) occurs in v. 4: יָגוּרוּ בָךְ; as protected citizens, in your midst, they ought to sojourn on Mount Zion. In Phoenician and Punic, גר designates someone protected by a deity, as is indicated by a multitude of personal names that use this term: גרעשתרת, "protected by Ashtaroth"; גרבעל, "protected by Baal"; גרמלך, "protected by Molech"; גרמלקרת, "protected by Melqart"; and so on. This concept is also not foreign to the OT: the question is posed in the entrance liturgy about who may abide in the sanctuary as a גר, as one being protected (Ps. 15:1; see also Isa. 33:14). In spite of all this, it is not directly said that the Moabites seek admission as members of the Yahweh community in Jerusalem, but rather that they seek protection in Jerusalem from the "devastator." However, whoever seeks protection in that place is included within the bounds of that over which Yahweh rules (on גר, see R. Martin-Achard, *THAT* I, 409ff.).

The enemy, from whom Moab's scattered ones seek to be hidden safely, is called שׁוֹדֵד (the devastator). That term might be a conscious borrowing from 15:1. The first time that שׁוֹדֵד is used to identify an enemy that is not mentioned by name is within the "Scythian songs" in Jeremiah (6:26; see also 12:12; 15:8). In the later oracle against the nations, this word practically becomes a technical term for the anonymous enemy, which breaks in against a people in almost apocalyptic numbers; see below, Isa. 21:2; 33:1. For the present passage, which furnishes a picture about what will happen in the future by abstracting from current historical circumstances, one has to assume that the term is meant in this special sense.

[16:4b, 5] If the interpretation that has been set forth to this point is correct, then one needs to give up trying to answer the question about who is sent, according to vv. 4b, 5, by seeking some specific historical situation that might fit. If that is true, however, it also makes no sense to separate vv. 4b, 5 from what precedes them. Indeed, it would have been grotesque if those from Moab who had been seeking help would have received the answer that, when all the danger was past, "in truth, a throne would be established." What is here is an expression of the eschatological, messianic hope held by Israel in the postexilic era. Moab would come to the mountain of God and seek protection there. The answer states that one would be able to find salvation for Moab when the hardship (or: the one bringing hardship; see above, textual note 16:4d) was past, when the devastation (or: the devastator) had come to an end, truly, when the assault (or: the assaulter) had been driven out of the land completely (perhaps one ought to translate here: from the earth). One would have to interpret this: not only Moab but also Jerusalem is in straits; there also, indeed, especially there, the people were waiting for a great change of destiny. One cannot get any closer to identifying what is meant by the difficult term מֵץ (hardship); the parallel word שֹׁד (devastation) points back to the שׁוֹדֵד (devastator) in v. 4a. The word has its roots within the vocabulary used by prophets who proclaimed judgment (Amos 3:10; Hos. 7:13; Hab. 1:3; Jer. 20:8, and often elsewhere), but here one should interpret it as a *nomen agentis* (actor noun). The other three verbs, אָפֵס (end), כלה (is gone), and הִמַּם (cleared out), which are virtual synonyms, show how eagerly the people hoped for the time of trouble to come to an end; on this, cf. 29:20: "for the tyrant shall be no more (אָפֵס), and the scoffer shall cease to be (כלה); all those alert to do evil shall be cut off." When that time finally arrives, then the time of salvation will make its appearance. The quality and stability of that time are assured by the fact that a throne will be established. One is reminded of the Egyptian depiction of the king's throne, which has a pedestal in the form of the hieroglyphic sign for *maat* (see *Isaiah 1–12*, p. 406). Corresponding to this, on the throne promised here, a שֹׁפֵט (judge, one who establishes righteousness) will sit, striving for justice, certainly proficient in righteousness. It is true that one technically needs to translate שֹׁפֵט as "judge," but this includes the idea that שָׁפַט, "judge," is used in the sense of "helping someone to get justice," and that שֹׁפֵט does not only mean "judge" but can also designate a "ruler" (Mic. 4:14; Dan. 9:12). There is no mention of the identity of the שֹׁפֵט.

In light of that, the addition of בְּאֹהֶל דָּוִד (in David's tent) provides a more detailed identification and should be treated as the earliest interpretive comment. But even if one looks beyond that note, it is still likely that the author expected that "the throne, on which one would sit permanently," would be located in Jerusalem. There—where else, anyway?—the messianic reign would be inaugurated, where the peoples, including Moab, would be able to find a place to hide in its shadows. One ought not ignore the point here, as is true for Isaiah himself (chaps. 7, 9, 11), that the Jerusalem kingship ideology is being used: the throne will be erected בַּחֶסֶד (in truth, stead-

143

fast love) and on it one will sit באמת (permanently, in truth). One might compare this with the kingship psalm, 89: חסד ואמת יקדמו פניך (steadfast love and faithfulness go before you) (v. 15); see also Ps. 89:3, 25; Isa. 55:3). Concerning באמת (permanently, in truth), when used alone, one is reminded of 2 Sam. 7:16, where the substantive אמת is not used; instead, the verb אמן *niphʿal* (be made sure) is used (and, parallel to that, כון, *niphʿal*, "be established"). The content also sounds much like Isa. 9:6 and 11:3-5. The ancient expectations, which were anticipated concerning the Davidic ruler and which Isaiah used at one time in his "messianic" predictions, were now activated once again in this passage. The ruler is depicted exclusively as one who protects justice and righteousness (cf. Isa. 11:4; Ps. 72:2-4). Attention is drawn to the extra details that are given as well: he strives for justice and is well versed in righteousness. In the entire OT, דרש משפט (striving for justice) is never used with reference to a king, although otherwise there is a general encouragement to seek justice (thus 1:17). Since, practically, the ruler is to be a "seeker of justice" according to the present passage, one is led to suppose that he is being characterized as someone who is knowledgeable in matters of jurisprudence. Ezra's job was לדרש את תורת יהוה (to study the law of Yahweh) (Ezra 7:10). The expression מהר צדק (proficient in righteousness), which is also unique, points in this same direction. It also reminds one of the way in which Ezra is described, namely, as ספר מהיר בתורת משה (a scribe skilled in the law of Moses) (7:6; cf. also Ps. 45:2). Therefore, by analogy, the messianic ruler is to be expected to perform the job of a ספר (scribe).

The addition is peculiar, suggesting as it does that this ruler will have his throne "in David's tent." Why not say simply that he will be a Davidide or at least that he will sit on the throne of David? It might be that the option was to be kept open that someone who was not of the family of David could still carry out the duties of the Davidic office in the coming time of salvation. It is even more amazing that a "tent" is mentioned. A throne belongs in a palace. No other OT passage speaks of David's residence as an אהל (tent); it is called the בית המלך (house of the king) (Jer. 36:12; 38:11; that phrase is used together with בית יהוה, "house of Yahweh," in 1 Kings 9:1, 10), and, like the sanctuary of Yahweh on Zion, his home is called a היכל as well. By contrast, the temple is sometimes called an אהל (tent) (Pss. 15:1; 27:5f.; 61:5; cf. also Isa. 33:20), and, in fact, specifically in those places where it talks about how those who are oppressed find a hiding place in the temple. Thus the word אהל (tent) is apparently borrowed from the temple ideology and inserted here into the messianic imagery, underscoring in the process what is fitting in that context, that the messianic hope includes the aspect that one can be hidden protectively.

Purpose and Thrust

The author of 16:1, 3-5 adds on to the songs that have been handed down, which lamented Moab's disaster, giving testimony about his own messianic hope. The Targ is not too far off the mark at this point when it paraphrases 16:1: "They shall bring tribute to the Anointed One [or: Messiah] of Israel, to the mount of the congregation of Zion." Isaiah also had expected a future king, one who would guarantee salvation. But the contrast is clear. Isaiah was obviously looking for a Davidide, and that ruler would have assured salvation only for Israel, whereas the שפט (judge) in this present passage is there for other peoples also, as illustrated clearly in the example furnished by Moab. In a sense, the picture sketched out here makes use of the notion that the king in Jerusalem was given authority over the peoples as well (Pss. 2:6ff.; 72:8ff.; cf. also 110:2). But the motif is transformed: the שפט (judge) is no longer the one who is victorious over the peoples, but is the sovereign who protects fugitives, not simply, as one might imagine from passages such as Isa. 11:3b-5, the one who guarantees that justice will be done in specific cases, but rather the one who knows how to effect justice and righteousness in an absolute sense. Here one finds motifs that clearly link the concepts about messiah with concepts from the theology of the temple. Most importantly, one notes that the concepts are set within the framework of an apocalyptic sequence of events: the time of distress, including a change of fortune leading to the time of deliverance. On the one hand, when speaking about Isaiah himself, one is correct to speak of his messianic predictions only if one is careful to avoid trying to impose a *temporal* sequence onto the passages; here, on the other hand, it would seem that 16:1, 3-5 are clearly on the path to a full-blown messianic expectation. Thus the section provides valuable evidence that messianic expectation was still alive in the postexilic era, but that it had undergone significant alterations.

The addition, v. 2, may at one time simply have been a marginal note, in which case it was inserted into the text at a most inappropriate place. As was noted above (p. 119), it is part of a reworking of the message about Moab, which sought to interpret these verses as a threat of judgment. In the context in which it presently stands, it no longer serves to announce disaster, but illustrates instead the distress that caused Moab to turn to Jerusalem for help.

[16:6f.] *Moab's Arrogance; Reason for Its Punishment*

Form
The songs in chap. 15 did not deal with the question about why such a great disaster had come upon Moab. In the present section we learn the reason: it is Moab's arrogance. One can ask whether v. 6 might be a reproach and v. 7 might be a threat of judgment; cf. the passage in Zeph. 2:8-10, which is constructed in a similar fashion. If that is true, then the verbs in v. 7 must be interpreted in a future sense. But it is likely that they are to be interpreted in the present tense; one might characterize this section as a reflection about Moab's destiny.

Meter: In both verses: five-stress cola (למואב, "on account of Moab," in v. 7a, is to be removed; קיר־חרשת, "Kir-hareseth," in v. 7b, is given one stress; אך־נכאים, "completely crushed," in v. 7bβ, is to be read with two stresses).

Setting

For the setting, see above, pp. 122f.

Commentary

[16:6] Wherever there is disaster, there must be guilt. The answer to the author's question about the nature of the offense is quickly identified: Moab's arrogance. It is a common assessment that the pride of the peoples brings them down; see Zeph. 2:10 (Ammon and Moab); Isa. 13:11ff.; cf. also 13:19; 14:11 (Babylon); Ezek. 30:13ff. (Egypt); Zech. 10:11ff. (Assyria); Zech. 9:6 (Philistia). Corresponding to this, the preexilic "prophets of judgment" accuse Israel/Judah of pride; see Amos 6:8; Hos. 5:5f.; Jer. 13:9; Ezek. 7:20ff., among other passages. Because of this, there is no reason to doubt that some people brought ruin on themselves because of high-mindedness. It is not as common to find the parallel points mentioned in the accusation: Moab's עברה (presumption) and its untrue בדים (idle babbling). Normally, עברה means simply "wrath," actually, "boiling up (of anger)." Passages such as Prov. 21:24 and 22:8 make clear that the word is used in wisdom contexts to describe one acting impulsively without any restraint, allowing oneself to be moved to speak words or act in a way that will have devastating consequences.

Its own insincere babbling is evidence enough of its presumptuousness, Moab somehow having come to the point that it no longer tried to evaluate its own actions. Precisely because they are not commonly found in the vocabulary typically used in the messages against the nations, these terms give some indication about the type of reception that the request from Moab enjoyed in Israel.

[16:7] The result of this behavior is apparent as well: Moab had experienced destruction, leaving the people with nothing but the chance to "howl" about it. According to "world order," it could not have come out any differently. It would seem that the double use of יליל (howl) established a link with יליל (howl) in 15:2, 3 and יללה (cry) in 15:8.

Verse 7b has traditionally been translated something like: "For the grape cakes of Kir-hareseth they whimper, completely shattered." The אשישי (grape cakes) are made with dried, pressed grapes (concerning raisins and their usage, see Dalman, *AuS* IV, 349ff.). One wonders why all of Moab would break out with such a great howling on account of such raisin cakes. The compiler of Jeremiah 48 must have asked the same question, since he replaced אשישי (grape cakes) with אנשי (men of). In Hos. 3:1, however, "love raisin cakes" parallels "turn to other gods," which means that the אשישים (grape cakes) played a role in the cultic meals of the heathen. According to 2 Sam. 6:19 and 1 Chron. 16:3, the אשישי (grape cakes) were consumed at an offering meal (not so in Song of Sol. 2:5). People must have treated them as very important; when they are given special mention, it points out that Moab has clearly lost its most valuable possession. But why grape cakes from Kir-hareseth? The form of the name itself causes problems. In v. 11 the reading

146

is קִיר חֶרֶשׂ (Kir-heres) (see also 2 Kings 3:25; Jer. 48:31, 36). In the Gk, the name has the form Δεσεθ (Deseth) (16:7; Ziegler corrects this to read Αδεσεθ, Adeseth) or Κιραδας (Kiradas) (Jer. 31:31, 36 = MT 48:31, 36), which means that it presumes the form קִיר חֲדֹשׁ(ת), "New City" (cf. קִרְתְּחֲדֹשֶׁת, "new city" = Carthage), which is what some MSS do read. However, that seems to be an attempt to find an easier reading; חֶרֶשׂ means "pottery, sherd(s)," thus "city of pottery sherds" or "sherd city," which one might think of it as a place-name (mocking nickname?). What remains is the question about the actual identification. Some have simply tried to interpret קִיר־חֲרֶשֶׂת (Kir-hareseth) as another name for קִיר־מוֹאָב (Kir-Moab) = *el-kerak*, without being able to furnish any proof. On the basis of 2 Kings 3:25, however, it seems to refer to the capital city of Moab, which alone defiantly sought to defend itself against King Jehoshaphat of Judah in his campaign to defeat them. This explanation seems plausible because *el-kerak* was situated so that it was in an excellent position to defend itself (see Abel, *Géographie* II, 418f.).

The verb הָגָה (whimper) can be used to describe the roaring of a lion standing over its prey (31:4) and the cooing of a dove (38:14), but also when someone would recite a text quietly (see Ps. 1:2), yet apparently always in the sense that one is expressing the desire for something that is very valuable (cf. Pss. 37:30; 63:7, among others), which makes excellent sense in this present context.

נָכָא (crushed) is a hapax legomenon; נָכֵא, which is a closely related term, always characterizes someone who is hurting deep within, and this is certainly the meaning of נָכָא as well.

Purpose and Thrust

The section is valuable, since it uses a very calm manner when suggesting that Moab would be well advised to ask probing questions about the real reasons why the misfortune had come upon it, rather than just spend its time blubbering and whimpering about it. The author betrays no awareness of the problems implicit in what he considers as "dogma," in the action-consequences sequence.

[16:8-11, 12] *Lament Concerning the Devastation of the Vineyard of Moab*

Form

It is apparently someone who came later, though possibly the author responsible for 16:6f. (see above, p. 120), motivated by the comment about the grape cakes of Kir-hareseth, who writes a more extensive description of Moab's pitiful condition. Moabite territories north of the Arnon set the stage for this passage. Verse 11, which focuses directly on Kir-heres (see Kir-hareseth, v. 7), shows that this passage presumes that vv. 6f. are in the text already. In contrast to vv. 6f., this passage is once again a lament; it is divided into two parts, each of which depicts the disaster (v. 8 and vv. 9b, 10, both introduced by כִּי, "truly," "since") and each of which provides some comment about how the individual was affected personally (v. 9a and v. 11, both introduced by עַל־כֵּן, "therefore"). It was established already that v. 12 must be a later addition.

Meter: The first line in v. 8 has to be read as a five-stress colon, the three additional cola as three-stress + three-stress bicola; their main purpose is simply to provide further details underscoring why the destruction of the vineyards in Heshbon and Sibmah, noted in the first line, was such a grave matter. Once again, the first colon in v. 9 is a five-stress colon (עַל־כֵּן, "therefore," is not to be considered when establishing the meter); the second line, clearly an expansion of the first, is once again a three-stress + three-stress bicolon. Verse 9b should probably be read as a five-stress colon (וְעַל, "and for," receives no stress). Verse 10a has 2 five-stress cola (מִן־הַכַּרְמֶל, "away from the grove of trees," has two stresses; the second לֹא should be altered to read וְלֹא, "and no longer," instead of לֹא, "no longer"; see above, textual note 16:10a). Since הַדֹּרֵךְ has typically been removed from the text of v. 10b, that line is also a five-stress colon. In v. 11 עַל־כֵּן (therefore) is once again not considered to be part of the metrical structure. Thus, as a conclusion, what remains is a heavy, six-stress colon (if כְּכִנּוֹר, "as a lyre," is removed from the second colon and the text is expanded to include a verb; see above, textual notes for v. 11). Verse 12, without a doubt, is a prose addition (contra *BHK* and *BHS*).

Setting
For the setting, see above, pp. 122f.

Commentary
[16:8] Concerning the location of Heshbon and Elealeh, see above, pp. 132f. Sibmah also must have been in the same vicinity (cf. Abel, *Géographie* II, 458; and Simons, *Geographical . . . Texts,* §298). Van Zyl suggests that it is at the site of *ḥirbet qarn el-kibš,* approximately halfway between *ḥirbet el-muḥayyiṭ* and *mādebā,* where evidence of occupation has been uncovered from both the Bronze and Iron ages.

The location of Jazer was long a puzzle, but this seems to have been cleared up by excavations led by R. Rendtorff on *tell ʿarēme,* about 5 km. northwest of *nāʿūr,* that now place it at that site (see Kuschke, FS Hertzberg, 100ff.; Rudolph, FS Driver, 137, and HAT 12³). Because of this identification, Jazer would be the northernmost of all the Moabite localities that are mentioned in these two chapters; no doubt it was right on the border with Ammon. Concerning Kir-heres, see above, pp. 146f.

At first, it is not clear just what type of destruction has been inflicted on Moab. If one ignores the conjectured reading שֻׁדְּדוּ (devastated) in v. 8a for the moment (see above, textual note 16:8a), which no doubt presumes that events have taken place that are connected with a war, then at least one might wonder whether the land had not been plagued by a devastating drought; אֻמְלָל (withered) in v. 8 would tend toward that interpretation (cf. the comparable uncertainty about the meaning of 15:6). But v. 9b, "for your harvest and your summer fruit, הֵידָד (cheering) has ceased," would lead one to the opposite conclusion; it is true that הֵידָד can describe the cheering that accompanies treading grapes in the winepress (see v. 10b), but Jer. 25:30; 48:33; 51:10 show that v. 9b can only mean that enemies have broken into the Moabite domain, shouting their hurrahs. The devastating effect of this invasion is illustrated by means of the depiction of the destruction of the vineyards.

First, the devastation of the שַׁדְמוֹת of Heshbon is mentioned. For שַׁדְמוֹת, KBL gives the meaning "terraces"; some have thus thought of vineyards formed by terracing a hillside (see Deut. 32:32; in other passages, grain fields are described in the same way, e.g., Isa. 37:27), a helpful insight, which gives more specific detail than does the generally accepted translation "open field" (see also Ugaritic *šdmt*, Gordon, *UT* no. 2388). It is common throughout the hilly region of Palestine to find terraces built and planted. Since these are not well-constructed, freestanding walls, they can be pulled down easily.

Based on the interpretation just given, the grapevines of Sibmah would have withered not because of lack of water but because someone wrecked them suddenly and destroyed whatever had been planted in the region. The magnificent vineyards were the pride of Moab, and the wine they produced must have been famous far and wide. This would be the only reason that it would be said: בַּעֲלֵי גוֹיִם הָלְמוּ שְׂרוּקֶיהָ (the lords of peoples had been overcome at one time by its choice grapes). The translation that has been offered for this line suggests that a story had made the rounds reporting that princes had been deplorably laid low by the Moabite wines. שְׂרוּקִים are red, very valuable grapes.

One notes the specific designation of the leaders as בַּעֲלֵי גוֹיִם (lords of [foreign] peoples), but one might compare this with בַּעֲלֵי עַמִּים (lords of peoples) in Ps. 68:31 (conjectured reading). The luxuriant growth in the Moabite vineyards is further depicted in the imagery connected with the grapevines of Sibmah, which spread so far to the north that they reached Jazer, on the Ammonite border, and whose tendrils grew eastward all the way to the desert (which is what the Moabite plateau soon becomes, just east of Medeba), and whose runners marched forth to the west as far as the sea (which naturally refers here to the Dead Sea; concerning grapevines that grow rapidly and produce abundantly, see Dalman, *AuS* IV, illuss. 88ff.).

[16:9] In v. 9a the author speaks about how so much of what has happened to Moab has affected him personally and deeply. Kaiser thinks that this can be interpreted only as a way to depict that the author was deeply moved, especially in light of his demeanor in v. 6. But a different author is speaking here, or else the same author in a different frame of mind. He passionately expresses his feelings of sympathy, with such great force, possibly because the northern Moabite cities mentioned in this section—none of them is south of Sibmah, and that is hardly south of the northern end of the Dead Sea—are all in a region that all the Israelites knew well. It may be that the inhabitants of that region were deeply affected by what had happened to them because they were related; cf. Ruth 1:1, 2; 1 Sam. 22:3, 4; Deut. 2:9. In any case, the author practically identifies himself as being one with those who were lamenting in Moab: אֲבַכֶּה בִּבְכִי יַעְזֵר (I will cry, as Jazer cries). Instinctively, he moves from the descriptive third person narration into the "you" of one who is personally involved: "for your קַיִץ (summer fruit) and your קָצִיר (harvest produce), cheering has ceased." Specifically, when קַיִץ, "summer (fruit)," is mentioned, one would think of figs. That is not inappropriate in the context, since fig trees are often found in vineyards (in the OT see 1 Kings 5:5; Mic. 4:4; Zech. 3:10; Isa. 36:16, and often elsewhere; see also Luke 13:6, and Dalman, *AuS* IV, 327f.). But one is more puzzled about קָצִיר (harvest produce) being mentioned. The text is suspect, since the parallel passage, Jer. 48:32, reads בָּצִיר, "vintage." However, it may still be that קָצִיר (harvest produce) is original, since the author's intention may have been to use the phrase קַיִץ וְקָצִיר because it was alliterative; see Jer. 8:20; Prov. 6:8; 10:5; 26:1. Nonetheless, v. 10 follows without mentioning the fields of grains, but does mention כַּרְמֶל (groves) and כְּרָמִים (vineyards).

[16:10] The word כַּרְמֶל (grove) seems to derive from כֶּרֶם (vineyard) (see KBL and cf. R. Růžička, *Konsonantische Dissimilation* [1909] 104: כֶּרֶם + the binding element ל, or originally כ). In any case, כַּרְמֶל describes a tract of land that has been planted with both vines and fruit trees (most importantly, fig trees). In gardens where one finds fruit trees and vines, happy shouts of celebration accompany the harvest (see Judg. 9:27; cf. also 21:19, 21), but now they resonate with a completely different type of הֵידָד (shout), the enemy's triumphant cry of victory in battle. One should note the attention to detail in the way this is formulated: harvesting is taking place, but not of fruit; rather, שִׂמְחָה (joy) and גִּיל (shouts of jubilation) are being removed by the harvesters. Isaiah 9:2 shows how closely these two terms were associated with the time of harvest. Just as these two terms are often linked, so רָנַן (joyful shouts) and רוּעַ (call for rejoicing) are also often used together as a word pair (see Zeph. 3:14; Isa. 44:23; Pss. 81:2; 95:1; 98:4; but most of these uses are in a cultic-religious sense). Naturally, the most basic reason for this joy is the simple fact that the harvest was adequate for providing the staples of life for another year. But a harvest is a chance for people to get together as well. The Mishnah (*Ta'anit* 4:8) reports that at one time, both on the 15th of Ab and on the Day of Atonement, daughters in white garments went out into the vineyards where they sang songs that encouraged the young men to make the choice of a wife. Now, however, such festivals were out of place: "for the cheering of the winepresser an end has been prepared." For בְּקִי, "winepress," see *Isaiah 1–12*, p. 181; concerning winepresses in general, see Dalman, *AuS* IV, 354ff. and illuss. 95–111; concerning trampling of the press (stomping on the grapes with the feet), one can refer to passages such as Amos 9:13; Lam. 1:15; Job 24:11.

[16:11] Once again, a lament is raised in v. 11, in fact, in such a way that it apparently picks up on the theme of vv. 6, 7. But one notes that the city is not called קִיר־חֲרֶשֶׂת (Kir-hareseth) in this passage, but rather קִיר חֶרֶשׂ (Kir-heres) (on this, see above, pp. 146f.). One might take this to be an indication that a different author is at work here, one who was familiar with this form of the name of the city. But what is most striking is that this city is mentioned here at all, since it is located a good distance south of the Arnon, whereas all the other localities in this section are in the far northern reaches of Moab. That can be explained when one recognizes that Kir-heres was the capital city, which would have been moved with sympathy by every blow that was struck, even out in one of the "provinces." This is supported by the fact that Kir-heres is also mentioned in parallel with what is simply called "Moab," the land as a whole.

The sympathetic feelings toward Moab are also expressed by the author, once again (see above, p. 138, on 15:5), by using terms that sound much like Jeremiah; cf. Jer. 4:19: מֵעַי מֵעַי אֹחוּלָה . . . הֹמֶה־לִּי לִבִּי (My anguish, my anguish! I writhe in pain! . . . My heart is beating wildly!) (see also Lam. 1:20 and 2:11). However, the comparison with Jeremiah also reveals the passionate tone of the prophet's words as he shows how he can personalize and intensify the words that had been passed down to him in the traditions.

In other passages as well, the "insides" are also considered to be the seat of the feelings (Ps. 22:15; Isa. 63:15; Jer. 31:20; Job 30:27; Song of Sol. 5:4; Lam. 1:20; 2:11); "they rage, they are red-hot, they are brought to the boiling point," whenever a deeply emotional experience affects an individual. In this type of situation, however, the verb המה (rile up) is used frequently (or the substantive המון, "roaring"). In other passages, it characterizes the raging or agitation of large amounts of water, the growling of a bear (Isa. 59:11), the yelping of a dog (Ps. 59:7, 15), and, with a transferred meaning (Ps. 55:18), also the unsettledness of the human heart or simply a human being's sighing (Pss. 42:6, 12; 43:5). The present context is unique in that the sound of the כנור (lyre) is included in the comparison (concerning this, see the reference to musical instruments in *Isaiah 1–12*, pp. 200f.); this, however, is simply the result of the ineptitude of a glossator (cf. above, p. 148).

[16:12] Once again, the expander who adds v. 12 reacts in a completely different way. It is likely that he had read about how Moab was climbing up to the cultic high places to lament (see 15:2), in the hope that they would be able to build a type of dam that would be able to stave off further disaster; now he felt compelled to establish that all of that effort would go for naught. Unfortunately, the text in v. 12aα is uncertain (see above, textual note 16:12a); however, נלאה (make the effort to get itself up) does fit well in the context; it could take considerable effort to participate in the cultic offerings (see Isa. 43:22ff. and cf. Mic. 6:6), and indeed was wearying, but the cult could also be very costly in terms of time and goods. In fact, v. 12b says simply that people went to the sanctuary to pray. But the prayers offered by the cultic community included bringing offerings forward, along with cultic singing, and could become a heavy burden, as Isaiah reported from the other point of view, remarking that Yahweh was worn out by all the cultic activities and could no longer tolerate all the praying (1:14f.).

מקדש does not necessarily refer to a temple structure only (see Josh. 24:26), although the term generally is used when referring to the temple in Jerusalem. When simple mention is made of Moab's sanctuary, referring to it as מקדשו, one might presume that there was an official sanctuary of the kingdom in the capital city (Kir-hareseth?), but it is more likely that this means merely that each resident of any particular Moabite city would visit one's own local sanctuary, i.e., one's own במה (high place) (see 15:2). Concerning all this cultic "tiresome effort," the verdict is issued: לא יוכל (it will not be able to make anything happen) (cf. 1:13; Zeph. 1:18). The reason is not given. The preexilic prophets would respond that cultic activity in the sanctuary, including prayer, would be a waste of time if one were not prepared to return to Yahweh. The author of this addition would most likely say that Moab deserved the trouble it got and that divine righteousness would have to take its course.

[16:13f.] *Renewed Announcement of Judgment against Moab*

The addition in v. 12 has already demonstrated that some in Israel considered the harsh destiny for Moab to be unavoidable and considered the sympathy that was clearly expressed in the songs of lament, concerning the fate of Moab, to be most inappropriate. Now the author of this final addition to the message against Moab, in the words of 16:13f., took the approach that the most appropriate message for Moab was that an inescapable, destroying judgment would come. The reason is not mentioned here either. According to Deut. 23:3, in terms of religious participation, the Israelites knew only that a complete prohibition, even to the tenth generation, applied to allowing the Ammonites and Moabites to become members of the Yahwistic community. In fact, Isa. 25:9-12 suggests that Israel must have suffered great trauma at the hands of Moab. It must be noted, however, that the reason for the judgment against Moab is not because of its treatment of Israel, and it would be a mistake for exegetical studies to conclude that the announcement of judgment was the result of pressure that developed into a nationalistic, Israelite spirit, with an aversion to this neighboring people.

At the time when this addition was inserted, Moab was still able to celebrate good times; כבוד (majesty) could suggest that they were still prosperous. However, the use of נקלה, "become despicable," which announced the coming change of fortune, would lead one to think rather of the honored position that Moab enjoyed over against its neighbors; note the contrast between "honored" (נכבד) and "despised" (נקלה) in Sir. 10:19. It is appropriate that המון, "noise, bustle," should be mentioned here, since Moab would consider that to be a good description of its present circumstances.

But all that would change within three years. No doubt, the author had specific political-military developments in mind; it may be that Moab had allowed itself to become part of a risky revolt against the ruling power. A remarkable comparison is made in כשני שכיר (as are the years of one who does day labor). שכיר can mean either "day laborer" (Lev. 25:53) or "mercenary" (Jer. 46:21) (see *Isaiah 1–12*, p. 324). Along with others, Fohrer suggests that the comparison means that a mercenary would normally sign up for a three-year stint. We know nothing about that; the term for a mercenary would usually either be longer than that or would not have any fixed term whatsoever. But the translation "day laborer" causes even more trouble. Why would the arrangements made with a day laborer last only three years? One ought to note carefully, however, that the Hebrew text does not say "as are the years of a שָׂכִיר (one who does day labor)," but rather, without the article: "as years of one who does day labor." The point of comparison is not the time of duration, but rather the drudgery of the life of a שָׂכִיר (day laborer). Job 7:1f. shows that this was a common comparison; in that passage, שָׂכִיר means "mercenary" in v. 1 and "day laborer" in v. 2. Apparently, the final solution to what שָׂכִיר means here cannot be determined (mercenary: Marti, Eichrodt, Fohrer, Kaiser, et al.; day laborer: Hitzig, Delitzsch, Procksch, Fischer, et al.).

The time of drudgery is assigned a period of three years. This is not the way prophets delivered their messages; it betrays more of the influence of an apocalyptic approach to history, which begins now to reckon with deadlines. Of course, no mention is made of a change of fortune that would be to Moab's benefit. A change that would bring salvation is in the future only for the people of God; for Moab, however, which is apparently serving as an example of a heathen nation (see above, p. 117), nothing but judgment awaits. It would be almost a totally destructive judgment; the author would not even be satisfied if only a "remnant" survives; he specifies: "a minute portion of a tiny bit" (cf. 10:25; 29:17), completely "powerless." One almost wonders why he would leave even that many of them; one supposes that he would have done so only because he was employing the commonly used terminology, which forced him at least to mention that there would be some type of remnant.

Purpose and Thrust

[15; 16] The exegesis of the individual passages has shown that these two chapters about Moab present a complex unit of material. Not all the individual sections belong to the same historical time period, and they also have been expanded by additional commentary. Of greatest importance, however, is that they are not the final result of an explicit, invariable viewpoint, on Israel's part, about its assessment of its neighbors. It is particularly noteworthy that no final redactor attempted to homogenize the various individual units and none attempted to cut out whatever might prove reprehensible to one's own views. The author of the final addition did not act as if it were not permissible to add a new message to what already had been delivered as a message from Yahweh—or, more correctly: directly to contradict a previous message. In spite of this, these two chapters are not just a hodgepodge of speeches about Moab, in which one message cancelled what had just been said. Overall, the greatest weight must be given to the voice that expressed deep sympathy for Moab, and that must be taken seriously. The theological center, pointed out by the way the two chapters are constructed, is found in 16:1, 3-5, the "messianic prediction," which gropes around awkwardly, looking for some way to point to a gateway of hope for oft-tormented Moab. Someday oppression and assault would be in the past and Moab's plaintive lament would fall silent. The end would bring a time of justice and righteousness, and the sovereign who would be ruling in the tent of David would be the guarantor that these would remain permanently in force.

The Downfall of Damascus
and the End of Israel

Literature

H. Donner, *Israel unter den Völkern,* VTSup 11 (1964). E. Vogt, "Jesaja und die drohende Eroberung Palästinas durch Tiglatpilesar," FS Ziegler II (1972) 249–255. *Concerning the text:* P. de Lagarde, "Kritische anmerkungen zum buche Isaias," *Semitica* 1 (1878). A. Jirku, "Niṭʿē naʿamanim (Jes XVII 10, c) = niṭʿē naʿaman-ma," *VT* 7 (1957) 201–202. G. Rinaldi, "לקט 'raccogliere,'" *BeO* 13 (1971) 210.

Concerning חמן: O. Eissfeldt, "Die Wanderungen palästinisch-syrischer Götter nach Ost und West im zweiten vorchristlichen Jahrtausend" (1934), *KlSchr* II, 58. H. Ingholt, "Le sens du mot ḥammān," FS R. Dussaud II (1939) 795–802. K. Elliger, "Chammanim = Masseben?" *ZAW* 57 (1939) 256–265. Idem, "Der Sinn des Wortes chammān," *ZDPV* 66 (1943) 129–139. R. Smend, "Altar," *BHH* I, 63–65. K. Galling, "Baʿal ḥammon in Kition und die ḥammanîm," FS Elliger, AOAT 18 (1973) 65–70.

Concerning אשרה: W. L. Reed, *The Asherah in the Old Testament* (1949) (not available to me). R. Patai, "The Goddess Ashera," *JNES* 24 (1965) 37–52. K.-H. Bernhardt, "Aschera in Ugarit und im Alten Testament," *MIO* 13 (1967) 163–171. H. Gese, *Die Religionen Altsyriens,* Die Religionen der Menschheit X/2 (1970) 3–232, esp. 149ff. Further literature is cited by J. C. de Moor, "אשרה," *TDOT* I, 438–444.

Concerning the "little Adonis garden": M. K. Ohnefalsch-Richter, *Die Bibel und Homer* (1893). Ch. Vellay, *Le culte et les fêtes d'Adônis-Thammouz* (1904). G. Maspero, *Führer durch das Ägyptische Museum zu Kairo,* German version by G. Roeder (1912). H. Sulze, "ΑΔΩΝΙΔΟΣ ΚΗΠΟΙ, I. Die kultischen Adonisgärtchen," *Angelos* 3 (1928) 72–91. A. Scharff, "Frühe Vorstufen zum 'Kornosiris,'" *FF* 21 (1947) 38–39. W. Baumgartner, "Das Nachleben der Adonisgärtchen auf Sardinien und im übrigen Mittelmeergebiet," *Zum Alten Testament und seiner Umwelt* (1959) 247–273.

Concerning the Hivites and Amorites: E. A. Speiser, "Ethnic Movements in the Near East in the Second Millennium B.C.: The Hurrians and their Connection with the Habiru and the Hyksos," *AASOR* 13 (1931–1932) 13–54. M. Noth, "Die syrisch-palästinische Bevölkerung des zweiten Jahrtausends v. Chr. im Lichte neuer Quellen," *ZDPV* 65 (1942) 9–67. R. de Vaux, "Les patriarches hébreux et les découvertes modernes," *RB* 53 (1946) 321–348. J. C. L. Gibson, "Observations on Some Important Ethnic Terms in the Pentateuch," *JNES* 20 (1961) 217–238. K. Kenyon, *Amorites and Canaanites* (1966). A. Kuschke, "Hiwwiter in ha-ʿAi?" FS Elliger, AOAT 18 (1973) 115–119. R. North, "The Hivites," *Bib* 54 (1973) 43–62.

[**Literature** update through 1979: N. Avigad, "Notes on Some Inscribed Syro-Phoenician Seals," *BASOR* 189 (1968) 44–49 (concerning צור in 17:10). P.

Hugger, "Jahwe, mein Fels: Vom Reichtum eines alttestamentlichen Kultwortes," *Laeta Dies*, Münsterschwarzacher Studien 9 (1968) 143–160 (on 17:10). G. F. Hasel, *The Remnant: The History and Theology of the Remnant Idea from Genesis to Isaiah* (1972). A. Tal (Rosenthal), "נרגר של צרורות. Un grain de caillou," *Leš* 37 (1972f.) 303–305 (on 17:6).

    Concerning חמן: R. Degen, "Der Räucheraltar aus Lachisch," *Neue Ephemeris für Semitische Epigraphik* 1 (1972) 39–48.

    Concerning the "little Adonis garden": J. A. Soggin, "'La sepoltura della Divinità' nell'iscrizione di Pyrgi (Lin. 8–9) e motivi paralleli nell'Antico Testamento," *RSO* 45/3–4 (1970) 245–252. M. Delcor, "Le problème des jardins d'Adonis dans Isaïe 17, 9–11," *Syria* 54 (1977) 371–394.]

Text

17:1 [The verdict[a] against Damascus]
    Behold, Damascus 'is eliminated,'[b] is a city no longer,
      and will become (nothing but) a pile of rubble.[cd]
  2 [[a]Abandoned are the cities of Aroer,[a]
      they are now the domain of herds;
      they will lie down there, and no one will scare them away.]
  3 [a]The fortress will disappear from Ephraim[a]
      and the monarchy from Damascus,[b]
    [c]and whatever is left of Aram[c] [d]will not be[e] more eminent
      than the majesty of the children of Israel;[d]
    that is the utterance of Yahweh of Hosts.

              * * * *

  4 [And it[a] will happen on that day:]
    The majesty of Jacob will become small,
      and the fat of its flesh will waste away.
  5 And it will happen just as when someone [during the harvest][a]
      hurriedly collects the stalks
      and he cuts the heads of grain with his arm;
    yes, it will take place as when someone leaves[b] heads of grain
      in the Valley of Rephaim.[c]
  6 And for it[a] a gleaning will remain,
      just as when someone beats olive trees:
    two, three ripe fruits[b]
      at the very top in the branches,
    four, five (of them)
      on the twigs[c] of the fruit tree;
    that is the utterance of Yahweh, [d]the God of Israel.[d]

              * * * *

  7 [On that day the human will look directly at the one who made him, and his eyes will view the Holy One of Israel. 8 However, he will not look upon <the altars[a]>, the botched work of his hands, and will not see that which his fingers made <[b]and the cultic pillars and incense altars[c]>[b]].

              * * * *

  9 [On that day his strong cities[a] will be like [b]the abandoned (cities) of the Hivites and Amorites,[b] which they abandoned in the presence of the children of Israel; and it will be a barren place.]

  10 Truly, the God of your help you have forgotten,
      and about the rock of your refuge you have not thought.

155

Therefore, you wish to plant little gardens for the lovely one,[a]
and sow[b] it with climbing plants of a foreign (god),

11 raised to maturity[a] (already) on the day[b] on which you planted,
made to sprout up[c] (already) on the morning[b] on which you
sowed it:
gone away is[d] the harvest on the day of weakness,[e]
[f]when your pain is unremitting.[f]

1a Concerning משׂא (verdict), see above, pp. 1f.
1b It is striking that, in conjunction with דמשׂק (Damascus), the masculine מוסר (is eliminated) is used, since the feminine verb והיתה (and will be) follows. According to Ges-K §121b, דמשׂק (Damascus) is in the accusative, i.e., the verb מוסר (is eliminated) is used in an impersonal sense, read thus by Dillmann, who makes reference to 8:22 and Pss. 22:16; 87:3; see also Feldmann; this view is rejected by Albrecht, *ZAW* 47 (1929) 281. Knobel tries to solve this in a different way: דמשׂק (Damascus) stands for עם דמשׂק (people of Damascus), a suggestion that takes into account that הסיר (remove) is never used to describe the destruction of a city. However, he has to admit that the following היתה (will be) must refer to Damascus as a city. One must conclude that the reading should be the feminine singular, either מוסרת or מוסרה (Duhm; Donner, 39; Kaiser; Vogt, 255; *BHK;* et al.). Donner (38f.) treats מוסחה as a *hophʿal* from the root יסר (is chastised) and the following word, מעיר (from [existing as] a city), as either a gloss or a dittography of מעי (pile of) in the second colon. But the *hophʿal* of יסר never occurs in the OT (and the single instance of the *hiphʿil,* in Hos. 7:12, must be changed into a *qal* form). After all this is considered, as most have concluded, it seems that this should be taken as a *hophʿal* form, מוסר, from סור (remove).
1c מעי is used only here in the entire OT. Instead of that reading, some suggest that מעיר (Damascus will change "from a city" into a pile of rubble) should be read (Schmidt; Ehrlich, *Randglossen* IV, 64; Procksch), but this would hardly be possible, since it would presume a repetition of the same word in the same line. Targ reads לכרך מחמרא (to a city of the heap) instead of מעי מפלה (Syr: *lḥwrbʾ wlmpwltʾ,* "to the desert and to the ruin"), which means it might have read לעי (to a heap). By contrast, the Gk (καὶ ἔσται εἰς πτῶσιν, "and there will be a calamity") apparently did not have מעי in its text at all. For this reason, some presume that it ought to be eliminated as a dittography of מעיר (is a city no longer; lit.: from [existing as] a city) (de Lagarde, *Semitica* 1 [1878] 29; Gray; Duhm; Marti), which is hardly an appropriate solution, since מעי does not directly follow מעיר. Vulg reads *sicut acervus lapidum* (just as a pile of stone), so that one might wonder whether it had a text that read כעי (as a pile of), but the text does not intend to say that Damascus will be *the same as* a pile of rubble. One must treat מעי as a less common form of the better-known עי (heap of ruins) (contracted, according to Gesenius, from מעוי; see Delitzsch, Naegelsbach, Knobel, Young), possibly chosen for this passage, even though it was not commonly used elsewhere, because the word sounded so much like מעיר (from [existing as] a city), which is the best solution, unless one chooses instead to assume that the Hebrew text was originally לעי (to a heap).
1d מפלה (rubble) occurs in this form only here; otherwise, the form מפלה is used (23:13; 25:2).
2a–a "Abandoned are the cities of Aroer" makes no sense in its present context. Three different localities were given this name in the OT: one is Moabite, south of Dibon, located at what is presently known as *ḥirbet ʿarāʿir,* high above the northern

bank of the Arnon (Num. 32:34; Deut. 2:36; Jer. 48:19, and often elsewhere); a
second is in Gad (Josh. 13:25; Judg. 11:33), "across from Rabbah" (= רבת בני עמון,
"Rabbah of the sons of Ammon," present-day *ʿammān*); the third is south of Beer-
sheba (1 Sam. 30:28, which certainly ought to be read as עֲרָרָה, Ararah, instead of
עֲרֹעֵר, Aroer), known today as *bīr ʿarʿara*, 20 km. southeast of Beer-sheba. There is
no known city with this name anywhere in the vicinity of Damascus. The name
seems to mean juniper thicket (de Lagarde, 30; the Arabic is *ʿarʿar;* see KBL); it
may be that other localities were given this same name. However, since "(daughter)
cities of Aroer" are mentioned, and the city is named along with Damascus, it would
have had to have been an important settlement in the region of Aram, and we would
certainly have had some knowledge of the place. Procksch suggests that one read
simply עָרֶיהָ (her cities) instead of עֲרֵי עֲרֹעֵר (cities of Aroer). The Gk seems to offer
some help (καταλελειμένη εἰς τὸν αἰῶνα, "abandoned forever"). Making use of this
reading, some link this with מפלה (rubble), at the end of v. 1, to read עֲזֻבָה עַד, "abandoned forever," at the beginning of v. 2. Most of the recent commentators emend
v. 2a, following de Lagarde (30): עֲזֻבוֹת עָרֶיהָ עֲדֵי עַד "its cities [those belonging to
Damascus] are abandoned forever"; cf. 26:4; 65:18, and often elsewhere (Steinmann,
Mauchline, Fohrer, Donner, Eichrodt, Alonso-Schökel, Kaiser, et al.). That emendation would help one to come up with an understandable text. However, that still
offers no explanation about how עֲרֹעֵר (Aroer) happened to show up here in this particular text. One notes that, although it was a rather important Moabite fortress, this
city is not mentioned in chaps. 15, 16 (though it is not missing from Jeremiah 48; see
v. 19). That would lead one to suspect that 17:2 is a verse that has been displaced
from some original location in chaps. 15f., or, even more likely, that it is a gloss that
belonged originally to those chapters. A reader had missed seeing Aroer mentioned
in the chapters about Moab and wanted to make up for the omission. In Jeremiah 48
Aroer is mentioned right after Dibon (= Dimon in Isa. 15:9), being located in the
same general vicinity as that city; this means that 17:2 most likely belongs somewhere in the context of 15:9. However, since Aroer is located high above the Arnon,
and the road down to the stream begins there, one must also consider the strong possibility that this belongs with the passages surrounding 16:2, where the fords of the
Arnon are mentioned. In any case, the words of the text, as transmitted, are to be
retained.

3a–a Scholars disagree about the interpretation of מבצר מאפרים. It has often been
translated "fortress *for* Ephraim," which would suggest that the Aramaic city of
Damascus would be a fortress for Ephraim because it would shield the Northern
Kingdom from the Assyrian might. Indeed, Israel's days were numbered after the fall
of Damascus (732) (Marti; Duhm; Procksch; Eichrodt; Vogt, 250). But the preposition מִן (from) prohibits this interpretation, no matter how much someone would like
to adopt it on the basis of the parallelism. For this reason, Donner's conjecture (39)
to read מֵאֲרָם (of Aram) still deserves serious consideration. However, since v. 3b
mentions the בני־ישראל (children of Israel), and the destiny of Aram and Israel is
viewed as one and the same at that point, it is certainly possible for the parallelism to
be between the מבצר (fortress) of Ephraim and the ממלכה (monarchy) of Damascus.
That there is parallelism means that the fortress of Ephraim must be considered as a
reference to Samaria, the capital city of the Northern Kingdom.

3b Qᵃ reads מדרמשק (from Darmesheq) (this form of the name also occurs in
1 Chron. 18:5f. and frequently elsewhere in the Chronicler's history, being a way to
avoid the doubling of the *mem;* cf. the Judean-Aramaic דרמסקוס [Darmasqus] and see

R. Růžička, *Konsonantische Dissimilation* [1909] 78; F. Rosenthal, *Die aramaistische Forschung* [1939] 15–18).

3c–c The Gk (καὶ τὸ λοιπὸν τῶν Σύρων ἀπολεῖται, "and the rest of Syria will be destroyed") might have used a text that read יאבד (will be destroyed) after ארם (Aram); many modern commentators accept this reading (Duhm; Marti; Feldmann; Donner, 39). If one keeps the *athnach* where it is, under ארם (Aram), then the first colon is too short. But it may be that the verse divider should be moved and placed at the end of the next word ככבוד (as the majesty of).

3d–d Targ reads: ויקרהון כיקר בני ישראל יהין (and their glory shall be as the glory of the sons of Israel), but this may be nothing other than an attempt to make the MT more understandable. Bruno is not comfortable with the "majesty" (glory) of the Israelites being mentioned, so he alters the text to read ככובד: "as the burden," but there is no reason for this change (see below, pp. 165, 169f.).

3e Qᵃ reads יהוה (Yahweh) instead of יהיו (they will be), an alteration suggested already by Ehrlich, *Randglossen* IV, 65. But שאר (remnant), technically a singular, can certainly be read with a plural verb as predicate. There is also no justification for Donner to eliminate יהיו (they will be) altogether.

4a Even though the shorter form ביום ההוא (on that day) is read in vv. 7, 9, there is no good reason for removing והיה (and it will happen) from the text (so Duhm, Marti; see 7:18, 21, 23; 10:20, 27; 11:10, 11, and often elsewhere).

5a קציר, "(grain) harvest," is difficult. Some have tried to solve this problem by suggesting that the word serves to designate a time period (Luzzatto, Naegelsbach, Cheyne: "at harvest"). Others think that קציר (harvest) is an abstract term used in place of a concrete term, קוצרים (= harvesters) (Gesenius, *Lehrgebäude der hebräischen Sprache* [1817] §163, 3; §164, 2); or, as is true of the words נביא (prophet), פליל (judge), among others, it might be a noun identifying the agent in this passage; see Knobel, von Orelli, Dillmann, and, much earlier, Qimḥi. Finally, one must at least suggest that קציר (harvest) might have to be removed as a gloss, in which case כאסף, in parallel with כמלקט (as someone leaves) in v. 5b, would have to be pointed כאסף (as one gathers). That solution would seem to be possible just because קציר (harvest) is used so near to יקצור (he cuts the heads of grain) in v. 5aβ. This would eliminate the need for the conjecture that is currently widely accepted, to change קציר (harvest) to read קצר (reaper of, reaping of) (Duhm; Buhl; Procksch; Kissane; Steinmann; Donner, 39; Vogt, 255, note 11).

5b Eichrodt suggests adding a substantive, from the same root, to מלקט (gleans) (probably לקט, "gleaning"; see Lev. 19:9; 23:22) (lost due to haplography). Following up on that observation, Vogt suggests reading מלקט as an abstract, i.e., either מלקט or מלקט, and thus translates v. 5bα: "so that only a gleaning of heads of grain remains" (see also Ges-Buhl: מלקט "might be intended as an abstract noun"). Vogt seems to offer the best solution, since the reader learns how harvesting is carried out in the grain fields: so that only very little is left for gleaning. But no one in ancient Jerusalem had to have that explained to them; thus there is no reason to alter the text.

5c One wonders why, at this particular point, mention is made of the Valley of Rephaim (located close to Jerusalem; see below, pp. 171f.), especially since the passage deals with the Northern Kingdom. It is obvious that they did not use unique methods of harvesting that would have differed from what was done elsewhere in the country. For this reason, Marti discussed changing רפאים (Rephaim) to אפרים (Ephraim). That would make good sense if a valley by that name were known. Others suggest that either בעמק רפאים (in the Valley of Rephaim) (Schlögl) or v. 5bα might be a gloss (Kissane), or that the text itself has been otherwise damaged (Gray), whereas Donner (39f.) takes the opposite approach, treating v. 5a as "an interpretive comment on v. 5b, resulting from a misunderstanding of the context and containing material that falls metrically outside the pattern of what surrounds it." It is certainly possible that the text might no longer be intact, but the reasons cited for making wholesale changes to the text are simply not justified.

6a Exegetes have been puzzled about the referent of the suffix on בו (for it). Some, like Vogt (253), who has revived the argument, believe that the referent must be to the זית (olive tree), at the end of the line. At the very least, that would be unusual. For this reason, others rearrange the text. Thus Gray and Procksch suggest that כנקף זית (as when someone beats olive trees) be placed at the conclusion of v. 5, possibly even inserting before these two words an או (or) as well (see Gk: ἤ, "or") (cf. also *BHS;* Kissane has another solution, placing כנקף זית, "as when someone beats olive trees," before בעמק רפאים, "in the Valley of Rephaim," in v. 5). But there is no serious reason why בו (for it) could not refer back to יעקב (Jacob) in v. 4.

6b To treat גרגרים (fruit, berry) as a gloss (Gray), so that a better balance can be achieved between v. 6b and 6c, is an example of the way someone can bring discredit to text-critical studies.

6c The suffix on מעפיה (branch) makes no sense, especially since זית (olive tree) is masculine. Long ago, it was suggested (Hitzig; see Driver, *JTS* 2 [1951] 25) that the ה on the end of this word should be taken as the article on the following word, פריה (fruit bearer), so that סעפי (branch of) would be in the construct state. In fact, Qᵃ reads סעפי (branches of) (though this reading is not completely assured), but it does not have the article before פריה (fruit bearer), which is appropriate, since one would not expect to find an article in such a poetic piece of literature. This concludes the discussion about attempts to find some way to resolve the problem of the suffix (Gesenius and Delitzsch refer to passages such as Prov. 14:13 and explain this as an anticipation of the genitive by use of a suffix, a style used in Aramaic and Syriac). It makes no sense that v. 6bα should be considered a "gloss that distorts the meaning" (so Donner, 40).

6d–d Duhm, Marti, et al. would like v. 6bβ to read נאם יהוה צבאות (utterance of Yahweh of Hosts). But there is no reason why this formula would have to match that in v. 3 exactly.

8a Without a doubt, מעשה (work of) is a play on words with עשהו (who made him) in v. 7. However, then המזבחות (the altars) interrupts the flow of the line. In addition, altars are never depicted anywhere else as the work of human hands (on Ezek. 6:6, see Zimmerli, BK XIII/1, 150 [Engl: *Ezekiel 1,* 187f.]), since this would mention the obvious. מעשה ידיו (the work of his hands) is parallel to אשר עשו אצבעתיו (which his fingers made), both of which naturally refer to idol figurines (cf. Isa. 2:8, and often elsewhere). Thus המזבחות (the altars) is a gloss, being inserted there by the same person who added references to the *asherah*s and the incense altars at the end of the verse.

8b–b See the previous note. The addition makes observations that come too late (which the Vulg also noted and was able to adjust, at least somewhat, by dropping the ו, "and," before האשרים, "the cultic pillars," *asherah*s). Everyone recognizes that this has all the characteristics of a gloss (Dillmann; Marti; Duhm; Procksch; Kissane; Donner, 40; Fohrer; Kaiser).

8c Concerning the translation of חמן, see below, pp. 176f.

9a Instead of ערי מעזו (his strong cities), the Gk reads αἱ πόλεις σου (your [sing.] cities), so that some alter the text to read ערי מעזך (your strong cities). But one ought not follow the inclination to adjust the suffix to agree with those found in vv. 10f. (additionally, Qᵃ supports the MT), since vv. 9 and 10 belong to different levels of the history of transmission; to alter עָרֵי מָעֻזּוֹ (his strong cities) to read עָרִים (cities) (Ehrlich, *Randglossen* IV, 66) is not recommended either. In addition, מָעֹו can hardly derive from עוז "take refuge"; rather, it comes from עזז, "be strong," even though it is true that a well-fortified locality would also be a place of refuge; see v. 10.

9b–b The word חֹרֶשׁ, which is of uncertain meaning, is given the meaning "forest, woody area"; the word אָמִיר, which appears elsewhere only in v. 6, probably means "summit" here. However, in addition to the uncertainty connected with whether these two words have been understood correctly, one is not convinced it is correct to translate this "and the cities of their refuge will be like the abandoned place of the forest and of the mountain summit"; the text must be damaged. The Gk reads: ἔσονται αἱ πόλεις σου ἐγκαταλελειμμέναι, ὃν τρόπον ἐγκατέλιπον οἱ Ἀμορραῖοι καὶ οἱ Εὐαῖοι (your cities will be ones having been abandoned, in the way the Amorites and the Hivites abandoned). On the basis of this reading, a long-standing suggestion has been that v. 9aα read: בַּיּוֹם הַהוּא יִהְיוּ עָרֶיךָ עֲזוּבוֹת כַּעֲזוּבַת הַחִוִּי וְהָאֱמֹרִי (in that day your cities will be abandoned, as the abandoning of the Hivites and the Amorites) (see *BHK³*). But since Qᵃ reads כעזובות, it would be better to read what is closer to the MT, as does Cheyne: . . . . עָרֵי מָעֻזּ כַּעֲזוּבוֹת (its fortified cities, as the abandoned of . . .).

10a נַעֲמָן (the lovely one) is frequently used to refer to the vegetation god (see below, pp. 182f.). נַעֲמָנִים is not a plural of quantity; instead, it is either a double plural, where two successive nouns in the plural express one compound idea (since the preceding noun in the absolute state is also plural, see Ges-K §124q; Joüon, *Gr* §136o), or as Jirku suggests (*VT* 7 [1957] 201f.), one could treat this as an incorrect pointing of a word that read originally *naʿaman-ma* (with mimation, as in Ugaritic; see Aistleitner, *WB* no. 1494).

10b The suffix נ - on a verb that is second feminine singular imperfect occurs nowhere else, for which reason some read simply תִּזְרְעִי (you will sow) (Duhm) or תִּזְרְעִי(ן) (you will sow) (Buhl, Procksch, Kaiser). But there is no reason to doubt that such a form existed (though one might not be sure exactly how it should be pointed). זרע (sow) can certainly be used with two accusative objects; see Judg. 9:45; Isa. 30:23; Ges-K §117ee. Naturally, the word ought not be eliminated as a "secondary way to fill out the parallelism" (Donner, here as elsewhere, is doomed to make mistakes because of his desire to establish a smooth metrical reading).

11a There is a wide divergence of opinion among scholars about whether תְּשַׂגְשֵׂגִי is from the root שׂגג (שׂגא, שׂגה), "to be big," or from שׂוג, "fence (about)" (see Song of Sol. 7:3) (שׂגג: Gray, Duhm, Marti, Fohrer, Kaiser, et al.; שׂוג: Hitzig, Procksch, Leslie, Ziegler, et al.). Since the salient feature of the little Adonis garden is that everything grows very fast there, the meaning "allow to become big" seems preferable.

11b Instead of בְּיוֹם (on a day), it has been suggested that the text read בְּיוֹם (on the day on which) (to coordinate with בְּבֹקֶר, "on the morning on which"; see *BHS*). This change would mean that נִטְעֵךְ (what you planted) becomes the object of תְּשַׂגְשֵׂגִי (you raised to maturity). One might do the opposite, pointing the second word בְּבֹקֶר (on a morning) (Bruno), and then translate it: "and, during morning time, when you plant." But one need not have perfect parallelism and one can hardly leave תַּפְרִיחִי (you made to sprout up) standing alone, with no object.

11c It is indeed tempting to follow Bruno, who reads תַּפְרִי, "who allows (it) to bear fruit," since this would allow for an advance in thought over that in v. 11aα (see יִפְרֶה, "will be fruitful," instead of what was originally יִפְרַח, "sprout forth," in 11:1), but even the most carefully done planting would not lead to someone expecting to get ripened fruit during the same morning on which one sows.

11d נֵד (dam, wall) makes no sense. The Gk and Targ seem to have read עַד (to, toward), which does not help either; Vulg reads *ablata est messis* (the harvest is taken away), which would seem to suggest that it read דָר (departed) (from נָדַד, "retreat, flee"). Maybe, at some point, אבד (perish) or a similar verb was read in the text.

11e נַחֲלָה is obviously not to be translated "inheritance" (Vulg: *hereditas*), but derives from חלה (be weak), as already noted by Ibn Ezra (*niphʿal* feminine participle, used as a substantive, or an abbreviation for מַכָּה נַחֲלָה, "grievous blow"; see Jer. 14:17). Perhaps it has simply to be emended to read מַחֲלָה (sickness) (so Donner).

11f–f For v. 11bβ the Gk reads: καὶ ὡς πατὴρ ἀνθρώπου κληρώσῃ τοῖς υἱοῖς σου (and, as a man's father, he will call to your sons); this means that it read כְּאָב אֱנוֹשׁ as if pointed כְּאָב אֱנוֹשׁ (as a man's father). According to Duhm², as the basis for τοῖς υἱοῖς σου (to your sons), there would have been a reading לבֵּנִיךָ (to your sons), which was an incorrect reading for what was originally לְפָנֶיךָ (before you), so that one would translate this something like: "even more bitter pains are still ahead of you," which, while paying due credit to Duhm's ability to reconstruct such a sequence, should still not be accepted, since the Gk is not all that trustworthy. One is still left with the question about whether וּכְאֵב אֱנוּשׁ (unremitting is your pain; lit.: and as human pain) is a second genitive phrase, governed by בְיוֹם (on that day), or whether, as is more likely, it is an independent noun clause, which gives more details about the situation ("during the time when the pain is most horrible").

Form

Verses 1-11 of Isaiah 17 are to be treated as a kerygmatic unit. It is misleading, however, to have all these verses introduced by the superscription מַשָּׂא דַמֶּשֶׂק (verdict against Damascus). Only vv. 1 and 3 deal with Damascus; from v. 4 on, the discussion is about "Jacob." The justification for treating vv. 1-11 as a unit, even if there are many levels within it, is that the destiny of Aram, mentioned in v. 3, is linked with that of Israel, so that there is a smooth transition in vv. 4ff. to the discussion about the end of the "majesty" of Jacob. Indeed, it is unlikely that the "you" [sing.] in vv. 10f. is also addressed to the Northern Kingdom, but the redactor certainly understood the referent in this way. Verses 12-14 lead one into a completely different setting, in which the issue is no longer threat, but rather being saved, and, even if it is not said in so many words, that message without question is directed toward the city of God, Jerusalem.

The stages of composition are very complex in vv. 1-11. That is seen already when one notes the introductory formulas in vv. 4, 7, 9, which make clear divisions in the text. But the prose nature of vv. 7f. and 9 (contrary to the attempt in *BHS* to read these as verse as well) also shows that the material passed through many stages before achieving its final form. There is still a wide divergence of opinion today about the way this material was composed, as can be seen by comparing the views of Fohrer, Donner, and Kaiser. Fohrer suggests that there are three main parts: vv. 1-6 are directed against Damascus and the Northern Kingdom, vv. 7 + 8 speak of a conversion at the end of time, and vv. 9-11 describe a sickness leading to death. Besides this, he treats vv. 1-6 as a conglomeration of six short messages from Isaiah: vv. 1f., 3, 4, 5a, 5b, 6. He considers vv. 7f. to be a late message from an unknown author, and presumes that vv. 9-11 are also "probably not from Isaiah." Donner's solution is radically different. Basing his views on Duhm's work, he considers vv. 1-11 as a single message from Isaiah, organized into three strophes: vv. 1-3, 4-6, and 10f. He treats v. 5a as secondary, has the same opinion about vv. 7f., 9, and believes that there are other additions, apparently glosses, which are to be removed. Still another, very different assessment is offered by Kaiser. He identifies four independent units: vv. 1-3 speak against Damascus and Israel, vv. 4-6 are about Israel's remnant, vv. 7f. are about the eschatological conversion, and vv. 9-11 are about the punishment for apostasy. He does not reject out of hand the possibility that vv. 10f. might be an authentic word from Isaiah, now in the wrong place, but he considers the other sections to be undatable material from the postexilic era. These are only examples of attempts to understand the way in which this group of passages, vv. 1-11, took shape; it will be necessary to discuss this question in further detail in the exposition that follows.

[17:1-3] The first section, vv. 1-3, is an announcement of judgment against Damascus, proclaimed as a message from Yahweh and separated from other material by means of the citation formula. The superscription was added by the redactor of the messages against foreign peoples. It has already been mentioned (see textual note 2a-a) that v. 2, which speaks of the "cities of Aroer," might originally have been part of the message addressed to Moab, since v. 2a has only one colon; the second one is missing. That in itself is an indication that the verse is no longer intact, which is not surprising if it has been misplaced from its original position within a different transmission complex. It also has long been noted that v. 2bβ, ורבצו ואין מחריד (they will lie down there, and no one will scare them away), sounds formulaic. The same little phrase is also used in Zeph. 3:13 and Job 11:19, and already Naegelsbach was of the opinion that this was an expansion to the text, based on its use in Job 11:19, later reproduced in Zeph. 3:13 (cf. Kaiser). One could be satisfied with the explanation that this is the only part of the verse to be treated as a later addition if v. 2a was intact and if v. 2bα did not also sound like a cliché (cf. 5:17; 27:10; 32:14; Zeph. 2:14). This means that all of v. 2 should be treated as an insertion.

[17:4-6] Verse 4 starts a new section once again, introduced by the formula והיה ביום ההוא (and it will happen on that day), and the citation formula is used still another time, at the end of v. 6, to bring this section to a conclusion. The phrase כבוד יעקב (majesty of Jacob) links this closely with the preceding message from Yahweh (see ככבוד בני־ישׂראל, "than the majesty of the children of Israel," in v. 3), but this part of the message has nothing more to do with Damascus; instead, it deals with a threat of disaster against "Jacob," intended here as another way to refer to the Northern Kingdom. Verse 4 uses imagery that makes a comparison to the way someone who is sick wastes away; v. 5 compares this to gleaning after grain has been harvested; v. 6 refers to the way one shakes fruit down from an olive tree. The rapid shift from image to image ought not lead one to look for what might be excised from the text.

Nonetheless, the introductory phrase, וְהָיָה בַּיּוֹם הַהוּא (and it will happen on that day), is not an original part of this message but is a redactional link, not as often happens (see בַּיּוֹם הַהוּא, "in that day," v. 7) only to serve the function of attaching a later comment, but correctly to show that the events described in both sections are identified as ready to happen at about the same time. Concerning the "authenticity" of v. 4, see below, pp. 169f.

[17:7f.] Without a doubt, in contrast to vv. 4-6, the prosaic material in vv. 7f. that comes between the poetic sections is certainly secondary. Someone from a later time speaks here, giving witness to his hope for the return of all human beings, not just Israel, back to God.

[17:9] It is also true that v. 9 is a later insertion; the phrase בַּיּוֹם הַהוּא (on that day) is a common indicator that one is dealing with an addition. The content of the verse depicts a harsh judgment for Israel. There is no doubt that still another author is speaking here. However, one must wonder if the prose v. 9 was originally linked directly to vv. 10 and 11, which are to be read metrically. The כִּי (truly) at the beginning of v. 10 seems to link the two parts together, with v. 10a providing the reason for the downfall that was threatened in v. 9. But it is highly unlikely that one would find a prose sentence linked together with what is otherwise poetic, to form one unit. In addition, v. 9 speaks about a "he" (see מָעֻזּוֹ, "his strong [cities]"), whereas vv. 10f. address a feminine singular "you," and v. 10b, introduced by עַל־כֵּן (therefore), has a threat of coming judgment that is much different from that originally formulated in v. 9. Thus one must also separate v. 9 from v. 10, with v. 9 being inserted secondarily, providing an introduction for vv. 10f.

[17:10f.] The question now follows whether vv. 10f., if one skips over vv. 7-9, might be the continuation of v. 6. Evidence to reject this suggestion is provided by the closing formula in v. 6 and also by the change from "he" to the feminine singular "you"; v. 10a is a message of rebuke; in vv. 10b, 11, one notes the threat that sets forth the consequences. This section is a unit all by itself; the כִּי at the beginning of v. 10 should be translated "truly," or something similar.

[17:1-11] A solution can now be proposed, one which is somewhere between that of Fohrer and that of Donner:

I. a. 17:1-3   The end of Damascus
    b. 17:4-6   The end of Israel
    c. 17:7f.   Addition to vv. 1-6. Humanity turns back toward Yahweh
II. a. 17:9   Secondary introduction to vv. 10f.
                 The destruction of strong cities
    b. 17:10f. The consequences of having forgotten God.

The reason why we do not conclude, as does Donner, among others,

163

that we can reconstruct these verses by peeling away what is later, so as to set forth an original single poem, will be discussed as we treat the setting of each individual unit and as we make further observations about the actual form of each.

[17:1-3] *The End of Damascus*

Form

If one eliminates the secondary superscription "the verdict against Damascus" and the inserted v. 2 (see above, pp. 156f.), then what remains is a prophetic announcement of judgment against the capital city of Aram.

> *Meter:* The poem begins with a seven-stress colon that, by the very length of the meter itself, conveys the gravity of the disaster (one also might note the darker sounds of the vowels in מוסרה, "eliminated," and מפלה, "pile of rubble," and the alliteration in the words that begin with מ). Verse 2 seems to begin with a five-stress colon, followed by a three-stress colon that does not have its second colon, another indication that the verse must have come from a different original context. Verse 3 is made up of 2 five-stress cola (in v. 3a one should once again note the alliteration formed by the many words that include the letter מ).

Setting

No reason is given for the downfall of Damascus, just as we are provided with virtually no information about why the destiny of Damascus is compared with that of Ephraim. Both of these problems are easily resolved when one is informed about the situation in which this message was delivered. There is no doubt that the Syro-Ephraimitic War provides the setting, as Rezin (or *ra'yān;* see *Isaiah 1–12,* p. 283) of Damascus and Pekah of Israel entered into an agreement to rebel against the mighty Assyria, which was pressing on into their territory under the leadership of Tiglath-Pileser, and who together wanted to convince Judah to join their anti-Assyrian coalition (see *Isaiah 1–12,* pp. 293ff.). There was hardly a time in their history when these two neighboring states were so closely allied with one another as they were then, when the end of the one unquestionably promised to mean a quick end for the other as well. Every attempt to date this material to a time later than the time when Tiglath-Pileser conquered Damascus in 732 runs into the problem that the monarchy of Damascus is mentioned. Kaiser's explanation, that the author clothed himself with "Isaiah's mantle," or that he would have been making observations about the city at a later time, when foreign rulers had restored the city to its former glory, could be accepted only if there were at least something in these two verses that would convince one to seek a time other than the general time period of 734. Of course, one might object that Damascus did not become a virtual desert in 732, turning instead, later on, into a lively center of activity as an Assyrian province. But Damascus certainly received a heavy blow in 732. In addition, one must keep in mind that

this passage deals with an announcement of judgment; it is not a description
of events as they took place (which is supported by the use of the verbal
forms ונשבת, "will disappear," and יהיו, "will be," in v. 3). It is on these
grounds that one can also explain why it apparently does not square with historical reality (Damascus fell in 732, Samaria not until 722/721), since this
text appears to suggest that Samaria would fall before Damascus. In reality,
as Tiglath-Pileser entered into the conflict, the Syro-Ephraimitic War, he first
"chastised" Israel and only then turned to engage Damascus. That is the only
way the second line of v. 3 makes sense, according to which the remnant of
Aram would have the same "majesty" as the sons of Israel; in 733 someone
in Judah could certainly have been of the opinion that the Northern Kingdom
of Israel would be defeated before the same would happen to Damascus,
since Israel was the weaker of these two states, which had united together.
Assyria's most important strategy was to open up the road to Egypt, which
Israel could easily blockade. Already in 733, with the establishment of three
Assyrian provinces on what was once their soil, the Northern Kingdom was
reduced to a level of absolute insignificance (see *Isaiah 1–12*, p. 394).

If this is a likely solution to the question about dating, then there is no
reason not to attribute this section to Isaiah. Almost everyone agrees that this
is authentic. Nonetheless, Kaiser suggests dating this section to a very late
(Hellenistic?) period. In light of the fact "that this city, which had once been
the chief Aramaic metropolis, continued to flourish, in spite of all the
onslaughts of time," it was expected "that it would also come to its final end
before the appearing of the era of salvation." It may be that such was the
mind-set of the redactor who brought these messages against the nations
together into a group, even though one still can hardly date this text that late.
Yet that does not alter the fact that vv. 1 and 3 are to be attributed to Isaiah.
If one would object that it was not Isaiah's style to threaten a judgment without including a mention of the reasons, then one should examine 14:28-32,
for just one example, where there is also no reason given for why the land of
the Philistines was to be held in the grip of plague after plague, each one
more destructive than the last. When studying the "authentic" messages of
Isaiah against the nations, one must keep in mind their intended function.
They were not supposed to summon whatever peoples were being addressed
to come to their senses, but also not to issue an oracle that would make
absolutely no demands of that people; rather, they were to protect Israel from
the illusion that Aram, Philistia, or whatever other people was being
addressed could successfully resist the well-planned assault by means of
which Assyria was steadily pressing on.

Commentary

[17:1] The message begins with the presentative הנה (behold), which is frequently chosen to introduce an announcement of disaster (see 3:1; 8:7;
10:33; 13:9, and often elsewhere), intending to draw attention to an unexpected event.

Damascus, as the capital city of the Aramean state to the northeast, was always in Israel's field of vision. At the time of Solomon, this city was instrumental in establishing the Aramean kingdom to the south of the Syrian high plateau. This new state's desire to expand is seen in efforts to advance into middle and even northern Syria, but also in attempts to expand the amount of land that it controlled to the south, at the expense of the Northern Kingdom of Israel. The Omri dynasty was able to stand up to the Aramean pressure to expand, but Hazael threatened to take away from Israel whatever power of resistance it had, at the time of Jehoahaz (2 Kings 13:3ff.), and was even able to advance to the point of being in a position to demand tribute payments from Jerusalem (2 Kings 12:18f.). It was only at the time of Jeroboam II that the attempt to win back the land east of the Jordan was successful, that which the Arameans had torn away from Israel (2 Kings 10:32ff.). But Amos already must have seen that the days of Damascus were drawing to a close (1:3ff.). If one looks at other passages besides this present one, both 7:8 and 8:4 show that Isaiah also expected that the end for Damascus was not far off. In that, he was not to be disappointed; the destiny in store for the Aramaic city of Damascus came upon it even more quickly than he expected.

The end of Damascus was so real for Isaiah that he uses the participle מוסרה, literally: "it is put out of the way," and takes a risk by stating plainly: מעיר, "it is no longer a city." What is left after that is מעי מפלה: "a scene of the wreckage of a collapse." Obviously, it would be enough to use either מעי (wreckage, pile) or מפלה (collapse, rubble), but linking both terms together underscores the totality and finality of the collapse. מעי is a hapax legomenon; it was probably selected because it contributed to the alliteration; the related term עי (heap of ruins) is also not all that common in predictions of coming disaster (see Mic. 3:12; Jer. 26:18 is about Jerusalem; Mic. 1:6 is about Samaria). מַפֵּלָה (rubble) is another hapax legomenon; the closely related מַפֵּלָה (ruin) is used otherwise only in 23:13 and 25:2, and the *hiphʿil* of סור (cause to turn aside, be eliminated) is never used anywhere else to describe the destruction of cities (which ought not lead one to conclude that the text should be questioned on text-critical grounds; contra Duhm, Marti, Donner). The vocabulary is not polished and smoothed, which speaks in favor of Isaiah as the source.

[17:3] It is surprising that v. 3aα mentions the destruction of the fortress from Ephraim. Rejecting the solution offered by some commentators, we have already explained (see p. 157) that this cannot refer to some place like Damascus or even to the Aramean empire as a whole. There is certainly no question that Isaiah had anticipated that Samaria would come to an end; see 28:1ff. and also 7:4ff. Concerning the usage of שבת (will disappear), see above, p. 56. מבצר is used to describe a "protected place" (cf. נִבְצָר, "inaccessible, be impossible," and בָּצַר, "make inaccessible"). It is often used in a genitive relationship with עיר (city), but can also, in and of itself, mean a "fortified city"; cf. the place-name Bozrah (see E. Jenni, *BHH* I, 269). In fact, Samaria is best able to fulfill the requirements for what is needed for a

מבצר (fortress), both because of its location and because of the measures that were taken to fortify it (cf. passages such as 1 Kings 20 and see K. Elliger, *BHH* III, 1655–1660). Shalmaneser V had to besiege the city for three whole years before it finally fell into his hands (2 Kings 17:5ff.; see *Isaiah 1–12*, pp. 419f.). Previous to that time, the Assyrians had taken the last king, Hoshea, as a prisoner, and the entire area, which had remained under the control of Israel/Ephraim after the bloodletting in 732, had already come into their hands. When Samaria fell, there was no hope left for Ephraim, just as the fall of Damascus sealed that country's fate and led to the downfall of the Aramean kingdom. It is Isaiah's style to speak of the Northern Kingdom as "Ephraim" (7:2, 9, 17; 9:8; 28:1, 3; on this, see *Isaiah 1–12*, p. 230), though Hosea uses this term as well.

Parallel to the "fortress from Ephraim," the phrase "monarchy from Damascus" is mentioned. It is one of the rules of Hebrew poetry that slightly different nuances are communicated by elements that stand in parallel, but it is most interesting to see *how* that is carried out here: On the one hand, in northern Israel the monarchy was an unstable institution; the dynasties changed, one after another, in quick succession; kings were always preoccupied with trying to hold onto their position. In Damascus, on the other hand, the monarchy was not up for grabs but was a very stable institution. During the roughly two hundred years that it lasted, only a few kings ruled over the Aramean Empire, and the only change in dynasty came at the time when Hazael took the throne. One could certainly entertain the possibility that Israel could survive without the monarchy, and there were some who thought that this would be the ideal (cf. Hos. 8:4), but the Aramean Empire would stand and fall with its monarchy.

In spite of the "complete" destruction of Damascus, Isaiah expects that there will be a "remnant" for Aram (concerning שאר, see H. Wildberger, *THAT* II, 844–855). Even for Israel, there was a remnant after the downfall of the state as an independent entity and after the deportation of the upper levels of society, of course one which lived in poverty and shame; and naturally one can speak about the "majesty of the children of Israel" only with irony or in bitterness. One can see in 16:14, in a threat of judgment, how one might try to portray how the "majesty" of a people could be turned into "contemptuousness" (see p. 152 for a discussion about כבוד, "majesty," in such contexts, and cf. also 10:16). In general, having כבוד, "majesty, honor, fame," would naturally be treated in a positive light in the OT. A people's כבוד would be shown in its size and in the wonderful way its cities developed, how its culture blossomed, how important its political might was, how it carried out its economic activity, and how it was viewed by the neighboring peoples. Israel was convinced of its own majesty (Mic. 1:15; cf. 1 Sam. 4:21f.), but part of its hope for the future was that it would become glorious (Isa. 62:2, 12). Here, however, the "majesty" is not just supposed to describe a shiny veneer, not just to show off one's luxury items, not simply a claim to be powerful, which would have no basis in fact; cf. 5:14. Isaiah also speaks of the

בני ישראל (children of Israel) in 31:6, there in reference to all of Israel. In this passage, the reference is intended primarily as a way to designate the inhabitants of the Northern Kingdom. But the double entendre inherent in this designation must be taken into account. The majesty of the בני־ישראל (children of Israel) was not all that safe for those who dwelt in Jerusalem, though there were some who thought so. Concerning the citation formula, cf. *Isaiah 1–12*, p. 66. There is no reason to deny that Isaiah is responsible for its being in the text.

[17:2] The message in v. 2, which has been incorrectly inserted here, speaks about the Moabite city of Aroer having been abandoned, known today as *ḥirbet ʿarāʿir*, located on the northern side of the Arnon, about 4 km. east of the present road, the one that runs from *mādebā* through *dibān* toward *er-rabba* and *el-kerak* (see the map, p. 130). This city controlled the route that led across the fords of the Arnon. Once it had belonged to the Amorite state of Heshbon; then it came under the control of Reuben or Gad (Josh. 13:9, 16; Num. 32:34), subsequently being conquered by King Mesha (Mesha Inscription, line 26; see also Jer. 48:19). Concerning the excavations at the *ḥirbe* (which have been confined to the area where the fortifications were constructed), see E. Olávarri, "Sondages à ʿArôʿer sur l'Arnon," *RB* 72 (1965) 77–94; idem, *ZDPV* 82 (1966) 283f. Since the present text speaks about the cities of Aroer, we have an indication that it played an important role at that time, which means it certainly could have been the capital city of a Moabite district (cf. ערי חברון, "cities of Hebron," in 2 Sam. 2:3, and ערי שמרון, "cities of Samaria," in 2 Kings 13:22; 17:24, 26; 23:19).

It is a favorite theme that one would speak about the abandonment of cities or territory in such announcements of disaster (see 6:11 and, in a passage that follows closely after this one, 17:9; cf. Jer. 4:29; Zeph. 2:4).

Concerning רבץ (lie down), see 11:6f.; 13:21; 14:30; and 27:10. It is usually said that herds of animals will graze on the ruins. It is another step to say that they would dwell permanently in that area. It means that it is as if they are going to be at home there, that they will feel safe and sound. The final little phrase intimates the same thing: ואין מחריד (and no one will scare them away); this same phrase is used in Lev. 26:6, but in a very different way, namely, to describe the rest that the people will be able to enjoy because they are protected from wild animals and enemies; similar thoughts about the remnant of Israel are expressed in Zeph. 3:13; Ezek. 34:28; 39:26; see also Mic. 4:4; cf. also Jer. 30:10; 46:27; Job 11:19. A passage that is still closer to what is said here is Nah. 2:12, which mentions the dens of lions, in which no one can startle them; cf. also Jer. 7:33, and especially Deut. 28:26. One has the impression that ואין מחריד (and no one will scare them away) was originally a phrase used in portrayals of the salvation that would come in the future, being used here in an unusual way to depict the very opposite. It has shock value when one finds a phrase, which spoke originally of peace and security in the future time of salvation, now being used to set the scene for a harsh announcement of disaster.

Purpose and Thrust

[17:1 + 3] The announcement that the end of Damascus was close at hand fits best into what Isaiah proclaimed during the era of the Syro-Ephraimitic War. It is apparent, from 7:1-9 and 8:1-4, that the goal of such a prediction of disaster was not to announce the downfall of a neighboring state, but rather to warn those who might have raised false expectations in light of the political-military situation. In the present circumstances that would mean the following warning: Do not consider it possible that the anti-Assyrian coalition can be successful in slowing down the Assyrian steamroller that was rolling their way. It is not stated in so many words here, but the idea is there anyway, that the only hope for Israel remains: entrust yourselves to Yahweh: "If you do not believe, then you will not remain."

[17:2] In spite of v. 2 being an intrusion in the flow from v. 1 to v. 3, in its own way, in the present context, it still underscores the finality of the end of Damascus. Its insertion into the text is characteristic of the tendency to intensify the message, something observed already in other passages in the book of Isaiah (cf. 2:23f.; 14:21-23; 16:13f.).

[17:4-6] *The End of Israel*

Form

[17:4] It has already been established above (pp. 162f.) that the introductory formula in v. 4 is a later addition. One must ask, however, whether the whole verse should be treated as secondary. One can hardly deny that the imagery is from a very different setting when compared with that in vv. 5f. But such a quick change from one image to another is not really a problem for an OT poet. One would come to a false conclusion if one would assume that v. 4, which speaks about the כבוד יעקב (majesty of Jacob), was written with v. 3 in mind, with its mention of כבוד בני־ישראל (majesty of the children of Israel); it is much more likely that the mention of כבוד (majesty) in both passages is the reason why the redactor linked them together, following the principle of linking passages that have a key word in common. In fact, Procksch thinks that it would have been difficult to have said that the Northern Kingdom was fat after the bloodletting in 734, which would mean that Isaiah would have used משמן (fat) and רזון (will waste away) to speak of fields (10:16), not of bodies. But there is no compelling reason to believe that this present message was delivered only *after* Tiglath-Pileser made his powerful advance into the territory that was under Israel's control in 733 (not 734, as Procksch maintains), so that this argument against the authenticity of the passage does not hold up either. Just because words are used both in 17:4 and 10:16, but speak in a different way about wasting away, does not in itself provide sufficient reason for denying the authorship to Isaiah, since metaphors can be used in different ways, depending on the circumstances. Contrary to the view of Procksch, however, we expressed in *Isaiah 1–12* that 10:16ff. could not have come from Isaiah. One frequently observes that the later expanders to the text do use Isaiah's imagery and way of speaking, but do not consider themselves precluded thereby from using such forms to suit their own purposes. In addition, the imagery that describes wasting away seems to be used more appropriately in 17:4 rather than in 10:16, since it refers not to lush stretches of land here, but to a personified version of Israel/Jacob. Thus no compelling reasons have been given for rejecting the notion that v. 4 and vv. 5f. form a single unit. Just on external grounds, one notes that the two parts of this passage belong together when it is observed that the suffix on בו (for it) can only have יעקב (Jacob) as a referent, in v. 4. The entire passage speaks about the destiny of the Northern Kingdom.

Meter: Verse 4a (after the introductory formula has been excluded from consideration) is to be read as a three-stress + three-stress bicolon, the same being true of v. 5a (if קציר, "during the harvest," is bracketed out); vv. 5b, 6aα, and 6aβ are all five-stress cola (though v. 6aα leaves one with the impression that it is rhythmically damaged). In v. 6b, excluding the closing formula, the section concludes with a two-stress + two-stress bicolon. One notes here how the verses become shorter, going from six-stress to five-stress to a two-stress + two-stress bicolon; the fall of the "majesty of Jacob" is virtually illustrated by the very rhythm of the verses.

Setting

Nothing speaks against Isaiah as the author, and, with the single exception of Kaiser, scholars agree that this is to be attributed to Isaiah, even though one might have to admit that there are a few expansions to the text (see above, pp. 162f.). One can be confident about dating this message to the time just before Tiglath-Pileser invaded the Palestinian arena in 733 (Donner, 41, between 735 and 733); on the one hand, it is likely a bit later than the confrontation between the prophet and Ahaz depicted in chap. 7; on the other hand, it would have taken place before 17:1, 3, since, according to v. 3, the כבוד (majesty) of the Israelites had been "heavily damaged," whereas, according to v. 6, it was apparently still intact.

Commentary

[17:4] "The majesty of Jacob will become small." In this case, "Jacob" does not refer to Israel as the people of Yahweh but to the Northern Kingdom, and it is certainly possible that Isaiah could speak this way (although בית יעקב, "house of Jacob," in 2:5; 8:17 would refer to all of Israel; concerning יעקב, Jacob, as a designation for Northern Israel, see *Isaiah 1–12,* p. 230). In this case also, כבוד (majesty) is used in a slightly ironic sense; it will now become apparent that the majesty of Israel was not nearly as majestic as one might have supposed at the time, within its own boundaries (cf. passages such as Amos 6:13). The Northern Kingdom was more important that little Judah, and those who lived in Jerusalem had certainly noted, with displeasure, the feeling of disdain with which the Northern Kingdom looked south, so that from time to time Judah also reacted to that opinion in a sarcastic and crabby way.

The comparison between a state whose claim to be in control rests on shaky ground and a heavyset man, whose "fat" disappears quickly when he is struck down by a sickness, hits the nail on the head. The text does not actually speak of his fat, but of the "fat of his flesh"; בשׂר (flesh) characterizes human beings on the basis of their weakness and with the view that they will one day pass away.

[17:5] Following the image of wasting away, that of the harvesting of a grain crop is used: "It will take place, as when someone hurriedly collects the stalks and (while doing so, with) his arm cuts off the heads of grain." By means of the inversion in the second colon, it is shown that the other activities connected with this harvesting are being described as well: the harvester gathers a bundle of the stalks with the left arm, using the sickle with the right hand—not directly at ground level, but somewhat below where the heads of the grain are formed—to cut the grain off. According to observations made in modern times, this technique leaves stubble about 20–30 cm. high, which provides the necessary nourishment for grazing herds. When one's hand is full, then one would set the bundle of heads of grain (*צבה, Ruth 2:16) to the side (see Dalman, *AuS* III, 37, 44, and illuss. 5 and 7ab). When such a technique is used for harvesting, the young girls who would go out to glean would not have much chance to find anything. Only a very little would be left for gleaning, whatever by some chance fell onto the ground. For this reason, Boaz instructed the harvesters: "You must also pull some handfuls for her [Ruth] from the bundles, and leave them for her to glean." Also, according to the regulations recorded in Lev. 19:9 and 23:22, one was not to harvest a field completely, all the way into the corners, so that there might be some left for the poor and the foreigners, which shows how little could have been gathered when someone went to glean. According to Mishnah *Pe'a* 4:10 and *Siphre Qedoshim* 87d, the young girl who was gleaning could not even claim what dropped from the hand of a harvester when he was stuck by a thorn or when a scorpion bit him (according to Dalman, *AuS* III, 42). Thus everyone who was listening to Isaiah clearly got the message about what the prophet wanted to say with his comparison: there is hardly anything left. But then he retraces his steps and says the same thing in still another way: "It will take place, as when someone leaves heads of grain in the Valley of Rephaim." (Concerning לקט, "glean," see G. Rinaldi, *BeO* 13 [1971] 210.) That goes one step beyond what was said in the previous line. There is not much left after the grain has been cut; moreover, after the young girls have finished their gleaning, then there is virtually nothing left to find. This is how thoroughly the enemies of Jacob/Israel will carry out their work.

When mention is made of the Valley of Rephaim, just as in Josh. 15:8; 18:6; 2 Sam. 5:18, 22; 23:13; 1 Chron. 11:15; 14:9, this use here also refers to the valley *el-baqʿa* (southwest of ancient Jerusalem; see Josh. 18:6; today, in the new city, it is situated between the train station and the city quarter *qaṭamōn*). The name רפאים (Rephaim) may have come from the fact that those who lived there made a connection between the archaeological remains, which were found in this valley, and the giants, who were known as the רפאים (Rephaim) (concerning the רפאים, Rephaim, as a pre-Israelite population who lived there, see above, pp. 60f.). It is possible that Isaiah speaks specifically about this valley because it was from there that the Philistines had once threatened Jerusalem (2 Sam. 5:18), but the explanation is probably much simpler, that all the inhabitants of Jerusalem and its environs were thoroughly familiar with this tract of land, and it was probably the only place anywhere around Jerusalem where any significant amounts of grain were planted and harvested (see Dalman, *Jerusalem,* illuss. 33ff.; and *AuS* I/2, illus. 31). This information is important for understanding this passage, since it shows that the message could have been spoken only in Jerusalem; indeed, it mentions "Jacob," but it is not addressed to the Northern Kingdom; rather, it is to be heard by the citizens of Jerusalem.

[17:6] Verse 6 continues with an image drawn from the life of the Palestinian farmers, the olive harvest. Grain, wine, and oil are the most significant products for those who lived on the land, being mentioned together time and time again (Lev. 23:13; Deut. 28:39; Amos 6:6, and often elsewhere). Every Israelite knew what happened when it came time to harvest the olives, in October. Deut. 24:20 states it clearly; "When you beat (חבט) (the fruit of) your olive trees, do not strip what is left; it shall be for the alien, the orphan, and the widow." This means that they did not only gather the olives that fell to the ground on their own, but they also beat the branches with a stick. A similar approach is still used today for harvesting the olives in Palestine (Arabic: *šdād ez-zētūn,* "the knocking down of the olives"). The men climb into the trees, use their hands to strip off from the trees whatever fruit they can reach, and then beat the fruit off the more distant branches with a stick or a thin pole. After this, the women and young girls pick up the fruit from the ground, normally from where it falls on top of a cloth that has been spread out on the ground (on this, cf. also Isa. 24:13). Jewish law distinguished between "picking off" (מסק, Mishnah *Peʾa* 8:1) and "knocking off" (נקף, *Giṭṭin* 5:8) the olives. To knock the fruit off the branches can damage the trees and reduce the crop the following year, but it has the advantage that one is able, one might say, to gather in the entire crop (see Dalman, *AuS* IV, 190–195 and illuss. 44–46; see also Pliny, *Natural History* 15.3: "*lex antiquissima fuit: oleam ne stringito neve verberato,*" "in fact there was a very old regulation for the olive harvest: 'Neither strip nor beat an olive-tree,'" [Loeb edition], and cf. Varro, *De Re Rustica* 1.55). Certainly, Isaiah speaks about knocking the fruit off on purpose; whatever is still left on the tree, to be gleaned, after this procedure is complete would hardly be worth mentioning. The present passage should certainly not be used as a source for understanding Isaiah's ideas about his "concept of a remnant"; the speaker clearly would not try to make a further point, as if to suggest that there would still be a turning back or that there would be a future in store for such a remnant, which would bring a time of salvation: no importance is attached to the עוללה (gleaning); cf. Mic. 7:1 and Jer. 49:9.

Normally, both the fruit of the olive tree and the tree itself are known as זית; here the hapax legomenon נרגר (ripe fruit) is used (but see Sir. 50:10). In rabbinic Hebrew the word is also used to refer to "berries, grape berries, little seeds, anything which is round," and thus it is not used only for olives (see Arabic *jirjir*, "beans," *jurjur, jarjar*, "very ripe olives").

Concerning the citation formula, see *Isaiah 1–12*, pp. 66f. That there is a different reading here, so that, instead of יהוה צבאות (Yahweh of Hosts), as in v. 3, it reads יהוה אלהי ישראל (Yahweh, the God of Israel), may have just happened by chance; in any case, one also ought not accept the suggestion offered by Duhm and Marti here—just because of the meter of the verse—that צבאות (of Hosts) be read here as well. It is possible, however, that Isaiah consciously used the designation "the God of Israel" in this passage dealing with Jacob/Israel, rather than the term צבאות (Sebaoth, of Hosts), which is a typical epithet within the context of Jerusalem theology. This usage makes the message even harsher: the God who had become known as the God of Israel announces here that the political state known as Israel was going to go out of existence.

Purpose and Thrust

As with the previous message about Damascus, one notices in vv. 4-6 that the reason for the announcement of disaster is completely missing. One might be even more puzzled that Isaiah of Jerusalem would not give any indication that he had feelings of sympathy about what was going to happen to these blood relatives. Based on what has been observed already, however, this message may have come into existence about the same time as the announcement of judgment now found in 9:7-20 and 5:25-29. There Isaiah made clear that Israel had ignored every opportunity which had been offered, so that finally nothing was left but a bitter end, to be dealt out by the irresistible enemy coming from afar. What was now waiting for Israel was the final phase of the unending, bitter tragedy, which had been played out between Yahweh, the God of Israel, and his people. To express sorrow at this point would show that Isaiah did not accept the verdict that the divine judgment, in all its severity, was deserved. One must also take into account that the present passage is not addressed to Israel; Isaiah is addressing Jerusalem. He has to speak in such graphic terms about the hopeless situation of the kingdom of their relatives so that no one would be so foolish as to believe that Judah's future might lie in making a treaty with the Northern Kingdom. There is apparently even a greater danger, namely, that the leaders of the Judean political community were in the position where they were making a false assessment about a possible relationship with the powers of the day, being ready to throw themselves into the arms of the Assyrians: that was a political decision which would make no sense for them, seeing as how the Northern Kingdom, just as Damascus, had no future. The majesty of Jacob had come to an end! Because of Isaiah's passionate desire to keep them from making such a fatal decision, it makes good sense that Isaiah would use a series of images which would confront his hearers in the harshest way possible, by depicting all hope for Israel's future as illusory. He had seen more clearly what was going on than had his partner in the discussion, "whose heart [at the advance of Aram and Israel] shook, as the trees shake in the wind" (7:2).

[17:7-8] *Addition to vv. 1-6; Humanity Turns Back toward Yahweh*

Form and Setting

For Isaiah himself, the message in vv. 4-6 was focused directly on the situation at hand. He did not consider himself to have been authorized to speak about what could happen to Israel in the distant future. But it is understandable that people who came later were no longer able to hear the announcement of disaster spoken against Israel and Damascus in its original, historical context and in the actual sense that the prophet intended when he spoke. They carried the thought still further: in spite of all the disasters that were anticipated, there would still be a time of restoration in the future. When all human attempts to help themselves had failed, that would then provide the greatest opportunity, namely, it would be time to turn back to their God. The author does not speak any longer about Damascus, says nothing more about Israel, but speaks simply about אדם (the human). For the individual, God is still the Holy One of Israel, but the reference to the Holy One of Israel is preceded by mentioning one of his names, one identifying him as creator. The final destinies that were in store for Damascus and Israel provided timeless examples to prove that godless human beings must finally fail in all they attempt. Whereas Fohrer is careful to say that the reference to the creator would permit one "to conclude that 'on that day' would not refer to the same time period as the judgment to which Isaiah's message has just referred, but should be considered a reference to the end of time," Kaiser considers it a "foregone conclusion that 'on that day' refers to the great Day of Yahweh, which was depicted so impressively in 2:6ff." But the end of time is not at issue, neither here nor there, at least not in so many words, and the emphasis placed on the creator and his work results from the fact that human beings in general are the topic of conversation, not Israel. ביום ההוא (on that day) serves here, just as in v. 4, to point to two events that will take place concurrently. Of course, one must still take into account that the author of vv. 7f. did not treat the message in vv. 1-6 in its original, historical context, but rather as it provided a fitting example of how all human solutions to problems ultimately fail. In this sense, one can treat ביום ההוא (on that day) as an eschatological designation of time, but one must then be aware that such an "eschatological" occurrence would be nothing other than the time when humans would turn back toward Yahweh, something that would take place within the framework of historical continuity. It is not said, and ought not be inferred, that Yahweh himself would set a new beginning in motion.

In Deutero-Isaiah, Yahweh is designated as the creator (עשׂה); see also Pss. 115:15; 121:2; 124:8; 134:3; 146:6 (creator of the cosmos); Hos. 8:14; Ps. 95:6 (creator of Israel); Prov. 22:2; Job 31:5; 32:22 (creator of human beings). Isaiah himself speaks of the "Holy One of Israel," as does Deutero-Isaiah, and the undertones perceived in Deutero-Isaiah seem to be heard here as well (Yahweh is the Holy One because he is the helper, the redeemer; see 41:14; 43:3; 49:7). One is also reminded of Deutero-Isaiah when the theology of creation is mentioned. Since the Holy One of Israel is the creator, it is not surprising that he is described here, without further clarification, as one who has a relationship with human beings (but see also Isa. 2:9, 11, 17, 20). This addition may have been inserted at about the same time that Deutero-Isaiah was taking shape.

Commentary

[17:7f.] In 5:12 Isaiah had lamented: "but they do not pay attention to (הביט) the activity of Yahweh, and they do not observe (ראה) the work of his hands." These two verses (vv. 7f.) sound even more like 31:1: ולא שעו על־קדוש ישׂראל (but do not look to the Holy One of Israel): the obstinacy of the human beings, which the prophet censures in that passage, would be overcome, according to the view of the author of vv. 7f., as the impression left by the judgment would lead them to see what they would have to do differently. On the one hand, when Isaiah spoke about the "activity" of Yahweh, he was thinking about his actions within history; on the other hand, the expander thinks of Yahweh as the creator, who would be recognized by human beings as such. In may be that שעה (look directly at) was chosen, superficially, because it made a wordplay with עשׂה (made) possible. But the meaning of שעה (look intently at), when compared with the parallel word ראה (see), furnishes a particular nuance: it refers not only to a dispassionate "looking" but to a "paying careful attention to," which purposely orients someone to observe exactly what is happening (Akkadian: *še'û*, "see, look around, search for, be on the lookout for someone"). In 31:1 the parallel phrase reads: ואת־יהוה לא דרשׁו (or consult Yahweh; lit.: and Yahweh they do not seek out). "Viewing Yahweh" is not far removed in meaning from דרשׁ יהוה (consult Yahweh) and ידע יהוה (know Yahweh) and has some connection to Isaiah's use of האמין (believe). In the present passage, nothing more is said about the implications of such a looking toward Yahweh.

What the human no longer would look toward is at least identified: no longer "upon the botched work of his hands" and not to "that which his fingers made." The terms מעשׂה ידיו (work of his hands) and אצבעתיו (his fingers; namely, Yahweh's) are used elsewhere in settings that deal with creation theology; see Pss. 8:4; 19:2; 102:26; 138:8; 143:5. In this passage, however, both the suffixes refer to a human being, characterized thereby as a pseudo-creator, that is, just as 2:8 should undoubtedly be interpreted, as a "creator" of "images" in which he places his trust.

The question about what is intended when these works of his hands and fingers are mentioned was also on the mind of the reader who furnished the glosses: המזבחות (the altars) and האשרים והחמנים (the cultic pillars and incense altars). Altars, *asherah*s, and incense altars are all located on high places where worship is conducted, which in this context would mean that they must refer to what was commonly used in the Canaanite fertility cult.

The designation חמן (incense altar) is used eight times in the OT, always in the plural, and is not used before the time of Ezekiel (6:4-6). It is possible that it refers to a cultic object that would have first been introduced into Judah in the late preexilic era (from the region of Arabia?). חמנים (incense altars) are mentioned only in contexts describing the destruction of heathen cultic installations. They are part of the inventory of the במה (high places) and are spoken about in Ezek. 6:4 along with the altars, in 2 Chron. 34:3ff. in a report about Josiah's reform, along with the מסכות (cast images), במות (high places), אשרים (*asherah*s, sacred poles), פסילים (carved images), and מזבחות הבעלים (altars of the Baals); see also Isa. 27:9. It is interesting to compare the passages in Chronicles with the notations made in the books of Kings, which served as its source. 2 Chron. 14:4 speaks of במות (high places) and חמנים (incense altars), which Asa removed, but the parallel passage 1 Kings 15:9ff. speaks about the banishment of the קדשים (male temple prostitutes), setting aside the גללים (idols) of his ancestors, and chopping down his mother's *asherah* image (מפלצת לאשרה); within the description of the cultic reform led by Josiah, the book of Kings does not make mention of the חמנים (incense altars). Thus the חמנים (incense altars), which first become known rather late in Israel, dislodged the older cultic objects that were listed in earlier texts.

The OT passages permit one to come to little more than hypothetical conclusions about how the חמנים (incense altars) looked and how they were used. One notes in 2 Chron. 34:4: החמנים אשר־למעלה מעליהם = "the חמנים, which are on them [namely, the altars]"; it is also possible that one could translate this: "those which are situated above them (on an elevated place)." Some commentators have taken this to mean that the חמנים (incense altars) were some sort of ornamental attachment placed on the normal altar. A number of different verbs are used to describe their destruction: כרת (*hiph'il;* cut off); שבר (*niph'al;* be broken); גדע (*pi'el, niph'al;* hew down, off, in two); סור (*hiph'il;* take away); נתץ (*pi'el;* tear down). There is never any mention of burning; the term must refer to objects fashioned of stone, which were set up on the cultic high places. The Gk translates this term with τεμένη (official place) (Ezek. 6:4, 6); ξύλινα χειροποίητα (wooden object made with hands) (Lev. 26:30); εἴδωλα (idol) (Isa. 27:9; 2 Chron. 14:4); ὑψηλά (high place) (2 Chron. 34:4, 7); and βδελύγματα (abomination) (Isa. 17:8); by this time, it is not understood as a reference to a specific object; the same is true in the Vulg (*simulacra,* "image," or *delubra,* "shrine"—or sometimes even *fana,* "holy place"; the translation in 2 Chron. 14:4 is very loose), a fact that should surprise no one.

Considering this state of affairs, one can understand why no one has been able to demonstrate clearly what was meant by חמנים. On the one hand, Rashi had already suggested deriving the word from חמה, "sun" (Job 30:28; Isa. 24:23; 30:26; Song of Sol. 6:10), and gave it the meaning "sun pillars." On the other hand, since the time of Grotius (*Annotationes*), the word also has been translated as "fire altar." Contemporary scholarship has vacillated, right up to the present, between these two meanings, either sun pillars or a particular type of altar. Some see a relationship between the OT חמנים and the Phoenician/Punic בעל חמן (Baal Hamon). In an earlier era, partially because of the supposition that "sun pillars" was the meaning of חמן, some thought it could have been a reference to a *Baal solaris* (Baal of the sun). But there is no place in the OT where any role is played by a cult of the sun, up on במות (high places). Others opt for בעל חמן being the local Baal of a place named *ḥammon* (or, as Eissfeldt suggests, of the Amanus mountain range; see *KlSchr* II, 58). Therefore the original setting for the OT term חמנים must have something to do with images of this deity. However, some call this solution into question, observing that it is most frequently mentioned in conjunction with altars. Ingholt (FS Dussaud II, 798) has called attention to the Palmyrene altar inscription, *CIS* II, 3978: "In the month of Elul, in the year 396, Lishamash and Zebida erected and dedicated this חמנא and this altar (עלתא) . . . for Shamash, the god of the house of their father." The altar includes a relief depicting the two who were the donors, Lishamash and Zebida, in front of an incense altar having the form of a candelabra, upon which a fire flames forth, into which the two of them are throwing little kernels of incense (at least Ingholt thinks he can detect that the scene depicts that this is happening; illus. in Ingholt, 798). Most of the recent scholars have tended to opt for treating חמן as an appellative for the incense altar, which certainly fits with the basic meaning of the root חמם (be warm, hot). This would mean that Baal, when called בעל חמן (Baal Hamon), would then be designated as the god who could typically be represented with the incense altar; he is perceived to be present in the fire that burns on it. This interpretation would not be invalidated by having חמנא mentioned in Palmyra in connection with Shamash; incense altars could be of service to a variety of deities.

The question about the specific form of the חמנים (incense altars) is still under discussion. According to Elliger, it refers to a four-sided altar, such as is found on the inscription mentioned above (with further reference to finds in Palmyra, Gezer, and Shechem; for Gezer, see *BHH* I, 63, illus. 1:2), whereas Ingholt thinks this would more likely refer to the stands in the shape of a candelabra, which are between Lishamash and Zebida on the relief of the altar, to which reference was just made. Galling (69f.) has suggested that חמנים are "small, four-footed incense boxes, decorated with geometric patterns," as have been found in Uruk, Babylon, Assyria, and Nippur. If this is the case, it would make good sense that the חמנים could have been placed on the altar, a situation one must presume according to the standard translation of 2 Chron. 34:4.

אשרה (*asherah*) is used in the OT both as the name of a female deity and as a designation for one of her cultic objects. Hebrew אשרה (*asherah*) corresponds to Ugaritic *aṯrt*, which is apparently the feminine form of Ugaritic *aṯr*, "holy place"; see Albright, *AJSL* 41, 100; Gese, 150. The word is clearly a personal name for a feminine deity; to personify a holy place is not all that uncommon. The deity is the consort of El, the head of the Ugaritic pantheon. She is listed right after Baal in offering lists. More specifically, she can be identified as *rbt aṯr ym* (Lady ʾAṯir[a]t of the Sea) (*UT* 49:16f., 19, 25; 51:I:14f., 22, and often elsewhere), but also as *qnyt ilm* (creatrix of the gods) (51:I:23; 51:III:26, 30, 35, and often elsewhere). This summarizes her basic functions: she is the mother of the gods and the goddess of the sea. One last point might be added, that, among her servants, she employed a fisherman (51:II:31; ʿnt VI:10). Her main role, however, was as the mother goddess, and she carried out maternal activities (52:24; 128:II:26, and often elsewhere).

In the OT, Asherah belongs with Baal (Judg. 3:7; 6:25ff.; 2 Kings 17:16; 21:3), which already seems to have been the way she was connected with the other gods by the Canaanites in Palestine. One supposes that this shift to Baal is linked to the gradual amalgamation of the Canaanite mother deities Astarte and Anat with Asherah. Since El was commonly identified with Yahweh in Israel, Asherah could no longer appear as El's spouse, so that it was a welcome step to get rid of her by linking her with Baal instead. Asherah took on the role that had been played by the Ugaritic Anat, who amazingly is never mentioned in the OT, except as part of a place-name or personal name, though she must have been known in Israel, since her name reappears in the Judean colony at Elephantine.

In the ancient Israelite era, Asherah was worshiped as the female fertility deity. That results from her being linked to Baal and explains why she received such harsh treatment and rejection (a subject, among other places, in the story about Maacah, the mother of King Asa, who constructed an image of Asherah that is referred to as a מפלצת, "an abominable image"). The women found themselves particularly drawn to the Asherah cult (cf. 1 Kings 15:13f.; 2 Kings 23:7); they went to special effort to weave בתים (coverings) for Asherah, in the part of the temple where the temple servants lived. What it had upon it is still under discussion; Murmelstein (ZAW 81, 223f.) thinks this term בה might be a euphemism for depictions of sexual intercourse. In this context, when בה is mentioned, most would think of a piece of clothing, one with portrayals of Asherah all the way around it.

It is not always clear whether a reference is to Asherah the goddess or the *asherah* as a cultic object. It is only in the OT that there is any mention of *asherah* with reference to a cultic furnishing. None of these passages include any clear description about the form and use of the *asherah*. The Gk also seems to give no clear indication that the translators had any concrete idea about what this was; otherwise, they would not have translated אשרה as ἄλσος, "sacred grove." Vulg translates לאשרה מפלצת in 2 Chron. 15:16 (cf. also 1 Kings 15:13) as *simulacrum Priapi* (image of Priapus [god of gardens]), which suggests that it was known that the אשרה (*asherah*) was a symbol of fertility.

When the OT mentions *asherah*s (sometimes also in the singular), this usually happens in contexts that speak of practices and cultic furnishings that were part of Canaanite religion (together with a Baal altar: Judg. 6:25ff.; with cultic high places: 2 Chron. 34:3; 1 Kings 14:23; with cultic pictures, פסילים, "carved images"/מסכות, "cast images": 2 Chron. 34:3; Deut. 7:5; 12:3; with *maṣṣebah*s: Exod. 34:13; 1 Kings 14:23; with altars: Exod. 34:13; Deut. 7:5; Jer. 17:2; with חמנים, "incense altars": Isa. 27:9; 2 Chron. 34:3f.). No passage in the OT provides detailed information about the function that the *asherah*s served in the cult. They are almost only mentioned in contexts discussing the removal of Canaanite cultic furnishings and practices: כרת (cut down): Judg. 6:25ff.; Exod. 34:13; 2 Kings 18:4; 23:14; גדע (hew down): Deut. 7:5; 2 Chron. 14:2; 31:1; שרף (באש) (burn [with fire]): Deut. 12:3; 2 Kings 23:6; the last passage also speaks of דקק לעפר (beat it to dust) (cf. also Judg. 6:26; נתש, "cut off": Mic. 5:13). It is important to note two other passages as well: Deut. 16:21 speaks about planting and 1 Kings 14:23 mentions building/constructing an *asherah*. These passages show that the word *asherah* did not always carry the same meaning for everyone: it can apparently be a shrub or (more likely) a tree (thus Mishnah ʿOrla 1:7, 8), but could just as easily be a dead stick of wood. Verbs such as נצב *hiphʿil* (set up) (2 Kings 17:10) and עמד *hiphʿil* (erect) (2 Chron. 33:19) would suggest it was a rather tall installation, most likely a pole, made of wood, since *asherah*s could be burnt. The way in which erecting or producing an *asherah* is described (cf. the verbs בנה, "build," 1 Kings 14:23 and עשה, "make," 1 Kings 14:15) leads one to conclude that the wood was worked by hand until it was judged to be fit to serve as a symbol of the divinity.

It makes no sense to try to harmonize all the various occurrences of the term to arrive at one common, general meaning (tree—pole) or to eliminate one specialized meaning in favor of another (thus Patai, who rejects the idea that this was a tree). Depending on the local conditions at a particular cultic site, a wooden pole would have to be used instead of having a live green *asherah* tree. The tree, or the cultic pole that took its place, is a symbol of "the power of life that survived through the changes that came during the course of a year, honored in a divine way through Asherah" (Maag, *BHH*). Most probably, this tree, at a holy place, would have been the symbol for a tree cult (so Gese); it is possible that Asherah herself was originally a goddess of the trees and thus, at the same time, a specialized type of vegetation deity (Bernhardt).

Concerning the manner in which this cultic object known as an *asherah* was depicted, the opinions are many and varied: Galling (*BRL*) considers it obvious that the cultic pole would have stood right next to a *maṣṣebah.* Numerous passages in the Bible would support this (Exod. 34:13; Deut. 7:5; 12:3; 1 Kings 14:23; 2 Kings 17:10; 18:4; 2 Chron. 14:2; 31:1); however, an even greater number of passages connect the *asherah*s and altars (Judg. 6:25ff.; Isa. 27:9; Exod. 34:13; Deut. 7:5; 12:3; 2 Kings 23:17; Jer. 17:2; 2 Chron. 14:2; 31:1; 34:4, 7), and ten other passages include other cultic objects, besides the *asherah*s, but none of them mention *maṣṣebah*s. That might explain why W. Helck (*Betrachtungen zur grossen Göttin und den ihr verbundenen Erscheinungen* [1971] 158) treats the *asherah* as a part of the altar (ornamentation on top of it), especially on the basis of what is said in Judg. 6:25ff. But that is not likely. The *asherah*s belong, as also altars and *maṣṣebah*s, to the common inventory of articles found on a במה (high place).

Purpose and Thrust

The expander considers turning away from worship of idols to be the same as turning toward Yahweh. He would consider that everything connected with restoration would result from that turning. Verse 8 is roughly the same as what one finds in the secondary additions to Deutero-Isaiah, in the polemic against the idol images. But the one who adds the glosses makes this much more rough sounding: it makes good sense to highlight the fact that idol images are simply the product of human effort and are not really gods (see Isa. 2:8), but to include an inventory of a cultic installation and say that humans produced it simply states the obvious. Yet to say that one who looks to Yahweh would be able to see through the emptiness of all cultic activities, focusing as they do on altars and *asherah*s, does point out that the spirit of prophecy was still alive.

[17:10f.] *The Consequences of Having Forgotten God*

Form

Since v. 9 is secondary (see above, p. 163), vv. 10f. should be considered first. Both verses deal with an announcement of judgment, for which the reason is given in v. 10a. The כי (truly) at the beginning serves now secondarily as a particle that links these verses with what precedes, but it may have originally been a deictic interjection (see above, pp. 131f., and see also H. W. Wolff, *Hosea* BK XIV/1, 173 [Engl: *Hosea*, Hermeneia (1974) 135]).

Meter: In vv. 10 and 11a, there are 3 three-stress + three-stress bicola (עַל־כֵּן, "therefore," in v. 10a, is outside the metrical structure). In v. 11b there are also six stresses, but these are to be divided into 3 two-stress cola.

Setting

There is no introductory formula; it is possible that it was eliminated when v. 9 was secondarily inserted. Since it is neither certain at the outset that v. 9 provides a correct indication about the setting for this section, nor apparent that these verses are connected in any way with vv. 1-3 and vv. 4-6, we must rely solely on internal indicators when attempting to establish the setting for this message of judgment. Unfortunately, there are almost no bits of evidence that can be used to give us even a most general feeling about how to date the passage. In addition, opinions diverge about the authenticity of the passage, and more recent exegetes express clearly just how uncertain they are. Kaiser is typical, as he observes that the addressee, source, and age of the piece are all uncertain, even though he does suggest that it could be a passage from Isaiah himself that has now been misplaced. By contrast, Fohrer does not believe the passage comes from the hand of Isaiah, "less because of the foreign cult mentioned in v. 10b than because of such a great number of expressions, some of which are most commonly found in the language used in the Psalms and some of which are not used before the time period beginning about 600." There are indeed words reminiscent of vocabulary from the Psalms: concerning אֱלֹהֵי יִשְׁעֵךְ (God of your help), see Pss. 18:47; 25:5; 65:6; 79:9; concerning צוּר מָעֻזּ (rock of his refuge), see Pss. 31:3; 71:3 (following a conjecture based on the Gk) and cf. צוּר מַחְסִי (rock of my refuge) in 94:22, צוּר יִשְׁעָתִי (rock of my salvation) in 89:27, צוּר יִשְׁעֵנוּ (rock of our salvation) in 95:1, and צוּר עֻזִּי (my mighty rock) in 62:8. But it would not be surprising to find such references in Isaiah. "Whoever has the name יְשַׁעְיָהוּ (Isaiah) would certainly be able to use אֱלֹהֵי יֵשַׁע [God of your help] as a designation for Yahweh" (Procksch). The Psalm passages cited show that one most likely would celebrate that Yahweh is a God of help in those passages where one is thinking within the framework of the ideology of kingship (cf. 2 Sam. 23:5). And it is in the same context that Yahweh is called "rock" (1 Sam. 2:2; Pss. 18:3, 32, 47; 89:27). When Isaiah, in 8:14, proclaims that Yahweh is the rock (צוּר) of stumbling for both of the houses of Israel, that in itself betrays his awareness that "rock" was used as an epithet for God. צוּר (rock) would seem to be an ancient Jerusalemite name for God (on this, see *Isaiah 1–12*, p. 359; and H. Wildberger, FS Shazar, 703f.). However, there are also other indications that Isaiah was very familiar with the language of the Psalms; cf. (even if one treats passages such as 14:32 as uncertain) 8:17f.; 30:2, 15; 31:1. The second major reason given by Fohrer that raises suspicions is the use of the pair of terms שׁכח (forget) and לֹא זכר (you have not thought about). It is clear to all that the verbs are favorite terms in Deuteronomy (6:12; 8:11, 14, 18, 19;

32:18; see also Judg. 3:7; 1 Sam. 12:9). Isaiah does not use them anywhere else, but Hosea is aware that they are used in a religious context (2:15; 4:6; 8:14; 13:6), and both terms are most common in Jeremiah.

A sense of uncertainty remains when one considers whether v. 10a comes from Isaiah, but one should clearly not follow the path that Marti has taken, suggesting that v. 10a is most likely a gloss, inserted by someone who lived later, though vv. 10b, 11 could still be attributed to Isaiah; v. 10a is absolutely necessary for v. 10b. If one would consider v. 10a to have come from someone other than Isaiah, then the entire section vv. 10f. must be treated as from someone other than Isaiah. But vv. 10b, 11 leave one with the definite impression that they are Isaianic. The language has an originality about it; the comparison with the "little Adonis garden" (or whatever it is that is specifically intended in vv. 10b, 11a) can be assessed in the same way. One ought not object by saying that Isaiah never polemicizes anywhere else against foreign cultic activities. Even if one is not satisfied that 1:29 provides evidence to the contrary, 2:8 still remains. In addition, the present passage is not intended as a polemic against a foreign cult; instead, the "little Adonis garden" serves only as a comparison that highlights the precarious situation of the "you" [sing.] who is being addressed, who had forgotten his God. Of course, it is appropriate to question whether "little Adonis gardens" were even known in Jerusalem at the time of Isaiah. There is no direct evidence for that. But certainly there is no reason to deny that, in addition to the Molech cult, other cultic customs had their source among the Canaanites, were still stubbornly held onto, and had some sort of continued existence in the pre-exilic era in Jerusalem—to say nothing of the fact that the land of the Phoenicians, where the little Adonis gardens were undoubtedly known, was not that far away from Judah. Isa. 57:3-13 might be preexilic (see Eissfeldt, *Introduction,* 345; Westermann, *Isaiah 40–66,* OTL, 325) and could provide important evidence, for this passage, that there was heathen cultic practice in ancient Jerusalem. 2 Kings 23:4ff. shows how entrenched the heathen cult had become, even within the confines of the temple environs; cf. also Ezekiel 8, especially, v. 14. Not long ago, not far south of the temple area, a heathen sanctuary was discovered that was probably established about 700, in which a fertility cult must have been a central focus (K. Kenyon, *Royal Cities of the Old Testament* [1971] 114ff.; cf. also her *Jerusalem: Excavating 3000 Years of History* [1967] 63–68, plates 31–35, XVII). There is no cogent argument for denying both of these verses to Isaiah, unless one argues from certain preconceived notions, and, for example, follows Kaiser's modus operandi (*Isaiah 13–39,* xii): "to deny on principle that any saying derives from the prophet himself, if it can be explained on the basis of a different period."

The section addresses a "you" [sing.], using the feminine. The addressee thus cannot be יעקב (Jacob), as in vv. 4-6. It is likely that Jerusalem is meant (cf. this feminine "you" in 1:21-26; 3:25; 22:1ff.; 29:1ff.), since one would hardly be right in supposing that this refers to Samaria (see 29:1-4). Nothing is said about which specific period of Isaiah's activity would provide the best date to identify when he spoke this message. Since this passage immediately follows vv. 4-6, it may indicate that it was correctly remembered that this passage also was uttered at the time of the Syro-Ephraimitic War.

Commentary

[17:10a] What the passage means is made more difficult because of the uncertainty about how one answers the questions that have just been posed. Thus one wonders whether one should interpret "forget God" and "not think about him" in the sense these expressions are used in Hosea and Jeremiah or in the way Deuteronomy uses the terms (cf. W. Schottroff, *THAT* I, 515ff.). It is possible, based on vv. 10b, 11, that Isaiah is thinking about idol worship. But it is more likely that one should interpret this forgetting of God, for which he reprimands them, in the way it is used in Hos. 8:14: "Israel has forgotten his Maker; Judah has multiplied fortified cities" (this is a passage about which Hosean authorship has been questioned); cf. Isa. 2:7f.; 22:9-11. According to this, Isaiah would be speaking about "forgetting God" in the sense of trusting in political-military might. Yet if one were to ask Isaiah for his opinion, he would say that the practices in which Jerusalem involved itself, in the attempt to ensure its security, had not been brought to a complete stop. The same is true as the prophet makes an observation using the imagery of that which quickly sprouts and just as quickly withers, נְטַע־נַעֲמָנִים (little gardens for the lovely one).

It was H. Ewald (*Die Propheten des Alten Bundes* I [1867²] 364) who first made a connection between vv. 10b, 11 and Adonis, and M. K. Ohnefalsch-Richter (*Die Bibel und Homer* [1893]) first used the wording in this passage to render the phrase "Adonisgärten" (Greek: οἱ Ἀδώνιδος κῆποι, "the gardens of Adonis"). The oldest textual example of this word and usage is found in Plato (*Phaedrus* 276b), after which time numerous other sources in Greek and Latin literature refer to the little gardens of Adonis. Depictions of such are found on Greek vases (with an early example already from about 400 B.C. in *AOB* 208; cf., in addition, reference works such as H. Haas, *Bilderatlas zur Religionsgeschichte* [1926] §§ 9-11, illuss. 105ff.). Baumgartner and others have followed the later development of such practices, and its expansion throughout the region of the Mediterranean, up to the present time.

These little gardens of Adonis make use of bowls, boxes, or earthenware vessels, which would have the seeds of fast growing types of plants planted in them. The fast sprouting and the withering, which took place just as fast, were supposed to symbolize the appearance and disappearance (or coming to life again and death) of the vegetation god. The prehistory of this story about the little gardens of Adonis, well known already in classical antiquity, has been difficult to trace. The name Adonis would suggest that its roots are in Phoenicia. But no Semitic sources available to us make any mention of the practice. In Ugarit the functions connected with the vegetation deity are split between Baal and Mot. The texts discovered there do indeed use some form of the root *nᶜm* (goodness, charm, loveliness) as an epithet for a variety of gods: Anat, e.g., 76:II:16; Yariḫ, 77:25; Baal, 2 Aqht VI:32; chiefly, Shahar/Shalim, 52:23, and often elsewhere. In addition, *nᶜm* is found as a (theophoric?) element in Ugaritic personal names, but to try to link this term to a particular vegetation deity is not possible, so that Ugaritic material is of no further help in trying to identify the deity to which Isa. 17:11 refers with נעמן (lovely one). That there is a close connection between the myths of Adonis and Osiris (on this, see W. Helck, "Osiris," *Wörterbuch der Mythologie*, I), and that both gods are connected with Byblos, poses the question about whether the "little gardens of Adonis" might possibly be explained on the basis of similar practices carried out in Egypt (thus Vellay, 142; W. Helck, *Betrachtungen zur grossen Göttin und den ihr verbundenen Gottheiten* [1971] 187; cf. also Scharff). Reference is made to little gardens of Osiris (Vellay, 142), grain mummies, Osiris beds, grain Osiris, and the like: for the Osiris festival on the 20th of Choyak, people would fill large stone troughs with earth and sow cereal grain in them. In the middle of the "little garden" one would set up a figure of Osiris. When the plants died, so did the god, and he was laid into a coffin after the harvesting, after which one intoned laments for the dead for him (a depiction of such a "grain corpse" is in *AOB* 205). Providing burial gifts for the one who died, the "little Osiris garden" was to assist the dead deity to become Osiris once again (for a complete description, see Maspero, 127f.). At the time of the Choyak festival, Osiris figures were constructed out of earth and seed kernels and then buried; when the seed germinated, then his resurrection was celebrated.

It is possible that a similar festival was also celebrated in the Tammuz cult, as might be inferred from a passage found in the Tammuz songs published by H. Zimmern (*BSGWL* 59 [1907] 206, 208, 214f.). Ezek. 8:14 gives evidence for the existence of the cult for this god in Jerusalem at the beginning of the sixth century. One will have to be content with being unable to solve the question about whether names such as אדנירם (Adoniram) (2 Sam. 20:24) and אדניקם (Adonikam) (Ezra 2:13, and elsewhere) furnish enough evidence to conclude that a god named Adon was known in Israel. Thus we are not in a position to say anything more specific about the background of Isa. 17:10b, 11. It is quite unlikely that the נעמן (lovely one), for whom these plantings are intended, could have been a deity named Adon. It is much more likely that it refers to Baal, who became known to Israel as a vegetation deity when the people entered into Canaan. Yet it should not be rejected out of hand that there might have been some influence from the Tammuz and Osiris cults. In the final analysis, the name of the deity is of no consequence; in any case: what we know about the little Adonis and Osiris gardens can be used when seeking the meaning of the passage.

[17:10b] One must ask whether v. 10b also speaks about this "little Adonis garden." זמורה has been translated with something similar to "vine branch, tendril of the grapevine," which seems correct in view of its use in Num. 13:23; Nah. 2:3. Although Ezek. 15:2 makes clear that the woody portion of the grapevine also can be meant when זמורה is used, this term then has a much broader sense: Ges-Buhl renders it something like "creeper, twigs, every bush which is similar to grape vine tendrils." If one removes the suffix from תזרענו (you will sow it) in Isa. 17:10b, then, when mentioned along with planting a little Adonis garden, it could refer to a second type of activity, which would result in a translation something like "tendrils of the clusters." However, grape tendrils are not known for growing fast and withering quickly, one does not sow vine tendrils, and this passage does not provide sufficient evidence to posit for זרע the meaning "set with vine slips" (so KBL). One would do better if one kept the suffix, just mentioned, as it is. But that would mean that the נטעי נעמנים (little gardens for the lovely one) would be planted with זמורה, which would therefore not be a type of grain, but rather another, amazingly fast growing type of plant. In fact, this plant would be symbolic of the זר (foreign [god]). According to Pss. 44:21 and 81:10, an אל זר is a strange god, whereby the term זר does not lay the stress on being a stranger, a foreigner, but rather on what is not permitted, what is illegitimate. The word אל (god) can even be missing, so that זר (strange, foreign) all by itself can serve as a designation for such a god, as in Deut. 32:16; Hos. 8:12; Jer. 2:25; 3:13; 5:19; Isa. 43:12. In Jer. 5:19 the זרים (foreign gods) are further described by use of a paraphrase, אֱלֹהֵי נֵכָר, gods who had been "imported"; this is a nuance that would apply just as aptly to the imported "little Adonis garden."

On the basis of Ezek. 8:17, it has been concluded that people held these tendrils of the deity or images of the god under their nose, in order to accomplish a transfer of their life power into their own bodies (on this, see Fohrer, *Ezechiel*, HAT [1955²]). Unfortunately, however, that passage is uncertain textually. In any case, one ought not suppose that there has been some influence from the cult of the Egyptian sun god (see Fohrer, *Jesaja*).

The activity in the little Adonis garden focused on setting life forces in motion. For that reason, plants that grew astoundingly fast were employed, so that these powers could be demonstrated to the naked eye: already on the very day that one planted them, "one would raise them to maturity"; on the very morning one planted them, one would get them to sprout.

By consulting Baumgartner (250ff.), one can learn more about the modern practice of "setting out shoots for propagation" in a contemporary version of a little garden of Adonis, known as a *nenneri* (also known as *nenniri* or *nennaru;* see M. L. Wagner, *Dizionario Etimologico Sardo* [1960ff.]), still planted in Sardinia. One of Baumgartner's descriptions of the practice reads as follows: "The *nenneri* is prepared for Maundy Thursday. We prepare it on the first day of the season of fasting, that is, on Ash Wednesday, six weeks earlier, in the following way: a person takes a large plate, made of porcelain or enamel. On the plate, one spreads out a thickness of wool, specifically, unwoven Sardinian sheep's wool, which is easy to spread out in loose flocks. The wool is dampened and then generously sprinkled with plant seeds. Normally, one takes the seeds from wheat, from chickpeas, or from lentils. It is most important that the container be placed in a dark location, either in a roomy chest or under a basket, so that no light can fall on the germinating plants, for the plants of the *nenneri* have to be as light-colored as possible. The person will water them, roughly every other day. The roots work their way into the damp wool and grow into the wool to form a nicely shaped cake. Before we take the *nenneri* to church on Maundy Thursday, we decorate it most beautifully. We stick flowers into it and tie a brightly colored silk ribbon around it. Sometimes, someone will also put a little burning light into it as well. But that is not necessary. In the church we place the *nenneri* close to the crucifix, on the ground. The priest blesses it. The *nenneri* is left in the church for three days, until the holy sabbath (Easter Sunday [*sic*]). Then we take it back home. However, those who have land carry it right out into the field, into the vineyard, or into the fruit garden, and leave it lying there. In that way, the land gets a blessing" (251f.).

That a light can be placed into this little garden, and in other cases an image can be used—sometimes it is customary that the figure would be of the crucified Christ (Baumgartner, 254; see also 265f.)—reminds one that an Osiris figure used to stand in the middle of the little Osiris garden in Egypt.

In Sardinia the people prepare their *nenneri* several weeks before they take them to church on Maundy Thursday; Plato and Hermes speak of eight days duration (Sulze, 75). It may be that it is a gross exaggeration for Isaiah to compress this into one day (Sulze, 88). However, since we are not informed about the type of plant and the technique that Isaiah had in mind, one must be cautious about how much one can say. For this reason, to translate הפריח as "to bring into bloom" makes no sense, nor is it necessary. There are proverbial expressions which point out that such artificial plantings do not produce any fruit; see, among others, Gregory of Nazianzus, *Carmina* [Poems] I, theol., *Patr. Graec.* 37, 888, line 53: Κῆπος Ἀδώνιδος ἤδε τεὴ χάρις ὠλεσίκαρπος (this delight of yours is a fruitless Adonis-garden) or Zenobius, *Cent.* 1:49: Ἀκαρπότερος εἶ Ἀδώνιδος κήπων (you are more fruitless than an Adonis grove) (cf. also the description of the Sardinian farmers mentioned above). It is not easy to figure out exactly which result was expected, in specific cases, when one set out a little Adonis garden. One can be sure that the basic point of having a little Adonis garden was that one might stimulate nature to wake up again, analogous to mourning for Baal in Ugarit, which was to effect a revivification of the dead god and thereby to bring about a reawakening of nature (*UT* 49:I:1*ff.; 67:VI:9ff.). Since mention is made here of long illnesses and pain, however, it may be that the prophet is thinking about a rite that was used to furnish a sick person with renewed strength. To be sure, such practices can be interpreted in many different ways, and one way of interpreting this does not mean that others are invalidated (cf. the material that Baumgartner collected).

Purpose and Thrust

Does Isaiah simply want to point out the futility of a type of magic that one sets in motion to deal with pain and sickness and finally death? If so, this would be a polemic against a foreign cult and we would then once again have to deal with the question about whether this passage comes from Isaiah, since he considered such polemics to be no more than a minor aspect of his mission. The study of v. 10a showed that אלהי ישע (God of help) and צור מעז (rock of refuge) were to be understood in political terms. For this reason, נחלה (weakness) and כאב אנוש (unremitting pain) provide images that describe military-political oppression. This is just as it was in 1:4ff., where the prophet perceived the oppression of Jerusalem in terms of an extremely dangerous sickness (cf. 10:16ff.), and אנוש (incurable) is also used elsewhere to describe military blows (Mic. 1:9). Most especially, by comparison, one ought to note what Jer. 30:12-15 says (take note of the vocabulary at the beginning: אָנוּשׁ שִׁבְרֵךְ, "your hurt is incurable" [emended], נַחְלָה מַכָּתֵךְ, "your

185

wound is grievous," and אָנוּשׁ מַכְאֹבֵךְ, "your pain is incurable," in v. 15aβ). In addition, Jer. 17:16 speaks about the יוֹם אָנוּשׁ (the day of disaster), on which the enemies of the prophet are to be crushed.

Would someone in Jerusalem have set in motion the "Adonis garden" magic, in order to bring the political-military malaise under control? That is most difficult to accept; the imagery about the plantings for the נַעֲמָן (lovely one) has to have been used in a metaphorical sense. The element that links the metaphor and what is really meant is the term זָר (foreign). The people had dealings with the זָרִים, the foreigners—in their pseudo-cult that they had adopted from the foreigners *and* in the politics of establishing treaties, by means of which the people sought salvation and life, instead of turning to the "rock of refuge" who dwelt on Zion. It is really the same problem, whether one joins cults or is "dealing the way foreigners do," from which one ought to keep one's hands far away. In terms of content, this message is not much different from words Isaiah spoke, in which he issued warnings about having nothing to do with foreign powers: 14:29-32; 18:1ff.; 20; 31:1ff.

[17:9] *Secondary Introduction to vv. 10f.: The Destruction of Strong Cities*

Form
Someone who was either reading or editing the transmitted words of Isaiah must have found v. 11b to be too vague. So he announces destruction "of his strong cities." The way he formulated this did not work out very well. The suffix on מָעֻזּוֹ (his strong [cities]) is left hanging in the air; he did not notice that the following material uses the feminine second person [sing.] form of address, "you."

Setting
See the discussion of the setting above, p. 163.

Commentary
[17:9] The author sees that a turn of events is coming that will be comparable to the time when the cities populated by those whom he groups together by using the terms Hivites and Amorites, those who dwelt in the land before the time of Israel, were turned to rubble by the hosts of Israel.

There is no doubt that he would have had only a "literary" knowledge of the Hivites, a pre-Israelite population group. It would seem that the center of their settlement was located in the mountainous region in central Palestine; yet they had a relationship with Gibeon (Josh. 9:1-7, 24) and Shechem (Gen. 34:2). Since a very different central location is presumed by Josh. 11:3 and Judg. 3:3, in which their population centers were located at the base of Mount Hermon or in Lebanon, one must be careful about the inferences one draws (cf. Kuschke, 118f.). We do not know where they came from, or to what group of people they belonged. Since Gen. 34:14f.

suggests that they did not know anything about circumcision, it has been presumed that they could not have been Semites. Some would replace the reading "Hivites" in Gen. 34:2 with "Horites" (Hurrians, חרי). This may be correct, but it does not mean that the Hivites should be equated with the Hurrians wherever they are mentioned (on this, see Speiser, 26ff.; North has recently reiterated that position). That the cities of the Hivites would have provided particularly good examples of "wastelands" does not square with historical information: Israel is supposed to have made a pact with Gibeon (Joshua 9), and even Shechem had certainly not been abandoned "before the coming of the Israelites." The author had his rigid viewpoint, which had already become dogma, about how the land had been taken; but he does not have any hard data or personal knowledge to describe how that actually took place.

As one of the subgroups of the population that were in the land before Israel came, the Amorites are much more frequently mentioned in the OT than the Hivites. The name is not always used in the same way: sometimes they are mentioned in lists of those peoples who were in the land already when the Israelites immigrated (e.g., Deut. 7:1; Josh. 3:10; 24:11), which means that they were *a* people, among others, in the land; sometimes the word is used as a generic term for the population that, as a whole, had been in the land for a long time (in the book of Joshua, in the Elohistic and deuteronomic sections of the Pentateuch, and in other scattered passages, such as Amos 2:9f.). In the Table of Nations in Genesis 10, they are mentioned right after the Canaanites (v. 16). The Canaanites are localized by Josh. 11:3 "in the east and in the west" (which means along the coast and in the Jordan Valley), the Amorites (along with the Hittites, Perizzites, and Jebusites) "in the hill country," and the Hivites "at the foot of Hermon" (see also Num. 13:29; concerning the division of the Amorites and Canaanites according to the biblical tradition, see the arrangement proposed by Kenyon, *Amorites*, 4). At the very least, that localization reflects the fact that these two groups were distinctive and separate from one another. Most recently once again, questions have been raised about the solution that de Vaux, among others (339; cf. also Noth, 34, 53), offered, positing two successive waves of Semitic nomads who came in from the Syrian-Arabian desert (Gibson, 220ff.). There is no way that one can distinguish the name Amorite from the Amurru (i.e., "the westerners"), who are mentioned in Sumerian, Babylonian, Hittite, Egyptian, and Assyrian texts. What can be said with greater specificity about the relationship between the Amorites in the OT and these Amurru is, once again, a disputed topic—it could be that the Amorites in Palestine had lived as members of the Amurru state but then relocated; this state played an important role in the region of Syria from the fourteenth century until about 1200 B.C.

In the present passage, the Amorites are mentioned along with the Hivites simply in a general description of the population that Israel encountered when it entered the land. When Isa. 17:9 speaks of these two peoples, but not of the Canaanites, that might indeed have correctly preserved a memory, which knew that when Israel entered the land as an entire group, the first altercations were with the Amorites and Hivites, whereas the integration with the Canaanites, who dwelt in the low-lying parts of the country, described in many different passages (see Josh. 17:16; Num. 14:25), did not take place until a later time.

Since the verse is linked to what precedes it by the phrase ביום ההוא (on that day), the author had the downfall of Israel in mind. One can presume that a Judean is speaking, one who is thinking about the fate of the cities of the Northern Kingdom. He might have lived at the time of Nehemiah, when

Judah was under terrible pressure from Samaria. In light of the accusation about having forgotten God, which Isaiah himself had once leveled against Jerusalem, it would have seemed an appropriate comment that the expander could now pick up and sharpen. But that remains in the realm of speculation.

The end is שממה (a barren place) (on this, see *Isaiah 1–12,* pp. 27f., 199, 315). Like the motif of the complete abandonment of the cities, this concept is also used regularly when such disasters are depicted, and Isaiah is also not unfamiliar with such terms (1:7; 6:11; cf. 64:9). The threat is frequently stated, in both Ezekiel and Jeremiah, that the land would become a שממה (barren place).

Purpose and Thrust: 17:1-11

Because 17:1-11 achieved its present form through such a complicated process, it is very difficult to determine exactly what major theme was in the mind of the redactor, since the variety of original sources for the specific units, and commentary about them, makes it seem that there is virtually no chance to discover some red thread that can be detected throughout. Yet one ought not miss the point that, when one studies the issue, vv. 7f. provide the key to the interpretation of vv. 1-11. Damascus will come to an end, Israel will fall apart, and this will indeed be so complete that nothing will remain but a שממה (barren place). But the expander balances this end by an observation: when "on that day" the absolute point is reached, so that all has been lost, then human beings will begin to reorient their lives toward Yahweh afresh. The hard road leading to judgment is the same path on which humanity must discover that each person must bid farewell to the "idol images" and seek salvation only in communal fellowship with Yahweh. Careful attention must be paid to the fact that Israel itself is no longer present in this vision of the future. Its history reached its final destiny in giving witness to the "Holy One of Israel," who alone is the creator and lord of humanity. At this point, Isaiah's words are recast, as part of an entirely new framework of thought, and are reused as the OT message embarked on a wholly new stage of development. But it is worth asking what the passage meant in the very beginning. The exegesis that has been set forth has shown that Isaiah publicly wanted to attest to the fact that his refuge was with the "rock of his salvation." The opinion of the final redactor of the message of the prophet was not all that different.

The Storming of the Peoples

Literature

Zion tradition/battle against peoples/battle against chaos: E. Rohland, "Die Bedeutung der Erwählungstraditionen Israels für die Eschatologie der alttestamentlichen Propheten," diss., Heidelberg (1956). G. Fohrer, "Σιων," *TDNT* VII (1971) 292–319. J. Hayes, "The Tradition of Zion's Inviolability," *JBL* 82 (1963) 419–426. J. Schreiner, *Sion—Jerusalem Jahwes Königssitz* (1963). R. de Vaux, "Jérusalem et les prophètes," *RB* 73 (1966) 481–509. G. Wanke, *Die Zionstheologie der Korachiten,* BZAW 97 (1966). H.-M. Lutz, *Jahwe, Jerusalem und die Völker* (1968). J. Scharbert, "Besprechung von G Wanke, Zionstheologie . . .," *BZ* 12 (1968) 274–275. H. Schmidt, "Israel, Zion und die Völker," diss., Zurich (1966). F. Stolz, *Strukturen und Figuren im Kult von Jerusalem,* BZAW 118 (1970). H. Barth, "Israel und das Assyrerreich in den nicht-jesajanischen Texten des Protojesajabuches," diss., Hamburg (1974).

Concerning המון: G. Gerleman, "Die lärmende Menge," FS K. Elliger (1973) 71–75. Concerning גלגל: Siegismund, "Ein Frühlingsritt am 'äussersten Meer,'" *PJ* 7 (1911) 127.

Concerning God's help during the morning: H. Schmidt, *Das Gebet des Angeklagten im Alten Testament,* BZAW 49 (1928). J. Ziegler, "Die Hilfe Gottes 'am Morgen,'" FS F. Nötscher (1950) 281–288. Ch. Barth, "בקר," *TDOT* II, 219–228.

Concerning the organizational structure of the Assyrian forces: W. Manitius, "Das stehende Heer der Assyrerkönige und seine Organisation," ZA 24 (1910) 97–149.

[Literature update through 1979: Concerning the Zion tradition: B. S. Childs, *Isaiah and the Assyrian Crisis,* SBT 2/3 (1967), esp. 128–136. S. C. Reif, "A Note on g'r," *VT* 21 (1971) 241–244.]

Text

17:12 Ha! A deafening noise from many peoples,
as the raging of the sea they rage!
And roaring from nations; as the roaring[a]
of mighty waters they roar.
13 [a][Nations, as the roaring of many waters they roar.][a]
[b]There he goes with his mighty rebuke therein,[b]
and (already) there is fleeing to what is far away,[c]
chased like [d]chaff upon the mountains[d] before the wind,

> as tumbleweeds before the storm.
> 14 At the time of evening—look, there is terror,
> before the morning (already)—it is all gone.[a]
> That is the destiny for those who plunder us,
> [b]and the lot of those who move in against us to commit robbery.[b]

12a ושאון לאמים (and roaring from nations), the first colon in the second line of v. 12, is too short metrically. For v. 12b the Gk reads: καὶ νῶτος ἐθνῶν πολλῶν ὡς ὕδωρ ἠχήσει (and the flat land, filled with many nations, roars as waters do), so that some (Schmidt, Procksch, et al.) suggest reading כבירים (many, mighty), right after לאמים (nations). Based on v. 13a (מים רבים, "many waters"), 8:7, and 28:2, but also because of the sense of the passage, this is not permissible; the Gk text has simply used πολλῶν (many) a second time; it had been used in v. 12a as well. Instead of this solution, one should transfer כשאון (as the roaring), to become part of the first colon of the line, rather than treating it as part of the second colon, as it is now.

13a–a This is missing in some MSS and the Syr (dittography of v. 12b).

13b–b Metrically, v. 13aβ is too short; some suggest that the reading should be וְנָעַר יְעַר בּוֹ (and he indeed rebukes therein). This change still leaves the hearer without a subject, which some commentators have furnished (Duhm: והוא, "and he [will indeed rebuke]"; Marti: ויהוה הוא, "and Yahweh, he [will indeed rebuke]"; Procksch, ויהוה, "and Yahweh [will indeed rebuke]"). It is possible that יהוה (Yahweh), shortened by the loss of a י, was then lost due to haplography, with only the ו left at the beginning of the next word.

13c For more on מן, in the sense of "far away from," when used in connection with fleeing, see Ges-K §119z.

13d–d I. Eitan (*HUCA* 12/13 [1937–1938] 65) suggests reading כְּמֹץ (as chaff), maintaining that מֹץ (chaff) is always used elsewhere in the OT in the absolute state and that הרים (here: mountains), which, on the basis of Arabic *harra*, could mean "waste, refuse," makes the line too long metrically; therefore he suggests that this second word is a gloss. He can hardly be correct in this. The idea of chaff being blown around everywhere, at the site of a threshing floor, easily blown by a strong wind up into the mountains, provides a particularly effective illustration when one wishes to describe enemies being scattered.

14a Because of the parallel with והנה (look; lit.: and behold), and also because of the readings found in many MSS and the versions, one should read ואיננו (it is all gone) at this point in v. 14a.

14b–b Syr: *wmnt' dbzwzn* (and the lot of those who despoil us); see also Gᴬ and MSS of the Lucianic recension (cf. Vulg and Arabic). For this reason, one should read וגורל בוזזנו (and the lot of those who move against us to commit robbery) (dittography of the ל).

Form

On the one hand, there is little doubt that this section is completely separate and in no way connected with the material that precedes it (contra Delitzsch). The threat is not to Aram/Damascus or to Israel/Samaria, but to Judah/Jerusalem (see below, pp. 192ff.), and the threat is not going to result in complete destruction; events are to change rather suddenly, since there is to be a deliverance. From time to time, it has been suggested that the "storming of the peoples" against Jerusalem deals with the approach of the Syrian-

Ephraimitic forces. Such a solution cannot be rejected out of hand, but it is not likely; a threat against Jerusalem, greater than any other that had ever taken place, would certainly not be equated by Isaiah with the "two smoking stubs from burning sticks" (7:4).

On the other hand, many commentators link 17:12-14 either very closely, or at least in a general way, with chap. 18. Like 17:12, 18:1 begins with הוי (ha, woe). That may have been the reason why the redactor inserted this message, addressed to Jerusalem, at this particular place within the collection of messages against the nations, but it gives no indication about how to determine the exact situation and who authored this passage (the peoples who storm Jerusalem are not the hosts of the pharaoh, contra König). But it is also most unlikely that this is instruction for the Ethiopian messengers (see 18:2), to teach them that Yahweh does not need any "exotic helper" (so Duhm). It is most apparent that 17:14b picks up the main point from the oracle that has just been uttered and makes sure that nothing more need be said. Yet one must give credit to the exegetes who want to consider 17:12-14 in conjunction with the following chapter (Ewald, Dillmann and Kittel, Duhm, Buhl, König, Kissane), for they have correctly recognized that this passage can be treated as authentic, as belonging to the corpus of messages from Isaiah; they have rightly noted what must be seen as the overall function of the passage.

The message begins with הוי (ha). In spite of this, one cannot treat it as if it were an actual woe oracle (on this, see *Isaiah 1–12,* p. 196), since, if it were such an oracle, the הוי would be followed by a participle or adjective, which would implicitly furnish the reason for the announcement of disaster. הוי (ha) is used here in an atypical way, as an interjection (which explains why it has been translated as "ha"), functioning much as הנה (behold), the point being to get the attention of those who are to be listening (cf. הוי, "woe," in 10:5). Schmidt thinks that this poem sounds "like the echo of an ecstatic experience"; see also von Rad, *OTTheol* II, 67. But there is no actual indication that this is a vision in the technical sense—just as it is not simply a stripped-down description about the advance of enemy forces; this is no prophet's visionary fantasy, delivered now as a dispassionate report. The way it is formulated reminds one of the report of a watchman, being similar to the type of material found in passages such as Jer. 4:11-13 (cf. v. 13 there: "Look! He comes up like clouds"; however, this is also much like Isa. 21:6-9a, which has the announcement: "Behold, there it comes, a procession of riders, teams of horses"; in addition, see 2 Kings 9:17). That the present passage has an "announcement from a watchman," which replaces the expected interjection הנה (behold) with הוי (ha), might be explained by the fact that the description of the enemy advance is recast to become a threat of disaster against the foreign army (v. 13aβ). It is for this reason that this section serves a legitimate function within the framework of the oracles against the nations. One comes to the end of the threat when ואיננו (it is all gone) is used, at the conclusion of v. 14a. After that, a generalizing reflection is added to the material: זה חלק שוסינו וגורל בזזינו (that is the destiny for those who plunder us, and the lot for those who move in against us to commit robbery). With reference to 14:26 (see above, p. 80), Childs (128f.) speaks of the "summary-appraisal form"; the oracle that precedes this statement would be summarized at this point and its importance would then be clarified.

As was done by F. Delitzsch (*Biblischer Commentar über die poetischen Bücher des Alten Testaments,* vol. 3 [1873] 54), we designate these summary statements that reiterate the main points as "epiphonemes." Except for Isaiah (see, in addition, only 28:29), the prophets do not otherwise use this form; it has its roots in wisdom (cf., e.g., Prov. 1:19: "Such is the end of all who are greedy for gain; it takes away the life of its possessors"; see also Ps. 49:14; Job 8:13; 18:21; 20:29; 27:13; constructed slightly differently: 5:27). Piled one on top of the other, even though somewhat modified, these epiphonemes are also used in Ecclesiastes (e.g., 4:4, 8, 16); the preacher uses them to articulate the results of his observations and reflections. Epiphonemes begin with a demonstrative, e.g., כֵּן אָרְחוֹת כָּל־בֹּצֵעַ בָּצַע (such is the end of all who are greedy for gain) (Prov. 1:19); זֶה דַרְכָּם כֵּסֶל לָמוֹ (such is the fate of the foolhardy) (Ps. 49:14); כֵּן אָרְחוֹת כָּל־שֹׁכְחֵי אֵל (such are the paths of all who forget God) (Job 8:13), and also elsewhere. The substantives used in these passages, אֹרַח (end, path) and דֶּרֶךְ (fate, road), are not all that far removed from what is meant when חֵלֶק (destiny) and גּוֹרָל (lot) are used in Isa. 17:14; in fact, the epiphonemes in Job 20:29 and 27:13 use חֵלֶק (destiny, portion) (and, instead of גּוֹרָל, "lot," the synonymous term נַחֲלָה, "heritage").

Meter: The passage begins with a weighty seven-stress colon (v. 12a). If one does not rearrange v. 12b, by moving כַּבִּירִים (mighty) (see textual note 12a), then one must overrule the present accentuation mark, so as to divide the verse after כִּשְׁאוֹן (as the roaring), which assumes that the reading is a six-stress colon (unless one would take this to be a five-stress colon, reversed so that it reads 2 + 3 stresses, which would be possible only if one would read כִּשְׁאוֹן מַיִם, "as the roaring of waters," as having one stress). The glosses in v. 13aα are prose. If one accepts the emendation suggested in the textual notes, then v. 13aβ is a two-stress + two-stress bicolon. Verse 13b is a seven-stress colon; v. 14a is a six-stress colon (לְעֵת עֶרֶב, "at the time of evening," receives only one stress); v. 14b is a five-stress colon. After having observed that there is a seven-stress colon in v. 12a, which announces the coming disaster, one notes that its counterpart is to be found in v. 13b, also a seven-stress colon, this time describing the flight of the enemy, though the completely unexpected change in fortune is depicted with the very short two-stress + two-stress bicolon in v. 13aβ.

Setting

Considerable disagreement exists about the historical setting of Isa. 17:12-14, and its authorship.

One must be careful about the way frequency statistics are used in a passage such as this, which is filled with so many terms that play an important role in the traditions. Nevertheless, the following can be said: הָמוֹן (deafening noise) is used in 5:13ff. (mythological concepts are also in the background in 5:14; yet no one has felt pressured to treat that passage as apocalyptic), in 29:5f., 7, 8 (הֲמוֹן זָרָיִךְ, "multitude of your foes," or else הֲמוֹן כָּל־הַגּוֹיִם, "the multitude of all the nations") and in 31:4; concerning הָמָה (raging), see 22:2; for שָׁאוֹן (roaring), see 5:14; for שָׁאָה (roar), see 6:11;

for the מִם כַּבִּירִים (mighty waters), see 28:2; cf. 8:7. For נַעַר (rebuke), the *terminus technicus* for describing the battle against chaos, cf. גְּעָרָה (threat) in 30:17. It is not of great importance that Isaiah also uses the word נוּס (flee), but one notes that he uses both נַעַר (threat, rebuke) and נוּס (flee) in the same sentence, in 30:17. מִמֶּרְחָק (to what is far away) is also used in 10:3 (also, in that passage, with נוּס, "flee") as well as in 30:27 (Isaianic?); מֹץ (chaff) is also found in 29:5, there also as an image of the הֲמוֹן (multitude) of the enemies. גַּלְגַּל (tumbleweeds), in the literal sense of "wheel," is used in 5:28 as well. Yet one should not overlook that the word is also used in that passage in combination with סוּפָה (stormwind). בַּלָּהָה (terror) is used only here, but it is not found in secondary parts of the book of Isaiah either. Though not frequently used elsewhere, בְּטֶרֶם (before) is a favorite term for Isaiah: 7:16; 8:4; 28:4. That חֵלֶק (destiny, portion) and גּוֹרָל (lot) are not found elsewhere in Isaiah is easily explained by the fact that these terms are traditionally used in epiphonemes. Concerning שָׁסָה (plunder), one can compare this with שָׁסַס (plunder) in 10:13 (within a quote of a speech by the Assyrians). Finally, בָּזַז (commit robbery) is used in 10:16, also with reference to the Assyrians. There is certainly no justification for agreeing with Marti, who says that this corresponds to a late Jewish way of thinking, as he makes the observation that the enemies of the Jews were called their plunderers and robbers, something that had been said already in Zech. 2:12f., and then, even more clearly, in Joel 4:2-6 (a passage in which neither of the verbs is even used).

At the very least, this survey of the vocabulary which has been used shows that nothing here would speak against Isaiah being the author. Beyond this, the uncertainty about the question of authenticity is simply tied to the fact that there are no indicators in this passage that would permit one to link this material to a specific historical situation. One can be certain only that enemies are mentioned, depicted as they march up against the city of God. Jerusalem is not mentioned in so many words, but one can be certain that this city must be meant, since the traditional material used here is widely used when reference is made to that city. Earlier commentators were convinced that Isaiah himself (no one else was even considered as a possible author) was the one who came up with this description about groups of peoples who were storming Jerusalem, just as the mighty roaring sea might have raged, created by him specifically at the time when Sennacherib invaded Judah in 701 (thus, Dillmann and, more recently, Bright, in Peake's *Commentary on the Bible;* Bright dates the material to the year 688, but still believes that it is to be attributed to Isaiah). In general, however, more recent scholars, whether or not they attribute the message to Isaiah, agree that the author makes use of preexisting traditions about the inviolability of Zion, traditions preserved in the Zion psalms (see the detailed commentary on each verse for the specific points of contact). If one has determined that there are connections with traditional material, passed down through the generations, then one is always faced with the question about which material is dependent on the other; in this instance, however, there is no doubt that the Zion psalms (46; 48; 76), if not chronologically earlier in their present form, at least contain traditions that predate the present depiction of the peoples storming Jerusalem. The material in Ps. 46:1-4, by itself, certainly does not give any indication that it is portraying battle forces that are storming Jerusalem; the section is reminiscent of the myth about the battle between the creator god and the forces of chaos, with the motif of battle against chaos being adapted for use in the depiction of the threat against the city of God. But "the peoples" appear then in the second section of Psalm 46, where, earlier, one would have found the mythic forces. It is difficult to know exactly when and how this recasting of the concept took place. But one would certainly be able to agree with Kraus's supposition (he refers to 2 Sam. 5:6) that the "complex of ideas which deals with the assault of the enemies, with the inviolability of Zion, and with God's awesome ability to intervene, had already been transferred over, as applicable, to the Jebusite city of Jerusalem in the pre-Israelite era" (*Psalmen 1–63*[4] BK XV, 344); cf. also Rohland, 140; Schreiner, 226, 235; von Rad, *OTTheol* I, 46; Lutz, 171ff.; Stolz, 88ff.; de Vaux, RB 73 [1966] 495ff.).

In more recent times, the explanation about how the traditions developed has been brought into question. Wanke, for example, has attempted to link "theology of Zion" with the group of temple singers known as the Korahites; this theory would mean not only that the psalms of Zion would have reached their present form initially during the postexilic era, but also that the essential concepts themselves came into existence during that time, obviously with the same assessment applying to the passages now in the book of Isaiah that would have made use of and reactualized this tradition. If this is true, not only would it mean that a large number of passages from the book of Isaiah that have already been questioned in terms of their "authenticity" would have to be assigned categorically to the postexilic era, but also a number of passages that clearly have been considered to have come from Isaiah would be denied him as well, e.g., 14:24-27; 28:1-4 (see, particularly, v. 2); 28:14-22; 29:1-7; 30:27-33; and the main body of the material in 31:4-9; only Kaiser has forged ahead, with abandon, and treated the text on the basis of such conclusions. But Wanke's thesis does not stand up to closer scrutiny. Many passages, besides those normally called psalms of Zion, include motifs about battles against other peoples and about peoples making the trek up to Zion; see Pss. 2:1ff.; 68:13ff.; 110:1ff.; cf. also 77:17. It is not true that these two motifs cannot be found in literature outside the OT (see Stolz, 72ff.; Schmidt, 41ff.).

The motif about the battle against chaos, with which the motif about the battle against the peoples is usually connected in traditio-historical studies, is used widely in the OT, in many different settings (see studies such as that by Stolz, 61ff.), and there is no way that such concepts first could have become part of what Israel believed only during the postexilic era and that such ideas would not have been integrated into the description of faith in Yahweh before this time. (Concerning those who speak against the views of Wanke, see, among others: Lutz, 213ff.; Scharbert, *RB* 12 [1968] 274f.; cf. also Hayes, *JBL* 82 [1963] 419f.) There is no doubt that the people of Jerusalem knew about the theological ideas connected with Zion during the time of Isaiah.

This conclusion does not, of course, establish with certainty that Isaiah himself is the author of the passage. B. Stade (*ZAW* 3 [1883] 16) already treated this as a redactional expansion, dated to the postexilic era. He found faithful followers for his position in Marti, Guthe, and E. Balla (*Die*

Botschaft der Propheten [1958] 470f.). Influenced by the knowledge that the section incorporated ancient material, which had its roots in themes transferred into Israel from the surrounding nations, the more recent phase of the study of the book, with rare exception, has attributed this section to Isaiah, dated most generally to the time of the Assyrian invasion into Judah in 701; however, most recently, even if one ignores the questions about the date of the theology about Zion, serious doubts about its authenticity have been expressed. Marti had already pointed out that the section talks about an event that is to occur at the end of time and that was formulated to give hope to the postexilic community. Fohrer has taken up these arguments once again, maintaining that this section speaks about an assault by the peoples against Zion that is to take place at the time when history would draw to a close. The threat of chaos and the battle against chaos would threaten once again, as the events surrounding the eschatological re-creation would unfold. Kaiser follows much the same argument: if one says that the prophet authored this type of material, then one would have to consider him to be the actual father of Jewish eschatology and apocalyptic. Apparently, this type of argumentation leads one into a hermeneutical circle: since one is convinced that this message is to be dated after the exile, one concludes that it is eschatological-apocalyptic, and since one believes that the material is eschatological-apocalyptic, one must therefore attribute it to the postexilic era. Maybe it would not be all that bad for Isaiah to be considered the "father of Jewish eschatology." In the first place, however, one must calmly assert that nothing in the passage would force one to interpret it only in an eschatological or apocalyptic sense. It may be that v. 12 describes nothing other than a very serious threat posed by an enemy. Nothing forces one to believe that vv. 13f. are speaking about anything other than sudden aid, coming in a time of great danger, and nothing, in principle, would hinder someone from assuming that the message was spoken within the context of a specific, historical series of events. The closing sentence does not seem to have a situation in mind that comes at the end of time, but seems to have the intent of applying a general confession of faith, applicable to all times, to a pressing threat in the present.

However, other reasons have been given that would argue against the authenticity of the passage, reasons that some believe cannot be refuted: the message is so unspecific, with no details about the identity of the people who will storm the city like rushing waters, none about the speaker, and just as little information about who is being addressed. Yet in a passage about which no questions have been raised, 10:28ff., the enemy is not named and the historical situation cannot be identified with certainty. We learn just as little about who is a threat to Damascus and Israel in 17:1ff. or about who, in 28:2, "is mighty and strong for the Lord," coming "like a storm of hail, a destroying tempest, like a storm of mighty, overflowing waters," or about the identity of "the overwhelming scourge" in 28:18ff. If none of the modern commentators has a problem with recognizing that this section speaks about Jerusalem, Isaiah would not have had to tell his hearers which city he had in mind either. One would not need specific details about the enemy, since every listener would know right away who the "he" was or who the "they" were. Besides all this, Barth, who has been so vehement in his rejection of the authenticity, has to concede "that the section does not simply formulate a general statement about what has ongoing validity, but deals with the circumstances surrounding a particular historical episode" (145). Possibly the most crucial objection to be raised by Barth, and others, points out that 17:12-14 does not fit the profile of what is known elsewhere about Isaiah's expectation of the future restoration (145), indeed, not just because Isaiah had never promised Jerusalem/Judah that there would be a specific and unending deliverance and a prosperous future in so many words; one cannot find any passages where he announces that king and people will enjoy an uninterrupted, settled future (37). This is the same objection that has been raised about passages such as 2:2-4 and 11:1-10 and that had to be dealt with critically when 8:9f. was discussed (at which point the absence of concrete details and the difficulty in dating the passage also tipped the scales for those who rejected its authenticity). In fact, it is not possible that Isaiah would have ever promised his fellow citizens unconditional protection and a settled future. The crux of the matter deals with whether he continually has to reiterate that his message has built-in contingencies, every time he speaks. Current scholarly efforts should be employed here as elsewhere in the effort to identify the exact circumstances in which a prophet delivered a message, but another issue must also be considered: to identify the function that such a passage is to serve. It is common for scholars to treat vv. 12-14 either as a message predicting disaster for Israel's enemies or as a message of salvation for Jerusalem, but the effort to force this passage to conform to this exact pattern simply does not work. Analyzing its actual function, this message—if one is willing to interpret it in light of the overall message of Isaiah—has a somewhat different purpose than to announce either a coming salvation or a disaster, namely: to summon fainthearted Jerusalem to trust confidently. That is why the final sentence is an expression of faith: even now, Jerusalem is still the city of God and ought to be assured thereby of Yahweh's protection (cf. 7:7, 8a, 9b). Even in the face of the onrushing flood of enemies, its inhabitants have no reason to despair or to undertake some questionable attempt to ensure their safety through diplomatic efforts. Jerusalem ought to be confident that its God would help. But even here, naturally, it would be important to add to this the *conditio fidei* (see *Isaiah 1–12*, p. 317): "If you do not believe, then you will not remain."

One of the real reasons for such a wide divergence of opinion about the authenticity of 17:12-14 is the predisposition that one brings to the study of the book, concerning the specific ideas one has about the nature of pre-exilic prophecy and, in particular, a specific notion about what Isaiah could have said or would not have said. It is a fact that "the boundaries that really define Isaiah's actual message" are still not yet clearly marked (see Karl Budde, *ZAW* 41 [1923] 154–203). But what has been mentioned just now should have made clear, at the very least, that one cannot deny 17:12-14 to Isaiah without, at the same time, eliminating some other passages as "inauthentic" that one normally would treat as from the prophet. But one thing can be said for certain: the reasons that have been given to reject the authenticity of the passage are not valid.

This leaves us with the problem of dating the passage within the time frame of the prophet's activity. It is doubtful that it was spoken during the time of the Syro-Ephraimitic War, so dated by some just because this passage follows the words that were directed against Damascus and Israel at the beginning of this chapter (see above, pp. 190f.). It would not help all that much if one considers this material to be either closely or loosely connected with chap. 18 either, since the date for chap. 18 is also just as disputed. During the time of Isaiah, there was only *one* time when masses of peoples stormed up against Jerusalem, that being when Sennacherib sent his field commander, the Rabshakeh, from Lachish to Jerusalem, against Hezekiah, with a large contingent of troops (בְּחֵיל כָּבֵד, emended) (2 Kings 18:17 = Isa. 36:2). But knowing about this event is not enough for one to conclude positively that this can be dated exactly to that time, since one cannot say for certain whether v. 12 describes an event that is taking place at that time or whether it is something that the prophet anticipates as coming in the future. If the latter were the case, this section of material could have come into existence basically in any time period in which one could presume that Jerusalem was under a severe threat. Content and specific vocabulary would lead one to make the closest connections with 29:5-7. But there are uncertainties about dating that passage as well, and links with some terminology and with general concepts certainly do not force one to conclude that the same date applies to both. On the basis of those similarities, the most one can argue is that the threat to Jerusalem described in 17:12-14 must have been a very real one for the prophet to have spoken so "uncautiously and directly" about how Yahweh would intervene. All this having been said, one has to be satisfied with a verdict of *non liquet* (nothing has been proved).

Commentary

[17:12] The prophet, who at this point issues a report as if he were a watchman stationed on the towers of his city, sees mighty masses of peoples marching up against Jerusalem. Those who consider this passage to be eschatological identify the "many peoples" as the heathen nations, at the end of time, who are going up against the city of God in the final battle (see Fohrer and Kaiser). But if this is Isaiah's message, then this host can only be the Assyrian army. Obviously, it is a problem that this term (עמים, "peoples") is in the plural; it has been explained that the Assyrian forces included auxiliary forces from other nations.

In ancient times, the Assyrian kings waged their wars with a people's army, which would have been called to service only when needed. All that changed during the time of Tiglath-Pileser III, under whom Assyria became a world power. Individual Assyrians still would have been liable for military service, but the largest percentage of the "Assyrian forces" now would have consisted of those who belonged to peoples who had been subjugated. The army was assembled by uniting the contingents of forces under the individual territorial governors (*paḫātu* or *šaknu;* cf. Sargon's Display Inscriptions, lines 112ff., 120; and Annals, lines 388ff., 408), but also from the troops that the vassal kings made available. Thus Ashurbanipal (Rm I, lines 68ff.): "During my march (to Egypt) 22 kings from the seashore, the islands and the mainland, servants who belong to me, brought heavy gifts to me and kissed my feet. I made these kings accompany my army over the land—as well as (over) the sea-route with their armed forces and their ships (respectively). Quickly I advanced as far as Kar-Baniti to bring speedy relief to the kings and regents in Egypt, servants who belong to me" (*ANET* 294).

Manasseh of Judah was also among those whose fate was to have to supply troops for the Assyrian king (Esarhaddon, broken Prism B, III, R 15, col. V, line 13).

In addition to these forces, which each could assemble whenever the need arose, each Assyrian king, during this late phase of its history, also had a standing army at his disposal, with which he would be able to carry out a lightning fast attack. The term that identifies these forces, *kiṣir šarrūti,* appears for the first time in Sargon's inscriptions. As the name itself informs us (*kiṣru* means "gathered together, assembled together," technically, "the 'united in readiness' members of the standing army," von Soden, *AHW*), this group is not made up of troops formed from any one specific nationality either. The Rassam Cylinder is informative on this point (VII, 58ff.): "The rebellious inhabitants of *bīt-imbī* . . . cast down the splendor of Ashur and of Ishtar, my lady. They fled from the mountains, to which they had earlier escaped, and they seized my feet. I assembled them together to draw the bow and added them into my royal armed forces, who fill my hand (*eli kí-ṣir šarru-ú-ti-ia šá ú-mal-lu-u qātu[ll]-u-a ú-rad-di*)."

Both the general army and the standing forces of the Assyrians were made up of a variety of ethnic groups during the latter part of the empire's history. It makes good sense that one would speak of the Assyrian army as עמים רבים (many peoples) (5:26 also speaks about the גוים, "peoples," though the text is usually altered to read the singular in that passage).

Thus the use of the plural is not enough to argue against this passage being dated to the time of Isaiah. A final reason for the plural being used is that Isaiah employs the terminology that has been transmitted in the Zion traditions, which speak about peoples (and royal empires; Pss. 46:7; 48:5ff.; cf. "multitude of all the nations" in Isa. 29:7ff.; see also 8:9). Concerning המון, cf. above, p. 20, on 13:4; there it clearly means "uproar," whereas here it is to be translated as "a mass of." According to Gerleman (72), the root meaning of the word is "a movement that takes place very noisily," and it is used originally to describe the sea and certain events that accompany being close to it and that cannot be separated from it: "the presence of noise and movement." המה is sometimes used to describe the roar of the sea: Jer. 6:23; similarly 50:42, or the waves as well: Isa. 51:15; Jer. 5:22; 31:35; 51:55.

מים (waters) is a plural of amplification: "the huge, mighty sea." The Sea of Gennesaret also can be identified as a ים. Parallel to this expression, one finds מים כבירים (many waters) in v. 12b (cf. 28:2). As is true of המון (deafening noise), שאון also means, on the one hand, the raging of the waters, and, on the other hand, a large group of people. According to KBL, the related verb שׁאה II is a hapax legomenon; it is probably used here only because of the parallelism. One also notes the imagery conveyed by the sound of the letters, with repetition of ה, מ, שׁ and the endings -וֹן and -וּן. The alternation between the dark-sounding *o* and *u* sounds, on the one hand, with the brighter *i* sounds, on the other, gives verbal expression to the sounds.

The traditions about Zion also mention that the one who fears Yahweh need not fear the waters that roar (Ps. 46:4). The crashing of the sea against the city of God uses imagery originally connected with the crashing of the sea that was present when the act of creation was carried out. Yahweh set firm boundaries for the raging sea (Jer. 5:22; cf. Isa. 51:15, which one should translate: "governs the sea [רֹגַע, emended text], as its billows roar"). The most important passage to consult is Ps. 65:7f.: מֵכִין הָרִים בְּכֹחוֹ נֶאְזָר בִּגְבוּרָה מַשְׁבִּיחַ שְׁאוֹן יַמִּים שְׁאוֹן גַּלֵּיהֶם וַהֲמוֹן לְאֻמִּים (By his strength, he established the mountains; girded with might; silencing the roaring of the seas, the roaring of their waves, and the tumult of the peoples), a passage that shows how central it is to the description of Yahweh's work of creation that he becalms the mighty and roaring sea, but one that also demonstrates how easy it is to move to the topic about how Yahweh exercises control within the historical realm, quieting down the raging of the peoples in this passage; see also Ps. 89:10: אַתָּה מוֹשֵׁל בְּגֵאוּת הַיָּם בְּשׂוֹא גַלָּיו אַתָּה תְשַׁבְּחֵם (you rule the raging of the sea; when its waves rise, you still them) (emended text; see *BHK*[3] and *BHS*).

[17:13] Instead of using שׁבח (still, becalm) in the *hiphᶜil* or *piᶜel*, as is true of the passages just cited, v. 13 uses the verb גער (rebuke) (cf. Ugaritic *gᶜr*, "call loudly, scold, shout down"; Arabic *jaᶜara*, "bellow") to describe Yahweh's intervention. In the OT this verb occurs in texts describing Yahweh's battle with the powers of chaos: Nah. 1:4; Ps. 106:9 (but with a transferred meaning, describing the damming up of the waters of the Sea of Reeds in the exodus). The substantive גערה (rebuke) is used in its original sense, describing the verbal rebuke uttered in the battle against the powers of chaos, in Ps. 104:7; Job 26:11 (cf. also Ps. 18:16 = 2 Sam. 22:16; Ps. 76:7).

The creator God's "scolding" is already a spiritualizing of what was originally a smiting with a magical club, with which Baal, according to the Ugaritic texts, displaces Yamm: "The club moved quickly in the hand of Baal, fast as an eagle. It smashed down violently, held by his fist, onto the forehead of the one who rules [Yamm], striking down to the bottom of the nose of the one who ruled over the floods. Yamm sank down, fell to the earth; the outer surface of his body shook, his foundation (?) was rattled" (*UT* 68:23-26; Aistleitner, *Die mythologischen und kultischen Texte aus Ras Schamra* [1964²] 51 [cf. *ANET* 131]).

Instead of using גער (rebuke), Ps. 46:7 uses נָתַן בְּקוֹלוֹ (he utters his voice); Job 38:11 is satisfied simply with using אמר (he said). Yahweh's דבר (word) is laden with mighty power (see *Isaiah 1–12*, pp. 229f.); even more so is his גערה (rebuke). When coming face-to-face with his fearsome scolding, the masses of the peoples flee away.

The verb נוס (flee) is also used in traditions about the creation: Ps. 104:7: "at your rebuke, they flee" (ינוסון), namely, the waters of the תהום (the deep); "at the sound of your thunder they take to flight" (יחפזו; cf. this with Ps. 48:6); this is used with a transferred meaning when the passage through the Jordan is depicted in Ps. 114:3, 5, and when portraying the enemies of Yahweh who flee when he appears in his theophany (Ps. 68:2).

Nonetheless, the use of ממרחק (far away) might correspond to the facts of the situation. The terrible storm that, according to 10:3, is going to seek out Israel for punishment will come ממרחק (from afar) and, according to 5:26, the sinister people (it is common that the singular is read here, instead of the plural, גוים, "peoples") is the Assyrians; in Jeremiah it is the "foe from the north" (4:16; 5:15; cf. also Isa. 13:5).

One learns no more about the original background of the battle against chaos in v. 13b, when observing the flight of these enemies: the enemies scatter apart from one another just as chaff is scattered all over the mountains when the wind blows (cf. 29:5ff. and Ps. 83:14). It is a common practice that one would build a threshing floor at a place where the wind can blow freely, but not right on top of a mountain (Dalman, *AuS* III, 69), since the wind would blow there with too great a force. If, in spite of that, Isaiah speaks of "chaff on the mountains," he has described the greater intensity of the wind on purpose: this will not be just like chaff blowing away from a typical threshing floor (see illus. 30 in Dalman, *AuS* III); instead, this depicts the way chaff blows away from a threshing place that is constructed out in the open, where the wind can blow across it from all directions, suggesting that the enemies will be scattered just as violently. This imagery is used elsewhere in the OT: Hos. 13:3 promises this end for Israel, caught up as it is with worshiping the idols; in Zeph. 2:2 this is for a shameless people; in Isa. 41:15 it is for Israel's oppressors; in Ps. 1:4 it is for the godless; and so on. But the word מץ (chaff) always occurs in reference to the imagery of enemies or evildoers being scattered.

Even this graphic image is not enough for the prophet; he comes at it from still another direction: "as tumbleweeds before the storm." It is difficult to determine exactly what is meant by גלגל (see also Ps. 83:14). Basically, the word means "wheel," generally being used for describing one that would be mounted on a war chariot, and this meaning must be somewhere in the background of what is intended here. But here it is more likely that one would be led to think about parts of a plant that are blown about by the wind.

In Ps. 83:14 the Gk simply translates the word as τροχός, "wheel"; however, in 17:13 it translates it: ὡς κονιορτὸν τροχοῦ, "as the dust from a wheel," which at least tries to make some sense of it. In fact, this expression refers to what is known as wind-driven brush, as tumbleweeds, which roll along on the ground like a ball (גלל means "roll, revolve"). This term most likely refers to a type of thistle, *Gundelia Tournefortii* (about this, see Siegismund, *PJ* 7 [1911] 127; Dalman, *AuS* I/1, 53; and Rüthy, *Die Pflanze und ihre Teile im biblisch-hebräischen Sprachgebrauch* [1942] 27ff.; idem, *Probleme der Bibelübersetzung* [1959] 5ff.; in addition, see illus. 2 in

Dalman, *AuS* I/1). In Arabic they are known today in Palestine as ʿ*akkūb;* when uttering a malediction, the Arabs might say: "May you be blown about as the ʿ*akkūb* is
blown by the wind, until you are stuck amongst the thorns or are cast into the sea"
(W. M. Thomson, cited by Rüthy, *Die Pflanze*, 28).

Concerning סופה, "storm wind," see, in addition to 5:28; 21:1; 29:6;
and Ps. 83:16, especially Nah. 1:3f., according to which Yahweh rides in,
within the storm, to rebuke the sea.

[17:14] When Yahweh strides forth, then a most surprising turn of events
takes place: in the evening there is terror, but, before the morning dawns, the
sinister threat has disappeared. This is expressed brilliantly in a pregnant
expression in v. 14a. Its shortness, of course, leaves many questions open:
exegetes have puzzled long and hard, trying to figure out whether it means to
say: in the evening the city is still utterly consumed with dread, but in the
morning the whole specter has disappeared; or, in the evening the mighty
fear of God falls on the enemies and in the morning they have already disappeared without a trace. Not only in the morning but also in the evening there
can also be a time for rejoicing, since Yahweh allows his might and majesty
to shine forth then as well; see Ps. 65:8ff.

בלהה is virtually always used in the OT to describe the kind of terror
that falls on the enemies (Ezek. 26:21; 27:36; 28:19); for this reason, it is
more likely that the second possibility is more correct, not the least of the
reasons being that the text does not mention "in the morning" but "before the
morning." בלהה is a very strong word; it is used when one depicts terror that
is disabling, an invasion that leads to a rapid, bitter end; in Job 18:14 death
is called the מלך בלהות (king of terrors); cf. also Job 30:15.

The sentence "before the morning (already)—it is all gone" corresponds very
nearly to what is said in Ps. 46:6: "God will help her [the city of God] לפנת בקר"
([when the night is] at the point of turning into morning). But also a number of other
passages in the Psalms mention that the one who prays awaits God's help at break of
day (5:3f.; 59:17; 88:14; 143:8; see also Lam. 3:22f.). H. Schmidt (*Das Gebet des
Angeklagten*, BZAW 49 [1928] 21–30) believes that this information is sufficient to
suggest that the person slept that night in the temple, which meant that the one who
prayed would be able to see "Yahweh's beauty in the morning" and would thus be
certain that Yahweh would help (Pss. 11:7; 17:15). This thesis has not stood the test
of time. If one wants to make sense of the stereotypical reference to expecting God's
help at break of day, within the context of the cult, then one might well take it as a
reference to the morning offering, which included a request for "help" or a plea that
the help would take effect. But no single cultic explanation would explain the usage
of the formula (see Barth, *TDOT* II, 219ff.). Ziegler thought that he could identify
three different aspects, any one of which could be intended: the rising sun furnished
an image of rescue and help, since, each time, God would certainly and reliably send
his help, just as surely as the sun rose every morning (284f.). But morning was also
the time when juridical decisions were handed down (Exod. 14:13f.; Jer. 21:12; Ps.
101:8), which means that it was that point in time when what was right finally got the
upper hand and was victorious. Finally, the morning was the time when Yahweh (dur-

ing battle) would intervene decisively, for the benefit of his people. "Thus Yahweh saved Israel, on the morning of that day, from the hand of Egypt," Exod. 14:30. Or: "when morning dawned, they were all dead bodies," 2 Kings 19:35 = Isa. 37:36; see also 1 Sam. 11:9 and cf. 2 Kings 3:9-20. The ideology of holy war is clear about morning being the time for the assault.

Based on this background, it would seem that the present passage should be interpreted as follows: the motif of "God's help in the morning" is apparently linked with the general theme of the battle against the peoples; Isaiah would have modified it (he actually says: בטרם בקר, "before the morning"), and then used it. But one ought not miss the point that the most significant factor in what he says deals with the suddenness of the change of fortune—a change of fortune that takes place against all expectations.

The most important point made by the prophet is now in what follows in v. 14b, something that he adds, which no longer simply makes use of the terminology that has its roots in the Zion tradition. The reason for confidence is based on what has been depicted, pointing out that all the masses of peoples disappear from Jerusalem. Jerusalem is to base its confidence in the knowledge that it will not be simply handed over to its enemies.

Concerning שׁסה (plunder), see *Isaiah 1–12*, p. 421; on בזז (commit robbery), cf. *TDOT* II, 66ff.

The two terms חלק (destiny) and גורל (lot), both of which are used regularly in wisdom settings, can be defined more exactly by observing their equivalents in the epiphonemes: Prov. 1:19 uses ארח (way) (the suggestion by *BHK*³ to emend this to read אחרית, "end," is mistaken); Ps. 49:14: דרך (fate, way) (the parallel word אחריהם, "after them," ought to be altered to read אחרותם, "their end"); Job 8:13: once again, ארח (path) parallels תקוה (hope). In Job 20:29 and 27:13, נחלה (inheritance) parallels חלק (destiny, portion). All of these terms are very close to what we would identify in modern times as "fate, destiny." In their basic sense, חלק and נחלה are used to identify the portion of land that fell to a particular tribe or clan, as, e.g., Num. 18:20: "You shall have no נחלה (allotment) in their land, nor shall you have any חלק (share) among them; I am your חלק (share) and your נחלה (possession) among the Israelites." The particular portion of land that a tribe received was determined by casting lots (cf. Greek κλῆρος, which means both "lot" and "destiny in life"). For examples of the use of the terms with a transferred meaning for גורל (lot) and/or חלק (destiny), see Isa. 34:17; 57:6; Jer. 13:25 (parallel to מְנָה, "portion"); cf. also Joel 4:3; Ps. 125:3; Dan. 12:13 (see J. T. Renner, "A Study of the Word Goral in the OT," diss., Heidelberg [1958] [typescript]).

Purpose and Thrust

The intended purpose of these three verses has been carefully explicated: Isaiah summons Jerusalem, at a moment when the people are under a severe threat, to trust calmly. To be sure, Kaiser has suggested that a prophet like Isaiah, functioning among a people whose history was still unfolding, would not have come to such conclusions; he thinks that the kings would rightly have rejected such notions as pie-in-the-sky fantasies, since they would not have had the luxury of even beginning to consider the possibility that Jerusalem could be delivered in the manner described here. But the prophets will not permit themselves to be pressed into the procrustean bed of a modern, rationalistic worldview. Concerning this problem of Isaiah's political views, much has already been discussed, rather thoroughly, about whether he was a thoughtfully realistic political thinker or whether he was a utopian (see F. Weinrich, *Der religiös-utopische Charakter der "prophetischen Politik"* [1932]; and K. Elliger, "Prophet und Politik," *ZAW* 53 [1935] 3–22 = *KlSchr,* TBü 32, 119–140). He was a utopian in terms of the faith and was still bold enough to position himself by confronting the harsh realities of his day, making use of the traditions that speak about salvation for Zion to summon his people to trust, at the very moment when the situation seemed most hopeless. He did the same in chap. 7: "Take care for yourself and remain calm! . . . It will not happen and will not succeed" (since, as one must mentally carry the thought to its logical conclusion, the head of Judah is Jerusalem, and the head of Jerusalem is the son of David, who has been chosen by Yahweh). In no way was that a free pass, permitting the listeners to have a blind faith that would rashly take deliverance for granted. Isaiah does not have a one-track mind when he speaks out; he proclaims neither announcements of judgment that would sacrifice belief in salvation nor promises of salvation that suggest that the people were to be released from being dependent on Yahweh. What he has to say is a message from Yahweh himself, from the God of Israel, who desires to establish his rule within the midst of his people.

Does that make Isaiah a daydreamer? The kings with whom he dealt were actually of the opinion that "it was not possible (to) really act on" what the prophet suggested to them, to shape their political decisions on the basis of the way the prophet had instructed them. Other prophets, such as Jeremiah, in their own unique situations, were not able to restate his message of promise in that exact way. It is a risky venture to have a "utopian" political stance, shaped by faith. But there are situations in which such a risky venture must be acted upon, and there are prophetic figures who have been given the ἐξουσία (empowerment) to press forth boldly in such risky ventures. One is not provided with a recipe for political action in 17:12-14, but this section points out that there are instances when the time is right for believing against all "reason," and when one must say as much at the very time that the pressures are apparently too great, during a time that one's very existence is threatened.

The eschatological-apocalyptic interpretation of this passage has to be rejected, as has been pointed out by the detailed analysis above. The only way that one could call the message in 17:12-14 eschatological is by noting that the prophet expects that Yahweh will intervene at a time when circumstances would be most threatening, and when he would anticipate that a radical turnabout in fortune was forthcoming. That it was not originally intended to refer to end times does not alter the situation that, in later times, this message was seen as providing evidence that there would be a battle at the end of time, pressed by the peoples, against the holy city and its inhabitants. What Isaiah called his contemporaries to believe, focusing on their despondent mood at that moment, was later reused and became a dogma that was considered to be valid at all times, altered so that this scene became the pivotal point at which there would be a major redirecting of history, set within the framework of the plans of the Lord of the world, who had unalterable plans for the way that history would unfold.

Isaiah 18:1-7

A Message about Cush

Literature

Concerning the vocabulary: on ל מעבר: E. Vogt, "ʿēber hayyardēn == REGIO FINITIMA IORDANI," *BZ* 34 (1953) 118–119. On בוא: L. Köhler, "Bāzāʾ = fortschwemmen," *TZ* 6 (1950) 316–317. On עלי־אור: E. Baumann, "Zwei Einzelbemerkungen. I. Jes 18,4," *ZAW* 21 (1901) 266–268. On צח: F. Montagnini, "Come caldo sereno al brillar della luce? (Is 18,4)," *RivBib* 11 (1963) 92–95. Y. Aharoni and R. Amiran, "Excavations at Tel Arad," *IEJ* 14 (1964) 142f. and plate 38. M. Weippert, "Archäologischer Jahresbericht," *ZDPV* 80 (1964) 182f. J. A. Soggin, "Zum wiederentdeckten altkanaanäischen Monat צח," *ZAW* 77 (1965) 83–86, and later note, 326. A. Lemaire, "Note épigraphique sur la pseudo-attestation du mois 'ṢḤ,'" *VT* 23 (1973) 243–245. On נצח יהוה: A. Wutz, "Abweichende Vokalisationsüberlieferungen im hebräischen Text," *BZ* 21 (1933) 7–21. On טל: A. Gonzáles, "El rocío del cielo," *EstBib* 22 (1963) 109–139, esp. 135.

Concerning the history of the era: A. Erman and H. Ranke, *Ägypten und ägyptisches Leben im Altertum* (1923). H. von Zeissl, *Äthiopen und Assyrer in Ägypten*, ÄF 14 (1955[2]). W. Wolf, *Die Welt der Ägypter* (1955). H. Tadmor, "The Campaigns of Sargon II of Assur: A Chronological-Historical Study," *JCS* 12 (1958) 22–40, 77–100. R. Borger, "Das Ende des ägyptischen Feldherrn Sibʾe = סוא," *JNES* 19 (1960) 49–53. E. Otto, Ägypten: *Der Weg des Pharaonenreiches* (1966[4]). B. Reicke, "Äthiopien," *BHH* I, 147–148. H. Brunner, "Äthiopien," *BL*[2], 125. K. A. Kitchen, *The Third Intermediate Period in Egypt (1100–650 B.C.)* (1973). D. B. Redford, "Studies in Relations Between Palestine and Egypt During the First Millennium B.C., II. The Twenty-Second Dynasty," *JAOS* 93 (1973) 3–17.

[**Literature update through 1979:** W. Janzen, *Mourning Cry and Woe Oracle*, BZAW 123 (1972).

Concerning the vocabulary: S. Duvdevani, "כחם עלי־אור, כעב־טל בחם קציר. נבואת ישעיהו על חילות אשור (Is 18: 4-5)," *Sepher J. Braslavi* (1971) 334–338. K. Seybold, "Zwei Bemerkungen zu gml/gmwl," *VT* 22 (1972) 112–117 (on 18:5).

Concerning the history of the era: O. Kaiser, "Der geknickte Rohrstab," FS K. Elliger (1973) 99–106. W. Zimmerli, "Jesaja und Hiskia," FS K. Elliger (1973) 199–208.]

Text

18:1 Ha! The land of the winged[a] boats
    [which is situated] [b]in the region[b] of the rivers of Cush,

205

2 which sends envoys[a] on the river,[b]
　　and [in] papyrus canoes[c] on the water.
Go,[d] you nimble messengers,
　　to a tall, smooth[e] nation,
　　to a people feared [far and wide,][f]
　　to a nation, which tramples down with muscle power,[g]
　　[whose land is cut through[h] by streams].
3 [All of you, who inhabit the circle of the earth,
　　and all of you who live on earth,
　　when someone raises a battle standard on the mountains, then look,[a]
　　when someone blows a horn, then listen carefully![a]]
4 Truly, thus says Yahweh to me:
　　In utter calm[a] I look on my place,
　　just like shimmering heat[b] in the (sun)light,[c]
　　just like a dew cloud on harvest day.[d]
5 Yes, at harvest time,[a] when the time for blooming is past
　　and the clusters of blooms[b] will have become ripening grapes,[c]
　　one cuts the suckers away with the pruning knife,
　　separates the wild grapes and pulls (them) out.
6 All of that will be left for the birds of prey from the mountains,
　　and for the animals of the field.
　　[And in summer the vultures will sit on it,
　　and all the animals of the earth will pass the winter on it.]

* * * *

7 [At that time, gifts will be brought to Yahweh of Hosts 'from'[a] a tall and smooth[b] people, and from a people feared far and wide,[b] from the nation which had trampled down 'with muscle power,'[b] whose land is cut through[b] by streams, to the place of the name of Yahweh of Hosts, to Mount Zion.]

1a According to KBL, צְלָצַל, in both the present passage and in Deut. 28:42, means "swarm of (crickets)"; H. Zimmern (*Akkadische Fremdwörter als Beweis für babylonischen Kultureinfluss* [1915²] 53) provides support for this with reference to Akkadian ṣarṣaru, "grasshopper, cricket," or something similar; cf. also Arabic ṣurṣūr, plural: ṣarāṣir (or ṣarāṣīr), "cricket, house cricket"; Arabic ṣalṣala, and ṣalla, "ringing, clanking, clattering," as well as II taṣalṣala; Syriac ṣrṣwrʾ, "*genus locustarum*" (so Brockelmann, *LS*). For this reason, the normal translation for אֶרֶץ צִלְצַל כְּנָפַיִם has been "land of the whirring wings," or something similar. Kaiser believes that he can find support for this translation in a reference from Herodotus 2.95, but that states plainly that much effort had to be expended in Egypt when attempting to guard against swarms of gnats. Nor can one be swayed by travelers who have observed that Nubia is still known today, though not in a favorable light, especially as a place that swarms with gnats, for that problem is certainly not unique to Nubia.

The meaning "harpoon," which is how צְלָצַל is translated in Job 40:31, cannot be used here, since the word is followed by כְּנָפַיִם (wings), in the genitive. According to Jerome (Latin: *umbra*, "shadow") Aquila linked צְלָצַל with צֵל, "shadows," and others have followed him in this, including Martin Luther, Dillmann, and Buhl, but shadows are also not uniquely characteristic of Nubia. Finally, the translation of the Vulg: *cymbalum* (cf. Hebrew צֶלְצְלִים, "clanging percussion instruments, cymbals") brings us no further. By contrast, the Targ rendered צְלָצַל as סְפִינָן, "ships," and, according to Jerome, Theod renders it with a word that would be the equivalent of the Latin *naves* (ships). In addition, the Gk translates בצלצל דגים in Job 40:31 as ἐν πλοίοις ἁλιέων (in boats of sailors). For these reasons, it would seem that the translation "light ship, boat" is justified, all the more so because of Ethiopic *salala*, "swim," and also Aramaic צלצל, "ship," which can be cited in support of this meaning, though not Arabic *zulzul* (something dangling) (see Lane, *Arabic-English Lexicon* 1 [1917]; Driver, FS T. H. Robinson [1950] 56; idem, *JSS* 13 [1968] 45; and Gesenius, *Thesaurus*, 1167f.)

1b–b Normally, מעבר ל means "on the other side of." Most commentators see no problem with that reading. Others (Duhm; Marti; Donner, VTSup 11 [1964] 122) treat v. 1b as a (scholarly) gloss. But this solution is too facile and there must be a more acceptable explanation. Apparently, this material deals with Cush, and this country's territory is not situated on the other side of the rivers. One might try to solve the dilemma by suggesting that, as far as Israel was concerned, Cush was situated on the edge of the inhabited world, so that one would not expect someone to have detailed knowledge about its exact geographical setting. Procksch suggests pointing this מעבר ל, "entrance, passage through" (cf. 16:2: מעברת לארנון, "at the fords of the Arnon," and see Gen. 32:23) and translates this "an entrance to the rivers of Cush." According to Vogt, (מ)עבר הירדן often means: "in the territory of the Jordan," which means that מעבר לנהרי כוש could mean "*in regione iuxta flumina Kus*" (in the region near the rivers of Cush), which would obviate the need for an emendation.

2a Since the time of H. Winckler (*Alttestamentliche Untersuchungen* [1892] 151f.), צירים (envoys) has often been altered to read צי־ים, "ships" (see 33:21 and cf. Ezek. 30:9), which would furnish us with a better parallel to כלי־גמא (papyrus canoes) (if correct, the ב would be eliminated). But there is no real parallelism in the verses that precede and follow this either, and it would be more difficult yet to interpret the passage if the suggested alteration were accepted.

2b Lightweight boats would undoubtedly be useless on the open sea, even if piloted by the most able of the Nubians; here ים (sea) refers to the Nile, just as in 19:5 and Nah. 3:8; in Jer. 51:36, the Euphrates River is called a ים. Still today, the Arabs speak of the *bahru-n-nīli* (*bahrun* = "sea, lake, river"; on this, see W. Schwarzenbach, 69 [see literature to 15:1—16:14]).

2c–c Gray and Donner suggest removing the ב before כלי (canoes, vessels), which also makes sense in terms of the meter. In other cases, כלי means "container, utensils, weapons," but here it means "ship" (see also 60:9, emended text); cf. Syriac *mʾnʾ* (the vessel, utensil) (which is how the Syr translates כלי here), which has the same range of meanings; French: *vaisseau*.

גמא is an Egyptian word (*qmʾ*, "rush, papyrus"; see E. A. W. Budge, *An Egyptian Hieroglyphic Dictionary*); Sym: δια σκευων παπυρινων (using papyrus vessels). For other instances where גמא = papyrus, see also 35:7; Exod. 2:3; and Job 8:11.

2d In this passage, לכו carries the sense: "goes back."

2e Some MSS and Qᵃ read וממורט (and smoothed) (on this, see G. R. Driver, *JTS* 2 [1951] 25), but the shorter form מורט (smoothed) of the *puʿal* participle as in MT is also possible; see Ges-K §52s; the uncommon form was adjusted later to conform to the normal pattern, as was often the case.

2f–f מן־הוא והלאה (far and wide) is found elsewhere only in v. 7, being part of that passage because it is dependent on this verse. Marti suggests removing מן־הוא (from this [place]) and takes הלאה to mean "in the distance." But הלאה means "from now on, furthermore," necessitating a reference to the place where one must begin. Thus הוא should be translated "there, in that place," in this passage, a meaning that is certainly seldom found elsewhere, but that makes sense when explained on the basis of the demonstrative usage of הוא (with the meaning: "that one"); on this, see the way הֵמָּה (NRSV: this is, lit.: they are) is used in Jer. 7:4.

2g קָו refers to a "(measuring) line." In Isa. 28:10 and 13, קַו לָקָו (line upon line) seems to have an onomatopoetic sense, intended to convey babbling speech. For this reason, Donner (122) explains that קַו־קָו is used here in order to convey the sense of someone speaking a foreign language, which no one can understand. Fischer speculates that it supposedly mimics the sound of the stomping of the boots of soldiers in an army, whereas Driver (*JSS* 13 [1968] 46) opts for a solution that treats קַו־קָו as a reduplicated adjective, with the meaning "very strong." Both K^(Or) and Q^a read קָוְקָו as one word, which would mean something like "sinewy muscle power," on the basis of Arabic *quwwatun,* "strength, power," and *qawiya,* "stretched tight, be strong."

2h There is uncertainty about בָּזְאוּ: one part of the Hexaplaric and Lucianic recension reads διηρπασαν (they plundered), which means that someone read this as if from the root בזז (spoil, plunder) or at least treated it as such, as did also the Targ, Syr, and Jerome (Vulg: *diripuerunt,* "they pillaged"), but this yields no acceptable meaning here. Köhler refers to Arabic *bazza,* "pull along forcibly," and suggests that it should be translated "pull along by floating," justifying this by presupposing that the traditionally accepted reading "cut through, across," would infer that the speaker would have had intimate knowledge of a detailed map of the region. But, at the very least, the meaning "pull along by floating" is just as problematic. Thus one does well in this instance to stay with the traditional rendering (cf. Syriac *bz',* "tear apart, cut apart").

3a For the imperfect, used in the sense of an imperative, see Joüon, *Gr* §113m.

4a אֶשְׁקוֹטָה (I will be utterly calm): concerning the way in which the short *o* sound was represented with a ו as a *mater lectionis,* see Joüon, *Gr* §7b, note 2. Ehrlich (*Randglossen* IV, 68) suggests that one should read אַשְׁקִיפָה (= "I will look out at"), but the text, as transmitted, conveys a more striking image.

4b Aharoni and Amiran believe that they can read ירח צח on an ostracon from Arad, which would provide evidence that צח is the name of a month (on this, see Montagnini, Soggin). But this reading is highly speculative (see Weippert and Lemaire), and, at the very least, there is no convincing evidence that one should look for the name of a month in the present passage. On the basis of the Arabic *ḍiḥḥ,* Eitan maintains that צח means "sun" in this passage and also suggests that אוֹר (on the basis of Arabic *'ry*) means "rain" or "dew" in this passage. But it is too adventuresome not to translate אוֹר as "light," and we also do best to stay with "shimmering," the traditional rendering for צח; see also רוּחַ צַח (a hot wind) in Jer. 4:11.

4c Literally, עֲלֵי־אוֹר: "above the light"; this has caused many difficulties in understanding what is meant; see below, p. 220. Baumann suggested altering the text to read עַל יְאוֹר (above the river [= Nile]). That is highly unlikely, but it certainly remains a possibility that אוֹר (light) is not the correct original reading.

4d Instead of בְּחֹם קָצִיר (in the heat of harvest), Donner proposes reading simply בְּקָצִיר (at harvesttime), but it would be better to follow those MSS that offer the reading בְּיוֹם קָצִיר (in the day of harvest) (as is apparently the way it was read also in the Gk, Vulg, Syr); it is unlikely that Isaiah would have used חֹם (heat) twice in the same line of the verse.

5a Here, as well, קָצִיר refers to a grain harvest; it ought not be interpreted as if it referred to a בָּצִיר, "harvest in a vineyard." לִפְנֵי is not to be taken in the sense of "*prae-*," in a temporal sense, but rather has the meaning "in the sight of, in the presence of"; at the time when the ripe grain is to be cut, that is the same time when the work mentioned here, which must be done in the vineyard, also presents itself as ready for the workers to harvest.

5b As in Job 15:33 and Gen. 40:10 (emended), נצה means "blooming, in full blossom" in this passage. Instead of יהיה נצה (clusters of blooms will have become), Wutz would rather read יְהֻֽה נֹצֵץ "throws off the blooms," an unnecessary emendation.

5c The grapes that are not yet completely ripe are called בסר (cf. Arabic *basara*, "handle before its time, earlier than one ought," and *busrun*, "ripening dates," and the equivalent terms in Aramaic, Syriac, and rabbinic Hebrew).

7a For עם, the Gk reads ἐκ λαοῦ (from a people), Vulg *a populo* (from a people); see also Qᵃ. For this reason, one should follow Ehrlich, *Randglossen* IV, 69; Dillmann; Marti; Feldmann; Procksch; Fohrer; Kaiser, et al., reading this מֵעַם (from a people).

7b One should consult the appropriate notes in v. 2 for information about מורט (smooth), מִן־הוא (far), קו־קו (muscle power), and בזא (cut through).

Form

As has already been mentioned (above, p. 191), in spite of other opinions to the contrary, 18:1 begins a new section, one that encompasses the entire chapter. There is no doubt that its message is about Cush. There is no discernible reason why a superscription מַשָּׂה כוּש (verdict concerning Cush) has not been placed at the beginning, but this probably could be explained if we were more informed about the earlier stages of the development of the material now found in chaps. 13–23.

[18:7] One must also deal with expansions to the original text of this unit of material. At the present time, it is rather generally accepted that v. 7 is a later addition, from another hand (but see Procksch, Fischer, Eichrodt, et al.), and even those who still speak in favor of Isaiah as the author of the verse assign it to a different time period and treat it as a later addition (Naegelsbach, Knabenbauer; cf. Hertzberg). As is true with the more common phrase ביום ההוא (on that day) (see 17:4, 7, 9), בעת ההיא (in that time) serves as a redactional link (cf. passages such as Jer. 4:11; 33:15; Zeph. 1:12; 3:20), and the fact that it is in prose betrays it as secondary; it directly contradicts what has just been said. Further evidence for this being a reinterpretation is found in the use of so many vocabulary items from v. 2 to describe the Cushites. Finally, מקום שם יהוה (the place of the name of Yahweh) sounds deuteronomistic.

[18:3] It is more difficult to arrive at a clear understanding of v. 3. In v. 2 the messengers from Cush are addressed directly; in v. 3 the listeners are "all who inhabit the circle of the earth." It is at least possible that all of those who hear this message were summoned, already within the original message, as witnesses to observe the intervention of Yahweh, which is announced in vv. 5f. However, v. 4 stands between vv. 3 and 5f., not really functioning very well as a continuation of what is said in v. 3. In addition, תבל (circle of the earth) is used elsewhere in secondary passages of the book of Isaiah (13:11; 14:17, 21, and often elsewhere), never being used in any of the passages attributed to Isaiah. תקע שופר (blow a horn) sounds much like 27:13, and

נֵס נָשָׂא (raise a battle standard) is commonly used by those who expanded the book of Isaiah (11:12; 13:2), another indication that this passage came into existence at a later time (so Marti, Buhl, Fohrer). It is possible that the same person who reworked the transmitted text of Isaiah by appending v. 7 also inserted v. 3.

[18:6b] There is also no doubt that v. 6b is a gloss, though of a different type. On the one hand, according to v. 6a, everything is to be left, all at once, to the birds of prey from the mountains and to the animals of the field; on the other hand, v. 6b divides this up: in the summer it will belong to the vultures, in the winter the animals will while the time away there. Some have spoken in favor of this verse fragment having been part of the original text, suggesting that the same point is stated in two different ways as a result of the poetic technique employed (Hitzig, Procksch; see also Kaiser); in reality, it is an ingenious way to expand on what is said in v. 6a.

[18:2bβ] Finally, v. 2bβ can hardly be original either. Because of the problems with the uncertainty about the translation (see above, pp. 207f.), one cannot be confident about any solution. That the relative pronoun is used already arouses suspicions. Both *BHK* and *BHS* treat v. 2bβ as the first colon of v. 3a, which does not help much; v. 3a has sufficient material to constitute a line of verse. Yet it also makes no sense that a relative clause would stand by itself as an entire line of a verse. Based on its content, it seems awkward; the streams of Cush have already been mentioned in v. 1. It is possible that it belonged originally with v. 7 and was relocated into v. 2 after v. 7 had been formed by appropriating elements from v. 2.

[18:5f.] There is a definite line of demarcation between vv. 4 and 5. Does this mean that vv. 5f. should be separated from their context and be treated as a separate unit of material? Marti favors this. He points out that difficulties are presented initially just by the change in person, followed by the problem of having to translate קָצִיר as "grain harvest" in v. 4, but as "grape harvest" in v. 5; besides this, questions are raised about the way in which ripening fruits are compared to the injustice that is to be imposed upon Judah. According to Marti, all these problems would be resolved by treating vv. 5f. as the continuation of 17:11. But vv. 5f. are needed because they develop what was begun in v. 4: it is true that Yahweh can look on for a time, he can even wait for a very long time, but he never gives up his hold on the reins of history: one day, the cloud heavy with dew turns into a storm cloud, from which the lightning flashes forth. The problems that Marti has identified are solved when one explains these verses appropriately, on the basis of the way they are connected with v. 4.

[18:1, 2a, 2bα, 4-6a] What remains is a woe oracle (on this, see below, p. 216). On formal grounds, it is addressed to "the land of the winged boats"; however, it is "the agile messengers" who actually hear the message, who are to go (back), bringing this message to the Cushites (in 2aα). At times, some have suggested (see Kaiser, based on Ezek. 30:9) that the messengers are those who are to be sent by Judah itself, to the land that lay south of Egypt, so that they could deliver the message now found in vv. 4ff. But v. 2a talks about the צירים (envoys) that Cush itself has dispatched, so that there must have been a delegation that had arrived in Jerusalem from Cush; as they were on their way, a message from Yahweh was given them as well. The rather extensive introduction (vv. 1f.) that precedes the actual message from Yahweh, in vv. 4-6, is needed, since little was known about the Cushites in Jerusalem.

Meter: The woe oracle in v. 1 is a seven-stress colon, whereas the way the Cushites are characterized in v. 2 (except for v. 2bβ) is cast in the form of two calm, three-stress + three-stress bicola and a concluding seven-stress colon. The insertion in v. 3 is apparently fashioned in the form of a five-stress colon and a three-stress + three-stress bicolon. The actual message from Yahweh begins, with the weightiness appropriate at the beginning of an official message, with a seven-stress colon, and then continues in v. 4b with a three-stress + three-stress bicolon; v. 5, which is the actual message predicting disaster, is constructed as two four-stress + four-stress bicola (במזמרות, "pruning knife," receives two stresses). The original message draws to a conclusion in v. 6a with a seven-stress colon (ולבהמת, "and to the animals of," receives two stresses). That it is difficult to try to read the last line metrically is another indication that v. 6b is a gloss.

Setting

Who is the author of this message, and what is the situation it addressed? If one removes v. 3 (and v. 6b) and eliminates v. 7 at the end, nothing in the passage would speak against Isaiah as the author; therefore the "authenticity" of the passage is generally recognized. Kaiser goes his own way with this passage, as with many others: "If one does not share the traditional view that the prophet looked forward to a direct intervention of Yahweh and the destruction of the Assyrians before the gates of Jerusalem during the revolt of the concluding years of the eighth century, a fundamentally new interpretation of the poem is required." But this passage does not speak of the destruction of the Assyrians encamped in front of Jerusalem; it describes an awesome blow that will strike Cush (on this, see below, pp. 218f.). One need not provide any additional proof that the prophets anticipated that Yahweh would intervene directly in world history, nor must one provide further details to show that this is the way Isaiah spoke. If one chooses to follow Kaiser by treating the passage, from the outset, as one scene from a proto-apocalyptic painting, depicting Yahweh's sweeping judgment against all the nations, then it is puzzling why the threat of judgment in vv. 4ff. is preceded by the introduction in vv. 1f. Ignoring the clear words in the text, Kaiser finds himself forced to describe an idealistic scene, defined by neither time nor space.

However, this does not solve the problem of how to answer the question about which phase of the prophet's activity would have provided the setting for this message. The only thing we know for certain is that the occasion was that of the arrival of a delegation from Cush to Jerusalem. What Cush was attempting with this move is left unstated, but it is not hard to figure out what was happening. Deputations such as this are sent in order to forge a political-military alliance or even to discuss details about how one might construct a united front against a common foe. A parallel to this would be the delegation of Philistines that came to Jerusalem, which occasioned the response in 14:29-32, and another would be the deputation that represented Merodach-Baladan before Hezekiah, 2 Kings 20:12ff. = Isaiah 39. This message must have originated during a time when Cush sought to effect a large-scale plan to guarantee that it could maintain its control over Egypt, against the encroachment of Assyria, by allying itself with a number of independent states on its northeast border, where it was the most vulnerable, and thus provide itself with a protective shield. That could have happened only at a time when Cush was definitely in charge within Egypt and when it would have found it necessary to ensure the security of Egypt along that border.

Cush (or Ethiopia, as the Greeks called that land since the time of Homer) is located in the region directly south of Egypt proper. About 2000 B.C., the territory covered roughly the region from the second cataract of the Nile as far south as Sai Island (so G. Posener, *Kush* 6 [1958] 39–68). When Egypt was not weakened by internal conflicts, it naturally sought to assert its influence by pursuing its interests in the land to the immediate south of its borders. Time and again, Egypt cast its gaze in that direction, with its wealth in gold being not the least of the attractions (see J. Vercoutter, *Kush* 7 [1959] 120–153). During the period of the Old Kingdom there were close trade relations; in the Middle Kingdom era the Egyptians established direct control over the region of Cush; at least the northern portion of its territory was actually annexed during the time of the New Kingdom.

The reverse was also true: it was possible at times for Cush itself to extend its control when Egypt was at a low point. After the downfall of the Middle Kingdom, a kingdom with a unique Ethiopian culture was developed, centered in Kerma. Its rulers made treaties with the Hyksos. At that time, the northern border was located at the first cataract, the southern border in the vicinity of the fifth series of rapids; later, that border was even farther to the south, in the middle of the Sudan. When the New Kingdom came to an end and Egypt came under the control of the Libyans, Cush once again was able to take its destiny into its own hands. With Napata in the center, a new kingdom was established; its ruler, Piankhy, who reigned 747–716 (dates when rulers were in power, here and in what follows, are according to Kitchen), had amazing successes also within Egypt. In the delta at that time, Tefnakhte (Egyptian: *T3f-nḫt[y]*) from Sais had been successful in seizing for himself a number of small principalities and, after the northern region was firmly under his control, turned his attention to the lands of the middle part of Egypt. At that point, Piankhy intervened and was able to defeat Egypt, but then he retreated back to his own homeland once again. It would seem that, after he pulled back, Tefnakhte prevailed once again and took control of Lower Egypt. After that ruler died in 720, he was succeeded by his son Bocchoris (Egyptian: *B3k-n-rnf*), whose reign apparently ended about 715, soon after the Ethiopian Shabaka [Tr.: younger brother of Piankhy] (716–702) led his people as they once again seized Egyptian territory. The Ethiopians were successful in solidifying their hold. But that brought them into the region that had been eyed by the Assyrians, meaning that they had to pursue all avenues which would ally them with the petty kings who ruled in the Palestinian region, in order to turn them into loyal vassals, since all of them would also be interested in seeking a way to protect themselves from their common threat. For this very reason, it was logical for those states that were part of this political nexus to seek help from the rear flanks by approaching the powers that were in control of Egypt at that time.

For Ethiopia to enter into the affairs of Palestine was nothing other than a reactivation of the political moves that had been made by many others who had earlier controlled Egypt. We are told in 2 Kings 17:4 that Hoshea of Israel had plotted a conspiracy against his Assyrian overlords and, in connection with that move, had sent messengers to סוֹא (K^Or סֵוא) (So), the king of Egypt. Scholars previously had sought to identify this pharaoh with a commander named Sib'e, mentioned in the annals of Sargon, who was defeated, along with Ḥanun of Gaza, at Rapiḫu (Greek: Raphia; presently: *refaḥ,* south of Gaza), suggesting that it should be pointed סֶוא instead of סוֹא (see that note, still found in *BHK*[3]). To arrive at such a solution, it was necessary that one ignore that the Bible speaks of a king (מֶלֶךְ), whereas Sargon speaks of a field commander (*turtannu*). In addition, it was demonstrated that the reading *sib'e* was incorrect and it should have been read as *re'e* (Borger). What that meant, in terms of the biblical reading סוֹא, was that some tried to read it as a reference to the city of Sais, situated in the western delta, instead of treating it as a personal name (Egyptian: *s3w;* Assyrian: *sa-a-a;* Arabic: *ṣā el-ḥagar;* see Hans Goedicke, *BASOR* 171 [1963] 64ff.). If this were correct, then one would have to insert an אֶל before מֶלֶךְ in the Hebrew text of 2 Kings 17:4, so that it could be translated: "(he sent) to Sais, to the king of Egypt." Then Tefnakhte would have been that king who extended his power into the delta from his original base in Sais and who was ready to unite all of Egypt under his control. In more recent times, this solution has been questioned as well. According to Kitchen (§334, note 751), סוֹא should be treated as an abbreviation for Osorkon (IV, 730–715), who was the last ruler of the Twenty-second (Tanite) Dynasty, headquartered at that time in Bubastis. In any case, at that time, Cush would not have been on the scene as yet.

Sargon relates another event that took place in 716: "Shilkanni, king of Musri, who[se residence is located far away], the terror-inspiring glamor of Ashur, my lord, overwhelmed him and he brought as *tâmartu*-present 12 fine (lit.: big) horses from Musri which have not their equals in this country" (see *TGI*[2], no. 33) [quoted, slightly altered, from *ANET* 286]. This Shilkanni has to have been Osorkon IV (not Osorkon III, from the Twenty-third Dynasty; concerning the identification of the two names, see Albright, *BASOR* 141 [1956] 24; and Tadmor, 78). This would mean that the Ethiopians were not as yet one of the parties in the conflict with the Assyrians in 716. But it was not much after that time that Sargon found himself involved in a confrontation with a much livelier Meluḫḫa, which was Sargon's name for Ethiopia, namely, as he engaged in battle against Ashdod (712 B.C.; concerning this date, see Tadmor, 79). Indeed, many commentators believe that the rebellion carried out by this Philistine city, under the leadership of the usurper Iamani, furnishes the appropriate background for the report in Isaiah 18 about the delegation from Egypt that came to Jerusalem (Schrader, *KAT*[2], 406; Procksch; Kissane; Eissfeldt, *Introduction,* 313f.; Vermeylen, 47). Yet this solution is doubtful, primarily because Ashdod, not Ethiopia, was the moving force in that rebellion. Broken prism A (H. Winckler, *Die Keilschrifttexte Sargons II* [1889] I, 186ff., II, 44f.; see *ANET* 287; *AOT* 351) states explicitly that Iamani had turned to the pharaoh and sought to make a treaty with him, and that Iamani, through lies, had instigated a revolt on the part of the rulers of

Isaiah 18:1-7

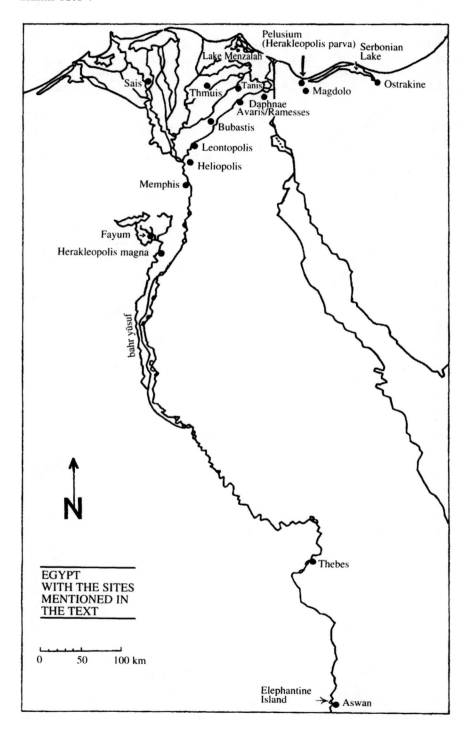

Pelusium
(Herakleopolis parva)
Serbonian Lake
Lake Menzalah
Sais
Tanis
Thmuis
Daphnae
Avaris/Ramesses
Magdolo
Ostrakine
Bubastis
Leontopolis
Heliopolis
Memphis
Fayum
Herakleopolis magna
bahr yūsuf

N

EGYPT
WITH THE SITES
MENTIONED IN
THE TEXT

0   50   100 km

Thebes

Elephantine
Island
Aswan

IDENTIFICA-TION ON THE MAP	HEBREW NAME	EGYPTIAN NAME	GREEK NAME	PRESENT-DAY NAME IN ARABIC
Aswan	סְוֵנֵה (OT) סְוֵן (Elephantine)	*śwn.w*	Συήνη	*aswān*
Avaris/ Ramesses	רַעְמְסֵס or רַעְמְסֵס	*ḥw.t wʿr.t*	Ἄυαρις	*tell ed-dabʿa/* *qanṭīr*
Bubastis	פִּי־בֶסֶת	*pr-b3śt.t*	Βούβαστις or Βουβαστία 𝔊: Βούβαστος	*tell basṭah*
Daphnae	תַחְפַּנְחֵס	*t3-ḥ(t)-(n-)* *p3-nḥśy* or *ṯbn.t*	Δάφναι/ Δάφνη 𝔊: Ταφνάς	*tell defenne* or *tell defne*
Elephantine	יֵב	*3bw*	Ἐλεφαντίνη	*el-gezīre*
Heliopolis	אוֹן/אָן or בֵּית־שֶׁמֶשׁ עִיר הַחֶרֶס ?	*iwnw* or *pr-Rʿ*	Ἡλίου πόλις	*maṭarīye*
Herakleopolis magna	חָנֵס ?	*ḥ(t)-nn-nśw(t)*	Ἡρακλεό-πολις Herodotus II 166: Ἄνυσις	*aḥnās* (on *baḥr* *yūsuf*)
Herakleopolis parva	חָנֵס ?	*ḥn-n-śtny*	Ἡρακλεό-πολις	*ḥnes* (by Pelusium)
Leontopolis	עִיר ההרס ?	*t3-rmw* or *ṯnt-rmw*	Λεοντόπολις	*tell el-yehūdīye*
Magdolo	מִגְדּוֹל	_____	𝔊: Μάγδωλος	*tell el-ḥēr*
Memphis	נֹף or מֹף	*mn-nfr* (*pypy*) from the end of the New Kingdom: *mnf*	Μέμφις	*mīt raḥīne*
Ostrakine	סרקאני (*Pesikta rab.* 17)	_____	Ὀστρακίνη	*ḥirbet* *el-flūsīyāt*
Pelusium (thus Vulgate)	סִין	*śwny*	Πηλούσιον 𝔊: Σάις	*(tell) faramā*
Sais	סוֹא ??	*s3w*	Σάις	*ṣā el-ḥagar*
Tanis	צֹעַם	*dʿn.t*	Τάνις	*ṣān el-ḥagar*
Thebes	נֹא or נֹא אָמוֹן	*nw.t*	Θῆβαι	*tell balamun*
Thmuis	_____	*ʿnp.t* (twin city of Mendes)	Θμοῦις	*tmai el-amdīd*

Philistia, Judah, Edom, and Moab, all of whom had been paying tribute to Assyria. Of course, it is reported in Isa. 20:4f. that there was hope at that time that one could count on the help of the Cushites, who had just then taken control over Egypt. However, since Shabaka had just taken control at the time when the rebellion was still in its infancy, it is highly unlikely that he would have initiated diplomatic contacts with Jerusalem already then. When the insurrection was put down, Iamani fled "into the territory of Musri—which belongs now to Ethiopia" (Sargon's Display Inscription, lines 102f., *AOT* 350; *ANET* 286; Akkadian: *a-na i-te-e* ^{KUR}*mu-ṣu-ri ša pa-at* ^{KUR}*me-luḫ-ḫa*), but the Ethiopian did not want this to lead to a serious confrontation with the Assyrians and thus delivered Iamani over to Sargon (cf. Donner, 123, note 4).

Sargon, who was so occupied with his desire to establish for himself free access to Egypt, died in 705. Hezekiah of Judah declared to Assyria that he would no longer remain a loyal vassal, removed the Nehushtan pole, and also removed Assyrian cultic symbols (2 Kings 18:4). The Philistine city-states, Ashkelon and Ekron, both joined him in the revolt against Assyria. Sennacherib's description of his campaign of 701, against the Phoenician and Philistine cities and against Hezekiah of Judah, includes reference to the fact that Ethiopia was right in the thick of this battle: "[They]—had become afraid and had called (for help) upon the kings of Egypt (*Muṣ(u)ri*) (and) the bowmen, the chariot(-corps) and the cavalry of the king of Ethiopia (*Meluḫḫa*) . . . In the plain of Eltekah (*Al-ta-qu-ú*) [אֶלְתְּקֵא, Josh. 19:24; אֶלְתְּקֵה, Josh. 21:23; אֶלְתְּקֹה, Josh. 19:44; certainly not to be identified with *ḥirbet el-muqanna*ᶜ but rather with *tell eš-šalaf;* see Y. Aharoni, *The Land of the Bible* (1967) 337f.; and B. Mazar, *IEJ* 10 (1960) 72ff.], their battle lines were drawn up against me. . . . In the mêlée of the battle, I personally captured alive the Egyptian charioteers with the(ir) princes and (also) the charioteers of the king of Ethiopia" ([Meluḫḫa]; Taylor Prism, col. II, lines 73–82; see *AOT* 353; *ANET* 287f.; *TGI*[2], no. 39). The Egyptian kings or princes mentioned by Sennacherib must have been vassal princes who had sworn allegiance to the Ethiopians. In the same period in which this coalition had been forged, it may be that Ethiopian messengers, mentioned in Isa. 18:2, appeared in Jerusalem (Delitzsch, Knabenbauer, Duhm, Feldmann, Bewer, Schmidt, Donner). There is no way to be certain about which of the two possibilities mentioned is correct, and this dilemma will not disappear until there is more information about the various changes in leadership and power in Egypt during this era. In addition, further problems that contribute to the difficulties in understanding this passage are connected with the difficult exegetical issues in 18:5f.; on this, see below, pp. 218f.

Commentary

[18:1-2] As was the case with 17:12, one must also ask the question about whether הוֹי is used in a special way, to introduce a woe oracle, or whether it is intended as no more than a common form of interjection. It has been noted that the participle הַשֹּׁלֵחַ (which sends) at the beginning of v. 2 is an element typically found in a woe oracle (on this, see *Isaiah 1–12*, p. 196). The classic woe oracle, which includes an identification of the person being addressed, after the initial הוֹי (woe) (v. 1), linked to a participial clause that briefly identifies the sinful action (v. 2aα), is expanded here, as often elsewhere, by means of a threat, vv. 4-6a. Because of the unique circumstances, the intervening material is needed, so that the messengers can be encouraged to return back to their own homeland.

When the Ethiopian delegation came to Jerusalem for an official visit, it must have been the talk of the town, and a response from Isaiah, making his reaction known, would have been eagerly anticipated. For that reason, there would have been no need for the prophet to make specific mention of the country about which he was speaking. The way in which Isaiah characterizes the land of Cush reflects the sensation that this would have caused in the capital city of Judah during the time when these messengers from that most mysterious land of Ethiopia were visiting.

Unfortunately, the translation used here, taking צלצל to mean "boat," is essentially based on the reading in the Gk and thus is not an assured rendering. But it is helpful to note that everyone who visited their country was most impressed by these speedy Nile boats. Even in present-day Nubia, life centers around events that occur very close to the rivers, and the boats furnish transportation. It is certainly possible that the sails on those boats are what is intended by the reference to "wings"; one might consult illuss. 313ff., 372ff., 407 in B. Landström, *Die Schiffe der Pharaonen* (1970). Yet it is also possible that "having wings" is a simple shorthand for describing the speed and maneuverability of the Ethiopians' boats. The "rivers of Cush" are probably the ʿAtbara, the White Nile, and the Blue Nile.

It was not only a very special, extraordinary event for the people of Jerusalem to have a visit from messengers who were sent by a land located so far away, but their method of travel was also out of the ordinary—not by means of an arduous journey over land, but coming as far as the Nile delta in swift watercraft "on the water." It has already been stated (textual note 2b) that ים refers here not to the sea but to the Nile.

The text mentions the כלי־גמא; apparently, this is supposedly a description of "those small skiffs built from papyrus reeds, which made such a big impression even on the Greeks when they visited Egypt, similar to the kind which are still used in the Sudan today. Actually, these were nothing more than little rafts, without borders around the edges, constructed by binding together bundles of papyrus reeds. These were slightly wider in the middle than at the ends; the rear end normally pointed steeply upward, whereas the front part rested flat on the water" (Erman and Ranke, 571f.; see also E. Otto, *Ägypten* [1966[4]] plates 7 and 9). They are so lightweight that it would have been no trouble for someone to portage them when one came to the cataracts.

Isaiah could not have reacted with anything but great consternation when he heard that the Ethiopians were in Jerusalem; his response was to send them packing, back to their own land, with what to them would have been a most unpleasant directive. Yet one detects in his words a certain measure of admiration for this exuberant, youthful people, which had so recently entered on the stage of world history. The messengers from Cush are "nimble" (קל) and thus swift.

Not much can be said about the original race to which the ancient Ethiopians belonged. They are Hamites, with dark skin (see Reicke). For the inhabitants of Judah, who were on the short side (see L. Köhler, *Hebrew Man*

[1956] 21–22), their tall, slender appearance would have been very impressive. Even Herodotus had heard of them: οἱ δὲ Αἰθίοπες . . . λέγονται εἶναι μέγιστοι καὶ κάλλιστοι ἀνθρώπων πάντων (The Ethiopians . . . are said to be the tallest and best-looking people in the world) (3.20; see also 114, where μακροβιώτατοι, "long-lived," is added as well).

In addition to מְמֻשָּׁךְ (tall), Isaiah also describes the people as (מ)מוֹרָט, "smooth." 1 Kings 7:45 speaks about נְחֹשֶׁת מְמֹרָט, "burnished bronze," Ezek. 21:14-16 of "a polished sword." In Akkadian, *marāṭu* means "scrape off, grind off"; cf. Arabic *mariṭa,* "without hair, being smooth," and Tigre *mrṣ,* "be smooth." It is likely that Isaiah has in mind the way one's body would have a shiny smoothness after it has been rubbed with oil, which would have been especially eye-catching when seen on the dark skin of the Cushites.

But he goes on further: they are "a people feared far and wide." The invasions into Egypt, which led to the Twenty-fifth (Ethiopian) Dynasty seizing control over the land, would undoubtedly have brought with it a respect for Cush from the surrounding countries that was commensurate with its power. קַו־קָו (here: muscle power) is a hapax legomenon; מְבוּסָה (tramples down) is found otherwise only in 22:5; these vocables might also have been used in an attempt to recreate the impression that the Ethiopians left on the Egyptians and their neighbors, as the sovereignty that the pharaohs enjoyed during the immediately preceding dynasties gradually ebbed away while they were edging closer to their demise.

See above, p. 210, for the reasons why v. 2bβ is treated as a later addition. Everyone who visits the country is impressed by the way the southern part of Cush is crisscrossed with mighty rivers.

[18:4-6] The interpretation of this message from Yahweh, delivered by Isaiah to the Ethiopian messengers, begins with the basic question about who is to be on the receiving end of the anticipated judgment from Yahweh that is mentioned in v. 5f.: the Ethiopians themselves or the Assyrians. The reason why the answer is not immediately apparent is explained by the fact that Isaiah is concerned only about one point, that is, he wants to stress: Yahweh is the only active subject who causes historical events to unfold as they do. That does not eliminate from Isaiah's understanding of history the fact that earthly powers appear on the stage of world history as the actors, but they are, one might say, virtual puppets in Yahweh's hand. For those who listened to Isaiah, there was no lack of clarity about what was meant; however, for those of us who are not sure about the exact situation in Jerusalem at that time and who cannot be confident that we know all the details about what was transpiring, understanding the passage is more difficult. For that reason, it is not a complete impossibility, as suggested by some commentators (Hitzig, Delitzsch, Kissane, Dillmann, Duhm, Procksch, Ziegler, et al.), that Isaiah is talking about the Assyrians, in which case, considering Isaiah's way of thinking during this confusing time, it would mean that Judah was being admonished not even to toy with thinking about entering into a treaty with Cush, since the Assyrian danger would be dealt a crushing blow from a different direction. This interpretation would seem to be correct because of what is said in 17:12-14. Nonetheless, there are significant problems with that solution: Ezek. 30:4 anticipates that "anguish shall be in Ethiopia, when the slain fall in Egypt," and the secondary passage in v. 9 explicates this still further: "On that day, messengers shall go out from me in ships to terrify the unsuspecting Ethiopians; and anguish shall come upon them on the day of Egypt's doom." This verse apparently picks up the theme expressed in Isa. 18:1ff., an interesting example of the "exegesis of scripture by means of scripture" (Zimmerli, BK XIII/2, 733 [Engl: *Ezekiel 2*, 130]). Obviously, this late example of reactualization, in and of itself, carries no greater weight than does the fact that Egypt, later on during the history of this Ethiopian dynasty, was actually under the control of Assyria, at the time of Esarhaddon. But chap. 20 also shows that Isaiah anticipated that a harsh blow would be struck against Egypt/Ethiopia, in fact, still more: Assyria would actually invade their land. What is decisive, however, as already noted in the discussion of the form (see above, pp. 210f.), is that we have a woe oracle concerning Cush in chap. 18, corresponding exactly to the formal characteristics elsewhere, which then leads into the issuance of a threat. One ought not object that it was impossible that Isaiah could have delivered such a message to the Ethiopian messengers, threatening their land with destruction. The audience that was hearing this woe oracle was not Ethiopia, but Judah, upon whom the prophet was trying to impress the fact that it would be foolish to join forces with the Ethiopian army, which was not nearly as powerful as it seemed, for better or for worse, the exact point which is also made in 20:5, in so many words. This interpretation does not force one, of course, to presume that chap. 18 is to be dated precisely to the same time period as 17:12-14. However, since that passage is set into the period when Jerusalem was experiencing intense pressure, brought on by the threat from Sennacherib, the present passage we are discussing is most likely from the time immediately preceding Hezekiah's revolt against the Assyrians, chronologically very soon after the death of Sargon.

[18:4a] The word from Yahweh, which Isaiah casts in the form of a message that the Cushite delegation is to bring back home, but that he really wants to use in order to influence current decisions being made in Judah, apparently presumes that Cush had, at that time, successfully seized control over Egypt, and nothing suggests that its demise was close at hand. In the time closely following 705, one might have countered Isaiah's argument by pointing out that his assessment of Cush, at the time of the rebellion of Ashdod (see chap. 20), had not proved to be correct. But those events in no way shook the prophet's confidence: Yahweh could also, from time to time, watch and wait, could simply observe the plans that earthly powers tried to carry out, until the moment came when he would intervene. Isaiah's summons to King Ahaz was to "remain calm" (השקט) (7:4), and he told the king that "in returning and rest (בהשקט) you shall be saved" (30:15); that was his encouragement during the time of the acute threat from Assyria. Yahweh himself can also "stay utterly calm" (cf. אֶשְׁקוֹטָה in v. 4), and, for him, that is certainly no sign of weakness or of a lack of interest in the affairs of the world, but expresses Yahweh's indisputable superiority, being above the pressures that drive earthly powers. That utter calm is paired with a keen observation about how these powers operate: אַבִּיטָה בִמְכוֹנִי (I look on my place). Yahweh's place, from which he looks out over all things, is obviously not Zion (which is presumed, however, in passages such as 8:18; 31:9; cf. Exod. 15:17; 1 Kings 8:13), but is rather his heavenly הֵיכָל (palace/temple) (see *Isaiah 1–12*, pp. 262f.). Isaiah would have known this concept from his acquaintance with the cultic songs; cf. Ps. 33:13f.: מִשָּׁמַיִם הִבִּיט יְהוָה רָאָה אֶת־כָּל־בְּנֵי הָאָדָם: מִמְּכוֹן שִׁבְתּוֹ הִשְׁגִּיחַ אֶל כָּל־יֹשְׁבֵי הָאָרֶץ (Yahweh looks down from heaven; he sees all humankind. From where he sits enthroned he watches all the inhabitants of the earth; cf. 1 Kings 8:39-42, 49 as well. One must also keep in mind that Psalm 33 speaks about Yahweh's righteous rule over all peoples: "Yahweh brings the counsel of the nations to nothing; he frustrates the plans of the peoples. The counsel of Yahweh stands forever, the thoughts of his heart to all generations" (vv. 10f.). In his unique role as the "judge of all the world," he is honored as the "one who looks down upon."

[18:4b] If Isaiah can make use of words from the liturgy in v. 4a, in v. 4b one sees the full extent of his mastery of language with his own unique use of imagery: "just like shimmering heat עֲלֵי־אוֹר (with [sun]light), just like a dew cloud on harvest day." The second image is easy to understand: in the first hours of the night, clouds of dew rise up over Palestine from the Mediterranean, "slowly at first, then frequently rising up faster and faster. By morning, as the sun rises, they hover without moving, up above the mountains, with the sun shining upon them, until they once again are evaporated as the daytime temperatures rise" (Dalman, *AuS* I/2, 311). The first image must be intended as a way of conveying the same idea. The חֹם, the heat itself, is obviously invisible, but it is possible to see the shimmering of the hot air (concerning the temperatures in Palestine, see N. Rosenan, *Atlas of Israel* [1970] section IV, 1: "Temperature and Humidity"). The intensity of the heat at harvesttime is proverbial; see the Yavneh Yam inscription, lines 10f.: הקצרם . . . בחם הי[ם] (those who were harvesting with me . . . in the heat of the [day]) (*KAI*, no. 200; [cf. *ANET* 568]). The difficult phrase עֲלֵי־אוֹר must mean "at the time of sunlight." H. Guthe reports: "On a few occasions, during harvesttime, I have observed that the clouds of dew, looking much like a veil, having been blown by the wind of the sea up into the heights of the central hill country around Jerusalem, would just hang there, like an immovable wall, facing the sun shining on them from the east, until its heat caused them to be pushed downward toward the ground, so that the plants there were besprinkled with countless shimmering drops of dew" (*Palästina* [1927²] 49).

[18:5] But the day comes, in the fall, when these little droplets of water do not dissipate, but form into heavy storm clouds; rain patters down from them or else they might even empty their contents in the form of a hailstorm, which damages what is growing in the fields and can even tear the leaves and fruit on trees to shreds (cf. 1 Kings 18:44ff.). It would have been possible for Isaiah to have stayed with this imagery and pushed it still further. But, as one observes in his technique again and again, with great ease he moves on to a different way of describing what will happen (see above, pp. 162f., on 17:4-6). One ought not follow Procksch at this point, linking the imagery in vv. 4 and 5: "The hot rays during harvesttime cook the grapes of the vineyard to the boiling point, so that the sweet fruit is readied for the picking"; nothing is mentioned subsequently about harvesting grapes, and the gathering of ripened grapes would hardly be an appropriate illustration for depicting the way God would carry out his judgment. Instead, v. 5a simply identifies the time period; this does not refer to the time when grapes were harvested, but rather to the time when the grains were gathered, which is also what is meant when קציר is used. At the time when the grain is harvested, which in Palestine comes during the month of May, the blooms on the grapevines have finished blooming; at that time, then, the clusters of blooms (נצה; see also *נץ, "clusters," in Gen. 40:10) begin to form the grapes that, during the process in which they gradually ripen (cf. the added word גמל, "ripening"), are known as בסר (unripe or sour grapes) (cf. Jer. 31:29f.; Ezek. 18:2). It is during that time that the vinedresser goes through to prune for the second time. The "farmer's calendar" from Gezer speaks of זמר (which, contrary to *KAI* II, 181; and A. Lemaire, *VT* 15 [1975] 15–26, one should translate not as "gathering the grapes" but as "pruning") and says this task is carried out between the grain (קצר) harvest and the fruit harvest (קץ). This particular activity was done in order to remove young shoots that were not going to produce fruit, as well as some leaves (see *Isaiah 1–12*, pp. 183f.), so that the juice of the grapevines would be as copious as possible and the ripening grapes would receive the benefits of the plant's production as much as was possible (cf. Dalman, *AuS* IV, 312). To achieve maximum success, it was crucial that this treatment would be carried out on the vines at just the right moment. It is probably this activity that is referred to in v. 5b. זלזלים (suckers) is a hapax legomenon, related to זלל; in the *qal*, it means "be light, worthless," in the *niphʿal*, "shake, quake"; the word is used to identify the shoots that grow wild, without any fruit forming on them; Gk: τὰ βοτρύδια τὰ μικρά (the very small clusters). On נטישות (KBL: "luxuriating shoots"), consult the usage in Jer. 5:10 and 48:32 (Gk: αἱ κληματίδες, "vine branches, brushwood"); on מזמרה (pruning knife), see *Isaiah 1–12*, p. 93. Apparently these terms refer to brand-new shoots, which would not even need to be cut off with a pruning knife, since one could simply tear them off or pinch them off with one's bare hand. The shoots that had been cut off from the vines in this way would normally be raked together and used to fuel a fire; according to John 15:6, they would simply be done away with by burning. But this passage refers not to vines that were woody but rather to green sprouts, which would be left for the birds of prey and animals of the field. That would make sense if the reference was about being beneficial for cattle, which appreciate anything green, but it does not make as much sense that it is good for the birds of prey (עיט), which, according to Gen. 15:11, swoop down on pieces of meat used in offerings and which, according to Ezek. 39:4, descend on the bodies of the slain (the verb עיט means "scream at, shriek as one swoops down on"). The prophet is apparently mixing imagery with reality. The tendrils that have been torn from the vines are the Ethiopians who have fallen in battle, upon whom the vultures will descend; cf. Deut. 28:26; Jer. 7:33; 19:7; and also 1 Sam. 17:44. In addition to that, Isaiah uses terminology that is employed in the imagery known to us from the curse formulas of the Assyrian treaties. One reads in one of the treaties of Esarhaddon: "May Ninurta, leader of the gods, fell you with his fierce arrow, and fill the plain with your corpses, give your flesh to eagles and vultures to feed upon" (*ANET* 538 and illus. 135 in O. Keel, *The Symbolism of the Biblical World: Ancient Near Eastern Iconography and the Book of Psalms* [1978]).

[**18:6b**] The expander who adds v. 6b seeks to give even more intensity to the imagery: in the summer, the vultures sit on the cuttings, in the winter, all the animals of the field do the same. In addition to the unfortunate division into winter and summer, the shoots of the vine, which had been torn off, are now said to cling tenaciously to life. "Vultures" and "all the animals of the fields" would have been finished with these already by this time. Once again, as earlier (e.g., 17:9, but also 17:2), one notes the technique used by the expander, furnishing additional details about the harshness of the judgment, but also showing that whoever adds this was not artistically sensitive.

Who is doing all this? The subject of כרת (cut away) is not mentioned. In the final analysis, it can be none other than the great "he," Yahweh. Yet the face of God is hidden behind an earthly "someone." Isaiah would have been thinking of the Assyrians. But that is not crucial as far as he is concerned; for him, it is important at this time only that he accentuate the point that the shoots, coming forth from Ethiopia, grasping at those far away and growing wildly, would be ripped from the ground when the time was right. One would do well to note that his reference ends at this point. There is no explicit comment about the downfall of Ethiopia. However, beyond the original borders of the territory where its own people had been born, it would not play an ongoing role as a leading power, and the glory that it enjoyed at the moment, as the Ethiopians exercised some control, would soon come to an end. For that reason, it would make good sense for Judah not to trust in the stability and durability of Ethiopia.

[**18:3**] Verse 3, a secondary addition (see above, pp. 209f.), addresses all inhabitants of the earth (concerning תבל, "circle of the earth," see above, p. 26); they should all look and listen when someone raises the battle standard (concerning נס, see *Isaiah 1–12*, p. 239) on the mountain heights and when someone blows the signal horn. Both terms can have a variety of meanings, with the most likely being that both signal to the forces to gather together for a military expedition, e.g., Isa. 13:2; Jer. 51:27; cf. also G.

Schumacher, *ZDPV* 9 (1886) 232, who himself experienced, up in the Golan, how erecting a harmless signal flag to be used in measuring the land brought together fully armed members of an extended family unit living in that region. Blowing a horn might at least have given those being threatened by an enemy the chance to be warned to flee to safety (Jer. 4:5; 6:1; cf. Hos. 5:8; Ezek. 33:3, 6). But in the present passage, which is addressed at the same time to all the inhabitants of the earth, the setting is neither that of calling them to come along on a military expedition nor that of a signal to flee; instead, the inhabitants of the earth are all summoned to see and hear, they are to function as witnesses—though, according to the opinion of this expander, not simply as witnesses who were to observe how Yahweh would look on his place (v. 4) and how he would let loose against Ethiopia (vv. 5f.), but to view the great events at the end of the age, which would come on the entire inhabited region of the earth. In that way, the message addressed to Ethiopia has been fully removed from its historical context, "dehistoricized," becoming instead an announcement about the final upheaval of all centers of power. It is easy to see how this type of interpretation could come out of this message from Yahweh, since vv. 4-6 contain a limited number of concrete details. Besides, one continues to be suspicious about the possibility that other concrete details, which were in the original message from Yahweh, have been sacrificed and eliminated in the present reinterpreted text.

[18:7] The other passage that is just as much a secondary addition, v. 7, is very different. Like ביום ההוא (on that day) (see above, p. 170), the introductory formula בעת ההיא (in that time) postulates that these events will all take place at the same time. However, let there be no doubt: it does not suggest that the events will be coterminous with the events that Isaiah has in mind, but rather with those envisioned in the eschatological drama described by the other reinterpretation (v. 3). When that took place, then Mount Zion would be the spiritual/political middle point of the entire inhabited region of the earth. That is where Yahweh resides, either directly or represented by his earthly regent, the Davidide (see 11:10), and all peoples would come there and would declare their loyalty to the ruler of the world. To this group of peoples—which is how the expander links this verse with vv. 1f.—the Ethiopians also belong, this nation far out on the edge of inhabited lands, whose appearance in Jerusalem had naturally made a deep impression.

The motif of "peoples paying homage on Zion," apparently being used in this passage, is itself old, and the motif is also known among Israel's neighbors. The goddess Inanna says to her consort Ur-Ninurta from Isin: "Since you [as lord] appeared shining forth in the holy heaven, since you [stand there] in the land of Sumer with all being astonished, my Ur-Ninurta, may all lands bring to you sumptuous (gifts)" (Falkenstein and von Soden, *SAHG* 109).

An inscription of Merodach-Baladan II, which deals with the rebuilding of the temple of Eanna in Uruk, closes with requests for the king: "the kings, his enemies, ought to bring to Eanna the overabundance of the four regions of the world, the produce of the mountains and the sea, as their heavy tribute. He will receive their gifts, he will let them enter into Esagila, into the presence of the lord of lords." (see P. Grelot, *VT* 7 [1957] 319–321; and H. Schmidt, 62f.; cf. also the longer text that Schmidt cites, 63ff.). But the same motif spread and was used in Egypt as well. In the Hymn of Victory of Thut-mose III, Amon-Re grants to the pharaoh rulership over the whole earth and, when he mentions the honors that will be accorded him by the peoples, he says: "I cause thy victories to circulate in all lands. The gleaming (serpent), she who is upon my brow, is thy servant, (so that) there shall arise none rebellious to thee. . . . They come, bearing tribute upon their backs, bowing down to thy majesty, as I decree" (see Erman, *Literature,* 320; [translation here from *ANET* 374]). Or: in a speech which is directed by Amon, king of the gods, to Amen-hotep III, he essentially announces to the pharaoh: "When I turn my face to the south, I *work a wonder for thee:* I make the princes of the wretched Ethiopia bestir themselves for thee, bearing all their tribute upon their backs" (*AOT* 20; cf. the longer passage in Schmidt, 45ff. [translation from *ANET* 376]). As Schmidt has pointed out in more detail, one notes a difference between the way the motifs are used in Mesopotamia and Egypt: on the Nile, the king is the representative of the divine world, for all human beings; in the land between the two rivers, the temple building fulfills this function. It is not just by chance that Isa. 18:7 speaks about neither king nor temple, but specifically about Yahweh himself; all the gifts of the peoples belong to him alone. Thus Ps. 68:29-32 also says: "Summon your might, O God . . . because of your temple at Jerusalem kings bear gifts (שַׁי) to you . . . let anointing oil be brought from Egypt; let Cush (!) hasten to stretch out its gifts [read, as here, by Duhm and the Zürcher Bibel, text emended] to God" ([Tr.: NRSV differs]; cf. also Pss. 76:12; 96:7-9; Isa. 19:21). But there are also instances in the OT when homage is paid to the personal representatives of the deity; see Pss. 72:10f., 15; 45:13.

The motif of peoples coming to pay homage was also known in Israel from ancient times. We encounter it once again, altered substantively, in Ezekiel (17:22f.) and in Deutero-Isaiah (45:14; 55:3b-5; 49:7), but then, even still later, in Zech. 2:15; 6:15; 8:20-22. The motif is used in Isaiah 60 in a very expanded form. The passage in the book of Zephaniah, 3:8-10, to be dated to the postexilic era, is amazingly similar to what is said in Isa. 18:7; cf. v. 10: מֵעֵבֶר לְנַהֲרֵי־כוּשׁ עֲתָרַי בַּת־פּוּצַי יוֹבִלוּן מִנְחָתִי ("from beyond the rivers of Cush, even to the remotest north, they shall bring my offering," text emended; see *BHK, BHS* [Tr.: NRSV differs]). That passage is a later addition to a "genuine" announcement of judgment (vv. 6f.; cf. the introductions by Eissfeldt, Sellin and Fohrer, and Kaiser). The designation of the place, מעבר לנהרי־כוש (in the region of the rivers of Cush), which corresponds exactly to the wording in Isa. 18:1 (cf. also the use of the verb יבל, "will be brought," in 18:7), makes it certain, however, that the Zephaniah passage is dependent on the one found in the book of Isaiah. One notes that the motif of the homage from the peoples is combined with the *assembly* of the peoples on Zion in Zeph. 3:8-10, but also that v. 9 expects there will be an actual conversion of the peoples, which could, at most, be implicit in Isa. 18:7. Psalm 68:32 is also not all that different from Isa. 18:7. The original wording of that psalm is undoubtedly very old, but vv. 31-33, under discussion in this connection, are dated by everyone to the postexilic era; see Kraus, *Psalms 60–150;* Gunkel, *Psalmen,* ad loc.; and Schmidt, 33 and 35. Therefore it is at least within the realm of possibility that Ps. 68:31-33 is also dependent on Isa. 18:7. One notices particularly in that passage that, when the motif "homage of the peoples" is employed, without much ado, Cush appears on the scene. There is apparently a desire to emphasize that Yahweh's sovereignty be recognized even to the "end of the world" (as has already been expressed explicitly in the verse from Zech. 3:10, where the emendation עַד־יַרְכְּתֵי צָפוֹן, "even to the remotest north," shows clearly what was to be emphasized).

For more on the later development of this motif, beyond the scope of the OT, see passages such as 1QM XII, 13f.: "O Zion, rejoice greatly, shine forth in jubilation, O Jerusalem, and shout with joy, all cities of Judah. Keep [your] ga[tes] open at all times, so that someone can bring to you all the riches of the peoples. And their kings shall serve you and all of your oppressors shall do homage before you" (the original German translation is that of E. Lohse, *Die Texte aus Qumran* [1964] 208f.; cf. also Rev. 21:24-26.).

The place where the presence of Yahweh would dwell is called מְקוֹם שֵׁם־יְהוָה צְבָאוֹת הַר־צִיּוֹן (the place of the name of Yahweh of Hosts, Mount Zion). It was a well-known theological emphasis in the deuteronomic-deuteronomistic stratum of the OT to say that the "name of Yahweh" dwells on Zion; Isaiah, who had no trouble saying that Yahweh himself dwells on Zion—in fact as יְהוָה צְבָאוֹת (Yahweh of Hosts) (see 8:18 and cf., on this, *Isaiah 1–12*, pp. 370f.)—did not know this other terminology, however. The way in which the expander formulates this addition appears to be intended as a way to modify (or maybe even correct theologically) the liturgical formula used by Isaiah: יְהוָה צְבָאוֹת הַשֹּׁכֵן בְּהַר צִיּוֹן (Yahweh of Hosts, who dwells on Mount Zion). מְקוֹם is, as often elsewhere, the holy place; cf. passages such as Jer. 7:3; Mic. 1:3; 1 Kings 8:30, and often elsewhere. The specific formulation מְקוֹם שֵׁם־יְהוָה (place of the name of Yahweh) is unique to this passage, even though Jerusalem is so often described elsewhere as the מְקוֹם (place) where Yahweh permits his name to dwell.

Purpose and Thrust

The original material in this chapter, vv. 1, 2, 4, 5, 6a, furnishes another example of Isaiah's political viewpoint about how Judah was to react in light of the danger with which Assyria threatened its people. The prophet sought to persuade Jerusalem not to venture into informal pacts, or maybe even formal agreements, with other powers, this time with the distant land of Cush, because of a false assessment about where real power was to be found, in the final analysis also because they had "forgotten about God," all in the name of what seemed to promise success in solving a problem they had at that moment. No matter how spectacularly Cush had made its appearance on the stage of world history, Isaiah does not trust them; their days are numbered. Yahweh could bide his time, but one day the moment would arrive when he also would settle accounts with this people, "having muscle power, which tramples others down."

Isaiah was correct in his assessment: Cush showed itself to be a "paper tiger": in the battle between Ashdod and the Assyrians, its soldiers abandoned the Philistines and left them on their own. In the military actions carried out by Sennacherib against Ashkelon and Ekron, into which Hezekiah was also drawn, the Egyptian and Ethiopian contingents did do battle at Altaqu against the Assyrians, but they were defeated.

One should take careful note of the understanding of history that lies at the root of this passage: for Isaiah, Yahweh is the absolute, superior Lord of history; however, the prophet does not speak about the way in which his decisions come to fruition in concrete, specific situations. The God of Israel is able to sit back calmly and observe the earthly plans and actions of the peoples: no one and nothing can escape the reach of his lordly power, and that would always become apparent at the appropriate time (on this, see H.-J. Kraus, "Prophet und Politik," TEH 36 [1952] 57).

The commentary that has been inserted into the text in vv. 3 and 7 radically alters the original ideas and is of great importance. The destiny of Cush becomes an object lesson that demonstrates the final judgment that will come to all powers that are at enmity with God (v. 3). But v. 7 goes even further and gives us a noteworthy example of the anticipation that belief in Yahweh would be universal in the eschaton. At the end of time, even so distant a people as the Cushites would acknowledge the lordship of Yahweh and would do an act of homage before him in the city that is at the center of everything connected with faith in Yahweh, in the "navel of the earth" (Ezek. 38:12): "'To me every knee shall bow, every tongue shall swear.' Only in Yahweh, it shall be said of me, are righteousness and strength" (Isa. 45:23f.; cf. Phil. 2:10).

Egypt's Confusion

Literature

Concerning the vocabulary: On יְאֹרֵי מָצוֹר: P. J. Calderone, "The Rivers of 'Maṣor,'" *Bib* 42 (1961) 423–432. On סוּף: N. H. Snaith, "יַם־סוּף: The Sea of Reeds: The Red Sea," *VT* 15 (1965) 395–398. W. A. Ward, "The Semitic Biconsonantal Root SP and the Common Origin of Egyptian ČWF and Hebrew SÛF: 'Marsh(-Plant),'" *VT* 24 (1974) 339–399. On עָרוֹת: N. Herz, "Isaiah 19,7," *OLZ* 15 (1912) 496–497. T. W. Thacker, "A Note on עָרוֹת (Is XIX 7)," *JTS* 34 (1933) 163–165. P. Sacchi, "Nota a Is. 19,7," *RivBiblt* 13 (1965) 169–170. On עַל־פִּי יְאוֹר: N. Herz, see above. A. Guillaume, "A Note on Isaiah XIX 7," *JTS* 14 (1963) 382–383. On שְׁתֹתֶיהָ: I. Eitan, "An Egyptian Loan Word in Is 19," *JQR* 15 (1924/25) 419–422.

Concerning the cultural history of Egypt: W. Wreszinski, *Atlas zur altägyptischen Kulturgeschichte* (1923). A. Erman and H. Ranke (see literature at 18:1-7). J. Vandier, *La famine dans l'Égypte ancienne*, Recherches d'Archéologie, de Philologie et d'Histoire 7 (1936). J. G. Wilkinson, *Manners and Customs of the Ancient Egyptians*, III (1937). W. Wolf (see literature at 18:1-7). Idem, *Kulturgeschichte des Alten Ägypten* (1962). A. Lucas, *Ancient Egyptian Materials and Industries* (1962[4]).

Concerning the history and geography of Egypt: A. Moret, *Le Nile et la civilisation égyptienne* (1926). J. Capart and M. Werbrouck, *Memphis: A l'ombre des Pyramides* (1930). J. H. Breasted, *A History of Egypt* (1909; reprint, 1964). P. Montet, *Tanis* (1942). A. Badawi, *Memphis als zweite Landeshauptstadt* (1948) (not available to me). J. von Beckerath, *Tanis und Theben*, ÄF 16 (1951). O. Kaiser, "Zwischen den Fronten," FS J. Ziegler II (1972) 197–206. Idem, "Der geknickte Rohrstab," FS K. Elliger, AOAT 18 (1973) 99–106. K. A. Kitchen (see literature at 18:1-7). F. Gomaà, *Die libyschen Fürstentümer des Deltas*, TAVOBeih B/6 (1974). W. Helck, *Die altägyptischen Gaue*, TAVOBeih B/5 (1974). M. Bietak, "Die Hauptstadt der Hyksos und die Ramsesstadt," *Antike Welt* 6 (1975) 28–43.

[**Literature update through 1979:** *Concerning the vocabulary:* J. Luzarraga, "Las tradiciones de la nube en la Biblia y en el judaísmo primitivo," diss., Pontifical Biblical Institute (1971). M. Dahood, "Isaiah 19:11 ḥkmy and 1QIs[a] ḥkmyh," *Bib* 56 (1975) 420.

Concerning the history and geography of Egypt: J. Yoyotte, "Fouilles à Tanis. Rapport sur la XXIV[e] campagne (1968–1969)," *ASAE* 61 (1973) 79–86. M. Bietak, *Tell el-Dabᶜa* II (1975) (on the cities Ramses, Avaris, and Tanis).]

Isaiah 19:1-15

Text

19:1 [Verdict[a] concerning Egypt]
  Behold, Yahweh travels[b] on swift clouds
    and comes to the land of Egypt.
  The false deities[c] of Egypt totter, when he draws near,
    and Egypt's heart melts away inside its chest.[d]
  2 And I goad on[a] Egyptian[b] against Egyptian,
    so that one battles against another,
  [and each one against his fellows,] city[c] against city,
    kingdom against kingdom.[d]
  3 And Egypt's spirit will be troubled[a] [within its own being],[b]
    since I disarrange its plans,
  so that they seek guidance from their false deities[c]
    and from the apparitions of the dead[d]
  [and from the spirits of the dead[e] and from the fortune-telling
    spirits[f]].
  4 I will deliver[a] Egypt over
    into the hand of a harsh overlord,[b]
  and a mighty king[c] will rule over her;
    this is [of the Lord][d] Yahweh of Hosts, a saying.

                    *   *   *   *

  5 [There the waters will dry up in the streambed,[a]
    and the (mighty) river [b]dries out, down to the bottom,[b]
  6 and the canals[a] give off a stench,[b] they will become (extremely)
    shallow,[c]
  indeed, the Nile branches[d] of Mazor[e] dry up.
  Reed and bulrush will become black,[f]
  7 'and' the rushes[a] [by the Nile][b] at the mouth of the Nile.
  And all the sown land by the Nile will become barren,[c]
    will be blown away, and it is gone.[d]
  8 Then the fishermen[a] will lament and mourn,
    [all[b]] who throw out[c] fishing tackle into the Nile[b]
  and those who stretch out the net above the surface of the water
    shrivel up on account of this (with worry).
  9 And those who work[a] flax will come to ruin,
    the women who comb flax[b] and the weavers[c] turn very pale,[d]
  10 and those who are weaving[a] it are disheartened,
    all who work for wages[b] are most dejected.[c]]

                    *   *   *   *

  11 The princes of Zoan are sheer fools,
    [a]the wise [advisers] of the pharaoh—their advice is stupid.[a]
  How could you say to the pharaoh:
    "I am a son of the wise, son of kings from antiquity?"[b]
  12 Where are they,[a] then, your wise?
    They ought to share with you and make known[b]
  what Yahweh of Hosts has planned
    for the land of the Egyptians.
  13 The princes of Zoan have become fools,[a]
    the princes of Noph have allowed themselves to be misled,[b]
  Egypt has been led astray
    by its territorial leadership.[c]

14 Yahweh has brewed[a] 'within their midst'[b]
a spirit, which creates confusion,[c]
so that they make Egypt stagger in everything that it undertakes,[d]
as a drunk stumbles around in his own vomit.
15 [And Egypt cannot undertake any more, that which has "head and
tail," [a]"sprouting vine and stalk."[a]]

1a Concerning מַשָּׂא (verdict), see above, pp. 1f.

1b Concerning the meaning "travel, drive" (not "ride") for רכב, see S. Mowinckel, *VT* 12 (1962) 287–299, esp. 299.

1c For אֱלִילִים (false deities), the Gk reads τὰ χειροποίητα (the things made with hands), Vulg: *simulacra* (image). Ehrlich (*Randglossen* IV, 69) suggests that an author who would call the Egyptian gods אֱלִילִים (false deities) would not be able to speak about their shuddering, and therefore he alters the text unnecessarily to read אֱלֹהִים (gods). Concerning the etymology and meaning of אֱלִילִים (false deities, idols), see *Isaiah 1–12*, p. 109, on 2:8.

1d Marti suggests that בְּקִרְבּוֹ (inside its chest) be removed, assuming that בְּקִרְבּוֹ (v. 3: within its own being) was brought into the text here from v. 3 (see also Kaiser); the other possibility is more likely, that it was inserted into v. 3 because it was read already in v. 1.

2a סִכְסַךְ (goad) is the *pilpel* of סוּךְ I (stir up, incite); cf. Arabic *šawkun*, "thorn."

2b The Gk and Theod read Αἰγύπτιοι (Egyptians) for מִצְרַיִם (Egypt), as does the Gk in v. 3. But it corresponds most closely to Israel's way of thinking collectively if one stays with the traditional translation "Egypt," even though the verb is in the plural in the second bicolon.

2c Qᵃ reads וְעִיר (and city), but the ו (and) is also missing in the ancient versions.

2d Gk: καὶ νομὸς ἐπὶ νομόν (and district over against district). νομός (district, province) is used here in the technical sense, to describe the districts of Egypt (see, e.g., Herodotus 2.4), but it can also be used, with a generic meaning, simply to identify a "region."

3a נָבְקָה (will be troubled) is a *niph‘al* perfect third feminine singular from בקק (empty); it is not recommended that one alter the pointing, by doubling the second root letter, to adjust this so that the text reads the "regular" form of נָבֹקָּה (see Ges-K §67dd). Others (see Marti) presume, on the basis of the Gk (ταραχθήσεται, "be agitated, disturbed") that the reading should have been נָבֹכָה (derived from בוּך, "wander around in a daze"); see Exod. 14:3; Esther 3:15; but בקק I *niph‘al*, "be devastated," in the sense of "be destroyed," makes good sense as it is.

3b בְּקִרְבּוֹ (within its own being) is probably a gloss.

3c Concerning אֱלִילִים (false deities), see above, note 1c. The Gk reads τοὺς θεοὺς αὐτῶν (their gods) (and, for וְאֶל־הָאִטִּים, "and to the apparitions of the dead," καὶ τὰ ἀγάλματα αὐτῶν, "and their idol images").

3d אִטִּים is probably a loanword from Akkadian (*eṭemmu* or *iṭemmu*, "spirit of one who has died"; Sumerian: *gidim*, "spirit, demon"; cf. Zimmern, *Akkadische Fremdwörter* . . . (1917²) 69; and *AHW* I, 263, which mentions this formula: "seek an answer from the *eṭeme*"). Vulg reads *divinos suos* (your own deities).

3e In this passage, the Gk translates אוֹב (spirits of the dead) as οἱ ἐκ τῆς γῆς φωνοῦντες (those calling out from the earth), though, in other passages, it generally translates it as ἐγγαστρίμυθος (ventriloquist), but that word is used here for its translation of יִדְּעֹנִי (fortune-telling spirits), which follows immediately after this term. For the etymology and meaning, see *Isaiah 1–12*, pp. 371f.; and cf. M. Dietrich, "Ugaritisch *ilib* und hebräisch *ʾ(w)b* 'Totengeist,'" *UF* 6 (1974) 450–451, et al.

3f As is always the case, ידעני is used in parallel with אוב (spirit of the dead). Thus one should question whether it means "fortune-teller" (so KBL²) and not rather "fortune-telling *spirit*." 1 Sam. 28:3 and 2 Kings 21:6 supply enough information for one to conclude that both words can refer not only to the "one who conjures up the dead" but also to "one who is possessed by a spirit of fortune-telling" (*HAL*: "fortune-telling spirit, spirit of the dead, one who possesses the same, fortune-teller"). That is not really a contradiction in terms: the fortune-teller is identified as being united with the fortune-telling spirit that is speaking through that person.

4a The word סכר (shut up), which occurs only here, has the same meaning as סגר. There is no need to make an emendation, since it is very possible that one could replace ג with כ. Targ reads אמסר I, "deliver up to, transmit to," but this hardly justifies following the suggestion that the word itself should be emended to read ומכרתי (and I will sell) (see Gray, Schlögl; cf. Ezek. 30:12).

4b Concerning the plural אדנים (overlord), cf. BrSynt §19c (an emphatic use when designating higher beings); on the use of the singular adjective with such a plural, see Joüon, *Gr* §148a. Hummel (*JBL* 76 [1957] 101) suggests that אדנים was intended originally as a singular, with an enclitic *mem* at the end.

4c Instead of מלך עז (mighty king), the Gk reads the plural βασιλεῖς σκληροί (harsh kings) and, corresponding to this, the plural of the verb as well, since it also had rendered the previous אדנים קשה (mighty king) in the plural. (This caused Schlögl to err, since he altered the Hebrew to read אדנים קשים, "mighty kings.")

4d האדון (of the Lord) is not read in either the Gk or Syr. It may have been intended, as in the similar case in 10:16, as a replacement word for יהוה (Yahweh), added into the text only secondarily.

5a As in 18:2 (see above, p. 207), ים does not refer here to the ocean but to the Nile (cf. Herodotus 2.97; see Pliny, *Natural History* 35.11: "*in Nilo cuius est aqua maris similis*" (in the Nile, whose water looks similar to that of the sea); and Seneca, *Natural Questions* IVA.2: "*continuatis aquis in faciem lati ac turbidi maris stagnat*" (it settles down in a continuous expanse of water with the appearance of a wide, muddy sea).

5b–b Literally: "dry up and dry out."

6a נהרות could refer to the branches of the Nile. However, designations such as נהרות בבל (rivers of Babylon) (Ps. 137:1) and נהר כבר (river Chebar) (Ezek. 1:1, and often elsewhere) make it likely that it should be translated "canals."

6b The א in והאזניחו has been explained as an *aleph prostheticum* (Ges-K §§19m and 53g), inserted simply to aid with pronunciation. However, Qᵃ reads this as והזניחו, which gives added support to the ancients who supposed that this was nothing but a copying mistake (see already J. Olshausen, *Lehrbuch der hebräischen Sprache* [1861] §255b; Marti; Gray; Duhm; et al.). It is also possible, however, that the transmitted text offers the choice between two ancient readings of the word: והזניחו and ואזניחו (see Ehrlich, *Randglossen* IV, 70).

6c For the use of both this form דללו (become shallow) and דלו (thus 38:14), see Joüon, *Gr* §82k.

6d Concerning יארי (branches), see *Isaiah 1–12*, p. 320, textual note 7:18a.

6e מצור III is the designation for Egypt (cf. Akkadian *muṣur*). Some suggest that this word, in contrast to מצרים, specifically refers to Lower Egypt (Delitzsch, Dillmann and Kittel). In any case, none of the ancient translations took מצור to mean "Egypt" (see also 37:25 = 2 Kings 19:24; Mic. 7:12). Calderone suggests altering the text to read צוּר יְאֹרִים (in which case the כ in יְאֹרִים is treated as an enclitic *mem*), meaning "channels of rock," that is, the cataracts. He thinks that מָצוֹר was probably chosen because the word could be understood to mean "oppression, siege," following the principle *nomen est omen* (the name tells the fate), which would therefore have pointed out to Egypt that its name proclaimed its destiny.

6f קָמַל is normally translated "wither." In Syriac the word means to "become black"; in Arabic *qamila* means to "have black spots," that is, after it rains. KBL begins its explanation with the Arabic substantive *qamlun*, "louse" (meaning: "to be overrun by lice"). One does better, however, if one stays with the idea of the Arabic *verb*, which, according to the context, clearly intends to describe what results after the Nile dries up.

7a For עָרוֹת [BDB: bare place], the Gk reads καὶ τὸ ἄχι (= "swamp grass") τὸ χλωρόν (and the pale/green swamp grass); Vulg reads this as *nudabitur* (it will be laid bare), which means it was thought that this was from the root ערר, "be stripped bare." As a general rule, the word was treated as if it were a substantive: "bare, open areas, without forestation"; cf. מַעַר and מַעֲרֶה*, "nakedness, clearing" (*HAL*); so also Ges-Buhl. However, that makes no sense. The Gk (but also Saadia and Qimḥi) detected more correctly what was meant. Behind עָרוֹת is Egyptian *ꜥr* (rush) or *ꜥrt* (stalk of a plant; according to Erman-Grapow I, 208, "stalk of a lotus blossom"); see Herz, 496; and Thacker. The parallel word סוּף is also an Egyptian loanword (*ṯwfy*; see W. F. Albright, *The Vocalization of the Egyptian Syllabic Orthography*, AOS 5 [1934] 65), as is also the Gk ἄχι (swamp grass) (*ꜣḫy* and *ꜣḫy*; cf. Hebrew אָחוּ, "reeds, rushes"). This eliminates the need of further attempts to emend the text, such as those of Marti, Reider (*VT* 2 [1952] 115), or Sacchi, who derives עָרוֹת from a root ערה = "be green" and translates this *"cose verdi"* (green things). But the καὶ (and) (preceding the τὸ ἄχι, "the swamp grass") in the Gk is most likely correct (lost by haplography of the ו) so that עָרוֹת has much the same sense as קָנֶה וָסוּף (reed and bulrush) in v. 6b.

7b עַל־יְאוֹר (by the Nile) should be removed from the text, as a dittography caused by עַל־פִּי יְאוֹר (at the mouth of the Nile), which follows immediately, also because it is not in the Gk. Herz suggests reading אֻלְּפוּ (faint) in the second instance (instead of עַל־פִּי, "at the mouth of") and eliminates the second יְאֹר (Nile), which results in his suggestion that v. 7a can be translated: "The עָרוֹת on the Nile shall faint." By contrast, Guillaume suggests that עַל־פִּי should be read as עֶלֶף; he uses Arabic *ꜥalafun*, which means "green or dried fodder for the animals" and translates: "the herbage of the Nile and all that is sown by the Nile shall become dry." However, these suggested emendations are too far-fetched for them to be accepted with any confidence.

7c Instead of יִיבָשׁ, Qᵃ reads יבֹשׁ.

7d The Gk does not have anything in its text corresponding to וְאֵינֶנּוּ (and it is gone); Qᵃ reads ואין בו (and there is nothing in it), but this is hardly correct.

8a Instead of הַדַּיָּגִים (the fishermen), Qᵃ reads הדגים (the fish), but the parallelism in the second half of the verse would favor the MT.

8b Schlögl favors eliminating בַּיְאוֹר (in the Nile). The line is too long, but it is more likely that כָל (all) should be removed.

8c Concerning the use of the construct state form מַשְׁלִיכֵי (who throw out) before prepositions, see BrSynt §70f.

9a The plural of פִּשְׁתָּה (feminine!), "flax," refers to the stalks of the flax, which have to be worked in order to extract the bast fiber.

9b The root שׂרק (not found anywhere else in biblical Hebrew) means, according to Judean Aramaic and Syriac, "comb," so that שְׂרִיקוֹת thus means "that which is combed," used with reference to flax: "that which is hackled, flax-combed." Thus

v. 9a would have to be translated: "Those who work the (flax) fiber to turn it into combed flax will come to ruin." But the length of the verse makes it likely that the *athnach* should be moved and placed under the previous word, פשתים (flax). Then, instead of שׂריקות (combed, carded), the active participle feminine plural שֹׁרְקוֹת (combers) (or masculine plural שֹׂרְקִים?) should be read (Vulg: *pectentes,* "combers"; Syr: *dsrqyn,* "of combers").

9c Hummel (98) treats ארגים (weavers) as being in the construct state, ארגי (weavers of), with an enclitic *mem.*

9d The hapax legomenon חורי is rendered in the Gk as βύσσος (linen) and should thus be translated something such as "white stuff"; cf. חור I, "white woven material, linen." However, Luzzatto had already come up with the suggestion to read this חורו (root חור), "bleach them, turn them pale" (see 29:22, also 24:6), which is now confirmed by the Qᵃ reading.

10a שתתיה is problematic. It has been traditionally interpreted as the plural of שת, "foundation," but this meaning does not fit in the context and does not agree with the masculine predicate מדכאים (those who are weaving). The Gk reads οἱ διαζόμενοι αὐτὰ ἐν ὀδύνῃ = "which it, as a chain in a weaver's loom, draws up." For this reason, some have suggested that שתתיה must derive from a verb related to the noun שתי, "weaving." Zimmern (28) concludes, on the basis of Akkadian *šatū,* "weave," that there also would have been a Hebrew root שתה, with the same meaning; cf. also Aramaic שְׁתָא, "weave," and שְׁתִיָא, "the warp in weaving." But Eitan refers to Coptic *štit,* "weaver," and, based on that word, suggests reading שְׁתִיתָהּ (so also *BHS;* cf. KBL²) and translates it "its weaver."

10b The Gk translates שׂכר as ζῦτος, "beer," meaning that it read שֵׁכָר, as did a few MSS; Syr: *škr˒* (liquor, strong drink). Some commentators accept this reading, since they think that, somehow, שתתיה in the first half of the verse must have been a derivative of שתה = "drink" (Schlögl: שֹׁתֵי יָיִן, "drinkers of wine"). Rashi treats עשׂי שׂכר as if it read עֹשֵׂי סֶכֶר, which is supposed to mean "something that dams up water" (for the purpose of catching fish, according to Delitzsch). But שׂכר means "compensation," just as in Prov. 11:18; yet it is possible that the pointing should be altered to read שָׂכָר (compensation, wages) (see below on meter, p. 245).

10c אגמי = עֲנֻמֵי (grieved); cf. Th. Nöldeke, *ZDMG* 40 (1886) 727; and M. D. Goldmann, *AusBR* 2 (1952) 50. Thus אגמי is not related to אגם, "bulrush pond," which has caused many problems in interpretation (Vulg: *lacunas ad capiendos pisces,* "ponds for capturing fish"; Ibn Ezra: "pools full of lively fish"), even though some follow certain Hebrew MSS and alter the text to read אגמי מים (pools of water).

11a–a Verse 11aβ appears too long. Thus it does not help much that G. R. Driver (*JTS* 38 [1937] 40) rearranges some of it and repoints some of it to read חכמי פרעה יעצו עצה נבערה (the pharaoh's wise men advise foolish advice); it is more likely that יעצו should be eliminated as a dittography of עצה (advice). In the OT, עצה hardly ever refers specifically to "advice" in the sense of someone consulting an "advisory board." נבערה (stupid) is not an attribute of, but rather a predicate to, עצה (advice), which means חֹ פֹ is to be treated as a *casus pendens.* Instead of עצה, it may be that, following the Gk (ἡ βουλὴ αὐτῶν, "their advice"), one should read עֲצָתָם (their advice). (Of course, one cannot completely eliminate the possibility that an emendation is more correct: חֲכָמָיו יָעֲצוּ עֵצָה נִבְעָרָה = "his wise ones pass out dumb advice.")

11b It is almost impossible to determine whether קדם means "an earlier time" or "east" here. It has traditionally been translated "an earlier time." In favor of "east," one need note not only the usage in 2:6, but especially 1 Kings 5:10, according to which the wisdom of the בני־קדם (sons of the east) was renowned (cf. Job 1:3).

According to Jer. 49:7, the wisdom of the Edomites and Temanites was proverbial. However, it is unlikely that the wise in Egypt would have lauded themselves as being the descendants of the kings of the east. Nevertheless, it was common for wisdom traditions to be placed into the mouths of kings who ruled in earlier times.

12a Hummel (102) suggests that the *mem* in אים (where are they) is an enclitic *mem*, but the suffix makes good sense here.

12b וידעו is translated: "and they should learn about a situation," but, at the very least, this should *precede* ויגידו (share with, tell about). The Gk reads εἰπάτωσαν (let them tell); Vulg: *et indicent* (and they will tell), which would lead one to conclude that the original would have been וידעו (and they shall make known), which is how it is treated by Gray, Duhm, Kissane, Kaiser, et al. The *athnach* on לך (to you) should be placed under this word.

13a and 13b Qᵃ reads the forms נאולו (also: have become fools) and נשאו (also: have allowed themselves to be misled). In addition to the root יאל I (be a fool), it is possible that there is also a root אול* I (be a fool) (see *HAL* and the adjective אויל, "foolish"; cf., e.g., שוא, "emptiness," and its similarity to נשא II, "deceive").

13c It has been suggested that one read the plural פנות (chief rulers) instead of פנת (chief ruler) (already suggested by Grotius, Duhm, Marti, Ehrlich, Kaiser, et al.); see Syr and Targ and cf. Judg. 20:2; 1 Sam. 14:38. It is possible that the singular is to be treated as a collective (Gray; cf. Ges-K §145bc).

14a Duhm suggests reading נסך, "pour out," instead of מסך (brew, produce by mixing) (see 29:10), an easier reading, which need not be adopted.

14b For בקרבה (in her midst), the Gk reads αὐτοῖς (to them), which would suggest that the original might have been בקרבם (in their midst). The third feminine singular suffix on בקרבה would have to refer to Egypt, which is a difficult reading, since the text speaks of those who are leading the land astray.

14c Concerning the plural עועים (confusion), cf. BrSynt §19b. Qᵃ reads עועים, which might be pointed עועים or in some similar way; in any case it would lead one to conclude that it is a reduplicated form from the root עוה (bend, twist) (see Ges-Buhl).

14d The masculine suffix on מעשהו (which it undertakes, its works) must refer back to Egypt, but שבטיה (v. 13b) has a feminine suffix (its [lit.: her] territorial [leadership]) and Aquila, Sym, Theod, Gkᵠᵐᵍ all read: τοῖς ἔργοις αὐτῆς (for her works), so that the word should be pointed מעשה (everything that it [lit.: she] undertakes).

15a–a The Gk translates כפה ואגמון (sprouting vine and stalk) freely: ἀρχὴν καὶ τέλος (beginning and end). On כפה (sprouting vine), see *Isaiah 1–12*, p. 221, textual note for 9:13.

Form

Chapter 19 is captioned by the (secondary) superscription משא מצרים (verdict concerning Egypt) (on this, see above, pp. 1f.). The entire chapter does, in fact, speak about Egypt. It makes sense that this message concerning Egypt would be inserted at this point, since chap. 18 also deals with Egypt and the author of chap. 20 sets his sights on this country as well.

Without a doubt, however, the present form of this chapter does not consist of one unified piece. In v. 16 poetry gives way to prose. The second part of the chapter is introduced by the well-known formula that the expander frequently used, ביום ההוא (in that day), which is repeated ad nauseam in vv. 18, 19, 21, 23, and 24. The content of the sayings in vv. 16ff. presumes a different situation and is occasioned by a different set of theological concerns. Thus it is virtually impossible that the additions in vv. 16ff. could have been produced by the same author as the one responsible for vv. 1-15, to function as later, additional comments. It is true that the chapter, as it now stands, is supposed to give the impression that it is a single unit. However, the break after v. 15 is such a major one that vv. 1-15 must first be treated separately.

That does not mean, however, that at least vv. 1-15 can be treated as one single original unit either. The citation formula נאם האדון יהוה צבאות (this is of the Lord Yahweh of Hosts, a saying) brings v. 4 to a conclusion, and v. 5 introduces a brand-new theme. Verses 1-4 are focused on a severe internal crisis in Egypt, during which it is to be delivered over to a "harsh overlord." However, vv. 5-10 describe an economic breakdown, caused when the waters in the "river" dry up, with no apparent relationship between this and the political crisis in vv. 1-4. Finally, vv. 11-14 deal with still another new theme: the foolishness and confusion of the princes of Zoan (and Memphis), who have given the pharaoh poor advice and must bear the consequences of the resulting desolate situation in which Egypt now finds itself. Verse 15 borrows from the phraseology of 9:13; the sentence is a prosaic expansion. The glossator felt compelled, in connection with מעשהו (which it undertakes, its works) (or מעשה, "her works"; see textual note 14d), to furnish further details about the hopelessness of Egypt's pitiful condition.

If one excludes v. 15 from consideration, this unit of material can be divided into three smaller sections: vv. 1b-4, 5-10, 11-14. A related question deals with whether these three parts are all from the same author and whether they form a unit by virtue of the fact that they all deal with the same historical situation. That question is not easy to answer. Verses 1b-4 anticipate a complete disintegration of the political structure of authority in Egypt. Local rulers battle with one another; a ruling government, which leaders want to install to coordinate these rulers, is not capable of getting the job done. The disarray in political orientation leads to an inner, personal disorientation as well. As always happens in such times, help is sought from advisers with questionable credentials, from conjurers and from fortune-tellers (v. 3). However, this same theme, dealing with the confusion that has affected those who claimed they were able to give intelligent advice, is continued in vv. 11-14. On the one hand, there are no indicators to suggest the exact nature of this confusion; however, since the pharaoh and the princes are involved in this, it must have something to do with political decisions. On the other hand, one does learn that the leaders of the administrative districts, especially the princes of Zoan and Memphis, play a crucial role. Consequently, one cannot be certain that vv. 11-14 deal with the same historical period as vv. 1b-4, but there are no convincing arguments against that viewpoint either.

A different conclusion must be reached concerning vv. 5-10. A natural catastrophe, of the type announced in this middle section of the piece, does not have to be linked to any coordinated, politically arranged show of force. The author demonstrates a detailed knowledge of the geography of the Nile delta region and has observed economic conditions carefully enough to be able to describe specific problems. This means that this author is someone who does not know about the land of Nile from secondhand reports only. He uses the name מצור (Mazor) when speaking of Egypt, which, except for 37:25, is not found elsewhere in the book of Isaiah and which is not used in any other preexilic writings. Even the terminology used betrays a detailed knowledge of Egypt: יאׁר (Egyptian: *ỉrw*) does not have to be considered in this list, since this way of referring to the Nile was known for a long time already (7:18) and סוף (bulrush) is one of the loanwords that Israel had borrowed from the Egyptian language (Albright, *Vocalization*, treats סוף as being related to the Egyptian word *ṭwfy*, "papyrus, papyrus thicket"; Ward suggests reading *čwf* [= *ṭwf*] and presumes, at the same time, that this is a Semitic loanword into Egyptian, not vice versa). But ערות (the rushes) (see above, p. 231), a foreign word borrowed from Egyptian, was known by so few in Israel that it did not take long for the time to come when no one knew what it meant. It also seems likely that שְׂתֹתֶיהָ (those who are weaving) (no matter how one finally decides to point it) in v. 10 is also an Egyptian word. Finally, it seems that זנח (give off a stench) is also based on an Egyptian verb (see below, p. 246). This type of detailed knowledge cannot be observed anywhere else in the OT; at most, one might detect a parallel of sorts in the Joseph story, which demonstrates some intimate knowledge of life in Egypt.

All of this excludes the possibility that the same author writes here and also speaks in the preceding and following sections of this unit. This portrayal is a secondary insertion between the two messages directed against Egypt, which now provide its framework, having been inserted and being most likely composed later than those two parts. However, one cannot move beyond the realm of conjecture in such a passage, which has so few datable referents; one has to be content with a relative chronology only.

Setting

Nonetheless, it seems possible to be more certain about the dating of the other two sections, vv. 1b-4 and 11-14. There is no doubt that they are making observations about a specific historical situation. It was a common recurrence that the centralized power of the pharaoh threatened to come apart and that there was a rivalry among local rulers, but it seems that a particular event resulted in this threat that Yahweh would deliver Egypt over to a harsh overlord, to a powerful king. Yet one could think of a number of times when this prediction could have been made. If one considers this passage to have come from Isaiah, this might refer to an Ethiopian (Piankhy or Shabaka?), but also could refer to an Assyrian (Sargon or Sennacherib?) (on this, see below, pp. 238f.). If one does not proceed from this presupposition, then every century up to the end of the Persian rule offers possibilities, with threatening countries located throughout the Near East. One might think of Esarhaddon, who pressed on into Egypt about 671, defeating the Ethiopian Tirhakah and conquering Memphis without fierce fighting. From then on, Egypt was ruled by territorial rulers who were accountable to an Assyrian overlord. A victory stele discovered in Zinjirli includes a picture of Esarhaddon, depicted larger than life, leading the king of Ethiopia and the one who ruled Tyre with a rope (*AOB* no. 144; *ANEP* no. 447). However, those who do not believe Isaiah authored this passage are normally of the opinion that it originates in the postexilic era. There were certainly enough times when centralized authority disintegrated, and there were also numerous times when there was inner, personal disorientation in Egypt (see Kaiser, AOAT 18 [1973]; and idem, FS J. Ziegler). The harsh overlord could have been Cambyses (Luzzatto) or Artaxerxes II or III (Duhm, Kaiser; see also Marti). Finally, Kaiser goes so far as to suggest that this prophecy should be dated in the period when it was expected that Antiochus III might invade Egypt, with the background to the passage possibly being furnished by events subsequent to the battle at Raphia, in 217, when the native-born citizens began to revolt against the Ptolemies, but without succeeding in breaking away from their control. Scholars have offered a host of other suggestions, and, no doubt, many more will follow.

Thus the discussion about the authenticity of 19:1ff., which has been carried on since the time of Eichhorn, Rosenmüller, and de Wette, has not yet resulted in any measure of agreement about a date for this passage that really makes sense and that is generally accepted, nothing beyond vague, possible solutions that are hardly worth mentioning. Just to show how opinions remain widely divergent about whether the passage is to be attributed to Isaiah, one can find the observation that vv. 1-15 are "quite generally" regarded as being from Isaiah (cf. Erlandsson, 76), but have the opposite point of view expressed rather abruptly by another, who contends that 19:1-15 cannot possibly be attributed to Isaiah (Fohrer). If one looks for the reasons, one sees quickly that the arguments are very shaky, if they are mentioned at all. Duhm finds fault with both style and meter. The meter does not cause any greater problems here than in many other Isaianic passages. Apparent stylistic problems are always noted in connection with the frequent repetition of מצרים (Egypt) in the first five verses. But that is caused chiefly by the fact that the author accentuates the deep inner conflicts within Egypt (v. 2), which one would thus almost anticipate stylistically (all the same, מצרים, "Egypt," in the superscription, ought not be considered here). However, Duhm takes the case still further: "Would Isaiah have been so thorough, as is to be noted in vv. 5-10, that he would have been concerned about how the Egyptian fishermen and weavers would be able to get enough bread?" Well, why not? Since it is hardly possible that vv. 5-10 come from Isaiah, however, one need not argue any more about that. "The chief argument against Isaianic authorship is the absence of any political motifs being given as reasons for the threats." However, it is a fact that Isaiah did deal with Egypt in connection with political issues (20:3; 30:2; 31:1, 3), not, of course, as Duhm suggests is the case about the author of this present passage, to keep up with the current "style," which was that one would hurl threats against the heathen; but simply because he did not want his people to stay in the dark about the weaknesses of Egypt, which ignorance would result in a terrible risk every time an agreement was concluded: "The Egyptians are human, and not God; their horses are flesh, and not spirit. When Yahweh stretches out his hand, the helper will stumble" (31:3). If one views 19:1-4 in this light, then Duhm's weighty observations also lose their force, though they have often been repeated by others. In addition to these arguments, Fohrer refers to connections with the vocabulary of Deutero-Isaiah and Ezekiel, but does not furnish evidence from specific verses. One might note the phraseology וייִדְעוּ לְךָ נָא וִיגִידוּ (they ought to share with you and make known) in v. 12, which might have a distant parallel in 41:26. But that passage uses terminology from a judgment speech, and it is certainly possible that the same would apply to Isaiah. Finally, when Kaiser observes: "The numerous verbal similarities to other passages in the book are evidence, not that Isaiah was the author, but that this is the work of a devout writer who drew all his ideas from the book," he also does not bother to provide any data to show just where these ideas were originally stated. It is possible that he is thinking of the designation of the "idols" as אֱלִילִים. But why would Isaiah be prohibited from using that designation more than a single time? A stronger argument could be made when noting the use of אֹבוֹת (spirits of the dead) and יִדְּעֹנִים (fortune-telling spirits) in v. 3bβ, but that is probably the result of a gloss written by a reader, who was reminded of 8:19. Finally, v. 15, which has vocabulary reminiscent of 9:13, is a later addition (so also Procksch). In conclusion, the points of contact that vv. 13f. have with 29:9f. do not leave one with the impression that a later individual filled in the details for Isaiah, but rather that Isaiah makes use of a particular motif in a completely new context. The same explanation holds true for 19:2, when compared with 3:5, where a reader noted the similarity of thought and felt compelled to insert וְאִישׁ בְּרֵעֵהוּ (and each one against the other) from 3:5.

Once one has eliminated the expansions and glosses, then the points of contact with the rest of the words of Isaiah are reduced to that portion of the material that helps to identify the actual author. A full discussion of the use of special vocabulary in vv. 1-4 and 11-14 can be found in Procksch. Here, one need only note that the *pilpel* of סוּךְ (goad on) is used in the OT only in 19:2 and 9:10, that נוּעַ (totter) is used in a similar contextual framework in 7:2, and that the princes of Zoan are also mentioned in 30:4 (and nowhere else in the entire OT); apparently, they played a significant role in Judah during Isaiah's lifetime. For these reasons, it is very likely that Isaiah himself is the source for 19:1b-4 and 11-14. The reason that this passage was suspect has to do with the fact that no one noticed that vv. 5-10 form an insertion and that v. 15 is also a secondary expansion, in addition to a significant number of glosses being added to the text.

It must be admitted that an exact dating for both of these sections of material has not yet been determined. Yet the answer to the question of the date can be given with some measure of certainty: the discussion is not about Ethiopia; Egypt would not yet seem to be under the rule of the Twenty-fifth Dynasty. If this is from Isaiah, the message would precede 18:1ff. chronologically. According to vv. 11ff., in spite of allusions to the questionable nature of the political activity, Zoan/Tanis was still important enough that

Isaiah took his mission seriously, that he had to warn others about the "foolishness" which had seized those who lived there. Osorkon IV (730–715) was still able to exert powerful influence in the Palestinian region. Apparently, he subscribed to the traditional political tactics developed by his dynasty: in the royal palace in Samaria, an alabaster vase was found, which included a cartouche of Osorkon II (874–850). In the battle of *qarqar,* against Shalmaneser III, in which Ahab of Israel played a leading role, one thousand soldiers from Egypt also participated, no doubt a contingent from the army of Osorkon II (cf. Kitchen, §§284f.). Hoshea of Israel had been encouraged by Osorkon IV to rebel, but then the latter disgracefully left the Israelite king in the lurch. He did come to the aid of *ḥanunu* of Gaza in 720 and tried to save him: Sargon reports that *reʾe* (which certainly ought to be read here instead of *sibʾe;* see above, p. 215), the *turtannu* (commander general) of Egypt, fought on the side of *ḥanunu.* This *reʾe* was apparently the commander of the forces of Osorkon IV. But Osorkon was still not willing to abstain from mixing in matters in the Near East (and probably had little choice in the matter, in light of the increasing size of the territory that was coming under Assyrian control). Sargon renewed his offensive against Philistia in 716 and pressed on further from there toward Egypt. He subjugated the Arabs in that region and installed a sheik who would be answerable to him in Laban (*tell abu selēme;* see Y. Aharoni, *The Land of the Bible* [1967] 290), so that he could keep the region in the vicinity of the *naḥal muṣri* under control. *Šilkanni,* the king of Egypt, was overpowered (concerning the identification of this *šilkanni* with Osorkon IV, see Albright, *BASOR* 141 [1956] 24) and was able to use the imposition of tribute to create external calm. With this, the political moves that the Twenty-second Dynasty attempted to carry out in Palestine finally came to naught. It is likely that the material in Isa. 19:1b-4 and 11-14 belongs to this period, since Tanis was still playing a role; yet a shrewd observer would be able to detect the relative strength of the various armed forces, as the greatly weakened coalition of princes sought to draw others into political activity that was most foolish. The nature of the situation would have led such a group to send out feelers in the direction of Jerusalem as well, just as there was deep interest in Jerusalem about what political moves Osorkon would make over against Assyria after Samaria fell. Isaiah had all the reasons in the world to make sure that the king and people were not uninformed about his views on the matter.

　　One final question remains. What is the identity of the "harsh overlord?" Some have thought this to be Piankhy (see above, pp. 235f.), who brought Egypt under his domination about 730 (Bright, though with reservations), or Shabaka, under whose leadership the Ethiopian dynasty attempted to bring the princes who ruled the delta under its control, between the years 716–712 (Kitchen, §125), who, according to Manetho, is supposed to have burned alive the last ruler of the Twenty-fourth Dynasty, Bocchoris (Procksch, Eichrodt, who also thinks this overlord might be Sargon). Viewing all this from a Palestinian perspective, however, when the Ethiopian dynasty conquered Egypt, it was treated as if it was nothing more than a conflict within Egypt's own borders, and the Egyptians themselves did not view the Ethiopians as if they were carrying out a foreign takeover, since they did not bring with them a foreign culture into the land and were meticulous about respecting the Egyptian deities (see the Piankhy stele, in Breasted, *ARE* IV, §§840, 848, 865, 871, etc.). Thus it is much more likely that the principal opponent for Osorkon IV in Syria/Palestine was the Assyrian Sargon II (722–705). There is no question that he was important enough to be described as a אֲדֹנִים קָשֶׁה (harsh overlord) and as a מֶלֶךְ עַז (mighty king).

[19:1b-4] *Yahweh Travels to Egypt*

Form

The threat against Egypt is introduced with the presentative הִנֵּה (behold) (cf. 3:1, הִנֵּה הָאָדוֹן יְהוָה צְבָאוֹת מְסִיר, "behold, the Lord, Yahweh of Hosts, takes away"; on this, see *Isaiah 1–12*, p. 128, and 8:7; 10:33; 17:1; 22:17; 28:2; 30:27). Just as in the threat in 3:1ff., where Yahweh himself speaks from v. 4 on, 19:1ff., already in v. 2, shifts to become a speech from Yahweh. In addition, a definite parallel in terms of content cannot be missed: there, Yahweh delivers Judah over to lacerating its own flesh; here, it is Egypt. However, lacerating one's own body, the breakdown within one's own land, forms only the prelude to the coming catastrophe described within the present passage. The actual threat follows in v. 4: Egypt will be delivered over to a "harsh overlord." Many have observed that a reason for the judgment of Yahweh is not included. In 8:6 the reason is given just before the announcement, introduced by the presentative, but 3:1 begins immediately with a הִנֵּה (behold). However, one ought not think in terms of what its form ought to be, since in both of those passages the criticism is implicit within the threat: the discord and confusion, seeking answers from the idols, and practicing fortune-telling. Isaiah frequently chooses to conclude a threat with the citation formula; cf. passages such as 3:15; 17:3, 6.

Meter: Verse 1bα: 3 + 2 stresses (הִנֵּה, "behold," as often with such particles, is not considered when identifying the meter of the verse). Verse 1bβ, by use of a heavy four-stress + four-stress bicolon, portrays the magnitude of the disaster that will come against Egypt. Verse 2a should probably be read as a three-stress + three-stress bicolon (bracketing out וְאִישׁ בְּרֵעֵהוּ, "and each one against his fellows"; see above, p. 237). Verse 2b: a two-stress + two-stress bicolon (one should note the gradual shortening of lines, from 4 + 4 to 3 + 3 to 2 + 2), suggesting at the same time the waves that are stirred up by Yahweh's appearance in Egypt). Verse 3: 2 five-stress cola (בְּקִרְבּוֹ, "within its own being," in v. 3a, as well as all of v. 3bβ, should be bracketed out; see above, p. 229; אֶל־הָאֱלִילִים, "from false deities," and אֶל־הָאֹבוֹת, "from apparitions of the dead," each receive two stresses). Verse 4: a three-stress + three-stress bicolon (וְסִכַּרְתִּי, "I will deliver over," receives two stresses; הָאָדוֹן, "of the Lord," is to be removed; see above, textual note 4d). It must be admitted, however, that one cannot be completely confident that the meter has been correctly analyzed, because the secondary insertions into the text may go deeper than one can determine with certainty.

Commentary

[19:1f.] In 18:4 Yahweh is compared to a dew-filled cloud, which hangs motionless up in the heavens, but here he travels or drives on swift-moving clouds. This formulation makes use of the ancient concept that Yahweh travels on clouds or even above the heavens: Ps. 68:5 רֹכֵב בָּעֲרָבוֹת (NRSV: who drives in the desert) (which some had earlier suggested should be altered to read ר׳ בֶּעָבוֹת, "who drives in the clouds," see *BHK³*; and others have suggested that it should be changed to read רכב בָּעֲרָפוֹת, "who drives in heavy clouds"; see *BHS* and H. L. Ginsberg, *JBL* 62 [1943] 112f.; W. F. Albright, *HUCA* 23/1 [1950/51] 18; which perhaps can be read in the form in which it is preserved; see G. R. Driver, *Canaanite Myths,* 128; H.-J. Kraus, *Psalmen BK* XV/1 [1960] 466 [Engl: *Psalms 60–150,* Continental Commentary (1989) 51], which, in any case, still means "cloud rider"). In addition, cf. Ps. 68:34: רכב בשמים (O rider in the heavens) (text emended). E. Ullendorff (*BJRL* 46 [1963] 242–244) suggests that there is a relationship between this epithet of Baal and that of Zeus, νεφεληγερέτα, "cloud gatherer" and S. Brock (*VT* 18 [1968] 395–397) sought to provide further argumentation to support this view; but this is simply not correct. Deut. 33:26 also praises Yahweh "who drives through the heavens to your help, in his majesty on the clouds (שְׁחָקִים)" [NRSV: "majestic through the skies"]; and Ps. 104:3 reads: הַשָּׂם עָבִים רְכוּבוֹ (who makes the clouds his chariot [NRSV: your chariot]). According to Ps. 18:11 = 2 Sam. 22:11, he rides (or drives onward) on the cherub. Since the discovery of the Ugaritic texts, it has been almost universally acknowledged that this concept must have its original roots in *rkb ʿrpt,* an epithet of Baal. Baal is the storm god, who presses forward on the rain clouds. But the passages just cited still make clear that the use of this terminology in connection with Yahweh is not simply limited to ideas about the god of rain when it speaks about him traveling through the heavens or on the clouds. He is the god who hurries to bring aid to his people (Judg. 5:4; Deut. 33:2; cf. also Ps. 68:8f.). When traveling about, above the heavens, he is proclaiming that he has power over the peoples (Ps. 68:34). There is no doubt that he also travels above the earth to bring judgment; cf. Hab. 3:8ff. Thus the ancient divine epithet has been combined with concepts connected with the theophany, Yahweh's appearing, to bring either salvation or judgment at whatever place he thinks it necessary to intervene (on this, see J. Jeremias, *Theophanie* [1965] 88, 159f.). It is obvious that the concept of God that is connected with this motif stands in tension with the other, which depicts Yahweh enthroned in his sanctuary (see esp. 6:1ff.), but this tension is part of the peculiar nature of the way in which Yahweh is spoken of in the OT, particularly when it comes to his rule as king.

The motif describing Yahweh as the one who rides on the clouds takes a specific form in the second colon: ובא מצרים (and comes to the land of Egypt). The coming is for the purpose of judgment (cf. Pss. 96:13; 98:9). At the same time, Egypt is also represented by its gods (here called אֱלִילִים, "false deities," the same term Isaiah used when speaking about the idols of Judah; on this, see *Isaiah 1–12*, p. 109). When Yahweh reveals himself in his theophany, "all worshipers of images are put to shame, those who make their boast in worthless idols (אֱלִילִים); all gods bow down before him" (Ps. 97:7). Nature itself is in uproar when Yahweh appears; see Judg. 5:5; Ps. 114:3ff. However, the present passage says that the gods begin to totter (נוע; the same verb is used to describe the reaction of those who experience Yahweh's appearance in the depiction of the theophany at Sinai, Exod. 20:18).

At a much earlier time, the Hadad hymn IV R 28, no. 2, spoke about how the natural world would shake when the gods tottered:

> Hadad, when he is furious, the earth quakes before him.
> The great mountains tumble down before him,
> before his wrath, before his rancor,
> before his roaring, before his thunder,
> the gods of the heavens flee up to heaven,
> the gods of the earth climb into the earth,
> the sun goes to the foundation of heaven,
> the moon disappears in the heights of heaven.

(A translation of the H.-P. Müller rendering: BZAW 109 [1969] 20; additional texts are cited there as well.)

One might compare this with the Hymn to Hadad-Rimmon (*Cuneiform Texts from Babylonian Tablets . . . in the British Museum* [1896ff.] XV, 15ff.; *AOT* 249):

> Father Ishkur, Lord, one who rides forth on the storm, that is your name, majestic god,
> Father Ishkur, one who rides forth on the hurricane, that is your name, majestic god,
> Father Ishkur, one who rides forth on the mighty lions, that is your name, majestic god,
> Ishkur, lion of the heavens, exalted steer, beamer, that is your name, majestic god,
> your name grips the world,
> your radiance covers the world like a dress,
> with your thunder, the great mountain totters, Father Enlil,
> with your roaring, the great Mother Ninlil shudders.

In addition, cf. *enūma eliš* IV, 65ff., 87ff., 107ff. (*AOT* 118; *ANET* 66f.).

If even the gods begin to totter, as drunks stagger around (cf. 29:9), then it is no wonder that Egypt completely loses whatever stability it had. Egypt's heart melts in its insides; so it reads in our text. In 7:2 Isaiah says that the heart of the people shook when the enemy came against them (also using the word נוע), and he warns in 7:4 that its heart ought not become soft (רכך). In that passage, Isaiah borrows from the formal terminology used in a war oracle (Deut. 20:3; cf. also *Isaiah 1–12*, pp. 297f.). A synonym for the heart "becoming soft" in a war oracle (see Deut. 20:8) describes how the heart "melts," which means that Isaiah is making use of the vocabulary of this genre here as well. In the wider sense, however, the war oracle is from the larger context of holy war. It would seem that it is also part of that concept that one need not engage in any real battle, since Yahweh confounds the enemy so completely that it will exterminate itself. In the present passage, this thought is formulated as follows: "I goad on Egyptian against Egyptian" (concerning the *pilpel* of סוך, "goad on," see *Isaiah 1–12*, p. 228); cf. Judg. 7:22; 2 Kings 3:23; Isa. 3:5; and Zech. 14:13; in addition, see Ezek. 38:21; 1 Sam. 14:20 (each one's sword against the other). In v. 2b "city against city and kingdom against kingdom" is an expansion of the traditional expression, furnished in light of the actual situation in Egypt at that time. Until the Ethiopian dynasty was able to consolidate its power, those who ruled from the Twenty-second to the Twenty-fourth Dynasties made life bitter, each for the other, and there were additional problems with princes ruling individual cities that, time and again, would declare their independence and battle one another. "The power of the dominant house rapidly waned until there was at last an independent lord or petty king in every city of the Delta and up the river as far as Hermopolis. We are acquainted with the names of eighteen of these dynasts, whose struggles among themselves now led to the total dissolution of the Egyptian state" (Breasted, *A History of Egypt* [1964] 448; cf. also 454).

[19:3] Verse 3 depicts Egypt's hopeless situation with a new image: Egypt's spirit is "agitated," literally "devastated." בקק can be used in a special sense to describe the "devastation" of a plan (עצה) (Jer. 19:7). Verse 3aβ thus declares that Yahweh devastates Egypt's עצה (plan). Note the parallelism between v. 3aα and 3aβ. This "devastating" of the spirit was to be seen plainly as they would propose muddleheaded plans. Naturally, עצה (plan), as elsewhere in Isaiah, when it speaks of the עצה (plan) of human beings (8:10; 29:15; 30:1), also refers to the type of political-military goals that humans set for themselves. The verb in the first bicolon is passive or intransitive; however, the verb in the second colon is active, with Yahweh as subject. One can come up with a rational explanation for Egypt's hopeless situation—but Isaiah sees deeper, noting that it is, at the same time, the result of divine intervening actions. In history itself, which can be understood and explained on its own terms (*etsi deus non daretur!* even though God would not be said to have been involved!), Yahweh still accomplishes what he plans to do. The subject, on the receiving end of this activity, in v. 3b is once again the Egyptians themselves. They turn toward אלילים (false deities) and אטים (apparitions of the dead). But it could just as easily be said that Yahweh delivers up the Egyptians to their false deities and to those who conjure up the dead. It is a judgment simply to be delivered over to worship of idols and to those who tell fortunes.

אטים (apparitions of the dead) is a hapax legomenon; cf. this with Akkadian *eṭimmu*, "spirit of a dead person." Concerning אובות (spirits of the dead) and ידענים (fortune-telling spirits), see *Isaiah 1–12*, pp. 371ff.

דרש (seek guidance), with a name of a god as the object, is virtually a technical term for seeking an oracle from a deity; according to 1 Sam. 9:9, this is accomplished through the mediation of a seer. In the OT one also would turn to Yahweh precisely in times of need that resulted from great political tensions: for example, when the dynasty itself was threatened because of the illness of the king (2 Kings 8:7-15; 1 Kings 14:1ff.). There were even situations where such circumstances motivated an individual to seek an answer from foreign gods, believing that such had particular restorative powers (2 Kings 1:2ff.; in that passage: ב דרש, "seek an answer from"). However, one would also seek an answer when war threatened (1 Kings 22; 2 Kings 3; cf. Jer. 21:1-10; 37:3-21). When one turned to seek help from spirits of the dead, then אל (toward) was used with דרש (seek an answer) (see 8:19; Deut. 18:11; cf. 1 Chron. 10:13); according to Gerlemann (*THAT* I, 464), one might suppose that this was because it originally took place when one physically went to the ancestral sites or to the grave site of one's forebears, so that one could establish contact with the dead. Saul (1 Sam. 28:7) goes to an אשת בעלת־אוב (BDB: a woman who was a mistress of necromancy); there were people who functioned as mediums, whose calling was to establish contact with the dead. Corresponding to this notion, in this passage דרש (seek an answer) is used with the preposition ב (v. 7). Isaiah presumes that the same results will come when Egypt seeks answers from the spirits of the dead as when the same practice was carried out in Israel. It does not matter to him that the activity of seeking answers from the dead did not, as in Israel, have only the most marginal legitimacy; it is nothing more than an indication that Egypt had long been rushing down a steep slope. Such "asking" was in no way simply an attempt to get information, but its purpose was to get the help of the gods or spirits of the dead, either by fighting against what threatened or by turning it back.

[19:4] The form of a war oracle appears once again in v. 4. As a general rule, Yahweh would promise Israel, in such a situation, that its enemies "would be given into its hand" (נתן ביד; see von Rad, *Holy War in Ancient Israel* [Engl: 1991], pp. 42ff.). Isaiah varies this by saying סכר ביד (on this, see above, p. 230). The verb has been commonly translated "deliver up to," since this is what the similar word סגר (*pi'el*) means. But Akkadian *sikkūru* means "crossbar"; no doubt, סכר ביד makes it even stronger than נתן ביד (give into the hand of), underscoring the utter finality, and means "lock someone up in someone's hand"; the fate of Egypt is sealed.

Concerning the identification of the "harsh overlord" and the "mighty king," see above, pp. 238f. The plural of majesty is used not only in the sense of a singular with reference to Yahweh, as is noted in the use of אדני (lord) (on this, cf. Wildberger, "Gottesepitheta," 710ff.; see above, p. 17), but also to refer to highly placed personages, of course only with a following genitive or suffix (e.g., Gen. 24:51, about Abraham; 42:30, 33, about Joseph; 1 Kings 1:11, 43, 47, about David). When he appears, Yahweh can rescue Israel from mighty enemies (איבי עז, "my strong enemy," Ps. 18:18), but when he comes in his wrath, he can also deliver someone over to a mighty enemy or king. Daniel 8:23 mentions a מלך עז־פנים (a king of bold countenance). In reality, עז

(strength) conveys not only the idea of abstract power, but also the subjective toughness in which "strength" is able to achieve its goals.

[19:5-10] *The Nile Dries Up*

Form

[19:5-10] For someone who read this, it was not enough that the announcement of the downfall of Egypt proclaimed that it would be accomplished through the actions of a foreign oppressor; a natural disaster would have to be concomitant with that—once again, one sees the tendency among some of those who insert expansions into the book of Isaiah to radicalize the sentence of judgment that has been announced—in the belief that this would provide even more objective evidence for the righteousness of Yahweh.

There is no use of the first person pronoun, with reference to God, in the entire passage; it is also never said that the catastrophe ought to be explained as having been sent by Yahweh, or by any other gods, and there is only a slight hint that Egypt deserved this fate. One can only arrive at the conclusion that Egypt was clearly at fault on the basis of the wider context. If one takes the section all by itself, then it is simply a depiction of what is actually happening, though it is cast in the form of a prediction about the future (note the frequent use of the perfect consecutive, with just one verb in the imperfect).

From the prophecy of the priest Nefer-rohu (more likely: Neferti), specific reference has already been made, in *Isaiah 1–12,* p. 399 (see also pp. 463f.), to the announcement that a king would come from the south, a passage that initially depicts the disaster that has come upon Egypt. Part of this description reports that the flooding of the Nile has not taken place: "THE RIVERS of Egypt are empty, (so that) the water is crossed on foot. Men seek for water for the ships to sail on it. Its course is [become] a sandbank. The sandbank *is against* the flood; the place of water *is against* the [flood]. . . . The south wind will oppose the north wind; the skies are no (longer) in a single wind. A foreign bird will be born in the marshes of the Northland. It has made a nest beside men, and people have let it approach through want of it. DAMAGED INDEED ARE THOSE good things, those fish-ponds, (where there were) those who clean fish, overflowing with fish and fowl. Everything good is disappeared, and the land is prostrate because of woes from that *food,* the Asiatics who are throughout the land. Foes have arisen in the east, and Asiatics have come down into Egypt. . . . No protector will listen" (*ANET* 445; see also the translation by Erman, *Literatur,* 154f. Some of the renderings are uncertain. See also *AOT* 47; text, with translation: W. Helck, *Die Prophezeiung des Nfr.tj.* [1970]). On the so-called Famine Stele, which claims to have been inscribed by King Djoser but which was certainly written during the Ptolemaic era, though it does deal with much older material (see Vandier, 38–42, 132–139), the pharaoh writes to the overseer of Nubians in Elephantine: "To let thee know. I was in distress on the Great Throne, and those who are in the palace were in heart's affliction from a very great evil, since the Nile had not come in my time for a space of seven years. Grain was scant, fruits were dried up, and everything which they eat was short. . . . The courtiers were in need. The temples were shut up;

the sanctuaries held [*nothing but*] *air.* Every[*thing*] was found empty" (*ANET* 31f.; for a rather different rendering, see also Roeder, *Urkunden,* 178f.; *AOT* 79; cf. also Erman and Ranke, 514; concerning a much later time period, see the depiction of the famine by Abd-Allatif, edited by de Sacy, 360ff.). Finally, one is naturally also reminded of the description in the story of Joseph about the seven lean years in Egypt.

Therefore, in the background of vv. 5-10, it seems likely that an Israelite author used an Egyptian portrayal of events, which included detailed information and knowledge about daily life in Egypt, employing Egyptian vocabulary (see above, p. 234). It is obvious that such texts do not furnish an exact description of a particular catastrophe, but are to be understood as typological and dramatic stories.

Meter: It would seem that, if one accepts the suggestions that attempt to clear up the textual difficulties, the poem has the structure of 8 three-stress + three-stress bicola, an absolute regularity of meter that one almost never finds in passages that come from Isaiah himself. Apparently, both times when מִם (waters) is used (in vv. 5 and 8), the stress falls on the second syllable; it was only later that the special accent to denote the dual form was introduced; see Ges-K §88d. In v. 6aβ it would seem that the break should first come after דלְלוּ (give off a stench). Metrical analysis confirms the need to eliminate עַל־יְאוֹר (by the Nile) in v. 7a. At the beginning of v. 8b, וּפֹרְשֹׂי (and those who stretch out) should receive two stresses. It is easier to read v. 10b as having three stresses if, as has often been suggested, one reads שֶׂכָר instead of שֵׂכֶר (both: wages).

Commentary

[19:5] The so-called Famine Stele, to which reference was just made, ends with the king issuing a "command" that determined the exact amount of gifts to be given to Khnum-Re, "the Lord of the Cataract Region." Estates were apportioned to the god, both in the region where the sun goes down and by the mountain where it rises; the farmers had an extra, a special, offering, a fixed amount of their harvest that they were to bring to the storehouses of the deity "after water had been brought to the newly established estates found at higher elevations"; the fishermen, trappers, and those who hunted in the waters were to tithe, and so on. That means: the overflowing of the Nile, at the appropriate time, which was responsible for maintaining life in Egypt, was a gift of the gods; if it did not come as expected, that had to be explained as the result of some deity being in ill humor. By means of offering gifts, people believed that they could ensure that what they needed would be given. Herodotus, a rationalist who was unwilling to accept the notion that the favor or wrath of the deity would explain whether the river rose or not, explained that he was not able to figure out the reason why the Nile, when it comes into the land, swells with water, beginning with the summer solstice, for approximately one hundred days; but then, when this number of days has passed, the water begins to ebb once again (2.19). It is now known, of course, that the swelling and diminution of the waters of the Nile, and the extent of this overflowing, is related to the amount of rainfall in the regions where the Nile begins, i.e., both in the territory where the great seas are located (winter rain) and in the Abyssinian mountain region (summer rain), so that both factors join together to have a cumulative effect on the amount of flooding (see Moret, 31–40).

Concerning נשת (dry up), one should consult Jer. 18:14 (emended text). The word is used rarely; more common are both חרב (dry out) and יבש (go dry down to the bottom), which parallel one another in other passages as well (44:27; Job 14:11; cf. also Gen. 8:13f.).

[19:6] The יהרות are the canals, which are used for irrigation (see above, p. 230), whereas the יאורים are the branches of the Nile (see *Isaiah 1–12*, p. 323, on 7:18), which form the Nile delta and provide such copious amounts of water as they flow through that region.

זנח I (*hiph⁽il*) is a hapax legomenon; it should be distinguished in usage from זנח II, "reject"; some have suggested (*HAL*) a connection with Arabic *zaniḥa*, "be rancid" (describing butter); it is possible that this is also a loanword from Egyptian (*ḫnš*; see F. Calice, *Grundlagen der ägyptisch-semitischen Wortvergleichung* [1936] no. 754; Coptic: *šnoš*, "stink"; see Ges-Buhl).

The ebbing of the waters results in the typical plants, which grow in the swampy areas, "becoming black," which means that they are dying off. There is no way to determine the exact meanings of קנה, סוף, and ערות, and it is furthermore unlikely that the author was trying to achieve technical accuracy. According to I. Löw, *Die Flora der Juden* I [1928] 664f., קנה (Ugaritic: *qn* I = tube: canals, esophagus, aromatic cane; see Aistleitner, *WB* no. 2423; Akkadian: *qanū*, "tube, arrow reed"; cf. Greek: κάννα, "pole-reed," and κανών, "straight bar"; Latin: *canna*, "reed pipe") is the arrow reed, *arundo donax*. Concerning סוף (bulrush) (= Egyptian *ṯwfy*), see above, p. 235. ים־סוף is generally translated by the Gk as Ἐρυθρὴ Θάλασσα, Red Sea (see Snaith).

[19:7] Concerning ערות (rushes), see above, p. 231.

מזרע is also a hapax legomenon, translated as "sowed land" (KBL²); such lands must also be irrigated in Egypt. The way this continues ("will become barren, will be blown away, and it is gone") points out, at the same time, that the standing grain that is growing on this land is what is really in the author's mind. Moreover, it is certainly not only cereal grains that are sown; cf. passages such as 28:25. Whatever dries up is blown away by the wind; cf. Ps. 103:16 and Isa. 40:6-8; in addition, see Ps. 90:5f.; Job 14:2; and Dalman, *AuS* I/2, 324f.

[19:8] Not only the farmers suffer when the rivers dry up; the fishermen are also affected. The *nomen agentis* (actor noun) דיג (the fisherman) is also a hapax legomenon, and דוג, which means the same thing, occurs only in the *kethib* form in Jer. 16:16 and Ezek. 47:10 (many Hebrew MSS read דיגים, "fishermen"). That did not happen just by chance. Those who were fishermen by trade were found only on the Sea of Tiberias (fishing was not possible on the Mediterranean, since the coast of Palestine, without any natural ports, was not conducive to such activity); by contrast, fishing played an important role in ancient Egypt, not only as a leisure, sporting activity practiced by the upper class (cf. Wilkinson, 52), but as a profession that provided a food source.

The people of high rank who went fishing were especially fond of using a long, thin spear, with barbs on the tip, so that, one might say, they could shoot the fish, but they could also fish with fishing hooks and tackle, whereas the fishermen who worked at this for a living would use a handheld net, a fenced enclosure, or a large dragnet (see illuss. 109–111 in Erman and Ranke; Wolf, *Kulturgeschichte*, diagram 3; Wilkinson, 41, 53; Wolf, *Weltgeschichte*, diagram 24). Fishing produced a copious amount of food. Fish (dried or pickled) play an important role in providing nutrition in one's diet. They are inexpensive, even cheaper than cereal grains. Thus they are one of the chief sources of nutrition for the poorer classes. But the upper levels of society also valued fish as a dish, if they were prepared in a tasty way. In later times, Egyptian theology treated fish as an unclean food (see the Piankhy stele, lines 150f., in Breasted, *ARE* IV, §882; cf. Herodotus 2.37). Yet even Herodotus mentions how important fish were as a staple of the Egyptian diet (2.77 and 92). Both Num. 11:5 and Ezek. 29:4 tell us that the people in Israel were aware of the important place that fish had in the Egyptian food supply.

The easiest way to catch fish was to use a hook, חַכָּה. According to Egyptian illustrations, hooks were used either with or without a fishing pole. Some fishing poles were outfitted with more than one line, and one Egyptian illustration (Wreszinski, no. 106) shows a fisherman using a spool with a hoop as a hook, upon which a fish is hanging. Therefore it is fitting that one could speak of "throwing out (הִשְׁלִיךְ) the hook."

It is possible that מִכְמֹרֶת or מִכְמֶרֶת (Hab. 1:15f.) refers to a large net (see Dalman, *AuS* VI, illuss. 66–69; and cf. Akkadian *kamāru* I, "hunter's snaring net"), which is thrown out from the shore and spread out over the surface of the water, though it is also possible that this term could refer to a dragnet. It is noteworthy that mention is made about how the fishermen, who now have neither work nor bread, are raising a lament (אנה I, used elsewhere only in 3:26; on this, see *Isaiah 1–12*, p. 159), which is exactly what one would do in cases where a death has occurred. Parallel to this, one finds אבל, "mourn" (also used in 3:26), which is a much more common word and which has a variety of nuances, and finally אמלל, "wither, fade away." Both of these verbs can be used in two ways, either to describe the drying up or withering of plants in nature or to depict humans who are sorrowing; i.e., no clear distinction is made between physical and emotional circumstances. A human being can wither away just as a plant does; see 1 Sam. 2:5; Jer. 14:2; 15:9; cf. Hos. 4:3. The very vocabulary used here gives evidence that those who lived in ancient times were resigned to not being able to fight off their destiny successfully, but rather they sought to adjust to whatever would come in the ebb and flow of life in the natural world.

[19:9f.] If the first stage, producing the raw materials, grinds to a halt, then those whose occupation is to process these materials are left with nothing to do. As an example of the problem, we are told about the dilemma for those who, as we would say, worked in the textile industry. The first to be mentioned are those who initially work the flax, then those who comb the flax, and finally those who weave it. The Egyptians were experts at producing extremely fine, white linen, the reason being that they had turned each step in the process into a subspecialty. On burial stones from the Twentieth Dynasty, from Abydos, we find depictions of people who identify themselves as weavers; their wives are members of singing groups who praise Osiris (see Erman and Ranke, 535ff.). They identify Tait as the goddess who discovered the art of weaving (cf. Sinuhe, 192, in *AOT* 59; *ANET* 20).

The עבדי פשתים are apparently the people who work the land, those who pull out the flax: the stalks of flax are not cut off but are pulled out of the ground in bundles, so that the long fibers are kept intact (see Erman and Ranke, plate 36, 1). Laid together in sheaves, these bundles are left on the ground to dry. Then the process of working them begins, starting with those who comb the flax; i.e., the stalks are pulled across a stationary device, affixed to the ground, which has a type of comb attachment, making it possible to detach the strands; see illus. 224 in Erman and Ranke (שׂרק actually means "to comb." The current technique is described by Dalman, *AuS* V, 20f., based on information from G. Crowfoot, *Methods of Hand Spinning in Egypt and the Sudan* [1974] 32f., illuss. 19–21).

It seems that this passage considers combing the flax to be work that women do, whereas the men do the weaving. Herodotus was surprised to find out that the women went to the market in Egypt and carried on commerce while the men stayed at home and did the weaving (2.35). One also wonders about the fact that there are different techniques for weaving, when compared with how it was done in Greece, but it can hardly be true that the same methods were used everywhere and in every time period in Egypt (cf. illuss. 222f. in Erman and Ranke).

There is no apparent reason for those who do the spinning to be mentioned only *after* the weavers. One possible reason is that this work was not considered to be as important, being work left to the women. Concerning the technical aspects of this activity, see Erman and Ranke, 535ff. and illus. 222; *ANEP* nos. 142f. All the various facets of linen production are finally identified together as עשׂי שׂכר (those who work for wages). The expression almost sounds as if it were used for describing aspects of a well-organized textile industry (on this, see Lucas, 140ff.). The workers' wages took the form of rations for the daily necessities. If one could not work, one could not acquire these necessities, or else fewer of them would be available. One can understand why these people would stand there, looking pale (חור), that they would be completely worn out and dejected (concerning the serfs, a poem says: "by the time he finally becomes a man, by then his bones are completely worn out" (Erman and Ranke, 144); they are אגמי־נפשׁ, "most dejected" (אגם is also a hapax legomenon). As elsewhere, the translation of בושׁ presents problems. The verb has both a subjective and an objective aspect (cf. M. Klopfenstein, *Scham und Schande nach dem Alten Testament* [1972] 49); in the objective sense it means simply "come to an end." However, an individual in ancient times was not, in the way we attempt it, able to objectify what happened; for such a person, these were also personally humiliating experiences.

Purpose and Thrust

This intervening material, in vv. 5-10, provides a fitting portrayal, one that furnishes a most interesting cultural and historical background for what would happen if the Nile did not flood. In and of itself, it is a moving depiction of human need, describing what transpired so many times in that land that was completely dependent on the water provided by the Nile. The passage does not contribute theologically until it is viewed within the larger context. For the author, the natural catastrophe is to be considered within the framework of the breakdown in the political realm; more specifically, it is the result of everything coming apart. For the ancients, whose thought was holistic, who were not able to distinguish between nature and history, that was not as much of a problem as it is for moderns, who treat natural catastrophes, as such, as irrational occurrences. For the ancients, such problems were the way that distortions of that which kept life ordered were manifested, with humans not being free of blame for the problems that resulted.

[19:11-14 (15)] *The Foolishness of the Princes of Egypt*

Form

Verse 3 said that Yahweh had "emptied, disrupted," the spirit of Egypt and had disarranged its plans. This motif is picked up here once again; an attempt is made to expand the depiction of the confusion that had befallen Egypt, in fact, especially because in other settings Egypt had been eager to praise its wisdom, for which it was indeed famous in the ancient world.

Based on its form, the section sounds like an announcement of judgment, or more accurately, an accusation speech. The blame is laid on the princes of Zoan, the advisers of the pharaoh. They are fools, they have given the pharaoh false advice; in v. 11a they are rebuked for their presumption. It would seem that אֵיךְ תֹּאמְרוּ (how could you [pl.] say) is a stock phrase within such an address; cf. Jer. 2:23; 48:14. In v. 12 the accuser directs attention to a specific "you" (sg.), which would be the pharaoh himself; he should see clearly that he has opened his ears to listen to advice from incompetent "wise ones." In the judgment speech, the accuser issues a summons to his opponents, with words something like: "tell it now, so that we might know" (Isa. 41:23; 43:9; 44:7). The scene has shifted now: the advisers are those who can make something known, instruct someone. But the accuser gets no answer, and thus he describes the situation once again in v. 13, now in even harsher tones, since the accused has said nothing in response. Obviously, the closing verse, v. 14, does not fit within the framework of a typical announcement of judgment: what appears at first glance to be human foolishness turns out to be the work of Yahweh. There is no reason to doubt, however, that it is precisely this last verse, which departs from the traditional form altogether, that articulates the main point.

Meter: (See the metrical delineation in *BHK*³; *BHS* is different.) It is likely that v. 11 consists of 2 three-stress + three-stress bicola; v. 12: a three-stress + three-stress bicolon (with the break after וידעו, "and they will make known") and a five-stress colon; v. 13: 2 two-stress + two-stress bicola; v. 14a: a five-stress colon; v. 14b: probably a heavy seven-stress colon, which attempts, as the piece is brought to a conclusion, to characterize the utter, inescapable confusion that has come upon Egypt. One should pay special attention to the beginning of the lines of the first three verses: אך (surely), איך (how), and אים (where are they).

Setting
See above, pp. 235f.

Commentary
[19:11] "The princes of Zoan are sheer fools." Zoan, *d⁽n.t* in Egyptian, Τάνις (Tanis) in Greek, was located in the northeastern corner of the delta, at the place known today as *ṣān el-ḥagar,* very close to Lake Manzala. Except for Memphis, it is mentioned more often in the OT than any other city in Egypt (Num. 13:22; Isa. 30:4; Ezek. 30:14; Ps. 78:12, 43). That is not just because of its location, being close to the border of the Sinai, which meant that it was often the preferred initial point of departure for expeditions setting out for the Near East, but also because of its historical importance.

The widely accepted opinion, that it was the location for the capital city of the Hyksos, *ḥw.t w⁽r.t* (Ἄυαρις, Avaris) and of the city of Ramses (רעמסס in Exod. 1:11), cannot be maintained any longer, based on the results of recent excavations, since these two places are both to be sought on the *tell ed-dab⁽a/qanṭīr* (cf. Bietak and the literature cited there; in addition, see B. Couroyer, "La résidence ramesside du Delta et la Ramsès biblique," *RB* 53 [1946] 75–98; J. von Beckerath, 29; L. Habachi, "Khatâ⁽na-Qanṭîr: Importance," *ASAE* 52 [1952–54] 443–562; R. Stadelmann, "Auaris," *Lexikon der Ägyptologie* I, 552–554; W. H. Schmidt, *Exodus,* BK II/1 [1988] 37f.; cf. also S. Herrmann, *A History of Israel in Old Testament Times* [1981²] 59). Yet, in a sense, Tanis is the successor of the city of Ramses, since the pharaohs of the Twenty-first and Twenty-second Dynasties used the stone monuments from there in order to build their residence.

During the time of the Twenty-first and Twenty-second Dynasties, Zoan played an important role, apparently as the point of departure from which the deputations went forth to the bordering countries in the Near East to foment rebellion against Assyria. According to v. 11aβ, the princes of Zoan are the wise ones, the advisers of the pharaoh. The pharaoh himself also might have resided in Zoan; in any case, he had strong ties with this city, which remained so during the entire reign of the Twenty-second Dynasty (see above, pp. 237f.). Since there are so many chronological uncertainties, however, one does well not to attempt to extract too much specific information. It is easy to understand that these princes would have been advisers to the pharaoh for political matters; it is logical that the advice from the princes of this city would have been carefully considered in matters of Near Eastern politics; indeed, one could not avoid considering it, since this city was still, in a sense, the gateway to the rest of the Near East. According to v. 11b, however, these advisers thought it very important that they were "sons," that is, students of the wise ones. Actually, the wisdom of Egypt is, generally speaking, nothing else but wisdom concerning official matters: "Imhotep, whose teaching is not preserved for us, we know to have been the highest official of King Djoser; Djedefhor, the son of Cheops, we know as a prince, one who was not legally in line for the throne. The 'father' of Kagemni, whose name has been lost, and Ptah-hotep are viziers, under the kings Huni and Issi, respectively" (Brunner, <i>HdO</i> I/2, 92). It was apparently a long-standing custom that the princely sons were placed under the tutelage of wisdom teachers. But the pretensions of these princes were greater yet: they thought that they were thereby legitimized, as if they were sons "of the kings of the <i>ancient</i> past." In this passage as well, בֵּן (son) is used in the transferred sense of "pupil." It is true that Egyptian wisdom teachers were assigned to kings (Merikare and Amenemhet) or were themselves high officials (Imhotep, Ptah-hotep). It is commonly assumed that special attention ought to be paid to wisdom that comes from the ancient times (קֶדֶם), which is the reason why the choice is often made to place wisdom instruction (such as is found in religious texts) into the mouths of important personages from times past.

Concerning אֵיךְ תֹּאמְרוּ . . . בֶּן־חֲכָמִים אָנִי (How could you say . . . "I am a son of the wise"), one should also consult Jer. 8:8: אֵיכָה תֹאמְרוּ חֲכָמִים אֲנַחְנוּ (How can you say, "We are wise?"); cf. not only Jer. 48:14; Ps. 11:1; but also Gen. 26:9, where Isaac, who comes close to being a party in a judicial dispute, is called on by Abimelech to answer charges.

The judicial process determines beyond doubt that these advisers are without wisdom; they are fools, and their advice is dumb. As elsewhere in Isaiah, עֵצָה is political advice; see above, p. 242.

If this passage has been correctly identified, in terms of its historical setting, then this advice was to lead to the construction of an anti-Assyrian front, which would also bring these princes into the battle that the states in Palestine would wage against the world power that was situated on the Tigris.

אֱוִיל (sheer fool) is a typical term in wisdom (out of twenty-six total occurrences, nineteen are in Proverbs, there chiefly in the more ancient proverbial collections), being the opposite of חָכָם (wise). The meaning of the root בער IV (stupid) (according to <i>HAL</i>, the verb is a denominative from בְּעִיר, "cattle"), can hardly be distinguished from אֱוִיל (sheer fool), but its use is not limited to wisdom materials. One must take into consideration that, according to the "synthetic" view about world history in ancient times, foolishness results in disaster and leads to death; one might compare this view with a passage such as Prov. 16:22: "Wisdom is a fountain of life to one who has it, but folly is the punishment of fools." "Foolishness" is more than a defect; it exists as a factor that produces disaster and is thus also assessed negatively when evaluated theologically; one notes a passage such as Jer. 4:22: "For my people are foolish, they do not know me."

[19:12] Those who are truly wise should be able to say what Yahweh has planned for Egypt. In a rather demanding way, the prophet turns toward the pharaoh himself: where are they, then, your wise, who are trying to make *this* happen (on this point, cf. Jer. 37:19, where Jeremiah is just as demanding of Zedekiah, saying: "Where are your prophets"; see also Judg. 9:38).

הגיד (share publicly) is a favorite term in Deutero-Isaiah's judgment speeches, summoning the opponent in the legal process to bring evidence out in the open that can exonerate that opponent: 41:22f.; 43:9; cf. also 43:12; 44:9; 45:21; 48:14 (surprisingly, these occurrences are limited to chaps. 40–48). However, one must also note what is said in Jer. 9:11: "Who is wise enough to understand this? To whom has the mouth of Yahweh spoken, so that they may declare it? Why is the land ruined?" The passage has not been attributed to Jeremiah (see the commentaries by Volz and Rudolph); however, it still gives evidence for a fixed pattern that was followed when such discussions were held and shows that the wise were trusted (differently than in Jer. 37:9, where it was expected of the prophets) to be able to give information about Yahweh's plans and the motivation behind them. Isaiah already polemicized elsewhere about the "wisdom" of the wise (see 5:21); it may be that he has politicians in mind in that passage too, those who did not listen to Yahweh but thought themselves to be sufficiently wise on their own (see *Isaiah 1–12*, pp. 208f.). The situation is about the same in 29:14; and, according to 31:2, the politicians who made the trek down to Egypt to seek help had, in their own way, brought about some good. As his remark in 10:13 demonstrates, on other occasions Isaiah took aim at the "wisdom" of foreign politicians. Those who are truly wise should be able to give correct advice, which according to Isaiah's understanding of wisdom would mean: they should be able to reveal the עצה (counsel) of Yahweh to those who heard them. For that reason, there could be no doubt that the wise ones or the advisers of the pharaoh were clearly out of their league. But this passage also shows clearly that Isaiah goes right to the heart of the matter, measuring the wisdom of each nation by how its actions square with the will of Yahweh, assuming as he does that Yahweh is also the lord over Egypt; his emphasis on Yahweh's will when making decisions brings one to conclude that it is not the Egyptians who are being addressed in this message against Egypt, but rather the political leaders in Jerusalem. Obviously, one also ought not look for this passage to present an all-encompassing plan for Yahweh, detailing how history will unfold, but rather to point out specific decisions that were geared toward dealing with what was being planned at that very time (see H. Wildberger, VTSup 3 [1963] 83–117, esp. 103).

[19:13] One might say that v. 13 picks up and underscores what was mentioned already in v. 11. Alongside the princes from Zoan, one finds their counterparts from Noph being accused as well, sitting on the same hot seat. Noph (Hos. 9:6 reads Moph) is that metropolis in Lower Egypt which the Greeks called Memphis, in Egyptian *mn-nfr(-pypy)*, often referred to by the shortened form of its name, from the time of the New Kingdom onward, as *mnf;* in Akkadian: *mempi* or *mimpi.* The name means: "the perfection (of Pepy) is ongoing"; concerning Egyptian *mn* (= אָמֵן?, "confirm, support"), cf. H. Wildberger, *THAT* I, 178. The city has that name because of the pyramid of Phios I (= Pepi I, Sixth Dynasty). It was situated on the west bank of the Nile, at the site of what is currently known as *mīt rahīne*, about 20 km. south of Cairo. The great temple to Ptah, *ḥ.t-k3pth*, was also located in Memphis; often, the city was referred to by this name as well (this name is the source of the Greek word Αἴγυπτος, Egypt). In 728 Piankhy conquered the city, which gave him de facto control over the entire delta; however, he then withdrew to Nubia once again. Later on, Memphis was able to enjoy the favor of both Shabaka and Shebitku. Kitchen (§333, note 75) believes that there is no problem with dating Isaiah 19 to the period of Osorkon IV, since Memphis had acknowledged the overlordship of the Tanite kings whose base of operations was in Memphis, which would mean that mentioning the princes of Noph and Zoan in parallel would make good sense for this period (concerning Memphis, see Badawi; Kees, Pauly-W 15, 1, 660–687; Capart and Werbrouck). However, Memphis was so important, also during later periods, that it could have been mentioned even if the present passage were to be assigned a later date.

The matter is carried still further in v. 13b: Egypt allowed itself to be deceived by the פִּנַּת (chief ruler) (a better reading would be the plural פִּנּוֹת, "chief rulers"; see textual note 13c above) of its שְׁבָטִים (territories). The basic meaning of שֵׁבֶט is "staff, scepter," with a transferred meaning of "tribal unit"; here it designates the Egyptian territory. For "territory," he could have used the term מְדִינָה, which is used in Ezra-Nehemiah as the way to designate the province of Judah; in the book of Esther, it designates the Persian satrapies. But Isaiah uses that particular term with which he is familiar, based on his own experience. The Egyptian territories consisted of the various regions over which the king exercised direct control, organized into this system at the time of the First Dynasty; this would have replaced the older organizational structure of "areas under the control of lesser officials" (concerning the way in which the country was divided into regions throughout the history of Egypt, cf. Helck, 204–211; for the period of the New Kingdom, map 7). The leaders of such a territory are known here as the פִּנּוֹת (leadership, chief rulers); this word is already used in this metaphorical sense in the ancient texts (Judg. 20:2; 1 Sam. 14:38), as a designation for the leaders of Israel (later, in the more technical sense, in Zech. 10:4). In Egypt, the mayor of a city and its surrounding region was called a *ḥ3.ty-ʿ* (= "the one in the top spot"; see Erman-Grapow III, 25). The accusation raised against these princes corresponds to what is said in v. 11: "they have become fools" (יאל I, "be a fool," is a less common form of אול I, "be a fool," to which אֱוִיל, "fool," is related), "they have allowed themselves to be misled." One ought not try

Isaiah 19:1-15

EGYPT/ETHIOPIA

	22. DYNASTY TANIS/ BUBASTIS	23. DYNASTY LEONTOPOLIS	24. DYNASTY SAIS	25. DYNASTY NAPATA
			Early Saite Rulers:	
760				
755				
750		OSORKON III 777–749		KASHTA ca. 760–747
745			(OSORKON) (Ruler of Mā) (ca. 755–740)	
740		TAKELOT III. 754–734 initially co-regent of Osorkon III.		
735	SHESHONK V 767–730		(TEFNAKHTE) (I.) (Ruler of Mā) (ca. 740–727)	
730		RUDAMUN 734–731 or possibly –715		
725		IUPUT II. 731–720 or until 715		
720	OSORKON IV. 730–715	SHESHONK VI. 720–715 (Existence doubtful)	TEFNAKHTE I. 727–720 BOCCHORIS 720–715	PIANKHI 747–716
715			Proto-Saite Dynasty	
710				
705				SHABAKA 716–702
700				
695			(AMERIS) (715–695)	SHABATAKA 702–690

254

PALESTINE		MESOPOTAMIA	
JUDAH	ISRAEL	ASSYRIA	

UZZIAH
767–739
from 792/1
co-regent of
Amaziah

JOTHAM
739–734/33

AHAZ
734/3–728/7
from 750/49
co-regent

HEZEKIAH
728/7–699

MENAHEM
753/2–742/1

PEKAHIAH
742/1–740/39

PEKAH
740/39–731

HOSHEA
731–722

TIGLATH-
PILESER III.
744–727

SHALMANESER
V.   726–722

SARGON II.
722–705

SENNACHERIB
704–681

The dates for the
reigns of the
Egyptian rulers
follow charts
compiled by
Kitchen; those for
the rulers of
Judah/Israel fol-
low Pavlovský/
Vogt (*Bib* 45
[1964] 321–347)

to interpret this as if the princes of Zoan misled those in Noph; rather, both groups had allowed themselves to be misled by their faulty analysis of the situation. At the same time, they had led Egypt itself astray. Isaiah already used the verb התעה (mislead) in 3:12 and 9:15, when he spoke about the leaders (מאשׁרים) of Israel, who were misleaders; on this, see *Isaiah 1–12,* pp. 138f.

[19:14] The most important theological statement follows in v. 14: what seems at first, to an observer, to be simply a human failure is in reality something effected by Yahweh (see above, p. 242, on 19:1ff.); *he* has "mixed within" their midst a spirit of confusion. Isaiah spoke earlier about mixing intoxicating drinks (שׁכר) in 5:22 (concerning v. 14bβ, see Prov. 9:2, 5; Ps. 102:10; concerning the "spirit that creates confusion," cf. 1 Kings 22:20ff.; 2 Kings 19:7 = Isa. 37:7; and Job 12:24). That this thought is certainly something which Isaiah himself could utter is seen by comparing this verse with 28:7ff., and especially with 29:9f., where he speaks of a "spirit of deep sleep" (רוח תרדמה), which Yahweh had poured out, and where he also compares those who lead others astray with those who are drunk (see שׁכר). There is no justification for saying that someone from a later time is speaking in 19:14, even though that might be a person who had carefully read Isaiah (Kaiser); what is said here is too unique for that. (A similar image is that of the cup whose contents cause the drinker to stagger, e.g., Jer. 25:15ff.; Isa. 51:17, 22; Nah. 3:11; Hab. 2:16.) This spirit of confusion causes all the politicians who seek to lead to make Egypt stumble "in everything that it undertakes." This imagery provides one with an excellent depiction of the dangerous euphoria that has led peoples, time and again, to get themselves tangled up in warmongering adventures.

Just the use of the word מסך (brew) would have made them think about "being intoxicated." תעה, "wander about trying to find one's way, stagger" (or be in such a condition, *hiph'il* or *niph'al*), is a graphic term for describing someone who is drunk; see 28:7. Verse 14bβ puts into words what is associated with this condition of not being in control of one's faculties, using a description that, for him, was drastic, though he had many ways to talk about this at his disposal: Egypt stumbles around, "as a drunk stumbles around in his own vomit." In a slightly different way, Isaiah uses the same imagery in 28:8; cf. also Job 12:25. He pulls out all the stops in order to stimulate all the emotions, hoping that something would work to keep them from concluding any agreements with Egypt. That would have been utterly foolish; in every respect it would have been an inexcusable risk of the highest order, which could result only in Judah being utterly ruined.

[19:15] *Addition: The Ineffectiveness of Egypt*

[19:15] Not only the prose form of v. 15 betrays that it is an addition; its awkward wording points this out as well. One reads in v. 14b that Egypt would stumble in everything that it would "undertake"; v. 15 says that it does not have anything to "undertake" (מעשׂה) that would make (עשׂה) "head and tail, sprouting vine and stalk." The same phraseology about head and tail occurs in 9:13 (on this, see *Isaiah 1–12*, pp. 234f.), though it makes much better sense in that context, showing clearly there that the judgment would be comprehensive, that it would affect every level of society (cf. the Eshmunʿazar Inscription, lines 11f.; *KAI* no. 14; vol. II, 20). Already in that passage (in the secondary addition in v. 14), commentary was added to that imagery which did not fit well in the context. That it does not belong with the rest of the present passage is shown by the puzzlement of the Greek translator, who did not know if ראש (head) and so on was to be treated as the subject or the object of יעשה (undertake). It is common for it to be taken as the object, with the result that עשה is translated: "have" (so Fohrer). If this is the correct interpretation, the point would be that Egypt was not in a position to complete any activity that would *have* "hand and foot," something that could be termed "a success in any way, shape, or form." One problem with such an interpretation is that עשה does not mean "have" but "make, do." But it also does not make any sense to take ראש (head) and so on as the subject. Kaiser translates this: "And there will be nothing for Egypt that head or tail . . . may do"; similarly, Hitzig, Dillmann, Duhm, Marti, Cheyne, Gray, et al., which means that, in the future, there would be no activity that the Egyptians would be able to do collectively, as a whole people, that would work out. But the point cannot be that the people of Egypt would never again be in a position to work together in a collective effort, but rather that it was letting itself be caught up in a foolish undertaking, in which one could be certain that only disastrous consequences would result; for this reason, it would be better to stay with the first alternative and treat this as an object. The expander was taken with the proverbial turn of phrase, "head, tail, sprouting vine, stalk," which he apparently knew from 9:13 and wanted to turn into an ingenious play on words when used with עשה/מעשה (undertaking/making); unfortunately, he could not pull it off.

In simple terms, what he wanted to say was that Egypt was simply not in any position to successfully carry out any plans.

Purpose and Thrust

[19:1-15] Both of the sections that can be attributed to Isaiah, 19:1b-4 and 11-14, are easily understood in light of the political circumstances that the people faced at the time when Isaiah spoke, as Assyria, from the time of Tiglath-Pileser III on, sought to fulfill its long-range plan of complete domination over all the lands of the Fertile Crescent. In light of this situation, Egypt must have been on its guard. Biblical, Assyrian, and Egyptian sources all furnish evidence that Egypt was following a political course that sought to construct a line of protection in the Palestinian territory that could stem this onslaught. Because Egypt was notoriously weak at that time, joining in a collective action with them was a suicidal undertaking for the countries in and around Palestine, most dangerous if they allowed themselves to be participants in Egypt's machinations. This is the reason for the excessively harsh reaction on Isaiah's part, which helps one recognize that he was much more qualified to weigh the various factors of relative political strengths and weaknesses than were the professional politicians in Israel, Judah, Philistia, and Moab. He was very perceptive in realizing that Egypt continually overvalued its ability to lead, particularly in light of deep internal tensions. He assessed its behavior as foolishness, confusion, in fact, as total delusion. Instead of encouraging Palestinian states to rebel—with promises of help that they simply could not or could only with great difficulty deliver—it should first have taken the steps necessary to unite itself internally, so that the vacuum of leadership could be remedied, a situation that the Assyrians must have noticed as well. Of course, Isaiah says nothing about that—he does not see it as his job to share advice with Egypt, but focuses more narrowly, as he attempts to bring Judah to realize that Egyptian promises are vacuous. The confusion that had befallen Egypt was seen by him as much more than a momentary weakness; it was the way in which Yahweh's judgment was going to be fulfilled. Yahweh "travels, drives" down to Egypt (v. 1), his עצה (decision) about Egypt has now been made, and what Yahweh plans is now going to take place (see 8:10; 14:27; cf. 7:7).

Without seeing this as an issue that needed to be clarified, and without discussing it thoroughly, the author presumes, and clearly understands, that the fate of Egypt is controlled by Yahweh, even as he makes use of the "harsh overlord" (v. 4) to be his tool for punishment—without either Egypt or Assyria being aware of what is going on. In this way, the power of Israel's faith is made plain, overcoming all obstacles that the world could throw in the way. If Judah is weak, that still gives it no reason to open itself up, in its time of need brought on by its self-assertiveness, to enter into political-military agreements. The deep confidence that his faith provides him is the secret that explains how Isaiah, with such an unbiased, calm attitude, can attempt to make plain the true circumstances about where real power is to be found in the various arenas where power has been exercised throughout world history, in this case, in the ridiculous foolishness of the "wise ones" from Egypt; and why he can be completely confident as he hopes to persuade Judah to come to a political assessment that his opponents would have had to view as a dangerous attempt to isolate themselves. It is consistent with this understanding of God that the problem is portrayed in terms of Israel's conflict with the deities of Egypt. Wherever Yahweh appears, the gods of that region go limp. The theme of monotheism lurks in the background, becoming a major theme later in Deutero-Isaiah. Thus to determine that this present passage about Egypt came from that exilic prophet "turns the problem upside down" (Eichrodt). The belief that Yahweh alone is the lord of history, that his plan is the only one that has any real meaning for the destiny of various peoples, is certainly Isaiah's own message. The same measuring line had been stretched out upon Assyria; see 10:5ff. Its "wisdom" was also labeled as intolerable presumptuousness (10:13). It is this understanding about Yahweh that brings about this conflict with the religions of foreign peoples (and no longer just with the peoples of Canaan); in a sense, this is where the conflict begins to take shape.

The wisdom of Egypt is dealt with plainly, in a much more visible way than with the assessment about their gods. Eichrodt does not quite catch the essence of this material when he says that Isaiah comes out, in vv. 11-15, "very forcefully against the wisdom teaching that was carefully crafted in Egypt, that was accorded much respect and wielded much influence in the neighboring population." It is true that Egypt was famous for its wisdom teaching, and this fame had not escaped the attention of people in Israel either, but Isaiah is not setting out to discount the wisdom that was carefully studied there. Its own lessons included calls for moderation and discretion, and it does warn against arrogance and against foolishly thinking of oneself more highly than one ought. More to the point, the prophet sets his sights on the politicians who offered advice that was nothing other than a distortion of true wisdom, against the wise, who were indeed justifiably proud of their ancestors, but who were getting caught up at that moment in committing fraud, about to lead their land to destruction. The wise are not condemned, but rather the proud wise, those who thought themselves wiser than they were, those who did not have the ability to see reality without any illusions—and that means that they would have been able to pay attention to Yahweh's עצה (decision) and take it seriously—the proud wise were the ones who had become fools.

The secondary verses 5-10 are of a completely different spirit. Here, in a most engaging way, the disaster that came upon Egypt is depicted—and it could come again at any time. The redactor, who inserted this passage at this point, also thought that a natural catastrophe such as this one was one way in which God carried out his divine judgment against the foolishness in which Egypt had been engaged.

Egypt's Future

Literature

Concerning the history of the Jewish diaspora in Egypt: General works: E. Schürer, *The History of the Jewish People in the Age of Jesus Christ,* III (1897–98) [Rev. Ed. 1986–87]. A. Causse, "Les origines de la diaspora juive," *RHPR* 7 (1927) 97–128. U. Wilcken, *Urkunden der Ptolemäerzeit* I (1927) 480, 485, 487f.; no. 110, lines 1–19. F. M. Abel, "Les confins de la Palestine et de l'Égypte," *RB* 49 (1940) 224–239. M. A. Beek, "Relations entre Jérusalem et la diaspora égyptienne au 2ᵉ siècle avant J.-C.," *OTS* 2 (1943) 119–143, esp. 121–132. *Corpus papyrorum judaicarum,* ed. V. Tcherikover and A. Fuks, vol. I (1957) no. 132, pp. 244–246. J. Harmatta, *Zur Geschichte des frühhellenistischen Judentums in Ägypten,* AAH 7 (1959) 337–409. V. Tcherikover, *Hellenistic Civilization and the Jews* (1959). M. Hengel, *Judaism and Hellenism,* 2 vols. (1974).

   Concerning Elephantine: C. Steuernagel, "Bemerkungen über die neu-entdeckten jüdischen Papyrusurkunden aus Elephantine und ihre Bedeutung für das Alte Testament," *TStKr* 22 (1909) 1–12. A. Jirku, "Die fünf Städte bei Jes 19,18 und die fünf Tore des Jahu-Tempels zu Elephantine," *OLZ* 15 (1912) 247–248. A. Cowley, *Aramaic Papyri of the Fifth Century B.C.* (1923). E. G. Kraeling, *The Brooklyn Museum Aramaic Papyri* (1953).

   Concerning Leontopolis: E. Naville, *The Mound of the Jew and the City of Onias,* Memoir of the Egypt Exploration Fund 7 (1890). M. Delcor, "Le temple d'Onias en Égypte," *RB* 75 (1968) 188–205.

   Concerning the theology: A. Causse, *Israël et la vision de l'humanité:* Études d'histoire et de philosophie religieuses publiées par la faculté de théologie pro-testante de l'université de Strasbourg 8 (1924), esp. 97f. A. Feuillet, "Un sommet religieux de l'Ancien Testament. L'oracle d'Is 19, 19–25 sur la conversion de l'Égypte," *RSR* 39 (1951) 65–87.

   [Literature update through 1979: *Concerning the vocabulary:* C. F. Graesser, "Standing Stones in Ancient Palestine," *BA* 35 (1972) 34–63. G. Wehmeier, "Der Segen im AT. Eine semasiologische Untersuchung der Wurzel brk," diss., Basel (1970). E. Stockton, "Sacred Pillars in the Bible," *AusBR* 20 (1972) 16–32.

   Concerning the theology: A. Feuillet (see above), now also in *Études d'exégèse et de théologie biblique* (1975) 261–279. W. Vogels, "L'Égypte mon peuple—L'universalisme d'Is 19, 16–25," *Bib* 57 (1976) 494–514.]

Text

19:16 On that[a] day the Egyptians[b] will be like the wives, will be terrified
and shake because of the swinging of the hand of Yahweh of Hosts,
which he will swing[c] over them.[d] **17** And the land of Judah will
become an insult[a] for the Egyptians; [b]every time when[b] someone
mentions it in their presence, they will be terrified because of the
decision of Yahweh of Hosts, which he determined to carry out
against them.

18 On that day, there will be five cities[a] in the land of Egypt, that will
speak the language of Canaan and that will promise with an oath to
give themselves completely to Yahweh of Hosts;[b] [c][one (of which)
will be named 'city of the sun.'[d]][c]

19 On that day there will be an altar for Yahweh in the midst of the land
of Egypt and a memorial stone[a] for Yahweh on its border. **20** And it
will serve as a sign and a witness[a] for Yahweh of Hosts in the land
of Egypt: when they cry out to Yahweh because of oppressors, he
will send them a deliverer;[b] that person will lead[c] the battle and free
them. **21** And Yahweh will make the Egyptians recognize him, and
the Egyptians will recognize Yahweh on that day. They will serve[a]
(him) with animal sacrifices and gifts of food, will make vows to Yahweh and will fulfill (them). **22** And Yahweh will [a]smite[a] the Egyptians
[a]with a restorative smiting.[a] Thus they will turn themselves toward
Yahweh, so that he will allow himself to be asked for help by them
and he will heal them.

23 On that day a highway will stretch all the way from Egypt to Assyria;
the Assyrians will come to Egypt and the Egyptians to Assyria, [a]and
the Egyptians will join together in a worship service with the Assyrians.[a]

24 On that day, Israel will stand as the third partner[a] along with Egypt[b]
and Assyria[b]—a blessing in the midst of the earth, **25** 'whom'[a] Yahweh of Hosts blesses, since he says: "Blessed be my people,
Egypt,[b] and the work of my hands, Assyria, and my hereditary possession, Israel!"

16a Q[a] reads only הוא ביום (in that day) instead of ההוא ביום (in that day), a case of
haplography.
16b Apparently, מצרים refers here to the people, not the land; Gk: οἱ Αἰγύπτοι; thus
"the Egyptians." Concerning the use of the verb in the singular, see Joüon, *Gr* §150e.
16c After מניף (swing), Q[a] adds ידו (his hand) again.
16d Q[a] reads עליה (upon her) instead of עליו (upon him, it); i.e., this manuscript read
מצרים (Egypt) as feminine, read the proper noun as referring to the land; see note 16b.
In spite of this, it reads both the verbs in the plural: וחרדו ופחדו (and they will be terrified and will shake).
17a חגא (Q[a]: חונא), a hapax legomenon, is translated by the Gk as φόβητρον (terror);
Vulg reads *erit in festivitatem* (there will be festivities), which means it connected
this with חגג, "celebrate a festival." This term is normally translated as "terror" or
some similar word. However, G. R. Driver (*JTS* 34 [1933] 378) connects this word
with Arabic *ḥajiʾa*, "to be ashamed" (as does KBL² and *HAL*), which would result in
the translation "shame" (in *JSS* 13 [1968] 46, he suggests that it could possibly be
better explained by Arabic *ḥajiʾa*, "to be struck").
17b–b כל אשר (on this, see Ges-K §143bβ) means "every time when" (see *BHK³*),

the subject of זכיר (someone mentions, remembers) remaining undesignated, not being identical with the subject of יפחד (will be terrified) (i.e., the Egyptians). Translations such as that of Duhm: "Whoever thinks about it, it trembles . . ." (*sic*), or: "each one, whom someone reminds about it, that one will be frightened" (Zürcher Bibel) are not likely.

18a Instead of חמש ערים (five cities), Jirku suggests reading: חמש שערים (five doorways), contending that this refers to the five gates of the Yahu temple in Elephantine (see the letter of Yedonya and his associates to Bagōhī; Cowley, no. 30, line 10; *AOT* 451); but gates do not speak!

18b "Promise in someone's name with an oath" is נשבע ב in Hebrew. Syr reads *wymyn bmryh* (and the right [hand] by his Lord['s name]), which has caused some to suggest that possibly ביהוה (by Yahweh) was read instead of ליהוה (to Yahweh). However, נשבע ל (= "swear an oath to someone," i.e., "enter into an agreement of mutual partnership with someone by means of an oath"; cf. 45:23; 2 Chron. 15:14) makes excellent sense.

18c–c The entire phrase עיר החרס יאמר לאחד (one [of which] will be named 'city of the sun') is to be treated as an addition; see below, p. 270.

18d הֶרֶס (a noun not attested elsewhere, derived from הרס, "tear down") would seemingly have to be translated "destruction," but this remains a puzzle. That there is such a great variety of evidence in the transmitted versions about the reading shows that the name of this city was not understood for certain, even by the ancient copyists. A number of Hebrew MSS, including Qᵃ, read חרס, which means "sun," on the basis of Job 9:7 (cf. also מַעֲלֵה הֶחָרֶס, "the ascent of Heres," in Judg. 8:13). Sym (πολις ηλιου, "city of the sun," according to Codex Marchalianus of the Syh, et al.), Vulg (*civitas Solis*, "city of the sun"), and Jerome all agree. But the Gk reads πόλις ασεδεκ = עיר הצדק, "city of righteousness" (see 1:26). Aquila and Theod do not seem to have understood what it meant and are content with simply transcribing הרס, as αρες, thus giving support to the MT, the same support also being provided by the Syr (*hrs*). Finally, Targ seems to have combined the readings: קרתא בית שמש דעתידא למחרב ("the city Beth-shemesh, which is about to be destroyed"). Jerome explains: "*quidam interpretantur in solem, et alii in testam transferunt uolentes uel Heliopolim significare uel Ostracinen*" (which some people understand to refer to the sun, while others translate it as referring to pottery, desiring thereby to signify either Heliopolis or Ostrakine) (*Onomastikon* 39, ed. E. Klostermann [1904]). (Ὀστρακίνη, Ostrakine, is a city in the eastern part of the delta; see the above map, p. 214.) Thus he had a text that read עיר החרס (city of the sun) and presumes that this is the Hebrew translation of Heliopolis, but he also considers the possibility that חרס (sun) is to be understood in the sense of חרש, "pottery sherd." Finally, the suggestion made by Ikenius is also worth mentioning (see Gesenius), that הרס should be explained on the basis of Arabic *haris*, "the one that tears apart" (= the lion), which would make עיר ההרס a reference to Leontopolis. This interpretation is made more difficult by the fact that הרס is never used in this way in the OT and because *haris* in Arabic is only a *nick*name for lions. One also has to eliminate the solution offered by the Gk, since it appears to be pure speculation, occasioned by a text that made no sense. It is best to stay with the reading in the MT, which is also supported by Aquila, Sym, Theod, and, to some extent, by Targ, Vulg, and Jerome. The Babylonian Talmud (*Menaḥot* 110a) has the reading עיר החרס (city of the sun); it does, however, interpret it as עיר ההרס (the city of destruction), explaining the original name on the basis of Job 9:7, as being בית שמש (house of the sun, Beth-shemesh). The confusing state of affairs arose because the meaning of the designation חרס as a reference to the sun had been forgotten and attempts were made to try to come up with some helpful solution. There is no doubt that the Egyptian city of Heliopolis is meant, known elsewhere in the OT either as אׇן or אׄן (On) (in Jer. 43:13, it is called בֵּית שֶׁמֶשׁ, Beth-shemesh, lit.: house of the sun).

19a For מצבה (memorial stone, *maṣṣebah*), Vulg reads *titulus*, "inscription, stele"; in the Vulg, this is a common translation for מצבה.

20a Gk: εἰς τὸν αἰῶνα (for ever) (= לְעַד), obviously a misreading of the consonantal text.

20b Instead of וישלח (and he sent), Qᵃ has ושלח (and he will send), certainly a preferable reading, as Procksch already suggested.

20c Instead of ורב (and will lead in battle, strive on behalf of), Qᵃ reads וירד (and [one] will come down), certainly not a correct reading, but interesting nonetheless, since it gives evidence that there was an expectation that someone would come from the heavenly world as rescuer. The Gk translates ורב וה׳ (one that will lead the battle and free them) as κρίνων σώσει αὐτούς (judging, he will save them) (Vulg: *et propugnatorem qui liberet eos*, "and, fighting on their behalf, will liberate them"); see Ges-K §104g. The MT also treats רב as a participle, which is unlikely immediately following מושיע (a deliverer). Here one should read וְרָב ("and he will lead," a perfect consecutive; so Kissane, Feldmann).

21a עבד (serve) is used in the technical sense of bringing cultic sacrifices.

22a Concerning both of the infinitives (the second action follows from the first), cf. Joüon, *Gr* §123m. Instead of ורפׁא (restorative, to restore), Qᵃ reads ונרפׁו (and they will be healed), showing that its copyists no longer knew that one could have a construction with two successive infinitives. For נָגֹף (he will smite), the Gk reads πληγῇ μεγάλῃ (with a great blow), so that it can continue with its reading καὶ ἰάσεται αὐτοὺς ἰάσει (and he will heal them with a healing).

23a–a The Gk translates this καὶ δουλεύσουσιν οἱ Αἰγύπτιοι τοῖς Ἀσσυρίοις (and the Egyptians will be servants to the Assyrians), not realizing that עבד (serve) is also to be treated here as having a cultic meaning (thus also Gray).

24a שׁלישׁיה (third) is used here instead of the more common form שׁלישׁית (as in 15:5).

24b and b The Gk reverses Egypt's and Assyria's positions in the text.

25a Instead of ברכו (he blesses him), the Gk reads εὐλόγησε ([Yahweh] blessed): the suffix on ברכו must have, as its referent, either ברכה (a blessing) or הׇאׇרֶץ (the earth), which means that it should be feminine. It should be read בִּרְכָהּ (her blessing); the suffix refers back to הׇאׇרֶץ (the land), which is read just prior to the relative clause (for an alternate view, see G. Wehmeier, *Der Segen im Alten Testament* [1970] 87f.).

25b It would seem that the Gk considers it an impossibility that Egypt could ever become the people of Yahweh, reading therefore ὁ λαός μου ὁ ἐν Αἰγύπτῳ (my people who are in Egypt).

Form

Practically all modern scholars have concluded that vv. 16-25 are later insertions, secondary in this text when compared with vv. 1-15 (cf., however, Mauchline; Erlandsson, 79f.; see above, pp. 1f.). On formal grounds, that is demonstrated simply by the fact that these verses are written in prose and because the formula ביום ההוא (on that day), used so frequently in other parts of the book of Isaiah in material that has been determined to be secondary, is used no less than six times (vv. 16, 18, 19, 21, 23, 24) in these ten verses. Using this formula as a guide, the material is to be divided into five subsections. These formal considerations result in divisions that are also diverse in terms of their content:

1. 19:16f.: The terror of the Egyptians in light of Yahweh's decision
2. 19:18: The "language of Canaan" in Egypt
3. 19:19-22: The Egyptians turn back toward Yahweh
4. 19:23: Egypt and Assyria find themselves within the cult of Yahweh
5. 19:24f.: Israel in a covenant relationship with Egypt and Assyria—a blessing in the midst of the earth

The theme of the fifth saying is apparently an expansion of the fourth saying, since the fifth would make no sense if the fourth were not there. However, one can also detect a connection between the other units as well. Thus if one surveys the entire group together, one can hardly avoid the conclusion that this is not simply a random collection of additions to the message about Egypt, which just happen to be together at this place; rather, this is part of a composition that was intentionally written as a unit. It starts out at the point where Egypt has to suffer from the frightening experience of Yahweh's raised hand passing over them; but, as v. 22 points out, this blow brings healing: the people turn (or, at least, some groups within the populace turn) to faith in Yahweh, which finally results in the two most important world powers, Egypt and Assyria, joining with Israel in a common faith in Yahweh. It is apparently expected that a logical sequence of events unfolds, occurrences that admittedly take shape over an extended period of time, so that the stereotypical ביום ההוא (on that day) has to be interpreted as a reference to a much more extended chronological framework. The entire unit of material appears to be a programmed series of events set within a time frame in which the future relationship between Egypt and Yahweh or Israel would develop. Of course, the question remains whether this portrayal has been sketched out by one individual and develops during particular, historically specific circumstances. It appears more likely that this message about Egypt underwent repeated expansions. Generally speaking, the five individual units, apart from the relationship between the fourth and fifth, are not so closely related that one would have to assume that they were composed sequentially. Their content is quite varied, which would speak against them having been composed for one and the same situation; the formal link, the repetition of ביום ההוא (on that day), would also be less likely if it were all composed at once. This assumption about the gradual development of the text would not automatically preclude the possibility that the same glossator added his additional observations from time to time, as the situation changed, putting down on paper new thoughts about Egypt, but this is also not likely. Most importantly, when one studies the individual sections carefully, there is no obvious, systematic attempt to give verbal expression to real prophecies; rather, in a way that contradicts the forms being used, the material voices reflections about specific events that had taken place in Egypt. Thus it is most likely that these are individual additions; at least some of these are written by different authors and at different time periods, within unique historical situations, which a redactor, who had all of these at his disposal, arranged in an order that he thought made sense. This individual may be the person who composed the fourth and fifth sayings.

Setting

Because of this conclusion, it must be pointed out that the historical circumstances behind these verses cannot all be studied at the same time. Yet the individual sayings are simply too short to be dated exactly, and concrete points of reference to historical circumstances are either lacking or cannot be identified by us with certainty. The only point about which there is general agreement is that Isaiah cannot be considered the author of these units; Isaiah never expected that the Egyptians would turn to Yahweh and become believers; not even 2:2-4 anticipates that the peoples would be converted. Some commentators forgo any attempt at dating or they satisfy themselves with vague statements calling these verses "post-Isaianic" or "postexilic." Some assume that these units of material might have come from students of Isaiah or from a circle of those who were familiar with Isaiah's message (Erlandsson, 79f.; Eichrodt), or at least that it might be possible to date them to the late preexilic era. But the most common solution has been to point, with greater or lesser confidence, to the postexilic epoch as most likely for the time of composition for 19:16-25, with most scholars thinking that they ought not be dated to the early postexilic era either. It is possible that v. 18 includes points of reference that could help with an exact dating. But what does the "language of Canaan" mean? Which are the Egyptian cities in which this language will be spoken, and how is one to interpret עיר ההרס (city of the sun) (or: how is one to emend the text of this passage)?

Verse 19 could also be important as one seeks to explain this passage, if one could be confident about identifying and explaining the meaning of the "altar for Yahweh in the midst of the land of Egypt" and the "memorial stone for Yahweh on its border." Finally, it would be helpful if one could be clear about what time period might have been appropriate for one to expect that Egypt and Assyria could have joined together in the way this event was anticipated in vv. 23ff. In the last verses, however, a hope is expressed that boldly goes beyond reality. At best, more detailed solutions to the questions about the dating cannot be offered until a detailed exegesis of the individual passages has been completed.

Form and Setting

[19:16f.] *The Terror of the Egyptians in Light of Yahweh's Decision*

This is a threat. It would be entirely appropriate for Isaiah to have spoken v. 16; the material in 19:1-4 does not say it any differently. However, that Egypt would have allowed itself to be shamed by the "land of Judah," as announced in v. 17, would certainly never have been said by Isaiah, who so frequently cites Judah's lack of "faith." It is just as unlikely that he would have said—if one translates חגא as "be terrified" or something similar—that the weak and endangered Judah of his own time could have caused Egypt any terror.

Commentary

[19:16] If one treats ביום ההוא (on that day) as having an actual referent, then it has to refer to that day on which v. 1 says Yahweh is going to travel to Egypt upon swift clouds. This author sees a decisive turn of events when Yahweh appears in Egypt, going way beyond what Isaiah expects according to what is said in vv. 1-4 and 11-15. This turn in fortune would bring about a change, so that Egypt would be led to have confidence in Yahweh and his decisions.

Comparing the Egyptians with women is surprising, since in no other place does the OT refer to women as being particularly frightened, though one finds frequent comparisons with the fears that come on a woman giving birth to a child, since that experience had made a very deep impression; see 13:8; Jer. 4:31; Mic. 4:10 (text emended).

The Egyptians are terrified "because of the swinging of the hand of Yahweh of Hosts, which he will swing over them." Concerning הניף (swing), cf. תנופה (battling with brandished arm) in 30:32. In this passage, one must consider it likely that the usage reflects on the way תנופה (swinging) and הניף (swing) are used in cultic settings, i.e., moving the pieces being offered back and forth, before Yahweh, a rite first encountered in the priestly writing, even though the practice itself might have been preexilic. "The meaning of this rite . . . can . . . only be that the portion given to the priest was acknowledged actually to be God's portion, as the one whose it really is and to whom it is dedicated, but which then reverts back once again to the priest" (W. Nowack, *Lehrbuch der hebräischen Archäologie* II [1894] 239, note 2); "moving the offered gift to and fro in the hands; this indicates the distributing of the food" (M. Noth, *Exodus,* OTL [1962], 232, on Exod. 29:24; on this, see also A. Vincent, "Les rites du balancement (tenoûphâh) et du prélèvement (teroûmâh) dans le sacrifice de communion de l'Ancien Testament," FS R. Dussaud I [1939] 267–272; and R. J. Thompson, "Penitence and Sacrifice in Early Israel Outside the Levitical Law," diss., Leiden [1963] 206f., note 4). When Yahweh "swings" his hand against Egypt, that means that he carries out the consequences of his sentence of judgment as he stretches forth his hand, but it also means that he claims Egypt for himself. It is likely that the author is thinking about the Egyptian plagues when this is said (or the miracle at the sea during the exodus), which would be repeated in a sense in the future, though the terminology used in that description ("with a mighty hand and an outstretched arm") may have been purposely avoided in this passage.

[19:17] Unfortunately, the meaning of חגא (here: insult) is unclear (see above, p. 261). But it must refer to something connected with being ashamed, shaming (or even being terrified; cf. Gk: φόβητρον, "terror"). It is even more difficult to determine the precise sense in which the "land of Judah" will impose such consequences on Egypt. Even the unique reference אדמת יהודה (actually: territory of Judah), instead of just יהודה (Judah) or possibly even ארץ יהודה (land of Judah), does not help. Was the author dreaming about his state of Judah having military might? Hardly: אדמה (territory) is "never a political term." אדמת ישראל (territory of Israel) (found only in Ezekiel) "sums up in a single expression the qualification that the land given by Yahweh is incomparable, which is accented especially in Deuteronomy" (J. G. Plöger, *TDOT* I, 93). It is more likely that the author moves in the direction that uses the mention of Judah to invoke the awesome might of Yahweh that will come against Egypt. Just being reminded of this land would cause one to think about terror, since that would zero in on the unalterable decision-making power of Yahweh of Hosts. הזכיר with the accusative plus אל means "(casually) mention something in someone's presence" (see W. Schottroff, *Gedenken im Alten Orient und im Alten Testament* [1964] 261f.).

With the use of עצה (decision) and יעץ (determined), the expander might be thinking of v. 12, which might also explain why the title יהוה צבאות (Yahweh of Hosts) is used; see also יעץ עצה (the decision, determined for . . .) in 14:26 and עוץ עצה (forge a plan) in 8:10. He apparently thinks that the עצה (decision) of Yahweh concerning Egypt, which had been envisioned in v. 12, had come to fruition as certain events had taken place. It is possible that members of the Jewish diaspora might have thought that these events could be interpreted as fulfilling the plans of Yahweh that had been announced so long before. One senses that one is being reminded of what is said in Deutero-Isaiah, which also accentuates that Yahweh had said long beforehand what would take place in the future (40:21; 41:26f.; 44:8, and often elsewhere), at which time the superiority of Yahweh over the gods would be manifested. Kaiser's viewpoint can hardly be correct, however, that the mention of the territory of Judah would have caused the Egyptians to be reminded in a terrifying way about the Egyptian plagues or about the downfall of the Egyptians who were caught in the sea during the exodus. It is possible that the author was thinking about the time when Cambyses defeated the Egyptians (with the decisive battle taking place at Pelusium in 525). Even though Herodotus, who portrays Cambyses as the offspring of cruelty and godlessness (3.16), may have depicted the mad frenzy of this Persian in Egypt in a distorted fashion, the loss of sovereignty must have been traumatic for the Egyptians, so that they could not find a way to settle themselves down and come to terms with it. But obviously, it is just as possible that it could refer to any one of a number of times when the Egyptians sought to throw off the yoke of foreign domination, only to be beaten back in failure (on this, see Kaiser, AOAT 18, 95–106).

Setting and Commentary

[19:18] *The "Language of Canaan" in Egypt*

This verse also takes the form of a prophecy, but it is clear in this passage that it is a *vaticinium ex eventu* (prophecy after the fact).

The author knows of five cities in Egypt that have all sworn allegiance to Yahweh of Hosts. This causes him to view this circumstance as the fulfillment of ancient predictions that the peoples, especially the Egyptians, would someday acknowledge Yahweh of Hosts as lord (cf. 45:22ff.). נִשְׁבַּע לְ (to [me every tongue] shall swear) is used in 45:23 when it is said that the peoples will turn toward Yahweh; cf. also 2 Chron. 15:14. It is not a novel solution to suggest, as some commentators have done (Duhm, Marti, Procksch, Hertzberg, Auvray, et al.), that this means nothing more than that diaspora Jews were living in just five Egyptian cities. If this were the case, then the construction נִשְׁבַּע בְּ (swear by) would have been used. This expression has to refer either to Egyptians who had associated themselves with Judaism or to Jewish communities that sought to win proselytes. According to Jeremiah 42ff., soon after the old city of Jerusalem was destroyed a group of Judeans fled toward Egypt and settled down in Migdol, Tahpanhes, Memphis, and in the land of Pathros (44:1). In addition, we learn in Jer. 24:8 that Jews were already in Egypt before that time (C. H. Cornill, *Das Buch Jeremia* [1905] 280: it is to be presumed "that, together with Jehoahaz, or in connection with his deportation reported in 2 Kings 23:34, a considerable number of Jews came to Egypt, which seems to be neither impossible nor all that unlikely"). That these emigrants did not simply gather together into communities located on the border (where Migdol and Tahpanhes are located), but also in Noph = Memphis and even in Pathros = Upper Egypt, leads one to conclude that they settled down with Jewish groups that were already established in those places. One might also consult Jer. 44:26-28, a passage that seems to suggest that the Jews in Egypt lived under extreme duress at times.

The Elephantine papyri furnish additional, new material about the presence of the Jews in Egypt during the time when the Persians ruled there. One learns from these that there was a Jewish colony in Elephantine (Aramaic: יֵב [Yeb], on the island of the same name, known today as *el-gezīre*, near Syene, present-day *aswān*) already at the time when Cambyses conquered Egypt, consisting of soldiers who were serving the Egyptians by functioning as watchmen on the southern border of the land. Deutero-Isaiah is also aware of the existence of a Jewish *gola* (group of exiles) in Syene (49:12, text emended; according to Qᵃ it should read סְוֵנִים, *sᵉwēnîm*). They had built a temple of Yahu (which is the way they refer to Yahweh), which was destroyed in about 410, at the instigation of the Khnum priest who functioned there (though at an earlier time Cambyses had spared it). It is unclear when this Jewish colony had been established; some suggest the time of Psammetichus I, 664–610, or Amasis, 570–526 (see Kraeling; dates are those suggested by K. Kitchen, *The Third Intermediate Period in Egypt (1100–650 B.C.)* [1973] 468 [table 4]). It would seem that the temple which the Egyptians destroyed was later repaired and put back into service. Apparently, the end of this colony coincides with the end of Persian rule.

We have no evidence that the author of Isa. 19:18 also had this Jewish community in mind. But it is not too daring, if one presumes that there were Jewish communities in other Egyptian cities already during the Persian era, which is certainly possible, that Egyptians might have joined in with these groups from time to time (cf. Schürer III, 38–40). The strong contingent of the Jewish diaspora in Egypt during the Hellenistic age (Philo speaks of about a million total; *Against Flaccus* §6.43) must have been preceded by a rather lengthy prehistory. It is well known that the Persians gave the Jews of Palestine extensive privileges and even supported their cultic activities financially. They would also have been favorably inclined toward the Jewish community in Egypt—which then must have resulted in severe oppression during the times when the native citizens rebelled against the Persians. It is obviously out of the question that there would have been any cities in which the entire population would have become believers in Yahweh. When, in spite of this, the author of 19:18 speaks of five "cities" that have sworn allegiance to Yahweh, he must have been thinking that particular gains in the number of those who converted to become believers in Yahweh constituted the initial wave of what would someday be a widespread realignment concerning what they believed.

In the five cities that had proselytes, the שְׂפַת כְּנַעַן (language of Canaan) would be spoken. שָׂפָה, meaning "language," is also used in 28:11 and 33:19, both times in conjunction with לָשׁוֹן (tongue). But what is meant by this unique designation "language of Canaan"? The documents from Elephantine are written in Aramaic. That is not surprising, since Aramaic had become the official administrative language in the western portion of the Persian empire (Imperial Aramaic, as it has been known since the term was coined by H. H. Schaeder, is the version of the language used in the Aramaic portions of the books of Ezra and Daniel). However, the Jews at Elephantine used Aramaic not only in their official correspondence but also in private communication; they had become so fully comfortable with Aramaic that they call themselves Arameans (on this, see Schürer III, 48: "'Judeans' is the narrower term, 'Arameans' the broader; at times, the latter term also can be used instead of the former"). There is no way to know for sure whether they immigrated there from a region of Palestine (or Syria) that had already switched over to Aramaic or whether they first became acquainted with Aramaic in Egypt. But it is easy to understand why one would normally think of Aramaic when hearing the phrase "language of Canaan."

Obviously, the fact that modern linguistic analysis considers Hebrew to be one of the Canaanite languages, but does not include Aramaic in the same category, is not a sufficient argument against this interpretation. In the OT, however, the Arameans are never subsumed under the general category of the Canaanites, and the two population groups and languages are never confused with one another. In Ezra 4:7; 2 Kings 18:26 = Isa. 36:11; and Dan. 2:4, Aramaic is explicitly identified as אֲרָמִית. However, Hebrew is identified specifically as יְהוּדִית in 2 Kings 18:26, 28 (= Isa. 36:11, 13), as well as in Neh. 13:24. The specific linguistic designation עִבְרִי (Hebrew) or לָשׁוֹן עִבְרִי (Hebrew tongue) is first found in the Talmud (*b. Yadayim* IV,

5; *j. Megilla* 71b). Sometimes, of course, the rabbis use עברי (Hebrew) to refer to Aramaic, not, as in most places, to Hebrew. It is even more common for Greek translations of the Hebrew text to use ἕβραιος to refer to the Aramaic language. This means that it is not completely impossible that Aramaic, the language used by the Jews in Egypt, could have been called the "language of Canaan," which would presume that Aramaic was already being spoken in the "land of Canaan" at that time. Unfortunately, the point in time when the language of the commoners in Palestine switched from Hebrew to Aramaic cannot be fixed accurately; in fact, no specific date can be identified (see M. Wagner, BZAW 96 [1966] 3–7) because this transition stretched across several centuries. It would have occurred sooner in the territory once known as the Northern Kingdom than in what was known as the Southern Kingdom. It was still considered surprising, at the time of Nehemiah, that the children no longer knew how to speak Hebrew (13:24). Thus if one is to understand "language of Canaan" as a reference to Aramaic, then 19:18 could not have been written before the Greek era.

In spite of this, it is more likely that Hebrew is meant. Even though there is a likelihood that the Jews of the diaspora who lived in the "five cities" in Egypt no longer spoke Hebrew on the street, it is certain that this continued to be known as the language of the cult (later, Hebrew is called לְשׁוֹן הַקֹּדֶשׁ, "the holy tongue"). And the very fact that the verse speaks about Egyptians joining the cultic community would make it natural that this cultic language is what is intended. (The associations that are still made today, if someone mentions the "language of Canaan," would point in the direction of recognizing Hebrew as an esoteric language used by the pious believers in their communal worship.)

Admittedly, nothing can be said with confidence about specific details concerning these "five cities." Just the use of the number 5 has resulted in differing opinions, whether the number 5 is literal or a round number. It has been noticed that many Egyptian things are counted with the number 5 (see A. Dillmann, *Genesis*, 2 vols. [1897], on 43:34; Buhl). But the number 5 is not a "round number" that has any particularly symbolic value. And when the author or expander also inserts the note that one of these five cities is עִיר הַהֶרֶס (city of destruction) (or עִיר הַחֶרֶס, "city of the sun," text emended), he must have had a specific mental image, with certain identifiable locations, in mind. Jer. 44:1, 15 mention four localities in Egypt, which might be in mind here as well: Migdol (see also Jer. 46:14; Ezek. 29:10; 30:6) is most likely to be sought at the site now known as *tell el-ḥēr*, 18 km. southwest of Pelusium (see K. Elliger, *BHH* II, 1215; J. Janssen, *BL²*, 1153; H. Kees, Pauly-W XIV, 1, 299–300); Tahpanhes (see also Jer. 2:16, text emended; 43:7-9; Ezek. 30:18), Egyptian *t3- ḥ(t)-(n) p3-nḥsy* ("fortification of the moors") is transcribed in Greek as Ταφνάς (Taphnas), which has generally been linked with Greek Δάφναι/η (Daphnai, Daphnē), which has been localized on what is known today as *tell defenne* or *tell defne,* west-northwest of *el-qanṭara.* It is quite plausible that the Jews would have formed and maintained communities in cities close to the Sinai Peninsula. That passage additionally mentions מֹף= Memphis (see above, p. 253; see also Hos. 9:6; Jer.

2:16; 46:14, 19; Ezek. 30:13, 16) and Pathros (see also Isa. 11:11; Jer. 44:15; and Ezek. 29:14; cf. *Isaiah 1–12*, p. 492). This last reference is not a city but rather the way to designate Upper Egypt; however, it can be used as an equivalent for סְוֵנֵה = Syene, *aswān*. However, one should note that the author speaks of five, not four, cities; it would seem that his information is based on a detailed knowledge of the situation of the Jews in Egypt during his own lifetime, which means that these "five cities" are not simply the result of a growing fantasy about how the faith would spread.

The insertion in v. 18b calls the fifth city עִיר הַהֶרֶס (city of destruction). Mention has been made already about the poor quality of the text and how unsure its interpretation remains (pp. 262f.); we believe it ought to be emended to read עִיר הַחֶרֶס (city of the sun). In favor of reading this as Heliopolis is that it is also known elsewhere in the OT; see Ezekiel 30 (v. 17, text emended). In one place this city, referred to elsewhere as אוֹן (On), is designated בֵּית שֶׁמֶשׁ (Beth-shemesh, lit.: house of the sun) (Jer. 43:13).

One must eliminate the possibility that this might refer to Ostrakine (which could be the meaning of Hebrew עִיר הַחֶרֶס), known today as *ḫirbet el-flūsīyāt* (see A. Alt, *ZDPV* 66 [1943] 68, note 2), which is located at the eastern end of Lake Sirbonis (cf. Abel, 230ff.).

One might wonder whether all these five cities were in the eastern delta (and east of that yet), which would suggest that Jewish influence in the Persian era was simply presumed. The material available to us is simply not detailed enough to allow us to draw any conclusions.

[19:19-22] *The Egyptians Turn Back toward Yahweh*

Form

It is likely that the author who wrote vv. 19-22 was stimulated by what was said in v. 18 as he gave expression to his hopes. He looks into a future when Egypt, after being inflicted with massive blows, would turn toward Yahweh; indeed, this would apparently not be only the Jews who were living there in the diaspora, but the Egyptians as a whole. Once again, this hope is anchored in actual events that had taken place, which the author seems to take as the initial stage of what would subsequently result in a completely new reality: construction of an altar in the midst of the land of Egypt and of a memorial stone on its border.

Setting

If this passage were taken out of context, one might speculate that these two cultic objects were expected first to be built sometime in the future. Yet one would then have to wonder why the author would specifically have mentioned only these two objects and would have anticipated nothing more than a *maṣṣebah* on the border of Egypt; if this were a prediction wholly separate from reality, there is no doubt that a much richer picture would have been painted.

It would provide significant help in dating this particular passage, as well as the additions to the book of Isaiah in general, if one were able to locate this altar and *maṣṣebah* both geographically and temporally. The only Jewish cultic installation in Lower Egypt about which we have any information is the temple in Leontopolis, modern *tell el-yehūdīye,* 18 km. north of Heliopolis; on this, see Naville; in addition, see Kees, "Leontopolis 8," Pauly-W XII, 2, 2055–2056. It was founded by a certain Onias who, according to Josephus, *Jewish War* 7.10.2, would have been the son of Simon, i.e., Onias III, son of the high priest Simon the Just. This is in agreement with the talmudic tradition (*b. Menaḥot* 109b; *j. Yoma* IV, 3:41c; see Michel and Bauernfeind II, 2 , note 202, on book 7; and cf. also L. Seeligmann, *The Septuagint Version of Isaiah* [1948] 92ff.). However, Josephus contradicts himself: according to *Antiquities* 12.5.1; 13.3.1-3, the construction of the temple "in the nome of Heliopolis" (Leontopolis is in the nome of Heliopolis) is attributed to the son of Onias III, the father himself having been the last of the Zadokite priests who was able to carry out the functions of his office in Jerusalem; i.e., it was built by Onias IV. Since, according to 2 Macc. 4:33f., Onias III had sought asylum in a sanctuary, Daphne near Antioch, but allowed himself to be tricked into being lured out, and then, "with no regard for justice," was put out of the way by being murdered, the details in the *Antiquities* are to be judged as more likely, which means that Josephus confused Onias III with Onias IV in *Jewish War* (see Delcor, 191). Unfortunately, not enough information is available to be certain about exactly when this Onias headed the project to construct the temple in Leontopolis. When Onias III was murdered (ca. 170), Onias IV was still a child. For this reason, the high priestly function was assumed by the brother of Onias III, Jason (174–172) (dates according to Delcor, 191); see 2 Macc. 4:7-15. This priest was followed by Menelaus (172–163), who was then succeeded by Alcimus (163–159), who, like his immediate predecessor, was not an Oniad family member. When this Alcimus was named high priest, Josephus reports that Onias IV fled to Egypt (*Antiquities* 12.9.7). It is likely that this information from Josephus has to be corrected as well: according to a letter, which can be dated exactly, having been found in the region near Memphis (see *Corpus papyrorum judaicarum,* no. 132, p. 244; see literature above), he must have already come to Egypt before the year 164, since the situation was already too hot for him to stay in the land of Judah even right after Jason's rule came to an end. According to the editors who published the *Corpus* just cited, the addressee in the letter, who is named Onias, could only be Onias IV (for a different view, see Wilcken, 487f.). In *Antiquities* 13.3.1, Josephus reports that Onias first bided his time for a while in Alexandria, but then was entrusted with the position of στρατηγός (civil and military governor) by the well-known Ptolemy II Philometor, a befriender of the Semites; cf. Delcor, 192. The important position that Onias could enjoy, according to the information provided in this text, fits very well with the role that Josephus tells us he played in Egypt, even though this historian certainly overstates the case when he reports that Onias, together with a certain Dositheus, was given the responsibility of ruling over the whole land of Egypt, as if he were a second Joseph. Even if one cannot accept the account by Josephus at face value, it certainly still remains possible that Onias had the chance to build a Jewish temple in the region that was under his authority. According to *Antiquities* 13.3.1, he did it for self-glorification, but also so that the Jews who lived in Egypt would be able to use it as their spiritual center. But this does not explain why the temple would have been built in insignificant Leontopolis; most of all, however: Why it was not constructed in a place where one would find a concentration of an Egyptian-Jewish population? In reality, this member of the Oniad family, shut out from exercising his function as the high priest in Jerusalem, probably simply wanted to create the possibility for his being able to carry out what he would have considered to be his legitimate function as high priest. No doubt, this plan would have met with the approval of the palace in Alexandria, keeping with its political strategy: in Jerusalem, the role of high priest was filled by those who were lackeys of the Seleucids (Jason and Menelaus). However, the Egyptian temple achieved its importance only as it served the military colony at Leontopolis (see Tcherikover, 280f.). At no time did the Egyptian Jews ever consider it to be their official temple (which falsely led Beek to conclude that the report about its establishment was to be considered as mere legend).

One ought not be surprised that the temple in Leontopolis would have been rejected, since a temple in Egypt clearly contradicts the deuteronomic law that there can be only one legitimate temple, the one located at the place that Yahweh would choose. In a letter sent to Philometor, however, Josephus reports that Onias writes: "Our prophet Isaiah foretold that there should be an altar in Egypt to the Lord God" (*Antiquities* 13.3.1; see also 3.2 and *Jewish War* 7.10.3). This report poses the question: Would Onias have been able to legitimate the construction of his temple by referring to Isa. 19:18? Or, taking the opposite stance, is this passage a later insertion into that text, added to justify the building (so Duhm, Marti)? There is no question that some, at times, found it necessary to legitimize an action by having a written passage lend support (one might refer to Deut. 11:29; 27:12, in connection with the construction of the temple by the Samaritans on Gerizim); and that, when it is difficult to prove that something is legitimate, traditions and documents can be manufactured in light of this need; many examples of this practice can be found in the history of religions. One has to admit that the time during which Onias IV exercised considerable influence in Egypt (Josephus almost goes so far as to say that there was a χώρα Ὀνίου, "country of Onias"; *Jewish War* 1.9.4; cf. 7.10.2; *Antiquities* 14.8.1) would provide a plausible background for 19:16-25.

This would even provide us with information that would demonstrate that a few additions were inserted into the book of Isaiah even far into the second century, which Kaiser has once again suggested as a likely possibility. However, if this is to give a legitimacy to the temple in Leontopolis, then why would one not find specific mention of a temple? In addition, why would the *maṣṣebah* be mentioned, since the occasions on which the *maṣṣebah*s for Yahweh would be mentioned in later times would only lead to accusations of unfaithfulness. However, that point aside, such a late dating for the final form of the book of Isaiah would presuppose a rather adventuresome process of development. The first manuscript of Isaiah from *ḥirbet qumrān*, which already has this reading in its text, is to be dated to a time soon after the temple of Onias was built (concerning the dating of Qᵃ, see F. M. Cross, "The Development of the Jewish Scripts," FS Albright [1961] 133–202, esp. 138). There is no doubt that the text of Isaiah had been so consolidated, into a fixed form, by this time that an insertion which would justify the sanctuary in Leontopolis would have fomented open rebellion—certainly in Jerusalem, where the text that has come down to us was preserved.

Finally, the Greek translation of the book of Isaiah, which also mentions both altar and *maṣṣebah,* had already been produced roughly in the middle of the second century (so Seeligmann, 91). Yet it would seem that the passage in Isaiah would make it possible for the temple built by Onias to be more than just a short-lived intermezzo; it survived long past the antagonism between the Ptolemies and Seleucids. It was only after the fall of Masada, A.D. 73, that the caesar Vespasian, who feared Jewish unrest in Egypt, ordered Lupus, the governor of Alexandria, to close the temple (*Jewish War* 7.10.4).

Based on what has just been said, Isa. 19:19 could be hundreds of years older than the temple that Onias built. Some have also suggested that this passage makes a veiled reference to the other temple in Egypt, about which we have some knowledge, the one at Elephantine (thus Steuernagel, Jirku). When, during the reign of Psammetichus I, and thus still within the seventh century, a Jewish military colony was established, to which reference might have been made when speaking of Pathros in Jer. 44:1; Ezek. 30:14; and possibly even Ps. 68:31 (see *BHK³*), it is not beyond the realm of possibility that the Elephantine temple was built before the basic form of the deuteronomic writings took shape under Josiah. However, present-day scholarship leans toward dating the temple to the time of Amasis II (570–526; dates according to Kitchen); see Kraeling, 47f. Admittedly, the only fixed date for anything about that temple is simply the information that Cambyses spared the sanctuary from destruction (Cowley, no. 30, lines 13f.; see also *AOT* 451). According to this text, however, the altar would be located בתוך ארץ מצרים (in the midst of the land of Egypt). But, of course, the *maṣṣebah* stands אצל־גבולה (on the border). However, when some person in Judah would say that, the thought would not be about the southern border of Egypt, by Elephantine, but rather about where the country of Egypt borders Philistia. Thus this thesis must be rejected as well. This means that every attempt to arrive at a precise date for 19:19 has come up short.

It might be just by chance that we know something about temples only in Elephantine and Leontopolis. Other places where Jews lived would certainly have had places for worship and *maṣṣebah*s "for Yahweh." The text recently studied by Harmatta (see Cowley, no. 81; dated ca. 310 B.C.) names ten localities between Migdal and Syene where Jews had settlements; in fact, two priests are even mentioned, one from Thmuis (where, according to Hengel, I, 16, the sanctuary mentioned in Isa. 19:19 could have stood). According to Josephus, Alexander supposedly employed Jewish mercenaries (*Against Apion* 1.192ff.). According to the Letter of Aristeas (lines 12–14), Ptolemy I deported 100,000 Jews to Egypt, some as military colonists, some as slaves. No doubt, this practice of the Ptolemies simply followed the practice carried out earlier by the Persians and, before them, by the last pharaohs of the Twenty-sixth Dynasty (on this, see Hengel, I, 15f.).

The section made up of vv. 19-22 must have come into existence at a time when Deuteronomy, which explicitly condemns setting up *maṣṣebah*s (see 7:5; 12:3; Exod. 23:24 and 34:13 are secondary insertions), would not, as yet, have made a significant impact on the consciences of the Jews. At least, it would not yet have been considered as having canonical scriptural status by the Jews in Egypt. Thus it would certainly have been part of the text by the time the Persian rule in Egypt came to an end (see Procksch, Bright, Schoors, Feuillet, 79–87).

Commentary

[19:19] "In the midst of the land" is too vague for one even to hazard a guess about which location the author had in mind. The same problem is posed by the notation that the *maṣṣebah*s were to be found "on its border." If one does not push the point too far, this could be a reference to Tahpanhes (see above, p. 270), Migdol (see above, p. 270) or even Zoan, which is mentioned in both 19:11 and 30:4 (concerning its location, see above, p. 250).

Since it speaks just about an altar, not a temple, this must be nothing more than a place where offerings were brought, a בָּמָה (high place, sacred place), of the type found in Dan; see A. Biran, *BA* 37 (1974) 40–43. When Cheyne suggests that, in reality, it was not just an altar which was built, but that it refers to a regular (synagogue) worship service which was established, which would have been just as meaningful as if one would have had a real altar, since it would also function as an אות (sign) and עד (witness) for Yahweh, then he also ought to be able to prove that מזבח (altar) (and מצבה, *maṣṣebah*) are used in other passages to refer to a synagogue or to a place of prayer. Egyptian obelisks can be referred to by using the Hebrew word מצבה (*maṣṣebah*) (Jer. 43:13; the *maṣṣebah* is also the ancient pattern that was replicated when fashioning obelisks). According to Gen. 31:45, *maṣṣebah*s also can serve to mark a border of a country. However, the context here would only allow one to identify the *maṣṣebah* as a specific reference to a cultic object; cf. Haag, *BL*², illuss. 71 (Gezer) and 72 (Hazor), often mentioned in conjunction with an altar (see also the *maṣṣebah* in the temple at Arad, *BL*², plate 21).

[19:20] The מצבה (*maṣṣebah*) is to function both as an אות (sign) and an עד (witness) for Yahweh. This means that the *maṣṣebah* is removed from its original close linkage with the altar, now becoming a symbol for Yahweh's claim to have power over Egypt; i.e., the *maṣṣebah* is now separated from its "context" of functioning as a cultic installation on a בָּמָה (high place). For this reason, the translation "memorial stone" is justified in this passage.

אות (sign) can refer back to former saving deeds of Yahweh (see, e.g., Josh. 4:6f.); here, however, it is a "sign" pointing forward to Yahweh's desire that he would establish control in the future (cf. Isa. 55:13; 66:19). After all, to translate it as "sign" is only an approximation; when one speaks of the אות (sign), what is intended has already been set in motion, that overarching order which God brings into existence, which eventually becomes real when Egypt turns toward Yahweh, though it had already been made visible in a limited way. A sign is the ἀρραβών (down payment) on the eventual full flowering of salvation; it "testifies" to the real presence of Yahweh. For this reason, it comes as no surprise that עד (witness) is parallel to אות (sign); on this, cf. Gen. 31:47f.; Josh. 22:26ff., 34; 24:27; Isaiah himself uses אות (sign) and מופת (marker, portent) in parallel (8:18; 20:3). Without a doubt, the author is thinking that the Egyptians would not be able to pass by this "sign" of faith in Yahweh either, without it making an impression. He himself identifies concretely that which the *maṣṣebah* (and certainly the altar as well) should give witness about: that someone who cries out to Yahweh when oppressors oppress does not cry for help in vain. Concerning צעק (cry out), see צְעָקָה (cry of helplessness) in 5:7, which, in the final analysis, is identical with זעק (cry out for help) in 14:31; 15:4, 5; and with זְעָקָה (downfall shriek) in 15:5 and 8; cf. also p. 98 above. The verb צעק is surprisingly common within the story of the exodus, when "crying out" to Yahweh is described (5:8, 15; 8:8; 14:10, 15; 15:25; 17:4; 22:22, 26). It takes on the status of a technical term when the "savior" Moses stands in the stead of Israel and "cries" to Yahweh. One cries because oppressors, לֹחֲצִים, are present, just as Israel had cried out to Yahweh in Egypt because of the לַחַץ (oppression) of its לֹחֲצִים (oppressors) (Exod. 3:9). The author of the present passage envisions some type of reenactment of the deliverance from Egypt, of course with one major and decisive modification: now it deals with the deliverance of the (Yahweh-believing) Egyptians themselves. Just as earlier, Yahweh would allow others to bring supplication to him and would send a deliverer, ושלח להם מושיע ורב והצילם ([and] he will send them a deliverer; that person will lead the battle and free them) (see above, p. 263, and cf. Exod. 3:10), a second Moses, whose activity would prove to be even more productive and expansive than the first. It is true that the Moses who led the exodus was never referred to as מושיע, "deliverer"; מושיע (deliverer) is the title used for the helper whom Yahweh sent time and again to Israel when its people suffered under the terrible oppression of enemies (Judg. 3:9, 15; 12:3; 1 Sam. 11:3; 2 Kings 13:5).

[**19:21**] It would seem that at least some remembrance of Moses can be detected once again in v. 21: ונודע יהוה . . . . וידעו . . . את יהוה (and Yahweh will make aware . . . and they will be aware . . . of Yahweh) (cf. נודע, "make oneself known," in Exod. 6:3 and ידע, "shall know," in 6:7; priestly writing). Just as Yahweh had reacted to the outcry and let himself be made known to the Israelites, and they recognized him and served him, thus he would also glorify himself in Egypt. נודע is one of the OT terms used in a technical way when describing the self-revelation of Yahweh (see W. Zimmerli, *EvT* 22 [1962] 15–31; and R. Rendtorff, ibid., 621–649). Yahweh makes it possible for himself to be detected in historical demonstrations of his power, after which one can know who he is. However, earlier still, Ezekiel also had the same understanding about how revelation took place; cf. 20:5: וָאִוָּדַע לָהֶם בְּאֶרֶץ מִצְרָיִם (and I made myself known to them in the land of Egypt); see also v. 9 and 35:11: "I will make myself known among you . . . so that you will know that I am Yahweh" (this passage speaks against Edom; 38:23 is similar); in fact, the recognition formula occurs even in the ancient accounts of the exodus (Exod. 7:17; 8:18), though naturally it refers to Israel in those passages. What is unique in this passage is that the prediction is not about a revelation of Yahweh's power when carrying out judgment, but rather the revelation of his might that will bring salvation to the Egyptians. One ought to note carefully that both Ezekiel and Deutero-Isaiah anticipate that the peoples will recognize Yahweh, with Ezekiel making explicit reference to the Egyptians

(29:6, 9, 16; 30:8, 19, 25f.; 32:15, 19). According to the passage at hand, the recognition of Yahweh would develop in such a way that the Egyptians would "serve" him with animal sacrifices and gifts of food. There had also been an opportunity for Israel to "serve" when the people embarked on the exodus from Egypt (Exod. 3:12; 4:23, and often elsewhere). In those passages, however, mention was always made about service to Yahweh. Only in this one instance is the verb constructed with the accusative, making mention of the gifts to be offered (but cf. Exod. 10:26; 13:5; and note the *hithpaʿel*, in the sense of "be offered," in Cowley, no. 33, line 10). In all likelihood, the story of the exodus probably does not have anything radically different in mind when it speaks about serving Yahweh than that offerings would be brought. Concerning זבח (sacrifice) and מנחה (gift), see *Isaiah 1–12*, pp. 41f., on 1:11. Unlike that passage, however, מנחה would not be used to refer to the general category of gifts given to the deity, but already in the special sense of "gifts of food."

In addition to offerings, vows and their fulfillment are mentioned. That is not a new point, however, since one takes vows to make "offerings." It is not likely that the present passage speaks, with a transferred meaning, about offering praise to God (cf. Pss. 50:12-14; 51:17-19). Oaths are part of prayers of lament; they reinforce the serious nature of the request being presented. There must have been times when they were not always "fulfilled," even after a favorable response, as is shown by the inclusion of warnings in Ps. 50:14; Eccles. 5:3; cf. Deut. 23:21.

[19:22] One is certainly somewhat surprised by the announcement in v. 22 that Yahweh would still smite these Egyptians, who had become so pious, with a "restorative smiting," and one might ask whether a redactor is at work here, trying to establish a link with v. 16. But v. 20 also had spoken about oppressors and yet had announced that a savior would appear. One might suppose that these two announcements, which seem to be so much at odds with one another, are to be taken together, so that the "salvation" takes place through another savior who would be sent by Yahweh, who would at the same time also be a second Moses. In favor of this solution, the verb עתר (he will allow himself to be asked for help), which occurs relatively seldom in the OT, appears surprisingly often in the stories in the book of Exodus that describe Moses' confrontations with the pharaoh (eight times out of a total of twenty, these in fact exclusively in Exodus 8–10), and always in a setting that includes Moses' plea on behalf of the pharaoh or the Egyptians that the plagues sent by Yahweh would be removed. That which could not have taken place at that earlier time, because the Egyptians remained hardened, would now take place: Yahweh would allow himself to be swayed. It is most interesting to note that the verb נגף (smite), which is found in widely divergent contexts, is also firmly anchored in the story of the exodus (7:27) and in the Passover pericope (Exod. 12:23, 27, describing the smiting of the firstborn in Egypt; see also מגפה, "plague," in v. 13).

Finally, the use of רפא (restorative healing) could be a reminiscence on

Exod. 15:26. Smiting Egypt could lead to restorative healing, since it would lead to turning toward Yahweh. One wishes to know more yet: what exactly are these blows from Yahweh? Ought one think of plagues here as well? Admittedly, the לחציט (oppressors) in v. 20 have to be enemies. What constitutes the restorative healing? The verb רפא (restore, heal) would fit well with "plagues," but could also be used, with a transferred meaning, for any type of peril. One also wishes to learn more about how the author envisions that one would see the evidence for turning to Yahweh. Translations such as "be converted" or even simply "repent" could lead one to have a wrong idea about what is happening. For the author, שוב in this case can hardly mean anything but that someone becomes a member of the Yahweh congregation and participates in its worship activities that can be expected to guarantee well-being, peace, and salvation in the widest sense.

When using the phraseology ורפאם ... נגף ורפוא ... ונגף (he will smite ... with a restorative smiting ... and he will heal them), the author, who is not a master with words, uses the infinitive absolute and is fortunate enough to formulate a perceptive thought, which is difficult to convey precisely in English: it is a blow that causes agony and, at the same time, restorative healing. The way this is formulated is not found elsewhere in the OT. However, the concept itself is found elsewhere in OT piety (cf. Hos. 6:1f.; Deut. 32:39; 2 Chron. 7:13f.; cf. also Isa. 30:26 and 53:5; 57:17f.): out of judgment, restoration comes forth, of course, as the passage from Hosea just cited makes clear, not automatically, but only in those cases where the "smiting" leads one to turn and go in the opposite direction. It is plain to see that רפא (heal) should in no way be understood in the sense of an apocalyptic turnaround, which results in salvation: this term deals with deliverance from the לחציט (oppressors), as Israel had been saved from its own oppressors (3:9). Because the text cannot be dated more specifically, one cannot be more precise about the details of what the author anticipates. Could it refer to the Egyptians being delivered from the Persians? Would מושיע (deliverer) point toward some leading figure who would be given the task of calling those who lived in Egypt to go into battle against the Persians—since Yahweh was willing to be swayed to bless the effort—with the confidence that this would finally lead to victory? Obviously, frequent attempts were made in Egypt to shake off the overlordship of the Persians. About 460, a certain Inaros the Libyan tried his luck, as did Amyrtaios of Sais after him, supported by a Greek flotilla (cf. Thucydides, *Peloponnesian War* 1.104; *FWG* 5, 92; Kaiser, "Der geknickte Rohrstab," 103; and idem, "Zwischen den Fronten," 198 [see literature at 19:1-15]). After them, rulers from the Twenty-ninth and Thirtieth Dynasties developed plans of their own. Nectanebo I (381/380–364/363; dates are from F. K. Kienitz, *Die politische Geschichte Ägyptens vom 7. bis zum 4. Jahrhundert vor der Zeitwende* [1953] 175) could point to some success against the satrap from Syria, Pharnabazus, but his dynasty finally met its end as well. However, vague guesses do not lead one confidently to any real conclusions.

[19:23] *Egypt and Assyria Find Themselves within the Cult of Yahweh*

Setting and Commentary

[19:23] An additional vision of the future: Egypt and Assyria come into contact with one another—not as world powers, but as fellow members of the same cult of Yahweh. One can presume that this utopian expectation was also occasioned by certain political relationships, but this is definitely the point at which all attempts to assign a date prove fruitless. Which "Assyria" is meant, anyway? The Assyrian Empire came to its end after Nineveh fell (612 B.C.); at the very latest, one might say it ended when Nebuchadnezzar defeated Pharaoh Necho II, who had hurriedly come to assist Assyria, in the battle of Carchemish (605 B.C.). It is most unlikely that this passage was written before that time. "Assyria" is thus the nickname for whichever particular power, in the course of world history, inherited what they once controlled, which would mean: the Persians. To be sure, some commentators (Hitzig, Duhm, Marti, Procksch, Kaiser) presume, almost as a foregone conclusion, that "Egypt" refers to the Ptolemaic Empire and "Assyria" to the Seleucid Empire. However, no adequate reasons have been offered to back this late dating. In the secondary passages of the book of Isaiah, a number of places have caused some to suppose that references to Assyria really point to Persia (Causse, *Les origines,* 108, suggests the middle of the fifth century, i.e., the time of the revolt of Egypt against Artaxerxes II, or the middle of the fourth century, when Artaxerxes III [Ochus] established firm control over Egypt once again; see also, idem, *Israel,* 97f.). One ought not say that there was no chance that anyone would have uttered the hopes expressed here during the Persian era. Rather, one ought to pose the question about whether this universalism within the Jewish community could have been hoped for after the time of Ezra—at least among groups that, like this author, were vigorously shaping their expectations in cultic categories. One might compare this text with Zeph. 2:11 and 3:8ff., even though those passages are also secondary additions to the words of that prophet (see also Isa. 55:3-5; 60; 62; 66:18-21; Ps. 47:10; Mal. 1:11; Zech. 8:20-23). As is also true for the Zephaniah passages, the expectation here is not for the "peoples" to stream to Jerusalem; one would pray to Yahweh in both Egypt and Assyria. This ability to pray to God in foreign lands also raised questions about the dogma that Zion was the only place where Yahweh could be worshiped.

There would be a מסלה (highway) between these two countries; on this, see *Isaiah 1–12,* pp. 295 and 497. Just as a מסלה (highway) would be available for the Jews who would be returning home to Jerusalem (40:3; cf. also 11:16; 62:10; Jer. 31:21), so now there also would be one for the Egyptians and Assyrians, to be used whenever they would want to visit back and forth. It would not have to be a highway for processions, as some presume (Fohrer, Herbert; cf. also Ziegler). Obviously, troops would not have to march over it any more. The author may be thinking of trade routes (but see K. Elliger, *Deuterojesaja,* BK XI/1, 18).

If taken all by itself, v. 23b could mean: "And the Egyptians will serve Assyria"; in context, however (see v. 21), עבד (serve) has to be treated as an intransitive here and את as a preposition (= with); to be sure, this is the only passage where the verb is used in the absolute sense ("join together in a worship service"). However, since עֲבֹדָה was used in a special way to describe "cultic worship" (see Josh. 22:27: עבד את־עבדת יהוה, "perform the service of Yahweh"; cf. "service," in English), this development makes good sense. According to v. 21, the "service" would be to bring offerings of animal sacrifices and gifts of food.

[19:24f.] *Israel in a Covenant Relationship with Egypt and Assyria—a Blessing in the Midst of the Earth*

It would seem that the author of these two verses was shocked by the boldness of the one who had spoken in v. 23 (possibly, that means: by his own boldness). He does not want to neutralize completely the hope expressed in v. 23, but rather seeks to put all these events back into their proper perspective. Verse 23 could leave one with the impression that Israel would be out of the picture. For this reason, it had to be said clearly that Israel would have its place within God's restored community as well.

Commentary

[19:24] It is true that one must wonder why the author, if he was not content to allow v. 23 to stand as it was, would not at the same time put Israel into the first place here. But שְׁלִישִׁיָּה (third partner) apparently has nothing to do with ranking. One would have to say: Israel would remain *primus inter pares* (first among equals). It would be a blessing in the midst of the earth. Does this refer to Gen. 12:3? G. Wehmeier (87f.; see above, p. 263) is of that opinion. At the very least, the passages are related in terms of content; the same ideas are expressed in Zech. 8:13. Many different answers have been put forth about the meaning of all these passages. Does it mean that Israel will be used as a proverbial example when words of blessing are spoken (see Scharbert, *Bib* 39 [1958] 25), or that Israel, as a people of בְּרוּכִים (blessings), will also serve as a source of בְּרָכָה (blessing) for others as well, i.e., the source of everything connected with life and its necessities, with physical and spiritual wholeness being fostered and multiplied? At the very least, the present passage has to be speaking of the second possibility; on this, see H. Junker, BETL (1953) 553, 557.

[19:25] Even if one accepts the emendation suggested above, v. 25 is appended in an awkward way. It is supposed to say that the entire earth is blessed by Yahweh of Hosts, the cultic deity of Jerusalem; the peoples of the earth, represented by Egypt and Assyria, stand in a direct relationship with

Yahweh, being under his blessing. Thus the author tries to have Yahweh characterize Egypt as "my people" and Assyria as "the work of my hands," in every way a unique assertion in the entire OT. If Egypt is "his" people, then Yahweh is its God. There is an apparent parallel in Ps. 47:9f.: "God is king over the nations. . . . The princes of the peoples gather as the people of the God of Abraham." The reading in that text has been disputed; the Gk itself had the reading: μετὰ τοῦ θεοῦ Αβρααμ (with the God of Abraham) (עִם, "with," instead of עַם, "people"!), but that might have been an unintentional misreading. For the present passage, however, the Gk apparently made a conscious alteration to the MT, correcting what it could not let stand: ὁ λαός μου ὁ ἐν Αἰγύπτῳ καὶ ὁ ἐν Ἀσσυρίοις (my people that is in Egypt and in Assyria), which means that the message was translated so that it applied only to the Jewish גָּלוּה (exiles) who were in those two countries. This correction in the Gk also shows that one is not forced to interpret this text as providing a typical example of the magnanimous treatment of others that is said to be characteristic of Hellenism. It is possible that the author is closer to Deutero-Isaiah than to Hellenistic Judaism. One cannot conclude that the epithet for Assyria, "the work of my hands," slights Assyria in relation to Egypt. Also in 64:7f., "work of your hand" parallels "your people"; see also 60:21 and the passages in Deutero-Isaiah that call Yahweh the creator of Israel (יָצַר, "shaper/former," 44:2, 24; 45:11; cf. also עָשָׂה, "maker," 44:2; and בָּרָא, "creator," 43:1, 15, in this sense). Israel is Yahweh's people, because Yahweh made, created, and formed it; cf. Deut. 32:6; Isa. 41:20; Ps. 100:3. If Yahweh is the creator, the unavoidable conclusion is that the peoples are also his work. Obviously, the author of the present passage acknowledges the validity of that assertion (as does Ps. 86:9 also). However, he also has to accord a title of honor to the "third party in the covenant," Israel, for which he uses נַחֲלָה (hereditary possession).

"When the Most High apportioned the nations . . . according to the בְּנֵי אֵל (number of the gods), Yahweh's own portion was his people (עַמּוֹ), Jacob his נַחֲלָה (allotted share) (Deut. 32:8f., emended text; see *BHK³*; cf. also Deut. 4:20; Ps. 47:5 and Pss. 28:9; 94:5; Mic. 7:14). There are also other passages where the "people of Yahweh" and the "hereditary possession of Yahweh" are parallel (e.g., Deut. 9:26, 29; 1 Kings 8:51; Ps. 78:71). One might conclude that נַחֲלָה (hereditary possession) could designate a closer relationship between Israel and Yahweh (thus Fohrer, following Duhm): it (Israel) is the chief possession; the other peoples are only like children of more distant relations (cf. Gen. 21:10 and see also Dillmann, Feldmann, Procksch).

Purpose and Thrust

These five messages appended to the מַשָּׂא (verdict) concerning Egypt appear to be aphorisms that give expression to certain truisms about Israel and Egypt. The attitude toward this neighboring people, and judgment about it, does not follow any consistent theme; instead, the author of each subsequent passage risks saying even more about his hopes—and, in the process, gets farther and farther away from the reality of circumstances and events that had

281

occurred, which doubtless had stimulated the writing of the additional message, until, finally, the one who speaks in vv. 24f. goes beyond all limits, past boundaries that no others ever crossed, and bestows on the peoples the highest titles of honor, which had applied previously just to Israel. Based on what has been said, to maintain that this "high point" (Feuillet) of OT faith could be explained only from a "distance," as possible only in the context of Hellenism, is not all that certain, though many exegetes presume so. "If one takes the prophetic element in these visions of the future more seriously, then one need not object to an earlier dating" (Eichrodt). The author(s), in the final analysis, have been deeply affected by the spirit that shaped Deutero-Isaiah, even if they are more caught up with speaking in cultic categories than the one who composed that material. Ought one say that the logical conclusions of Deutero-Isaiah's universalism have been drawn out here? Or is the *proprium Israeliticum* (uniqueness of Israel) mentioned, only to be given up? One detects the struggle with that question in vv. 24f., wondering whether Israel would not still have a unique place in what was to come. The answer is that it would be "a blessing, in the midst of the earth," which is added parenthetically. The advantage that would remain with Israel was that it has the promise that it would be the source of blessing for all the others. In this way, Israel's election would not be made null and void, but the knowledge that Yahweh is sovereign over the peoples is treated with utter seriousness—indeed, not only that he is the lord over all peoples as a judge, but that he claims them as his own possession and puts them into the stream of blessings, which had been made visible to Israel at first, but which now would spread out over the "heathen" as well. One is not far from Paul's "to the Jew first and also to the Greek" (Rom. 1:16).

Isaiah 20:1-6

Isaiah Goes Naked and Barefoot

Literature

Concerning the text: C. F. Burney, "The Interpretation of Isa XX 6," *JTS* 13 (1912) 417–423. F. Nötscher, "Entbehrliche Hapaxlegomena in Jesaja," *VT* 1 (1950) 301. D. M. Beegle, "Proper Names in the New Isaiah Scroll," *BASOR* 123 (1951) 28. G. R. Driver, "Notes and Studies: Hebrew Scrolls," *JTS* 2 (1951) 17–30.

Concerning the tartan: A. Ungnad, "Joseph, der Tartan des Pharao," *ZAW* 41 (1923) 204–207. P. Koschaker, "Fratriarchat, Hausgemeinschaft und Mutterrecht in Keilschriftrechten," *ZA* 41 (1933) 1–89, esp. 35f. W. Baumgartner, "Beiträge zum hebräischen Lexikon," FS O. Eissfeldt (1958) 25–31. G. Wilhelm, "Ta/erdennu, ta/urtannu, ta/urtānu," *UF* 2 (1970) 277–282.

Concerning the history of the era: H. Winckler, *Die Keilschrifttexte Sargons* (1889). R. F. Harper, *Assyrian and Babylonian Letters* (1892ff.) no. 1037. R. C. Thompson, "An Assyrian Parallel to an Incident in the Story of Semiramis," *Iraq* 4 (1937) 35–43. H. Tadmor, see the literature for 18:1-7.

Concerning Ashdod: F. M. Cross and D. N. Freedman, "The Name of Ashdod," *BASOR* 175 (1964) 48–50. M. Weippert, "Archäologischer Jahresbericht," *ZDPV* 80 (1964) 155. M. Dothan, "Ashdod: A City of the Philistine Pentapolis," *Archaeology* 20 (1967) 178–186. Idem, "Ashdod: A City of the Philistine Pentapolis," *ADHL* (1967) 129–137. M. Dothan and D. N. Freedman, "Ashdod I," *ʿAtiqot* 7 (1967) 1–171. H. Tadmor, "Fragment of a Stele of Sargon II from the Excavations of Ashdod," *ErIsr* 8 (1967) 241–245. J. Kaplan, "The Stronghold of Yamani at Ashdod-Yam," *IEJ* 19 (1969) 137–149. M. Dothan, *Ashdod II/III, ʿAtiqot* 9–10 (1971). For further literature references, cf. E. K. Vogel, "Bibliography of the Holy Land," *HUCA* 42 (1971) 12.

Concerning the symbolic actions of the prophets: L. Suarez, "La realidad objectiva de las acciones simbolico-profeticas," *Illustración del clero* 36 (1943) 53–58, 132–136. A. van den Born, "De symbolische handelingen der oudtestamentische propheten," diss.: Nijmegen (1935). Idem, *Profetie metterdaad: Een studie over de symbolische handelingen der profeten* (1946). R. Criado, "Tienen eficaria real las acciones simbolicas de los Profetas?" *EstBib* 7 (1948) 167–217. G. Fohrer, "Die Gattung der Berichte über symbolische Handlungen der Propheten," *ZAW* 64 (1952) 101–120 (also BZAW 99 [1967] 92–112). Idem, *Die symbolischen Handlungen der Propheten,* ATANT 25 (1953).

Concerning אות: C. A. Keller, *Das Wort OTH* (1946). F. Stolz, "אוה," *THAT* I, 91–95. F. J. Helfmeyer, "אות," *TDOT* I, 167–188.

Isaiah 20:1-6

[**Literature update through 1979:** *Concerning the symbolic actions of the prophets:* E. R. Fraser, "Symbolic Acts of the Prophets," *Studia Biblica et Theologica* 4/2 (1974) 45–53.]

Text

20:1 [In the year in which the tartan[a] came to Ashdod, when Sargon,[b] the king of Assyria, sent him and he waged war against Ashdod and took it:[c]]
2 At that time Yahweh spoke through[a] Isaiah,[b] the son of Amoz:[c]
"Go, loose the sackcloth
    from your hips,
and take off your shoes[d]
    from upon your feet."[e]
This is exactly what he did, and he went about [f]naked and barefoot.[f]
3 Then Yahweh spoke:
"Just as my servant Isaiah[a] has gone about naked and barefoot, for three years,[b] as a sign and word of admonition concerning Egypt and Cush,
4 thus will the king of Assyria take away the prisoners out of Egypt and the deported ones[a] from Cush, young ones and old ones, bare and barefoot [and with uncovered vessel,[b] [c]the humiliation of Egypt[c]].
5 Thus they are horrified and shame themselves[a] because of Cush, their hope,[b]
and on account of Egypt, their honor.
6 [And the inhabitants of this coast will say [a]on that day[a]: "Behold, so it is with our hope,[b] that to which we fled[c] for help, that we might be saved from the king of Assyria! How shall *we* run away from there?"]

1a תרתן (Qᵃ: תורתן; see Dewey M. Beegle, *BASOR* 123 [1951] 28) is an Akkadian loanword (*tardinnu, tirtānu, tirtannu,* or something similar; see *RA* III, 245) and is normally considered to be a title for the field commander of the Assyrian army (cf. 2 Kings 18:17). Ungnad derives the word from *redû,* "follow after"; it refers to the second one, that is, the one most important after the king himself, actually a reference to the field marshall who held the highest rank. According to W. Baumgartner (FS O. Eissfeldt [1958] 27), with reference to Bezold and Deimel, it has an even older history, since that word itself is a loanword from Sumerian, though Wilhelm has suggested more recently that *tann-* or *tenn-* has a background as a Hurrian morpheme. In Akkadian cuneiform texts from Ugarit, however, *tartennu* is a title for the heir to a reigning prince; see J. Nougayrol, *Le palais royal d'Ugarit IV* (1956), texts 17.227, line 28 (p. 42); and 17.159, lines 23, 30 (p. 126), which is easy to explain on the basis of its connection with the root *redû;* cf. also Koschaker, 35f.
1b L reads סַרְגוֹן (with a *metheg*); compare this with Aquila, Theod σαραγων; by contrast, B reads סַרְגוֹן (with a *dagesh* in the ג; compare this with Sym σαργων (Gkᑫ); Gk: αρνα or σαρνα (Ziegler opts for reading this as Σαρναν instead!). According to Chrysostom, Aquila, Sym read σαργουν. Akkadian reads the name (according to Weisbach, Pauly-W 1A, 2, 2498) *šarru-kīnu,* "the king is lasting," pointing out that it was later recast into the form *šarru-ukīn,* "he (a certain deity) has chosen the king."
1c Qᵃ reads וילכודה instead of וילכדה (a more ancient stage in the development of the vowel letters).

284

2a The Gk translates ביד (by the hand of) with a simple πρὸς (to).

2b In this verse, as well as in v. 3, Qᵃ reads ישעיה instead of ישעיהו; on this, see *Isaiah 1–12*, pp. 4f. Syr adds *nbyᵓ* ([the] prophet) after ישעיהו (Isaiah).

2c בן־אמוץ (son of Amoz) is missing in the Gk, but is in Gk^B and in Gk^L.

2d Instead of ונעלך (and your shoe), the Qᵃ reading ונעליך (and your shoes) should be followed here; cf. Gk: τὰ σανδάλιά σου (your sandals); Sym, Theod (according to Codex Marchalianus and Eusebius): τα υποδηματα σου (your shoes); note also that נעלך (your shoe) is used in Josh. 5:15, though נעליך (your shoes) is used in Exod. 3:5.

2e L and other Hebrew MSS read the dual. However, some Hebrew MSS read רגלך ("your foot"; see the preceding note). In both cases, what has happened is that this way of writing the word without the ' reflects a defectively written dual form, not a singular.

2f–f ערום ויחף are accusatives describing a state or condition; see Joüon, *Gr* §126a.

3a Qᵃ reads ישעיה; see note 2b.

3b Based on the sense of the passage, the *athnach* should be placed under שנים (years) instead of under ויחף (and barefoot).

4a Qᵃ reads גולת (deported ones) instead of גלות (deported ones), which does not alter the meaning in any way, though גולה in the construct state is never used elsewhere in the OT.

4b חשופי (uncovered) has been explained as a form constructed on the basis of a pattern found in Aramaic, from the root חשף (strip, lay bare) (Knobel; Procksch, who refers to de Lagarde, *Nominalbildung*, 192; Donner, 114; Ges-Buhl), though no other example of the same form has been shown to exist. Ehrlich (*Randglossen* IV, 73) alters the text to read וחשפתי את (and I will strip off the . . .). The Gk (ἀνα-κεκαλυμμένους τὴν αἰσχύνην Αἰγύπτου, "those who have uncovered the shame of Egypt") does not provide a word that would directly translate שת (vessel), though it might be that the word was considered offensive or that it was a rarely used vocable (see, elsewhere, only 2 Sam. 10:4), and therefore that its meaning was not known. Yet the emendation provided by Ehrlich is inadequate, purely on the grounds that חשף (strip off) is never used elsewhere with ערוה (nakedness) as an object. The emendation suggested by Bruno, to read חָשִׂיף שֶׁה עֶרוֹתָם, which supposedly means: "he will pull for them the skin over the ears," is more of a fantasizing stab in the dark than a serious suggestion. No doubt, it simply should be read in the construct state as חֲשׂוּפֵי (stripped of) (Gray).

4c–c ערות מצרים (the humiliation of Egypt) has often been considered an explanatory gloss on שת (vessel) (Duhm, Buhl, Marti, Gray, Procksch, Fohrer, Donner, Kaiser); however, one might consider the possibility that חשופי שת (uncovered vessel) is also a later addition to the text; on this, see below, p. 294.

5a As often elsewhere, Qᵃ replaces the perfect consecutive ובשו (and they shall shame themselves) with the imperfect ויבושו (and they have shamed themselves).

5b מבט occurs only in this verse, in v. 6, and in Zech. 9:5: "that toward which one (greatly desiring help) would look." At this point, Qᵃ reads מבטחם, "their trust" (though it does not make this alteration in v. 6); on this, see Nötscher; Driver, 25. Although it had been conjectured long before the discovery of the Qumran texts that מבטח (confidence, trust) should be read in all three passages, מבט ([their] hope) should be considered the original reading, following the *lectio difficilior* rule. Isaiah is fond of using the related *hiphᶜil* הביט (look): 5:12; 8:22; 18:4; 22:8, 11.

6a–a ביום ההוא (on that day) is missing in the Gk. Many commentators are suspicious about whether the time designation is original, and, for this reason, it is often removed from the text; but it is frequently used by those who expanded the text of the book of Isaiah as a formula to introduce an addendum (see passages such as 19:16ff.). Since the entire v. 6 is a later addition (on this, see below, p. 297), it is to be left as is.

6b See above, note 5b.

6c For נסנו, "we fled," Qᵃ reads נסמך. This suggests that it intends to say: "that upon which one has supported oneself." That would make good sense, particularly since נוס (flee) has made the interpretation of the passage very difficult (see below, p. 297). However, the *niphʿal* of סמך (support oneself) is always accompanied by על (upon) in the OT.

Form

Within the context of the oracles against the foreign nations in the book of Isaiah, chap. 20 presents a type of material that is unique. It is a report of an unknown person about a symbolic action, concluding with a message from Yahweh that interprets the action. One also finds a report from an unidentified individual in 7:1-17, there within the framework of the memorial record that recounts the Syro-Ephraimitic War. One must also pursue the question about whether chap. 20 has been appropriated from a larger unit of material, because this section of material could be adapted so as to be used as a message against the Philistines. Gray thinks this might have been a fragment from a biography of Isaiah, while Eichrodt suggests that it might "possibly be a little book similar to that which we can still detect in chaps. 6–8." He thought of this possibility after pondering the questions raised by the way v. 2 fits into its context, leading one to suspect that the original textual form has been damaged in some way. According to v. 1 (cf. בעת ההיא, "at that time," in v. 2, which presupposes that the time period for the events in vv. 1 and 2 is the same), the command to go naked and barefoot would have been issued in the year that Ashdod fell. According to v. 3, however, Isaiah had already been going about in this condition for three years before Yahweh explained the reason for his command, which therefore would have come long after the fall of Ashdod; and, in spite of all this, v. 6 reports that the inhabitants of the Philistine territory still had to be warned, even after all that time, not to place confidence in Cush/Egypt. For this reason, scholars have generally concluded that v. 2 was inserted at a later time, by someone who wanted to describe the circumstances that surrounded the message from Yahweh, now recorded in vv. 3-6. If that is right, בעת ההיא (at that time) would have to be taken in a loose sense: at the time of the rebellion of Ashdod. If this suggestion is adopted, one would favor translating the text as a pluperfect (as, e.g., the Zürcher Bibel). However, v. 2 is essential for understanding what follows and has to be part of the original wording of the account. At the very time when such an extraordinary, indeed shocking, activity has begun to take place, as is related in this passage, it must be made clear that the prophet was not following a capricious course of action but was carrying out Yahweh's own injunction. Not only the content but also the form of this type of report, which describes a symbolic action, can hardly be complete if v. 2 is not included. One might compare this with passages such as Jer. 13:1ff.: "Thus said Yahweh to me, 'Go (הֲלֹוךְ) and buy yourself a linen loincloth, and put it on your loins. . . .' So I bought a loincloth according to the word of Yahweh, and put it on my loins. . . . Then the word of Yahweh came to me: . . . This evil people . . . shall be like this loincloth" (cf. also Jer. 18:1ff. or Hosea 3). The parallelism between this passage and Isaiah 20 is striking; this latter passage had to take the specifics of the actual situation into account in constructing the text. There are three sections that are all part of this genre: (1) a command to carry out a symbolic action; (2) a report about how this was accomplished; and (3) the meaning of the action (see Fohrer, *ZAW* 64 [1952] 103). If v. 2 belongs to the original text, however, then v. 1 must be treated as a secondary dating, first inserted at the beginning of the text at a later time, though this does not mean that the dating was pulled out of thin air (see 14:28); however, this also does not mean that בעת ההיא (at that time) is to be interpreted solely within the time frame indicated by v. 1. By its very nature, "at that time" would have been further identified by the original context of the story: at that time when some in Jerusalem mulled over the possibility that they should risk joining with the Philistines, more specifically, hazard joining with Ashdod to place their trust in Cush/Egypt, and thus quit being under the overlordship of Assyria. The redactor, who placed v. 1 at the beginning, thought wrongly that the command was issued at the time when Ashdod fell. That cannot be right: when Ashdod fell, there is no doubt that Isaiah would have quit his strange behavior.

There are also problems with the way that the material in v. 5 fits into the sequence of events in this section as it now stands. The verse gives every indication that it is basically a doublet to v. 6. Marti and Fohrer treat it as secondary, with Fohrer suggesting that its purpose is to expand on the phrase "the humiliation of Egypt," which had been added at the end of v. 4. The question about what is original is most difficult to answer because no mention is made of the intended subject in v. 5. On purely formal grounds, it would have to be the Egyptians and Cushites, in v. 4, but the content of the passage makes that impossible. Could it be that the "inhabitants of the coast" speak in v. 6? If that were true, why would ישׁב האי הזה (inhabitants of this coast) not already be mentioned in v. 5? Thus v. 5 seems to be a marginal gloss to v. 6, which was mistakenly made part of the original text. However, the other possibility must also be considered, that v. 5 might be speaking about the Judeans, more specifically, about those circles in Judah who had spoken favorably about taking part in the Ashdod rebellion. If one considers the motivation that can be detected for recording the genuine so-called oracles against the foreign nations in the book of Isaiah, this explanation is certainly plausible, if not indeed demanded: most of the time, Isaiah speaks about other peoples only because he wants to dispute Judah's political decisions or wants to make it harder for its leaders to make decisions that would lead to worse problems. Here, as well, he would want his actions, which were intended to symbolize the gloomy future in store for Cush and Egypt, to demonstrate how ludicrous it was to follow Judah's anti-Assyrian policy.

There is a clear and close parallel between this and what is stated in chaps. 18 and 19.

If v. 5 is part of the original text of the report, then there is still tension between it and v. 6, even if the interpretation that relates v. 5 to Judah is accepted. There are also other problems in interpreting this verse. "The statement that the inhabitants of the coast fled to the Egyptians for help in order to be delivered from the emperor is certainly ambiguous; in any case, it conflicts with the concluding question, about how they are to escape. For if they had in fact fled to Egypt, they would automatically have been affected by the occupation of Egyptian territory. But if they had done no more than to send petitions to Egypt, as hastily as if they were fleeing, it is strange that the Assyrians should attack first Egypt and then the Philistine cities" (Kaiser). Verse 6 must be a later addition and is to be attributed to a redactor, who took the transmitted account and recast it so that it would serve a new function, as a message directed toward a foreign people.

What remains then is that only vv. 2-5 belong to the original text, and the symbolic action has no other function than to warn Judah not to enter into an imprudent relationship with Egypt. One might suppose that the description has been taken from a larger context. It is certainly possible that other alterations to the original text were intentionally made during the course of the transmission of this section. These will be discussed in further detail as the individual verses are discussed (see below, pp. 291ff. and pp. 296f.).

Meter: Fohrer (BZAW 99, p. 97) suggests that there are four strophes, each with six short lines (in vv. 3, 4, and 6); the view expressed in his commentary is much the same; see also Lowth and Skinner. There is at least some evidence for the rhythm of poetic speech in vv. 3 and 4: עָרוֹם וְיָחֵף (naked and barefoot) — אוֹת וּמוֹפֵת (sign and word of admonition) — עַל־מִצְרַיִם וְעַל־כּוּשׁ (concerning Egypt and Cush) — אֶת־שְׁבִי מִצְרַיִם וְאֶת־גָּלוּת כּוּשׁ (the prisoners of Egypt and the deported ones from Cush) — נְעָרִים וּזְקֵנִים (young ones and old ones) — עָרוֹם וְיָחֵף (bare and barefoot). As a whole, however, the verse cannot be divided metrically, which indicates that the message from Yahweh has not come down to us intact. By contrast, the closing verse, v. 5, is a four-stress + four-stress bicolon, highlighting the gravity of what it has to say: וְחַתּוּ וָבֹשׁוּ מִכּוּשׁ מַבָּטָם וּמִן מִצְרַיִם תִּפְאַרְתָּם (Thus they are horrified and shame themselves because of Cush, their hope, and on account of Egypt, their honor). There is no point in trying to read v. 6 metrically.

Setting

This passage, just as that in 14:28-32 and the call narrative in chap. 6, is dated specifically. It is true that analysis has shown that it is likely that the sentence has been inserted as part of a later redaction and is not precisely correct concerning the date that it furnishes. It is evident, however, that this material is to be understood within the context of the time when Ashdod rebelled.

As is true elsewhere, Kaiser has expressed an opinion about this passage that goes against the mainstream of interpretation. Since there was no invasion of Egypt in the year 711, the prophet would have been disappointed that his expectations had not come true. Questions about whether Isaiah would have gone about naked for three years (or, at the very least, fourteen months, if one would presume that the rebellion began at the end of the first year and that it was brought to a halt in the beginning of the third year) are raised, simply if one considers climatic changes. In addition, the passage deals apparently not only with a military defeat but also with an invasion of Egypt and a deportation carried out on a large scale. One might date this to the time of Esarhaddon's campaigns against Egypt—if one does not opt for concluding that this passage was formulated in the postexilic era. The first argument, namely, that the proclamation was never fulfilled, does not carry any weight. As is well known, at many other times prophets were "disappointed," if one measures the predictions on the basis of the bare details of what actually happened (on this, see E. Jenni, *Die politischen Voraussagen der Propheten* [1956] 79–82). Furthermore, the decisive point being made, that one could not rely on or trust in Cush/Egypt, in no way missed the mark. As far as we are concerned, even though we find the symbolic action as presented to be unsettling, we must still watch out that we do not judge the phenomenon of prophetic activity on the basis of our own standards of whether this could have taken place. One cannot help but get the impression that the original account was made more grotesque by the additional note that this lasted "for three years" (on this, see below, pp. 294f.). In closing, concerning the third argument, one must note that Egypt was certainly conquered from time to time, but the relationship between Judah and Cush/Egypt that is assumed in chap. 20 never happened the same way again. There is no doubt that this passage comes from the time when the questionable decision was being considered by Judah and Philistia, that they would declare their independence from Assyria, as is also the case in 14:28-32.

We do have good information about the historical events that took place during that time, as they are recorded in Sargon's inscriptions (on this, see Tadmor, 79ff.), especially on the Display Inscription (see H. Winckler, I, 96ff.; II, 30ff.; translations are in *AOT* 350ff.; *ANET* 286; *TGI*[2] no. 35). Azuri, the king of Ashdod, had proved himself to be unreliable and was deposed by Sargon in favor of his brother Ahimiti. However, this family member did not prove himself capable of staying in control, and the people of Ashdod replaced him with a certain Ia-ma-ni, "who did not have any claim to the throne," usually identified today as an Ionian/Greek (Hebrew: יון; for a different view, see Tadmor, 80, note 217). Sargon could not tolerate such an act of insubordination; infuriated, he intervened immediately with his own standing army (see above, pp. 213, 216). Ia-ma-ni did not even wait for it to reach the point of open war, but fled into the border region of Muṣuri (which, in spite of the contrary opinion that this refers to an Arabian territory, refers to Egypt), "which belongs (now) to Ethiopia [Meluḫḫu]—and his (hiding) place could not be detected. I besieged (and) conquered the cities Ashdod, Gath [*Gi-im-tu*], Asdudimmu" (*ANET* 286) (Asdudimmu is certainly *ʾašdod-yam*, Ashdod-by-the-Sea, probably to be identified as *mīnet el-qalʿa*, known as Ἄζωτος Πάραλος on the Madeba Map; see M. Weippert, *ZDPV* 80 [1964] 155; Honigmann, *RLA* I, 167; and J. Kaplan). The city was completely plundered and its territory was placed under direct Assyrian control.

Sargon saw to it that the population was hauled off to Assyria while exiles from other parts of the realm were resettled in this region. This impressive decision by Sargon, to put in a quick appearance, made a deep impression on the king from Meluḫḫa: "The awe-inspiring glamor of my kingship blinded him and terror overcame him. He threw him (i.e. the Greek [*Ia-ma-ni*]) in fetters, shackles and iron bands, and they brought him to Assyria" (*ANET* 286). Sargon's report leaves one with the impression that he took this personally and that he himself went into the battlefield against Ashdod. However, Isa. 20:1 speaks of the tartan, his field commander, which is most likely correct; more than once the Assyrian kings are known to have taken for themselves the glory of the accomplishments of those who served under them. The action against little Ashdod was too insignificant for him to have led the expedition personally. Tadmor (79, note 208) believes that he can garner enough information from other texts to conclude that Sargon stayed at home in Assyria during the year of the campaign against Ashdod, because it was important for him to be present to supervise the construction of his new residence, *dūr-šarrukīn*. Furthermore, the campaign would have had to have already taken place in 712, not, as is usually presumed, in 711 (see Tadmor, 79). The king of Meluḫḫa, mentioned by Sargon, would have had to have been Shabaka (see above, pp. 212f.).

Apparently, Judah would have also been affected by these events. According to a broken prism (Winckler I, 186ff.; *ANET* 287), Ia-ma-ni had sent gifts not only to pay homage to the pharaoh of Egypt, "a potentate, incapable to save them," but additionally to a large number of countries, Judah included, to incite revolt (see above, p. 216). Sargon does not tell us how successful Ashdod was in Jerusalem, and the OT does not report on the matter either. It is generally supposed that Judah had distanced itself from that relationship in sufficient time. It would seem that Isaiah's "sign" was not performed without some effect.

Tadmor (80) reexamined a damaged text that Winckler had already published (*Altorientalische Forschungen* 2, 570). The fragment mentions a campaign led by an unnamed Assyrian king against a city named *azaqā*, which was extraordinarily well situated and extremely well fortified so as to be able to defend itself. In spite of all this, the attempt to conquer it was successful and the city was completely plundered. Since that text immediately goes on to mention a march against the Philistines, Tadmor suggests that this city ought to be sought in the vicinity of Philistia, which would lead to this *azaqā* being identified with the biblical Azekah (= *tell zakarīye*). In addition, he believes he can make a strong case for the unnamed Assyrian king who led this strike being none other than Sargon, who thus would have also conquered the Judean city of Azekah when he went on his campaign against Ashdod, even though he would not have advanced inland to make a direct assault against Judah. However, this interpretation of the fragment, which unfortunately is badly damaged, is constructed on the basis of too much guesswork for one to accept it without superimposing a huge question mark on the whole effort. It is always possible that a document will be found some day that will shed more light on the specifics of Judah's involvement in the Philistine rebellion of 713/712, which might explain just how much reason the inhabitants of Jerusalem would have had for holding their breath when Sargon's troops began to put down the Philistine revolt—which would clarify why Isaiah went to such great extremes in trying to keep Judah from getting involved in the matter.

In any case, chap. 20 fits very well into the events that surrounded Ashdod's rebellion. Yet when one examines the description of these events carefully, certain observations point to this report being somewhat different from Isaiah's own way of speaking. The message from Yahweh in v. 3 speaks of "my servant, Isaiah," even though one would have anticipated that Yahweh would have addressed the prophet as "you," as in 6:7ff.; 7:3f.; and 8:1f. According to the way v. 3 is presently written, one would have to assume that Yahweh was speaking to an unknown prophet *about* Isaiah. In fact, there is a "you" in v. 2, but why in that verse does it say that Yahweh spoke ביד ישעיהו (through [or: by the hand of] Isaiah) and not simply that he spoke *to* him? Most importantly: authentic messages of Isaiah are consistently transmitted in metrical form, though we were able to show above that one is hard-pressed to find evidence here for a metrical structure. The vocabulary itself does not appear that different from what Isaiah would use. On אות ומופת (sign and word of admonition), see 8:18; on חתת (be horrified), see 7:8; 30:31; 31:4; on בוש מן (shame themselves because of), see 1:29. מבט (hope), which occurs elsewhere only in Zech. 9:5, and is not known to have been used after that time, might easily be understood as a term that Isaiah could use (see above, p. 286).

This study results in the following: the basic form of chap. 20 is that of a report from an unknown individual, which follows the usual format for describing a symbolic action of Isaiah and its meaning. It must come from an author who was well informed, but one who turned Isaiah's message from Yahweh into a prose form and who likely modified certain aspects of the material in some other ways that we can no longer identify with confidence. The report from this unknown individual was "reworked" still later by another (or several) redactor(s), taking on thereby the form of an oracle against a nation, in this case, the Philistines.

Commentary

[20:1] Enough has already been said about v. 1 in the discussion of the setting concerning the dating and historical situation behind v. 1. One can compare the phraseology בשנת בא תרתן אשדודה (In the year in which the tartan came to Ashdod) with the corresponding form for reporting dates in 6:1 and 14:28 (there are no other parallels in the OT). Concerning תרתן (tartan) (without the article), see above, textual note 1a. Thompson has expressed the opinion that the tartan mentioned here could have been a man named Zer-Ibni (see R. F. Harper, *Assyrian and Babylonian Letters* [1892ff.] no. 1073), a close friend of Sargon. The passage in 2 Kings 18:17 (though not its parallel passage in Isa. 36:2) mentions the tartan of Sennacherib.

Ashdod, along with Ashkelon, Gaza, Ekron, and Gath, is one of the five cities of the Philistine pentapolis. In Assyrian, the city is given the name *asdudu;* in Late Babylonian, it is *ašdudu;* in Ugarit, the city appears in Babylonian cuneiform with the name *ašdadi;* also, on an Egyptian list of names from the early eleventh century, it is transcribed as *ỉsdd,* which would lead one to conclude that the name would go back to an older Canaanite form *ʾatdādu;* Ugaritic cuneiform uses a gentilic that derives from the name of the city, *aḏḏy.* It is possible that the name should be connected with Old Akkadian *šadādu,* "to measure" (on this, see Cross and Freedman, 48–50). The ancient city of Ashdod was situated on what is now an Arab village, *isdūd (esdūd),* approximately 7 km. south-southeast of the present city *ʾašdod.* Excavation of the site began in 1962, resulting in information that it had been settled since the Early Bronze Age, which means it was there long before the Philistine immigration (ca. 1180). In the middle of the thirteenth century, the Late Bronze Age settlement came to an abrupt end. Whether that was the result of being conquered by Israelites cannot be determined on archaeological grounds. But there are clear indications that the Philistines took control of it during the twelfth century and eleventh century. Toward the end of the eighth century, the city once again suffered massive destruction, with the inhabitants being murdered and later laid to rest together in mass graves. There is every reason to believe that these events followed Sargon's campaign against Ashdod. During the 1963 season of digging, three fragments of a basalt stele were discovered that spoke of Sargon's victories (the only evidence of this type that we possess to give witness to the Assyrian presence in Palestine). It must have been erected sometime between 712 and 705, and it served as the base for an obelisk or a statue of the Assyrian ruler (see Freedman, *BA* 26 [1963] 138; for further literature, see above). The territory of the Philistines proved itself to be a most difficult buffer zone for the Assyrians, who needed to penetrate it before pressing on into Egypt. In the long run, however, all resistance was pointless. The Philistines had apparently been just as remiss as were many circles in Israel/Judah when it came to taking into account the radical changes in the political landscape in the Near East that developed after Tiglath-Pileser made inroads into Syria-Palestine. The period in world history in which the small states in this region—among them Israel as well—could profit from the weakness among the foreign powers or, whenever the situation presented itself, could play off the forces stationed along the Nile against those in Mesopotamia, had at last come to an end.

[20:2] Verse 2 provides the reason why Isaiah engaged in his shocking behavior: Yahweh had commanded it. The formula . . . דבר (יהוה) ביד ([Yahweh] spoke by the hand of . . .) is used here in a most clumsy way. It is normally used only when describing the circumstances in which the prophet served as a mediator, but is not used in cases, like this one, when he is addressed, being given a direct message from God. Since we have evidence in 1 Kings 12:15 (see also Exod. 9:35 and 1 Sam. 28:17), one can hardly maintain that this formula is first used only in later times. However, the way it is used here betrays the opinion that the prophet's activity is perceived as if he merely plays the role of being some apparatus that receives instructions sent out by the deity.

One cannot help but notice that Isaiah is once again identified here (see 1:1; 2:1; 13:1) as the son of Amoz, betraying at the same time the fact that literary activity (and zeal to establish a link with Isaiah) has now begun. Concerning the name of the father, see *Isaiah 1–12,* p. 5. One might note that the name has also been found in written form (though certainly not referring to the same person) on a piece of pottery from *tell el-qāḍi,* the OT city of Dan (A. Biran, *BA* 37 [1974] 50).

The interpretation of the entire section depends very much on what one understands שׂק to mean, that which Isaiah is to "open" from his loins, i.e., that which he is to lay aside (פהה, "take off," as the opposite of חגר, "put on," in 1 Kings 20:11; concerning אזר, "clothe, gird," see Ps. 30:12). This word seems to be an Akkadian loanword, which has also found its way into Greek (σάκκος = "rough cloth made of hair, especially goat's hair"; derived sense: "any object that is manufactured using this type of cloth"). For most of the passages, KBL gives the meaning "loin-covering," adding the note: "worn upon the naked body around the hips"; Ges-Buhl: "a piece of material made of hair, worn around the hips"; a similar meaning is given by W. Hönig, *Die Bekleidung des Hebräers* [1957] 102–109. But it is not easy to be satisfied with this translation for all the occurrences. It is said not only that one girds oneself around with שׂק, but also that one can clothe oneself with such material (לבשׁ, "wear," Ps. 35:13; 69:12; Esther 4:1f.; Jonah 3:5), one can cover oneself with one (כסה *hithpaʿel*, 2 Kings 19:1f. = Isa. 37:1f.; Jonah 3:8), and one can sleep in one (1 Kings 21:27). One can lie down in sackcloth and ashes; one spreads the שׂק out (2 Sam. 21:10). The imagery in Isa. 50:3b ("and [I] make שׂק [sackcloth] their [the heavens] covering") could hardly be used if the term referred only to a loincloth. Maybe Fohrer is right (*BHH* 1638) when he suggests: "The form of the sack . . . was . . . apparently different, depending on the time period and gender. At times, one must assume it refers to an outer garment with holes for head and arms, which would be wrapped around to cover the whole body, . . . at other times, it was a piece of cloth of the type that would be used as a loincloth, which one would bind on." In any case, one would do well not to prejudice the issue in advance by translating this as "loincloth," or something similar, but ought to stay with the word "sackcloth" in English, which would in principle be based on the present and similar passages, suggesting essentially that this is a simple cloak, roughly woven, usually made of the hair of black goats.

Isaiah was also supposed to take off his shoes/sandals. Concerning נעל (shoe), see *Isaiah 1–12*, p. 240. That is another sign of mourning or abasement. In general, footwear belonged to the traditional clothing worn by an Israelite male. When mourning, however, one would forgo wearing them (Ezek. 24:17, 23), a practice also followed even by a king (2 Sam. 15:30). When Hezekiah was buried, a tradition reports that the entire group of mourners went barefoot (*Lam. Rab.* 24).

If one would have worn the שׂק (sackcloth) on the naked body, then the human being who "opened" it would have been naked in the fullest sense of the word. Said in another way: if ערום refers to being completely unclothed, then one would have to understand שׂק (sackcloth) as a specific reference to a loincloth. Neither of these conclusions is likely. One ought not too quickly counter with the argument that complete nudity would have clashed with normal sensitivities; we know little about these matters and are not able to use such assumptions when deciding how much freedom one would have been ready to grant a prophet in such circumstances. That some boundaries were not to be transgressed is shown by 2 Sam. 6:20. Even the objection raised by Kaiser, that the climatic conditions in Jerusalem would not have permitted complete nakedness over a longer period of time, has some merit, though he is not justified in drawing from this the conclusion that this passage speaks about a legendary Isaiah figure, rather than about the historical person. One also notes that the Greek equivalent γυμνός means not only "naked" but also "lightly (only with undergarments) clothed." A number of OT passages suggest this meaning for עָרוֹם: Isa. 58:7; Job 22:6; 24:7, 10. In addition, David, who is scolded by Michal because he has stripped himself of clothing, was not naked but had girded himself with a linen ephod (2 Sam. 6:14). The most important objection to taking this term to mean complete nakedness is raised by the meaning that this symbolic action is to convey. Isaiah's behavior is not motivated in the same way as was Saul's, who, having come into the company of the prophets, tore his clothing from his body while in an ecstatic trance (1 Sam. 19:24). Isaiah's purpose was to portray the way the Cushites and Egyptians would have to travel on foot into exile. One might think of such depictions as the naked prisoners on the ivory plaques from Megiddo (*ANEP* no. 332; cf. also *AOB*² no. 128), though those who were deported during the Assyrian era are not portrayed as being without any clothing (see how prisoners are represented after Tiglath-Pileser's troops conquered Astartu in *ANEP* no. 366 and cf. *AOB*² no. 141). Now it is said that the Egyptians are to go into exile חֲשׂוּפַי שֵׁת (with uncovered vessel). But then it would also have to have been said that Isaiah went around with a חֲשׂוּף שֵׁת (uncovered vessel) as well. חֲשׂוּפַי שֵׁת (uncovered vessel), as also the following phrase עֶרְוַת מִצְרָיִם (the humiliation of Egypt), is an addition in that verse, an addition furnished by a reader who was not satisfied with the predicted degradation of Egypt. But how did Isaiah come to wear sackcloth? Some explain that this would have been the typical clothing for a prophet (Kissane, Ziegler, Eichrodt, et al.), and some refer to 2 Kings 1:8, which identifies Elijah as an אִישׁ בַּעַל שֵׂעָר, "a man clothed with a pelt" (NRSV: a hairy man, with a leather belt around his waist); or, in addition, Zech. 13:4, according to which the prophet wore an אַדֶּרֶת, a "pelt coat" (NRSV: hairy mantle); thus Duhm and Marti. However, a שַׂק could hardly be designated as an אַדֶּרֶת (pelt coat, hairy mantle), and we have no information to suggest that the writing prophets would have demonstrated their claim to be among those who were to proclaim the message of Yahweh in that they wore a unique costume. In reality, we cannot say for sure why Isaiah wore the שַׂק (sackcloth); it is possible that he did so because he wanted to give expression to his mourning about the future destiny of Judah (or the Philistines?). Taking off the sackcloth would have to be understood as a way to elevate, still another notch, his desire to depict this mourning, in order to prevent Judah from going off on such political adventures. If it is correct, as has been suggested, that chap. 20 was originally part of a larger complex of material, it could be that the reason for wearing the sackcloth would have been mentioned there.

[20:3] The prophet receives the command and carries it out. This is certainly proper and has parallels with other symbolic actions of the prophets. According to what has been mentioned, this would not have involved being completely naked, and the "three years" would not have covered a full three years either (see above, p. 289). It is also not said that he would have gone about "naked" all the time and everywhere; it would be enough to presume that he did this from time to time, in particular circumstances. One must add, however, that there is also no reason to consider that this behavior was only legendary and never happened. The sign was to be so grotesque that no one could have missed the point. The symbolic actions that Ezekiel was to carry out were no less strange, such as when he was to bake his bread using human excrement or, being granted a dispensation, by using cow dung (4:12ff.), or to lie thirty days on his left side in order to bear the burden of Israel's guilt and then forty days on his right side because of the guilt of Judah (4:4ff.). The only point that remains difficult to understand is that the meaning of this action would have first come to him after he had been going about naked for the "three years." If one were to go about "naked" for three years without being able to say what it was supposed to mean, that would have made him into a comical figure. To speak of forced actions, which a person feels an inner compulsion to carry out, without knowing the reason why (G. Hölscher, *Die Profeten* [1914] 30), simply will not do. But it has already been demonstrated above that the message from Yahweh to Isaiah in v. 3 that is to explain the meaning of the action does not completely correspond to what really happened. Undoubtedly, the message that explained the reason would have come to Isaiah at the beginning of the rebellion and might have been phrased something such as: "As you go about naked and barefoot as a sign and omen . . . thus. . . ." One might suppose that the length of time "for three years" was also first inserted by the redactor, who knew how long it took for these events to unfold.

Isaiah is identified here as an עבד (servant) of Yahweh. That is unique. Eliakim is entitled a "servant of Yahweh" according to 22:20, called to be head over the palace. Without a doubt, Isaiah would not have called himself an עבד יהוה (servant of Yahweh). However, it is clear from 1 Kings 18:36; 2 Kings 9:7; 10:10 (Elijah); 1 Kings 14:18; 15:29 (Ahijah of Shiloh); 2 Kings 14:25 (Jonah ben Amittai), and Amos 3:7 (on this, see H. W. Wolff, BK XIV/2, 218 [Engl: *Joel and Amos,* 181]) that people considered the prophets to be servants of Yahweh, though these passages, with the exception of 1 Kings 18:36, belong to the deuteronomistic reworking of the text. Whether Deutero-Isaiah would have thought of himself as an עבד יהוה (servant of Yahweh) is obviously related to the interpretation of the servant of God songs, but in any case the עבד יהוה (servant of Yahweh) refers basically to one who functions as a prophet. One would hardly presume that designating Isaiah as an עבד (servant) in this present passage would make it "deuteronomistic"; it more likely demonstrates the opposite, that the deuteronomistic vocabulary had a precedent. In any case, it is noteworthy that the disciple of Isaiah who is at work here found it appropriate to use the title עבד (servant) when he recorded the story about how his master was sent to do this. The prophet is Yahweh's servant, because he had the job of carrying out whatever his own master assigned him. The analogy between this and the function of the "servant" of a king is unmistakable.

Isaiah's behavior was to be an אות (sign) and a מופת (word of admonition) about Egypt and Cush. The symbolic actions of the prophets are rooted originally in magical practice (cf. Fohrer, ATANT 25, 70ff.). The signs "have magical power; they do not only depict what will happen in the future, but they also force it to take place" (Keller, 55). For example, when the pharaoh, according to the so-called Execration Texts, smashes the image of an enemy king or a vessel on which the name of an enemy city had been inscribed, he would assure his domination thereby as well as the success of future military ventures; by means of the action that released these magical powers, he set these events in motion. In a state treaty between *bar-gaʾyā* of *ktk* and *matīʿel* of Arpad, among other threats, the last one reads: "[And the same way thi]s (?) [will be stripped naked], in the same way the wives of *matīʿel* and the wives of his descendants and the wives of his great ones shall be stripped naked!" (see *KAI* 222A:37ff.). In the ritual connected with concluding the treaty, wax figures that depict the wives are apparently "stripped naked," which would set in motion the corresponding disaster for the wives of the rebels in case the treaty were broken.

The symbolic actions are used as signs that aid in the proclamation; they have no additional meaning beyond that of a signal which attracts attention (cf. the names of Isaiah's children, 8:18, or Jeremiah, when he carries a yoke, Jeremiah 27). Yet the translation "sign" is chosen only as a last resort; in the *signum*, the event that is intended is somehow present as well; this sign underscores that this message corresponds to reality.

[20:4] Finally, with v. 4, explicit mention is made about what Isaiah is to proclaim via his odd behavior: Egyptians and Cushites are going into exile. It is not said that virtually all of them are going (so Kaiser), and it is certainly also not intended—even when considered separately from the fact that the Assyrians never deported entire peoples. But it is clearly presumed that Assyria would conquer Egypt/Cush. Since the Ethiopian Shabaku had himself conquered Egypt, about 715 (on this, see above, pp. 212f.), it is proper that Egypt would not be mentioned alone. What is more surprising is that Cush and Egypt are mentioned together as if they were two separate national entities, whereas Cush, in chap. 18, and Egypt, in chap. 19, each appears alone. (In addition, one notes that Egypt is mentioned before Cush in vv. 3 and 4; however, in v. 5 Cush is placed first.) One could certainly conclude that, at the time when this message went forth, the people in Jerusalem were not yet clear about who was actually in control in Egypt. In any case: if Egypt were affected, Cush would have suffered as well; the reverse would also have been true.

[20:5] In light of the downfall of Cush/Egypt, which seemed to have been such a mighty people, those who were in Jerusalem would be shaken to the core (concerning חתת, "horrified," see *Isaiah 1–12*, p. 352; on בוש, "shame themselves," ibid., p. 77). The whole world would fall apart for those who were so confident that they could find support from those who were in power on the Nile. One was very proud (תפארת!, "honor!") to have a renowned ally such as Egypt, without noticing that those who were in power on the Nile would treat the little states in Syria-Palestine as good friends only as long as they would serve their own purposes by being willing to be sent to the Assyrian front. For Judah, its real honor could only be Yahweh; to look toward Egypt in pride was just as idiotic and disastrous as when "the drunkards of Ephraim" praised themselves (28:1-4).

It would be tempting to read מבטחם (their confidence) with Q^a instead of מבטם (their hope) (see above, textual note 5b); this would provide a perfect contrast to 30:15, according to which those who בטחה (trust) in Yahweh are reminded that he is "your strength." In light of 5:12 and 22:11b, however, מבטם (their hope) is also appropriate, where what is to be done is commanded clearly: one must look to (הביט) Yahweh, to his deeds, if one does not want to come to a ruinous end. It is also stated in Zech. 9:5 that one suffers shipwreck if one places confidence in earthly powers.

[20:6] The message comes to an end with v. 5 (on this, see above, p. 287). Verse 6 is an addition, by means of which the material is recast to become a message addressed to the inhabitants of the coastlands. Burney believes he can show that ישב האי הזה (inhabitants of this coast) refers to the residents of Cyprus or even a specific Cypriot (namely, Ia-ma-ni). According to the context, however, the ישב האי (inhabitants of the coast) have to be the Philistines, even though the OT never refers to their territory as an אי (coast). In 23:2, 6, the ישבי אי (inhabitants of the coast) are the Phoenicians; both Jer. 2:10 and Ezek. 27:6 speak of the איי כתים (coasts of Cyprus [Kittim]); Jer. 47:4 of אי כפתור (coastland of Caphtor). Since אי means simply "coastal region," ישב האי (inhabitants of the coastland) is an acceptable way to designate the area. But it could be that the expander used the vague "residents of the shore" on purpose, instead of "Philistines" (or "inhabitants of Ashdod," or something similar). That would have made it possible to redirect the message so that it would apply to a completely new situation. In addition, one cannot be sure that the expander was actually thinking of the historical Assyria; אשור (Assyria) is used elsewhere as a pseudonym for a subsequent world power.

Purpose and Thrust

This section gives further evidence for the intensity and consistency with which Isaiah attempted to protect Israel from going down the path of destruction by making peace treaties with world powers. In this specific case, it deals with Cush/Egypt, just as is the case in chaps. 18f. Yet one must also keep in mind that Isaiah issued just as sharp a warning, during the Syro-Ephraimitic War, counseling Israel not to seek the support of Assyria. For Isaiah, the issue is not about being friends or enemies with Egypt, but about the ongoing stance that Israel continually had to maintain as the people of Yahweh.

Military and political events did not directly give Isaiah the impetus to speak; at this time, Egypt/Cush had not yet had to endure an invasion of Assyrian troops. Still, his warning was certainly appropriate: Egypt had in fact shown itself to be a "broken reed of a staff, which will pierce the hand of anyone who leans on it" (36:6). In the final analysis, Isaiah was not interested in issuing a political assessment, but rather wanted Israel to recognize that Yahweh alone is its הפארת (honor) and its מבט (hope), the "place" toward which it ought to orient itself. Because of this, it is no real μετάβασις εἰς ἄλλο γένος (transition from one subject to another) when the expanders make use of Isaiah's message, even though the situation would now have been radically altered. There was no other מבט (hope), to which one could turn to look for help, except Yahweh. What is new is that, according to their way of thinking, "on that day" the "inhabitants of the coast" would also see that trust in earthly powers always leads to the helplessness and hopelessness of death. For all times and for all peoples there is only one hope: turning decisively to "Yahweh of Hosts, who dwells on Mount Zion." That Isaiah himself, by going about naked and barefoot, had witnessed to Israel—"for three years"—shows once again how this situation must have seemed to him to be most dangerous, how intensively he must have fought to be given a hearing, and how ready he was to act with resolve with his life on the line to plead on behalf of his God.

Isaiah 21:1-10

The Fall of Babylon

Literature

Concerning the text: F. Buhl, "Jesaja 21, 6-10," *ZAW* 8 (1888) 157–164. P. Lohmann, "Die anonymen Prophetien gegen Babel aus der Zeit des Exils," diss., Rostock (1910) 61. P. Dhorme, "Le désert de la mer (Isaïe, XXI)," *RB* 31 (1922) 403–406. H. Torczyner, "Biblische Kleinprobleme II. 3. Ein verkannter Volksname in der Bibel," *MGWJ* 75 (1931) 15–17. J. Carmignac, "Six passages d'Isaïe éclairés par Qumrân," FS H. Bardtke (1968) 37–46, esp. 43.

Concerning general background: W. H. Cobb, "Isaiah xxi. 1-10 reëxamined," *JBL* 17 (1898) 40–61. W. E. Barnes, "A Fresh Interpretation of Isaiah XXI 1-10," *JTS* 1 (1900) 583–592. P. Lohmann, "Zur strophischen Gliederung von Jes 21:1-10," *ZAW* 33 (1913) 262–264; see also idem, *ZAW* 32 (1912) 49f. Ch. Boutflower, "Isaiah XXI in the Light of Assyrian History," *JTS* 14 (1913) 501–515. E. Sievers, "Zu Jesaja 21:1-10," *BZAW* 41 (1925) 262–265. R. B. Y. Scott, "Isaiah XXI 1-10: The Inside of a Prophet's Mind," *VT* 2 (1952) 278–282. K. Galling, "Jesaja 21 im Lichte der neuen Nabonidtexte," FS A. Weiser (1963) 49–62.

Concerning history: S. Smith, *Babylonian Historical Texts Relating to the Capture and Downfall of Babylon* (1924). F. W. König, "Geschichte Elams," AO 29/4 (1931) 1–38, esp. 23; cf. also idem, *RA* II, 336–338. H. H. von der Osten, *Die Welt der Perser* (1956). H. Schmökel, "Keilschriftforschung und alte Geschichte Vorderasiens," *HdO* III, 2 (1957). W. Hinz, *Das Reich Elam* (1964).

Concerning visionary experiences: G. Hölscher, *Die Profeten: Untersuchungen zur Religionsgeschichte Israels* (1914) 70–72. J. Hänel, *Das Erkennen Gottes bei den Schriftpropheten* (1923). I. Seierstad, *Die Offenbarungserlebnisse der Propheten Amos, Jesaja und Jeremia* (1946). M. Eliade, *Shamanism: Archaic Techniques of Ecstasy* (1964). E. Benz, *Die Vision, Erfahrungsformen und Bilderwelt* (1969). G. Schüttler, *Das mystisch-ekstatische Erlebnis: Systematische Darstellung der Phänomenologie und des psychopathologischen Aufbaus* (1968).

Concerning the shield: H. Droysen, *Heerwesen und Kriegführung der Griechen* (1889) 12f. I. Benzinger, *Hebräische Archäologie* (1907²). H. Bonnet, *Die Waffen der Völker des Alten Orients* (1926) 181–201. R. de Vaux, *Ancient Israel: Its Life and Institutions* (1961) 244f. E. Salonen, *Die Waffen der alten Mesopotamier,* SOr (1965).

[Literature update through 1979: *Concerning the text:* G. Wilhelmi, "צפה הצפית Polster in Babel? Eine Überlegung zu Jesaja 21, 5 und 8," *VT* 25 (1975) 121–123.

Concerning general background: D. R. Hillers, "A Convention in Hebrew Literature: The Reaction to Bad News," *ZAW* 77 (1965) 86–90.]

Text

21:1 [Verdict[a] "[b]'from the desert'[b]"]
  [c]Like storm winds,[c]
    which sweep away[d] through the southland,[e]
  it comes[f] out of the desert,
    out of a horrifying[g] land;
2 [a]a harsh vision[a]
    was made known to me.[b]

                    * * * *

  With cunning the cunning one acts,
    and the devastator devastates.
  [c]"Up, Elam!
    Close up the (siege-)enclosure, Media![c]
  All of its 'arrogance'[d]
    I will shut down."[e]

                    * * * *

3 Therefore my hips are
    jerked about throughout with cramps,
  pains have seized me,
    as pains of a woman who is giving birth.
  Because of the hearing,[a] I am (thoroughly) agitated,
    because of the seeing,[a] aghast.
4 [a]My heart is bewildered,[a]
    dread has seized me.
  The evening twilight[b] [or: hours] for pleasure,
    he has made for me into horror.

                    * * * *

5 Someone makes preparations for the table,[a]
    [b]spreads out the cushions,[b]
    [c]someone eats and drinks.[c]
  "Up, you commanders!
    anoint[d] the shield!"

                    * * * *

6 Indeed, thus spoke the Lord[a] to me:
  [b]"Go, post the lookout![b]
  He is to report[c] what[d] he sees!
7 And if he sees war chariots,
    teams[a] of horses,
  [b]a procession of donkeys,
    a procession of camels,[b]
  then he should keenly observe,
    [c]with utmost attentiveness[d][c] he is to pay attention!"

                    * * * *

8 Then 'the seer'[a] called out:
  "On watch,[b] O Lord,
    I[c] stood
    without a break during the day,

and at my post
I kept watch
all the night long.[d]
9 And behold, there it came:
a procession of men,[a]
teams of stallions."

* * * *

Then one commenced[b] and spoke:
"Fallen,
fallen[c] is Babylon,
and all depictions[d] of its gods
'are' smashed[e] on the ground."
10 [a]"You, my thrashed (people),
my threshing floor son!"[a]

* * * *

What I have heard [b][from Yahweh of Hosts, the God of Israel],[b]
I have announced it to you.

1a Concerning translating משׂא as "verdict," see above, pp. 1f.

1b–b The content of the passage treats 21:1-10 as a message about Babylon; it is most unusual to find the phrase מדבר־ים (wilderness of the sea) serving to describe the משׂא (verdict) more explicitly. The truth of the matter is that Babylon is not situated in a wilderness of the sea, not even in a desert that borders on the sea. In spite of this, some have still tried to find a way to explain מדבר־ים (wilderness of the sea) as a reference to Babylon. For example, Qimḥi suggests that מדבר refers to the steppe between Media/Persia and Babylon and ים means "west." This would mean that the author would have had to have been at home in the territory of Media/Persia. Or Gesenius: מדבר־ים means "level ground by the sea," with "sea" referring to the Euphrates in this case. Solutions based on such suggestions are not satisfactory. Nonetheless, it is worth noting that southern Babylonia is referred to in Akkadian as *māt tāmti(m)*, "sea land" (noted already by Delitzsch; see also Dhorme; and more recently Auvray, and Erlandsson, 82; see above, p. 1). However, מדבר (desert) is not used to refer to a "land, country." For this reason, there is no way that this (as suggested by Young) could refer simply to the flat plain on which Babylon is situated, through which the Euphrates flows. If one wants to stay with the MT, then one might consider this as a reference to "the Syrian-Arabian desert that is located to the west of the lower Euphrates valley" (through which one travels to get to the sea) (so Fohrer) or to the desert southeast of Babylon, on the Persian Gulf (so Dillmann and Kittel). But there seems to be no possible reason why a message announcing judgment against Babylon would be described initially as an utterance against some undesignated desert. The reading מדבר־ים (deserts), which, according to Gesenius, is in one codex, does not help much either, especially since the plural of מדבר (desert) is never used elsewhere in the OT. Qᵃ reads דבר ים. Is that supposed to mean "message about the sea" or should one point these two words as one, reading דְּבָרִים (words), resulting in the translation: "words like storm winds" (so Scott)? It is strange that words would travel along. Targ (משרין דאתין מן מדברא כמי ימא) does not really provide a translation, but rather a suggested meaning ("Armies, which come out of the desert as the water from the sea"). It is worth noting that the Gk (τὸ ὅραμα τῆς ἐρήμου, "the vision of the desert") seems not to have read ים (sea), which still leaves it an open question about what the title "message about the desert" would mean at the head of a message that has nothing to do with a desert. Taking a different ent tack, Cobb (48) suggests the following solution: יָם is the perfect form of a lost verb, יָמַם, "to rage." Considering that same possibility, Marti suggested that יָם should be altered to read הֶמְיָה, "a roaring," then taking this word with the next, resulting in: "a roaring as from storms, which travel through the Negev"; so also Gray, et al. A similar solution is posited by Procksch in the reading יֶהֱמֶה (there is raging, as storms); see also *BHK*[3] and *BHS*. Schlögl prefers to take the substantive נַהַם to mean "roaring." Driver (*JSS* 13 [1968] 46f.) also comes up with a unique suggestion here: יָם should be read as יוֹם, which would permit one to translate it: "(Stormy) weather, like tempests in the south." Fischer discusses reading מִדְבַּר־צִיִּים and translates: "Message concerning the steppe of the desert animals." Sievers opts for inserting שְׁמוּעָה (report), and then alters בָא, "comes" (masculine), to read בָּאָה, "comes" (feminine), which is simply too much changing of the original text. It would be an attractive solution for one to read כַּשְׂדִּים (Chaldeans) instead of מִדְבַּר־יָם (desert of the sea) (so Cheyne; see Marti) if one could only explain how this simple and obviously preferable reading could have been damaged or altered.

With all of this uncertainty among the possible explanations, one might choose to stay with the MT reading (as Fohrer has done), even though one realizes that the text makes no sense whatever. However, the solution might be found in the superscription notice in 21:13, מַשָּׂא בַּעְרָב, "verdict in the desert." In that comment, בַּעְרָב (desert plain) has apparently been borrowed from the first line of that poem (a similar thing happens in 22:1). This must be what happened here as the redactor, who inserted the superscription in 21:1, took the word מדבר (desert) (or ממדבר, "out of the desert," which would mean that the מדבר form came about through haplography in copying; see the Gk) from v. 1bβ (as had been suggested earlier by Hitzig, Dillmann, Marti, and, more recently, by Kaiser). The circumstances that would have caused יָם (sea) to be inserted, or what the intention might have been, must remain in the realm of the fantasies spun by textual critics.

1c–c Targ reads בעלעולין (in the whirlwinds), which would suggest that the original was בסופה (in storm winds), but this does not give much help.

1d I. Eitan (*HUCA* 12/13 [1937/38] 66) suggests taking the ל in לחלף (sweep away) as an emphatic *lamed,* reading לְיַחֲלֹף (indeed, it will sweep away). In reality, the form should be interpreted on the basis of the explanation in Ges-K §114o ("Finally, the infinitive with ל is very frequently used in a much looser connexion to state motives, attendant circumstances, or otherwise to define more exactly"); see also BrSynt §47, and cf. Isa. 38:20 and 44:14.

1e Gk: δι' ἐρήμου (through the desert) is apparently just a paraphrase; Targ: באורח דרומא, "upon the way of the south"; Vulg: *ab africo,* "from the southwest" or "from the southwest wind"; Syr: *mn tymn',* "out of the south"; this means that the versions all treat נגב (Negev) as a designation for one of the points of the compass. One wonders whether the MT intended rather to speak of the region to the south of ancient Judah, known once again today as נגב (the Negev). It might be that Syr and Vulg are correct, since they presume the reading מִנֶּגֶב (from the Negev/south) as being in parallel with the following ממדבר (out of the desert); there is no way to decide between the two. A much more radical alteration has been proposed by Torczyner: that the ל in לחלף (sweep away) should be read with the previous word. This would then be a reference to a country or a territory through which the Elamites and Medes would have to travel; e.g., Gambulu (according to Torczyner, read as Gunbula by the Arabic geographers), located in the swampy regions of the Euphrates and Tigris deltas, directly on the Elamite border, so that one could translate: "As the storm wind, he traveled through Gambul," a most tempting solution, but one that is a bit too clever to accept.

1f Since perfect forms are used in v. 2a, בא (comes) should also be treated as a perfect.

1g Syr reads *rḥyqtʾ* (remote); announcements of disaster frequently state that the enemy comes from a *distant* land, but for this very reason נוראה (horrifying) should be treated as part of the original text; see S. Talmon (*Textus* 4 [1964] 103f.). Qimḥi explains that this refers to the land of the Medes and Persians, since the distant regions would be frightening precisely because they were located in the realm of the unknown.

2a–a Schlögl would alter חזות קשה (a harsh vision) to read חזון קשה (also: a harsh vision), an unnecessary alteration; see 29:11.

2b Technically, a vision is not made known, but rather observed. In fact, Syr reads *ʾtḥzy (ln)* (appeared [to us]). Ehrlich (*Randglossen* IV, 74) refers to Gen. 41:28, which picks up הגיד (revealed) from 41:25 and uses הראה (shown); cf. also Isa. 2:1: "The message, which Isaiah . . . saw."

2c–c The Gk reads ἐπ᾽ ἐμοὶ οἱ Αἰλαμῖται, καὶ οἱ πρέσβεις τῶν Περσῶν (upon me, the Elamites, and the honored ones of the Persians), which means that it read עלי (upon me) as a preposition with suffix, read צורי (close up the [siege-]enclosure) as צורי (honored ones of), and finally, used "Persians" as a shorthand way of describing the Medes—not a stellar example for demonstrating the care with which the Gk was translated! Yet the Syr hardly does any better, as it reads *wṭwry,* "and the mountains" (of Media) instead of צורי (close up the [siege-]enclosure). It would make it a lot easier if one were able, with Schlögl, to insert על־בבל (against Babylon) after מדי (Media), but no hard evidence supports such a change, and the meter of the verse would clearly be overloaded.

2d The form of אנחתה (arrogance) is unusual. Many Hebrew MSS read אנחתה (her arrogance), which suggests that the Masoretes, who provided the ה with a *raphe* (see *BHK,* 1906 edition), were also of the opinion that the ending ה־ was to be taken as a suffix; on this, see Ges-K §91e, and Joüon, *Gr* §94h, but see also Vulg: *gemitum eius* (his groan); this results in the suffix being virtually left hanging in the air. Marti treats the entire line as a gloss. Whereas Cobb (41f.), picking up once again a suggestion from B. Ruben (*Critical Remarks upon Some Passages of the Old Testament* [1869]), was so daring that he altered the text to read כלי השבתי אנחמתה (destroy, annihilate, O Ecbatana!), Eitan (66) connects the word with Arabic *naḥwat* (pride), or better yet, as far as he is concerned, with the Syrian-Palestinian dialectical form *naḥā,* "to swell with pride," since "sighing" makes no sense in the context. One is never told the reason why the seer should have experienced his vision in such a harsh way (v. 2a) and why he was so deeply moved by utter terror (vv. 3f.) when what it predicted was that all sighing would come to an end. Boldly making radical changes with the help of the Gk, Duhm ends up with the suggestion that the text should read: כל־גאון עתה השבתי (I will now cause all exaltation to cease).

Since all these emendations are flights of fancy rather than efforts that evoke confidence in their conclusions, one does best here to stay with אנחתה (groaning), explaining the rare form as having originally been אנחה (groaning), now with a double feminine ending (cf., e.g., ישועתה, "help," in Ps. 3:3; though, on this, see Ges-K §90g, which treats such a form not as double feminine but as one that is often used in poetry). Yet maybe Duhm was on the right track. For על־כן (therefore) at the beginning of v. 3 to make any sense, there is no possible way that the previous line could have been speaking about the final end of all sighing. The text must have been dam-

aged. Both Isa. 13:11 and Ezek. 7:24 use the phrase הִשְׁבַּתִּי גְּאוֹן (I will bring haughtiness to an end), so that the emendation that reads גַּאֲוָתָהּ (her pride) (thus Buhl and
*BHK*³) or at least גְּאוֹנָהּ (her exaltation) would have caught the correct sense of what
the passage intended, in which case the suffix would naturally refer to Babylon.
2e Some commentators (Cobb, Procksch) suggest reading הִשְׁבַּ(יֹ)תִי (exterminate)
instead of הִשְׁבַּתִּי (I will close down), based on an analogous relationship this verb
supposedly has with the previous imperatives עֲלִי (up!) and צוּרִי (close up!); but, in
the light of references to 13:11 and Ezek. 7:24, this alteration to the text is most
likely not correct.
3a Gk: τὸ μὴ ἀκοῦσαι (not able to hear) and τὸ μὴ βλέπειν (not able to see); Targ:
מלמשמע (cannot hear) and מלמחזי (cannot see); Syr: *dlʾ ʾšm‹* (which I did not hear) and
dlʾ ʾḥzʾ (which I did not see). This means that these versions treat מן as a מן privative
([be apart] from), so that the sense of the passage is: "hearing and seeing left me";
see Marti, Ehrlich (*Randglossen* IV, 74), Kaiser, et al., though the context would suggest that מן causative is more likely: the seer is thrown into confusion by the things
that he has to see and hear; see Duhm, Feldmann, Fohrer, Eichrodt, et al.
4a Instead of תעה לבבי (my heart is bewildered), Qª reads תועה ולבבי (going astray
and my heart), which makes no sense.
4b The Gk reads: ἡ ψυχή μου! (my spirit); Syr: *šwprʾ* (beauty, fairness). נשׁף refers
to that time when the wind howls (cf. נשׁף, "blow," as a less frequently used form
related to נשׁב, also: "blow"). One must admit readily that "twilight of pleasure"
sounds strange. However, G. R. Driver's suggestion (BZAW 77 [1958] 44), based on
the Arabic *nasafa* and its derivatives, to translate this: "my faintest (*i.e.* scarcely
breathed) wish has been turned into anxiety for me," is not convincing enough for it
to be read instead of the way that the passage has traditionally been translated.
5a Galling (FS Weiser, 57) alters הַשֻּׁלְחָן (the table) to read וְשֶׁלַח, "(one gets ready)
the throwing spear and . . ."; he believes that offensive weapons should be mentioned.
But there is a good reason why only the defensive weapon κατ᾽ ἐξοχήν (par excellence), the shield, is listed.
5b–b צפה הצפית obviously gave trouble to those who worked on the ancient versions.
Targ (אקימו סכראין, "set the watchmen"), Syr (*dqw dwqʾ*, "watchmen watch"), and
Vulg (*contemplare in specula,* "look carefully, in a watchtower") all relate this to צפה
I (look out); Gesenius and Delitzsch believe that צפית should be translated as "sen-
tinel" or "watch," and Galling (57) still translates this "one spies out the spying."
Qimḥi refers to *Gen. Rab.* (on Gen. 35:34), according to which צפית supposedly
means "candlestick"; one should read צפה הצפית as meaning סדר מנרתא (one should
arrange the candlestick), concerning which S. Krauss (*ZAW* 27 [1907] 292f.) refers to
Epiphanius, who mentions the Syrian name (σαβιθά) for a winepress dipper, which
would not automatically be contradictory to the meaning "lamp" in the Midrash.
Also original, but unlikely, is the interpretation suggested still by Ewald (*Propheten*
III, 11f.) and Dillmann that צפית means "horoscope." In reality, this term is most
likely connected with צפה II, a root that is admittedly found only here in the *qal*. One
cannot be sure of the exact meaning; KBL, Fohrer: "arrange the rows of tables";
Hitzig, Duhm, Procksch: "spread the tablecloths"; Zürcher Bibel: "spread out the
cushions." Thus it has something to do with preparations for a festive mealtime, part
of which included spreading out blankets, mats, or cushions, upon which one would
sit or lie when eating. (The Gk has no equivalent for צפה הצפית, "spreads out the cushions." That is no reason to eliminate these words; it may simply be that the translator
was skipping these words of the text because they were so difficult.)

5c–c Duhm, Marti, Guthe, et al. treat אכול ושתה (someone eats and drinks) as glosses, but, at best, the reason for accepting this solution would be based on metrical grounds.

5d Instead of מֹשחו (anoint), B reads ומֹשחו (and anoint). The Gk translates the colon as ἑτοιμάσατε θυρεούς (prepare the oblong shields), which is a loose translation, just as is that of the Targ: מריקו וצחצחו זינא, "polish and shine the weapons."

6a Targ: יהוה (Yahweh) instead of אדני (Lord).

6b–b לך העמד המצפה (Go, post the lookout) causes some significant problems for understanding exactly what is meant. Is it not true that the prophet himself is the lookout? What then would be the reason for him to go somewhere and post someone for this task? On the basis of v. 8, B. Stade (*ZAW* 8 [1888] 165) suggests reading: לכה עמד המצפה, "Go, set yourself up at watch" (on this, cf. Hab. 2:1); similarly, Buhl, 161: לכה עמדה מצפה, "Go, take your position, lookout," which is what *BHK*³ adopted as its preferred solution. If that is correct, however, then one cannot avoid making textual alterations in v. 8 as well. In that passage, Buhl (162) alters ויקרא (and he will call out) to ואקרא (and I will call out) and emends MT אריה (the lion) to אויה (woe). But one can hardly make allowances for the text being altered this extensively, so that it is best, also in v. 6, to stay with the transmitted text, especially since this is supported by the Gk as well.

6c Qᵃ: ויגד (and he reported), instead of יגיד (he is to report).

6d Hardly anyone agrees to eliminate אשר (what, that which) because it is "objectionable metrically and because of the way it sounds" (Sievers, 263).

7a After צמד (teams), Qᵃ inserts איש (each [made up]) (see v. 9a).

7b–b Buhl (163) (see also Stade, 166) suggests reading רכב חמור (riders of donkeys) and רכב גמל (riders of camels) (Gk: ἀναβάτην ὄνου καὶ ἀναβάτην καμήλου, "mounter of donkeys and mounter of camels"), and Procksch has taken up this suggestion once again. Now Qᵃ does read רוכב גמל (rider of camels) and, concerning חמור רכב (rider of donkeys), at least inserted a ו after the ר, after the text had been copied. In both places, Targ and Syr read רכיב, "riding." In spite of all this, the text is to be left as is.

7c–c Joüon (*Gr* §141b) thinks that רב־קשב (many attentive actions) should be read as having the adjective in the first position; in reality, this is a genitive construction, specifically: "much as regards attentiveness"; cf. passages such as 1 Sam. 2:5, רבת בנים, "with numerous sons."

7d Ehrlich (*Randglossen* IV, 74) wants to point קשב (attentiveness) as קשֵּׁב (an intensifying infinitive absolute). That is unnecessary; a substantive from the same stem can take the place of and serve the function of the infinitive absolute in such cases; see Ges-K §113w; BrSynt §93d.

8a Admittedly, "and the lion called" makes no sense within this context. No help is provided by the Gk as it reads this expression as a personal name, Ουρία, but it does show that this textual error must have been a very ancient one. Ibn Ezra thought this should be read כאריה (as a lion) (see also Rev. 10:3), and Delitzsch used this interpretation to suggest: "then he called with the voice of lions." Ehrlich (*Randglossen* IV, 74) conjectured אֲהָהּ (alas) (cf. 2 Kings 3:10), and Buhl (162) thought that the interjection אויה (woe) (see Ps. 120:5) might originally have been read here. Marti altered it to read אראה (I will see), which would have been continued in והנה (and behold) in v. 9, while von Orelli and König thought this might have been a call of alarm, which had been borrowed from the vocabulary used by shepherds. The correct solution was seen by Lohmann (*Anonyme Prophetien*, 61) when he suggested that it should read הָרֹאֶה, "the seer." Q[a] (הראה, "the seer") gave the necessary textual support for his emendation, which has resulted in almost universal acceptance (Fohrer, Eichrodt, Young, Auvray, Schoors, Kaiser, et al.).

8b The Gk reads σκοπιὰν κυρίου (lookout place of the lord), and Ehrlich (*Randglossen* IV, 74) suggests on this basis that it should be pointed מִצְפֶּה אֲדֹנָי (the place of waiting commanded by YHWH).

8c To posit reading אֲנִי (I) instead of אָנֹכִי (also: I), just because of meter, is much too presumptuous, limited as we are in our knowledge of the intricacies of Hebrew meter.

8d Procksch treats יוֹמָם (by day, continually) as a variant reading for תָּמִיד (without a break), which then resulted in כָּל־הַלֵּילוֹת (*sic*) (all night) being added. For this reason, he would remove both phrases, which he justifies because of the metrical overload. Once again, at this point, we see how the metrical pattern, which he believes he can detect, leads him to eliminate phrases from the text arbitrarily.

9a Stade (167) thinks that אִישׁ (of men) should be removed and, also on metrical grounds, he would eliminate the entire phrase רֶכֶב אִישׁ (a procession of men). Q[a] once again reads רֹכְב (riders of) (see also above, note 7b–b); however, the matter is settled by staying with the MT.

9b Q[a] reads וַיַּעֲנֵי (and he answered me). On the basis of metrical considerations, Sievers would remove וַיַּעַן (then he commenced; lit.: and he answered); Guthe would remove וַיֹּאמַר (and spoke).

9c Gk, Ethiopic, Arabic all have a textual reading that does not include the second נָפְלָה (fallen); unjustifiably, both Procksch and *BHS* suggest it should be eliminated.

9d Still once more, some exegetes suggest that metrical reasons are sufficient to warrant the text being shortened: Marti would leave out פְּסִילֵי (depictions, idols); Guthe and Procksch choose rather to eliminate אֱלֹהֶיהָ (its gods) and read וְכָל פְּסִילֶיהָ (and all its images). A different approach is followed by Lohmann (*ZAW* 33 [1913] 263), based on a suggestion by Gray, using the Gk (καὶ πάντα τὰ ἀγάλματα αὐτῆς καὶ τὰ χειροποίητα αὐτῆς, "and all her images and all that her hands have made") to read כָּל פְּסִילֶיהָ וֵאלֹהֶיהָ (all her depictions and her gods); however, though one can smash images of deities, one cannot do the same to the actual gods.

9e Based on the Gk (συνετρίβησαν, "they were crushed to bits"), Procksch would read שֻׁבְּרוּ (they were smashed) here, and Q[a] (שברו) now seems to give textual support for the reading. Bruno has the sentence end with שֻׁבְּרוּ (they were smashed), places אֶרֶץ just before מְדֻשָׁתִי, and translates: "land of my threshing," which is impossible.

10a–a One must admit that v. 10a is very short and that מְדֻשָׁתִי, "my thrashed [one]" or, in a more neutral sense, "my threshed," would seem to anticipate that some type of substantive would follow. But it does not help to adopt either the reading of Sievers (263), עַם־מְדֻשָׁתִי (people of my threshing) or that of Procksch, בֶּן מְדֻשָׁתִי (son of my threshing).

Instead of גָּרְנִי (my threshing floor), Q[a] reads גִּדְרִי (my wall, hedge, enclosure). Carmignac takes this to be the original reading and suggests for בֶּן־גִּדְרִי the translation "fils de mon bercail" (son of my fold). This means, of course, that מְדֻשָׁתִי (my thrashed) no longer provides a close parallel, so Carmignac also suggests, instead of that, to read מַרְעִיתִי, "mon pâturage, mon troupeau" (my pasture, my flock). It is true that Israel is called "people of my pasture" but never simply "my pasture"; the translation "mon troupeau" (my flock) obscures this difficulty. The suffix in the genitive clause בֶּן־גָּרְנִי (my threshing floor son) correctly must be linked with the more dominant word בֶּן (son), so that this does not mean "son of my threshing floor," but "my threshing floor son" (see Weingreen, *VT* 4 [1954] 50–59).

10b–b מֵאֵת יְהוָה צְבָאוֹת אֱלֹהֵי יִשְׂרָאֵל (from Yahweh of Hosts, the God of Israel) is likely a secondary addition (thus Marti; Guthe; Lohmann, *ZAW* 33 [1913] 263; Sievers, 265), intended to underscore further the trustworthiness of the message; this phrase interrupts the parallelism between the two halves of the verse.

Form

The superscription מַשָּׂא מִדְבָּר (a verdict from the desert) (concerning this emendation, see above, textual note 1b–b) is most likely secondary; it places the passage that follows into the framework of the *Massa* collection in the book of Isaiah. The next superscription of this type, מַשָּׂא דּוּמָה (verdict concerning Dumah), follows in v. 11. Boutflower has theorized that vv. 1-5 deal with Sargon's campaign against Babylon during the year 710, whereas vv. 6-10 look beyond this to the destruction of Babylon brought about by Sennacherib in 689. A long time ago, Barnes (pp. 589, 591) also suggested this same dividing point, though he read vv. 1-5 as an oracle of Isaiah against Judah, while he treated vv. 6-10 as the same type of oracle, but this one concerning the time when Sargon conquered Babylon. In spite of this, there is no doubt that vv. 1-10 form a single unit. The way that the reader is first notified, toward the end of the section, in v. 9, that this message deals with Babylon finds its parallel in 13:1ff., where one waits until v. 19 before the catchword Babylon appears. However, the Elamites and Medes, who give every appearance of being the powers who can bring an end to Babylon, are mentioned already in v. 2. The mention of these two peoples causes many problems for exegetes, since the assault on ancient Babylon was attributed to the Persians. But this difficulty is not a good enough reason for questioning whether this material forms a single unit.

When attempting to treat this poem as a whole, in terms of how it breaks down into smaller sections, and concerning the inner connections between its individual parts, problems are posed for the reader that are not insignificant, that in the final analysis can hardly be solved in a satisfactory way.

[21:1f.] What comes "like storm winds from the desert"? Who is the "cunning one" and the "devastator" in v. 2bα? Who commissions that Elam and Media should be summoned in v. 2bβ? Who is the "I" who announces the end of "his arrogance" in v. 2bγ? It is clear already at this point that this vague and secretive style is used intentionally. This passage deals with circumstances filled with intrigue, which are hidden in the nether reaches of the future, revealed at first only in an obscure way in the vision.

[21:3f.] In vv. 3f. the seer surprisingly turns to describe his own personal perplexity in reaction to what he must see and/or hear. He is shaken, down into the depths of his soul, and his psychological burden eats away at him until it causes him physical discomforts; he feels completely bewildered and discovers that it does not let up even in the evening hours, which are otherwise so soothing.

This passage also presents problems with specific details about what is happening. Why does the seer experience such harsh spiritual and physical shock waves when one would expect that he, as an Israelite, would take a breath of fresh air as the mighty earthly enemy and oppressor stands face-to-face with its own catastrophe? In fact, both vv. 3 and 4 function to portray the utter harshness of the disaster that will break out against Babylon by reflecting on the horror in terms of personal emotions. One must also take into account that the author may be making use of the traditional vocabulary employed when describing such visions.

[21:5] Unexpectedly, the seer now continues in v. 5 with a further description of what has been seen. After the voice has spoken in v. 2, another image is now inserted abruptly: someone prepares for a festive meal. We once again learn nothing about who does that, the reasons why, or for what purpose. Just as little is said about who the commanders are, those who are summoned in v. 5b. Are they Babylonians? Or are they enemies of Babylon? And what is the meaning of the command that they are to anoint the shields?

[21:6f.] Again in vv. 6f., one is surprised by another completely new topic: Yahweh commissions the seer to post a lookout, who is to report about what he has seen. Who is this lookout? For what reason ought a seer, who is himself a "lookout" (cf. Hab. 2:1), receive orders to "post" such a one? In the final analysis, is the lookout the alter ego of the seer himself?

[21:8, 9a] In vv. 8 and 9a, this lookout, who at this point is called a "seer," reports about how he stood on watch and did observe the approach of an army coming to wage war. One would have to presume that these are the Elamites and Medes, mentioned in v. 2bα, and that this was the occasion when the announced end of the "cunning one" entered the phase when it would begin to play out in history.

[21:9b, 10] Finally, in vv. 9b and 10, the actual message is stated. Even here one cannot be sure who is speaking, but the message itself is clear: The end has come for Babylon. Particular accent is given to the fact that this is accompanied by the end of its gods. But, once more, the proclamation that this major cosmopolitan city will fall moves immediately into direct address to Israel (!מדשתי ובן־גרני, "my thrashed people and my threshing floor son!"). The downfall of Babylon—without it being stated in such explicit terms—is a message that brings good news for the people of God. But it is stated in a most restrained way; nothing in the passage suggests how this will affect the future destiny of his people. At the very end, the seer reasserts that he has proclaimed absolutely everything that had been revealed to him. Even the interpretation is nothing more than a hint about what lies ahead. The person who reads or hears this report will have to expend personal energies when trying to make sense out of the voices that abruptly follow one another and the images that flash briefly across the screen during the vision.

[21:1-10] Yet if one surveys the entire passage, starting at the conclusion, no one could disagree that these ten verses, in spite of all the jagged transitions, form an original unit; and, to state it once again, in spite of all the obscurities, form a passage that was transmitted intact, one that makes sense as well. The difficulties are stylistic; however, this style is not clumsy or poor, but is adequate for conveying what has been seen and heard. The passage as a whole is a little work of art, preceded by much skill and practice in the art of putting such experiences into words.

The author describes what he has seen by terming it a חזות (vision). Other passages of the same type in the OT are in Hab. 2:1-4; the night visions of Zechariah, especially the first and last ones (1:7-17 and 6:1-8); but also Job 4:12-21. In some respects, one is reminded of aspects of the Balaam stories (see below, pp. 323f.). If one takes into account the complexity of the construction of the passage, the present account is without parallel. The above analysis results in the following structure:

1.	21:1b, 2a	Introduction: the seer is overcome by a harsh vision
2.	21:2b	1. First scene: the cunning one is driven out
		2. First message: summons to the actors who are to set God's judgment in motion
3.	21:3f.	The bewilderment of the seer himself
4.	21:5	1. Second scene: setting the table
		2. Second message: summons to the commanders to get themselves ready
5.	21:6f.	Appointment and charge given to the seer
6.	21:8, 9a	The report of the lookout (or, as the case may be, the seer)
7.	21:9b, 10a	The meaning of the vision
		1. v. 9b: Babylon's fall and the end of its gods
		2. v. 10a: Hint about the deliverance of Israel
8.	21:10b	Assurance of the trustworthiness of the communication

Meter: There is no question that this report about the vision is to be read as a metrically composed poem. If one removes the introductory formulas, which are not constructed metrically (vv. 1a, 6a, 8a, and the words ויען ויאמר, "then one commenced and spoke," in v. 9bα), and (as was explained above in textual note 10b–b) removes from v. 10: מאת יהוה צבאות אלהי ישראל (from Yahweh of Hosts, the God of Israel), then there are twenty-four lines of verse. Of those, a good half (thirteen) are clearly to be read as two-stress + two-stress bicola. Six more lines seem to have three stresses, as is seen immediately in the first line, v. 1bα, in the word כסופות (like storm winds), which in the first colon is all that remains. Some (see above, textual note 1b) have sought passionately and perceptively, by trying to reconstruct what apparently would have been the subject of the following בא (comes), to recover the stressed word that is now treated as missing. One must certainly consider the possibility that some of the text could now be lost. Based on the style of the poem, however, that is not likely, particularly in five other cola that all manifest the same problem: הגד־לי (was made known to me) and השבתי (I will close down) in v. 2; רב־קשב (with utmost attentiveness) in v. 7; בבל (Babylon) in v. 9; and מדשתי (my thrashed) in v. 10. There is no way that the text could have been damaged in all these cola. One must consider the possibility that, at least in some of these passages, some words are to be read with two stresses. But it would be more likely in these places that an individual word is important enough in these instances that it could carry the weight of two accented syllables, highlighted by the fact that it stands alone. If one glances over the passages under discussion, the deeper meaning of those words becomes evident in a striking way. There is no doubt that the irregularity in the meter, which jumps out as this is read, is fully intended and is an effective stylistic technique. Every place where it has been suggested that the text be altered on metrical grounds shows that the uniqueness of this carefully crafted passage has gone unnoticed. An analogous situation holds true for the five lines that apparently are composed of six-stress cola, v. 5a (3 + 3), vv. 6b, 7b, and both the lines of v. 8b (each 2 + 2 + 2). In all these cases, text critics have looked for ways to shorten the verses (see the appropriate textual notes). But the seer expends just a little bit more effort in each of these longer lines, so that what was seen can be sketched out with a broader stroke and by taking his time; the only place where this explanation does not hold true is in v. 6b, but even here there is no doubt that the colon should not be shortened.

Setting

Verse 9bα announces that Babylon will fall, and v. 2bβ appears to presume that the Elamites and Medes are going to be the ones who will bring about the utter ruin of the city. When the fall of Babylon is being discussed, as was the case also with chap. 13, from the outset it is unlikely that Isaiah is to be considered the author. It may be true, as is reported in chap. 39, that he had warned his contemporaries against having any dealings with Babylon. During his lifetime, however, Judah was never *oppressed* by Babylon and there would have been no reason for him to predict its ruin when he was still alive. It is true that Cobb (59f.) suggests that vv. 6-8 could reflect a time when Hezekiah sent a delegation to Merodach-Baladan, and v. 9 could be their response upon their return, including the macabre report that Babylon had fallen. Erlandsson (*The Burden of Babylon* [1970] esp. 86–92) has gone to great effort to interpret the passage within the context of historical events that occurred around the year 700. At that time, primarily Elam, but Media also, attempted to mount a rebellion against the Assyrians (i.e., the שודד, "devastator," in v. 2). Were this the case, Isaiah would want to point out that it would be worthless to rely on Babylon, since the Assyrians would bring them down as well. The truth of the matter is that Babylon was under severe pressure from the Assyrians more than once during the time of Isaiah, and one must acknowledge the correctness of H. Winckler's assertion (*Alttestamentliche Untersuchungen* [1892] 125) that the *only* time Babylon was destroyed was in 689 (cf. the portrayal of these events in *FWG* 4, 74). But this interpretation of the poem does not square with the whole text. The "devastator" and "cunning one" in v. 2 has to be identical with that power whose demise is announced in v. 9, and this power must once again match up as that force which "threshed" Israel. For this reason, it still seems most likely that this vision, as is true also for chaps. 13 and 47 and Jeremiah 50f., is to be attributed to the time of the Babylonian exile. It is not enough to point out that the deities of Babylon were certainly not smashed to the ground when the city was conquered (on this, see *FWG* 4, 110; and the Cyrus Cylinder, Rawlinson, V, 35, lines 22–35; *AOT* 369–370; [*ANET* 315f.]) since this text is not dealing with a *vaticinium ex eventu* (prophecy after the fact) and it is commonly stated in descriptions about the downfall of a world power that the gods also fell (cf. Isa. 46:1f.; Jer. 50:2; 51:44, 47; cf. Isa. 19:1). In the final analysis, the depiction of the future that the author of Isaiah 40–55 set forth matches what took place still less than this passage; in spite of that, Deutero-Isaiah belongs to the time of the exile.

Other grounds are even more substantive for calling Isaiah's authorship into question. According to everything that we know about Isaiah, the son of Amoz, he was not a visionary of the type that describes the author of this passage. Finally, the vocabulary also speaks against its authenticity.

It may be just by chance that Isaiah never mentions מדבר (the desert). חזות (vision) is used in 28:18, but with the meaning "agreement," or something similar (in 29:11 its use is not attributable to Isaiah). הגיד, in the sense of "reveal," is never so used by Isaiah (but see Jer. 16:10; 42:4, 20f., among other passages). Concerning הבוגד בוגד (with cunning the cunning one acts), one might compare 24:16; 33:1; and 48:8; concerning השודד שודד (the devastator devastates), see 16:4 and once again 33:1; see also 15:1. Isaiah uses השבית (close down) in a completely different sense in 30:11, whereas it does carry the same meaning in 13:11 and 16:19 as is found in 21:2. חלחלה (cramps) is used elsewhere only in Nah. 2:11 and Ezek. 30:4, 9; ציר (pains) together with the verb אחז (have seized me) is elsewhere in Isaiah only in 13:8, in the rest of the OT only in 1 Sam. 4:19 and Dan. 10:16. To see another use of יולדה ([one] who is giving birth), one can examine 13:8 (cf. also 26:17), and 13:8 also uses the verb בהל (be aghast). פלצות (dread) is found elsewhere in the OT only in Ezek. 7:18; Ps. 55:6; Job 21:6. בעת (*piʿel*) (has seized) is not found anywhere else in the book of Isaiah but is used in Job, precisely at the point where the dreams and visions of the night are described, in 7:14; cf. also 9:34 and 13:21. צפה I (*piʿel*), "be on the lookout," is not found elsewhere in Isaiah 1–39; the *qal* participle is used in Ezek. 3:17 and 33:7 as a paraphrase to describe the prophet's task, of course serving a different function than that of the מצפה (lookout) as depicted in the present passage. מצפה (watch), in the sense of the lookout post for a visionary, is used only here, but see the parallel משמרת (watchpost) in Hab. 2:1. In laments for the dead, Isaiah never uses the technical term נפל (fallen), but see 14:12. Again with פסילים (depictions), one encounters its use only in secondary passages (10:10; 30:22), and the phrase פסילי אלהים (depictions of its gods) occurs elsewhere only in Deut. 7:25 and 12:3. In this particular case, the results of the examination of the vocabulary are especially clear. The vocabulary used in 21:1-10 is not Isaiah's, and one cannot agree with the assessment by Barnes (591) that the style and phraseology would speak more for than against Isaiah as the author. Taking the opposite approach, one sees striking connections with chap. 13, with the poetry in Job, and also with some passages in Jeremiah, Ezekiel, Habakkuk, Deuteronomy, and Deutero-Isaiah. At the least, these findings do not contradict dating this passage in the exilic or late Babylonian period.

Some have more recently expressed the opinion of assigning a still later date. At least, Kaiser poses the question about whether this might not be by a prophet who comes late, later than the time of the Neo-Babylonian Empire. If this were true, then Babylon would be the pseudonym for another world power, i.e., the Persians or maybe even the Seleucids. One cannot deny that Babylon, sometimes in the form Βαβυλών, is used later as a code name for describing world power in general, serving as the antitype of the new Jerusalem. Israel had apparently learned how to generalize about any power that opposed God by observing the concrete example of Babylon. One can easily understand why: Babylon had plunged ancient Israel into a crisis that was without parallel in its history, and the trauma associated with being under the rule of the foreign country of Babylon had made such a deep impression in its collective memory that it would not go away. One might say that, in light of the situation, expectations that Babylon would fall were necessary manifestations of Israel's desire to continue to exist; the belief that its gods would fall gives expression to the way in which the people of God expressed itself in religious terms. For this reason, one can certainly understand why the fall of Babylon was mentioned with relative frequency in the OT, and there is no doubt that prophecies of that type would have fallen on the willing ears of the people in spite of the great caution exercised by both Jeremiah and Ezekiel. Therefore, there is no reason to categorize these passages as apocalyptic instead of historical.

But that leaves the question about why Elam and Media are identified as powers, as the source of the threat to Babylon's existence. In 13:17 the Medes (without Elam being mentioned) are called the enemies who will go against "the pride-filled magnificence of the Chaldeans" (v. 19). It has been explained already (above, pp. 13f., 17f., 28f.) that it is not nearly so automatic that one should presume, as is commonly done in scholarly circles, that this text refers not to the Medes but to the Persians. In any case, one ought not be surprised that the Medes are mentioned here once again. But who are the Elamites?

The Elamites' monuments, which celebrate their own history and which include their own style of writing, come from a relatively late period. Besides artifacts found in archaeological excavations, what we learn about their history comes from the inscriptional material of the Assyrians and Babylonians. When they appear on the historical scene, these inscriptions portray them primarily as the opponents of the peoples of Mesopotamia. Already at an early time the Elamite leader known as *šutruk-nahhunte* (ca. 1185–1155) conquered Babylon and in the process carried off the well-known law stele of Hammurabi to Susa, where it was discovered in the excavations during 1902. In the Neo-Assyrian era, the Elamites were the natural antagonists of Assyria and were frequently allied with Babylon in a common purpose when they rebelled, though they were far and away the more powerful in their ability to put up a resistance. Ashurbanipal seems to have been the first to have come up with a final solution to the irritating Elamite problem. After a series of campaigns, Susa was conquered in 646, then plundered and destroyed. A collection of princes from the region around the Zagros Mountains, from Urartu, Media, and Persia, sent envoys to Ashurbanipal in 639. Among them was also *kuraš* (Cyrus) from *parsumaš* (which at least to some extent is the same as *anšan*, the name of one of the ancient Elamite territorial subdivisions). *Anšan* also was apparently lost to the Achaemenids when the Elamite power waned. In a sense the Persians were the heirs of Elam. They gradually extended their rule farther and farther south, until finally the eastern region of Elam, known by the name *pārsa*, became virtually the "motherland" of the Persians (see König, *RA* II, 337). That Elam never recovered from the defeat when Ashurbanipal crushed them and never afterward was able to play a major role in world history has much to do with the efforts of the Medes and, soon after that, the Persians, as they attempted to exercise control over the Iranian region.

Yet the ongoing existence of Elamite culture during the time of the Persian Empire is very apparent. Even though the Elamites were not able to set the tone, this does not mean that they simply disappeared. In spite of everything, one notes that during the entire span of Achaemenid rule, a special attempt was made to keep Elamite as the second official language of the realm. At the time of Cyrus the Great, in a region between Susa and the Persian Gulf, there were Elamite "kings." Even as late as the era of Darius I, that king was confronted three different times with Elamite rebellions, and the revolts that took place when he first came to power show that, even then, families with Elamite names had power and commanded respect. Elamite family groups are still known at the time of Alexander the Great, and one still comes across Elamite dynasties at the time of the Seleucids (see König, 23; Hinz, 132f.). It is certainly not correct to declare summarily: "From this point on ([the year] 639, that is, after Ashurbanipal's conquest of Susa), there is no longer an Elamite history" (Schmökel, 281).

We would be able to be more certain of what was happening if we could more confidently date the message against Elam in Jer. 49:34-39. In its introduction, it is assigned to the year when Zedekiah began to reign (ראשית מלכות). Some exegetes, at least as far as it applies to the message as a whole, presume that this date is accurate and treat the message as one that originated with Jeremiah (Rudolph, HAT 12; Weiser, ATD 20/1; Eissfeldt, *Introduction,* 364), whereas many others treat it as inauthentic (Fohrer, *Introduction,* 400, et al.), though still being unable to cast any light on the historical background. Regardless of how one settles that issue, Jer. 49:34ff. gives evidence that, from time to time, Elam still played a somewhat significant role even after Ashurbanipal brought about the fall of Susa. Unfortunately, one cannot be sure, at the point in the Babylonian Chronicle that discusses events of the ninth year of Nebuchadnezzar (Wiseman, 36), whether "king of Elam" should be read. Anyway, we do know that Elamites brought problems to Uruk in 540 (see Kaiser). All of this shows that it would have been possible that the author of 21:1-10 could have expected an attack by united Median and Elamite forces against Babylon. If this is the case, then the vision would have to be dated in the early years of Neo-Babylonian rule, when the Medes were still sitting firm in the saddle and the Persians had not yet made their entrance on the stage where the big events in world history were acted out.

One admits that this solution would not be supported by Ezek. 32:22-26, where Elam is mentioned, between Assyria and Meshech-Tubal, as a dead power, buried in the depths of the underworld. Finally, Elam is also mentioned in Isa. 22:6, along with Kir, in fact, as a people that was storming Jerusalem at the time of Isaiah. But in that passage, Elam and Kir could only be referring to contingents of the Assyrian forces. Analogously, one might suppose that Elam and Media in 21:2 are just some of the peoples who are mentioned by the seer, because they were the neighbors who bordered directly on Babylon, who would have to be first in line in bearing the brunt of the battle when the Persian attack against the city commenced. If that be true, we are at the time in which Deutero-Isaiah also was anticipating that the Persians would go against Babylon and, consequently, that the exiled Jews would be set free, that is, at the time of the Babylonian Nabonidus (see Galling, *Studien zur Geschichte Israels im persischen Zeitalter* [1964] 20; and cf. P. R. Ackroyd, *Exile and Restoration*, OTL [1968] 223). There is obviously no reason to doubt that עֵילָם refers to the Elamites and מָדַי to the Medes.

Commentary

[21:1a] The vision is designated a מַשָּׂא (verdict), and this labeling serves to classify it as one of the oracles against the nations in the book of Isaiah. It may be that it is not specifically called a מַשָּׂא בָּבֶל (verdict concerning Babylon) because chap. 13 already carries that superscription and one would avoid repeating it here because it would leave the impression that it is merely a repetition. In reality, it does deal with a further message of judgment concerning Babylon, even if v. 10a hints at the possibility that this passage's real function is as a message of good news for downtrodden Israel.

[21:1b] The main problem with interpreting v. 1b seems to be the question about who one understands to be the subject of בָּא (comes out). As was mentioned in the text-critical discussion, the shortness of the first line has led to the assumption that the subject has been lost from the text. But what has been said about the style of a report concerning a vision would suggest that this is not likely. According to many exegetes, that which is coming, that which is compared to the onrush of the storm wind in the נֶגֶב (Negev), is the power that is preparing to bring about the demise of Babylon (cf. 5:28; Jer. 4:11-13). That view causes troubles then with the interpretation of מִמִּדְבָּר (from the desert) and מֵאֶרֶץ נוֹרָאָה (out of a horrifying land): Elamites and Medes do not come out of the desert, but rather out of the Elamite and Median mountain regions; and the territory around Babylon was not desert either, but was well-developed land, crisscrossed with a network of canals. According to other exegetes, however, mention is already being made about the "harsh vision" in v. 1b, which has come upon the seer. Concerning this vision, one can compare it with the description of the night vision in Job 4:15: וְרוּחַ עַל־פָּנַי יַחֲלֹף תְּסַמֵּר שַׂעֲרַת בְּשָׂרִי, "a spirit glided past my face; the hair of my flesh bristled"; see also Job 27:20f. But one must also take into account that the OT speaks frequently of Yahweh's coming in or as the storm wind (Pss. 18:11; 104:3b; Job 9:17; Nah. 1:3; cf. Ps. 83:16; Job 40:6). And when the discussion is about the storms in the בָּב (Negev), the desert, the frightening land, that might be a play on words referring to Yahweh's place of residence in the southern desert (Deut. 1:19; cf. 33:2; Judg. 5:4; 1 Kings 19:4ff.).

[21:2] Whatever it is that roars in tumultuously, as does the storm in the land of the south, in any case it causes the seer to be deeply shocked. The seer speaks of a "harsh vision." Much effort has been expended by commentators in trying to understand why it is termed "harsh." Fohrer bolsters his own case with the explanation: "It is not the content of what has been heard that fills him with horror and shock, since it is in fact a message that brings joy for his downtrodden and thrashed people. . . . It is rather the experience of the hearing, which makes him shake physically and gives him pains that can hardly be endured." In addition to these considerations, one would also need to take into account that the description of how visions of this type were experienced would be presented using stereotypical phraseology. In spite of all this, it is noteworthy that the vision does not betray any hatred toward Babylon. One gets the impression that the seer is very much aware of the tragedy that would be in store for the proud and shining world power when it finally fell.

Just as is true of the much more commonly used form חָזוֹן (vision) (see also חִזָּיוֹן, vision), חָזוּת serves to designate a visionary experience. It is true that the corresponding verb חזה, at least in late texts, can also be used when speaking about normal acts of seeing, just as, conversely, ראה can also be used, though relatively infrequently, when reporting the seeing of a vision. Thus it ought not cause one to wonder what is happening when v. 3 uses the verb ראה (see) and when v. 8 speaks of a ראה (seer) (text emended) and not a חזה (also: seer). In some passages the visionary aspect of חזה (see a vision) and its derivatives apparently fades into the background; it does little more than to say that a prophet has received a message, underscoring thereby its revelatory character (see *Isaiah 1–12*, pp. 5f.). At times, חָזוֹן can be used almost synonymously with דבר (speak); cf. 29:11, where חָזוּת (vision) is used in a vague, generic sense. But there is no doubt about this passage—it refers to an actual visionary experience, even though the brief descriptive elements in the text do not give enough background for one to employ the categories of modern psychology to explain precisely what happened. One must first pay attention to the fact that the חָזוּת (vision) is *made known* to the seer (הֻגַּד־לִי). That should not be any big surprise. Even in its earliest uses, חזה (have a vision) deals with a realm of experience that includes both visual and auditory experiences at one and the same time. It is thus entirely appropriate that v. 3 mentions both hearing and seeing.

What is special about the vision portrayed here is that it tells of the deep shock it caused for the seer himself. A rather close parallel occurs in Job 4:13ff. The poetic writer of Job describes the חֶזְיֹנֹת לַיְלָה, "night visions," which come upon a person who is sound asleep. One is also reminded of Zechariah's night visions, which also include the appearance of chariots and horses (6:1ff.), though they do not relate that the person seeing it all was deeply upset. But that aspect is included in the visions that come within dreams in the book of Daniel: 4:2; 7:1; 10:8f., 16f.; cf. also Gen. 15:12 and Jer. 4:19. In Ethiopian (1) Enoch 60:3, an apocalyptic figure reports: "(Then) a great trembling seized me. Fear took hold of me; my hips were bent and loosened themselves, my complete 'I' melted thereunto (lit.: and my kidneys lost control), and I fell on my face." Naturally, visionary experiences of this type are not limited only to groups somehow linked to the OT. When Muhammed prayed during the battle of Badr, he received a vision from the angel Gabriel. "He shook mightily, then he came to his senses and said to Abu Bakr: 'Receive happy news! God's presence has arrived'" (*Das Leben Muhammed's nach Muhammed Ibn Ishâk* [in Arabic], ed. Abd el-Malik Ibn Hischâm [1858] vol. 1, 444; German translation from Arabic: G. Weil [1864] I, 331). Such experiences can also come upon present-day individuals. W. James (*The Varieties of Religious Experiences* [reprint 1961], 63f.) reports the experience of one of his friends: "It was about September, 1884, when I had the first experience . . . I lay awake awhile . . . when suddenly I *felt* something come into the room and stay close to my bed. It remained only a minute or two. I did not recognize it by any ordinary sense, and yet there was a horribly unpleasant 'sensation' connected with it. . . . The feeling had something of the quality of a very large tearing vital pain spreading chiefly over the chest, but within the organism—and yet the feeling was not *pain* so much as *abhorrence*. . . . I was conscious of its departure as of its coming: an almost instantaneously swift going through the door, and the 'horrible sensation' disappeared."

In the description about what happened to Muhammed, it says that he came to his senses once again (*nabaha* VIII, "being awake, awaken, be conscious, come to one's senses again"). One would have to treat this as an ecstatic experience in the strict sense. In addition, wherever night visions are mentioned, the sequence of events—somewhat differently than in passages such as the one describing Isaiah's call vision (see *Isaiah 1–12*, pp. 260f.)—apparently take place outside the bounds of one's normal conscious experiences. Some try to describe this as an "inner" seeing and hearing, in which the visionary is able to be confident about what is truly real in contradistinction to what appears real in external experience. In such cases, one might speak of pseudo-hallucinations. However, since in this present passage there is talk of posting a lookout, one is probably more correct if this is called an actual hallucination.

Initially, the seer perceives in this vision that the cunning one acts with cunning and the devastator devastates. שׁוֹדֵד (devastate) and בּוֹגֵד (be cunning) are also used together in 33:1, and there is also a play on words, using שֹׁד (devastate) in 16:4 (with בגד, "be cunning," in 24:16; see also 48:8). Since both of these terms are traditionally used in depictions of enemies, one ought not expect to discover specific, detailed, precise information about the opponent. As is typical, scholars disagree about the interpretation. Does the seer visualize the advance of the enemies of Babylon or does he observe how Babylon itself does such things to others? One might suppose that he would probably not use the verb בגד (be cunning) when portraying Babylon's enemies; at least *something* in this phraseology, though lacking elsewhere, hints at the reason why the world power Babylon must come to ruin. But the truth of the matter is that the modern reader wants to know more than the seer is willing, at first, to disclose. However, concrete details are provided in his report, in the third line of v. 2, where Elam and Media are summoned to go into battle against Babylon. For details about the historical situation, see above, p. 310.

The imperative עֲלִי (up!) is used as a simple interjection (cf. 1 Kings 20:22); Elam does not have to "go up" when it sets out against Babylon. This is the typical summons in the "call to battle" (Jer. 46:9; 49:28, 31; 50:21; 5:10; 6:4f.; Joel 4:9, 12). The normal pattern follows up this call with a verb that describes the specifics about how the battle is to be waged (see R. Bach, *Die Aufforderungen zur Flucht . . .* , WMANT 9 [1962] 62ff.). In this passage, that would be צוּר, "surround, besiege (a city)"; cf. Deut. 20:12, 19; 2 Sam. 11:1; 20:15, and often elsewhere. It has been noted that this is the only passage where the verb is used in an absolute sense. The one who is on the receiving end of this military expedition is not to be identified yet.

As is well known, this did not result in the siege of Babylon, but instead, Gobryas, the governor of Gutium, entered into the proud capital of the Chaldean empire on 16 *tešrīt* 539 (*FWG* 4, 110).

Babylon's נַאֲוָה (?) is to come to an end. It is common in the messages against the foreign peoples that someone is accused of having "pride, arrogance," and this in no way describes something unique about Babylon (see above, p. 146, on 16:6). Nonetheless, its arrogance served as the example par excellence for describing the eschatological world power (see H. Ringgren, *TDOT* I, 469; K. G. Kuhn, *TDNT* I, 515).

Everyone has noticed that the announcement of the end of Babylon's arrogance includes an "I," which can refer only to Yahweh. Under no circumstances should הִשְׁבַּתִּי (I will close down) be changed (see above, textual note 2e); this corresponds precisely to how the OT understands history, that the divine "I" appears suddenly, completely unexpectedly. The actors on the stage of history are peoples and powers; Yahweh and Yahweh alone is the lord of history. He makes sure that such trees do not grow up into the heavens; there is nothing so repulsive to him as the arrogant pride of the peoples.

[21:3f.] As has just been explained, when the seer speaks of the violent shock, that refers to his psychological experiences. One notes that this inner shock does not refer, as in 15:5; 16:9, 11; and Ezek. 21:11 (see also Jer. 4:19), to sharing in the suffering of those who are about to be on the receiving end of an unfolding catastrophe—sympathy for Babylon is out of the question—but rather underscores the severity of the events that have been predicted. It is characteristic of the OT that matters which upset one's inner being are manifested in physical pain (or ought one say that the human being in the OT has no other way to portray psychological agitation than to describe the effects that such an experience has on the body? In any case, it does not operate within the framework of the distinction we make between soul and body).

In v. 3aγ, the visionary compares himself with a woman giving birth. But v. 3aα already had used this imagery; חַלְחָלָה derives from חִיל I, "have labor pains, be in labor." In other places in the OT, the imagery is used when describing wrenching pains, which come on suddenly, to a people who are overtaken by disaster (Isa. 13:8: Babylon; Ezek. 30:4, 9: Egypt; Nah. 2:11: Nineveh; see also Jer. 6:24 and 30:6). The phrases in v. 3aβ-γ have a striking parallel in 13:8; concerning ציר (cramps) and יולדה (one giving birth), see above, p. 23.

Besides the physical pains, there is also a spiritual disillusionment, vv. 3b and 4a. That about which the seer is being informed shocks him to the depths. Parallel to בהל (be agitated), the *niphʿal* נעוה (be aghast) vacillates in the way it is used, meaning either that someone is (physically) bent over or that someone is (spiritually) bewildered; cf. Ps. 38:7: "I am utterly bowed down." In v. 4a the verb seems to be at home in the psychological realm, but פלצות can just as regularly refer to shaking or quaking of the body (Job 21:6; see also the verb פלץ, "tremble," in Job 9:6). בעה (seize, terrify) is a strong expression; it is used when speaking of an evil spirit, 1 Sam. 16:14f.; it is said about נחלי בליעל (torrents of perdition), 2 Sam. 22:5; it describes a solar eclipse, Job 3:15; 15:24; it is used with dreams and visions, Job 7:14; however, it also refers to God in his majesty, Job 9:34; 13:11. Thus it ought not appear strange that "wander around, be bewildered" (תעה) is mentioned. Isaiah uses the word to describe those who are drunk, 28:7; cf. also 19:14; however, Ps. 95:10 does speak of an עם תֹּעֵי לֵבָב, "a people with a wandering spirit" (as this is translated in the Zürcher Bibel).

The seer comes up with a vivid and unique formulation in v. 4b: "The evening twilight of pleasure he has made for me into horror." One might conclude from this that the vision had come upon him at night (when sleeping?). The identity of the actual subject of שׂם (he has made) is once again not immediately apparent. One could link this with פלצות (dread), though then one would have expected the feminine form שׂמה. Hitzig suggests translating it "someone," noting here the same problem as with בא (it comes) in v. 1; Marti reads: "the vision"; Feldmann: "the sum total of all that affects him, . . . which has incessantly bombarded the prophet during the vision"; Fischer: "certainly, Yahweh"; Procksch: "hardly God, but rather all the circumstances of his inner torment." It is probably best that the subject not be identified specifically; it deals with the overall impression that the vision had left.

After the evening twilight time comes (נשׁף, actually: "blow"), a cool wind begins to blow in the hill country of Palestine, which brings longed-for relief to humans, animals, and plants. One can easily understand that someone would eagerly anticipate its arrival (נשׁף חשׁקי, "evening twilight of pleasure"), but in other places in the OT (Job 7:3, 14) those who are suffering spiritually or have physical troubles could have horrible experiences during the time they otherwise would have had a refreshing night of sleep.

[21:5] The visionary does not stop after relating his deep shock; new images are pressed upon him. Someone prepares a table before him. One should note the infinitives absolute: ערך (make preparations for), צפה (spread out), אכול (eat), שׁתה (drink): that which appears glides by so fast that the seer has no time at first to formulate his impressions in the form of sentences; he cannot tell us anything about who sets the table and the reason why. One can fully understand Kaiser when he sighs: "We would have been grateful to him [the poet] for expressing himself less cryptically." But the poet can say no more than what he observed. Quite likely, these would have been upper-crust Babylonians, unaware of any dangers, who were having a relaxing time at a table that has been festively prepared, suddenly then being frightened by the cry: "Up, get the weapons." Herodotus (1.191, Penguin edition [1954]) is able to provide some information: "But as it was they were taken by surprise [by the Persians]. The Babylonians themselves say that owing to the great size of the city the outskirts were captured without the people in the centre knowing anything about it; there was a festival going on, and even while the city was falling they continued to dance and enjoy themselves, until hard facts brought them to their senses"; cf. also Xenophon, *Cyropaedia* 7.15; and Dan. 5:30. One ought not object that "a prophet could hardly have known anything about this beforehand" (Kaiser). Why not, since such assaults were often depicted by focusing in on the exact moment when the enemy is paying less attention to the threat than would be appropriate? To be sure, others have attempted to explain what was happening. Marti (who considers אָכוֹל שָׁתֹה, "eat, drink," to have been inserted by a reader or copyist) thinks "that the commanders . . . have been summoned to anoint themselves to partake of a richly provisioned festive meal, which in this case would have followed a victorious battle against the enemy," referring to the same imagery in Zech. 9:14f. and to the portrayal of the harvest and treading the winepress in Joel 4:13. But one can hardly use that passage in the strict sense to help here; that meaning would simply not work here; it is unlikely because the commanders, if one follows the train of thought, seem to need to be encouraged, to have to be invited: "eat and drink," whereas this text apparently suggests that eating is already in progress (Duhm and Marti, with reference to Cheyne, eliminate both infinitives).

Concerning עָרֹךְ הַשֻּׁלְחָן (make preparations for the table), see 65:11; Ezek. 23:41; Pss. 23:5; 78:19; Prov. 9:2. People of high standing eat at a table, on which food and drink have been placed; cf. passages such as 1 Sam. 20:29, 34; 2 Sam. 9:10, 11, 13; 19:29.

Concerning צָפֹה הַצָּפִית (spreads out the cushions), see above, textual note 5a–a. Unfortunately, one cannot arrive at a satisfactory explanation about what this phrase means exactly. One might consider that this refers to blankets which one would spread out on the ground in order to sit on them; cf. depictions such as *AOB* no. 551; *ANEP* no. 451.

In the middle of the festive meal, the call rings out: קוּמוּ הַשָּׂרִים (Up, you commanders). The imperative קוּמוּ (rise up) (often used together with a second verb) is frequently chosen when summoning one to prepare for imminent battle; see Deut. 2:24; Judg. 7:15; Jer. 6:4, 5; 49:14, 28, 31; Obad. 1, among others.

The "anointing" or "lubricating" of the shields is apparently one of the tasks performed immediately before a battle. Before a festival meal, one would anoint one's head with oil (Ps. 23:5); in contrast to that, it may be that here the call is for one to lubricate the shields (see also 2 Sam. 1:21, text emended). But why would one anoint shields before the battle?

That is related to the question about what kind of material was used to make the shields. At this point, Targ speaks of polishing and making the weapon shine. Virgil (*Aeneid* 7.626f.) tells about the outbreak of a battle: *leves clipeos et spicula lucida tergent arvina pingui* ([some] with rich fat burnish shields smooth and javelins bright), which would presume that the shields were metal, as when Aristophanes (*Acharnians* 1128) speaks about this, saying that when one would pour oil on a shield, one could see one's reflection in it. According to 1 Kings 10:16f., Solomon ordered that two hundred large shields (צִנָּה) and three hundred smaller round shields (מָגֵן) were to be made, each overlaid with hammered gold. But those were apparently more ornamental pieces in the collection of royal weapons than real implements to be used to protect oneself in actual battle (on this, see de Vaux; Benzinger, *Hebräische Archäologie* [1927³] 300–302). Rehoboam, when replacing them, had bronze shields made (1 Kings 14:27), which were apparently also more of a luxury item. According to Homer, the Greek form of the ἀσπίς (shield) was constructed using skins, layered one on top of the other, along with a metal plate, which in historical times was made of bronze; besides this there were also shields made of wickerwork, wood, and leather (Droysen, 12f.). In Egypt massive shields were made of wood or had a wooden framework on which leather was stretched (Bonnet, 186). In Mesopotamia as well, the shields were normally made of wood or leather, to which a variety of metals could be added for decoration or for strengthening (Salonen, 183). But there were also shields in use that were made of sticks of wood, interwoven and joined with leather (Bonnet, 194; *ANEP* no. 372; see Keel, *Symbolism of the Biblical World*, illuss. 306f.).

The description in 21:5 would lead one to think this refers to the wood-and-leather shields. The anointing can hardly have been for the purpose of "shining up" metal (as Knobel and Bredenkamp surmise), but to lubricate the leather—in order to make it pliable, so that "the leather would not cut in," suggests Marti, or "presumably . . . to avoid their being split when struck by a stone, spear or other missiles," says Kaiser. But that type of care for the leather would seem to make more sense at the time when the weapons were stored after a battle, so Fohrer is more likely correct in suggesting that anointing a shield was a dedicatory action, offered to the deity, "for whom they were thereby offering themselves and for whose land they were engaging in a holy war." He points out that מָשַׁח (anoint) "consistently [refers to] anointing that accompanied a dedication" (cf. also E. Kutsch, BZAW 87 [1963] 7–9). When, according to Jer. 22:14, houses were smeared red (with red lead) (also using מָשַׁח, "anoint"), that was probably intended, at least originally, to serve an apotropaic function, to ward off evil. In fact, one can certainly anoint oneself in order to increase the chances that one would stay well (Amos 6:6; see H. W. Wolff, BK XIV/2 [Engl: *Joel and Amos*, 276f.]), but a magic rite would also have been behind this: one uses this means to enhance one's life forces. With all this in the background, "anointing the shield" would have been a (possibly no longer understood) ritual, intended to give the weapons magical power (this, according to Gesenius,

had already been suggested by the Jewish exegetes discussing 2 Sam. 1:21),
in which case the dedicatory action toward the deity would also have been a
secondary interpretation of the action (on this, see A. Lods, "Magie
hébraïque et magie canaanéenne," *RHPR* 7 [1927] 1–16, esp. 15. Concerning
the apotropaic power of oil, see Zeph, *Handwörterbuch des deutschen Aberglaubens* VI, 1240f.).

[21:6] One cannot know for sure who is speaking in v. 5b; it could be watchmen or envoys who had become aware of the news about the advance of the
enemy. But now, once again most abruptly, the seer hears the voice of Yahweh himself.

Yet at this point, as is so often the case in such situations, one is in a
dilemma about how to translate כִּי at the beginning of v. 6; the common rendering "because" is not appropriate, since there is no logical connection
between this and what has preceded; to translate it as "indeed" is nothing
other than a last resort.

The voice of Yahweh commands the seer to post a "lookout." For this
reason, it would seem that this person would be another individual, not the
visionary who had experienced the חָזוּת קָשָׁה (harsh vision). When battles are
taking place, or in times of danger, one would post צֹפִים ("watchers" or
"lookouts"), whose job is to make a report when they observe anything out
of the ordinary or when messengers come who are able to bring news about
how things are going on the battlefield (see 2 Sam. 13:34f.; 2 Kings 9:17ff.).
This would be the reason why the prophet is commanded, during his trance,
to post such a lookout and is then to be informed about what he has to report.
Disagreeing with this simple explanation, some have objected (Hitzig; cf.
Fohrer) that this does not square with "without a break during the day" and
"all the night long" in v. 8, since the vision could not have possibly lasted
that long—as if, in a vision or a dream, one were not able to generalize when
talking about the passing of time! Perhaps one would not be forced to think
in these terms if one were not drawn to compare the motif with what is in
Hab. 2:1. There, the prophet is himself the lookout who has to stand watch.
For that reason, as was shown above in the text-critical notes, it has been
suggested that the wording of the MT has to be altered—but suggested alterations simply have not proved convincing. Some have also tried the risky tactic of explaining this psychologically. Hölscher (70ff.) speaks of a split in the
prophetic "I"; the "spirit" becomes a separate, active being, being separate
and at a distance from the human being who sees the vision, appearing with
the ability to see visions. It is this one who is said to have become the "lookout," commissioned by the prophet, and to whom he would make reports in
a supernatural way. Hölscher thus equates the events in this passage with
entrancing experiences, like those describing what happened to Ezekiel (8:3;
11:24; 40:1f.; see also 1 Kings 18:12) or to apocalyptic figures (2 [Syriac]
Apoc. Bar. 6:3). Even earlier, Duhm had tried to explain this text similarly,
noting that psychics in ancient times and still today are able to separate
themselves from their bodies "so that they can get information about what is

happening at a distance, being in a more or less deep catatonic state, during which, according to their opinion, their 'soul' . . . leaves the body, transfers itself to the desired location, and there observes what is to be observed"; cf. also Weiser-Aall, *Handwörterbuch des deutschen Aberglaubens* III, 1849, 1851. Duhm even considers it possible that the הַדֹּבֵר בִּי מַלְאָךְ (angel who talked with me) could be most properly understood to be an alter ego. But there is no way that Zechariah considers himself to be identical with the angel speaking to him. In the same way, the seer in 21:1-10 does not treat the "lookout" as his second "I." The questionable nature of Duhm's solution was recognized already by Hänel (92ff.). Apparently the only reason so many have accepted the idea that this refers to an alter ego is that such well-known scholars have favored it. For this reason, one has to conclude that this passage is dealing with hallucinatory images and voices. It would seem that the emendation, to read הָרֹאֶה (the seer), at the beginning of v. 8, would cause certain problems for this interpretation. But the seer in that verse can be none other than the imaginary מְצַפֶּה (lookout) who has been posted as watchman.

[21:7] Yahweh himself gives the orders about what the lookout should be observing on his watch: war chariots, which, when an enemy force draws near, raise a cloud of dust, as well as the charioteer corps, who cannot be camouflaged as well as a company of foot soldiers could be (concerning war chariots, see *Isaiah 1-12*, pp. 108f.; in addition, see H. Schäfer and W. Andrae, *Die Kunst des Alten Orients* [1925] 392). Chariots drawn by horses are known in the Near East already in the second millennium B.C. They became widely used as a result of the expansionist activities of the Hyksos, and the Aryan nobility of the Hurrians apparently inaugurated the training of horses. It is common knowledge that Solomon had formed a special charioteer corps for himself, along with a line of well-fortified cities as bases for them (cf. עָרֵי הָרֶכֶב, "cities for his chariots," in 1 Kings 9:19; 10:26). Thus the Judean population was not ignorant about chariots. But it is most surprising that רֶכֶב חֲמוֹר (a procession of donkeys) and רֶכֶב גָּמָל (a procession of camels) are also mentioned. In ancient Palestine, loads on wagons were pulled by either oxen or cattle; cf. the wagon from Lachish (*BRL* no. 532; *ANEP* no. 367). We hear nothing in the OT about wagons being drawn by donkeys or camels. Thus it is certainly tempting to accept the emendation already suggested by Buhl, that רֶכֶב (wagon) be changed to read רֹכֵב (riders of), especially since we now also have רוֹכֵב (riders of) as the Qᵃ reading. But this would mean that we would have to follow that line of reasoning and also translate פָּרָשִׁים as "rider" (or "cavalier"; see Procksch). However, since פָּרָשִׁים (horses) is in a dependent relationship with צֶמֶד (team), this has to refer to a team of horses, and thus one must realize that this speaks of chariots. It is possible that, in both of the uses in v. 7aβ, רֶכֶב means "procession" (of beasts of burden); see Vitringa, Hitzig, Delitzsch, Knobel, Dillmann, Duhm, Zürcher Bibel, KBL, Kaiser (the camel as a beast of burden: 1 Kings 10:2; 2 Kings 8:9; Isa. 30:6; 60:6, among others). Fohrer, though, thinks this refers to wagons that haul heavy equipment, which would be drawn by donkeys or camels.

The lookout is to see what is coming, but is also to listen attentively, in fact, to give that as much attention as he can. That would be valuable in trying to ascertain what this procession of forces has up its sleeve.

[21:8] Unfortunately, some questions about the text in v. 8a remain. Since the מְצַפֶּה (lookout) in v. 6bα is designated as a רֹאֶה (seer), understanding the vision is made more difficult. One would have expected v. 8a to read something such as: "Then *I* heard the lookout calling: . . ."; something such as this must be meant, but it is not stated in so many words.

The seer reports how he stood at watch, מִצְפֶּה or מִשְׁמֶרֶת, in order to be on the lookout. In the sense of a "lookout post," מִצְפֶּה is used as a technical term elsewhere only in 2 Chron. 20:24, but Sir. 37:14 also speaks of seven watchmen (צוֹפִים) on the watchtower (מִצְפֶּה).

מִצְפֶּה (Mizpeh), as well as מִצְפָּה (Mizpah), which means the same thing, is a rather common place-name (cf. the German geographical designation for a lookout point or elevated lookout point and the many cities that include the element of "waiting," such as Wartburg), which leads one to conclude that it was common, in times of unrest, for lookouts to be posted in locations that were suited for the purpose. מִשְׁמֶרֶת (post), parallel to מִצְפֶּה (watch), has a broader range of usages, and can be used, as here, in the special sense of identifying the place where one would post a watch; thus Hab. 2:1. Moreover, the parallelism between the subject matter and actual wording that is common to Hab. 2:1 and Isa. 21:8 is striking:

Hab. 2:1 (emended text):	Isa. 21:8aα
עַל־מִשְׁמַרְתִּי אֶעֱמֹדָה	עַל־מִצְפֶּה אֲדֹנָי אָנֹכִי עֹמֵד
וְאֶתְיַצְּבָה עַל־מָצוֹר	תָּמִיד יוֹמָם
וַאֲצַפֶּה לִרְאוֹת מַה־יְדַבֶּר־בִּי	וְעַל־מִשְׁמַרְתִּי אָנֹכִי נִצָּב
. . . :	כָּל־הַלֵּילוֹת:

I will stand at my watchpost,	On watch, O Lord, I stood
and station myself on my rampart;	without a break during the day,
and I will keep watch to see what	and at my post I kept watch
he will say to me,	all the night long.
. . .	

In the Habakkuk passage, v. 2 follows this by specifically calling what the seer will see a חָזוֹן (vision). This parallelism cannot have happened just by chance. There must have been certain circles of seers where it was common practice to understand their function by analogy to what a lookout did. Such ecstatics would apparently have taken position at a particular place, such as on a mountaintop, where they would await their visions. The Balaam narrative mentions a lookout field (שְׂדֵה צֹפִים [NRSV: field of Zophim]), which was located at the top of Pisgah (Num. 23:14). The description of how the revelation was received in Num. 24:1ff. is also worth comparing: "[Balaam] set his face toward the wilderness. Balaam looked up and saw Israel camping tribe by tribe. Then the Spirit of God came upon him, and he uttered his oracle, saying: . . . ." (Apparently, the office of lookout for the house of Israel, which was entrusted to Ezekiel, functioned on a different plane; cf. 3:17, and often elsewhere.)

One often sought to use certain stimuli (music, dance, narcotics) to bring on a vision (cf. 2 Kings 3:15; Eliade, 375ff., 394ff., and often elsewhere; Benz, 37–82); by contrast, the seer in the present text was simply to remain at his post night and day, at the highest level of readiness, just as is appropriate for any lookout at his post; cf. 62:6. No provisions were made for using any special techniques to bring on special revelatory experiences, but he was to wait patiently for the time when something could be perceived (on this, see Seierstad, 150).

[21:9] But then, all of a sudden, processions of men and teams of horses appear. The זֶה (there), after the הִנֵּה (behold), underscores how, after such a long time of waiting, in a flash all could be recognized with surprising clarity.

The seer recounts what he has experienced; this means that בָא (came) should be treated as a perfect form. On the basis of v. 7, it was expected that he would see teams of horses; but it is surprising that there is a רֶכֶב אִישׁ (procession of men). Apparently, the seer first sees a procession of warriors and then the charioteer corps afterward. Donkeys and camels are not mentioned here, possibly because they were not crucial for explaining the meaning of the vision.

The seer tells not only about what he saw, but, in keeping with his orders, also about what he could hear; the reason for the vision is found in the message that is now delivered. Its importance is underscored by the introductory וַיַּעַן וַיֹּאמֶר (then one commenced and spoke). Again, one has to wonder about the identity of the subject of the verb. One might suppose it is the seer himself, but it would be strange if the comment וַיִּקְרָא (and he [the seer] called out) in v. 8 would then be continued by וַיַּעַן וַיֹּאמֶר (then one commenced and spoke). There must be another who serves as the subject of these two verbs, who *interprets* for him what he has just seen. Who is this person? In Zech. 4:1ff. the prophet sees a vision, the interpretation of which is left open for the moment. Then he poses the question: "What are these, my lord?" The answer is given him by מַלְאָךְ הַדֹּבֵר בִּי (the angel who talked with me) (v. 5). One should note that the answer that interprets this vision is introduced by the formula וַיַּעַן . . . וַיֹּאמֶר (and he answered . . . and he said), that is, the same way the interpretation is given in Isa. 21:9; see also Zech. 1:10 (concerning the original wording, see K. Elliger, *Das Buch der zwölf kleinen Propheten*, ATD 25 [1964[5]] 103); 3:4; 6:5; cf. also 5:6. This means that one would have expected the question: "What do these [the chariots] mean?" In the hearer's own mind, he or she has to insert these thoughts, since only then does the introductory ויען ויאמר (then one commenced and spoke) make any sense. In analogy to the visions in Zechariah, the subject must be the "angel who gives an explanation." In Zech. 2:4 it seems that such a function is performed by Yahweh, who himself gives the answer. This should also be assumed in this passage, as the suffixes on מדשתי (my thrashed [people]) and בן־גרני (my threshing floor son) in v. 10 help one to recognize.

Now, however, to the content of the answer: this sounds like a lament for one who has died, in which נפל (fallen) is a specialized formal term; see above, pp. 50f.; and cf. Amos 5:2; Lam. 2:21; and Jer. 9:21. Babylon is not simply besieged, humiliated, and weakened, but dead, robbed of all life in the same way that a dead person is robbed of life for ever.

Babylon's power and splendor were symbolized in its gods, but even the imagery of its deities lay smashed on the ground, their potency exposed as being totally impotent, their splendor totally illusory; on this, cf. 19:1bβ. Deutero-Isaiah expects the same thing: "Bel bows down, Nebo stoops, their idols are on beasts and cattle" (46:1); and the author of the massive poem about Babylon's downfall in the book of Jeremiah, in 50:2, anticipates it too; cf. 51:44, 47.

Concerning the parallelism between נפל (fallen) and שבר (smashed) niphʿal, one can compare Isa. 8:15 and Jer. 51:8. Note that the perfect of both verbs is used. What the seer has seen in a vision lies first of all in the future, but still it already exists as a completed reality.

[21:10] It corresponds to the abrupt style of the report about the vision that, right after the decisive message about the fall of Babylon has been stated, in v. 10a, unexpectedly and with few words, Israel is now addressed, and even at that with terminology that does not immediately make sense: "you, my thrashed, my threshing floor son!" The "I" in the suffixes on מדשתי (thrashed) and בן־גרני (threshing floor son) can be none other than Yahweh.

In Amos 1:3 an accusation is raised against Damascus, that it had threshed Gilead with threshing sledges of iron. It has actually happened from time to time that prisoners of war have been mutilated by "threshing" (see Judg. 8:7, 16). In other places דוש (tread, thresh) is used to depict the horrible way in which a defeated enemy was treated (2 Kings 13:7; Mic. 4:13; Hab. 3:12; Isa. 25:10; 41:15; cf. H. W. Wolff, BK XIV/2, 187f. [Engl: *Joel and Amos,* 154]). בן־גרני (my threshing floor son) means essentially the same: Yahweh had given Israel over to his enemies, just as a farmer brings his grain to the threshing floor, because there it was to be tread under foot (pictures are in Dalman, *AuS* III, illuss. 13–24). But Israel remained his people, and, in the destruction of Babylon, the day came when he showed that he had not forgotten them in their humility and in their suffering; now the day had come on which it would be known that he was also their Lord. One ought to note carefully that virtually no details are provided about the specifics of what is to come in the future; this is far removed from the vast array of images used by someone such as Deutero-Isaiah. This one had been given a glimpse into the future, but what that would mean in a concrete sense for Israel remained sealed, in spite of that glimpse, within the mystery of Yahweh's counsel. It seems almost as if the seer can already hear someone posing a question, naturally because of wanting to know more, and that in more detail. He fends that off: "What I have heard I have announced to you." What he said had not been the product of his own fantasizing, but had been revealed to him. But he had in no way overstepped the bounds arbitrarily, in order to satisfy someone's curiosity, just because that would have been expected and anticipated.

The additional מֵאֵת יְהוָה צְבָאוֹת אֱלֹהֵי יִשְׂרָאֵל (from Yahweh of Hosts, the God of Israel) is supplied in order to remove any uncertainty about who had been speaking in vv. 9b, 10a. Naturally, the seer himself also treated this vision as a revelation from Yahweh. When the expander underscores that point with these words, it reflects on a requirement of faith that seeks absolute certainty—understandable insofar as the "redemption" of Israel had been postponed and, even though Babylon had fallen, the end of all the troubles had not yet appeared on the horizon.

Concerning יְהוָה צְבָאוֹת (Yahweh of Hosts), see *Isaiah 1–12*, pp. 29ff.

Purpose and Thrust

The report of the vision in 21:1-10 gives moving testimony to Israel's hope while they were under the oppressive domination of Babylon and to the heavy spiritual burden for the faith of Israel that resulted from the destruction of Jerusalem and the loss of their political freedom. The seer promises: the world power, which had seemingly prepared for Israel nothing less than total dissolution, would disappear. Totally unexpectedly, the destructive events would unfold; the enemy would fall victim because of the Babylonian leadership, with its self-assured fanciful notion that it did not have a care in the world. As he portrays his own perplexity, he shows that this upheaval within the power ranks will be massive, the consequences harsh. Nothing can be seen of hate and a desire for vengeance, and when commentators speak of jubilation because of the fall of Babylon, one must at least point out that this would be a most subdued jubilation. The visionary is far removed from using a large brush and harsh colors to depict the severity of Babylon's destruction. For him, prime importance is attached to the unavoidable end that will come upon the city itself and that it will become clear therein that its gods are nothing. This knowledge would give hope to the people of God, for which the address in v. 10a would shine as a comforting light. Israel is still Yahweh's son; the father's face bends down low to them. They can breathe a sigh of relief, not so much because of Babylon's fall, but because Yahweh would once again turn toward them. That the future is not illustrated in detail alters nothing when it comes to the great import of what is communicated in this message, though it does protect Israel from expecting something previous to the time that God would see fit to accomplish it, in his own good time.

We have refused to agree with the exegetes who think that the seer does nothing more than paint a picture about the end of the "world city," and that this, as the onset of the pains, would immediately precede the coming

326

final salvation. This passage just speaks of Babylon and Israel; salvation for the world is not within the field of vision. In spite of this, there is no doubt that this section contributed to the way in which apocalyptic views about history were depicted. Just the call itself, פָּתְאֹם נָפְלָה בָבֶל וַתִּשָּׁבֵר (suddenly Babylon has fallen and is shattered) in Jer. 51:8 might be a reminiscence of this deeply moving outcry that the seer had perceived. "Thus more and more Babylon appears to represent pride which is hostile to God, and which the Almighty will humble" (Ringgren, *TDOT* I, 467). At the appropriate place, there will be a discussion about whether Babylon is in view in the Isaiah apocalypse. In any case, the Johannine apocalypse took up the call: ἔπεσεν ἔπεσεν Βαβυλὼν ἡ μεγάλη (Fallen, fallen is Babylon the great), Rev. 14:8; 18:2 (concerning the OT background of μεγάλη, "great," see Dan. 4:27). There, Βαβυλών (Babylon) certainly refers to Rome (on this, see Str-B III, 816). But finally it goes even deeper than the fall of Rome; Babylon is the typological example of power directly opposed to God, with its titanic arrogance, that must finally come to judgment, so that the reign of God can be established. From the viewpoint of history, Isa. 21:1-10 has achieved an interpretation that far transcends its own historical parameters.

A Message about Dumah

Literature

Concerning the text: F. Buhl, *Geschichte der Edomiter* (1893). P. Lohmann, "Das Wächterlied Jes 21:11, 12," *ZAW* 33 (1913) 20–29. Ch. Rabin, "An Arabic Phrase in Isaiah," *Studi sull'Oriente e la Bibbia,* FS G. Rinaldi (1967) 303–309.

Concerning Arabia: J. Euting, *Tagebuch einer Reise in Inner-Arabien* I (1896), II, ed. E. Littmann (1914). N. Abbott, "Pre-Islamic Arab Queens," *AJSL* 58 (1941) 1–22. E. Täubler, "Kharu, Horim, Dedanim," *HUCA* 1 (1924) 119–123. W. Caskel, *Lihyan und Lihyanisch,* Arbeitsgemeinschaft für Forschung des Landes Nordrhein-Westfalen 4 (1952). I. Rabinowitz, "Aramaic Inscriptions of the Fifth Century B.C.E. from a North-Arab Shrine in Egypt," *JNES* 15 (1956) 1–9. H. St. Philby, *The Land of Midian* (1957). A. Grohmann, *Kulturgeschichte des Alten Orients: Arabien,* HAW 3, 1, 3, 3, 4 (1963).

Sources: M. Streck, "Assurbanipal," VAB VII, 1–3 (1916). R. Borger, *Die Inschriften Asarhaddons, König von Assyrien,* BAfO 9 (1956). C. J. Gadd, "The Harran Inscriptions of Nabonidus," *AnSt* 8 (1958) 35–92.

[Literature update through 1979: *Concerning Arabia:* A. van den Branden, "ʾUmmᶜattarsamm, re di Dûmat," *BeO* (1960) 41–47. M. Weippert, "Die Kämpfe des assyrischen Königs Assurbanipal gegen die Araber: Redaktionskritische Untersuchungen des Berichts in Prisma A," *WO* 7 (1973) 39–85. Idem, "Abiyateʾ," *WO* 8 (1975/76) 64.]

Text

21:11 [Verdict[a] concerning Dumah[b]]
 [c]To me it calls[d] from Seir[c]:
  [e]"Watcher, how far along is it in the night?[fe]
  Watcher, how far along is it in the night?"[g]
12 [a]The watcher says[a]:
  The morning has come,
  [b]and still[b] it is night.
  If you will [c]ask, ask,[dc]
   come once again!

11a Concerning משא (verdict), see above, p. 1f.
11b The Gk translates דומה (traditionally: Dumah) as Ιδουμαία (Idumea) (Gk[534]: ιουδαια, Judah!), Aquila: *duma,* seeking to explain the word (according to Jerome)

to mean *silentium* (silence) or *similitudo* (resemblance). Two Hebrew MSS have the reading אֱדֹום (Edom) in the margin (see Gesenius), and some Hebrew MSS, dating to the time of Jerome, read רומה (Rome) (see Gesenius), thus being of the opinion that this message was about either Edom or Rome. It has apparently seemed obvious to many that this should be read as אדום (Edom) (haplography of the א), as is done by Marti, Guthe, Buhl, Feldmann, Procksch, Leslie, et al. In favor of this reading, one must also consider that the call to the watcher comes "from Seir." Seir is the name of the mountain range east of the *ʿaraba* depression, where Edom was situated. Since the superscription מַשָּׂא דוּמָה (verdict concerning Dumah) is likely secondary, the more important question is whether the redactor even knew any more about who had been the original recipient of the message. But then, how would he have just happened to identify this message as one spoken concerning Dumah, located off the beaten path, a rather unimportant place? If one can find texts that read this even as Judah or Rome, then it is not hard to understand that the translator of the Gk, who would have hardly known anything about the oasis Dumah, in Arabia, would have thought it referred to the much better known Idumea. The most important point in favor of reading this as a reference to Dumah is that the following section, vv. 13-15, which speaks of the Dedanites and of the people from Tema, also deals with the destiny of Arabian oases. Since, according to our knowledge of the history of Arabia (see below, pp. 331f.), it is certainly possible that Israel had dealings with Dumah during particular periods, there is no compelling reason to alter the text.

11c–c There is just as little justification for *BHS* to suggest the text be altered, on the basis of Aquila, Sym, Theod (according to Eusebius), to read אֵלַי קֹרֵא הַנֹּדְדִים (προς εμε καλει [τους φευγοντας]) (to me he calls [the fleeing ones]).

11d Just as in v. 1 above, with the verb בא (it comes), one should assume that the subject is not specifically identified; see Joüon, *Gr* §155f; BrSynt §37.

11e–e In place of v. 11bβ, the Gk reads φυλάσσετε ἐπάλξεις, "watch the battlements," and some minuscules (see Ziegler) also insert τι ολολυζεις φυλασσων (what do you lament, watcher?) (or something similar) as well, in which case ολολυζεις (you lament) is apparently the result of misreading מלילה (from the night) (as if from הליל, "howl"). These readings that offer alternatives to the MT do not provide evidence for a better original text, but rather show plainly that even those who worked with the text in ancient times were puzzled about the meaning of these obscure lines.

11f Already here, the first time it is used, Qᵃ reads the shorter word מליל (in the night). Ehrlich (*Randglossen* IV, 75) had already suggested this reading, since the effect of repeating the question with such a minor alteration would not have been caught anyway. It is not worth the effort to argue about this point.

11g לֵיל (night) can be in the absolute state; see Joüon, *Gr* §96Am.

12a–a Procksch thinks the line is too long, suggesting that אָמַר שֹׁמֵר (the watcher says) should be removed, which makes sense also because the prophet himself speaks in the first person (see אלי, "to me," in v. 11); however, cf. v. 8.

12b–b Instead of וגם (and still), Procksch suggests reading וְגָמַל (haplography of the ל) and translates it: "The morning comes; thus the night has come to an end." Admittedly, one is surprised by the reading in the MT. Buhl (68) thinks he has solved the problem by translating it: "The morning comes, when it is also night"; Kaiser recently did the same. But this translation ignores the perfect אָתָה (has come). Even if one would like to treat this as a prophetic perfect, it would still make no sense with this interpretation that someone would repeat the summons to come again to seek an answer.

12c–c Concerning the unique forms of תִּבְעָיוּן (you will ask) and בְּעָיוּ (ask), see Ges-K §75h.

12d Instead of the imperative בְּעָיוּ (ask), Ehrlich (*Randglossen* IV, 75) would read the infinitive absolute בָּעוֹ (ask), a completely unnecessary alteration.

Form

Even though there is a certain relationship between these two verses and those which follow (see below, p. 336), they should still be studied initially by themselves; this treatment is primarily justified by the new superscription in v. 13.

Lohmann has tried to demonstrate that this little poem is basically a profane, popular watcher's song (see also H. Gunkel, *Die israelitische Literatur* [1963], reprint from *Kultur der Gegenwart* I, 7: *Orientalische Literaturen* [1925], 36, and the footnote on p. 52). In order to make this proposal appear believable, he suggested that the first line at one time read: בָּעֶרֶב אֵלַי קָרָא מִשַּׁעַר, "at evening time [= already in the evening, an exaggerated way to say: in the middle of the night] it called (up) to me from the gate" (26). But that is a radical alteration to the text, and the interpretation is also forced. In addition, Lohmann has to assume that this is a playful little song. The people want to know whether the nighttime will soon be past so that the gates can be opened, "but he [namely, the night watcher], in a surly mood, sends the jokesters away with a spiteful reply" (24). The prophet would have then altered the original מִשַּׁעַר (from the gate) to read מִשֵּׂעִיר (from Seir) so that this popular secular song would have been recast as an oracle against the heathen nation of Edom. As this took place, the answer of the watcher would also have taken on a new meaning. The visionary sight, which the prophet possessed, would have focused on two separate events, advancing on the horizon. For Israel, it was the dawn of a bright day; for Edom, the darkness of a gloomy night. This explanation pushes the fantasizing too far; in reality, just as is true in vv. 1–10, this is a report of a vision or, as the case may be, an audition. The seer hears a voice; he has a hallucination, and this voice calls to a שֹׁמֵר (watcher). This term is apparently parallel to מְצַפֶּה (lookout) in v. 6 and רֹאֶה (seer) in v. 8 (text emended); this means that, with the use of שֹׁמֵר (watcher), a seer is addressed directly (it would be better not to speak of a "prophet" in this connection). But a measure of uncertainty results, because such a person is identified either as a מְצַפֶּה (lookout) or as a צֹפֶה (also: lookout) elsewhere in the OT when the work of a seer is depicted, but the same cannot be said for שֹׁמֵר (watcher). Nevertheless, one can compare this usage with Isa. 62:6 (unfortunately, that passage is very difficult to understand, but see Muilenburg, *IB*, who points to direct links between that passage and 21:11f.—though he incorrectly refers to it as vv. 12–13). However, if in v. 8 the author uses מִצְפֶּה (on watch) parallel to מִשְׁמֶרֶת (at one's post), then he can just as easily call the "watcher" שֹׁמֵר instead of מְצַפֶּה (lookout). Therefore, at least keeping the fiction alive, 21:11f. depicts a question being put to a seer, whom one would have to seek out in Jerusalem. Seers could become so widely known as being expert in their calling that they could be summoned to come from a great distance (Balaam: Num. 22:5; Samuel: 1 Sam. 9:6; Elisha: 2 Kings 5:3; 8:7ff.). This means that one need not assume that people from Dumah (or even from closer by, from the mountains of Seir) had sent a delegation to Jerusalem in order to seek someone who would announce their future to them. The text says: אֵלַי קֹרֵא מִשֵּׂעִיר (to me it calls from Seir); that is the way visions are described; see, e.g., קוֹל קוֹרֵא (a voice cries out) in 40:3 and קוֹל אָמַר (a voice says) in 40:6.

Meter: If one disregards the introductory formulas, the poem is composed of 3 two-stress + two-stress bicola: vv. 11bβ-γ, 12aβ-γ, 12b.

Setting

We saw no reason to change דּוּמָה (Dumah) to read אֱדוֹם (Edom). But דּוּמָה (Dumah) is not only a place-name; it also means "be silent." Thus in earlier times, even if the text was not altered, דּוּמָה was often treated as a symbolic designation of Edom, which would serve to indicate something about its future destiny: destruction and the stillness of death (Vitringa, Delitzsch, Knobel). Concerning this, Dillmann notes that a superscription such as "verdict about silence" would not be inappropriate, since the prophet would be hiding more than he is revealing when he affixes such a mysterious title. But מַשָּׂא (verdict) is virtually always linked with a designation of some locale (or people). "Remain still" does not fit well in terms of the content either; the inquirer does get an answer right away. דּוּמָה (Dumah) must be a *nomen loci* (place-name). A settlement bearing this name (today: *ḥirbet dēr ed-dūma;* see Simons, *Geographical Texts,* §319) is situated about 15 km. southwest of Hebron, but surely this would not have been important enough to be the subject of this oracle. Thus there is no doubt that דּוּמָה (Dumah) is the same as *adummatu* in the Akkadian inscriptions (Δουμαίθα, Doumaitha, in Ptolemy 5.18; Domata or Domatha in Pliny, *Natural History* 6.157), which is the present-day oasis *el-jōf,* also known as *dūmat el-jandel,* "Dumah of the Rock," located on the northern border of the *nefūd* desert. In Gen. 25:14f. Dumah is also mentioned at the same time as Kedar and Tema, among others. A significant number of settlements are linked to the oasis *el-jōf* (see Simons, §121.6), stretching a day's journey toward the northeast (Euting I, 124).

Now that the location of Dumah has been settled, the question arises about whether there is a period in Israel's history when there would have been enough interest within Judah/Jerusalem about the destiny of this far-removed oasis that a seer who dwelt in Judah/Jerusalem would have found sufficient reason to pursue this interest.

The history of Dumah (and that of Dedan and Tema, which are mentioned in the next unit of material, as well as that of the people of Kedar) is known only in a fragmented form. Tiglath-Pileser III, when reporting on the year 738 in his annals (line 154; *AOT* 346), mentions a queen from Arabia who owed him tribute by the name of *zabibē,* whose kingdom would have been located around Dumah (see

Abbott, 4). In the same annals (lines 210–217), *samsī,* also identified by the title "queen of Arabia," is mentioned as well, apparently having joined a coalition organized by Damascus against Assyria, but who was then once again forced to subjugate herself afterward. She also seems to have ruled in Dumah. Along with her, the inhabitants of Tema (and other clans) declared their loyalty to the Assyrians by delivering their tribute. Sargon (Display Inscription, line 27, *AOT* 349) also counts *samsī* among his vassals and praises himself that he struck a blow against the distant Arabians and deported them to Samaria (Annals, lines 120–123, *TGI*[2], no. 34). In 703, at the time of Sennacherib, Arab auxiliary forces who are serving Babylon appear for the first time. The queen *iatiʾe* sends her brother *basqānu* with Arab troops, with the support of Merodach-Baladan (British Museum 113,203; see *ARAB* II, §259). Concerning the same period, we also learn of a certain *ḫazāilu,* king of [KUR]*aribi,* who also rules over the land of *qidri* (K 3087 and K 3405; see Streck, VAB VII/7, 216ff. and 222f.; in addition, see Ashurbanipal's Annals, cylinder B, col. VII, line 81; in Streck, 130f.). Thus it is not surprising that, when Babylon fell in 689, the Arabians also suffered under the harsh response meted out by the Assyrians. Sennacherib attacked the queen, *telḫunu,* who then fled to *ḫazāilu,* who was at [URU]*adummatu* (Winckler, *Die Keilinschriften und das Alte Testament* [1902[3]] 47), and inscriptions of Esarhaddon report that Sennacherib conquered Dumah ([URU]*adummatu*) and as spoils of war, in addition to the idols, deported *iskallatu,* the wife of *ḫazāilu,* to Assyria (Nineve. Klasse A, IV, 1ff. in R. Borger, *Die Inschriften Asarhaddons, Königs von Assyrien* [1956] 53). *ḫazāilu* seems to have worked out some deal with the Assyrians; in 676 he came to Nineveh, during the reign of Esarhaddon, at which time he succeeded in getting his idols returned. According to the same text, when he died in 675, the Assyrians installed his son *iataʾ* (*iatiʾe, uaiteʾ, iaʾlū*) as king. Someone tried to plot a revolt against him, and Esarhaddon came to his defense. But finally *iataʾ* himself tried to gain his independence. So then he himself was overthrown by Esarhaddon, and his gods were taken back to Nineveh (VAT 5600, lines 3ff.; in Streck, 376f.). Yet *iataʾ* somehow survived and was later even able to risk asking Ashurbanipal if he could get his idols back. He had "to declare the name of the great gods," i.e., swear his allegiance, and when that was done he got his *atarsamain* back (cylinder B, VII, 87ff.; in Streck, 130f.). Soon after that, *iataʾ,* sensing that fresh breezes were blowing, revolted against his overlord and plundered his lord's vassal territory [KUR]*amurru.* Ashurbanipal sent the troops that he had stationed in Arabia against him; the curses of the covenant that had now been broken were inflicted on him and *iataʾ* had to flee to [KUR]*nabaiti.* Ashurbanipal installed in his place a king who was beholden to him alone; *iataʾ* was brought to Nineveh and was locked up in a cage with animals (Rm VIII, 10–13; in Streck, 66f.). Also during the time of Ashurbanipal, the same fate was met by *ammuladi,* the king of [KUR]*qi/adri* (Rm VIII, 15–29; in Streck, 68f.), who, according to cylinder B VIII, 31–39 (Streck, 134f.), suffered a defeat at the hands of the loyal Assyrian vassal *ka[ma]shaltā,* the king of Moab (see above, p. 116). "At the bidding of the great gods of my lord, I made for him a dog leash and left him to be guarded in the prisoner's cage" (Rm VIII, 27–29; in Streck, 68f.). After *šamaššu-mukīn* had been conquered, Ashurbanipal installed this man as king of *aribi* (Rm VIII, 40–47; in Streck, 68f.). But that brought no peace to Arabia. In 645 Ashurbanipal besieged the [LU]*qidrai* of *iataʾ,* the son of *bir-dadda,* the king of *aribi* (this *iataʾ* is a nephew of the *iataʾ* who was mentioned above, who was the son of *ḫazāilu*). They were deported, along with their families, their idols, and their possessions, to Assyria (Rm VIII, 73–IX, 8, 42f.; in Streck, 70ff.): "As for *uaiteʾ,* along with his troops, which had not stayed faithful to the agreements, who fled before the weapons of *aššur,* my lord, and who were made to disappear because of them, the mighty *gira* (*ura*) made them lie prostrate on the ground" (Rm IX, 53–57; in Streck, 76f.). He experienced a fate similar to that of *ammuladi.* Ashurbanipal had him brought to Assyria, had a hole bored into his jawbone, had a string pulled through the jaw, attached to it a dog leash, and left him to be watched in the prisoner's cage at the east gate in Nineveh. He had to pull the king's chariot in a procession (Rm IX, 102–111 and X, 21–29; in Streck, 80f. and 82ff.).

With this account, the Assyrian reports fall silent. According to Josephus (*Against Apion* 1.19), Nebuchadnezzar, laying claim to all the territory that had been under Assyrian control, set forth on a campaign against Arabia, specifically against Kedar (cf. Jer. 49:28); however, the historicity of this notation has not gone unquestioned. Most importantly, it was under Nabonidus (556–539) that Arabia stood, as never before, in the center of historical events, indeed because of the decade-long sojourn of the last ruler of the Neo-Babylonian Empire, out in the desert, the reason for which still remains a puzzle (normally dated to 550–540; Galling: 553–546, in *Studien,* 16; see above, p. 299). An insulting poem about Nabonidus (II, 18–26; *TGI*[1] no. 40, and *ANET* 312–315) reports that he transferred power over Babylon itself to his son Belshazzar and, to quote what is then said: "And, himself, he started out for a long journey. . . . He turned towards Tema (deep) in the west [lit.: in *amurru*]. . . . When he arrived there, he killed in battle the prince of Tema [*tema*ᵓ], slaughtered the flocks of those who dwell in the city (as well as) in the countryside" (*ANET* 313). In listing the cities over which he ruled, in addition to ᵁᴿᵁ*tema*ᵓ, it also mentions ᵁᴿᵁ*dadanu* (Dedan!), ᵁᴿᵁ*padakku* (*fadak/el-ḫuwayyiṭ*), ᵁᴿᵁ*ḫibrā* (*ḫaibar*), ᵁᴿᵁ*yadiḫu* (*yadīᶜ/el-ḥāyiṭ*), and *yatribu* (*yatrib/*Medina) (H 2, I, 24–25; *TGI*[2] no. 47; concerning the location of these places, cf. Gadd, 81ff.; *FWG* 4, 352, note 18; and the map of Arabia, p. 335); he selected *tema*ᶜ itself as the location for his residence. The stele in Haran reports that Nabonidus made a triumphant return to Babylon, but, by that time, the territory over which he had ruled lay under the lengthening shadow of the newest world power, Persia, which soon would be ready to bring Babylon down. With this, Arabia sunk once again, almost completely, into the dark reaches of history.

During the many fluctuations of Arabia's history that we can follow between 740 and 540, particularly in light of the continual stubborn efforts of the Arabian kings to reassert their independence, it is impossible for one to date with certainty the events that are in the background of 21:11f., which speak of the oppression of Dumah. During the time of Isaiah himself, Dumah had played a relatively important role. Those commentators who cannot see any reason in vv. 11f. and vv. 13ff. for rejecting Isaian authorship cannot be faulted from the outset, based on our knowledge of the history. Yet there is little doubt that the song does not come from Isaiah. אתה (come) in v. 12aβ is an Aramaic word, and the form אָתָיו (come) in v. 12b is also an Aramaic form. Isaiah never uses the word; it appears for the first time in the book of Jeremiah (3:22; 12:9). Right next to it, the typical Aramaic verb בעה, "ask," is found as well, used elsewhere (in the *niphᶜal*) only in Obad. 6. There are also other reasons why the text must be dated later than Isaiah. A certain relationship between this and 21:1-10 is noted (1) in the metrical pattern (two-stress + two-stress bicola; see above); (2) in the sketchy content, which does little more than provide hints and does not say anything clearly; and (3) in

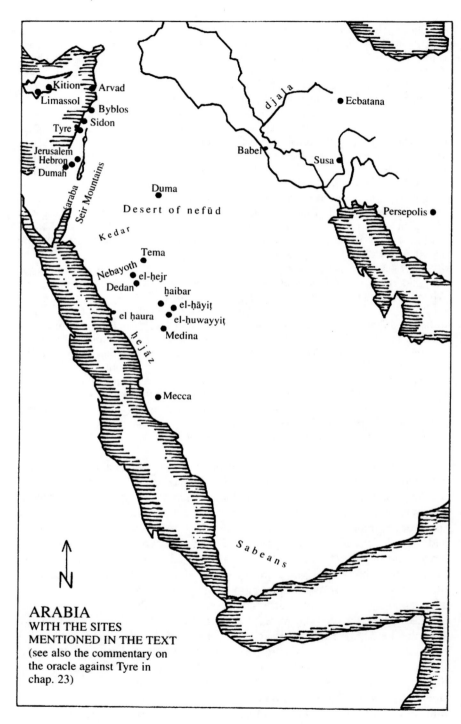

ARABIA
WITH THE SITES
MENTIONED IN THE TEXT
(see also the commentary on
the oracle against Tyre in
chap. 23)

IDENTIFICATION ON THE MAP	HEBREW, OLD SOUTH ARABIC, OR PHOENICIAN NAME	AKKADIAN, OLD PERSIAN, OR ELAMITE NAME	GREEK OR LATIN NAME	PRESENT-DAY NAME
Arvad	אַרְוַד	^{URU}*aruada/i* or ^{URU}*arw/mada/i*	Ἄραδος	*ruād*
Byblos	גְּבַל	^{URU}*gubla*	Βύβλος	*jbēl*
Dedan	דְּדָן	^{URU}*dadanu*	ᵴ: Δεδαν	*el-ᶜulā*
Dumah (15 km. sw. of Hebron)	דּוּמָה	^{URU}*udumu*	ᵴ: Ρουμα	*ḥirbet dēr-ed-dūmah*
Duma (in Arabia)	דּוּמָה	^{URU}*adummu*, ^{URU}*adummatu* (or something similar)	Δουμάδα, Δυμάθα	*el-jōf* or *dūmat el-jandel*
Ecbatana	אַחְמְתָה	^{URU}*agmatanu* Old Persian: *hagmatana*	Ἀγβάτανα Ἐκβάτανα	*hamadān*
ḥaibar		^{URU}*ḥibrā*		*ḥaibar*
el-ḥāyiṭ		^{URU}*jadiḥu*		*el-ḥāyiṭ*
el-ḥaura			Λεύκη Κώμη	*el-ḥaura*
el-ḥejr	OSA *ḥgrᵓ*		Ἔγρα, Hegra, Hagra, Egra	*el-ḥejr*
el-ḥuwayyiṭ		^{URU}*padakku*		*el-ḥuwayyiṭ*
Kedar	קֵדָר	^{KUR}*qidri*, ^{KUR}*qadri*, ^{LU}*qidrai* (or something similar)	Cedrei	
Kition	Phoen.: (י)כתן Cf. Hebr.: כתי(ם)	^{URU}*qartiḥadasti ?*	Κιτ(τ)ιον	*larnaka ?*
Limassol	Phoen.: קרתחדשת ?	^{URU}*qartiḥadasti ?*	Neapolis	*limassol*
Medina		^{URU}*jatribu*		*medīna*
Nebayoth	נְבָיוֹת	^{KUR}*nabaiti* (or something similar)	ᵴ: Ναβαιωθ	
Persepolis		Old Persian: *pārsa*	Περσέπολις, Πέρσαι	*taḥt-i-jamšīd*
Sidon	צִידֹן, צִידוֹן	^{URU}*ṣidun(n)u* or ^{URU}*ṣaᵓidunu*	Σιδών	*ṣaida*
Susa	שׁוּשָׁן	^{URU}*šušan*, ^{URU}*šuši* Old Persian: *šūšā* Elamite: *šūšun*	Σοῦσα	*šuš*
Tema	תֵּמָא, תֵּימָא	^{URU}*temaᵓ*, ^{URU}*temai* (or something similar)	ᵴ: Θαιμαν	*taimā*
Tyre (island)	צֹר, צוֹר	^{URU}*ṣurru/i*	Τύρος, Σώρ	*ṣūr*
Tyre (mainland)		^{URU}*ušu*	Παλαίτυρος	*tell maᶜšūk* or *tell rešidīye*

the way it speaks of the שֹׁמֵר (watcher), which in the final analysis must be identified as being the מְצַפֶּה (lookout) in vv. 1-10 (see above, pp. 322f.). However, if one does not treat this passage as the work of Isaiah, then there are many possible historical events with which one might connect it. But it seems most probable that this should be related to the same period to which vv. 1-10 have been assigned (Duhm, Marti). Galling (FS Weiser, 60) gets even more specific, dating it to the time after 545, when (at least according to his dating) Nabonidus left the oasis, and the question had to have been posed by those living there: "What does the future have in store? Will a change in fortunes come, which will mean freedom from the Babylonians? Tensions between the Babylonian troops and their collaborators, on the one side, and the Arabs, who had freedom on the mind, on the other, could have led the latter, beginning with Edom (cf. Seir in v. 11!) to turn to consult the Jewish prophet" (similarly, Fohrer). It must be said again: This historical dating is possible; it is not assured.

Commentary

[21:11] Concerning מַשָּׂא, see above, pp. 1f. For the historical discussion about Dumah, see the excursus above, pp. 331f. One might ask whether a seer in Jerusalem would have considered it to be his task to give an opinion about the destiny of the oasis in Dumah in Arabia. That is probably the most important reason why so many exegetes quickly abandoned that reading in favor of אֱדוֹם (Edom). Besides, Edom shared a common border with Judah. But as is shown by Obadiah or Isaiah 34, those who lived in Jerusalem were in no rush to offer any sympathy to Edom during the exilic-postexilic era; it is unthinkable that this people, which had profited from the demise of Judah, would have chosen Jerusalem of all places to ask for news about the end of its "night"—and that would have to mean: news about the breakup of the Babylonian Empire. This was a sufficient reason for Procksch, who treats this as a message about Edom, to date the passage in the preexilic era. There have already been others who have thought it likely that Jews were living in the Arabian oases during the time of Nabonidus who would have kept up their contact with their homeland (Gadd, 86; R. Meyer, *Das Gebet des Nabonid,* Sitzungsberichte der Sächsische Akademie der Wissenschaften zu Leipzig, Philosophische-historische Klasse 107, part 3 [1962] 72ff.; Galling, FS Weiser, 60). About that we know nothing. This presupposition is not important either. The historical overview pointed out that the oases had achieved an importance during the late exilic age that had not been theirs up to that point, so much so that those living there looked for every opportunity to throw off the foreign domination. "Watcher, how far along is it in the night?" poses a question that was no doubt just at the surface of what was a burning issue, as signs were detected about the weaknesses in the Babylonian overlordship. In this regard, the frame of mind in Dumah was certainly no different than that in Jerusalem, so that an exchange of information, indeed a reciprocal expression of sympathy, would have been natural.

The seer hears the voice coming from Seir. שֵׂעִיר (Seir) (also הַר־שֵׂעִיר,

Mount Seir, or אֶרֶץ־שֵׂעִיר, "land of Seir") is used in the OT to refer to a land in which the Horites were first known to have dwelt (Gen. 14:6, and often elsewhere; Gen. 36:21 virtually identifies this population group as the בְּנֵי שֵׂעִיר, "children of Seir"), but which later became the central territory that the Edomites occupied (see Gen. 32:4, where אֶרֶץ שֵׂעִיר, "land of Seir," and שְׂדֵה אֱדוֹם, "country of Edom," are used synonymously; see also Num. 24:18; Deut. 2:5; Josh. 24:4, among other passages, in addition to which come all the passages that identify Seir as the home territory of Esau). It is the mountainous area east of the ʿaraba, which means it is the depression of land running from the Dead Sea to the Gulf of ʿaqaba). שֵׂעִיר (Seir) means "hairy, wooded"; Dalman tells how he encountered wide areas covered with forests (*AuS* I/1, 81). There is disagreement about just how much land west of the ʿaraba could also be included under the designation שֵׂעִיר; in any case, in ancient times, the Edomites had their main area of occupation south of Moab, and the road that led from Jerusalem to Dumah went through their territory (see map, p. 334), so that it makes sense when the seer hears a voice from Seir while seeing a vision that deals with Dumah. It is certainly possible that someone could ask a watcher, let us say somewhere near the city gate: מַה־מִלַּיְלָה (How far along is it in the night?)—so that one would have some idea how long it would be until one could leave the city. But here, of course, the question is posed with a transferred meaning in mind. "Night" is used to convey the image of oppression and lack of freedom, in this case, no doubt, when one is under foreign rule; cf. חֹשֶׁךְ (darkness) and צַלְמָוֶת (a land of darkness) in 9:1 and the vocabulary used in 8:22f.

The repetition of the same question, with the small variation that uses לֵיל (night) instead of לַיְלָה (also: night) highlights the urgency and intensity of the hope, wishing that the great change in fortune would not be long in coming.

[21:12] Since the voice poses the question to the seer himself (see אֵלָי, "to me," in v. 11), one would expect that the answer in v. 12 would begin with וָאֹמַר (and I said), or something similar. Instead, the third person is used; in just the same way, that is what happened with the מְצַפֶּה (lookout) and then רֹאֶה (seer); here also, as in vv. 1-10, the שֹׁמֵר (watcher) seems all of a sudden to be a different person than the seer.

The answer, אָתָה בֹקֶר וְגַם־לָיְלָה (the morning has come, and still it is night), is most surprising. That exegetes translate this verse in a variety of different ways reflects the uncertainty about what it means. Yet it is certain that the perfect אָתָה (has come) is not to be taken in a future sense; the change in fortune is already a reality, at least according to the seer's convictions. The seats of power, which held control, were now less in charge; significant cracks on the stage of world history were now showing up. But nothing more specific could be said about how these cracks would look when they spread; for this reason, the questioner is encouraged to come again, in case something more might be known at a later time. (שֻׁבוּ, "come once again," is not used in the sense of "repent," as suggested by Gesenius, Delitzsch, Steinmann, et al.) The time is not ripe for a more detailed assessment, but the situation could become clearer in the near future.

Both verbs in this answer, אתה (come) and בעה (ask), which show Aramaic influence, are also originally from Arabic, which means one might suppose that the author tries to allude to the language spoken by the people of Dumah (see Rabin).

Purpose and Thrust

It has been noted when examining the oracles against the nations that are from Isaiah himself that they were always basically directed at Judah/Jerusalem, since they were intended as a way to keep them from entering into dangerous treaties or embarking on false hopes. Even the message about Babylon in vv. 1-10 turns to Israel in the end. One would also expect that the same is true about these two verses concerning Dumah; in actuality, it is Israel that is addressed, apparently at a time when information was obtained that there were initial indications of a major shift in power in the region of Arabia, a report that would have motivated many in Jerusalem to boldly hope for massive change. The seer counsels them to take it easy. For the time being, in spite of everything, it is still "night." It would be good for those in both Dumah and Jerusalem to rein in their impatience.

That is exactly what this little message has reiterated down through the ages. There are situations in which the community of believers, even when new movements are afoot, must dampen its expectations, until the new events and relationships become clearer.

In addition, this also shows that a seer in the OT was no simple predictor, able to describe specific future events in detail; Yahweh is unbound as he acts within history and he does not bind himself to predictions, a fact that faith ought to acknowledge respectfully.

Dedanites and Kedarites

Literature

See literature on 21:11, 12.

Text

21:13 [ªVerdict "in the desert"ª]
In the scrub,ᵇ in the desert, pass the night,
ᶜcaravans of the Dedanites!ᶜ
14 To the thirsty ones
offer water,ª
inhabitants of the land of Tema!
'present'ᵇ to the ones fleeingᶜ their bread!ᵈ
15 Far they flee because of swords,ª
ᵇbecause of the unloosed sword,ᵇ
and because of the stretched bow,
and because of the pressureᶜ of the war.

* * * *

[16 For thus said the Lordª to me: "ᵇIn a yearᵇ [harsh] ᶜas the years of a
day laborer,ᵈᶜ the entireᵉ majesty of Kedar will be gone. 17 And the
remainderª ᵇof the number of bows of the soldiers of the Kedaritesᵇ
will be (very) few, for Yahweh, the God of Israel, has said it."]

13a–a משא בערב (verdict in the desert) is missing in the Gk. Syr reads *mšgl* *dᶜrby*,
thus "verdict concerning Arabia," but this is unlikely; here as well, a key word from
the text is used in the superscription (see בערב, "in the desert," in v. 13b; and cf.
above, p. 302). It has traditionally been assumed that ערב (desert) is used here as a
secondary masculine form of the common ערבה, "desert," though this word is never
used elsewhere with this meaning (but see Hab. 1:8, text emended; cf. *BHS*). If the
preposition were not ב, then it would be worth considering the possibility that this
could mean "Arab" or "Arabian"; see Jer. 25:24; Ezek. 27:21, among other passages;
but ב משא in the sense of "verdict concerning . . ." never occurs in the OT. Since ערב
in v. 13b is translated by the Gk as ἑσπέρα (at nightfall) (see also Syr, Targ, Vulg),
some (Guthe, Cheyne) have suggested that it be pointed בָּעֶרב, "in the evening," but

one does not pass the night in the evening. If it is not possible to alter v. 13b, then one should stay with בָּעְרָב (in the desert) in v. 13a as well.

13b It is hard for exegetes to make sense of יער (scrub) as long as they think this term refers to a beautiful European or American type of forest. Some suggest eliminating יער (scrub), since the verse is too long anyway (Schlögl), or treat the word as a dittography of בערב (in the desert) (Ehrlich, *Randglossen* IV, 75; cf. Marti), whereas still others alter the text (e.g., Bruno: כִּי עוֹד, "for yet," instead of בִיער, "in the scrub"). But Arabic *waʿrun* designates "track covered with stones, boulders and wood" (KBL) and יער can also describe the *macchia,* the "brushwood" commonly found in Palestine [see Dalman, *AuS* I/1, 73–89; cf. illus. 25). This type of undergrowth, which can serve the military purpose of providing cover, is also found in some places within central Arabia.

13c–c Gk (ἐν τῇ ὁδῷ Δεδαν, "on the road of Dedan") might have read בְּאֹרַח דדן (on the path of Dedan). The gentilic דדנים (Dedanim, the Dedanites) is used only here (being otherwise always דדן, Dedan), but for that very reason one should stay with the MT reading, especially since the fact that the preposition ב is missing in the MT shows that the Gk cannot be correct when it reads ἐν τῇ ὁδῷ (on the path].

By writing a דודנים (Dodanim) as it does, Qᵃ seems to be showing a particular way that this was pronounced. Aquila, Sym read δωδανιμ (Dodanim); however, cf. Akkadian ᵁᴿᵁ*dadanu.*

14a Qᵃ reads האתיו, with the א; concerning the MT form, see Ges-K §76d and §75u; Bauer-Leander §59g.

14b Instead of קדמו (they presented before), the Gk reads the imperative συναντᾶτε (present before); corresponding to this, in parallel with התיו (offer), it is normally pointed קַדְּמוּ.

14c Gk: τοῖς φεύγουσι (to those fleeing); Syr: *lmbdrʾ* (for those scattered); yet there is no reason not to follow the MT.

14d Qᵃ בלחם (with bread); Gk: ἄρτοις (with bread); it is true that the suffix on בלחמו (their [his] bread) seems out of place, but it does make good sense: "the bread, which they need."

15a Some exegetes are bothered that חרב, "sword," is used twice in the same line. For this reason, Fischer suggests reading הֹרְגִים, "murder," while Kissane reads חֲרָבוֹת, "desolate lands"; however, neither reading is likely.

15b–b Ehrlich (*Randglossen* IV, 75) treats this colon as a gloss to what precedes. He, along with others, is bothered by the traditional translation of נטושה, "drawn," saying that this would have meant either "expanded far and wide" or "cast away," neither of which would make any sense (see Procksch). Some, therefore, would follow Luzzatto and read לְטוּשָׁה (smoothed, sharpened); see Gen. 4:22; Ps. 7:13; this alteration is unnecessary, however, since נטש also means "let loose of, allow to go about freely." For more on the concept of a raging sword, moving about freely, see Isa. 34:5f.

15c For כבד (pressure), Qᵃ reads כבוד (glorious), a reading one can certainly understand, but nevertheless one that is unlikely. כבד, with this transferred meaning, is also used thus in 30:27.

16a Along with many other Hebrew MSS (see Gesenius) and also the Targ, Qᵃ reads יהוה (Yahweh); on this, see above, p. 305, textual note 6a.

16b–b Qᵃ: בעוד שלוש שנים (in yet three years); however, the number 3 has been inserted here to coordinate this with 16:14. Duhm thinks that the actual number was left out on purpose, since the author himself was not sure about the specific duration.

For this reason, his suggestion is that one ought not translate "in a year"—well, why not?

16c–c If שׂכיר כנשׁי (as the years of a day laborer) is supposed to mean: just as long as a mercenary is obligated to serve his tour of duty (which, according to 16:14, was three years), then it is hard for one to make much sense of the present text. As was explained in detail above (pp. 152f.), however, what is intended is that this will be as wearing as are the years of a שׂכיר (day laborer). The text should not be altered, on the basis of the Gk ὡς ἐνιαυτὸς μισθωτοῦ, "as the yearlong time period for a worker hired for pay"; cf. Vulg: *quasi in anno mercenarii*, "just as a year for a mercenary") to read כשׁנת שׂכיר, (as a year for a day laborer).

16d Concerning the translation of שׂכיר (day laborer), see above, pp. 152f.

16e כל (entire) is missing in both Qᵃ and the Gk, probably due to haplography.

16f For קדר (Kedar), Targ reads the very general term ערבאי, "Arab."

17a I. Eitan (*HUCA* 12/13 [1937/38] 67f.) suggests reading וּשׁאר (and the remainder) as a verbal form, pointed וְשָׁאַר; and then he translates v. 17a: "and there will remain few archers [which is the way he believes he can translate קשׁה, 'bow,' in a loose sense], the mighty men of Kedar shall be diminished"; this is an unnecessary alteration; see also 16:14.

17b–b On purely grammatical grounds, מספר (number) is the subject of ימעטו (will be very few); however, the logical subject is the plural גבורי בני־קדר, and the phrase means: "the warriors of the Kedarites with their bows . . ."; see Ges-K 146a; it is too easy a solution if one just eliminates מספר־קשׁה (number of the bow[s]) as a gloss (Schlögl). Concerning the reading גבורי קדר (warriors of Kedar) in Qᵃ, with the inserted correction that added בני (sons of) [before: Kedar], see S. Talmon, *Textus* 4 (1964) 119.

Form

The superscription משׂא בערב (verdict in the desert), which is certainly a secondary addition, correctly separates vv. 13ff. from what precedes. It is true that the region where Arabs lived is also the center of attention here, and thus it is fitting that vv. 13ff. are appended to vv. 11f., though both form and content show that vv. 13-15 form a separate unit; the message deals no longer with Dumah but with the Dedanites and Tema. This also makes clear that the original form of the passage concludes with v. 15. Verse 16 starts off with another messenger formula, though it is linked to vv. 13-15 by כי (for), meaning that vv. 16f. are to be treated as an addendum. Someone who came still later searched in vain for a message about Kedar, maybe because its fate was of more interest than that of the oases of Dumah, Dedan, and Tema. The prosaic nature of the passage itself shows that these two verses supply an addition to the text, but beyond this there is a whole different attitude over against Arabia: in vv. 11f. and 13ff., there is a certain solidarity and sympathy. These must come from a time when Israel and the Arabian clans were experiencing the same fate of being under oppression and must have had the same hope for liberation; in addition, the voice of one who is sharing the burden can be detected in vv. 13-15. The postscript, however, is interested only in Kedar's power being taken away (just as is true concerning Moab in 16:13f.).

Verses 13-15 offer encouragement to the Dedanite caravans, to get themselves to safety (v. 13), and to the Temanites, to give them aid when they come (v. 14), closing with the motivation for such behavior (v. 15). Verses 16f. are an announcement of disaster; no specific reason is identified.

Meter: Verse 13b is a five-stress colon; v. 14a is a two-stress + two-stress bicolon; v. 14b and the two lines in v. 15 are each three-stress + three-stress bicola; vv. 16f. are prose.

Setting

The overview of the history of the Arabian oases (see above, pp. 331f.) gave some indication of how the fate of the Arabian clans was both changeable and harsh during the time of the Neo-Assyrian and the Neo-Babylonian empires. On the one hand, one can certainly presume that some situations could furnish the background for vv. 13-15 even after the downfall of Babylon. On the other hand, the situation depicted here also could have taken place at such a time that Isaiah could have been the author (see Kissane, Procksch, Auvray, Young; cf. also Wright, Mauchline). Little can be concluded by a study of word usage, but there are some hints: Dedan is first mentioned in the books of Jeremiah and Ezekiel (Jer. 25:23; 49:8; Ezek. 25:13; 27:15, 20; 38:13) and in P (Gen. 10:7; Gen. 25:3 is a later addition), which means that Dedan appeared relatively late as a topic for discussion in Israel. One would be no more convinced that the *hiphᶜil* of אתה (offer) is Isaianic than that Isaiah used the *qal* of this verb in v. 12.

There is no need to discuss any further that the vocabulary used in vv. 16f. does not come from Isaiah. However, the content itself speaks most convincingly against Isaianic authorship; there is no parallel for this type of oracle against a nation by this prophet. But if Isaiah is not the author, then the determination of the dating is also wide open. Since, at least as far as we know, Israel had little to do with Dedan, Tema, and not even much contact with Kedar before the exile, one should probably assign to vv. 13-15, as to vv. 11f., a date late within the period of the exile (see esp. Galling, FS Weiser, 60ff.). Nothing in the text suggests that this message speaks about the eschatological threat of "unnamed enemies coming from the north" (thus Kaiser).

According to what has been said above, vv. 16f. would had to have come into existence still later than vv. 13-15. It is immediately apparent that this material closely parallels 16:14f. in both form and content. One would presume that the same glossator was at work in both passages, unless a still later reader thought that the gloss in 16:14f. aptly referred to Kedar as well and inserted the phraseology from that text at the end of this passage.

Commentary

[21:13] The "caravans of the Dedanites" are addressed, not the Dedanites as a whole. Since the residents of Tema were summoned to provide help, according to v. 15, the caravans must have been situated close to their oasis (as the crow flies, Tema is a good 130 km. northeast of Dedan).

The Dedan referred to in the OT is presently called *el-ʿōlā* (*el-ʿulā*). The identification of this oasis as the ancient Dedan (Akkadian: URU*dadanu*) has been confirmed by a Minean inscription from *el-ʿōlā*, which calls the place *ddn* (see M. Lidzbarski, *Ephemeris für semitische Epigraphik* III [1915] 273), and the same name is also used in Himyaritic inscriptions; cf. examples such as recorded in *CIH* 287, lines 5, 9. This oasis is in the northern *ḥejāz*, on the "incense road" between *medīna* and *taimā* (see the map, p. 334). It is surrounded on both sides by rock walls made of red sandstone that are 100 to 200 m. high (cf. Euting II, 218; and Caskel, 16; see also the pictures in Euting II, 241f., 244; in addition, see Simons, *Geographical Texts,* §60; and Abel, *Géographie,* I, 291).

As is true also of Dumah and Dedan, Tema (תימא; in Job 6:19 תמא is among the most ancient settlements in Arabia mentioned in recorded history. The cuneiform texts call the city URU*temaʾ* or URU*temai;* today it is the oasis *taimā* (see Simons, §121.9). It is situated in a deep basin, the level of which descends in elevation as one travels from south to north; it has underground streams of water, apparently copious, which flow out into the world-renowned well in this city, the *el-haddāj* (see the plan of the oasis in Euting II, 148; cf. also 164; in addition see the pictures, p. 153).

[21:14] Thus the Temanites were certainly in a position to provide water for those who were fleeing; one might even assume that 21:14 is itself a play on words, referring to the well itself (thus Euting; see his *Beschreibung der Oase,* II, 146–163).

The caravans of the Dedanites are encouraged to spend the night in the יער (scrub) (concerning the "undergrowth" in Arabia, cf. A. Musil, *Arabia deserta* [1927] fig. 66). It would seem that an element from the "encouragement to flee" form is being used; cf. Jer. 48:6-8, 28, and often elsewhere.

Apparently, this verse describes a situation in which the caravans would have to avoid staying at the desert outposts where their needs normally could be met, since the enemy is hard on their heels. If they stay out in the open desert during the night, they would be more difficult to find or would have a better chance of holding their own if attacked. But this strategy means that they are in danger of not getting the needed supplies. For this reason, the inhabitants of Tema are encouraged to bring supplies out to them— obviously on carts they could pull out to them surreptitiously at night. It is natural to assume that the ישבי ארץ תימא (inhabitants of the land of Tema)— this would also include the population from the general surrounding area and not just the residents of the city who are addressed—are well disposed toward the Dedanites. The caravans deserve all the sympathy they can get, fleeing as they do from before what is apparently a very strong enemy (cf. כבד מלחמה, "pressure of the war," in v. 15).

Up to this point, the text generally makes sense. To be sure, the detailed interpretation is more difficult. Since this verse does not address the Dedanites as a whole, but rather talks about problems for their caravans, one would have to disagree with those who suggest that this passage deals with an attack against Dedan itself or discusses an actual battle fought against this oasis; it is more probable that it deals with a threat to the procession of goods being transported by the Dedanites. That is bad enough for Dedan. A somewhat comfortable existence could be provided for those who lived by these desert oases only if they engaged in commerce; specific mention of that activity by Dedan occurs in the OT: Ezek. 27:20f.; 38:13 (whereas Job 6:19 speaks of the caravans of Tema and Ezek. 27:20 names the princes of Kedar as being part of the same procession in which Dedan is to be found). It is not just by chance that Saba is also mentioned in close proximity to these passages. The commercial highways led from the South Arabian kingdom of the Sabeans up along the incense highway toward the Mediterranean Sea. At *el-ʿōlā* one of the caravan paths branched off toward the port city of *el-ḥaura* on the Red Sea (known to the ancient authors as λευκὴ κώμη, "white village," and another path went off from *taimā* toward Babylon, with still another branching off toward the Persian Gulf. Fohrer presumes that they were coming from the Persian Gulf or from the north, fleeing on a road that would get them back to their homeland, but it just as well could have been that they were attempting to escape from the territory of Dedan since it was being threatened. In either case, they are called fugitives (נֹדֵד).

[21:15] We learn nothing about which enemy motivated them to take flight; nothing more is said than that this was flight from the sword, the bow, and the "pressure of the war." One can conclude from כֹּבֶד מִלְחָמָה (pressure of the war) that it was not simply one of the all too common attacks carried out chiefly in order to plunder a caravan procession. Marti thought this verse might refer to Persian troops who, after the fall of Babylon, may have sought to solidify control over the caravan routes of Arabia for the Achaemenid Empire as well, while the oases would naturally have been trying to preserve their newly won independence. Galling (FS Weiser, 61) thinks that this also should be dated to the year 545 (see above, p. 336), at a time when the garrisons of the Babylonians would have gotten into a small-scale war after Nabonidus pulled out of Tema. But it is also possible that this verse reports on a conflict among various Arabian groups; if the Kedarites tried to take over the trade in the area where the commercial activity crossed through Arabia, that could explain why the expander in vv. 16f. felt constrained to predict the downfall of the splendor of Kedar.

[21:16f.] Among the places named in Gen. 25:13ff. (P), Kedar is treated, along with Dumah and Tema, as belonging to the children of Ishmael (cf. also 1 Chron. 1:29f.). The earliest mention of Kedar might be in Jer. 2:10, a passage showing that there were indeed ties between Judah and Kedar at that time. Unfortunately, scholarly research has resulted in widely divergent opinions about the authenticity of Jer. 49:28-33; see the commentaries of Rudolph and Weiser, on the one hand, who believe there is at least a basic core of genuine material, and those of Duhm and Volz, on the other hand, who treat the entire passage as inauthentic. No matter how one settles that question, that passage is evidence for some in Judah having had intensive contact with Kedar, though this relationship does not seem to have been one of mutual admiration. In Isa. 42:11 the Kedarites are among those who raise

joyful shouts as they give witness to the greatness of Yahweh, and 60:7 actually anticipates that the צאן (flocks) of Kedar will be brought before Yahweh,
up on Zion (one should note that this is immediately preceded by an
announcement that the Sabeans would offer gifts of gold and incense).

The Himyaritic inscriptions use Kedar (*qdr, CIH* 493, line 2; and 495, line 2) both as
a clan name and as a tribal name. The *qidri* (*qadri, qidrai*) were always causing trouble for the Assyrians. (Concerning Nebuchadnezzar's campaign against Arabia, see
above, p. 333.) In the Persian era, it seems that the Kedarites had progressed to the
point of forming an entity, as a state. At least an Aramaic dedicatory inscription from
the fifth century, from *tell el-mashūṭa* (12 km. west of Ismalia), mentions a king from
Kedar by the name of קינו בר גשם (*qynw br gšm*) (Rabinowitz, 2), which leads some
to conclude that there was a time when the rule of the Kedarites extended even as far
as the Nile delta. According to Isa. 42:11 (see also Jer. 49:28), the Kedarites lived on
farmsteads; according to Ps. 120:5, in tents, which were unique because of their
brown color (Song of Sol. 1:5). Since they were bedouin, their actual place of residence cannot be determined specifically. In Jer. 49:28 they are equated with the
"people of the east"; in addition, they are mentioned parallel to Nebaioth (Isa. 60:7).
Pliny (*Natural History* 5.11) mentions the Cedreians as the neighbors of the
Nabateans (there is disagreement about whether the Nebaioth and the Nabateans are
two names for the same group of people). The center of Nebaioth was Hegra (Hagra,
Egra, known today as *el-ḥejr,* southwest of *taimā* near *el-ʿölā;* see the map, p. 334).
The area where the Kedarites roamed was northwest of them, on toward the *ʿaraba.*
Thus Israel stood shoulder to shoulder with Kedar and may have been bothered by
them from time to time.

During that period of their independent existence, when the Kedarites
controlled territory all the way to the southeastern border of Palestine, in the
postexilic era, and when they were financially well off because of their commercial successes, there might have been reason to speak of the כבוד
(majesty) of Kedar; see above, p. 152.

One ought not be surprised that v. 17 speaks about shooting arrows as
characteristic of this bedouin people; the bow was the most effective weapon
if one were attacked in the desert. The complete annihilation of Kedar is not
predicted, either, just as a small remnant was to be left for Moab according
to the gloss at the end of the Moab oracle (see above, p. 153).

The oracle says nothing about who will bring the power of Kedar to an
end; one has the impression that the author spent little time wondering about
that, just as he did not feel it necessary to explain why Kedar deserved the
fate that was to come. The most one can say, following hints in the phrase
כל־כבוד קדר (the entire majesty of Kedar), is that Israel had to fight feelings
of inferiority when measuring themselves against these proud people who
lived in the desert. It is not just by chance that the author calls for the support
of Yahweh, the God of Israel; it would seem that deep-seated nationalistic
animosities were surfacing against Kedar (cf. Jer. 49:28-33).

Purpose and Thrust

[21:13-15] One is deeply moved that the author of 21:13-15 would identify with the fate of the fleeing Dedanites and appoint himself as one who would speak on their behalf, even though one could also assume that Israel would have felt itself part of the events that were unfolding southeast of its border and would have had every reason to follow the events, because of how it might affect them. One needs to realize that the journey over land to Dedan and Tema would have taken many, many days (as the crow flies, the distance between Dedan and Jerusalem would have been about 650 km.!). One can hardly believe that the author from Judah would have sent a message to the Dedanite caravans. It is just as unlikely that he himself would have spent time in Arabia. The actual addressee is once again Israel, which was being summoned to pay attention to what was happening in Arabia.

[21:16f.] It is clear that the additional material was meant for the author's own people to hear. Both verses express Israel's trust that Yahweh was already making sure that the trees would not grow up to reach the heavens, which means that Israel did not need to be dazzled by the כבוד (majesty) of its adversary. One would have to wait only a little while: only a year, though it would be a year filled with hardships, as is that of a שכיר (day laborer); then the proud might of Kedar would be broken, its glory would fade.

Negligence and Delusion in Jerusalem

Literature

Concerning the text: G. H. Box, "Some Textual Suggestions on Two Passages in Isaiah: i. Isaiah 22:5b," *ExpTim* 19 (1908) 563–564. H. Torczyner, "Dunkle Bibelstellen," BZAW 41 (1925) 276. M. Weippert, "Mitteilungen zum Text von Ps 19:5 und Jes 22:5," *ZAW* 73 (1961) 97–99. A. Guillaume, "A Note on the Meaning of Is 22:5," *JTS* 14 (1963) 383–385.

    Concerning the historical background: W. Rudolph, "Sanherib in Palästina," *PJ* 25 (1929) 59–80. O. Eissfeldt, "Ezechiel als Zeuge für Sanheribs Eingriff in Palästina," *KlSchr* I (1931) 239–246. H. L. Ginsberg, "Gleanings in First Isaiah," see esp. V. "The Valley of Vision," M. M. Kaplan Jubilee Volume (1953) 251–252. W. Baumgartner, "Herodots babylonische und assyrische Nachrichten," *Zum Alten Testament und seiner Umwelt* (1959) 282–331. J. A. Brinkmann, "Elamite Military Aid to Merodach-Baladan," *JNES* 24 (1965) 161–166. L. L. Honor, *Sennacherib's Invasion of Palestine* (1966). W. von Soden, "Sanherib vor Jerusalem 701 v. Chr.," FS H. E. Stier (1972) 43–51. G. Brunet, *Essai sur l'Isaïe de l'histoire* (1975).

    Concerning the topography of Jerusalem: J. Simons, *Jerusalem in the Old Testament* (1952). L.-H. Vincent and A.-M. Steve, *Jérusalem de l'Ancien Testament* I (1954). A. Kuschke, *ZDPV* 78 (1962) 116ff. M. Weippert, *ZDPV* 79 (1963) 164ff. K. Kenyon, "Excavations in Jerusalem, 1962," *PEQ* 95 (1963) 7–21. N. Avigad, "Excavations in the Jewish Quarter of the Old City of Jerusalem, 1970," *IEJ* 20 (1970) 129–140. Idem, "Excavations in the Jewish Quarter of the Old City of Jerusalem, 1971," *IEJ* 22 (1972) 193–200. M. Broshi, "The Expansion of Jerusalem in the Reigns of Hezekiah and Manasseh," *IEJ* 24 (1974) 21–26.

    Concerning the Day of Yahweh: See the literature cited in *Isaiah 1–12*, p. 97, and above, literature on 13:1—14:2. F. C. Fensham, "A Possible Origin of the Day of the Lord," *Biblical Essays* (1960) 90–97 (not available to me). J. Jeremias, *Theophanie*, WMANT 10 (1965) 97–100. H. D. Preuss, *Jahweglaube und Zukunftserwartung*, BWANT 87 (1968) 170–179. A. J. Everson, "The Days of Yahweh," *JBL* 93 (1974) 329–337.

    [Literature update through 1979: *In general:* H. W. Hoffmann, *Die Intention der Verkündigung Jesajas*, BZAW 136 (1974).

    Concerning the topography of Jerusalem: J. Wilkinson, "Ancient Jerusalem: Its Water Supply and Population," *PEQ* 106 (1974) 33–51. A. D. Tushingham, "The Western Hill under the Monarchy," *ZDPV* 95 (1979) 39–55.

    <Additional reference added at the time of proofreading: J. A. Emerton, "Notes on the Text and Translation of Isaiah XXII 8–11 and LXV 5," *VT* 30 (1980) 437–451>].

Text

22:1 ^a[Verdict concerning "valley of vision"]^a
 ^bWhat happened to you anyway,^b that you^c all together
  have climbed up on the roofs,
 2 ^ayou, filled with noise,
   raging city,
   rejoicing stronghold?^a
  Your pierced ones have not^b been pierced with the sword
   and ^cnot^b fallen in battle.^c
 3 [All of] your leaders have fled together,^a
  ^bwithout bow(shot) softened up;^b
  [all] ^cof you whom anyone met^c were taken prisoner, all together,
   even if they had run far^d away.
 4 Therefore ^aI say^a: "^bLook away from me,^b
  I must weep bitterly,
  you should not go to any trouble to comfort me
   concerning the devastation of the daughter of my people!"
       *   *   *   *

 5 For a day ^aof confusion and of trampling and of consternation^a
  (came) from^b the Lord,^c Yahweh of Hosts.
  The valley of vision^d ^ewas traversed quickly by noise,^e
   and outcry^f (halted) opposite the mount.
 6 And Elam had raised^a the quiver ^b[men on the chariot (harnessed
  with) steeds],^b
   ^cand Kir had taken out the shield.^{ac}
 7 And the specially [well-cared-for area]^a of your valley floor
  was^b filled with chariots and steeds.^c
  Someone took up a position opposite the gate
 8 and laid bare^a the protection^b of Judah.
       *   *   *   *

  ^cOn that day^c 'you glanced out'^d
   toward the armaments in the House of the Forest.^e
 9 And toward the cracks^a in the city of David—
  you^b looked (shocked), ^cthat they were so many.^c
  And the waters you collected in the lower pool,
 10 and the buildings of Jerusalem you counted,^a
  and the houses, tore down,^b
   so that the wall could not be traversed,^c
 11 and have made a collection pool between the two walls^a
   for the waters of the old pool.
  But toward the one who makes such things happen you did not
  glance,^b
   and to the one who fashioned it from afar^c you did not look.^d
       *   *   *   *

 12 Then [the Lord]^a Yahweh of Hosts called
  ^bon that day^b for weeping
  and for a lament for the dead and for shaving bald
  and for being wrapped about with sackcloth.
 13 But behold there, jubilation and joy,
  killing of cattle and slaughtering of sheep,^a
  ^beating of flesh
   and ^adrinking of wine—

"Let us eat and drink^a
for tomorrow we are dead!"^b
14 But^a in my ears ^bYahweh of Hosts^b revealed:^a
"Truly, this offense
cannot be forgiven you,^c
even until you die!"
^d[says Yahweh of Hosts, the Lord].^d

1a–a For חזיון גיא משא (verdict concerning valley of vision), Gk reads: τὸ ὅραμα τῆς φάραγγος Σιων, "the vision concerning the Zion slaughter." Apparently it read this as a reference to the Hinnom Valley, to the west of Jerusalem. Schmidt would replace חזיון (vision) simply with הנם (Hinnom), which is no doubt too easy a solution to the problem posed by this superscription. Another unconvincing solution is offered by Guillaume, who connects חזיון (vision) with Arabic *ḥaḍwa* ("opposite"; here: "the valley opposite").

1b–b For מה-לך (what happened to you then?), Qᵃ reads: מלכי (my king); Targ: מא לכון (what was wrong with you then?), but the MT is correct; at first, Jerusalem is addressed in the feminine singular, then, in what follows, in the second masculine plural, a shift that poses no problem here and elsewhere for Hebrew sensitivities about language usage.

1c Qᵃ: כי עליתי (for I went up); Gk: ὅτι ἀνέβητε (for you had gone up); Targ: ארי סליקתון (that you went up) (correspondingly, the Gk reads כלך as πάντες, "all"; Targ has כולכון, "all of you").

2a–a H. Donner (127; see literature on 17:1-11) states the following: "2a, according to its Masoretic wording, is syntactically untenable." For this reason, he removes מלאה (filled) and places תשאות (noises) after עיר (city), so that he can translate it: "noisy city of turmoil." Schlögl thinks the colon is too long, so he removes המיה (raging) and reads תשאות מלאת עיר (noises filling a city). But what other exegetes know about syntax leads them to be satisfied with the text as is, and המיה (raging) should be retained because it is needed with עליזה (rejoicing).

2b and b Concerning לא (not), when used to negate a nominal clause, see BrSynt §32a.

2c–c For ולא מתי מלחמה (and not [all] fallen in battle), Gk reads: οὐδὲ οἱ νεκροί σου νεκροὶ πολέμου (and your dead have not died in battle), which makes the second colon match the wording of the first exactly, but in Hebrew poetry the second colon is often shorter than the first.

3a יחד (together) would seem to be superfluous, since כל (all of) is read as well. Duhm treated it as part of the next colon, using the מ (from) from מקשה (without bow[shot]), altering that to read אחזם (seizing), but that is too radical an alteration of the textual evidence. One should not use the adventurous translation of the Gk either (οἱ ἁλόντες σκληρῶς δεδεμένοι εἰσί, "those taken are bound harshly"). It would be more likely that כל (all) was added to this colon, rather than יחד (together).

3b–b According to the MT, v. 3aβ supposedly makes the observation that it did not even take an attack by archers in order to take the leaders into custody. That would be remarkable; the original wording of the text seems to have been disturbed. The versions apparently had trouble with the text as well. It has often been suggested that the order of the four cola should be rearranged: aα, bβ, bα, aβ (see Schlögl and Donner), but that still does not get rid of the troublesome מקשה אסרו (without bow[shot] they were taken prisoner). Torczyner (276) suggests switching the first אסרו (they were taken prisoner) with ברחו (they had run far away), but the solution

349

probably lies in a different direction. Targ reads גלו (they were taken into exile) instead of אֻסָּרוּ (they were taken prisoner); following this, some have suggested that one read סָ(א)רוּ (they turned aside) (Procksch, Bruno, *BHS*) or הֻסְרוּ (they were taken away) (*BHS*), which would permit one to translate the text as it is rendered above.

3c–c Instead of נִמְצָאֵיךְ ([all of] you whom anyone met), the Gk (οἱ ἰσχύοντες ἐν σοί, "the strong among you") seems to have read אַמִּצַ(יִ)ךְ (your strong ones) (according to Driver, *JTS* 41 [1940] 164, נֶאֱמָצִיךְ) and some (Duhm, Guthe, Feldmann, Procksch, Kissane, et al.) believe this reading ought to be followed. However, the MT makes good sense as soon as one recognizes that v. 3bβ should be read as a concessive subordinate clause.

3d Gk, Syr may have found the reading לְרָחוֹק (to a distant place) (see Donner and cf. *BHK³*), but מֵרָחוֹק can certainly be translated "far away" (see *HAL* 565).

4a–a It has been said that אָמַרְתִּי (I say) is "technically incorrect and metrically superfluous" (Donner, 127), but one should question whether either of these observations is correct.

4b–b Qᵃ reads שׁוּעוּ מִמֶּנִּי (also: look away from me).

5a–a After the three genitives that are dependent on ἡμέρα (day) (ταραχῆς, "of upheaval," ἀπωλείας, "of destruction," καταπατήματος, "of trampling"), the Gk reads additionally: πλάνησις (of wandering). However, some commentators believe that the MT itself has already been expanded. Thus Procksch, Donner, Fohrer, and others, along with some Hebrew MSS (see *BHS*) eliminate מְבוּכָה (consternation) (as a partial dittography of מְבוּסָה, "trampling"?). The colon does seem to be too long, but it may be that the three genitives, which sound so similar (note the alliteration and the dark, sinister effect caused by the *ū* sound), were written this way on purpose. Eichrodt attempted to recreate the alliteration with the translation: "a day of *Sturm, Sturz, und Bestürtzung*," though this attempt, as is true also of other similar efforts, loses something of the precise meaning of the words.

5b לַאדֹנָי . . . יוֹם can hardly be translated: "(There was) a day . . . *for* the Lord." As is also true in Ugaritic (see, e.g., Gordon, *UT* 10.1), לְ can also mean: "from—far off, from—far away"; see *HAL* 483.

5c Procksch and Donner want to remove אֲדֹנָי (Lord); one cannot be sure if that would be correct.

5d See above, textual note 1a. The *athnach* in חִזָּיוֹן (vision) should be under צְבָאוֹת (of Hosts), at the end of the previous line.

5e–e Ges-Buhl and KBL do not think מְקַרְקַר makes any sense. Gk and Syr have readings that are so different that they are of little help. Since, in rabbinic Hebrew, קִרְקֵר means "tear down," or "break off" and קַ might be a defective way of writing קִיר, "wall, battlement," some suggest translating this something such as: "he throws down the bulwark" (Qimḥi, Ibn Ezra, Dillmann, Marti, Zürcher Bibel, et al.). Donner and others make no attempt to translate it. But in Aramaic, Syriac, Arabic, and rabbinic Hebrew, the root means "bellow, snarl, screech, cackle," or something similar. Recently, in Ugaritic texts, it has been noted that *qr* is used in similar situations (Krt 120 = 222f.). קַרְקֵר קֹר is thus a periphrastic construction and possibly means something such as "noise a noise" (Weippert).

5f If קֹר means "noise," then one can no longer treat שׁוֹעַ II, with Ges-Buhl and KBL, as the name of a people living east of the *diyala* river, namely, the Sutaeans (Akkadian: *sutū*), a group of people about whom some scholars also believe reference is made in Ezek. 23:23 (see W. Zimmerli, BK XIII/1 548 [Engl: *Ezekiel 1*, 488]; and cf. Rm 8333 in E. Dhorme, *Mélanges syriens* I [1939] 204). Rather, שׁוֹעַ is a secondary masculine form of שׁוְעָה (cry for help) (= שׁוֹעַ, "cry for help," in Job 30:24; 36:19). Naturally, one would have to come to a different conclusion if one would follow scholars such as Bredenkamp, Klostermann, and H. Winckler (*Alttestamentliche Untersuchungen,* 177f.) in reading קֶר (noise) as קוֹעַ (Koa) (in Ezek. 23:23, קוֹעַ, Koa, parallels שׁוֹעַ, Shoa), which has often been connected with Akkadian *qutû* (also the name of a tribe, also living in the region east of the *diyala* river). Duhm, Marti, and Box (563) take a stab in the dark with their thesis that מקרקר is a denominative from קִיר, supposedly with the privative sense "take away a wall."

Donner reads עַל (upon) instead of אֶל (opposite) (cf. Qᵃ), which might be correct.

6a and a Donner switches the position of the two verbs נָשָׂא (raised) and עָרָה (taken out), a change that is worth mentioning but too uncertain to be accepted.

6b–b בְרֶכֶב אָדָם פָרָשִׁים (here: men on the chariot [harnessed with] steeds) is very hard to understand and interrupts the train of thought between v. 6aα and v. 6b, where a particular national group is identified. The Gk (ἀναβάται ἄνθρωποι ἐφ᾽ ἵπποις, "men went up on horses") helps little. Houbigant and Lowth suggest reading אֲרָם (Aram) instead of אָדָם (man); cf. also *BHK*³. In order to justify this reading, it has been pointed out that אֲרָם (Aram) is also mentioned next to קִיר (Kir) in Amos 9:7, but that does not help to make any sense of the passage either. Based on Ezek. 23:23 and the Gk, Winckler (177f.) suggests reading: וְרֶכֶב אֲרָם עַל־פָרָשִׁים, "and Aram mounts the horses." Driver (*JTS* 38 [1937] 40) suggests it be read: בְרֶכֶב אֲרָם פָרָשִׁים (in the chariot of Aram, horsemen). But this should be treated as a gloss (Duhm, Marti, Gray, Fohrer, et al.). If one eliminates this, then v. 6b furnishes a parallel colon for v. 6aα, a parallel that is obvious also on the basis of the content. Correspondingly, then, vv. 7a + bα form one line of verse, and vv. 7bβ + 8a another.

6c–c It is baffling why the Gk would translate v. 6b with καὶ συναγωγὴ παρατάξεως (and a formed line of battle).

7a B. E. Shafer (*CBQ* 33 [1971] 389f., 394f.) translates מִבְחָר, both here and in other passages, as "fortress" ("your valley fortresses were full of chariotry"). But then it would have to be speaking about the charioteer corps of Judah, which would disturb the train of thought.

7b Qᵃ reads וְהָיָה (will be) instead of וִיהִי (was); Guthe and others simply want to eliminate וִיהִי (was) altogether; but, based on what seems right in the Hebrew language, it belongs where it is. It is even more unnecessary to follow Bruno and alter וִיהִי מִבְחָר (and the specially [well-cared-for area]) to read וְיֶהֱמוּ בָהָר (and they will roar on the mountain).

7c The article should be removed from before פָרָשִׁים (steeds) (Duhm, et al). It is not recommended that one take the word with the next colon (see Gk, Targ), since the language shows a preference for using "chariot" and "steeds" together.

The *athnach* should be placed under וְהַפָרָשִׁים (and [the] steeds). It is not appropriate to translate פָרָשִׁים as "cavalry" (Donner, 126; see K. Galling, *ZTK* 53 [1956] 132ff.); this is not talking about a cavalry corps, but about horses harnessed to the chariots of a charioteer corps.

8a Procksch suggests that the *niphᶜal* וַיִּגָּל (and it was uncovered) should be read, in which case מָסָךְ יְהוּדָה (the protection of Judah) would be the "logical subject." Others think that Yahweh would be the subject of וַיְגַל (and [he] laid bare), though it would be more likely that an unnamed "someone" is the subject. Since the plural שָׁתוּ (they took up a position) is used just before this, it makes sense to read וַיְגַלּוּ (and they laid bare) (see Gk). Bruno is a little too original once again for one to approve his suggestion that וַיִּגֹּלּוּ (and they rolled forward) be read.

8b One can understand how exegetes are suspicious of the present wording in v. 8a. מסך means "blanket, curtain," so that נלה מסך seems, at this point, to mean "spread out the curtain." The Gk reads: καὶ ἀνακαλύψουσι τὰς πύλας Ιουδα (and they removed the gates of Judah); Duhm thinks that the Gk translators read פתחי (gates of) instead of מסך (covering, protection), but it is more likely that the Gk translators took a guess at what the general sense of the MT might be. Duhm might be right when he alters מסך (curtain) to read מְסָד (foundation). But since this is another passage where one cannot be sure of what the emendation to the text means either, it is better to stay with מסך; on this, see below, pp. 366f.

8c–c Some have been suspicious about the originality of the way this refers to the time period as ביום ההוא (on that day). Procksch thinks that it must be a connecting link inserted secondarily; Duhm would eliminate it altogether, since it, as in v. 12, must be dealing with the future, whereas v. 11b cannot be a prediction. It is true that there is no prediction here, though ביום ההוא (on that day) does not have to have been used here in the same stereotypical sense in which it is employed in the later expansions to the book of Isaiah.

8d In general, the plural וַתַּבִּיטוּ (and you glanced out) is read here; see vv. 9a, 11b, but see also textual note 8a (so Guthe, Procksch, et al.).

8e For אל־נשק בית היער (to the armory of the House of the Forest), the Gk reads: τοὺς ἐκλεκτοὺς οἴκους τῆς πόλεως (the select houses of the city). But the MT reading is correct; בית היער (House of the Forest) is a shortened form of בית יער הלבנון (House of the Forest of Lebanon).

9a According to Ehrlich (*Randglossen* III, 136) the verb בקע is used primarily "in connection with the formation or creation of water sources" (thus Judg. 15:19), so that בקיע would mean "natural spring" (IV, 77); however, no one has followed his suggestion, first of all because the people at that time would not have had to search for long if they wanted to know whether there were many or only a few springs in the city of David. Ehrlich also would have to presume that a לא (not) fell out of the text between כי (that) and רבו (they were so many)!

9b Qᵃ: ראיתָ[מ]ה (orthographic addition of ה; no change in meaning); on this, cf. Meyer, §64.2b.

9c–c That Procksch wants to eliminate כי־רבו (that they were so many), because of meter, shows once again that the schematic he tries to impose metrically is most suspect.

10a ספרתם (you [pl.] counted) is missing in the Gk. Was the word simply missing from its text or did its translators, as well as some exegetes today, have trouble understanding why there would be any point in knowing the number of the houses?

10b Concerning the *raphe* in וַתִּצוּ (and you tore down), see Meyer §14.6; Qᵃ writes this as ותתוצו (also: and you tore down).

10c Qᵃ: לבצור (to make inaccessible). Some have tried to translate בצר *piʿel* here as "reinforce, strengthen," but that is not really what the word means; see below, p. 369.

11a Qᵃ reads the simple plural: בין החומות (between the walls).

11b Qᵃ: הבטחמה (orthographic addition of ה; no change in meaning); see textual note 9b.

11c מרחוק (from afar) is missing in both Sym and Theod; Donner treats it as an expansionary gloss from v. 3. One can hardly agree with this solution here either. In v. 3 מרחוק needed to be translated "far away"; there the Gk translated it πόρρω (far [from]) but here it reads ἀπ᾽ ἀρχῆς (from the beginning). One must wonder whether מרחוק should be taken in the temporal sense (as, for example, in the Zürcher Bibel "from way back when"; and cf., e.g., מרחוק, "of old," in 25:1). However, it is not clear what a temporal sense in this passage would mean, within the context of Isaiah's understanding of history.

11d It is incomprehensible why ראה, "see," should be corrected here to read יִרָא "fear for oneself" (A. Sperber, *A Historical Grammar of Biblical Hebrew* [1966] 647).

12a אדני (Lord) is missing in the Gk, Ethiopic, Arabic, and is also correctly treated as a gloss by some exegetes (Duhm, Donner). Schmidt wants to go still further and remove יהוה צבאות (Yahweh of Hosts). But there is a good reason for this epithet being used here to refer to Yahweh. It is to call to mind for the hearers just exactly *who* this God is, whose workings they ignore so carelessly, with such punishing consequences.

12b–b The authenticity of this ביום ההוא (on that day) (see above, textual note 8c–c) has also been questioned (Duhm, Marti, Procksch). However, to take up the refrain ביום ההוא (on that day) from v. 8 once again makes sense. The actions of Jerusalem "on that day" will be set off over against the actions of Yahweh on that same "day."

13a and a–a According to Donner, the verse has "been secondarily filled extra full." Because of metrical considerations, he thinks it appropriate first to eliminate ושחט צאן (and slaughtering of sheep) and ייין אכול ושתו (wine—let us eat and drink), but once again here he did not operate satisfactorily with his metrical scissors. No doubt, the admittedly expansive way this is described was intended and is effective in illustrating how Jerusalem made sure that its high standard of living was not affected to any great extent.

13b–b Ehrlich (*Randglossen* IV, 78) would treat all four infinitives in the first half of the verse as infinitives construct, which is possible because the first three verbs are written defectively, and this analysis is suggested even more by the form שתות (drinking of). But *scriptio defectiva* is no rarity with infinitives absolute. The form שתות (drinking of) in v. 13a, used with שתו (drink) in v. 13b, might have been chosen because it sounded so similar to the previous שָׁחט (slaughtering of) (see Ges-K §75n).

14a The ו (but) before נגלה (revealed) is disjunctive (Ehrlich, *Randglossen* IV, 78); thus there is no reason to remove it, though Donner wonders whether that should be done. It would be even less satisfactory to move ונגלה (but it has been revealed) (the option chosen by Ehrlich and Schlögl) to the previous line or to eliminate it altogether and to read באדני (by my Lord) instead of באזני (in my ears) (oath formula!).

14b–b Naturally, יהוה צבאות (Yahweh of Hosts) ought not be removed (contra Procksch).

14c One is well advised not to follow Qᵃ in moving לכם (to you) directly after יכפר (be forgiven).

14d–d The closing formula is missing in the Gk; Ehrlich (*Randglossen* IV, 79) treats it as a variant reading to באדני יהוה צבאות (by the Lord, Yahweh of Hosts) (which is the way he would read v. 14a). This formula is probably an actual later addition (Duhm, Gray, Fischer, Procksch, Donner, et al.).

Form

Without any link to what immediately precedes it, 22:1 begins a new section. No reason is apparent for why this material, which deals with Jerusalem, would have been inserted into a collection of oracles against the nations. But by means of the (secondary) superscription, משא גיא חזיון (verdict concerning valley of vision), the passage is placed on the same level as the other units of material that precede it. It is possible that the redactor wanted to emphasize that Judah/Jerusalem stood under divine judgment just the same as all the peoples. It is also possible that the mention of Elam in v. 6 (cf. Elam in 21:2) motivated its being placed here. There is no need to spend much time discussing that another obvious break occurs just before v. 15—even if one removes the closing formula from v. 14bβ; in spite of that, vv. 15ff. do deal with the topic of Jerusalem as well and belong to roughly the same period.

A much more difficult problem relates to whether vv. 1-14 were composed originally as a single unit in the form in which the text now stands. Duhm and Procksch divide this section into two parts, vv. 1-8a and vv. 8b-14, both of which they consider to be Isaianic. Cheyne would draw the line of division between vv. 5 and 6; Marti considers vv. 6-11 to be a secondary insertion; he treats vv. 1-5 and vv. 12-14 as two separate messages; however, both would have come into existence under the same circumstances. More recently, Kaiser set forth an analysis very similar to that of Marti, though he also treats v. 5 as secondary and links vv. 1-4 and vv. 12-14, to be considered as one original unit. He divides vv. 5-11 into three separate additions: vv. 9-11a would be a "historical" portrayal by a reader, composed during the sixth century, describing the measures taken in Jerusalem to fortify the city's defenses in 588, as the Babylonians closed in; and vv. 7, 8 + 11b would have been an expansion from the early exile, just after the fall of Jerusalem in 587. Finally, vv. 5f. would be an eschatological postscript written by a "protoapocalypticist," leading to 22:1-14 being assigned a new function as a prediction of the coming and maturing day of judgment. Only after this time period would this passage have fit appropriately into the collection of oracles against the nations in chaps. 13–23.

Procksch justifies dividing the material into two parts by suggesting that, on the one hand, vv. 2b-8a describe what would happen in the future; Isaiah's prophetic foresight would have been able to forecast the siege and defeat that was going to overtake Jerusalem, during a period when the people of Jerusalem would have perceived nothing (similarly, Skinner, Gray). On the other hand, vv. 8b-14 record a description identifying the measures that had been taken for defense, just prior to the expected onslaught against the city. If one ignores the threat in v. 14, the entire passage looks back on events that have already taken place, not to that which is coming in the future, and offers a highly critical assessment of what has happened.

There is also no apparent reason for suggesting that vv. 9b-11a have to have been an insertion by another hand. Duhm thinks that these verses would have interrupted "the bicola in vv. 8b, 9a, and 11b, which so obviously show that they are to follow one another directly." But that fails to explain why v. 11b could not also logically follow v. 11a. When Duhm goes on still further to say that it is apparent "that the prophet cannot bother with the fine points of the historical details when looking back on what happened," then he as much as admits he has no sound reason for his conclusion. There is a good reason for this detailed description: the author purposely depicts the hectic activity that resulted when the threatening danger was acute, when one would have tried all sorts of protective measures, without doing the one thing needed. Marti and Kaiser are more consistent from the outset, declaring the entire section from vv. 6-11 (Kaiser: vv. 5-11) to be an interpolation. At least Kaiser noted, no doubt correctly, that the first major break does not come after v. 5, but already after v. 4. The only question is whether v. 5 is from another author; put another way: whether the כי (for) that links vv. 5ff. to what precedes it has to be considered a redactional technique or whether vv. 5ff. were linked with vv. 1-4 from the very beginning, in spite of this break. Verse 4 speaks of the deep pain that has come over the prophet. The depiction of the "day . . . of Yahweh the Lord" in vv. 5f. furnishes a continuation that is excellent: the verses describe vividly and in detail "the devastation of the daughter of my people" that was discussed in v. 4. This portrayal reaches its high point in v. 11b. In spite of everything that we learned about its fate in vv. 2b, 3, Jerusalem basically came out of all this rather well; in the final analysis, the prophet's pain is not the result of what his city had to endure, but rather that the people of Jerusalem were not able to read the signs of the times; they did not get the point of the reason for the Day of Yahweh. When the second part concludes with v. 11b, this provides an excellent summary for the reason why Isaiah was under obligation to bring his message, as is also stated elsewhere. The use of ולא הבטתם (you do not glance) picks up והביטו (you glanced out) from v. 8b and, using the other visual term, ולא ראיתם (you did not look) in v. 11b, picks up ראיתם (you looked [shocked]) from v. 9a (which, in addition, shows that it would make no sense to follow Sperber's suggestion that this second ראיתם should be adjusted to mean "you feared"; see above, textual note 11d; it also would speak against Kaiser's solution, which places v. 9 and v. 11b at different stages in the development of the text).

Finally, when v. 12 uses ביום ההוא (on that day), it forms a link with "a day of confusion and of trampling and of consternation" in v. 5. Admittedly, ביום ההוא (on that day) is often chosen as a formula in the book of Isaiah for introducing secondary interpretations that are being inserted. But it does not serve that function in this passage, as can be seen from the fact that it is not at the beginning of the message; its meter also shows that it functions as an integral part of the prophetic message. ביום ההוא (on that day) is linked with יום . . . ליהוה (a day . . . from Yahweh) in v. 5, just as ביום ההוא (on that day) in 2:17 picks up the phrase יום ליהוה צבאות (a day comes for Yahweh of Hosts) from 2:12 once again. One simply cannot treat vv. 5-11 as a secondary insertion while still maintaining that Isaiah is responsible for vv. 12-14. Whether, at the very least, vv. 9b (or also v. 9a)-11a might have to be eliminated as secondary will have to be determined by whether one can explain the reason for Elam and Kir being mentioned, as far as that affects the understanding of the entire passage. That vv. 12-14 particularly belong to the original form of the text is demonstrated by the fact that they are to be understood on the basis of the same situation that is discussed in vv. 1-4. Those who were in Jerusalem had good reason to mourn, but instead they allowed themselves to engage in exuberant, booze-induced hilarity. And the actual climax of the passage is not stated explicitly until v. 14, introduced within a revelation from Yahweh, with vv. 4 and 11b serving only as intermediate steps.

355

To summarize, vv. 1-14 can only be treated as an unbroken unit because the attempt to treat vv. 2b-8a as a prediction about a disaster that will come soon and suddenly simply cannot be right. The perfects, and even more so, the imperfect consecutives, cannot be interpreted as futures. Verses 1b and 2a have the form of an invective against the exuberant city, and there is no doubt that these lines deal with the present; the partying crowd is confronted with hard facts in vv. 2b and 3, and in v. 4 the prophet goes head to head with the people, whose interpretations had directly caused his response, as he issued a rebuttal. In the second part, he gives the reasons for his violent response by first describing the day that had come upon Jerusalem from Yahweh, following that up with a reference to Israel's complete refusal to do what they must have known was called for in such a situation, that they were to look to Yahweh, pointing out that they did no more than hurriedly come up with measures to strengthen their own capabilities for defending themselves, working under the illusion that they could ward off the danger in this way. Verse 12 shows that the events that took place were a divine call to turn back, a summons that, as v. 13 illustrates, was totally ignored.

In terms of form, in the final analysis, the entire passage is an announcement of judgment, with vv. 1-13 serving as a reproach, giving the reasons why this judgment was inevitable.

Meter: Donner breaks this passage down into three strophes (vv. 1-4, 5-8a, 8b-13), each having 7 five-stress cola (v. 14 would be a "chant," consisting of a prose introduction and a six-stress or seven-stress colon; see his chart IX, 183f.). Admittedly, he knows that uncertainties remain in his textual reconstruction, and one needs to recognize that there could be places where alterations or damage to the text could have distorted the original metrical structure. However, also here, one cannot find any regular pattern, neither within the strophes nor within the meter of the individual lines.

Verse 1b: a five-stress colon; v. 2a: a six-stress colon (2 + 2 + 2); v. 2b: a six-stress colon (3 + 3, חלל, "pierced with," is not accented); vv. 3a and 3b: each a five-stress colon (3 + 2; in both cases, כל, "all," is a later addition); v. 4: על־כן אמרתי (therefore I say) is not part of the metrical structure; beyond this, 2 two-stress + two-stress cola; the first line of v. 5, as far as צבאות (hosts), is a ponderous seven-stress colon, the second line is a five-stress colon (קר, "noise," is not accented); v. 6: (after removing ברכב אדם פרשים, "men on the chariot [harnessed with] steeds"): a three-stress + three-stress bicolon; v. 7a (after eliminating the ה, "the," in והפרשים, "and *the* steeds"): a six-stress colon; vv. 7b + 8a: a three-stress + three-stress bicolon; v. 8b: a three-stress + three stress bicolon; v. 9a: a five-stress colon; vv. 9b + 10a: a four-stress + four-stress bicolon; v. 10b: a two-stress + two-stress bicolon; v. 11a: a seven-stress colon; v. 11b: a three-stress + three-stress bicolon (the second לא, "not," is unaccented); v. 12a: a three-stress + three-stress bicolon (אדני, "the Lord") is to be removed, and the *athnach* is to be placed under לבכי, "to weep"); v. 12b: a two-stress + two-stress bicolon; v. 13aα: a three-stress + three-stress bicolon; v. 13aβ and b: each a two-stress + two-stress bicolon; v. 14a functions as an introductory formula, not being part of the metrical structure; v. 14b: (after removing the concluding formula): three-stress + three-stress bicolon.

One notes that this division of the verses diverges in various places from that found in *BHS*. It is also easy to see here that the length of the verse depended on how the events were unfolding. Thus the four-stress + four-stress bicolon in vv. 9b + 10a underscores the painstaking preparations to defend themselves; the two-stress + two-stress bicolon in v. 10b shows how speedily they set to the task after the decisions were made; in addition, the 2 two-stress + two-stress bicola in vv. 13bα and bβ show the vigorous bustle of activity at a friendly banquet, before the macabre morning comes when all joy is at an end.

Setting

Even exegetes such as Marti and Kaiser, who are willing to use the slightest reason to reject any passage as Isaianic, accept the conclusion that Isaiah is responsible for vv. 1-4 (except for the superscription in v. 1a) and vv. 12-14 (except for the concluding formula v. 14bβ; but see C. H. Cornill, *ZAW* 4 [1884] 96f.). As has just been shown by the study of the structure of this passage, vv. 5-11 not only fit well into the context but are absolutely necessary if one is to make any sense of vv. 12ff. These verses are also to be attributed to Isaiah, and not only on formal grounds. The main point of the passage deals with a central theme of Isaiah: Jerusalem was plunging ahead, by preparing to defend itself in any way possible, instead of realizing that Isaiah was issuing a call to the people to reflect on their relationship with Yahweh and to return to him; cf. 5:12 but also 7:3ff. (where a threatening time for Jerusalem finds the king checking out their readiness to defend themselves, especially, at that time, the safety of the water supply "at the far end of the water conduit for the upper pool"). Finally, not only did Isaiah speak regularly about how Yahweh was using national disasters to call the people to return to him; but he also knew from bitter experience that this summons had absolutely no effect on the people (see 9:7-20), so that his God had to bring on further disasters, those being unrelentingly harsh (5:25-29). If vv. 5ff. are not attributed to Isaiah, then the view that the Day of Yahweh was something that would be coming in the future (though the actual wording reads . . . יוֹם לַאדֹנָי יְהוִה צְבָאוֹת, "a day . . . from the Lord, Yahweh of Hosts") would play a much more decisive role, leading one in fact to treat this passage as apocalyptic, which would obviously exclude Isaiah from consideration as the author. However, יוֹם (לַ)יהוה (a day [for, from] Yahweh) is not always, not even in Isaiah, a technical term that speaks of the "last day." Chapters 2, 12ff. do speak of a future יוֹם יהוה (Day for Yahweh), but it is called that only because Yahweh will be more clearly seen and will act to intervene in a more momentous way than would be seen during the normal times of his people's history (see P. A. H. de Boer, *VT* 24 [1974] 235). It is not problematic that Isaiah looks *back* on such a day at this point, though Everson (334f.) has energetically argued that it is.

It is Kaiser's opinion that, in addition to material in vv. 7f. speaking against Isaiah's authorship (what speaks against Isaiah here, anyway?), v. 11b would also speak against it, "with its comment that the events which had come about were planned long ago by Yahweh." However, besides the fact that מֵרָחוֹק (from afar) is hardly used here temporally (see below, p. 371), there seems to be no good reason why Isaiah could not have uttered these statements, since the prophet specifically mentions the עצה (plan) of Yahweh in other passages, after those historical events had transpired. Thus there are no compelling reasons for suggesting that vv. 5-11 had to have been written after the time of Isaiah.

Having concluded that Isaiah is the author of the material, one must still ask which situation is being addressed in this message. Procksch thinks that v. 3 describes a vision, which would not have had to play out in history in exactly that way. To summarize his views: this passage comes from a time of wild excitement and partying that gripped Jerusalem when they decided to declare that they would no longer be vassals of their political leader Sargon, having concluded an agreement with Ashdod that they would oppose Assyria. For this reason, he dates this passage earlier (along with vv. 8b-14 and vv. 15-23), to 713; Eissfeldt comes to a similar conclusion (*Introduction*, 314), though he suggests that it could also be from 705. Cheyne and Fischer date it way back to 722/721. However, since the arguments for concluding that this is a vision of the future do not hold, the most likely date is just after Sennacherib left Jerusalem. Behind this message are events implying that a terrible threat to the city has been turned back and that the enemy's power has been badly damaged, which leaves no other choice if dated to the period when Isaiah was active. Even today, the reasons for Sennacherib's withdrawal are still not completely clear (see S. Herrmann, *A History of Israel in Old Testament Times* [1981[2]] 258f.); in any case, for Jerusalem, the suspension of the siege must have come as a total surprise, which would explain psychologically why there would have been such an exuberant mood in spite of the heavy losses that Judah as a whole had suffered.

Admittedly, one should not overlook the fact that assigning this date to the passage does not solve all the problems with certain specific details, such as what situation is behind vv. 2b, 3; the most critical issue, however, deals with the question about why v. 6 would speak of Elam and Kir if Jerusalem was being threatened by Assyrian forces (see the commentary notes on these specific verses). One can certainly understand why Childs (26) believes that one seeks to answer the wrong question if one tries to determine which specific historical events are behind this text; the chapter simply does not provide sufficient information. However, if this passage comes from Isaiah, that does not prevent a commentator from trying to do the best one can in determining as closely as possible what actual situation is behind this, even if more information is desirable for one to be sure of standing on solid ground.

Commentary

[22:1a] גיא חזיון (valley of vision) is a superscription that uses a keyword from the text itself (see above, p. 302). The real question is why the redactor of the משא (Verdict) collection would have selected this particular keyword. If, as is often supposed, the "valley of vision" is the Hinnom Valley, where Jerusalem celebrated festivals for its Molech (or Melech) cult (2 Kings 23:10; Jer. 32:35), then one might conclude that the redactor thought that the judgment against Jerusalem was, in the final analysis, a judgment against this Molech cult—which essentially would miss the point about what concerned Isaiah.

[22:1b-4] This section describes Isaiah's "mourning." According to what has been said above, Jerusalem's populace was overjoyed because it thought that it was the perfect time to celebrate the most unexpected change in the political-military fortunes. Kissane, for one, thinks that the transition between v. 2a and v. 2b is too abrupt; hence he would rewrite the text, similar to 1:21, to say: "How sad it is now, for the once happy city!" Ginsberg (251f.) agreed, and both are of the opinion that vv. 1-4 focus on the future. But the present wording simply cannot be rearranged so radically.

The question that opens this section is clearly a reproach; cf. Judg. 18:23 and see I. Lande, *Formelhafte Wendungen der Umgangssprache im Alten Testament* [1949] 43f., according to which מה־לְּךָ means: "What is the matter with you (that you are behaving so strangely)?" Isaiah is beside himself about the way these "senseless" people are acting, as they completely miss the point of it all, showing how entirely deluded they are, which will finally result in their complete destruction. When the prophet speaks in v. 4 about how he mourns, that description about his sadness certainly has a sarcastic undertone, since he does not want the populace in Jerusalem to know where his real sympathies are—in light of the insensitivity of the people this mourning would not be appropriate anyway—so he uses this method rather as a way to announce the שׁד (devastation) that will have to come on a people who are so disillusioned and unrepentant. Verses 2b and 3 are also sarcastic. Some had been wounded and had died, but not in open battle; rather, it was those who wanted to get out of that hot spot, their own city, as quickly as possible, so that they could save their skin. That the קְצִינִים (leaders), who were responsible for the protection of the people and city, who of all people would have been expected to stay at their posts when threats were most severe, had slipped out instead, only to run right into the hands of the enemy anyway, shows vividly how pathetic they were in living by their convictions; but it also shows that they were simply incapable of determining whether even they themselves had much of a chance to make an escape. The enemy has certainly departed; the city seems to have been freed, but the events shockingly demonstrate that there was rottenness to the core in this state, especially among its leaders.

We have a good deal of information about the military and political events that occurred in 701, first in what is recorded in the addendum to the first part of the book of Isaiah (chaps. 36–39; in the main, this is identical with 2 Kings 18:13—20:19), but also in Assyrian reports, with the most important being the Oriental Institute Prism of Sennacherib (*AOT* 352ff.; *ANET* 287f.), though important further information comes from the so-called Bull Inscription (D. D. Luckenbill, *The Annals of Sennacherib* [1924] 68:18–70:32) and from little comments within other inscriptions of this same king (ibid., 77:17-22 and 86:13-15; cf. also the texts in *ANET*

287f.). In addition, there is also information in Herodotus (2.141), from a much later time of course, about Sennacherib's tragic experience when he attacked Egypt. It would seem that we are fortunate enough to be well informed about what happened. But at significant points the sources contradict one another. With materials of this type, that is not surprising. In the final analysis, the biblical text is not as much interested in history as it is in its portrayal of Isaiah, and it includes a significant amount of legendary material. Herodotus's report was obviously written down long after the events took place (see Baumgartner, 305–309). But even the Assyrian inscriptions must be used by historians only with the greatest degree of caution. They are also biased; their goal is to demonstrate the magnificence of the king and thus they magnify all his successes, hush up or never mention the debacles that he had to endure, and are selective about what they summarize, so that even setbacks look like victories. Comparing the Bull Inscription with the longer report written on the Taylor Prism shows that the latter is a newer redaction of the shorter Bull Inscription, by means of which it was intended that both the real and purported successes of Sennacherib were to be depicted with greater clarity (see von Soden, 44).

This is not the place for an intensive study of the sources, or for a comprehensive attempt to provide all the details of the events (see the presentations in the histories of Israel written by Noth, Bright, Metzger, Herrmann; in addition, see the presentation by S. Smith in *CAH* III, 71ff., as well as the articles cited in the literature section above, especially that of von Soden, plus the commentaries on the book of Isaiah and on I, II Kings). Only some details that help explicate the present text can be stated with certainty. At the beginning of his rule, Sennacherib had to deal with many problems in the eastern part of his empire. His chief opponent, Merodach-Baladan of Babylon, apparently tried to build a strong second front against Assyria in the southwestern part of the realm (see Isaiah 39 = 2 Kings 20:12-19). Hezekiah was certainly not the only head of state in the Syro-Palestinian region who received a visit from the envoys of Merodach-Baladan. In this revolt, the chief opposition to Assyrian power was centered in the Philistine cities of Ashkelon and Ekron. Before dealing with these cities, Sennacherib had to neutralize the power of his most dangerous enemy, Merodach-Baladan, which he succeeded in accomplishing in 703 when he conquered Babylon and banished Merodach-Baladan. Then he could set out on a campaign against the lands to the west.

The coastal regions belonging to Syria and Phoenicia did not stand a chance when trying to stop his advance; the Philistine cities were the first to make a concerted effort to resist, believing that Egypt would not leave its allies in Palestine in the lurch. But Sennacherib defeated the Egyptian relief forces at Eltekeh (Akkadian: *altaqū;* concerning its location, see above, p. 216). That sealed the fate of the two Philistine cities, and Sennacherib turned his attention toward securing access along the eastern flank of the road that led down to the border of Egypt, hence Hezekiah of Judah was being called to pay the consequences for his part in the rebellion. The entire countryside of Judah was defeated, right up to Jerusalem, control of which was then transferred to the Philistine rulers who had not joined the rebellion. Sennacherib reports that forty-six walled cities, together with smaller villages, were taken from Hezekiah. "Himself [Hezekiah] I made a prisoner in Jerusalem, his royal residence, like a bird in a cage" (Taylor Prism III, 20f.). Isaiah himself describes the pitiful conditions in the city in 1:8: "Yes, Zion's daughter is left like a booth made of foliage in a vineyard, like a shelter for the night in a cucumber field, like an ass's foal 'in a pen.'" But Jerusalem was never conquered, though that certainly would have been

the crowning achievement of this campaign of Sennacherib, which seemed to have
been so successful until then. For reasons that we do not know, the siege was lifted;
the answer usually given, that news about revolts in the eastern part of the realm
caused the pullout, is probably not accurate. It is possible that there is a kernel of
truth to what some suppose, based on a combination of information from the biblical
account and that of Herodotus, that a plague so decimated the Assyrian forces who
were camped outside the city that they had to give up their attempt to take the city
(on this, see von Soden, 45ff.).

Even though Jerusalem did not fall, the losses throughout Judah were
catastrophic. The entire countryside was lost; Hezekiah had to prove his loyalty by paying tribute; he had to hand over control of his elite troops to the
Assyrians, "those whom he had brought in to increase protection for his res-
idential city, Jerusalem, and whom he employed as auxiliary forces" (Taylor
Prism III, 32f.); to this he had to add significant sums of treasures from the
temple and the palace. If Sennacherib did not exaggerate, this even included
the king's own daughters, the palace ladies, and male and female singers, all
of whom he had deported to Nineveh. Even if Sennacherib overstated the
case when he described his campaign as a triumph of his own power, those
in Jerusalem who perceived the situation could do nothing but be depressed
and deeply concerned about the future.

[22:1b] In spite of this situation, Jerusalem was celebrating. Just as people
would go up onto roofs at other times to mourn (see 15:3; Jer. 48:38), now it
was for celebrating. Even today it is common in Palestine that one builds a
little room up on the roof, which can serve as sleeping quarters for guests but
which also can be used for banquets (see Dalman, *AuS* VII, 59); that is also
where one would set up the סֻכּוֹת (booths) when celebrating the Feast of
Booths (ibid., 84), Neh. 8:15f. According to *t. Pesaḥim* 6.11 *j. Pesaḥim* 35b
(ibid., 86, note 8), the Passover meal also can be eaten up on the roof (see
ibid., illuss. 14f.; cf. also Judg. 16:27).

[22:2a] The city, in which justice and righteousness was to dwell (1:21),
was filled with תְּשֻׁאוֹת (noise) instead. According to Zech. 4:7, תְּשֻׁאוֹת specifically describes shouts of joy, expressed when one becomes aware of happy
circumstances. The related verbal root שׁאה II [BDB: I] describes the roaring
sound made by rushing waters; see passages such as 17:12f. Elsewhere,
Isaiah uses הָמוֹן ("tumult," derived from הָמָה, "roar, be boisterous") with שָׁאוֹן
("uproar," derived from שׁאה II [BDB: I], "make a din, crash"); see 5:14,
where the same line refers to עָלֵז (rejoice) also. Isaiah also speaks of
Jerusalem as a קִרְיָה עַלִּיזָה (jubilant city) in 32:13, in a message that probably
comes from about the same time period (concerning the meaning of עלי, see
Brunet, 290–292). Isaiah is fond of using the word קִרְיָה (city), though it is
not used often overall in the OT: 1:21, 26; 29:1; the expanders of the book
were especially fond of it as well, using it ten times in chaps. 1–39, four
times in the Isaiah apocalypse alone.

[22:2b, 3] Some leaders (קָצִין; see *Isaiah 1–12*, p. 39) judged the situation to be so hopeless that they decided to abandon the sinking ship. They scattered in all directions, some getting quite far away as they fled, but finally even they were captured by the Assyrians anyway; one might think of the comparable experiences of Zedekiah (2 Kings 25:4ff.), who was fleeing in the wilderness near Jericho when he was caught by the Babylonian security forces and was transported to the headquarters where he would meet his fate. The texts that have come down to us in the OT do not describe any such attempts to flee during the time when Sennacherib was besieging the city. Nevertheless, one reads on the Taylor Prism (III, 22f.) that Sennacherib had a rampart built, "so as to hinder those who might attempt to flee his [Hezekiah's] city" (though this translation is not assured). One can assume that the instigators of the war had forsaken the city, a cowardly action that would have given the Assyrians sufficient reason to carry out whatever measures were necessary to take them into custody. Prisoners of war were shackled (see, e.g., p. 333 above; Zedekiah was also put in chains: וַיַּאַסְרֻהוּ בַנְחֻשְׁתַּיִם, "they bound him in fetters," 2 Kings 25:7; cf. also 2 Kings 23:33). One should take what is suggested, when יַחַד (all together) or יַחְדָו (also: all together) is used, with a grain of salt; the secondary insertion of כֹּל (all) in two places shows how ready someone was to exaggerate about such cases. Obviously, נָדַד (flee) and בָרַח (run far away) mean much the same thing, though with בָרַח (run far away) it is more likely that either the destination or the point of origin would be in mind, whereas נָדַד (flee) seems to convey more that one is roaming around with no place to call home.

[22:4] In this passage, Isaiah uses בַת־עַמִּי (the daughter of my people) to describe Jerusalem's populace, though elsewhere he calls them the יֹשֵׁב יְרוּשָׁלִַם (inhabitants of Jerusalem), sometimes also speaking of the בַת־צִיּוֹן (daughter of Zion). One sees how ambivalent he is about his feelings for this people at this very point, where he is disappointed and forcefully denounces his fellow citizens for being unaware of what was going on, but is still able to use this tender description: "the daughter of my people." But those who notice him should not go out of their way to comfort him, for he knows that the actions of the people will lead to most bitter consequences (see v. 14), and yet he does not doubt for a second that Israel is still Yahweh's people and will remain so. At this point, Isaiah comes close to saying what we read in some of Jeremiah's poetic laments; see 4:19-22; 14:17f.

Whenever someone is in trouble, they expect that others will sympathize. Here, however, Isaiah asks the people to quit paying attention to him, since it would be completely inappropriate, in his case, for them to comfort him and tell him that things would get better.

Concerning אֲמָרֵר בַּבֶּכִי (I must weep bitterly), one might compare 33:7: מַר יִבְכָּיוּן (weep bitterly) and also ἔκλαυσεν πικρῶς (about Peter: he wept bitterly) in Matt. 26:75.

[22:5-11] The Day of Yahweh: Isaiah describes that which had come upon

Jerusalem as a יום . . . . לאדני יהוה צבאות (a day . . . from the Lord, Yahweh of Hosts), which he had announced in 2:12 as a יום ליהוה צבאות (a day for Yahweh of Hosts) over all that is haughty and lifted up. This passage shows that the prophet does not only announce a coming day for Yahweh, but also can portray the way in which he observes that it has come already. Though the first line in v. 5 summarizes all of this with a type of superscription, the following lines describe the attack of actual, identifiable troops against Jerusalem, apparently describing the most acute threat to the city in v. 8a: the city had no protection against the enemy.

The second part of this section, vv. 8b-11a, describes the way the inhabitants of Jerusalem acted "on that day," while v. 11b points out the most important response that should have been forthcoming, but just never was: that they should have looked to Yahweh, the one whom Israel could thank for its existence, and the one from whom the people would also have to expect deliverance to come.

[22:5a] The Day of Yahweh is identified as a יום מהומה ומבוסה ומבוכה (a day of confusion and of trampling and of consternation). מהומה (confusion) is clearly used when holy war is discussed: "But Yahweh your God will give them over to you, and throw them into great panic (והמם מהומה גדולה), until they are destroyed" (Deut. 7:23; see also 1 Sam. 5:9, 11; 14:20). That type of massive destruction is not surprising, since the ideas linked with the Day of Yahweh are closely connected to the concept of holy war (see the excursus, *Isaiah 1–12*, pp. 112f., the literature cited there; and E. Jenni, *THAT* I, 723–726). מבוסה (trampling) probably also has a special meaning within the context of the discussion about the Day of Yahweh; see Mic. 7:4. מבוכה (consternation) is a hapax legomenon; yet one might refer to the way בוס (tread down, trample) is used in Isa. 14:25; 63:6; Zech. 10:5. According to the way the original concept of the Day of Yahweh had developed, it would have been the enemies of Yahweh and Israel who would have been overcome with consternation. But just as the Day of Yahweh is envisioned as coming against Israel in Amos 5:18-20, and against the people (in effect, also against Israel) by Isaiah in 2:6ff., this passage also speaks of a day of confusion *for* Israel/Judah; on this, see Ezek. 7:7: "The time has come, the day of confusion (מהומה) has drawn near and not for celebrating upon the mountain (based on the Zürcher Bibel translation, text emended). But one notes in the curses included in the covenant formulary that they also mention the threat that Yahweh will also send forth מהומה (confusion), when he allows the curses to come upon the people (Deut. 28:20).

[22:5b] Now to the specifics, where one naturally no longer would expect to find the formulations and specific terms from the vocabulary describing the Day of Yahweh: "The valley of vision was traversed quickly by noise and outcry (halted) opposite the mount" (v. 5b). Concerning the designation of the place known as גיא חזיון (valley of vision), see textual note 1a–a and pp. 358f. When an armed force makes preparations to besiege a city, it naturally does not happen without a lot of noise; in fact, noise is often used during a battle as a way to intimidate; cf. Judg. 7:16ff.

One wonders whether this description has anything to do with the concept of the peoples storming the city of God (Kaiser refers to Isa. 17:12 and Ps. 46:7). But none of the terms commonly used in the traditions about the mount of God are used here; and, if they were used, one would have to have concluded this description by speaking about the deliverance of Jerusalem.

Though one would think of the outcry of the attackers when קֹר is used, one cannot be sure about how שׁוּע is used, since שׁוּע and its derivatives are always used when one calls for deliverance. In addition, שׁוּע (cry out for help) and שַׁוְעָה (cry for help) are both typically used in the liturgical vocabulary of the temple. וֹשׁוּע אֶל־הָהָר could thus mean: a call for help rings out in the direction of Mount Zion, where Yahweh dwells.

[22:6] It is most surprising that Elam and Kir are identified as the enemies who are going to storm Jerusalem, providing the most important reason why some commentators treat vv. 5-11(or 6-11), or at least v. 6, as secondary. Naturally, these two peoples could not have had the reason or opportunity to go up against Jerusalem on their own. Only Assyria could be the real enemy of Jerusalem; Elam and Kir could have done no more than provide contingents to help the Assyrians (which would not change matters at all if one reads שׁוּע as the name of a people; see above, textual note 5f.; and if אָדָם, "men," should be read in v. 6aβ as אֲרָם, "Aram"; see above, textual note 6b–b).

The Assyrian forces included ancillary troops from many different places; see above, pp. 197f. Conquered groups especially had to supply contingents for the standing army of the Assyrian kings, known as the kiṣir šarrūti. It is true that Elam was not incorporated as an integral part of the Assyrian Empire until Ashurbanipal (see above, pp. 312f.). Until then, it had always sided with the chief opponent against the Assyrians within Mesopotamia, that being Babylon, and went to battle along with marduk-apla-iddina II (Merodach-Baladan) and šamaš-šum-ukīn against the might of Assyria, about which we have explicit information. But that does not exclude the possibility that, previous to that time period, some Elamites served the Assyrian kings. One might compare this situation with that of David, who was served by the כְּרֵתִי (Cherethites) and פְּלֵתִי (Pelethites), 2 Sam. 8:18, and often elsewhere; cf. also 2 Sam. 15:18ff. (on this, see R. de Vaux, Ancient Israel: Its Life and Institutions [1961], 123, 221). An inscription on a stele mentions kabābu (shield)-carriers (catapultists), whom Sargon assembled in Hamath and installed as a contingent within the kiṣir šarrūti (Manitius, ZA 24 [1910] 125f.). The Rassam Cylinder (VII, 58–81) reports that Elamite fugitives seized the feet of Ashurbanipal and declared their allegiance to him. These would have been the individuals whom he could have used to form a contingent of archers and would have made part of his royal forces (kiṣir šarrūti). Other information apparently also suggests that the largest percentage of the Assyrian forces would have been archers (LUṣabē MEŠ GIŠqašti) (see Manitius, 127ff.; see above, p. 189). Seemingly, Elamite archers were among the most proficient (cf. G. Walser, Die Völkerschaften auf den Reliefs von Persepolis [1966] 72f. and plates 4, 35, 36); thus it would not be surprising to find them among the contingents of Assyrian troops who spearheaded the operation against Jerusalem. When Merodach-Baladan of Babylon revolted right after Sennacherib came to power, it was public knowledge that Elam encouraged the action, and šutruk-naḫḫunte II of Elam energetically supported Babylon by sending support troops (see Brinkmann, 161ff.). Babylon was defeated, so it is not unlikely that Sennacherib also formed for himself an Elamite archer corps at that time, made up of the Elamites who had fled or who were taken prisoner; we are told that Ashurbanipal did the same in a similar circumstance. (Concerning the conflict between Sennacherib and Babylon, see *CAH* III [1970³] 61ff.)

Our information about Kir, mentioned along with Elam, is paltry. In Amos 1:5 the Arameans are threatened with the punishment that they will have to go into exile in Kir, and, according to Amos 9:7, Kir was their country of origin. Specific information is available in 2 Kings 16:9 about how Tiglath-Pileser III took the inhabitants of Damascus into exile to Kir. However, this reference seems dependent on the Amos 1:5 passage, and that reference may have been composed with Amos 9:7 in mind (see V. Maag, *Text, Wortschatz und Begriffswelt des Buches Amos* [1951] 7). Kir is apparently never mentioned in Akkadian texts. The most we can say is that Kir must have been located somewhere in southern Babylon, somewhere near Elam.

Psalm 127:5 uses the image of a warrior who has a quiver full of arrows; one would anticipate that it would speak here about how the quiver would be emptied (see above, textual note 6a and a). But one lifts the quiver also when one wants to take out the arrows. It is more surprising when it is said that the shield is uncovered. These must have been covered when they were transported.

The Code of Hammurabi praises Inanna as a goddess "who uncovers my weapons" (*pa-ti-a-at* ^{GIŠ}*kakkī-ya*). Information is available that both the Greeks (from the time of the Peloponnesian War up to the Hellenistic era) and the Romans had covers for their shields: both Euripides (*Andromache* 617) and Aristophanes (*The Wasps* 1142; and in *The Acharnians* 574) speak about the "case for the shield," the σάγμα; Xenophon (*Anabasis* 1.2.16) mentions the ἀσπίδες ἐκκεκαλυμμέναι (shields uncovered); Diodorus Siculus (20.11) speaks of the shield covers, the ἔλυτρον. As for the Romans, one might consult Caesar, *Gallic War* 2.21 (*scutis tegimenta detrahere*, "the coverings were to be drawn off the large square shields") and Cicero, *On the Nature of the Gods* 2.14 (*ut clipei causa involucrum vaginam autem gladii, sic praeter mundum cetera omnia aliorum causa est generata*, "just as a shield-case is made for the sake of a shield and a sheath for the sake of a sword, so everything else except the world was created for the sake of some other thing" [trans: H. Rackham, LCL]). Beyond this, further information is available in "Schild," Pauly-W (IIA, 1, esp. 425).

[22:7] Archers can move around with ease; their power can be used anywhere. By contrast, chariots are generally confined to rather flat stretches of land; cf. 1 Kings 20:23, 28. For that reason, chariots were of little use as a weapon up in the hill country of Judah, at least insofar as the opponent did not get forced into fighting a battle out in the open. But the Assyrians brought their chariots along; the "valleys" around Jerusalem are practically filled with them. One should note that the Hebrew text speaks of עמקים, which refers to broad (valley) plains. The עמק רפאים (Valley of the Rephaim) is located by Jerusalem; on this, see above, pp. 171f. Sennacherib's troops had come not from the north but rather from the west, as they made their way up to Jerusalem, a tactic which would certainly not have precluded the charioteer corps from setting up headquarters in the relatively flat area to the north of the city. It may be that Judah engaged in a battle against Assyria in the vicinity of Lachish, one in which chariots played an important role. In any case, in the battle near Eltekeh, the Egyptians/Ethiopians made use of some chariots (Taylor Prism III, 73–82).

The troops of Sennacherib took their positions "opposite the gate," but this is hardly, as Kaiser suggests, "the cavalry vanguard." Duhm is certainly right in suggesting: "even if the riders wanted to let the foot soldiers break down the doors, so that they could then storm the city, it is hard to see how they could have done anything much in the narrow and crooked . . . streets except block the way for their own soldiers who were on foot." The word פָּרָשִׁים (steeds), along with רֶכֶב (chariot), belongs to v. 7a, as has been explained already. In spite of the presence of the article on הַשַּׁעְרָה (the gate), one ought not think of a specific gate; "the gate" serves as a *pars pro toto* (one part serving to identify the whole thing) for the entire wall that encircles the city.

But what is really meant by מָסָךְ יְהוּדָה (protection of Judah)? Sennacherib reports only that he erected temporary barriers which would make it more difficult to flee the city. Of course, when he was conquering the cities of Judah, which had been protected by thick walls, in addition to constructing ramps for the siege, he also set up battering rams and used techniques such as undermining the foundation, making breaches in the walls, and scaling ladders (?) to bring the siege to a successful conclusion. One can easily understand why Duhm suggested changing מָסָךְ (protection) to read מָסָד (foundation); the tactic involved digging under the foundation stones into which the gates were set, in order to free the gates and pull them down; on this see Hab. 3:13 and cf. גַּלֵּה יְסוֹדִים (uncover foundations) in Mic. 1:6. One could certainly agree with that change, if mention had been made of the foundation of Jerusalem. In other places, מָסָךְ means "blanket" (2 Sam. 17:19; Ps. 105:39) or "curtain" (Exod. 26:36f.; 27:16, and often elsewhere). Making reference to the related term מַסֵּכָה II (shroud) in Isa. 25:7, Procksch, in a way similar to what Hitzig suggested, thinks that when it says the "curtain of Judah" will be taken away it means: "All of a sudden Judah will be able to see; just as scales would fall from their eyes—when it is too late." That interpretation would be nice if it were correct, but he has obviously been influenced by 2 Cor. 3:12ff., and he presumes that Yahweh is the subject, which is highly unlikely. But most importantly: the "curtain of Judah," in this sense, never fell from them—not even after it was too late. That it never sunk in was the very reason for Isaiah being so deeply disappointed about Judah. Since the other points Isaiah mentions all deal with concrete measures, מָסָךְ יְהוּדָה must as well. Some think that the "curtain of Judah" might have been border strongholds, such as Lachish. But Sennacherib's troops are positioned right outside Jerusalem. Thus there is hardly another possible solution, except to assume that the "blanket of Judah" refers to

Jerusalem itself. Numerous times in history, it had become apparent that Jerusalem was the real, and last, bastion of Judah. Without Jerusalem, Judah had no future. As Samaria was the "bastion" of Ephraim (17:3), thus Jerusalem was the "blanket" of Judah. If it has now come to the point that Jerusalem has been "exposed," with all the other fortified cities now fallen and all ties cut off, then the situation for Judah is most grim.

[22:8b-11a] In light of this most precarious position, some were still trying to improve their defensive installations, literally right down to the wire.

[22:8b] The first step was to check out the נשׁק (armaments) in the "House of the Forest." The "House of the Forest" has to be the building that Solomon constructed on the palace grounds in Jerusalem, otherwise known as the "House of the Forest of Lebanon"; see 1 Kings 7:2; 10:17, 21. We have good information about the building specifications. It was one hundred cubits long, fifty wide, and thirty high (a cubit = 50 cm.), with four rows of cedar pillars, having cedar rafters on top of the pillars, topped by a roof of cedarwood. It was called the "House of the Forest of Lebanon" either because it was constructed using the cedarwood from Lebanon or because its numerous pillars made it look like a forest (see M. Noth, *Könige*, BK IX/1 [1964] 134ff.). When the Hall of Pillars and the Hall of the Throne were taken together, the House of the Forest of Lebanon was larger than the temple. Nothing more specific can be said about its defensive capabilities. According to 1 Kings 10:17, expensive shields were stored there (see above, pp. 319f.). According to Möhlenbrink (BWANT 4, 7 [1932] 98), it supposedly served as "barracks for the palace guard and their horses," but this is completely wrong; more likely, it would have been the place where the representatives of the state government carried on business, later being used for a purpose that was not intended originally, serving as an arsenal. This is what one must conclude if נשׁק, as has been customary, is translated "armaments." But it is questionable whether that is the correct meaning. Although *ntq* seems to mean "projectile" in Ugaritic, in Akkadian *nisqu* or *nisiqtu* means "choice, the best," and the Gk translates it in this passage as ἐκλεκτοί (picked out, select). In 1 Kings 10:25 the Gk translates the same word with στακτή, "myrrh oil." Were choice, expensive items stored in the House of the Forest of Lebanon? In the final analysis, is this the same place as what is called the בית נכות, the treasury (Akkadian: *bīt nakamti*), in Isa. 39:2 (= 2 Kings 20:13)? That would mean that a search took place to see if the necessary provisions for a harsh war were on hand. Yet this interpretation is not without its own difficulties either. Nevertheless, one must remember that when Rehoboam was forced to collect the treasures that were to be turned over to Shishak right after he invaded, he had the golden shields brought from the House of the Forest of Lebanon, where Solomon had stored them (1 Kings 14:25ff.).

"The cracks in the city of David" are those in the walls of the Davidic-Jebusite part of Jerusalem. When the leaders checked out how solid they were—too late to do anything about it—they discovered many cracks.

Scholarly research has uncovered solid evidence that Hezekiah expanded the ancient Jebusite city, the one that David had conquered, to include what is referred to in 2 Kings 22:14, Zeph. 1:10, and Neh. 11:9 as the מִשְׁנֶה, the "second city." Recent excavations apparently confirm the note in 2 Chron. 32:5 that says: "Hezekiah set to work resolutely and built up the entire wall that was broken down (הַחוֹמָה הַפְּרוּצָה), and raised towers on it, and outside (לְחוּצָה) it he built another wall; he also strengthened the Millo in the city of David, and made weapons and shields in abundance." To some extent, this note reflects the same construction measures about which Isaiah speaks. The excavations led by N. Avigad make it possible to observe the course of the new western wall in greater detail. These excavation results seem to suggest that some portion of the southwest hill was also included within Hezekiah's city wall (concerning the course of this wall, see N. Avigad, *IEJ* 20, 135; and *IEJ* 22, 195). Further excavations will provide still more information to help resolve this problem. That the prophet makes no mention of the second city—no doubt it is to be located west of the area where Solomon built the temple (see H. Kosmala, *BHH* II, 831–832, 842, and illus. 2)—is probably explained by the fact that it was not first built at the time when the threat of an Assyrian advance was acute. It might be that the city wall had to be expanded earlier, as many arrived in the city after escaping from Samaria when it fell (see Broshi). But it is also possible that some settlements in the area had just recently been fortified by the addition of a city wall; Hezekiah, considering the possibility that someone could besiege the city, then could have decided that he better provide that area with even stronger fortifications.

[22:9a] The cracks in the wall of David's city, which Isaiah mentions, should be considered to be the same as what is called the חוֹמָה פְּרוּצָה (wall that was broken down) in 2 Chron. 32:5. Recent excavations have clarified much about the expansion of the ancient Jebusite/Davidic city; see Kuschke, Weippert, Kenyon. The early view that the city of David never expanded beyond the southeastern hill on the plateau that drops in elevation as one goes to its southern end (cf. views, such as that in Galling, *BRL* 301–302) must now be rejected on the basis of newer information.

[22:9b] "And the waters you collected in the lower pool" must be referring to measures taken to assure a water supply in time of siege. Reference was made to the "upper pool" in 7:3, which also mentioned a water conduit that led to it. Some (thus Simons, 191; Vincent and Steve, 293–295) believe that the lower pool is the same as the (ancient) pool of Shiloah—*birket el-ḥamra*. This means that they presume the upper pool mentioned in Isa. 7:3 must be somewhere in the northern part of the city. But that is problematic also; see M. Burrows, *ZAW* 70 (1958) 221–227, where he, most likely correctly, locates the upper pool at the southern end of the Kidron Valley (on this, see *Isaiah 1–12*, pp. 295, 343; and H. Kosmala, *BHH* II, 825–827). The lower pool may have been very close to the upper, which does not mean that it has to be south of the other, but rather, deeper down into the valley, that is, actually beneath the *birket el-ḥamra*. But it is important to remember that we are not presently in a position to identify the location of the various pools with certainty (see the very different solutions offered by Simons, 157–194; Vincent and Steve, 289–297; and Brunet, 168–171, 293–295).

[22:10] One cannot be sure of the meaning of v. 10a either. Why count the houses in the city? The context suggests that this is somehow connected with the preparations for the expected siege. This count would not have been merely to find out the total number of the houses, but to take an inventory to determine how many people could be housed in the buildings located inside the city walls. How many escapees from the countryside and from the immediate surrounding area could be squeezed in? Where could supplies be stored? Where would one find place for the livestock? Most importantly: how could one find enough space for what the military required? (According to Sennacherib's prism inscription, Hezekiah brought in troops to strengthen his capital city; see above, p. 361.) It has generally been assumed that counting the buildings was directly related to tearing down houses, as mentioned in v. 10b. One would want to determine which of them could be torn down to strengthen the walls since, because of the immediate pressures, they would not be in a position to go outside the city to get construction materials for strengthening the damaged wall. But this solution is not very satisfying. Why would one first have to count the houses, if such emergency preventative measures needed to be undertaken? לבצר החומה hardly means "strengthen the wall," but rather "make it hard to get by." There must be another interpretation for v. 10b, totally unrelated to the counting. The houses (note the article) that are to be torn down would probably have been in the way of those defending the city, whether built on top of the city wall or adjacent to it. They would have made it hard for the defenders to have a clear view of what those besieging the city were doing or might have allowed the attackers to climb up onto the wall undetected. Thus they were to be torn down so that a clear field of vision was created. The only link, then, with counting the houses might have been the need to know how many people were in the houses being torn down, since they also would need some place to stay.

[22:11a] Verse 11a describes still another emergency measure. "A collection pool between the two walls" was built as well. It would be very easy to find out where this reservoir was located if we knew what was meant by the reference to "two walls." 2 Kings 25:4 (see also Jer. 39:4) speaks of a "gate between the two walls, by the king's garden." From the dual form חמתים (two walls) one must infer that there was at least some specific area in the city that was protected by two courses of walls. It has already been noted that, according to 2 Chron. 32:5, Hezekiah had another wall "outside" (the original one). Would this מקוה (pool) have been located between the old (Jebusite) and the new (Hezekiah) wall? The answer to that question would obviously depend on where the old pool was constructed; according to v. 11aβ, this new מקוה (pool) was built to hold the water from that old pool, and one must also take into account that the water from the Siloam tunnel, another project attributed to Hezekiah in 2 Kings 20:20, would have had to empty into some pool as well. In fact, this same passage in the book of Kings adds that Hezekiah installed a ברכה (pool, reservoir) (cf. also 2 Chron. 32:2ff.), which also is mentioned in the Siloam Inscription (*KAI* 189:5; *ANET* 321). Can it be any clearer that this is the new pool? This would mean that the old pool in the present passage would be the one that collected the water that flowed through canal II (see *Isaiah 1–12*, p. 343) from the Gihon spring toward the south before the new tunnel was built; this means that the "old pool" is none other than the upper pool of 7:3. It could no longer be used as a reservoir after the water tunnel was constructed, because it was outside the city wall. For this reason, a new collection point for the water had to be built, for the water that once had flowed into the "old pool." It has long been a problem for scholars that, according to 2 Kings 20:20, Hezekiah "brought water into the city" with his tunnel from the Gihon. In fact, this notation says much in and of itself. Why would someone construct such an expensive tunnel if not for the purpose of assuring that the city would have a water supply available, also during times of siege? But the pool at the end of the tunnel is outside what had always been assumed was the course taken by the ancient city wall. Now it would seem that the second wall, built by Hezekiah, also in the area around where the tunnel ends, which we have suggested is what the מקוה (pool) refers to, would have enclosed this area; cf. Avigad, *IEJ* 20, 133f. Thus "between the two walls" refers to the area between the old city wall and the new one, built by Hezekiah (concerning the path followed by Hezekiah's wall, cf. fig. 3 in Avigad, 135).

[**22:11b**] According to Isaiah, the hectic activities that went into Jerusalem's preparation for a harsh and long siege were a glaring contradiction to the only action that would have made any real difference: turning toward Yahweh; but this did not happen, no matter how great the external threat. The suffix on both of the participles עשׂיה (the one who did such a thing) and יצרה (the one who built it) refers to Yahweh's actions within history, not to the מקוה (pool), for which Brunet (169f.) believes he has made a good case (with Brunet being of the opinion that the יצר, "doer of such a thing," and עשׂה, "one who built it," was Isaiah himself, which is obviously ludicrous). Isaiah is operating from his understanding of history at this point also. History is the territory where Yahweh is active. The Assyrians were not in front of the gates of the city of Jerusalem just by chance and not simply as a consequence of Assyrian efforts to expand the area over which they exercised control; Yahweh had caused it to happen; when it comes to whatever happens, he is the יצר (doer) and עשׂה (maker, builder). In other places Isaiah uses the related substantives to express the same idea as is conveyed with these two participles, with 5:12 offering a particularly close parallel: וְאֵת פֹּעַל יְהוָה לֹא יַבִּיטוּ וּמַעֲשֵׂה יָדָיו לֹא רָאוּ (but they do not pay attention to the activity of Yahweh, and they do not observe the work of his hands). Apparently, whenever anyone in Israel spoke of Yahweh's "work," that would originally have referred to his activity when he created and then sustained the creation. But Isaiah adopted the vocabulary used for speaking about the theology of creation and made use of it when unfolding his view of how history worked (see *Isaiah 1–12*, pp. 202f.). The evidence for the use of this link between creation and history in the present passage is seen most clearly when Isaiah pairs עשׂה (do) here with יצר (build, shape), a word that is deeply embedded in descriptions about creation (יצר, "shape, create," used parallel to עשׂה, "do, make," to describe the actions of Yahweh in creation: Isa. 43:7; 44:24; 45:7, 9, 18; Jer. 33:2; Ps. 95:5; but Genesis 2 already uses יצר [vv. 7, 8, 19] interchangeably with עשׂה [vv. 4, 18]; concerning the use of יצר, "shape," to describe Yahweh's involvement within history: 2 Kings 19:25; Isa. 37:26; 46:11; Jer. 18:11). Thus history is "the creation" of Yahweh. The way Deutero-Isaiah associates the two main areas in which Yahweh is active, in both creation and history, is certainly already present in what Isaiah says; he simply is not, per se, as interested in using the creative activities of Yahweh to make his point.

Since Yahweh is the "creator" of history, one can and must find a way to recognize his intentions through observation, so that one can come to the proper decisions about one's own actions. It is true that history unfolds according to Yahweh's עצה (plan) (cf. above, pp. 82f.). But this is not destiny, which rolls on automatically; it is rather a summons to Israel to reevaluate its own situation in light of the way in which God guides the events. That is all part of what is meant with הביט אל (you did [not] glance toward) and ראה (יהוה) (you did [not] look [to Yahweh]). These ideas are not far removed from what Isaiah says in a slightly different way in 7:9 and 28:16 when using האמין (believe). It was just as important to keep calm and have confidence, in 701, as it had been important in 733; indeed, in the light of the incomparably more dangerous situation, it was even more important. No doubt, "look to Yahweh" means basically to place confidence in him, but always in such a way that one would be able to comprehend what he intended one to learn when he acted within history and that one would respond appropriately. In Isaiah's mind, that would mean political decisions should be made on the basis of this trust. If anyone had looked to Yahweh, such a person would not have concluded that it would take only a couple of improvised measures to turn back the deadly threat to the besieged city successfully.

The question has already been raised about what it might mean that Yahweh directs the events of history מרחוק (from afar). It is explicitly stated in Jer. 23:23 that Yahweh is not a God מקרוב (near by) but is מרחוק (far off). Some have compared this statement with the Hymn to the Sun, by Akh-en-Aton: "Thou has made the distant sky in order to rise therein, in order to see all that thou dost make" (*ANET* 371; see Erman, *Literatur,* 361), and they believe that the passage in Jeremiah speaks about God's omnipresence (see Rudolph, HAT 12³, 153). But it would be better not to try to impose that meaning on the passage here in Isaiah. For Isaiah the important point is that God is present, but hidden, within history. On the surface, the Assyrians and the authorities in Jerusalem seem to be in charge; "from afar," however, Yahweh is the one who creates history and is its lord. It would pay dividends to recognize what is far off, what is in the background, what finally is the only factor in determining reality. Thus מרחוק (from afar) also deals with a qualitative dimension, not a spatial one.

[22:12f.] Verse 12 begins by trying to explain the meaning of the events that unfold on that Day of Yahweh. Yahweh had called "for a lament for the dead and for shaving bald and for being wrapped around with sackcloth," that is, for a service of penitence, just as would have been considered appropriate in any time when war threatened; see above, p. 98 (on 14:31) and pp. 133f. (on 15:3f.); however, see also Joel 1:13f.; 2:12-17. It is not surprising that Yahweh is also given the epithet צבאות (Sebaoth, of Hosts) at this point (on this epithet, see *Isaiah 1–12*, pp. 29f.), especially because he uses an amazing number of terms that are common in passages describing elements of cultic piety in Jerusalem; even the insertion of אדני (Lord) fits well with the general tenor of the discussion.

Summoning people to come to a penitential service is specifically introduced by קְרָא עֲצָרָה (call a solemn assembly) in Joel 1:14; 2:15. Concerning בְּכִי (weep), used in connection with such a penitential service, see Isa. 15:2, 3, 5; 16:9; in addition, see Joel 2:12; cf. Jer. 3:21; 31:9, 15, 16. מִסְפֵּד (lament) is also used in conjunction with בְּכִי (weep) in Joel 2:12, which does not have to mean that it is being used just to describe mourning for someone who has died (see above, pp. 107 and 133f.). As in 15:2, קָרְחָה, "baldness," also serves here as a mark which points out that someone is mourning; see previous notes on 3:24 and 15:2. Finally, wrapping שַׂק (sackcloth) around oneself is also part of this ritual of mourning; see above, pp. 292f. This garment is used not only when one mourned for someone who died but generally, any time one wished to find a way to express that one was deeply upset (so, e.g., 1 Kings 21:27).

While lamenting that Jerusalem was deluded, so that it did not allow itself to be moved by this summons to repentance, Isaiah uses the vocabulary commonly employed when summoning attendance for a day of repentance, about which we learn the most from its usage in Joel and Jeremiah, also having been encountered in the Moab passages in the book of Isaiah. This vocabulary might raise suspicions about its authenticity. But then one also would have to treat vv. 13f. as coming from someone besides Isaiah, a conclusion that no one would reach. Certainly such days of repentance happened in Isaiah's time already, and the practices that are highlighted here are, in and of themselves, very ancient: weeping, mourning, shaving the head, and wrapping around oneself a mourning garment. Up to this point, the suspicions about the text's authenticity cannot be supported. But elsewhere Isaiah never attaches any importance to cultic services; cf. particularly 1:10-17; this is at least true insofar as they are only "customs," human activities that are substitutes for a real turning toward Yahweh. But here it is Yahweh himself, not the priests and not the political leaders, who calls for penitence. He issues this summons through the events of history, in language plain enough that no one could miss the point. Of course, v. 12 is not to be interpreted as if disconnected from v. 11b; i.e., Isaiah uses the language of the cult, but he uses it, one might say, as a vehicle for delivering his prophetic summons, calling for a return to Yahweh.

However, instead of getting people to follow him, the people celebrate.

One can hardly say that the prophet is speaking of what the people are doing here as if he were describing how they were holding special cultic celebrations; these are wild parties, with drinking, about which Isaiah also expressed his disdain elsewhere (see 5:11-13; 28:1ff.; cf. 29:9). Some believe that they can even hear, in Isaiah's words, just how irritated he was with this completely decadent feasting when he laments that so many cattle and sheep had to die. There may still be something here that reflects the hesitation of primitive human beings to kill an animal, based on the fear that it might avenge its death. The ancient Israelite ate meat only on special occasions (see N. Bratsiotis, *TDOT* II, 320). But the people whom Isaiah was watching were not reserved in the least; there was no holding back. To be sure, the precarious nature of the situation had been generally acknowledged. But the little bit of true knowledge that was still there brought about the completely opposite reaction from what should have been. If the future is that unsure, savor the moment! Isaiah characterized the mood of these revelers by attributing a quote to them, just as at other times he used this technique to show what these people were really thinking (see H. W. Wolff, *Das Zitat im Prophetenspruch,* BEvT 4 [1937] = TBü 22, 36–129): "Let us eat and drink, for tomorrow we are dead!" This must have been a well-known quotation (which Paul cites in 1 Cor. 15:32).

The ancients used many similar expressions. In Sumerian wisdom, there are two possible ways to look at life, depending on the situation:

> We all die; therefore let us carouse!
> We are going to live a long time;
>   therefore, let us be thrifty!

(See H. H. Schmid, BZAW 101 [1966] 228 and 104.)

In the Gilgamesh Epic (X, III, 6f.), Sidiru advises the hero, who is on a quest to find eternal life:

> Thou, Gilgamesh, let full be thy belly,
> make thou merry by night and day.

(Quoted from E. A. Speiser's translation in *ANET* 90. See also A. Schott and W. von Soden, *Das Gilgamesch-Epos* [1972^2], 75.)

Similar views are expressed in A Song of the Harper, which was to be played at a banquet when someone died:

> Let not thy heart flag. Follow thy desire and thy good. Fulfill thy needs upon earth, after the command of thy heart, until there come for thee that day of mourning.

(Quoted from John A. Wilson's translation in *ANET* 467. See also W. von Bissing, *Altägyptische Lebensweisheit* [1955] 141.)

373

Let there be before you song and music,
cast all evil behind you and think about joy
until the day comes when one lands in the land which loves quietness!

(This translation is based on von Bissing, 142.)

From a pylon in the grave of [an otherwise unknown] Petosiri, one reads:

Drink and get drunk!
Do not cease (to celebrate) a beautiful day.
Follow your heart during the fleeting moment on earth.

(This translation is based on S. Schott, *Altägyptische Liebeslieder* [1950] 138.)

There is even a Coptic hymn that says:

Our life is a shadow, which passes by;
there is no return for death.
Therefore, satisfy yourselves with the good things, which are there. . . .
Let us satisfy ourselves with good wine and pleasant fragrances.

(This translation is based on von Bissing, 144.)

Similar thoughts are expressed also in Ecclesiastes:

This is what I have seen to be good: it is fitting to eat and drink and
find enjoyment in all the toil with which one toils under the sun the
few days of the life God gives us; for this is our lot.

(This is from 5:17; see also 5:18f.; 3:12f., 21f.; 9:7ff.; Wis. 2:1ff., and often elsewhere.)

Naturally, the Greek world also had a similar philosophy of life. This verse is
handed down from Asclepiodotus:

Come, let's take our cup! We drink! The day is short.
Are we going to delay, until torches to light the way home are glowing?
Come, we cup! We drink! There's no time for falling in love.
How soon we will already, my stupid friend, have rest in the eternal night.

(This is translated from *Anthologia Graeca*, XII–XVI, ed. H. Beckby, n.d.[2], 36f.)
See also the Alcaeus quote in Kaiser.

A proverb advises:

Think about the end of life. Therefore, joke and indulge, as long as the
world lasts. (*Epigraphie Graece*, ed. G. Kaibel, 344.3.)

Similar wisdom for living is also found on the Goblet Inscription (see A.

Deissmann, *Light from the Ancient East* [1965] 129f.; cf. 295) and also in inscriptions from graves, such as that which is purported to be from Sardanapalus:

> Eat, drink, and sport with love; all else is naught.

(Plutarch, *Moralia* 336c; quoted from the Frank Cole Babbitt translation in the Loeb Classical Library.)

The quotation used in Isaiah apparently summarizes a view of life that was held by many throughout the ancient Near East.

[22:14] Since the utter seriousness of the situation was shockingly misunderstood, Isaiah reacts by delivering an extremely harsh announcement of judgment. That can be seen even by observing the form that he uses for the introduction. The common messenger formula, which already by that time had an air of politeness about it, יהוה אמר כה (thus says Yahweh), was not strong enough; he says: צבאות יהוה באזני ונגלה (in my ears Yahweh of Hosts revealed). This formula is unique, but cf. 5:9: צבאות יהוה באזני נשמע (or) נשבע (truly, Yahweh of Hosts has made an oath [or: was heard] in my hearing) (concerning this textual emendation, see *Isaiah 1–12*, p. 190, textual note 9a; and cf. ibid., pp. 198f.; in that passage as well, an oath formula follows the opening formula). Isaiah wants to make sure that the message of judgment is heard not only as simply a message from God, but in its full sense as an oath that God swears. Apparently, he also had to fight against those who would minimize the message the prophet delivered.

גלה (reveal) is one of the words used in the OT to describe revelations; see H. Haag, "'Offenbaren' in der hebräischen Bibel," *TZ* 16 (1960) 251–258; and cf. H.-J. Zobel, *TDOT* II, 476–488. The introductory formulas that Isaiah uses are very similar to those in passages such as 1 Sam. 9:15: שמואל את־אזן גלה ויהוה Yahweh had revealed to [lit.: uncovered the ear of] Samuel); see also 2 Sam. 7:27; 1 Chron. 17:25; Job 33:16; 36:10, 15. In a prayer to Nusku (Ebeling, *AGH* 40, 4), the oppressed person pleads: "Open my ears." In the final analysis, this expression comes originally from secular contexts: "to open someone's ear" means "tell someone something that is secret" (1 Sam. 20:2, 12, 13, and often elsewhere).

The content of this oath makes clear that it is impossible for Jerusalem to get out from under the guilt that it has brought on itself. If, as is common elsewhere, one translates כפר with "be forgiven," then one will quickly come to false conclusions about what the text means. עון, "guilt because of sin" (see *Isaiah 1–12*, p. 22), implicitly includes the idea that the consequences would follow according to a predetermined plan, as this is explained by the so-called synthetic view of life, automatically bringing the "punishing consequences" along with the deed, so that an action itself actually causes the disaster to follow. Thus one would have to try to intervene and deter the automatic consequences, which means, try to "cover" the guilt (כפר, "cover"; see *Isaiah 1–12*, p. 270). Means were available whereby one believed it would be possible to expiate the offense and interrupt the built-in consequences, so that the former situation of settled peacefulness could be restored. Another approach would be to try to avert one's doom by making a כֹּפֶר ("expiation payment"; concerning these concepts, see V. Maag, "Unsühnbare Schuld," *Kairos* 8 [1966] 90–106). In the OT, it is generally clear that God is the one who is in charge, the one who is responsible for expiation (see F. Maass, *THAT* I, 853ff.). But in the passive sense, this older meaning of כֻּפַּר is still visible. This does not mean: I (Yahweh) will not forgive you your guilt; לֹא כֻפַּר means: the natural consequences of guilt will take their inevitable course; the offense will follow the predetermined path, with full force. In addition to the present passage, three places in the OT explicitly announce that there is no chance for expiation. In 1 Sam. 3:14 Yahweh swears that no expiation will be possible, ever, for the offenses committed by Eli's family. Jeremiah pleads that the offenses of those who are causing him grief would not be expiated (18:23). And the prophet who speaks in Isa. 47:11 asserts that Babylon's wickedness would not be expiated, which means, no actions to work out a reconciliation would divert the consequences. The present passage is to be interpreted in the same way as the Deutero-Isaiah reference. The corruption that had been brought about by the false, unrepentant attitude of those in power in Jerusalem was not to be removed by attempts to expiate the guilt—"even until you die" is added by Isaiah, which means: as long as you live, this doom hangs above your head. The "you" who are abruptly addressed here are not further identified; it must be people who thoughtlessly presume that order, peace, and settledness are once again assured, now that Sennacherib has withdrawn.

The closing formula (see above, textual note 14d–d), which is certainly secondary, underscores once again that this is the way it will stay.

Purpose and Thrust

Along with 1:4-9, 22:1-14 is probably among the last messages that have been passed down to us from Isaiah. Deep indignation, in fact, bitterness, is expressed here. One can understand why. Isaiah was deeply involved in the political situation in Judah in 701. Without a doubt, he opposed the decision to break off their subservient relationship with Assyria by joining with the Philistines who had issued a plea to Ethiopia/Egypt, hoping to get a promise of help. He had done all he could to arouse confidence that God would intervene at the appropriate time, which meant not only that diplomatic actions and military preparations would no longer be necessary, but that they actually would be signs of unbelief (see 14:24-27; 17:12-14; cf. also 29:1-8). Once again, those in Jerusalem apparently faced a dilemma: the real-world politics of those who understood the way things *really were* was being played off against the utopia of *faith*. And it was demonstrated once again that those who were real-world politicians did not understand reality clearly at all. They were mistaken about their chances to revolt against Assyria; Judah had been able to see the frightening consequences of their miscalculations. What upset Isaiah so deeply was his awareness that those living in

Jerusalem refused to see the seriousness of the situation. Instead of making a sober evaluation of the circumstances, admitting the mistakes that had been made, and gaining the appropriate insights about what to do now that the catastrophe was over, they were blind to their own failures and once again started living in a world of illusions. Thus the truth of the matter was that only one response was possible, namely, to announce that their real destiny would even now continue on its course and that "stubbornness" would bring with it bitter vengeance.

Against Shebna's Claims

Literature

Concerning the text: A. von Gall, "Jeremia 43,12 und das Zeitwort עטה," *ZAW* 24 (1904) 105–121. H. L. Ginsberg, "Some Emendations in Isaiah," *JBL* 69 (1950) 55–56.

Concerning the entire section: A. Kamphausen, "Isaiah's Prophecy Concerning the Major-Domo of King Hezekiah," *AJT* 5 (1901) 43–74. K. Fullerton, "A New Chapter out of the Life of Isaiah," *AJT* 9 (1905) 621–642. E. König, "Shebna and Eliakim," *AJT* 10 (1906) 675–686. K. Fullerton, "Shebna and Eliakim: A Reply," *AJT* 11 (1907) 503–509. H. L. Ginsberg, "Gleanings in First Isaiah: VI. The Shebna-Eliakim Pericope, 22:15-25," M. M. Kaplan Jubilee Volume (1953) 252–257.

Concerning סכן *and* אשר על־הבית: R. de Vaux, "Titres et fonctionnaires égyptiens à la cour de David et Salomon," *RB* 48 (1939) 394–405. A. Alt, "Hohe Beamte in Ugarit" (1953): *KlSchr* III (1959) 186–197. H. J. Katzenstein, "The Royal Steward (*Asher ᶜal ha-Bayith*)," *IEJ* 10 (1960) 149–154. C. Rabin, "Etymological Miscellanea," *Scripta Hierosolymitana* 8 (1961) 395–396. M. J. Mulder, "Versuch zur Deutung von sokènèt in 1. Kön. I 2,4," *VT* 22 (1972) 43–54. E. Lipiński, "SKN et SGN dans le sémitique occidental du nord," *UF* 5 (1973) 191–207.

Concerning שבנא: D. Diringer, *Le iscrizioni antico-ebraico Palestinesi* (1934). S. Moscati, *L'epigrafia ebraica antica* (1951).

Concerning the inscription from the grave in silwān: N. Avigad, "The Epitaph of a Royal Steward from Siloam Village," *IEJ* 3 (1953) 137–152. E. Vogt, "Sepulcrum praefecti palatii regum Iuda," *Bib* 35 (1954) 132–134. H. J. Katzenstein, see above. D. Ussishkin, "The Necropolis from the Time of the Kingdom of Judah at Silwan, Jerusalem," *BA* 33 (1970) 34–46.

[**Literature update through 1979:** *Concerning* סכן *and* אשר על־הבית: A. A. Wieder, "Three Philological Notes," *Bulletin of the Institute of Jewish Studies* 2 (1974) 103–109.]

Text

22:15bβ   ᵃ[Againstᵇ Shebna, the one in charge of the palaceᶜ]

15a   Thus said the Lord,ᵈ Yahweh of Hosts, 'to me':

15bα   "Up, go on in to this administrator there,
       ᵉ'and say to him'ᵉ:

16   'ᵃWhat do you haveᵃ here, and *whom* have you here,
      that you are having a grave hewn out here for yourself,
      that you hew outᵇ for yourself, ᶜhigh up,ᶜ a grave,ᵈ
      are having a residence chiseled outᵇ of the rocks?

17 Behold,[a] Yahweh [b]stretches you out full length,[b]
   with full force,[c] you man,[d]
   and seizes you[e] with a strong grip,
18 and flings[a] you with a mighty step,
   as a ball, into [b]a land
   that lies open on both sides.[b]
   There you will die,
   and that is where your fancy chariots[c] will be,
   you disgrace to the house of your lord!
19 [I oust you out of your position
   and [a]"pull you" down[a] from your place.'"]

15a Concerning the rearrangement of the text here, see below, p. 382.

15b The preposition עַל (here: against) before Shebna clashes with אֶל (to) before הַסֹּכֵן (administrator). Schlögl would smooth this out by reading אֶל־שֶׁבְנָא (to Shebna) (which is also suggested by *BHK³*). If the rearrangement of the verses noted above is acceptable, this alteration is not necessary. עַל־שֶׁבְנָא (Against Shebna) is a superscription, in which case עַל (against) is quite appropriate.

15c Literally: "the one who is over the house (= the king's palace)." Yet Vulg reads here: *qui habitat in tabernaculo* (who dwells in the tabernacle) and then translates הַסֹּכֵן as *praepositus templi* (the one who is placed before the temple); on this, see below, pp. 388f.

15d אֲדֹנָי (lord) is missing in 2 Hebrew MSS, Gk, Theod, Syr. Many consider it to be secondary and remove it, though it probably would have been skipped in the Gk, since κύριος (lord) already had to be used there to translate יהוה (Yahweh).

15e–e According to Gesenius, 2 Hebrew MSS read וְאָמַרְתָּ אֵלָיו (and he said to him) at the end of the verse; Gk: καὶ εἶπον αὐτῷ (and he said to him); Targ (at the beginning of v. 16): וְתֵימַר לֵיהּ (and say to him); and Vulg: *et dices ad eum* (and you shall say to him). This directive to the prophet is apparently original.

16a–a Qᵃ reads MT מַה־לְּךָ (what do you have [here]) as one word, מְהַלֵּךְ, "walking around here."

16b and b For both חֹצְבִי (hew out) and חֹקְקִי (chisel out), the ־ is the so-called *ḥireq compaginis* (connecting *ḥireq*); see Joüon, *Gr* §93n (this is actually the old genitive ending). Concerning this construction (with a genitive separated from the word in the construct state by a locative adverb), see BrSynt §70f.

16c–c Schlögl suggests altering מָרוֹם (high up) to read בַּמְּרוֹם (in the heights), a completely unnecessary change; cf. Meyer, III, §106.2a.

16d Based on the context, the Gk translated the suffix on קִבְרוֹ (his grave) as σεαυτῷ (your own), whereas O. Schroeder (*ZAW* 32 [1912] 302–303) wrongly suggests moving the ו (his) to serve as the copula before חֹקְקִי (chiseled out); in addition, he then transposes the לוֹ (for himself), which follows מִשְׁכָּן (residence), to the beginning of v. 17 (vocalizing it as לֹא, "indeed").

17a Schlögl suggests inserting אֲנִי (I) after הִנֵּה (behold), or reading הִנְנִי (Behold, I) instead of הִנֵּה יהוה (Behold, Yahweh), which would make Yahweh the speaker here, as in vv. 19ff. But one ought to be careful about making alterations would result in smoothing the reading by eliminating the uneven places that actually preserve some of the evidence to show how the text developed historically.

17b–b There is disagreement about the exact meaning of the *pilpel* טִלְטֵל (from טוּל). It is usually translated the same as one would the *hiphᶜil*, as "throw a far distance." It has been objected that one would have to continue the idea when translating v. 18aαβ.

I. Eitan (*HUCA* 12/13 [1937/38] 68f.) thinks that the *pilpel* has an iterative (repetitive) sense, meaning "shake back and forth"; cf. Judean Aramaic טלטל, "shake out." However, it is probably better to follow Ehrlich (*Randglossen* IV, 79), who shows that טלטל also can mean "stretch something out full length."

17c The use of the substantive טלטלה (a stretching out) is surprising here; in parallel with the following עטה (to be strong; here: strong grip), one would expect the infinitive absolute טלטל (to stretch out). Following Duhm, Procksch, et al., we think the ה on the end of טלטלה should be treated as the article for גבר (man); in fact, it is used as a vocative. Kaiser, however, thinks a more radical error has crept in, and, following both Ginsberg (*JBL* 69: כְּטַלְטֵל הַבֶּגֶד, "as the clothing is shaken") and G. R. Driver (*JSS* 13 [1968] 48f.), he suggests it should read כְּטַלְטֵלָה בֶּגֶר (as one shakes out a garment). But this conjecture is not needed and causes different problems when translating עטה in the next colon.

17d גבר (hero) or הגבר (the hero) must have been used in an ironic sense; Fohrer simply translates it as "you plain fool." It is not necessary to repoint גֶּבֶר as גֻּבָּר, with the supposed meaning "O you robber" (Michaelis, according to Gesenius).

17e The exact meaning of עטה II is also in doubt. Based on Arabic ʿaṭa, KBL suggests that it should be translated "grasp" for this passage, translating it in Jer. 43:12 (following von Gall), however, as "louse, get rid of lice," which is the way Kaiser would also translate the verb in the present passage. But it does not make any sense that a man who is to be hauled far away would first have to be deloused! The meaning "seize" is also supported by Sir. 34:16 (see Smend's discussion of the text). It also does not make any sense to translate this verb as if it is עטה I, "cover up," so that it is translated something such as "wrap up altogether" here (see Marti).

18a צנף has traditionally been assigned the meaning "wrap around." Galling (*BRL* 239) assumes that this text has something to do with the Egyptian custom of wrapping corpses. But why should someone accord so much honor to such a bumbler? Rinaldi (*BeO* 5 [1963] 205) believes that צנפה should be removed from the text and then translates the rest: "*Girando (il braccio) ti mette in moto [ ] come un cerchio*" ("turning (the arm), start moving you [ ] as if in a circle"); however, the decisive words for this interpretation, namely, *il braccio* ("the arm"), are the very words that had to be added into the text. Instead of יצנפך, the Gk reads: καὶ ῥίψει σε (and he will fling you), and Eitan suggests linking this verb with Arabic ḍafana, "to kick." The *Lisān al-ʿArab* suggests "give someone a kick" as a meaning for ḍafana, which describes how the instep of the foot is used on the rear end of an animal or human being. It specifically cites the phrase ḍafana bihi l-àrḍa (kick him to the ground). Eitan essentially has the right idea. But one should still make note of the fact that Lane IV, 1702, when referring to Arabic ṣafana, comes up with the meaning "he flung him upon the ground" for ṣafana bihi l-àrḍa.

It is hard to "wrap up" a person into a lump; with the traditional meaning, one also notes that there is no verb in v. 18aβ (Zürcher Bibel expands this with: "he drags him"). Thus צנף is used here in the same way as הטל (hurl) in Jer. 22:26 (see also v. 28), a passage with very similar content. After Yahweh takes hold of him, the consequences are portrayed graphically with this term. Yahweh throws the hated Shebna to the ground, jumps on him, and hurls him away.

18b–b Literally: "into a land, broad toward both hands (sides)"; cf. the translation of v. 18aβ in Vulg: *quasi pilam mittet te in terram latam et spatiosam* (he throws you, as one would a ball, into a land that is broad and spacious). Kissane proposes reading וְשָׁמָּה קִבְרַת כ׳ instead of כ׳ ושמה מרכבות (and that is where your fancy chariots will be), which leads him to translate this clause: "and thy splendid tomb shall be desolate." However, this change is neither necessary nor likely.

18c The same holds true for Bruno's brainstorm that רְקָבְךָ, "you will rot," should be read instead of מרכבות (fancy chariots). One might wonder if the Gk does not supply the more original reading, having a text that read the singular מרכבה (τὸ ἅρμα, "war chariot"); "*one* chariot is certainly enough" (Duhm). However, since the author is trying to depict Shebna's arrogance in the worst light, it is more effective for him to speak about many chariots.

19a–a Targ, Syr, Vulg reflect a reading that presumes that the original was in the first person, אהרסך (I oust you), and most scholars accept that as the original reading (it is common in the ancient Hebrew script for ' and א to be mistaken for each other; see also *BHK*[3] and *BHS*). The Gk reads only one verb in v. 19 (ἀφαιρεθήσῃ, "you will be pulled down"), but there is no problem with the parallelism in the MT, and the second person is used here so that it matches v. 18.

Form

No more need be said about the fact that a new section begins with v. 15. A link with the preceding threat against Jerusalem could exist, insofar as the "leader" who is accused so harshly and who is threatened with Yahweh's judgment might be one of those responsible for the faulty political reasoning that led to the debacle of 701. This would mean that he could have been the leader of the pro-Egyptian party, which pressed for a rebellion against the Assyrians. One might presume, if this is true, that v. 18 speaks of a deportation to Mesopotamia.

Some commentators express doubts about whether the administrator (סכן) is the same as Shebna, the one who was in charge of the palace. Some have pointed out that the title "one in charge of the palace" is not used in the same circumstances where one finds the designation סכן (administrator). But it is conceivable that the correct title for the one in charge of the palace was not used in this passionate attack against his person. That was not necessary, either, since there is no doubt that those who lived in Jerusalem knew the identity of the סכן (administrator) very well, the one who was being grabbed here by the scruff of the neck.

On the other hand, a clarification about usage is not enough to explain על (upon, against, concerning), which cannot be used as a preposition with בא (go), though the solution to this problem has long since been known. The superscription for the whole section is in v. 15bβ; it was probably written in the margin and then inserted at the wrong place in the text. Most of these superscriptions were supplied when the texts were assembled together (see, e.g., 21:1, 11, 13; 22:1). But that does not mean that they are automatically in error (cf., e.g., 6:1 or 20:1). However, this question is linked to others that deal with authorship and dating, at which point one also must remember that Shebna is not the one in charge of the palace according to 36:3, 22, and 37:2 (and the corresponding passages in 2 Kings 18f.), but is the secretary (ספר).

If one sets the superscription aside, this section begins with the messenger formula in v. 15a. What is surprising is that v. 15bα is not for public consumption but is a private message directed at the prophet. One would have expected that, somewhat analogously to that found in 7:3, this directive would have been introduced with the formula ויאמר יהוה אל ישעיהו (or: אלי) (and Yahweh spoke to Isaiah [or: to me]) and that the message from Yahweh addressed to the administrator would have been introduced by . . . ואמרת אל (thus you shall say to . . .). In fact, Gk, Targ did read ואמרת אליו (and you shall say to him), and hints still remain that this formula was used in the Hebrew text as well (see above, textual note 15e–e). If, contrary to what we presume to be the case, it so happened that the words were not in the original, then the idea would still have formed in the mind of those who were hearing this message (on this, see Kaiser).

Furthermore, one wonders whether the messenger formula in v. 15aα might originally have *followed* this directive to the prophet, coming just before v. 16. Based on an analogy with 7:4, however, this change is not necessary. Some minuscules (see Ziegler), Sa, Syhᵐᵍ do read καὶ εἶπεν κύριος (σαβαωθ) πρὸς με (λέγων) (and the Lord [of Hosts] spoke to me [saying]).

Some have already suggested (see *BHK³*) that the order of the cola in v. 16a and b should be reversed; then the two participles in v. 16b would both be in apposition to הסכן הזה (this administrator) in v. 15bα. But this alteration would not be needed if one were to insert ואמרת אליו (and say to him) between vv. 15 and 16; v. 16b is direct speech to the person being addressed, an analysis supported by the parallels noted in 22:1f.; one might compare: 22:1f.: מה־לך אפוה כי עלית . . . תשאות מלאה עיר הומיה (What happened to you then, that you all together have climbed up . . . you, filled with noise, raging city) with 22:15: מה־לך פה . . . כי חצבת לך . . . חצב מרום קברו (What do you have here . . . that you are having hewn out for yourself . . . that you hew out for yourself, high up, a grave); see also passages such as Isa. 3:15 (text emended); Ps. 50:16; Jonah 1:6.

Thus the structure of the passage is clear (see C. Westermann, *Basic Forms of Prophetic Speech* [1967] 137–142)

1. 22:15bβ Superscription
2. 22:15a   Introductory formula
3. 22:15bα Instruction to the prophet, (commissioning the prophet), namely:
   a. go . . .   b. and say to . . .
4. 22:16   Reproach, beginning with the reproachful מה־לך (what do you have)
5. 22:17f. Threat or announcement of judgment (introduced with הנה, "behold," which is often used instead of a messenger formula)

Only v. 19 is now left. The verse is quite different from what precedes it, using the first person style and leaving a bland and harmless impression, right after the vitriolic threat in vv. 17f. It is also hardly the job of a prophet to threaten someone with removal from their position in the government. Without any doubt, v. 19 is a later addition; it provides a transition to the passage that describes how Eliakim is to be installed into his official position (vv. 20ff.) and was probably not made part of the text until that passage was inserted.

Meter: The superscription v. 15bβ and the introductory formula in v. 15a are not part of the metrical structure. Verse 15bα (with אליו ואמרת, "and say to him") is a five-stress colon. In v. 16a the accusation is delivered using a heavy seven-stress colon (מַה־לְךָ פֹה וּמִי לְךָ פֹה כִּי חָצַבְתָּ לְּךָ פֹה קֶבֶר, "what do you have here, and whom do you have here, that you are having a grave hewn out for yourself"); in v. 16b the direct address takes the form of a six-stress colon (לֹ [left untranslated] is not given a stress). The announcement of judgment in vv. 17 and 18 has three lines, each of which has three parts (vv. 17 and 18a, each: 3 + 2 + 2; v. 18b: 2 + 3 + 3), and the later addition in v. 19 is a heavy two-stress + two-stress colon (note the alliteration: מִמַּצָּבְךָ and מִמַּעֲמָדְךָ).

Setting

Based on what has been said to this point, in general, the message that is delivered to the administrator is from Isaiah. Since the superscription is secondary, this conclusion provides no support for the notion that the Shebna mentioned here is the same Shebna who was the contemporary of Isaiah, to whom reference is made in chaps. 36f. Thus Fohrer, for one, thinks that this סֹכֵן would have to have been some lesser official. But even if this argumentation were correct (though, on this, see the following excursus), it would not change the fact that Isaiah is to be considered as the author, which is recognized even by scholars who lean in the direction of being highly critical of what should be attributed to Isaiah. Even Kaiser has to admit that 22:15-18 is to be attributed to Isaiah, "for lack of sufficient reason to the contrary"; there could have been an administrator in Jerusalem at the time of Isaiah who "had certain particular duties in the administration of Jerusalem or Judah."

No "sufficient reasons" argue against its authenticity, but many good arguments are in its favor. It is constructed much like 22:1ff., as has been noted already. The language, which includes so many images, some even grotesque, is Isaiah's; the passionate interplay is Isaiah's style, as he pronounces a judgment on this man's behavior; it is Isaiah's style to chastise him vehemently because he was hewing out a fancy grave for himself and selecting for himself such fancy chariots.

Of course, it is difficult to answer the question about the specific dating of the message against Shebna. We have stated already that it might be possible that it was placed right after 22:1-14 because it comes from the same time period. If the סֹכֵן (administrator) is a separate person, not connected specifically with the Shebna who was in charge of the palace, then there would be no grounds for coming to this conclusion. But there are no good reasons to reject the validity of the superscription.

סֹכֵן is a hapax legomenon and one cannot be completely sure of its exact meaning. The feminine form, סֹכֶנֶת, designates a "maid, nurse, guardian" (of the king), in 1 Kings 1:2, 4, but the meaning of סֹכֵן would not have to equal precisely whatever masculine functions would correspond—ignoring for the moment the recent suggestion by Mulder, who argues that the translation "nurse, guardian," should be replaced with "second woman in command" (that is, the old queen). The verb סכן means "bring a benefit, be useful." It is certain that this is related to *sakānu ana,* "care for," in the Amarna Letters (285:26, and often elsewhere). Besides this, in these letters the substantive *zukinu* is also used, as a Canaanite gloss to the Akkadian term *rabizu* (= *rabiṣu*). One would have to translate this term something such as "administrator, second-in-command" (see Mulder, 45). The Ugaritic texts also use a word *skn,* which supposedly means "governor, administrator," or something similar (see Alt). The Ahiram Inscription speaks of a סכן בס‹כ›נם, a "governor among governors" (*KAI* 1:2; *ANET* 661). An inscription found in Limassol, Cyprus (see map, p. 334), mentions a סכן קרתחדשת, that is, a governor from *qarthadašt* (*KAI* 31). The identification of this city is still under discussion. Some think it might be Kition, but other suggest Amathus or Limassol, which was called Neapolis in the Roman era (see G. Hill, *A History of Cyprus* I [1940] 107f., 251, 262f.). The most helpful inscription is an Aramaic one from *ḥama* that speaks about a סכן.בית.מלכה, an "administrator of the house of the king," which would have invested the person holding the office with very important authority, if it were not actually the highest position after that of the king (thus *KAI* 203). All these references fit nicely with סכן in the present passage to show that סכן could very well serve as a synonym for אשר על־הבית (one who is in charge of the palace). Based on his survey of the inscriptional material, Lipiński says briefly: "The term *skn* designates the king's second in command" (the relationship between this סכן and Akkadian *šaknu* is still disputed; see Rabin, Mulder, Lipiński).

When Isaiah says הסכן הזה (this administrator), he uses it in a disparaging way (just as when he speaks of Israel as העם הזה, "this people"; see *Isaiah 1–12,* p. 342 and cf. König, *Syntax* §48 [=*Lehrgebäude* 2.2]). No doubt, it was because he wanted to heap up as much scorn on this man as possible that he does not use his actual title, על־הבית (one who is in charge of the palace). As already mentioned, the prose narrative in Isaiah 36f. refers to a secretary named Shebna, Eliakim being in charge of the palace. Even though that is certainly not a blow-by-blow historical account of the events during 701, still one would hardly be right in assuming that the titles of the two most important officials serving at that time in Jerusalem would have been switched. It is not a foregone conclusion that there could not have been two different men named Shebna. But it would be more likely to assume that Shebna was "reduced in rank" to the position of secretary or that some other unknown reasons caused the men who occupied the two highest governmental positions to switch places, which would mean that 22:15-18 should be dated just a little before the dialogue with the Rabshakeh took place, as reported in chap. 36. In other words, unfortunately, one cannot determine any more exactly when to date vv. 15-18.

Commentary

[22:15] The form of the name שבנא (Shebna) (written with ה rather than א in 2 Kings 18:18, 26) is rather unusual. The Gk reads Σομνας (Somnas), Vulg *Sobnas* (whether the pronunciation after *b/m* would have been either *u/o* does not present a problem;

cf. Brockelmann, *VG* I, 75a; there is also no problem with the letters *b* and *m* being interchangeable). R. de Vaux (400) suggests that it might be the Egyptian name *šbnw.* But according to H. Ranke (*Die ägyptische Personennamen* [1935] 325, nos. 11f.), references to this name are found only during the Middle Kingdom era; since Shebna is found so often in inscriptions in Palestine, this thesis must be rejected. Rather, there is little doubt that this form of the name is a hypocoristicon for the full form שבניהו (Shebnayahu) (1 Chron. 15:24), sometimes spelled שבניה (Shebnayah) (Neh. 9:4f.; 10:11, 13; 12:14); on this, see Noth, *Die israelitische Personnennamen,* 258; a name with the theophoric element יהוה (Yahweh) cannot be Egyptian. There is no reason to conclude, as does König (676), that Shebna had an Aramaic background, making his suggestion on the basis of the א at the end of the name; there are many good Israelite names, such as עזרא (Ezra), בארא (Beera), עמשא (Amasa), and the like, which have the same letter at the end; in addition, one finds with relative frequency this form of the name (בעלא, אלא, אחא) on inscriptions. Akkadian also has the name *šubunuyama* (*PSBA* 15, 15). The name is found on seals and seal impressions, either in the form שבנא (Shebna) or שבניה(ו) (Shebnayah[u]); see Diringer, 122, 123, 179, 214, 218; in addition, see Moscati, 72, 78, 79. Furthermore, Diringer (123f.) depicts a seal impression that uses the hypocoristicon שבני. One notes with particular interest the inscription on the Louvre seal no. 106216: לשבניו עבד עזיו (belonging to *sbnyw,* servant of *ʿzyw*). Unfortunately, its provenance is unknown and there is no agreement about when it should be dated. According to Dalman (*PJ* 2 [1906] 46f.), it clearly belonged to a servant of King Uzziah; on this, see also Ginsberg, FS Kaplan, 253.

Concerning the form of the title אשר על־הבית (the one who is in charge of the palace), one might compare it to the ס רש = Akkadian *ša rēši* (*šarri*) "the one who is the head (of the king)"; (see *AHW* II, 974, 9c; and H. Zimmern, *ZA* 34 [1922] 91f.); in addition, note that *ša bitāni* is sometimes used as a designation for the one who is in charge of the palace (see *AHW* I, 132). But one also ought to note Arabic *kny ʿly byt ʾlmlk,* Tab. 1, 2440, 1. In addition to Shebna, others in the OT are given this title: Ahishar, an official under Solomon (1 Kings 4:6); Arza, an official under Elah in Tirzah (1 Kings 16:9); and Obadiah, a high-level official who served Ahab (1 Kings 18:3). Epigraphic evidence for the title has been found in an inscription in *silwān,* about which more will be said in a moment, dated approximately to 700 (Avigad, 43), as well as on a seal from *tell ed-duweir* (see S. H. Hooke, *PEFQSt* 67 [1953] 125f.; and Katzenstein, 153), which reads: לגדליהו אשר על הבית (belonging to Gedalyahu, who is over the hou[se]). It very likely belonged to that Gedaliah who was put in charge over Judah by Nebuchadnezzar after the fall of Jerusalem (2 Kings 25:22). An official with this title would have been the person in charge of the royal palace. This is exactly the position held by Ahishar (see above) in the list of officials in 1 Kings 4:1ff., but he is certainly not in charge over everyone else (see Noth, BK IX/1, 65). However, R. de Vaux has pointed out that Joseph, when in Egypt, was installed by the pharaoh "over his house" (אתה תהיה על־ביתי, Gen. 41:40), functioning exactly as would a vizier (the Egyptian equivalent of the Hebrew אשר על־הבית, "one who is in charge of the palace," is *ḥry pr,* "chief of the house"). For this reason, de Vaux believes that a case can be made for supposing that what formerly had been a position as chief over the palace, with time became a role in which one functioned as the second in command for the king. In the account in chaps. 36f., the אשר על־הבית (one in charge of the palace) led the delegation that was authorized by King Hezekiah to make official contact with Sennacherib's Rabshakeh. When one goes so far as to include the description of the dignity and the functions that Eliakim the son of Hilkiah performed in vv. 20ff. (though this must be done with caution), then one cannot avoid coming to the conclusion that the one who was in charge of the palace had become the first in importance after the king in the Davidic kingdom (cf. Katzenstein, 144f.). Duhm is correct when he expands on this idea: "For the minister of the house to be, at the same time, the head minister of state corresponds to those who were functioning at the patriarchal level within a state, which was formed by leading nobility, with the ruling chief being the one who has the most land, getting his income from his domains and from taxes paid on assessments for what is grown in the soil, but one must note that one would not have been able to identify 'independent civilians' as separate from those who would provide income to the state." It has been common for this function to be compared with that of the majordomo from the time of the Merovingian and Carolingian dynasties.

Some have tried to identify the Shebna mentioned in 22:15 with those of the same name found in Palestinian inscriptions. The inscription found in a grave in *silwān,* which was just noted, from the site of the necropolis of ancient Jerusalem, also speaks of one אשר על הבית (one who was in charge of the palace). This inscription was found by Clermont-Ganneau in 1870 on a burial installation that was hewn out of rock, written above the entrance to the inner chamber of the grave (see *IEJ* 3 [1953] plate 11; and *Bib* 35 [1954], just after p. 132). He had it chiseled out and sent to London, where it now can be seen in the British Museum. Even Clermont-Ganneau thought that it was possible to read the words אשר על הבית (one in charge of the palace), but he thought the rest of it was illegible. However, Avigad (137ff.) has now been able to decipher more of it. Donner and Röllig (*KAI* II, 189) translate it: "This is [the grave of . . .]ihw, who was in charge of the palace (אשר על הבית). There is no gold or silver here, [but] only [his bones], and the bones of his slave girl are with him. Cursed be the man who opens *this*" (see plates 8–10 in Avigad). Some words obviously cannot be read with certainty, but אשר על הבית (who was in charge of the palace) is correct, as is also the theophoric element -יהו. Paleographic analysis has not made it possible to assign an exact date to this short inscription, but it is obvious that the way the letters are shaped is very close to those on the well-known inscription from the Siloam tunnel, so that Yadin dared to suggest that -יהו should be filled in to read שבניהו (Shebanyahu) (see *IEJ* 3, 150, shared orally with Avigad). By contrast, Katzenstein (153) supposes that the name could originally have been חלקיהו (Hilkiyahu), in which case he thinks this would have been the Hilkiah who was the father of the Eliakim who is mentioned in v. 20. These suggestions are certainly within the realm of possibility. However, many names at that time ended in -יהו, and we know precious little about the variety of officials who served the king in Jerusalem. It does not help the case for linking this to the שבניהו (Shebnayahu) mentioned in this section that the inserted phrase describes Isaiah referring to a grave "high up," while the grave in *silwān* is on a slope in the middle of the present-day village, which forced Avigad to have to argue that an observer down in the Kidron Valley would still be able to speak of a "grave that is high up."

In his comments about Shebna and Eliakim, Ginsberg (FS Kaplan, 525) concludes that the Shebna mentioned in 22:15 is to be differentiated from the secretary Shebna in chaps. 36f. According to him, the one who was in charge of the palace in 22:15 would have been the owner of the seal now preserved in the Louvre, mentioned above, with the wording לשבניו עבד עזיו (belonging to *sbnyw,* servant of *ʿzyw*). It would have been possible that everything Isaiah predicted about this man could have come true (253). As evidence, he suggests that the title עבד (servant) (along with the name of a king) would be practically the same as אשר על־הבית (one in charge of the palace). One also must act cautiously and not hurry to accept this suggested identification.

The prophet is given the command to go in to "this administrator there." It is common that the imperative is used twice when instructions of this type are given to prophets or messengers. לֵךְ, "go," is actually no more than an interjection at this point; קוּם (come) in Jer. 18:2 is similar. For this reason, a second verb has to be supplied, here בֹא (go on in), to furnish the specific details of the command; see Ezek. 3:4, 11; however, cf. also Hos. 1:2; 3:1; Amos 7:15; Jonah 1:2; 3:2, and often elsewhere. Some commentators believe that the use of the verb בֹא betrays the fact that the prophet went looking for the one who was in charge of the palace in his own house. Others think it is more likely that Isaiah would have to go meet Shebna out by the grave that he had hewn out. In favor of that solution, פֹּה (here) is used three times in v. 16. In either case, one must assume that Isaiah avoided confronting this administrator so harshly out in public. The message about this man would possibly have been "published" by one of Isaiah's disciples, sometime afterward.

[22:16] The accusation begins with מַה־לְּךָ פֹה (what do you have here), which means something such as: to what are you treating yourself here, anyway? What are you doing so boldly? This ordinary phrase is given a unique twist right after that: מִי לְךָ פֹה (whom have you here), a formulation not used anywhere else, makes it especially ominous. It would seem that one would have to interpret it to say: You do not have anyone (no ancestors, no relatives) whose background could make it appropriate for you to erect such an elaborate grave site.

One could infer as much from the fact that Shebna was a *homo novus* (self-made man), not having belonged to the aristocracy in Jerusalem, which could be the reason why his father's name is not mentioned. As the descendant of a family that had neither rank nor fame, the wider circles of the population in Jerusalem may have viewed him as a usurper who had gotten to a level of power to which he was not entitled.

Shebna had this grave hewn from the rock. Akkadian *haṣābu* means "break off, cut out from something." Even if it might not be the grave of the Shebna we are discussing, the grave of the one in charge of the palace in *silwān*, to which reference had just been made, gives us a good idea about the way a grave of an important man from Isaiah's time would have looked. It is not a grave in a cave, but it was made by hollowing out a rocky wall, shaping it externally to resemble a house, carving out a room within to form a chamber for a grave (see the plans furnished by Avigad, 138f.; and cf. Ussishkin, fig. 6). Since the grave is about the size of a small house, it is certainly possible that the word קֶבֶר (grave) could be used parallel to מִשְׁכָּן (residence).

[22:17f.] Both the terseness and force of Isaiah's language comes through especially in the way he uses the infinitives absolute טַלְטֵל (stretch out), עֹטֶה (seize), and צָנוֹף (fling), but this cannot really be translated accurately and adequately into English.

גֶּבֶר (man) describes a man in terms of his strength, but what does it really matter if one is a גִּבּוֹר (strong man, hero) if Yahweh goes to work against him? Cf. Ps. 52:7: "But God will break you down forever; he will snatch and tear you from your tent; he will uproot you from the land of the living" (based on NRSV; Zürcher Bibel is similar). M. Klopfenstein (*Die Lüge nach dem Alten Testament* [1964] note 319) wonders whether, in addition to Ps. 101:7, Ps. 52:4-6 might not also have been addressed to palace officials who were misusing their authority; cf. the announcement of judgment Psalm 101:7, which reminds one of Isa. 22:17f.

"The land that lies open on both sides" would be that land into which Shebna would be exiled, i.e., the Mesopotamian lowlands (concerning the Assyrian custom of exiling the leading figures within population groups that opposed them, see the historical excursus above, pp. 331ff., but also 2 Kings 17:6; Amos 7:17). Fohrer, however, thinks this expression refers to the Palestinian coastal region where the Philistine cities are located, but the Assyrians would never have deported a rebellious Judean to Philistia. Shebna would die in that faraway land, which was particularly crushing, because land in a country one does not know at all is unclean; see Amos 7:17; cf. Jer. 22:26-28; Ezra 9:11. Not only was the land of Israel Yahweh's land; it was also the land where the patriarchs were buried; cf. the phraseology "be gathered to his people," and the like; see B. Alfrink, *OTS* 5 (1948) 118–131. One can resign oneself to the fact that one will die if one is sure that an orderly burial will take place, in one's homeland; however, the prospect of having to die far from one's family is deeply unsettling, since one would consider it possible that, without protection, one could be given over to demonic forces. It is thus highly ironic that Shebna, who is having a burial house hewn out for himself from rock, which seemingly would last forever, would never be able to look forward to being laid to rest there.

Yet constructing such a majestic grave was also a prestigious affair. When observing his burial chamber under construction, one could get the feeling that this man had a swelled head, which is also intimated when it is mentioned that the man in charge of the palace has also arranged for fancy chariots. מֶרְכָּבָה is normally used when referring to a war chariot, but Gen. 41:43 says of Joseph that he traveled through the land in the pharaoh's "second" bedecked chariot, showing everyone thereby that he was in a highly honored position. 1 Sam. 8:11 assumes that all kings travel about in fancy chariots; and, according to 2 Sam. 15:1, the king's son Absalom surrounded himself with chariots and horses so that he could make it publicly known to the people that he aspired to his father's throne. Thus it would seem that Shebna had virtually usurped the special privileges due to the king alone. Isaiah castigates him, fuming with indignation: "you disgrace to the house of your lord!" The "house of his lord" is obviously not the temple here (it is a misunderstanding about this point that led to the translation of אֲשֶׁר עַל־הַבַּיִת as *qui habitat in tabernaculo*, "who dwells in the tabernacle," and the rendering of הַסֹּכֵן as *praepositus templi*, "the one who is placed before the temple," in the Vulg), but instead, this is the palace of the king; cf. 1 Sam. 25:28; 2 Sam.

12:8, among other passages. There is no doubt that it has been stated this way on purpose: Shebna seems to have forgotten that the king is the אָדוֹן (lord); Shebna is not functioning in his proper role as עֶבֶד (servant). The king is often given the designation אָדוֹן (lord); quite plainly, he is the אָדוֹן (lord) over human beings (cf. particularly Jer. 22:18; 34:5).

[22:19] We do not have any information about whether Shebna was actually exiled, as is threatened here. Because Shebna appears as the secretary in 2 Kings 18f. (= Isaiah 36f.), with Eliakim serving as the one in charge of the palace, many have supposed that Hezekiah dropped him down to a position of lesser importance. It makes sense that the danger in Shebna's political moves might have been so obvious that it was natural that the positions of power within the cabinet be reassigned. That change is clearly something very different from what Isaiah had threatened at this point.

Verse 19 stands in direct contradiction to what Isaiah has proclaimed, since this verse does not speak of being exiled, only of being removed from office. Regardless, this later addition attempts to point out that Isaiah's prediction came true. And that was an important point to make, since the expander who writes in vv. 20ff. wants to make clear that Eliakim was installed in Shebna's position.

מַצָּב and מַעֲמָד, both having the meaning "position, office," in this passage, are used only here in that sense. Otherwise, these two vocables refer concretely to the place where someone puts something. However, a specific place is also needed for someone who holds an office, to which the office-holder goes to carry out public duties; cf. 1 Chron. 23:28; 2 Chron. 35:15.

It is also to be noted here that the one who expanded the text by adding v. 19 has Yahweh speak in the first person. Those who expand the text are careful to clothe their own thoughts within the authority that a direct message from Yahweh affords.

Purpose and Thrust

At first glance, it seems that the mere fact that Shebna was having a grave hewn out brought about a harsh condemnation from the prophet, so that one wonders whether the announcement of judgment is appropriate. The elegant grave must have been just one symptom which showed that this official was arrogant to the core. Even if what is described in this message did not happen exactly as stated, it still shows that it is his גָּאוֹן, his arrogance, that is so harshly condemned in this man. Shebna did not see that there were limits which were imposed by custom and position. Some commentators suggest that Isaiah had a basic aristocratic disposition, which would have made it difficult for him to endure watching someone who was a Johnny-come-lately put on the airs of a great noble.

The message provides indirect evidence that Isaiah openly acknowledged that he was convinced that the Davidic family had been chosen to rule. One might remember what was said in 3:4: "Then I will make lads their princes, and mischievousness shall rule over them." Was Shebna some sort of venerable figure of importance who was pressing Hezekiah to make danger-ous, if not suicidal, decisions? One might remember the analysis in chap. 3 at this point as well: "Your leaders are misleaders, and the path on which you ought to go, they mess it up" (v. 12). For Isaiah, when Shebna showed off with his grave and fancy chariots, it was a sign of the kind of arrogance that led Israel astray in its political decisions, leadership that never looked for guidance from the one who was actually in charge, to the one who created all history from afar (22:11)—making political judgments that would bring ruin for all to see, born here, as so often elsewhere, of personal ambition and of seeking to have power.

Eliakim's Call and Fall

Literature

W. F. Albright, "The Seal of Eliakim and the Latest Pre-exilic History of Judah, with Some Observations on Ezekiel," *JBL* 51 (1932) 71–106. E. Jenni, *Die politischen Voraussagen des Propheten*, ATANT 29 (1956) 42–48. R. Martin-Achard, "L'oracle contre Shebnâ et le pouvoir des clefs, Es. 22, 15–25," *TZ* 24 (1968) 241–254. See also the literature for 22:15-19.

[**Literature update through 1979:** H. J. Katzenstein, "The House of Eliakim, a Family of Royal Stewards," *ErIsr* 5 (1958) 108–110. A. Phillips, "The Ecstatics' Father," FS D. W. Thomas (1968) 183–194.]

Text

22:20 And it will happen on that day
    that I will appoint my servant,
      [a]Eliakim, the son of Hilkiah,[a]
  21 and I will clothe him with your robe[a]
    and wrap[b] your sash[c] around him,
      and I will place your authority into his hand.
  And he shall be father
    for the population of Jerusalem
      and [d]for the house of Judah.[d]
  22 And I will lay the key
    of the house of David on his shoulder,
  and he will open and no one will close,
    and he will close and no one will open.
  23 And I will drive him in, like a tent peg,[a]
    at a place where he will remain secure.
  And he will be a 'throne of honor'[b]
    for his father's house.

            * * * *

  24 [Then, the entire weight[a] of the house of his father will hang on him, [b]the sprouts and the leaves,[b] all the small vessels,[c] both the basins and all types of pitchers. 25 On that day, says[a] Yahweh of Hosts, the nail, which has been driven into that place, which holds firmly,

**will give way, break off, and fall, and the load, which is hanging on it,
will break into sherds, for Yahweh has declared it.]**

20a–a Schlögl suggests, because of the metrical length, that בן־חלקיהו (son of
Hilkiah) should be removed. While there may be other reasons why one should consider this notation secondary (but see below, pp. 394f.), the metrical reasons are not
sufficient to justify this action.

21a No English word is the exact equivalent of כתנת (here: robe); this refers to a
long, shirtlike garment, here apparently some type of clothing that would make clear
that its wearer has an office which carries with it much honor.

21b Concerning the meaning given here for חזק (wrap around), Eitan (68) refers to
Arabic ḥazaqa, "to bind around one with (a rope)."

21c אבנט should not be translated "belt, girdle"; a belt is used with everyday clothing, whereas an אבנט is always worn as a symbol of high office.

21d–d One ought not remove ולבית יהודה (for the house of Judah) on account of the
length of the meter (as Schlögl suggests, based on the Gk); vv. 21f. both have three
parts.

23a יתד seems to refer to a (tent) peg here, one that would be hammered firmly into
the ground. In v. 25, however, one must translate the same word as "nail."

23b כסא כבוד, "throne of honor," corresponds well to the other imagery used elsewhere in the text. There is no reason to accept changes that have been suggested,
both by Eitan (68), who thinks that כסא means "glory," based on Arabic kasā᾽ (treating כבוד, "honor," which follows, as an explanatory gloss), and also by Bruno, who
thinks כסא ought to be pointed כסא, "moon," and then proposes that the reference to
the moon in this case would be speaking about the (silvery) head of a nail.

24a In v. 23 כבוד meant "honor, dignity"; here, however, the word is used in its basic
meaning: "weight." One ought not follow Schlögl and point it כבד (heaviness), since
then it would disturb the link between it and כבוד (honor) in v. 23.

24b–b צאצאים means "shoot, what comes later." Since the following word צפעות (sg.
צפיעה) seems to mean "leaves" (KBL refers to Mehri ṣġāf, ṣġafōt, "leaf, petal"; Ges-
Buhl analyzes it differently: "probably the wild shoots of a tree"), but both would
still analyze צאצאים as having a connection with the other imagery in the text, which
speaks of growth. Shoots spring forth from the ground; W. Caspari (*ZAW* 49 [1931]
67), with help from 34:1b, thus thinks that if humans are referred to as sprouts, that
must have some connection with a mythical view of the world that pictured humans
as coming forth from the ground. That could be, but here the word is chosen in order
to show that the relatives of Eliakim appear contemptible. Fullerton (*AJT* 9, 628)
suggests that צאצאים might have been chosen because some type of play on the word
צאה (excrement) was intended; see Isa. 28:8.

　　According to Procksch, both vocables are to be treated as glosses; the imagery
about something hanging on a nail would fit well when speaking about small vessels,
but not in reference to descendants. True, but this is only making a comparison. Just
as small vessels hang on a nail, thus the family members hang on their hero.

24c כלי הקטן refers to pottery vessels that are small. But Eitan (69) is not satisfied
with that; קטן is supposedly connected here with Arabic qaṭana, "to reside in a place,"
but also with a meaning "to serve another person," so that it really means "household
vessels" here. But such a meaning for קטן is not suggested by any of its uses in the
OT.

25a Qᵃ: נואם; see E. Y. Kutscher, *The Language and Linguistic Background of the
Isaiah Scroll (IQIsaᵃ)*, STDJ 6 (1974) 498ff. (which henceforth will be referred to as
"Kutscher").

Form

As it now stands, the passage is a unified treatment, dealing with Eliakim, the servant of Yahweh. It is introduced by the formula והיה ביום ההוא (and it will happen on that day); it closes with כי יהוה דבר (for Yahweh has declared it), at the end of v. 25. However, there is a definite break between vv. 23 and 24. Verses 20-23 have a metrical structure, whereas there is no doubt that vv. 24f. are simple prose. It is also clear that the content of the two parts differs. The first discusses Eliakim's call to his office and rank; the second is about his downfall. The first part has a certain elegance but the second is cumbersome and thrown together. There is no possibility that these two parts were composed in one sitting. If one would hope to keep the possibility open that the same person was speaking both times, then a rather long time would have had to have elapsed between vv. 20-23, when great expectations were attached to the call of Eliakim, and the much later time, reflected in vv. 24f., when these hopes were shown to have been unwarranted, false hopes. Dillmann comes to the dubious conclusion that vv. 24f. are a continuation of the discussion about Shebna (so also Alexander, Kamphausen, and, much earlier, also Calvin; see Fullerton, *AJT* 9, 626). But that is not likely. The same negative assessment must be given to Ginsberg's attempt to rearrange large portions of the text and to alter the text itself extensively, in order to restore a presumed unity in vv. 15-25 and to salvage the entire passage as a single message from Isaiah. Another hand is responsible for vv. 24f., providing a later addition to vv. 20-23.

Setting

The introductory phrase "and it will happen on that day," used in v. 20, links this section with the previous message concerning Shebna; i.e., based on the present relationship to the preceding, the day on which Yahweh appoints Eliakim to his office is the same day as that on which Shebna is either exiled or—according to v. 19—removed from office. If this connection were original, then Isaiah would have to have been the author of vv. 20-23. But serious questions are raised about whether this is correct. We have already noted above (p. 389) that v. 19 is composed in the form of a direct message from Yahweh, whereas Yahweh is spoken of in the third person in the preceding verses. In vv. 20-23, identified as a distinct unit by the introductory phrase, Yahweh also speaks directly; v. 19 is thus not original to either section, though it serves to link the two sections, and so it makes little difference whether it is considered the conclusion of vv. 15-18 (in the third person) or the introduction to vv. 20-23 (also first person but preceding the introductory phrase; see Kaiser, but also earlier comments by Fullerton).

In addition to these arguments about form, however, even more convincing reasons are based on the content. No doubt it fits within the realm of prophetic activity that Isaiah could threaten a royal official with being hauled off to a strange land. But it is hardly possible that Isaiah could encroach on the domain of the king, using the authority of a message from Yahweh to select Eliakim to be the highest government official. Could Isaiah have characterized an official in the palace, the "prime minister" no less, as "servant of Yahweh"? On the one hand, in the political sphere, the עבד יהוה (servant of Yahweh) can be none other than the king. The Davidic ruler is Yahweh's counsel in the city of God and in Israel as a whole; according to the ideology of kingship, this function extended throughout the nations, to the ends of the earth. On the other hand, a minister of the king can be only an עבד המלך (servant of the king) (see, e.g., the seal from Megiddo with the inscription: לשמע עבד ירבעם, "belonging to Shema, servant of Jeroboam," or that found at *tell en-naṣbeh*, ליאזניהו עבד המלך, "belonging to Yazanyahu, servant of the king"; see *BHH* III, 1787f., no. 3; and cf. W. Zimmerli, *TDNT* V, 658, note 14; the Israel Museum recently acquired a seal impression with the inscription: ליהוזרח בן חלקן׳יהו עבד חזקיהו (belonging to Yehozeraḥ, son of Hilq[i]yahu, servant of Hezeqyahu) (see Ruth Hestrin and Michal Dayagi, *IEJ* 24 [1974] 27ff.).

Since Isaiah was basically a faithful supporter of the Davidic dynasty, it is impossible that he would have blundered so badly by attributing such honor to the position held by one in charge of the palace. Within the context of the entire message about Eliakim, this term עבד (servant) is not an offhand comment and cannot be interpreted as a simple slip of the tongue. This passage, vv. 20-23, is in the form of an oracle of investiture; nowhere else in the OT can one find a description of a royal official being invested. Even if one ignores the reference to עבד (servant), this installation of Eliakim, with all the powers the office entailed, makes bold use of terms otherwise connected with royal ideology. In 9:5 Isaiah had given the future David ruler the name "father" (more correctly: אבי־עד, "everlasting father"). Here the one in charge of the palace is called אב (father). In 9:5 the sovereign authority (משרה) is placed on the shoulder of the new ruler from the house of David. Here Yahweh places the ממשלה (authority) into Eliakim's hand. When the location where this one will be set securely in place, just as a tent peg, is called נאמן (secure), that could reflect the promise to David that his house would be נאמן (made sure) (2 Sam. 7:16; 1 Kings 11:38; cf. Ps. 89:29).

In light of all this evidence, Fullerton (*AJT* 9, 630) theorized that this text was not dealing with the call for Eliakim to be in charge of the palace at all, but that he would be king. This interpretation fails, since it cannot explain: "I will clothe him with *your* robe and wrap *your* sash around him," but it is significant that this viewpoint can be suggested in the first place. Procksch has another way to solve the problem. He would eliminate אליקים בן־חלקיהו (Eliakim, the son of Hilkiah), since Isaiah would never have looked for help from a minister of the king, but rather from one who would be an official, serving God himself (עבדי, "my servant"), who would be able to give counsel to both king and people better than could someone like Shebna. "As the עבד [servant] . . . he was totally responsible to Yahweh, but is also installed in a most honorable, unique position. . . . Just as Isaiah hoped for a king in the messianic era . . . so also he hoped for a counselor, in addition to the שֹׁפְטִים [judges] and יֹעֲצִים [advisers] at the end of time (1:26), which would fit very well into his idea of what the future would be." Jenni (44) carried this interpretation still further: this predicted (anonymous) servant would serve as an eschatological antitype to the official who was threatened with judgment from God in vv. 15-18. Kaiser agrees with this eschatological viewpoint, but thinks that Jenni did not apply fully what he had noticed, because he was trying to hold to the view that Isaiah wrote the passage. One cannot fail to notice how much this text sounds like the messianic predictions and, even more, the servant of God songs in 42:1ff. and 49:1ff. He is correct on that point, but the reference to Eliakim in v. 20 cannot simply be removed, since the sentence that would then remain, "I will appoint my servant," would then be nothing but a torso, immediately putting the question into one's mind about who this servant might be; one might compare this with 43:1: "I have called you, using your own name." And when these exegetes believe that they can make their eschatological interpretation more secure by removing this name, they are simply under an illusion, which they have allowed themselves to entertain because of their unfortunate opinion that "that day" is the day on which the events of the end of time will make their appearance. והיה ביום ההוא (and it will happen on that day) is nothing other than the well-known phrase that the expanders of the book of Isaiah used when they added something to the text, without engaging in deep reflection about what that meant. Indeed, it would have been most remarkable if someone would have taken an oracle, initially intended to convey something about the eschaton, and then would have recast it to apply to Eliakim, when in fact the historical Eliakim never aroused much enthusiasm in Jerusalem. The expander who added vv. 24f. was certainly not of the opinion that vv. 20-23 were promising that there would be an antitype to the historical majordomo Shebna at the end of time; if that were true, he would have had nothing to add.

To summarize: vv. 20-23 do not come from Isaiah, but must have been spoken originally with reference to Eliakim, the son of a certain Hilkiah. If Isa. 36:3ff. is correct when it speaks of a certain Eliakim who was in charge of the palace in Jerusalem in 701. The conclusion seems unavoidable that a prophetic contemporary of Isaiah is speaking these words, one who might have suggested to the king that Eliakim be appointed and who wanted to bolster his claim that this was the right person for the job by quoting religious statements. But even if this is all true, there is still the question about which prophet could have acted in this way and would have been able to play a significant role in what was actually the king's domain. It is more likely that some prophet wanted to solidify this person in his position by speaking this word, but said this after the actual event, maybe even long after Eliakim had been appointed. This might mean that the oracle was not intended for Eliakim personally but concerned his family (somewhat like the promise through Nathan in 2 Samuel 7, at least in its present form, which is technically addressed to David, though it speaks about the Davidic family line). It is obvious that one must presume that certain palace positions in Jerusalem were passed on through inheritance.

Kaiser refers to Gedaliah, who was installed as governor in Judah after Jerusalem was conquered in 587 (2 Kings 25:22; Jeremiah 40f.). He is supposedly the same person as that Gedaliah who was in charge of the palace, mentioned already, in reference to a seal found at *tell ed-duweir* (= Lachish) (see above, p. 385); and cf. R. de Vaux, "Le sceau de Godolias, maître du palais," *RB* 45 (1936) 96–102. His father was Ahikam, who, as one can probably conclude from 2 Kings 22:12, also served as the one in charge of the palace (cf. Katzenstein, 153f.). Ahikam's father, to take it one step further yet, was Shaphan, who, as Kaiser supposes, based on 2 Kings 22:8, served in the capacity of secretary of state. Katzenstein (154) ventures an opinion that the office of the one in charge of the palace was basically controlled by *one* family in the last days just before the exile, that being the family of Hilkiah. In a sense, that view is supported by the seal impression mentioned above (p. 394), now located at the Israel Museum, that speaks of יהוזרח (*yhwzrḥ*), son of Hilkiah, עבד (servant) of King Hezekiah, who must have been a brother to Eliakim.

There may be another way to fix the time period historically, as one tries to determine when the Eliakim oracle was uttered. From both *tell beit mirsim* and *tell er-rumeileh* (Beth-shemesh) (near ʿen šemš, En-shemesh), we know of impressions from a seal that were made toward the end of the kingship period that read: לאליקם נער יוכן (belonging to Eliaqim, lad of Yokin). Albright offers extensive comments concerning its date and meaning. He believes that נער (lad) is a parallel term for אשר על־הבית (one in charge of the palace of the king) and believes that יוכן (Yokin) is a shorter version of (King) Jehoiachin. Of course, this view leads directly to the question about whether it would be likely that we would possess several seal impressions, from different locations, all belonging to this particular man who was in charge of the palace of Jehoiachin, when that king did not rule for much more than three months. Albright gets himself out of this dilemma by presuming that Eliakim was still in charge of that king's property even long *after* he went into exile. This thesis depends on another, that Jehoiachin was still considered by many to be the legitimate ruler and was treated as such by the Babylonians, even after he had been deported to Babylon (see J. Bright, *A History of Israel* [1981³] 328 and note 53). If this assumption is valid, it would explain why this man, who one might say was the legal representative of the Davidic dynasty while the king was being held, would have been accorded such titles as are reserved for the king alone; v. 22, where he appears as the one who possesses the power of the keys over the house of David, would make much more sense in light of these circumstances. It must be repeated, however: we can do no more than engage in speculation.

Commentary

[22:20] The call or installation oracle for Eliakim begins with the verb קרא (appoint); cf. 42:6; 45:3f.; 49:1. Yahweh appoints Eliakim to be his servant. עבד (servant) can be used in the OT as the way a pious person would humbly speak about oneself; here, however, it is a title of honor. The עבד (servant) is Yahweh's agent on earth. This title is not used for one particular office alone. The patriarchs are Yahweh's servants; see Exod. 32:13. Moses is obviously Yahweh's servant. The king is Yahweh's servant, and thus David is the עבד יהוה (servant of Yahweh), emphasizing thereby that his kingdom is the center of operations for God's rule over the whole earth; see 2 Sam. 3:18; 1 Kings 11:34; Ps. 89:4, 21, among other passages. But the צמח (branch) mentioned in Zech. 3:8 is also the servant of Yahweh, as is Zerubbabel in

Hag. 2:23. In addition, the prophets are "servants" in service to their God as well; see references to this phrasing as early as 1 Kings 14:18 and 15:29. In the deuteronomistic writings, references to "my (your, his) servants, the prophets," shows that this practically became a formalized title (see above, pp. 295f.). Finally, the special figure known as the עבד יהוה (servant of Yahweh) in Deutero-Isaiah must be listed as well. However, in spite of all the variety of offices held by those who can be identified as servants of God, no passages in the OT accord this title to those who have governmental positions within the palace. And that should come as no surprise, since they are not standing directly before God. When, in spite of all that, this title is bestowed on Eliakim, that must have taken place during extraordinary historical circumstances—the king being either weak or unable to carry out official duties.

The name Eliakim, meaning "God sets up," was also the original name of the king whose name was changed to Jehoiakim, and Neh. 12:41 also mentions a priest named Eliakim. The name Hilkiah, meaning "Yahweh is my portion," is even more common; it must have been used originally within priestly circles (see 2 Kings 22:4; Jer. 1:1; cf., in addition, Num. 18:20; Pss. 16:5; 73:26; 119:57).

[22:21a] When the investiture takes place, the one in charge of the palace is shown to have been given new authority by being clothed with the special robe of his office. The first term for this garment is כתנת. The word is related to Akkadian *kitītu*, "linen robe," and to *kitinnū*, "linen"; cf. *kitū*, "flax, linen"; being used also in Ugaritic, *ktn*, "coat"; in Greek, χιτών (Ionic: κιθών); and in Latin, *tunica*. That the same word is used throughout does not mean that it always refers to the same type of garment, which means one should be cautious when using examples from the Greek and Roman period; in addition, the כתנת does not always have to have been made of linen (see the illustrations in the *Lexikon der Alten Welt*, 1535f.; and cf. Hönig, 30ff.). The כתנת is not worn only by those holding an official position; the same word describes clothes worn by men and women in private life. In spite of this, it sometimes refers to a certain type of special priestly clothing (Exod. 28:4, and often elsewhere). One notes that the text speaks of *your* כתנת, which means that it was made using a special technique or had special decorations that would identify it as the special garment worn by the one in charge of the palace.

The special garments worn by priests included an אבנט, a sash. The word comes from Egyptian (*bnd* = "wrap up in, clothe"; see Erman-Grapow I, 465); that garment is never referred to as one that would be worn by private male citizens, which means it is exclusively used as a decorative piece, separating the one wearing it from all the other citizens; cf. Elisabeth Staehelin, "Amtstracht," *Lexikon der Ägyptologie* I, 230–231, which gives some information about the *ḥry ḥbt*, the Heriheb (see Mohamed Saleh, "Cheriheb," ibid., 940–943), that is, the reciter of cultic songs, saying that he wore "a wide band on a slant across the breast."

The insignias publicize that Shebna's authority has been transferred now to Eliakim. Certainly this text does not say that full authority is now his, but when the word ממשלה (authority) is used, which is used elsewhere when the full authority of the king is being discussed, it shows that he is empowered to do much more than just what one in charge of the palace or what one who was responsible for the king's possessions would do.

[22:21b] What is predicated next is even bolder and more comprehensive: "He will be *father* for the population of Jerusalem and for the house of Judah." Here, as well, as is so often the case, Jerusalem and Judah are linked together; in the final analysis, this line refers to the different legal status held by each of these two parts of the kingdom in their relationship with the Davidic dynasty (see M. Noth, *GesS*, TBü 6 [1966³] 181f.).

Isaiah also speaks about the יושב ירושלם (inhabitants of Jerusalem) in 5:3, but instead of בית יהודה (house of Judah), he calls them the איש יהודה (inhabitant[s] of Judah). He does not use this terminology anywhere else either (but see 2 Sam. 2:4, 10, 11; Hos. 5:12, 14; thus it is possible that it was in use already in preexilic times, but otherwise it is found in later passages). Maybe a number of members of other tribal units had gone into the territory south from Jerusalem, in the region that was controlled later by Judah, living as sojourners there (M. Noth, *The History of Israel* [1960²] 55ff.).

As in 9:5 (see *Isaiah 1–12*, pp. 404f.), the idea conveyed by אב (father) is primarily that of the one who gives protection as he provides care. The pharaoh is given the title "father." Thus, e.g., Rekh-mi-Re, a vizier who served under Thut-mose III, says: "What is the king of Upper Egypt? What is the king of Lower Egypt? He is a god, through whose authoritative policies people live; he is the father and mother of all human beings, one of a kind, with no one like him" (G. Lanczkowski, *Numen,* Suppl 4 [1959] 272). In the Kilamuwa Inscription, the king boasts: "I, however, to some I was a father. To some I was a mother. To some I was a brother" (*ANET* 654; see also *KAI* 24:10f.). In one of the Karatepe inscriptions, אזתוד (Azitawadda) (who assigns himself the title עבד בעל, "servant of Baal"!) says: "Baʿl made me a father and a mother to the Danunites" (*ANET* 653; *KAI* 26: I: 3).

In these texts, it is the king who is given the title "father." It is a different story in the Elephantine Papyri, concerning the wise man Ahiqar; he is described as אבוהי זי אתור כלה, "father of all Assyria" (*ANET* 428; see also J. Zobel, *Der bildliche Gebrauch der Verwandtschaftsnamen im Hebräischen* [1932] 7ff.); see also Gen. 45:8: "God made me [namely: Joseph] לאב לפרעה ולאדון לכל־ביתו ומשל בכל־ארץ מצרים (a father to Pharaoh, and lord of all his house and ruler over all the land of Egypt)" (on this, see H. Ringgren, *TDOT* I, 8). One is left with the impression that the office of the one in charge of the palace for the Davidic family far surpassed, in the level of importance, the responsibilities of the Egyptian vizier; yet one can imagine that the author of the message about Eliakim had Gen. 45:8 in mind (indeed, the entire role that Joseph had played in Egypt), and viewed Eliakim as a second Joseph, though this one now fulfilled the same function in Israel.

[22:22] Questions about Egyptian influence have also been raised in light of this v. 22. R. de Vaux has noted the passage in *ARE* II, §§679–680, which tells us that the vizier declares to the head of the treasury every morning: "It has been reported to me by all of the responsible officials that the rooms were closed at such-and-such a time and they were opened at such-and-such a time." After this conversation between the two officials, one reads: "The vizier should order that every gate of the house of the king be opened, to make it possible for all who go in to go in (and) [for all who go out] to go out in the same way." There is no doubt that the אֲשֶׁר עַל־הַבַּיִת (one in charge of the palace) was responsible for the security of those who lived in the palace. This one is responsible for the keys of the house of David. Already in ancient times palaces and temples were locked up; see Judg. 3:25; 2 Sam. 20:3 (צרר, shut up); 1 Chron. 9:27. Concerning what keys looked like and the way they worked, see K. Galling, *BRL* 460; R. Knierim, *BHH* III, 1703f. (with illuss.); Hug, Pauly-W II, A, 1, 557–567; Dalman, *AuS* VII, 70ff. (with illuss. 12f.). In those days, the keys were so large that they could be placed on a shoulder. The power of the keys, which is given to Eliakim at this point, apparently goes far beyond the literal meaning; it means the overall responsibility and authority for the dynasty of the Davidic family, their possessions, and all their affairs. The magnitude of this responsibility can be detected in the assertion in v. 22b: וּפָתַח וְאֵין סֹגֵר וְסָגַר וְאֵין פֹּתֵחַ (and he will open and no one will close, and he will close, and no one will open). One gets the feeling that this is intended to ward off any attempts to question the authority of Eliakim. However, since we know so little about the circumstances behind this oracle, it is hard to give any credence to such conjectures whatsoever.

[22:23] With v. 23 there is a transition to a different image. Eliakim is like a tent stake, which is driven firmly into solid ground. In 33:20 Jerusalem is compared with "an immovable tent, whose stakes will never be pulled up, and none of whose ropes will be broken." Also in 54:2 Israelites living in the time of salvation are encouraged: "strengthen your stakes!" Therefore this imagery means that the city could count on complete security and protection during Eliakim's administration over the city and country.

But now comes the final attribution: "He will be a throne of honor for his father's house." Eliakim would have belonged to an aristocratic family in Jerusalem, from which the king's family would have selected certain members on an ongoing basis, who would have been available as senior officials. In this senior level position he would bring particular honor to his father's family. Because a member of the family served in such an important post, the relatives also would have felt honored, as if they themselves were all ruling from a throne. In other passages, it is God or the king who sits on a throne, once in a while, the priest as well (1 Sam. 1:9; 4:13, 18; cf. also Zech. 6:13). Obviously a senior official or a visitor to the king's palace could have been accorded the honor of being offered an expensive chair in which to sit. It is not intended that this term would refer to the place of honor in a tent, near the corner stake (thus Procksch).

[22:24] The expander who adds vv. 24f. follows up what was said in v. 23b. It did not turn out the way the prophet in vv. 20-23 expected. The clan of Eliakim not only had felt honored because of the high status that had been accorded their family member, but they wanted to profit richly through his position of power. That which could have been כבוד = "honor" for his father's family, and was to *stay* that way, had become כבוד = "weighty importance" for Eliakim. Unfortunately, a wordplay of this type cannot be rendered in German or English in all its force; if need be, one could translate כסא כבוד as *Würdenthron* (throne of honor) and כבוד in v. 24 as *Bürde* (burden). A German proverb says that worthiness brings burdens [responsibility brings responsibilities]; in just this way, Eliakim proved that the honor accorded him was a heavy weight around his neck, a real handicap that got in the way of carrying out his official duties. His family members are described disparagingly as "sprouts" and "leaves." Then the author immediately uses an even more disrespectful image. These family members have no importance; they are just like everyday dishes one uses in the kitchen. Duhm catches the flavor of what is said: "intentionally counting all these ordinary, little pots is ridiculous; every last one of the members of the whole clan of Eliakim fashions himself to be a great lord and desires an important job." The author is even more specific about what types are included in the reference to the "small vessels." There are both אגנות (basins) and all sorts of נבלים (pitchers). The word אגן (*HAL:* "large and deep bowls") corresponds to Akkadian *ag(g)annu,* "basins"; Ugaritic: *agn,* "kettle, bowl" (see Driver, *Canaanite Myths*); Egyptian: *ikn,* "bowl, basin"; Arabic: *ijjāna,* "urn, amphora." The word is also common in other Semitic languages. It may originally have been a loanword from Akkadian; see Zimmern, 33. (Concerning their shapes, see J. Kelso, *The Ceramic Vocabulary of the Old Testament* [1948] 15ff. and also illus. 2; in addition, see A. M. Honeyman, "The Pottery Vessels of the Old Testament," *PEQ* 71 [1939] 76–90, who thinks this refers to a vessel that looks much like a κρατήρ, "krater"; cf. also C. H. Gordon, *Before the Bible* [1962] 216.)

In addition to this, "all types of pitchers" are mentioned (see the illustrations in *BRL* 325f.; and Honeyman, 84f.). Neither the אגנות (basins) nor the נבלים (pitchers) have to be particularly small; in that sense, to refer to them all together as כלי הקטן (small vessels) is hardly justified if one looks at the actual size of the crockery, but this language is intended as a way to highlight that all of those hangers-on who have grabbed onto Eliakim are utterly worthless.

[22:25] In v. 25 the expander uses יתד (v. 23: tent peg; here: nail) once more, but once again he gives the word a different meaning. Here it refers to a nail on which one can hang all sorts of useful things that one wants close at hand—but sometimes so much is hung on a nail that it cannot bear all the weight, even if it has been pounded into some object that is sturdy. The entire collection of things falls to the ground and breaks. The imagery is not particularly apt in this case either. At least, one does not hang up basins. Nonetheless, the comparison with a nail that has too much weight hanging on it is not a bad one and it agrees with what the author wants to say. More than once a well-meaning and qualified politician has been doomed by the "hanging on" of relatives and friends. In ancient Israel, where more importance was attached to the clan in both good times and bad than is true in our own experience—though today, politicians in the Far East still rely heavily on the strength of their own family—"the downfall of Eliakim" certainly could not have been all that unique, but it serves as an example of a basic evil that comes with the territory, just because each country must be governed somehow, and it seems very difficult to surmount the problems.

One wonders whether still another expander added a note, beginning with ביום ההוא (on that day) in v. 25. But no satisfactory conclusion would then have been reached at the end of v. 24. Here is another case showing that ביום ההוא (on that day) is a throwaway expression, meaning virtually nothing, much like our "then," which by no means should be used as the primary evidence for interpreting a passage eschatologically. But also there is no evidence to support Kaiser's "suspicion" that the author "was holding up the mirror to a hated contemporary, perhaps a Jewish tax official working on behalf of the Ptolemies and responsible for the finances of Judaea and the Temple, thus seeking to prophesy his fall with impunity."

It is surprising how the expanders bluntly present their judgment as the unalterable decision of Yahweh. נאם יהוה (utterance of Yahweh) is not enough; כי יהוה דבר (for Yahweh has declared it), at the very end, is intended as a final addition, to heighten the impact that this message was intended to make.

Purpose and Thrust

Verses 20-23 paint the picture of a trustworthy official, fully aware that his task is to promote the welfare of the people. Eliakim did not seek out the position on his own, but he was appointed by God and installed into his office, and the anonymous prophet is not hesitant about according him the high title of being a servant of Yahweh. This passage gives us at least a hint about what someone in Israel would look for as the ideal way the country should be run. One might say that Eliakim is portrayed as the model of a good father of the country, having been legitimized in his office by God, but who still knows that he is a "servant," meaning that he remains answerable to God, someone who also knows, at all times, that there are limitations to the authority that God has given him.

In the real world, this ideal can come crashing down, as is seen in vv. 24f. Duhm wonders: "How did the public react to such an oracle, at the time when the expanders so blatantly spoke in the name of Yahweh of Hosts, letting loose as they expressed their hate and jokes?" And Marti offers his view about these last two verses: "a later . . . addendum, inserted by someone who was envious that the family of Eliakim had the honor of having such a famous ancestor." There is certainly some joking, hatred, and envy involved as this addition is composed. However, that does not do justice to the author. He knew of many individuals, brilliant and legitimately chosen by God, who had tragically come to ruin, just as it is described—though in a very different, momentous way—in the story about the call and fall of Saul. The concrete details about his demise are furnished in such a way that one detects that someone was skilled in making careful observations about the careers of such men.

The passage about the power of the key of Eliakim is most interesting because it finds its echo in an important way in the NT. In Rev. 3:7 the Christ is presented as the "true one (ἀληθινός, Hebrew: אָמֵן?), who has the key of David, who opens and no one will shut, who shuts, and no one opens." It would seem that, during the early Christian era, Judaism did not treat Isa. 22:22 as messianic (see J. Jeremias, *TDNT* III, 748), with good reason, since one in charge of the palace technically does not prefigure the messiah. But the author of the Apocalypse came up with a very important, though hardly noticeable, alteration. The Christ does not carry the key that opens David's house, but the key of David himself. He has at his disposal the full power of the royal עֶבֶד יְהוָה (servant of Yahweh). That this message to Eliakim could have been appropriated for use in NT christology, making just this one, apparently minor, alteration, shows once again that the functions attributed to Eliakim were definitely royal functions, as described in OT kingship ideology. According to Rev. 1:18, this same Christ carries the keys of death and the underworld (ᾅδης, Hades). It is not at all contradictory that the key which the new David holds in his hand (3:7) is apparently the key to the kingdom of God.

Throughout the history of the church, Isa. 22:22 has played an even more important role elsewhere; this verse, significantly altered in Matt. 16:19, is used to paraphrase the full authority accorded to Peter: "I will give you the keys to the kingdom of heaven, and whatever you bind on earth will be bound in heaven, and whatever you loose on earth will be loosed in heaven." This passage is quoted "correctly" insofar as it is not applied to Christ himself but directed toward Peter, who, one might say, is elevated to serve as the one in charge of the palace, the vizier of Christ, and as such is to carry on the affairs of his ascended Lord on earth. R. de Vaux (*Ancient Israel*, 130) calls him the "Vizier of the Kingdom of Heaven." Obviously the NT passage must be understood within its context. The power of the keys is reinterpreted here, so that the authority no longer entails opening and closing, but binding and loosing. That is to be interpreted in the light of the halakic tradition, according to which those who were trained in the law would be able to explain whether one was to be bound by or freed from having to obey a particular law (see E. Schweizer, *The Good News According to Matthew* [1975] 343; for a different interpretation, see J. Jeremias, *TDNT* III, 750f.). But one must not overlook that the charge to Peter occurs within a tradition according to which the vizier of the king, in a most unique way, was granted expansive powers (see Martin-Achard, 253f.).

Isaiah 23:1-18

A Message about Tyre

Literature

Concerning the entire passage: J. Linder, "Weissagung über Tyrus, Isaias Kap. 23," *ZKT* 65 (1941) 217–221. W. Rudolph, "Jesaja 23:1-14," FS F. Baumgärtel (1959) 166–174. J. Lindblom, "Der Ausspruch über Tyrus in Jes. 23," *ASTI* 4 (1965) 56–73.

Concerning the text: S. Grünberg, "Exegetische Beiträge: Jesajah 23, 15," *Jeschurun* 13 (1926) 50–56. M. Dahood, "The Value of Ugaritic for Textual Criticism: Isa 23:9," *Bib* 40 (1959) 160–164. Idem, "Textual Problems in Isaiah: Is 23:2," *CBQ* 22 (1960) 400–404. W. G. E. Watson, "Tribute to Tyre (Is. XXIII 7)," *VT* 26 (1976) 371–374.

Concerning Canaan: F. Böhl, "Kanaanäer und Hebräer," BWAT 9 (1911) 1–11. B. Maisler, "Canaan and the Canaanites," *BASOR* 102 (1946) 7–12. S. Moscati, "Sulla storia del nome Canaan," *Studia biblia et orientalia* 3 (1959) 266–269. C. L. Gibson, "Observations on Some Important Ethnic Terms in the Pentateuch," *JNES* 20 (1961) 217–238, esp. 217–224. J. Gray, *The Canaanites* (1964). M. C. Astour, "The Origin of the Terms 'Canaan,' 'Phoenician,' and 'Purple,'" *JNES* 24 (1965) 346–350.

Concerning Phoenicia: O. Eissfeldt, "Phoiniker und Phoinikia," Pauly-W XX, 1 (1941) 350–380. M. Noth, "Zum Ursprung der phönikischen Küstenstädte," *WO* 1 (1947) 21–28. D. Harden, *The Phoenicians* (1962). D. Baramki, *Die Phönizier* (1965). S. Moscati, *Die Phöniker* (1966). E. A. Speiser, "The Name Phoinikes," *Oriental and Biblical Studies* (1967) 324–331. "L'espansione Fenicia nel Mediterraneo," *Studi Semitici* 38 (1971) (various authors).

Concerning Tyre and Sidon: E. Honigmann, "Sidon," Pauly-W IIA, 2 (1923) 2216–2229. O. Eissfeldt, "Τύρος," Pauly-W VIIA, 2 (1948) 1876–1908. H. J. Katzenstein, *The History of Tyre* (1973). M. Elat, "The Political Status of the Kingdom of Judah within the Assyrian Empire in the 7th Century B.C.E.," *Lachish V* (1975) 61–70, esp. 64f.

Concerning Tartessos: A. Schulten, "Tartessos," Pauly-W IVA, 2 (1932) 2446–2451. FS J. Maluquer de Motes, *Tartessos y sus problemas* (1969) (not available to me). K. Galling, "Der Weg der Phöniker nach Tarsis in literarischer und archäologischer Sicht," *ZDPV* (1972) 1–18.

Concerning Cyprus: G. Hill, *A History of Cyprus* I (1949).

Concerning the "seventy years": C. F. Whitley, "The Term Seventy Years Captivity," *VT* 4 (1954) 60–72. A. Orr, "The Seventy Years of Babylon," *VT* 6 (1956) 304–306. O. Plöger, "Siebzig Jahre," FS F. Baumgärtel (1959) 124–130. P. R. Ackroyd, "The 'Seventy Year' Period," *JNES* 17 (1958) 23–27. R. Borger, "An Additional Remark on P. R. Ackroyd, *JNES* XVII, 23–27," *JNES* 18 (1959) 74.

Isaiah 23:1-18

[**Literature update through 1979:** H. J. Katzenstein, "צור־היסטוריה, מִשָׂא
גיאוגרפיה, ארכיאולוגיה. Onus Tyri—historia, geographia, archeologia," *HaMiqra'
weToledot Yiśra'el* (1972). M. Dahood, "UT 128 IV 6–7, 17–18 and Isaiah 23:8-9,"
Or 44 (1975) 361–374. E. Lipiński, "The Elegy on the Fall of Sidon in Isaiah 23," H.
L. Ginsberg Volume (1978), non-Hebrew section.
Concerning the text: G. J. Wenham, "Bᵉtûlāh, a Girl of Marriageable Age," *VT*
22 (1972) 326–348. A. Fitzgerald, "*BTWLT* and *BT* as Titles for Capital Cities," *CBQ*
37 (1975) 167–183.
Concerning Canaan: G. Dossin, "Une mention de Canaanéens dans une lettre
de Mari," *Syria* 50 (1973) 277–282.
Concerning Phoenicia: B. Oded, "The Phoenician Cities and the Assyrian
Empire in the Time of Tiglath-pileser III," *ZDPV* 90 (1974) 38–49.
Concerning Tyre and Sidon: P. Compermolle, "L'inscription de Salmanassar
III, IM 55.694 du Musée de Bagdad, la chronologie des rois de Tyr et la date de fon-
dation de Carthage (806/05 av. n. è.)," *AIPh* 20 (1968/72) 467–479. G. Pettinato,
"I rapporti politici di Tiro con l'Assiria alla luce del 'trattato tra Asarhaddon e Baal,'"
Rivista di studi fenici 3 (1975) 145–160.]

Text

23:1 [Verdict concerning Tyre]

Scream,[a] you Tarshish ships,[b]
for [c]'your refuge'[c] is destroyed!
On the return voyage[d] from the land of the Kittim
it was made known to you.
2 Bewail,[a] you coastal dwellers,
'you merchants'[b] from Sidon,[c]
[d]'whose messengers travel there'
3 'over' water in great numbers.[a]
The seed on the Shihor was 'his' harvest[b] [of the Nile],[c]
and his income [was][d] the profit from trade with the peoples.
4 Go away in disgrace, Sidon,
for the sea says[a] [b][the stronghold of the sea actually][b]:
"I am not in labor
and I bear nothing,
neither raise young men to maturity
nor do I bring up daughters."
5 [a][When one gets the news[b] in Egypt, then one shudders][a] [c][just as
by the news about Tyre].[c]
6 [a]Travel across[a] to Tarshish,[b]
scream, [c]those of you who live on the coast![c]
7 Is this your exuberant[a] (city),
whose origin[b] is in the distant past,
whose feet carried her,
to let herself be settled, to settle[c] [d]in a distant land?[d]

* * * *

8 Who made that decision
concerning Tyre,[a] the bestower of crowns,[b]
whose 'merchants'[c] are rulers,
whose tradespeople[d] are honored throughout the (whole) earth?[e]
9 Yahweh of Hosts decided it,
[a]to disfigure[a] the 'pride' of all majesty,
to make all the honored in the world despicable.
10 [a]'Build up' your land,

404

'since (for) the Tarshish ships'[a]
there is no longer a shipyard![b]
11b Yahweh[a] gave a command concerning Canaan,
to destroy its fortresses,[b]
11a stretched out his hand over the sea,
to shake kings' realms violently.

* * * *

12 [And said:][a]
From now on you will be exuberant no longer,
you mistreated[b] [c]maiden, daughter[c] Sidon!
Up, to the Kittim,[d] travel over there!
Even there, there will be no rest for you!
13 [a][Behold, the land of the Kittim—[b]that is the people which exists no
(longer);[b] Assyria[c] has designated it for ships.[d]
Someone erected[e] siege towers (?),[f] destroyed[g] its palaces, has
made it into a pile of rubble.][a]
14 Scream, you Tarshish ships,[a]
for your refuge is destroyed.

* * * *

[15 And on that[a] day it will happen [b]<<that Tyre[c] [d]will remain forgotten[d]
for seventy years. In the days of 'another'[c] king, (but) after seventy
years,>>[b] then it will happen for Tyre, just as it says in the song
about the prostitute:
16 "Take your lute,
traverse the city,
forgotten prostitute!
Play well,
[a]sing a lot,[a]
so that someone will remember you!"]

* * * *

[17 But after seventy[a] years Yahweh will take notice of Tyre, and she will
once again return to her prostitute's wages,[b] [c]and she will play the
prostitute with all[d] the kingly realms of the earth,[e] which are on the
face of the earth.[c] 18 Yet her profits from trade and her prostitute's
wages will become Yahweh's holy possession. It will neither be
hoarded nor stored up, but it will become the acquisition of those
who dwell in the presence of Yahweh, so that they eat until satisfied
and clothe themselves in finery.[a]]

1a Q[a]: אילילו (also: scream) (a ה is read instead of an א at the beginning, a common
occurrence in the Qumran materials).
1b Gk: Καρχηδών; Lat: *Carthago;* Vulg reads *naves maris* (ships of the sea) for
אניות תרשיש (Tarshish ships).
1c–c מבית (from the house) cannot be right. I. Eitan (*HUCA* 12/13 [1937/38] 69)
suggests מְבִית, which is supposedly somehow connected to the idea conveyed by
Arabic *mabit,* "shelter for the night," and would mean the same thing as מבוא
(entrance) and מעוז (place of safety) (in reality, designations for a "port"). But one
would expect to find a substantive with a suffix, which would refer back to אניות
(ships); thus בֵיתם (their house) has been suggested (*BHS;* cf. Targ מחוזהון, "their
havens"; Vulg reads: *vastata est domus,* "[the] house is devastated"). The Gk has no
equivalent term, which causes Duhm to regard it as a variant reading for מבוא (from
coming, on the return voyage), which follows it. Ehrlich (*Randglossen* IV, 80) treats

it as a dittography. However, when the same refrain is used at the end of the poem (v. 14), instead of מבית (from the house), it reads מעזכן (your refuge), which presumably ought to be read here as well (Marti, Ziegler; cf. Procksch).

1d If need be, מבוא can mean "when returning home" (*HAL* 566), but it would probably be better to point this מבוא (entering, on the return voyage) and to treat it as an adverbial accusative.

2a It is surprising to find the imperative דמו, "be quiet," since both vv. 1 and 6 call for the people to scream. The Gk reads τίνι ὅμοιοι γεγόνασιν (to whom have they become similar), which means it analyzed the word as a perfect from דמה I, "be like, resemble." Some (Marti, Guthe, Kaiser, et al.) would rather read the *niphʿal* from דמה II, that is, נדמו (may they be ruined), whereas others think it should be analyzed as the *niphʿal* of דמם (be silenced, destroyed), and still others (Schlögl, Bruno, *BHS*) treat it as the *qal* of that same root, reading דמו (they were silent). Already in 1884, the Assyriologist F. Delitzsch had suggested that דמם was related to the Akkadian verb *damāmu*, "grieve" (see *Prolegomena eines neuen hebräisch-aramäischen Wörterbuchs zum Alten Testament* [1886] 64, note 2). Since then, as has been pointed out by Dahood (*CBQ*, 400ff.), a Ugaritic word *dmm* has been discovered, meaning "mourn." This meaning results in a good parallel to הילילו (scream) in v. 1 (see *HAL*, which also postulates the meaning "howl, lament" for Pss. 4:5; 31:18; Lam. 2:10).

2b It is surprising to find the singular סחר (merchant from), especially when it immediately follows the plural ישבי אי (coastal dwellers). Here one must follow the Gk, Targ, Vulg and read the plural (סחרי, merchants of) (*BHS*, Kaiser).

2c The Gk translates צידון (Sidon) as Φοινίκη (Phoenicia).

2d–3a These lines make no sense. For עבר (crossing over), Qᵃ reads עברו (they cross over), a reading adopted by Rudolph (168); instead of עבר ים (crossing the sea), it is more probable that one should read the plural participle עברים (crossing, traveling over) (Procksch, *BHS*). After the word had been divided incorrectly, resulting in the singular עבר, what originally was the plural סחרי (merchants from) might have been altered to match this reading. The Vulg translated עבר ים מלאוך as *transfretantes mare repleverunt te* (crossing over the sea, they fill you up again), but one must recognize that this particular מלאוך is not to be analyzed as a form of מלא (fill, be full). Ps. 107:23 speaks of יורדי הים באניות עשי מלאכה במים רבים (Some went down to the sea in ships, doing business on the mighty waters). Based on this passage, Ehrlich emends v. 2bβ and the beginning of v. 3: עברים מלאכיו במים רבים (its messengers travel there over many waters) (similarly: Duhm; Marti; Procksch; Rudolph, 168; Auvray; Kaiser; et al.). The parallel noted in the psalm passage shows right away that the messengers are not like the צירים (envoys) in Isa. 18:2, who were fulfilling a diplomatic function when sent; instead, these are merchants. This interpretation is at least partially supported by the reading in Qᵃ: מלאכיך (your messengers). Since the suffix has to refer back to צידון (Sidon), it should probably be read מלאכיה (lit.: her messengers) (thus Kaiser); see תבואתה (lit.: her income).

3b Duhm and Kaiser consider קציר (harvest) to be a parallel word for זרע (seed) and remove it; in reality, it corresponds to תבואתה (lit.: her income) in the second colon. To be sure, one expects a suffix, so some have followed Marti and read קצירו (his harvest) (thus also Ehrlich, Schlögl, Procksch, et al.). It would be better to read a feminine suffix here as well, with Sidon as the referent.

3c יאור (stream, canal of the Nile) is missing in the Gk; it is widely considered to be a variant reading for שחר (Shihor) (Duhm, Marti, Ehrlich, Procksch, et al.). Concerning the meaning of the word, see *Isaiah 1–12*, p. 320.

3d There is no corresponding word for ותהי (and there was) in the Gk. It makes no sense to read it here, so most modern scholars eliminate it.

4a Q^a reads אמרה (she says); Kaiser suggests altering כִּי־אָמַר יָם (for the sea says) to read הָאֹמֶרֶת (the one who says), since the lament, that one had not given birth, would be possible only if a married woman would say it, whereas יָם (sea) is masculine (on this, see K. Albrecht, *ZAW* 16 [1896] 61). In a transferred sense, however, one cannot forbid males to speak about becoming pregnant.

4b–b מָעוֹז הַיָּם (stronghold of the sea) has been treated by many as a gloss on יָם (sea), which itself then caused לֵאמֹר (saying) to be added as the introduction to the following speech (see Marti, who accepts the interpretation of Olshausen, Duhm, and Cheyne).

5a–a This is a later addition; see below, p. 412.

5b שֵׁמַע (the news) does not seem to fit, since כַּאֲשֶׁר (when) is used when introducing a subordinate clause; the Gk reads ἀκουστὸν γένηται (= יִשָּׁמַע, "it will be heard"); Syr *(d)ʾštmʿ* (= נִשְׁמַע, "it was heard"); Vulg: *cum auditum fuerit* (when it will be heard). Presumably, the Gk preserves the correct original reading (Marti, Guthe, Feldmann, Procksch, Ziegler).

5c–c כְּשֵׁמַע צֹר (just as by the news about Tyre) is very likely a later insertion into the text; see below, p. 427.

6a–a Q^a reads the participle עֹבְרֵי (those [of Tarshish] who are crossing over) in the construct state. Kissane had proposed that reading before this text was found; the MT need not be altered, especially since both the Gk and Targ presume a reading with the imperative. One would be even less inclined to follow Ehrlich, who reads עָבְרוּ (they crossed over) and inserts, in addition, אֳנִיּוֹת (ships of), so that the verse will have acceptable meter. It is at least worth noting that some scholars point it עָבְרוּ (they crossed over), as Bruno suggests also, but that does not mean the suggestion is convincing.

6b The Gk reads εἰς Καρχηδόνα (to Carthage).

6c–c The Gk translated יֹשְׁבֵי אִי (those who live on the coast) as οἱ ἐνοικοῦντες ἐν τῇ νήσῳ ταύτῃ (those who are living on this island), which means they were thinking this referred to the city of Tyre, which was built on a rocky island. Although אִי can mean not only "coast" but also "island," יֹשְׁבֵי אִי (those who live on the coast) seems to have been used specifically as a way to refer to the Phoenicians; see above, pp. 115f.

7a Q^a reads הָעֲלִיזָה (*the* exuberant [city]), possibly correctly.

7b Q^a: קַדְמוֹתָהּ (origins, former times); the plural is also used in Ezek. 36:11.

7c Vulg: *ad peregrinandum* ([for the purpose of going] to foreign places), though this is not about temporary stops in foreign countries or about pilgrimages; instead, it refers to places where the Phoenicians established commercial outposts. Watson (372) argues for a completely different understanding of the verse: "Can this be your joyful city, to whom, since ancient times, they brought her tribute to her at her feet, obliged to reverence at a respectful distance?" But one can hardly agree with him.

7d–d Q^a מרחק; such a usage, which would likely be pointed מֶרְחָק, would have to be interpreted as an adverbial accusative, meaning "in the distance." But that meaning also can be intended when מֵרָחוֹק (usually: from a distance) is used; on this, see Exod. 2:4; 20:18, 21; 2 Kings 2:7.

8a Duhm and Kaiser suggest replacing צֹר (Tyre) with צִדֹן or צִידוֹן (Sidon), since that is the only city mentioned either before or after this. Admittedly, it is surprising that Tyre is referred to here, especially if v. 5 is treated as a gloss. On text-critical grounds, however, there is no reason to remove צֹר (Tyre).

8b Q^a המעטרה (the crowned one) seems to support reading either a *piʿel* or *puʿal* participle, as Procksch had suggested. Vulg translates this *coronata* (having been crowned); Lindblom (166) assumes that the *hiphʿil* has an intransitive meaning and thus translates this "the one wearing crowns, the crowned one." Finally, Ehrlich and Schlögl think that the MT is contradictory and that it also should read הַמְעֻשָּׁרָה, "the rich ones"—but that is their problem; if "rulers" are mentioned in v. 8b, it is certainly possible that v. 8a can speak of Tyre as the "bestower of crowns!" For further discussion, see below, pp. 417f.

8c As pointed, סֹחֲרֶיהָ makes no sense; it should be read סֹחֲרֶיהָ (whose merchants).

8d In suggesting an explanation for the unusual form *כִּנְעָנֶיהָ (here: tradespeople), KBL presumes it may have been formed by mixing parts of two words: כִּנְעָה (load, pack) and כְּנַעַנִי (tradesman); cf. also Bauer-Leander, §564, which assumes that there was a less common form כְּנַעַן; note also Egyptian *kynʿnw* (Maisler, 9). It is not right to follow Duhm and Marti in eliminating the word simply because it is difficult to explain; it is not a variant, but rather a necessary parallel to סֹחֲרֶיהָ (whose merchants).

8e The article on אָרֶץ ([whole] earth) in Qᵃ is a prosaicising element that has been inserted into the text, as one frequently notes in this copy of the scroll. But one ought not eliminate אֲשֶׁר, "whose," at the beginning of v. 8b, as do Schlögl and Kaiser, even though the relative particle is sometimes used in such a way that it causes a prosaicising of the text; on this, see L. Köhler, *Deuterojesaja,* BZAW 37 (1923) 58.

9a–a Qᵃ reads כֹּל (all) before גָּאוֹן (pride) instead of כֹל (all) before צְבִי (majesty). *BHS* suggests this reading should possibly be followed, with גָּאוֹן (pride) being pointed so that it is in the absolute state. In such a case, צְבִי (majesty) would be in a dependent relationship with לְהָקֵל (to disfigure). Duhm and Marti had already suggested that כָּל־צְבִי (all the majesty) be placed *after* לְהָקֵל (to disfigure); similarly, Schlögl. By contrast, Procksch reads לְכַלּוֹת צְבִיָּהּ (to eliminate her majesty) instead of כָּל־צְבִי (all the majesty); cf. also Kaiser. The end of the verse also has aroused the suspicions of many exegetes. Duhm considers נִכְבַּדֵּי־אָרֶץ (the honored of the world) to be an unneeded repetition of the conclusion of v. 8, eliminates both words, and replaces them with עִבְרִי אַרְצֵךְ (cross through your land), from the beginning of v. 10, though he then alters this to read עָבְרָה אָרֶץ (arrogant of the world); the same is done by Schlögl and others. That involves too many textual alterations. Verse 9 has three parts: 9a, 9bα, 9bβ; this removes the need for any textual alterations; repeating נִכְבַּדֵּי־אָרֶץ (honored in the world) is an effective stylistic technique.

10a–a Targ reads וְלָא מֵאַרְעֵיךְ (go into exile from your land), which means it already had this version of the text, which is so difficult to understand, and had attempted to make some sense of it. Concerning suggestions by Duhm and Marti, see textual note 9a–a. Ehrlich (*Randglossen* IV, 81) suggested reading עָבְרוּ (they invade): "the enemies that are invading overflow the land, just as the Nile overflows Egypt." Kissane leaves עברי (cross over, through) but alters אַרְצֵךְ כַּיְאֹר בַּת־ (your land as the stream of the daughter of [Tarshish]) to read (*sic*) אֶרֶץ כִּתִּים אֳנִיָּה (land of Kittim, ship of [Tarshish]). However, Qᵃ reads עבד (serve) instead of עברי (cross through) and thus supports the Gk reading, which translates the whole verse: ἐργάζου τὴν γῆν σου, καὶ γὰρ πλοῖα οὐκέτι ἔρχεται ἐκ Καρχηδόνος (you shall work your land, since the ships will no longer come from Carthage). This means that the Gk has no term equivalent to כַּיְאֹר (as the stream of). There seems to be no good way even to begin to explain what this word means here, and it has been treated, as is commonly done is such cases, as a gloss. Even if that gloss is presumed, the verse is still very difficult to understand, which might suggest that a more radical alteration has taken place in the text. It is odd that the distant city of Tarshish would be addressed without any further ado, and one must admit that Kissane is likely correct in treating בַּת־תַּרְשִׁישׁ (daughter of Tarshish) as a mistake. It really does not help if one follows Procksch's solution, which rearranges the text so that v. 10 follows right after v. 6. It would seem that this time, the Gk approximately reflects the correct text; following it, one might read: עִבְדִי אַרְצֵךְ כִּי אֳנִיּוֹת תַּרְשִׁישׁ (work your land, since the Tarshish ships), which would mean that the first two consonants in כיאר should be separated from the rest, forming the word כִּ, "since." The rest of the word, אר, is then to be taken with the following בה, which probably originally formed the word for "ship," possibly even אֳנִיּוֹת (ships of) (see v. 1), which was damaged later.

10b The Gk did not understand מָעוֹז and thus left it out of the translation; Procksch suggested it be altered—because of πλοîα (ships) in the Gk—to read מַלָּח, "sailor"; Duhm, et al., *BHK*, and *BHS* read מָחוֹז, which is supposed to mean "harbor"; Kissane proposes מְחָ, which also is supposed to mean "harbor"; finally, in attempting to explain the word, KBL cites Egyptian *mdḥ*, "build ships," and *mdḥ.t*, "carpenter's work," and thus offers "shipyard" as a translation for מָעוֹז (which would then suggest that מָחוֹז, in Ps. 107:30, also means "shipyard"; see also *HAL*).

11a Procksch, Rudolph (169), Steinmann, Eichrodt, and Kaiser (see also *BHS*) all reverse the order of vv. 11a and 11b, since the common subject in both halves of the verse, יהוה (Yahweh), is first mentioned in v. 11b. That makes sense, even if one would wonder how such a switch could take place. However, it seems there also are other places in the chapter where parts of the text have been moved around.

The Gk reads σαβαωθ (of Sebaoth) after κύριος (Lord, Yahweh); based on the meter of the verse, that can hardly have been original.

11b מָעֻזְנָה is a rare form. There have been a variety of suggestions, such as the possibility that the two consonants נה are used together to avoid the duplication of letters, which originally would have been ה (Dillmann), or that the נ is an archaic form of the plural ending (Eitan, 70); these are little more than useless attempts to defend the MT. S. Talmon (*Textus* 4 [1964] 124) might be correct here, suggesting that it could have been written by combining מָעֻזֶּיהָ (her place of safety) with a parallel term מָעֹן (dwelling place) (see Ps. 90:1). For a long time already, it has been read as מָעֻזֶּיהָ (her place of safety), which has now been shown to be correct on the basis of Qᵃ.

12a וַיֹּאמֶר (and he said) should probably be removed from the text (Duhm, Procksch, Rudolph, Kaiser, et al.); not only does it make the meter too long, but it is not correct in terms of what it says. It is not Yahweh but the author who speaks.

12b Qᵃ does not read the article on מְעַשֵּׁקָה (one who mistreats), which is probably more accurate. Ehrlich (*Randglossen* IV, 82) considers מְעַשֵּׁקָה (one who mistreats) to be an impossible reading. He notes that this is the only time that the word is used with an intensive stem, and it does not make any sense in the context either, since it characterizes the way the Phoenicians are treated as unjustified, which would be impossible, since Yahweh is the one who carried it out. But this argumentation is not convincing (see below, p. 431).

12c–c It seems that we have too much of a good thing when בְּתוּלַה (maiden) is read just before בה (daughter); it is not found in the Gk, which is reason enough for some exegetes to leave it out of their text (Duhm, Procksch, Kaiser, et al.). But (contra Procksch) the meter does not require that this term be eliminated; it is simply a stylistic technique, used with the lament; see below, p. 415, and note the alliteration: בַּ בְּתוּלַה.

12d One notes right away that כִּתִּים (the Kittim) (which, following the *Qere*, is certainly the correct reading, instead of כתים; see v. 1), which is an accusative indicating the direction, is at the beginning of the clause, separated from עֲבֹרִ (travel over there). Haupt (see Marti) would move it so that it *follows* עֲבֹרִי (travel over there); Cheyne (see Marti) mentions the possibility that it be changed to read כִּתִּמָה (toward the Kittim) (cf. כַּשְׂדִּימָה, "into Chaldea," in Ezek. 11:24). The meaning is not changed in either case.

13a–a If one wants to stay with the MT in v. 13, then one would have to translate this something such as: "Behold, the land of the Chaldeans, that is the people that exists no longer—Assyria has established it for ships. They have erected its [referring back to a masculine] siege towers (?), they have destroyed its [referring back to a feminine] palaces. He has made it [referring back to a feminine] into a pile of rubble." No one but König has believed it possible to make sense of the passage as is; the text, if left as it is, would show that the author is a very poor excuse for one. Thus no one will make any sense of this without some textual adjustments. The most significant problem deals with אֶרֶץ כַּשְׂדִּים. Why is there a reference to the "land of the Chaldeans" in a message about the Phoenicians? H. Ewald thought that כַּשְׂדִּים (Chaldeans) was a copyist's mistake for כְּנַעֲנִים (Canaanites) (*Göttingische gelehrte Anzeigen* [11 Nov. 1837] 1799), and von Orelli and Cheyne follow his suggestion. Others (Procksch; Kissane; Rudolph, 170, *BHS*) remove אֶרֶץ כַּשְׂדִּים (land of the Chaldeans). However, since the Kittim had been mentioned already, Meier (see Duhm) had earlier suggested reading כִּתִּיִּים (Kittiim), and many have agreed with this solution (Marti, Guthe, Kaiser, et al.). Actually, this verse should be interpreted as a gloss to כתי(י)ם (Kittiim or Kittim) in v. 12.

13b–b There are also problems with understanding the meaning of זה העם לא היה (lit.: this the people not was). Since the time of Bredenkamp, the preferred solution to this problem has been simply to eliminate this portion of the verse altogether (Procksch; Kissane; Rudolph, 170). But that is the easy way out; at times it is just not easy to get into the mind of the glossators.

13c Another surprise comes when Assyria is mentioned. Duhm (followed by Marti) suggests replacing אַשּׁוּר (Assyria) with אֲשֶׁר (that which), which gives him the chance to point the following word יסדה as יְסָדָהּ (foundation), and he assigns the meaning "seafarer" to צִיִּים (BDB: wild beast, either desert dweller or crier, yelper) (to be translated: "This is the people, which is a commercial enterprise for sailors")—very creative, as is normal for Duhm, but unlikely nonetheless.

13d צִי means "demon"; see 13:21 and the textual note 21a there. In addition, however, there is apparently another צִי with the meaning "ship"; it seems to be an Egyptian loanword (Egyptian *ḏ3y* refers specifically to the riverboat). One notes that Num. 24:24 speaks about ships that come from the Kittim and humiliate the Assyrians, and Dan. 11:30 specifically mentions Kittim ships. Because there were close ties between Egypt and the Phoenicians, and thus also very likely with the Phoenician colonies on Cyprus, it is not surprising that the word צִיִּים (ships) would be selected when the Kittim were involved. This interpretation comes later in the text, but still substantiates the emendation above, which changed כַּשְׂדִּים (Chaldeans) to read כתי(י)ם (Kittiim or Kittim); it also makes it impossible that the other meaning for צִיִּים, either as "demons" or "desert animals," could be involved here.

13e One Hebrew MS (see *BHS*) reads the singular הֵקִים (someone erected); Kissane follows this, which means that the singular must be used in place of עֹרְרוּ (they destroyed). However, the text is probably correct as it is; the subject is an unidentified enemy that defeats Kition/Cyprus.

13f Qᵃ reads בחינה instead of בחיניו, supporting the *Kethib* reading here, not the *Qere* [בחוניו]. When used in conjunction with אַרְמְנוֹתֶיהָ (her palaces), the feminine suffix in Qᵃ might also be correct. It is not clear what בחון/בחין actually means. KBL says only that this is "obscure"; the Gk translates from a text with a different reading; Targ reads חֲזיתהא, "its watchtowers"; Syr: *bṣwyʾ*, "waiting tower (?)," which leads *HAL* to suggest this be translated "siege tower."

13g Duhm and Marti conclude that עֹרְרוּ (destroyed) resulted from damage to the text, which originally read עֵרָיו, "his cities"; this would have to be taken, along with the following אַרְמְנֹתֶיהָ (her palaces), as the object of הֵקִימוּ (they erected). However, these emendations are all based on the view of those particular exegetes that v. 13b speaks of the way in which the "seafarers" had been active in establishing colonies; in reality, this is about how the land of the Kittim was conquered and devastated.

14a The Gk also refers to Carthage here (see above, textual notes 1b, 6b, 10a–a).

15a Qᵃ reads הוא instead of ההוא, omitting the article because of haplography.

15b–b In Qᵃ the entire text between הוא (that [day]) and לצר (for Tyre) is missing (*aberratio oculi* [the eyes wandered]; note that צר, "Tyre," is used twice).

15c–c "Seventy years, as the years of a king" sounds odd; on this, see below, pp. 433ff. Having been left with this same impression, the Gk reads ὡς χρόνος ἀνθρώπου (as the time of a human being), which also cannot reflect the original text. Procksch and Kaiser alter the text to read בִּימֵי מֶלֶךְ אַחֵר (in the days of another king). In this case, one would have to move the *athnach* to the preceding word שָׁנָה (year). That does not radically alter the consonantal text, but one must admit that this emendation is also questionable, since there has been no previous mention of a king, after whom another one is to follow. But there is no better solution anywhere.

15d–d נִשְׁכַּחַת (will remain forgotten) is a third feminine singular perfect, used instead of the more common נִשְׁכְּחָה (also: will remain forgotten). Not many will agree with Feldmann that it should be treated as a participle. The ת is explained as an old feminine ending (Joüon, *Gr* §42f).

16a–a It is not necessary to change הַרְבִּי ([sing] a lot), for metrical reasons, to read הַרְעִיבִי (Schlögl)—it is not impossible for two stressed syllables to follow right after one another, and he does not let us in on the reason why he translates הַרְבִּי שִׁיר as "sing sweetly."

17a Qᵃ reads [שׁ]בעין (seventy), using the Aramaic plural ending (note that Qᵃ uses צִיִּין instead of צִיִּים in v. 13, both meaning "ships").

17b The Gk translates וְשָׁבָה לְאֶתְנַנָּה (and she will return to prostitute's wages) as: καὶ πάλιν ἀποκατασταθήσεται εἰς τὸ ἀρχαῖον (and again it will be reestablished as it was in former times); Targ: לְאַתְרָהּ, "to her place"; they may have felt uncomfortable with having to translate "prostitute's wages." Instead of אֶתְנַנָּה (prostitute's wages), one should accept the reading of many Hebrew MSS, Syr, Vulg, which have the suffixed form נָהּ- (*her* prostitute's wages).

17c–c The Gk also was not willing to speak about playing the whore; it translates this: καὶ ἔσται ἐμπόριον πάσαις ταῖς βασιλείαις τῆς οἰκουμένης (and it will be a trading station for all the queens of the earth).

17d כל (all) is missing in Qᵃ.

17e Bruno thinks that the verse has one accented syllable too many and thus suggests removing הָאָרֶץ (the earth) (then pointing מַמְלְכוֹת [in pause]; still: kingly realms). When one is dealing with those who interrupt the text by inserting additions, however, it is better not to cover their tracks for them by trying to make this appear to be in verse form by eliminating some words. To be sure, הָאָרֶץ (the earth) does not fit well with הָאֲדָמָה (the face of the earth); however, the "style" used by this expander should be left as it is.

18a עָתִיק is a hapax legomenon. Besides this, one does find *עָתִיק, "old" (1 Chron. 4:22); for this reason, Vulg translates עָתִיק as *usque ad vetustatem* (all the way back to antiquity). Arabic *'tyq* also means "precious," for which reason עָתִיק should be translated "choice, excellent." That does not suit Procksch; he alters this to read לְמַכְסֶה עָתִיק and translates "for clothing the old people"—but the youngsters in Jerusalem would not have been satisfied with this type of prediction.

Isaiah 23:1-18

Form

[23:1-14] This chapter has the superscription צֹר מַשָּׂא (verdict concerning Tyre). Like the other superscriptions in chaps. 13–23, it is probably also a redactional element. In similar instances, in 13:1; 21:1, 11, however, there was no reason to doubt whether the title was correct. For chap. 23, by contrast, its correctness has often been questioned. Whereas vv. 5 and 8 speak of Tyre—there is no doubt that vv. 15-17 are about Tyre—v. 2 deals with the merchants of Sidon and v. 12 addresses daughter Sidon. It has been suggested, and it seems to be supported by the evidence, that not only vv. 15f. and 17f. are later additions to the text—everyone agrees with that—but that even vv. 1-14 did not come into existence all at the same time. Therefore attempts have been made to recover an original basic text, an approach used particularly by those exegetes who believe that such an analysis at least will be able to "salvage the core" of the message for attribution to Isaiah. Thus Procksch treats the middle section, vv. 5-11, which mentions Tyre, as having been inserted in what is now vv. 1-4 and vv. 12-14, which directly address Sidon, in his opinion Sidon as a city. The inserted material, concerning Tyre, would have been followed still later by vv. 15-18.

By contrast, Rudolph (170) has argued in favor of vv. 1-14 being a single unit. He presumes that there were three parts: (1): vv. 1b-4, 6, which speak about the Phoenicians; Sidon in v. 2 would not be a reference to the city, but would be another way to designate the Phoenicians as a group (as reflected in the Gk here, which reads צִידוֹן as Φοινίκη, "Phoenicia," though it does have a different way of translating it in v. 12); (2): vv. 7-9 with v. 5, which is to be moved so that it follows v. 9; here Tyre is addressed; (3): vv. 10-14, which speak about the Phoenicians, especially about the city of Sidon.

Still another version is offered by Kaiser. He also considers vv. 1-14 to be basically a single unit, but suggests that the entire message is about the destruction of Sidon. He considers v. 5, which refers to Tyre, to be an apparent gloss, and he follows the suggestions of Duhm and Marti in v. 8 when he alters צֹר (Tyre) to read צִידוֹן (Sidon). Verse 5 is to be eliminated altogether; in his view, this verse does not come up to the high standards that are appropriate in poetry and it interrupts the flow of the text in a way that cannot have been original. (One will have to consult the commentaries and introductions for further suggestions about how to analyze the text.)

It is true that no good reason exists for questioning the unity of vv. 1-14 (except for vv. 5 and 13). Disagreeing with Kaiser, I also see no good reason to question the superscription. It is no problem that Sidon is mentioned along with Tyre; Sidon serves basically as a general designation for the Phoenicians. Homer himself sometimes referred to the Φοίνικες (Phoenicians) as the Σιδόνες (Sidonians) (*Iliad* 23.743f.). Verse 11 mentions כְּנַעַן (Canaan), which is virtually the same as Sidon in this passage, meaning that it also serves as a designation for the Phoenicians (see below, pp. 430f.). On coins one can find the phrase לצר אם צדנם (for Tyre, with the Sidonians) (C. F. Hill, *Catalogue of the Greek Coins of Phoenicia* [1910] CXXXIII).

412

Ethbaal from Tyre is called the "king of the Sidonians" in 1 Kings 16:31 and, in Gen. 10:15, where Sidon appears as a son of Canaan, there is no doubt that it refers to the Phoenicians in general, rather than being used as a way to identify the city. The same is true for בת־צידון (daughter Sidon) in v. 12 (see below, pp. 431f.).

In addition to the gloss in v. 5, numerous questions are raised about v. 13. It is so poorly preserved that there is no way to explain it accurately. Numerous attempts have been made to sift through the words to reconstruct an original text, one that would fit well into the context without difficulty and would also have a satisfactory metrical structure (see attempts such as Rudolph's and Kaiser's). But the alterations that one has to make to achieve the desired result are so complicated, and the final result is so arbitrary, that the best solution is to alter it as little as possible. The entire verse should be treated as a gloss (thus Dillmann; Cheyne, *Introduction;* Fohrer; Schoors; cf. Feldmann).

One will have made significant progress in figuring out who wrote this and the time when it was written once one determines whether vv. 1-14 is in the form of a prediction, i.e., an announcement of judgment, or whether the material looks back on a terrible calamity that struck the Phoenicians. If this is a prediction, then one is freed from having to expend the energy to discover what historical situation is behind this, one that would roughly correspond to the way the fate of Phoenicia is depicted. The notion that this points to the future has been suggested more recently once again by Rudolph (173) (see also Feldmann, Fischer, Eichrodt). He admits that the text describes this as if it has already taken place, but maintains that it is simply prophetic anticipation, which means that we have the right to interpret 23:1-14 as a threat. But we do not in fact have this right. The catastrophe has begun already; one can call on others only to lament Phoenicia's fate. Only v. 12 speaks about the future. Daughter Sidon will not be able to rejoice any more, *because* it has been struck with such a destructive blow. This verse in particular shows that the author is looking back on events that have occurred already (see the details provided by Lindblom, 56ff.).

In terms of its form, what we have is a "summons to lament." One might say that הילילו (scream) (vv. 1, 6, 14) is the identifying mark. In a song of lament, one would naturally speak about the fact that one has suffered disgrace in the national catastrophe; here, however, in the summons to lament, it is said: "Go away in disgrace!" (v. 4). Or one might otherwise lament that one has to leave one's native land, that one has been driven out of one's home (Jer. 9:18); here, there is a summons to emigrate—in fact, toward Tarshish (v. 6)—but even there, in that foreign territory, one would discover that there would be no place to find any rest. Since there would be no rest anywhere, one detects that the summons to lament is filled with sarcasm; this passage does not come from someone who is suffering along with everyone else, as one finds in passages such as the songs of lament concerning Moab in chap. 15.

In vv. 8-11 the poem moves on to a reflective stage; the author is not just an observer, one who is enjoying that it is finally time for the Phoenicians to get what they have coming, and it is not simply a poet who is trying to depict the severity of the calamity that has struck the Phoenicians; this author serves as a witness that these events have been determined beforehand by the decision of Yahweh and that Yahweh has his good reasons for causing this particular turn of events in Phoenicia's history. This is the real reason the poem is written.

In v. 12, however, the author once again turns back to address Phoenicia. He does not see any comforting dawn's early light for this neighboring country anywhere on the horizon. It is thus very effective that v. 14 brings the poem to a close with a repetition of the call to "scream."

Concerning vv. 15-18, see below, pp. 433ff.

Meter: The original material that formed this chapter, vv. 1-4, 6-12, 14, should be analyzed as a metrically constructed poem. Admittedly, there are not many places where one finds *parallelismus membrorum,* the clearest indication that one is dealing with poetry, and one cannot speak of any sort of regular metrical pattern. In some places it is difficult to identify the metrical structure exactly because one cannot be sure of having correctly reconstructed the original text. However, it is wrong to work the text over and over until one is able to splice together some sort of passable version of the procrustean bed of what supposedly is the original meter. With all these problems, one can do nothing more than be as careful as possible when trying to determine the metrical structure.

Verse 1a is not constructed metrically; it is a secondary superscription. Verse 1b is written as 2 five-stress cola.

Verse 2, along with ובמים רבים (over water in great numbers) at the beginning of v. 3, shows itself to be 2 two-stress + two-stress bicola (יֹשְׁבֵי־אִי, "coastal dwellers," is to be read with a single stress). The rest of v. 3, based on the textual corrections that have been proposed, is a three-stress + three-stress bicolon. It is difficult to determine what is in the first line of v. 4 (even if מָעוֹז הַיָּם לֵאמֹר, "the stronghold of the sea actually," is bracketed out). It is possible that this also is a three-stress + three-stress bicolon: בּוֹשִׁי צִידוֹן כִּי־אָמַר יָם לֹא־חַלְתִּי וְלֹא־יָלַדְתִּי should be accented as shown here. The second line of the verse is to be read as a five-stress colon. Verse 5 (later addition!) is prose. Verse 6 is once again a two-stress + two-stress bicolon (יֹשְׁבֵי אִי, "those of you who live on the coast," has only one stress, as above). Verse 7 has a five-stress colon and a two-stress + two-stress bicolon. Verse 8a should probably be read as a three-stress + three-stress bicolon (מִי יָעַץ זֹאת). That this short colon has three stressed syllables, followed immediately by two more stressed syllables, shows that this question is very important—which makes sense also on the basis of the content; see below, p. 428. הַמַּעֲטִירָה should be read with two stresses, which means that it also is highlighted. Tyre, so proud, carrying itself so high and mighty, has to learn that Yahweh also makes the final decisions about its existence. Verse 8b also should be analyzed as a two-stress + two-stress bicolon (second colon: כְּנַעֲנֶיהָ נִכְבַּדֵּי־אָרֶץ; see also v. 9); it may be that the uncommon form נִכְבַּדֵּי (honored) may have been used so that two stressed syllables would not be used together, one right after the other.

Verse 9 has three parts (see the way this is arranged in the translation). This variation to the pattern once again is used to underscore the importance of the answer.

Verse 10 (if one treats כִּיאֹר as a gloss) contains 1, and v. 11, 2 five-stress cola.

The first line of v. 12 (after ויאמר, "and said," is removed) is composed as a seven-stress colon. It is difficult to analyze the second line of v. 12; it is possibly a three-stress + three-stress bicolon: לך (*sic*) כתים קומי עברי גם־שם לא־ינוח. If כתים (Kittim) was placed *after* עברי (up, cross over to), one would keep two accented syllables from colliding, but putting כתים (Kittim) (*casus pendens* [as a nominative absolute]) in the initial position was obviously done on purpose; the author wants to arouse tension for the listener, who wonders what will be said about the Kittim. For that reason, it is proper that there should be a pause in speaking, right after כתים (Kittim) is mentioned. Because of this, the stress on שם (there) in the second colon is followed immediately by לא (no [rest]), also stressed; the latter word receives a particularly strong accent, which is proper in light of the content.

Since it is very difficult to be sure about the original wording in v. 13, it is best not even to offer an opinion about the metrical questions raised there.

Verse 14 = v. 1b, first line.

Verse 15 is a prosaic introduction to v. 16, which itself is composed with 2 six-stress cola, each with three parts (each 2 + 2 + 2).

Verses 17f. cannot be read metrically.

Setting

[23:1-14] The authenticity of 23:1-14 has been discounted by most, since the poem in vv. 1-14 does "not have anything in common either with Isaiah's style or with his ideas" (Duhm); even Eissfeldt, who is usually much more cautious than most, offers this assessment in the second edition of his *Einleitung* (389): "In any case, the passage does not contain anything that is characteristic of Isaiah's style, and for this reason one should no longer give serious consideration to the possibility that this comes from the time of Isaiah, even though that is not completely impossible." It has been determined already that this same judgment no doubt applies to vv. 15ff. as well. As mentioned above, some scholars, in more recent times, have used a variety of approaches to try to recover at least some of the material from vv. 1-14 that they believe could be assigned to Isaiah (Dillmann and Kittel, Procksch, et al.), in which case a variety of solutions have been offered about how much can be salvaged. By contrast, Rudolph has recently championed the cause for vv. 1-14, not only that it is a complete single unit, but also that the entire section is to be attributed to Isaiah, including vv. 5, 13, about which many questions have been raised. His view is that the poem makes complete sense as a prediction, uttered in the time "of the massive resistance movement against Sennacherib, after the death of Sargon," between 705 and 701 (173f.). But it has already been explained that this passage cannot be analyzed as a prediction. If it looks back on what already happened, then even more importance is attached to the discrepancy between this and historical reality. At the outset, this makes no sense as a correct way to date the passage, since neither Cyprus nor the geographically still more distant Tarshish would have been summoned to offer sympathy. Rudolph adds other arguments: mention of Assyria in v. 13 would preclude a late dating, in either the Persian or the Greek eras. But this verse seems to be a gloss, and questions have been raised, textually as well, about whether אשור (Assyria) is even the correct textual reading (see above, textual note 13c); yet, even if one would treat the present text as original, the dating of the text would still fit most likely in the century between Isaiah and the time when Assyria's might came to an end. When v. 9 raises the accusation against the Phoenicians, that they are filled with גאון (pride), that would certainly fit with Isaiah's way of thinking; but it has been noted above already, in comments about 16:6 (see p. 146; see also 14:11), that this reproach is a stock phrase that can be used in any of the oracles against the nations. The overall vocabulary is simply not typical of Isaiah; see Cheyne, *Introduction,* 142f. The ideas are not those which follow Isaiah's interests. The closest to Isaiah would be the use of the verb יעץ (decide) in v. 9, which reminds one of the עצה (counsel) of Yahweh, a concept that was very important to him; but the thought that God makes decisions about the future is also a regular feature of oracles against nations generally; see Jer. 49:20; 50:45.

Two observations are decisive in concluding that this is not from Isaiah. When this prophet deals with other peoples, he is actually always addressing Jerusalem/Judah (see above, pp. 101f.); he is concerned about the fate of other nations only when that is demanded because he cares so deeply about his own people; Isaiah is not a prophet who views his task as being called to offer an opinion about all the events that take place in world history. The other argument, which deals more with formal considerations, is connected with what has just been said. Isaiah's messages concerning the foreign nations never furnish observations after the fact about events that unfold within world history; in his case, they are always "predictions"—and their function always must be to issue a warning to Israel. For these reasons, one must conclude that 23:1-14 (18) are not to be attributed to Isaiah.

In any case, the historical circumstances behind 23:1-14 are difficult to determine and have been the subject of great disagreement. No doubt, Tyre/Phoenicia was often exposed to attacks, which could supply details to explain the background of the passage if we knew the specifics. But, at the very least, the text does give one rather significant bit of information that can help with the dating. Isaiah himself spoke about Tarshish ships, and this type of vessel was mentioned already in 1 Kings 10:22; see also 1 Kings 22:49; Ezek. 27:25; and Ps. 48:8. The only time they are mentioned in postexilic passages is in Isa. 60:9. Of course, Tarshish itself is mentioned specifically in passages that are clearly late (Jonah 1:3; 4:2). However, in passages in the priestly writings (Gen. 10:4), the city and the country are linked to the sons of Javan, as is also the case with the כתים (Kittim); here, in the present passage, it is linked specifically to Tyre and the Phoenicians. In the seventh century, however, Tarshish was lost to the Phochaean Greeks (cf. Herodotus 1.163 and 4.152).

The seafaring people who lived in Phoenicia had long had contact with Kition/Cyprus; it had possibly been colonized by residents of Tyre already about 800 B.C., or still earlier (see Moscati, 198), though it declared its independence while under kings who had Phoenician background (Moscati,

203); finally, the Greeks seized control of Cyprus as well—insofar as the Persians did not contest their claims. The observations in our present passage refer back to a time when the power of the Phoenicians had not been interrupted yet, that is, before the Assyrians finally incorporated Phoenicia into their realm and before the Greeks became that empire's chief rival in carrying on trade throughout the Mediterranean region.

When attempting to date the passage, however, some have pointed out that the only time periods that could come into question would be those in which attacks against Phoenicia actually led to a total catastrophe and that it could not have been an event in which Tyre was in the middle of all the action. For these reasons, many have been attracted to Duhm's solution, pointing to the radical destruction of Sidon by Artaxerxes III Ochus (ca. 346). Cyprus also joined in the rebellion against the Persians at that time, with Nectanebo II of Egypt spurring them on from behind the scenes. But the report about these events by Diodorus Siculus (16:41–46) does not even mention Tyre. For this reason, Lindblom, who treats this passage as a message about Tyre, argues that it was set in the time when Alexander conquered it: "No one can disagree that Tyre is thought of as completely destroyed in our poem. We hear nothing about a destruction of the city in the days of Alexander the Great" (58). But he bases his interpretation on the meaning of מִבַּיִת (lit.: from the house) in v. 1, that all the houses of Tyre are reportedly destroyed (61). מִבַּיִת is textually suspect, however, and all portrayals of this type are to be taken with a grain of salt. It is also not necessary that שֻׁדָּד (destroyed) must mean that Tyre was completely leveled. According to this text, the worst problem is posed by the threat to the maritime trading activities of the Phoenicians. Those who believe that this text should be assigned a late date acknowledge indirectly that Tyre would not have been described as a "bestower of crowns" in the late postexilic era as they offer their suggestion that the *hiph'il* מַעֲטִירָה (crown) has to be intransitive (be crowned). But even if they were right on this point, this epithet would make the most sense during a time when Tyre still played a central role as the leading merchant in a maritime empire. That observation also applies to what is said in v. 11, which mentions how violently the royal kingdoms located across the sea are shaken when Phoenicia is conquered. This sentence could never have been written in Persian or, still less, in Greek times. Finally, it does not make any sense that this message about the Phoenicians would have been composed so much later than the Moab passages in chaps. 15f. and also subsequent to the sections about Babylon and Dumah in chap. 21. Besides, one cannot fail to notice a certain connection between this and the chapters about Moab. The vocabulary and ideas in vv. 1-14 simply do not sound similar to passages in the OT that are definitely written later. Verses 15ff. show how one would actually have thought in the postexilic era. Thus this message cannot have come into existence all that long after the time of Isaiah, i.e., in the late Assyrian era. Apparently, it recounts the events connected with the downfall of the Tyrian domination in the region surrounding the Mediterranean Sea. Most likely, this would have happened during the reign of Esarhaddon.

Isaiah 23:1-18

The catastrophes that befell Phoenicia during the time that this Assyrian ruled (681–669) came in two phases, about which we have excellent information from Esarhaddon's own documents. Even though this king had demonstrated his power by launching a campaign against Philistia in 679, *abdi-milkutti*, the king of Sidon, shaking himself free from the Assyrian yoke, established an alliance with *sanduarri*, the king of URU*kundu:* "They trusted in their own power; I [namely: Esarhaddon], however, trusted in Ashur, Sin, Shamash, Bel, and Nebo, the great gods, my lords" (Borger, *AfO* 9 [1956] 50). The expedition to punish *abdi-milkutti* resulted in the city being destroyed: "As to Sidon, his fortress town, which lies in the midst of the sea, I leveled it as (if) an *abûbu*-storm (had passed over it), its walls and foundations I tore out and threw (them) into the sea destroying (thus) its emplacement completely. I caught Abdimilkutte, its king, who fled before my attack into the sea, upon an oracle-command of Ashur, my lord, like a fish on high sea and cut off his head. I carried off as booty: his wife, his children, the personnel of his palace, gold, silver, (other) valuables, precious stones, garments made of multicolored trimmings and linen, elephant-hides, ivory, ebony and boxwood, whatever precious objects there were in his palace, (and) in great quantities. I led to Assyria his teeming subjects, which could not be counted, (and) large and small cattle and donkeys in great quantities. (There), I called together all the kings of the country Hatti and from the seacoast and made them build a town (for me) on a new location, calling its name Kar-Esarhaddon" [thus far: *ANET* 291] . . . I reorganized this region. I installed one of my eunuchs as ruler over it. I demanded from him increased tribute and more gifts than previously. From the cities which belonged to him, I transferred URU*ma᾿rubbu* and URU*sariptu* to Baal, the king of Tyre" (cited completely by Borger, 48f.). The kings who were natives of the Phoenician region, Baal (Akkadian: *ba᾿lu*) of Tyre included, then settled down and cooperated and served well as vassals of Esarhaddon. Manasseh of Judah is mentioned within the same context, and, in a list of ten kings from KUR*yadnana* (Cyprus), *damusi*, the king of URU*qartihadasti*, is mentioned also (on this, see above, p. 384; and Katzenstein, 207).

We have a copy of a treaty between Esarhaddon and Baal of Tyre from this same time period (Borger, 107ff.) that helps us to see that the overlordship of Assyria was very humiliating for Tyre: Baal was permitted to open letters from Esarhaddon only in the presence of the Assyrian governor. If any ships belonging to Baal suffered shipwreck in Assyrian waters, the entire cargo belonged to Esarhaddon. Mention is made of piers in harbors in Assyrian territories where Tyrian ships could dock and from which they were permitted to carry on trade with the other territories that were also under Assyrian control (text uncertain; concerning this treaty, see Elat, 64f.). Because of all this, it is no surprise that Baal of Tyre allied himself with Tirhakah the Ethiopian, after Esarhaddon had conquered the latter in 674, even though, not long before this, *abdi-milkutti* had been destroyed completely when he rebelled.

It does not seem to have cost much energy for the Assyrian leader when he acted to conquer Tyre in 671: "I conquered Tyre, which is located in the midst of the sea; I took away from its king Baal, who had trusted in *tarqu* (Tirhakah), the king of KUR*kusi* (Cush), all his cities and all his possessions. I conquered Egypt, KUR*paturisi* (Pathros) and KUR*kusi* . . . all the kings, who dwell in the midst of the sea, from Cyprus (KUR*yadnana*) and Javan (KUR*yaman*), even as far as Tarshish (KUR*tarsisi*); [they all] placed themselves under my feet" (Borger, 86). Some (see Moscati, 56f.; Katzenstein, 278f.) doubt that Esarhaddon actually conquered the island portion of Tyre, but rather think he simply coerced them into paying tribute. It might be that he had to satisfy himself at first with just placing the island under siege and that Baal had to capitulate when Esarhaddon was on his return trip, following his magnificent campaign against Egypt. The region was divided into three provinces: Simyra in the north, Sidon (or: *kār-ᴵᵈaššur-aḫu-iddina* = Esarhaddon's harbor) in the middle, and ᵁᴿᵁ*ušu* (the solid land of Tyre) in the south (Moscati, 59).

It would seem that the expeditions of Esarhaddon, for the purpose of inflicting punishment on the Phoenicians, provide the most likely background for 23:1-14. Particularly in favor of this view, one notes that Cyprus also came under the control of Assyria, so that Esarhaddon could boast that he had brought under his control "all the kings who dwell in the midst of the sea, from Cyprus and Javan, even as far as Tarshish (!)." But this was also the time when he defeated Egypt, so that the once booming trade that the Phoenicians had established with the land of the Nile was also placed under the control of Assyria. The Assyrians must have attached great importance to having Phoenicia firmly under its control if it were to be successful in containing Egypt. Thus the Phoenicians could not simply slip away to Cyprus; in fact, the relationships with its western colonies were severed as well (cf. v. 11). Another reason why this message cannot possibly have come from the Persian era is the great interest in the fate of Phoenicia in the passages in the book of Ezekiel that deal with Tyre (and Sidon).

Commentary

[23:1a] According to the superscription (see above, pp. 1f.), chap. 23 presents a משא (verdict) about the Phoenician city of Tyre. In fact, it discusses the fate of Phoenicia in general and must have come from a time when Tyre played a central role in Phoenicia. Time and again, Tyre was the last line of defense for the Phoenicians. If it fell, Phoenicia was done for.

צר (also צור), Phoenician and Ugaritic: *ṣr*, Akkadian: ᵁᴿᵁ*ṣurru/i*, Egyptian: *d3r*, Greek: Τύρος (Herodotus 2.44), rarely also referred to as Σωρίος, Ζωρ(ος), known today as *ṣūr*, is without doubt a Semitic name, meaning "rock," so called because the city was situated on a rocky island that was located very close to the coastline; cf. the wordplay in the threat in Ezek. 26:4: "I will . . . make it a bare rock (צחיח סלע)."

It is situated about 75 km. south-southwest of Beirut, 55 km. north-northeast of Haifa. The name would suggest that it was settled by a group of Semitic immigrants who had crossed over the Lebanon range and advanced to the Mediterranean coast.

The area where the Phoenicians lived is limited to a remarkably isolated area, quite inaccessible. On the east are high mountains; on the north and south are a series of foothills that go right down to the seashore and isolate access as they drop off precipitously (in the south, one might mention particularly the *rās el-abyaḍ* and the *rās en-nāqūra;* in the north are foothills above the *nahr el-kelb* and also the *rās eš-šeqqa*). In this protected region, the Phoenicians were able to develop their own unique culture. The land is open only toward the sea, and the Phoenicians in Tyre, Sidon, and other cities were industrious in their use of this doorway, particularly since its western coastline is dotted with excellent natural harbors, which served well in promoting maritime traffic throughout the ages.

Isaiah 23:1-18

Since the time of Alexander the Great, who tried to break the resistance of the city by pouring huge amounts of dirt into the sea to build a land bridge, the island of Tyre, lying about 600 m. from the mainland, has been a peninsula. Directly opposite is mainland Tyre; Egyptian: ʿt, Akkadian: ušu, known by the Greeks both as ἡ πάλαι Τύρος or Παλαίτυρος (Old Tyre), which often has been identified as tell rešidīye (about 6 km. south of ṣūr), though it is really to be found on tell el-maʿšūq (directly east of ṣūr; see E. Honigmann, ZDPV 47 [1924] 26; M. Noth, Aufsätze zur biblischen Landes- und Altertumskunde II [1971] 29; Eissfeldt [1948] 1881f.).

Numerous mythological accounts have been passed down describing how the city came into existence, but none of these can be trusted to provide accurate information. Tyre is mentioned already in Ugaritic texts and in the Amarna Letters. According to the latter, it was harshly oppressed, along with its king abimilku, by zimrida of Sidon, the inhabitants of Arvad, and the Amorite leader aziru, but the king stayed faithful to Egypt even when ušu was conquered and the city was cut off from all supplies from the mainland (Knudtzon, nos. 146–155). That Tyre had been under the overlordship of the Egyptians at some point in time is shown in the close ties that existed between the two countries, as the present text still demonstrates (v. 3; see also v. 5). Although Sidon had been the most important city of the Phoenicians at first, at the turn of the millennium that role shifted to Tyre, which then became Phoenicia's center.

The OT mentions one of the contemporaries of David and Solomon, Hiram (I), 969–936 (see 2 Sam. 5:11; 1 Kings 5:15-26; the dating is made possible by using the Tyrian list of kings passed down by Menander and recorded in Josephus, Against Apion 1.18). This is the same Hiram who expanded the surface of the city by filling in certain areas and who had two harbors constructed, the Sidonian in the north, which is still in use today, and the Egyptian in the south, presently covered once again by the sea. Today, about 12,000 inhabitants live there; in ancient times, it could have had 25,000 residents, and the city out on the island could have served as a refuge for a significant number of inhabitants from the mainland during wartime.

Ittobaal I, known as Ethbaal in 1 Kings 16:31 (887–856), presented his daughter Jezebel to Ahab, the crown prince of Israel, as his wife. Although the OT calls him the "king of the Sidonians," Josephus is a bit more specific, calling him either the "king of Tyre and Sidon" or the "king of the Tyrians and Sidonians" (Antiquities 8.13.1 and 9.6.16). As is the case with Hiram, who had made a treaty with Solomon (1 Kings 5:26; see also 9:10-14), Ittobaal also was on good terms with Omri and Ahab, showing that Israel and Tyre, in some sense, often looked for ways to work in partnership (even though this leader caused disharmony against the Omrides within their own country). But Tyre finally also wielded its power against its neighbor to the south, as is seen in Amos 1:9 (the authenticity of this passage has not gone unquestioned; see H. W. Wolff, BK XIV/2, 170, 193f. [Engl: Joel and Amos, 140, 158f.], though there are insufficient reasons to deny it to Amos). After that, the Tyrians expanded their territory at Israel's expense, thereby eliminating Israelite citizens without mercy. Still later, there were tensions between Israel or Judah and Phoenicia. When Isa. 23:9 makes the point that Yahweh has concluded that the arrogance found in all majestic places had to be brought down, the citizens of Israel would have been able to point to concrete examples of the גאון (arrogance) of Tyre.

At first, Tyre was cautious in its dealings with Assyria. From time to time, it had paid tribute, though it generally had been able to maintain its independence. Thus Tiglath-Pileser reports: "ḫirimu, the Tyrian, who conspired with raḫianu [known as Rezin in Isa. 7:1ff.; see *Isaiah 1–12*, p. 283], [. . .] I conquered *maḥalab*, his fortress, in addition to the great cities; I plundered them [. . .]. He submitted himself to me and kissed my feet; [I received] 20 talents [. . .] of colorful types of clothing and linen, generals, male singers, female singers [. . .] Egypt" (*TGI²*, no. 26). In spite of all this, the indigenous kingdom remained untouched, and Tyre could even still claim to have control over its colonial possessions. Thus the Cyprian governor during this time could identify himself, on two bronze bowls found in Kition, as the "servant of Hiram, the king of the Sidonians" (*KAI* 31:1; see above, p. 384). Because Tyre was able to remain flexible, and also probably because Assyria did not see any advantage in trying to destroy Tyre's control over its colonies, for a time it was able to keep itself from suffering the fate that was in store for both Aram and Israel. It would even seem that it was given a portion of the land of Israel that was taken when that territory was conquered (cf. A. Alt, *PJ* 33 [1937] 66f., note 3). However, harsh conflict resumed at the time of *lulī*, also identified by Sennacherib, in his report about the campaign during 701, as the "king of Sidon" (*TGI²*, no. 39), but who is referred to as the "king of Tyre" according to Josephus, *Antiquities* 9.14.2. His decision to join with the other Syrian-Palestinian leaders to rebel against Assyria ended with the complete loss of the Phoenician cities, all the way from Greater Sidon in the north to Acco in the south. Tyre itself was able to resist invasion and was able to survive a siege that lasted five years; *lulī* "fled into the distance, in the midst of the sea, and disappeared from the surface of the earth" (*TGI²*, no. 39). Another source (*ARAB* II, §309) tells us that he fled from Tyre to Cyprus—which would show that Cyprus had been in a subservient relationship; according to Josephus, *Antiquities* 9.14.2, Elulaios (*lulī*) once again brought the Kittim under his control, though they had rebelled. To be sure, Tyre was able to recover from this harsh blow, but then got drawn once again into the later revolt against Esarhaddon, which was mentioned above, pp. 417f., and which apparently provides the background for the present material.

[23:1b] The message against Tyre begins with a call to lament; cf. 13:6; 14:31; Jer. 48:20; 49:3, and often elsewhere. These passages show that the call to lament is frequently included as a stylistic element in oracles against the nations (see also Jer. 4:8). Beyond the literal sense, not only cities, peoples, and individual human beings can be called on to "scream"; so can (city) gates (Isa. 14:31), as well as juniper trees and oaks of Bashan (Zech. 11:2).

H. Jahnow (BZAW 35 [1923] 195) has pointed out a passage in a Romanian lament for someone who died:

> Whine, house and table, go on, whimper,
>   N. has left you alone now forever!
> Mourn as well, you old cold walls,
>   for you, as well, can only bawl!
> Lament, O field, make a fine speech,
>   you'll be unplowed now, beyond his reach!

In this present situation, the ships of Tarshish are called to raise a lament; no doubt, they are summoned at this point because they were the pride of the Tyrian sailors.

They also knew about Tarshish ships in Jerusalem; Solomon was a partner with Hiram in engaging in trade with Tarshish (1 Kings 10:22; the translation and interpretation of the passage is uncertain, however; see Noth, BK IX/1, 232f.). There is no question that תרשיש (Tarshish) is the same as Ταρτησσός (Tartessos) in Greek. Both Diodorus Siculus (5.35.4) and Pseudo-Aristotle (*De mirabilibus auscultationibus* 135) report that the Tyrians had traveled to Tartessos and had brought back such a quantity of silver that they had no place to store it and thus were forced to make everything they needed for daily life out of silver, even replacing their lead anchor with a silver one.

The exact location of Tartessos has still not been identified to everyone's satisfaction; on this, see *Isaiah 1–12*, pp. 117f.; and Galling, 6. In addition, it would seem that Tartessos sometimes refers to a city but at other times encompasses an entire region in southern Spain (e.g., Esarhaddon, in the inscription mentioned above, speaks about ^KUR^*tarsisi*); on this, see Galling, 1f. Albright (see *Isaiah 1–12*, p. 117) suggested that the name means "refinery [fleet]," but that must now be rejected.

At the very latest, the Phoenicians must have established a presence in the western half of the Mediterranean Sea by the twelfth century, founding settlements in Gades (Ethiopian: *gādīr* [*Jub.* 8:23]; Greek: Γάδειρα [Gadeira] or Γήδειρα [Gedeira]; today this is Cádiz, in Spain) and in Lixus (now: Larache), in Morocco. This Gadez served as the harbor where goods were transferred, to be shipped to Tarshish, which was located at the mouth of the Guadalquivir River, for transport to the city and farther inland. Phoenician trade with this city and the surrounding countryside must have taken on huge proportions, and it continued on into the sixth century. One might note Ezek. 27:12: "Tarshish did business with you [namely, Tyre] out of the abundance of your great wealth; silver, iron, tin, and lead they exchanged for your wares" (text emended; translation from NRSV, following Zürcher Bibel as well; see also Ezek. 38:13). Phoenician dominance in the west came to an end when the Assyrians seriously damaged their power; in that power vacuum, left when Tyre no longer had control in the west, Carthage was able to take over some regions, but most of the territory came under the control of the Greeks. As a result, the Phochaean Greeks founded a kingdom on the southern coast of Spain, one that extended all the way up into the North Sea, held together by commercial contacts. Thus it is fitting when Tarshish is called a son of Javan in Gen. 10:4 and 1 Chron. 1:7 (where תרשיש should be read instead of תרשישה; concerning the dating of the passage—the end of the seventh century—see H. Gese, *RGG*³ VI, 1423f.).

This period, which was apparently a high point for Tartessos, came to an end when Carthage destroyed the city about 500 (Schulten, 2450). After that, there are fewer and fewer bits of news about Tartessos in Greek writings; finally, its location was not even known exactly, so that it was confused with Gades, even in modern times (on this, see Galling, 6).

Considering this history of Tartessos, it makes sense that someone in Israel in later times would still speak of Tarshish, but it would not be possible that an Israelite prophet during the postexilic era would encourage people to flee there, as is mentioned in v. 6. This point provides further evidence for the correctness of the view set forth above, that 23:1-14 should be dated to the late Assyrian period.

The Tarshish ships, which are addressed in vv. 1 and 14, come "from the land of the Kittim." While on a return voyage, they are forced to discover that their safe haven in their homeland has been destroyed, deeply upsetting news for sailors in any age. Based on information about the treaty between Esarhaddon and Baal of Tyre, noted already (pp. 418f.), if they could not enter port to deliver their commercial wares to Tyre, the inventory on the ship would then belong to the power that now exercised control over the Phoenician coast, and there is little doubt that the sailors' lot was that they then would have to become slaves.

The כתים ארץ (land of Kittim) is Cyprus, more specifically, the southern portion of the island; the city of Kition possibly got its name from the Kittim (in Phoenician, it is called כת (Kit); the gentilic is כתי, Kitti). The Hebrew כתים (Kittim) or כתיים (Kittiim) is always used as a designation for the people or the region (later, in 1 Macc. 1:1; 8:5, the word refers to the Greeks, and the Romans are the referent when it is used, first in Dan. 11:30, then later also in the Qumran texts). According to Gen. 10:4 (P), as is also true of Tarshish, it belongs to the בני יון (children of Javan), Javan being a son of Japheth. Thus this passage comes from a time when the Greeks were already exercising control over Cyprus.

All available information suggests that Kition is to be found somewhere near where Larnaca is today (see the map, p. 334). Archaeological excavations at the supposed site (see V. Karageorghis, *Studi Semitici* 38, 161ff.) have shown that the city was founded about 1300 B.C., destroyed about the year 1000, and then rebuilt once again very close to the sea, since the inner harbor had filled up with sand. There is disagreement about just how far back one can assume connections linking Kition to Phoenicia; it would appear, however, that Hiram I of Tyre had to put down a rebellion of Kition against him in the tenth century (see Moscati, 198), and one already notes Phoenician influence on the pottery of Kition in the eleventh century, which would suggest trade relations, at least. A Phoenician presence also is substantiated by epigraphic material. In an inscription from Pula that is presumably from the ninth century, Tyre is called the "mother of Kition" (*KAI* 46:5f.); in addition, cf., among other evidence, the inscription mentioned on p. 385, which refers to a certain סכן (governor) of Cyprian Carthage, servant of Hiram, the king of the Sidonians.

In a list of his vassals, Esarhaddon mentions, among others, ten kings of Cyprus (Borger, 60). Kition is not mentioned there, but the list does include ^{URU}qar-*tiḫadasti* (Carthage) (which some use to argue that these are two different names for the same place; cf. Moscati, 203). The same rulers who served as vassals in Cyprus are mentioned in another list, using the same information, from the time of Ashurbanipal (Streck, VAB VII/2, 138ff.). After that time, Phoenician domination of Cyprus was apparently broken.

It is most puzzling that כתים (Kittim) is mentioned on various sherds found in Arad in the Negev. The following command is included on a letter found there, addressed to אלישב (*’lyšb*) (certainly the commander of the fortress): "Give to the כתים (Kittim) three (?) baths of wine and write the name of the day." This is apparently about Cyprian mercenaries serving Judah (see Y. Aharoni, *IEJ* 16 [1966] 1ff.).

Some kings of Cyprus are known from the Persian era, having Phoenician names, whereas Esarhaddon already lists some kings of Cyprus who have Greek names. No doubt, a Phoenician cultural presence remained on Cyprus even after the political ties with the motherland had been cut; commercial relations would have continued between Phoenicia and Cyprus at all times.

[23:2f.] Both the coastal dwellers and the merchants of Sidon are summoned, in vv. 2f., to utter cries of lament. On the one hand, the יֹשְׁבֵי אִי (coastal dwellers) could refer to the inhabitants of Tyre, but since this expression is parallel to סֹחֲרֵי צִידוֹן (merchants of Sidon), it must refer to Phoenician merchants in general; cf. above, p. 297. On the other hand, this close parallelism also would argue in favor of סֹחֲרֵי צִידוֹן (merchants of Sidon) being a general term for the merchants of all of Phoenicia.

Akkadian *saḫāru* means "turn oneself, go about, stay on someplace." As a meaning for the Hebrew participle, Ges-Buhl suggests "traveling merchant"; KBL believes one can be more precise: "buyer (who looks about for goods to buy)"; cf. passages such as 1 Kings 10:28. However, this specialized meaning is not always appropriate. One learns from v. 8 that the סֹחֲרִים could be great merchant barons. These are actually the Phoenician merchants, as one can conclude from vv. 2f.

One also finds the word סֹחֵר in Phoenician, and it is certainly not just by chance that this root, which is not used very often in Phoenician, is purposely included in Ezekiel's message against Tyre: 27:12, 15, 16, 18, 21, 36 (and in 27:12, when mentioning Tyrian trade with Tarshish; cf. also 38:13).

Trade is the means by which the Phoenicians gained a livelihood, the reason why their kingdom was formed, the material basis for their culture. Phoenicia did have some products that they could offer their partners. First of all, they had wood from the forests of Lebanon, both cedar and pine; when Hiram delivered wood to Solomon, that was only one small example of such trade. A relief from the time of Sargon II shows huge tree trunks being transported out of Phoenicia by ship (see Meissner, *BuA* I, illus. 206). In connection with his description of a campaign against Lebanon, Nebuchadnezzar says: "I . . . opened passages and (thus) I constructed a straight road for the (transport of the) cedars. I made the Arahtu flo[at] (down) and carry to Marduk, my king, mighty cedars, high and strong, of precious beauty and of excellent dark quality, the abundant yield of the Lebanon, as (if they be) reed stalks (carried by) the river. Within Babylon [I *stored*] mulberry wood" (see *AOT* 365; cited here from *ANET* 307). In addition, they provided expensive fabric; the chief Phoenician industry was that of producing woven goods and dyed goods. The colored garments of Sidonian wives were mentioned with high praise by Homer (*Iliad* 6.289f.). Their best-known product was Phoenician purple dye (see below, pp. 430f.). It is also worth noting that they had produced glass at least from the seventh century on, earlier if Pliny's assertion (36.190–193) would prove correct, that the Phoenicians were the ones who discovered glass; see Moscati, 149. One can see that the ancient Phoenicians were very skilled if one examines what has been preserved from their work in stone, metal (especially copper), and ivory. A lively and detailed picture about their commercial activities, trading partners, and wares is found in Ezekiel 26f.

Based on all this, one can easily understand vv. 2b, 3: Phoenicia sends its מַלְאָכִים (messengers) over the sea. The substantive, which derives from this same root word, מְלָאכָה, means "undertaking, business, wares." מַלְאָךְ (messenger) is a good parallel to סַחַר (profit from trade), referring to what someone today might call a "(commercial) representative." "Across many waters" is not an exaggeration, especially when one remembers that evidence of Phoenician contact has been found not only along all the coastlands of the Mediterranean, but also on the islands: Cyprus, Malta, Pantelleria, Sicily, and Sardinia, among others, and even farther out, on the Atlantic coasts of southern Spain and of Morocco. There is no need to explain more about why Egypt is mentioned as an example, in v. 5, since close ties existed between these two countries throughout the ages. The contacts between these two lands are reflected already in the travel narrative of Wen-Amon (*AOT* 71–77; *ANET* 25–29), providing a graphic description. That is a story about a purchase of cedarwood, a problem having been caused when twenty Egyptians ships sent to transport the goods were intercepted just outside Byblos. Among other products, Egypt was transporting gold and silver vessels, but also textiles and foodstuffs, lentils and fish.

The present passage speaks about the "seed on the Shihor." שִׁחֹר (also: שִׁיחוֹר/שְׁחוֹר) is Egyptian *š(y)-ḥr*, the "Pool of Horus"; see Erman-Grapow IV, 397. It is not clear whether, in this text, it refers to a lake in the vicinity of the Suez Canal, to one of the branches of the Nile, to a canal in the delta, or simply to the Nile itself. The last suggestion is the one that the expander thought was correct, since he glossed שִׁחֹר (Shihor) with יְאוֹר (of the Nile).

When זֶרַע (seed) is used, that must mean the harvest of what had been planted; cf. Job 39:12, where the word means the grain itself. Egypt would pay the Phoenicians for the goods that they delivered by trading them for agricultural products; whatever one would sow along the Shihor, one might say that the Phoenicians could gather it in as a harvest. The second colon generalizes this specific example: "And his income was the profit from trade with the peoples." תְּבוּאָה is used primarily to describe what is harvested from a field, but here the word is used in an expanded sense, which is fully understandable, to refer to income in general. סַחַר (profit from trade) is what one earns by סָחַר (trading). The discussion in 1 Kings 10:15 is about the סַחַר (business) of the merchants (the meaning of that passage, which has textual problems, is uncertain; on this, see Noth, BK IX/1, 204, 228f.); it would seem that it is referring to taxing profits on trade.

But what exactly is meant by סְחַר גּוֹיִם in this passage? The expression can hardly be taken to mean that the profits from trade, which the people trading with them earn, would be income for the Phoenicians; instead, it must refer to that profit which comes to the Phoenicians when they engage in trade with the other peoples. If אֵימַת מֶלֶךְ, in Prov. 20:2, means "fear *in the presence of* the king," and זַעֲקַת סְדֹם, in Gen. 18:20, means "the outcry *concerning* Sodom," then סְחַר גּוֹיִם also can mean "the profit gained through trade *with* the peoples."

[23:4] Concerning the summons to בּוֹשׁ (go in in disgrace), a concept that is difficult for one to communicate today in German or English, see *Isaiah 1–12*, pp. 76ff., on 1:29. One might be surprised to find the imperative, but Lindblom has correctly sensed what this means. It is used here not to give a strict order, but in the well-known, common way, pointing out that a certain individual must realize, in a particular transaction or situation, that the person being addressed does not have a choice about what is going to happen. In plain words, here is what is being said: "You, Sidon, disappointed and stripped of all honor, have no other choice than to take whatever is coming to you." Misfortune is always experienced in ancient Israel as shame and disgrace (cf. passages such as Job's lament in chaps. 29f.), just as there are always some who pile insults and mockery onto those whom fate has struck a severe blow.

The depiction of the completely hopeless condition that had come on the Phoenicians is presented in a most original way, in the form of a speech uttered by the sea, to which Phoenicia owed almost everything. The sea compares itself to a woman who could not give her husband any children. The use of the perfect in the speech does not refer back to past events—if one looked back to the past, the sea would have been much more like a mother who could enjoy life with a whole host of children. This is an emphatic or affirmative perfect (Lindblom, 65; cf. Ges-K §106.3). The sea announces that, from now on, one can no longer expect her "productivity" to continue; the merchant activity of Phoenicia on the seas has been struck through the heart; this prediction of their downfall as merchants corresponds to the way it really happened historically.

גִּדַּל (raise to maturity) and רוֹמֵם (bring up) also are used in parallel in 1:2; on this, see *Isaiah 1–12*, p. 12. This imagery makes sense only when one recognizes the actual situation throughout the entire ancient world (and throughout much of the East yet today), that a woman's value and worth depend directly on how many children she had provided for her husband. It was a deep disappointment for a husband if he had no children, and that was the greatest shame a wife could suffer (Sarah, Leah, Rachel, Hannah); also, cf. 54:1ff. One can be pleased that בְּתוּלוֹת (daughters) are mentioned along with בַּחוּרִים (young men) (1:2 speaks only about בָּנִים, "sons"). It is to be noted that both גִּדַּל (raise to maturity) and רוֹמֵם (bring up) refer to the daughters and to the young men. Concerning בָּחוּר (young men), see *Isaiah 1–12*, p. 234.

[23:5] Verse 5 makes no sense within this context; it has to be a gloss. Even as a gloss, there are problems with the verse. What type of news is it supposed to be that would cause someone in Egypt to shudder, as when the report about Tyre came? Kaiser is possibly right in thinking that the gloss developed in two stages, meaning that the first gloss did not have the phrase כַּשֵּׁמַע צֹר (just as by the news about Tyre). One would shudder in Egypt when hearing about what had happened in Phoenicia. One might consider the possibility that this verse, when reduced to its original form, might have been part of the original message about Tyre. Against this conclusion, however, one notes that חִיל (be in labor) is used in a very different way immediately before this, in v. 4; in addition, the way v. 3 describes the relationship between Phoenicia and Egypt matches very poorly with v. 5. Kaiser suggests the following possible historical situation: "The first glossator clearly had in mind the connection between the conquest of Sidon by Artaxerxes III at the beginning of the year 343 and his victorious attack upon Egypt in the autumn of the same year. This brought an end to the independence of Egypt which had been regained by the revolt of Amyrtaios in 404, and which since then had been repeatedly defended against all Persian attempts to reconquer the country." It may well be the background, but it is *not* at all that "clear." If Kaiser is correct, then one might agree with him that the second glossator, who added צר כשמע (just as by the news about Tyre), would have been thinking about Alexander's defeat of Tyre, which would have been the last obstacle in the way of still another world power that was being hindered by Tyre as it made its way to Egypt.

שמע (news) is vague information, not a detailed report that can be trusted implicitly; it is hearsay, but this is just the type of thing that gets one upset.

[23:6] In v. 12 flight to Cyprus is advised, though at the same time it is said to be pointless. *Here* one is encouraged to go *to* Tarshish. According to Esarhaddon's report (Borger, 86), that region also came under Assyria's control, but there is little doubt that such was only nominally the case. However, the response called for here is naturally also meant as ironic, just as in v. 12. Tarshish was much too far away for anyone seriously to consider an evacuation to that location.

[23:7a] Now, one can do little but "scream" in the city that once was so exuberant and happy-go-lucky. Concerning עלי (exuberant), see *Isaiah 1–12*, p. 204, and above, p. 361; however, see also 32:13 and Zeph. 2:15. Obviously, one ought not doubt that there were times when vigorous activity filled the port city of Tyre; yet, as can be seen in the passages just noted, עלי (exuberant) is frequently used in portrayals of disaster. It is a common stylistic technique in laments for an author to play off, one against another, what once was and what is now or what is now versus what once was; see Lam. 1:7.

This city was not just exuberant, it also could boast that it was very old; thus it seemed that it had been built on a solid foundation. The wordplay between קֶדֶם (origin) and קַדְמָתָה (distant past) can be replicated to some extent when juxtaposing the German words *Urzeit* and *Ursprung* and the English "antecedent" and "antiquity." What one would intend to say when using מקדם (from one's origin) would normally be conveyed by מעולם (from of old). Cities make a point to boast about their great age; note accounts such as that of the founding of Babylon, by the gods, in *enūma eliš* VI, 38–53. Justinus (*Epitome* 18.3.5) reports the following about Tyre: *urbem ante annum Troianae cladis condiderunt* (they founded the city even before the Trojan destruction); and Herodotus, when he made his trip to Phoenicia, learned from the priests of Tyre that 2300 years had passed since the city had been founded (2.44); cf. also Ezek. 36:11 and Lucian, *De dea syria* 3, who says that the temple of Heracles in Tyre was as old as his temple in Egypt, and much older than those within Greece itself.

[23:7b] Verse 7b naturally refers to Tyre's colonies. The first stage was for the Phoenicians to establish outposts for commercial ventures; then later, there were times when they went further and exercised political control over the coasts along the Mediterranean—naturally, as is also true of modern colonial history, chiefly for the purpose of ensuring that their commercial contacts would be kept open.

It is fitting that one could paraphrase the time one would spend in the various mercantile outlets of the Phoenicians by using the verb גור (settle, sojourn). The Phoenicians would spend some time there as "foreigners," but of course as those who had made sure that they had the right to stay there. Except for some areas, such as the Punic kingdom of Carthage, it could not be said that these various regions actually became Phoenician. For that reason, it would not have been a significant interruption of their normal life when they were claimed by a new naval power, here, the Greeks.

[**23:8, 9**] For the author, the downfall of proud Tyre is not simply an event that has taken place as characters took new positions of power on the stage of world history; Yahweh of Hosts planned this (concerning יעץ, "make a decision," see above, pp. 82f.; cf. *Isaiah 1–12*, pp. 202f.). Moreover, this decision by Yahweh did not just happen because he acted on a passing impulse, though it also was not such an obscure puzzle that human beings could never figure out what was going on; rather, it was a "disfiguring" of the "pride of all majesty." That corresponds exactly to what Isaiah himself once noted as the reason why the judgment against Judah had to happen; see, above all, 2:12-17 (one notes particularly that Tarshish ships are also mentioned as a symbol of pride in that passage). But furthermore, one must keep in mind what has been stated already in the discussion concerning 21:2 (text emended), namely, that the announcement of judgment precipitated by arrogance is a stereotypical motif in oracles against that nations (see also 13:11 and cf. 2:12ff.; 16:6; Jer. 13:9, et al.). Of course, it is said not only that Yahweh determines that the arrogance will come to an end, but also that he will "disfigure" (חלל) it; the halo that surrounded Tyre would be torn away. One must recognize that the rulers of this city thought of themselves as having been enveloped by a divine halo, as one can see in both of the magnificent poems about the downfall of the rulers of Tyre in Ezekiel 28; the second one resorts to depicting its demise by using the mythology about the fall of the original human and, in its own unique way, sketches out what is stated here when חלל (disfigure) is used. Finally, the traditional keyword גאון (pride) is used, more clearly defined by כל־צבי (of all majesty), which makes it look still worse (on this, see 13:19, where צבי, "elegant," parallels גאון, "pride-filled"). The גאון כל־צבי (pride of all majesty) is manifested in Tyre in the way it carries itself with pomp and circumstance. Herodotus talks about this when speaking of the sanctuary of Heracles, filled to overflowing with votive offerings (here that would be a reference to the city god Melqart), using the words: "Not the least remarkable [were] two pillars, one of pure gold, the other of emerald, which gleamed in the dark with a strange radiance" (2.44).

It is important to the author that he takes one more opportunity to describe how particularly beautiful the now-fallen Tyre once was: its "merchants are rulers." One can hardly take this to mean that the "rulers" in Tyre belong to the merchant class of people, but rather that powerful heads among the merchant class actually wielded such political power in the colonies that they worked hard at establishing principalities. This interpretation is strongly suggested even by the parallelism with "whose tradespeople are honored throughout the (whole) earth." They have (political) clout and enjoy the prestige that those who have been successful seek to cultivate.

The *hiphᶜil* of עטר is a hapax legomenon; there is no question that this word is related to the substantive עֲטָרָה, "crown, diadem." As was explained above, one ought to reject the suggestion that it has an intransitive meaning; Duhm is correct: if one translates this as "crowned," then the king of every little city-state in the ancient Near East could identify himself the same way. But Tyre had created principalities and kingdoms among its colonies, responsible to the city, that probably had gained independence when the opportunity presented itself and then were able to defend themselves. Verse 11 mentions kingdoms that are apparently possessions of Tyre that are located across the sea.

For just one example of this, one might remember what was said above, p. 384, about the inscription found at Limassol, Cyprus, which speaks of a certain governor of קרתחדשת (*qrthdst*), a servant of Hiram, the Sidonian king.

This interpretation is valid only if 23:1-14 is dated to a time when Tyre had not been able to assert its independence within its recent past or at least when the memory of its imperial glory was still fresh.

As a parallel word for סֹחֲרֶיהָ (its merchants), כְּנַעֲנֶיהָ (its tradespeople) is used in v. 8b (concerning the pointing, see above, textual note 8d). The same meaning for כְּנַע, "trader," is found in Zeph. 1:11, in fact also in a disrespectful sense. This meaning is even clearer in Hos. 12:8; there כְּנַע refers to contemporary Ephraim, which has been brought down by the Canaanite spirit of playing the whore and by mercantilism. Both Ezek. 16:29 and 17:4 speak of the אֶרֶץ כְּנַע, the "land of tradespeople," a designation that already had been transferred, in that context, from its original referent, the Phoenicians, to identify Babylon; moreover, this shows in what type of light Israel had viewed the commercial activities of the Phoenicians. The gentilic כְּנַעֲנִי (Canaanite) is used in a similar way in Job 40:30, though it does not have a negative ring about it when used in Prov. 31:24. The entire way its meaning developed gives us evidence for the great importance attached to commercial ventures in Phoenicia; in addition, see the excursus concerning כְּנַע Canaan) below, pp. 430f.

[23:10] All the ancient brilliance of Tyre, its easy manner, its prosperity and high standard of living, that is all gone. Based on the textual emendation suggested above, v. 10 fits very well within the context: "For the Tarshish ships there is no longer a מֵזַח." Unfortunately, the meaning "shipyard" is uncertain, but even if one would read מָחֹז and translate this as "harbor," the meaning is still clear. From now on, if it wants to survive, Tyre is going to have to culti-vate its land like every other people. One cannot miss the Israelite author's way of trumpeting his joy at their tragedy.

Concerning the use of עבד (build up, work), when speaking about agri-cultural activities, see Gen. 2:5; 4:2, 12, and often elsewhere.

[23:11] Verse 11 picks up the theme that had been the subject of v. 9, stress-ing once again: Yahweh is behind what has happened to the Phoenicians. Instead of using the verb יעץ (decide), which has theological overtones in that passage, here the author uses the simple צוה (command)—a warning, nonetheless, one that might not immediately come to mind when one hears יעץ (decide); here one thinks right away that it is an unalterable decision or a plan of God that has existed from eternity concerning how world history will unfold.

The homeland of the Phoenicians is affected just as much as its pos-sessions overseas, which fits right in with what was said in Esarhaddon's report, as cited above, p. 421.

The phraseology ידו נטה על־הים (stretched out his hand over the sea) reminds one of the exodus tradition (Exod. 14:26, and often elsewhere; cf. also Ps. 89:26), the only difference being that there it is Moses who stretches out his hand, though this should be compared with Exod. 15:12 and the deuteronomistic formula that Yahweh had brought Israel out of Egypt בְּיָד חֲזָקָה וּבִזְרֹעַ נְטוּיָה (by a mighty hand and an outstretched arm), Deut. 4:34, and often elsewhere.

הרגיז (to shake violently) is frequently used when mention is made of a quaking (of the earth, or even of the heavens; Isa. 13:13; 14:16; Job 9:6; cf. Jer. 50:34). As if by an earthquake, if not due to a cosmic catastrophe, the imperial power of Tyre is shaken.

Here the Phoenician territory is called כנען (Canaan). The Israelites must have known that the Canaanites in their own land had close family ties to the neighboring Phoenicians. As was shown above, pp. 412f., Israel normally called its northern neighbors צידונים (Sidonians), sometimes simply using the collective צידון (Sidon) (Judg. 10:6), or else it specifically mentioned the cities of Sidon, Tyre, etc. (see, e.g., Joel 4:4; Zech. 9:2; Amos 1:9). כנען (Canaan) is used only here in the entire OT as a way to refer to Phoenicia (but cf. Gen. 10:15; Num. 13:29; Josh. 5:1; 1 Chron. 1:13). Both lists of the nations, in Genesis 10 and in 1 Chronicles 1, use the term "Canaan" in a broader sense, one that includes heterogeneous population groups; however, even there Sidon is listed as the firstborn of Canaan. It is apparent that there is a close family relationship between the Canaanites of Palestine and the Phoenicians; it is most clearly detected in their language and in their religious concepts.

First, we find the following on both a stele of Amenophis II from Memphis (see *Or* 20, 381) and on the statue of Idrimi (see S. Smith, *The Statue of Idrimi* [1949] 14, lines 18f.): *māt kinanim*. The Amarna Letters often speak of the land *kinaḫḫi* (or *kinaḫna/i*) and mention cities in Phoenicia in that connection (the only Palestinian city named is Hazor; see Gibson, 218). Even Augustine reports: *interro-gati rustici nostri, quid sint, punice respondentes Chanani* (our farmers having been asked who they are, responding in Punic, say "Chananians") (*Patrologia Latina*

430

XXXV, 2096). According to Sanchuniathon (in Philo of Byblos), Χνα (Chna) is the ἥρως ἐπώνυμος (eponymous hero) of the Phoenicians (quoted by Eusebius, *Praeparatio evangelica* 1.10.39). In earlier times, the name כנע was frequently treated as if a derivative from כנע (bow down), so that Canaan supposedly meant something like "low ground." But texts discovered in Nuzi inform us that *kinaḫḫu* has the same meaning as φοῖνιξ, which means "red purple" (cf. φοινός = "red"; φοίνικες certainly has nothing to do with Egyptian *fnḫ-w; see* Speiser, 325ff.). The name was already used by Homer; indeed, it seems that it was used already in the texts that employed the Linear B script on Crete. Yet it is most likely that כנע (Canaan) was originally the name of a people, with the meaning "dark purple" only derived from that name in later times, since the Canaanites had gathered the purple snails and then had produced cloth goods dyed with this color, which became such a common item for export from Phoenicia that "Canaanite" and "dark purple" became terms that were used interchangeably; on this, see Speiser; Eissfeldt; Gray, 15ff.; Maisler. In Ugarit (*rās eš-šamra*), work stations that handled dyeing were unearthed, with evidence that purple snails had been used, in fact, most surprisingly, in the Mycenaean quarter of the city, showing that purple was an item in demand as an export already then; see Speiser, 330.

[23:12] The ויאמר (and said) is completely out of place at the beginning of v. 12. Yahweh does not speak in what follows; rather, it is most likely that the author himself calls Tyre to lament. Naturally, לא־תוסיפי עוד לעלוז (from now on you will no longer be exuberant), based on the sense of the passage, is also no direct command (cf. above, pp. 425f.); instead, it is to say that there will be no more chances for Phoenicia to celebrate, so that it will have to bury its arrogance for ever.

Once again, it seems to disrupt the flow when the topic of the verse is Sidon, since Tyre has just been addressed, and it is that city which is meant when עליזה (exuberant) is used in v. 7. However, בת־צידון (daughter Sidon) (epexegetical genitive [a genitive of characterization]; cf. Ges-K §128k) does not refer to the population of the city of Sidon in an exclusive sense. If בת־אדום (daughter Edom) (Lam. 4:21f.) refers to the Edomites and בת־יהודה (daughter Judah) (Lam. 2:2, 5) can refer to the Judeans, then בת־צידון (daughter Sidon) can refer to the Sidonians (= Phoenicians).

בתולת בת־צידון (maiden, daughter Sidon) uses more words than needed, but in spite of this one ought not shorten the phrase. In a lament, one speaks to the one who is uttering the lament in the most tender way possible. Using בת־צידון (daughter Sidon) is itself a sign of affection; placing בתולת (maiden) before it elevates the feeling still more. In the present passage, however, there is a subtle ironic tone. This is the same way one should understand מעשקה (mistreated). Ehrlich (*Randglossen* IV, 82) has stated correctly that this address includes a sadness that the offering has to take place. In reality, a מעשק (mistreated one) suffers an injustice. But just as one can find an ironic lament for one who has died, so also one may detect irony in the lament about the downfall of a people. Naturally, it is also ironic that the people are encouraged to travel over to where the Kittim are (v. 12b). One would not find any place to rest there either—simply because Esarhaddon also had brought Cyprus under his control. One should consider how the verb נוּח (rest) is used when studying the substantives מָנוֹחַ and מְנוּחָה. Both mean "resting place" (cf. passages such as Ps. 23:2); a בֵּית מְנוּחָה is a house of rest (1 Chron. 28:2). When someone in Israel expresses trust that salvation will come, one of the central motifs is that one is filled with a longing to have a place of rest, where one can live in safety and can let life progress without disruption (see 28:12; 32:18; Deut. 12:9), expressed also when one hopes that the messiah will come (11:10). Yet it was nothing but an illusion that one might find a place where one could stop being on the run simply by fleeing to the land of the Kittim.

[23:13] Every attempt to make some sense of v. 13 stands on shaky ground, since the text itself is so uncertain. If one agrees that כַּשְׂדִּים (Chaldeans) should be replaced with כתים (Kittim), then this would furnish a continuation of v. 12b: There is no point in looking for "rest" among the Kittim since that people does not exist any longer either. Assyria has completely destroyed it—its palaces have been leveled. The suggestion from L. Köhler (*Kleine Lichter* [1945] 30–32) that אַרְמְנוֹת be translated "homes in towers" fails because it is wrong to derive it from רוּם (be high). The word belongs to the root רמה I, "throw, establish (a dwelling)"; cf. Akkadian *ramū*, "cast forth, throw up and occupy (a house)" (Speiser, *JQR* 14 [1923–1924] 329). In contrast to the normal word בֵּית (house), however, this word means a spacious, strongly fortified house, which one always could defend in time of need, even if the city walls had fallen. If the suggested translation of בחון or בחין (both: siege towers), as noted above, is correct, then it would seem that Kition had come under siege, and it was necessary for the Assyrians to build towers in front of the wall so that their advance force could use that as a point of departure when going up against the defenders.

The most difficult part to understand is the sentence אַשּׁוּר יְסָדָהּ לְצִיִּים. This cannot possibly mean that the Assyrians had first "founded" Kition, or any other city of the Kittim either. Yet *HAL* suggests that יסד means "determine, allot" in the present passage, with supporting evidence from Hab. 1:12; Pss. 104:8; 119:152. Thus one would have to suppose it means: Assyria has, so to speak, made the land of the Kittim into a naval base of operations, so that it could further extend its control, from there, throughout the Mediterranean Sea region. Since the verbs in v. 13b (except for שׂמה, "[someone] has made it into") are in the plural, it is likely that the subject changes. "They" have destroyed the naval base of operations. Unfortunately, after the Assyrian era, no further information is available concerning Cyprus. The Persians took control of the island in 449, its having been a bone of contention, up until that time, between the Persians and the Greeks. Does the author have the events of 346 in mind (cf. Hill, 146f.)? The Cypriots rebelled in that year, along with the Phoenicians, against the Persians. But Artaxerxes III sent his treaty partner Idrieus, the prince of Caria, to take bloody revenge. Thus it is possible to think of situations into which v. 13b might fit without too much trouble, but to come to a conclusion that assigns the date of v. 13 with certainty is hopeless, since so little is known about the volatile history of Cyprus.

[23:14] Verse 14 repeats what was said in v. 1, thus bringing the entire poem to a close. This conclusion shows that the author saw the decisive result of these events in the complete destruction of the maritime commercial activities of Tyre. To be sure, the Phoenician ports were too important, and their positions were too advantageous, for them to have been put out of commission forever because of any particular wartime catastrophe. But the old splendor of the "bestower of crowns" was gone for good.

Form and Setting

[23:15f.] It has been determined already (see above, p. 412) that vv. 15-18 are made up of two separate additions. Both speak about Tyre, thus being intended as additional comments on what has just been said; moreover, one notes that these expanders of vv. 1-14 both thought that this text was providing a message about Tyre. Verses 15f. betray their nature as a later addition with the introduction: "and on that day it will happen." Based on all the other analogous situations where the phrase is used, "that day" must be the time when the disaster spoken about in vv. 1-14 comes upon Tyre. However, though vv. 1-14 look back into the past, both the expansions look to the future. This perspective recasts vv. 1-14 into the form of an announcement of disaster. To be sure, neither the misfortune in store for Tyre nor its pitiful situation is described in detail, with sober reflection; rather, the future destiny for Tyre is characterized only indirectly, but therefore even more effectively, as the residents of the city are confronted with a mocking song about a forgotten prostitute, one who wants to be remembered once again. The situation will be so pathetic for this commercial center, which once had so many customers, stepping over each other to take care of her every need, that she is compared here to a prostitute who, once the fancy of many, must now ply the streets and use her little theatrics just to get someone even to look her way.

But just what kind of "that day" is in the mind of those who expand on vv. 1-14? There is no point in trying to give an answer, since this deals with a prophecy that does not have to be fulfilled exactly as portrayed. In spite of this, one might think of the time when Nebuchadnezzar besieged Tyre, which also caused Ezekiel to expect that Tyre would be completely destroyed—though that, of course, never happened.

This interpretation means that the material which begins with the phrase וְנִשְׁכַּחַת צֹר (that Tyre will be forgotten) and continues through the second שִׁבְעִים שָׁנָה (seventy years) in v. 15 has to be a still later addition. The text as we now have it in v. 15 is absolutely impossible. That which is to take place "on *a specific* day," even if one interprets "day" in the broadest possible sense, cannot take place over a period that needs to last for seventy years. This insertion must have been placed into the text after vv. 17f. were added on.

[23:17f.] Based on what has been suggested about the meaning of vv. 15f., it is clear that vv. 17f. are an addition to the addition. According to the opinion of this expander, the city would have to suffer the fate of the forgotten prostitute for seventy years, but then Yahweh once again would begin to "take notice of" the city.

Hebrew פקד (take notice of) can have two meanings; it is normally translated "punish," but this English word no longer conveys the double entendre of the Hebrew expression which can introduce the idea of help that is coming for the downtrodden as well as punishment for oppressors. In the present passage, the expander picks up on זכר (remember) from v. 16. It will work out that Yahweh once again will "remember" the forgotten prostitute Tyre after seventy years. That means that vv. 16ff. are essentially to be treated as an announcement of salvation. Tyre once again will rise to life and experience a renewed period of prosperity. But it must be said: its commercial ventures, afterward as well as beforehand, are whoring, and the profits from its business will not belong to the city but will belong to the Yahweh community up on Zion. Thus this is an announcement of salvation for both Tyre *and* Israel, though for Tyre it is, as such, filled with bitter irony, whereas for Israel, at least according to the opinion of the expander, a very bright and happy future is in store.

Seventy years is a round number; from the outset, one ought not even try to match this up with historical events, since the effort will not bear fruit; one might think of the way seventy years is used in Jer. 25:12 and 29:10 to determine the length of the Babylonian exile; cf. also Zech. 1:12; Dan. 9:2; 1 Chron. 36:21. With all this in mind, since vv. 17f. also look on into the future, this could be looking toward the time when the Phoenicians, who had been struck severely by both Assyria and Babylon, once again would reach a level of prestige in the Persian era.

Commentary

[23:15] Based on the analysis offered above, v. 15 was originally nothing more than a short introduction to the song about the prostitute in v. 16. Here, obviously, שירה (song) is used in the sense of a mocking song. In this way, the sarcastic tone of the preceding call to lament (cf. passages such as v. 10: "build up your land . . .") is picked up once again and made harsher yet. Did the author know something about the prevailing techniques being used as the prostitutes plied their trade in the port city of Tyre, thus already having some idea from that knowledge about how this comparison could be made (see Procksch)? Even if true, that is nothing but a surface point of departure; the point of comparison is much more clearly the fact that she is forgotten. No one looks twice at this city that once was so ravishing, just as no one desires an old or sick prostitute.

[23:16] The mocking song itself provides us with an unexpected insight into the ways of a prostitute; indeed, one would hardly guess that the author is quoting a song from Tyre, but doing so in Israel. Israel was allergic, throughout its history, when it came to cultic prostitution. But common prostitution was apparently tolerated—as was true throughout the ancient world. Jephthah was the son of a prostitute (Judg. 11:1); Samson took no time at all, when he got to Gaza, to find a prostitute (Judg. 16:1); 1 Kings 3:16 describes a disagreement between two prostitutes, without the text making any official statement that prostitution was wrong; Prov. 5:1ff. warns more than once that one ought not allow oneself to be taken in by a whore; such advice would have been necessary. For more on the subject, see F. Hauck and S. Schulz, *TDNT* VI, 584ff.

[23:17] The expander who adds vv. 17f. picks up the theme of vv. 15f. The imagery of the prostitute is taken still further, though within an entirely new framework. Now the point of comparison is no longer that the prostitute is forgotten, but it focuses on the prostitute's wages, which means the profit that Tyre received from its commercial ventures with other peoples.

All that would happen after seventy years. "It happened after . . . years" (or "days," or something similar) is a common formula in the OT (cf., e.g., Deut. 9:11; 31:10; Judg. 11:39). Looking toward the future, it is used in Ezek. 29:13. The reason this passage uses the number seventy goes back to the fact that, traditionally, this was a round number for how many years one would be oppressed. Of course, one is not bound to this number literally. Ezek. 4:6 announces that there were to be forty years during which Judah would have to be penitent because of its offenses; Ezek. 29:13 mentions forty years that Egypt would be "scattered"; the Moabite Stone (line 8) recounts forty years of punishment for Moab. But the number seventy is also used by Israel's neighbors. Borger has pointed out that in an inscription of Esarhaddon, Babylon, after it was destroyed by Sennacherib, was supposed to remain desolate for seventy years because of a decision by the god Marduk. But whether or not the tablet which described the destiny that Marduk had determined for Babylon had said that there would have to be seventy years before it could be resettled, merciful Marduk, once his heart calmed down again, "altered the numbers" and commanded that the city be rebuilt already in the eleventh year.

No one has yet figured out why seventy years was chosen as the period a city or a people had to be punished. It could be that this punishment was to last as long as someone normally would live, if one lived a full life (cf. Ps. 90:10). A new beginning could be made when all the people who were living at the time when a great offense had been committed had been blotted out. In Num. 14:29-34, it is presumed that, after forty years, virtually all those who had been at least thirty years old when Israel rebelled against Moses would have died. When compared with that, seventy years of punishment, instead of the typical forty years, would have been a significant increase. This would mean that it would affect not only those who had been grown up—realistically, the only ones who were actually responsible for the trouble—but would apply to everyone who was alive; all would have to be gone before a new chapter in its history could begin.

The expander who added vv. 17f. also wanted to include vv. 15f. in this new period, after seventy years had passed. He does not say, as one might anticipate: Tyre will lie desolate for seventy years, but rather: . . . it will remain forgotten. He chose these words because of the song about the forgotten prostitute.

But what he would have been thinking when he uses the comparison כימי מלך אחד (as the days of one king) has yet to be explained by any exegete. Kings are not in the habit of being older than typical human beings. Even if this might be talking about the length of one's reign and not the length of one's life, one could object that kings are not in the habit of ruling that long either (even Ramses II did not make it past sixty-five years). Nonetheless, one must admit that the emendation to the MT suggested above is not certain. Beyond that, exactly how the king whom this expander might have had in mind would be different is best left alone, without speculation.

The expander expects that Tyre will once again assume its ancient role as a commercial center. He says a mouthful. It will seek to reestablish its ties with all the kingdoms of the world and will pocket the profits from all of them.

אתנן, "gift," always refers to a "prostitute's wages," and Deut. 23:19 and Mic. 1:7 are even more explicit, mentioning אתנן זנה (wages of a prostitute); in these cases, the reference is to the payment for cultic prostitution. In v. 18 סחר (profit) is used with אתנן (prostitute's wages). At best, the only other passage in the OT that compares commercial activity with whoring and commercial profit with a prostitute's wages would be found in Nah. 3:4; otherwise, זנה (whoring) is used metaphorically only when describing idol worship; but one might compare this with Rev. 18:3: "the kings of the earth have committed fornication with her [Babylon/Rome], and the merchants of the earth have grown rich from the power of her luxury" (see also Rev. 18:9f.). The portrayal is not a bad one; it shows that Israel did not think much of commercial activity, as one can detect already in vv. 1-14. One is tempted to ask whether what is really behind this is jealousy on the part of a nation that itself does not have the chance to profit from commercial activity.

[23:18] What has just been said seems to be the source of a new problem, according to what is described in v. 18. The riches that Tyre will acquire cannot be hoarded by them; instead, these will become קדש (holy) for Yahweh. קדשים are the votive offerings; the singular קדש is a designation for that which has been dedicated to the deity; in practical terms, these gifts would pay the expenses of the cult; cf. passages such as Lev. 27:10, 33; Num. 18:17. These holy treasures, which belong to the deity and thus to the sanctuary, are not to be distributed only among the Levites (apparently as a financial settlement, because the local sanctuaries had been done away with according to the deuteronomic law), but also among the sojourners, the orphans, and the widows (Deut. 26:10f.). According to the present text, this dedicated treasure is for the benefit of "those who dwell in the presence of Yahweh." Concerning ישבים לפני יהוה (those who dwell in the presence of Yahweh), cf. also Judg.

20:26; 2 Sam. 7:18 = 1 Chron. 17:16; 1 Sam. 1:22; Ezek. 44:3; cf., in addition, יֹשֵׁב בְּבֵית יהוה (one who dwells in the house of Yahweh), Pss. 23:6 and 27:4, text emended. In the same way as is true of the formula "see the face of God" (see *Isaiah 1–12*, p. 43), this phraseology presupposes that one would have one's devotions before the image of the deity. One presumes that this does not speak in general, just about those who believe in Yahweh, but refers specifically to the priests at the sanctuary, whose livelihood is provided by the votive offerings that are brought to the deity. The offerings that would come from Tyre would not just help those in Jerusalem to eke out a meager existence, but the people would be able to eat until full and, beyond this, they would also be in a position to clothe themselves splendidly, just as is fitting for priests. Is the author thinking about the fact that Tyre had been known to export expensive material?

The promise expressed in vv. 17f. probably originated in priestly circles. One might excuse this wish, as they expressed hope that the "prostitute's wages" from Tyre would be brought over to fill their coffers, by understanding that, during the wretched era just after the exile, when this addition would have been inserted, they would have lived more often than not in extreme poverty; in any case, there was certainly no guarantee that they would have been able to eat until they were full. One might remember that Nehemiah had to take care of providing income for the priests and other temple personnel (Neh. 12:44-47).

Besides this, the thought that a foreign people would bring its gifts to Jerusalem, to the Lord of all peoples of the earth, is a rather widely used motif, linked with Israel's hope for salvation and connected with the sanctuary in Jerusalem, one element of that hope being that the peoples also would come to worship (see above, pp. 223f., on 18:7, which is also an addendum supplied by a later hand); 19:21 expects that the Egyptians will participate in the Yahweh cult, and, when they do that, they are expected to be ready to obey the command that no one is to come before the deity with empty hands (Exod. 23:15; 34:20).

Purpose and Thrust

[23:1-14] This analysis has shown that the call to lament, in vv. 1-4, 6-12, 14, was supplemented by a variety of added comments. The author is quite indifferent to the harsh destiny that has come upon Phoenicia. The call to lament is merely a literary form; its only purpose is to portray effectively the way in which the power of Tyre, once renowned and praised throughout the world, came to an end. One detects no compassion; what is there is clearly an expression of satisfaction that the end has come now for this country that seemed to have gotten used to living a charmed life, in a location that enjoyed the special benefits of both nature and history. But the fall of Tyre is not simply an example of *sic transit gloria mundi* for the poet; the hermeneutical key is found especially in vv. 9 and 11. Yahweh decided on this; it is his deed. Here as well, the action of the God of Israel is driven by his will that righteousness should be carried out. This deals with the uncovering "of the pride of all majesty." Human arrogance, even when embellished with the trimmings of religious ideology (cf. Ezekiel 28), finally has to be exposed, to show that it is really powerless and empty. But this author does not try to offer a positive plan from God about how to deal with all the peoples in general.

[23:15f.] The expander who adds vv. 15f., who looks toward the future, also knows that Tyre has come to its end; it would fall into the dustbin of forgottenness, where no hope could be visualized. Here the mocking of the city, which once was rich and full of life, is readily apparent.

[23:17f.] The glossator who supplies vv. 17f. was not willing to leave it alone, with Tyre sinking into forgottenness. There would still be a future for the once famous city. But he does not presume that their character would change all that much after the many years of humiliation; just the opposite: when he calls the commercial ventures between the city and other peoples "playing the whore," used otherwise as a technical term for idolatry, the harshest possible judgment is assessed against Tyre. The aversion to all profit that comes without effort and that comes through constant cheating is characterized eloquently. But he takes a risk and suggests, with a bold turn in his own thinking, that he expects this newly acquired wealth in this city to bring glory to the God of Israel. One might laugh at that, since the author thus had not forgotten himself and his priestly companions. But bringing gifts to Jerusalem is a *signum* that the universal rule of Yahweh, as king, was coming near.

One wonders what could have given this man the courage to think that there would be such a change in the course of history—there is certainly not much that would have been happening in the daily events of life to stimulate such an idea. This is the utopia of faith, which expects that God will show his majestic honor, in spite of all external troubles, overcoming all obstacles, even when the fulfillment of that expectation sometimes seems in doubt. That this hope appears so boldly, if one might not even say casually, in the face of so many troubles of the day, brings out both aspects: the power and the danger of this faith, in the arena in which the world of apocalyptic makes its statement. One must see that this passage is much different from 2:2-4, so as to recognize that this way of thinking is far removed from the substance and sober judgment that would express the hopes of a prophet such as Isaiah.

The Isaiah Apocalypse

Literature

Concerning the entire subject: A. Hilgenfeld, "Das Judentum in dem persischen Zeitalter," *ZWT* 9 (1866) 398–488, esp. 437–488. R. Smend, "Anmerkungen zu Jes. 24–27," *ZAW* 4 (1884) 161–224. M.-J. Lagrange, "L'apocalypse d'Isaïe (24–27)," *RB* 3 (1894) 200–231. E. Liebmann, "Der Text zu Jesaja 24–27," *ZAW* 22 (1902) 285–304 and *ZAW* 23 (1903) 209–286. E. Sievers, *Jesaja 24–27*, Verhandlungen der königlichen sächsischen Gesellschaft der Wissenschaft zu Leipzig, philosophische-historische Klasse, vol. 56 (1904) 151ff. (not available to me). J. van Gilse, "Jesaja XXIV–XXVII," *NTT* 3 (1914) 167–193. P. Lohmann, "Die selbstständigen lyrischen Abschnitte in Jes 24–27," *ZAW* 37 (1917/18) 1–58. G. Hylmö, *De s. k. profetiska liturgiernas rytm, stil och komposition,* LUÅ, N. F. Avd. 1, vol. 25, no. 5 (1929). N. Dominguez, "Vaticinios sobre el fin del mundo," *CTom* 51 (1935) 125–146. W. Rudolph, *Jesaja 24–27*, BWANT 62 (1933). L. Aubert, "Une première apocalypse (Esaïe 24–27), *ETR* 11 (1936) 280–296. J. Lindblom, *Die Jesaja-Apokalypse,* LUÅ N. F., Avd. 1, vol. 34, no. 3 (1938). M. A. Beek, "Ein Erdbeben wird zum prophetischen Erleben," *ArOr* 17 (1949) 31–40. J. Lindblom, *Die Jesaja-Apokalypse (Jes 24–27) in der neuen Jesaja-Handschrift,* K. Humaniska Vetenskapssamsfundets i Lund Årsberättelse (1950/51) 2, 79–144 (not available to me). E. S. Mulder, *Die teologie van die Jesaja-apokalipse* (1954). O. Ludwig, *Die Stadt in der Jesaja-Apokalypse: Zur Datierung von Jesaja 24–27* (1961). A. H. van Zyl, "Isaiah 24–27: Their Date of Origin," *OTWSA* 5 (1962) 44–57 (not available to me). G. Fohrer, "Der Aufbau der Apokalypse des Jesajabuches (Is 24–27)," *CBQ* (1963) 34–45 = BZAW 99 (1967) 170–181. G. W. Anderson, "Isaiah XXIV–XXVII Reconsidered," VTSup 9 (1963) 118–126. M.-L. Henry, *Glaubenskrise und Glaubensbewährung in den Dichtungen der Jesajaapokalypse,* BWANT 86 (1966). W. E. March, "A Study of Two Prophetic Compositions in Is 24:1–27:1," diss., Union Theological Seminary (1966) (not available to me). O. Plöger, *Theocracy and Eschatology* (1968) 53–78. P. Redditt, "Isaiah 24–27: A Form-Critical Analysis," diss., Vanderbilt (1972). G. Brockhaus, "Untersuchungen zu Stil und Form der sogenannten Jesaja-Apokalypse," master's thesis, Bonn (1972), typescript. G. Rochais, "Les origines de l'apocalyptique," *ScEs* 25 (1973) 15–50, esp. 36–40. H. Ringgren, "Some Observations on Style and Structure in the Isaiah Apocalypse," *ASTI* 9 (1973) 107–115. W. Elder, *A Theological-Historical Study of Isaiah 24–27* (1974). J. Vermeylen, "La composition littéraire de l''apocalypse d'Isaïe,'" *ETL* 50 (1974) 5–38. B. Otzen, "Traditions and Structures of Isaiah XXIV–XXVII," *VT* 24 (1974) 196–206.

Concerning apocalyptic: J. Fichtner, *Prophetismus und Apokalyptik in Protojesaja* (1929). O. Plöger, see above. K. Koch, *The Rediscovery of Apocalyptic*, SBT

2/2 (1972). P. D. Hanson, "Jewish Apocalyptic against Its Near Eastern Environment," *RB* 78 (1971) 31–58. Idem, "Old Testament Apocalyptic Reexamined," *Interpretation* 25 (1971) 454–479. G. Rochais, see above.
[**Literature update through 1979:** *Concerning the entire subject:* G. N. M. Habets, "Die grosse Jesaja-Apokalypse (Jes 24–27): Ein Beitrag zur Theologie des Alten Testaments," diss., Bonn (1974). A. Feuillet, "Les oracles (d'Is) dont l'origine est discutée," in *Études d'exégèse et de théologie biblique* (1975) 69–80.
Concerning apocalyptic: W. W. Hallo, "Akkadian Apocalypses," *IEJ* 16 (1966) 231–242. P.-G. Müller, "Entstehen und Anliegen der Apokalyptik," *BiKi* 4 (1974) 110–115. P. D. Hanson, *The Dawn of Apocalyptic* (1975). W. R. Millar, *Isaiah 24–27 and the Origin of Apocalyptic,* HSM 11 (1976). J. Coppens, "L'Apocalyptique. Son dossier. Ses critères. Ses éléments constitutifs. Sa portée néotestamentaire," *ETL* 53 (1977) 1–23.]

Text
First of all, a complete translation of the entire text will be presented, taking into account all the textual emendations. The reasons for the alterations to the text will be given in the discussion of the individual units. Numbers along the margin identify the various levels:

   I: the so-called original level
  II: the eschatological images
 III: the songs about the city
 IV: the later additions

(Cf. the analysis that follows and the overview that is summarized on p. 459.)

I,1 24:1 Behold, Yahweh ravages the earth
   and devastates it,
disfigures its face
   and scatters its inhabitants.
  2 Then the same thing happens to the priest as to the (man from among) the people,
   to the servant as to his master,
    to the maid as to her mistress,
to the buyer as to the merchant,
   to the one who loans as to the one who has to borrow,
    to the debtor as to his creditor.
  3 The earth will be ravaged completely,
   plundered completely, until there is nothing left to plunder.
       * * * *
For it is Yahweh who has spoken this message:
  4 It is withered, the earth is wilted,
   it is disintegrated, the world is wilted,
    it is disintegrated, that which is above, together with the earth,
  5 for the earth is desecrated beneath its inhabitants,
   for indeed they have transgressed the laws, stepped over the bounds of the commandment,
   broken the eternal covenant.
  6 For this reason a curse has consumed the earth,
   those who live on it must suffer the consequences.

For this reason the inhabitants of the earth disappear completely,
and what is left of human beings, that is quickly counted.
* * * *

I,1a [7 The wine (branch) is wilted,
the grape tendrils have disintegrated,
everyone groans, each one who used to have a happy heart.
8 The jubilant sound of the kettledrums is silenced,
the (festive) noise of those who are celebrating is stilled,
the jubilant sound of the zithers is silenced.
9 No one drinks wine any longer with songs,
the drunken drinking of the heavy drinkers leaves a bitter taste.]
* * * *

I,1b [10 The nothing city is destroyed,
every house is closed; no one comes on in.
11 Lamenting about the wine (rings out) in the side streets,
all joy is vanished,
the jubilation of the earth has moved out.
12 Only devastation still remains in the city;
the smashed gate lies there in (complete) desolation.]
* * * *

I,1c [13 Truly, thus will it be on the earth,
in the midst of the peoples of the world:
as when one knocks off olives,
as when one goes gleaning,
when the wine harvest has come to an end.]

I,2 14 They all will raise their voice,
they rejoice about the supremacy of Yahweh,
exult, even from the western sea.
15 "Therefore, honor Yahweh in the east,
on the coasts of the sea, the name of Yahweh,
the God of Israel."
16 From the farthest edge of the earth (in fact)
we heard songs of joy:
"to the righteous one, majesty."
* * * *

But I thought: "I am done for, I am done for,
woe is me": cunning ones deal cunningly,
in cunning the cunning ones act cunningly.
17 Horror and hole and holder,
that is for you, inhabitant of the earth!
18 And it will happen:
whoever flees from the sound that strikes horror,
that one will fall into a hole,
and whoever climbs out of a hole,
will get caught in someone's holder.
Truly, the windows in the heights open themselves wide,
and the foundations of the earth quake.
19 Bursting, the earth bursts apart,
splitting, the earth splits open,
swaying, the earth sways back and forth,
20 staggering, the earth staggers just as would one who is drunk,
tottering, just as does a hut for the night, in a field.
Its foolishness weighs down heavily on itself,

and it falls—it will never stand up again.

II,1   21   And on that day it will happen that Yahweh will call to account the host of the heights in the heights and the kings of the earth on the earth. 22 And they will be imprisoned as one confines a prisoner in a hole, and will be confined under strict watch, and will be summoned to give an account after many days.
    23 And the moon will be red with shame,
and the sun will be white with humiliation,
    for Yahweh of Hosts will have become king
upon Mount Zion
    and in Jerusalem,
      and in the presence of his elders is glory.

III,1
  25:1 Yahweh, you are my God,
    I want to exalt you, I want to praise your name.
For you have carried out wonders regarding plans,
    trustworthy and immovable, even from a distance.
  2 Truly, you have made the city into a pile of stones,
    made the inaccessible fortifications into a mass of rubble,
so that the fortress of the impudent is no longer a city,
    for all eternity it can never be built up once again.
  3 Therefore the strong nation will honor you,
    [the city of] the brutal peoples will fear you,
  4 for you were a refuge for the unimportant,
    a refuge for the poor in their oppression,
a shelter from the downpour,
    a shade from the scorching (sun).
For the snorting of the brutal ones is as a downpour in winter,
5 as the scorching (of the sun) in a parched land.
You will put a damper on the fuming of the "impudent,"
    [heat by means of a cloud's shadows]
      the (triumph) songs of the brutal ones will be stifled.

II,2   6 There Yahweh of Hosts makes preparations
    for all peoples on this mountain,
      a banquet with rich foods,
a banquet with aged wine,
    with highest quality, rich foods,
      with aged, full bouquet wines.
  7 And he destroys on this mountain
the mask, with which the face of all peoples is masked, and the covering, which is spread out as a cover over all the nations together.
  8 And he will destroy death forever.
And the lord Yahweh will wipe away the tears from every face, and the humiliation of his people he will remove completely from the whole earth.
Truly, Yahweh has said this.

II,3   9 And on that day one will say:
Look, there is our God,
    in whom we hope and who will help us.

Yahweh is the one in whom we hope,
we will exult and will cheer ourselves because of his help;
10 truly, Yahweh's hand rests on this mountain.
* * * *

[But Moab will be trampled in its own place,
as one stomps straw down into a dung pit.
11 And if it spreads its hands out,
as a swimmer spreads them, when one wants to swim,
thus will one bring down its pride,
no matter how practiced it is in moving its hands.]
* * * *

12 And your towering stronghold, with its walls, someone pushed down,
cast it down, knocked it down, right to the ground, into the dust.

III,2
26:1 On that day this song will be sung in the land of Judah:
We have a strong city;
for protection he makes
walls and embankment.
2 Open the gates,
so that the righteous people can come in,
those who maintain faithfulness.
3 Its frame of mind is held fast; you preserve (for it) salvation,
salvation, because it trusts in you.
4 Trust in Yahweh forever [in Yah],
since, at all times, Yahweh is a rock.
5 Truly, he has brought down those who inhabit the heights;
the towering city, he pushes it down,
he pushes it flat down to the ground,
he knocks it down into the dust.
6 The foot stomps it in,
feet of one who is miserable,
footsteps of an insignificant people.

I,3a 7 The path for the righteous is flat,
the beaten track that you prepare for the righteous is straight.
* *

8 Also on the path of your judgments,
O Yahweh, we trust confidently in you.
To name your name, to call on you,
the heart is yearning.
9 Indeed, my heart, it yearns for you in the night,
also in the morning my spirit (still) longs for you.
* *

For your judgments (come) on the land,
thus the inhabitants of the earth learn righteousness;
10 if the wicked person finds mercy,
then that one never learns what justice is,
twists what is straight on the earth,
and never sees the supremacy of Yahweh.
* *

11 Yahweh, your hand is raised high,
yet they do not see it;

thus they have to see and be thwarted, because of the zeal for the people,
  and the fire against your enemies will consume them.
                    * *
12 Yahweh, you will provide us peace,
    since you have accomplished all our deeds for us.
13 Yahweh, our God, other lords besides you ruled over us,
    yet only about you, we thought only about your name.
14 Dead will not again be alive,
    shades do not rise up.
  Indeed, you have punished and exterminated them
    and obliterated whatever would remind someone of them.
15 You have multiplied the people, Yahweh,
    you have multiplied the people, have glorified yourself,
    have expanded all the borders of the land.
                    * *
16 Yahweh, in need we sought you,
    we called out, since your chastisement pressed us hard.
17 As a pregnant woman, when her hour comes,
    writhes about, cries out when her pains come,
    that is how we, Yahweh, have become before you.
18 We were pregnant, we writhed about; when we gave birth, it was wind.
    We can provide no help for the land,
    and those who dwell within the earth do not come into the world.
                * * * *
I, 3b 19 Your dead will live, [my dead body] will rise up,
    the inhabitants of the dust will wake up and will rejoice.
  For the dew of the lights is your dew,
    and the earth will give birth to the shades.
                * * * *
I, 3c 20 Now then, my people, go on into your chambers
    and close your doors behind you.
  Hide yourself for a brief moment
    until the malediction has passed by.
21 For behold, Yahweh moves out from his dwelling place,
    in order to bring the consequences of the transgressions of the inhabitants of the earth upon them.
  Then the earth will expose their blood
    and will no longer hide those whom they have struck dead.
IV, 1
27:1 On that day, with the sharp, huge, and strong sword, Yahweh will inflict punishment on Leviathan, the fleeing snake, and Leviathan, the twisting snake, and will kill the dragon that dwells in the sea.

IV, 2 2 [On that day]
    vineyard of pleasure, sing about it!
   3 I, Yahweh, am your protector,
    every moment I drench it.
  So that it experiences no damage,
    I protect it night and day;
   4   I bear no anger.

444

> If I would find thorns, thistles,
> I would go charging right in against them,
> would set every one of them on fire—
> 5 unless one takes advantage of my protection,
> makes peace with me,
> peace makes with me.

IV, 3   6 In the coming (days) Jacob will take root,
> and Israel will flourish and sprout up,
> and the whole world will fill itself with fruit.
> 7 Did he strike it, as he strikes the one who struck it,
> or did he murder it, as his murderers were murdered?
> 8 By startling, by driving away, he disputed with her,
> drove her out using his storm, the strong one,
> on the day of the east wind.
> 9 Truly, the guilt of Jacob is covered *by that means*
> —and *that* is the entire fruit coming from the distancing of its
> sins—:
> so that all the stones of the altar
> will be made just like crushed limestone
> [Asherim and incense altars will not arise ever again].
> 10 For the fortified city lies all alone,
> a depopulated place
> and abandoned like the steppe.
> There the young bull will graze,
> there he will bed down
> and eat the undergrowth bare.
> 11 If its branches are dry, then the wives will break them off
> when they come to set them on fire,
> for it is a people that has no insight.
> For that reason its maker does not deal mercifully with it,
> and it finds no grace from the one who established it.

IV, 4   12 And it will happen on that day
> that Yahweh will beat out the ears, from the (Euphrates) river on,
> even as far as the brook of Egypt.
> There you will be gleaned,
> one after the other, you children of Israel.

*   *   *   *

IV, 5
> [13 And it will happen on that day
> that there will be blowing into the large horns.
> Then they will come, those lost in the land of Assyria
> and those scattered in the land of Egypt.
> And they will fall down before Yahweh
> on the mount of the sanctuary in Jerusalem.]

Chapters 24–27, within the book of Isaiah, are not attributable to Isaiah the son of Amoz. This assertion, which is more sure than virtually any other conclusion established by the modern analysis of the written material of the OT, is one of the concrete results of literary criticism; it hardly needs to be discussed further. The reasons for the "inauthenticity" have been summarized convincingly by Rudolph (60f.) (see, earlier, Smend, 193–224; for the opposite viewpoint, cf. the representative views of Lagrange, 230f.). In any case, it is virtually indisputable that these chapters, in a particular way that must be discussed in greater detail, form a unique part of the book of Isaiah that clearly stands out as being quite different from the rest. The collection of oracles against the nations concludes with chap. 23, and chap. 28 opens a new section of the book, one that plainly has no connection with chaps. 24–27; in that material, Isaiah himself is once again the speaker. It must be admitted that, in a sense, one that somewhat follows the pattern of chaps. 13–23, chaps. 24–27 announce Yahweh's judgment to other peoples; however, these chapters are not to be classified as oracles against the nations, as is plain to see as one notes that the typical superscription, אשׂמ (verdict), is missing altogether. Except for the mention of Moab in 25:10b-12, no enemy of Israel's or Yahweh's is named; no people, except for Israel/Jacob; and no places, with the exception of Zion and Jerusalem (Assyria and Egypt are named in 27:13, but only as lands in which Israel was living while in exile). It is true that there is a reference to a "city," which has fallen, but we do not learn its name, and what we learn about it is not so specific that its identity becomes immediately apparent. While it is correct that Yahweh's judgment concerning the peoples is described, no longer is there mention of a judgment against any *specific* people, even if that group were not to be identified by name. To be sure, one need not doubt that the prophecies, songs, and prayers, which have been assembled together in these four chapters, are each directed toward a particular, historical situation, but the events about which the authors speak are apparently to be understood as focusing on the time when a *universal,* eschatological-apocalyptic *turn of events* would be taking place. Jerome himself already had noted that a different type of material in chaps. 24–27 clearly separated it from the previous chapters: "*Post specialem singularum gentium correptionem . . . nunc quid totus orbis in consumatione passurus sit, propheticus sermo describit et nequaquam de singulis gentibus, sed de cunctis pariter prophetatur*" (After individual nations each have been reproved . . . now, a prophetic sermon describes what is going to be revealed to the whole world at the end of time; this is no longer prophesied about individual nations, one at a time, but about all nations, as if they formed one large group) (CCSL, LXXIII, 316).

In spite of this, these chapters were certainly placed here intentionally, into a position immediately following the materials connected with the nations in the book of Isaiah—certainly not with the intention of integrating them into the oracles against the nations, but for just the opposite reason, in order to put the previous oracles into their own proper eschatological context. The exegetical study of chaps. 13–23 gave us no reason to suspect that the main point of those messages, directed against individual peoples, was that apocalyptic events were anticipated, or even that someone expected that the entire inhabited world would come to an end all at once. It is likely, however, even if one finally cannot prove it, that the redactor who positioned chaps. 24–27 right after these oracles wanted to use them as evidence for a worldwide conflagration, in truth, as pointing to the complete breakdown of the order that existed within the world among the peoples up until that time. At the same time, when chaps. 24–27 are added, a new context is provided, indicating a new way to interpret the previous collection of material.

Chapters 24–27 were appended to the corpus in chaps. 13–23 after that material had already reached its final form. However, that does not prove that the "apocalypse" would have to have been written later than the "verdict" collection; of course, that sequence is likely. Even though it is true that the greater portion of material in the oracles against the nations cannot be attributed to Isaiah, it is certain that none of what is in chaps. 24–27 would have come from him, so that, if the large majority of inauthentic passages in chaps. 13–23 belong to the exilic era, chaps. 24–27 would be postexilic. However, that assumption must be examined more carefully and explained more specifically wherever possible.

Form

In the first place, one must deal with the question about the unity of these four chapters. In the present form, in which they have come down to us, it is evident that they are offered as a unified composition, seeking to provide a witness to the coming events that would take place during the great turning point in history that was soon to follow, though one must put particular stress on the designation "composition." But as soon as one discusses the question about the history of the stages of development for this composition, opinions vary widely. It is composed using radically disparate elements, and one cannot expect to sketch out, to everyone's satisfaction, the exact way in which this material took shape. None of the many efforts to demonstrate the "structure" of the chapters has yet had the good fortune of receiving the general approval of a significant number of scholars. Yet one cannot give up on the attempt to comprehend how the entire section fits together and makes sense, also in light of its structure. The results will be affected significantly by the care with which the detailed analytical work is carried out.

One cannot provide an entire history of the study of the text at this point (but see Brockhaus, 1–31). But reference can be made to some significant attempts to understand the development and structure of the "apocalypse."

Duhm suggests that the original body of material included 24; 25:6-8 (except for בלע המות לנצח, "and he will destroy death forever"); 26:20—27:1, 12, 13. According to him, material added later would include the song in 25:1-5, a song of praise to God, occasioned by the destruction of a fortified city, as also the mocking song spoken against Moab in 25:9-11, as well as the poem in 26:1-19, with which he links 25:12 too, and finally the song of Yahweh's vineyard in 27:2-5. The original body of material is to be considered an apocalypse. Thus Duhm recognized that one must differentiate between announcements of coming judgment and salvation on the one hand and songs and poems on the other; the original body of material would have been expanded afterward, by another hand. In studies that followed, his viewpoint underwent significant alterations and his analysis has been modified and refined in some respects, but it remains his contribution that he pointed to a substantive difference between the prophecies and the songs.

447

Procksch attempted to divide the chapters into sections on the basis of differences in the metrical patterns. One section of the material was said to have a characteristic seven-stress colon structure; the other, even though it was not consistent throughout, generally followed a three-stress + three-stress pattern. The first block of material—he practically terms this the seven-stress apocalypse, because he sees that it is dominated by observations about the world judgment—would include 24:1-7, 18b-23; 25:6-10a (10bff.); 26:7ff.; and 27:1, 12f. The second block he titles the song cycle; this has none of the identifying features of apocalyptic, but deals with the downfall of a great city. He includes in this 24:8-18a; 25:1-5; 26:1-6; 27:2bff. (thus on p. 306, differently on p. 310).

One must certainly pay attention to the meter when analyzing the text, but determining the exact metrical divisions is so difficult, as will be demonstrated, that it cannot be used as the determining factor in carrying out the analysis. In addition, the text-critical studies will show that Procksch, as others have done also, makes significant alterations to the received text in his quest to force the text to fit his theory about the meter.

In a study of the Isaiah apocalypse that still deserves careful attention, Lindblom comes essentially to a conclusion rather similar to that suggested by the previous two scholars. He also differentiates between "eschatological poems" or "apocalyptic oracles," on the one hand, that is, 24:1-6 (worldwide catastrophe); 24:16aβ-20 (the same); 25:6-10a (festive banquet on Zion); 26:20f. (worldwide judgment); and 27:12f. (return from the diaspora), versus the noneschatological songs, that is, 24:7-16aα (song of thanks: the destroyed city); 25:1-5 (the same); 26:1-14 (communal lament); and 27:2-11 (song of jubilation: the good fortune of the Jewish community). Further, he suggests that there were three additions: 24:21-23 (incarceration of the princes and the kingdom of Yahweh); 25:10b-12 (concerning Moab); and 27:1 (destruction of the kingdoms of the world). Beside these additions, he also considers the communal song of lament in 26:15-19 to be secondary, so that what remains of the original material in the apocalypse includes the five eschatological poems and the remaining four songs. What particularly occupied his attention was the question about how one was to interpret the alternation between oracles and songs. Already before his study, Hylmö had suggested that chaps. 24f. should be interpreted as a prophetic liturgy. However, Lindblom (69ff.) rejects using this term; he finds no conversation and response between God and human beings or between priests and laity, typical elements in this type of liturgy. But he still does follow Hylmö's lead in treating all the oracles and songs as having an inner and original unity, not just in the first two chapters, which Hylmö suggested; and he believes that the alternation between the two types of material can be explained by showing that this material takes the form of a festival cantata. The major focus would be on "the destruction of a foreign city," which the Jews would have interpreted as a miraculous act of Yahweh, but which at the same time ushered in a new world epoch, in fact, the beginning of the eschatological end time. The author would have been a Jerusalem cult prophet and the various parts would have been divided between a prophetic choir and a choir from the worshiping community. Even more importantly, he made an attempt to identify the "setting in life" for this festival cantata. The key point for him is found in the admonition: "Open the gates, so that the righteous people can come in" (26:2). The celebration, after the fall of the enemy city, would supposedly have been connected with a festival procession, which would have entered through the city gates; some of the participants in the cantata would apparently have been positioned at various places along the route, others in the procession itself, still others at the sanctuary.

Recently, Fohrer ("Aufbau") combined these two ideas, liturgy and cantata, although his analysis of the four chapters differs significantly from that of Hylmö and Lindblom. He treats the entire block of material as a cantata, which has three liturgical units, 24:1-20; 24:21—25:10a; and 27:1-6, 12f., held together by two linking sections (26:1-6 and 26:7-21). Of course, he is aware that it is questionable to use the term "liturgy" and that the term "cantata" is not much of an improvement over simply suggesting that this is essentially an artistic cycle of poems of different types. According to him, therefore, one also has to deal with secondary compositions that once were independent units of material. Thus, in spite of his use of the terms "liturgy" and "cantata," Lindblom's attempt to explain the apocalypse as a block of material that was essentially one unit from the very beginning is now abandoned. The time when scholars sought to identify liturgies in the OT in every place possible (see Rudolph, 35f., note 9), is no longer in vogue.

Even before Lindblom, Rudolph had completed a study of the apocalypse, one that has been frequently cited. He clearly rejected Hylmö's interpretation. But he also noted that there was a difference between eschatological prophecies and hymns (which he also wanted to interpret eschatologically). However, he also suggested that some passages be removed from both groups: 24:7b-12, 14-16, which is the depiction of the conquered city; 27:2-5, which is the song of Yahweh's vineyard; and 27:7-11, which is "a song of lament concerning the despicable condition of Jerusalem." Still later additions are found in the little oracle against Moab in 25:10b, 11 (but see Rudolph, 48f.) and the glosses in 24:7a; 25:11a; and 27:6.

The more recent attempts by Plöger and Kaiser are based on Rudolph's work. According to Plöger, the essential block of material that gives form to the apocalypse is contained in chaps. 24–26; chap. 27 consists of obviously later additions, and chaps. 24–26 have been enriched by songs in 25:1ff.; 26:1ff.; and the message about Moab in 25:10b-11 (12) (though the song against the city in 24:10-12 belongs to the original body of material that formed the apocalypse). Yet even what was part of this original unit made use of disparate material that had existed in independent form.

Even more than Plöger, Kaiser attempts to delineate layers of material in his commentary. He considers the original material to have been in what is now 24:1-13, 16aβ-20. He thinks it possible that the author, a protoapocalyptic theologian, also might be responsible for 26:1-18, 20-21. According to him, a second layer of material consists of eschatological songs of thanksgiving: 24:14-16aα and 25:1-5. A third layer, with more advanced apocalyptic speculations, would include 24:21-23 and 25:6-8, as well as 25:9-10a. He assigns the resurrection passages, 25:8aα and 26:19, to a fourth reworking of the text. According to him, chap. 27 has its own history of development, though v. 1 and vv. 12f. could still belong with 24:21-23 and 25:6-8. He makes no effort any longer to divide the material in the apocalypse, as others had done, into prophecies and songs; he suggests that a better hypothesis would be that there was a gradual expansion of the original material, one that took considerable time.

Vermeylen comes to essentially the same conclusion in his article. He makes careful note of the numerous points of tension in this rather short body of material, which of course would not have to mean that it is nothing but a conglomeration, making no sense in its present form. One must posit steps in the development of the whole: he finds the oldest basic form of the material in 24:2-13, 18b-20, and 26:8-9*, 11-13, 16-18, 20-21. In this material he finds a close parallel to Isaiah 13 and suggests that this is another instance where the fall of Babylon is discussed, his view being that it refers to its destruction at the hands of Xerxes in 485. According to him,

449

this basic material was expanded in two stages, though he does not believe that the most recent layer has the marks of a single unit; he assigns that layer to the Greek epoch. He believes that the latest insertions are the notations about death and resurrection in 26:14, 19, and 25:8. Thus, according to Vermeylen, every generation expanded on the original text, each for its own reasons, thus commenting on what was before them. He himself admits that his analysis, which cannot be discussed in greater detail at this point, might be no more than guesswork in some places and that it is beyond our abilities to establish the exact chronology of the individual sections. One notes that his analysis does agree substantively with that of Kaiser, though one must also note that two contemporary scholars, both of whom have the same basic idea about how the text developed, came to such radically different conclusions when working with the specifics that deal with the exact nature and dating of this process.

Thus scholarly activity, beginning with Duhm and continuing through the work of Rudolph up to the present time, typified by Kaiser and Vermeylen, seems to be guided by the opinion that these chapters developed into their present form gradually, with a significant number of additions and insertions resulting in the text as we now have it. If one surveys the work of those who write in languages other than German, however, one cannot miss the point that the common opinion, beginning with Lindblom, is quite the opposite; many of these scholars maintain that there is an original unity to the material. Though Anderson does not accept Lindblom's cantata designation for the material, he does argue forcefully that the apocalypse formed one block of material from the beginning. He thinks that it is set within a time frame which is not far removed from Deutero-Isaiah, Haggai, and Zechariah, which means that he would assign roughly the same date as Lindblom did.

Ringgren has come out most vociferously in favor of the view put forth by Lindblom, in fact directly in response to Fohrer's thesis that the text underwent many modifications, as summarized above. He would certainly have been even more opposed to the ideas of Plöger, Kaiser, and Vermeylen. In his opinion, the chapters are constructed as a coherent composition, in which case he is not even willing to eliminate the message against Moab, 25:10f., though almost everyone else does so.

One more attempt to argue for the unity of the material in these chapters was set forth in the massive study by Redditt. He identifies four sections (319f., 395ff.):

1. 24:1-20:   Dissolution of the present world order
2. 24:21–26:6: The place of Jerusalem in the coming world order
3. 26:7-21:   The necessity of Yahweh's judgment
4. 27:1-13:   Conditions for Israel's rescue

This overview is by no means complete, but it must suffice. Scholarly activity in recent times concerning the study of the problem of the Isaiah apocalypse has reached almost the same proportions as the effort that has been expended concerning the question of the identity and nature of the servant of God in the second major part of the book of Isaiah, unfortunately without coming to any generally accepted solution. Because of this state of affairs, everyone who seeks to speak about the apocalypse should be careful not to suggest that one's own conclusions are final. However, based on all the most recent research—disagreeing with both Anderson and Ringgren—two points must be made:

1. One can no longer work with the thesis that there is a basic unity to

the apocalypse, not even if one presumes that there have been some later additions. Even the attempt to solve the problem by describing the form with a flexible term, such as liturgy or cantata, as a way to deal with the tensions and inner contradictions must be judged a failure. The alternative offered is what one might call an expansion- or growth-hypothesis. It is very difficult to show how this process of development took place, as can be seen when comparing the views of Plöger, Kaiser, and Vermeylen. That does not mean that the thesis itself is invalid. Since it has frequently been observed that comments have been inserted into passages elsewhere in the book of Isaiah, both in the form of expansions and of insertions, it would actually have been more surprising if the chapters that we are presently studying would have proved to be an exception to the rule (one might compare passages such as 4:2ff.; 7:17-25; 10:16-23; 11:10-16; 12, etc.).

2. More recent scholars who presume that there was some such process of growth all agree that what they suppose to have been the "original text" must always be kept in mind when they speak of the "commenting," and the "commenting" ought not be read without the "text." This means that these scholars also have the same concern as do those who argue for the unity of the text. They would say that the uneven points within the text are to be treated as tensions, which developed as the hermeneutic process took its course and which provide evidence that there was an ongoing effort to reapply what had been passed down to them for their own situation. In its favor, this viewpoint argues that there was a text which spoke about a great turn of events, close at hand, a message that occasioned intensive reflection, adaptation to new situations, and thus new interpretations.

[24:1-13] With current scholarship being in the position that has been described, allowing no one to begin from any starting point that has achieved a measure of consensus, there is no way around proceeding with an individual analysis of each of the chapters. No matter what has been suggested to have been the original body of material, there has been general agreement that one would begin to discuss it by studying 24:1-20. Of course, even these twenty verses do not form one single unit, without interruptions. The chapter begins with the presentative הנה (behold) with participle. As is true elsewhere (3:1; 8:7; 10:33; 22:17; 26:21aα = Mic. 1:3a; Amos 6:11), this formula introduces an announcement of judgment; this one applies to the entire earth. It would seem that the reason is not provided, since v. 2 does not announce that the coming judgment is going to smooth out what had become permanently differentiated social levels, so detested by God; instead, it says that the borders, which had been functioning until that time and which had made it possible to have social order, would fall by the wayside. It would seem that a conclusion has been reached already at the end of v. 3 with the sentence: "for it is Yahweh who has spoken this message." The accusative object in this formula (את־הדבר הזה, "this message") is unique; besides here, כי יהוה דבר (for Yahweh has declared it) is found at the end of a section also in 22:25 and 25:8; in 1:2 and Jer. 13:15, however, it is used at the beginning of a message.

451

Thus it is not nearly as sure, as some would make it, that the oracle in vv. 1-
3a comes to a conclusion with v. 3b. In terms of content, v. 4 takes up the
theme of v. 1 once again (in which two verbs that sound alike, אבל, "withered," and נבל, "wilted," provide variations on the two similar sounding verbs
in v. 1, בקק, "ravages," and בלק, "devastates"). Then v. 5 provides the missing reason for the announcement of judgment, and על־כן (for this reason), at
the beginning of v. 6, underscores that the worldwide judgment is a result of
the entire earth having been defiled. This means that the accusative phrase
את־הדבר הזה (this message), mentioned above, apparently refers to vv. 4-6.

Verses 7-9 form the first insertion, or else later addition, in vv. 1-6.
Thus, by itself, the vocabulary in these verses does not provide evidence that
a world catastrophe is being envisioned. Verses 10-12 are once again motivated by still another concern: the destruction of the city. That section also is
likely a later addition; on this, see below, p. 485.

Rudolph suggests linking v. 13, which now follows, to vv. 1-6 and has
found many supporters, but also detractors. Just as the verse could have been
written because of ונשאר אנוש מזער (and what is left of human beings, that is
quickly counted), which comes at the end of v. 6, it also could have been
written because of נשאר בעיר שמה (only devastation still remains in the city) in
v. 12. In either case, it is a gloss: some reader was reminded of 17:6 and
wanted to point out that that prophecy of Isaiah was now coming to its fulfillment.

[24:14-20] Verse 14 begins a new section: jubilant celebrating is announced,
"from the western sea," "from the farthest edge of the earth" (vv. 14-16aα).
There are many problems with how to interpret this section: *who* are the המה
(they), who exult even from the sea? *Why* do they do it? And why is it that
they specifically do so *from the* sea? It may be that identifications were once
provided before v. 14, now lost, which would have clearly identified the המה
(they). However, המה also can be used when one wants to use the indefinite
"someone." In actuality, Israel comes to mind when this is said. "From the
sea" is simply the parallel term for בארים, used in the sense of "in the east,"
and it is further clarified in v. 15bα, which speaks of באיי הים (on the coasts
of the sea). From all azimuths, from every direction one could scan on the
horizon, praise to the great God would go forth when hearing the news that
the judgment of God was going on throughout the earth (or throughout the
"city of chaos"). If that interpretation is correct, then the המה (they) would
have to be the Jews scattered throughout the world in the diaspora, who
imagined that their day of deliverance had come. According to v. 16aα, a certain group, known as the "we" group, heard the songs of the המה (they). With
this, what is being said takes a turn, since now the צדיק (righteous one) is
acknowledged as the one who has צבי (majesty), an obvious reference to Yahweh (see below, pp. 497f.). According to the context, this rejoicing about
Yahweh and the majesty of his community can have been set in motion only
by means of the announcement of this worldwide judgment, or, as the case
may be, by the destruction of the "chaos city." It is possible that vv. 14-16aα

once stood in a completely different context. To speculate about what this might have been will prove fruitless; the verses make good sense as a continuation of vv. 1-6 and would never have been intended to serve any other purpose.

In opposition to Israel's rejoicing, the prophet, who according to v. 16aα (cf. שמענו, we heard!) knows that he is surrounded by a circle of those who think just as he does, issues a protest. How can one break out into such rejoicing when the entire earth is split wide open or is engulfed by a brand new flood. He sees nothing but the harsh nature of God's judgment, which should cause Israel to be introspective as well. "Compared with a superficial . . . eschatological expectation the severity of eschatological catastrophe must be taken seriously" (Plöger, 59).

Thus this description of a dangerous time shows that vv. 14-20 belong with vv. 1-6. This section makes good sense in connection with that announcement of judgment. It means that this is also part of the original body of material. The original link was broken by the expansions now found in vv. 7-13.

[24:21-23] A completely new section of material begins with the well-known introductory formula והיה ביום ההוא (and on that day it will happen). For almost all occurrences in the book of Isaiah, it serves as a marker, one that points to later additions. Another item that would suggest that it has been added later is the observation that vv. 21f. can hardly be read metrically (concerning v. 23, see below, p. 505). In no way is this an attempt to minimize the importance of what is said; just the opposite: it is very important. The expander felt compelled to illustrate the announcement of the worldwide judgment and to expand on it: not only the kings of the earth, but at the same time, first off in fact, it would affect "the host of the heights in the heights." Verse 22 already seems to presume that there are phases through which things would pass on the way toward the end of time. According to v. 23a, it is not only the earth that totters; instead, the entire order within the cosmos is coming unglued. But far and away more important than anything else: Yahweh's rule as king would finally come out from its position in hiding, and the mount of God in Jerusalem would be the place from which the indescribable glory of Yahweh's own majesty would shine forth. If one takes all this into consideration, vv. 21-23 would be much closer to real apocalyptic thinking than would vv. 1-20. This section is not part of the original body of material. It remains to be seen whether this short passage should be connected with other similar passages.

[25:1-5] Isaiah 25:1-5 has all the markings of a song of thanksgiving; it is not a prediction, but looks back on what has happened already. The thanks that are directed toward Yahweh are specifically linked to "the city," which has become a mass of rubble. It would seem that this psalm belongs with 24:10-12, which also discusses the destruction of a city. But that hardly can be the case. Isaiah 24:10-12 is not a song of thanksgiving, but is part of the eschatological announcement of judgment; one cannot miss the point that there is a certain sympathy in that passage for those who have to go through the experience with that city. Here, however, in 25:1-5 (and the same is true for 26:5f.), there is a sense of satisfaction with the destruction of the enemy city. If one considers the song by itself, one cannot say that it is eschatological. That does not mean that the redactor, who inserted this material here, may not have understand it as anticipating what one would sing in an eschatological song of praise. The mention of a destroyed city in 24:10ff. would have motivated him to insert this song here, serving, one might say, the function of expanding that passage. But one ought to note that there are no three-part lines here in these five verses, a distinctive feature of the rest of the Isaiah apocalypse (see below, pp. 473, 494f.), a circumstance that itself points to this song being a secondary addition within its present context. As Plöger (69) has suggested, this could in fact be older than the present depiction of the eschatological event (see below, p. 518). According to Vermeylen (36), the song belongs to his second level, and most would treat the songs in the Isaiah apocalypse as later than the rest of the text. However, as Plöger correctly points out, that remains an open question. Later, one will once again have to ask whether other sections in the Isaiah apocalypse would be similar to 25:1-5.

[25:6-8] The following section, the passage about the eschatological celebratory meal, 25:6-8, cannot function as a continuation of vv. 1-5. It is clear that this is, once again, a prediction. It goes way beyond anything that had been expected by Israel in the future when it says that Yahweh prepares a celebratory meal on Zion for all nations, which were to assemble at the same time, and that the mask would be taken away from all the nations. Obviously, that fits in with the announcement that death itself will be removed completely. Of course, v. 8aα, which speaks of that, has been treated by many exegetes as an insertion. That is unavoidable if one considers this section to be part of the original body of the material in the apocalypse. However, this way of treating the text is unlikely: "on this mountain" in vv. 6 and 7 refers to בהר ציון (on Mount Zion) in 24:23. Just as in that passage, eschatological concepts are clearly used very exactly, so that they become part of a specific apocalyptic depiction. One can identify a certain rhythm in the speech, but no more can be said than that this is elevated prose, unless one can justify making massive alterations to the form of the received text. This analysis suggests that 25:6-8 belongs to the same layer as 24:21-23.

In a way that is different from 24:3 (see above, pp. 451f.) כי יהוה דבר (truly, Yahweh has said this), at the end of v. 8, clearly points out that this is the end of the section.

[25:9-10a] To the special cycle of material in 24:21-23 and 25:6-8 belongs a third part, 25:9-10a: "On that day" makes use once again of the same formula used in 24:21; "on this mountain" (v. 10) refers back to vv. 6 and 7, where the same way to identify a specific geographical place is used (see also "on Mount Zion" in 24:23). One can hardly object, however, that the celebratory meal is for the peoples, whereas the "we" in v. 9 refers to the Israelites; the people of Yahweh were mentioned already in v. 8. To be sure, those phrases which echo what has just been mentioned in the preceding verses are further indications that an expander has inserted this, as a conscious addition; however, see the discussions about the relationship between vv. 9, 10a, and the section that precedes them, in Lindblom (35), Procksch, and Fohrer ("Aufbau"). The verses present themselves as a rich conclusion to the little cycle of eschatological-apocalyptic visions in 24:21-23 and 25:6-8.

[25:10b, 11 (12)] A sharp break comes right in the middle of v. 10: vv. 10b, 11, (12) speak about Moab, the type of concrete reference that does not fit within the framework of the apocalypse. Within these verses one finds an emotionally aggressive demeanor, which is not like anything else in the apocalypse. This is a later addition, accepted as such by most scholarly studies. Later on, there will be a discussion about whether this section is actually about Moab. In its present context, which depicts events that are to occur at the end of time, it could be a code name for ungodly power as such.

A particular problem is posed by v. 12: though there had been mention of the people of Moab previous to this, now the reference is to a stronghold, which is to be knocked down to the ground. It is hardly likely that v. 12, skipping vv. 10b, 11, is a direct continuation of v. 10a (so Rudolph, 17; see Lindblom, 39; Plöger, 62–63; Fohrer, *Kommentar* and "Aufbau," 173, et al.); the verse is formulated much like 26:5 and can justifiably be treated as an addition to an addition.

[26:1-6] There is no doubt that 26:1-6 is, once again, a separate section, which must first be examined by itself. The introduction in v. 1a: "On that day this song will be sung in the land of Judah" causes one to treat these verses, as a whole, as an eschatological hymn. But if one disregards this phrase—and it is certainly secondary—then it also speaks about the fall of a city (vv. 5f.), an event that lies already in the past. Of course, in contrast to that city, mention is made in the first place concerning the strong city Jerusalem, in which Yahweh, as an eternal rock, continually provides refuge. Both formally and in terms of content, this passage is a parallel to 25:1-5. Repeating the point, it is to be treated as an eschatological unit of material only if viewed within the context into which it has now been placed. Whereas it could be inferred only from the context in 25:1ff., it is stated in no uncertain terms here, in the introduction in 26:1a: "that day" is *the* day, the one about which the previous prophecies had spoken. One might compare this with the introduction in 12:1a, by means of which it is almost possible to identify that chapter as an eschatological song of thanksgiving.

[26:7-21] There is no question that a new section begins with 26:7, even though some consider vv. 7ff. to be a continuation of vv. 1-6, as does Duhm, though he does speak of vv. 1-19 as a "very artfully contrived poem, crammed full of assonance, plays on words, and the like." At first glance one would agree with this assessment, but it is premature and, no matter what conclusions one finally reaches, vv. 7ff. should be distinguished from the preceding. It is a much more difficult question to resolve where the section that begins with v. 7 comes to its conclusion and how it is to be classified in terms of its form-historical genre. Lindblom (40ff.), who views vv. 7ff. as a continuation of vv. 1-6, considers it to be a song of thanks, which first reaches its conclusion in v. 14; the following verses, 15-19, are then assigned to the category of a song of communal lament, which is clearly to be distinguished from the other poems in the apocalypse and would not have been composed until very late (after 145, when the Maccabeans were successful in expanding the territory of Judah; cf. Lindblom, 64ff.). This very late dating sounds suspicious. Besides, vv. 7-14 and 15-19 are intertwined so thoroughly that one ought not divide the two parts unless forced to do so. Rudolph (46ff.) thinks that he can recognize elements which would make vv. 7-19 a relatively self-contained piece, of course only after paying the price of removing vv. 14a, 18bβ, and 19, and rearranging some of the other passages as well. One should not decide that such radical changes must be made in the text until virtually every other solution has proved fruitless. Yet Eissfeldt (*Introduction,* 324) is probably right when he suggests that vv. 7-19 contain "a prayer, rather like a national lament, asking for the removal of the distress which is oppressing the people and which it cannot avert of itself, and for the restoration to life of dead compatriots." In terms of the form-historical genre, the entire passage presents itself as a communal lament, even though the form has been altered significantly, admittedly one in which the "we" alternates with the "I" and correspondingly thus also includes motifs that are typically found in an individual song of lament. In addition, certain points have a reflective character (vv. 7, 9b, 10), but it is not impossible that one should find influences from wisdom in cultic lyrics. For a specific description about the individual elements in a song of lament, see below, p. 558.

[26:19] Of course, already at this point, something special needs to be said about v. 19. It is the absolute antithesis of the lament in vv. 17f., which expresses resignation to one's fate. Is this an addition, from another hand and from a different time period? That has been suggested often enough (cf. Rudolph, 48, 61ff.; and Lindblom, 63f.), but one ought not resolve the tension with the immediately preceding verses so quickly. Other explanations are possible as to why there is such a sharp discrepancy between vv. 18 and 19: one can note the same type of "alteration of mood" in the psalms; cf. Pss. 6:9ff.; 28:6ff.; 31:20ff.; 56:10ff., among others (see O. Kaiser, *Introduction to the Old Testament* [1975] 334–335). Then it would seem one could presume that the author's "your dead" might correspond to Israel—to that Israel which was under oppression. Just as he had heard reported from ancient times, he also would have had the confidence: even if Israel's actions, and the sufferings that followed, did not achieve their intended purpose, in any case: its dead would live, they would rise again. It is more likely, however, that v. 19 is intended as an "oracle of salvation," which is certainly appropriate when it follows a lament (see Kaiser, *Introduction,* 263, 335; Rudolph, 21f.; Plöger, 76–77; Lindblom, 50; Ringgren, 111; et al.). Yahweh answers the one who prays: "your (i.e., Israel's) dead" are in fact "my dead body" (unless נבלתי is a gloss). The most important question about the content concerns whether "resurrection" means resurrection of individuals after death or that the collective group Israel would come to life once again after a time of most severe oppression. No matter how this question is finally answered (see below, pp. 566ff.), v. 19 certainly should not be separated from vv. 7-18.

[**26:20f.**] It is clear that the form of the two verses which follow, vv. 20f., has nothing in common with the preceding song of lament and the oracle of salvation that is connected with it. In spite of this, the link in thought between the two sections is unmistakable: Israel is suffering in a severely oppressive situation; it is in no position to bring about its own deliverance; what it can bring forth is nothing but "wind." It is true that it has been promised "resurrection," but what is Israel supposed to do in the meantime, as the oppression gets more and more severe? These two verses offer the answer: hide oneself for a brief moment, until "the wrath" has passed by. The lament, along with the oracle of salvation that belongs with it, is not to be treated as a self-contained unit of material. Within those words, the author picks up on the objections and doubts connected with his eschatological message and provides them with an answer; however, the actual ending point for the entire section is first reached in v. 21: the great turning point is close at hand; Yahweh sets forth from his places; the eschatological judgment is set in motion. Yet Israel, encouraged by its hope for a resurrection, must wait trustingly, until the storm of judgment has roared on by. Thus vv. 7-21 form a single kerygmatic unit.

When one follows this understanding of the passage, it is at least likely that the entire section of material in vv. 7-21 belongs to the original body of the material in the apocalypse and that it provides the continuation of 24:1-6, 14-20. There, in 24:16aβff., the author warned against starting the rejoicing too quickly; here, in what is certainly a later phase of his activity, he already had opportunity to deal with the disappointment that some experienced, since Israel's salvation was still only anticipated and the impression had been left that it itself could be pulled under by the crashing waves, as the judgment against the nations roared on through. However, this individual apparently said all he wanted to say when he finished 26:20f. From then on, the events would speak for themselves.

[**27**] Now, however, on to chap. 27. On formal grounds, one notices right away that the individual units are once again introduced by the well-known introduction or linking formula, ביום ההוא (on that day) (27:1, 2, 12, 13). In v. 6 one finds a similar designation for time, (בימים) הבאים ([in] the coming [days]). Based on these formulas, the events announced here are also to be set within the eschatological horizon of the apocalypse.

In terms of content, there is no particularly close connection between the five individual units, and one can hardly assume that they have all come from the same hand.

[27:1] The first section, v. 1, makes use of mythological viewpoints, set within a creation framework, which thus have eschatological-apocalyptic markings from the outset: the powers of chaos, which Yahweh had driven back at the beginning of what initiated the present state of affairs in the world, would be completely eliminated in the end.

[27:2-5] The second section, the "new song of the vineyard" (vv. 2-5), actually does not speak about the future; it is apparently included to provide a contrast to the song of the vineyard in 5:1-7; and, in the present context, the intention is to say that Israel would live under different conditions in the future than those which were there at the time of 5:1-7.

[27:6-9] Verses 6-9 also speak about restoration for Israel; its guilt has been expiated; its sins removed.

[27:10f.] In a contrast to what immediately precedes, vv. 10f. speak of the pitiable circumstances in the devastated "strong city," having been given no special treatment.

[27:12, 13] The traditional depiction of the coming time of restoration included the motif that those who had been dispersed in the exile would be gathered and returned home, which is also promised in vv. 12f.

One might ask whether these two verses, 12 and 13, in spite of the ביום ההוא (and it will happen on that day) at the beginning of v. 13, do not indeed belong together as a separate unit and whether both were composed by the same author. But one might suppose that there was a reader who read the announcement in v. 12 and found it too vague, since he knew exactly what was to be expected: the large horns would announce the day of salvation; those who had been scattered would return home both from Assyria and Egypt, and the holy mountain in Jerusalem would finally come into its own as the chief place for worship. With this material, a rich finale is provided for the apocalypse.

The analysis just summarized has shown that these four chapters went through a rather complicated process of development. The individual units were certainly not all composed by the same author and not during the same time period either. It is not enough simply to divide the passage into two parts, into eschatological prophecies and songs, as has so frequently been the solution of choice in the past. Among other things, the complicated textual history certainly explains why all the efforts to achieve a consensus about the date of the passage have met with little success. It is only appropriate that one might seek to determine the age of the individual layers of material or that of later additions—to be sure, it is very difficult to find an answer and often enough one simply will have to give up.

The analysis has thus determined that the material contains the following layers and later additions:

I. The original body of material, which provides the crystallization point for attracting all that follows
    Theme: The world judgment. It breaks down into the following sections:
    1. 24:1-6:   Announcement of the ravaging of the entire earth (break after v. 3a)
       Additions: a. vv. 7-9:   The wilting of the branch of the vine and the silencing of the festive noise made by the revelers
                    b. vv. 10-12:   The destruction of the chaos city, to be understood as the decisive event, by means of which the events at the end of time are set in motion
                    c. v. 13:   The gleaning among the nations
    2. 24:14-20:   The premature jubilation of Israel (vv. 14-16a) and the deep shock experienced by the seer because of the horrible events that were coming on the earth
    3. 26:7-21:   Yahweh's people in the oppressive circumstances at the end of time
                    a. vv. 7-18:   The communal lament of the people; its inability to find deliverance
                    b. v. 19:   The oracle of salvation: the resurrection of the dead
                    c. vv. 20f.:   Israel at the time of Yahweh's breaking forth for the judgment of the world
II. Eschatological images
    1. 24:21-23:   The end of world kingdoms and the breaking in of the reign of God
    2. 25:6-8:   The celebratory meal on Zion
    3. 25:9-10a: An eschatological song of thanksgiving
    Additions, concerning Moab: a. vv. 10b, 11: Moab in the dung heap
                                b. v. 12: The destruction of its fortifications
III. The city songs
    1. 25:1-5:   A hymn: The destruction of the strong city (vv. 1-3) and the protection of those faithful to Yahweh (vv. 4f.)
    2. 26:1-6:   A hymn: Yahweh, the lordly protector of Jerusalem (vv. 1-4) and the destroyer of the towering city (vv. 5f.)
IV. Later additions: eschatological impressions
    1. 27:1:   The defeat of the chaos dragon
    2. 27:2-5:   The new song of the vineyard
    3. 27:6-11:   A time of flourishing for Israel; devastation of a fortified city
    4. 27:12:   The gathering of those faithful to Yahweh
    5. 27:13:   The return to Zion

Some points must be noted about this overview:

a. There is no way to determine whether it was textual group II or III that was inserted before the other into the original body of material. One might suppose that the eschatological images were the first to be added. It is possible, however, that the city songs are considerably older than the original body of material, even if they were first inserted into this text at a later time.

b. In the exegetical study that follows, we will not take each of the individual layers one at a time, not primarily because one must remain aware that the analysis offered above has a hypothetical character about it; but rather because, as one must continue to maintain, the Isaiah apocalypse is to be treated as a single unified prophecy about an eschatological turn of events, even though it might have a complicated history of development, and because each individual layer, each section, and each expansion is to be given its proper interpretation only in light of the overall scope of the entire work.

Setting

The question about assigning a date to the Isaiah apocalypse was discussed already in a preliminary way above (p. 447).

There continue to be those who wish to attribute all of chaps. 24–27, or at least a basic core of original material, to Isaiah, dated therefore to the eighth century. Thus Beek tries to show how it was possible to believe that Isaiah was the author. He begins with the Moab passages (25:10-12, which he considers to have been part of the original body of material in the apocalypse) and combines what is said here with what is now found in chaps. 15f., material that he is convinced is authentic. He thinks that the catastrophe which came upon Moab, as described in those chapters, provides the background for 24:18b-20 as well, a passage that he believes could refer only to an earthquake. It must have been an earthquake that would have deeply shaken the peoples in Palestine, and that only could have been the one to which reference is made in the date provided at the beginning of the book of Amos (see Amos 1:1). This is a haphazard reconstruction; the most important objection one might raise is that it does not take into account how very different this thought world in the apocalypse is, when compared with that of Isaiah the son of Amoz.

Eissfeldt (*Introduction*, 326) also begins with these same words about Moab and believes that every reference to the destroyed city, in all the passages of the apocalypse, speaks of the capital city of Moab, and he also mentions the connection between the apocalypse and the chapters about Moab in Isa. 15f.—naturally without trying to convince anyone that Isaiah wrote them! However, both of the chapters about Moab are later additions; besides this, the way a Jew in Palestine would have looked at history would not have been so narrow that one would have interpreted the downfall of the capital city of their small neighboring country to be an event of such importance that it would have been interpreted as the beginning of the worldwide judgment and the onset of the time of salvation.

One can understand why thoughts about the identity of that city have returned again and again to Babylon; since its downfall was so important, it would certainly be possible for someone to have interpreted such an event as the beginning of the reign of God. But *which* time that Babylon fell? Ewald thought it would have been

the time when Cyrus defeated Babylon. And even Henry (33) leans in that direction
and agrees. Recently, Elder set forth arguments that all these chapters would have
come into existence at a time when the downfall of Jerusalem and the destruction of
the temple would still have been a living reality for the exiled Jews (215); the entire
section of material would have been directed against Babylon and its royal cult, and
the author could have been none other than Deutero-Isaiah (216). Even Rudolph
(62f.) has continued to opt for Babylon, though he thinks it refers to the time when
the city was conquered by Alexander in 331. According to Lindblom (77ff.), the
damage would have been too minimal at these times when Babylon was conquered
for such events to have provided the historical background for the city songs. He
focuses instead on the time when Xerxes I conquered Babylon in 485, since this was
the only time when the city was actually destroyed. In his own study, Procksch
begins with 24:14f., which speaks of the exultation "even from the west." In his view,
that phrase could refer only to the area surrounding the Mediterranean, in which
there are only two world-class cities, namely, Rome and Carthage. Since Rome never
suffered defeat during the period in question, that would "leave only Carthage,
Rome's archenemy, whose fall at the hands of C. Scipio Aemilianus in the year 146
B.C. must have aroused such feelings."

Hilgenfeld (437ff.) once suggested that this material was about Tyre, in fact,
dated to the time when it was conquered and destroyed by Alexander the Great; he
suggested that the reference to "even from the west" also could refer to island fortifications.

The interpretation mentioned above, connecting it with Moab, had other supporters as well, and recently found another passionate advocate in Mulder (78ff.). He
zeroes in specifically on the city of Dibon, thinking that the vocable מדמן (dung pit)
(25:10) is a play on this name (90f.). He dates the passage to the first half of the third
century B.C., when the Nabateans pressed on into Moab (93).

Duhm (followed by Marti) thought this passage was about the destruction of
Samaria by John Hyrcanus (about 107 B.C.). Support for this solution has been
sought in 26:6, a passage which presumes that Jews had, at the very least, supported
the conquest of the enemy city. That dating is very late. Of course, it is not the latest.
Only to satisfy one's curiosity, it must be mentioned that van Gilse opts for dating
these chapters in the second *post*-Christian century (more specifically, to A.D. 119;
see 186).

Ludwig has put forth a new theory: maybe all the city songs are references to
Jerusalem, though this would not mean that the background for all of them would
have been the same event. On the one hand, he reaches no final conclusion about
whether 24:8-12 and 17:10-11 refer to the conquest of Jerusalem by Nebuchadnezzar
(587) or by Antiochus Epiphanes (168/167) (64, 74f.). On the other hand, he thinks
that 25:1-5 and 26:1-6 refer to Jerusalem's conquest of the Syrian fortification Acra,
led by the Maccabean Simon, in 141 (or: 142)—which Procksch had already suggested in connection with 26:1 (in favor of this view, one might note the reference to
the festive entry by the Jews into the recaptured city of Jerusalem after the city had
fallen and the vocable קריה, "city," which is supposed to be a play on the word
"Acra").

These are not all of the suggested solutions; new ones will continue to
crop up and old ones will be pulled out of the files once again. Those which
have been cited, as examples, show how, over and over again, scholars have
maintained tenaciously that one could date the apocalypse on the basis of the

461

downfall of a city. But, in light of the analysis set forth above, that approach will obviously be unproductive for arriving at the right answer. There is no way one can presume that the same situation provides the background for all the city songs. In light of these difficulties, it would seem necessary that one should give up every attempt to clarify the historical background. Delitzsch once offered the opinion: "All attempts to historicize will fail, since everything which seems to be set within a historical context serves only as an eschatological emblem . . . its base of operations in on the other side of all the history which has happened until now." The "failure" is apparent, but that does not mean that the question about the historical background is not worth pursuing, even when one cannot answer all the questions satisfactorily. That is because the message in these passages is not in the realm of what is "on the other side of all history which has happened until now." Yet it is true that proclamations of this type can easily be reapplied to new situations and the aspects that are timeless and typical are more important than those that refer to a specific situation, one that cannot be repeated.

This being true, one can understand why recent scholars (Fohrer, Plöger, Kaiser) make no attempt to identify the situation exactly. One will have to review each specific block of material to see if one cannot at least offer some informed guesses. Already at the very beginning, however, one can say the following: one should certainly reject the late dates suggested by Duhm (107 B.C.), Ludwig (141 B.C.), and Procksch (146 B.C.), but also those of Mulder (93) (just before 270 B.C.), Plöger (77) (who concludes: "Hence, the century of Ptolemaic rule may be suggested as the general period and more specifically the latter part of this period"), and Kaiser (who fixes the time period between 167 and 164 as a terminus ad quem for the latest material).

In expressing opposition to all these late dates, according to our present conceptual framework, it is most difficult to presume that the book of Isaiah, even if one ignores the relatively unimportant glosses, would not have achieved its present form already before the year 200 B.C. (see above, p. 273). The book of Daniel, which came into being about 164, is not even considered to be a prophetic writing. Neither the texts found at Qumran nor the Septuagint give any indication that chaps. 24–27 were missing in their version of the book that carries the name of Isaiah. No other substantive portion of the book of Isaiah offers any reason to believe that it came into existence later than 300, not even the material in 19:16-25, which is undoubtedly late. At most, 200 B.C. would be the latest terminus ad quem for the last additions, with the terminus a quo for the earliest sections certainly at the time very soon after Deutero-Isaiah. In order to seek to verify these assumptions, and at least to attempt to narrow this broad period of time somewhat, three approaches are possible: to examine the way the words are used, to examine the eschatological concepts (which would mean how close or far they are from apocalyptic thinking), and to examine the way in which earlier written passages from the OT are reused.

1. Word usage: Lindblom (111ff.) devoted a special section in his

study of the Isaiah apocalypse to language usage. He concluded that there is
a close connection between the language in these four chapters and the rest
of the book of Isaiah. The only way to explain this would be "that the author
of the cantata had become so absorbed in the style and language usage in the
book of Isaiah that one could say that the cantata actually imitates it. There
is no way for us to determine whether this imitation was done consciously
and on purpose or whether it happened completely spontaneously" (115).
Indeed, he can cite a significant number of vocables that occur elsewhere
only (or almost only) in the rest of the book of Isaiah or are among the words
frequently chosen in this book, in fact, in Proto-Isaiah and yet also in
Deutero-Isaiah. According to Lindblom (116), links in vocabulary usage are
found everywhere except in chaps. 36–39; except for this material, the author
of the apocalypse would have to have had Proto-, Deutero-, and Trito-Isaiah
all in front of him already. Like Lindblom, Mulder also spent time specifically studying the vocabulary usage and style in the apocalypse (67–77). His
conclusions match those of Lindblom, except that he also thinks that the
author knew chaps. 36–39 as well.

One can be thankful to Mulder for assembling all the hapax legomena (72),
namely: אמן (trustworthy), 25:1; אכפה (confining), 24:22; ארבות (in moving), 25:11;
the plural ארים (the east), 24:15; גר (lime), 27:9; חרה (disappear completely), 24:6; לוט
(mask), 25:7; מדמנה (dung pit), 25:10; ממחים (rich foods), 25:6; מתבן (straw), 25:10;
נסך (covering), 25:7; נפל (in the sense of "be born"), 26:18, 19; סאסאה (driving away),
27:8; עקלתון (twisting), 27:1; צות (set on fire), 27:4; פשע (go charging), 27:4; רזי (be
done for), 24:16; שאיה (desolation), 24:12.

In those passages that we have suggested belonged to the original block of
material, only four of these vocables are used: ארים (the east) (note, however, that Isaiah uses this in the singular אור, "fire," in 31:9; the other occurrences are in Deutero-
Isaiah); נפל (fall) (Isaiah is naturally familiar with the normal way in which the word
is used); חרה (disappear completely). There is no reason to assume that any of these
three appears first in the late postexilic era. That point could be made only with reference to the fourth, רזי (be done for), if indeed this word is to be treated as a derived
form of the Aramaic (actually Middle Persian) word רז, "secret." But it should probably be connected with the root רזה (waste away), which also was known to Isaiah.
Beyond this, however, not a single one of the hapax legomena cited by Mulder would
give any proof that this material has to be dated to the very latest of the suggested
time periods; the Hebrew that is used in the Qumran writings is very different from
this; in fact, one would have to say that Job, Ecclesiastes, and the books of Chronicles all speak a very different language. In 24:19 one does come across רעע II (bursting), which is an Aramaic word, instead of the proper Hebrew word רצץ (BDB:
crush), but רעע (burst, break) is used already in the preexilic Psalm 2 (v. 9). Typical
Aramaic words, to say nothing of loanwords from Greek (as can be found in the book
of Daniel), are not to be found in the Hebrew of the Isaiah apocalypse. Endings that
follow Aramaic patterns, such as חבי instead of חבי (hide yourself), in 26:20 (חבי is not
to be analyzed as an imperative feminine singular or something similar, as suggested
by Ges-K §75qq and *HAL*, but was simply pointed by the Masoretes following Aramaic patterns; cf. the preceding imperatives לך, "go," and סגר, "close"; this is correctly explained in Ges-Buhl; see also Marti); and ממחים (rich foods), in 25:6, can be

found already in Deutero-Isaiah, as is also true of the particles לָמוֹ (them) (26:14, 16), בַּל (not) (26:10, 11, 14, 18), and כְּמוֹ (as) (26:17).

The results of the statistical study of the vocabulary are clear and cannot be refuted: the language used in the apocalypse belongs in the Persian epoch and generally fits better into the earlier rather than the later part of the Persian era. Lindblom's assessment is not specific enough, since he does not differentiate between the various layers, but one ought to pay attention to his conclusion, even if one does not accept his solution to the question about where the city songs are to be assigned historically, namely, that the results of the vocabulary study would in no way conflict with his thesis that the downfall of the city refers to the conquest of Babylon by Xerxes in 485.

2. The eschatological concepts: One of the chief problems that must be dealt with in any exegesis of Isaiah 24–27 is whether the eschatological concepts used in these chapters are still in tune with the postexilic prophets or whether they are already to be treated as apocalyptic. The dissension within scholarly ranks is uncomfortably obvious concerning this issue as well. Duhm asserts vehemently: "The oracle is an apocalypse through and through; one will not go wrong in using the Sibylline Oracles, Daniel, Enoch, and the like in seeking to explain it," or: Isaiah "just as easily [could] have written the book of Daniel as this material." On the other side, to cite just one example, Fohrer is just as apodictic, explaining that it has been known for a long time already "that there are no characteristics of apocalyptic here." But Lindblom (7) also stresses that he was using the term "apocalyptic" here only because it has become so entrenched within scholarly circles, and Rudolph (59) thinks that one must speak about an Isaiah apocalypse only with great caution, though he goes on to say that one certainly hears echoes of various apocalyptic motifs (24:22; 27:1, 13; similarly, Plöger, 77).

In order to bring clarity to this issue, it is also important to take note of the form-historical indicators commonly found in the apocalypse genre. Koch (23ff.) has worked extensively on this point: great cycles of speeches, the apocalyptic speaker is emotionally very upset, paranetic speeches, pseudonymity, richly symbolic mythical figures, having the character of a composition. As far as this list concerns chaps. 24–27, it would seem that the last indicator comes closest. But that is the extent of it. These chapters do not present themselves as a pseudonymous, but rather—just as is the case for passages such as those in the Deutero-Isaianic section of the book of Isaiah—as an anonymous production. It is true that there are mythical concepts here, but these are not in the baroque or grotesque style found in actual apocalypses. The other identifying features are simply not there at all.

If one applies Koch's categories to chaps. 24–27, the conclusion is unavoidable: this is not an apocalypse. Evaluated on the basis of its form, this body of material is far removed from the book of Daniel.

However, now to the individual apocalyptic motifs: Plöger (77) identifies the concept of a world judgment, taking the form of a universal-cosmological event, as an apocalyptic motif and points to the resurrection of the dead as an identifying mark which shows that the eschatological turning point has been reached. One can look at some others as well: not only the earth but even the heights of heaven disintegrate (24:4); the host of the heights are called to account and are imprisoned also, along with the kings of the earth (24:21f.); the battle against chaos becomes an eschatological theme (27:1); the large horns are blown (27:13). Admittedly, these are motifs that receive extensive treatment in apocalyptic; however, if one sets aside the discussion about the resurrection of the dead (the mention of which has caused some to arrive at an impossibly late dating, whereas others treat the mention of these topics as very late insertions), then these topics expand on ideas that one finds discussed in prophetic contexts as well (for the specifics, see the commentary on each passage). This is most clear in the passages such as Isaiah 13; 21; 33f., but it is also noted in the messages about Moab in chaps. 15, 16, and in both Deutero- and Trito-Isaiah. There is, however, *one* point where a basic formal distinction has been noted above: no longer is there a mention of a specific world power; neither are we informed about which other power this God-hating nation (or, as the case may be: this "city") has destroyed. Yahweh *alone* is the one who carries out the judgment; he no longer needs an earthly tool. Nevertheless, some essential factors that are part of the worldview and conceptual models in actual apocalyptic materials are missing here: the differentiation between העולם הזה (this world) and העולם הבא (the world to come); those which discuss the ages of the world; a Satan figure who is the personification of evil; an actual angelology (if one does not consider the "host of the heights" to fit this criterion); visions, with the key to their interpretation being allegorical; an assessment about when the end will come or even simply speculations that use numbers, a son of man or messiah figure; and finally, there is nothing of the esoteric here, as is typical in apocalyptic. Thus one might offer this judgment: the so-called Isaiah apocalypse is probably farther removed from apocalyptic than is Proto-Zechariah.

3. The dependent relationship with earlier writings: One of the most surprising things about preexilic prophecy is that those who were at work during that era hardly ever referred to one another. There are no direct quotations from one another, and though it is clear, for example, that Jeremiah and Hosea are "related," it is not even possible to be sure that Jeremiah knew of Hosea. By contrast, Zech. 1:4 mentions specifically the preaching of the נביאים ראשונים (former prophets). As has been stated already, the authors of Isaiah 24–27 must have been familiar with the other parts of the book of Isaiah, and with other prophetic books as well, and must have spoken their language. The exegesis of the individual passages will point out these connections in detail.

Just to cite a few examples that jump out as one reads this material:
The parable of the vineyard, 27:2-5, without any doubt whatsoever, assumes that Isaiah 5:2-7 is known; in fact, it purposely seems to take the completely opposite point of view.

24:13 apparently intends to say that the prophecy in 17:6 has now been ful-filled.

Concerning 24:16: בגדים בגדו ובגד בוגדים בגדו (cunning ones deal cunningly, in cunning the cunning ones act cunningly), see 21:2b: הבוגד בוגד והשודד שודד (with cunning the cunning one acts, and the devastator devastates); cf. also 33:1 and 48:8.

Concerning 24:2aα: והיה כעם ככהן ([and] the same thing happens to the priest as to the people), see Hos. 4:9a: והיה כעם ככהן (and the same thing happens to the priest as to the people).

Concerning 24:17: פחד ופחת ופח עליך יושב הארץ (horror and hole and hold-ing, that is for you, inhabitant of the earth), see Jer. 48:43: פחד ופחת ופח עליך יושב מואב (horror and hole and holding, that is for you, inhabitant of Moab); cf. also Isa. 24:18 with Jer. 48:44.

Concerning 24:20bβ: ונפלה ולא־תסיף קום (and it falls—it will never stand up again), see Amos 5:2aα: נפלה לא־תוסיף קום (it falls—it will never stand up again).

Concerning 24:23b: מלך יהוה צבאות בהר ציון (for Yahweh of Hosts will have become king on Mount Zion), see Mic. 4:7: ומלך יהוה עליהם בהר ציון (for Yahweh will have become king over them on Mount Zion).

Concerning 26:21a: כי־הנה יהוה יצא ממקומו (for behold, Yahweh moves out from his dwelling places), see Mic. 1:3a: כי־הנה יהוה יצא ממקומו (for behold, Yahweh moves out from his dwelling places).

A comprehensive study no doubt would verify that the authors of Isa-iah 24–27 were very familiar with the prophetic writings of the preexilic, exilic, and early postexilic eras. One already notes here the type of scholarly research efforts that characterized the apocalypticists.

It also has been noted frequently that parts of the apocalypse also seem to presume a knowledge of P: 24:5 speaks about how the peoples have broken a ברית עולם (eternal covenant). This is almost certainly a reference to the Noachian covenant in Gen. 9:16. Isa. 24:18: ארבות ממרום נפתחו (truly, the windows in the heights open themselves wide) reminds one of Gen. 7:11: וארבת השמים נפתחו and the windows of the heavens were opened). Isa. 24:23bβ reminds one of Exod. 24:9f. However, that does not mean that these passages have to be dated later than the priestly writing, which first would have been promulgated shortly after the year 400, since the time when it came into exis-tence and the time when it was publicly put in force need not be coterminous and there is no doubt that some of the material in P has a lengthy prehistory; for more, one is referred to the exegesis of the individual passages that have been mentioned, which will show that the links with P are clearly not as cer-tain as some suggest.

When one takes all the results from the three types of questions that have been addressed into account, on the one hand it seems even more cer-tain that one should accept the conclusion that the chapters did not come into existence initially in the second, but—except for later additions—also not initially in the third pre-Christian century. On the other hand, the exilic era does not come up for consideration either, nor do the first decades of the postexilic epoch. At the very least, however, the original body of material came into existence quite possibly—and this is said with great caution—in the fifth century B.C., indeed, more probably in the first rather than the second half. It is possible that the two city songs, at the beginning of chaps. 25 and 26, might be older. The other layers would have to be dated somewhat later. A careful study of 27:6-11 (see below, p. 590) will demonstrate how that section probably anticipates the conquest of Samaria. It belongs possibly in the general period of Nehemiah, but it is also possible that it came into existence first during the early Ptolemaic era. But that would be one of the latest additions. This means that the so-called Isaiah apocalypse developed during various phases between the years 500 and 300—we might possibly say: between the years 500 and 400.

The Judgment on the Earth

Literature

J. deGroot, "Alternatieflezingen in Jesaja 24," *NThS* 22 (1939) 153–158. J. C. M. Neves, "A Teologia da Tradução Grega dos Setenta no Libro de Isaías" (on chap. 24), diss., Lisbon (1973) (not available to me).

[**Literature update through 1979:** J. P. Floss, "Die Wortstellung des Konjugationssystems in Jes 24," FS G. J. Botterweck (1977) 227–244.]

Text

24:1 Behold, Yahweh ravages[a] the earth[b]
and devastates[a] it,
disfigures[c] its face
and scatters its inhabitants.
2 Then the same thing happens to the priest as[a] to (the man from among) the people,
to the servant as[a] to his master,[b]
to the maid as[a] to her mistress,
to the buyer as[a] to the merchant,
[c]to the one who loans as[a] to the one who has to borrow,[c]
to the debtor as[a] to his creditor.[d]
3 The earth will be ravaged completely,[a]
plundered completely, until there is nothing left to plunder.
* * * *

For it is Yahweh who [b]has spoken this message[b]:
4 It is withered, the earth is wilted,[a]
[b]it is disintegrated,[b] the world [b]is wilted,[b]
[c]it is 'disintegrated,' that which is above, 'together with'[c] the earth,
5 for the earth is desecrated beneath[a] its inhabitants,
[b]for indeed they have transgressed the laws, stepped over[c] the bounds of the commandment,[b]
broken the eternal covenant.
6 For this reason a curse has consumed[a] the earth,
those who live on it must suffer the consequences.[b]
For this reason the inhabitants of the earth disappear[c] completely,
and what is left of human beings, that is quickly counted.

468

* * * *

[7 The wine (branch) is wilted,
   [a]the grape tendrils have disintegrated,[a]
   everyone groans, each one who used to have a happy[b] heart.
 8 [a]The jubilant sound of the kettledrums is silenced,
    the (festive) noise of those who are celebrating is stilled,
    the jubilant sound of the zithers is silenced.[a]
 9 No one drinks wine any longer with songs,
    the drunken drinking of the heavy drinkers leaves a bitter
    taste.[a]]

* * * *

[10 The [a]nothing city[a] is destroyed,
    every house is closed; no one comes on in.
 11 [a]Lamenting about the wine (rings out) in the side streets,[a]
    all joy is vanished,[b]
    [c]the jubilation of the earth[d] has moved out.[c]
 12 Only devastation still remains in the city;
    the smashed gate lies there in (complete) desolation.[a]]

* * * *

[13 Truly, thus will it be[a] [b]on the earth[b]
    [b]in the midst of the peoples of the world[b]:
    as when one knocks off olives,
    [c]as when one goes gleaning,[c]
    when the wine harvest has come to an end.]

1a and a The range of meaning for the verbs בקק (ravage) and בלק (devastate) is quite similar: KBL and *HAL* assign the meaning "ravage" to both. The Gk translates בוקק as καταφθείρει (he destroys, brings to naught) and בולקה as ἐρημώσει αὐτήν (he will strip it bare, lay it waste). G. R. Driver (*JTS* 38 [1937] 41f.) suggests that both בקק and בלק are derivatives of the same biradical root בק. He believes it is possible to translate these lines: "Behold! Yahweh doth crack the earth and doth cleave it." But according to Ibn Ezra, בקק means "empty out" in this passage, and Gesenius treats it in much the same way, assigning to it the basic meaning "open up, pour out" (cf. בקבוק, "flask, bottle"). Delitzsch explains that when בקק is used, it is because that is "the natural sound which is made as the fluid gradually drains out"; cf. Arabic *baqbaqa*, "bubble, chatter, coo," which means "gurgle" (water) in Palestinian Arabic. Still today some exegetes translate it as "empty" or "empty out." However, both parallelism and the other instances where the verb is used make this highly unlikely. *HAL* compares it with Arabic *bāqa(w)*, "mishandle," and relates the use of בקק to a root בוק* (Maltese: *bewwaq*, "hollow out"; see J. Aquilina, *JSS* 3 [1958] 65); the substantive בוקה in Nah. 2:11 means "waste, void."

The meaning of בלק is not completely certain either. The substantive מבלקה in Nah. 2:11 seems to mean something such as "ravaging, devastation." However, Syr translates בולקה as *mtrˁ lh*, "he opens it," and *HAL* refers both to Arabic *balaqa*, "open and close" (a door) and to Old South Arabic *blq*, "opening." However, that information does not help to make sense of it. Driver may be right when he postulates that both verbs are somehow connected with the biradical root בק*. The two verbs would have been used together for reasons of alliteration.

1b Qᵃ reads אדמה (ground) for ארץ (earth); see Kutscher, 216.

1c One wonders whether the *piˁel* עוה is to be read in its concrete ("turn back") or its transferred ("disfigure") sense. Depending on how one solves that question, פניה will be translated either "surface" or "face" (see the translations). Ehrlich's suggestion (*Randglossen* IV, 83) to read שָׁוֶה (smooth, level) instead of עוה (turn back or disfigure) is just as unlikely as that of Hitzig, who wants to alter עוה to read שִׁנָּה (he changed); at least he can find support for this in the clause שִׁנָּה פָנָיו (change their countenance) in Job 14:20.

2a Verse 2 announces that the traditional sociological structures will be leveled out, using, in fact, six pairs of opposites. As often elsewhere (see BrSynt §109d), the particle of comparison כ precedes both the subject and predicate here, which means that at times it is hard to know which one is the subject. In the text we are studying, the subject precedes the predicate in the first pairs of words: the priest will be the same as a man from among the people, the master as his servant, the mistress as her maid. The first part of v. 2b would seem to follow the same pattern: the one who is still in a position to sell something will be the same as the one who (in time of need) has to make a purchase. With the last two pairs, however, it is clear that the comparison goes in the other direction: whoever has to borrow will be the same as the one who can make a loan, and the one who has incurred a debt will be the same as his creditor. Those two examples show how the first part of the line is to be interpreted: the one who is forced to sell something will be the same as the one who has enough means to be able to make a purchase.

2b Auvray suggests reading כַאדֹנוֹ (as his master) instead of כַאדֹנָיו (as his masters), but the plural suffix is also used elsewhere with אָדוֹן (lord, master); cf. אֲדֹנִים קָשֶׁה (lit.: harsh overlords) in 19:4 or בְעָלָיו (lit.: his owners) in 1:3; on this, see BrSynt §19c; and Joüon, *Gr* §136d.

2c–c Procksch agrees with Sievers (see also deGroot, 156; and *BHS*) and removes כַמַלְוֶה כַלֹּוֶה (to the one who loans as to the one who has to borrow) as a variant of what follows, based on metrical considerations, but v. 2a also has three parts, and a certain overabundance of comparisons is no doubt intended.

2d Duhm and Marti suggest reading נֹשֶׁה instead of נֹשֵׁא (both: lend, be a creditor). Admittedly, it is surprising that the spelling with א would follow right after the spelling כַנֹּשֶׁה. However, Qᵃ also spells it כנושא; on this, see Arabic *nasaʾa*, "delay of payment, grant (more) credit."

3a According to Bauer-Leander §58p' (see also Duhm and Marti), the unusual pointing of the *niphꜥal* imperfect was chosen in analogy to the pattern used in the ע″וי verbs and because it sounded just like the infinitives הבוז (plunder) and הבוק (ravage).

3b–b It is possible that the accusative אֶת־הַדָּבָר הַזֶּה (this message) is not part of the original (thus Procksch, *BHS;* but see below, p. 473); however, one ought not try to make a case for this on the basis of the meter.

4a Once again, because of the meter, Procksch suggests removing the first נָבְלָה (wilted), and deGroot (156) also considers possible alternate readings here. But the way אָבַל (withered) is supplemented by נָבֵל (wilted) is the same here as the way בָּקַק (ravages) was supplemented by בָּלַק (devastates) in v. 1; this is part of the style of writing used by the author. If נָבְלָה (wilted) is missing in the Gk, that is simply because the translator did not have three different verbs available that had roughly the same meaning (which is a problem in modern languages as well; אֻמְלַל is translated with "disintegrate" only as a last resort).

4b–b On the one hand, Schlögl suggests removing נָבְלָה (is wilted); on the other hand, Procksch thinks that אֻמְלְלָה (it is disintegrated) is too long for the meter.

4c–c Qᵃ, Syr, Vulg, and one Hebrew MS read the singular אֻמְלַל (it is disintegrated), which is what one would expect with the substantive מָרוֹם (that which is above).

As the text stands now, one would have to take עַם (people) as the subject (which certainly can be used with a plural form of the verb), with מרום functioning as an adverbial accusative: "In the heights, the people of the earth wilt," but that is impossible. The Gk reads οἱ ὑψηλοὶ τῆς γῆς (the lofty of the earth) and Syr: *dlʾ rwmh dʾrᶜʾ* (which are not the lofty ones of the earth), which suggested to S. Talmon (*Textus* 4 [1964] 118f.) that עם functioned as some sort of parallel to מרום (above) (in Qᵃ עם is inserted as if the copyist missed it the first time). But עם would be a very poor parallel to מרום (that which is above). It would be better to read עם as עִם (with) and הַמָּרֹום (that which is above) instead of מרום (above). One ought not object to אמלל (it is disintegrated) being used twice (contra Gray, who considers that the line, as it now reads, has a "serious corruption"). Thus it should be translated: "It is disintegrated, that which is above, together with the earth."

5a The Gk translates תחת (beneath) as διά (on account of), though Sym reads ὑπό (from under); תחת is certainly correct; the earth has to carry the burden of its inhabitants.

5b–b Some commentators think that v. 5 seems to be too long. Thus *BHS* suggests removing עברו תורת חלפו חק (for they have indeed transgressed the laws, stepped over the bounds of the commandment) (cf. Schlögl and Procksch). But here we have another example of a verse with three parts. In an impressive way, this verse gradually becomes more and more inclusive. First the individual תורת (laws) are mentioned, then the חק (commandment) itself, and finally the ברית (covenant), to which the חק (commandment) belongs.

5c It is striking that חלף (stepped over) plus accusative is used parallel to עבר (transgressed). Otherwise, when the verb is used in the *qal,* it means "travel on by," or something similar, and is not furnished with an accusative object. For this reason, KBL and *HAL* read the *piᶜel* חלפו (they have altered), followed by Kaiser. But the suggested translation "alter" is even more strange as a parallel to עבר (transgress) than it would be if one posited, for the *qal,* a meaning something such as "ignore something" or "disregard something." In Hab. 1:11 חלף (transgress) and עבר (become guilty) also are parallel and can certainly be treated as synonyms.

6a Syr and some Hebrew MSS read אבלה (mourns) (see Gesenius). It is Ehrlich's opinion that v. 6aα is "decidedly non-Hebraic"; he alters על־כן אלה אכלה (for this reason a curse has consumed) to read על כָּל־אֵלֶּה אָבְלָה, "on account of all this the land goes bad." But the idea that the curse "consumes" is not all that foreign to Hebrew thought patterns.

6b Qᵃ reads וישמו instead of ויאשמו. Even earlier, Ehrlich had suggested reading יָשַׁמּוּ (they were desolated, appalled). But the reason for this particular way of writing, as in other passages in the Qumran MSS as well, may be because the א had become silent; on this, see Kutscher, 292.

6c There are problems with understanding what חרו means. The root meaning of the word is "be hot, glow." The Zürcher Bibel still follows this by translating it "consumed by glowing heat," but the OT uses the verb elsewhere only in the transferred meaning ("be angry with"), and "be hot" is still very different from "consumed by glowing heat." Qᵃ has the reading חורו, "they are pale" (see 19:9); but, in light of what follows, this meaning is not strong enough. G. R. Driver (BZAW 77 [1958] 44) makes use of the Gk: ἐκτρυχωθήσονται, "be thoroughly exhausted," and posits that this might suggest that there was an original Hebrew word חרו (root: חור), which, in light of Arabic *ḥāra(w),* would mean "be weak" or "be emaciated." KBL suggests a root חרה II, which is to be linked with Arabic *ḥarā(y),* meaning "take away, remove"; and *HAL* agrees, finding support in the Old South Arabic *ḥry* ("injury"); see also G. R. Driver (*JTS* 2 [1951] 26). That suggestion is probably correct, meaning that one can translate this as "they disappear completely"—an excellent parallel to v. 6bβ: ונשאר אנוש מזער (and what is left of human beings, that is quickly counted).

7a–a Schlögl considers אמללה־גפן (the wine [branch] is wilted) to be an explanatory gloss. If he is right, then a whole host of parallel terms will have to be removed from the OT as glosses!

7b Instead of שמחי (happy of), Qᵃ reads שומחי (the rejoicers of), which is a form constructed by analogy, following the pattern of the participle of transitive verbs; see Kutscher, 340f.

8a–a Within v. 8, deGroot (156) thinks he can identify three alternative readings; this is certainly not acceptable. In addition, he believes that vv. 8aα, 8b, 11bβ should be inserted before v. 8aβ (cf. also *BHS*). But this rearrangement is not likely either. The three parts of v. 8 speak about how musical instruments fall silent; v. 11b speaks about how the jubilation of the earth falls silent.

9a Instead of ימר (leave a bitter taste), Qᵃ reads וימר (and . . . leaves a bitter taste); see Kutscher, 416. One frequently notes a tendency in Qᵃ to link sentences into series.

10a For קרית־תהו (nothing city), the Gk reads πᾶσα πόλις (every city), intimating that this announcement of judgment applies far and wide.

11a–a F. Hitzig (*ZWT* 18 [1875] 201f.) suggested that one read צוחה עלה בין החוצות (laments will be raised in the side streets); he thinks that it would be obvious, in the midst of a completely devastated city, that there were more important things to worry about than wine. But this type of objection misses the point; these descriptions make use of traditional phraseology.

11b The reading ערבה has been challenged. It must be from ערב IV, "become evening" (cf. Akkadian *erēbu*, "enter in, go down"). Houbigant has suggested reading עָבְרָה (passes by). Some act as if they leave the text as is, but still translate it as "disappear, vanish," or something similar. The Gk reads πέπαυται (has ceased, stopped); Targ: שלימה (be at an end); Syr: *bṭlt* (has ceased); Vulg: *deserta est* (is deserted); thus it would seem that one has to presume that it originally read עברה (pass away).

11c–c See above, textual note 8a–a.

11d הארץ (the earth) is missing in Gkᴮ.

12a Some problems are created by the transmitted text. שאיה is a hapax legomenon; there is no reason why it should not derive from שאה I, "be devastated." But the construction is also difficult to figure out. שאיה (desolation) is probably a *casus pendens*, so that it should be translated, literally: "As for how that relates to desolation—the gate is smashed." One should not even bother with some suggested alterations, such as that of Ehrlich, who reads תושיה (BDB: sound, efficient wisdom, abiding success) instead of שאיה (desolation), and then reads this half verse: "And one will strike down comfort at the city gate."

13a There is no doubt that the subject of יהיה (will be) is the indefinite "it," not Israel (as suggested by Ehrlich, who wonders as well whether it should be read יהיו, ("they will be").

13b–b Once more, בתוך העמים (here: in the midst of the peoples of the world) and בקרב הארץ (here: on the earth) are not alternative readings (deGroot, 157) but parallel terms; the only problem is with the translation, since we do not have two different vocables to translate "midst."

13c–c *BHS* suggests that one should read כעולל עוללות (as when the gleaner goes gleaning) here, with reference to Jer. 6:9. This reading does provide a better parallel for כנקף זית (as when one knocks off olives), and it is immediately clear that v. 13b has three parts; otherwise, there would be problems with the meter.

Form

As has been explained already, vv. 1-6 belong to the original body of material in the apocalypse, whereas both vv. 7-9 and vv. 10-12 are later additions, and v. 13 is probably also. The structure is clear: introduced by הִנֵּה (behold), vv. 1-3a are an announcement of punishment in which the author himself speaks. Even though the first person "I" of Yahweh is not explicitly included, vv. 4-6 are to be treated as a message from Yahweh, introduced by v. 3b, which serves to give the announcement of punishment its authority and furnishes the reason for it.

Meter: Verse 1a can probably be treated as a five-stress colon (הִנֵּה, "behold," is not considered part of the metrical structure, and וּבֹלְקָהּ, "devastates it," receives two stresses).

Verse 1b: two-stress + two-stress bicolon.

Verse 2a: 3 + 2 + 2 (כַּאֲשֶׁר, "as," should be read without a stress; perhaps the text originally read כַּנֹּשֶׁה בּוֹ כַּנֹּשֶׁא, "to the debtor as to his creditor").

Verse 3a: a five-stress colon.

Verse 3b: the same as v. 3a (unless it is a two-stress + two-stress bicolon, with no stress on כִּי, "for").

In v. 4 one has a verse with three parts once again: 3 + 3 + 3 (disagreeing with the textual arrangement in *BHS*, but following *BHK*); the same is true for v. 5: 4 + 4 + 3 (once again, with *BHK*, against *BHS*).

In v. 6 the text should probably be read as having 2 seven-stress cola.

Verse 7, once again, has three parts: 2 + 2 + 2 (כֹּל, "each one," is possibly a secondary expansion; שִׂמְחֵי־לֵב, "having a happy heart," has one stress only).

Verse 8: 3 + 3 + 3 (against both *BHK* and *BHS*).

Verses 9 and 10: three-stress + three-stress bicola (לֹא, "no one," receives a stress; יִשְׁתּוּ־יָיִן, "drinks wine," once again has just one stress).

Verse 11 also has three parts (3 + 3 + 3); one should note the different way this verse is printed in *BHK* versus *BHS*.

Verse 12: this is most likely a five-stress colon (יֻכַּת־שָׁעַר, "smashed gate," has just one stress).

Verse 13a: 3 + 3 + 3; v. 13b: 2 + 2 + 2 (כְּעוֹלֵלֹת, "as one who goes gleaning," has two stresses).

It is to be noted—both here and in many passages in the rest of the apocalypse—that many verses have three parts (as also in chaps. 23 and 21). In this section, they are used where there is a transition, with the focus shifting from the announcement of judgment to an expansive, sweeping depiction of what will happen. As one comments on the material, it is important to recognize that the longest part of any verse is in v. 5, where what has been done wrong is being discussed, explaining the reason for the great catastrophe that was to come on the earth. The closing two lines in v. 13, also having three parts each, give sufficient authority to this addition, which closes the section. Attempts by some exegetes to eliminate these three-part verses by manipulating the text, so that a regular metrical structure can be attained, have led the study of the text down a wrong path.

There is no question, and the observation has often been made, that the blocks of material in the apocalypse lack the pliability, the aptness, and the precision found in what Isaiah himself says. The frequent repetition of the same verb, or of those which are closely related, or of those which sound very similar, is a distraction for the modern reader. But one ought not simply apply our personal discomfort as a measuring stick. The author tries to find his own way to stress the importance of his message and is very competent in the way he uses the stylistic technique that was available to him. He loves alliteration; see v. 4: אֻמְלְלוּ מְרוֹם עַם־הָאָרֶץ אֻמְלְלָה תֵבֵל נָבְלָה אֻמְלְלָה הָאָרֶץ נָבְלָה אָבְלָה or v. 6: אֵלָה אָכְלָה אֶרֶץ. He also likes to use expressions that are very similar to one another: v. 1: בקק (ravage) and בלק (devastate); v. 4: אבל (withered), נבל (wilted), and אמלל (disintegrated), and then follows this by repeating נבל (wilted) and אמלל (disintegrated). The expander who composes v. 8 repeats שבת (silence), varying this by using חדל (still). One should also note the constructions such as הבוק תבוק (will be completely ravaged) and הבוז תבוז (completely plundered) (v. 3a). The authors show that they have engaged in scholarly study when they use rare expressions, such as בקק (ravage) and בלק (devastate) or שׁאיה (desolation), and are not shy about using daring renderings such as כנשה כ(אשר) נשׁא בו (to the debtor as to his creditor) or שׁאיה יכת־שׁער (the smashed gate lies there in complete desolation). This results in a style that seems to us to be a bit forced at times.

Setting

Concerning the time when this was written, see above, pp. 460f.

Commentary
[24:1-3a] *The Complete Devastation of the Earth*

[24:1] This section starts out in the middle of the story, and begins with the announcement that the entire earth will be completely devastated, and it does not matter much whether one agrees that בקק means "empty completely"; see above, textual note 1a. In v. 3 the verb בקק (plunder) parallels בזז (here: ravage). The devastation follows after everything has been plundered.

One should note that participles follow after the introductory word הנה (behold): Yahweh is about the business of setting the worldwide judgment in motion. One can be sure that these events are still in the future because the participles are then followed by perfect consecutives (one does not look back into the past, as one does in the "city songs"). Thus it is certainly anticipated that it will come very soon, but the exact time is not known, which means that this author does not function like those who compose the apocalypses, who can virtually take out their watches in order to tell the exact time when everything will begin to fall apart.

הנה (behold), followed by God as the subject, and then continuing with a participle, is used surprisingly often in the book of Isaiah: 3:1; 8:7; 10:33; 19:1; 22:17; 26:21 = Mic. 1:3; beyond these, it is found in the OT only in Gen. 28:13; 1 Kings 19:11; 2 Kings 7:19; Amos 6:11; 2 Chron. 21:14. This means that more than half of all the passages are in the first part of the book of Isaiah. Those who argue for the Isaianic authorship often use this fact as

474

support that, in their opinion, carries great weight when they argue in favor of chaps. 24–27 being from Isaiah. But the reason for this usage can be explained by noting that this is simply one more indication that the apocalypse generally demonstrates a dependence on the ideas found in the rest of the book of Isaiah.

Both verbs, בקק (ravage) and בלק (devastate), are probably used here after being gleaned from Nah. 2:11 (cf. also בקק, "ravage," in Nah. 2:3; note, in addition, בזז, "plunder," in Nah. 2:10). In that passage, the object of the ravaging is the world-renowned city Nineveh, but here it is the entire earth.

It is not stated how or through whom Yahweh brings this judgment to completion. It is doubtful that it takes place at the hands of enemy powers, as in Nineveh; the author of vv. 1-6 seems to have some sort of a drought in mind. In v. 21 the host of the kings of the earth is accompanied by the "host of the heights in the heights," but one ought not try to interpret the text before us in light of that very late passage; besides, the only important point is that Yahweh is at work.

Verse 1bα states that the face of the earth will be disfigured (concerning this translation, see above, textual note 1c). That would fit in with what happens in floods, earthquakes, and drought. The *piᶜel* עוה (disfigure) occurs elsewhere only in Lam. 3:9: גָּדַר דְּרָכַי בְּגָזִית נְתִיבֹתַי עִוָּה; it means something such as: "He has blocked my ways with blocks of stone, has made my paths crooked" (cf. also Job 19:8). This motif thus seems to be rooted in songs of lament and is used in a situation in which the one who prays sees absolutely no way out of trouble. Thus, in the present passage, it would mean that the ravaging of the earth will make it impossible to travel around in it. Admittedly, this idea does not square exactly with the expression that follows, הפיץ ישביה, according to which the occupants of the earth are not going to perish in particular places and locales but, rather, are scattered about. One wonders whether, instead of reading הפיץ (scatters), one should rather read הפיץ, "crushed." But the motif that the inhabitants of a country are scattered is a traditional element in these types of depictions of disaster (Gen. 11:8f.; Lev. 26:33; Deut. 4:27; 28:64; Jer. 9:15; 30:11; Ps. 44:12, etc.). Of course, here it describes the inhabitants of the whole earth. In that light, this way of using the expression is unique. And just where are the inhabitants of the earth to be scattered? When this motif is applied to the new situation of a worldwide judgment, it no longer fits into the new setting. But one ought not try to press this description to the point that it would be expected to provide even minor details. According to v. 6, in fact, the inhabitants of the earth are not scattered, but are decimated.

[24:2] In v. 2 the author adds more information, speaking of a complete flattening out of all the previous distinctions between human beings. He first borrows from Hos. 4:9: "And it shall be like people, like priest." But then, this reminiscence is expanded by the word pairs servant/master, maid/mistress, buyer/merchant, loaner/borrower, debtor/creditor. At first, one might think that this pairing means that some sort of leveling out would take place

475

among social classes. It would seem that all the differences in importance and all the privileges that would have appertained thereunto would have gone by the wayside, authorities and positions of power would be discarded, and the kingdom of God would come, in which a perfect righteousness would finally become a reality. But that would hardly be much of an improvement if the population of human beings had been decimated so that scarcely any people remained. Thus some offer an interpretation of this passage based on 3:1ff.: the authorities will be put out of the way, young boys will become princes, and then, any facet of what one might know as orderly existence, necessary if one is to have שלום, "peace, welfare, success, prosperity, good fortune," would be lost as well; each person would distrust the other, indeed, each person would rise up in opposition to the other (see 3:5). But priests, masters, and mistresses are certainly not authorities, buyers, creditors, and debtors. In reality, this is simply intended as a way to say that high and low, well-to-do and poor, are all going to be caught in the same misery; every one of them will be just like the rest.

This motif is known far and wide. Thus one reads in the Admonitions of Ipu-wer: "It is really true: the insignificant now possess majestic things; the one who once could not even make a pair of sandals now has treasures. . . . It is really true: the important ones are filled with laments and the insignificant are filled with joy. . . . It is really so: the son of an important person cannot even be recognized any longer; the son of the woman of a house becomes the son of the woman who served him. . . . It is really so: those who built the pyramids have become field workers, and those who once were in the ship of god are now harnessed. . . . It is really so: the dead and living are just the same; the natives have become foreigners. It is really so: one has every hair fall out. The son of a man of importance cannot distinguish himself any longer from the one who is nothing. . . . It is really true: very high-ranking wives have it just the same as female slaves. Those who play music in the chambers in the middle of the houses sing their song to the music gods as laments, and those who tell wonderful stories sit on top of the millstones. It is really so: the servant women have power over their mouth, but yet, when their mistresses speak, it is annoying to them. . . . Look, . . . the one who never even slept on a couch now has a bed. Look, the rich sleep thirsty; the one who used to be concerned about every desire now has beer, enough even to waste some. Look, those who had clothes go about now in rags; the one who could not even weave for oneself a single thing now possesses the finest linen" (W. von Bissing, *Altägyptische Lebensweisheit* [1955] 130ff.; cf. also *ANET* 441ff.).

This is obviously no description of an apocalyptic scene but is just a depiction of a time when the traditional order has fallen apart. But in no way does that passage speak about a time when righteousness put everyone on the same level. It is possible that Isa. 24:2 comes from the description of a time of degeneracy.

In the Erra Epic IV, 7–11, one reads: "One who does not know weapons draws a sword; one who does not know arrows, his bow is full; one who does not know battle, he leads war; one who does not know strength(?) flies away from it like a bird; one who limps passes one who moves easily; the cripple overpowers the strong one" (see L. Cagni, *L'Epopea di Erra*, Studi Semitici 34 [1969] 104f.).

The Bahman Yašt is different, being clearly an apocalyptic writing, but it has a very similar description about the confusion within the fixed order of society: "those who are of lower standing marry the daughters of nobles, great ones, and priests, and the nobles, great ones, and priests sink into poverty and bondage. The misfortun(at)e of the common people will attain greatness and respect and the helpless and common person will get to the first place and have honor" (II, 38f.). "The most insignificant slaves strut in with the demeanor of the nobles" (II, 36; see A. von Gall, *ΒΑΣΙΛΕΙΑ ΤΟΥ ΘΕΟΥ* [1926] 130).

One might also compare this with the sentences from the Syriac Writing About Young Daniel 3:41-44: "And the son will be bitter toward his father, and he will say: You are not my father. And the servant will make himself an equal of his master. The maidservant will take a seat and the mistress will provide what is needed. The young boy will lie down (at table) before the old man" (quoted from H. Schmoldt, "Die Schrift 'vom jungen Daniel' . . . ," diss., Hamburg [1972] 42f.).

In this enumeration, the priests are listed first; unlike chap. 3, no political authorities are mentioned. That lack confirms that this section comes from the postexilic era, at which time the priestly group could carry out only spiritual (and, to some extent, also worldly) functions; this means that the only nobility which remained as a separate group, distinct from the people, was a priestly one. The list of those affected in the economic sphere is surprisingly all-encompassing. It betrays something about the structure of Israelite society at that time. The common citizen had no political power; it would seem that something like a gold aristocracy had developed. עבד and שפחה have traditionally been translated "servant" and "maid"; more correctly, these terms refer to male and female slaves. But עבד (servant) has a wide variety of meanings, since it simply designates anyone who has a master over him. By contrast, according to A. Jepsen, the word שפחה refers to the chaste, subjugated young girl, especially one who serves the woman of the house (*VT* 8 [1958] 293). גבירה (mistress) also seems to have a rather wide range of meanings; yet this word first of all refers apparently to the position held by the wife within the family and is thus a precise, complementary opposite term for שפחה (maid).

לוה, "loan, borrow," and נשה, "loan, borrow," would seem to be two words for the same activity, but נשה technically means loaning something in order to make a profit; cf. Exod. 22:24 and Ps. 109:11, where נשה (give credit) parallels בזז (plunder). Thus one is correct when seeking to translate נשה as "usurer" in that passage. By contrast, לוה is a very general term and can certainly refer to a loan offered because someone seeks the welfare of the person who is in need.

[24:3b-6] *The Downfall of the Earth and Its Cause*

[24:3b] The reasons for treating v. 3b as the introduction to what follows have been given already. To be sure, the announcement of judgment that follows is not constructed using the pattern of a direct speech of Yahweh; still, the author intends that the introduction will simply state that his announcement of judgment against the world "aims to draw upon the sphere of Yahweh's revelation" (so Plöger, 55).

[24:4] Verse 4 reuses v. 1, now, of course, using the images of wilting and withering. אבל (wither), נבל (wilt), and אמלל (disintegrate) are all verbs that describe how vegetation dies out in a time of drought. With the passing of the seasons, everyone who lived in Palestine got used to watching plants dry up and die, but that the whole earth should "wilt" describes an incomparable catastrophe (ארץ has to be translated "earth" in this context, especially since it parallels תבל, "world," and is then contrasted with מרום, "that which is above"). Once again, this verse sounds much like Hosea: האבל הארץ ואמלל כל־יושב בה (the land mourns, and all who live in it languish) (4:3aα); obviously, in that passage, ארץ is to be translated as "land"; cf. also Jer. 12:4, where ארץ (land) and עשׂב כל־השׂדה (grass of every field) parallel one another. Isa. 24:4 is very similar to Jer. 4:23-28. Once again, it is not hard to recognize that types of material which were first used to depict the judgment against Israel are now reused without any significant changes when the worldwide judgment is portrayed. It is possible that this reinterpretation which expands the scope of judgment to a universal level is to be detected already in Jer. 4:23-28: על־זאת תאבל הארץ וקדרו השׁמים ממעל (NRSV: Because of this the earth shall mourn, and the heavens above grow black) (v. 28); however, if this is correct, אבל should not be translated—as has commonly been done—as "mourn" in that passage either. There are other close similarities between Jer. 4:23-28 and other parts of the Isaiah apocalypse, especially in this passage with which we are now dealing: mountains and hills quake (cf. Isa. 24:18b-20); based on the passage from Jeremiah, the seer must make clear that no human beings are left (cf. Isa. 24:6bβ). The Jeremiah passage also declares that the gardens which produce their fruits and vegetables are now desert; where the earth was, now there is nothing but תהו ובהו (a formless void) (note that the term תהו, "nothing," is used in 24:10); what this means is that the creation once again has fallen back into its primordial chaos. With reference to this passage, Volz (KAT X²) also discusses a coming "worldwide catastrophe" and places this section into the category of that material which conveys an apocalyptic viewpoint. Following this through logically, he thus does not believe this passage is from Jeremiah (see also G. Fohrer, *Introduction to the Old Testament* [1968] 399f.).

In spite of the great similarity in the concepts, one cannot be sure whether Isa. 24:4 is dependent on this passage from the book of Jeremiah; it also could be an independent effort, further developing the old concepts that described judgment so that these images would apply to a worldwide judgment.

In Jer. 4:23-28 the world above the earth is also drawn into the catastrophe. This also happens according to Isa. 24:4b. The "heights" dry up just like the earth. מרום (heights) is a paraphrase for שׁמים (heavens). It is not immediately apparent what is meant when it says that the heavens also wilt and dry out. But one ought not press these words in an attempt to arrive at some literal meaning; it is enough to recognize that it says the heavens also are affected by the catastrophe; cf. Isa. 13:13; 34:4; Hag. 2:6. The situation would be very different if one were not to follow the emendation that changes this reading from עַם (people) to עִם (together with). Then, with Rudolph (1), one would have to translate this something like: "The most highly placed of the peoples of the earth pine away" (Gk: ἐπένθησαν οἱ ὑψηλοὶ τῆς γῆς, "the high ones of the earth mourn"). Based on the parallels that have been mentioned, however, this reading is unlikely; it must also be noted that the prophet does not wish to say that only the highest level of society is going to be summoned for judgment.

[24:5] That the judgment is more extensive can be seen already when one looks at how this continues in v. 5: "for the earth is desecrated beneath its inhabitants." It is a common viewpoint throughout the OT that the land is desecrated by the godlessness of its inhabitants, particularly due to their worship of false gods, as, for example, when a wife who has been sent away is taken by another man and then returns back to her first husband (Jer. 3:1f.), or when Israel plays the whore (Jer. 3:9), or when they offer children in sacrifice to the idols of Canaan (Ps. 106:38); according to Num. 35:33, the land is desecrated if no expiation is made for a murder. Thus this means that the sins of its inhabitants bring a terrible curse that hovers over the land (see v. 6); it is no longer a blessed land and no longer will be able to offer its inhabitants what they need for their daily existence. World order and the settled situation which is linked with that order cannot be separated. The godlessness of human beings also disrupts the order of the cosmos, which a human being must trust to continue to function well if life is to go smoothly. One notes that all these passages just cited describe Israel as having desecrated the land; once again, the author of the apocalypse has taken a common description and has transferred it so that it applies to the אֶרֶץ, with reference to the whole "earth."

In v. 5b the reason for the desecration is then given. It is stated in general terms: transgressing the commandments, stepping over the bounds of the law, and breaking the eternal covenant. These are accusations that have been directed against Israel from time to time; here, however, they apply to all the inhabitants of the earth. The last of these three terms is the most striking, since it speaks of a בְּרִית עוֹלָם (eternal covenant). It would seem impossible for this expression to be a reference to the covenant at Sinai, since that one is based on the unique relationship that Yahweh has with Israel. It has normally been assumed that the author is thinking here about the covenant with Noah, in the priestly writing, which is identified specifically as an "eternal covenant" (Gen. 9:16; cf. also 9:12). In fact, the covenant with David also can be called a בְּרִית עוֹלָם (everlasting covenant) (2 Sam. 23:5; cf. Isa. 55:3), but that one is certainly not the subject of the discussion in this passage. As has been observed over and over again, since this passage also has other motifs that have been used concerning Israel and that are now transferred so as to apply to the earth and/or its inhabitants, it is not completely impossible that the author might have been thinking of other covenants besides the one with Noah, and might once again be using expressions, when speaking about all humanity, that were directed originally toward Israel. One can come to this conclusion based on the following considerations: the Sinai covenant is constructed in such a way that there are obligations for both partners, correctly interpreted by means of what has been called the covenant formulary: "You will be my people, and I will be your God," or by similar expressions. A covenant of this type can be broken, which means that the divine partner is no longer bound to keep his side of the bargain either. By contrast, the Noah covenant is similar to the covenant with Abraham (Gen. 17:7, 13, 19; Ps. 105:10), with the promise coming from one covenant partner only, thus making it an eternal covenant. The expression "break the eternal covenant"—this is the only place in the OT where it is used—actually does not make sense. The surprising way in which this is formulated has to have been the result of a mixing of the concepts connected with the covenant with Noah, which is an eternal covenant, and that from Sinai, which could be broken, since the premise there is that a relationship exists between partners. That the concepts connected with the covenant at Sinai must be somehow involved here is also suggested when there is mention of a curse in v. 6. Yahweh's covenant with Israel always stands under the threat of the curse (Leviticus 26; Deuteronomy 28; see also Exod. 23:21ff.). Still another indication that the concepts connected with the Sinai covenant are being used here shows up in that תורה (laws) and חק (commandment) are spoken of in parallel with ברית (covenant). The covenant with David includes a provision for חסדים (steadfast, sure love) (Isa. 55:3; 2 Chron. 6:42), the covenant with Noah makes a promise, but the covenant at Sinai includes stipulations that the laws were to be obeyed. In regard to the present passage, it is a waste of time to speculate about how one might differentiate between תורה (laws, torah) and חק (commandment) (concerning חק, "commandment," see *Isaiah 1–12*, p. 213; concerning תורה, "law, torah," see ibid., pp. 38, 371). It is surprising that the plural תורת (laws) is used here. It is rarely used in passages that one knows to be preexilic (one cannot be sure about Exod. 18:20).

It is also noteworthy that this text does not mention the תורת (laws of) Yahweh and also does not speak about his חק (commandment), but that these are discussed without any other referent, simply being called תורת and חק. That is fitting, since Yahweh knows only Israel and gave only that one people his commandments. But, in spite of this, it is assumed that all human beings know something about תורת (laws) and חק (commandment) and are still responsible for their actions and failings. Even though the peoples might not know Yahweh personally, his *will* is still not completely hidden from them. It is inherent, within every human being's conscience, that there is a general knowledge of basic rules about how life is to be lived, which can have no other outcome than to put one under a curse if ignored. At this point, ברית עולם (eternal covenant) apparently refers to this general order, which cannot be violated without suffering the consequences. The specific deeds that the author has in mind are not stated, but it is presumed, once again, that everyone knows the details about how the actual destruction of the basic order of existence would take place.

[24:6] Breaking the covenant brings on the curse. One might compare this text with Jer. 23:10: "For the land is full of adulterers; because of the curse the land mourns, and the pastures of the wilderness are dried up" (text uncertain); see also Jer. 11:3, 8. According to Zech. 5:3, the curse goes out עַל־פְּנֵי כָל־הָאָרֶץ (over the face of the whole land), because thieves and perjurers (text emended) have carried on for too long a time already, without being punished. Even Dan. 9:11 says that the curse, which is written in the law of Moses, has been poured out on Israel; see also 2 Chron. 34:24. Again, the only point that is new in the present passage is that the curse consumes the entire earth. In 1:20 the sword "consumes" unrepentant Israel, just as a wild animal would, and, just as the sword is made into a personified power that brings disaster in that passage, so here the curse consumes the earth. The curse that is on the earth falls back on the human beings; the earth is the place where it lives, and an earth that has been struck by a curse will not give those human beings any chance to survive. Human beings can do nothing more on the earth after it has been desecrated because of their transgression, can do nothing but "endure the consequences." In keeping with the synthetic view of life that is found throughout the OT, אשם does not mean only "be guilty," but also "bear the punishment for it, bear the consequences of the transgression." One ought not try to read into this expression that it is possible for the transgression to be cleared away by some action; instead, the consequences will continue to be played out without any mercy until everything is completely destroyed. The inhabitants of the earth will continue to diminish in number (concerning חרה, "disappear completely," see above, textual note 6c). They will want to eat but will not be able to be satisfied, just as Hosea (4:10) describes what will happen in a similar context. The great wave of death will sweep over humanity, and those who are left will be nothing but a מזער, "a littleness" (concerning מזער, "quickly counted," see 16:14). The traditional idea that at least a small remnant would survive, this time not from Israel and not from any particular foreign people, but from humanity (אנוש) as a whole, is another element of what was expected, and that is not skipped over here either. It may be that, after the end, there would be a new beginning, but we learn nothing about that.

Among the groups that lived near Israel, we come across portrayals of a complete breakdown of the established order most frequently in Egypt. The chief interest for Egyptian religion was that the established order could be preserved, so that its writers do not concentrate on reflecting about how order might come to an end. However, that such a final end could happen was somehow always in the background as a threatening possibility (see E. Hornung, *Zeitschrift für ägyptische Sprache und Altertumskunde* 81 [1956] 28–33; and L. Kákosy, "Schöpfung und Weltuntergang in der ägyptischen Religion," *Acta Antiqua Academiae Scientiarum Hungericae* 11 [1963]

17–30): "Just as the rising of the sun means that the creation has been renewed, each sunset is a preview of the final downfall of the world" (Kákosy, 22). However, at times during the course of Egyptian history some of those depictions and portrayals were especially prominent. That was clearest during the First Intermediate Period (Kákosy, 28). In this context, one might mention A Dispute over Suicide, The Proverbs of Kha-kheper-Re-seneb, The Protests of the Eloquent Peasant, and The Admonitions of Ipu-wer, all of these being wisdom texts. However, this concept also found its way into the mortuary texts; above all, see the Book of the Dead, chap. 175 (the Papyrus of Ani version, Kha's version, and a Leiden Papyrus version). According-ing to the Myth of the Heavenly Cow, the sun god descends once and for all—not just for the night, as he does daily—into the primordial waters (Kákosy, 19). However, the most frequent references to the threats about the final downfall of the world are found in the Magical Texts (S. Sauneron, *BSFE* 8 [1951] 11–21), such as in Papyrus Salt I, 1–7 or in Papyrus Turin, 137:2-4).

Some portions of the following texts are quoted, insofar as they include state-ments that sound very much like what is in the Isaiah apocalypse:

From A Dispute over Suicide: "One's fellows are evil; the friends of today do not love. To whom can I speak today? Hearts are rapacious: Every man seizes his fel-low's goods. (To whom shall I speak today?) The gentle man has perished, (but) the violent man has access to everybody. To whom can I speak today? (Men) are con-tented with evil; goodness is rejected everywhere. To whom can I speak today? (Though) a man should arouse wrath by his evil character, he (only) stirs to laughter, (so) wicked is his sin. To whom can I speak today? Men are plundering; every man seizes his fellow's (goods). . . . The land is left to those who do wrong. To whom can I speak today? There is lack of an intimate (friend); one has recourse to an unknown to complain to him. . . . The sin which treads the earth, it has no end" (cited from *ANET* 406f.; see also W. von Bissing, *Altägyptische Lebensweisheit* [1955] 126f.).

From the Sayings of Kha-kheper-Re-seneb: "The land is in an uproar and is devastated; justice has been turned aside; injustice dwells in the deliberation halls. The thoughts of the gods are trampled down, their decrees are not observed. The land is in misery, there is mourning in every place. Cities and villages lament. Every sin-gle person is a wicked person. People turn their backs on respect. People revolt against the Lords of Silence; there is suffering every day, and justice is dismayed by all of what happens. . . . Behold, the affairs of the servant are just like those of the master" (von Bissing, *Lebensweisheit*, 122f.).

From the Protests of an Eloquent Peasant: "Note carefully that righteousness does not go forth from your hands, since it has been pushed away from its own place; the advice causes displeasure, the speech takes a path that leans to one side, the judges grab to seize what he has taken. The one who holds his breath languishes down on the ground; the one who himself hopes that others will leave him alone causes others to tremble violently. The arbiter is a robber; whoever is supposed to do away with want arranges for more of it. The city is its own storm flood; whoever is supposed to fight against injustice makes hardship" (von Bissing, *Lebensweisheit*, 159; see also *ANET* 407ff.).

From the Admonitions of Ipu-wer: "It is really true: the land spins around like a potter's wheel; the robber possesses treasures; everyone has become a plunderer. It is really true: the stream is blood, and if one drinks from it, then, as a man, one rejects it, since one thirsts for water. It is really true: the gates, posts, and walls are scorched. Only the chambers of the king's palace are sturdy and lasting. It is really true: the southern ship is in confusion, the cities are hacked in pieces, and Upper Egypt has become a wilderness. It is really true: the crocodiles are satisfied by what they have pounced on. The human beings go to them willingly. Things are bad all over the earth. People say, 'Don't come here; it is dangerous.' But the people swarm about like the fish, the fainthearted act that senselessly because of terror. It is really true: the human beings are few; everywhere one looks, one sees someone placing his brother into the earth. . . . It is really true: laughing has disappeared; one simply does not do it any more. Mourning travels throughout the land, mixed with cries of lament. . . . Look, no office occupies its proper place any more; they are just like a flock without shepherds. . . . One says: he is the shepherd of all people; no evil dwells in his heart. His flock gets smaller and smaller even though he spends his time every day trying to gather it together. Ah, if only he had recognized their nature in the first generation, then he would have set evil aside. He would have stretched out his hand against it and would have destroyed the seed from it and its heirs. . . . Now it will be no better, as long as the gods prolong it. . . . There is no pilot at this time" (according to von Bissing, *Lebensweisheit*, 129ff.; see also above, p. 476; in addition, see *ANET* 441ff.).

In chap. 175 of the Book of the Dead, Atum says, "The land [according to Kha and Ani: this land] will become Nun, will become the primordial flood as at the time of its origin. I am the one who will still be left, along with Osiris, (after which) I will have changed myself to become another serpent [Ani: other serpents], which no human being knows, which no god sees [variants: those which human beings do not know and which no gods see]" (E. Otto, *Chronique d'Égypte* 37 [1962] 243).

From a Ptolemaic Hymn concerning Osiris: "He is the only one who still survives, along with the majesty of Re, whereas the land of Nun is [that which gushes forth from?] the primordial flood, as it was at the time of its original beginning and (during which time) there was no god nor goddess; (he) made himself into another serpent" (Otto, ibid., 252).

Finally, in Papyrus Salt, now in the British Museum (10.051), one can read: "at nighttime. It was not day . . . gods and goddesses [put] their hands on their heads. The earth. . . . [the sun] did not rise. The moon stayed away. . . . The heaven fell into darkness. . . . The earth was ruined, the water was changed. It did not go downstream. . . . The whole world lamented and cried, the souls . . . [gods] and goddesses, human beings, spirits and dead, cattle and flocks" (S. Schott, AnBib 12 [1959] 321f.; see also P. Derchain, "Le Papyrus Salt 852 [B. M. 10051] rituel pour la conservation de la vie en Égypte," Acad. Royale de Belgique, classe des lettres, Mémoires LVIII [1965] 137).

For further examples from the magical texts, cf. S. Sauneron, *BSFE* 8 (1951) 11–21; in addition, see Asclepius 24 in the Corpus Hermeticum.

The similarity between some of these motifs and those in the Isaiah apocalypse can be seen right away. Viewed structurally, these are not prophecies, but are laments about the terrible course the world was taking. It is possible that the wretched condition could be the result of the negligence of the gods, but the judgment is not what the deity summons; instead, it comes as the disastrous consequences that affect human beings when they fail to act as they ought. One also notes that this text focuses just on Egypt; the foreign peoples are not in the picture at all in these laments; rather, they anticipate that there will be a return to the primordial chaos. From these texts, one would not learn anything at all about the way in which the kingdom of God, to its full extent, would develop.

[24:7-9] *The Wilting of the Vine Branch and the Silencing of the Jubilant Shouts of the Heavy Drinkers*

These verses, 7-9, provide a supplement to vv. 1-6. In and of themselves, these verses do not show that a worldwide catastrophe was envisioned, but in the present context they are supposed to portray the way in which this catastrophe would begin to take place. Of course, it is an inadequate portrayal, one that actually minimizes the problem. If the entire earth has been devastated and its surface has been disfigured and even the heights of the heavens have been wilted and have disintegrated, what is so bad about the prospect that the vine branches would wither? And if there is to be only a pitiful few people who will survive the catastrophe, what is the point of the announcement that no one will sing any longer when they have their wine? These concepts were simply appropriated from the huge storehouse of material that had been used in previous times to depict periods of disaster, without the author putting forth the necessary effort to adapt this material to the new situation.

[24:7] In v. 7 the author links what he says with what was in v. 4 (cf. אבל, "wilt," and אמלל, "disintegrate"). It was probably those very verbs which suggested to the expander that these sentences should be inserted, first about the wilting of the vine branches and then also about the end of the joy with which the heavy drinkers celebrate at festivals.

אבל also has to be translated as "wilt" here, not as "mourn." To be sure, תירוש (new wine) does not wilt; instead, the vine branches do that, but it is not hard for the Hebrews to make this mental jump, in order to understand the new meaning; cf. Joel 1:10: הוֹבִישׁ תִּירוֹשׁ אֻמְלַל יִצְהָר (the wine dries up, the oil fails).

Concerning תירוש (new wine), see L. Köhler, *ZAW* 46 (1928) 219, who links it with a root ירשׁ, "tread, press grapes," and sees it as the Semitic word that corresponds to the foreign word יין (wine). Isaiah himself uses only the word יין (wine) (5:11, 12, 22; 22:13).

When one searches for parallels to v. 7 elsewhere in the OT, in addition to Joel 1:10, there are other passages in Joel: 1:12, 16. The motif that joy comes to an end, שבת שמחה, occurs also in Lam. 5:15, and in Hos. 2:13 Yahweh issues a threat to Israel that all joy will come to an end (וְהִשְׁבַּתִּי כָּל־מְשׂוֹשָׂהּ, "I will punish her for all the festival days"). Concerning the use of שׁיר (song), תֹף (here: kettledrums), and כנור (zither) together, see Gen. 31:27; 1 Chron. 13:8; concerning the musical instruments כנור (there: box-lyre) and תֹף (there: tambourine), see *Isaiah 1-12*, pp. 200f.; in addition, see illuss. 35f., 71, 74 in *Music in Ancient Israel*, Haifa Music Museum (1972/73).

[24:9] Concerning v. 9, cf. 5:11 and Amos 6:3. In addition to all the traditional phraseology used by the author, some of the formulations are unique: חָדַל שְׁאוֹן עֹלְזִים (the [festive] noise of those who are celebrating is stilled) (concerning עָלַז, "celebrating," see Brunet, 190, 192; see above, p. 361) and יֵמַר שֵׁכָר לְשֹׁתָיו (the drunken drinking of the heavy drinkers leaves a bitter taste) (on שֵׁכָר, "heavy drinkers," see *Isaiah 1–12*, p. 200).

Just as in 5:11f., the present passage informs us somewhat about the way the drinking rites of that time period were viewed, apparently not having changed much since the time of Isaiah. As part of a festival celebration—there is no doubt, concerning this passage as well, that the author is not thinking about a cultic festival—one would find wine and song, in fact, singing accompanied by music. While young girls would have been involved in playing the music at such festivals, wives would have been there as well, along with wine and singing (depictions of dinner parties that included music and singing are provided by W. Wreszinski, *Atlas zur altägyptischen Kulturgeschichte* [1923], plates 10, 39, 91; see also Ashurbanipal, Annals, Cylinder B, V, 65f., in VAB VII/2, 116ff.; in addition, see the clay tablet inscription L⁴, Rm III, 9–11, in VAB VII/2, 265ff.).

Whereas Isaiah, in the passage to which reference has been made, engages those who are celebrating at the festival by offering a biting criticism and threatens Israel, for its part, with exile, the expander of this particular passage simply uses the fact that all festive noise will be silenced as an additional way to describe the distress that will come at the end of time; for him, festivals are completely legitimate ways to express one's joy in life; these are worldviews that separate the apocalyptic writers from the prophets.

[24:10-12] *Addition: The Destruction of the Chaos City*

These verses now deal with a new theme. Verse 11 admittedly speaks once again about the disappearance of joy at festivals, but now with the additional specific detail that people in the streets of the city were lamenting because of a lack of wine. However, v. 11bβ speaks once again about the end of the "joy of the earth" (though this does not mean, as suggested in *BHS*, that v. 11bβ should be moved and placed right after v. 8). Still, when the earth is mentioned once again, that is a hint that the author views the destruction of the city in connection with the worldwide catastrophe, so that here, more clearly than in vv. 7-9, the verses have been more adequately integrated into the depiction of the ravaging of the entire earth. But with the adaptation of the traditional expressions, some absurdities are included as well. One who is in a city that lies in complete ruins has better things to do than to complain about the lack of wine.

[24:10] Analysis has shown that the city discussed in vv. 10ff. can hardly be the same as the enemy city mentioned in 25:1ff. and 26:1ff., nor can it be the

Moabite city in 25:12 nor the one referred to in 27:10. Perhaps the author was motivated by having experienced personally the downfall of a city and thus included this addendum, since he thought that it happened as a fulfillment of or was the ἀρραβών (down payment) for the fulfillment of the prophecy that precedes these verses. There is every indication that these verses reflect on something that had just happened (כֹּה, "smashed," in v. 12, describes an event that took place at the same time; it is not an anticipated future event).

The city is called a קִרְיַת־תֹּהוּ (here: nothing city). קִרְיָה (town, city) is much more common than עִיר (city) in the various layers that now make up the first part of the book of Isaiah, though עִיר is much more common elsewhere (קִרְיָה: 1:21, 26; 22:2; 29:1; additionally, in 32:13; 33:20; and 25:2, 3; 26:5; thus altogether it occurs ten times, with only eighteen other occurrences in the entire OT; this is once again a small indicator that there must have been something like an Isaiah school; it is from this group that the Isaiah apocalypse would have come). Some have tried to link this word with קָרָה (happen), so that the basic meaning would be "meeting place"; see KBL, Ges-Buhl. It is difficult to differentiate clearly between עִיר and קִרְיָה. What is more interesting is that the city is more specifically defined by תֹּהוּ (here: nothing).

In some places, תֹּהוּ can simply be used, much like Arabic *tīh,* to designate a waterless, impassable desert (Deut. 32:10; Ps. 107:40; Job 12:24, etc.), where one would meet death if one ventured in. In addition, the word also means "unreal, empty." In Isa. 40:23 it is used together with אַיִן (naught); in 41:29 with אַיִן (delusion), אֶפֶס (nothing), and רוּחַ (wind); in 49:4 with רִיק (in vain) and הֶבֶל (vanity); in 59:4 with שָׁוְא (lies); cf. also 44:9; 45:18f. All told, the word occurs twenty times in the OT, eleven of them in the book of Isaiah. It must have been fitting that this vocable would have been used to describe the chaos that was about to begin, just as it was used with בֹּהוּ (void) in Gen. 1:2. But one cannot say that this word was used originally within the context of descriptions about creation; it did not begin as a mythological term (though that is possible in the case of בֹּהוּ, "void"). But that fact does not change that it is appropriate that the word is used to designate chaos, as the opposite of the orderly cosmos of creation; cf. 45:18: "who created the heavens . . . he did not create it a תֹּהוּ (chaos), he formed it to be inhabited"; and Jer. 4:23: "I looked on the earth, and lo, it was תֹּהוּ וּבֹהוּ (waste and void)"; on this, see above, p. 478. Concerning תֹּהוּ (nothing, void), cf. C. Westermann, *Genesis* BK I/1 [1974], 141ff., including more literature citations [Engl: *Genesis 1–11,* Continental Commentary (1984), 102ff.]).

By means of the creative work of Yahweh, the chaos was shaped to form a structured worldwide order; when the world would come to an end, then this order would sink back down into the amorphous, gloomy situation in which it existed before God intervened to separate it and arrange it. A קִרְיַת־תֹּהוּ (nothing city) would thus have to be a city that had just experienced the reintroduction of the primordial chaos. One cannot assume that the use of תֹּהוּ (chaos, void) presumes that the priestly writing was a source, since the word is also used already in Deutero-Isaiah.

No other passage in the OT speaks about a city being "broken," though it is said from time to time that שֶׁבֶר (downfall) comes upon a city; see above, p. 138. The way it continues is more original and specific: "every house is closed; no one comes on in." That line certainly does not mean that the occupants carefully locked up their houses before they fled, and one should also reflect on what is said in the stipulation in Lev. 14:38 that a house has to be closed up if it has become unclean because of some sort of dangerous growth; the entryway is to be closed up by having a pile of stones thrown in front of it.

[24:11] In the side streets of the city, people are complaining about wine. Apparently, wine was so dear to the ancient Hebrews that they were excessively agitated if they were forced to do without it. According to Hos. 7:14, Israel howled concerning the storehouses and cut themselves in their quest for grain and wine, and, according to Isa. 16:7, Moab, completely crushed, was whimpering about not having the grape cakes from Kir-hareseth; cf. also Joel 1:5.

The observation is common that joy and jubilant shouting had disappeared when a city had suffered destruction: Jer. 16:9 (קוֹל שָׂשׂוֹן וְקוֹל שִׂמְחָה, "the voice of mirth and the voice of gladness"); Jer. 48:33; Joel 1:16 (שִׂמְחָה וָגִיל, "joy and gladness"); Ezek. 24:25 (תִּפְאַרְתָּם מְשׂוֹשׂ, "their joy and glory"); Joel 1:12 (שָׂשׂוֹן, "joy"); Hos. 2:13 (כָּל־מְשׂוֹשָׂהּ, "all her festival days"). However, when he used the verbs עָרַב (vanish) and גָּלָה (here: move out), the author created his own unique formulations.

One might compare this lament about the city with that which described the downfall of Akkad (*SAHG* 192f.), in which its earlier good fortune was described in the following words:

> The inhabitants of Kish,
> with rattles in their left [hands] they danced,
> the center of the city is filled with the sound of kettledrums,
> outside, the double-reeds and tympanies resound.

The streets of such a city in the ancient Near East would apparently have been filled normally with happy activity.

[24:12] Whatever is finally left of the קִרְיַת־תֹּהוּ (nothing city) is just שַׁמָּה (devastation). It had been threatened in 5:9 that many houses would become שַׁמָּה (there: deserted); otherwise, שַׁמָּה is a favorite word in the book of Jeremiah; cf. a passage such as 19:8: וְשַׂמְתִּי אֶת־הָעִיר הַזֹּאת לְשַׁמָּה (and I will make this city a horror) (this word is used twenty-four times in the book of Jeremiah, with only fifteen other uses in the rest of the OT). One might wish to translate this word as "desert"; however, the accent is on the horror of it all; one ought not ignore the emotional undertone that is intended here.

At the conclusion, the author illustrates what has happened by making a specific observation: שְׁאִיָּה יֻכַּת־שָׁעַר (the smashed gate lies there in [complete] desolation). Concerning שאיה (desolation), see above, pp. 463, 472. שער (gate) should certainly be treated as a collective, even though it is true that some smaller cities would have had only one gate through which people entered. That the gates are mentioned would suggest that the city had fallen into other hands, after a fierce defensive struggle on the part of those who were being besieged.

[24:13] *A Later Addition: The Gleaning Among the Peoples*

An expander might have been reminded of 17:6aα when reading v. 6 (ונשאר בו עוללת כנקף זית), "and for it a gleaning will remain, as when someone beats olive trees") and thought that it was fitting to reuse the passage here. "What is left of human beings, that is מזער (quickly counted)" is the way it reads in v. 6bβ, and v. 13 goes on from there. In fact, this is what has now happened; this situation is illustrated by means of a depiction of a gleaning in which little has been left on the olive tree, after someone already has knocked off its fruit (see above, pp. 172f.). He does not go on to include the description of the remnant in 17:6aβ-b, but he does insert אם־כלה בציר (when the wine harvest has come to an end) at the end. That seems to be an ordinary agricultural term, but we do find virtually the same little phrase in 32:10bα (כי כלה בציר, "for the vintage will fail"), even though there is no real reason why one would be speaking about harvesting in that context. "The wine harvest has come to an end" means that the happy time is now past, the utter earnestness of the judgment has now come. This deeper meaning must certainly be taken into account here.

Verse 13a confirms that it was correct, in the interpretation offered above, to assume that this refers to the worldwide judgment, since בקרב הארץ (on the earth) parallels בתוך העמים (in the midst of the peoples of the world). This expansion that now puts the whole world into view sets the final seal on the reinterpretation of the traditional material, which was used originally in reference to the land and/or to Israel.

Purpose and Thrust

[24:1-6] The original body of material, vv. 1-6, is clearly an announcement of God's judgment against the entire earth. The judgment is imminent; Yahweh himself presides over the judgment, and he himself placed the message into the mouth of the prophet. Though it is not stated in so many words, the author is thinking that a far-reaching drought is soon to come (the expanders expect a catastrophe brought on by war). The soil would no longer produce its fruit, human beings would die, and those who were left would be scattered throughout the world—looking for places where they might be able to procure something to eat. Prominent and insignificant, poor and rich, all would experience the same fate. Where there was simply nothing more to be found, every privilege that had come with one's position and every advantage that came with a preferred status would lose all importance.

The earth would produce no more of its fruits because it had been des-

ecrated, since the earth can promise human beings that life will go well only
if it remains blessed. The earth itself was under the curse because of what
humans had done, doing what simply ought never to have been done, so that
the eternal covenant was violated. The human beings had departed from the
faithful relationship with God, had ignored the fixed order; only within that
context could settled life be enjoyed, and now they would have to bear the
consequences. It is true that it says: "Yahweh empties out the earth," but this
must be considered in the light of the other references about how the curse,
which human beings have set in motion with their actions, would now consume the earth—destiny would take its course, without any chance of stopping it and without anyone being shown mercy.

Some believe that this speaks about worldwide judgment. The detailed
discussion of this passage has shown that a new level indeed has been
reached, as this concerns the efforts of the prophets to deliver the message of
judgment. In many different places it could be shown that the motifs and formulations which had once been spoken concerning Israel or another people
were now elevated to the status of portraying a universal catastrophe. This is
about the entire earth, concerning all its peoples, about אֱנוֹשׁ (human beings)
(v. 6) as a whole. Yahweh is the one who establishes and guarantees the system of order, but it is also obviously presumed that all human beings know
about the covenant and have no excuse (cf. Rom. 2:14f.). Some hints in the
direction of this type of announcement of judgment occur already in preexilic prophecy. It is remarkable, however, that Israel does not appear in this
passage at all, neither having to assume some share of the responsibility nor
having been excluded from the judgment. This is why this passage differs
from passages such as 14:26, which mentions that Yahweh has made a decision about the whole earth and about all peoples, but which zooms in on the
downfall of Assyria, the great enemy of Israel.

Nothing is mentioned about what will happen after the judgment,
though the passage also does not seem to be interested in saying that humanity is facing an end, after which there will be nothing left but the deep emptiness of nothingness. It is clear that the prophecy leaves many unanswered
questions, for which some answers are provided by the prophet himself and
some are also supplied by those who expanded his text.

[24:7-9] The glossators who add vv. 7-9 and vv. 10-12 do not really add
anything new. The one who supplies vv. 7-9 pulls out the motif that describes
how joy, at a festival time, would fade in silence, drawn from his storage bin
of reminiscences, as he tries to spruce up the passage with a few observations
of his own, but he did not understand that his words did little except minimize the weighty issues with which his master had been dealing.

[24:10-12] The expander who adds vv. 10-12 is deeply moved by the downfall of some city. He wants to shows that the things which are to come at the
end of time are now being set in motion. This observation sets a precedent.
The downfall of the great city later became the decisive event in some apoc-

alypses, seen as that decisive moment which set the coming of the end in motion (cf. Rev. 18:1ff.).

For all that has been said, the message of this section seems at first glance to be far removed and foreign to most human beings who are alive today, since it deals with the world of apocalyptic and its understanding of history—yet, at the same time, it is uncomfortably close and apt. Human beings overstep the bounds of the order that God has established, and it is not all that much different from the way things are now that the earth, the only home base for human existence and enjoyment, emptied and disfigured, no longer will do what it is supposed to do. It might just prove true:

עַל־כֵּן אָלָה אָכְלָה אֶרֶץ וַיֶּאְשְׁמוּ יֹשְׁבֵי בָהּ
עַל־כֵּן חָרוּ יֹשְׁבֵי אֶרֶץ וְנִשְׁאַר אֱנוֹשׁ מִזְעָר

For this reason a curse has consumed the earth,
 those who live upon it must suffer the consequences.
For this reason the inhabitants of the earth disappear completely,
 and what is left of human beings, that is quickly counted.

The Premature Jubilation of Israel and the Seer's Deep Shock

Text

14 They all will raise their voice,
   they rejoice^a about the supremacy of Yahweh,
      ^bexult,^c even from the western sea.^{db}

15 "Therefore,^a honor Yahweh in the east,^b
   on the coasts of the sea, the name of Yahweh,
      the God of Israel."

16 From the farthest edge of the earth (in fact)
   we heard songs of joy^a:
      "to the righteous one, majesty."
         * * * *
   But I thought: ^b"I am done for, I am done for,^b
   woe is me": ^ccunning ones deal cunningly,
      in cunning the cunning ones act cunningly.^c

17 ^aHorror and hole and holder,^a
   that is for you, inhabitant of the earth!

18 And it will happen:
   whoever flees from the sound^a that strikes horror,
      that one will fall into a hole,
   and whoever climbs out of^a a hole,
      will get caught in someone's holder.
   Truly, the windows ^bin the heights^b open themselves wide,
      and the foundations of the earth quake.

19 Bursting,^a the earth^b bursts apart,
   ^csplitting, the earth splits open,
      swaying, the earth sways back and forth,^c

20 staggering, the ^aearth staggers ^bjust as would one who is drunk,^b
   tottering,^c just as does a ^dhut for the night,^d in a field.
   Its foolishness weighs down heavily on itself,
      and it falls^e—it will never stand up again.

14a The *athnach* under ירנ (they rejoice) should be moved, to be placed under יהוה (Yahweh) instead (Procksch).

14b–b צהלו מים (exult, even from the western sea) should not be taken with v. 15, as some commentators do. Once again, we are dealing with a three-part verse.

14c One notes that the two imperfects, יִשְׂאוּ (will raise) and יָרֹנּוּ (rejoice), are then followed by the perfect צָהֲלוּ (exult). The Gk may have read the imperfect (ταραχθήσε-ται τὸ ὕδωρ τῆς θαλάσσης, "the water of the sea will be stirred up"); beyond this, however, either its translators did not understand the text or else they translated the text very loosely. Since the time of H. Ewald (*Die Propheten des alten Bundes* III [1868²] 169), some scholars (Fischer, Procksch, Fohrer) have read the imperative צַהֲלִי (cry shrilly in praise) instead of the perfect צָהֲלוּ (they cried shrilly in praise) (adjusting the reading on the basis of the following כַּבְּדוּ, "honor") and then, along with מִיָּם (water, sea), they commonly have treated this word as part of the next verse. However, then one runs into trouble with how to interpret עַל־כֵּן (therefore) at the very beginning of v. 15. The text is fine as it is. One cries out in praise in the west and calls for those in the east who share the faith to give honor to Yahweh.

14d Does מִיָּם mean "from the sea" or "from the west?" Or should one go so far as to accept Kaiser's translation (who refers to Ges-K §133e): "(they) rejoice (more loudly) than at the sea" (cf. also Kessler)? Since the word that is paired with מִיָּם in the other part of the line is בָּאֻרִים (here: in the east), obviously used in a local sense, the same can be assumed for מִיָּם (here: from the western sea). Because of the parallelism, this time יָם (sea) is used simply in a way to designate one of the points on the compass: from the western sea (or: in the west; see BrSynt §111a, and M. Dahood, *Bib* 48 [1976] 427).

15a Unlike someone such as Fohrer, at least Procksch recognizes that, after one has changed צָהֲלוּ (they exulted) to be an imperative, then עַל־כֵּן (therefore) does not fit; thus he suggests that עָלֵזוּ (shout for joy) should be read here as a further parallel to צַהֲלִי (cry shrilly in praise) and כַּבְּדוּ (honor); see also *BHS*. This is the way that a questionable textual change forces an even more questionable change!

15b בָּאֻרִים is a *crux interpretum* and has caused the most varied interpretations and "improvements." אוּר I means "brilliance, luster"; the plural is used only here and is certainly a suspicious reading. Qimḥi and Ibn Ezra think that this word is related somehow to אוּר כַּשְׂדִּים (Ur of the Chaldeans) in Gen. 11:28 and to מְאוּרַת צִפְעֹנִי (hole of a viper) in Isa. 11:8 and believe that they can justify the meaning "valley, flat lowlying land." However, no modern scholars have accepted this solution. The Gk does not even have a term that would correspond to בָּאֻרִים—presumably because they did not know what to make of the word—whereas Vulg translates it: *in doctrinis*, "in teaching"; this means that they thought the word referred to the well-known practice of obtaining an oracle by lot, using the Urim (see Exod. 28:30; Lev. 8:8; Deut. 33:8). Houbigant suggested that the text be altered to read בָּאֻמִּים, "among the peoples" (see Gesenius), as is read also by Liebmann (*ZAW* 23 [1903] 234), Ehrlich, et al. But these emendations do not fit very well when one matches them up with מִיָּם (from the western sea); one is even less inclined to agree with Perles (*Analekten* [1922] 56), who thinks he has found a reference to "the people of Beirut" (בָּאֻרִים). Ewald had explained the term already, in this context, as meaning "in the direction of the light," that is, "the east," and many have followed him in this (Duhm, Marti, et al.). Procksch, however, on the basis of a reference to Ps. 136:7, maintains that the אוֹרִים are the stars; but admits that this meaning does not fit; he thinks the easiest solution would be to read בָּאִיִּים, "on the islands" (*BHS*: בְּאִיֵּי הַיָּם, "on the islands of the sea"). While one ought not reject that solution completely, Kaiser has made reference to a possible root אוּר II; according to M. Jastrow, *Dictionary of the Targumim* I (1950), this means "the break of day," which shows that one can indeed follow Ewald's interpretation.

16a Based on 12:2, Ehrlich suggests pointing זמרת as זִמְרָה (melody, song), an unnecessary alteration, particularly since both the text and the meaning of זמרת (in *Isaiah 1–12: my strength*) are in question. It would be less satisfactory still if one were persuaded to follow Schlögl and eliminate זמרה as a gloss. Most surprisingly, the Gk translates the word as τέρατα (signs, wonders). On the basis of Syriac *dmyr,* meaning "surprising, wonderful," G. R. Driver (*JSS* 13 [1968] 50) was convinced that he had sufficient grounds to postulate the existence of a Hebrew word זמירות, meaning "strange things," which also would make better sense in Ps. 119:54. One would have to admit that this interpretation would provide a good parallel to צבי (majesty), which follows it, but צבי (majesty) is not used in parallel with זמרה (song of joy); instead, it is a quote from the song of praise.

16b No one knows for sure what is meant by רזי. KBL is resigned to saying "unsure." For v. 16a the Gk reads καὶ ἐροῦσιν Οὐαί (and they say, "woe"), which means the translators simply skipped over both occurrences of רזי־לי; Sym: τo μυστήριον μου εμοι το μυστήριον μου εμοι (my mystery to me, my mystery to me) (as read in Codex Marchalianus and in a reference in Eusebius, though Eusebius does not identify Sym specifically as the source); Sym, Theod: το μυστήριον μου εμοι (my mystery to me) (according to the readings recorded in the Syh); Theod: *mysterium meum mihi* (my mystery to me) (quoted and translated thus by Jerome in his reference to this text as recorded by Theodotion); Vulg: *secretum meum* (my secret); thus, they all thought that this referred to Aramaic רז (secret) (see Dan. 2:27ff.). Even Procksch agreed, thinking it seemed that the prophetic secrets were supposed to be revealed in the events surrounding the last times. That cannot be right, since the cry of woe אוי לי (woe is me) follows immediately, which forced Procksch to alter אוי לי בגדים (woe is me, cunning ones) to read אוי לבגדים (woe to the cunning ones) (so also *BHS* and Kaiser). Liebmann (*ZAW* 23 [1903] 239) thinks that this was a "gloss, from a time when the Aramaic was the dominant language." But even earlier both Hitzig and Delitzsch (see also Ges-Buhl) had suggested that this could be a substantive form of the root רזה (make to disappear), to which they assigned a meaning something such as "disappearance, downfall" (similarly Knobel, Duhm, Feldmann, Fohrer, et al.).

16c–c It is understandable that some scholars think this text is too long (e.g., deGroot, 157), especially because the Gk has a shorter text, but in this case also their mistaken view comes because they have not detected the style of the apocalypse.

17a–a פחד ופחת ופח (horror and hole and holding) is a proverbial expression (see Jer. 48:43; cf. also Lam. 3:47) and, for this reason, the accuracy of the text should not be questioned.

18a To suggest that קול (sound) and תוך (out of) are superfluous, or even burdensome, and ought to be removed, as they are from the Gk and Jer. 48:43f. (so Duhm), puts this solution into the category of textual alterations offered by someone who wants to treat the author as a pupil needing instruction.

18b–b There is no question that ממרום means "in the heights"; see above, textual note 14d. Thus it is not necessary (following Guthe; see also *BHS*) to insert השמים (the heavens) after ארבות (the windows of) (see Gen. 7:11; 8:2), but it is also not necessary to follow H. D. Hummel (*JBL* 76 [1957] 98), who treats the first מ in ממרום (here: in the heights) as an enclitic *mem* that belongs on the previous word, ארבות (windows).

19a P. Wernberg-Møller (*ZAW* 71 [1959] 61) treats רעה as a participle and translates: "With a breaking the earth is broken"; it would be better to treat רעה (bursting) as an action noun that takes the place of an infinitive absolute (cf. 22:17), but that is less likely in light of the following infinitives פור (splitting) and מוט (swaying). רעה

(because the accent is placed on the first syllable!) is treated by Delitzsch, Duhm, Marti, Gray, *BHS*, et al., as a copying mistake for the infinitive form רֹעַ (dittography of the ה), a reading now supported by רוֹע in Q^b.

19b It is surprising to find the article on the word אָרֶץ (earth), since it is missing the other two times it is used here. Possibly the ה is a dittography, just like the ה in רעה (bursting) (Gray, Feldmann, et al.).

19c–c It is out of the question that v. 19bα (or all of v. 19b) should be treated as an alternate reading to what precedes. That the Gk translates this ἀπορίᾳ ἀπορηθήσεται (it will be perplexed by perplexities) is an interesting way to imitate the Hebrew wordplay and is close to the exact way the words sound, but the translation is too free.

20a Q^a reads the article on אָרֶץ (earth) here as well; see Kutscher, 411.

20b–b Ehrlich suggests reading כַּסֻּכָּה = כְּסֻכָּה (like a booth) instead of כְּשִׁכּוֹר (just as would one who is drunk), citing 1:8 as support, where סֻכָּה (booth made of foliage) is used in parallel with מְלוּנָה (shelter for the night); however, this alteration is not necessary.

20c Q^a: והתנודדא (also: tottering); concerning the way ה is switched to א, see Kutscher, 163.

20d–d In 1:8 the מלונה is the hut (or the framework) under which the same one who was guarding a field would spend the night; something like this certainly is not built very solidly and could easily begin to sway. Some translate this word in the present passage as "hammock" (Delitzsch, Knobel, Naegelsbach, Duhm, Zürcher Bibel). Gesenius had already suggested this might be a hanging "swinging bed, which the watchman might have fixed up for himself, up in the trees, in a garden or vineyard in the Near East, to protect himself against wild animals." But it would be better to interpret this as a reference to a hut that one could quickly throw together, possibly constructed on top of trees, that also would serve to protect one against rain. Besides this, Q^a reads וכמלונה (and just as a hut for the night); see Kutscher, 423.

20e Q^a reads the masculine ונפל (and it falls). In light of the fact that this is a quotation from Amos 5:2, it is a mistake to eliminate the word because of metrical considerations (so Schlögl).

Form

Concerning the limits of the passage and how it is to be divided into its constituent parts, see above, pp. 451f. Verses 14-16a and vv. 16b-20 each form separate units. The text begins by mentioning a group of people who are referred to only as המה (each one, they), who join in singing a euphoric זמרת (song of joy). It would seem that this is a reaction to the events announced in vv. 1-6. But the response is entirely inappropriate, since the announcement of the punishment that is to come upon all the inhabitants of the earth had not offered a way out for Israel; Israel would have been included in that generic term המה (each one, they) as well. For this reason, the author of v. 16b contrasts this questionable song of joy with his own deep shock, as he repeats the announcement of disaster from vv. 1-6, though with different words and images.

Meter: At the outset, v. 14 furnishes still another example of a three-part verse (3 + 3 + 2), as is also the case in v. 15 (4 + 3 + 2).

Verse 16aα seems to be constructed using 2 + 2 + 2 stresses (unless the verse should be read as prose).

Verse 16aβ-b is hard to analyze, which might be because of a textual corruption that cannot be fixed. It is possibly a three-part line of verse, each with three stresses, something such as: ואמר רזי־לי רזי־לי / אוי לי בגדים בגדו / ובגד בוגדים בגדו

Verse 17: three-stress + three-stress bicolon.

Verse 18: 3 five-stress cola (והיה, "and it will happen," is not part of the metrical structure).

Verse 19, once again, is a three-part verse (3 + 3 + 3), which is probably to be read with the stressed syllables as follows: התרועעה, התפוררה, and התמוטטה.

Verse 20 is constructed using 2 three-stress + three-stress bicola (נוע, "staggering," is not stressed at all; by contrast, והתנודדה, "tottering," has two stresses).

This material generally follows the pattern of composing verses with three constituent parts. One might wonder whether the two-part verses could have been inserted into the text at a later time. However, since other passages also alternate between three-part and two-part verses, this type of literary-critical elimination of material could certainly not be justified solely on the basis of an uneven metrical structure. Using the criterion of content, there is no justifiable reason for eliminating those verses; however, see below, pp. 499f.

Setting

Verses 14-20 are set virtually in the same situation as vv. 1-6; the passage must certainly have been composed by the same author, though it is possible that it was written somewhat later. Thus these verses also belong to the original body of material in the apocalypse.

Commentary

[24:14f.] The news about the great turn of events within history caused the המה (each one, they) to engage in excessive celebrating. The joyful celebration could be heard from the western sea (concerning מים, see above, textual note 14d) and could be heard at the very same time from the region where light first could be seen at daybreak (concerning ארים, see above, textual note 15b). It was heard also among those who inhabited the coastlands (concerning אי, see above, p. 297); finally, it could be detected even at the farthest edge of the earth. It seems that this language suggests that it could be heard in all the places where those scattered in the worldwide diaspora of Judaism were living at the time when Persia was in control.

Three verbs are used to describe this jubilation: רנן (raise [a voice]) is usually found within cultic contexts; the rare term צהל (exult) originally described the neighing sound made by a horse, but is also used together with רנן (there: be glad) in 12:6, in the summons to praise God; כבד (honor) is also used with God as the object in 25:3, as well as in 1 Sam. 2:30; Isa. 29:13; 43:20; Ps. 22:24. One cannot be sure whether this verb refers to the cultic celebrations of victory or whether it describes a spontaneous outburst of jubilation when one hears the good news. Even if the latter solution is correct, however, the honor would still have been accorded to Yahweh, more specifically, according to v. 14b., to the גאון, to the supremacy, to the grandeur, of

Yahweh. The OT does not speak about Yahweh's גאון (supremacy) often, but it is appropriate to say that this terminology is characteristic of Isaiah; see 2:10, 19, 21, used in parallel, all three times, with פחד, the awesome fear before Yahweh. The song of the sea in Exodus 15, a song of victory, is dominated by the theme that the גאון (supremacy) of Yahweh, or the fullness of his גאון (supremacy), has thrown his enemies down. That song begins with encouragement to one's self: אשירה ליהוה כי־גאה גאה (Let me [NRSV: I will] sing to Yahweh, for he has triumphed gloriously) (15:1b; see also v. 21b). According to Mic. 5:3, the messiah shall feed his flock in the גאון (majesty) of the name of Yahweh. Yahweh's גאון (supremacy) shows itself in the way he uses his power (see also Job 37:4 and cf. Isa. 26:10), especially when he strikes down the enemies of Israel in wartime. His גאון (supremacy) causes widespread terror. According to H.-P. Stähli (*THAT* I, 380), the word was not used in everyday speech, but rather in poetic compositions. Similar terms speak of the majesty of the deity or of the king, capable of causing widespread terror, in both Mesopotamia and Egypt; see, e.g., Ashurbanipal's Annals (Rm I, 85f.: VAB VII/2, 8ff.): "The glamor (or the majesty) of my kingdom . . . dazzled him (*melammu šarrūtiya iktumušu*)" [quote from *ANET* 294]; cf. also the Taylor Prism II, 34ff., III, 29ff., in *AOT* 352, 354; and Gilgamesh IV, V, 45 (Schott and von Soden); or: "The (terror-inspiring) splendor of Ashur and Ishtar blinded (lit.: overwhelmed) him (thus) that he became a madman" (Rm I, 84: VAB, VII/2, 8f. [quote from *ANET* 294]); see also AOAT 11 (1971) 74f.; and, for Egypt: S. Morenz, *Der Schrecken Pharaos: Religion und Geschichte des alten Ägypten* (1975) 139–150.

In parallel with גאון יהוה (supremacy of Yahweh), one finds the phrase שם יהוה אלהי ישראל (the name of Yahweh, the God of Israel) in v. 15b. This formula, which is used in exactly this form elsewhere only in 1 Kings 8:17, 20 (and the passages in 2 Chron. 6:7, 10, which quote from 1 Kings), is directly linked to the deuteronomic שם (Name) theology. As is well known, the phrase שם יהוה (name of Yahweh) can be used interchangeably with Yahweh's own name within the cult, in which cases its use can be attributed simply to the need to have another way to say the same thing. Of course, much more is behind its use in the present passage. When a name is used, power goes forth, that power which is inherent in the person who goes by that name. The שם (name), as a dynamic dimension, is the essence of the deeds and accomplishments of a person, and thus also of the respect and praiseworthiness which that person deserves. The present passage thus specifically calls for honoring that name, because the fullness of the power and majesty of Yahweh has become clear in the events that the author has in view, thus manifesting the full importance of his שם (name).

The way the points of the compass are identified is interesting. ים, of course, is used also in other passages that speak about the west, since Israel immediately would have thought of the Mediterranean, and only that referent, when the sea was mentioned. Based on what has been said above (textual note 15b), אֻרים is used as a way to designate the east. The coastal regions would have to be sought farther north then, e.g., one might identify them with those situated north of Israel along the coast of Syria and Asia Minor, possibly also those on the island of Cyprus.

[24:16a] If that interpretation is correct, then the כְנַף הָאָרֶץ (farthest edge of the earth) would have to be as far south as one could go, which means Upper Egypt, where some of the Jews from the diaspora (at Elephantine) were living. The OT speaks otherwise about the (four) כַנְפוֹת הָאָרֶץ (farthest edges of the earth) only in the plural, as in 11:12, which mentions gathering Israel from the four farthest edges of the earth; cf. also Ezek. 7:2; Job 37:3; 38:13. This would seem to be a term used initially during the exilic-postexilic era.

The author went to a lot of trouble to use terms that were not overworked. One might compare this idea that the Jews were on the move in every part of the world with that in Zech. 6:1ff., which speaks of the four chariots, which "are the four winds of heaven going out": the black steed toward the north, the white toward the east, the dappled toward the south, and the red toward the west (text emended). As in that passage, here also it is a crisis within the Persian Empire that provides the historical background for this hope, as it is expressed here in the Isaiah apocalypse. Hopes were apparently fanned time and again in the various parts of that huge realm, as many Jews in the diaspora wished for a great change in the state of affairs, accompanied by the further hope that one could return home soon. There were most likely even more Jews in the diaspora during the Greek era, but they were no longer all under one and the same worldwide power, and what had once been such a burning hope for a return later seems to have been put on the back burner.

The זמרת (song of joy), which was heard coming from all four cardinal points, was heard by a group of people that included the author, who speaks about "we," presumably an assembly of those faithful to Yahweh who lived in Jerusalem and who followed not only the events transpiring within world history but also the reactions of the people of God to what was happening, even in lands that were far from Jerusalem.

The content of the song is summarized as צְבִי לַצַדִּיק (to the righteous one, majesty). For us, that is a difficult piece of information to interpret. What does צְבִי mean and who is the צַדִּיק (righteous one)? Since Yahweh is apparently the one who is to be praised, it seems likely that the צַדִּיק (righteous one), to whom צְבִי (majesty) is attributed, is God. Some have objected that הַצַדִּיק (the righteous one), without any further clarification, is never used elsewhere about God, so that they understand the reference to "the righteous one" to be about "the people of the Torah" (Duhm), "the pious people of God" (Procksch), "the righteous or pious Israelites" (Feldmann), "the pious Jews" (Kaiser), or something similar. Justifiably, Henry has raised questions about this solution; it would seem "rather strange that, in a hymn which praises the God who rules over the whole world, without any transition . . . at the highpoint of the song, a new term would appear all of a sudden, which . . . would take the song in an entirely unexpected new direction" (49). There is no denying that הַצַדִּיק (the righteous one) never became a divine epithet, as did terms such as הקדוש (the holy one). But some OT passages certainly come close to this usage, such as יהוה הצדיק (Yahweh is in the right) in Exod. 9:27; אל־צדיק ומושיע (a righteous God and a Savior) in Isa. 45:21; אלהים צדיק (O righteous God) in Ps. 7:10; צדיק יהוה (Yahweh is righteousness) in Ps. 11:7, and often elsewhere; חנון יהוה וצדיק (gracious is Yahweh, and righteous) in Ps. 116:5. Finally, in Job 34:17, God is identified as צדיק כביר, the "righteous mighty." Thus on the one hand it is certainly possible, within the confines of the OT, that הצדיק (the righteous one) can be used as a term for God. And on the other hand there is no place in the OT where Israel or even the "true Israel" is addressed in an abbreviated way as הצדיק (the righteous one). In later apocalyptic, "the righteous one" is a designation for the savior who will come at the end of time, Ethiopic (1) Enoch 38:2; 53:6, but that work is located "beyond the horizon" (Kaiser) of the prophet who is speaking here.

Now, of course, one has to explain the way צבי (majesty) is used so that it fits with the use of הצדיק (the righteous one). The word can be used in such a way that it describes the land of Israel more specifically (Dan. 11:16, 41: ארץ־הצבי, "beautiful land"). Jeremiah already spoke of אֶרֶץ חֶמְדָּה נַחֲלַת צְבִי צִבְאוֹת גּוֹיִם (a pleasant land, the most beautiful heritage of all the nations) (3:19; cf. also Ezek. 20:6). Zimmerli thinks that the word practically became "an apocalyptic code word for the 'promised land'" (BK XIII/1, 445 [Engl: Ezekiel 1, 408]). Modifying this observation somewhat, Kaiser thinks that "the poet may have been thinking of the renewal of the country, serving the Jews as an adornment." The most direct reference to the land as הצבי (the beautiful) is in Dan. 8:9 (though that text is unfortunately not without problems). It is clear that, if one interprets צבי in reference to the land, then "the righteous one" has to be Israel, but that is quite unlikely, based on what has just been said above. Therefore some think that צבי refers to the beautiful ornaments (see Ezek. 7:20) that the pilgrims or representatives of the peoples were bringing to Yahweh in Jerusalem. Now it is true that ancient Israel repeatedly lived in the hope that the peoples would come to Jerusalem with their gifts (see above, pp. 223f.), but these are never designated צבי. It is possible that the author might have used this term precisely because it did not refer only to material gifts but to everything that could proclaim the majesty of Yahweh.

[24:16b] The prophet is deeply upset by the reaction of those who shared the faith with him. Up to that point, he himself had not been made aware of any details about restoration for Israel, but simply knew that a catastrophe was coming upon the earth, one that would cause a most gruesome terror.

Unfortunately, the double use of רזי־לי (I am done for, I am done for) cannot be explained with complete confidence (see above, textual note 16b); thus one must start with אוי לי (woe is me), which the prophet uses to express his shock at what he has detected is happening; on this, see previous discussion about both 16:11ff. and 21:2ff. According to what we can figure out, he was shaken to the point that he hurt physically and was completely upset inside, so that to speak about losing all strength (on this, see above, on 17:4) would certainly fit well. He is not concerned about singing hymns; instead, he feels that he is virtually at the end of his physical existence.

It is hard to say what is meant specifically by בָּגַד (here: deal cunningly). The author apparently adapts this from 21:2, where the prophet's חָזוּת (vision) is experienced as קָשָׁה (harsh), because he has been forced to observe that "with cunning the cunning one acts." It is possible that one should adopt "rob" as the meaning, as suggested by Ges-Buhl. But, one way or another, this is a bitterly evil time. It is not enough for the prophet to use this formula הַבּוֹגֵד בּוֹגֵד (with cunning the cunning one acts) just once; he wants to do 21:2 one better and thus he writes וּבָגָד בּוֹגְדִים בָּגָדוּ (in cunning the cunning ones act cunningly). One cannot conceive of, and plumb the depths of, how horrible this event really is.

Other passages in the OT are plays on words, with a certain vocable being repeated; cf., e.g., Isa. 29:14: הַפְלֵא וָפֶלֶא לְהַפְלִיא (amazing things, shocking and amazing), but cf. also passages such as Maqlū I, 126–130:

LÚ*kaššapu ikšipanni kišpi ikšipanni kišipšu*
MÍ*kaššaptu takšipanni kišpi takšipanni kišipši*
   ēpišu ipušanni ipšu ipušanni epusu
   epištu tepušanni ipšu tepušanni epusi
   muštepištu tepušanni ipšu tepušanni epusi

The enchanter who has enchanted me: with the enchanting,
   with which he has enchanted me, may you enchant him!
The enchantress, who has enchanted me: with the enchanting,
   with which she has enchanted me, may you enchant her!
The conjurer, who has conjured me: with the conjuring, with
   which he has conjured me, may you conjure him!
The conjuress, who has conjured me: with the conjuring, with
   which she has conjured me, may you conjure her!
The bewitcher, who has bewitched me: with the bewitching,
   with which she has bewitched me, may you bewitch her!
   (BAfO 2 [1937] 12).

One might wonder whether these wordplays could have been used originally in texts in which oaths were uttered.

[24:17f.] The next two verses, 17f., would seem to fit better in the context of Jeremiah 48 and frankly seem to have been inserted here by the prophet (or an expander?) after having been "gleaned" (see above, the chart on p. 129).

Obviously פַּחַד (horror), פַּחַת (hole), and פַּח (holder) are used together here because of alliteration. The rare word פַּחַת can be used to describe a hole where someone would hide from enemies (2 Sam. 17:9). But here it is probably used in the sense of the kind of hole or pit one would have dug in order to catch animals. Nonetheless, Dalman (*AuS* VI, 335) thinks it describes a hole that would be useful to a bird catcher who was trying to stay out of sight. פַּח (holder) (translated as *Garn,* "yarn," in the German [along with *Grauen* and *Grube*] only because of the attempt to replicate the alliteration)

499

is probably a type of net used by the fowler, which claps together when sprung (see H. Wildberger, "Schlinge," *BHH* III, 1702f.; and illus. 63, which depicts nets that clap together, in Dalman, *AuS* VI).

[24:18a] Concerning the thought that one would not be able to escape from judgment, Amos uses similar images in 5:19; 9:1ff. (cf. also Ps. 139:7-12); in Amos, however, once again it obviously deals with judgment on Israel. See also Erra Epic IV, 75ff., in P. F. Gössmann Oesa, *Das Era-Epos* (1955) 30f.

[24:18b] Verse 18b switches to a completely different line of thought (as often elsewhere, כִּי, "truly," at the beginning, is not a causal conjunction but is used as a particle of emphasis). As mentioned already, the sentence "The windows in the heights open themselves wide" could be a comment reminiscent of Gen. 7:11; 8:2 (P), or even a prototype of P. Is the prophet expecting a new flood? One cannot be sure of that; the vocabulary in 2 Kings 7:2, 19 also speaks of אֲרֻבּוֹת בַּשָּׁמַיִם (windows in the sky) and Mal. 3:10 of the אֲרֻבּוֹת הַשָּׁמַיִם (windows of heaven), without either passage suggesting that there would be another flood, but simply that a violent rainstorm was expected. The second half of the verse seems to be speaking of an earthquake. However, neither a worldwide flood nor an earthquake fits well with the concepts that are usually mentioned when speaking of the coming worldwide judgment. When dealing with this type of material on a literary-critical level, one ought not allow oneself to be led in the wrong direction just because these images do not seem to fit together well. A whole host of concepts hit the prophet, in a disorganized way, more than one could handle all at once; the modern exegete has to come to the conclusion that images are brought together here that occur originally in very different contexts. Their unity is found in the way they portray the unspeakable terror of what is to come by using the wealth of the disparate material that went through the author's mind.

When one says that the heavens have windows, then, from the commonly accepted view of the world, one is assuming that the heavenly ocean is located above the firmament (see B. Meissner, *BuA* II [1925] 107ff.; and T. Jacobsen in H. A. Frankfort, et al., *Before Philosophy* [1949] 194f.). It is true that the prophet says "heights" instead of "heaven," but that is simply part of his own unique style of speech (see above, p. 478). It is another aspect of the same worldview that the earth rests on foundations (Mic. 6:2, and often elsewhere). More than once the OT speaks about the earth quaking when Yahweh goes forth in power against the enemies: Judg. 5:4; 2 Sam. 22:8, similarly in Ps. 18:8; Isa. 13:13; Jer. 10:10; 51:29; Pss. 68:9; 77:19.

[24:19] As Yahweh takes care of this matter, the cosmos itself falls to pieces. This is the same thing that the following verses, 19, 20, have to say, even though other passages do suggest that the whole earth stands firm and does not sway (Pss. 93:1; 96:10) or say that it is founded on sturdy bases (Job 38:6). When, in spite of that, the earth is in motion, it shows that the chaos had been subdued, yet it had not been rendered completely powerless. Even though Yahweh has carried out the work of creation, chaos could gain the upper hand once again. The first two parts of v. 19 fit in at this point: "Bursting, the earth bursts apart, splitting, the earth splits open." One senses how much effort is expended by the author to go beyond traditional ideas so that something can still be said about that which seemingly cannot be discussed any further. The same is true about the comparison that relates the way the earth staggers to the staggering of a drunk; this is daring and unique, just as is the following depiction, which refers to a hut, built for the night in a field, that takes almost no time to throw together. It can totter even when a light gust of wind hits it, and a watchman would spend some uncomfortable hours if in it during a storm. מלונה (hut for the night) is used elsewhere only in 1:8; see *Isaiah 1–12*, p. 31.

[24:20] Verse 20bα does not furnish any new details for the description of the worldwide catastrophe, but gives the reason why the judgment is going to be so severe: "Its foolishness (פֶּשַׁע) weighs down heavy on itself." It is not immediately apparent what should come into one's mind when פֶּשַׁע is mentioned; however, one might relate this with what is said about breaking the covenant, in v. 5, as was explained in the discussion of that verse. "Whoever commits *pæšaʿ* . . . breaks with him [Yahweh], takes away from him what is his, embezzles it, misappropriates what is there. Even though this always implies that a conscious act has been committed, the concept as such does not refer to one's intentions, but to perpetrating a deed, which insinuates that possessions have been ripped off or that a break has occurred between some individuals who are part of the same group. Therefore, according to the OT, the worst aspect about sinning is committing that deed which causes a split within a group" (R. Knierim, *THAT* II, 493). Concerning the way sins are a burden loaded on a fool, cf. Ps. 38:5.

Now, at the very end of it all, in v. 20bβ, the point is driven home once again that the break cannot be reversed; this little verse matches the wording in Amos 5:2, right down to the ו (and) that precedes וְנָפְלָה (it falls), though that passage refers to maiden Israel. It is characteristic of the freedom exercised by those who are at work in this type of prophecy, when they employ the "scriptures," that such verses can be used, one might say, without any second thoughts, the written material serving as a quarry from which individual pieces can be used to construct one's own argument. Duhm thinks it unfortunate that this little phrase was quoted this way, since it gives trouble to a reader: "How is one to picture the downfall of the earth, and how might v. 23 make sense in the way it is linked with 25:6ff., if it is never going to come back into existence again." Now, according to the above analysis, 25:6ff. comes from a different author. Besides this, one might indeed admit that one would have trouble understanding the passage when it says that the earth will fall and will rise no more, but the issue is not to be resolved just so we feel satisfied with it; see what is said about the concept of the downfall of the earth in Papyrus Salt (cf. above, p. 483).

In connection with נָפְלָה (it falls), one also should recheck the information that is supplied about the fall of Babylon in 21:9. The verb נָפַל (fall) is used in a specialized way in laments for the dead (see above, p. 325). But the author is not satisfied yet; he also inserts וְלֹא־תֹסִיף קוּם (it will never stand up again). Within all the OT songs of lament for the dead, this little phrase is used elsewhere only in Amos 5:2. Thus one can be confident about saying that this is a direct citation from Amos. This text intends to say: the fall is an irreversible fact; the downfall of the earth is depicted as an event that no longer can be altered, one that is set in motion already.

Purpose and Thrust

The section of material in 24:14-20 forms a most remarkable passage. Indeed, maybe the most important reason behind this statement is that the text takes such a sharp and serious position against the simplistic expectation, held by a variety of groups who formed (diaspora) Judaism at that time, which presumed that the end of the present world order would include, right off the bat one might say, a restoration for Israel that was already on the way. In what follows it will become clear that the prophet did not think that the promises which had been given to Israel were no longer in force, nor that נָפְלָה וְלֹא־תֹסִיף קוּם (it falls—it will never stand up again) was the last word about the destiny of his people. But he did seem to want to prevent Israel from grinning from ear to ear, or possibly even stop them from enjoying the view, as the earth was about to experience incomparable destruction because of God's judgment. Initially, he simply speaks about how horrible what is going to come upon the earth will be. Israel as well, precisely Israel, was then supposed to pay attention to this message and be deeply moved, and thus was supposed to lay its songs of celebration aside.

The exegesis of the individual verses shows how much, specifically in this section, traditions that had been passed down were now reused. There is hardly a phrase that cannot be interpreted as an echo from some prophecy that had been spoken long ago. In spite of this, the material as a whole conveys something quite different from the sum total of the individual concepts, since these have been assigned a new function, used now to speak about the "earth" as a whole. In vv. 18b-20, where the prophet tells about how everything will completely break apart, he comes the closest to using his own words. The reason for the coming of the end—though one should note that he never uses that terminology himself—is discussed only in a very short but very important phrase in v. 20bα. A preexilic prophet would have offered more expansive and discriminating arguments. However, it would make no sense to try to identify the hardships point by point if one were convinced, as was this prophet, that the basic disrespect for the order that God established in the world had brought on this hopeless situation; every attempt to enumerate the specific details would serve no other function than as a digression, actually weakening the argument.

It might be worth noting that neither the word "Yahweh" nor the word "God" is used in this relatively expansive description in vv. 16b-20. This lack does not mean that one should not think of this as a judgment from Yahweh, but rather: the events can take their natural course; Yahweh does not have to do anything else. The פֶּשַׁע (foolishness) was weighing down, already now, on human beings and the world at large. One does not need to speak of God (should one say: one does not even need to know who Yahweh is?) in order to see how critically dangerous the situation had become.

The End of the World's Kingdoms and the Breaking In of the Reign of God

Literature
[**Literature update through 1979:** N. Perrin, "The Interpretation of a Biblical Symbol," *JR* 55 (1975) 348–370.]

Text
21 ^aAnd on that day it will happen^a that Yahweh will call to account the host of the heights ^bin the heights^b and the kings of the earth ^bon the earth.^b 22 And they will be imprisoned ^aas one confines a prisoner in a hole,^a and ^bwill be confined under strict watch,^b and will be summoned to give an account after many^c days.
23 And the moon^a will be red with shame
and the sun^a will be white with humiliation,
    for Yahweh of Hosts will have become king
on Mount Zion
    and in Jerusalem,
        ^band in the presence of his elders is glory.^{cb}

21a–a והיה ביום ההוא (and on that day it will happen) is missing in the Gk; however, there is no good reason for eliminating the formula.

21b–b and b–b The Gk has no parallel term for במרום (in the heights); the same is true of על־האדמה (on the earth). One can understand how the Gk text might have shortened the reading; it would be a mistake, however, to suggest that these two phrases are alternate readings.

22a–a It is difficult to explain the relationship between אספה (here: as one confines) and אסיר (prisoner); אספה is a hapax legomenon. Since one would expect a noun in the construct state to precede אסיר (prisoner), it would have to be altered to read either אספת (confining of) (Ewald) or אֹסֶף (also: confining of) (thus Duhm, with reference to 33:4; in addition, Guthe, Gray, Ehrlich, Feldmann, *BHS*, et al.; it might be that the ה on the end of אספה should be read as an article on אסיר, "prisoner"). However, since אסיר (prisoner) is missing in Qa, Gk, and probably also in Targ, it is possible that S. Talmon is correct (*Textus* 4 [1964] 123; see also *HAL*) when he suggests that אסיר (prisoner) was inserted later.

22b–b וסגרו על־מסגר (and will be confined under strict watch) is obviously not simply a "repetition of the preceding sentence" (contra Guthe).

504

22c According to H. D. Hummel (*JBL* 76 [1957] 102), רב (many) is an accusative expressing the passage of time; thus he suggests that the מ is an enclitic *mem,* which is to be moved to the end of מבצר (under strict watch). But there is no problem with using מן (from), immediately before designations of time, to mean "after."

23a and a The Gk translates הלבנה (moon) with ἡ πλίνθος, "brick, unbaked clay brick," and החמה (sun) with τὸ τεῖχος, "wall"; it treated these words as if they were pointed הלבנה and החמה (thus *BHS*). However, the Gk certainly made a mistake here; it simply did not know that the rare word חמה referred to the sun, and thus it also gave the wrong meaning to לבנה. Support for the fact that "moon" and "sun" are correct translations is furnished by 13:10, which uses שמש (sun) and ירח (moon) in a similar context. Kaiser translates לבנה as "the pale one" and חמה as "the hot one"; others interpret them in a similar fashion, but the edge has been taken off the original sense of this terminology. Fohrer translated חפר as "blush" and בוש as "grow pale"; this translation causes the sharp imagery of these terms to be lost.

23b–b At the end of v. 23, Schlögl suggests reading הגיד לזקניו כבודו (declare to his elders his glory), and *BHS* also proposes כבודי (his glory); however, these emendations also are completely unnecessary.

23c In place of כבוד (glory), the Gk reads δοξασθήσεται (he was glorified); thus it presumes that the verb form יכבד should be read here, which *BHS* also recommends as an emendation; in addition, it also left out צבאות (Hosts) and הר (mount), which is certainly not justified; cf. הר ציון (Mount Zion) in 4:5; 8:18; 10:12; 18:7; see also 25:6, 7, 10 (see above, p. 454). Wherever Zion is mentioned, it is common for the divine epithet צבאות (of Hosts) to show up as well (10:24; 18:7; 31:4; 37:32).

Form and Setting

The analysis presented above (see p. 453) has shown that an expander has inserted his own material at this point. However, good reasons can be offered for why this material is placed precisely here. The prophet has just objected to having Israel sing triumph songs. The expander does not contradict that; he is not speaking about Israel's triumph either, but rather is offering an announcement about Yahweh's total and final victory, at which time his rule as king over every place will come into full bloom. He testifies to the fact that only then will the worldwide catastrophe have reached its final goal.

Meter: It has been noted above already, on p. 453, that it is difficult to detect a meter here. Possibly v. 23 was made up of 2 three-part verses (each 2 + 2 + 3; וּבִירוּשָׁלַם, "and in Jerusalem," has two stresses).

Commentary

[24:21] Since the previous passage looks toward the eschatological turn of events, "that day" is obviously the day on which the great collapse takes place. However, once again, when it is used here, the formula conveys an eschatological sense only because of its context.

In 10:3, Isaiah speaks about the יוֹם פְּקֻדָּה (day of affliction), and the root פקד (call to account, afflict) is used frequently in the first part of the book of Isaiah when Yahweh's judgment is mentioned (see *Isaiah 1–12,* pp. 214f.), even though, apart from 10:3, none of the passages comes from Isaiah himself. In chaps. 24–27, it is clear that there is a surprisingly frequent use of the verb (in addition to 24:21, also 26:14, 16, 21; 27:1, 3). Already 13:11 mentioned that the evil of the world (תבל) would be requited, but that was with specific reference to Babylon. Here, however, virtually all the kings of the אדמה (earth) were to be called to account. Kings were not discussed at all in vv. 1-20, and it would seem that the author of that material was not thinking that the catastrophe would come in the form of a war. One also notes that those verses always refer to the ארץ (earth), whereas here the word אדמה (lit.: ground) is used. Both of these factors confirm that another author is at work in vv. 21-23. In the present passage, there is apparently one final struggle between Yahweh and the powers, who are evil personified. It is a battle that will be fought not only on the earth (על־האדמה) but also in heaven (במרום, in the heights). It is apparently not anticipated that the heavenly powers themselves would be involved in the battle on the earth—a concept used elsewhere in the OT (Judg. 5:20). It would seem that this refers to a battle in the heavens that would parallel that on earth; indeed, the heavenly battle is mentioned first, meaning that the battle with the kings that takes place on the אדמה (earth) describes earthly events that correspond to the heavenly struggle, the stage on which the decisive battle would actually be fought. Concerning מרום, "heights" = "heaven," see above, pp. 478f.

But who belongs to the צבא המרום (host of the heights)? Not all agree on the answer. Procksch, Rudolph (33), and others think it refers to angels and the heavenly leaders and protective angels of the peoples, just as they are referred to in the book of Daniel (see Dan. 10:13: "the prince of the kingdom of Persia," שׂר מלכות פרס, who opposes Michael, the guardian angel of Israel, who also has to do battle against the princes of the Greek lands according to 10:20f.). This is clearly a battle in the realms above the earth, the only difference being that it speaks of a שׂר (prince) in Daniel instead of a צבא (host). In addition, the book of Daniel also speaks about an angelic host (חיל שׁמיא, "host of heaven", 4:32; צבא השׁמים, "host of the heavens," 8:10), but that is a host which clearly stands at Yahweh's side. Josh. 5:15 knows of the existence of a שׂר־צבא יהוה (commander of the army of Yahweh). One also might remember that Luke 2:13 mentions the πλῆθος στρατιᾶς οὐρανίου, "multitude of the heavenly host," which certainly refers to hosts of angels, but, once again, these are some of the angels who glorify God. By contrast, the NT speaks of angelic beings who are going to be opponents of God in the last battle; see Luke 21:26 (δυνάμεις τῶν οὐρανῶν, "powers of the heavens"). Jer. 19:13 mentions צבא השׁמים, "the host of the stars" (see also 7:18, Gk), which were being worshiped; correspondingly, Acts 7:42 refers to the στρατία τοῦ οὐρανοῦ (host of heaven), to which God had delivered the idol-worshiping people of Israel. In other OT passages "host of heaven" also refers to the stars (Ps. 33:6; Isa. 45:12; Neh. 9:6; cf. also Jer. 33:22), but in all these passages they are "creations" and do not function as powers that oppose God at all. Among the peoples who lived in the regions around Israel, however, the stars were not simply viewed as harmless natural powers, but rather as forces that could determine one's destiny (see Meissner, *BuA* II [1925] 247ff.). This is why the star cult was forcefully rejected in Israel (see

Zeph. 1:5; Jer. 19:13, among other passages), though, according to Deut. 4:19, Yahweh allotted the stars to the other peoples. Except for Jer. 19:13, the stars are not treated as serious opponents for Yahweh in the OT, as those which would have to be "punished" in the final decisive battle.

Unfortunately, it is still impossible to discover specifically what was meant by the title יהוה צבאות (Yahweh of Hosts) (see H. Wildberger, FS Z. Shazar, 715–722); however, no matter what one determines the meaning of צבאות to be, whether it refers to the heavenly household of Yahweh (cf. scholars such as F. M. Cross, *HTR* 55 [1962] 256) or to the mythical natural forces of Canaan, which have had their powers taken away (thus V. Maag, *STU* 20 [1950] 50), in any case, here as well, one need not assume that Yahweh would be forced to engage in one final battle against them. In apocalyptic, however, the stars are treated as formidable opponents to the reign of God. Lindblom, along with Kaiser, points to Ethiopic (1) Enoch as the "best commentary" (Lindblom, 27); cf., e.g., 90:24: "Then his judgment took place. First among the stars, they received their judgment and were found guilty, and they went to the place of condemnation; and they were thrown into an abyss, full of fire and flame and full of the pillar of fire. Then those seventy shepherds were judged and found guilty; and they were cast into that fiery abyss" (trans. E. Isaac, in J. H. Charlesworth, ed., *The Old Testament Pseudepigrapha: Apocalyptic Literature and Testaments* I [1983] 70f.). Obviously one wonders whether this passage in Isaiah can be interpreted on the basis of the much later text in the Enoch apocalypse. In light of Jer. 19:13 and the Septuagint reading in Jer. 7:18, however, one can certainly take that chance. One must consider the possibility that this material has been shaped to some extent by influences from outside Israel proper. Even Gesenius suggested that this could have been an assimilation of ideas that originated in Zoroastrianism.

The Bundahish [a late Zoroastrian text] describes a final battle between the heavenly powers: "Then Ahura Mazda struck Angra Mainyu, Vohu Manah [struck] Akem Manah." At the end, Angra Mainyu is thrust "into the darkness" and plunges into "the darkness (of hell)"; see K. F. Geldner, *Die zoroastrische Religion,* Religionsgeschichtliche Lesebuch I (1926) 49 [Engl: *The Zoroastrian Religion in the Avesta,* trans. Jehangir C. Tavadia [1933]). Unfortunately, it is hard to say how old such Iranian concepts are. The so-called Oracle of Hystaspes (Lactantius, *Institutiones divina* 7.17.9-11) is certainly to be dated in the pre-Christian era. That writing depicts, first of all, general despotic activity, lawlessness, and the dissolution of all set order: "So, in one common game of freebooting, as it were, the whole world will be destroyed. When these things take place, then, the just and the followers of truth will separate themselves from the evil and will flee into the deserts. Upon hearing of this the impious one, inflamed with wrath, will come with a great army and, with all the troops he has summoned, he will surround the mountain in which the just are staying in order to seize them. And when they see themselves surrounded and besieged on all sides, they will cry out to God with a loud voice and will beg heavenly aid. God will hear them and will send a great king from heaven who will save them and set them free, and destroy all the impious with fire and sword" (G. Widengren, *Die Religion Irans,* RM 14 [1965] 201 [quoted from the Mary Francis McDonald translation of *Lactantius. The Divine Institutes,* Books I–VII, Fathers of the Church 49 (1964) 519]). Furthermore, another passage depicts the deliverance as having been brought about by the actions of "the great king" with the words: "Suddenly a sword will fall from the heavens so that the just may know that the Leader of the holy warfare is about to descend, and He will come down in the company of angels to the middle of the earth. There will come before Him an inextinguishable flame, and the power of angels will draw into bands that multitude of just souls which have surrounded the mountain. Then there will be slaughter from the third hour until evening, and blood will flow in the manner of a torrent. And after all his forces have been destroyed, that impious one alone will flee and his power will perish from him" (Lactantius, ibid., 7.19.5; Widengren, 202 [translation, McDonald, 521]).

Obviously, one cannot suggest that there is any direct dependence here. Yet such "parallels" show that, at the time when apocalyptic thought began to make its appearance, Israel lived in a world in which such concepts were certainly accessible.

[24:22] A rather uncommon motif is used in v. 22 as well: "And they will be imprisoned as one confines a prisoner in a hole, and will be confined under strict watch and be summoned to give an account after many days." One almost has to presume that the subject of אספו (they will be imprisoned) would include both the representatives of the heavenly hosts and the earthly powers that fought battles, those who were going to defend themselves against the rule of God in the final battle. בור (hole) might be a parallel term to שאול (Sheol). According to 14:15, the great leader of the world would be brought to שאול (Sheol), to the uttermost distant region of the בור (hole). There, others who formerly wielded power on earth, the kings of the nations, would be waiting for him. In the present passage, however, בור is to be treated as a reference to a hole that would have been used as a prison (cf. Gen. 37:20ff.; Jer. 38:6; in addition, see בית הבור, "the dungeon," in Exod. 12:29). In any case, after many days, those who were incarcerated would be "punished." Thus the events at the end of time would take place in two phases, so that only after an interim period would the final reckoning actually be carried out. At this point, we are encountering one of the first traces of what developed into the concept of a drama at the end of time, one that would unfold in various phases. This passage is apparently related to Rev. 20:1ff., according to which Satan would be in chains for one thousand years and would be cast into the underworld, which the angels of heaven would then lock and seal, "so that he would deceive the nations no more." Afterward, he would be let loose again for a short period of time; see the passage above quoted from Ethiopic (1) Enoch. According to the Apocalypse of Ten Weeks (Ethiopic Enoch 93 + 91:12-17 [being treated as one continuous original unit]), during the tenth week, in the seventh part, the great eternal judgment would take place "and it [the eternal judgment] shall be executed by the angels" (trans. E. Isaac; see above; see also the translation by Kautzsch; the text is uncertain). "The first heaven shall depart and pass away; a new heaven shall appear" (91:15f., Isaac translation). It is possible that the OT concept is in the background, since Yahweh, at an earlier time, at the creation, was victorious over his great opponent, the great sea monster, and had sealed it in the abyss. In addition to the OT passages, one might compare this with the Prayer of Manasseh, vv. 2f.: "you who made heaven and earth with all their order; who shackled the sea by your word of command, who confined the deep and sealed it with your terrible and glorious name" (NRSV; see H. Gunkel, *Schöpfung und Chaos in Urzeit und Endzeit* [1921²] 95). But there may be Iranian ideas behind this as well. In the Zoroastrian eschatology, the dragon Azhi Dahāka is bound on Mount Damawand, but he escapes from his fetters at the end of days and fills the world with his crimes. After a short time he would be conquered forever by Keresaspa, who had been slumbering until that time, being awakened then by two messengers of Ahura, at which point the time of salvation could begin (see Bahman Yašt 3:52-62; cf. Bundahish 29:8f.; F. M. Müller, *Sacred Books of the East* V [1880] 233ff., 119).

However, the question remains: just how far one can go in interpreting this short section in Isa. 24:21-23 by trying to fill in the gaps in its brief presentation with material from later times? This text says nothing about a prince or leader of the hosts of the heights, says nothing about how the "punishment" will be carried out, nothing about where "the hole" is to be found, nothing about how many days the powers are going to be confined there, and reports nothing about an interim kingdom during which the messiah would rule. Does the author really say nothing about all this because he can presume that his readers were already in the position of being able to fill in the details of his little picture in just this particular way? Hardly. What was later developed in apocalyptic thinking is simply in an embryonic form here. Yet the beginning of what later would come to the birth has now begun its gestation.

[24:23a] During the course of time, when everything was falling apart, the moon and sun would lose their former appearance. It is surprising that the moon is mentioned before the sun; in the rest of the OT that happens elsewhere only in Isa. 30:26; Ps. 104:19; Song of Sol. 6:10, though this is the normal sequence in Akkadian. לבנה is a designation for the moon only here, in Isa. 30:26, and in Song of Sol. 6:10; in both of the other passages, the designation for the sun is also חמה.

Why are the stars to be ashamed (בוש/חפר)? Kaiser thinks that the כבוד (glory) of Yahweh, mentioned in v. 23b, shines so brightly that it lights up the entire earth, not only the holy city, which then makes the light of the moon and sun pale by comparison (Isa. 60:19; Zech. 14:7; Rev. 21:23; 22:5). However, the word that is used is not "pale by comparison" but חפר (here: be red; lit.: be put to shame) and בוש (here: be white; lit.: be ashamed). Steinmann thinks that this expression is connected somehow with the star cult, whose stars themselves must now be ashamed. It would be more likely that the moon and sun, which had been understood to be those powers which ruled over the history of the peoples and over the destiny of each individual people, would now be shown publicly in their nothingness (see M. Klopfenstein, *Scham und Schande nach dem Alten Testament*, ATANT 62 [1972] 82). When one of these is unmasked and its meaninglessness exposed, then its self-respect is deeply affected, is ruined, so that the one affected is ashamed. It is possible, however, that the text does not want to say any more than that the cosmos itself is brought into the overall upheaval of all things. The concept is used in many contexts and is connected with the idea that eclipses of the sun and moon got the people thinking about the destruction of the world; on this, see the description of the frightening end of the world (see above, p. 483) to which reference was made in Papyrus Salt; cf. also the interpretation offered by Derchain, 24ff. To be sure, this text is not yet eschatological; it describes a crisis situation, one that had recurred time and again (e.g., at the death of a pharaoh), but that could be rendered harmless if the proper rites were observed. However, the material that originated in this setting was then used to portray apocalyptic events.

[24:23b] Only at the very end is the promise finally given, though it was because of what was to come that the end of the world and the cosmic upheaval were even mentioned in the first place; this is about the establishment of Yahweh's rule as king on Mount Zion. Concerning the royal titles of Yahweh, see *Isaiah 1–12*, pp. 261f. According to that Isaianic passage (6:1), Yahweh is enthroned in the temple or possibly in his heavenly sanctuary. The very ancient Psalm 29 already had declared that Yahweh was enthroned as king forever (v. 10); Psalm 93 declares: "Your throne is established from of old; you are from everlasting" (v. 2). The identifying mark, which denotes a song of ascent to the throne, יהוה מלך (Yahweh [is] king), thus should not be translated in a preterite sense; certainly Yahweh must not ascend to his throne again and again; he *is* king. Various scholars have already shown that the translation "Yahweh has become king" or some similar rendering is an inaccurate translation, even on philological grounds (see J. Ridderbos, *VT* 4 [1954] 87–89; D. Michel, *VT* 6 [1956] 40–68; and cf. L. Köhler, *VT* 3 [1953] 188). In this passage, however, the order of the words is reversed: מלך יהוה (Yahweh rules), and the phrase at the beginning of this section, which introduces it all, is והיה ביום ההוא (and on that day it will happen), which means that מלך יהוה is a *futurum exactum* (Yahweh will rule).

The point is that כבוד (glory), in the presence of his elders, is not a condition that exists already either, but is one aspect of the eschatological hope; this means: the divine rule of God is projected here into the future; the teleological-dynamic character of faith in Yahweh has transformed the static structure that shaped the ancient Near Eastern concept of the kingdom of God; see V. Maag, VTSup 7 (1960) 129–153, esp. 151, note 1: "The magical-mythic formula is given a new meaning, an eschatological one." The confession concerning the royal rule of Yahweh is thus altered to become an eschatological-apocalyptic faith statement. That is certainly not intended to

deny the present aspect of the βασιλεία τοῦ θεοῦ (kingdom of God). However, because human beings broke that relationship of trust, its status was
uncertain and it was challenged by the "powers." In its full extent, and in a
way that could not be challenged or reversed, it would have to become clear
just exactly who is lord and master over all humanity and over the cosmic
forces. (One should note that the Jerusalem ideology of kingship is recast
into an eschatological framework in the same way in the messianic prediction.) This observation shows a clear line of development from Isaiah,
through Deutero-Isaiah, to apocalyptic. For Isaiah, Yahweh sits as king on
his throne, which is elevated up into the heights, and the seraphim sing: "His
כבוד (glory) shouts out, that which fills the earth" (6:3). Deutero-Isaiah
announces to the messenger who brings joyful news about Zion: מלך אלהיך,
"Your God (has become) king" (52:7; one should note the word order here as
well). He is not functioning in this role already, but will become king, in the
fullest sense of the word, when the time of salvation dawns. This reinterpretation can be explained on the basis of Deutero-Isaiah's understanding of
God; see a passage such as 40:9ff.: "Say to the cities of Judah, 'Here is your
God!' See, Yahweh God comes (יבוא) with might, and his arm rules for him.
. . . He will feed his flock like a shepherd" (though רעה, "shepherd," is a royal
title). Isa. 24:23b is not far from what is said in Deutero-Isaiah. If there is any
difference, at most it would be in the fact that the royal rule of Yahweh follows here, after the virtually complete ruin of the world powers. It is also not
far from this concept when Haggai anticipates that Yahweh will shake heaven
and earth and will throw down kings' thrones, the only difference being that
the change of rule in that passage would lead to the Davidide Zerubbabel ruling, instead of Yahweh ruling directly. It was already part of the ancient ideology of kingship that the Davidides would rule "to the ends of the earth"
(Ps. 72:8; cf. also v. 11; Zech. 9:10). It is an element of belief concerning creation that Yahweh is lord both of the cosmos and of history, and Deutero-
Isaiah systematically reflects on what this means (see H. Wildberger, "Der
Monotheismus Deuterojesajas," FS W. Zimmerli [1977] 506–530). In addition, one element within "songs of ascent to the throne" is that there is a celebration because Yahweh is king. The present passage thus bundles a variety
of traditions together within an apocalyptic context.

There is no alternative to Yahweh exercising his dominion from a base
in Zion, in Jerusalem, at the end of time. The songs of Zion already state that
Yahweh has a permanent residence on Zion (cf., e.g., Ps. 76:3: "His abode
has been established in Salem, his dwelling place in Zion"); cf. also Psalm
87; Exod. 15:17f. Isaiah also can make use of traditional phraseology to say
that Yahweh dwells on Zion (8:18) and that he has a fire on Zion and an oven
in Jerusalem (31:9). All of that means much more than that Jerusalem was
the site for the main sanctuary of the tribes that worshiped Yahweh, the place
to which Israel would come when making pilgrimages. Zion inherited and
made use of the ancient concepts about a divine mountain; that mountain—
according to the teaching about Jerusalem—has the highest possible magnificence (Ps. 78:68f.; see also Isa. 2:2); it is situated in the far north (Ps. 48:3),

and thus it brought the power of the ancient divine mountain to the north of Ugarit to nothing. From that particular place Yahweh would call to the earth, from the rising of the sun until its setting (Ps. 50:1f.); it is the navel of the world (Ezek. 38:12). After Yahweh conquered all the powers that would rise against him, then Yahweh's royal rule, which the people firmly believed would become reality, would finally reach the stage where it would be visible.

However, now there is one more surprise at the conclusion of the section: "And in the presence of his elders is glory (כבוד)." It could be that the expander chose the word כבוד (glory) on purpose, as the antithesis of וכבד עליה פשעה (its foolishness weighs down heavy on itself) (v. 20). In that passage, the foolishness of the people weighs heavily on them; here, the complete and visible "weightiness" of the presence of God is on Zion, in the presence of the elders (concerning the כבוד יהוה, "glory of Yahweh," see *Isaiah 1–12*, p. 267). Where Yahweh is king, there כבוד (glory) is also to be found; the only part that is surprising is that it will be "in the presence of his elders." Isa. 40:5 mentions the כבוד (glory) being revealed in the presence of all flesh. One would expect the same to be said here. According to Ezek. 10:4, 18, 19, the כבוד (glory) of Yahweh leaves the temple and, according to 11:22f., the city as well, though in the time of salvation it returns once again (43:2), in fact returning to the temple itself: "and lo! the כבוד (glory) of Yahweh filled the temple of Yahweh" (44:4; cf. 43:4). In addition, the כבוד (glory) of Yahweh is mentioned numerous times in the priestly writing, in the very contexts that discuss the establishment of the cult at Sinai (Exod. 24:16, 17; 40:34f.; Lev. 9:6, 23). The main topic there deals with the tabernacle, but it is obviously intended as a discussion about the temple in Jerusalem. The כבוד (glory) ensures the holiness of this holy location, indicates the presence of the holiness of the holy God, and makes it possible to carry out all the actions connected with worship, which then guarantees the holiness and the salvation of the people of Yahweh. When the prophet speaks here in 24:23 about the elders, before whom the כבוד (glory) is to be displayed, it shows that this passage also uses concepts linked to the covenant at Sinai; see Exod. 24:9-11 (E) and vv. 16f. (P). Based on the importance accorded to these traditio-historical themes, one can draw the conclusion that the presence of Yahweh on Zion would mean that unhindered cultic activity could be reinstituted on the mount of God, that is, on Zion, once the restoration had occurred. However, it has been noted at other times that the texts which form the apocalypse insert ancient traditions into completely new situations, which results in instances where one cannot be sure about how to interpret the passage. One wonders whether the elders in this passage are the representatives of Israel, as they are in the Sinai pericope, or whether they possibly appear on behalf of the peoples of the world in general. As explained above, p. 454, that 25:6-8 is thought to be the continuation of 24:21-23, and speaks there about a festival banquet (covenant banquet) for the peoples, would favor this latter suggestion. However, Israel also comes into view at the end of that section as well, which means that salvation for the nations does not prevent Israel from keeping its unique status.

The Revelation to John speaks about twenty-four elders, dressed in white garments, themselves seated before the throne of God on twenty-four thrones, whose task is to sing the song of praise to the creator and redeemer (see Gunkel, *Schöpfung,* 302ff.; W. Bousset, *Die Offenbarung Johannis,* KEK [1906[6]] 245ff.; H. Kraft, *Die Offenbarung des Johannes,* HNT 16a [1974], 96f.). There is also uncertainty concerning that passage about who the elders sitting before the throne represent.

Purpose and Thrust

This short section offers a brief summary of the apocalyptic message about the end of the worldwide empires and of the coming of the מלכות יהוה (kingdom of Yahweh). It includes a variety of concepts, such as the one about the host of the heights in the heights, the one about the confinement of the enemies of Yahweh in a pit, and the one that says there would be the two phases of the judgment, all of which depict eschatological events in summary fashion. The author had done a good job of reading the preceding prophecies in vv. 1-20. But he took the announcement about the great downfall, which was before him, a step further, even to the point of including some foreign (Iranian?) ideas. Verses 21-23 are closer to apocalyptic than is the preceding section, which forms part of the original body of material; one would almost be inclined to identify this as a tiny apocalypse. The most important contribution of the author is that he has taken the announcement of disaster, which he treats in his own unique way, and makes it flow into a prediction which declares that salvation will come. For him, only one matter is important: that Yahweh will be acknowledged as king. He still speaks—how could it be otherwise—about Zion, as the place where the divine action of salvation first would be seen, as the point in the world where the divine presence is concentrated. However, Zion is the source of salvation for the world, which will come as soon as it is freed from the powers who controlled and oppressed everyone. It is readily apparent that vv. 21-23 are very important for the NT message in general, and for the announcement of the coming of the βασιλεία τοῦ θεοῦ (kingdom of God) in particular, and it is not easy to accord to these insights the great importance that they deserve.

The Refuge for the Unimportant

Literature

G. B. Gray, "Critical Discussions: Isaiah 26; 25:1-5; 34:12-14," *ZAW* 31 (1911) 111–127. P. Lohmann, "Zu Text und Metrum einiger Stellen aus Jesaja. II. Das Lied Jes 25:1-5," *ZAW* 33 [1913] 256—262. J. Coste, "Le texte grec d'Isaïe XXV 1-5," *RB* 61 [1954] 67–86. J. A. Emerton, "A Textual Problem in Isaiah 25:2," *ZAW* 89 [1977] 64–73 [not yet studied].

[**Literature update through 1979:** H. J. Stoebe, "Anmerkungen zur Wurzel plʾ im Alten Testament," *TZ* 28/1 [1972] 13–23 (on 25:1).]

Text

25:1 Yahweh, you[a] are my God,
   I want to exalt you, I want to praise your name.[b]
For you have carried out wonders regarding plans,[c]
   [d]trustworthy and immovable,[d] even from a distance.
   2 Truly, you have made the city[a] into a pile of stones,[b]
   made the inaccessible fortifications into a mass of rubble,
so that the fortress of the 'impudent'[c] is no longer a city,[d]
   for all eternity it can never be built up once again.
   3 Therefore [a]the strong nation[a] will honor you,
   [b][the city of] the brutal peoples[b] will fear you,
   4 for you were a refuge[a] for the unimportant,
   a refuge[a] for the poor in their oppression,
   [b]a shelter from the downpour,
   a shade from the scorching (sun).[b]
   [c][For the [d]snorting of the brutal ones[d] is as a downpour in 'winter,'[e]
   5 as the scorching (of the sun) in a parched land.][a]
You will put a damper on the fuming[b] of the "impudent,"[c]
   [d][heat by means of a cloud's shadows][d]
   the (triumph) songs[e] of the brutal ones [f]will be stifled.[f]

1a Ehrlich (*Randglossen* IV, 88) suggests that אתה (you) belongs with the second half of the verse, treats יהוה אלהי (Yahweh, my God) as a vocative, and translates this (with reference to Gen. 49:8): "YHWH, my God, I will glorify you." That suggestion will not work; even the metrical structure does not allow it.

1b Gray wonders whether שִׁמְךָ (your name) was used on purpose, because it rhymed with אֲרוֹמִמְךָ (I will exalt you).

1c I. Eitan (*HUCA* 12/13 [1937/38] 71) suggests reading the verbal form עָצוֹתָ (you have planned) (root עוּץ = יעץ plan) Instead of עֵצוֹת (plans). If this were the case, then the *athnach* would have been placed correctly, under פלא (wonder). However, this change is not likely, both because of the meaning and the length of verse, besides the fact that the verbal form עצות (you have planned) (with a long *ō* as the "linking vowel") would raise suspicions as well. The *athnach* should be moved from פלא (wonders) and placed under עצות (plans). It is not clear what Q^a intended with its reading עצית, instead of עצות (plans) (see Kutscher, 221).

1d–d It is characteristic of this type of text to have words such as אֱמוּנָה אֹמֶן (trustworthy and immovable) used together, a style that uses more words than needed. Both words are objects of עשית (you have carried out): "things that are trustworthy and immovable." None of the versions did justice to the Hebrew wording of this text.

2a מֵעִיר (from the city) cannot be correct here; it does not help to refer to 17:1. The Gk reads πόλεις (cities) and might have found the reading עָרִים (cities) here; Targ: קִרְוֵי, also means "cities." By contrast, both Syr *qryt*ʾ (city) and Vulg (*civitas*) reflect a singular reading in the original. מֵעִיר (from a city) must have been influenced by part bα of this verse, as has been recognized for a long time already (Houbigant, Lowth, Döderlein, et al.). In light of the singular קִרְיָה (fortifications; BDB: town, city) in part aβ of this verse, the plural reading is probably not correct (contra *BHS*). Following most exegetes and *BHK*, הָעִיר (the city) should be read, which, if true, suggested to *BHK* that it was possible that the ה belonged originally with the preceding word שַׂמְתָּה (you made).

2b The Gk reads εἰς χῶμα (into a heap of rubbish); Targ: לְגַלִּין (into heaps). Presuming an analogy with לְמַפֵּלָה (a mass of rubble) In v. 2aβ, one might follow *BHS* and read לְגַל (into *a* heap of rubble).

2c The meaning itself raises suspicions about זָרִים (strangers). Instead of אַרְמוֹן זָרִים (fortress of the strangers), the Gk reads τὰ θεμέλια τῶν ἀσεβῶν (the foundations of the ungodly). For this reason, it has been suggested that one read זֵדִים (impudent) instead of זָרִים (strangers) (see two Hebrew MSS that already read it thus).

2d Gray (118) thinks that a different noun should be read here instead of מֵעִיר (from [being] a city), having a meaning much like גַּל (pile of stones) and מַפֵּלָה (mass of rubble), or (which is more likely) that a verb has been lost here, one that would parallel לֹא יִבָּנֶה (it can never be built up). However, מֵעִיר (here: is no longer a city) provides a good parallel for גַּל (pile of stones) and מַפֵּלָה (mass of rubble); see 17:1. Admittedly, the repetition of עִיר (city) is not very artistic; one wonders whether the text is still intact.

3a–a Instead of עַם עָז (strong nation), Kaiser suggests reading עַמִּים (peoples), which would have been changed to the present reading after קִרְיַת (the city) was inserted into v. 3b; but there is no way one can do without the adjective עָז (strong) as a parallel to עָרִיצִים (brutal).

3b–b Verse 3b, which has to be read as a four-stress colon, looks suspicious because it follows right after a three-stress colon in v. 3a. Most importantly, however, it is not likely that the reading "city of the brutal peoples" is correct. Gray (*Commentary* and *ZAW* 31 [1911] 119f.) suggests following the Gk and eliminates גּוֹיִם (peoples). However, one cannot remove גּוֹיִם (peoples) when it is used parallel to עַם (nation). It is better to follow Procksch, Hylmö, *BHS*, and Kaiser and to eliminate קִרְיַת (city of).

4a and a According to the way we would think this should have been written, it does not seem right that מעוז (refuge) is used twice. Even the Gk does not have an equivalent for the first occurrence. Gray thinks (based on a reference to 11:5) that the one מעוז (refuge) was used to replace a term that originally was a parallel word. But it is not the task of exegetes to "improve" the text.

4b–b Verse 4bα should be read as a two-stress + two-stress bicolon, as in both *BHK* and *BHS*, but Procksch would rather read a three-stress + three-stress bicolon, inserting הָיִיתָ (you have been) before מחסה (shelter), and he replaces מחרב (as the scorching [sun]) with v. 5aα: either כְּחֹרֶב בְּצָיוֹן (as the scorching [of the sun] in a parched land) or מחרב בצ" (from the scorching [of the sun] in . . .), but this suggestion should not be followed.

4c–5a With this gloss, an attempt is made to explain why "the poor" would need a מחסה מזרם (shelter from the downpour), which, of course, each reader can figure out on one's own.

4d–d רוח עריצים is translated, e.g., by Kaiser, as "the mind of the ruthless"; others read it "the angry breathing of the ruthless." Neither of these is any more satisfactory than the way רוח is usually translated, as "spirit." What is meant is that the conduct of the brutal ones, which comes forth from their spiritual nature, is "an excited breathing, 'snorting,' in which the psychic vitality (rage) explodes" (R. Albertz and C. Westermann, *THAT* II, 735).

4e קיר, "wall, city wall," is an impossible reading, even if one would try to preserve it by translating: "as a downpour against a city wall." For a long time already, it has been presumed that קוֹר or קֹר "winter," should be read instead of קיר (wall); see J. Carmignac, FS H. Bardtke (1968) 42.

5b Instead of reading שָׁאוֹן (fuming), Duhm, Marti suggest וּגְאוֹן (and the pride of) (see also *BHK*), looking to 13:11 for support. One will have to admit that this term would fit better with the verb כנע (subdue, humble) (*hiphʿil*); one can bend pride, but the same is not true of an uproar and fuming. Yet, since the author is so imprecise in his use of words, a textual change is hardly appropriate. One simply will have to translate הכניע with a word such as "dampen."

5c See textual note 2c for an explanation about changing זרים (strangers) to זדים (impudent ones).

5d–d Vulg translates this as *et quasi calore sub nube* (and just as heat under a cloud) (see also Targ: כְּטַלַל כֵּיף מְקַר, "as the shadow of a cool rock"), Zürcher Bibel: "as the heat through the shadows of clouds." But Procksch is justified in asking about just how apt it is for Yahweh to be compared to heat as clouds cast shadows when he humbles the enemies. No doubt this must be a gloss inserted by a "spirit-filled" reader.

5e For זמיר, Theod reads κληματίδα (little branch) (according to Marchalianus and Syh), which means that he read it as זְמוֹרָה, "tendril, climber" (see above, p. 183). זמיר II means "prune," זָמִיר I means "songs of joy" (see 24:16). One might wonder whether זמיר means "strength," which is the meaning of זִמְרָה in 12:2 (see *Isaiah 1–12*, p. 500, textual note 2b). On the one hand, that meaning would make better sense with the verb ענה (be put down, stopped), but, on the other hand, זמיר, "song of joy," furnishes a better parallel for שָׁאוֹן (fuming).

5f–f Targ reads יְמָאכוֹן, "they will be humbled"; Syr: *ttmkk* (you [or: she] will be humbled), which caused *BHS* to suggest the pointing יֵעָנֶה. Others (Guthe; Gray, ZAW 31 [1911] 118; see also *BHK*) change the person: תַּעֲנֶה (you humble), which would be supported by the parallel term הכניע (you put a damper on), but it is possible that it should be changed to read the passive form noted above.

516

Form

Concerning the extent of the section, and the form, see above, pp. 453f. The song has received many glosses: קִרְיַת (the city of) in v. 3; from the second כִּי (for) in v. 4 as far as צָיוֹן (parched land) in v. 5; and חֹרֶב בְּצֵל עָב (heat by means of a cloud's shadows) in v. 5. The arrangement is clear:

> v. 1a: Announcement of the intention to praise God
> v. 1b: Overarching reason: the wonderful actions of Yahweh
> v. 2: The destruction of the city
> v. 3: Calling to the peoples to honor Yahweh
> v. 4: The special reason for thanks: Yahweh is the shelter for the insignificant
> v. 5: The future expectation, which flows from learning about the help: Yahweh will dampen the fuming of the brutal ones

Some have tried to call this a city song. It is true that v. 2 directly announces the downfall of a city, but that is just the initial stimulus to praise Yahweh's פֶּלֶא עֵצוֹת (wonders regarding plans) with all one's heart. Yet the praise of God is not to be rendered for its own sake, but serves the function of providing the confidence for the "insignificant" that Yahweh is working on their side, in opposition to the brutal ones.

It is also clear that the song cannot be given an eschatological interpretation. It can be shown that it does not belong to the original body of material and, even more obviously, that its original context was not in a location between 24:21-23 and 25:6-8. The attempt to identify the downfall of the city historically has usually been tied to the attempt to discover some event that took on apocalyptic proportions. Thus it is not surprising that these attempts have been fruitless. However, it is true that the song was actually placed here by the compiler, because it was to testify that the Yahwistic community could remain confident in the oppressive climate at the end of time. Maybe it was the material that was inserted in 24:10-12, which also discusses the destruction of a city, that motivated him to use this section as paranesis for the community that would still exist at the end.

Meter: The entire poem is composed using three-stress + three-stress bicola (if one presumes that the passages noted above are glosses). The only exception would be the two-stress + two-stress bicolon in v. 4bα; its uniqueness also shows that this verse contains the main theme of the song. Three-part verses, which are typical in the rest of the material in chaps. 24–27, are completely missing—another indication that the material we are studying had its own history before it was inserted here.

Setting

When one is dealing with a song such as this, with all the contact points with cultic traditions, every attempt to identify the date is questionable from the outset. The vocables and phrases make it possible to find many links to the literature in the Psalms, as one would expect. However, the language has features that are unique to Isaiah. Concerning פֶּלֶא עֵצוֹת (wonders regarding plans) in v. 1, see 9:5 and 28:29; cf. also 29:14; in addition, עצה (plan) is obviously a typical Isaianic term; concerning אמונה (trustworthy) and אמן (immovable) in v. 1, cf. the special meaning for the root אמן in Isaiah (see *Isaiah 1–12*, pp. 302ff.) and, concerning אמונה (trustworthy), see 11:5; cf. also 26:2; 59:4. Concerning the use of two derivatives of the same root, cf. מִשְׁעֵן וּמַשְׁעֵנָה (support and staff) in 3:1 or גַּאֲוָתוֹ וּגְאוֹנוֹ (its haughtiness, its pride) in 16:6. Concerning the privative use of מן (away from, departing from being) (v. 2) in מֵעִיר (is no longer a city), see מֵעָם (will have ceased to be a people) in 7:8 and מֵעִיר (is a city no longer) in 17:1. קְרִיָה (city, town) is used twenty-nine times in the OT, ten of those being in Isaiah 1–33 (Isaianic: 1:21, 26; 22:2; 29:1); concerning מַפֵּלָה (pile of stones) in v. 2, see מַפֵּלָה (pile of rubble) in 17:1; however, cf. 23:13. It is surprising that so much of Isaiah's specialized vocabulary is used here or can be found elsewhere in the book of Isaiah: מַחְסֶה (shelter); זֶרֶם (downpour); צֵל (shade); חֹרֶב (scorching sun) (v. 4) are all used together also in 4:6; צָיוֹן (parched land) is used elsewhere in the OT only in 32:2. The statistical evidence for word usage indicates nothing that would contradict Plöger's assumption that the song is older than the original body of material in the apocalypse, and it is certainly possible that the conquest of the city refers to the conquest of Babylon by Xerxes, as has been suggested, most forcefully, by Lindblom.

Commentary

[25:1a] As is common in cultic songs, the name of God is at the beginning, and is in the vocative. In fact, one addresses God בשם יהוה (in the name of Yahweh). It is necessary to mention the name specifically, since human beings would pray to so many gods, but also because the deity would tune in only when personally addressed. It is common for יהוה (Yahweh) to be identified more exactly with the use of אלהי (my God) in apposition; here it turns into a short confessional statement: "You are my God"; cf. Pss. 31:15; 40:6; 86:2. In Babylonian psalms of this type, after the name of the god, a whole chain of epithets would follow that were supposed to sway the deity to act favorably toward the one praying (the OT is more cautious in this; "you are my God" is all one needs to say). The apposition "my God" or the confession "you are my God" is supposed to awaken the deity's interest in that particular person—it is to remind the deity that the one who is praying gives precedence to this deity, but also that one could legitimately count on the deity's faithfulness toward the one praying (see O. Eissfeldt, "'Mein Gott' im Alten Testament," *KlSchr* III [1966] 35–47 [Engl: "'My God' in the OT," *EvQ* 19 [1947] 7–20]). This text does not say "our God," and, for this reason, the verbs that follow are in the first person singular; thus this is not some form of Israelite victory song, but is the song of thanksgiving of an individual.

The verbs רום (exalt) *pil'el* and ידה II (praise) *hiph'il* belong to the introduction of a song of thanks. Concerning ידה (praise) *hiph'il,* cf. 12:1; of course, in that passage the verb means "thank," but here, with the object שֵׁם (name), it means "praise," and the meaning frequently comes quite close to what one might translate as "confess." All these ideas are interrelated here;

the confession is not simply a recitation of statements of faith, but is praise
and thanksgiving.

[25:1b] One does not praise Yahweh out of the clear blue, but because one
has experienced his help (see ישועה, "salvation," in 12:2). In the present case,
the poet formulates it as follows: "You have carried out wonders regarding
plans" (concerning פלא עצות, "planner of wonders," cf. *Isaiah 1–12,* p. 403;
and H. Wildberger, *TZ* 16 [1960] 316, 325; concerning עצה, "plans," see
Isaiah 1–12, pp. 202f.). When one speaks of פלא עצות (wonders regarding
plans), these are not *miracula,* but acts of salvation, deliverance from troubles during wartime, being freed from oppression, but also are the kinds of
help that the one who is praying can experience for oneself. Even though this
is a song of thanks of an individual, in the present case—the Isaianic term
עצה (plan) already points in this direction—the context suggests that this is
about deliverance from political oppression; in the eschatological perspective
into which the song is *now* inserted, that would be deliverance from the
oppressive pressures of the last times. Also, that this takes place "even from
a distance" (see 22:11 and 37:26) apparently uses a term that belongs to the
specialized vocabulary one would use when depicting the way in which the
deeds performed by Yahweh unfold according to a set "plan." For this same
reason, it is customary that one would use אמונה (trustworthy) when praising
the reliability of God's ability to offer help; cf. passages such as Ps. 33:4,
כל־מעשהו באמונה (and all his work is done in faithfulness). One can entrust
oneself to Yahweh (concerning אמונה, "trustworthiness," see H. Wildberger,
THAT I, 177ff., esp. 196ff.).

[25:2] Whereas Yahweh is praised through the use of formulas in v. 1b,
those commonly found in every song of thanksgiving, v. 2 furnishes more
specific details, at least for the author's contemporaries. What is said about
the city is roughly comparable, sometimes even on the level of actual vocabulary, to what is threatened will happen to Damascus in 17:1. It is common
for someone to speak about an עיר (city) or a קריה בצורה (inaccessible fortification), since that terminology points out the actual nature of a city, that it is
not very accessible (concerning the root בצר, "fortified," see above, p. 369).

In v. 2b the city is further characterized as ארמון זדים (the fortress of the
impudent) (text emended). Frequently, sections that deal with this particular
topic speak about palaces that have been destroyed; see 13:22; 23:13. But
here the word ארמון (fortress) is used metaphorically, with reference to the
city itself. By and large, the OT expresses an aversion to palaces and, by
extension, is also not favorably disposed toward those who live in them (cf.
Amos 3:9ff.), since palaces make a statement about the arrogance of their
owners. Concerning זד (impudent), see above, p. 26, on 13:11, where this
word parallels ערי־ן (high-mindedness).

According to Judg. 9:45, Abimelech scattered salt all over the
destroyed city of Shechem, in order to make it uninhabitable; and, according
to Deut. 13:17, a city that worshiped idols was forever to remain a תל (tell,

ruin) and was never to be rebuilt again; cf. also Ezek. 26:14. Over and over again, attempts were made to eradicate cities completely, even though those attempts did not last לעולם (for all eternity). One would try to obliterate a city because, as Deut. 13:13-18 points out beautifully, one would want to prevent its corrupting influence—in other cases its political-military might—from extending still farther. In the present case, לעולם (for all eternity) fits in very well as this text is given a new purpose in an apocalyptic context.

[25:3] As it now stands, v. 3 is practically incomprehensible; "the strong nation" likely refers to the residents of the destroyed city or at least the national group whose capital city had just been demolished. It is more difficult to figure out what קרית גוים עריצים ([the city of] the brutal peoples) means, since, in fact, this קריה (city) no longer exists. If קרית (the city of) is removed, as has been discussed already (textual note 3b–b), then what is being said is that the downfall of the city did not just make a deep impression on the "strong nation" alone, but on brutal peoples worldwide. In this way, a subtle distinction is made. The עם עז (strong nation) will recognize the greatness and majesty of Yahweh, will acknowledge him, and will give him honor. At the very least, the brutal peoples will fear him. The thought that people, including those who up to that time knew nothing of Yahweh, would turn to him, after they had witnessed his astounding works, shows up in other passages in the OT as well and is high on the list of Deutero-Isaiah's expectations; cf. 55:5. This viewpoint presumes that Yahweh's control within history would be rather easy to detect as the events unfolded, but also that the peoples and their gods were linked closely. On the one hand, if a people were subdued, that would have shown that its gods were powerless, and the people would have been ready to offer tribute to the gods of an opponent who had successfully defeated them; on the other hand, one would have feared a people whose gods had shown their power impressively; cf. passages such as the one describing the arguments used by the Rabshakeh in 36:13ff.

[25:4abα] Verse 4 shows that the author thought it most important to point out that Yahweh had shown that he was a refuge for the insignificant. As in 14:30a, where both vocables דל (insignificant) and אביון (poor) are used together (in an addition to the text), it is likely that they should be interpreted here as references to the Yahweh community, which sought and found protection in its God. מעוז (refuge) is a technical term, used in cultic contexts connected with Jerusalem; see Pss. 27:1; 28:8; 31:3, 5; 37:39; 43:2.

Two images should be highlighted further: Yahweh is מחסה מזרם (a shelter from the downpour) and צל מחרב (a shade from the scorching [sun]). A זרם, "downpour, cloudburst," can be most unpleasant in Palestine; cf. passages such as 28:2 or 30:30. However, the chief problem with heat is not just that it can be annoying at times, but that it can actually be life threatening. The basic meaning of the root form of the word חרב means "dryness," but it also is used at times to mean "heat." Shade is always most appreciated (cf. Jonah 4:5ff.); for this reason, the imagery is often chosen when one wants to depict the protection that the pious enjoy from Yahweh; e.g.: 'hide me in the shadow of your wings, from the wicked who despoil me" (Ps. 17:8f.; cf. Pss. 36:8; 57:2; 63:8; in addition, see Dalman, *AuS* I/2, 504ff.).

[25:4bβ-5aα] A glossator felt obligated to try to explain this imagery, which was already easy to understand: "for the snorting of the brutal ones is as a downpour in winter, as the scorching in a parched land." The עָרִיצִם (brutal ones) had been mentioned already in v. 3; there, however, the word referred to the brutal peoples; here it points to enemies who threaten an individual. The רוח (wind; here: snorting) can be very dangerous; one might note 30:28: "his [Yahweh's] רוח (breath) is like an overflowing stream that reaches up to the neck." This dynamic character of the spirit fits the comparison with the torrential downpour in winter better than the one that follows, which speaks of dry conditions in a parched region of the country, above which the summer heat hovers and which puts what is below it at the mercy of the intense heat of the sun, without the benefit of trees.

[25:5aβ-bβ] The antithesis to protection being provided for the poor is that a damper will be put on the impudent. Isa. 24:8 spoke of the שְׁאוֹן עַלִּיזִים (festive noise of those who are celebrating). There, as in 5:14, it referred to the שָׁאוֹן, the noise heard at a joyous festival; here, it is about the fuming of infuriated tyrants. Isaiah speaks about the שָׁאוֹן (crashing) of powerful masses of peoples, who storm on ahead like cascading water. It seems that a reference to the "noise" of a massive enemy army is intended in the present passage as well. שָׁאוֹן is to be interpreted as an expression of prideful behavior (cf. Job 40:12); for this reason, it is to be brought low or dampened (הַכְנִיעַ).

In 24:16 זמרת, the triumph or victory songs, were mentioned; here it is announced that the זמיר ([triumph] songs) of the brutal ones "would be stifled"; the pride of victory, which is given expression in the singing, would be wiped out completely.

The glossator tried to make things clearer here as well; he inserted חרב בצל עב (heat by means of a cloud's shadows); apparently he wanted to point out that the "heat" of the brutal ones would be rendered harmless by the shadows cast by a cloud. That line does not provide helpful insight. "Shadows" were just mentioned, to portray the protection that the pious find in Yahweh; here, however, the צל עב (cloud's shadows) are the means used to dampen the scorching rage of his opponents.

One ought not try to defend the viewpoint that such confusing glosses are really part of the original text.

Purpose and Thrust

The analysis and study of the individual verses has shown that one must be very careful, when examining 25:1-5, to distinguish between the original sense of what once was a discrete unit of material, a song of thanks, and the interpretation that has been imposed on it after it has been inserted into the apocalypse. As one sees in the way it ends, the song of thanks was supposed to move the community, in general terms, to place quiet trust in Yahweh. It is true that the downfall of a city is mentioned, which one would not expect to find in the song of thanks of an individual. Once again, one might ask the question about the use of "I" in the Psalms. Is this a king or commander or the collective "I" of Israel? One can presumably stay with the interpretation offered above, that a pious person, who had no special status, was moved by the downfall of a city, instead of by some normal type of personal deliverance, to portray for the fellow members of his community the way in which Yahweh was a helpful, protecting power.

Within the eschatological-apocalyptic framework, the city now becomes a symbol of the mighty power that opposes Yahweh, sounding much like what is said about Babylon in chaps. 13 and 21. Within this context, the זדִים (impudent) and עריצִים (brutal ones) are the enemies who storm Jerusalem, the city of God, at the end of time, who will experience a defeat that will end opposition to the reign of Yahweh on Zion, once and for all. The finality of this event is shown clearly in the use of מעִיר (is no longer a city) and most clearly in לעולם לא יבנה (for all eternity it can never be built up once again), in v. 2bβ. That Yahweh is the refuge for the insignificant and the shadow for the poor shows that the community that exists at the end of time will be safe, even in the midst of all the distress that is going to befall the whole world, and it can know that it will survive in good shape. Thus we have an interesting example of how a text is given a new interpretation and how traditional themes are reused. The answer to the question about whether such a text is to be interpreted eschatologically depends on one's presuppositions about whether one ought to look at individual units of material by themselves or only within the overall context in which they now stand, into which they have been inserted secondarily; said another way, one must decide which level in the process of the transmission of the material is to be treated as the decisive stage. However, there can be no doubt that the second alternative is the most important from a theological point of view.

The Celebratory Banquet upon Zion

Literature

F. Bammel, *Das heilige Mahl im Glauben der Völker* (1950). S. Virgulin, "Il lauto convito sul Sion," *BeO* 11 (1969) 57–64.
[**Literature update through 1979:** P. Grelot, *De la mort à la vie éternelle. Études de théologie biblique*, LD 67 (1971). G. von Rad, "Statements of Faith in the Old Testament about Life and about Death," in *God at Work in Israel* (1980), 194–209; M. Delcor, "Le festin d'immortalité sur la montagne de Sion à l'ère eschatologique en Is 25,6-9 à la lumière de la littérature ugaritique," *Salmanticensis* 23 (1976) 87–98. U. Kellermann, "Überwindung des Todesgeschicks in der alttestamentlichen Frömmigkeit vor und neben dem Auferstehungsglauben," *ZTK* 73 (1976) 259–282. H. Wildberger, "Das Freudenmahl auf dem Zion: Erwägungen zu Jes 25, 6-8," *TZ* 33 (1977) 373–383.]

Text

6 There Yahweh of Hosts makes preparations
   [a]for all peoples[a] on this mountain,
      [b]a banquet with rich foods,
   a banquet with aged wine,[b]
      with highest quality, rich foods,
         with aged, full bouquet wines.
7 And he destroys on this mountain
   the mask,[a] with which [b]the 'face of all peoples' is masked,[b] and the covering, which is spread out as a cover over all the nations[c] together.
8 [a]'And he will destroy' death forever.[a]
   And the Lord Yahweh will wipe away the tears from every face, and the humiliation of his people[b] he will remove completely from the whole earth.
   Truly, Yahweh has said this.

6a–a לכל־העמים (for all peoples) is missing in MSKen[23] (Gray), but that has to be a simple copying mistake.
6b–b "A banquet with rich foods, a banquet with aged wine," is missing in the Gk. If one wishes to follow Procksch and Sievers, reading 2 seven-stress cola in v. 6, then

one would have to shorten the text. But it seems that three-part verses are being used once again.

Ehrlich explains that there is no verb מחא or מחה with the meaning needed here, suggesting that ממחים is the result of a dittography of מחים, the plural of מֶח, "mark" (v. 8). But to read the participial form ממחים (here: rich foods) is shown to be correct by the parallel participle מזקקים (here: aged).

7a Since the root לוט means "cover," the lexica suggest that the hapax legomenon לוֹט means "covering, mask" (Arabic: *lāṭa*, "adhere to, smear over with clay"; Akkadian *lī/ēṭu* II seems to refer to some type of cloth, some form of covering). Ehrlich relates לוט to Aramaic לְיַט, postulating that the meaning thus would be "curse." But Hebrew has no such root לט with this meaning. The ancient versions apparently did not do justice to the word. Since לוט parallels מסכה (covering), however, one can stay with the traditional meaning of the word: "mask." Exegetes also have had trouble with the phrase פני־הלוט (lit.: the face of the mask). Houbigant and Lowth already had suggested, on the basis of a Hebrew MS, that פני (face of) be moved to the position just before כל־העמים, so that it would read: "the covering, which is covered over the face of all peoples." Admittedly, this suggested alteration has not won much of a following. Based on Job 41:5 (פְּנֵי לְבוּשׁוֹ, "outer garment"), some have posited a meaning such as: "that which is turned toward the face, the outer side of a veil" (Delitzsch), whereas others have followed the suggestion of Naegelsbach, who says this is a genitive of identity, which means the לוט (mask) itself is פָּנִים, "the outer side." These are nothing but random attempts to make some sense of a perplexing phrase. Houbigant and Lowth have possibly come the closest to what was intended.

7b–b An extended discussion has ensued about the way the second הלוט (here: masked) should be pointed. Qimḥi had already suggested that לוט was a passive participle (used here instead of the normal form לוּט, "is masked"). Ges-K §72p treats לוט as an active participle (having been used instead of the normal form לָט), followed by Delitzsch, von Orelli, Duhm, et al. However, still others stay with the passive interpretation, in which case it is assumed that לוט is pointed as it is because that way it rhymed with the preceding substantive. 1 Sam. 21:10 (see the feminine passive participle לוּטָה, "wrapped," in that passage) demonstrates that the passive can be used in this sense, and it is quite likely that it should be pointed לוּט. This suggested way to understand the verb seems to bring up another issue which is so problematic that it has caused some commentators to opt for still reading לוט as an active participle. A mask—so the argument goes—is not itself covered, but something is covered by a mask. But the solution to this problem is easy. "The verbs that describe covering can treat the covering as the object when used in the active sense and can treat it as the subject when in the passive sense" (Ehrlich)—just as one can see is clearly the case in the following phrase, המסכה הנסוכה (the covering, which is spread out as a cover)!

7c Qᵃ reads נואים (also: nations); see Kutscher, 511, who explains that the extra letter is added to separate the two vowels, so that they would be spoken separately (known as dissimilation).

8a–a On the one hand, the Gk translates this: κατέπιεν ὁ θάνατος (death swallows up); on the other hand, Aquila reads καταποντισει τον θανατον (he will throw death down); Sym: καταποθηναι ποιησει τον θανατον (he will make death to be swallowed up); Theod: κατεποθη ὁ θανατος (death will be swallowed up), the same reading as is found in 1 Cor. 15:54. Since the verb parallels ובלע (and he destroys) (v. 7), it is quite unlikely that the passive was read originally. Indeed, one must wonder whether ובלע (and he destroys) should be read here as well, just as previously; in fact, some MSS do have the ו (and); Syr does read the passive, but still reads the word with the copula (*wntblᶜ*, "and will be swallowed up").

There is no reason to doubt that לנצח means "forever." Sym (according to Eusebius) correctly reads εἰς τέλος (to the end), but Aquila (according to Marchalianus) and Theod (according to Marchalianus and Syh) and 1 Cor. 15:54 read εἰς νῖκος (in victory) (Gk also translates לנצח in 2 Sam. 2:26 as εἰς νῖκος (in victory). By contrast, Targ reads לעלמין (for ever); Syr combines both translations: *bzkw lᶜlmyn*, "through the victory forever." The reason for translating נצח as "victory" is because נצח means "be victorious" in both Aramaic and Syriac—Jews who spoke Aramaic took the meaning of the word with which they were familiar and used it when they were dealing with the Hebrew terminology. Concerning the problem about whether this little phrase was in the original, see below, p. 530.

Ehrlich suggests that מות supposedly means "pestilence" but that it is to be interpreted with a transferred meaning: "the plunderer and destroyer, which was as ruinous for the peoples as pestilence." That is not likely, but it is symptomatic of the fact that the phrase about death being swallowed up forever has been treated by exegetes as if it were completely out of place and ought not be left there.

8b The Gk has τοῦ λαοῦ (of a people), which is the reason why Ehrlich suggested that only עם (people) be read, since that would fit better in the context; no one else has adopted his reading.

Form

Analysis of this material (see p. 454) has shown that it furnishes a continuation for 24:21-23. The reference to בהר הזה (on this mountain) picks up בהר ציון (on Mount Zion) in 24:23. One might object that the author's contemporaries would already have known that ההר הזה (this mountain) could have brought only Zion to mind, but the formal argument is augmented by points of contact between the content of 24:21ff. and 25:6-8; both passages deal with promises, whereas the material that comes between these two sections is a song of thanksgiving, 25:1-5, which looks back on the past. If vv. 6-8 are the continuation of 24:21-23, however, that has consequences for the interpretation of the material, especially concerning the traditio-historical background of this short passage. In this case, the celebratory meal on Zion is to be interpreted in light of Yahweh establishing his rule on the mount of God.

This passage is unique in the OT when it promises that there would be a festive meal in which all peoples would participate; one must treat this idea as a brand new one, which the author himself composed. That does not exclude the possibility that certain motifs from the traditions at hand could have stimulated this grandiose and theologically very important vision that depicted an eschatological sacrificial meal. At first, one might think of ties with the tradition about the "pilgrimage of the peoples to Zion," portrayed most clearly in 2:2ff.; in addition, see especially chap. 60. However, Isa. 2:2ff. itself already furnishes us with a significant reinterpretation of what was apparently a much older tradition complex, elements of which can be detected also in some of the other passages in the OT; see *Isaiah 1–12*, pp. 89–92; see above also, pp. 223f. Isaiah 2 specifically mentions a pilgrimage to Zion, with the goal of that pilgrimage to the house of Yahweh being that there would be instruction concerning justice, with the related hope that there would be a lasting peace. In other passages, such as 18:7 (see above, pp. 223ff.), it is expected that the peoples would bring their gifts to Jerusalem; cf. also Pss. 96:7f.; 72:10; Zeph. 3:9f.; Isa. 45:14; 60:3ff., etc. (see H. Schmidt, "Israel, Zion und die Völker," diss., Zurich [1966], who differentiates among the motifs of a pilgrimage of peoples, an assembly of peoples, and the peoples bowing down in homage, though these types of themes are obviously closely related). The present passage assumes that the people and/or their representatives have come to Jerusalem; however, this is not mentioned explicitly, nor are the gifts that they have brought along, nor is it said that the reason they have appeared is for worship; they are there simply because they have been invited to a festival. To aid in interpreting this passage, one also can use Zech. 14:16, where it is expected that the peoples have come up "to worship the King, Yahweh of hosts, and to keep the festival of booths." That passage specifically mentions Yahweh's kingdom, possibly also suggesting there would be a meal. If one spends time "on this mountain," however, then one naturally would take part in a sacrificial meal; offerings are part of every religious festival and of every visit to the temple, particularly if someone has come from some distance: "You prepare a table before me in the presence of my enemies; you anoint my head with oil; my cup overflows" (Ps. 23:5). Yahweh is a most generous host and those who visit the temple are to share his company at the meal. Ps. 22:27 announces: "The poor (or: afflicted) shall eat and be satisfied"; cf. also 1 Sam. 1:9; Neh. 8:10; Ps. 36:9; Jer. 31:14. When "all peoples" are to gather at the same time for a sacrificial meal on Zion, however, then there must be a special reason; according to the context, it is because God has taken control of the kingly dominion (24:23). Yahweh of Hosts, who has triumphed over the earthly and supernatural powers, now invites the peoples to a celebration of his decisive victory. This connection is confirmed by Ps. 22:27ff., in which the reason for the celebration is given in v. 29: כִּי לַיהוָה הַמְּלוּכָה וְהוּא מֹשֵׁל בַּגּוֹיִם (For dominion belongs to Yahweh, and he rules over the nations) (according to the Gk, Syr, הוּא, "he," was inserted later). Already quite some time ago, H. Gressmann (*Der Ursprung der israelitisch-jüdischen Eschatologie* [1905] 300) used the passage before us to suggest that this was a coronation meal, a sacrificial meal that would have accompanied Yahweh's eschatological ascent to the throne. Since this ascent to the throne was not just about Yahweh's rule over Israel but signaled his taking power over the peoples as well, naturally the peoples also would have had to have been present (and because this was the complete, lasting dominion, it would have to be said: "all peoples").

There were sacrificial meals when the kings in Israel ascended to the throne: 1 Sam. 11:15; possibly 2 Sam. 6:18f. S. Mowinckel (*Psalmenstudien* II [1922] 126) also refers to 1 Kings 8:62-66.

In order to interpret this passage, Mulder brings the Baal festival into the discussion, at which the dedication of Baal's palace was celebrated (*UT* 51:IV:35–59).

More instructive yet are the "Rephaim" texts from Ugarit. El summons the gods to assemble in order to honor Baal:

> Listen well, [princes of the gods]
> .... [dei)ties:
> Upon the top of [the head of Aliyan Baal ....]
> Oil of the (divine) decision (?) will be [shaken].....
> ....he praises them.
> [Aliyan Baal] takes control [of] the king[dom] because of my decree,
> He takes [possession of the throne of his administration],
> the seat of rest, the seat [of his dominion].
> I call the princes of the gods [and goddesses]
> in my palace ....!

Great crowds of gods come, cattle and small livestock are slaughtered, there are bulls and fattened oxen, rams, yearling calves, frisky lambs and kids, cups are filled with the choicest of wines "from the highest quality, which flows from the breast of Lebanon" (Aistleitner, *Texte*, 85f.)—and that goes on for seven days. This is a celebration of Baal's ascent to the throne.

There is a similar report in the Creation Epic, *Enūma eliš*, as the gods assemble together to enjoy festivities when Marduk is enthroned. They kiss one another and sit down to a banquet (III, 134ff.):

> They ate festive bread, poured [the wine],
> They whetted their drinking-tubes with sweet intoxicant.
> As they drank the strong drink, [their] bodies swelled.

After this, they praise Marduk and state explicitly (IV, 5ff.):

> Thou, Marduk, art the most honored of the great gods.
> . . . .
> O Marduk, thou art indeed our avenger.
> We have granted thee kingship over the universe entire.

Then he has to pass a test successfully; he is to allow a garment to disappear and then cause it to reappear. He does this also; the gods rejoice among themselves and honor him (28):

> Marduk is king!

After Marduk has achieved victory and has built Esagila in Babylon, the gods assemble there once again, for a celebratory banquet. This time it no longer deals with creation, but with stabilizing what has been brought into order (*Enūma eliš* quotes are from *ANET* 66; see also *AOT* 116f.).

Thus there is no doubt that Isa. 25:6-8 employs very ancient concepts that were used when describing the enthronement of the deity, who is supposed to show, or already is supposed to have shown, power in the creation battle; these ideas are transformed now so that they fit the description of what takes place at the end of time (on this, see Elder, 31–34 and 58–60). In addition to putting this material into an eschatological context, there is another important modification: the participants at the banquet in 25:6-8 are not the gods (nor are they representatives from Israel!) but they are "all peoples." With these two alterations, the ancient mythology is now recast and used for a completely new kerygma.

Bammel points to the way in which kings were chosen among Germanic clans: according to the chap. 16 of the Hervœr saga, Sweyn, who wants to become king of the Swedes, offers "to perform the offering before them. After that was completed, Sweyn was accepted as king. Someone brought a steed to the assembly [lit. "to the *ting*"), divided it up so that it could be eaten, and used the blood to stain the offering trees a reddish color. The sacred action of the sacrificial banquet authenticates the agreement: the rightful establishment of a new kingdom and the duties incumbent upon a new group of adherents." In this case, of course, it does not deal with a god taking control in order to rule as a king, but with someone who is the leader of a clan. But the text is helpful in showing that the coronation meal functions in some sense as a covenant meal, by means of which both partners, king and people, enter into a reciprocal agreement, pledging their faithfulness to each other. David also became king over the tribes by making a covenant agreement (2 Sam. 5:3). Even if that passage does not say anything specifically about a sacrificial meal, there is no doubt that such a covenant agreement would have been accompanied by this type of meal. Mowinckel (*Psalmenstudien* II, 296f.) supposes that the sacrificial banquet of Yahweh, as described in Zeph. 1:8; Ezek. 39:17ff., is the horrendous event (Gressmann, 300, reads: "consumed in hideousness") where just the opposite takes place when compared with what happens at the sacrificial meal for the peoples that is depicted in this passage. It is appropriate for one to question this; what is depicted in those passages has nothing to do with a coronation meal. Gressmann (140) and Mowinckel are probably more on the mark when they relate this to such passages as 4 Ezra 6:52; Syriac Apocalypse of (2) Baruch 29:3; Ethiopic (1) Enoch 60:24; *b. Baba Batra* 74, according to which Yahweh would use the flesh of Behemoth and Leviathan to prepare a banquet for those who had survived down to the beginning of the messianic era. Finally, one is reminded of Matt. 22:1-10, the parable about the royal wedding, and Luke 14:15-24, the parable about the great banquet. In fact, neither of the versions of this parable says that such a banquet will be celebrated in the kingdom of God, but rather that the kingdom of God is *like* such a banquet. In the introduction to the parable in Luke 14:15, however, the phrase is preserved: "Blessed is anyone who will eat bread in the kingdom of God"; cf. also Matt. 8:11f.; Luke 22:24-30; Rev. 19:9, and, on this subject, A. Schweitzer, *The Mysticism of Paul the Apostle* [1931] 236ff.; and L. Goppelt, *TDNT* VIII, 212.

Not only does the author of 25:6-8 take the concept of a coronation banquet and make it eschatological, but he also expands the idea: in v. 7 he inserts a new motif: the removal of the masks that have been spread out over the peoples—an example of the way in which apocalyptic thinkers could assemble thoughts together in their "paintings" that had originated in a wide variety of settings. Since the masks are evidence for mourning (see below, p. 532), if one would skip over the phraseology in v. 8aα, then v. 8aβ could provide a fairly good continuation for v. 7. For this reason, some exegetes think that v. 8aα is a later insertion into the text; their reason is usually that the little phrase interrupts the flow of the passage in its present context in a way that cannot be left to stand; the real reason more likely is that they think it is impossible, within the context of vv. 6-8, that the destruction of death could be mentioned all of a sudden in such a matter-of-fact and radical manner. The question about when the apocalypse is to be dated plays a role here as well, since it is believed that it would be easier to date the apocalypse rela-

tively early if v. 8aα were not there. However, the stage of textual development to which vv. 6-8 belongs is simply later than the original body of the
material in the apocalypse anyway; besides this, before one makes a decision
about how to date this passage by using this little phrase as the determining
factor, one must ask what the phrase means within the framework of the
entire prediction. It could be that some belonged to small groups which,
within their own little circles, held onto a private hope that death would be
overcome, long before that hope entered into the consciousness of the general Israelite populace. The concept is involved already in Ezek. 37:1-14,
which presumes that the dead will come back to life, even though it is true
that that passage does not speak about the resurrection of the dead but about
the restitution of Israel.

The decisive point in favor of v. 8aα being part of the original text is
provided by comparing it with Ps. 22:27-31, a passage consulted above
already when looking for parallels to vv. 6-8. After mentioning eating and
being completely satisfied and all the tribes of the peoples turning to Yah-
weh, that passage continues in v. 30a: אָכְלוּ וַיִּשְׁתַּחֲוּוּ כָּל־דִּשְׁנֵי־אֶרֶץ לְפָנָיו יִכְרְעוּ
כָּל־יוֹרְדֵי עָפָר (lit.: They have eaten and indeed, all the fat ones in the earth
bow down; before him shall bow all who go down to the dust). Unfortunately, the beginning of this verse has raised problems; יְשֵׁנֵי (all who sleep)
should certainly be read instead of דִּשְׁנֵי (all the fat ones in). אָכְלוּ (they have
eaten) has been changed by some to read אַךְ לוֹ (indeed, to him), with the following verb pointed as a simple imperfect instead of an imperfect consecutive. However, no substantiating evidence can be found in the versions. Thus
one must ask whether this also refers to the time of an apocalyptic banquet.
However that might be resolved, the dead are brought into the relationship
where they would be under the control of Yahweh: "In Psalm 22 . . . a specific apocalyptic theology is discussed, which views the time when the
βασιλεία τοῦ θεοῦ [kingdom of God] would break in as the moment when
a particular individual would be delivered completely from deadly peril: it is
the moment when there is a conversion of the world, explicitly established
with the onset of the βασιλεία [kingdom], in its special theological sense,
the resurrection of the dead, even if this still is conceptualized in a very cautious way as a deliverance from trouble so that one could take part in cultic
activities in the presence of Yahweh." One must be much more careful about
the way one uses the term "resurrection" than is Gese, the source of this quotation (H. Gese, *Vom Sinai zum Zion* [1974] 192), but it is readily apparent
when working with the problem that is being discussed here, which deals
with waiting for a מלוכה (kingdom) of Yahweh that would stretch out over the
whole world, that the problem of the dead—and death itself—has to be mentioned. As far as this is related to the history of traditions, it is completely
appropriate that the topic of "death" should be dealt with in 25:6-8. When the
מלוכה (kingdom) truly comes to belong to Yahweh, then he also has to be the
lord of those who have died. But that means, once and for all, that he must
overcome the power of death as well—whatever form that might take (see

below, pp. 532f.). Thus there is no valid reason for treating this little phrase as an insertion by a later hand.

Meter: As also was the case concerning 24:21-23, it is possible to identify a metrical pattern only in some of the verses. One can still detect a three-stress + three-stress bicolon in v. 6aα; the same is true in v. 6aβb. But it is better not to try to find a metrical structure in vv. 7 and 8, and the possibility of identifying a pattern does not improve if one removes v. 8aα (see Virgulin, 63).

Nonetheless, it is worth noting that the author has artfully used a style that employs repetition:

משתה שמרים	משתה שמנים
שמרים מזקקים	שמנים ממחים
a banquet with *rich foods*	*a banquet* with *aged wine*
with highest quality, *rich foods*	with *aged,* full bouquet *wines*

Cf. also בהר הזה (on this mountain) in vv. 6 and 7; the two times ובלע is used, in vv. 7 and 8 (destroy, swallow up); as well as the formulations הלוט הלוט (the mask, with which is masked) and המסכה הנסוכה (the covering, which is spread out as a cover) in v. 7; in addition, compare לכל־העמים (for all peoples) in v. 6 with על־כל־העמים (of all peoples) and על־כל־הגוים (over all the nations) in v. 7.

Setting

The present section of material is similar to 24:21-23 in that it uses apocalyptic concepts that are quite advanced. It has been shown that the correct date must be at a time following the composition of the original body of material in the apocalypse. One might suppose that some groups were deeply dedicated to fleshing out such thoughts, among whom what truly can be called apocalyptic literature developed.

Commentary

[25:6] The host at the "coronation meal" here is Yahweh, unlike the setting in 1 Sam. 11:15, where the people set up the festival. This itself is different from the Hervœr saga, mentioned above, where the king who is to be crowned is himself the one who offers the sacrifice for his subjects. The festival banquet on Zion is a divine offer of grace to the peoples. As in 24:23, here also Yahweh is identified more specifically by means of the epithet צבאות (of Hosts), which has its roots in the Jerusalem cultic tradition (except for these two passages, יהוה צבאות, "Yahweh of Hosts," is not used in chaps. 24–27). The banquet is not just for Israel and not even just for the eschatological community of the chosen; simply stated, it is for the peoples. That v. 6 speaks of the עמים (peoples) and v. 7 also mentions the גוים (nations) should not be pressed, in an attempt to differentiate between the two terms; it also would be wrong to translate גוים with the traditional word "heathen." Concerning the way in which עם (people) and גוי (nation) are used in parallel, see *Isaiah 1–12*, p. 90. There is no question where the banquet would take place; it would be on Zion, the focal point of Yahweh's rule, just as it is clear that the מלכות יהוה (kingdom of Yahweh) is not a transcendent type of rule. As can be seen at the end of the section, that the invitation goes out to all the peoples would not automatically exclude the people of God from maintaining their own unique relationship with God.

The celebratory meal is called a מִשְׁתֶּה (banquet), not, as one might have expected, a זֶבַח (sacrifice). At a real מִשְׁתֶּה (banquet), one naturally would have had wine, and, if there is wine, it would be a happy celebration.

The term מִשְׁתֶּה (banquet) is not used originally in connection with the cult; a מִשְׁתֶּה is a feast held on the happy occasions of one's life; see Gen. 21:8; 29:22; 40:20; Isa. 5:12; Job 1:4, 5, etc. It is an important concern in Deuteronomy that everyone would be happy when a cultic festival was held at the sanctuary. There would be every reason to celebrate if Yahweh had become king on Zion. For that reason, שְׁמָנִים, "rich foods," are served up; for people today these are not necessarily the most desired portions, but they were for the ancient Israelites.

For the ancient Arabs, the fatty humps of the camel were the choicest part of the slaughtered animal (G. Jacob, *Altarabisches Beduinenleben* [1897] 94), and one can still say in Arabia today: "N. N. is so hospitable that the wall of his tent is rigid, made so because of putting on and taking off fat" (J. J. Hess, *Von den Beduinen des Innern Arabiens* [1938] 122). Text 130:2-17 from Ugarit tells about how one would provide food for a divine guest:

> Prdmn [subject?] serves Aliyan Baal;
> he provides service for the prince (*zbl*), for the lord of the earth;
> he got himself up, nimbly he furnished him food;
> he hurriedly set before him the breast portion.
> With an open knife he cut off a fatty portion,
> swiftly served it and offered him something to drink.
> He put the drinking cup into his hand,
> the goblet into his fist,
> the immense bowl, which the person who looked on watched
>   while trembling,
> the majestic drinking cup, the likes of which no wife had ever seen,
> the goblet, the likes of which (even) Atrt had not seen.
> It held a thousand *kd* of wine,
> ten thousand mixed drinks could have been made in it
>   (Aistleitner, *Texte*, 24f.; cf. also the portrayal of the banquet
>   of the gods in *UT* 51:IV:39–59, in Aistleitner, 44f.).

When שְׁמָנִים (rich foods) is used (this plural form occurs only here), one ought not think it refers to meat, but rather to foods that have been prepared using a lot of oil. For an extraordinary festival, one also needs to have an excellent wine, in this case one that has been prepared carefully, with special effort to strain it meticulously so as to make it clear, without sediment. What is described is the opposite of what was presumably the popular notion in Israel, that Yahweh would prepare for the peoples a drinking feast at which he would "make them drunk, until they become merry and then sleep a perpetual sleep and never wake" (Jer. 51:39; cf. Jer. 25:15ff. and Ps. 75:9).

531

[25:7] And once again, it is also "on this mountain" that the mask or covering will be "swallowed up," that which had been over the peoples until then—not just taken away but completely destroyed, so that there would be absolutely no danger that it could be placed over the peoples once again. But what is really meant by לוֹט (mask) and מסכה (covering)? According to Procksch (following Delitzsch, von Orelli, et al.) this is "the removal of spiritual blindness . . . so that it would be as if scales fell from their eyes, since they then were able to see Yahweh; the result of having been called to the royal banquet was that they then would have the knowledge of God. The revelation that is first made known to the elders in Israel (24:23) is now extended to all peoples, who at the present time no longer would have to drink the divine cup of wrath, as this is described by Jeremiah (Jer. 25:15ff.); instead, they would get the cup of the joy of the true knowledge of God." This beautiful exposition is certainly what is said in 2 Cor. 3:12ff., but not in the present text, where the issue is not about the knowledge of God that is to be given to the peoples, but rather about comfort and restoration. The commentators who suggest that the mask and covering are used as symbols of mourning are undoubtedly right; cf. 2 Sam. 15:30; 19:5; Jer. 14:3f.; Esth. 6:12 (see the reasons given by Kessler, but also by Duhm, Lindblom, Fohrer, Kaiser).

[25:8aα] Now to the famous phrase about which there has been so much discussion concerning its original setting: "And he will destroy death forever." If this passage belonged to vv. 6-8 from the beginning, then the mourning that causes the peoples to cover their faces would be the mourning for those who had died. That fits nicely with the comment about wiping away tears. Is this mourning for those who have fallen in battle, so that this death deals specifically with death on a battlefield? It is possible that this idea is included, but it would be better to take the phrase in a more general, comprehensive sense. No longer would there be any mourning for the dead at all, since death has been swallowed up.

Why was the verb בלע (lit.: swallow up) used? One does not normally try to "swallow up" masks and coverings; furthermore, it is also striking that it speaks about "swallowing up" death. It is worth the effort to study just exactly *who* "swallows up" what according to the OT: the earth (or the underworld; אֶרֶץ, "earth, underworld," can be used synonymously with שְׁאוֹל, Sheol; e.g., Exod. 15:12; Num. 16:32, 34; 26:10; Deut. 11:6; Ps. 106:17); the מְצוּלָה, "the deep, the abyss" (Ps. 96:16); Nebuchadnezzar כַּתַּנִּין (like a monster) (Jer. 51:34); also note: the great fish swallows Jonah (Jonah 2:1). בלע (swallow up) is thus used primarily when human beings find themselves in the realm of the powers of death. The human being not only suffers death, but experiences it as a force that pounces on and overpowers one, much as one would be attacked by an animal that rips flesh apart. Also at times the term מות (*mot*, death) tends to take on some personal characteristics; Canaan's worldview has not completely disappeared, in which Mot is a deity; cf. *UT* 67:I:5, where Mot threatens to consume Baal. But now death itself will experience the very thing that it had been doing to human beings until that point: Yahweh swallows it up.

However, one must also remember that Hebrew מות (*mot*) and English "death" do not have the same range of meaning. A person is in the realm of *mot* or in שאול (Sheol) already when being afflicted by a terrible illness. *Mot* is anything that causes trouble during one's life, is that which limits the way in which one lives life, is that which takes something away from one's prosperity and gets in the way of fellowship with other humans or with God (see C. Barth, *Die Errettung vom Tode* [1947], esp. 53ff.). The present passage is to be interpreted in light of this background. When Yahweh is king on the mountain of God at the end of time, then no limitations will be imposed on where his power can reach. At that time, *mot*, as a power that threatens life and that causes one to have doubts about one's ability to go on living, will have played its last hand. At that point, even the peoples who are under Yahweh's dominion but thus also under his protection will never go through any more disasters. Mourning will be swallowed up, just as death itself. This text is not speaking directly about resurrection but says, rather, that there are no longer any limits to how far Yahweh wishes to go in bringing restoration. We can see that this interpretation is on the right track because of what has been recognized already, that the traditio-historical background of 25:6-8 is to be found within the framework of a description of the deity being enthroned after winning the battle against chaos. In Babylon, Marduk, joyously acclaimed as "king," has destroyed Tiamat; Baal becomes king because he was victorious over either Yamm or Mot. Thus one ought not be surprised that this recasting of the ancient tradition includes the idea that מות (*mot*, death) will be swallowed up. Though it is clear that מות (*mot*, death) is not to be considered here as a person, it is just as true that the idea about Yahweh being victorious over the opposing power has still left some traces. In this light, a parallel occurs in 27:1.

Some questions have still not been resolved. What does that text mean for the practical realities of daily life? Will a person no longer actually have to die? What then will happen to those who are dead already? This matter needs to be discussed further. But it is clear from what has been said already that the actual source of the idea of resurrection in the OT is connected with the confession of faith that anticipates that Yahweh would rule without any limitations, even if one holds to the view that some of the stimuli for the development of this notion might have come from sources outside Israel proper (Iranian religion).

[25:8aβ-b] Yahweh will wipe the tears from every face. It is most surprising, in this passage that focuses intensely on universal salvation, that the people of Yahweh have such a unique position at the conclusion of this description, in v. 8b. It is almost as if the author had heard anxious voices, wondering: What was Israel to get from all this? One might think that this is simply a later addition, inserted by someone who wanted to carve out a little spot for Israel in this magnificent painting. However, hardly any description in the OT about what is expected in the future does not have a special place for the people of God, indeed, specifically in the Pauline sense of "the Jews first, and then also the Greeks." What is more remarkable is that the author is reserved when speaking of Israel's salvation, almost to the point that one might say: "first the heathen, then also the Jews." The return from exile is never even discussed; that may be another indication that this message comes from a time, or from a milieu, in which the return to the land of the fathers was no longer a burning issue for the Jews of the diaspora.

However, whatever Israel was suffering in the dispersion could be called חרפה (humiliation). This term, as is true of similar terms (בוש, "be ashamed"; כלם, "be humiliated"; חפר, "be abashed"), has both a subjective and an objective side: one feels one has been abused already, mocked, discriminated against; yet one is still living, at the same time, in prejudicial circumstances, sometimes having lost all rights. It is hard to say exactly what חרפה is supposed to mean in this setting. Possibly the loss of the homeland and independent national existence is less of an issue now than in earlier times; maybe it is not even about existing as a minority among the nations as such, but rather that they had experienced rejection by those among whom they lived, caused by the fact the Judaism sought to be different, which might even have led to "anti-Semitic" tendencies. That such problems existed has to be acknowledged on the basis of the book of Esther, even if the actual story is not historical (see Eissfeldt, *Introduction,* 507f.). When, at the end of time, all troubles come to an end, when all life-threatening injuries that can be caused by the powers of death will have been taken away from all the peoples, and when tears will have been washed away, then the most pressing problem for Judaism, its disgrace, would be removed as well, that humiliation which was caused by its unique position, if not by the fact that it truly sought to live on the basis of the faith of the fathers.

Purpose and Thrust

In a grandiose way, the material recorded in 25:6-8 describes more specifically what would result from that which was announced in 24:21-23; there it was promised that the final rule of Yahweh on Zion would soon make its appearance. Enough had been said clearly already, in 24:21f., about the harsh way accounts would be settled with the powers of the heavens and the earth. But that accounting did not mean that all the peoples would cease to exist; instead, the accounting would make it possible for them to be included in the salvation that would go forth from Zion. The author depicts this salvation by using the imagery of a festival banquet for all peoples, apparently within the context of a coronation celebration for Yahweh. It would be a banquet that would be much more extravagant than a typical sacrificial meal. But even that picture was not enough for him; he includes the comment that all suffering would finally come to an end. And Israel could be assured that it could live out its faith with the full guarantee that it would remain the people of Yahweh, even though it was now spread out among the peoples, since all peoples would be united now under Yahweh's control. They would be scorned and ridiculed no longer; no longer would they serve as targets for those who wanted to heap on derision and mockery; thus they could be confident of full support as they lived out their faith, publicly being known as the people of Yahweh. Finally, the author dared to enunciate one last confession, stated abruptly, without further comment; it is thus difficult for us to assess the specific meaning that he would have attached to that comment. He makes an almost casual remark to his hearers or readers: Yahweh will "swallow up" the powers that bring the types of disasters which lead to death.

With this section, the author ascends to a level of expectation that is hardly matched anywhere else in the OT. The thought that there would be an eschatological celebratory banquet aroused enthusiasm; later apocalyptic did not want to let go of the idea, but never was quite able to replicate the boldness of the statement. In Qumran there was mention of a banquet at which the messiah would participate (1QSa II, 17-21), though that was obviously prepared not for all the peoples, but only for the "sons of light." Jesus also described the βασιλεία τοῦ θεοῦ (kingdom of God) in terms of a great banquet. Synoptic passages make it possible to conclude that the idea of a banquet at the end of time was a common theme in contemporary Judaism. The community formed around Christ made use of it and modified it in certain ways; see Luke 22:24-30. The most important corrective to the imagery, compared with the way it had been used up to that point, occurs in Matt. 8:11f.: "Many will come from east and west and will eat with Abraham and Isaac and Jacob in the kingdom of heaven, while the heirs of the kingdom will be thrown into the outer darkness."

After this, never again was Judaism able to forget that the rule of God at the end of time would also include, of necessity, the victory over death; there could be no complete joy in the kingdom as long as the power of death had not been broken. And the Christian church took this message for itself and filled in the details about what was meant. However, it can be only for the good when, within the context of the Christian proclamation about the resurrection, death is dealt with in the widest sense of what is meant by the OT term מות (death) and when the hope for eternal life is not separated from the expectation that God will establish his rule over everything.

535

Israel's Thanks and
Moab's Final Downfall

Text

9 And on that day one will say[a]:
Look,[b] there is our God,
   [c]in whom[c] we hope [d]and who will help us.
Yahweh is the one in whom we hope,[d]
   we will exult and will cheer[e] ourselves because of his help;
10 truly, Yahweh's hand rests on this mountain.

   * * * *

   [But Moab will be trampled[a] in its own place,[b]
   as one stomps[c] straw[d] down into a dung pit.[e]
11 And if it spreads its hands out,
   as a swimmer spreads them, when one wants to swim,
thus will one bring down its pride,
   [a]no matter how practiced it is in moving[a] its hands.]

   * * * *

12 [[a]And your towering stronghold, with its walls,[a] someone pushed down,
   [b]cast it down,[b] knocked[c] it down, right to the ground, into the dust.]

9a Q[a] reads the second person: ואמרת (and you will say), and the Syr reads the same: *wt'mr* (and you will say). But it is not clear who this "you" is supposed to be. The subject is an unnamed "someone."

9b Between הנה (look) and אלהינו (our God), Q[a] reads יהוה (Yahweh) as well.

9c–c The Gk translated this: Ἰδοὺ ὁ θεὸς ἡμῶν, ἐφ᾽ ᾧ ἠλπίζομεν (behold our God, in whom we hope), which means it treated זה as a relative pronoun, which is probably correct; on this, see BrSynt §150b; Joüon, *Gr* §145c.

9d–d This material is not in the Gk. Some believe that the MT has too many words, but, here as well, repetition is one of the stylistic techniques: if ויושיענו (and who will help us) would be missing, this passage would make no sense, though one also ought not remove v. 9bα, as do Duhm, Marti (see also Procksch, et al.), since it is not the task of exegetes to change the style to suit their fancy.

9e Q[a] reads the cohortative נגילה (let us exult); yet it reads ונשמח (and we will cheer ourselves) right after that. The Hebrew used in the Qumran texts no longer shows a sensitivity for modal differences.

536

10a Qᵃ reads ונדש (also: but will be trampled), going against the tendency elsewhere in the manuscript to use vowel letters wherever possible by employing the *plene* reading. Sym translates: και αλοησομεν (and we will crush), which means it treated the form as a *qal*. Aquila reads correctly: και αλοηθησεται (and it will be trampled); the Gk translates it more loosely: και καταπαθήσεται (and it will be made to suffer).
10b The ancient versions themselves had trouble understanding what תחתיו meant. There is no equivalent in the Gk; Targ reads באתרהין (in their place). One could translate this "under him" or even "instead of him," but what would that mean? This must be an example of a passage where תחת is still used as a substantive, so that one could translate it: "in its places," which means, in the land in which it lives (cf. 2 Sam. 7:10).
10c Qᵃ כחדוש (as it is renewed) is probably a simple copying mistake. It is surprising to find this *niphʿal* infinitive construct form הדוש instead of what one would expect, הדוֹש; see Bauer-Leander §56u".
10d מתבן (hapax legomenon) is a derivative of the word תבן (straw); thus it means "pile of straw." It is obviously used here on purpose, as a play on words with מדמנה (dung pit); for this reason also, the suggestion offered by H. D. Hummel (*JBL* 76 [1957] 104) that the מ should be connected with the previous ש is ill advised.
10e The Kethib for this verse reads בְּמֵי, "in the waters of," instead of בְּמוֹ. Yet, according to König (who refers to Job 9:30 and Isa. 30:22 [?]), מוֹ also means "water," used apparently because it furnished a wordplay on the name Moab. If one accepts this interpretation, however, one also would have to translate מדמנה (here: dung pit) correspondingly, as a geographical reference. But this word, a derivative of דמן, "manure, dung," like Arabic *dimn*, "manure pile," should apparently be translated rather freely in this passage to mean something such as "mushy manure pond." Isa. 10:31 does mention a city named מדמנה (Madmenah), but it is clearly not located in Moab. However, Jer. 48:2 does refer to a locality by the name of מדמן (Madmen) in the land of Moab. For this reason, Qimḥi also wanted to treat the occurrence of מדמנה in this passage as a reference to the name of a city. That is not correct, even though it might be possible that there is a play on words which involves the name of a Moabite city מדמן (Madmen) (concerning מדמן, "Madmen," see A. H. van Zyl, *The Moabites*, POS 3 [1960] 80). There is no doubt that בְּמוֹ is the correct reading; its meaning corresponds to Ugaritic *bm* (in it) and it is also found at times in other OT passages, instead of the simple ב (in).
11a–a There is disagreement about both the correctness of the form and the meaning of ארבות (here: how practiced it is in moving). Marti wonders whether this should read: עם הרבות ידיו (in spite of the multiplying of its hands). But one should think twice about adopting that reading.

אֹרֵב or אָרַב* means "ambush." Guthe chooses to read ארבותיו instead of ארבות ידיו (moving its hands) and translates: "together with its tricks," whereas Ehrlich refers to Arabic *ʾrb*, "have practice," and suggests the translation: "in spite of the practice of its hands." G. R. Driver (*JTS* 38 [1937] 42f.) also refers to Arabic *araba* I, "tied (a knot)"; *aruba*, "was crafty" II; and III, "went obliquely"; *ariba* IV and V, "exerted oneself, strained oneself"; and believes it is possible to translate this phrase "in spite of the struggles of his hands." There is no way to be sure about how to resolve this; one might adopt the meaning "dexterity" for ארבות, which is the reason for the translation suggested above.
12a–a Literally, ומבצר משגב חומתיך means: "and the fortification of the heights of your walls," which once again leaves one with the impression that the line is too full; for this reason, *BHS* suggests removing מבצר (stronghold). But here also one should

let the overly wordy style stay as it is. It is certainly possible to have a series of such genitives; cf. passages such as 28:1. The suffix on the last word in such a chain of genitives governs all the words in the expression (see above, p. 306). Some of the MSS in de Rossi (see Gesenius) point this as חֹמוֹתָיִךְ (your walls), whereas Guthe and Schlögl favor reading the third masculine singular (= its walls). However, it is certainly possible to have such transitions into direct speech. Another possibility is that the person of the verbal suffix switches back and forth because v. 12 is secondary in its relationship with vv. 10b, 11.

12b–b הִשְׁפִּיל (cast it down) is missing in the Gk; contra *BHS*, this is not a good enough reason to remove it.

12c Qᵃ reads יניע (he will knock down), without changing the perfect forms of the words הִשְׁפִּיל (cast it down) and הֵשַׁח (pushed down) in the immediate context. The point is that the writer of Qᵃ wanted the present passage to say: Moab *is* humiliated, but its final complete destruction has not yet fully taken place. Procksch should also not be followed when he suggests that all three verbs should be pointed as infinitives absolute, thus הָשֵׁחַ (push down), הַגֵּיעַ (cast down), and הַשְׁפֵּיל (knock down), arguing that the subject is missing and that the perfect forms seem strange anyway; v. 12 is a later addition, providing information which stated that Moab's downfall had actually occurred now; the perfects are correct as they stand.

Form and Setting

[25:9-10a] As has been explained above, vv. 9-10a should still be treated as having a close connection with vv. 6-8. Indeed, v. 9 opens with the formula ואמר ביום ההוא (and on that day one will say), which seems to point to these lines being an expansion of the text. However, one should note that it does not say והיה ביום ההוא (and it will happen on that day), which is the common way such additions are inserted by a later writer.

Verses 9, 10a are in the form of a song of thanksgiving. One cannot find direct and obvious eschatological motifs; once again, the only reason why one would treat this eschatologically is because of the connection with the preceding section of material. "That day" is *the* day, on which Yahweh would begin to rule, at the end of time, and on which the peoples would be fed sumptuously on Zion. Since Yahweh is addressed as "our God," one must conclude that someone from Israel is speaking.

Meter: Verse 9aβ: three-stress + three-stress bicolon (?). Verse 9b: probably a seven-stress colon. Verse 10a has four stresses, without a break, and thus provides a full-sounding conclusion.

Commentary

[25:9-10a] The song begins with the presentative particle הנה (look), but this time it is not at the beginning of a threat of judgment; instead, it points to a restoration that is going to occur at any time. הנה (look) is a way to express the deep surprise that, against all hope, even in light of the great catastrophe that was now in the past, Yahweh had once again acted to provide help, this time as well (and thus, naturally, would act in the same way in the future also).

Concerning the rest of this short song, one can easily find parallels in the cultic poetry: concerning v. 9aβ, see 33:2; Pss. 25:5; 40:2; cf. also Gen. 49:18; Jer. 14:22; concerning the use of גיל (exult) and ישועה (help, restoration) together, or similar wording, cf. Hab. 3:18; Pss. 9:15; 13:6; 21:2 (here שמח, "rejoice," is also used in the same context; גיל, "exult," and שמח, "rejoice," are often used together as synonyms; see Pss. 14:7; 16:9; and often elsewhere).

In v. 10 the author writes down his own thoughts; nowhere else does one find it said that Yahweh's hand "rests on this mountain," though this idea does correspond to Zion theology. "Hand" is a symbol of strength, might; it deals with the certain protection that Israel can find on the mountain of God.

Form

[25:10b, 11] Concerning separating vv. 10b, 11 from the preceding, as a later addition, and treating v. 12 as an addition to this addition, see above, p. 455.

Meter: Verses 10b and 11a are constructed parallel to one another; each verse is formed as a seven-stress colon, inverse to the normal structure (3 + 4).

Verse 11 has four stresses and its shortness shows clearly that it is intended as a conclusion.

Verse 12 can be read as a four-stress + four-stress bicolon.

Verse 10b is linked to v. 10a by means of a ו (here: But), as if the train of thought is to continue uninterrupted. It would seem that a reader found it necessary to contrast the way in which Israel was protected on the mountain of God with Moab's hopeless situation. Moab is "trampled" (lit.: "threshed"), in fact, "in its own place," which means, right where it is now living, without any possibility that it still could find a way to escape its fate. Concerning דוש (tread, thresh) as an image that describes the harsh fate of a people, see above, p. 325. Threshing takes place on a threshing floor, but the author pushes the common imagery to grotesque dimensions: as straw is threshed into a dung pit. He was filled with a bottomless hatred against Moab and, in his efforts to depict these feelings, the manure pile now becomes a mushy manure pond, from which Moab tries to swim out to save itself, though unsuccessfully (but remember what was mentioned above, that both the text and translation are uncertain). Moab's pride is smitten to the core. One can hardly threaten a people with a more insulting demise than that they would drown in a mushy manure pond. Kaiser speaks of its "remarkably original portrayal," but it is not so much remarkable as tasteless.

In threats of this type, against foreign peoples, pride (here: גאוה) is frequently offered as the reason and this rebuke is used also in chaps. 15f. (see above, p. 146, on 16:6). Nevertheless, one should probably take into account the fact that the author reacts so violently against Moab because Israel has been so deeply hurt by this neighboring people.

Setting

[25:10b, 11] Now one comes to the question about what situation might have caused this addition. Duhm thinks that this seems to put into words the hope that finally became a reality when Moab was subjugated by Alexander Janneus (Josephus, *Antiquities* 13.13.5). Even though the passage is a later addition, this dating is much too late. There might be a connection with Neh. 13:1, a passage that could lead one to suppose that, at the time of Nehemiah, there was suffering among the Jews who were living in proximity to the inhabitants of what earlier had been known as the territory of Moab and that these people were doing all they could to stop Jerusalem from being restored. But we do not know enough about the relationship between Judah and the peoples living in the former territory of Moab for us to settle on any specific date with a degree of confidence.

Commentary

[25:12] According to v. 11, Moab's pride had to be cut down to size; in the addition to the addition, in v. 12, the walls of a Moabite city have fallen, in fact, "right to the ground." In this situation, the glossator makes use of the same verb, הִשְׁפִּיל (here: cast down), as was used in v. 11, but also inserts הֵשַׁח (pushed down). It would seem that he had read his Isaiah very well, since these two verbal roots also had been used together in 2:9, 11, 17. In 2:11 and 17, the verb שׂגב (human pride) is used as well, with that root being represented here in the form of the substantive מִשְׂגָּב (towering). Concerning מִבְצָר (stronghold), see above, pp. 166f. הִגִּיע לָאָרֶץ (knocked it down, right to the ground) occurs also in Lam. 2:2, but the glossator in the present passage is not content to use לָאָרֶץ (to the ground) to get rid of the deep tensions caused by his feelings of hatred against Moab; he adds עַד־עָפָר (into the dust) to this, just as he had added מִשְׂגָּב (towering), because it was not enough for him simply to mention מִבְצָר (stronghold). It is clear that some pressure had built up inside him, so that he sought to intensify what was commonly threatened when disaster was discussed.

Does this verse speak about one stronghold or many? Some have suggested already that מִבְצָר מִשְׂגַּב חוֹמֹתֶיךָ (here: your towering stronghold with its walls) is merely illustrative of the גַּאֲוָה (pride) of Moab; however, it is likely that this verse was occasioned by the fall of a particular dwelling place, most probably the capital city of the Moabite territory. But it is idle speculation to try to determine what city is meant and when it might have fallen. Whatever specific situation is actually behind this, the fall of Moabite walls was enough to prove to the expander that Moab and its pride had come to an end.

Purpose and Thrust

The author of the original body of material had painted a gloomy picture about events that were to come and issued an explicit warning not to break out in rejoicing. Nevertheless, the man whom we can thank for the magnificent eschatological portrayal in 24:21-23 and 25:6-8 indicates clearly that

Israel would not be forgotten by Yahweh, even though his gaze was directed toward peoples living throughout the whole world. It is different here: vv. 9 and 10a, which are closely linked to vv. 6-8, demonstrate that Israel itself will have reason to rejoice. But the expanders who add vv. 10b-12 are not satisfied with leaving it at that. Apparently as the result of a terrible trauma, which Judah must have experienced as a consequence of a conflict with "Moab," they want to pull out all the stops as they try to show that Judah's restoration cannot be wrecked by "Moab's" pride ever again. "Moab" will be brought down, all the way into the "mushy manure pond," down "into the dust."

"Moab" cannot possibly refer to the Moabite people any longer, to those who had continued to be a close neighbor of Israel until the downfall of Jerusalem; here it is the name for the peoples now living in what once was called the land of Moab. Some have suggested the possibility that the name had come to be used symbolically to designate the powers who oppose God at the end time. The text itself does not include any phraseology which would justify that view. But it is clear that one would have to interpret "Moab" in that way, at a later time, within the context of the apocalyptic expectation. In this manner, the Moab material is used to express the hope that the God whose hand was resting "on this mountain" would remain the victor over all hostile peoples and demonic forces.

The Strong City of the Faithful and the Downfall of the Towering Fortress

Text

26:1 On that day this[a] song [b]will be sung[b] in the land of Judah:
  We have a strong[c] city;
    for protection [d]he makes[d]
      walls and embankment.
 2 Open the gates,[a]
    so that the righteous people can come in,
      those who maintain faithfulness.
 3 [a]'Its' frame of mind is held fast; you preserve (for it) salvation,
    salvation,[a] because it trusts[b] [c]in you.[c]
 4 Trust in Yahweh forever [a][in Yah],
    since,[a] at all times, Yahweh[a] is a rock.
 5 Truly, he has brought down[a] those who inhabit the heights;
    the towering city, [b]he pushes it down,
  he pushes it flat down[b] to the ground,
    he knocks it down into the dust.
 6 The foot[a] stomps it in,
    feet of one who is miserable,
      footsteps of an insignificant people.

1a Qᵃ reads הזואת ("this," feminine) instead of הזה ("this," masculine).
1b–b Instead of יושר (will be sung), Qᵃ reads the *qal* ישיר (someone will sing).
1c Qᵃ reads עז (strength). Von Orelli already had suggested the possibility that עז (strength) should be read instead of עַז (strong). Based on the meter, the MT reading is preferable.
1d–d The Targ reads יהסם (shall be set upon) instead of ישית (he makes); Vulg: *ponetur* (is placed); both presume that a passive form was in the original. For this reason, Procksch follows Buhl and suggests יושׁת (is placed). However, since the *hophʿal* of this verb occurs otherwise only once in the OT, this emendation is questionable; the subject of ישית (he makes) is Yahweh; see below, p. 546.
2a Instead of שערים (gates), Qᵃ reads שעריך (your gates).
3a–a It is difficult to understand exactly what is meant in v. 3a, though this is not necessarily the result of a faulty transmission of the text. Ibn Ezra interprets it מי שיצרו סמוך עליך אתה השם תצרנו בשלום, "those whose mind depends on you, you pre-

542

serve, Yahweh, in salvation." The Hexapla transcribes יצר as ιεσρο, on the basis of which Guthe, Gray, Feldmann, Procksch, Fohrer, et al., read (ו)יצרֹ, "(and) he protects him"—which is possible, but too uncertain. Procksch is suspicious about the direct address to Yahweh; he alters תצֹר (you preserve) to ונֹצֵר (and preserving). As one can well imagine, that שלום (peace; here: salvation) is used twice has aroused suspicions, especially since one of the two is missing in the Gk, Syr. But it must be reiterated once more: such repetitions are not uncommon in the Isaiah apocalypse. J. Carmignac (FS H. Bardtke [1968] 42) thinks that Qᵃ reads שלֵם שלום, and translates v. 3a: "la disposition soutenue tu conserves, parfaite la paix" (you preserve a steady frame of mind, perfect the peace). However, it is not certain that it should be read שלֵם; it is often difficult to differentiate י and ו in Qᵃ.

3b בָּטוּחַ (lit.: is trusted), which, according to its form, appears to be a passive participle, has raised many questions. The Gk translates only בטחו, at the beginning of v. 4 (as ἤλπισαν, "they trusted"); it may be that בטח was lost due to haplography. Vulg: *quia in te speravimus* (because we will trust in you); Hexapla transliterates: χι βακ βατου (because of trusting you); Aquila: οτι επ αυτω πεποιθασι (for in him they have believed); Targ: אֲרֵי במימרך אתרחיצו (because they have trusted in thy Memra). *BHK* suggests reading the infinitive absolute בָּטוֹחַ (trust). According to Ps. 112:7, however, בָּטֻחַ means "filled with trust, secure," a meaning found in rabbinic Hebrew as well (*HAL*). Marti might be right in suggesting that בָּטוּחַ, corresponding to סָמוּךְ (held fast), would accentuate the aspect of the firmness of faith, its steady character.

3c–c Procksch, along with Lohmann, replaces בָּךְ (in you) with בְיָה (in Yah), a form found in v. 4; it is suggested that it is superfluous in that passage. But there are many instances in the cultic lyrics of the OT in which third person speech moves to direct address without any transition.

4a–a Commentators have been bothered by the fact that בְיָה (in Yah) and יהוה (Yahweh) are right next to each other. For v. 4b, the Gk reads: ὁ θεὸς ὁ μέγας ὁ αἰώνιος (God, the great, the eternal), but could hardly have had a different original text. Aquila: οτι εν τω κυριω κυριος ο στερεωσας τους αιωνας (for in the Lord, the Lord, the one who firms up the ages). The exegetes opt for removing either one or the other (see *BHK*, *BHS*), but it is more likely that כי (since) and בְיָה (in Yah) should be switched; i.e., בְיָה (in Yah) should be considered part of v. 4a. It would be a mistake to adopt the suggestion offered by A. Guillaume (*JTS* 13 [1962] 322f.), who points בָּיָה as בְיָה (he remembered, he was mindful of), on the basis of the Arabic verb *bāha*.

5a Qᵃ reads השח instead of השׁח (he has brought down), which can be explained only as a copying mistake.

5b–b Many have found it problematic that יְשׁפִילֶנָּה (he pushes it down) and יַשׁפִּילָהּ (he pushes it flat down) are right next to each other. Targ refers to the first by using מאך (he will bring it down), the second by using רמה (he will cast it), which is the reason why *BHK* suggests reading יַפִּילָהּ (he will bring it down) instead of יַשׁפִּילָהּ (he pushes it flat down). But that is not an appropriate solution when one considers the style of this text; that neither the Gk nor Syr translates יַשׁפִּילָהּ (he pushes it flat down) and that this word is also missing in Qᵃ is hardly decisive, since these texts all display a tendency to shorten the text. It is much more likely that יְשׁפִילֶנָּה (he pushes it down) should be taken with v. 5a, the mistaken positioning due to the *athnach* being placed wrongly on the preceding word (Gray, Ehrlich, Fohrer, Kaiser, et al.). If this is the case, then v. 5a is composed as a three-stress + three-stress bicolon, v. 5b as a two-stress + two-stress bicolon.

6a The Gk does not have any equivalent for רגל (foot), which is enough reason for many to eliminate it from the text (Marti, Feldmann, Ehrlich, Procksch, et al.). But

רֶגֶל (foot) conforms perfectly to the style of restating in order to make something more precise, here with the phrase רַגְלֵי עָנִי (feet of one who is miserable), just as the preceding יַשְׁפִּילֶנָּה (he pushes it down) was given more specificity by adding יַשְׁפִּילָהּ עַד־אֶרֶץ (he pushes it flat down to the ground). One must also consider it highly possible that the singular is stylistic and thus should be read as conveying the plural sense, just as עָנִי (one who is miserable) is used in parallel with the plural דַּלִּים (here: an insignificant people) (the plural דַּלִּים might have been chosen on rhythmic grounds, since two stressed syllables would clash if it had read פַּעֲמֵי דַל).

Form

Concerning how the extent of the passage and its classification was determined, see above, pp. 455f. As is generally acknowledged, its form and content are very close to 25:1-5, and this material is assigned to the same stage of development. This is a hymn, beginning with a song of praise about a city, which could be interpreted only as a reference to Jerusalem. In reality, the praise is obviously directed toward the lord protector of the city, Yahweh; cf. Psalms 48 and 87. In contrast to Isa. 25:1ff., it is not an "I" but a "we" who is speaking, that is, Israel; more specifically, as v. 2 phrases it, Israel, גּוֹי־צַדִּיק שֹׁמֵר אֱמֻנִים (the righteous people, those who maintain faithfulness), which means, the true people of Yahweh. In the second half, the poem moves on and speaks about the destruction of an enemy city. Accordingly, this portion of material is divided into two subsections: vv. 1-4 and vv. 5, 6.

To be sure, the structure does not follow the common form of a hymn. After the introduction in v. 1a, the author begins with a confessional section in v. 1b, without providing information about what specific benefit Israel received from God. In vv. 2f. a surprising turning point is reached: someone is supposed to open the gates for the people who believe in Yahweh. This summons reminds one of an entrance liturgy; cf. also Ps. 100:4. Therefore, this would seem to be the type of song that has its "setting in life" in a procession that moves up to the sanctuary. Verse 4 issues a call to trust—apparently displaced, coming as it does right after it has been said that the people are שֹׁמֵר אֱמֻנִים (those who maintain faithfulness) and are בָּטוּחַ (trusting) already. But such encouragements are not uncommon in hymns; cf. Ps. 46:9; 11; and H. Gunkel and J. Begrich, *Einleitung in die Psalmen* (1933) 56, no. 34.

The narrative part then follows, in v. 5, introduced by כִּי (truly), which gives the concrete reason for the praise of God. This looks back to the destruction of an enemy city. The imperfect forms in v. 5b do not contradict this analysis; they describe the results of the humiliation which was reported in v. 5a.

Some believe that v. 6 conveys a jussive sense, which is possible, since one also can express wishes and petitions in a hymn, because the need to look to God for help can never be satisfied once and for all; cf. passages such as Ps. 104:35; see also Ps. 139:19. However, because it follows the imperfects in v. 5b, which have the same form and are understood as indicatives,

v. 6 should be interpreted analogously as the description of something that happened already.

Meter: Verse 1b: 2 + 2 + 2; the same holds true for v. 2. Verse 3: 4 + 3; the same is true of v. 4 (following the suggestion that transposes כִּי, "since," and בְּיָהּ, "in Yah"). In v. 5a one should probably read a six-stress colon (3 + 3) (after the *athnach* has been moved and placed under יַשְׁפִּילֶנָּה (he pushes it down). Verse 5b: 2 + 2. In v. 6, it would seem that the poem once again concludes with a three-part verse (2 + 2 + 2). Here also one should note the artistic style: יצר (held fast) and תצר (preserve) in v. 3, יַשְׁפִּילֶנָּה (he pushes it down) and יַשְׁפִּילָהּ (he pushes it flat down) in v. 5b, רֶגֶל (foot) and רַגְלֵי (feet of) in v. 6.

Setting

It has been explained above already that the enemy city cannot be identified. There is also virtually nothing in the specific vocabulary that would help to set the piece in any particular epoch; generally, it uses the relatively timeless vocabulary of cultic lyric. Concerning the content, one could say much the same as was said above concerning 25:1-5. Taken by itself, this material is also not apocalyptic; the destruction of a towering city does not qualify as an apocalyptic event; besides this, it is unlikely that this refers to a capital of one of the world empires, which in certain circumstances could be viewed as the personification of evil in the world. Some commentators have observed correctly that v. 6 says it is the poor and insignificant who have trampled this particular city. To be sure, that designation could refer only to some of the people who belonged to Israel, but Israel never conquered world-class cities. Thus it is at least not completely impossible that this also refers to the city of the Moabites that was discussed in 25:12, but we have no knowledge about such an event. There was mention of the insignificant and poor (here: עָנִי and דַּלִּים) also in 25:4 (דַּל and אֶבְיוֹן).

Commentary

[26:1a] By using the introductory בַּיּוֹם הַהוּא (on that day), this material is inserted into the context of the apocalypse; once again, "that day" is the great turning point, so that the hymn becomes an eschatological song only secondarily.

It is labeled simply with the general term שִׁיר (song), though one could describe it more specifically as a תְּהִלָּה (song of praise). The word שִׁיר, which is itself a neutral term, also can be used when identifying a cultic song: Isa. 30:29; Amos 5:23; Pss. 30:1; 92:1, etc. It might have been chosen for this passage in order to be able to use the phrase יוּשַׁר הַשִּׁיר (a song will be sung). Ps. 137:3 speaks of a שִׁיר צִיּוֹן (song of Zion), which would be a correct way to describe at least the first part of this piece. There are unmistakable connections to the so-called psalms of Zion. It already has been determined above that the song was composed for use in a procession formed to celebrate a victory in war.

[26:1b] Jerusalem, the city about which the שִׁיר (song) is to be sung in the land of Judah, is as strong as it is, according to v. 1b, because Yahweh had provided it with walls and an embankment for יְשׁוּעָה (here: protection). This is a remarkable phrase, since there is a lot more to יְשׁוּעָה than the protection that walls and ramparts can provide. Jerusalem was certainly a well-fortified city in its prime and was capable of putting up strong resistance against its opponents in a hard and protracted siege (concerning defensive measures in general, see Haag, *BL*[2], 179ff. and illus. 16, col. 181). In reality, according to the faith of Israel, its security was due to the presence of Yahweh in the holy city. Conversely, while the presence of Yahweh did offer external protection, it really guaranteed יְשׁוּעָה (salvation) in a much broader sense.

It is surprising that the subject of יָשִׁית (he makes) is not named; it cannot be anyone but Yahweh; in no case should one alter the pointing to read יוּשַׁת (is established) or (with Kaiser) to treat חוֹמוֹת וָחֵל (walls and embankment) as the subject. Yahweh, and Yahweh alone, makes Jerusalem a shelter for Israel.

[26:2] When reading the command to open the gates, so that the people of God can enter, one is quickly reminded of Ps. 24:7ff., where the gates of the sanctuary are challenged to lift up their heads, there, of course, not so that the people could come in, but rather that Yahweh, the מֶלֶךְ הַכָּבוֹד (king of glory), could enter. The most important comparison one can make is between this and Ps. 118:19f., since that passage also is part of the song of thanksgiving of an individual:

אָבֹא־בָם אוֹדֶה יָהּ׃   פִּתְחוּ־לִי שַׁעֲרֵי־צֶדֶק

צַדִּיקִים יָבֹאוּ בוֹ׃   זֶה־הַשַּׁעַר לַיהוָה

(Open to me the gates of righteousness,
that I may enter through them and give thanks to Yah.
This is the gate of Yahweh;
the righteous shall enter through it).

The way in which the two passages match so closely, even to the point of the specific wording, is plain to see. Here we learn about why the gates are to be opened. The righteous want to enter so that they can praise Yahweh. The one who prays this psalm had experienced יְשׁוּעָה (salvation) when death threatened and now wants to proclaim the מַעֲשֵׂי יָהּ (the deeds of Yah) (v. 17).

Concerning the activity that would take place in the temple after a victory, see Ashurbanipal, Annals, Rm X, 17–39 (VAB VII/2, 83ff.). Once one passes through the gates, one is in the holy precinct. Not everyone could gain access; it was a common practice throughout the ancient Near East that one might approach the deity only if one was in a state of holiness; see H.-J. Kraus, BK XV/1, 111f. (Engl: *Psalms 1–59*, 227); and K. Galling, ZAW 47 (1929) 125–130. According to the entrance liturgy in Psalm 15, entrance into the sanctuary was possible for: הֹלֵךְ תָּמִים וּפֹעֵל צֶדֶק וְדֹבֵר אֱמֶת בִּלְבָבוֹ׃ (those who walk blamelessly, and do what is right, and speak the truth from the heart). It is true that there are other qualifications as well, but the essential requirements are contained in the terms צֶדֶק (right) and אֱמֶת (truth). Isa. 33:15 formulates it . . . הֹלֵךְ צְדָקוֹת וְדֹבֵר מֵישָׁרִים (those who walk righteously and speak uprightly . . .). According to Ezek. 18:5 (a passage also to be interpreted within the context of the entrance liturgy tradition), it is the צַדִּיק (righteous one) who performs what is מִשְׁפָּט (lawful) and צְדָקָה (right); and, according to Psalm 118, which was just cited, it is for the צַדִּיקִים (righteous ones) that the gate will open itself up; cf. also Ps. 1:5.

With all of this in the background, it is not surprising that the present passage speaks about the גּוֹי־צַדִּיק (righteous people); they are the legitimate members of the Yahweh community. This people is not justified because it had been without sin, but because it had done enough to satisfy the requirements that were imposed on someone who was paying a visit to the temple. As in the passages just cited, in which the overarching term צַדִּיק (righteous) is accompanied by terms that define the concept in greater detail, the same is true here as well: the גּוֹי־צַדִּיק (righteous people) are the ones who שֹׁמֵר אֱמֻנִים (maintain faithfulness). The OT speaks of a צִיר אֱמוּנִים (faithful envoy) (Prov. 13:17), an עֵד אֱמוּנִים (faithful witness) (Prov. 14:5), or an אִישׁ אֱמוּנִים (one worthy of trust) (Prov. 20:6), which means that the accent is on one's reliability. In the abstract, however, אֱמוּנִים naturally carries a whole range of meanings that are connected to the root אָמַן (BDB: confirm, support); see H. Wildberger, *THAT* I, 177ff. The standard is not stated primarily in terms of the inner relationship with Yahweh or in subjective piety, but rather concerns whether one has fulfilled specific basic requirements connected with the faith in Yahweh, and these stipulations essentially lie in the realm of ethics.

[26:3] In v. 3 the confessional element is front and center. The formulation stands on its own: Israel has experienced and can confess that Yahweh preserves שָׁלוֹם (peace) for one who has a "solid frame of mind." Ps. 24:5 promises that the righteous person will have בְּרָכָה (blessing) and צְדָקָה (vindication), and Isa. 33:16 states that the fortresses of rocks will be their refuge. Ezek. 18:9 says it in the broadest way possible: such a person will have life.

Then another point is added: "because it trusts in you." As already explained above, בָּטוּחַ (trust) points to what is inherent in one's nature; trust is not just an action that happens by chance, but it is an ongoing, reliable way of life. One might say that this phrase provides an interpretation of גּוֹי־צַדִּיק (a righteous people). The right way of acting, that which is the foundation for belonging to the Yahweh community, on a deeper level than that of fulfilling ethical requirements, is ultimately a genuine trust in Yahweh. In this sense, this passage is close to what is said in Hab. 2:4: "The צַדִּיק (righteous) will have life (יִחְיֶה) by virtue of his/her אֱמוּנָה (faith)"; on this, see H. Wildberger, *ZTK* 65 (1968) 139ff. Here, however, the cultic community can still hope for שָׁלוֹם (peace).

[26:4] Among the consequences, the help that the one who has been trusting has experienced will itself cause even more trust, thus providing the reason for the encouragement: "Trust in Yahweh forever." Israel *can* trust, since Yahweh is the עולמים צור (rock at all times). Concerning the divine epithet צור (rock), see above, p. 180; now also F. Hugger, *Jahwe, mein Fels,* Münsterschwarzacher Studien 9 (1968) 143–160. A "rock" in itself is a symbol of reliability and durability, but the author places even more stress on this here: Yahweh is an eternal rock (עולמים צור occurs only here; however, cf. passages such as Ps. 62:8: God is צוּר-עֻזִּי, "my mighty rock").

[26:5f.] Immediately after the call to faith has been issued, based on this timeless statement of faith that Yahweh is the eternal rock, specific reasons for believing are given in vv. 5f., explaining why Israel is to go into the sanctuary at this very time to praise God. It had been possible for the "poor" and "insignificant" to bring down "those who inhabit the heights," i.e., a towering city. In the final analysis, it was obviously Yahweh who had done it, but the host of believers also had done what they could.

It is surprising how much v. 5 reminds one of the vocabulary in 25:11b. If one treats that passage as a very late addition, then one would have to assume that that author already knew 26:5 well. It is impossible to prove that assumption, since it is always possible that the author was using traditional vocabulary.

מרום (heights) was used earlier (24:4, 18, 21) as an alternate way to refer to the heavens; here it simply describes a city that was established on high ground, though "heights" serves at the same time as a symbolic expression to describe the pride of its inhabitants.

Purpose and Thrust

26:1-6 is a hymn sung after a victory; an enemy city had been conquered and that conquest was being celebrated now by means of a procession to the sanctuary. However, the central theological point is not about the praise of God, but is a call to trust עדי-עד (forever), in v. 4a. Starting with this central point, the special emphases in the psalm take on their meaning. Judah *can* trust, because its God is an eternal rock. His city, Jerusalem, *is* a strong fortress, whose walls assure one of salvation, ישועה. The people of God could verify that they did indeed belong to him and could expect that Yahweh would keep שלום (peace) ready for them. That these are not just statements of faith hanging out there, detached, in the middle of nowhere had been proved when the inhabitants of the heights were brought down.

The terms עדי-עד (forever) and עולמים (at all times) might have been exactly what the redactor needed to justify inserting the song here, into the apocalypse, and thus to give it the new function that it now serves. Within the new world order, the strong city would be the center of that kingdom of God which would extend over the whole earth. When the enemy stronghold was conquered, that was, at the very least, the firstfruits of the triumph that the people of God would win as they went up against all the powers of this world. Thus this song is a promise that the גּוֹי־צַדִּיק (righteous people) would be able to survive all the storms of the end time and would be able to be preserved in שָׁלוֹם (peace). The way in which the meaning of עַד and עוֹלָם underwent a change in the postexilic era might have been the reason for this reinterpretation: "*ʿōlām* becomes the code word . . . for God's activity; only his rule would be in effect in the eschaton" (E. Jenni, *THAT* II, 239).

Yahweh's People during the
Oppression of the End

Literature

Concerning the text: A. F. L. Beeston, "The Hebrew Verb *špt*," *VT* 8 (1958) 216–217. G. Schwarz, "'. . . Tau der Lichter . . .'?" *ZAW* 88 (1976) 280–281.

Concerning resurrection: F. Nötscher, Altorientalischer und alttestamentlicher Auferstehungsglauben (1926), esp. 154–159. H. Birkeland, "The Belief in the Resurrection of the Dead in the Old Testament," *ST* 3 (1950) 60–78. L. Rost, "Alttestamentliche Wurzeln der ersten Auferstehung," *In memoriam E. Lohmeyer* (1951) 67–72; reprint: *Studien zum Alten Testament*, BWANT 101 (1974) 61–65. E. Zolli, "Il canto dei morti risorti e il ms. DSI[a] in Isa 26,18," *Sefarad* 12 (1952) 375–378. J. de Savignac, "La rosée solaire de l'ancienne Égypte," *NC* 6 (1954) 345–353. R. Martin-Achard, *De la mort à la résurrection* (1956); esp. 101–112. [Engl: *From Death to Life* (1960), esp. 130–138]. G. H. Botterweck, "Marginalien zum atl. Auferstehungsglauben," *WZKM* 54 (1957) 1–8. P. Humbert, "La rosée tombe en Israel," *TZ* 13 (1957) 487–493. F. König, *Zarathustras Jenseitsvorstellungen und das Alte Testament* (1964), esp. 214–240. G. Fohrer, "Das Geschick des Menschen nach dem Tode im Alten Testament," *KD* 12 (1968) 249–262. E. Haenchen, "Auferstehung im Alten Testament," *Die Bibel und wir* (1968) 73–90. H. D. Preuss, "'Auferstehung' in Texten alttestamentlicher Apokalyptik (Jes 26,7-19, Dan 12,1-4)," *Linguistische Theologie* 3 (1972) 101–172, esp. 107–124. G. Stemberger, "Das Problem der Auferstehung im Alten Testament," *Kairos* 14 (1972) 273–290, esp. 279f. S. Virgulin, "La risurrezione dai morti in Is 26,14-19," *BeO* 14 (1972) 49–60. J. F. A. Sawyer, "Hebrew Words for the Resurrection of the Dead," *VT* 23 (1973) 218–234.

[Literature update through 1979: *Concerning the text:* F. J. Helfmeyer, "'Deine Toten—meine Leichen.' Heilszusage und Annahme in Jes 26,19," FS G. J. Botterweck (1977) 245–258. J. Day, "טַל אוֹרֹת in Isaiah 26:19," *ZAW* 90 (1978) 265–269.

Concerning resurrection: J. Kammerer, "Die Auferstehung der Toten im AT als Element der eschatologischen Restauration des Bundesvolkes Israel," diss., Vienna (1968). E. B. Keller, "Hebrew Thoughts on Immortality and Resurrection," *IJPR* 5 (1974) 16–44.]

Text

7 The path for the righteous is flat,[a]
   the beaten track that you prepare[b] for the righteous[c] is straight.

* * * *

8 Also on the ^apath of your judgments,
    O Yahweh, we trust confidently in you.^a
  ^bTo name your name, to call on you,^b
    ^cthe heart is yearning.^c
9 ^aIndeed, my heart, it yearns for you^a in the night,^b
    also in the 'morning'^b my spirit (still) longs for you.

          * * * *

  ^cFor your judgments (come) on the land,
    thus the inhabitants of the earth learn^d righteousness;^c
10 if the wicked person ^afinds mercy,^a
  ^bthen that one never learns what righteousness is,
  ^ctwists what is straight on the earth,^{bc}
    and never sees the supremacy of Yahweh.

          * * * *

11 Yahweh,^a your hand is raised high,
    yet they do not see it;
  ^{bc}thus they have to see and be thwarted,^c because of the zeal for
the people,^{db}
    and the fire against ^eyour enemies^e will consume them.

          * * * *

12 Yahweh,^a you will provide^b us^c peace,^d
    since you also have accomplished all our deeds for us.
13 ^aYahweh, our God, other lords besides you ruled over us,
    yet only about you, we thought only about your name.^a
14 Dead^a will not again be alive,
  ^bshades do not rise up.
  Indeed,^b you have punished and exterminated them
    and obliterated^c whatever would remind someone of them.
15 ^aYou have multiplied the people, Yahweh,
    you have multiplied the people, have glorified yourself,^a
  ^bhave expanded all the borders of the land.^b

          * * * *

16 Yahweh, ^ain need 'we' sought you,^a
  ^b'we called' out, since your 'chastisement' pressed 'us' hard.^c
17 As a pregnant woman, when her hour comes,
    writhes about,^a cries out when her pains come,
      that is how we, Yahweh, have become before you.
18 ^aWe were pregnant, we writhed about;^a ^bwhen we gave birth, it was
wind.^b
  We can provide no help^c for the land,^d
    and those who dwell within the earth ^edo not come into the
world.^e

          * * * *

19 Your dead will live, [my dead body]^a will rise up,
    the inhabitants of the dust 'will wake up^b and ^cwill rejoice.'^c
  For the dew of the lights^d is your dew,
    and the earth will give birth^e to the shades.

          * * * *

20 Now then, my people, go on into your chambers
    and close ^ayour doors^a behind you.
  ^bHide yourself^b for a brief moment
    until the malediction has passed by.

21 For behold,ᵃ Yahweh moves out ᵇfrom his dwelling place,ᵇ
   in order to bring the consequences of the transgressions of the
   inhabitants of the earth upon 'them.'
   Then the earth will expose their blood
   and will no longer hide those whom they have struck dead.

7a There is no word in the Gk corresponding to ישר (here: straight), and it is considered to be superfluous by many of those who work with the text; however, the Gk ought not be followed at this point. ישר is obviously not direct address to Yahweh, as suggested by Procksch, but is a predicate for מעגל צדיק (the beaten track for the righteous). One also need not be troubled about the meter, since the construct phrase מעגל צדיק (the beaten track for the righteous) can be read as having just one stress.

7b תפלס (that you prepare) functions as a relative clause (Fohrer, Kaiser, et al.); Qᵃ reads this word as תפלט (you bring to safety), presumably because it did not understand the rare verb פלס (make level).

7c Qᵃ writes צדיק (righteous) without the vowel letter.

8a–a One would have an easier time making sense of this colon if one followed Schlögl, removing ארח (path), but that is too easy a solution to be acceptable. One also should reject Ehrlich's suggestion that this word ארח (path) is nothing but a dittography of the same word from the beginning of v. 7. Gray might be closer to the truth when, following Lowth, he suggests that קוינו (we trust confidently) should be read instead of קוינוך (we trust confidently in you), especially since Qᵃ also has the same reading. That would mean that ארח משפטיך (path of judgments) would be the direct object of קוינו (we trust confidently). In spite of all these suggestions, it would be better to leave the text unaltered and to treat ארח משפטיך as an adverbial accusative: "on the path of your judgments."

8b–b Literally: "according to your name and according to your thought." Instead of לזכרך (here: to call on you), Qᵃ reads לתורתך (according to your torah), a significant alteration; this change might even have been introduced purposely.

8c–c The Gk does not translate תאות־נפש (the heart is yearning); once again, this can be attributed to the fact that it clearly tends to simplify the text. It would seem that Syr and MSS of the Targ had a reading נפשנו (our inner beings, hearts), but this most likely is not correct, in light of the singular נפשי (my heart) used at the beginning of v. 9. There the author uses נפש (inner being, heart) once more, the first time obviously without any further specificity, the second time with the suffixed form נפשי (my heart). It would be a mistake to translate נפש with "soul" in this passage; although "heart" is not an exact translation either, it will have to do.

9a–a Ehrlich does not think it possible that a speech with the singular pronoun could be used here, so he alters the text to read נפשנו אותך (our heart, it yearns for you) (and later, to read רוחנו, "our spirit"). Admittedly, it is surprising to find the singular after the plural קוינו (we trust confidently) in v. 8. In light of the nature of such texts, however, one ought to be careful about expressing the view that it is "impossible."

9b and b On the one hand, Marti believes that בלילה (in the night) makes no sense and has removed it. On the other hand, Guthe wonders whether this word בלילה shows that בבקר, "in the morning," should be read in v. 9aβ instead of בקרבי (in my midst). Metrical reasons suggest that בלילה (in the night) should be retained, and the change Guthe suggests makes good sense.

9c–c The Gk reads διότι φῶς τὰ προστάγματά σου ἐπὶ τῆς γῆς (because your commands are light upon the earth). Procksch (following Oort), Rudolph (18), et al., thus reads כ[ב]אר ([as] light) instead of כי כאשר (for just as) and translates it: "when light shines. . . ." Some have argued that כאשר (just as) needs to be followed by a verb, but it is just as possible that this could be there instead of the copula, which is missing from the Hebrew, so that it would be translated "come," as has been done above.

9d Targ translates למדו (lit.: they learned) as יתאלפין (they shall be taught); that might have been done in order to match it to the surrounding imperfect forms.

10a–a Qᵃ: יחן (he will be gracious to). One notes the tendency, already in Chronicles, to replace the passive with the active (for examples in Qᵃ, see Kutscher, pp. 402f.). If Qᵃ is correct, then רשע (wicked person) would have to be considered as an accusative. For יחן (MT: was treated with mercy), the Gk reads πέπαυθαι (will be stopped), which has caused Procksch and Gray to suggest that it may originally have read יחדל (will come to an end) (Procksch, possibly יחת, "will be shattered"; Gray: חדל, "has come to an end"). Marti would rather insert the negative particle בל (not) before יחן (he will be gracious to) (based on haplography due to the previous תבל, "earth"); none of this is likely. It is also impossible to agree with Siever's suggestion, which Guthe has accepted, based on Ps. 1:4, that one read לא כן רשע (the wicked are not so) in this passage.

10b–b Ehrlich suggests changing למד צדק בארץ (learn justice in the land) to read עָמַד צַדִּיק בָּאָרֶץ (a righteous one will stand in the land). There is no evidence to support this change; nevertheless, it should be pointed בָּאָרֶץ (in the land) (see Gk, Targ, Syr, Rudolph, Kaiser, *BHS*, et al.).

10c Duhm wonders whether one should possibly add עָוֶל (injustice), since the colon is too short—nothing more than a wild guess. It is even worse to remove בארץ נכחות (what is straight on the earth) altogether (Schlögl).

11a Duhm thinks that יהוה (Yahweh) is an "inadvertent repetition" (see the end of v. 10), but the vocative is necessary in the transition to second person speech.

11b–b The Gk has expanded the text: γνόντες δὲ αἰσχυνθήσονται· ζῆλος λήμψεται λαὸν ἀπαίδευτον (however, knowing, they will be put to shame; zeal will destroy a rude people)—most imaginative, but not faithful to the text.

11c–c Apparently, *BHS* treats יחזו ויבשו (they have to see and be thwarted) as a gloss to the preceding יחזיון (they do not see it), which is thus to be removed (though Guthe, at least, would eliminate only ויבשו, "and they would be thwarted"). Once again, this is another example of the well-known lack of understanding about how such a text is constructed.

11d Because it is followed by צריך (your enemies), Marti chooses to agree with Cheyne and read עמך (your people); cf. Ps. 69:10. That change is not necessary.

11e–e The very opposite (see note d) is found in the Gk, which has no suffix to match צריך (your enemies), but it is absolutely necessary there.

12a Duhm wants to treat יהוה (Yahweh) as part of the preceding verse; Procksch agrees, but wonders whether יהוה (Yahweh) should be read at the beginning of v. 12 as well (because of the meter).

12b There is disagreement about the meaning of תשפת; KBL: "get ready for" (with reference to Ugaritic *tpd*, "lay, put in the right place," and Old South Arabic *špt*, "give"). Beeston points out, however, that Old South Arabic *š* corresponds to Hebrew שׁ and thus opts for changing the present passage to read תשפה ("decree, ordain," denominative of שָׂפָה, "lip"). The word was not understood even when Qᵃ was copied; it reads השפוט (you will judge). But the Gk reads δός (give); Theod (according to Marchalianus) θήσεις (you will give); Vulg: *dabis* (you will give); thus, in spite of the uncertainty about the linguistic interpretation, one should translate this "lay down, give."

12c Liebmann (*ZAW* 22 [1902] 302) removes לנו (us), which is totally unnecessary.

12d *BHS* follows Bruno in suggesting שׁלּוּם, "retaliation, vengeance," should be read instead of שׁלוֹם (peace) and כִּגְמֻל (as recompense) instead of גַּם כֹּל (also all), with reference to Syr, but the Syr does not really support this unnecessary alteration.

13a–a The Gk translates v. 13: κύριε ὁ θεὸς ἡμῶν, κτῆσαι ἡμᾶς· κύριε ἐκτὸς σοῦ ἄλλον οὐκ οἴδαμεν, τὸ ὄνομά σου ὀνομάζομεν (Lord our God, you acquired us. Lord, we have not known others apart from you; we have named your name). Based on this, Gray suggests reading v. 13aβ-b: בְּעָלֵנוּ אֲדֹנִי / זוּלָתְךָ בַל-נֵדַע / נַזְכִּיר שְׁמֶךָ (O our ruler [or: O our *ba'al*], O Lord / besides you, we have not known / we have remembered your name); that can hardly be right. In any case, the line is surprisingly long, though it is not obvious where any part of it could be eliminated. If the text is correct as is, then both בָּךְ (you) and שְׁמֶךָ (your name) are dependent on נַזְכִּיר (we thought only about). Instead of בְעָלוּנוּ (here: have ruled over us), Ehrlich proposes נָעַלְנוּ, "we despise, reject." That does little to make the text more understandable. It is certainly possible that there is some error here, but none of the many suggested alterations (see scholars such as Duhm, Marti, Procksch) is convincing.

14a Guthe wants to read מְתֵיהֶם (their dead), but that is impossible; the phrase is simply an apodictic statement that there is no hope for any who are dead (see also רְפָאִים, "shades").

14b–b There are problems with לָכֵן, if it has the meaning "therefore." But it is not a good solution to eliminate everything (so Guthe) from רְפָאִים to לָכֵן (shades . . . to [what is usually translated]: therefore); v. 14aβ is absolutely necessary for the parallelism. As is often the case, לָכֵן ought probably to be assigned an asseverative meaning: "truly, indeed"; see *HAL*.

14c Q^a reads וַתֶּאְסֹר (and you have imprisoned) instead of וַתְּאַבֵּד (and you have destroyed), but there is no doubt that the MT is correct (Gk: καὶ ἦρας, "and you have taken away"; Targ: וְתוֹבֵיד, "you shall make to perish"; Syr: *w'wbdt*, "and you destroyed"). אבד (obliterate, perish) is used with זֵכֶר (memory) in Ps. 9:7 and with שֵׁם (name) in Ps. 41:6.

15a–a The second יָסַפְתָּ לַגּוֹי (you have multiplied the people) is missing in one Hebrew MS; Guthe suggests that it be removed, and Gray would eliminate the preceding יהוה (Yahweh) at the same time. In fact, it is simply a haplography in that particular MS; besides, repetition is a characteristic of the style here as well.

Ehrlich suspects something is wrong with יסף (multiply) and would rather read יִסַּרְתָּ (you disciplined) both times, as well as read לָנוּ (us) instead of לַגּוֹי (the people); instead of נִכְבַּדְתָּ (you have glorified yourself), he suggests הִכְבַּדְתָּ (you made heavy), which results in his translation: "You have disciplined us, O YHWH, disciplined us very severely." If one follows this approach, one very likely can write a whole new OT. Procksch follows Oort and alters נִכְבַּדְתָּ (you have glorified yourself) to read נִכְבָּדוֹת, "glorious things" (Ps. 87:3); thus also *BHS* (see also Gk); this is possible, but too uncertain.

15b–b Ehrlich considers it impossible that רִחַקְתָּ could mean "you have expanded" (saying that it then would have been הִרְחַבְתָּ in the Hebrew); in other passages, רחק means "remove." He expands the text by adding to it the object "us," based on what has just preceded it, and treats כָּל-קַצְוֵי-אָרֶץ (lit.: all the ends of the earth) as an accusative that identifies the goal to be reached (maintaining that קַצְוֵי-אָרֶץ never means "boundaries of the land"). This would make the sense of the passage: "you have placed us far away into all the parts of the world." Based on the meaning required for רחק (send away), one cannot reject Ehrlich's suggestion out of hand, but his translation simply makes new problems as one tries to understand the meaning of the entire verse.

16a–a פְּקָדוּךְ (lit.: they visited you) is questionable, just from the fact that two Hebrew MSS read פְּקַדְנוּךְ (we visited you); also some MSS of the Gk, Ethiopic, and Arabic presume the first person plural reading. In addition, it is strange that פקד would be used here in the presumed sense "seek," but, as demonstrated by Judg. 15:1; Ezek. 23:21, it is not completely impossible. It seems better to alter the text to read פְּקַדְנוּךְ (we sought you) rather than to follow other suggested emendations that involve more extensive changes. Thus Kaiser's alternate reading בְּצַר פְּקֻדָּתֶךָ, "in the distress of thy visitation," is troubling; one cannot dispense with the verb.

16b צָקוּן is a strange form. Gk: ἐν θλίψει (in tribulation); Vulg: *in tribulatione;* Syr: *bḥbwšyʾ* (in the distress); thus they all thought this word was a substantive. Some believe that it is a substantive and point it צָקוּן (construct state), "pressure of a spell" or something similar (see Dillmann; cf. Duhm, Ehrlich, et al.). One might presume, in spite of this, that it is supposed to be a verbal form. Gesenius and Delitzsch think that it is a perfect form of צוק (BDB: constrain, press upon), to which a paragogic *nun* has been appended; see Deut. 8:3, 16. There is a root צוק I, "pour out," and there are at least *hiphʿil* forms of the root צוק II, "press upon," but these meanings do not help to make sense of it. Some (Marti, following Cheyne; Kaiser) alter it to read צָעֲקוּ (we cried out) and follow this with either מִלַּחַץ (from distress) or בְּלַחַץ (in distress).

16c In other places, לחשׁ means "exorcism, adjuration"; since that meaning is problematic for this passage, G. R. Driver (*JTS* 38 [1937] 43) explains the word on the basis of Akkadian *laḥāšu*, "to be bowed down," and, since he alters the preceding word to read צָקוּן and alters לָמוֹ (for him) to read לָנוּ (for us) at the end of the line, he translates: "Thy chastisement (has been) a humiliating constraint to us." It is true that the Gk presumes an original לָנוּ (for us). That change should be adopted, since previous alterations were adapted for the text, to read פְּקַדְנוּךְ (we sought you) and צָעֲקוּ (we called out). But the postulated meaning offered by Driver, based on Akkadian *laḥāšu*, is highly unlikely, so that it will have to be read as מִלַּחַץ ([your] chastisement) (see 19:20).

17a No word in the Gk corresponds to תָּחִיל (writhes about); Duhm, Marti, Gray, Ehrlich, et al., remove it, partially with reference to the meter, but one could find better reasons for saying that it is essential to the meter!

18a–a According to Duhm, metrical considerations and the parallelism make it necessary to move the first two words from v. 18 to v. 17. That is an arbitrary suggestion; once again, we have a three-part verse before us.

18b–b Procksch is not pleased with the description of how the birth took place (the verbs do not lead one to conclude that wind was being born). Instead of יָלַדְנוּ (we gave birth), he would rather read יֹלְדָה (giving birth), and he takes רוּחַ (wind) with יְשׁוּעוֹת (here: help) (cf. Gk: πνεῦμα σωτηρίας, "saving wind"). Guthe thinks that כְּמוֹ (just as), which is missing in the Gk, makes no sense. Duhm and Marti remove the entire phrase כְּמוֹ יָלַדְנוּ רוּחַ (when we gave birth, it was wind); it is too bad that one finds such a long list of births of wind in the text-critical observations!

18c Q^a: יְשֻׁעָתֶךָ (your help); however, one should still stay with the MT reading.

18d Gk: ἐπὶ τῆς γῆς (upon the earth). Some, like Procksch, thus believe that one ought to read בָּאָרֶץ (*upon* the earth). We simply do not have enough of a feel of the language to determine for sure whether the MT offers a reading that is possible syntactically. However, it is more likely that the Gk, in spite of its expanded translation that includes the preposition, had only the word אֶרֶץ (earth) in its text.

18e–e According to C. F. Whitley (*ZAW* 84 [1972] 215f.), בַּל conveys a positive meaning in this passage (like Ugaritic *bl*), and he says that נָפַל does not mean "be born" but rather "disappear." It is impossible, however, that בל would have two different meanings in the same sentence.

Qᵃ: יפולו instead of יפלו (here, both: come into [the world]) (according to Kutscher, 331, cases of this type should not be treated as pausal forms; these are accented on the penultimate syllable, a practice that he maintains was still followed by Qumran circles).

Procksch thinks that ובל (and not) is a dittography of the following three letters [ו]יפלו (and . . . come), for which reason he wants to remove it. He translates v. 18bβ: "the inhabitants of the earth sink down"; see textual note 19e below.

19a נבלתי (my dead body) seems strange when it follows מתיך (your dead). Syr reads wšldyhwn (and their corpses), which is why it would be altered here to read נבלתם (their dead bodies) (*BHS*), though one would expect the second singular suffix here; it is most likely that one must treat this as a gloss (Duhm, Marti), added by a reader who wanted to identify himself specifically among those who were included in the hope of the resurrection.

19b It is surprising to find the imperative הקיצו (wake up). The Syr (wntt ʿyrwn, "and they will be aroused") leads one to presume that its text read a perfect consecutive, whereas Qᵃ reads יקיצ (they will rise). They might be right; in any case, whichever is right, it has to be translated as a future (Gk: ἐγερθήσονται, "they will be raised").

19c–c The imperative ורננו (and rejoice) is impossible. Qᵃ reads וירננ (and they rejoiced), Aquila: αινεσουσιν (they will praise). Here one has to follow Duhm, Marti, Cheyne, and Procksch in pointing this as a perfect consecutive, ורננו (and they will rejoice) (Gk: εὐφρανθήσονται, "they will be made joyful").

19d "Dew of light" is a *crux interpretum*. For כי טל אורת טלך (lit.: for dew lights of your dew), the Gk reads ἡ γάρ δρόσος ἡ παρὰ σοῦ ἴαμα αὐτοῖς ἐστιν (for dew that is from you is soothing for them); this means it seems to have read ארוכה (healing).

In 2 Kings 4:39, one finds ארת (herb) used in the sense of "mallow" (chelidonium majus), but that is no help in the present passage; the same is true of the suggestion proposed once again by Schwarz that this should read טל אבוה, "dew of the spirits of the dead." One would do best to stay with the translation "dew of lights"; particularly since the singular אורה (light) appears in Ps. 139:12, it is certainly possible that a plural אורות (lights) could be used. Humbert (491f.) believes that one can take this in the special sense "particules lumineuses" (luminescent particles).

19e Ehrlich argues vehemently in favor of the viewpoint that נפל in the *hiphʿil* can mean "give birth"; since Sheol would give birth, one would have to start with the idea that it would mean something like "cast upward." Thus it would have to be translated: "Thus (Yahweh) allows it—your dew—to fall on the land of shades [that is, Palestine]." However, one can hardly doubt that נפל has the meaning "give birth"; cf. καταπίπτειν (was born) in Wis. 7:3, πίπτειν (fall [between feet], be born) in *Iliad* 19.110, and Arabic saqaṭa IV, "have a miscarriage," but note also Hebrew נפל, "miscarriage."

20a–a The pointing on דלתיך permits one to choose between דלתיך (both your doors) (*Kethib*) and דלתך (your door) (*Qere*) or דלתך (your door). As has generally been done in the past, the dual form should be read.

20b–b Concerning חבי (hide yourself) (an Aramaism), see above, p. 463. Everywhere else, the Hebrew uses the written form חבא (in fact, in the *niphʿal*); on this, see G. Bergsträsser, *Hebräische Grammatik* II (1929) §29e.

21a הנה (behold) is missing in Qᵃ, but this can hardly be right.

21b–b In place of ממקומו (from his dwelling place), the Gk reads ἀπὸ τοῦ ἁγίου (lit.:

from the holy), which would fit the context, but this is certainly not a good enough reason to emend it to read מִקְדָשׁוֹ (from his holy place) (Schlögl).

Form

Concerning the analysis of this section, see above, pp. 455ff., and the overview on p. 459.

Meter: Verse 7: no doubt a three-stress + three-stress bicolon (מַעְגַּל צַדִּיק, "the beaten track . . . for the righteous" should be read as having one stress). Verse 8a: a five-stress colon. Verse 8b: a two-stress + two-stress bicolon. Verse 9a: a three-stress + three-stress bicolon. Verse 9b: a four-stress + four-stress bicolon. Verse 10aα: a two-stress + two-stress bicolon. Verse 10aβ-b: a three-stress + three-stress bicolon (וּבְלִי־יִרְאֶה, "and never sees," has one stress; possibly the ו should be removed). Verse 11a: a five-stress colon. Verse 11b: a three-stress + three-stress bicolon.

From v. 12 on, it is extremely hard to identify the metrical structure with confidence. Verse 12: possibly a four-stress + four-stress bicolon (כִּי גַם כֹּל, "since also all," has one stress). Verse 13: ? Verse 14a: most likely a three-stress + three-stress bicolon, in which the stress is on בל (not) both times it is used, placing special emphasis on the negation of what follows. Verse 14b: three-stress + three-stress bicolon. In v. 15, for variety, a three-part verse is used (3 + 3 + 3). Verse 16 can hardly be read metrically, which, as in v. 13 above, might be because the text as we have it has been damaged. Verses 17 and 18 seem to have three parts, but the meter can hardly be identified. Verse 19: four-stress + four-stress colon (if נְבֵלָתִי, "my dead body," is not to be removed). Verse 19b: three-stress + three-stress bicolon. Verse 20a: this is likely also a three-stress + three-stress bicolon (לֵךְ־עַמִּי, "my people, go," should be read as having only one stress). Verses 20b and 21 are also very difficult to analyze exactly.

The disjunctures in the flow of thought in this material and the fact that the genre has been "broken apart" can also be detected throughout, for it is impossible to identify the metrical pattern with any measure of confidence.

Concerning the stylistic techniques: note the arrangement in vv. 7, 8a:

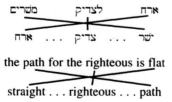

In vv. 8b, 9a:

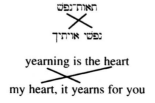

557

In vv. 9b, 10a:

righteousness they learn

never learns what righteousness is

Setting
According to the above analysis, vv. 7-21 belong to the original body of material; the poem was composed not long after 24:1-20.

Commentary

[26:7-18] *The Song of Lament*
[26:7] The first part, vv. 7-18, is a song of lament that has been massively "broken apart" in both form and content. It is to be subdivided as follows:

- a. 26:7   The fundamental statement of faith
- b. 26:8, 9a   The longing for God
- c. 26:9b, 10   Reflective interlude
- d. 26:11   Request that the enemies be obliterated
- e. 26:12-15   Confidence about being heard (with a reflective look back at Yahweh's faithfulness in the past)
- f. 26:16-18   The lament: Israel's condition is hopeless

The oracle of salvation follows in v. 19 and then, in v. 20, there is a challenge to Israel to act appropriately as the judgment is effected.

a. 26:7: The Fundamental Statement of Faith
It has been noted again and again that this verse has a wisdom character. It could easily belong in the book of Proverbs; cf. 4:18: "But the path of the righteous is like the light of dawn"; or 15:19: "But the path of the upright is a level highway"; see also 1:19; 2:20; 3:6; 5:6; 15:24, etc. The verb פלס (prepare) is used in Proverbs as well, in fact with מעגל (beaten track). In 4:26, within the context of wisdom instruction, the "son" is encouraged to keep the path for his feet going straight. By contrast, 5:21 says virtually the same thing as Isa. 26:7b: Yahweh is the one who keeps human beings on a straight path, and even Prov. 4:26 infers that God-given wisdom will keep those who are adept at it on the path of life. One should not translate v. 7b as a parallel to v. 7a: "the way of the righteous is straightness," but literally: "for the righteous. . . ." This means it is Yahweh who puts the righteous one on the right path. For this reason, a pious person would plead: "lead me on the אֹרַח מִישׁוֹר (level path)" (Ps. 27:11), or such a person confesses: "All the paths of Yahweh are חֶסֶד וֶאֱמֶת (steadfast love and faithfulness)" (Ps. 25:10). But one also reads about the king on the Babylonian Princes' Mirror (reverse, 7): "But if he has paid attention to the guidance of Ea, then the great gods will (contin-

ually) lead him into insight and upon the path of justice (*ṭūdat mīšari*)" (MAOG 11 [1937] 4, 8). Yahweh is the lord over destiny in life; the believer can place trust in the fact that God makes that person's way straight, spares that person hardship, and does not lead that person astray. As an incontrovertible confession of faith, the author presumes this statement when discussing the destiny of Israel during the terrifying end times. But, said the other way around: if one starts out from this basis of faith, then it would be difficult for one to argue theologically against the appropriateness of the way history was unfolding.

b. 26:8, 9a: The Longing for God

[26:8] Verse 8 fits very well with v. 7. Israel knows that the way of the righteous is that of a level path (the proverbial saying originally addressed to an individual is now applied to all Israel; now it refers to the people as a whole as righteous), for which reason the path of judgment cannot pose a threat; the people can trust in their God even on that path. In this context, משפטים (judgments) must refer to experiences in which Israel recognized the judging hand of its God. Even though such experiences proved harsh, they could not drive Israel away from God; the judgments could not render its confession useless; even within the context of the judgments, the people stretched out their hands in hope toward God; one might say: from the *deus absconditus* (hidden God) toward the *deus revelatus* (revealed God).

The verb קוה (trust confidently, hope) is usually connected with קו (measuring line). Some raise questions about that. The basic meaning of the verb could well be explained as: "be stretched as tightly as a measuring line." The Arabic vocable *qawiya* means "stretched, be strong" (see above, p. 208). The Hebrew vocables that one usually translates with the words "wait" or "hope" are close in meaning to what is involved in trusting, especially בטח; see R. Bultmann, *TDNT* II, 521–523. The word קוה is never used in the secular sense to describe placing confidence in a human being, but always refers to waiting for some event; in the theological context, however, this almost always speaks about hoping in God. Human beings hope in Yahweh, even though one would leave it an open question about the specific way in which his help would manifest itself; see Ps. 73:25ff. and cf. C. Westermann, *THAT* II, 621f.; in addition, see J. van der Ploeg, "L'Espérance dans l'Ancien Testament," *RB* 61 (1954) 481–507; and T. C. Vriezen, "Die Hoffnung im Alten Testament," *TLZ* 78 (1953) 577–586.

The assurance that one can hope in Yahweh comes from the context of songs of lament. This action of turning toward God is not just a habit linked to cultic "orthodoxy," but is rather a deep yearning from the heart (תאות־נפשׁ). There is a good reason why there is no suffix on נפשׁ (here: heart); נפשׁ is used to identify the intensity of deep emotions (see C. Westermann, *THAT* II, 77ff.); one almost could translate תאות־נפשׁ as "greedy demand." It is not a piety, "sicklied o'er with the pale cast of thought" [*Hamlet* 3.1] and dulled by running on idle until exhausted, but is rather a submission characterized by ardor and passion. If the text has been transmitted correctly, this expectant longing is for the שֵׁם (name) of Yahweh and for זֵכֶר (calling upon) him, which obviously means yearning for Yahweh himself, though the very mention of his name establishes contact with the God who is far off; indeed, the God who is able to restore is there already. There are other passages where זכר (call upon, remember) parallels שֵׁם (name) (Exod. 3:15; Prov. 10:7). In the present passage, זכר means "the appeal to, the cultic adoration of."

[26:9a] Verse 9 takes up the thought once again. נַפְשִׁי (my heart) is in a *casus pendens* relationship and is picked up once again when the first person is used as part of the following verb. Yet here also it means much more than a simple "I," but specifically: "I, in the totality of my being a unique individual."

אַוָּה (yearn), which picks up תַּאֲוָה (yearning) from v. 8, is defined further by the use of the parallel word שָׁחַר (long for), just as, when it occurred earlier in v. 8, קִוָּה (trust confidently) clarified what was meant. These are synonyms that can hardly be distinguished from one another in terms of shades of meaning; placing them together serves the purpose of intensifying what is being said. But it is noteworthy that קוה (trust confidently) is in the first person plural, whereas the verbs in v. 9a are in the first person singular. The poet first identifies himself as one with his associates, with those who thought as he did, by using "we"; then he goes on to speak for himself, using "I."

שָׁחַר (long for) is used rather infrequently, though it does have a set role within the poetry of the Psalms: Pss. 63:2 (parallel to צמא, "be thirsty"); 78:34 (parallel to דרשׁ, "seek [God]"); Job 8:5 (parallel to התחנן, "make supplication"); cf. also Hos. 5:15 (parallel to בקשׁ, "seek").

נַפְשִׁי (my heart) is picked up again in the second half of the verse by the use of רוּחִי (my spirit). One does not get the sense of this Hebrew word if one uses the traditional, hardly avoidable English terms "ghost, spirit." Corresponding to its dynamic character (רוח means literally "wind"), it can be used to designate the whole range of human states of mind; see above on 25:5 and cf. D. Lys, *Rûach: Le souffle dans l'Ancien Testament*, EHPR 56 (1962). In the present passage, one should not try to show how this term is differentiated from נפשׁ (here: heart). Even in the morning, the longing for God is still there. It is noteworthy that לַיְלָה (night) is mentioned first; the ancient Israelite especially must have experienced nighttime with great anxiety (cf. Pss. 6:7; 77:7, etc.), whereas one would experience Yahweh's help in the morning. For this reason, longing for God during the loneliness and defenselessness throughout the dark night would have brought on particularly intense emotions. Obviously, it would be normal for "night" to be linked with "day." When, as an exception to the rule, "morning" is used with "night," that means: still in the morning, when fear is taken away from human beings, even then longing for God is very much alive.

c. 26:9b, 10: Reflective Interlude

[26:9b] Verse 9b seems to begin—apparently quite abruptly—all over again, though כִּי (for) does show that the intention is for vv. 9b, 10 to be understood within the context of the song of lament. Verse 8a had stressed that hope in Yahweh need not dissolve into nothing, not even when the events connected with judgment are taking place; vv. 8b, 9a then continued by showing how passionately the author still longed for Yahweh. Verse 9b now picks up the theme of v. 8a once again (as is shown by the reuse of מִשְׁפָּטֶיךָ, "your judgments"), in order to amplify the thought that hope also remains when one is "on the path of your judgments." Judgments are necessary, since that is the only way in which the inhabitants of the earth learn that one is to respect צֶדֶק (righteousness).

[26:10] Verse 10a underscores this knowledge by stating that the wicked person never learns what righteousness is, even if he or she finds mercy; besides this, the wicked person is blind to Yahweh's נֵאוּת (supremacy). It is worth noting that צדק (righteousness) is used without any other terms that define it more carefully; this is not about "righteousness before God" and is not about righteousness among human beings either, but is about righteousness pure and simple, about a recognition of order in the world and the rules by which one lives, about an existence that cannot thrive without שׁלום (peace); further details about what this means can be found in the discussion above on 24:5f.

The pedagogical character of divine judgment is pointed out here very clearly (note that למד, "learn," is used twice in the section). It is a terribly painful way, but it is the only way available when one wants to combat the actions of the רשׁע (wicked person) and when one wants to prevent נְכֹחוֹת (what is straight) from becoming "twisted" on earth. Even the peoples (the text says יֹשְׁבֵי תֵבֵל, "the inhabitants of the earth") can know what צדק (righteousness) is and what נכחות (straight paths) are all about; in actuality, that is exactly what is meant in 24:5 when that passage refers to the בְּרִית עוֹלָם (eternal covenant). נכחות refers to what is set out in a straight line, that is, that which is right; see passages such as Amos 3:10, where חמס (violence) and שׁד (robbery) are direct opposites of נְכֹחָה (what is right).

The verb עָוַל I (twist) is used elsewhere only in Ps. 71:4 (parallel to רשׁע, "wicked," and חוֹמֵץ, "cruel"); the substantive עַוְלָה (unrighteousness), which is from the same root, is used more often, but is found almost only in the later writings of the OT and is frequently used in the Qumran texts as a way to identify godless behavior; the Manual of Discipline (1QS) virtually states that the רוח (ה)עול(ה) (spirit of unrighteousness) is the exact opposite of the רוח (ה)אמת (spirit of truth). As important as it is, on the one hand, to appeal to a human being to use the knowledge one has been given concerning justice and order, it is just as important to recognize that salvation is a possibility only when one recognizes that Yahweh is the one who installs and preserves this order. In the final analysis, the misery of the godless is linked to the fact that they do not know Yahweh or, as it is said in a more picturesque way in v. 10b: "they never see the נֵאוּת יהוה (supremacy of Yahweh)." The נֵאוּת יהוה (supremacy of Yahweh) was mentioned in 24:14 as well, and, no matter what specific word is used, in the entire book of Isaiah "supremacy" is one of the chief characteristics of Yahweh's nature (cf. passages such as 6:1); it is close to what is meant when the term "holiness" is used. Whereas Yahweh's גאון (supremacy) is clearly seen in his action of judgment in 24:14, here the גאות (supremacy) of Yahweh concerns his role as protector of world order; finally, this characteristic is related even to his activities in creation; see also Ps. 93:1.

It is frequently mentioned that one would expect a person to turn back toward him when under the judgment of God, and this idea plays a central role not only in the deuteronomic-deuteronomistic theology, but also in Hosea (though the phraseology למד צדק, "learns what righteousness is," is used only in this passage). The thought is drawn out to its logical conclusion. To offer mercy gets in the way of the educational objective; thus God has to give up on the approach that offers mercy in place of justice. The author was apparently very perceptive about the actual problem posed when Yahweh, who is truly אל חנון ורחום (a God of grace and mercy), does not act consistently with his true nature in this case. But he comes to the conclusion that God, if he does not want צדק (righteousness) to disappear altogether, has no other choice than to deny mercy to the רשע (wicked person).

d. 26:11: Request That the Enemies Be Obliterated

[26:11] One of the main features of a song of lament is a prayer that asks for the enemies to be obliterated. In this passage the request is, one might say, given a theological basis: Yahweh has raised his hand, but his opponents do not see it. One is reminded of the refrain in the cycle that includes 9:7-20 and 5:25-30: "In all this his wrath did not turn away, and his hand is still stretched out." Once again, Yahweh's judgment did not accomplish what was intended; Yahweh's hand was raised, but it was not taken seriously, as a warning sign. There is only one harsher way to intervene: "the fire against your enemies will consume them." They will collide with the קנאת־עם (zeal for the people). That is not the zeal of Israel, not really that of the enemies either, but is Yahweh's own zeal *for* his people; cf. Isa. 9:6 (on this, see *Isaiah 1–12*, pp. 406f.); 37:32; Zech. 1:14.

The request that the opponents might be destroyed completely is fleshed out even more with the harsh phrase אש האכלם (fire will consume them); cf. Ps. 21:10. One must wonder whether "fire" should be taken literally. Kaiser might be right that the ancient concept of a theophany, in which Yahweh comes on the scene in the midst of fire (cf. Pss. 50:3; 97:3), might have been resurrected here; see also Deut. 4:24; 1 Kings 18:38; 2 Kings 1:10; Isa. 29:6; 30:30; 33:14; and also Heb. 12:29. Whatever it might mean, one need not suppose that this concept has been influenced by Iranian eschatology, according to which the enemies of Ahura Mazda are destroyed by fire (by contrast, cf. 2 Pet. 3:7, where it is much more likely that one might have to take Iranian influences into account; see W. Grundmann, *Der Brief des Judas und der zweite Brief des Petrus*, THK XV [1974], 114); "fire" is most likely just a metaphor for Yahweh's furious rage. However, the apocalyptic expectation that there would be a worldwide conflagration at the end of the times, which has no roots in the OT, could have used passages such as this one as a point of departure; cf. 1QH 3:29-36; 1 (Ethiopic) Enoch 1:6-9; 4 Ezra 13:10f.; (Ethiopic) Apoc. Pet. 5.

e. 26:12-15: Confidence about Being Heard (with a reflective look back at Yahweh's faithfulness in the past)

[26:12] Following the request that the enemies be obliterated, v. 12 continues with an expression of the confidence that Yahweh would provide "us," that is, Israel, with שׁלום (peace). Since the people had been dealing with enemies (צרים) just then, the first thing that שׁלום (peace) would bring to mind is that there would be a cessation of the political-military pressure under which Israel had been suffering. But certainly the entire range of meaning connected with this term is involved as well. The rarely used verb שׁפת means "put on, set on" (2 Kings 4:38; Ezek. 24:3) or "lay in" (Ps. 22:16); here it is similar: Yahweh—of this faith is sure—would "lay in" the peace, so that one would need to do no more than take hold of it and rejoice that it is available for use. The causal clause that is appended makes the point that such a situation had always been their experience in the past. Time and again Yahweh had done for Israel what it should have done for itself, but which it had not been able to accomplish on its own. One might think of the victories of Israel described in the book of Judges, which are in fact depicted as Yahweh's victories; cf. also Exod. 14:14. Thus it had been in the past; why would it be any different in the future! The verb פעל (accomplish) is used most pointedly in the Psalms and in Job; it is used almost solely in exilic-postexilic texts and in elevated poetic speech. Like the substantive פֹּעַל (BDB: doing, deed, work), it is used when Yahweh intervenes in history or when it refers to the way he interposes in the life of an individual; see J. Vollmer, *THAT* II, 461ff. (14 times with a divine subject out of a total of 57 occurrences).

[26:13] The one who prays gets more specific in v. 13. The deeds about which the author is thinking had become necessary because foreign אדנים (lords) controlled Israel. Note the wordplay in Hebrew between פעלת (deeds) and בעלונו (ruled over us). The action of Yahweh (פעל) was necessary because of the ruling (בעל) of other lords. In the OT בעל usually means "take someone as wife, marry," which resulted in its being used with a transferred meaning in Jer. 3:14 and 31:32 to describe Yahweh as the husband of Israel. A בעל could be an owner, e.g., of cattle (see Isa. 1:3) or of a house, with all the rights at his disposal that are available to someone who was an owner, to make decisions about those who were under him. According to Josh. 24:11; Judg. 9:2; 20:5; 1 Sam. 23:11f.; 2 Sam. 6:2, and often elsewhere, the בעלים (citizens) of a city are those who own property and as such are the politically influential persons.

In contrast to בעל (owner), אדון is a designation that has less to do with someone who has a possession than it does with someone who is a master; a בעל is over possessions (even if that refers to a wife), but an אדון is someone who is over עבדים (servants). One cannot be sure about exactly what the author had in mind with his reference to "lords," but it is likely that they were exercising political power. If the following word, זולתיך (besides you), is not a later addition, this would have meant: in spite of everything, Israel declares its allegiance only to *one* אדון (lord), its God. Some have suggested that this might be a reference to the exodus from Egypt or to what is recounted in the books of Joshua and Judges. The way the passage continues in v. 13aβ-b would make good sense in connection with the book of Judges. Israel fell under the power of lords, came to its senses, called on the name of Yahweh, and then also experienced his help.

[26:14] The one who is praying continues now with a completely surprising thought: "Dead will not again be alive, shades do not rise up." The interpretation of this verse has been hotly debated. If it is to be interpreted within the context of vv. 7-19, then there is hardly any other solution than that those who are dead and who will not rise again refers to those "lords" who at one time had exercised control over Israel. That would mean that v. 14 continues the look back that began in v. 12b. As it states there, Yahweh had acted on Israel's behalf. For its part, Israel had directed its thoughts to the name of Yahweh (v. 13b). Thus Yahweh had punished those lords to whom the people had been delivered, had exterminated them and obliterated them, until not even a memory about them survived. Yahweh intervened—and the unprecedented oppression was gone. Verse 14 backs up this statement with what is apparently a familiar quotation. The enemies are dead and the dead do not come back to life again; they vegetate as shadows in שאול (Sheol), and no one had yet returned from that place (concerning רפאים, "shades," see above, pp. 60ff.).

The realization that there is no return from death was noted again and again in the ancient Near East. In Akkadian the underworld is the *erṣet lā tāri,* the "land of no return." In front of the body of his dearly loved friend Enkidu, Gilgamesh has to confess that all the crying will do no good: "I would not give him up for burial—in case my friend should rise at my plaint" (10.2.6f.). But there was nothing left for him to do but to acknowledge that Enkidu had gone "to the fate of mankind" (*illikma ana šimatu awīlūtim,* 10.2.4), and the barmaid instructs him concerning his lament: "When the gods created mankind, death for mankind they set aside" (10.3.3f.; the passages are quoted from *ANET* 89f.; see also A. Schott and W. von Soden, *Das Gilgamesch-Epos* [1972]). Human beings are prohibited from eating of the tree of life; Genesis 3 states it plainly: "you are dust, and to dust you shall return" (v. 19). Israel knew that it had to come to terms with that fact: "For there is hope for a tree, if it is cut down, that it will sprout again," but the same was not true for a human being: "But mortals die, and are laid low; humans expire, and where are they? . . . so mortals lie down and do not rise again; until the heavens are no more, they will not awake or be roused out of their sleep" (Job 14:7, 10, 12, text emended). Even in such a late book as Ecclesiastes, one can find the statement: "All go to one place; all are from the dust, and all turn to dust again" (3:20). One might also read once again from

564

the texts quoted above, on p. 373, particularly the passage from the Coptic hymn: "Our life is a shadow, which passes by; death lets no one return."

[26:15] Verse 15 continues what is said in v. 14 without any break. The oppressors have been exterminated; that is the one side of the story, but at the same time Yahweh had dealt faithfully with his people, had multiplied them and had provided a broad area in which they could live. It is the essence of the divine blessing that the people would multiply; the promise had been in effect from the very beginning, when it was spoken to the patriarchs, even down to the latest era, which certainly makes sense in light of the fact that the physical existence of Israel was threatened again and again by war, epidemic, catastrophes caused by drought, and deportation. For little Judah, which still existed after the exile, with a total population that was undoubtedly very small, it would have posed just as much of a problem as it had for the nomadic clans who were poised at the border of Canaan during its early period. It is also possible that the author was focused on the circumstances in the diaspora communities, which never consisted of more than a minority of the population no matter where they lived, for whom it was and always would be a harsh challenge to attempt to maintain their identity in the midst of the overwhelming number of people in the indigenous population among whom they lived.

There also would have been pressure, from time to time, because of the narrow geographical borders within which Israel had to live. However, it is asserted here: "You have expanded all the borders of the land." Here as well, this is probably a reference to the past, maybe even to the distant past. And Israel was supposed to learn from its reflection on the past that the same types of blessings were still possible in the present. One cannot know for sure exactly what the author had in mind. It is unlikely that the historical setting would have been at the time of Judah's expansion during the Hasmonean era. Verse 15b is obviously to be taken with a grain of salt; people were fond of looking at the past with rose-colored glasses, as if the description corresponded to the way things had really been. In any case, there once was a time when it looked as if Israel could become a great empire: at the time of David, when the territory of Israel was extended and the neighboring kingdoms were subservient to the monarchy. Since v. 13 might be a reference to the situation during the time of Joshua/Judges, it is not impossible that this look back on the past focused on the time of David.

f. 26:16-18: The Lament: Israel's Condition Is Hopeless

[26:16] Once again, with v. 16, the problem concerning the relationship that the passage has with the surrounding material can hardly be resolved with any certainty. An additional handicap is obviously imposed by the difficulties with text and translation, both of which are very hard to resolve. One might try to interpret this verse as a reflective look back to the past as well. Over and over again, there were troublesome times when Israel turned back again and sought Yahweh, cried out to him when "chastisement pressed hard," and his intended purpose was achieved. It is more likely, however, that v. 16 should be taken together with vv. 17f. To be sure, that would work only if one altered פְקָדוּךְ (they sought you) to read פְקַדְנוּךְ (we sought you) and לָמוֹ (either "for him," or "for them") to read לָנוּ (for us), as was suggested above. If one agrees with these emendations, then v. 16 speaks about the present or the immediate past. Once again there had been trouble for Israel; because of the pressure of an unusually harsh chastisement, the people cried out to Yahweh once again during this time of trial, though help had not been detected as yet. Concerning פקד in the sense of "turn oneself toward, seek," see above, textual note 16a–a, and cf. 1 Sam. 17:18. צעק (call out) comes from the standard vocabulary for such situations; one might compare this with 19:20, where Israel cries out to Yahweh מִפְּנֵי לֹחֲצִים (because of oppressors).

Israel understands that its trouble (צר) was Yahweh's מוּסָר (chastisement); however, this מוּסָר (chastisement) placed the people into the type of terribly oppressive situation in which an enemy showed them no mercy whatsoever.

[26:17] Verse 17 moves on to completely different imagery. The trouble that Israel had been suffering is compared with that of a woman giving birth; cf. 13:8; 21:3. The way a wife would writhe around and cry out when the birth pangs came upon her had made a deep impression on the ancient Israelites. Once the birth had taken place, however, then the pains were forgotten, and the mother would have been deeply satisfied as she held a child in her arms; cf. John 16:21. However, the author complains here that when Israel finally seems to be at the point of giving birth after such painful labor pains, all that comes out is רוח, "wind" (concerning such "births of wind," see Gesenius and the description of ancient and medieval authors, to whom he refers). In a way similar to how הבל is used, רוח also can mean "nothingness"; cf., e.g., Jer. 5:13 (describing the נביאים, "prophets"); Isa. 41:29 (describing deities, used with אָוֶן, "delusion"; אֶפֶס, "nothing"; and תֹּהוּ, "empty"); Job 16:3; sometimes it simply means "nothing"; see Prov. 11:29; Job 6:26; Eccles. 5:15.

One might compare this verse with comments such as those found in the Akkadian setting, Maqlû VII, 22: "The enchanting that you have enchanted, may it [become] wind"; VIII, 57: "Your sorceries are wind! Your sorceries are storm win[d]!" (BAfO 2 [1937] 47, 56); or words from Ashurbanipal, who had someone write down: "Your gods and goddesses I consign to the wind" (*Annals*, Rm VI, 64 in VAB VII/2, 54f.); cf. also Gilgamesh II, v, 141–143, in Schott and von Soden, 31.

"And inhabitants of the earth do not come into the world" (v. 18bβ). This phrase also must be understood, as Plöger (67) suggests, in a metaphorical way, namely, in the sense used in v. 18bα: יְשׁוּעֹת בַּל־נַעֲשֶׂה אֶרֶץ (we can provide no help for the land). In spite of all the crying to Yahweh, the oppression is still there; Yahweh no longer seems to be the God whom Israel had experienced in its history. The song of lament ends in total resignation, indeed, with an accusation against Yahweh that is hardly even disguised (cf. passages such as Psalm 39 or the ending of Psalm 74). The words of confidence uttered in vv. 7, 8a, full of faith and with a positive disposition, now seem to have been shown to be pure illusion. The author seems to be moving close to putting into words the same questions that are posed in the book of Job.

[26:19] *The Oracle of Salvation: "The Resurrection of the Dead"*

[26:19] The alternatives presented to a commentator in v. 19, whether this is just a change in mood or an oracle of salvation, have been discussed above; see pp. 456f. If this is an oracle of salvation, as we believe we can assume, then טלך (your dew) in v. 19bα causes some problems. If Yahweh is speaking, one would expect טלי (my dew). Kaiser explains the second person suffix by suggesting that Yahweh is no longer speaking in v. 19b, but that the community is confessing already that God has accomplished that which was impossible, doing it by means of his dew. At this point, however, one might follow Rudolph, who interprets טלך: "the dew that falls on you." For the overall interpretation of the text, it really does not matter which view one accepts. But it is important that v. 19 be interpreted in close connection with that which has taken place just previously. One way or another, the verse is to be understood as the great "however," over against vv. 17f., and under no circumstances should this part of the text be cut apart from what precedes it by using the scissors of literary criticism, since it belongs together form critically.

נבלתי: (my dead body) does not seem to belong to the original form of the text; based on where the word is placed now, however, it is supposed to make the point that the "dead" of Israel are, at the same time, Yahweh's corpses, which means that Yahweh does not stay off at a distance, undisturbed by the death of his people. At this same time, Israel is the apple of his eye (Deut. 32:10), his firstfruits, from which one cannot eat without being punished (Jer. 2:3). Whoever tries to destroy Israel will have to deal with Yahweh himself.

That is what is meant by this oracle of salvation. It cannot be otherwise; Israel can count on that. His dead will live, will rise to life, will awake, and those who live in the dust will be able to rejoice. If the interpretation offered above means that vv. 7-18 are to be understood as a communal song of lament, which came out of the context of a period when Israel's very existence was threatened, then the oracle that is offered as an answer to the lament must be speaking about the removal of this threat and about how the sound of distress shifts to sounds of rejoicing. The author had nothing else to say than to state clearly: all of our miserable writhing brought forth nothing but wind and ישועת בל־נעשה ארץ (we can provide no help for the land); now mention can be made about the radical shift in Israel's fortune, which had not been expected at all any more. At the same time, this new future for Israel as a whole means that the reference is not to the resurrection of individuals but is a metaphorical reference to the reestablishment of Israel (see Kissane; Fohrer in *KuD* 14, 31, and in his commentary; Haenchen, 85; Virgulin, 59). There is no room within the context for any other interpretation. Because the wider context demands that Israel be restored, not just individuals, Rudolph interprets this verse in its literal sense, as a reference to the resurrection of the dead, treating v. 19 (along with vv. 14a and 18bβ) as an "interposed piece." In the same way, Kaiser takes the verse all by itself and considers it a very late insertion. But discussion has reached the point already that Preuss (111) suggests: "The numerous attempts that have been made, as the text has been studied, to move it elsewhere, split it apart, or remove it, have the effect of encouraging a person to try once more to interpret the text just as it stands."

After the chastisement and hopelessness had been described in such vivid detail, the portrayal of the radical change in fortune had to be depicted by using the most radical imagery one could find. It speaks about the resurrection of the dead (a corpse coming to life once again) and about those who had taken up residence in the dust being awakened.

עָפָר (dust) is used at that time in the same way as אֶרֶץ is sometimes selected, as a way to describe the "underworld"; cf. עֲפַר־מָוֶת (dust of death) in Ps. 22:16 and יֹרְדֵי עָפָר (who go down to the dust) in Ps. 22:30 (parallel to יְשֵׁנֵי אֶרֶץ, "who sleep in the earth," text emended); cf. also the phraseology יֹרֵד בּוֹר or יֹרֵד שַׁחַת (both: [someone] goes down to the pit). In a communal lament, people would use the verbs חָיָה (revive) and קוּם (raise up) when speaking about the people as a whole coming to life once again, as is shown by Hos. 6:2; cf. also Amos 5:2. When the verb הֵקִיץ (awake) (ἐγείρεσθαι in the NT) is used, it comes from the background of the widely accepted notion that death is sleep (cf. Jer. 51:39-57; Matt. 27:52; 1 Cor. 15:20; Eph. 5:14).

Kaiser refers to Plato, *Apology* 32, 40. In connection with Mesopotamia, Gilgamesh VIII, ii, 13-16 should be mentioned, where Gilgamesh speaks to dead Enkidu: "'What, now, is this sleep that has laid hold on thee? Thou art benighted and canst not hear [me]!' But he lifts not up his head; he touched his heart, but it does not beat" (*ANET* 87f.; see also Schott and von Soden, 67). For Ugarit, cf. the words of Danel to Baal: "May Baal break the pinions of them [the vultures], as they fly over the grave of my son, rousing him from his sleep" (*ANET* 154 [Aqht C, 150f.]; see I Aqht 151, Aistleitner, *Texte*, 78).

In the Egyptian Book of the Dead (chap. 178), the dead person is challenged: "wake up then! Wake up, you who sleeps! Look, one now brings the offering" (translation based on: G. Kolpaktchy, *Ägyptisches Totenbuch* [1970²] 286); see also the address to dead Horus: "Wake up," on the Metternich stele, 232 (Roeder, *Urkunden*, 96).

A high priest from Memphis provided for his wife the following song as the inscription on her grave: "The West is a land of sleeping, filled with oppressive darkness, the stopping place of those who have taken leave, who sleep there in their coffins. They do not wake up, in order to see their brothers" (H. Bonnet, *Reallexikon der ägyptischen Religionsgeschichte* [1971²] 353f.).

The phraseology used to describe Israel in its state of death and in its deliverance goes beyond the traditional phraseology found in songs of either lament or thanksgiving. The unprecedented situation of the oppression that is being experienced at the end of time calls for articulating just how it would be resolved by using extraordinary language. At that point, Israel stands on the threshold of a type of faith which expects that there will be an actual return to life once again, after death has come. The metaphors חיה (live), קום (rise up), and הקיץ (wake up) are used as if the concept about the dead coming to life again was essentially common knowledge, as is seen even more clearly in Ezekiel 37; in that passage, cf. both the description about coming to life again when breath is given and the depiction about graves being opened.

How can that which is impossible become possible? Verse 19bα explains it as follows: "the dew of the lights is your dew." It is clear that this is to be taken as a reference to Yahweh's power to make alive, and the phrase makes perfect sense in this context.

During the long period when there is no rain, dew plays a decisive role for vegetation in Palestine; it is the sole reason why the plant world does not completely die out during the heat of summer. An Arabic proverb states: "Dew causes the parched land to be fruitful"; cf. Sir. 43:22. The concerned farmer can pray: "O God, (give us) dew when the grain stalks sprout." And at harvest, God is praised: "God has blessed the dew! If there had been no dew, the seed would have shriveled and been for nothing"; and the women who harvest in Jerusalem sing: "O grain of God, O blessing of the dew!" (Dalman, *AuS* I/2, 310). Within the Eighteen Benedictions, God is celebrated as the giver of rain during the time from the Feast of Booths until Passover, whereas from Passover until the Feast of Booths he is the one who provides dew (Dalman, ibid., 312; *j. Ta'anit* 63d). Correspondingly, Elijah announced not only that there would be no rain in "these years" but also that the dew would cease (1 Kings 17:1; cf., in addition, 2 Sam. 1:21; Mic. 5:6; Ps. 110:3, etc.). In terms of quantity, dew comes in copious amounts in Palestine. One can get very wet from it (Song of Sol. 5:2). When someone is planning to set off on a trip at break of day, then another person might say to that individual: "Do you want to carry the dew away on your back?" (E. Baumann, *ZDPV* 39 [1916] 186 no. 239). With this background, one can easily understand the pictorial significance of referring to dew as a means by which something is brought to life again. The Arab poets even speak of buried corpses being brought back to life because of the revivifying effects of dew or rain. In the Hamāsa one reads: "Go visit the Ma'an and say to his grave: 'May the morning clouds moisten you with rain on top of rain'" (see Gesenius); or: "May a rain moisten the hill that conceals Arib, the son of Asa, coming from clouds that richly pour it out, that empty themselves without thunder."

By contrast, David says in his lament over Saul and Jonathan: "You mountains of Gilboa, let there be no dew or rain upon you" (2 Sam. 1:21). From that time onward no plant was to grow and flourish in the place where Israel's heroes had fallen. And in the Targum to Psalm 68 one reads: "As the Israelites heard your booming voice, their spirits fled; immediately you allowed a revivifying dew come down upon them" (according to Gesenius).

The Ras Shamra texts speak frequently about a daughter of the rain god Baal, *ṭly.* This name has been formed from the Ugaritic word *ṭl,* "dew," with the afformative *y,* the mark that identifies relationship; it has generally been translated "cover with dew." But this daughter of Baal has an epithet as well, *bt rb,* which clearly means "daughter of the rain" (Hebrew: רבבים, "copious showers"); see *Welt der Mythologie* I, 312. In addition to this *ṭly bt rb.,* the Ugaritic texts being quoted here also refer regularly to a sister of *ṭly* named *pdry bt ar.* No one has been able to make any sense of *pdry* (see *Welt der Mythologie* I, 103; and J. C. de Moor, *The Seasonal Pattern in the Ugaritic Myth of Baʿlu,* AOAT 16 [1971] 82); but *ar* has been linked either to Hebrew אור (light) or to Arabic *ary* (moisture, rain cloud). The pointing would speak against its having the meaning "light"; for that, one would have expected *ur;* cf. the Ugaritic personal names *uryy* and *uryn.* For this reason, the better solution would be to connect it with Arabic *ary,* which also has been translated regularly as "dew." De Moor (83) thinks that it refers to a special type of dew, one that would be differentiated from both *ṭl* and *rb.* Since Arabic *ary* also means "honey," one might presume that the inhabitants of Ugarit used this word to describe a dew that was somehow similar to honey. Since these connections have been noted, one cannot immediately refuse to consider the possibility that it might be correct to translate אורת טל as "dew of lights" or that it might refer to a certain type of dew, possibly something like a misty rain. However, since that meaning for אורת (= misty rain) is not found elsewhere in the OT, one can hardly assume that someone who read this passage would have thought it meant anything other than "dew of lights." Concerning the usage in the OT, consult Humbert. A number of Egyptian texts say that the nighttime dew comes from the heavens, that it is formed by the tears of Horus and Thoth, and thus that the power of resurrection is included within the moisture (Savignac, 345ff.).

Like "dew," "light" is also used symbolically for life and prosperity, blessing and salvation (cf. also 9:1; 42:6, 16; 58:8, 10; Mic. 7:8f.). Where light no longer shines, there a person is surrounded by disaster (Amos 5:18, 20; Isa. 13:10). The theophoric proper names that have a word for light as their second element, (אוּרִיָה[וּ], Uria[hu]; אוּרִיאֵל, Uriel; אֲבִינֵר, Abiner; אַבְנֵר, Abner; נֵרִיָה, Neriah), and similar names in Akkadian (used in conjunction with *nūru, namāru,* etc., "bright, glowing"), all praise the deity as the dispenser of good fortune and salvation (cf. Noth, *Israelitische Personnennamen,* 167–169; J. J. Stamm, MVAÄG 44 [1939] 56f.; concerning the meaning of light, cf. J. Hempel, "Die Lichtsymbolik im Alten Testament," *Studium Generale* 13 [1960] 352–368). Based on what has been said, טל אורת means something such as "life-providing, salvation-bringing, good-fortune-creating dew." The sentence that furnishes the reason, in v. 19bβ, also shows that this does not refer to life after death, but that it speaks about someone who will rise up again, to enjoy full life.

[26:20-21] *Israel at the Time When Yahweh Rises Up for Worldwide Judgment*

[26:20] That Israel faces a new future does not alter the fact that a storm of judgment would sweep on through to cover the entire earth. The author of the original body of material pointed out forcefully in 24:16aβff. that there would be no cause for Israel to begin rejoicing right away. Thus the concern for Israel was that it would be careful so that it would not be swallowed up by the coming events. This is the reason for the admonition: "Hide yourself for a brief moment until the malediction has passed by" (v. 20b). Concerning זעם (malediction), see *Isaiah 1–12*, pp. 416, 442f.; cf. also 30:27. It is obviously Yahweh's "malediction" that is meant, but once again it should be noted that it does not say specifically זעם יהוה (malediction of Yahweh). Just as there are other passages where "anger" is an objective, almost personified power that, once set in motion, cannot be restrained afterward, until it has spent its energy completely, so here, in the same way, the "malediction" or "curse" is a power that carries on its activity automatically. It would strike Israel also, if the people got in its way.

Concerning מעט רגע (for a brief moment), cf. Ezra 9:8 and Isa. 10:25: מעט מזער (only a short time). This expression is to be taken with a grain of salt. When considered in light of all eternity, the time of oppression would be condensed into a very short time, just as the length of time it would have taken the community to pass through the misery of the end times would seem minimal at the actual moment that they returned to life again. This phraseology is not used solely within apocalyptic, but is also found in a song of thanksgiving (Ps. 30:6).

Verse 20a uses ideas that are a bit more specific: לך is to be translated with something such as "now then"; there is no more time to delay. It is worth noting that Israel is addressed as "my people." The election remains in force. Israel remains under Yahweh's protection (nonetheless, cf. how Isaiah himself speaks of Israel as העם הזה, "this people"; see *Isaiah 1–12*, pp. 342f.).

If one uses Dan. 12:13 to aid in interpreting the present passage, then one is tempted to think that the "chambers" in which the host of believers are to hide themselves refer to actual graves, so one could explain it as follows: when the writhing comes at the end of time, do not be reticent about suffering death; God can and also will wrench the dead from the grave. However, that explanation is not justified. *We* speak today about "burial chambers," but the OT never uses חדר in reference to the grave. "Chambers" is to be taken literally. Yet it is unlikely that this refers to the side chambers in the temple (see 1 Chron. 28:11); these are simply inner rooms of a house; cf. Gen. 43:30; Judg. 16:9; or Exod. 7:28; 1 Sam. 4:7 (a room where a person sleeps); or Judg. 15:1 (wife's room). Since these rooms would open up toward a central courtyard within a large house (see Galling, *BRL,* 266f.; and Haag, *BL²,* 670ff.), they would provide excellent protection. It goes without saying that people would hide themselves here in time of war, which means one can hardly agree with the suggestion (as offered by Lindblom, 52) that this is a direct reference to the statements in Isa. 2:10, 19. It is more likely that the background is furnished by the story about how those faithful to Yahweh were spared during the great flood, when "every living thing" was handed over to destruction; see Gen. 7:1–16 (so Procksch; Kessler; Fohrer; Mulder, 52). Others suggest that it points to the Passover night when Israel was spared while the firstborn of Egypt all were being struck down (Exod. 12:23). Kaiser also refers to Ezekiel 9, which mentions protecting the pious ones in Jerusalem from judgment. The motif about closing the door (Gen. 7:16) favors the flood story as the likely background. Concerning closing houses with a key, see above, p. 399.

[26:21] The judgment is very close at hand; note the presentative with participle at the beginning of v. 21. It explicitly mentions that it will be all-encompassing. It will spread out upon עון ישׁב־הארץ (the transgressions of the inhabitants of the earth). The author already had talked about a יושׁב הארץ (an inhabitant of the earth) in 24:17; concerning פקד (bring the consequences [on someone]), see above on 24:21. Yahweh moves out from his own dwelling place (מקום) to act in judgment. That belongs to the terminology used when describing a theophany. Yahweh goes forth from Seir (Judg. 5:4; cf. also Ps. 68:8f.). הנה יהוה יצא ממקומו (behold, Yahweh moves out from his dwelling place) is found, using this exact wording, in Mic. 1:3; there, על־במותי־ארץ (upon the high places of the earth) parallels ממקומו (his dwelling place), which likely refers to the heavens in that passage; see J. Jeremias, *Theophanie*, WMANT 10 (1965) 12. In the postexilic passage Isa. 63:19bα, the author prays: "O that you would tear open the heavens and come down." In 26:21 the מקום (dwelling place), considered within the entire context, more likely refers to Zion. When one considers that this passage has a proto-apocalyptic character, however, it is surprising that the author has all the inhabitants of the earth in view. The motif one would expect to be adequate for this purpose, which would speak about how all nature was in uproar (see the passages noted above that deal with Yahweh rising up), is transformed; it states that bloodguilt will be exposed throughout the earth. The blood of those who were struck down unjustly cries to Yahweh for vengeance (cf. Gen. 4:10; in addition, Ezek. 24:7f.; Job 16:8; Heb. 12:24); the time for divine forbearance is past. The events have been set in motion; there is no turning back (לא־תכסה עוד, "will no longer hide"). The settling of accounts would be final and irrevocable.

No doubt, the mention about bloodguilt provides just an example of the עון (iniquity) of human beings; the account had come due now; all the deeds had been totaled up. But bloodguilt points to the deepest level of עון (iniquity), to the type of sin that causes someone's death, which can never be forgiven; see V. Maag, "Unsühnbare Schuld," *Kairos* 8 (1966) 90–106.

Purpose and Thrust

In 26:7-21 the author struggles with the question about Israel's destiny during a time when there would be a catastrophe without equal, one that would come upon all people in the very near future. If the analysis presented above is correct, the author of the original body of material reaches the conclusion of his prophecy with this section. Israel's dead would live again; the earth would give birth to its shadows once again. That is the great hope which he offers to his people as they traverse the dark path leading through the judgment of God. This message was apparently spoken at a time when Israel had been sorely tempted to renounce the faith. At the beginning of this section, the deep level of despair that had gripped the people as they sank down after a time of euphoria (24:14ff.) is contrasted by the author with the thesis that one could be confident if one believed that Yahweh's ways for the righteous are straight (v. 7). And from the beginning he lifts up the people to share his hope: "Also on the path of your judgments we trust confidently in you . . ." (v. 8); in fact, he lays his own soul bare for those who listen to him. He had apparently learned by experience that in some situations a person can deal with another person who is tempted to give up on believing only by proclaiming one's own confession (v. 9a); in this case, it is a confession that his own deeply burning desire is directed toward Yahweh. Judgments must come, but that does not contradict directly the fact that Israel can expect that שלום (peace) would come as well. At times in Israel's history the people had experienced Yahweh's faithfulness (vv. 12-15). But then, once again, ever more piercingly, the voice of doubt rang out. Even if it were true that Yahweh had demonstrated his covenant relationship with Israel in the past, the situation was in doubt *in the present*. One could strive to live within that framework, but no restoration was in sight (vv. 17f.). But at that very point the poet plays off a message from Yahweh against this mood of resignation. Israel's need had become so horrible that there was nothing to which it could be compared; yet Yahweh's help would be just as incomparable, would be so surprising that nothing could describe the wondrous nature of divine faithfulness except to use the imagery that the dead would come back to life. Salvation is coming to life out of death. This help had not become visible as yet, but Israel should and could draw back in quietness until the time of trouble had passed.

Having said all that, this section affords stirring testimony that the "however" of faith can be expressed, even in light of a complete breakdown that would seem to deny everything that one had ever experienced from God in history and that thus brought into question every one of the statements of faith that had been treated as sure and certain.

Eschatological Impressions

Isaiah 27:1

The Defeat of the Chaos Dragon

Literature

C. Rabin, "BĀRI^AḤ," *JTS* 47 (1946) 38–41. H. Wallace, "Leviathan and the Beast in Revelation," *BA* 3 (1948) 61–68. G. R. Driver, "Mythical Monsters in the Old Testament," *Studi orientalistici in onore di G. L. della Vida*, I (1956) 234–249. V. Maag, "Lewjathan, die Vorweltschlange," *Neue Zürcher Zeitung* no. 1775 (1959) 43. C. H. Gordon, "Leviathan, Symbol of Evil," *Biblical Motifs*, ed. A. Altmann (1966) 1–9. J. Francke, *Veelkoppige monsters: Mythologische figuren in bijbelteksten* (1971) (not available to me). M. K. Wakeman, *God's Battle with the Monster* (1973).

[Literature update through 1979: M. K. Wakeman, "The Biblical Earth Monster in the Cosmogonic Combat Myth," *JBL* 88 (1969) 313–320. E. Ruprecht, "Das Nilpferd im Hiobbuch," *VT* 21 (1971) 209–231. P. Cepeda Calzada, "El Leviatán, símbolo bíblico," *Crisis* 21 (1974) 5–46. J. V. Kinnier Wilson, "A Return to the Problems of Behemoth and Leviathan," *VT* 25 (1975) 1–14.]

Text

27:1 On that day, with the sharp, huge, and strong sword, Yahweh will inflict punishment on Leviathan, the fleeing[a] snake, [b]and Leviathan,[b] the twisting snake, and will kill the dragon [c]that dwells in the sea.[c]

1a בָּרִחַ (here: fleeing) is not used elsewhere in the OT. One would expect that an adjective from the root ברח (flee) would be written בָּרִיחַ. Q^a reads the active participle: בורח. If, in spite of some hesitations, one still derives this from ברח (flee), then one would have to translate it something like "fleeing" (Gk: φεύγων, "fleeing"), which is what KBL suggests as the meaning. Aquila (μοχλος) and Vulg (*vectis*) took the original to be בְּרִיחַ, "bar," but this translation does not merit serious consideration. Besides this, there is the personal name בָּרִיחַ (1 Chron. 3:22), which according to *HAL* means "without hair." Albright (*BASOR* 83 [1941] 39f., note 5) proposed that נחש ברח meant "primordial dragon." The word is used also in the Ugaritic texts, in fact, as part of the phrase *ltn bṯn brḥ* (Lotan [Leviathan] dragon *brḥ*) (parallel to *bṯn* *ʿqltn*, "crooked dragon"). Thus with the use of נחשׁ ברח (and the same is true of נחשׁ עקלתון, "the twisting snake"), one is dealing with words that have been linked together far back in antiquity. However, saying this does not help with determining a meaning for ברח. Both Gordon (*UT,* no. 515) and Aistleitner (no. 577) argue in favor of linking it with Arabic *barḥ,* to mean "evil, destructive," but that is a unique development of the meaning within the Arabic language itself (see H. Gese, in *Die Religionen Altsyriens, Altarabiens und der Mandäer,* RM 10/2, 59f., note 44); Rabin suggests that it means "slippery." With this uncertainty, it is best to stay with "fleeing," knowing full well that the final solution to this problem has not yet seen the light of day.

1b–b Guthe, Schlögl, and Procksch think that ועל לויתן (and Leviathan) should be removed; it is true that *ltn* is used only once in the Ugaritic phrase just mentioned, but one should think twice before removing repetitions of this type from the Isaiah apocalypse.

1c–c אשׁר בים (which dwells in the sea) is missing in the Gk; for this reason, Marti and Guthe suggest eliminating it. It is not impossible that there is a dittography of what follows: ביום ההוא (on that day). It is most likely, however, that the reverse is true: בים (on the day) at the beginning of v. 2 is more likely a dittography caused by אשׁר בים (which dwells on the sea), something already assumed by Gray (ההוא, "that," would have been inserted still later).

Form and Setting

Verse 1 stands there all by itself (see above, p. 458), even though it obviously also has to be treated as a component of the apocalypse, as one can see just by the fact that it is introduced by the phrase ביום ההוא (on that day). "That day," as the content of the verse also indicates, is the day on which the events at the end of time will transpire. The verse is an announcement of judgment, though not directed against a specific people, also not against neighboring peoples, and not even against world powers, but against the powers of chaos, represented by לויתן (Leviathan), in the two forms in which he appears, and by תנין (dragon). This is the reason why the threat of judgment has taken on apocalyptic dimensions. Along with other passages, לויתן (Leviathan) is mentioned in Ps. 74:14, a reference that comes closest to preserving the original concept; the conquest of Leviathan is one aspect within the description of Yahweh's activity in creation; more specifically, it is connected with the battle against chaos: "You crushed the heads of Leviathan; you gave him as food for the creatures of the wilderness." Parallel to this, it says in v. 13: "You divided the sea (ים) by your might; you broke the heads of the תנינים [which certainly should be read as a singular, "dragon"] in the waters." Thus here is another passage where לויתן (Leviathan) and תנינים (dragons) are mentioned together. Yahweh made it possible for life and success to exist on earth only after they were defeated. If one looks carefully, this text actually speaks about three figures, since, as is shown also in the Ugaritic texts, Baal went up against ים (the sea), which was itself depicted in a personified way, and defeated him. The creation psalm, 104, as well, which also deals specifically with the concept of battle with the primordial flood (see vv. 7ff.), refers to

575

Leviathan, who is no longer an opposing power; there he has become a harmless creature that God had made so he could play with him. Finally, Leviathan is mentioned also in Job 40:25, but in that passage he is also no longer a chaos monster, but a powerful creature living in water, which some think refers to a crocodile (see G. Fohrer, *Hiob*, KAT XVI [1963], 528ff.). The Babylonian Talmud (*b. ʿAboda Zara* 3b) goes so far as to say that God plays with Leviathan three hours every day. It is also said in the Talmud, though chiefly in apocalyptic, that Leviathan remains alive so that the pious can enjoy consuming his flesh (*Baba Batra* 74b, 75a; Syriac Apocalypse of [2] Baruch 29:4, see above, p. 528; cf. 4 Ezra 6:49, 52).

Leviathan, originally the primordial monster and great opponent of Yahweh (who also can be called by the name Rahab in other passages), has been changed in some passages to become just a harmless creature, even though it is still known for its great size and strength. The primordial flood or, as the case may be, the sea, which once had covered the entire surface of the earth, is now pushed back; God assigned borders to it (Ps. 104:9; Job 26:10; 38:8ff.). But the ordered world of the creation is still threatened. In spite of everything, Leviathan hangs on tenaciously to life; if its heads are smashed, new ones grow back. Some magicians know how to rouse up Leviathan (Job 3:8); and, just as at times the earth, which has been firmly established by the creator, starts to shake apart, so also at times the ancient dragon bestirs itself once again. However, now, at the end of time, a new battle against chaos takes place, which is not going to lead merely to the dragon being pushed back, but which will result in its being killed.

It has been a long-standing exegetical tradition to consider the monsters in 27:1 as symbols for world powers. Once again, it would seem that mythological concepts are "historicized," as is also the case in 14:12ff., where the downfall of Helel ben Shachar leaves one with the impression that it is describing the demise of great tyrants. In spite of considerable effort, scholars have not come to any agreement about which world power or which world powers are meant. לויתן (Leviathan) is never used elsewhere in the OT with this type of a transferred meaning. By contrast, in both Ezek. 29:3 (conjecture) and 32:2 (conjecture), תנין (dragon) is used as a designation for the pharaoh. In Egypt itself, the crocodile is symbolic of the power of the king (as is seen in hieroglyph I 3, which uses the image of the crocodile in duplicate as a way to refer to the pharaoh); a hymn says about Thutmose III: "I permit them to see your majesty as a crocodile, which is feared in the water, which a person does not approach too closely" (*AOT* 19).

For these reasons, it has been common for תנין (dragon) to be treated as an epithet for Egypt in this present passage. This approach would seem to force one to link the two references to Leviathan to some historical event as well. However, that linkage has proved problematic. Hitzig suggests Babylon and the Medes, with support for the latter in Herodotus 1.102, which states that Phraortes was killed in the year 635. That reference might have given us a fixed point to help with dating the Isaiah apocalypse, but that would be a very early date, one which finds hardly any proponents any more. Delitzsch thinks this might be a reference to Assyria and Babylon and even has some support: ברח (fleeing) supposedly speaks of the swiftly flowing Tigris, עקלתון (twisting) to the winding Euphrates. But Assyria and Babylon never stood together as world powers; besides this, the references to *brḥ* and *ʿqltn* in the cited Ugaritic passages certainly do not allude to these two rivers. Duhm, who was not willing to assign such an early date to the passage, thought it could refer to the Parthians; as supporting evidence, he noted that the נחש ברח (fleeing dragon) also could signify the northern constellation of the fleeing dragon (the Parthians come from the north), whereas the twisting snake would have referred to Syria, "which had surrounded most of Judah and threatened to crush it" (לויתן, "Leviathan," is frequently treated as a derivative of לוה, "surround"; *HAL:* "wreathed creature"); Marti suggests much the same. If one brings the Parthians into the picture, one must of course conclude that the present passage would have been written very late; in addition, even though it is not used together with לויתן (Leviathan), in Job 26:12f. נחש ברח (fleeing serpent), in parallel with ים (Sea) and רהב (Rahab), undoubtedly refers to chaotic power (see Fohrer). Cheyne (see Gray) links the three dragons in the chapter with Egypt, Babylon, and Persia, but it is also unthinkable that one would have Babylon and Persia mentioned together as world powers. Procksch suggests still another solution, that the two Leviathans are the Ptolemaic and Seleucid kingdoms, whereas the dragon in the sea is a reference to the Macedonian homeland, which was the home for the dragon in Greek mythology. However, aside from the fact that it is unlikely that someone in Palestine would have known about this as a reference to Macedonia, serpents and dragons are simply not the type of creatures commonly found in Greek mythology. Finally, Eissfeldt (*Introduction,* 326) also suggests that this speaks of the Seleucid and Ptolemaic kingdom, without speculating about who the third power might be.

Other solutions have been proposed, but the uncertainties mean that little productive information is available. Scholarly research has focused intensively on the historical background because it has been hoped that this could help to arrive at a date which could be used confidently to fix the time when the apocalypse came into existence. However, our study has shown that it would not have helped all that much, even if one had been able to come up with a satisfactory conclusion, since 27:1 does not belong to the original body of material in the apocalypse and very well could have come from a much later time.

If one takes the sum total of what is to be learned from the history of the study of the text, one is left with the simple conclusion that the discussion has bogged down. In most recent times, it has gone, by and large, in a circle. Because scholars have been convinced that the Leviathan and the dragon were being interpreted correctly if one could fix a historical point in time, that being roughly during the period following Alexander the Great, the entire apocalypse was then treated as a work composed during the Hellenistic era of Israel's history; then, since it was thought that the apocalypse was to be dated well into the Hellenistic era, Isa. 27:1 was interpreted within that context. It is possible that the very ancient concept about the chaos monsters had been brought back to life when the various parts of the book of Job were composed. But it is worth noting that the historical interpretation of the passage has been treated recently with much more caution, if not actually rejected (Fohrer, Kaiser, Auvray). In spite of all this, the author would have had his own precise ideas about just who these forces of chaos represented for his own era. In many places in the OT תנין (dragon) refers to Egypt. One also should take into account that the chaos monster Rahab is used with reference to Egypt, according to information in Ps. 87:4 (see also Isa. 30:7) (see H.-J. Kraus, BK XV/2, 604 [Engl: *Psalms 60–150*, 188]; E. Hertlein holds a different view, *ZAW* 38 [1919/20] 113–154). The OT provides no evidence that would support interpreting these powers of chaos as references to any of the other world-class kingdoms. That is not surprising; from the outset it is wrong to try to divide the designations נחש ברח (fleeing snake) and נחש עקלתון (twisting snake) and תנין (dragon) so that they refer to two or three different powers. Wherever לויתן (Leviathan) and תנין (Tannin, "dragon") (as well as רהב, Rahab, ים, Yam, "sea," and תהום, Tehom, "the deep") are used in parallel, the terms all point to a single power, opposed to Yahweh, which has been defeated by him; the names are interchangeable; the scene stays the same (see Fohrer). The many different terms simply illustrate the variety and fearsome nature of these powers that oppose Yahweh. Based on what has been noted above, one can presume that the three powers of chaos all describe Egypt. With as much caution as possible, one might at least offer the observation that the background for this passage could be assigned to the time of the campaigns of Artaxerxes III against Egypt, which led to the land being recaptured by him in 342, which meant that Egypt's independence came to an end. However, the possibility that the author had in mind another political situation, or even an entirely different world power, must remain an option. The only other important point to make is that the power which goes up against Yahweh in what would be the final battle is so dangerous that it could be described only by using mythical categories and that this battle would be so decisive that it would be interpreted as a renewed battle against chaos.

Meter: It would be better not to try to discover a metrical pattern here, even though על לויתן נחש ברח (Leviathan, the fleeing snake) and ועל לויתן נחש עקלתון (and Leviathan, the twisting snake) are obviously used in parallel.

Commentary

[27:1] Based on what has been said above, this verse speaks about how Yahweh would avenge the world power that personified opposition to him. The three names for the opponents correspond to the three attributes of Yahweh's sword, קשה (sharp), גדולה (huge), and חזקה (strong). Naturally it would have to be an extraordinary sword if it were to be capable of winning a victory over such a powerful foe. Other passages in the OT that discuss Yahweh's battle against the powers of chaos mention his arm (Isa. 51:9; cf. Pss. 77:16f.; 89:11, 14), unless it is simply stated that he would do them in with his rebuke (see above, p. 199). By contrast, Yahweh's sword is mentioned primarily in prophecies against the nations (Isa. 34:5f.; Jer. 47:6; 48:10; Zeph. 2:12; Ezek. 32:10), but also can be mentioned within threats of judgment issued against Israel (Deut. 28:22; Ezek. 21:8ff.; Amos 9:1; 1 Chron. 21:12). This means that the motif which refers to Yahweh's sword has been brought into the tradition about the battle against chaos from its original place in the messages against the nations.

Enough has been said above about לויתן (Leviathan) and תנין (dragon) and the symbolism connected with them. But unique in itself, and without parallel in the OT, is mention of Leviathan here as having two different aspects, being identified as a ברח נחש (fleeing snake) and as a נחש עקלתון (twisting snake). One should clearly not think that this is about a normal snake, even though the Gk translates נחש with ὄφις (serpent). In Amos 9:3, which also speaks about a נחש in the sea, that is, a sea monster, the Gk translates it as δράκων (dragon), and the same is true for Job 26:13. Identifying something specifically as ברח (fleeing) in Job 26:13—without לויתן (Leviathan) being mentioned—shows that Israel apparently knew of that terminology as well; however, no other passage in the OT speaks about עקלתון (twisting). But we have known since the Ugaritic texts were discovered, as has been explained above, that this attribute (which was usually translated, with reference to Arabic *ʿaqala*, "twist, be crooked," as "crooked") provides another link to the Canaanite tradition.

In the Ugaritic Baal myth, Mot threatens Baal concerning what will happen if he does not accept his invitation:

> *ktmḫṣ ltn bṯn brḥ*
> *tkly bṯn ʿqltn*
> *šlyṭ d šbʿt rašm*

> Just as you struck down *Ltn*, the fleeing serpent,
> as you prepared an end for the serpent which twisted itself,
> the ruler with seven heads
> thus you also will be struck and will sink down.

(67:I:1ff. = 27ff.; the translation follows that of Aistleitner, *Texte*, 14 [see also *ANET* 138]).

Here Baal is the deity who was victorious over the chaos monster (*bṯn* corresponds linguistically to Hebrew פתן (BDB: venomous serpent, perhaps cobra), but its meaning corresponds to נחש, "serpent," in the present passage). In addition, one must consider the vocabulary. One should note that "Lotan" (which is how scholars have usually chosen to vocalize Ugaritic *ltn*) is not repeated. That omission makes clear that "the fleeing snake" and "the snake that twists itself" do not refer to two different powers. The same is true about the text ʿnt III:35–39, in which Anat praises Baal with the words:

> Did you not then crush Ym [= ים], the beloved one of El?
> Did you not prepare an end for *Rbm*, the flood (god) of El?
> Did I not muzzle the *Tnn* [= תנין] . . .?
> Indeed, you shattered the writhing serpent [*bṯn ʿqltn*],
> The ruler with the seven heads
> (Aistleitner, *Texte*, 27–28 [cf. also *ANET* 137]).

It is surprising that the vocabulary used to describe the battle against chaos survived down into the postexilic era—an indication that speaking about the battle of Yahweh against the powers of chaos was more intense and varied in the Jerusalem cult than one would be led to believe on the basis of what might be assumed just by reading the Psalms, even though the motifs are to be found there as well.

Purpose and Thrust

It is significant for that moment in time when the great shift in fortune was to take place that the ancient group of motifs that had described the battle of Yahweh against the powers of chaos, which Deutero-Isaiah still treated as references to ancient times, is used now to portray the eschatological intervention of Yahweh. It corresponds to the final establishment of Yahweh's kingdom on Zion that his opponents would be done away with once and for all. The passage set a precedent (see Wallace). According to Dan. 7:2ff., the animals that symbolize the various world powers rise up out of the sea. To be sure, they are not chaos monsters, but that they come up out of the sea points to their having their origin in that mythology. By contrast, Rev. 13:1f. speaks of an animal (which also comes forth from the sea) that had been given its power and its throne and its great might by the δράκων (dragon). As 12:9 explains, the dragon is "that ancient serpent, who is called the Devil and Satan." In actuality, he delegates his power to his earthly embodiment, to that "animal" which depicts world power at enmity with God. The ancient serpent would be bound for one thousand years, but then once more it would be able to rage upon the earth until, at the end, it would be cast into the lake of fire and sacrilege and would be tormented there for all eternity (Rev. 20:1ff.). In this way the chaos monster, identified with Satan, finally becomes the last enemy of God.

This passage makes clear that evil in the world has a metaphysical background; the victory over evil could not be won simply on an earthly battlefield, but could come to a full and final victory only in the metaphysical battle at the end of time, fought between God and the powers that were inimical to him. This battle would finally result in the reign of God becoming a complete reality and would finally be able to bring about full salvation.

Isaiah 27:2-5

The New Song of the Vineyard

Literature

E. Robertson, "Isaiah XXVII 2-6," *ZAW* 47 (1929) 197–206. L. Alonso-Schökel, "La canción de la viña. Is 27, 2-5," *EstEcl* 34 (1960) 767–774. E. Jacob, "Du premier au deuxième chant de la vigne du prophète Esaïe, réflexions sur Esaïe 27, 2-5," FS W. Eichrodt (1970) 325–330.

[**Literature update through 1979:** B. Jongeling, "L'expression *my ytn* dans l'AT," *VT* 24 (1974) 32–40 (on 27:4).]

Text

2 ᵃ[On that day]
  ᵇvineyard of pleasure,ᶜ ᵈsing about itᵉ!ᵇ
3 I, Yahweh, am your protector,
  ᵃevery momentᵃ I drench it.
  ᵇSo that it experiences no damage,ᵇ
  I protectᶜ it night and day;
4   I bear no anger.ᵃ
  ᵇIf I would findᵇ thorns,ᶜ thistles,ᵈ
  I would go chargingᵉ right in against them,
   ᶠwould set every one of them on fireᶠ—
5 unless one takes advantage of my protection,
  ᵃmakes with me peace,ᵃ
  ᵇpeace makes with me.ᵇ

2a Marti and Guthe (cf. also Duhm, *BHK, BHS*) suggest adding וַיֹּאמֶר (and he said) at the beginning; Schlögl would add וְהָיָה (and it will happen), which he proposes for v. 12 as well (in addition, see above, p. 575, textual note 1c–c).

2b–b Procksch thinks that, at one time, the verse might have read אֲנִי יהוה נְטַעְתִּי כֶרֶם חֶמֶד עֵנָב לָהּ (I, Yahweh, I planted a vineyard; special grapes were in it), but this type of fantasizing does not qualify as serious textual criticism.

2c The Gk reads καλός (good); *BHS*: חֶמֶד (delight); *BHK*: חֶמֶר (wine) (according to the Leningrad text)—this being one of the very few places where there is a difference in the consonantal text of the manuscripts that have been transmitted through the Masoretes; in fact, Qᵃ reads חוֹמֶר (fermenting; see Kutscher, 375); cf. חָמַר I, "ferment," in Hab. 3:15 [NRSV: churning]; Syr: ḥumrā᾽ (the fermenting). Since it does speak about a vineyard, it seems right that one should read חֶמֶר, "wine," but the correct form is still חֶמֶד (delight); see כַּרְמֵי־חֶמֶד (pleasant vineyards) in Amos 5:11.

2d Ehrlich (*Randglossen* IV, 94) suggests reading the *qal* imperative instead: עֲנוּ (you, [pl.] sing) since he thinks that the *piʿel* does not have the requisite meaning for this passage; this is a somewhat rash observation.

2e The suffix on לָהּ (lit.: to her) can refer back only to כֶרֶם (vineyard), which is masculine everywhere else it is used. It could be that it should be pointed לֹה (to him) or לֹה (to him), but כֶרֶם (vineyard) might also be in the feminine in Lev. 25:3. Rudolph (23) suggests that the feminine form of the suffix comes from the fact that the author was thinking about the whole scene, i.e., that he has אֶרֶץ יִשְׂרָאֵל (land of Israel) in mind.

Isaiah 27:1-13

3a–a לרגעים means "all moments, over and over again"; see Ezek. 26:16; 32:10; Job 7:18. Since the Gk seems to read μάτην (in vain), Gray thinks it possible that the original text might have had the reading לריקם (for emptinesses), but there is nothing wrong with לרגעים (every moment).

3b–b Verse 3bα is hard to understand with the present pointing. The subject has to be the indefinite "someone"; Vulg translated the verb as a passive (so also Gk); some exegetes lean toward pointing it יִפָּקֵד (be visited upon it); see Num. 16:29; cf. also Prov. 19:23. One should not choose to adopt Duhm's translation: "so that its foliage will not be missed." Procksch reads אני אפקד, resulting in his translation: "I assign watchmen over it," which is possible only because he replaces פ (so that . . . no) with אני (I), which is completely arbitrary.

3c Qª: אצורנה (also: I protect it). Just as is true sometimes in the MT, there are times in Qumran where a *hateph*-vowel is written *plene;* see Kutscher, 148.

4a The Gk (τεῖχος, "wall," at the end of v. 3) and Syr (šwrʾ, "the wall") apparently read this as חֹמָה (wall) instead of חֵמָה (rage); however, there is no evidence to support that suggestion (contra Umbreit); the same assessment applies to Robertson's (200) interpretation; based on Arabic cognates, he translates this: "I have no tent (namely, for a night watch)." Furthermore, it is unacceptable to follow G. R. Driver's observation that חמה should be understood to mean not "hot anger" but rather "fiery wine" (*TZ* 14 [1958] 133–135); one should stay with the MT as is.

4b–b Qimḥi notes that מי־יתנני (who will find [for] me) is used here in place of מי יתן לי (also: who will find for me), the suffix on נתן (find for, give) being used quite often as an alternative to employing the dative (see Job 9:18; Josh. 15:19). The Gk seems to have had a text that read the suffix as a second feminine singular, but (contra Procksch) there is no other support for following that reading.

4c Qª reads שומיר (according to Kutscher, 385, שׁימיר, which he terms "simply a mechanical error").

4d Qª, some Hebrew MSS, Targ, Syr, Vulg: ושית (and thistles), which has been commonly accepted because of 5:6; as is shown by the meter, however, the MT is to be left as is, here as well (see below, p. 583).

4e במלחמה (in battle) is surprising; to go to war against thorns is about the same as bombing ants. However, it would be too easy a solution to eliminate it by citing its absence in the Targ, which translates the entire text rather freely anyway (see also *BHS*). Duhm changes מלחמה (war) to read מְלֵחָה, "salty soil" (see Jer. 17:6; Ps. 107:34; Job 39:6), since the godless, about whom the author was thinking, would have been like shrubs in the steppe and would have been living in the land of salt; however, almost no one has followed his suggestion. Because of the accent, it is better to take במלחמה with אפשעה (= I go charging right in) (see Delitzsch); since v. 5 speaks of peace, מלחמה (battle) seems to be mentioned appropriately in v. 4.

4f–f Qª: ואציתנה יחדו (and *have* set every one of them on fire) shows how carelessly whoever copied this manuscript treated the text. The way אֲצִיתֶנָּה (I will set on fire) is pointed seems to presume that there was a lesser-used form of יצת (BDB: kindle, burn), namely, צות; Delitzsch rejects this solution (*OLZ* 19 [1916] 165f.). *BHS* suggests that it should be read אַצִּיתֶנָּה (I will cause it to be set on fire). Since צות is not used anywhere else, that may be correct.

5a–a The Gk reads ποιήσομεν εἰρήνην αὐτῷ (we will make peace with him); Syr: wʾ ʿbd lh šlmʾ (and he will make peace with him). But the subject of יעשה (will make) is an unnamed "someone"; indeed, this someone points to the enemies of Israel, who also are Yahweh's enemies; peace with Yahweh also includes being at peace with his people.

582

5b–b One hardly could expect otherwise: some think this is a dittography. Once again, in this passage that solution is out of the question.

Form

Compared with v. 1, the theme of vv. 2-5 is completely different; there is no conceivable way that the passage functioned originally as the continuation of v. 1. As it is now, it is linked to the introductory phrase ביום ההוא (on that day), even if that would prove simply to be a dittography (see above, p. 575, textual note 1c–c). In any case, this section, which taken by itself contains nothing that one would be forced to label eschatological, is now placed within an apocalyptic framework because of the context. This means that this passage also, much as passages such as the "songs of the city," must be interpreted first in its own right and then as an element within the context of apocalyptic expectation.

There is a difference of opinion about whether v. 6 also belongs with vv. 2-5. The verse does not deal specifically with the imagery of the vineyard any more, but one could consider it to be a rich-sounding conclusion to the section (possibly having been inserted there by a later hand). But הבאים (in the coming) is a remnant from a new introductory formula; this means that the passage concludes impressively with a double use of שלום (peace). Even without including v. 6, it is a message of promise for the people of God.

As with 5:1-7, some have attempted to title this a song of the vineyard. It is true that Israel is compared to a vineyard here as in 5:1-7. Additional commonalities between the two passages jump out immediately: 5:1 uses שיר (sing), 27:2 uses the root ענה (sing), *piʿel*, which means about the same; the vineyard in 5:1ff. is situated on a fine piece of land, that in 27:2ff. is כרם חמד (a vineyard of pleasure). Here, as there, Yahweh, the owner of the vineyard, does everything possible to care for what he planted. שמיר (thorns) and שית (thistles) threaten these plants, just as they also posed a threat in that passage (one also finds that same merism in 7:23-25; 9:17; 10:17, but nowhere outside the book of Isaiah). According to 27:3, Yahweh provides moisture for his vineyard every moment. According to 5:6, he forbids the clouds to rain upon it. The vintner in chap. 5 expects משפט (justice) and צדקה (righteousness); the one in chap. 27 announces שלום (peace). In spite of all this, 27:2-5 cannot be interpreted as a simple imitation of 5:1-6. Taken as a whole, Isaiah's song of the vineyard is a judgment speech, whereas what we have here is a message of promise. It would be much more accurate to say that this is the antithesis of 5:1ff., as is especially clear when noting how חמה אין לי (I bear no anger) is used in v. 4; there is not the slightest hint of criticism directed against Israel; the opposite is true, since the vineyard is promised unconditional protection. Kaiser suggests that this passage makes the first song null and void. This passage seeks to describe Israel in the time of salvation; the judgment that had been promised in 5:1ff. would be in the past; the people of God would be reconstituted with a new start on the future and would live in a time of restoration, during which no one would worry that it could come to an end. Judgment had had its day; "on that day" refers now to the time of salvation.

Meter: The poem is consistently constructed according to the pattern of three-part verses: vv. 2, 3a (after ביום ההוא, "on that day," has been bracketed out): 3 + 3 + 3. Verse 3b, 4a: 3 + 3 + 2 (read לי אין חמה, that is, as having two stresses; since אין, "no," comes right after the tone syllable on חמה, "anger," it is especially emphasized). Verse 4b: 3 + 2 + 2 (read שׁיּת שׁמיר, "thorns, thistles," with one stress only; שׁמיר שׁיּת is a hendiadys; based on the meter, it is not recommended that one read שׁמיר ושׁית, "thorns and thistles," because of 5:6; בה, "against them," should not receive a stress). Verse 5: 3 + 2 + 2 (שׁלום לי, "with me peace," and יעשׂה־לי, "makes [peace] with me," each get one stress).

Setting

Since the poem should be studied initially as a separate piece, one must look for information within the passage itself that might help us to arrive at a date. Jacob (328) has expressed the view that the author was focusing on the antagonism between the Jews and Samaritans in the postexilic era, recalling what is said in Hag. 2:10-14; Ezra 4:23; Neh. 1:3; 2:3. According to him, the author did not simply want to write the Samaritans out of the restoration altogether; they were like others who had been judged as deserving the death sentence, but it would be possible for them to find asylum or peace at the holy shrines. That is a plausible solution, but only one of many possibilities (see below, pp. 585f.). Even if the Samaritans are the unnamed referent, the exact dating of the passage is still an open question.

Commentary

[27:2] Concerning ביום ההוא (on that day), see above, p. 575, textual note 1c–c. The vineyard of pleasure, about which Yahweh calls for a song, can be none other than Israel itself: that Israel which had faith—living when the first eschatological indications of a new start were being detected, the Israel that was alive at the beginning of the time of restoration. A rich previous history depicts how Israel is compared with a vineyard, certainly not limited to 5:1-7. A vineyard benefits from careful attention, produces wonderful fruit, and is the pride of its owner. An Arabic proverb says: "The vine is a lady, . . . the olive is a bedouin, the fig is a farmer's wife" (Dalman, *AuS* IV, 311). The "vineyard of Yahweh" is thus a fitting image for describing that particular Israel which had been chosen. Israel is a luxuriant vine that produces wonderful fruit (Hos. 10:1); it has been planted in its own land by Yahweh as an excellent vine, a plant of the purest stock (Jer. 2:21; see also 5:10 and Ezekiel 15). The passages just cited show also that this image could be used without any problem as one element within an announcement of judgment. It does not take much for a vineyard to be damaged; the woody vine can be set on fire quite easily, and a brand new planting of vine tendrils is exposed to dangers that are hard to fend off. Yet, according to the present passage, Israel is כרם חמד (a vineyard of pleasure). Amos 5:11 speaks of כרמי־חמד (pleasant vineyards), Isa. 32:12 of שְׁדֵי־חֶמֶד (pleasant fields); חֶמֶד describes both what is beautiful and what is expensive; thus it always identifies that which is the most desirable, a possession about which one can feel nothing but joy. This is why the summons is there: "sing about it!" There is no way to determine exactly how to distinguish between ענה (sing) *pi'el,* used here, and שׁיר (sing) in 5:1.

The author takes great pains to stress that Yahweh protects his vineyard. The imagery is easy to understand. In 1:8 Isaiah speaks about the booth in the vineyard (see *Isaiah 1–12,* p. 31), which serves as a shelter for the watchman. This person would have much better lodging if the owner of the vineyard would have gone so far as to build a tower (5:2; see *Isaiah 1–12,* p. 181).

[27:3] In addition to having it located on a good site, with rich soil (5:1), it is also important that the vineyard does not lack the proper moisture. As for Yahweh's own vineyard, Israel, he waters it "every moment," whereas working with actual vineyards in Palestine could involve the dangers that result from having to endure long periods of drought. Of course, לִרְגָעִים (every moment) is not meant literally; it does not rain in Palestine during the summer months, but, if the vines are planted in good soil and have gotten enough moisture during the winter, the plants certainly can survive to grape harvest (which takes place in August/September). The more moisture one gets, however, the closer one can plant the rows of vines and thus the larger the harvest.

Verse 3b repeats the same idea with slightly different words. So that no dangers can come upon his vineyard, Yahweh protects it night and day.

[27:4] As one can see just by looking at the meter, the central message now follows in v. 4a: "I bear no anger." It would seem to make no sense at all that one would be angry with a vineyard. However, the owner of the vineyard who is mentioned in 5:5f., in the midst of his disappointment, does not hold back from giving the vineyard over to destruction. The author is obviously mixing the imagery together with what he wants to say, which is that there is no longer any anger against Israel. In contrast to this message, Isaiah speaks emphatically and passionately about the wrath of Yahweh against his people and hardly can imagine that God's indignation would ever end: "In all this his wrath (אַפּוֹ) did not turn away, and his hand is still stretched out" (9:11, 16, 20; 10:4). Isaiah never uses the word חֵמָה (anger), though it is used commonly in Jeremiah, Ezekiel, Deutero-Isaiah, and Trito-Isaiah.

If, in spite of all of the special care that is given, thorns and thistles sprout anyway (on שָׁמִיר, "thorns," and שַׁיִת, "thistles," see *Isaiah 1–12,* pp. 183f.), then Yahweh would immediately attack them aggressively, going to war. פָּשַׂע (go charging) is a hapax legomenon; however, see the substantive פֶּשַׂע (a step) (1 Sam. 20:3), which derives from this root. The imagery, which looks at first to be poorly chosen, depicting Yahweh at war with thorns and thistles, expresses nicely how Yahweh would go forth against any possible enemy of his people, with every ounce of his might (cf. Yahweh as a warrior in Ps. 24:8; Exod. 15:3). שׁמיר שׁית (thorns, thistles) could be invaders who intended to devastate the land of Israel.

One aspect of the battle involves burning, which fits best with the imagery about the thorns and thistles which are composed of easily combustible materials; see 9:17; 10:17. For the author, this imagery involves the threat of a complete (יחד, "every one") destruction.

[27:5] There is an alternate solution, however: that the enemies would want to turn toward Yahweh. Verse 5 states it this way: "Unless one takes advantage of my protection." The oppressors of the people of God provide the subject for יחזק (here: take advantage of). This sentence is to be explained in light of the asylum function that a sanctuary served. One would use חזק (take advantage of, take hold of) when someone who was being followed would seize the horns of the altar in the sanctuary (Adonijah, 1 Kings 1:51; Joab, 1 Kings 2:28; in addition, cf. also Pss. 17:8; 31:3; 36:8; 57:2; 59:10, etc.; concerning the concept of seeking asylum, see M. Löhr, *Das Asylwesen im Alten Testament* (1930), L. Delekat, *Asylie und Schutzorakel am Zionheiligtum* (1967). But the concept is raised to a more sublime level. Protection is to be found with *Yahweh;* in fact, Yahweh himself *is* protection for those who are his. It is obvious, however, that one ought not try to make a sharp distinction between seeking protection from Yahweh and looking for it in the temple. The sanctuary is the place where the fellowship with God becomes real and actualized.

To find shelter with Yahweh means that a person achieves שׁלום (peace). Admittedly, it is hard to be sure about the exact sense conveyed by the grammatical constructions in v. 5. יחזק (take advantage of, take hold of) is jussive, but it is not clear whether one is also supposed to treat the two occurrences of יעשׂה (make) in the jussive sense. Does this verse intend to say: the enemies of Israel should hurry up and make peace with Yahweh? Hardly; it is more likely that it is intended as an indicative statement: They will get peace as a result. This means that the peace is not actually the "work" of those who are seeking protection, but the result of their having turned toward Yahweh.

Jerusalem, most specifically, the temple, is the place where שׁלום (peace) dwells; see 26:3; 54:13; Ps. 122:7f.; cf. also Isa. 2:2-4. In the eschatological sense and similar to the NT εἰρήνη, שׁלום (peace) expresses the all-encompassing salvation at the end of time, though even within that context it still should not be described falsely as something that is only internal; even at that time, it is always to be characterized as complete protection from attack, as prosperity, well-being, being blessed, success (see W. Eisenbeis, *Die Wurzel שׁלם im Alten Testament,* BZAW 113 [1969]). One should note that this includes a conditional promise when it is spoken to these opponents of Yahweh; the polarity between making peace and being able to go away in peace should not be reduced to a single continuum.

Purpose and Thrust

The way in which Isaiah's song of the vineyard is played off against this passage, with the content of this passage describing the very opposite situation,
clearly attributable to an author who was undoubtedly steeped in the traditions of Isaiah, shows once more that the statements in the OT are definitely
bound to a specific historical setting. In the earlier song, it was an announcement of judgment; here, it is a promise of salvation, with the explicit assurance that the people of God are no longer standing under the wrath of God.
We do not have any more information about the exact situation in which this
was spoken originally, as a noneschatological message. According to its
present context, however, it speaks about the end of time, in which Yahweh's
judgment would be in Israel's past and in which the only continuing relationship would be with God's חסד (mercy).

In this passage, unlike the passage that speaks about the joyous meal
on Mount Zion, the salvation is promised to Israel and not specifically to all
peoples of the world. Yet, even in this passage, it is not an exclusive relationship; even Israel's enemies could place themselves under Yahweh's protection and could allow themselves thus to be included in the peace offered
by the Lord of Zion.

Isaiah 27:6-11

Time of Flourishing for Israel; Devastation of the Fortified City

Literature

J. Herrmann, "סאסאכ Jes 27:8 und שאשא Hes 39:2," *ZAW* 36 (1916) 243.
[**Literature update through 1979:** P. J. Becker, "Wurzel und Wurzelspross: Ein Beitrag zur hebräischen Lexikographie," *BZ* 20 (1976) 22–44.]

Text

6 In the coming (days)[a] Jacob will [b]take root,[b]
   and Israel will flourish and sprout up,
      and [c]the whole world[c] will fill itself with fruit.[c]
7 Did he strike it, as he strikes the one who struck it,[a]
   or did he murder it, as [b]his murderers'[b] were murdered?
8 By startling,[a] by driving away,[b] 'he'[c] disputed with her,
   drove 'her'[d] out using his storm, the strong one,
      on the day of the east wind.
9 Truly,[a] the guilt of Jacob is covered *by that means*
   —and *that* is the entire fruit coming from the distancing of its[b] sins—:
      so that all the stones of the altar
         will be made just like crushed limestone
      [Asherim and incense altars will not arise ever again].[c]
10 For the fortified city lies all alone,
   a depopulated place
   and abandoned like the steppe.
There the young bull will graze,
   [a]there he will bed down
   and eat the undergrowth bare.[a]
11 If its branches[a] are dry,[b] then the wives will break[c] them off
   when they come to set them on fire,
   for it is a people that has no insight.
For that reason its maker does not deal mercifully with it,
   and it finds no grace from the one who established it.

6a Many expand הבאים (the coming) by adding הימים (days) (Marti) or בימים (in [the coming] days). Procksch, among others, proposes altering MT to read the well-known form ביום ההוא (in that day), whereas *BHS* and Kaiser suggest reading בָּא הַיּוֹם ו (that day has come, and . . .) (though one should rather expect that it then would have been יָבוֹא הַיּוֹם ו, "that day will come, and . . ."). Ehrlich takes the cake with his pointing: הֲבָאִים, the line being translated: "Will Jacob take root in the coastlands?" In this instance, even he himself has to admit that this phrase would be a fragment then, which has absolutely no connection to what precedes it. When G. R. Driver proposes the translation: "Jacob shall give roots to the coming generations" (*JSS* 13 [1968] 50f.), one has to admit that he was able to propose this without recourse to emendations, but there is no doubt that he is mistaken. The truth of the matter is that הבאים is a shorthand way (Gray) of saying הימים הבאים (the days are coming when), which is grammatically another way to express an accusative of time (see Joüon, *Gr* §126i; and see Eccles. 2:16).

6b–b One's attention is drawn to יְשָׁרֵשׁ (lit.: may he take root) being used just before יָצִיץ (will flourish). Qᵃ reads the indicative ישריש (he will take root) (see also ριζωσει, "will take root," in Aquila, Sym, Theod). It is also possible that it should be pointed יְשָׁרֵשׁ (he will take root); cf. Isa. 40:24. In any case, it is to be translated in an indicative sense.

6c–c and c Procksch wants to remove either פְּנֵי־תֵבֵל (lit.: the face of the world) or תְנוּבָה (with fruit); he translates it: "and they will be full of fruit." That change would make the interpretation of the passage easier, since it is not immediately apparent why the entire face of the earth would be filled with fruit when Israel blooms. However, textual criticism should not be used to remove all the problems in interpretation.

7a The Gk reads πληγήσεται, καὶ (he will strike, and) instead of הַכֵּהוּ (he will strike him), which leads *BHS* (see also Gray, Procksch) to suggest reading הֲכֵה וְ (has someone ever struck as a striker struck him?). Admittedly, it is difficult to make any sense of the passage (but see the parallel word הֹרָג, "were murdered," in the second colon). However, the Gk translation is not very literal and the suggested alteration does not help much to make sense of the passage.

7b–b Qᵃ reads הורגיו (his murderers), which means it is treated as if it is an active participle, a reading that has been presupposed for a long time already by many scholars (Guthe, Gray, Duhm, Marti, Ehrlich, Procksch, Fohrer, Kaiser, *BHK*, *BHS*), who display a rare degree of unanimity.

8a בְּסַאסְּאָה has caused many problems for the interpretation. It would seem that even the Masoretes had trouble with it, since the Leningrad text reads it with the pointing בְּסַאסְּאָה (*sic*) (see *BHK*). The *Qere* of some Hebrew MSS reads בְּסָּאָה (see *BHK*). The ancient translations (Aquila, Sym, Theod, Targ, Vulg, but not the Gk) apparently thought this term referred to a measure of grain, the סְאָה (seah), and Delitzsch still translates it "with measures"; von Orelli translates it "moderately," and Gesenius thinks that the word was a contraction of בְּסָאָה סְאָה (measure by measure). Dillmann questions this solution; he says (based on the Gk, which does translate this very freely) that this would have to be analyzed as an infinitive with a third feminine singular suffix or else a noun expressing action, סַאסְּאָה (BDB: by driving away). Scholars have generally followed his suggestion. Of course, that still does not assure one that its meaning is clear. G. R. Driver (*JTS* 30 [1928] 371f.) thinks that it is a *pilpel* infinitive that, based on the Arabic, means "in shooing her away" (*saʾsaʾ* = "he drove on with cries," used originally to describe how one would force donkeys to move on). F. Schulthess (*ZS* 2 [1923] 15f.) believes that it is to be related to a verb used in connection with trying to get the attention of small animals, *ša* or *sa*, resulting in a meaning something like "startle." The solution offered by Feldmann, that it is to be related to Arabic *zʾzʾ*, "move far away," does not merit serious consideration. Even if one cannot be sure of the derivation, one should opt for a meaning something like "startle" because of the parallelism with שָׁלְחָה (send away). It is likely that the ה at the end of the word should be furnished with a *mappiq* and treated as a suffix.

8b It is a mystery why שלחה (send away) should be treated as a gloss (*BHS*).

8c Marti follows Oort and wants to read יְרִיבֶהָ (*he* disputed with her). Since it is not possible to be sure of the interpretation of the passage in this context, there is no way one can show that this change is correct, but it may be that Marti is right in this case.

8d Instead of הָגָה (she drove), one should read הֲגָהּ (he drove her) (Marti, *BHK*, and *BHS*, which also mentions הֹגָהּ, "driving her," as a possible pointing). In any case, that reading is more likely than what Procksch proposes, emending the text to read הֹוָה, "misfortune."

9a Guthe and Schlögl suggest reading לֹא כֵן (not thus) instead of לָכֵן (truly), which would make the text mean the exact opposite of what it does now, a most unlikely solution.

9b Qᵃ: חטאו (they sinned); see Kutscher, 374. A. C. M. Blommerde (*Bib* 60 [1974] 551) suggests treating חטאתו (its sins) as a genitive, dependent on כל־פרי (the entire fruit) (as an example of a "broken construct chain"), and thus translates v. 9aβ: "and this is: removing every fruit of his sin, . . ." but this would be a most unlikely construction anyway.

9c Following the Gk, Procksch suggests adding [מרחוק] נכרתים כיער (one knocks them down, as the forest, [from afar]). That reading is possible, but tenuous.

10a–a Concerning v. 10b, Duhm proposes that one would read וְשָׁמִיר וָקוֹץ יַעֲלֶה סְעִפֹּת, "and thorns and thickets will sprout twigs," right after עגל (young bull). Once more, one has to wonder about the self-confident boldness displayed in such textual criticism.

11a Vulg reads *messis illius* (of that harvest), but there is no doubt that the MT has קָצִיר II in mind, "twig, shoot" (which is to be understood in the collective sense).

11b Concerning the infinitive of יבש (be dry), see Ges-K §70a.

11c *BHS* suggests reading תִּשְׁבְּרֶנָּה (you broke her), a form that includes an energic *nun;* but when a collective is used, it is common to find a grammatical form that differs from its semantic significance. Ehrlich points it תִּשְׁבְּרֶנָה (they will break them off) and takes the following נשים (wives) as the subject of the verb. He may indeed be right this time. קָצִיר (branches) is a collective and is treated as a feminine.

Form

There is great disagreement about the limits of this section and its divisions. Verse 6 functions as a type of superscription for the entire passage. Unlike what immediately precedes them, vv. 10f. do not deal with Israel but rather, once again, with a fortified city. It is understandable that many commentators treat v. 10 as the beginning of a new section. However, it is still more likely that these verses are to be interpreted as offering a contrast to the preceding promise of restoration, which the author appended to the songs about the city that were already in the text he had before him. One should also note that the verses in 26:1-6, which have been treated by everyone as a single unit, also begin with a description about protection and peace for Israel, but then go on to talk of the enemy city being thrown down.

As a superscription for his discussion of 27:7-9, Kaiser uses "A Difficult Text." "One can read these verses again and again without knowing exactly to whom they are referring and how they fit into their context." When studying these verses, particularly if one includes vv. 10f., the truth of the matter is that it is not easy to identify the basic theme. Nevertheless, attempts have been made to make some sense of the train of thought, attempts that include both v. 6 and vv. 10f. in the discussion. Verse 6 is a promise of restoration to Israel; because of הבאים (הימים) (in the coming [days]), this passage, like others, is placed within the context of an eschatological event. Verse 7 asserts that Yahweh did not deal with Israel in the same way he struck their opponents, whom he had put to flight with a strong storm wind from the east. Of course, it is problematic that the reference to these opponents comes in the form of a feminine singular suffix, which would have to refer to a city or to its inhabitants. However, the greatest difficulty involves how to classify v. 9: "Truly, the guilt of Jacob is covered by that means (בזאת)." *Through what means* is it covered? And can the "fruit" of having placed the sins far away be that the altars are knocked down? One would expect the very opposite, that Jacob would destroy its own altars and in that way would make reparations for its guilt. In order to make sense of this, one has to figure out first who is meant by "Jacob." If one treats the mention of the "city" as a reference to Samaria (which is what both Plöger, 74, and Kaiser have suggested recently), then one would be inclined toward treating "Jacob" as a reference to the inhabitants living in what once was the Northern Kingdom, people who would be expected to acknowledge their cultic mistakes at this time and, as "fruit" of the mild treatment they received from Yahweh, finally figure out what appropriate actions they should take. As will be discussed in further detail below, this interpretation does have a certain plausibility about it. בזאת (by that means) does not point back but rather forward; it can certainly mean: "with the following conditions"; see *HAL* (254) and cf. passages such as Gen. 34:15. In this case, the condition under which Jacob's guilt can be covered would be fulfilled if the altars (v. 9bα) would be destroyed. However, v. 9aβ does not say anything else about how the guilt is covered, but basically explains v. 9aα. When Jacob's guilt is covered, that is a result of its sins having been removed far away, which means that the illegitimate altar is actually a way to refer to an illegitimate cult.

Verses 10f. add further comments: in any case, the fortified city is to be feared no longer; it will be destroyed until nothing is left.

Meter: Verse 7: three-stress + three-stress bicolon. In v. 8 ביום קדים (on the day of the east wind) should be treated as the third part of the verse (3 + 3 + 2), with particular stress laid on that part, since it is so short. Verse 9a should be read as a four-stress + four-stress bicolon (in which case לכן, "truly," is outside the metrical structure). Verse 9bα is very likely a five-stress colon (in which case כאבני־, "like crushed limestone," is to be read as having *one* stress). Verse 9bβ is certainly a later addition; see below, p. 594. Verse 10a probably has three parts (3 + 2 + 2); the same is true for v. 10b (presumably also 3 + 2 + 2). Verse 11abα: 4 + 3 + 3. Verse 11bβ-γ: a three-stress + three-stress bicolon.

Setting

As explained above, this is also a later addition. In order to identify the background historically, it also would be nice if one could know which city is the "fortified city." However, there is great difference of opinion about that here, as in the other passages within chaps. 24–27 that speak about an enemy city; the same is true for the other major question, the identity of the "imperceptive people" for whom its maker can show no mercy, in v. 11. If that is a reference to Israel/Judah, then the fortified city could be none other than Jerusalem (Duhm; Fischer; Rudolph, 53ff.; Fohrer); however, this would be a contradiction to what is said in vv. 6f., one that could not be resolved, since there it speaks clearly about restoration. If this were true, it would mean that one would be forced to conclude that vv. 10f. form a self-contained unit that must be treated separately. However, even if one does not consider that option for the moment, it is still most difficult to see how there could be a prophecy in the postexilic era that would announce such a total destruction of Jerusalem. In any case, there is no parallel for such a statement anywhere in the OT. Besides this, every reference to the destroyed city within the rest of the Isaiah apocalypse speaks about an enemy city. For this reason, others think this refers to a world-class city, as is the case with the city songs in 25:1ff. and 26:1ff., some city on the same level as Babylon. Yet, once again, this interpretation stands in contradiction to v. 11, according to which Yahweh is the creator and shaper of the people without insight, molder of those whose dwelling was in this city, which is an apparent reference to Israel. As a way to get out of this dilemma, some commentators (Marti; more recently Plöger, 74; Kessler; and Kaiser) think it refers to Samaria. However, chronological reasons would preclude this from being a reference to the destruction caused by John Hyrcanus (108 B.C.). It would be just as impossible to conclude that the background for this reference is the destruction of Samaria by the Assyrians in 721 (so Fischer). More recently, Kessler has expressed the opinion that it might refer to the destruction of Samaria by Demetrius Poliorcetes in 296.

After the subjugation of Asia Minor, the battle at Issus (333) opened the way for Alexander into Asia. But he chose to go south first, so that he could take control of Egypt. In the process, he experienced bitter opposition in the Phoenician city of Tyre and was able to conquer it only after a siege of seven months. As he proceeded along the coastline, where he was delayed by opposition in Gaza as well, he also was able to take control of the central region of Palestine, including Samaria and Judea. It is possible that there is a reference to Alexander's campaign in Zech. 9:1-8 (see K. Elliger, *ZAW* 62 [1950] 63–115; and M. Delcor, *VT* 1 [1951] 110–124). We are poorly informed about exactly how these events affected the Israelite territory proper; it would seem that there were no major battles along the way. Eusebius (*PG* 19, 489f.) does report that there was opposition by Samaria and tells of the measures taken to punish them afterward. Unfortunately, there is no way to verify this comment. While Alexander remained in Egypt, the inhabitants of Samaria murdered the prefect of Coele-Syria, Andromachus. "Ob quae ab Aegypto reversus Alexander magnis eos suppliciis affecit, et urbem eorum captam Macedonibus ad habitandum dedit anno regni sui quarto" (in return for which, Alexander, after returning from Egypt, punished them severely and, having taken their city, he gave it to the Macedonians to live in, in the fourth year of his reign). Thus Alexander allowed some of his veterans to settle in Samaria, which quickly must have brought about a Hellenization of the city. One certainly also can trust the information that Alexander caused the city to be expanded, a project headed by his general Perdiccas.

We also learn something more about what happened to Samaria from Diodorus Siculus (19.93.6f.). According to him, Demetrius (the son of Antigonus) suffered a terrible defeat at Gaza in a battle against Egypt, which resulted in all of Syria coming under the control of Ptolemy. But Antigonus himself intervened, which caused Ptolemy to retreat back to Egypt. Before he did so, however, he is reported to have demolished the cities of Acco, Jaffa, Samaria, and Gaza (κατέσκαψε). This remark poses a dilemma for the historian. What is the reason for this "scorched-earth policy" (see J. Seibert, MBPF 56 [1969] 151)? In addition, Eusebius mentions that there was another conquest of Samaria, in 296: "Demetrius rex Asiae cognomento Poliorketes Samaritarum urbem vastat, quam Perdiccas ante construxerat" (Demetrius, king of Asia, surnamed Poliorcetes, demolished the city of Samaritans that Perdiccas had built previously) (*PG* 19, 496). This reference does not betray any awareness of the destruction in 312; otherwise, the city would have had to have been rebuilt very quickly. Some historians (see V. Tcherikover, *Hellenistic Civilization and the Jews* [1959] 47f.) thus believe that this reference must be treated as a mistake on the part of Eusebius, particularly since Plutarch (*Demetrios Poliorketes*) does not seem to have known anything about that event; but others lean toward accepting it on its own merits. One certainly could suppose that the destruction caused by Ptolemy I, son of Lagos, might not have been particularly severe and that enough was left from the fortifications and other structures that Perdiccas built for a further destruction to have taken place.

Since information about these "conquests" of Samaria remains inconclusive and scanty, one has to admit that one cannot be confident that the present passage should be dated to the era of the battles of the Diadochi at all. One might also remember that reference was made above to the viewpoint of Jacob that 27:2-5 also deals with the Samaritans. It is possible that the present passage deals with Samaria, even if one cannot be sure about the dating. In this case, "Jacob" or, as the case may be, "Israel" would refer to the population living in what was once was the Northern Kingdom, a suggestion supported by the fact that "Jacob" is never mentioned anywhere else in chaps. 24–27. Thus, in Jerusalem, where the author of this section must have been living, it would have been expected that heathen Samaria was going to fall. One result of that event would have been that the rest of the people still living in what had once been the Northern Kingdom would have found their way back to Yahweh and thus would have begun to bloom and sprout. When one could speak about the future time of restoration, then it is easy to understand how the reunification of Israel and Judah could have been expected (Jeremiah 30f.; Ezekiel 37; Hos. 2:2). The same hope is here as well. Jacob would place those items that it had used in its idol worship far away and its guilt would be covered.

If this "city" is Samaria, it is possible that this text should be dated in the early Hellenistic era—particularly since this passage is a later addition to the apocalypse. The harsh blows that are in the background would refer to the fact that the city had been a bone of contention between the heirs of Alexander during that era. Yet it is also plausible that those who lived in Jerusalem might have cherished such dreams from time to time during the Persian era as well, possibly at the time of Nehemiah. It does not matter that we do not have information about Samaria being destroyed during the Persian era, since it is a prediction, which would not have to have been fulfilled; some certainly were not.

Commentary

[27:6] It is important for the author to point out that the inhabitants of the Northern Kingdom also would be included in the restoration "in the coming days." Other passages in the OT use the imagery of sending out roots; see Ps. 80:10; Job 5:4; Isa. 40:24; the closest to this passage is Job 14:7-9, but see also Isa. 11:1. As a tree that appears to have died off can send forth shoots once again "at the scent (רֵיחַ) of water" (Job 14:9), so also Israel, which seems to be lost, can still have a future, and not only that: it would bloom and sprout, and the whole earth would be filled with its fruit. In Hos. 14:6 Yahweh promises: "I will be like the dew to Israel; he shall blossom like the lily, he shall strike root like the poplar" (text emended); see also v. 8: "they shall blossom like the vine," and where it sprouts and blooms, there one also would expect fruit. The text refers to the תְּנוּבָה, the produce that the soil of the earth (פְּנֵי־תֵבֵל) would yield; see passages such as Lam. 4:9; Deut. 32:13.

One wonders whether מָלְאוּ is transitive or intransitive. Since the preceding verbs are in the singular, פְּנֵי־תֵבֵל (the whole world) must function as the subject, which means that מָלֵא (will fill itself) must be intransitive. One would expect that there would be some mention of Israel in connection with the fruitfulness of the land of Israel, but the phraseology פְּנֵי־תֵבֵל (lit.: the face of the world) does not permit this interpretation. Therefore, this is what it intends to say: when Israel flourishes again, at that very time the whole earth will be full of good gifts, with material goods being the first to come to mind. The use of תֵבֵל (world) clearly has the end of time in view: when everything is in order in Israel once again, then the affairs of the whole world will be in their proper place.

[27:7] In the past, Israel had suffered greatly when Yahweh acted upon them in judgment. Yahweh had "struck" them, *but* still not with the same level of severity with which those who struck them were struck, and it was not wiped out through murder in the same way as those who did the murdering were treated. Admittedly, it is difficult to translate this text and be confident about the result. Another possible translation would be: "Did he (God) strike him, as his striker struck him? Or was he murdered, as his murderer murdered him" (Kessler)? But that is not likely. When God strikes someone severely, he does that through the earthly tools he chooses to use; when he strikes, that is no different from the blows of the "striker."

[27:8] But who are these enemies who have struck, who have murdered? Since this text looks back to events in the past, one could suppose that this reference is to the Assyrians, who had disappeared ingloriously from the stage of world history in the meantime. Or might it be the Persians, whose governor was residing in Samaria, but who had to surrender their control to Alexander the Great? Or is this maybe speaking about the time when Samaria was a bone of contention between the successors of Alexander? Unfortunately, v. 8 is hardly the type of passage that would allow this question to be answered unequivocally. It speaks about the "day of the east wind," which frequently has been interpreted as a reference to the Assyrian invasion, but קָדִים (east wind) could simply be a metaphor for describing the destruction that has come over Jacob, comparable to the hot east wind (Arabic: *eš-šerqīye*, sirocco), which is so hot that all the vegetation dries up in almost no time and is blown away then by that wind; cf. Ps. 103:15f.; Jer. 18:17; Job 27:21 (see H. Guthe, *Palästina* [1927] 50). If this is a reference to the Assyrians, then the startling, the driving away, and the driving out would be about the exile of the inhabitants of the Northern Kingdom. However, the suffixes on these verbs just mentioned are feminine singular, which means they cannot refer directly to Jacob. If vv. 10f. speak about Samaria, then the reference here might be to the populace in this city; the author sees Israel and Samaria as one and the same. Concerning the fate of those who once lived in Samaria, one might refer to 2 Kings 17:6 and *AOT* 349f. (cf. *ANET* 284f.). Thus on the יוֹם קָדִים (day of the east wind) a strong storm (רוּחַ קָשָׁה) struck Samaria/Israel; Yahweh had not been at all lenient in the "dispute" (רִיב), but that was now in the past.

[27:9] Now, when the strong city (v. 10), in which some heathen group had been entrenched in both ancient and recent times, would be demolished, so that Israel's guilt could be covered over, then the possibility existed that a new beginning could be made. According to the deuteronomistic approach to writing history, the basic error of the Northern Kingdom was that it permitted itself to be caught up in heathen cultic practices: "They walked in the customs of the nations. . . . They built for themselves high places at all their towns . . .; they set up for themselves מַצֵּבוֹת (pillars) and אֲשֵׁרִים (sacred poles)"; see 2 Kings 17:7ff. (concerning the *asherim* and *maṣṣebot*, see above, pp. 177ff.). Deuteronomy also called for their destruction (7:5; 12:3). In the present passage, there is discussion about tearing apart the altars (which were up on the heights; concerning אַבְנֵי מִזְבֵּחַ, "an altar of stones," see Deut. 27:5f.; Exod. 20:25). In Deut. 7:5; 12:3, altars are mentioned along with *asherim* and *maṣṣebot*. It may be that some reader thought they should be included here and then expanded the text to include the comment that the *asherim* and incense altars (see Isa. 17:8 above, pp. 176f.) were never to be built again. It needs to be said once again that חַמָּנִים (incense altars) are mentioned only in the relatively late documents of the OT; they are not listed as part of the inventory at a בָּמָה (high place) in the preexilic era (see above, p. 176).

If Israel finally would be at the point of bridging the long-standing gap with its own past, then the guilt would be withdrawn, that which had weighed it down like a heavy curse during all these past centuries and which had not allowed it to live in freedom and prosperity as the people of God. Concerning כִּפֶּר (cover), see *Isaiah 1–12*, p. 270; and above, pp. 375f.

[27:10] One notes that vv. 10f. are connected with the preceding material by means of the כִּי (for). The hope that Israel would be restored is now interrupted by comments which anticipate that the fortified city is to be demolished—based on the proposed interpretation set forth above, this demolition would come after the destruction of Samaria. The description of the fortified city uses stock phrases for predicting that enemy cities will be destroyed, meaning that one cannot press it for exact historical and geographical details. Nevertheless, nothing would preclude Samaria being identified as the city. A piece of land that has been devastated is often described after time has passed as a נוה, "delightful pasture" (Jer. 9:9), in order to bring out the contrast between what once was and what now is. Here, in fact, the city is compared with an abandoned steppe. Once again, comments about the ruined heights being abandoned are part of the standard vocabulary used when depicting such scenes (concerning עזב, "abandon," see Isa. 7:16; Ezek. 36:4); the same is true also of the comparison with the desert (Isa. 14:17; Jer. 9:11; Zeph. 2:13). At most, the only "original" comment would be the announcement that the bushes, which still might poke up, would be eaten by animals, right back down to the surface.

[27:11a] One cannot be sure if the same author is speaking in v. 11; in any case, the same thing is said in another way. It is not enough that the bushes will be grazed right back down to the ground; the dry branches that remained standing are going to be destroyed as well. Women will come, will break them off, and will set them on fire; this phrasing likely means that they are looking for whatever can be used as fuel for cooking or baking; see Dalman, *AuS* IV, 1–29.

קציר, "branches," is a very general term, one that is not used specifically to identify certain types of plants. Ps. 80:12 speaks of the קציר (branches) of the vine; in Job 14:9; 18:16; 29:19, קציר (branches) is used simply to describe the opposite of the root of a plant. That usage refers to whatever part of the plant is visible above ground. Thus, when the women who are looking for something to burn gather the קציר (branches) together, there is nothing left to see afterward except bare hillocks. This means that an end has been prepared for the fortified city that makes no allowance for a single ray of hope; Samaria, the "heathen" city, has been destroyed so completely that it poses absolutely no further threat to Israel.

[27:11b] Bringing this section to a conclusion, v. 11b furnishes the reason why this dismal fate for the city is completely justified and why one cannot count on the possibility that divine mercy will come. The inhabitants of the city were לא עם־בינות (a people that has no insight). In this context, בינה (insight) must be interpreted in a religious sense. In the OT way of thinking, this people can be said to have departed from knowledge of God and from the fear of God. The inhabitants of the city do not understand God's ways and are not aware of what his promises are all about. It is striking, nonetheless, that בינה (insight) is used, a term found primarily within wisdom contexts, rather than דעת אלהים (knowledge of God) or יראת יהוה (fear of Yahweh).

It is expected that every human being would have בינה (insight); when someone cuts oneself off from it, that person is a fool. For a long time already, the residents of Samaria were no longer just Israelites (A. Alt, "Der Stadtstaat Samaria," *KlSchr* 3 [1959] 258–302; and 2 Kings 17:24); Alexander the Great pushed things even further in the same direction when he settled Macedonian war veterans in the city (see Schürer, II, 160f.). However, since Yahweh, and no other God, was the creator, one has a right to expect בינה (insight) from these groups of peoples as well.

Now, when it is said that this people without insight will find no mercy, that once again points to the way in which order was understood in the OT and in the ancient world (see the extensive discussion about this matter in remarks concerning 22:14). Radical grace, which is great enough to include the godless as well or which actually reaches its high point in bestowing grace on sinners, is simply not to be found in the OT. However, one must understand the concern that forms the background to this way of thinking, namely, the fear that the entire scale of values could fall apart if unconditional grace were proclaimed. One can see impressive evidence in 26:9f. for the fact that some in Israel had wrestled with the question about whether the godless could still find grace. In the present context, however, there is no deep reflection concerning this problem; v. 11b simply serves the function of pointing out that the demise of the city is irreversible.

Purpose and Thrust

The section of material in 27:6-11 is very important. Once again, it shows that the split which resulted in the formation of the Northern Kingdom after the time of Solomon continued to be most traumatic for those in Judah who believed in Yahweh—completely justified if one analyzes this event on the basis of the presuppositions linked to faith in Yahweh. Yahweh is the God of Israel, not the God of Judah. As long as "Jacob" does not put forth any new shoots, Israel's faith is called radically into question. Now, however, if the interpretation presented above is considered correct, the prospect that Samaria was going to be destroyed had awakened fresh hopes that the old wounds would be healed. The author believes that the earlier predictions that the fortified city would be destroyed (25:1ff.; 26:1ff.) would in fact be fulfilled, but he gives a new meaning to those predictions at the same time. Now, atonement could be made for the guilt of Jacob; now, there was nothing standing in the way of Israel being reunited with Judah. In this possibility, the author sees a triumph for the divine faithfulness, for which reason "Jacob," in spite of its burdensome history, simply could not be written off; instead, it also would have to be prosperous along with Judah when the fullness of salvation came at the end of time.

Isaiah 27:12, 13

Gathering and Return Home

Text

12 And it will happen on that day
   that Yahweh will beat out the ^aears, 'from' the (Euphrates) river on,
   ^beven as far as the brook of Egypt.^b
   There you^c will be gleaned,
   ^done after the other,^d you children of Israel.

           *   *   *   *

[13 And it will happen on that day
   that there will be blowing into the large horns.
   Then they will come, those lost^a in the land of Assyria^a
   and those scattered ^ain the land of Egypt.^a
   And they will fall down^b before Yahweh
   on the mount of the sanctuary in Jerusalem.]

12a–a Instead of מִשִּׁבֹּלֶת הַנָּהָר (from the ears of the river), it is likely that one should follow Lindblom (60), Kaiser, et al., and read שִׁבֳּלִים מֵהַנָּהָר (the ears from the river) (*BHS*: שִׁבֹּלֶת מֵהַנָּהָר, "ear from the river"); עַד (as far as), which precedes נַחַל מִצְרַיִם (the brook of Egypt), needs a מִן (from) just before הַנָּהָר (the river) in the first half of the verse, to balance it.

12b–b The Gk reads ἕως Ῥινοκορούρων (as far as Rhinocolura). A city by this name was located at what is known today as *el-ʿarīš* (the city that gives what once was known as the נַחַל מִצְרַיִם, "brook of Egypt," its current name, the *wādi el-ʿarīš*).

12c As happens frequently, Q^a reads the more expanded form אתמה instead of אתם (both: you [pl.]); on this reading, see Kutscher, 433ff.

12d–d לְאֶחָד אֶחָד means "to one still another one"; thus it has to be translated: "one to the other" or "every other one."

13a–a It is wrong if textual criticism is used to remove בְּאֶרֶץ אַשּׁוּר (in the land of Assyria) and בְּאֶרֶץ מִצְרַיִם (in the land of Egypt) because of metrical considerations (Sievers; see also Procksch); the same holds for Sievers's attempt to insert בְּצִיּוֹן (in Zion) before הַר הַקֹּדֶשׁ (the mount of the sanctuary).

13b Q^a: והשתחו (and bow down).

Form and Setting

Concerning the limits and division of this material, see above, pp. 457f. For Israel to come back into existence at the end of time, it is not enough that the two kingdoms which were related as brothers should be reunited; those who had been scattered needed to be reassembled in one place and the Jews of the diaspora needed to return to the land of the ancestors or back to Jerusalem and its sanctuary on the mount. That necessity would have moved the authors of these two pieces to append them as expansions. If the people of Israel were reunited in the land of the ancestors, then the goal of what was expected at the end of time would have been realized, and this reestablishment of Israel as a nation could bring the "apocalypse" in chaps. 24–27 to its conclusion as well, which also shows that these chapters are to be understood as a unit in spite of the complicated way in which this material came together.

In terms of the time period, these two sections would not have been written that far apart from one another. However, v. 13 is clearly secondary in its relationship with v. 12. Concerning the dating, one also might think here in terms of the late Persian era or the early Hellenistic period.

Meter: It is difficult to determine with relative certainty just how these two verses are to be analyzed metrically; in any case, the phrase from ובאו (then they will come) to מצרים (Egypt) (v. 13b) can be treated as a seven-stress colon.

Commentary

[27:12] Verse 12 discusses gathering together those who have been scattered, initially by using the imagery of knocking kernels out of the ears of grain; on this imagery, see Judg. 6:11; Ruth 2:17; and cf. Isa. 28:27. Normally, grain that had been harvested would be processed at the threshing floor. Beating grain out would work only with very small portions (as is the case with Ruth) or would be handled this way only in cases where someone would have good reason to stay away from the threshing floor because it was visible from such a distance (as with Gideon). This method takes a lot of time; for this reason, less is lost than would be the case in the traditional threshing process. This means: Yahweh carries out his saving action of gathering with the greatest possible care; he spares no effort, since not a single little kernel is to be lost.

הנהר (the river) (with the article!) refers here, as often elsewhere, to the Euphrates. It is still striking, however, that it is not mentioned in conjunction with the Nile, but with the נחל מצרים (brook of Egypt). Based on all the parallels in the OT, the "brook of Egypt" must refer to what is known today as the *wādi el-ᶜarīš* (Akkadian: *naḥal*KUR*muṣri*). In ancient times, it was known as the border between Palestine and Egypt; see Num. 34:5; Josh. 15:4, 47, etc. This would mean that הנהר (the river) would identify one of the borders at which one would begin to gather or free the people of God from their surroundings, which were mostly heathen. "From the brook of Egypt to the Euphrates" is technical phraseology that describes the borders of what once identified the limits of the Davidic empire and thus designates the ideal borders for Israel's land (cf. 2 Kings 24:7). In this territory, therefore, the בני ישראל (children of Israel) would be gathered together (לקט) like ears of grain out in the open field. Thus the geographical territory envisioned in v. 12 does not match with that in v. 13—corroborating evidence that shows that v. 13 does not belong originally with v. 12. Specifically, v. 12 does not deal with bringing Israel home from its surroundings, but rather with extracting Israel from among those who lived around them, who were either largely heathen or largely unbelieving. It would be proper to return their land to them, since they had been promised a portion as an inheritance. Just as ears that the cutter had missed when he grabbed for a bunch of stalks, which were left lying on the ground and could have gone to waste, the children of Israel were threatened with the danger that they could become extinct among the masses of those who were either indifferent or who had some other belief system. As is asserted here, however, that demise would not come. Yahweh would keep them together and would beat them out; he would be very careful to separate the kernels from the chaff. This message supplies us with a stirring insight into how things were for the Jews, circumstances that could apply only to the late postexilic era.

[27:13] The situation is different with v. 13, which is clearly speaking about Jews who are actually in the diaspora, who will be returning from Babylon and Egypt. נדחים (the scattered) is a common expression describing the *Gola* (see *Isaiah 1–12*, p. 493). This is parallel to אבדים (those lost). One ought not presume from the way this is stated that the Jews in Egypt were scattered, whereas those in Babylon were threatened with destruction; these are simple variations required by the parallelism. In addition to this, אבד does not mean only "go to ruin," but also "wander around, lose one's way" (see Jer. 50:6; Ezek. 34:4, 16; 1 Sam. 9:3, 20). There is no doubt that it was dangerous to "lose one's way" within the surrounding heathen culture; this situation resulted in most of the ethnic-religious groups settling for some form of Hellenistic syncretism. That was not to be Israel's fate. The large horn (שופר, actually, "ram's horn") would be blown so that Israel could begin to make preparations to return home. One would usually blow the horn in order to gather an army (Jer. 51:27, etc.), but also when a people was to be called to take flight (Jer. 4:5; 6:1, etc.). However, "on that day" the ram's horn would be blown as a sign that the eschatological era was breaking in; cf. Zech. 9:14. This passage caught the attention of others; see Pss. Sol. 11:1; Matt. 24:31: "And he will send out his angels with a loud trumpet call, and they will gather his elect from the four winds"; cf. also 1 Cor. 15:52; besides this, see 4 Ezra 6:23; see also Str-B I, 959f.; III, 481. It was going to be a שופר גדול (large horn) since it was an incomparable event that was being set in motion. It is possible that one should think of this as being blown on Zion, as is mentioned specifically in Pss. Sol. 11:1. But its sound would be so loud that those who were scattered would be able to hear it and come, no matter where they were living. The author was not worried that there would not be enough room in little Palestine, to say nothing of Jerusalem, for all the Jews living in the worldwide diaspora to assemble; in the future, new parameters would be established that would make the impossible possible. Those who were returning home would want only one thing in their old homeland: to worship Yahweh on the holy mountain. The ancient concept is at work here once again, that Zion was the dwelling place of Yahweh or at least the place where his name dwelt and where his כבוד (glory), which had filled the temple, had come to rest (1 Kings 8:11; Ezek. 43:5; 44:4). Theoretically, one could praise Yahweh anywhere the sun shone (Mal. 1:11), but it would be an incomparable advantage if one could do so on the mount in Jerusalem where the sanctuary was located. One cannot know for sure whether הר הקדש should be translated as "holy mount" or "mount of the sanctuary"; in any case, קדש (holy) can be used all by itself as a designation for the temple.

Purpose and Thrust

It was an irrevocable aspect of Israel's hope in the postexilic era that the Jewish people would be gathered and would return home—and that remains true still today. Some might think that this expectation takes the low road after the high road taken in some of the other statements in the apocalypse; all the peoples of the world are not in view in this scene and there is absolutely no mention of the reign of Yahweh over the whole earth. However, one is moved by the fact that yearning to be able to honor Yahweh in his sanctuary is at the center of this hope. The scope of Israel's hope and the extent of that hope can be seen at the same time (cf. Rev. 7:9ff.). If one surveys the four chapters as a whole, then of course this hope for Israel is just one particular aspect of the hope that Yahweh's reign, which was to encompass the whole earth, would be established on Zion in all its fullness.

Postscript: Isaiah 24–27

The final word about the development, structure, and meaning of the Isaiah apocalypse has not yet been uttered. However, the *communis opinio* of scholars, that this is a postexilic work, has been demonstrated by the exegesis of the individual passages. The viewpoint that has been taking shape only very recently is also irreversible; the apocalypse is not one literary unit.

Not only because of the form but also because of the content, there are good reasons for one to have to speak about levels and later additions. One cannot say that this is one single, unified product, satisfied that its thoughts are organized systematically; these are impressions that have been woven together and have been placed together, one after the other. Not just motifs and single traditions but also sections of material from different backgrounds are brought together to provide a richness to these eschatological-apocalyptic predictions. Additions were supplied to expand the material so as to fill in details and from time to time to reactualize what had been said earlier.

In this very way, however, this section became a magnificent document, one that came to show how Israel struggled with its hope for the future, more specifically, with its faith, since both its future and that of all peoples lay in the hands of Yahweh; and, at the end, even though the harshest judgment would come to fruition, salvation alone could remain. There is no doubt that the final word is said in 24:21-23 and 25:6-8: in the announcement of the full breaking in of the reign of God, which would stretch out over all the peoples of the world, in which death also would be swallowed up, along with all the suffering connected with it. It is understandable not only in human terms but also grounded deep within the faith of Israel that Israel is warned with utter seriousness that it should not start rejoicing too quickly, but the true Israel is also described in great detail, showing how it would appear as those coming events unfolded. This depiction was not based on what humans could comprehend but was founded deep within Israel's faith. In this way, a single, long, complex body of material came into existence, in a process of transmission that we certainly cannot visualize down to the specifics. One might compare its development with the book of Job and its various levels. It presents what might be compared with a majestic symphony, having as its leit-motif the faithfulness of Yahweh, manifested in his desire that restoration would be made visible in the end. The variations on the theme portray the depths and heights of judgment and deliverance. In this way, the apocalypse makes a respectful effort to pick up the theme of Isaiah's own depiction of the future in 2:2-4 (though it is easy to see that the accents are placed differently). With respect to these chapters, Delitzsch offered the following opinion: "The author is not Isaiah himself, but one of Isaiah's disciples, one who outdoes the master here. Isaiah is great all by himself, but even greater through his disciples, just as the rivers are greater than the source from which they flow." These are bold statements, to which not everyone would subscribe, but they are true insofar as they show that a section of material has been brought into the book of Isaiah that depicts once again the thoughts describing the מלכות יהוה (kingdom of Yahweh) by expanding considerably on the ancient Israelite faith. One might say that the oracles against the nations are bundled together with this material to form one single ray of light, to demonstrate the goal that God has as he deals with the peoples as well as with Israel.

We have stated clearly that there are problems with identifying these chapters as an "apocalypse," as is frequently done. That scholars have come to such a variety of conclusions when dealing with the question about whether this designation can be properly used is connected with the issue about the development and structure of these chapters. That this material comes together gradually prohibits one from making generalizations about its development. One encounters motifs that one certainly could call apocalyptic, and yet entire sections have nothing whatsoever to do with apocalyptic thought. It is not an apocalypse, but the beginnings of an apocalyptic understanding of the world and an awareness of history are there. Isaiah 24–27 stands at the beginning of a powerful movement, one in which the faith of Israel once again showed that it had surprisingly creative power.

Manuscript Sigla

Aquila	Aquila
B	Bombergiana
Gk	Greek (Septuagint)
Gk^Q	Codex Marchalianus
Kethib	*Kethib* (so written)
L	Codex Leningradensis
MSS	Manuscripts
MT	Masoretic Text
OL	Old Latin
Q^a	First copy of Isaiah from Qumran cave 1 (1QIsa^a)
Qere	*Qere* (so read)
Sa	Sahidic
Syh	Syro-Hexapla
Syr	Syriac
Targ	Targum
Theod	Theodotion
Vulg	Vulgate

Hebrew Grammars Cited

Bauer-Leander   H. Bauer and P. Leander, *Historische Grammatik der hebräi-schen Sprache des Alten Testaments* (Halle, 1922).

BrSynt   C. Brockelmann, *Hebräische Syntax* (Neukirchen, 1956).

Ges-K   *Gesenius' Hebrew Grammar*, edited and enlarged by E. Kautzsch, 2nd English ed. revised in accordance with the 28th German ed. (1909) by A. E. Cowley (Oxford, 1910).

Joüon, *Gr*   P. Joüon, *Grammaire de l'hébreu biblique* (Rome, 1947²).

Abbreviations

AAH	Acta antiqua academiae scientiarum Hungaricae
AASF	Annales Academiae Scientiarum Fennicae
AASOR	*Annual of the American Schools of Oriental Research*
ADHL	M. Noth, *Abhandlungen des heiligen Landes*
ÄF	*Ägyptologische Forschungen*
AfO	*Archiv für Orientforschung*
AGH	*Die Akkadische Gebetsserie* "Handerhebung," ed. Erich Ebeling
AHW	W. von Soden, *Akkadisches Handwörterbuch* (1966f.)
AIPh	*Annuaire de l'institut de philologie et d'histoire orientales et slaves*
AJSL	*American Journal of Semitic Languages and Literature*
AJT	*American Journal of Theology*
ANEP	J. Pritchard, ed., *Ancient Near Eastern Pictures Relating to the Old Testament* (1969²)
ANET	J. Pritchard, ed., *Ancient Near Eastern Texts Relating to the Old Testament* (1955²; 1969³ with supplement)
AnSt	*Anatolian Studies*
AO	Der alte Orient
AOAT	Alter Orient und Altes Testament
AOS	American Oriental Series
AOT	*Altorientalische Texte zum Alten Testament*, ed. H. Gressmann
ARAB	*Ancient Records of Assyria and Babylonia*
ARE	*Ancient Records of Egypt*, ed. J. H. Breasted
ARM	Archives royale de Mari. Textes Cuneiformes
ArOr	*Archiv Orientální*
ARW	*Archiv für Religionswissenschaft*
ASAE	*Annales du service des antiquités de l'Égypte*
ASTI	*Annual of the Swedish Theological Institute* (in Jerusalem)

Abbreviations

ATANT	Abhandlungen zur Theologie des Alten und Neuen Testaments
ATD	Das Alte Testament Deutsch
AuS	G. Dalman, *Arbeit und Sitte in Palästina*, 6 vols. (1928–1942)
AusBR	*Australian Biblical Review*
AUSS	*Andrews University Seminary Studies*
BA	*Biblical Archaeologist*
BAfO	Archiv für Orientforschung, Beihefte
BASOR	*Bulletin of the American Schools of Oriental Research*
BDB	F. Brown, S. R. Driver, C. A. Briggs, *A Hebrew and English Lexicon of the Old Testament*, repr. 1953
BeO	*Bibbia e Oriente*
BETL	Bibliotheca ephemeridum theologicarum lovaniensium
BetM	*Beth Miqra*
BETS	*Bulletin of the Evangelical Theological Society*
BEvT	Beiträge zur evangelischen Theologie
BHH	*Biblisch-Historisches Handwörterbuch*, ed. B. Reicke and L. Rast
BHK	*Biblia hebraica*, ed. R. Kittel
BHS	*Biblia hebraica stuttgartensia*, ed. K. Elliger and W. Rudolph
Bib	*Biblica*
BibLeb	*Bibel und Leben*
BibOr	Biblica et Orientalia
BiKi	*Bibel und Kirche*
BK	Biblischer Kommentar zum Alten Testament
BL	*Bibel-lexikon*, ed. H. Haag
BRL	*Biblisches Reallexikon*, HAT I, 1, ed. K. Galling
BS	*Bibliotheca Sacra*
BSFE	*Bulletin (trimestrial) de la société française d'égyptologie*
BuA	B. Meissner, *Babylonien und Assyrien*
BWANT	Beiträge zur Wissenschaft vom Alten und Neuen Testament
BWAT	Beiträge zur Wissenschaft vom Alten Testament
BZ	*Biblische Zeitschrift*
BZAW	Beihefte zur *Zeitschrift für die alttestamentliche Wissenschaft*
CAH	Cambridge Ancient History (1970^3)
CB	*Cultura bíblica*
CCSL	Corpus Christianorum, Series Latina
CIH	*Corpus Inscriptionum Himjariticarum* (= *CIS*, IV)
CIS	*Corpus inscriptionum semiticarum*
CTM	*Concordia Theological Monthly*
CTom	*Ciencia Tomista*
EHPR	Études d'histoire et de philosophie religieuses
Epigr.Gr.	Epigrammata Graeca

ErIsr	*Eretz Israel*
Erman	A. Erman, *Die Literatur der Ägypter* (1923)
EstBib	*Estudios Bíblicos*
ETL	*Ephemerides theologicae lovanienses*
ETR	*Études Théologiques et Religieuses*
EvQ	*Evangelical Quarterly*
EvT	*Evangelische Theologie*
ExpTim	*Expository Times*
FF	*Forschungen und Fortschritte*
FRLANT	Forschungen zur Religion und Literatur des Alten und Neuen Testaments
FWG	*Fischer Weltgeschichte*
Ges-Buhl	W. Gesenius and F. Buhl, *Hebräisches und aramäisches Handwörterbuch zum AT* (1921ff.[17])
GesSt	*Gesammelte Studien* (collected studies)
GSAI	*Giornale della societa asiatica italiana* (Florence)
HAL	W. Baumgartner et al., *Hebräisches und aramäisches Lexikon zum Alten Testament*
HAT	Handbuch zum Alten Testament
HAW	Handbuch der Altertumswissenschaft
HdO	*Handbuch der Orientalisk* (Leiden)
HNT	Handbuch zum Neuen Testament
HSM	Harvard Semitic Monographs
HTR	*Harvard Theological Review*
HUCA	*Hebrew Union College Annual*
IB	*The Interpreter's Bible,* ed. G. Buttrick, 12 vols. (1952–1957)
IEJ	*Israel Exploration Journal*
IJPR	*International Journal for Philosophy of Religion*
JAOS	*Journal of the American Oriental Society*
JBL	*Journal of Biblical Literature*
JCS	*Journal of Cuneiform Studies*
JNES	*Journal of Near Eastern Studies*
JPOS	*Journal of Palestine Oriental Society*
JQR	*Jewish Quarterly Review*
JR	*Journal of Religion*
JSS	*Journal of Semitic Studies*
JTS	*Journal of Theological Studies*
KAI	H. Donner and W. Röllig, *Kanaanäische und aramäische Inschriften,* 3 vols.
KAT	Kommentar zum Alten Testament
KBL	L. Koehler and W. Baumgartner, *Lexicon in Veteris Testamenti Libros* (1953)

Abbreviations

KD	*Kerygma und Dogma*
KEK	*Kritisch-exegetischer Kommentar über das NT*
Ken	B. Kennicott, ed., *Vetus Testamentum Hebraicum cum Variis Lectionibus* (1776)
KlSchr	*Kleine Schriften*
LCL	Loeb Classical Library
Lehrg.	*Lehrgebäude* (Eduard König, *Historisch-kritisches Lehrgebäude der hebräischen Sprache.* 2 vols. in 3 [1881–1897])
Leš	*Lěšonénu*
LS	*Lexicon Syriacum*
LUÅ	Lunds universitets årsskrift
MAOG	Mitteilungen der altorientalischen Gesellschaft
MBPF	Münchener Beiträge zur Papyrusforschung und antiken Rechtsgeschichte
MGWJ	*Monatsschrift für Geschichte und Wissenschaft des Judentums*
MIO	*Mitteilungen des Instituts für Orientforschung* (Berlin)
MVAÄG	*Mitteilungen der vorderasiatisch-ägyptischen Gesellschaft*
NC	*Nouvelle clio. Revue* . . . (Brussels)
NF	Neue Folge (new series)
NRSV	New Revised Standard Version
NS	New Series
NTD	Das Neue Testament Deutsch
NThS	*Nieuwe theologische studien*
NTT	*Norsk Teologisk Tidsskrift*
OLZ	*Orientalische Literaturzeitung*
Or	*Orientalia* (Rome)
OTL	Old Testament Library
OTS	*Oudtestamentische Studiën*
OTTheol	*Old Testament Theology*
OTWSA	*Ou testamentiese werkgemeenskap in Suid-Afrika*
PG	J. Migne, *Patrologia graeca*
Pauly-W	A. Pauly and G. Wissowa, *Realencyclopädie der klassischen Altertumswissenschaft* (1894ff.)
PEFQSt	*Palestine Exploration Fund Quarterly Statement*
PEQ	*Palestine Exploration Quarterly*
PJ	*Palästina-Jahrbuch des deutschen evangelischen Instituts*
POS	Pretoria Oriental Series
PrJ	*Preussische Jahrbücher*
PSBA	*Proceedings of the Society of Biblical Archaeology*
RA	*Reallexikon der Assyriologie und vorderasiatischen Archäologie*
REJ	*Revue des études juives*

RGG[3]	*Religion in Geschichte und Gegenwart*, ed. K. Galling, 6 vols. (1957ff.[3])
RHPR	*Revue d'histoire et de philosophie religieuses*
RHR	*Revue de l'histoire des religions*
RivBib	*Rivista Biblica*
RivBibIt	*Rivista Biblica Italiana*
RLA	*Reallexikon der Assyriologie*
RM	Religionen der Menschheit
Rm	Rassam Cylinder
RSO	*Revista degli studi orientali*
RSR	*Revue des sciences religieuses*
RTP	*Revue de théologie et de philosophie*
SAHG	A. Falkenstein and W. von Soden, *Sumerische und akkadische Hymnen und Gebete* (1953)
SBT	Studies in Biblical Theology
ScEs	*Science et esprit*
SOr	Studia Orientalia
SOTSMS	Society for Old Testament Study Monograph Series
ST	*Studia Theologica*
STDJ	Studies on the Texts of the Desert of Judah
Str-B	H. Strack and P. Billerbeck, *Kommentar zum Neuen Testament*, 6 vols. (1921ff.[4])
STU	*Schweizerische Theologische Umschau*
Suppl.Calv	*Supplementa Calviniana*
TAVOBei	*Tübinger Atlas des Vorderen Orients*, Beihefte
TBü	Theologische Bücherei
TDNT	*Theological Dictionary of the New Testament*, ed. G. Kittel and G. Friedrich, 10 vols.
TEH	Theologische existence heute
TDOT	*Theological Dictionary of the Old Testament*, ed. G. Botterweck and H. Ringgren
TGI	*Textbuch zur Geschichte Israels*, ed. K. Galling (1950)
THAT	*Theologisches Handwörterbuch zum Alten Testament*, ed. E. Jenni and C. Westermann, 2 vols. (1971–1976)
THK	Theologischer Hand-Kommentar
TLZ	*Theologische Literaturzeitung*
TStKr	*Theologische Studien et Kritiken*
TQ	*Theologische Quartalschrift*
TT	*Theologisch tijdschrift*
TZ	*Theologische Zeitschrift*

Abbreviations

UF	*Ugarit-Forschungen*
UM	C. H. Gordon, *Ugaritic Manual*
ÜP	M. Noth, *Überlieferungsgeschichte des Pentateuchs* (1948) (Engl: *A History of Pentateuchal Traditions* [1981])
UT	C. H. Gordon, *Ugaritic Textbook*
VAB	Vorderasiatische Bibliothek
VAT	Vorderasiatische Abteilung, Thontafelsammlung
VG	Carl Brockelmann, *Grundriss der vergleichenden Grammatik der Semitischen Sprachen*
VivPen	*Vivre et penser*
VT	*Vetus Testamentum*
VTSup	*Vetus Testamentum*, Supplements
WB	J. Aistleitner, *Wörterbuch der ugaritischen Sprache*
WMANT	Wissenschaftliche Monographien zum Alten und Neuen Testament
WO	*Die Welt des Orients*
WZKM	*Wiener Zeitschrift für die Kunde des Morgenlandes*
ZA	*Zeitschrift für Assyriologie*
ZAW	*Zeitschrift für die alttestamentliche Wissenschaft*
ZDMG	*Zeitschrift der deutschen morgenländischen Gesellschaft*
ZDPV	*Zeitschrift des deutschen Palästina-Vereins*
ZKT	*Zeitschrift für katholische Theologie*
ZNW	*Zeitschrift für die neutestamentliche Wissenschaft*
ZS	*Zeitschrift für Semitistik und verwandte Gebiete*
ZTK	*Zeitschrift für Theologie und Kirche*
ZWT	*Zeitschrift für wissenschaftliche Theologie*

Index of Biblical
and Related References

Index of Biblical and Related References

Apocrypha and Pseudepigrapha

Index of Biblical and Related References

Canaanite and Aramaic Texts

Greek and Latin Authors

Index of Biblical and Related References

Index of Names and Subjects

Index of Names and Subjects

Forces, Assyrian, 197f.
Forgetting God, 182
Foundations of the earth, 500
Function of the world, understanding, 57, 75, 251

Gadez, 422
Garden of God on the top of the Lebanon, 59, 62
Gath, 96
Gaza, 93, 96
Gedaliah, 385, 396
Ghosts, demons, 31f., 134
Gidiria, 115, 126
Gleaning, 172f., 488
God's intervention in the morning, 201f.
God's reign, see Kingly Rule of Yahweh
God, dying, 183
Gola, 38, 268, 599
Grace, 596
Grave, 70, 387

ḥaibar, 333ff.
Hanun (Hanno) of Gaza, 93, 213, 238
Hatred, 76, 540
Haughtiness, hubris, 37, 59f., 75f., 119f., 145f., 259, 317f., 388ff., 428, 438, 521, 539f.
ḥazāilu, 332
Heaven, 65, 506
ḥejaz, 334, 343
Helel, son of Shachar, 62ff.
Heliopolis, 214f., 271
Hell, 62
Herakleopolis magna, 214f.
Herakleopolis parva, 214f.
Heshbon, 114, 132f.
Hezekiah, 84, 92f., 99, 102, 197, 216, 219, 255, 360f.
Hiram of Tyre, 420
Historicizing of myths, 63, 576ff.
History, 20, 38, 40, 49, 76f., 82f., 85, 153, 218, 226, 242, 249, 258, 317, 327, 371
Hivites, 186f.
Holistic thinking, 249
Holy war, 19f., 320, 363
Homage of the peoples, 225, 437, 525f.

Hope, 326
eschatological-messianic, 143
messianic, 144
Horonaim, 137
Hoshea of Israel, 238, 255
Host of heaven, 506
Hosts of angels, 506
House of the Forest of Lebanon, 367
Humiliation of Israel, 534

Iamani, 216, 290
iata', 332
iata' (son of *ḥazāilu*), 332
iati'e (Arabic queen), 332
Imperial Aramaic, 269f.
Inaros the Libyan, 278
Integration into the Yahweh Community, 35
Interim period, 508
iskallatu, 332

Jacob, 590, 592
Jahaz, 133
Jason, 272f.
Jazer, 148
Jehoshaphat, 115
Jerusalem, 83f., 100f., 355, 358, 362f., 366f., 461, 511, 544, 546
Jerusalem theology, 67, 173
John Hyrcanus, 461
Jonah ben Amittai, 122
Joram of Israel, 115
Joseph, a second, 398
Judgment, 26, 162f., 174, 188, 356, 500, 559ff., 593
Judgment of the peoples, universal, 85
Judgment of the whole earth, 25, 220, 226, 464, 474, 478, 488, 571f., 578

ka|ma|shaltā, 117, 332
kamusunadbi, 117
Kashta, 254
Kedar, 116, 333, 344ff.
Keys (power of), 396, 399, 402
King, 388f.
Kingly rule of Yahweh, 37, 240, 282, 438, 505, 510f., 513, 525ff., 530, 534, 548, 600f.

Index of Names and Subjects

Index of Names and Subjects

Index of Hebrew Words

Index of Hebrew Words

624

CPSIA information can be obtained at www.ICGtesting.com
Printed in the USA
242606LV00001B/4/P

9 780800 695095